THE 1972 Compton Yearbook

A summary and interpretation of the events of 1971 to supplement Compton's Encyclopedia

F. E. Compton Company

William Benton
PUBLISHER

CHICAGO · LONDON
TORONTO · GENEVA
SYDNEY · TOKYO
MANILA

THE 1972 COMPTON YEARBOOK

Editor in Chief   Dean H. Schoelkopf
Editor   Patricia Dragisic
Assistant Editor   Sharon Barton
Staff Editor   Dave Etter
Consulting Editor   Richard Pope
Contributing Editors   Samuel Allen, Judy Booth, David Calhoun, Katharine Quinn Cohen,
Daphne Daume, Herbert Glaettli, Barbara Gordon, Mary Alice Molloy, Orville Snapp,
Karen Strueh, Margaret Ziemer, Joseph Zullo

Editorial Production Manager   J. Thomas Beatty
Production Coordinator   Grant Disney
Production Supervisor   Rita A. Piotter
Layout Supervisor   Emily A. Friedman
Production Staff   John Atkinson, Susan Alison Bush, Charles Cegielski, Gerald Fisher,
Barbara Wescott Hurd, Marilyn Klein, Lawrence Kowalski, Lois C. Lantz, Lynn K. McEwan,
Lila H. Morrow, Janina Nalis, Richard O'Connor, Ruth Passin, Frank A. Petruzalek, Mary Reardon,
Julian Ronning, Madolynn Scheel, Linda G. H. Schmidt, Harry Sharp, Elliott Major Singer,
Valerie Walker, Penne L. Weber, Anita K. Wolff

Art Director   Will Gallagher
Associate Art Director   Cynthia Peterson
Senior Picture Editor   James Sween
Picture Editors   Florence Scala, Adelle Weiner
Layout Artists   Richard Batchelor, David Alexander
Quality Control   Richard Heinke
Illustrator   Ron Villani
Cartographers   Chris Leszczynski, supervisor; Eugene Tiutko
Art Staff   Martina Daker, Bernard Holliday

Index   Frances Latham, supervisor; Virginia Palmer, assistant supervisor;
Gladys Berman, Grace Lord, Mary Neumann

Geography Editor   Frank J. Sutley
Research Geographers   William A. Cleveland, supervisor;
Gerald E. Keefe, Joseph R. Sturgis

Copy Control   Felicité Buhl, supervisor; Gurtha McDonald, recorder; Mary K. Finley

Manuscript Typists   Rosebud Gainer, Mary Hunt, Judith Lukens,
Allena McCorvey, Eunice Mitchell

Secretary   Marie Lawrence

Compton's Encyclopedia
Donald E. Lawson, Editor in Chief

Catherine McKenzie, Senior Vice-President and Director of
Editorial, F. E. Compton Company

Library of Congress Catalog Card Number: 58-26525
International Standard Book Number: 0-85229-169-8
Copyright © 1972 by F. E. Compton Company.
All rights reserved for all countries.
Printed in U.S.A.

Contents

Hope for the Future

by Senator William Benton, Publisher

With every passing year, the task of improving *The Compton Yearbook* becomes more challenging. How do our editors continue learning to bind the past to the present and the present to the future? "If you do not think about the future," said Nobel prize-winning novelist John Galsworthy, "you cannot have one."

We are not content to offer merely an inventory of the past and the present—a chronology of events and conflicts laced with occasional dramas of high human achievement. Not only its errors, but also its surprises, inventions, and ideas mark our time. Taken as a whole, they give our time a character and will some day be seen as providing a tradition for it. "Character is destiny," wrote Heraclitus, the Greek philosopher, and it is our intent in *The Compton Yearbook* to suggest our time's destiny by capturing its particular character.

To do so, we seek to recount the events of the year in such a way as to transform them from isolated fragments of contemporary history into a cohesive and intelligible whole. "To be able to be caught up into the world of thought— that is [to be] educated," said Edith Hamilton, the interpreter of Greek civilization. To serve education in this highest sense is the task we have set for ourselves.

Through it all, our aim is to promote understanding. We hope to harmonize what seem to be the irreconcilable elements of the modern world into a vast, if tremulous, balance. Our intent is not merely to repeat and review but also to enlarge and inspire. We hope, like the poet, to give each man his own view of the world—to show him what he sees but does not know that he sees. We seek something triumphantly individual in the yearbook, what poet John Masefield once called "the old, proud pageant of man."

My own response to the cluster of feature articles is highly personal, as always, and I hope yours will be.

Until I read Walt Kelly's article on cartoons, for example, I was not aware that William Hogarth, the great 18th century innovative painter, was among the earliest commentators-through-comics. Or that Henry Ford, the industrialist, was one of those who sent a telegram to have Sandy, the dog, returned to the "Little Orphan Annie" comic strip when it was once "lost."

John V. Lindsay's thoughtful article on urban problems reminded me again how rural was the environment of the Founding Fathers of the United States—living as they did in a group of colonies that boasted only six cities with populations of as much as 8,000. Today that size "city" would be considered small for a "farm town," and almost miniscule even for the suburbs that have erupted outside of the cities of the present. Mayor Lindsay's proposal for "national cities"—communities free to seek direction and survival independent of state authority—had its roots in an obscure 1937 report from a committee headed by an old friend of mine, Harold Ickes, the secretary of the interior under President Franklin D. Roosevelt.

Until I read the article on invasion of privacy by Ralph Nader and John Spanogle, I was not aware of the deviousness of some of the explorations of the private lives of some of us, for example, the use of the "welcome wagon" lady as an investigator-in-disguise by certain credit agencies. Or the sales by certain income-tax services of information they gather while helping to make out your return. Or, again, the sale by a federal agency, for $1.50 a copy, of its estimate of the marital stability of a couple who apply to it for home loans. The implications of such activities stretch far into the future. For, as Nader suggests, it is possible that the lifetime of a child could be darkened by a single report of an eighth-grade teacher who says that the child has been a disciplinary problem, and this remark is recorded in a data bank. How important are such stories now being generated by these new activities? I cannot believe the results are widespread, nor do I believe they have as yet had any appreciable effect on American life. Let us hope that the tocsins of warning, such as Nader's, will help prove me right, and that I may continue to be right.

But as fascinating and provocative as such information in the feature articles may be, it cannot compare—in historic terms—with the deeper and more subtle rhythms that emerge from reading this yearbook. For in that reading one catches a certain tone, a specific quality in the character of our times. "Character is an historical fruit," wrote Henri Frédéric Amiel, the Swiss poet and philosopher. And it is as apparent today as yesterday that we must preserve a sense of history—and must do it with insight, with purpose, with a feeling for its nourishing nature for the future.

As I see it, the quality of character is not just in the clamor of our times but in the growing concern about them. In going through the articles and special features of this yearbook, you will become aware not only of the enormous variety of problems facing mankind but of the varying responses to them. It is that perspective

which prompts me to conclude that we should not feel as pessimistic about our time as many headlines suggest. We of Compton's seek to be realists. It is because of our quest for reality, we feel, that we are better able to identify the problems around us and to focus on both the need for, and the means of, solving them. We do not throw up our hands in dismay or despair. "All interest in disease and death is only another expression of interest in life," wrote Thomas Mann.

The range of concern expressed in *The Compton Yearbook* is immense and the implications are enormous. In Senator Edward Kennedy's article on Indochina refugees and war victims, we see a microcosm of the problems of the age. The problems will become more acute for *all* of us if, because of the violence and oppression of this century, we casually come to accept suffering and injustice.

Similarly with Dr. Alex Gerber's article on America's health care problems. It embraces a vast irony: great scientific progress existing along with the societal failures of medicine. It indicates the imperatives for ending this irony by finding a way in which medicine can match its social responsibilities with its scientific achievements. The reason is clear: there are few social ills that do not reach upward as well as downward and, while it is the poor who are denied the full spectrum of medical help today, it may be the middle income families who find they cannot afford full medical care tomorrow.

We are not simply besieged with somber problems but stimulated by their solutions. The problems create the pessimism; the solutions, perhaps as yet only dimly perceived over the horizon, give solid grounds for hope. If there is anything that characterizes our times, it is the bombardment of problems and the fertility of ideas to solve them.

To present all this adequately demands editorial discretion. It is our conviction at Compton's that the people of these times will soar to a more fulfilling destiny if they achieve better understanding of both problems and ideas. The way to do this is to draw upon the knowledge resources of the age in order to better define the epic character of the years through which we are now passing.

Compton's Pictured Highlights and Chronology of 1971

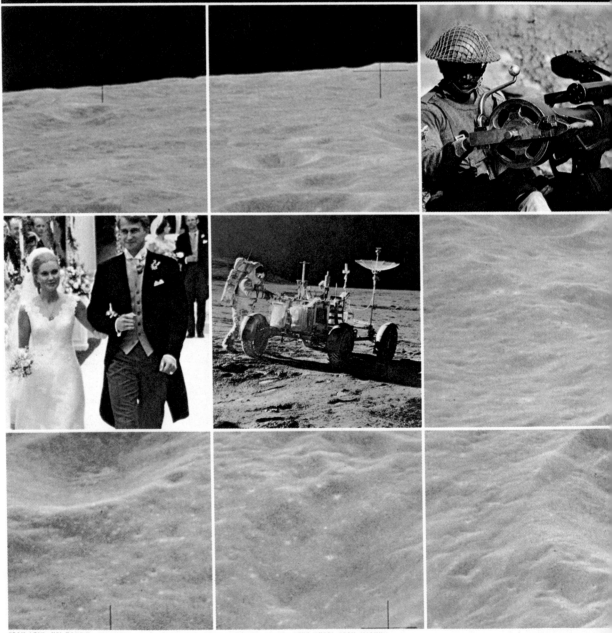

FROM LEFT: UPI COMPIX; COURTESY, NASA; PHOTOREPORTERS; FLETCHER DRAKE; RENE BURRI FROM MAGNUM

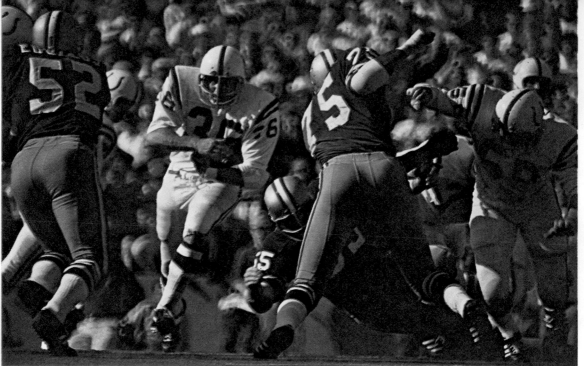

Norm Bulaich, number 36, star running back of the Baltimore Colts, carries the ball in a running play against the Dallas Cowboys in the fifth annual Super Bowl game played in Miami, Fla., January 17. The Colts won the world championship in a contest full of errors.

JANUARY

2 The final session of the 91st U.S. Congress adjourns after the Senate extends the funding of the supersonic transport (SST) program for three months.

A steel barrier collapses after a soccer match in Glasgow, Scotland, causing 66 deaths and scores of injuries.

3 The Swiss Supreme Court authorizes tax officials to give the U.S. government information on bank dealings of U.S. citizens suspected of tax fraud.

East Pakistani leader Sheikh Mujibur Rahman pledges to seek full autonomy for East Pakistan in the constitution to be written by the new National Assembly.

4 A Montreal, Que., court holds four separatists criminally responsible for the death of Pierre Laporte, Quebec's minister of labor and immigration.

5 Egypt, Israel, and Jordan resume indirect peace talks with United Nations (UN) mediator Gunnar V. Jarring.

6 The U.S. command in Saigon, South Vietnam, announces a drive to combat the abuse of drugs among U.S. military personnel in that country.

8 The British ambassador to Uruguay, Geoffrey Jackson, is kidnapped in Montevideo by Tupamaro guerrillas.

9 UN mediator Jarring concludes a two-day visit to Jerusalem for talks on a new peace proposal.

11 Bolivia's president, Gen. Juan José Torres Gonzales, announces that he has put down a rightist military coup.

The U.S. secretary of the navy, John H. Chafee, signs an agreement to end the Navy's use of Culebra Island, off Puerto Rico, as a missile target area.

12 Six persons, including Roman Catholic priest Philip Berrigan, are indicted on charges of conspiring to kidnap U.S. presidential adviser Henry A. Kissinger and to bomb the heating systems of federal buildings in Washington, D.C.

14 A truce agreement ends a week of clashes between Jordanian troops and Palestinian commandos north of Amman, Jordan.

15 Egypt's Aswan High Dam is formally dedicated by Egyptian President Anwar el-Sadat and Soviet President Nikolai V. Podgorny.

16 The Swiss ambassador to Brazil, Giovanni Enrico Bucher, is released 40 days after being kidnapped by Brazilian terrorists.

17 The Baltimore Colts defeat the Dallas Cowboys 16-13, in the Super Bowl.

18 Northern Ireland's prime minister, James D. Chichester-Clark, meets with British Home Secretary Reginald Maudling to request more help in curbing disorders.

20 British postal workers begin the first nationwide postal strike in Great Britain's history.

25 A coup d'etat led by Maj. Gen. Idi Amin deposes Uganda's President Milton Obote while he is returning from a meeting of the Commonwealth heads of government.

Charles Manson and three female companions are convicted of first-degree murder in the California slayings of actress Sharon Tate and six others.

28 U.S. President Richard M. Nixon asks Congress for pay increases and other benefits for servicemen as a step toward the creation of an all-volunteer army.

FEBRUARY

3 The Soviet Union accuses the U.S. of negotiating in bad faith by refusing to include certain curbs on fighter-bombers in discussions at the strategic arms limitation talks (SALT) in Helsinki, Finland.

Clashes between Roman Catholics and British troops break out in Belfast, Northern Ireland.

4 Egyptian President el-Sadat confirms his nation's acceptance of a 30-day extension of the Middle East cease-fire and proposes to reopen the Suez Canal if Israel agrees to begin partial troop withdrawal from the canal's east bank in that period.

5 The lunar module of U.S. manned spacecraft Apollo 14 lands on the moon after a flight marked by engineering problems.

7 Wladyslaw Gomulka, former first secretary of the Polish Communist party, is suspended from membership on the party's Central Committee.

8 South Vietnamese troops with U.S. air support sweep into Laos in a move to cut North Vietnamese supply routes.

In March South Vietnamese marines (left) set up firebases in Laos. This gun crew is firing 105mm howitzers from a hilltop position. The Veterans Administration Hospital in San Fernando, Calif., (below) collapsed, causing a heavy loss of life, during the earthquake that hit the Los Angeles area on February 9.

WIDE WORLD
CURT GUNTHER FROM CAMERA 5

Joe Frazier (left) lands a damaging left hook on Muhammad Ali. Frazier defeated Ali and became undisputed world heavyweight champion at the March bout in Madison Square Garden in New York City. India's Prime Minister Indira Gandhi (facing page, top) receives garlands of flowers while campaigning near New Delhi. In March she won a clear mandate to lead her country for another five years. In 1971 the "Jesus Movement" spread in many parts of the U.S. One group of "Jesus people" (facing page, bottom) started the Love Inn Christian Communal Farm in Freeville, N.Y.

CURT GUNTHER FROM CAMERA 5

The U.S. Senate confirms the nomination of John B. Connally as secretary of the treasury.

10 Cambodian Premier Lon Nol is reported to have suffered a paralyzing stroke.

11 Ceremonies in London, Moscow, and Washington, D.C., mark the signing by more than 60 nations of a treaty banning nuclear weapons from the ocean floors.

14 Persian Gulf oil-producing nations and Western oil companies sign an agreement settling their dispute over oil prices and marketing conditions.

15 The Polish government announces that the food price increases that had precipitated rioting in December 1970 would be withdrawn on March 1.

16 A highway between West Pakistan and China is formally opened.

17 President Nixon indicates at a news conference that he has ruled out use of tactical nuclear weapons in Indochina, but that no limits have been placed on U.S. air support of South Vietnamese offensives.

Israeli Foreign Minister Abba Eban says his country's retention of some occupied territory will be a condition of any peace settlement with the Arab states.

20 An emergency warning of a nuclear attack is broadcast by mistake in the U.S. in place of the usual Saturday morning test alert.

King Abdul Halim Muazzam is installed as chief of state in Malaysia.

21 Brazilian diplomat Aloysio Dias Gomide is released by Uruguayan Tupamaros almost seven months after he had been kidnapped.

23 U.S. sources report that after five days the South Vietnamese invasion into Laos has not seriously lessened activity on the Ho Chi Minh Trail.

24 Algerian President Houari Boumédienne announces the take-over of 51% interest in French oil companies in Algeria and the nationalization of natural gas facilities.

25 East German officials, in a letter to West Berlin Mayor Klaus Schütz, propose negotiations to permit West Berliners to visit East Berlin and East Germany.

26 The Colombian government declares a state of siege after rioting breaks out in the city of Cali.

28 U.S. tanks assume positions along the Laos-South Vietnam border to block the expected advance of a North Vietnamese tank force into South Vietnam.

MARCH

1 The National Assembly meeting to draft a new constitution for Pakistan is postponed indefinitely; East Pakistani leader Sheikh Mujib calls a general strike in protest.

A bomb explodes in the Senate wing of the U.S. Capitol.

2 Norwegian Premier Per Borten and his coalition government resign following a political scandal.

3 China is reported to have launched its second earth satellite.

4 Canadian Prime Minister Pierre Elliott Trudeau marries Margaret Sinclair in North Vancouver, B.C.

7 Egyptian President el-Sadat says the cease-fire with Israel will not be extended.

8 Four U.S. airmen kidnapped on March 4 by Turkish leftists are freed unharmed.

U.S. Army Capt. Ernest L. Medina is ordered court-martialed on murder charges stemming from the My Lai incident in South Vietnam in March 1968.

10 William McMahon is sworn in as prime minister of Australia following a Liberal party vote of no confidence in Prime Minister John G. Gorton.

12 Israeli Prime Minister Meir says that Israel will keep various occupied sites around Jerusalem and will demand the demilitarization of the Sinai Peninsula in any peace settlement.

Syria's premier, Lieut. Gen. Hafez al-Assad, is elected president of Syria in a national referendum.

15 The U.S. government lifts restrictions on travel to China by U.S. citizens.

17 The minority government of Premier Trygve M. Bratteli takes office in Norway.

Finnish Prime Minister Ahti Karjalainen announces the resignation of his government after the Commu-

BALDEV FOR TIME © TIME INC. 1971

nist faction of the coalition votes against a government bill.

19 Nihat Erim is named to be the new prime minister of Turkey.

20 Northern Ireland's Prime Minister Chichester-Clark resigns under pressure from Protestants demanding stronger action against Roman Catholic demonstrators.

22 Argentina's president, Brig. Gen. Roberto Marcelo Levingston, is deposed in a bloodless coup d'etat by armed forces chiefs.

JOHN ROBATON FROM CAMERA 5

NORMAN WEBSTER FROM THE "TORONTO GLOBE AND MAIL"

The United States table-tennis team poses at the Great Wall of China in April. The team members and three U.S. journalists were the first Americans invited to visit China since Mao Tse-tung gained control of the mainland 22 years before.

23 Brian Faulkner wins leadership of Northern Ireland's Unionist party and is asked to form a government.

24 The South Vietnamese invasion into Laos ends after 44 days with the removal of all but about 500 of the 20,000-man task force.

The U.S. Senate votes to end all further funding of the development of the supersonic transport.

25 Fighting between Pakistani army units and East Pakistanis breaks out in East Pakistan following the collapse of talks on self-rule.

26 Finnish Prime Minister Karjalainen withdraws his government's resignation.

Lieut. Gen. Alejandro Agustín Lanusse is sworn in as president of Argentina.

27 The Pakistani army is reported to have killed more than 10,000 East Pakistanis and to have arrested East Pakistani leader Sheikh Mujib.

28 A North Vietnamese force raids a fire base south of Da Nang, South Vietnam, killing 33 U.S. military personnel, the highest death toll for a single attack since July 1970.

29 A U.S. Army court-martial finds First Lieut. William L. Calley, Jr., guilty of the premeditated murder of at least 22 South Vietnamese civilians at My Lai.

30 The Pakistan central government announces that the East Pakistan independence movement is crushed.

APRIL

1 Egyptian President el-Sadat offers to reinstate the Middle East cease-fire and permit the reopening of the Suez Canal if Israel will agree to a partial withdrawal of troops from the east bank of the canal.

Argentina announces the legalization of political parties outlawed since 1966.

2 Palestinian guerrillas announce their intention to fight in Jordan until King Hussein I replaces Prime Minister Wasfi el-Tal and army officers hostile to their cause.

4 Senator J. W. Fulbright (D, Ark.) asserts that the U.S. obsession with Communism permits countries such as Israel and South Vietnam to manipulate U.S. foreign policy.

5 U.S. Rep. Hale Boggs (D, La.) calls for the resignation of Federal Bureau of Investigation (FBI) Director J. Edgar Hoover, citing the tapping of telephones of Congressmen.

6 A letter to President Nixon from U.S. Army Capt. Aubrey M. Daniel III, prosecutor in the Calley trial, states that the president's interference in the case compromised the judicial process.

7 President Nixon announces a further 100,000-man reduction in U.S. troops in South Vietnam by December 1.

A Catholic funeral takes place in Belfast, Northern Ireland, in April. Violence increased in Ulster during 1971, and feelings hardened between Catholics on the one hand, and British soldiers and Protestants on the other.

U.S. Secretary of Defense Melvin R. Laird announces plans to increase U.S. military aid to Jordan.

8 The Paris peace talks, suspended since March 18, resume.

9 A truce between Jordan and Palestinian commandos, arranged by Syrian mediators, is announced.

12 Chinese Premier Chou En-lai endorses Pakistani President Agha Mohammed Yahya Khan's efforts to curb the East Pakistan independence movement.

13 The U.S. Council of Economic Advisers issues its third inflation alert, warning the steel industry against excessive wage and price increases.

15 The Yugoslav ambassador to Sweden, Vladimir Rolovic, dies of gunshot wounds received a week earlier when he was attacked by Croatian separatists.

16 President Nixon says U.S. air power will continue to be used in Vietnam as long as North Vietnam holds U.S. prisoners.

17 Egypt, Libya, and Syria announce agreement to form a confederation of Arab republics.

19 Sierra Leone declares itself a republic within the Commonwealth of Nations.

Unemployment in Great Britain is reported to have reached 3.4%, the highest level since May 1940.

20 The U.S. Supreme Court issues four unanimous decisions supporting the imperative of school desegregation.

Cambodian Premier Lon Nol resigns for reasons of health, creating a government crisis.

22 The death of Haitian President François Duvalier is announced; his son Jean-Claude is sworn in as president-for-life.

23 U.S. jets carry out their sixth attack in six days on North Vietnamese missile sites, the heaviest series of such bombing raids since 1968.

24 Mass rallies calling for an immediate end to the war in Indochina are held in Washington, D.C., and San Francisco, Calif.

26 A U.S. presidential commission recommends the admission of China to the UN.

27 South Korean President Park Chung Hee wins reelection to a third term.

28 The Soviet Union is reported to have proposed at the SALT meetings a five-year treaty limiting missile defenses.

29 The U.S. combat death toll in Vietnam is reported to have passed the 45,000 mark.

30 The Canadian government allows antiterrorist legislation to expire.

13

MAY

1 Amtrak, the National Railroad Passenger Corp., takes over operation of most U.S. passenger trains.

3 Erich Honecker is named first secretary of the East German Communist party, replacing Walter Ulbricht, who resigned, citing as reasons old age and ill health.

The Cambodian government crisis is resolved with an agreement that Lon Nol will serve as titular premier and Sisowath Sirik Matak will hold the principal executive power.

Massive antiwar protests took place in Washington, D.C., in April and May. Vietnam veterans (below) used guerrilla theater as part of a week-long demonstration. A large contingent of active-duty GI's (right) later participated in a march and rally.

RIGHT: NANCY PALMER AGENCY
BELOW: MICHAEL ABRAMSON FROM BLACK STAR

Antiwar protesters in Washington, D.C., fail in their attempt to close down the U.S. government; more than 7,000 arrests, a record for the city, are made.

4 Mexico urges nonaligned members of the Geneva Disarmament Conference to draft their own ban on biological and chemical warfare.

6 Greece and Albania resume diplomatic relations, broken off since 1940.

8 A demonstration calling for military victory in Vietnam is led in Washington, D.C., by the Rev. Carl McIntire.

9 West Germany, Switzerland, the Netherlands, Austria, and Belgium, in moves to stem the monetary crisis, announce either upward revaluations of their currency or its floating against the fixed price of the U.S. dollar.

11 Great Britain's Prime Minister Edward Heath orders an investigation of reports that businesses and foreign embassies are buying confidential government information.

13 North Vietnamese forces are reported to have made two strong attacks on South Vietnamese forces in the A Shau Valley.

14 Egyptian President el-Sadat announces the foiling of an attempted coup and the formation of a new cabinet.

17 Laos reports the loss of its last major positions on the Bolovens Plateau to North Vietnamese forces.

18 The U.S. Congress passes legislation ending a two-day nationwide strike of railroad signalmen.

20 Nine Soviet Jews are found guilty of anti-Soviet activity in Leningrad, U.S.S.R.

21 French President Georges Pompidou and British Prime Minister Heath conclude two days of summit talks in Paris with an agreement to promote Great Britain's entry into the European Economic Community (EEC).

23 Viet Cong infiltrators blow up aviation fuel supplies at the U.S. air base at Cam Ranh Bay, South Vietnam.

The body of Ephraim Elrom, Israeli consul general in Istanbul, Turkey, is found six days after Turkish leftists had kidnapped him and demanded the release of political prisoners.

28 The residents of Filicudi Island, Sicily, begin leaving the island rather than remain with Mafia leaders exiled there by the Italian government.

Sicily's Mount Etna, the highest volcano in Europe, began a series of eruptions in April that became severe in May. Orchards on its slopes and a volcanological observatory near its peak were destroyed, and the threatened village of Sant' Alfio was evacuated.
KEYSTONE

KEYSTONE

UPI COMPIX

Evonne Goolagong of Australia (above) won the coveted women's title at the Wimbledon tennis competition, which began in June. Also in June, Patricia Nixon and Edward Finch Cox were married at the White House (right). Titian's masterpiece 'The Death of Actaeon', (facing page, top) was sold at auction for $4,032,000. Daniel Ellsberg (facing page, bottom) admitted releasing the Pentagon papers to the nation's press.

JUNE

1 Palestinian refugees charge Jordanian police with firing on demonstrators at a refugee camp in Amman, killing ten persons.

2 U.S. bombers and helicopters attack North Vietnamese troops in Cambodia in response to a South Vietnamese call for help.

A Yuba City, Calif., court arraigns Juan V. Corona on murder charges in connection with the slayings of 23 men whose bodies were discovered recently.

3 The South Vietnamese National Assembly passes election reform legislation requiring presidential candidates to have the endorsement of a specific number of legislators and councillors.

4 The North Atlantic Treaty Organization (NATO) foreign ministers meeting in Lisbon, Portugal, approves Soviet proposals for talks on troop reductions in Central Europe.

8 Chile's President Salvador Allende Gossens declares a state of emergency in Santiago Province after the assassination of former cabinet minister Edmund Pérez Zukovic.

9 The "big four" negotiators are reported to have reached a consensus on controls over traffic between West Berlin and West Germany.

10 President Nixon removes the 21-year-old embargo on trade with China.

12 Tricia Nixon, elder daughter of President Nixon, is married to Edward Finch Cox in the White House Rose Garden.

13 *The New York Times* begins publishing excerpts from secret Pentagon papers on the history of U.S. involvement in Vietnam.

15 *The New York Times* complies with a court order to halt temporarily the publication of the Pentagon papers.

16 The U.S. Senate defeats two amendments that would have set deadlines on withdrawal of U.S. troops from Indochina.

17 The U.S. and Japan sign a treaty to return Okinawa and the southern Ryukyu islands to Japan in 1972.

21 The International Court of Justice at The Hague, Netherlands, advises that South Africa's administration of South-West Africa (Namibia) is illegal and should be surrendered to the UN.

Chinese Premier Chou tells U.S. newsmen that U.S. military support of Taiwan is a major obstacle to easing U.S.-Chinese relations.

23 Great Britain and the EEC reach final agreement on the major issues related to Britain's membership.

The Organization of African Unity (OAU) annual heads of state conference ends in Addis Ababa, Ethiopia, with the passage of a resolution opposing dialogue with South Africa.

30 The U.S. Supreme Court rules, 6-3, that the government has failed to prove that reasons for prior suppression of the Pentagon papers outweigh the constitutional guarantee of freedom of the press.

Three Soviet cosmonauts are found dead in their Soyuz 11 reentry capsule after completing a flight that set a new space endurance record.

JULY

1 The U.S. Postal Service is inaugurated as a semi-independent government agency.

3 Maltese Chief Justice Sir Anthony Mamo is named governor-general for Malta, replacing Sir Maurice Dorman, who had resigned at Malta's request.

4 An Egyptian-Soviet communiqué from Moscow maintains that the Suez Canal will reopen only if Israel withdraws from all occupied territories.

5 Former West German Chancellor Kurt Georg Kiesinger announces he will not seek reelection as chairman of the Christian Democratic Union.

6 H. Kamuzu Banda is sworn in as Malawi's president-for-life.

Barend W. Biesheuvel is sworn in as premier of the Netherlands, heading a right-of-center coalition.

Louis Armstrong, famed jazz trumpeter, dies in New York City.

7 The British government issues a White Paper urging public approval of EEC membership.

West German Foreign Minister Walter Scheel begins a visit to Israel, becoming the highest ranking German official to do so.

10 Three Moroccan generals and the Belgian ambassador are killed during an attempted coup at the summer palace of King Hassan II.

11 U.S. labor leader George Meany indicates his support of direct controls on wages and prices to curb inflation.

The despair of the Bengali people is reflected in the face of a man carrying his dying wife. He was trying to take her to a hospital in a refugee camp near Calcutta, India, for treatment of cholera, but she died en route. Millions of East Pakistani people had fled to India.
KEYSTONE

13 The Jordanian army begins a campaign to remove Palestinian guerrillas from their bases in northern Jordan.

14 A coalition government with Olafur Johannesson as premier takes office in Iceland.

15 President Nixon announces that he will visit China before May 1972.

16 U.S. Secretary of Agriculture Clifford M. Hardin promises federal aid to help halt the spread of Venezuelan equine encephalomyelitis in the southwestern U.S.

The United Transportation Union begins selective strikes against U.S. railroads.

Northern Ireland opposition party members announce they will boycott Parliament because the British government refuses to inquire into the July 8 killings of two civilians by British troops in Londonderry.

18 Iraq closes its border with Jordan and asks for the withdrawal of the Jordanian ambassador.

20 The Soviet Union states its support of China's admission to the UN and its opposition to an international conference on Indochina.

23 Egyptian President el-Sadat warns that he will not allow 1971 to pass without decisive action against Israel unless agreement is reached on withdrawal from Arab territories.

Liberian President William V. S. Tubman dies in London; Vice-President William R. Tolbert is sworn in as his successor.

27 U.S. Secretary of Commerce Maurice H. Stans warns Congress that the U.S. may experience a balance of trade deficit in 1971 for the first time in this century.

28 William J. Porter replaces David K. E. Bruce as chief U.S. delegate to the Paris peace talks.

29 Yugoslavia's President Tito is reelected to a new five-year term.

30 A Japanese air force fighter collides with a passenger jet airliner killing 162 persons, the highest air disaster toll on record.

31 Apollo 15 astronauts make the first of three planned excursions on the moon in their lunar rover.

AUGUST

1 American steel companies and the United Steelworkers reach a contract agreement, thus averting a nationwide strike.

2 The U.S. announces its support for Chinese membership in the UN and continues its opposition to the expulsion of Taiwan.

U.S. railroads and the United Transportation Union reach an agreement, ending strikes against ten railroads.

5 The Soviet Union and the U.S. submit a draft treaty to the Geneva Disarmament Conference to ban biological weapons.

U.S. Assistant Secretary of State Joseph J. Sisco ends six days of talks in Jerusalem in a new initiative to reopen the Suez Canal.

7 Four cabinet members resign in Chile in disagreements over party policies.

9 Northern Ireland invokes emergency powers of preventive detention without trial and begins arresting suspected leaders of the outlawed Irish Republican Army (IRA); at least 12 persons are killed in rioting.

The Soviet Union and India sign a 20-year friendship treaty during a visit to India by Soviet Foreign Minister Andrei A. Gromyko.

10 Pakistan cancels permission for U.S. Senator Edward M. Kennedy (D, Mass.) to visit refugee camps in East Pakistan.

11 New York City's Mayor John V. Lindsay announces he is switching from the Republican to the Democratic party.

12 Alabama Gov. George C. Wallace launches a challenge of the federal busing policy.

13 NATO announces that its Mediterranean naval headquarters will be moved from Malta in compliance with Malta's request.

14 Bahrain declares its independence from Great Britain.

15 President Nixon announces a 90-day freeze on wages, prices, and rents; an import surcharge; and suspension of convertibility of the dollar into gold; he also proposes tax reductions and repeal of the 7% auto excise tax.

Massive air and artillery assault on North Vietnamese concentrations near the demilitarized zone is reported.

16 In a Los Angeles federal court Daniel Ellsberg pleads not guilty to charges of illegal use of the secret Pentagon papers.

18 New Zealand and Australia announce withdrawal of their combat forces from Vietnam by about the end of the year.

20 Malawi's President Banda ends an official five-day visit to South Africa and urges other black leaders to make similar visits.

The heads of state of Egypt, Syria, and Libya sign in Damascus, Syria, a constitution forming the Confederation of Arab Republics.

The life sentence of Lieutenant Calley is reduced to 20 years by a reviewing general.

21 Great Britain announces it will investigate charges that its troops had beaten and terrorized political prisoners in Northern Ireland.

22 Col. Hugo Banzer Suárez takes office as president of Bolivia, ending four days of civil war.

23 South Vietnamese Vice-President Nguyen Cao Ky withdraws his presidential candidacy.

26 Netherlands Queen Juliana begins her first official visit to Indonesia since its independence.

27 Japan announces provisional floating of the yen.

29 South Vietnamese President Nguyen Van Thieu retains control of the lower house of the National Assembly despite substantial gains by opposition party candidates.

31 U.S. Chief Justice Warren E. Burger says courts ordering busing to achieve racial balance in every individual school are misreading Supreme Court opinions.

SEPTEMBER

1 Referendums in Egypt, Syria, and Libya approve the formation of the Confederation of Arab Republics.

3 The "big four" representatives sign an agreement on the status of Berlin, to take effect when East and West Germany reach agreement on its implementation.

6 A young girl caught in a gun battle between British troops and snipers is the 100th person killed in the Northern Ireland violence since 1969.

7 Ireland's Prime Minister John Lynch and Britain's Prime Minister Heath end two days of talks on the strife in Northern Ireland without reaching agreement.

8 Senator Edmund Muskie (D, Me.) says that if a black is chosen as the Democratic vice-presidential candidate, the ticket will be defeated.

11 South Vietnamese President Thieu opens his presidential campaign by declaring he will resign if he receives less than 50% of the vote; he is running unopposed.

13 EEC finance ministers agree on a trade and monetary policy intended to get the U.S. to devalue the dollar and revoke the import surcharge.

Nine hostages and at least 28 prisoners are killed when approximately 1,000 state troopers, sheriff's deputies, and guards regain control of the state prison at Attica, N.Y., held for four days by 1,200 inmates.

15 Northern Ireland's Prime Minister Faulkner announces he had authorized the indefinite internment without trial of 219 persons.

16 President Nixon announces at a news conference that the U.S. will vote to give the People's Republic of China a seat on the UN Security Council.

17 U.S. Supreme Court Associate Justice Hugo L. Black retires after 34 years on the court, citing health problems as the reason.

18 Egypt and Israel exchange rocket fire across the Suez Canal for the first time since August 1970.

20 EEC foreign ministers decide in Brussels, Belgium, not to invoke immediate reprisals against U.S. trade policies.

Astronaut James B. Irwin salutes the flag on the moon's surface during the Apollo 15 mission in July. To the right is the lunar roving vehicle. In the background is the lunar module "Falcon." The spacecraft landed in the Hadley Rille area at the edge of the Sea of Rains.

21 The 26th session of the UN General Assembly opens in New York City; Indonesian Foreign Minister Adam Malik is elected president, and Bahrain, Bhutan, and Qatar are admitted.

22 Malta accepts the offer of $22.8 million a year to permit British and NATO forces to continue using military facilities there.

U.S. Ambassador to the UN George Bush submits two resolutions bearing on the seating of China; Japanese Premier Sato announces that Japan will co-sponsor the U.S. resolutions.

A U.S. Army court martial acquits Captain Medina of all charges in connection with civilian deaths at My Lai.

23 Canadian Prime Minister Trudeau warns that Canada will be forced to reassess its relations with the U.S. if current U.S. economic pressures on Canada become permanent.

U.S. Supreme Court Associate Justice John M. Harlan retires after 16 years because of ill health.

24 The British government orders the permanent expulsion of 105 Soviet representatives in Great Britain, charging them with espionage activity.

26 Japanese Emperor Hirohito is greeted in Anchorage, Alaska, by President Nixon on the first stop of the first trip abroad by a Japanese emperor.

Israel announces that it will ignore the UN Security Council call for a halt in its development of occupied Jerusalem.

28 Joseph Cardinal Mindszenty arrives at the Vatican, ending 15 years of exile in the U.S. embassy in Hungary.

A Greek military court finds five persons, including Lady Amalia Fleming, widow of the discoverer of penicillin, guilty of plotting the escape of a Greek prisoner.

Prisoners stand with clenched fists held high at Attica Correctional Facility in New York, where 1,200 inmates took over part of the state penitentiary for four days in September. An armed force rushed the prison to put down the rebellion, and 43 people were either killed outright or died later from wounds.

WIDE WORLD

OCTOBER

1 Great Britain's Defense Secretary Lord Carrington issues orders permitting British troops to use automatic weapons against terrorists in Northern Ireland.

3 South Vietnamese President Thieu wins uncontested reelection to a second four-year term.

4 Egyptian President el-Sadat is selected to be the first president of the Confederation of Arab Republics.

6 NATO foreign ministers appoint former NATO Secretary-General Manlio Brosio to explore with the Soviet Union the possibility of mutual troop reductions in Europe.

7 President Nixon outlines Phase II of his program of wage and price controls in a televised address.

The British government announces that an additional three battalions will be sent to Northern Ireland to tighten border controls.

8 The Soviet Union orders the expulsion of 5 British subjects, prevents the return of 13 others, and cancels high-level exchange visits, including one planned by British Foreign Secretary Sir Alec Douglas-Home.

10 Austrian Chancellor Bruno Kreisky receives in parliamentary general elections the first majority to be gained by an Austrian government since World War I.

11 British Prime Minister Heath, in a televised speech, asserts his government's intention to maintain control of Northern Ireland.

12 Simultaneous announcements in Moscow and Washington, D.C., state that President Nixon will visit Moscow in May 1972.

15 A three-year agreement to limit the export of Japanese textiles to the U.S. is initialed by Japan.

The British Parliament passes legislation curbing nonwhite immigration into England.

17 British Prime Minister Heath orders an official inquiry into allegations of the torture of internees in Northern Ireland.

The Pittsburgh Pirates win the World Series by defeating the Baltimore Orioles 2-1 in the seventh game.

18 Soviet Premier Aleksei N. Kosygin is assaulted on the Parliament grounds in Ottawa, Ont., during his tour of Canada.

20 The Nobel peace prize is awarded to West German Chancellor Willy Brandt for his efforts to lessen East-West tensions.

U.S. presidential adviser Kissinger arrives in Peking for talks to arrange an agenda and itinerary for President Nixon's China visit.

21 President Nixon announces his surprise choices of Lewis F. Powell, Jr., and Assistant U.S. Attorney General William H. Rehnquist as associate justices of the U.S. Supreme Court.

'Mass', composed by Leonard Bernstein and conducted by Maurice Peress, was performed at the grand opening of the John F. Kennedy Center for the Performing Arts on September 8. Performers included the Alvin Ailey American Dance Theatre and the Norman Scribner Choir.

FLETCHER DRAKE

24 South African police stage predawn searches of more than 100 homes of prominent persons, many critical of the country's apartheid policies.

25 The UN General Assembly approves, 76-35, an Albanian resolution calling for the admission of China to the UN and the expulsion of Taiwan; earlier it defeated a U.S. resolution to call the expulsion of Taiwan an important question requiring a two-thirds majority vote.

27 The Democratic Republic of the Congo (Kinshasa) announces the country is to be known henceforth as the Republic of Zaire.

28 The British Parliament approves plans for membership in the EEC by a 112-vote margin.

Yugoslav President Tito receives a warm official welcome on his first state visit to the U.S.

29 The U.S. Senate refuses to authorize funds to continue the foreign aid program.

NOVEMBER

1 A South African court sentences the Anglican dean of Johannesburg, Gonville A. ffrench-Beytagh, an opponent of apartheid, to five years in prison on charges of subversion.

3 Northern Ireland announces the arming of the Royal Ulster Constabulary reserve forces, which had threatened to strike in the face of mounting terrorist attacks.

5 Cuban sugar technicians return to Havana ten days after landing unannounced in New Orleans, La., to attend a conference for which they had been denied visas.

6 The U.S. Atomic Energy Commission conducts a controversial hydrogen bomb test on Amchitka Island, hours after a special session of the U.S. Supreme Court denied an appeal for an injunction against the test.

7 The coalition government of Belgium retains its majority in parliamentary elections although militant French- and Flemish-language parties make substantial gains.

8 Reports of a shuffle of the Chinese leadership raise speculation that Defense Minister Lin Piao has been ousted and possibly slain.

9 British troops sweep through three Roman Catholic sections of Belfast, arresting 43 suspected IRA members.

10 The U.S. Senate ratifies the treaty returning Okinawa and the southern Ryukyu islands to Japan.

Cuban Premier Fidel Castro arrives in Chile on his first visit to another Latin American country since 1959.

11 Japan reports its first official overture to open communications with China had been spurned by Chinese Premier Chou.

Walt Disney World opened in October 1971. Located 15 miles from Orlando, Fla., it combines fantasy and business in 27,400 acres of attractions.

12 President Nixon announces that U.S. troops in Vietnam will be reduced by 45,000 men by February 1972.

14 Phase II of the U.S. economic program goes into effect.

15 The Chinese delegation takes its seat in the UN General Assembly.

A French counterespionage official and one of his former aides are indicted by a U.S. grand jury on charges of conspiracy to smuggle $12 million in heroin into the U.S.

16 A commission in Great Britain clears British troops of charges of torturing and brainwashing internees in Northern Ireland but reports some evidence of ill treatment.

17 Thailand's Premier Thanom Kittikachorn and a "revolutionary council" seize full power in a bloodless coup d'etat.

18 Indian Prime Minister Indira Gandhi reports she has rejected UN Secretary-General U Thant's proposal to help relieve tensions between India and Pakistan, saying Thant should work toward ending Pakistan's civil war.

19 Israeli Prime Minister Meir says she will "demand" that the U.S. supply Israel with more jet fighter-bombers to correct the military imbalance in the Middle East.

22 Pakistan claims Indian divisions have launched a four-pronged attack on East Pakistan.

23 Rhodesian Prime Minister Ian D. Smith and British Foreign Secretary Sir Alec Douglas-Home reach an agreement for accepting Rhodesian independence.

25 Denmark and Norway become the first NATO members to establish full diplomatic relations with North Vietnam.

27 A Chilean congressional committee rejects President Allende's reform legislation and moves to prevent Allende from dissolving the Congress.

28 Jordanian Prime Minister el-Tal is shot to death in Cairo by Palestinian guerrillas.

29 Simultaneous announcements in Washington, D.C., and Peking say that President Nixon will begin his China visit on Feb. 21, 1972.

DECEMBER

2 Cambodian defenses near Phnom Penh are reported to have collapsed in the face of a heavy North Vietnamese thrust.

Israeli Prime Minister Meir confers with President Nixon at the White House.

3 India declares that full-scale war with Pakistan has begun in response to Pakistani air strikes on Indian airfields.

6 India recognizes the Bangla Desh rebel government as the government of East Pakistan; Pakistan breaks diplomatic relations with India.

The U.S. Senate confirms the nomination of Powell to the Supreme Court.

South Korean President Park proclaims a national emergency to cope with a possible invasion by North Korea.

7 India reports its troops have taken the city of Jessore, East Pakistan, after heavy fighting, giving India control of half of East Pakistan.

The Soviet Union announces that a capsule launched from its Mars 3 space probe on December 2 soft-landed on Mars.

8 Chilean President Allende announces that the government will take control of food distribution in the wake of demonstrations protesting food shortages.

9 President Nixon vetoes legislation to set up a national system of child development and day care.

10 West Germany agrees to increase its payment toward maintaining U.S. troops in Germany.

The U.S. Senate confirms the appointment of Rehnquist to the Supreme Court.

Portugal and the U.S. announce an agreement permitting continued U.S. use of air and naval bases in the Azores.

12 Northern Ireland Unionist party Senator John Barnhill is killed and his home bombed.

14 The East Pakistan government in Dacca resigns, dissociating itself from any further actions of the central Pakistan government.

The U.S. Congress completes action on the Economic Stabilization Act extending presidential authority over wages, prices, and rents until April 1973.

15 Pakistani Foreign Minister Zulfikar Ali Bhutto walks out of the UN Security Council, protesting its failure to take effective action to halt the India-Pakistan war.

17 Pakistan accepts a cease-fire along its West Pakistan-India border, ending 15 days of war.

18 President Nixon announces that an agreement on a general realignment of currency exchange rates has been concluded by the Group of Ten ministers meeting in Washington, D.C.

Greek Premier George Papadopoulos announces that martial law, in force since the 1967 coup, will be eased beginning Jan. 1, 1972.

20 Pakistan President Yahya Khan resigns and is replaced immediately by Bhutto, returning Pakistan to civilian rule for the first time since 1958.

President Nixon, in Bermuda for talks with British Prime Minister Heath, announces termination of the U.S. 10% import surcharge.

24 Giovanni Leone is elected president of Italy.

28 President Nixon signs legislation requiring able-bodied welfare recipients to register for jobs or job training.

29 Great Britain's foreign office orders the withdrawal of British forces from Malta rather than pay an additional $11 million demanded by the Maltese government.

30 The U.S. command in Saigon announces the end of intensified bombing of North Vietnam after five days of raids.

War broke out between Pakistan and India in December. The body of a soldier is half-buried in the sand in Kashmir (facing page). Indians were imprisoned in Pakistan (left), but later, after India's victory in the war, jubilant Bengali rebels (above) occupied the East Pakistani police headquarters.

PHOTOREPORTERS INC.

The tragedy of Indochina
Ten million civilian victims

by Senator Edward M. Kennedy

The Tragedy of Indochina

SENATOR KENNEDY is chairman of the U.S. Senate Judiciary Subcommittee on Refugees.

The Indochina war confronts the world with a very serious regional crisis of people—millions of people—refugees, civilian casualties, war victims of all kinds. Over the years nothing has more accurately documented the intensity and spread of the conflict and the level and nature of military operations than the number of civilians killed or wounded or made refugees. By this measure, even today, the war is scarcely winding down for the peoples directly involved.

In South Vietnam, with an estimated population of 18 million, the United States Agency for International Development (AID) estimates that some 5.4 million persons have become refugees and war victims since 1964. This figure is based on an estimated 2.4 million refugees from 1964 to 1966—a period prior to the time that a registration procedure for refugees was developed—and the actual registration of war victims since then. As of mid-1971, the toll was continuing to climb. During the first six months of 1971 the flow of newly registered refugees and war victims averaged more than 33,300 per month. And despite the claimed resettlement of tens of thousands, the active case load of those still receiving benefits rose dramatically from some 433,300 in January to more than 587,200 in June. These 1971 figures represented a sharp increase in the flow of new refugees and war victims. It should be noted that over the years the General Accounting Office—the investigating agency for the U.S. Congress—has consistently reported that official statistics on the number of war victims are understated. The real toll is undoubtedly much higher.

The same is true concerning the number of civilian casualties in Vietnam. The official figures are based solely on hospital admissions. As of mid-1971, official figures reported 373,910 admissions since 1965. This is a misleading figure, although it is usually cited as the total figure by our government, because it omits civilian casualties treated elsewhere, those not treated at all, and those who are killed outright. If these additional numbers are added to hospital admissions, civilian casualties from 1965 through mid-1971 number some 1.1 million—including 335,000 deaths. These unofficial estimates represent the conclusions of the U.S. Senate Judiciary Subcommittee on Refugees after extensive inquiry over more than six years.

As of mid-1971 the toll of civilian casualties continued to climb. During the first six months

With a wrecked bridge in the background and debris covering the burial grounds, a Vietnamese woman mourns at the grave of her husband.

PHILLIP JONES GRIFFITHS FROM MAGNUM

"Confronted with the inability to tell friend from foe, yet required to achieve some quantitative measure of 'success' . . . U.S. and South Vietnamese forces unleashed a firepower that displaced millions of Vietnamese from their lands and homes."

of 1971, civilian casualties—based on hospital admissions alone—averaged more than 3,600 per month for a total of 22,035. The actual occurrence of civilian casualties, however, was probably at least 50,000, including as many as 10,000 deaths. In contrast to the sharp increase in the rate of new refugees and war victims during this period, the rate of civilian casualties had decreased, but was still comparable to the rate during 1967, one of the peak years of U.S. combat.

Inevitably, tens of thousands of the civilian casualties who have survived are physically disabled. Again, not all of them are reflected in official statistics. But as of late 1969 some 79,-600 civilian amputees and paraplegics were registered with the Vietnamese government, as well as some 25,600 civilians who had become blind or deaf from war causes. Additionally, the official registration listed some 258,000 orphans and some 131,000 war widows.

In Laos, with an estimated population of some 2.8 million, at least 700,000 persons have become refugees over the years. As of mid-1971 the toll was continuing to climb. Despite the claimed resettlement of thousands, the official refugee relief case load rose from 283,000 in January to 317,000 in June. Estimates on the number of civilian casualties have always been

difficult to determine for Laos. Conveniently or otherwise, few official records have been kept until recently. In what can only be called an understatement in response to my inquiry in April 1970, officials in the U.S. Department of State called the casualty situation "serious and getting worse." In September, after a field investigation and additional inquiry, the subcommittee on refugees estimated that from early 1969 through the summer of 1970—a period of intensive conflict and U.S. bombing—civilian casualties probably numbered some 30,000, including at least 10,000 deaths. During the first six months of 1971, civilian casualties—based solely on admissions to U.S.-assisted medical facilities—averaged some 160 per month for a total of 1,960. As in the case of Vietnam, however, the actual occurrences of civilian casualties undoubtedly were much higher.

In the simplest human terms the story of the Meo tribespeople in Laos is a profoundly tragic one. Nearly the entire Meo population has become refugees—either as civilians fleeing from battle or as paramilitary forces, under U.S. tutelege, taking flight from defeat. The Meo have been running since 1962. Some families, if they have survived, have moved as many as 18 times. The mortality rate caused by their constant dislocation over rugged terrain, and by the

There were few survivors when a group of Vietnamese residents of Cambodia, held in a compound by Cambodian troops, were caught in a crossfire between the government troops and the Viet Cong.

general hardship and endemic malnutrition the war precipitated, has been incalculable. U.S. officials estimate, for example, that during a long move, such as the evacuation from the hills along the Plain of Jars in early 1970, one out of every family of five dies en route. Of an estimated Meo population of 400,000 in 1960, some observers conservatively estimate that some 50% of the men have been killed and some 25% of the women and children have fallen as casualties. After long years of fleeing and fighting, of moving and dying, Meo ranks are demoralized and tragically thin. The cost to the Meo for services to U.S. interests has been nothing short of the decimation of their tribe.

In Cambodia—as of mid-1971, after little more than a year of war—estimates on the number of displaced persons ran as high as 2 million, nearly a third of Cambodia's population. The capital city of Phnom Penh and the provincial capitals and district towns were bulging with refugees from the countryside. Medical facilities were overburdened with civilian casualties. Although both Cambodian and U.S. officials were long aware of the widespread dislocation of people, there was little evidence to suggest that they were much concerned about the situation. This attitude was hauntingly similar to attitudes voiced by the South Vietnamese and Laotian governments on the same subject. If such attitudes—and the conflict—continue in Cambodia, there is little doubt that human priorities will again get lost in the tide of war.

It is difficult to comprehend the aggregate statistics—more than 10 million—of civilian war victims in Indochina. It is even more difficult to comprehend the *implication* of these statistics—let alone some other aspects of the war—on the social fabric, economic viability, and political organization of nations confronted with massive upheaval and total war.

But the vast human costs of the war do tell something about its unique character and the nature of U.S. involvement. Why have the costs been so great? How could such a massive human tragedy develop—almost unnoticed by our national leadership? How have U.S. military practices and political strategies contributed to it? What must we understand about our obligations to a people devastated by a decade of war? And what are we to understand about our responsibility to salvage a broken society?

THE "PEOPLE'S WAR"

The basic problem and central question that has troubled the U.S. over its role in the Indochina war was stated in testimony before the U.S. Senate Judiciary Subcommittee on Refu-

"Of the estimated 6 million tons of bombs dropped over Indochina, about half have fallen during the last two or three years—a tonnage equal to the explosive force of more than 100 Hiroshima-type atomic bombs."

PHILLIP JONES GRIFFITHS FROM MAGNUM

gees by Ambassador William E. Colby, former deputy for pacification to the U.S. Military Assistance Command in Vietnam, on Apr. 21, 1971: "The nature of the war waged in Vietnam has imposed a heavy burden on the population of that country. . . . it has been a 'people's war'!"

What Ambassador Colby said about the war in Vietnam is equally true about the conflict in neighboring Laos and Cambodia. And today there can be little doubt that the Indochina war has indeed been a war of the people, tragically dramatized in the horrendous toll it has taken in the lives and spirit of civilians throughout the region. In such a war, a revolutionary "people's war," the key to "victory" is the political allegiance of people, not the amount of territory captured. The people become both the primary objective and the first target of this unconventional conflict. The people are the "hearts and minds" to be won. They are the "water" in which the insurgent "fish" swims. They are the "population resource" to be "denied the enemy." People become the focal point of "pacification" and "civic action" and all those other proliferating strategies, tactics, and slogans that are associated with U.S. involvement in Vietnam and in all of Indochina. For the other side, the people are the object of "national liberation" and "political reeducation." In traditional warfare "the people" have always been considered noncombatants, to be victimized as military targets only inadvertently. But in the "people's war," the people inevitably become the focus of the conflict.

The first "people's war" in Indochina was directed against the French colonial regime. The

PHILLIP JONES GRIFFITHS FROM MAGNUM

U.S. Army soldiers transport Vietnamese refugees after they were caught in the middle of an artillery barrage.

seeds for the second "people's war" were unfortunately buried in the settlement of the first—a fact of history that has been too little understood in the U.S. or, for that matter, in the South Vietnamese government or elsewhere.

One of the first manifestations of the unsettled character of the first conflict in Indochina was the large movement of refugees from North to South Vietnam in 1954. In the months following the partition of Vietnam by the Geneva accords of July 1954, approximately 7% of the population of the North, about 900,000 persons, sought refuge in the southern part of this former French colony. It is certain that additional numbers would have come, had they not been prevented from leaving by the authorities of North Vietnam after the end of the 300-day period for free departure permitted by the Geneva accords.

The refugees, mostly peasants who had experienced a harsh life in Viet Minh-controlled areas during the first Indochina war, fled mainly for political reasons. They were fleeing from Communism. A substantial number were Roman Catholic, often led into exile by their religious leaders. By 1957 the government of South Vietnam, with the assistance of the U.S. government and several private voluntary agencies, had largely completed the important task of caring for these refugees and integrating them into the society and economy of their new country. With that, the South Vietnamese, like many Americans, considered the Indochina conflict settled and began, again with U.S. assistance, to consolidate their government and to develop their country.

The perception of the North Vietnamese, under Communist leadership, was fundamentally different. To them the "people's war" could not be considered concluded until all the people of Vietnam were unified under one government. And so, while the task of integrating refugees from North Vietnam was underway in the south, the North Vietnamese initiated a second phase of the "people's war." This was done through the political and guerrilla activities of the indigenous South Vietnamese Viet Cong. By 1959 this second phase of the "people's war" was well under way, as a growing level of terrorism began to claim an increasingly heavy toll in the lives of local officials and ordinary citizens. It gnawed at South Vietnam's village structure and precipitated a deterioration in the political, economic, and social stability of the countryside. Inevitably this situation produced refugees, who moved in growing numbers from insecure areas

American soldiers point the way to safety to frightened women and children during the battle at Hue, South Vietnam, where fighting was prolonged and intense. Only 7,000 of 17,000 homes were left standing after the battle.

CLAUDE JOHNER FROM PHOTOREPORTERS

South Vietnamese residents of Cambodia fleeing atrocities and repression board a military vessel for Vietnam.

age villager began to find himself squeezed from both sides. His life was being disrupted by Viet Cong activities—from forced labor and coercive taxation to political terrorism and guerrilla warfare. But to this disruption of rural life was added the new pressure of increased retaliatory military operations by South Vietnamese government forces. Each year ground operations and, more particularly, artillery fire and aerial bombardment increased. In 1965, with the introduction of U.S. ground combat troops, this military activity dramatically escalated. No longer were Vietnamese fighting Vietnamese.

It is not without significance that within nine months of the arrival of U.S. combat units, nearly a million refugees flowed out of the countryside. During those few months the U.S. had introduced a level of firepower and ground combat activity never seen before in South Vietnam. And as this activity continued, a truly massive shift from the countryside to the urban centers occurred in the Vietnamese population. Also, a new rationale was introduced to explain this movement. No longer did we hear that the refugees were "voting with their feet." Refugees, it was now said, were really a "population resource" that could and should be *denied the enemy* and used to the advantage of the South Vietnamese government. It was explained that if the Viet Cong could not rely upon the food and protection of the population—if the proverbial "water" could be drained away from the Viet Cong "fish"—then the Viet Cong would be defeated. Although such refugees might pose a short-term relief burden to the government, the war, it was confidently stated, would be shortened. But the refugees were not cared for, and the war was not shortened. And so, in the main, Vietnamese civilians became merely pawns to be exploited by all parties to the conflict.

When I visited Vietnam for a second time, in early 1968, the condition of the people was deteriorating rapidly, mainly as a result of our military practices—such as "search and destroy," "free fire zone," "free strike zone," "H & I fire" (harassment and interdiction), and "forced relocation." Implicit in these practices, and more, was the basically indiscriminate, and often careless, treatment of civilians. In a "search and destroy" operation, for example, things were more "destroyed" than "searched."

Confronted with the inability to tell friend from foe, yet required to achieve some quantitative measure of "success"—such as enemy "body counts" and the number of Viet Cong "neutralized"—U.S. and South Vietnamese

to seek safety and relief assistance in district and provincial towns.

Initially, Americans were told by their government that these refugees were simply people fleeing from Communism—that they were making an ideological choice and "voting with their feet." Both U.S. and South Vietnamese officials declared that these refugees were really an opportunity—a sign of good faith in the South Vietnamese government. And of course, to a degree, these officials were right.

But to most refugees the experience was far more complicated. By the early 1960's the aver-

forces unleashed a firepower that displaced millions of Vietnamese from their lands and homes. In pursuit of our "people's war" strategy—of trying to kill Viet Cong on a massive scale while also "winning the hearts and minds" of other Vietnamese—the U.S. really achieved neither. There was, and still is, a deadly incompatibility between programs of winning the hearts and minds of villagers and simultaneously killing or capturing many of the villages' young men. In the final analysis, in our use of the modern technology of war—of heavy bombing and extensive artillery support, of trying to do from the air what we can not do from the ground—the U.S. has been destroying the very land and people it set out to save.

To anyone who has spent a night in a Vietnamese district town, where 105-millimeter howitzer cannon continuously shatter the night's silence, it comes as no surprise that a majority of the refugees surveyed in Vietnam have, over the years, complained most about bombs and artillery fire as their principal reason for fleeing their villages. From pilots dumping leftover bombs into "free strike zones" to the all too frequent use of "H & I fire," it is little wonder that the Vietnamese continue looking to the sky with trepidation.

The same can be said for the people of Laos and Cambodia. In Laos, especially, aerial bombardment has contributed heavily to the displacement, injury, and death of civilians and to the destruction of the countryside. A key element in our government's military activities in Laos has been the U.S.-sponsored and -controlled air war to support Laotian ground forces and to interdict North Vietnamese materiel and personnel moving down the Ho Chi Minh trail.

According to most observers, the bombing of Laos evolved in four escalating phases. The first ran from the spring of 1964 into the fall of 1966. Bombing during this period was rather sporadic, carried out mainly by Laotian T-28's and directed mainly against enemy troop concentrations in jungle areas. Very few civilians were involved. In the second bombing phase, from the fall of 1966 to the early months of 1968, targets began to include enemy-held or enemy-threatened villages and towns. U.S. aircraft became increasingly prominent, refugee movements occurred in many areas, and the occurrence of civilian casualties was frequent. The third bombing phase began in 1968, shortly after a partial bombing halt over North Vietnam in March, with U.S. aircraft outnumbering Laotian T-28's for the first time. Bombing began to be conducted on a more regular basis and was directed increasingly against populated areas. Many villages and towns in the northern part of the country were evacuated during this period.

Some refugees are able to escape with household goods and livestock, but others are left completely without possessions when their homes are destroyed.

PHILLIP JONES GRIFFITHS FROM MAGNUM

"The people become both the primary objective and the first target of this unconventional conflict. The people are the 'hearts and minds' to be won."

In the fourth bombing phase, which began very early in 1969, the most significant bombing increase occurred. It followed a complete bombing halt over North Vietnam in November 1968. Numerous records of interviews with refugees report that during some of this bombing phase aircraft came over the countryside daily—dropping napalm, phosphorus, and anti-personnel bombs. In summarizing a series of interviews with refugees, one observer reported to the subcommittee:

They [the refugees] say the jets bombed both villages and forests, that they spent most of their time in holes or caves, and that they suffered numerous civilian casualties. They say that everything was fired on, buffaloes, cows, ricefields, schools, temples, tiny shelters outside the village, in addition to, of course, all people.

Over and over again in recent years such reports by qualified private observers and former U.S. government personnel in the field have been filed with the subcommittee. The thrust of these reports, summarized in the comment above, is fully substantiated in the findings of surveys conducted by the U.S. mission in Vientiane, the Laotian capital. The findings in a survey conducted in July 1970 among refugees from the Plain of Jars were dramatically instructive. Some of these findings were as follows:

—97% of the refugees questioned said that they had seen a bombing attack—32% as early as 1964;
—68% said they had seen someone injured by bombing;
—61% said they had seen a person killed;
—75% said their homes had been damaged by the bombing;
—99% said the bombing made life difficult for them;
—87% said they built a shelter in the woods after they first saw a bombing raid;
—23% said the bombing was directed at people.

Over the years U.S. bombing of Laos undoubtedly achieved some of the goals of interdicting and harassing Pathet Lao and North Vietnamese forces—even though, in purely military terms, it did not prevent these forces from seizing more government-controlled territory. It is equally clear, however, that the bombing took a heavy toll among civilians and brought much devastation to the countryside.

U.S. forces have dropped nearly three times the tonnage of bombs over Indochina as they dropped during all of World War II. Of the estimated 6 million tons of bombs dropped over Indochina, about half have fallen during the last

Senator Edward Kennedy (center) speaks with a Vietnamese family at Thuong Duc, a refugee village in the Da Nang area of South Vietnam.

two or three years—a tonnage equal to the explosive force of more than 100 Hiroshima-type atomic bombs.

All of this underscores how tragically counter-productive much of our military and political strategy has been in Indochina. As I stated in a speech in Boston, Mass., more than four years ago: "The kind of war we are fighting in Vietnam will not gain our long-range objectives; the pattern of destruction we are creating can only make a workable political future more difficult." I felt that "if the current policies relating to the nature of the war were not changed, and the assumptions underlying civilian programs not revised, then the prospects of Vietnam . . . were dim."

Just how dim, we can see only now.

THE TRAGIC RESULTS OF FORCED RELOCATION

The scene is familiar. The army trucks arrive early in the morning near a village in the highlands of South Vietnam. The villagers, all Rhade tribesmen, have been told by the authorities that the trucks would come. Hurriedly, the villagers assemble as many of their few belongings as they can carry—small bags of clothes, some pots and pans, a few precious religious objects. Everything else must be left behind.

Slowly the soldiers begin to pile men, women, and children onto the waiting trucks. People squirm together in the hot dry sun, the red dust of the highlands baked on their clothes. A flash of flame adds to the heat as the soldiers begin to burn the village's longhouses and their furnishings.

A few hours later the villagers arrive at their new "resettlement" site—a barren hill near a provincial road. The villagers are given only tin roofing. All other building materials for makeshift huts they must find by themselves. They search the nearby woods and, in a few days, put together an assortment of shabby structures made of gnarled logs, weathered planks of wood, and old tin sheetings—all topped by sparkling U.S.-supplied tin roofing.

Some refugees are able to find enough wood to construct their huts on piling, as is their tradition. But they bear only a sad resemblance to the well-constructed hardwood longhouses of their native village. The only food they are given is a few days' worth of cornmeal and bulgur wheat, neither of which they know how to cook.

This movement of Montagnard tribespeople in Darlac province a year ago is an example of forcibly relocating people in Indochina—for *our* strategic reasons rather than the interests of the people themselves. In the first six months of 1971 at least 40,000 Montagnard villagers were forcibly moved in the highlands of Vietnam.

Additional numbers of people were moved elsewhere in the country. For years such forced relocations occurred in countless villages throughout all of South Vietnam. And always it was done in the name of bringing "security to the people."

The scenario for such operations was graphically portrayed in a statement submitted to the Senate subcommittee on refugees early in 1971. Written by a U.S. refugee official in central Vietnam—long after the policy of forced relocation was discredited by most observers—the statement said:

> Each year the farce of "taking security to the hamlets" is blandly outlined in the official Pacification and Development Plans —and each year no such thing happens. Instead, the Hamlet Evaluation System (HES) shows a certain number of hamlets evaluated as "insecure." Some general then says Darlac province will have no more low-rated hamlets. The province chief, knowing his forces are not about to take security to the hamlets, decides to bring them in under an "artillery umbrella," usually along one of the main roads in the province. At this point all [South Vietnamese] Ministry of Social Welfare regulations are violated and a group of hamlets are moved in, presumably at "their own volition," but with no planning either for the move or adequate provisions for their health or welfare.

About the time the statement was submitted to the subcommittee, Gerald Hickey, U.S. anthropologist with nearly two decades of experience in Vietnam, called forced relocations "one of the unlearned lessons of the Vietnam War." In a memorandum for the subcommittee's record he concluded, as have many other expert observers, that "the gains in population and resource control resulting from such relocation projects are, for the most part, outweighed by the social and economic disruptions that affect the whole of Vietnamese society. The ever growing number of shoddy settlements of Montagnards who have forcibly, or even willingly, been relocated is a stark reminder of this disruption."

Unfortunately, the capricious movement of people has been one of the more tragic themes of America's participation in the war—repeated constantly throughout all of Indochina and with official blessing from nearly all quarters. Over the years these movements were always justified in the name of bringing "security" to the people. But the fact is that the meaning of "security" to a villager was dramatically different from its meaning to a U.S. or South Vietnamese official.

To most officials in South Vietnam, security is whether the computerized Hamlet Evaluation System rates a hamlet as "secure." Such a rating is based upon the extent and frequency of enemy presence. If government officials cannot go there, it is deemed "insecure." To the villagers, however, such enemy presence may not repre-

"Little progress will be made in rehabilitating the peoples of Indochina if war continues to tear at the very fabric of their society. The war must end—not just the most visible symbols of our participation in it."

ROBERT J. ELLISON—EMPIRE FROM BLACK STAR

GUS CORAL—CAMERA PRESS FROM PIX

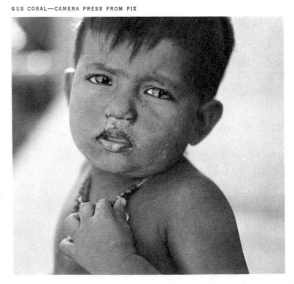

Some private U.S. groups maintain refuge areas and hospitals to help civilians who are ill or crippled. This wounded child and her mother have found help at the Quaker Center in Quang Ngai, Vietnam.

sent insecurity, even though they have to give some rice or service to the guerrillas. To the villagers this is a form of accommodation, not insecurity. And above all, they are not uprooted from their ancestral lands—one of their main concerns.

Indeed, as anthropologist Hickey and others have documented so well, far worse conditions of security are usually created for the villagers by the poverty and hardships imposed by forced resettlement. For example, of the more than 2,500 Montagnards relocated in a single resettle-ment area near Pleiku province early in 1971, nearly 10% died of diseases related to conditions at the new site. These were just some of the distressing findings of a U.S. medical official in the field. Yet, by official statistics the resettlement site was defined as "secure"—even though too many villagers had nothing but the security of the grave.

The same bankrupt policy of forced relocation has been pursued in Laos—less obviously, because the "secret war" in Laos was hidden so long from public view. However, in part as a result of the subcommittee's inquiry and field visits, a number of things came to light—including official internal memoranda of the U.S. mission in Vientiane, which commented on relocation practices and made abundantly clear the tie between refugee movement and military objectives. One memorandum, written in early 1970, stated that "military considerations and decisions by our own friendly military commanders have been dominant in the actions that have triggered refugee movements."

Just how manipulative U.S. officials have been when discussing the options involved in the forced relocation of people is evident in another memorandum, cited in a subcommittee report issued in September 1970. This memorandum discussed in some detail the arguments for and against the "mass evacuation" of tens of thousands of refugees from the Plain of Jars area in Laos just *prior* to a Pathet Lao attack against

Laotian government forces in early 1970. Listed in favor of mass evacuation were such points as these:

—to prevent the people from being captured by the Pathet Lao and North Vietnamese army and being used as porters;

—to give the people a chance to live under RLG (Royal Lao Government) administration; specifically so that their children will be educated and indoctrinated in the RLG school system and grow up as loyal citizens of Laos;

—such refugee evacuation would clear the Plain . . . for unrestricted military strike operations against the enemy;

—it will deny the enemy control over a considerable population of villagers and their services under Communist forces.

Arguments listed against mass evacuation included the following:

A Cambodian refugee family sleeps in the space allotted to them in the Phnom Penh Detention Center. Many refugees have been forced to relocate to satisfy military objectives and not because they were in a battle zone.

"We are conditioned, in the world we have created, to accept much suffering and injustice—especially in our time when violent conflict and oppression are active in so many areas."

The memorandum concluded—indeed, recommended—that "mass evacuation" from the Plain of Jars area was not a sound idea. Nonetheless, as so often before, a decision was made contrary to the recommendation, bringing with it much hunger, misery, disease, and death among the thousands of people involved.

For years our national leadership spoke solemnly of defending the right of self-determination for the peoples of Southeast Asia. This, Americans have been told, has been our principal objective in Vietnam, Laos, and Cambodia. Yet with each passing day of war, it became clearer that the kind of war we were waging really served to all but destroy the possibility of accomplishing this end in any meaningful way for the bulk of the people caught in the conflict. Because for the refugees and other war victims, a very significant cross section of the Indochinese people, "self-determination" is less a political aspiration than a simple human urge to return to their native villages in peace. This, a more fundamental kind of self-determination, was defeated by our officially sanctioned strategies and policies calling for, among other things, the forced relocation of people—an activity which has, over the years, produced masses of displaced and yet unsettled refugees.

WHAT CAN BE DONE TO END THE BLOODBATH

The record is clear on where the U.S. stands in Indochina. In 1971, as in earlier years, each day brought new violence. Each day escalated the human costs for all involved. There were more refugees. There were more casualties, both military and civilian. There were more prisoners of war and more missing in action. Our national leadership has used the specter of a highly dubious Viet Cong "bloodbath" to justify the continuance of the war. We must not allow this to blind us to the bloodbath going on every day in Vietnam and so much of Indochina. This bloodbath started long ago and our country has been part of it. And the bloodbath will continue as long as the war continues, and so long as efforts to end that war are avoided and delayed for whatever excuse.

Few will disagree that the North Vietnamese, the Viet Cong, the Pathet Lao, and others have also been contributing to the bloodbath. But the question for most Americans in 1971 was: How much longer would we tolerate policies by our government that make easy the killing and maiming and dislocation of millions?

The devastation the war has brought to the peoples of Indochina is painfully clear. Less

—the move would further aggravate already crowded refugee conditions and pose a major socioeconomic problem for which there is no immediate solution nor sufficient time to alleviate the personal deprivations of the refugees before they are properly resettled;

—in the case of the Communist indoctrinated Plain villagers, or in the case of the tribal peoples, if Vang Pao (Commander of irregular Lao forces supported by the U.S.) loses prestige and control, the dissension created by undesirable refugee conditions will soon reach a state *in extremis*. From an insurgency/security viewpoint, this can become a powder keg in areas under our control;

—the possibility of the fact that ethnic Lao of the Plain are of questionable loyalty would put them deep in "RLG territory" and would aid an insurgency effort being made on the Vientiane Plain;

—if there be loyal elements within the group they can serve as a source of friendly intelligence as well as tying up enemy resources needed to control them;

—if the refugees are moved a possible vacuum will be created that the enemy will populate . . . by default.

clear, however, is what we, as a nation, are going to do about it.

First and foremost, our country must help to end the violence, not simply "Vietnamize" it. Little progress will be made in rehabilitating the peoples of Indochina if war continues to tear at the very fabric of their society. The war must end—not just the most visible symbols of our participation in it.

Secondly, we must not permit the slogan of "Vietnamization" to submerge compassion and a sense of national responsibility towards helping substantially to ameliorate the truly massive social and humanitarian problems caused by the war. Our government's concern in this area has been meager all along. In fact, for Cambodia it has not existed. And in South Vietnam the limited concern built up over the years was being reduced in 1971. Not only were significant cuts being made in funds allocated to support South Vietnamese government programs for war victims but supplementary programs by private voluntary organizations were being phased out. At the same time, however, our national leadership was stating unequivocally that our government was allocating $1.5 billion for a new pacification program, which included absolutely no provision for social welfare and the rehabilitation of people.

Until priorities in U.S. policies and programs for Vietnam and all of Indochina are changed—until these priorities are reflected in the policies of the South Vietnamese government and the Cambodian and Laotian governments—until programs for people have the same concern and resolve as programs for security—little progress will be made towards rehabilitating the human debris of the Indochina war and repairing the fabric of a damaged society.

Thirdly, all channels of assistance to Indochina must be explored and, hopefully, utilized. The U.S. must not dominate the socioeconomic development of Indochina, even though we have an obligation and responsibility to participate in it heavily. Our government must do more to encourage and support international participation. Over the years a measure of such participation has occurred. And it is gratifying to note that in recent months, especially, concern and offers to help have grown—on the part of private agencies, international organizations, and individual governments.

Today the highest priority should be given to involving the United Nations (UN) in the relief effort of the entire area, including North Vietnam. I have long believed that the UN secre-

JOHN ROBATON FROM CAMERA 5

"How much longer would we tolerate policies by our government that make easy the killing and maiming and dislocation of millions?"

tary-general should be requested to convene as soon as possible an international conference on Indochina relief. The immediate and long-term needs of the people in Indochina can never be met through existing relief mechanisms or by the political authorities that finally assume effective control in the countries involved. Such a conference would lend fresh perspective on the possibilities of expanding emergency relief operations—especially in Cambodia—and on the approaches to the eventual task of social rehabilitation and reconstruction. Through the good offices of the secretary-general, the conference should make an effort to establish an international relief mechanism for Indochina. It should be the function of this body to receive and channel relief contributions, to appeal for the safe-conduct of mercy missions into difficult areas, to supervise and coordinate general relief operations, and to involve additional humanitarian and developmental agencies, including the Red Cross.

In this connection, a general comment should be made regarding the long-standing need for better international machinery for responding to human suffering as it occurs anywhere in the world. There is today no broadly based and continuing mechanism to render massive emergency assistance to populations ravaged by conflict and oppression or natural disaster. Although a large number of international public and private organizations—including those within the UN—exist for this purpose, the fact remains that these organizations are too often limited in what they can do, by their individual mandate, tradition, political or regional association, and small resources.

In light of distressing developments involving humanitarian aid to victims of the conflicts in Vietnam, Nigeria, and East Pakistan, new initiatives must be taken within the UN to establish a UN Emergency Service, supported, perhaps, by a declaration on humanitarian assistance to the civilian population in armed conflicts and other disasters.

To establish a UN Emergency Service is a logical extension of UN activities in humanitarian questions—and, we hope, it would also be a means to blunt and overcome some norms of international conduct, bureaucratic inertia, and diplomatic complexities now reflected in the erratic and timid international response to massive human suffering in so many troubled areas. The distressing experiences in Indochina and elsewhere should compel all men of good will to do all they can to enlist the support of their governments in helping to accomplish this objective.

Fourthly, we must learn from our experience in Indochina a lesson regarding the use and deployment of our military power. The time is long overdue for our nation, at the highest levels of government, to take stock of policies and attitudes that have contributed so heavily to the massive flow of refugees, the occurrence of civilian casualties, and the inexcusably low priority attached to the care and protection of civilians in combat zones. The record of hearings and inquiry of the subcommittee on refugees has confirmed time and again that the forced relocation of civilians, aerial bombardment, free fire zones, and similar practices have had a devastating impact on the civilian populations of Vietnam, Laos, and Cambodia. There has been a vast gap between our government's official policy of concern for the welfare of civilians and the performance of our forces in the field. Events at My Lai come immediately to mind. Our nation must finally come to grips with this issue. We must finally come to recognize and understand the flagrant abuses of American power. And we must resolve that what has been done in Indochina, in America's name, must never happen again.

I have believed for some time that the president should create a permanent Military Practices Review Board to advise the Joint Chiefs of Staff on standards and procedures designed to keep U.S. military policies and practices within the bounds of simple humanitarian and international legal obligations, and to monitor the implementing of the rules of engagement governing U.S. armed forces in active combat.

America's policies and actions in Indochina have too often made moral and humanitarian principles expendable. I, for one, believe that these principles—however elusive they may be—still matter. In the long run, the practice of such principles shapes international esteem and goodwill, and they represent those important foreign policy variables that diplomats may try to but cannot really ignore in the councils of government.

CONCLUSION

America is great and powerful. And as the recent history of Indochina illustrates so well, we freely use our influence and power in many ways and for many ends. But the power to heal, to salvage, and to rehabilitate the hapless victims of conflict—and the responsibility to minimize our contribution to the inevitable human toll of war—has never been exercised in a measure commensurate with the other uses of our power in Vietnam, Laos, or Cambodia.

We are conditioned, in the world we have created, to accept much suffering and injustice—especially in our time when violent conflict and oppression are active in so many areas. But the newer world we seek will not evolve if we ignore these challenges to leadership and take comfortable refuge in the mundane patterns and attitudes of the past.

There is much to be done for the war victims in Indochina. And there is much more our country must do to help.

GULP!! NEVAH AGIN!

The FUNNIES
Are Relevant
BY WALT KELLY

With Superman battling the polluters and Archie and Veronica out picketing, comics have seemingly taken on a new "social awareness" in the 1970's. To place these recent developments in perspective, Walt Kelly, creator of "Pogo" and one of America's best-known cartoonists, takes a personal look at the history of comics in the United States—from Rube Goldberg and his cartoons mocking the national passion for industrial gadgetry to the avant-garde Robert Crumb, whose "Fritz, the Cat" exhibits a dark fantasy of introspective sex, politics, and "now" philosophy.

The comic artist has always been a compulsive, irrepressible, and sometimes irresponsible commentator. From the beginning, such brashness has very often put the cartoonist squarely into trouble.

George Perry and Alan Aldridge, in their study, 'The Penguin Book of Comics', display a print of an Egyptian papyrus comic strip about 3,000 years old. They surmise that the intent of the work was "perhaps to ridicule the Egyptian convention of showing gods as animals by showing animals as men." The artist's work is charming, but his fate, if he was caught, can be guessed at when it is remembered that the subject was sacrilegious. Less than lovely rewards often have been the only largesse reaped by the comic artist.

William Hogarth of England, in the 18th century, was one of the first to comment with comic illustrations in anything like the modern sense. His broadsides were published as sheets and sold individually. In a later period Thomas Rowlandson, another Englishman, indulged in the same sort of comic commentary. He was among the first to use "balloons" of speech in his compositions.

Other artists in England and the United States carried on this tradition of self-expression, oftentimes voicing social and political criticism of the societies of which they were part. Most, until the latter part of the 19th century, made only modest money from their efforts. None of these comic artists had more than one editor; each artist was his own source of ideas. When the brickbats came from an outraged individual or the public in general, the artist got his lumps as in ancient times. Hogarth's work, for example, was so pirated (copyright laws being then little known), and the bile of his critics so pronounced, that he died an embittered man.

The Early Years of Cartooning in the U. S.

In the United States some of the first comic features appeared in the early 1890's but continuity cartoons really became popular in the early part of the 20th century. The two most admired U.S. cartoon artists around this period were Rube Goldberg and Harry (Bud) Fisher. Prior to 1907, comics in newspapers were more or less a Sunday feature. Fisher really started the public craze for the daily comic strip with his "A. Mutt," a racing-type strip later renamed "Mutt and Jeff" in which he caricatured vulgar race-track bamboozlers. Rube started as a sports cartoonist but added enough of the sidelight material at sports events in his work to start a dozen separate comic art features. He became best known for his cartoons mocking the national passion for giant industrial gadgetry. Both Fisher and Goldberg were absolutely individualistic in their approach and drew what interested them. They were able to do so because each worked for just one publisher. Their public popularity was great enough to allow them to demand and get large sums of money for their work from publishers. They managed to do equally well when they joined the syndicates and became "syndicated."

The term "syndicate" is actually a misnomer. Syndicates originated before the turn of the century when groups of newspapers banded together to share copy and sometimes newspaper art. These groups of newspapers could properly be called "syndicates." Since the mailing and distribution duties of such syndicates were onerous, they were eventually passed on to outside agencies that retained the name of "syndicate."

Syndicates performed a useful function. Not all papers could afford high-priced, special writers and artists. The syndicates provided for a sharing of the cost, which kept the individual newspaper prices down. That is still an essential function of the syndicate people. At the same time, however, syndicates induced a period of puritan hibernation in the cartooning field. Because of the commercial demands of the system, the artist's emphasis was shifted from self-expression to staying in business.

This became particularly apparent in the early 1920's when the syndicates decided to take a hand in developing comic strips by deciding what the public wanted and using that information to direct the work of comic artists. The syndicates took on a formidable task—weighing the phobias and tastes of dozens upon dozens of editors and publishers and the reading desires of millions of newspaper subscribers in order to develop comic strips that sold and stayed sold. As is usual when men judge other men, the estimates of the intellectual strength of the reader were medium low. As time went on, the editors' and the readers' whims and strictures were guessed at, analyzed, and appealed to. Over the years, by trial and prayer, the syndicates all arrived at one bedrock conclusion: the comic features should be "safe," that is, acceptable to all walks of life. The cartoonists should stay within prescribed bounds, and no controversial subjects such as religion or politics should be discussed. To further ensure their investment, the syndicates began the practice of hiring versatile artists of less than creative powers to fill in for the original artist when necessary. Thus if anything untoward happened to the original cartoonist, such as a case of malingering, loudmouthing, steady drunkenness, or death, the continuity of the strip was not interrupted, and money for the syndicates continued to flow in.

Thus during the 1920's and 1930's comics in general reflected the American willingness to enjoy complacency, to accept handout emotions through radio, movies, and magazines, and to respect the spitball wisdom of any number of public commentators. The funny-paper air was filled with young, wedded couples, innocent and sweet, with children, somewhat innocent and somewhat sweet; cute puppy dogs, kittens, and rabbits, all in red or blue pants; stern and more or less handsome defenders of law and order; goofy old fathers with lovely daughters; and raffish, far-flung adventurers. A great number of these characters were born in committee and presumably reflected sure judgments of what the public was dying to see. Many were the conceptions of Captain Joe Patterson of the *New York Daily News*.

The Early Renegades: Herriman, Sterrett, Tuthill, Smith, and Crosby

In spite of this success formula of safety, which admittedly made money for the syndicates, artists were inclined to be strongly individualistic. One such cartoonist was George Herriman, who in his cartoon strip, "Krazy Kat," portrayed the irony of life and of love. Krazy Kat was of indeterminate sex to many, but at least one dog in another comic strip once said, "I thought all cats were girls." Krazy was infatuated with Ignatz, a mouse described by Perry and Aldridge as "the cynic, the anarchist, the scoffer—he was totally defeated by the Kat's

love—an all-conquering force that could be deterred by nothing and no one."

The Mouse, who apparently was married and the father of a number of tiny sprats, was male enough. He threw bricks at the Kat, usually hitting him or her on the brain. For this he was usually thrown in the "calabozo" by Offissa Pup, who, in turn, was in love with Krazy. This cast of characters formed a basis for a mélange of puns, strange language, and inside-out thinking. As to the Kat's actual gender, it was all cleared up by a Hearst editor one time when he remarked, "Krazy Kat? I always thought of him as a female."

Other lights glimmered briefly between 1918 and 1935. Women were being emancipated, but editors were incensed if the cartoonist helped uncover her. Cliff Sterrett, a master compositor of graphic black and white frames, lampooned women's fashions, prohibition, and the American search for a health elixir in his cartoon strip, "Polly and Her Pals." He once remarked that editors were hard on him, even after World War I, when they received letters condemning Sterrett's use of the fashions of the day. Steven Becker, in his book 'Comic Art in America', quotes him as saying, ". . . all I did was show a girl's ankle . . . ," but Cliff's concept of an ankle extended very often to mid-thigh.

In 1918 one very real hero, Harry Tuthill of St. Louis, Mo., created an image, not too caricatured, of the U.S. male, a woman-beset and beleaguered head of household named George Bungle. His strip was full of rantings and fury. By the mid-1920's, Bungle's constant frustration at female relatives, female neighbors, and female strangers cast intimations of James Thurber. Tuthill was an iconoclast who defied the committee approach to acceptability. His dour, almost bitter humor and occasionally scathing satire on domestic life became so popular that by 1934 "George Bungle" was an anti-household word. Tuthill's true nature, his skep-

ticism and his inclination to overt indignation, led him in 1939 to part with his syndicate in a fury, throw his strip overboard, and retire to a spot called Ferguson, Mo., where he lived out his life, angry but quiet. Bungle was not seen again.

Sparkings of comment came from a smattering of other strips. Sidney Smith used his strip, "The Gumps," to make occasional dissections of the bumptious qualities of the politician and, especially, the candidate. His lead male, Andy Gump, a chinless loudmouth, was another caricature of the great American husband. But Andy's "Oh, Min," a call for help directed to his wife, fell into what might be called "The Saturday Evening Post" theory of humor, i.e., "Man is ineffectual and needs Woman's help." This is a safe idea, readily acceptable to most wives and endured sheepishly by most husbands. It is a motivating force behind much funny business in all fields of entertainment. The concept can accurately be described as committee humor.

Through the 1920's and 1930's, Percy Crosby, an exquisitely fine draftsman, drew one of the finest of kids' strips ever—"Skippy." The hero of the strip was a knowledgeable, slightly larcenous child through whom Crosby was able to relate his thoughts on the times, men's minds, and other down-to-earth comment. It was tolerated because it featured kids and was thus presumed cute. The strip skirted the edges of iconoclasm, but Crosby retained his most burning remarks for books and pamphlets.

"Little Orphan Annie"

By the mid-1930's Harold Gray had established a platform for right-wing views in his strip, "Little Orphan Annie," through Annie and her in-and-out benefactor, Daddy Warbucks. Gray's view in general was that only the righteous should be strong and win. Troubles with unworthies were very often solved by wiping out the unworthies. Muscles and guns ran hand-in-hand with wealth, to the evident satisfaction of

In the comic strip "Krazy Kat," by George Herriman, the cat and Ignatz the mouse are engaged in a running conflict.

PAW WASN'T **FOOLIN'**, FOLKS. THE LITTLE LIAR'S BEEN **TELLIN'** THE **TRUTH!**

Gray and the syndicate people, and they found millions of hard-nosed readers to support the strip's views.

Despite sporadic cancellations by newspapers, Gray's work was usually taken back to the fold. After all, Annie was an orphan and had a dog named Sandy. In one episode the dog was lost for a spell, and some evidence of Gray's kind of readership came, when, in the mass of letters imploring that Sandy be restored, there was one strongly worded demand for the dog's safe return—a telegram from U.S. industrialist Henry Ford.

Milt Caniff

In the early days of the Depression Captain Joe Patterson dreamed up a "safe" comic strip of adventure that involved a youth—an American—and his elder soldier-of-fortune companion operating on the mainland shores of China. Such a setting amid the exotic breezes of Oriental fantasy and derring-do, it was reasoned, would take the mind of the public off the besetting desperations of the day. A young man who was drawing something quite different for the Associated Press was chosen to be the comic strip's originator and artist. His name was Milton Caniff.

Caniff hailed from Ohio, which in those days was a hotbed of Norman Rockwellism. Ohioans firmly believed in the church and the Boy Scouts and got their sense of the exotic from readings of H. Rider Haggard, Sax Rohmer, and the *National Geographic Magazine*. It was largely for readers of a similar background that the first "Terry and the Pirates" strips were produced quite successfully.

Then the make-believe action of the strip began to reflect actual world events. The Japanese began making menacing noises in the direction of China that culminated in the invasion of the mainland in 1937. Cartoonist Caniff found

himself, through his characters, in a fight and eventually in a war against Japan. Although the U.S. was officially neutral at this time, Caniff was decidedly not. From this point on, through World War II, Milt's work showed him to be thoroughly and honestly respectful of the factories, the dogged courage, the idiosyncracies, and the spirit of America. During the war there was all applause, but after, serious thinkers decided that some of the stuff was corny. In the late 1940's some people even felt that Caniff was fronting for the China Lobby. Others said no, he was a propagandist for the U.S. Air Force.

Milt's straight, middle-of-the-road thought produced not one but two of the most successful strips in history. The second was "Steve Canyon," which had the same mixture of sophisticated dialogue, action, and beautiful girls as "Terry and the Pirates." This strip, unlike "Terry," however, belonged to Milt himself. Although Caniff had not been too rigidly hampered by editorial supervision in producing the earlier, controlled strip, he wanted the freedom to express himself as he saw fit. With "Steve Canyon," Milt was able to continue a philosophical train on occasion without having some supervising personality suggest that it was time to leave the brain behind and use the muscles.

Al Capp

One of the most famous, admired, notorious, and reviled U.S. cartoonists is Al Capp. He is also one of the best paid. Like Rube Goldberg, he has an abhorrence of idiocy in all forms, of everyday damfools, and of determined ignorance.

Almost from Capp's start in 1934, syndicate people have been alarmed by his barbarous caricatures of politicians and other blimps. His strip, "Li'l Abner," began innocently enough, featuring a mere bumpkin and his beautiful sweetheart, but, after a short time, Capp came on strong, savaging dance crazes, business tycoons, politicos, and other entertainers, popular songs, and the zoot suit. Mostly, he has been against heroes and those who consider themselves heroes. His own hero is not a hero, nor an antihero, but a kind of nonhero.

Editors ask with regularity that this tyrannosaurus rex of cartooning be curbed. The syndicate people just shrug and sigh. "What can we do?" they say, "He's a genius." It might be added, with no disrespect to Al's standing, that any cartoonist whose work sells to more than 300 newspapers is considered the office genius.

One instance of Capp's ability to create a national uproar took place over 20 years ago when Capp produced a gourd-shaped animal called the Schmoo. It was a small creature that was good to eat and was happy to be eaten. It multiplied so fast there was never a scarcity. It also laid eggs and bottles of milk—all marked Grade A. Outraged by the implications of such a creature's productivity, congressmen and other intellectuals embarked on a Schmoo probe, concluding that the Schmoo meant the economy of plenty and was anticapital and antilabor, for it meant the abolition of both.

Liberals came to think of Capp as one of their own, largely because he tilted at many of the same monsters they detested. Thus they were stunned when, in the mid-1960's, Capp turned his scorn on the young new left. Much as he had earlier lampooned the zoot suiter, he now raged against the mod dress of the youthful rebel. He was against the guitars and general habits of the group and violently wrathful about their mores. He lampooned a popular young girl singer, labeling her a phony. His new tirade won him a few more enemies and threw the dust of doubt in the eyes of those who had not previously noticed that Al had never been a member of a party.

Crockett Johnson's "Barnaby"

It was after World War II that more or less outspokenly antiestablishment, yet commercially oriented, strips came into a kind of vogue. "Barnaby," by Crockett Johnson, was an outstanding example. Johnson perpetrated a kind of magic in his strip that railed in the main

Cliff Sterrett's character Polly (right) was a sultry, fashionable woman of the 1920's. Her adventures were often fast paced in the strip "Polly and Her Pals" (facing page).

© KING FEATURES SYNDICATE, INC.

Marital conflict is an enduring theme in comic strips. Andy and Min Gump (above) carry on an involved argument in Sidney Smith's "The Gumps." Other popular husband-and-wife protagonists were Maggie (right) and Jiggs (facing page) from the strip "Bringing Up Father," by George McManus.

against the belief of most parents that the imaginations of most children should not be taken seriously. "Barnaby" was started in 1942 in the left-wing newspaper *PM* in New York City and was geared to the limited audience of the sophisticated East Coast. Unfortunately though, Johnson grew tired of the work and turned the strip over to a committee: an artist, a writer, and an editor. Though the strip lasted another few years, the original spark was gone.

PM, being the kind of paper it was—iconoclastic and desirous of not aping the established press—put no editorial pressure on Crockett Johnson's writing or drawing. He was completely on his own. This attitude began to emerge more and more often in the big syndicate offices.

"Pogo"

At about the same time that "Barnaby" began appearing Pogo entered the scene [drawn by the author]. After five years of guess and grab in comic books, the strip was accepted as a daily feature by the *New York Star,* the immediate successor to the by then defunct *PM.* The original approach was to tell American-oriented fairy stories using animals that were indigenous to the Okefenokee Swamp in Georgia, but eventually social and political interests crept in. The *Star*'s liberal attitude allowed that freedom. After the *Star* folded, Robert M. Hall, head of the New York Post Syndicate, decided to syndicate the strip, having the refreshing attitude of disregarding the political commentary and deciding that the strip was funny enough on its own. No suggestions nor editorial chastisements ever came from management, despite the occasional outraged cries from wounded editors and publishers across the land. Hall's position—allowing the artist complete artistic autonomy—represented a major breakthrough in spirit on the part of syndicate editors and owners.

"Pogo" ran into many difficulties through its career. In the time of Joe McCarthyism in the early 1950's there came warnings, always from outside the syndicate, that the strip was "skating on thin ice" with its political commentary. A caricature of Senator McCarthy as a cat called Simple J. Malarkey caused some to announce that the author had finally fallen through. A hasty assessment.

So Pogo has continued to enter unabashed into political controversy. When Virginia and other Southern states were closing public schools in order to stave off the U.S. Supreme Court's order to integrate, Pogo offered speakeasy

schools in caves and education delivered in an unmarked plain brown paper sack, despite indignant cries of protest from the South. When a pig appeared in Pogo who resembled the then premier, Nikita Khrushchev, the Soviet Union officially called on the Japanese newspaper the *Asahi Evening News* to drop the strip. In recent years readers have been exposed to a Western steer who bore a strong resemblance to the then U.S. president, Lyndon B. Johnson, and, currently, a hyena-type character speaking in alliteration who has been taken by some readers to be our esteemed vice-president, Spiro T. Agnew.

Pogo makes fun of whatever is at hand. The guiding principle is that there is little use in trying to display a public buffoon by means of a generality. In the cartoon strip as in the editorial cartoon field, the people being lampooned must be recognizable and completely identifiable or the point is not made. There is no reason to disguise the great nuggets of delightful comic material drawn from public leadership in church, state, education, or pool hall. It is through such comic depiction that we recognize the foibles and frailties of our lives. As Pogo once said, "We have met the enemy and he is us."

"Peanuts"

Very shortly after the Pogo strip first appeared as a nationally syndicated feature in May 1949, United Feature Syndicate uncorked the pent-up wisdom and magic of Charles "Sparky"

"Little Orphan Annie" (right) and her trusty dog Sandy have been reader favorites for years. In the 1920's another popular strip starring a child was "Skippy" (below), by Percy Crosby. In contrast to the mellow aura of childhood, "Terry and the Pirates" (facing page) evokes a sense of danger and excitement.

RIGHT: © CHICAGO TRIBUNE-NEW YORK NEWS SYNDICATE, INC. BELOW: © KING FEATURES SYNDICATE. FACING PAGE: © CHICAGO TRIBUNE-NEW YORK NEWS SYNDICATE, INC.

Schulz with a quiet blockbuster of a strip—"Peanuts." Through quiet understatement Charles Schulz has the children who are the characters of his strip delve into the painfully hilarious secret mind of most adults.

The strip did not start out like this. Originally, United Feature Syndicate took it on because it was simple, funny, about kids, and its physical layout was shallow in depth, which was desirable for subscribing newspapers that needed to conserve space. Even then Schulz's gags had a unique originality. One of the earliest has Charlie Brown declaring himself the winner of a boxing match because his opponent has not come out of his corner. The last panel reveals that Charlie Brown's opponent is a baby, unable to walk. That kind of innocence was what the syndicate bought. What finally evolved and continues to develop in Schulz's strip is a world of children with all the ego, eccentricity, and brash whim of the adult world. Charlie Brown cannot get a kite into the air, but for years he has continued to try despite criticism, advice, adverse weather, or the perversity of inanimate objects.

He plays baseball in what is evidently a perpetual rainforest and continues to pitch from a rain-shrouded mound until it clears enough for him to realize that everybody else has gone home. From these sequences and many others come Schulz's comments on man himself.

The syndicate did not hold Schulz to the original simple surface humor of 1951. The world has grown since then, and the ability of the public—including syndicate minds—to comprehend the gentle and the subtle has grown with it.

One last point on "Peanuts." Schulz is constantly being interpreted by many who would like to get into a successful act. Shading and subtle intimations of the Christian gospel have been read into his work. If they are there, they are writ by no bold finger and are not a blatant or overt message.

Jules Feiffer

Another instance of the passing of syndicate control over the artist is found in the work of the brilliant Jules Feiffer. Feiffer's cartoon technique is a series of caricature portraits with dialogue; the speech is lettered in loosely beside the character's face without resort to balloons.

Feiffer has produced some of the most introverted mod thought in print, delving into politics, the troubles of the up-to-date young, man's insignificance to himself, war, peace, parties, booze. Most of this stems from a Greenwich Village background, and the feature was, for a long time, a vital part of *The Village Voice,* an early "liberated" journal. The Hall Syndicate experimented with this far-out treatment of life

by Feiffer and, despite its unusual format and style, it picked up a number of newspaper subscribers. Feiffer's work appears infrequently now since he has turned to other pursuits, among them, playwriting ('Little Murders') and movie scriptwriting ('Carnal Knowledge').

Comic Books

One interesting development in the field of comic satire was the advent, in the early 1950's, of *Mad* magazine, a monument of parody engendered by Harvey Kurtzman. Through such avid and able artists as Jack Davis, Mort Drucker, George Woodbridge, and Al Jaffer—to name just a few—the periodical has lampooned the mighty, the lowly, and the merely high. *Mad* deals with the current frivolities that pass as the events of the day. Although it is not a "straight" comic magazine, it has opened the way for some of the "real" comic books to venture timidly into commentary of a type.

In general, the history of comic books in this area has been a negative one. Comic books as such sprang to a stumbling life in the early 1930's. At first there was some attempt to have them live up to their name, but by the 1940's, this sally toward fun had fallen to the level of committee humor and adventure continuities. Action continuities were the easiest to hack out: Good guy meets bad guy and BOFF! Gore and violence eventually became flamboyant. In the 1950's the books came under sustained attack by the "nice people"—educators; Parent-Teacher Associations; social workers; and indignant parents—to clean up or shut up. As a result of a U.S. Senate investigation into the question of whether comic books were corrupting the young, the comic industry adopted a "Comics Code," which pressured national distributors not to sell those books not carrying the seal of approval. The result, if anything, was that the books became less original and more dull.

In recent years, perhaps because of the seminal influence of *Mad,* some of the comic books have, in a bumbling fashion, turned to "good works" as a means of fostering excitement. Lately the superheroes have been fighting for ecology and the domestic comedy continuities have involved themselves in the social problems of the city. But none of these "good works" stories read as if they were ground out in a white fury by a cartoonist aghast at his surroundings. They look like the work of a committee. A writer or editor apparently has seen the public mood and decided that, for example, the threat to the environment is the thing for their superheroes to battle. But the superheroes solve problems of trash pollution with their muscles; vandals and other miscreants are pursued, captured, and thwarted with the same old violence. Unctuous messages in side panels of lettering make sure the "do-good" idea is driven home. And the domestic comedy routines read like poor imitations of old Lucille Ball situation television shows, where through haphazard chance, the good intention to clean up the backyard is finally realized. None of these comic books demonstrate the vibrance or vitality of the angry efforts of an individual cartoonist.

This is an unfortunate state of affairs because the comic books have nobody to answer to. They exist practically without advertising, thus they are not subject to censorship by advertising clients. The comic books are perfectly free to comment boldly, loudly, discerningly, and cleverly, but the committee mind blocks such action. The artists are told by three or four people what is expected of them.

Underground Comics

Totally unlike the above product are the undergound comics, which exploded into garish and somewhat ghastly life in the late 1960's. These have been described in the introduction to an article by Jacob Brackman in *Playboy* of December 1970 as being "obscene, anarchistic, sophomoric, subversive, apocalyptic . . . [they] attack all that middle america [sic] holds dear."

Despite that analysis, the undergrounds are popular with the young. They are not distributed through normal channels, that is on the newsstand, but in special "head" shops, many of which stock antiestablishment periodicals. Such head shops and their wares are closely in touch with the long hair, the beard, the guitar of youth.

The drawings and continuities in these books are often—not always—cluttered, disorganized, and purposely ugly. The term used to describe them, "comix," indicates part of their purpose: to co-mix. As Brackman puts it, "A reference

The author's "Pogo" (above) and Al Capp's "Li'l Abner" (facing page) are two of
the most popular and successful strips in the history of comics.   A full
cast of Pogo's animal friends are displayed, including several based on well-known
political figures.

point, an attitudinal acid test, comix are precisely the kind of medium over which young people come together, discover one another."

Ugliness in this case is a plain sign of how
large numbers of youths view the world around
them: not alone the tin cans and slop in the
streams but also the attitudes of public figures,
parents, and educators. As a young man in a
recent cartoon said to his agitated father,
"What's all this about the Secret Pentagon Papers? That's what I've been telling you all
along."

In these illustrated stories pot is the smoke,
hypodermics are more common than bicycles,
fornication abounds, and there is much tendency toward bloodletting. The language ranges
up to and including four-letter words. Pornog-
raphy aside, the undergrounds are the real thing
of protest. Angry, strident, bold, cruel, sadistic,
masochistic, vengeful, and sophomoric, as
Brackman says, but also real, unrelenting, and
rebellious.

The comix movement flowered largely
through the work of Robert Crumb, who is under 30 and somewhat of a genius in the field of
self-expression. Crumb's work is a dark fantasy
of introspective sex and a running satirical and
sarcastic comment on profits, politics, and frilled
philosophy.

Crumb has created three outstanding characters. Two of the three are actually one; that is,
the pair constitute a man talking to himself.
One of these two is a bushy bearded old-timer
in a nightgown, the caricature of an ancient god
or an old Hebrew sage. The other is an ordinary
appearing young man who resembles a listless
shoe clerk. The first, Mr. Natural, is a no-non-
sense pragmatist who knows all the ways and
words of the world. The other, Flakey Foont,
is apparently sane, though not completely
square. His knowledge of the world is what he's
last heard on the radio. Mr. Natural considers
the universe insane and is afraid Foont is on
his way to joining it. Flakey's mind worries
about two things—the first one, sex; the other,
Mr. Natural's taking ways with the food in
Foont's refrigerator. The continuity is an enjoy-
able, exasperating, and upside-down dialogue of

The sophistication of Jules Feiffer's strip (below) is in marked contrast to the plain-folks appeal of Charles Schulz's "Peanuts" (above). R. Crumb produces some of the most well-known underground "comix" characters (facing page).

the common man within himself, his dogmatic ego in constant clash with his fears.

Fritz, the Cat, is R. Crumb's frontline creation. The artist describes him as "a sophisticated, up-to-the-minute young feline college student who lives in a modern 'supercity' of millions of animals . . . yes, not unlike people in their manners and morals." Fritz is, like Percy Crosby's Skippy, larcenous and charming, but there the resemblance ends. Fritz's ways with girls are numerous. When Crumb undresses these nubile female animals, their bodies are chubby, cute, and human, not very often voluptuous. Crumb does have the ability to use restraint. His depictions of a sex orgy do remain funny.

It should be pointed out that for all Fritz's endearing qualities and Robert Crumb's description of his hero as an ordinary, up-to-date student, this Cat is not for the kiddies. Steve Krantz, who is currently producing a film featuring Fritz, has announced that "it will probably be the first animated cartoon to be rated X."

It is the feeling of freedom and the knowledge that most obscenity laws are mushy, and thus vulnerable to legal attack, that enables many printer-distributors and originators of comix to operate with what they consider impunity (although head shops have been known to be busted by the police). Most cartoonists feel that the only valid censorship occurs when nobody will buy their product.

Mention should be made of another comix cartoonist, a man who signs himself Foolbert Sturgeon. He has taken the heady step of lampooning Jesus Christ. His interpretation is probably an apoplectic experience for most people calling themselves Christians, for his Christ relies on mystic magic in a funny inversion of Christ's reputation. As a comic structure the work does have one fault; it is a "one joke" continuity. Once Sturgeon's Jesus is shown to have human frailties, the mysticism definitely wears thin.

Conclusion

Ominous as these signals from the young may seem to those of us grown old in the salutary exercise of saluting, it should be remembered that the artist or cartoonist is hardly ever more than a reporter. He is not more of a clairvoyant than any other similarly informed and aware observer. He may be relieving current tensions, fulfilling daydreams, or in the phrase of a few days ago, telling it like it is. He does all this with exaggeration, the method of attack used by all cartoonists.

Like that ancient Egyptian cartoonist who ridiculed the sacred cows of his time, these new cartoonists are simply expressing their attitudes on the events and ideas of the day. And as such, they are merely performing what has always been the natural role of comic artists.

Bibliography

Becker, Stephen. 'Comic Art in America'. New York: Simon and Schuster, 1959.

Brackman, Jacob. "The International Comix Conspiracy." *Playboy,* December 1970.

Craven, Thomas, ed. 'Cartoon Cavalcade'. New York: Simon and Schuster, 1943.

Murrell, William. 'A History of American Graphic Humor'. Published for the Whitney Museum of American Art, New York: Macmillan, 1938.

Perry, George, and Aldridge, Alan. 'The Penguin Book of Comics'. Harmondsworth, England: Penguin Books, Ltd., 1967.

Waugh, Coulton. 'The Comics'. New York: Macmillan, 1947.

A PROPOSAL FOR 'NATIONAL CITIES'

by John V. Lindsay

Environmental blight takes many forms in the city. Garbage piles up (left) in an urban renewal area; neighborhood services often deteriorate when renewal begins. Industrial wastes poison the nation's waters (facing page) while the industrial complexes add visual pollution to the landscape.

JOHN V. LINDSAY completed his sixth year as mayor of New York City in 1971. He served in the U.S. House of Representatives from 1959 to 1965.

It is time we rethought the role of the cities in the American governmental system. It is time, because our present federal system, which makes literally no provision for cities, threatens the very life of the urban nation we have become.

Today, the great urban centers have a national role. They are financial, commercial, and communication centers for whole regions or for the nation itself. They are, in fact, "national cities" and not only merit but require a more realistic political status if they are to survive.

HISTORICAL BACKGROUND

The failure of our present federal system to provide proper powers to cities did not result from any oversight on the part of the nation's early leaders. Quite the contrary, our first statesmen deliberately chose to discourage the creation of large urban centers. They regarded their society as materially, morally, and aesthetically superior to that of Europe and attributed much of this superiority to the fact that 95% of the U.S. population then lived in rural areas.

Thomas Jefferson wrote to James Madison in 1787: "Our governments will remain virtuous for centuries as long as they are chiefly agricultural. . . . When they get piled upon one another in large cities, as in Europe, they will become as corrupt as Europe."

That same year the Northwest Ordinance of 1787, one of our first declarations of national policy, encouraged westward migration and fulfilled the provision of an earlier federal ordinance providing free land for schools. New York City, however, could not establish a public school system until more than 50 years later— with no federal assistance at all.

Even though the authors of the Constitution hoped that the United States would remain rural and even though they omitted from their great document any reference to cities, we have become an urban nation. One can no longer think of America without thinking of its major cities. Our commerce and industry exist almost completely within cities like New York, and the current system of urban centers is more complex than anything imaginable in the 1700's.

Urban Growth

Starting with a population that was 95% rural, the nation has become almost 75% urban. A colonial country having six cities with popu-

lations of 8,000 or more has grown into an industrialized country with 26 central cities of more than 500,000 each—and each is the core of a larger metropolitan area. While all the U.S. urban centers once contained only 5% of the population, the 29 largest metropolitan areas in 1971 held more than one third of the people. From an overwhelmingly agricultural economy we have changed—despite the most productive agriculture in world history—to an economy that concentrates the bulk of its productive capacity in metropolitan areas, and half of it in the 29 largest.

Every major city reaches beyond the state that contains it, controlling vital services for whole sections of the nation. The Federal Reserve Banks are located in 12 major cities, and federal circuit Courts of Appeals in 11. Such cities are regional centers for the distribution of money, credit, and justice. Similarly, cities like Atlanta, Ga.; Denver, Colo.; and Boston, Mass., are regional hubs of transportation, communications, and commerce. They perform economic and social functions for a much broader geographic area than the states in which they are located. It is no longer reasonable to say that cities like Chicago, Ill.; Baltimore, Md.; and Philadelphia, Pa.—whose budgets are each larger than those of 15 of the 50 states—must

still be treated as inferiors by their state governments.

The Concentration of Social Problems

Moreover, the major cities carry the nation's heaviest burden because they contain and must deal with most of America's social problems. During the past century the Industrial Revolution has concentrated job opportunities in the central cities attracting the people most desperately in need of work—but most unlikely to find it. The poor, the unskilled, the immigrants, and the victims of discrimination came to the cities because that was where the most jobs were. Many of them came because mechanization and agricultural controls wiped out farm employment.

The most recent arrivals often lacked the skills needed in cities or were barred from jobs by discrimination. They and their families often fell into a cycle of unemployment and welfare that now threatens to create a permanent underclass in the cities.

By the late 1960's the Industrial Revolution had created in our cities the kinds of problems that the Constitution's authors had hoped to avoid when they reserved to the states all powers not specifically designated as federal. Still the law said that these great cities existed solely at

Choked with automobile traffic and poisonous fumes, Madison Avenue (facing page) in New York City looks more like a messy parking lot than the prestigious thoroughfare it is thought to be. Many city dwellers, conscious of the dangers of pollution and of the problems of traffic congestion, are riding bicycles to work or to school; however, they find that the experience can be dangerous (right) and disappointing.

the mercy of those states and that they had no right to national power or authority.

Problems in City-State Relations

Denying cities a place in the federal system did not, of course, stop the growth of the cities. What it did accomplish was to give power over the cities to state legislatures dominated by rural interests and often unwilling to understand, much less deal with, the complex problems common to every city.

The states hold the power to tax, to borrow, to lend, to impose fees, to negotiate with neighboring jurisdictions, to deal with the federal government, to set priorities, to regulate commerce and public service utilities, to establish civil service rules, even to manage municipal services. Most cities are not allowed to perform any of these essential functions without specific state legislative approval. Few have ever won an increase in local power without a battle against rural, and sometimes suburban, state representatives who are hostile to urban needs, goals, and residents and who are capable of using their leverage to block action or exact major concessions from urban legislators.

The absurdities of city-state relations are legion. In one major city all police policy—including hiring, promotion, and pay—is set by a commission named by the governor of the state. Another city must get state approval to shift the responsibility for sidewalk inspection from one city agency to another. Just recently the New York state legislature eliminated our city's careful system of rent controls while strengthening similar controls elsewhere in the state.

When at last the national government awoke to the problems in our cities, the weaknesses of the present federal system became painfully evident. Under the domestic thrust of the Administration of President Lyndon B. Johnson in the 1960's, approximately 180 federal programs were started, ranging from education to sewage treatment.

The new legislation encouraged greater state-city cooperation, metropolitan integration, and more cooperation between separate taxing authorities (for example, school districts) and local government. Federal financing of some of these programs was channeled through state governments, so that states often became involved in urban problems for the first time.

But for any number of reasons—the war in Vietnam and the accompanying cuts in domestic spending, racial tension, and urban racial disorders, as well as the tangle of federal, state, and local bureaucracies—the great federal initiative faltered by the end of the sixties.

At the same time the inflationary recession of 1969–71 imposed on the cities rising expenditures with little increase in revenue from their principal taxes. State and local governments depend upon a brisk growth in the national economy to meet their fiscal needs. When that growth ceased at the same time that unemployment and inflation increased the need for revenue, the cities were the prime victim. Faced with the same pressures as the cities, states cut back their budgets, and the first item to go was usually aid to localities.

WANTED: "NATIONAL CITIES"

Taken together, these events of the past decade have clearly shown the need for a new look at the cities' role in the federal system. I have proposed that the federal government charter a certain number of "national cities," granting them the power to act independently on critical issues of local concern and urban development.

National cities should have essential economic powers: to raise taxes, to set fees, and to issue bonds and notes. They should have the right to chart their own financial course.

Recreation in the crowded city can mean building and painting a colorful wall (facing page, left), or it can mean playing in the water from a fire hydrant (facing page, right) because there is no swimming pool available. Disturbed by the ugliness and harshness of ghetto life, actors and artists conducted a special summer street program (right) to introduce the arts to children in Staten Island, N.Y.

National cities should have the freedom to deal directly with the federal government and to cooperate on joint federal-city programs in such areas as manpower training, child care, education, and health. Under the present system, federal programs in these vital areas go through the state governments, so that city officials and Washington agencies have to deal through remote state bureaucrats.

National cities should have additional powers: the right to manage and direct urban services; the right to a voice, at least equal to the state's, in the regulation of local industry, collective bargaining, utility monopolies, and franchised public services; the right to decentralize certain functions to local neighborhoods; and the right to resist unjustified mandated state costs.

These are the rights and powers that cities must have if they are to deal decisively with the problems of urban America today. The national cities charter would constitute a direct grant of national home rule in those areas where state governments have failed to act.

National cities would create a new federal-city relationship alongside the present federal-state system. These national cities would still remain politically part of their states, but they would have a relationship with the national government consistent with their national burden.

There need be no set size for national cities, although the 26 urban centers with populations greater than 500,000 would seem logical choices for that designation. However, national functions and national responsibilities, not size, should make cities worthy of national status.

The pressure of these past few years has given many of us the sense that the futures of our cities are linked one to another. We have only recently discovered that Seattle and Baltimore, Atlanta and Phoenix, San Francisco and Chicago—all the big cities—have inherited a common national legacy. Despite state differences, despite a long history of regional competition for national resources, we have learned that the things that unite us in the cities are more important than the things that divide us. The mayors of America's major cities have thus mounted an unprecedented campaign to persuade the Congress and the public of the priority of urban needs.

The Case for Federal Innovation

There is sound precedent for a national charter for major cities. In the past the government has granted similar special status and corporate charters to other bodies from the Tennessee Valley Authority to the Federal Deposit Insurance Corp. to Amtrak.

Employment and housing are two problem areas for the cities.
The Model Cities program employs local residents (below) on its
construction projects, which are designed to create a new environment
in a designated area of the city. An unemployed man reads notices
of available jobs (facing page, bottom); there were dramatic job shortages
in most fields in 1971. Puerto Ricans in New York City use community
organizations (facing page, top left) to work for solutions of problems
like poor housing. The sign that says in Spanish, ''Power to the Poor'' and
''Viva the Squatters,'' (facing page, top right) is evidence of
community support for people who took matters into their own hands
and occupied suitable housing.

ARNOLD HINTON FROM NANCY PALMER AGENCY

JAN LUKAS FROM RAPHO GUILLUMETTE

ALLEN GREEN FROM NANCY PALMER AGENCY

WERNER WOLFF FROM BLACK STAR

Social problems are legion in the city. Confrontations between the police and members of minority groups are common (right), but many cities are making efforts to improve police-community relations. Many poor people, especially the elderly (facing page, left), are trapped in the ghetto and never see the world beyond their doorsteps. Young children (facing page, right) generally do not have the opportunity to enjoy the cultural resources of the city. They never get the chance to visit the zoo, play in parks, or go to the movies.

The creation of national cities with substantial powers might require a constitutional amendment, though careful legislation could accomplish the task. Most important, it demands a concentrated national focus on urban needs. The National Commission on the Causes and Prevention of Violence, chaired by Milton S. Eisenhower, called for an Urban Constitutional Convention to consider such questions. However, that suggestion went almost unnoticed, certainly unheeded.

The notion of national cities is hardly radical. In 1937 the National Resources Committee, headed by Secretary of the Interior, Harold L. Ickes, sent a brief for city home rule to President Franklin D. Roosevelt. The committee concluded:

In spite of this vital and growing significance as the principal instrument of public service and community control, the American city is still the legal creature of higher authorities, subject to their fiat for the most minor power and procedures, reaching out in one State to the legislature to perform the peddling of peanuts on a municipal pier. The city is in many ways the ward of a guardian who refuses to function.

The committee recommended the establishment of a direct relationship between the federal government and the major cities. But like so many other important, far-sighted reports, it was ignored—and only now, more than 30 years later, have we come to appreciate its wisdom.

The national cities proposal is susceptible to great improvement, refinement, and elaboration. In any case, a change of this scale is essential—and even that is no guarantee that our cities will be free or able to do what they must. The national functions and national burdens of the major U.S. cities also demand much greater national financial support. They must receive federal assistance for the unique burden of caring for so many of the country's poor, untrained, and uneducated.

Only a meaningful program of federal revenue sharing directly with cities and a national reform of our archaic welfare system will meet that national obligation. They are long overdue responses to national conditions of poverty, unemployment, discrimination, and migration that have so burdened the cities.

Of course, there has always been one "national city"—Washington, D.C.—directly run by the federal government. Unhappily the kind of support and leadership provided that city by

BELOW: GEORGE LOVE FROM RAPHO GUILLUMETTE.   RIGHT: BURT GLINN
FROM MAGNUM

successive Congresses has been as backward and antiurban as the support provided by any state legislature in the nation.   So the national cities idea by itself is no cure-all.   It will require a new national attitude and new national commitment to our great cities if it is to have real impact.

An Urgent Need for Change

For years America has poured billions of dollars into cities and villages and jungles in all parts of the world, under the guise of protecting our national security.   It is now time for us to admit that the greatest threat to American stability in the 1970's comes from within our own borders.   Continued neglect of the cities can only lead to more despair and bitterness and violence.   Today our national security urgently demands the same kind of multibillion-dollar commitment at home that we gave the great cities of Europe through the Marshall Plan after World War II.

The very survival of the nation depends upon a willingness to innovate and to act on the urban crisis.   We have only just emerged from almost two centuries of neglecting urban problems.   We must, as a nation, be willing to make changes in our most basic arrangements if we are to deal with the urban civilization we have created.

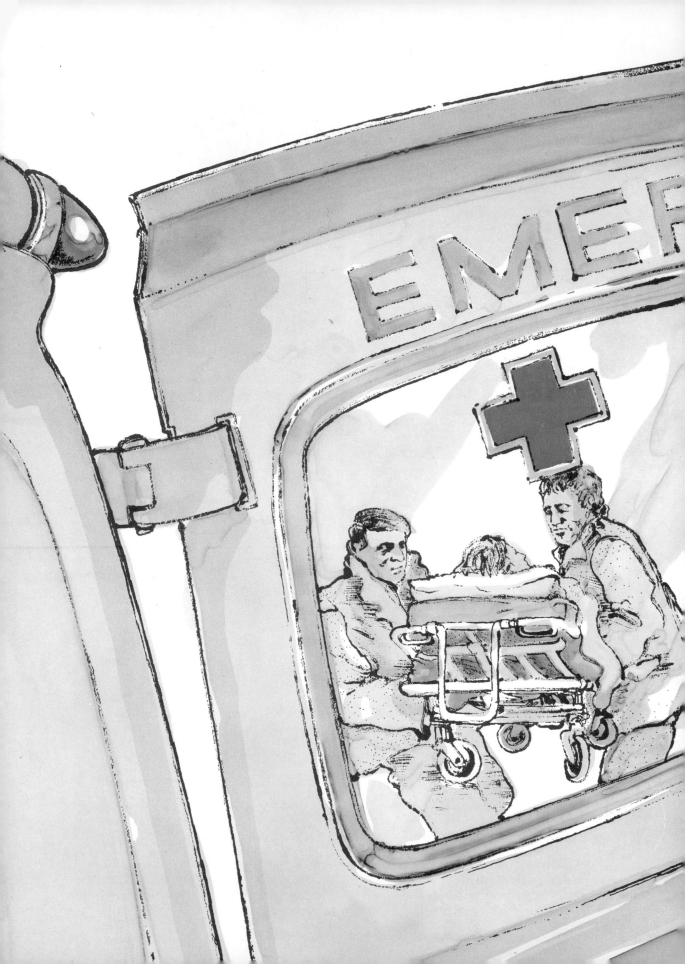

THE HEALTH CARE CRISIS

by Alex Gerber, M.D.

DR. GERBER is associate clinical professor of surgery at the University of Southern California School of Medicine. His book 'The Gerber Report: A Doctor's Diagnosis and Prescription' was published in 1971.

A century ago, British statesman Benjamin Disraeli declared, "The health of the people is really the foundation upon which all their happiness and all their powers as a state depend." The late Indian leader Mohandas K. Gandhi, in a similar vein, was even more succinct: "It is health which is real wealth." If we agree with these dicta, the United States is not the most powerful and richest country in the world as is commonly believed, for we are not the healthiest. True, we spend relatively more for health care than any other country. But the U.S., which ranks first in almost every field of human endeavor—from Nobel prizewinners to electric toothbrushes—lags seriously behind many nations in accepted World Health Organization indexes of health.

The domestic health picture is equally disquieting. Infants in rural and urban slums are dying three and four times as often as their more affluent neighbors; in some of the depressed counties of the South, the maternal mortality rate for blacks is six times higher than for whites; and on some Indian reservations the incidence of tuberculosis is seven times the national rate. The story is the same for malnutrition, narcotics addiction, and numerous other health problems. Indeed, the health level of many areas in the U.S. all too closely resembles that of the poverty-stricken, disease-ridden *barriadas* of Latin America.

Laymen and health authorities alike have been growing more concerned about this situation as well as about other aspects of health care in the U.S. And U.S. President Richard M. Nixon gave credence to their concern when he announced, during the early days of his Administration, that this country was on the verge of a "massive crisis" in health care. The president's gloomy message must have come as an icy shock to Americans who had been assured year after year that "we receive the best medical care in the world."

If there is a health care "crisis" in this country, surely it is not due to lack of progress in medical science and technology. The last few decades have seen the U.S. rise to a preeminent position in medical research and development. The resulting scientific and technological breakthroughs have appreciably enhanced the phy-

sician's ability to diagnose and treat disease. New procedures, new tools, and new drugs appear on the medical scene with breathtaking rapidity, so that it is now possible to alleviate suffering and save lives by means unheard of only a generation ago. We clearly have come a long way since the physician's entire therapeutic armamentarium could be carried in a little black bag, and Oliver Wendell Holmes could truthfully say that if all medicines, as now used, were cast into the sea, "it would be all the better for mankind and all the worse for the fishes."

But unfortunately, the fruits of these medical advances are not enjoyed by all segments of our population. The fabric of health care in the U.S. is of an uneven texture chiefly because of the inherent socioeconomic distortions of our society, but also because the distribution of our health care services is dependent upon a system that is undermanned and without adequate quality controls. At the same time, confidence in our health care system, now the second largest industry in the U.S., is being undermined by skyrocketing medical costs that threaten all but the higher income groups.

In its long and turbulent history, American medicine has been beset with many challenging problems, but never has it faced such widespread criticism as at present. The clamor for change is growing louder. The public is seeking an answer to the thorny question of inadequate health care, and the debate has spilled over to the halls of the U.S. Congress and the Oval Room at the White House. Every phase of medical education, organization, service, and financing is coming under close scrutiny.

Medical Education

The human body is a delicate and complicated mechanism that requires a well-organized health team for its maintenance. This team is made up of doctors, nurses, technicians, and a host of other allied health workers. The central role is played by the physician, because he is the one who is sought out by the sick and who usually must account for their well-being. In keeping with this responsibility, medicine demands of its followers a long and vigorous education.

The period of preparation for a career in medicine is longer than for any other profession. Prospective physicians usually spend four years in college, four years in medical school, and one year in hospital apprenticeships as interns. The great majority then continue their hospital training for an additional three to five years in order to become medical specialists. Upon passing a specialty board examination, the physician is certified as professionally competent and deemed ready to hang out his shingle.

Medical educational facilities have increased slowly over the past 40 years and, indeed, have hardly kept up with the population growth, much less the vastly increased demand for physicians. In the 1970–71 school year, there were 103 medical schools with a total enrollment of 40,377, and a graduating class of 8,996. These schools admitted 11,360 first-year students but turned away one fully qualified applicant for every one they accepted. The obvious lack of a sufficient number of medical schools in the U.S. is forcing many qualified candidates to either study abroad or give up the career of their choice. These options seem inimical to the aims of a democratic society—especially one that is as wealthy as the U.S.

Critics of medical education contend that the curriculum places too much emphasis on individual disease and not enough on social problems. Medical schools are currently under tremendous pressure to remedy this alleged shortcoming by steeping their students more fully in the social and behavioral sciences. Medical educators are constantly reminded that today's medical student is of a "new breed," far more socially aware and responsive to the ills of society than his counterpart of yesteryear. There are, of course, no objective statistics to substantiate this claim. But the call for sweeping away the "irrelevancies" of medical education is allowing fledgling medics to spend less time in the basic physical and biological sciences so that they may pursue elective courses in combating such admitted enemies of health as war, ignorance, and poverty.

Medical educators have even more immediate concerns. The high costs of medical education have placed many schools in a tight financial squeeze. During fiscal year 1970, no fewer than 60 medical schools applied for special federal funds because of economic distress; half of these were in such a precarious financial position that their continued operation was jeopardized (the financial burden has actually led to the closing of two dental schools in recent years despite the shortage of dentists).

Our investment in medical education has escalated from $10,000 per student 50 years ago to more than $120,000 today. Less than 10% of this amount, however, is covered by student tuition and fees. For many years, a major part of medical school income has been derived from governmental granting agencies for research

projects and training programs. The federal out-lay of research funds rose from $45 million in 1940 to $2.3 billion in 1967. The slowing of this exponential growth in the past few years and the shrinkage of federal subsidies have precipitated the dollar crisis now threatening many of the medical schools.

The only workable solution to these financial woes is more federal aid; medical schools have simply become so expensive to run that most of them no longer can depend upon private endow-ments. The federal government is sympathetic to the medical schools' plight and hopes to brighten their economic outlook by allocating funds under the Health Profession Education Act, a piece of legislation that will provide vari-ous medical educational facilities with approxi-mately $3 billion in the next three years in the form of construction and educational grants, stu-dent loans, and scholarships.

To make a real dent in the problem, however, the federal government must make a more sub-stantial monetary commitment. The stifling of career opportunity that results when qualified students are denied entrance should be reversed by rapidly expanding existing medical schools and building new ones. Moreover, there is no way of knowing how many equally qualified stu-dents would apply if money was not a factor. Only about 10% of medical students come from the economically lower 50% of the population. Since tuition and fees account for so minor a fraction of the $1.3 billion spent on medical education annually, the government would suffer no great hardship if it picked up the bill for *all* qualified students unable to afford medical school.

Increased government subsidies to medical students would help to rectify another grave in-justice. The affluent who are denied admittance to medical school can seek a medical education abroad, but the poor do not have this choice. The economic factor, among others, has pre-vented members of minority groups from study-ing medicine in the past. For example, only 2.2% of our physicians come from the black minority, though blacks comprise 12% of the general population; the record for Mexican-Americans is even worse. Medical schools are doing their best to correct these inequities and currently are engaged in a furious competition to recruit students from minority groups. In 1971, 6% of the freshmen in medical schools were black.

Medical schools are also slowly overcoming their former prejudice toward female doctors.

In the past year, the number of women admitted to medical schools has risen from 9% to 11%. Stanford University School of Medicine is ac-tually engaged in a policy of "open recruitment" and admitted 16 women in 1971, twice as many as in the preceding year. The women's libera-tion movement may have been partly responsible for prying open a few doors formerly reserved for men. At any rate, it will be some time be-fore we catch up with the rest of the world where it has long been recognized that medicine is a legitimate field for women. The 7% of women in our physician population compares poorly with the Soviet Union's 75%, England's 30%, and France's 26%. Indeed, only a handful of countries have a smaller ratio of female to male doctors than the U.S. has.

Medical Care Organization and Service

Illustrator Norman Rockwell's portrait of the old family doctor working alone in a dingy of-fice over the corner drugstore bears little sem-blance to the doctor of today. The modern physician practices in a well-equipped office building or group clinic, usually in close prox-imity to a hospital, surrounded by many differ-ent kinds of allied health personnel. He has adjusted well to scientific medical advances and, as an individual, commands the respect and con-fidence of his patients. Public opinion polls re-veal that doctors are usually held in higher re-gard by the community than members of any other profession—even the ministry. But medi-cine's image has tarnished a bit in recent years, and this is a matter of growing concern to all physicians. Why has the once lofty position of the medical profession suffered a decline? For the answer, we must look at the way medicine is organized, how medicine is adapting to chang-ing patterns of health care, and what medicine is doing to contain inflated costs.

Hovering over all physicians and deeply en-meshed in their daily activities is the symbol of organized medicine, the American Medical As-sociation (AMA), founded in 1847 "to promote the science and the art of medicine and the betterment of public health." Through its satel-lite state and county medical societies, the AMA holds a power over its members matched by few other organizations. The AMA's Council on Medical Education is responsible for the ap-proval of medical schools and hospital intern-ships and thus exercises considerable control over medical education and training. This con-trol extends over to physician licensure, since in most states there are close ties between the state

Medical care costs have risen drastically since 1960; the aged are most affected

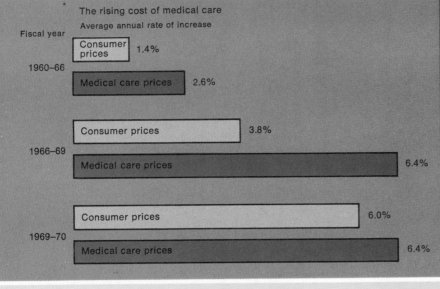

The rising cost of medical care
Average annual rate of increase

Fiscal year

1960–66
- Consumer prices 1.4%
- Medical care prices 2.6%

1966–69
- Consumer prices 3.8%
- Medical care prices 6.4%

1969–70
- Consumer prices 6.0%
- Medical care prices 6.4%

During the 1960's the rate of increase for medical care prices was nearly double that of prices for all consumer items. Factors contributing to this rapid rise in costs included salary increases for hospital personnel, rearranged pricing structures by hospitals, and increased demands for services.

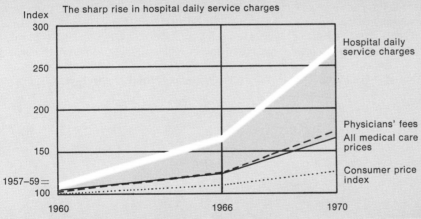

The sharp rise in hospital daily service charges

Index
300
250
200
150
1957–59 = 100

1960   1966   1970

- Hospital daily service charges
- Physicians' fees
- All medical care prices
- Consumer price index

Daily service charges by hospitals have risen faster than any other single medical care expense. A significant part of this rise can be attributed to the inclusion of hospital personnel under minimum wage laws.

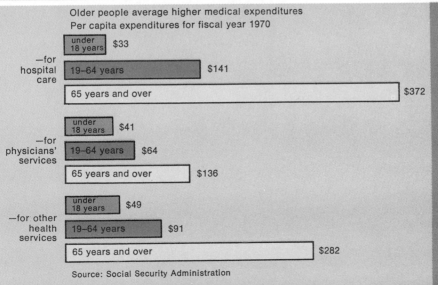

Older people average higher medical expenditures
Per capita expenditures for fiscal year 1970

—for hospital care
- under 18 years $33
- 19–64 years $141
- 65 years and over $372

—for physicians' services
- under 18 years $41
- 19–64 years $64
- 65 years and over $136

—for other health services
- under 18 years $49
- 19–64 years $91
- 65 years and over $282

Source: Social Security Administration

The average personal health care expenditure in the United States for 1970 was $280. Broken down by age group, however, the averages were $123 for youth, $296 for those in the intermediate age group, and $790 for those over 65. The greatest differential exists for hospital expenses, where the per capita expenditure by the aged is more than 11 times that for youth.

medical society and the licensure agency, the state board of medical examiners. Finally, the AMA's general policies, and the requirement of most hospitals that a physician must be an AMA member before he is granted staff privileges, greatly influences the physician's mode of practice.

In the past few years, many physicians have become increasingly critical of the AMA. The disenchanted are strange bedfellows. On the one hand are the liberals, unhappy because of what they consider the AMA's reactionary attitude on socioeconomic issues. On the other are the conservatives, who have strongly resisted the recent move of the AMA from the far right to a position closer to center. The liberals are increasingly turning to the American Association of Public Health Physicians to espouse their progressive health care views. The conservatives have attempted to maintain their viewpoint by forming new organizations dedicated to preserving the traditional economic status quo of medicine.

Continued vibrations within the ranks of organized medicine may be anticipated as physicians react to new forms of health care delivery. The time-honored doctor-patient relationship is being profoundly affected by the apparent demise of the general practitioner (GP) and the trend away from solo medical practice. Most doctors have adjusted to these changes with little trouble, but some are finding it difficult to fit into the new molds.

The backbone of the medical profession in the first quarter of this century was the general practitioner. He practiced empirically rather than scientifically, because most of the specific remedies that are commonplace today were not available to him. In 1931, GP's outnumbered specialists five to one. But the difficulty with keeping abreast of jet-age advances in medicine has forced doctors to specialize, and specialists now far outnumber GP's. The 20% of active physicians who remain in general practice includes an appreciable number over the age of 65, so that the GP is rapidly becoming the vanishing American. Meanwhile, the number of certified specialists has risen from 14,000 in 1939 to 120,000 in 1971, and there are many more specialists yet to be certified.

The reversal of the GP-specialist ratio has been a natural outgrowth of proliferating medical knowledge. Realizing this, the GP's are now seeking specialist status themselves. The plan is to gradually replace the GP by a new family-practice doctor who will be groomed in the broad perspectives of family and community medicine. A recently inaugurated, three-year family-

practice hospital training program will qualify the graduate for the latest specialty board— the American Board of Family Practice. The pressures for resurrecting the general practitioner are so great that several states have mandated by law the establishment of family-practice departments in their tax-supported medical schools.

Unfortunately, specialist practice has brought along some inherent problems of its own. The changeover has often been accompanied by depersonalized, fragmented, inconvenient, and more expensive medical care. Some patients are unhappy about consulting a multiplicity of doctors as is sometimes necessary for complicated medical problems. But, in the balance, the advantages of specialist care far outweigh the disadvantages.

The ultimate answer to the deficiencies of fragmented specialist care is group medical practice. The pooling of talent and resources under one roof for the sharing of personnel and expense is now widely accepted by both physicians and patients. Thus there has been a steady rise in the numbers of group-practice clinics that has paralleled the slow demise of the general practitioner. Many physicians learned at firsthand the value of medical teamwork during World War II, and they have been largely responsible for the flourishing of group practices. A recent survey revealed that 40,000 physicians were members of more than 6,000 group practices in the U.S. Group practice is especially popular on the West Coast.

Medical Manpower Shortage

Sick people may not be as concerned about the organizational pattern of medical care as they are about finding a doctor when they need one. For there no longer is any doubt that the U.S. is facing a doctor shortage that has become so acute it borders on the critical. This problem is compounded further by a serious maldistribution of practicing physicians. Most medical authorities no longer question the existence of a medical manpower shortage, and they are actively seeking alternatives for alleviating it.

By latest count there are 334,028 physicians in the U.S., of whom 19,621 are inactive or retired. Almost 85% of the physicians are involved in direct patient care. The remainder are engaged in such other activities as research, teaching, and administration. This seemingly large number of physicians is much more productive than in preceding years because of technical advances, greater use of ancillary personnel, and urbanization of the population. It is abundantly clear, however, that these factors that enable the physician to practice more efficiently have been overbalanced by the general population growth, an "explosion of demand" for health services due to higher income and education levels, greater availability of health insurance, the aging of the population with the attendant increase in chronic diseases, and added demands upon the physician's time because of highly complex diagnostic and therapeutic procedures that were completely unknown only two decades ago.

The imbalance between the supply and demand for physicians is having a deleterious effect on medical care. More than 500,000 Americans live in rural counties without a single physician. In desperation, some of the 5,000 doctorless communities have strung banners across their main streets pleading, "We Want a Doctor!" In urban areas the problem is scarcely less serious. Patients have difficulty getting an appointment with their doctor and, when they see him, spend long periods of time in the aptly named "waiting room." Some seek more immediate attention at hospital emergency rooms that are overflowing with nonemergency cases.

It has been estimated that there is a deficit of 50,000 physicians in the U.S. Much of the blame rests with the AMA which, 20 years ago, derided government predictions of a coming medical manpower shortage. To its credit, the AMA about-faced in 1966 and now vociferously favors medical school expansion programs. A fair start has been made in this direction; the physician population is currently increasing 3% per year while the general population growth rate is 1%. But the "lead time" for turning out physicians is more than ten years (including time for planning and building new medical schools), and the doctor shortage will not be corrected for at least a decade.

The manpower shortage has been accompanied by a maldistribution of doctors that is easy to understand in a free and competitive society. Life is too unpleasant in the ghetto and in Appalachia for a physician to settle voluntarily in those places. It is not merely a question of making more money elsewhere. The depressed areas rarely offer physicians the facilities or the free access to competent consultation so necessary for optimal care of patients. Doctors and their families find it far more desirable to move to the suburbs where the educational and social opportunities are more rewarding. The exodus of physicians from the inner city is the reason that the East Garfield Park section of Chicago has been left with only 13 doctors to serve 65,-000 poor people, and this is a story that could be repeated over and over across the country.

One distressing consequence of the sagging medical manpower structure in the U.S. has been an increasing influx of foreign-trained doctors. Only about 25% of these foreign imports are U.S. citizens, who by necessity or choice have studied abroad. Many of the foreign medical school graduates come to the U.S. for postgraduate study, but eventually they obtain a license to practice here permanently. These licentiates have increased rapidly so that foreign graduates must now be reckoned with as a force in American medical care; the 3,000 added in 1970 brought the total number of foreign graduates practicing here to 55,000—almost one fifth of the active physicians in the U.S.

In some quarters, a good deal of faith is being placed on automation as the solution to the doctor shortage. But predictions of a large-scale replacement of physicians by computers seems premature at this stage. Important attributes of a practicing physician—judgment, intuition, compassion, morality, and ethics—cannot be fed into a machine, and computer output depends upon human input. Automation, although of increasing importance in hospital laboratories, pharmacies, and bookkeeping departments, is still in its infancy as an aid in clinical diagnosis. Multiphasic screening methods may in time add to doctor productivity, but even this time-saver is being approached with caution. In view of universal complaints about hurried, depersonalized medical care, many doctors are reluctant to place yet more mechanized equipment between the patients and themselves.

More widespread use of paramedical personnel, the growth of group practice, and automation are sure to have a favorable bearing on the medical manpower problem. But many health authorities insist that the only effective answer to the doctor shortage is to augment the number of medical school graduates by far greater expansion of educational facilities than we have seen thus far. Simply put, when there is a scarcity of a commodity or service, and the demand cannot be lessened, the supply must be increased. In the case of medical care, there is ample evidence that the demand will grow rather than lessen.

How many more medical schools do we need, and how soon do we need them? By all indications, we should double the present doctor output, and we should start this herculean task immediately. In the first place, we must reduce the 50,000 doctor shortage from which the country is now suffering. Second, we must anticipate greater demands for medical services in the near future from several sources: medical care is sought more frequently on the higher rungs of the economic ladder, and the 20% of our population in the poverty class are slowly extricating themselves from the socioeconomic morass in which they are mired; and we may be due for another upsurge in population growth as the seeds of the post-World War II "baby boom" flower in the next decade. Third, this country must reverse the unconscionable "brain drain" and begin exporting doctors rather than importing them from underdeveloped countries that can ill afford the loss of their scientific personnel. Last, we must provide additional freshman slots in medical schools so that the aspiring physicians whom we are now turning away can be admitted.

Perhaps all we need now is a stimulus to our sense of national purpose. There are comparisons to be made with the Soviet Union other than numbers of nuclear submarines and intercontinental ballistic missiles. The Soviets, with a population only 20% greater than ours, already boast twice as many physicians; in addition, they are graduating three times as many medical students yearly. Instead of importing 3,000 doctors annually, as we do to shore up our weak medical manpower foundations, the Soviet Union is developing a humanitarian image by emphasizing medical foreign aid to underdeveloped countries in Africa and Asia. In the preceding 20 years, the Soviets have built clinics and hospitals in Iran, Ethiopia, India, Iraq, Algeria, Yemen, Pakistan, Jordan, and the Congo, and they have staffed these and other facilities with thousands of physicians. Their current medical construction and staffing program in underdeveloped parts of the world is even more ambitious. This is a record that the U.S. will not soon duplicate.

Before leaving the subject of the medical manpower shortage, a word must be said about the equally frustrating maldistribution of physicians. Although there will always be a few medical missionaries eagerly seeking personal and professional gratification in the urban and rural slums, the missionary approach is irrelevant to the needs and hopes of the poverty class. While admiring the selflessness of these dedicated men, the overwhelming majority of doctors will be less than enthusiastic about joining them. Health services in undesirable slum areas will only be

How the medical care dollar was spent* and who pays for health care

1950 Total＝$11.0 billion

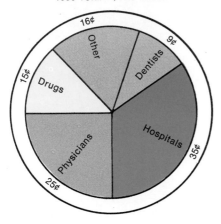

Although the total expenditure for health care increased rapidly between 1950 and 1970, the relative distribution by type of expenditure changed very little. The category showing the largest change was that of hospital care, which increased from 35% to 44%. Private financing has always constituted the largest share of medical care expenditures, but new government programs have begun to shift the balance toward more public financing. Before the Medicare and Medicaid programs, public funds provided 26% of the medical care dollar, but by 1970 the public share had reached 37%.

Public funds finance a growing share of medical care

1960 Total＝$23.7 billion

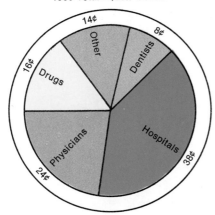

Fiscal Year 1966
Total Spent ＝ $42.3 billion

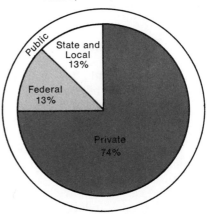

1970 Fiscal Year
Total＝$58.5 billion

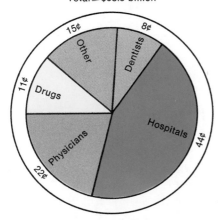

Fiscal Year 1970
Total Spent ＝ $67.2 billion

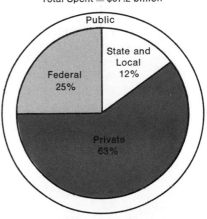

*Personal health care expenditure.

Source: U.S. Department of Health, Education, and Welfare

Source: Social Security Administration

fully provided when young physicians are regimented to serve tours of duty among the disadvantaged. (Mexico and other Latin American countries have such a mandatory rule.) Since the federal government is now paying for almost the entire cost of a medical education, it does not seem unreasonable to ask a young medical graduate to repay his debt by briefly serving the unfortunate. The newly created National Health Service Corps is attempting to recruit physicians to fill the need, but the voluntary approach almost certainly is doomed to failure.

Medical Care Costs

Looming over the controversies that surround education, organization, and service is the specter of rising medical costs. Indeed, it is concern about the "staggering costs" that has focused attention on other aspects of health care in the U.S. All sectors of our economy are sharing the heavy financial outlay for medical care. Private patients often resent out-of-pocket expenditures for medical services after paying high premiums for health insurance, and costs of Medicaid have gotten so out of control that demands for junking this government health insurance program are heard from all sides.

In the past decade, the U.S. health bill rose 170%—from $26 billion and 5.3% of the gross national product (GNP) in 1960 to nearly $70 billion and 7% of the GNP in 1970. The rise in medical expenditures has been paced by the federal government, which in 1971 spent $21 billion, almost one third of the nation's total outlay for health care.

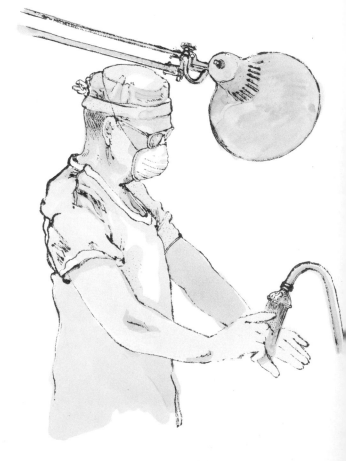

Medical care costs have been especially hard hit by the general inflationary trend in the U.S. Since 1960 these costs have increased twice as fast as the Consumer Price Index. Hospital charges have led the way, going up five times faster than the cost of living. Providing one day's hospital care in 1971 averaged $92.32— 184.8% higher than the $32.42 daily hospital cost ten years earlier. The end, evidently, is not in sight, for the American Hospital Association (AHA) gloomily predicts an average daily hospital charge of over $150 by 1975. This may not be wide of the mark in view of current daily hospital costs of $130–$150 at many metropolitan centers. Mushrooming hospital costs have not been uniquely an American experience. In Great Britain, National Health Service expenditures for hospitals climbed from $470 million in 1949 to $4.35 billion in 1969.

Hospital charges of $27.4 billion were responsible for the largest fraction of total national expenditures for health in 1970. The next largest item was physicians' fees—$14.4 billion, followed by drugs, $7.2 billion, and dentists' services $4.1 billion.

The reasons for so large a jump in health care costs are easily discerned. Total population growth during the 1960's, plus the increased amount and quality of services per capita, explains roughly 50% of the increase. But increased prices of health services accounted for the other 50%. In other words, only one half of increased health care costs were reflected in added health care services; the remainder was wiped out by inflation.

Hardest hit of all by inflation have been the hospitals, meeting zooming payrolls that make up some two thirds of total hospital expenses. The higher hospital wages are well justified, because in the past hospital workers were cruelly exploited. Nurses, for example, have long earned less than garbage collectors; this inequity is now being rectified. Interns at the Los Angeles county hospital who once worked slave hours for $10 per month now make 100 times that much. Other hospital workers are also commanding much higher wages than in the past. But the wage-scale increases have pushed up hospital room costs significantly—as much as 30% in one year.

Physicians' fees have also risen, though far more modestly than hospital charges. The increase in fees has been necessary to cover employee wage boosts in the doctor's office and the generally higher cost of practicing medicine. Some physicians in the surgical specialties, for example, have seen their malpractice insurance rates soar 1000% in the past six years. The high cost of insurance indirectly leads to higher medical costs because doctors are forced to practice "defensive medicine"; many unnecessary tests and examinations are performed with an eye toward some day satisfying a jury in a potential court case.

The prospects for containing medical costs in the near future are not bright. Hospital charges and physicians' fees will continue to spiral upward as long as inflation remains unchecked. Diagnostic procedures will become more complex and more costly. New therapeutic breakthroughs portend sharply higher payments for such procedures as organ transplants and open-heart operations. Finally, people over age 65 account for one fourth of total health expenditures, and this group will make up an increasing percentage of the total population in the next two decades. There is comparatively little

on the horizon that will offset these threats to a new wave of higher medical costs.

Rising medical costs, like other forms of inflation, place an especially severe hardship on people with fixed salaries. The aged, with stagnant incomes and comparatively more frequent visits to the doctor and hospital, are doubly penalized by higher medical prices, though this burden has been partially lifted by Medicare.

Organized medicine, private groups interested in health, and government are all searching for ways to contain medical care costs. Greater efficiency for physicians is hoped for in the further growth of group practices and the more widespread use of physicians' assistants. The prescribing of generic drugs rather than brand names is being advocated as a money saver. Fixed fee schedules for government insurance plans will help hold the line on rising physicians' fees. Private health insurers are being urged to increase their out-of-hospital medical benefits and thus cut down on the necessity for more costly in-hospital care. Operating budgets are being squeezed in an effort to encourage amalgamations and cooperative business arrangements among hospitals. All of these steps may help, but their total impact on medical costs will not be appreciable.

Even less can be anticipated from the oft-repeated exhortations for a greater emphasis on preventive medicine—especially by means of automated multiphasic screening. These "annual exams" cannot prevent such major illnesses as coronary thrombosis, cancer, stroke, or arthritis. Occasionally, diseases are picked up at an earlier stage, but the total effect on medical costs of this gain in time is quite negligible. And from a professional standpoint, the returns would be greater if the efforts spent on annually examining healthy people were diverted to taking care of the acutely ill who are receiving inadequate medical attention.

If medical costs are to be reduced by preventing disease, far more could be accomplished by changing the eating, drinking, smoking, and driving-to-work habits of the American society than by urging people to check in at a doctor's office for a multiphasic screening examination. Preventive medicine for adults is largely a do-it-yourself thing.

The only answer to unexpectedly high medical bills is prepaid health insurance that spreads the risk over the largest possible group. This idea, introduced by Prince Otto von Bismarck in Prussia nearly 100 years ago and implemented in Great Britain in 1912, is now universally accepted in the U.S. There has been a phenomenal growth of various types of private health insurance since World War II, and the federal government has entered this field with Medicare and Medicaid. Today about 90% of our population is covered by some form of health insurance. Hospital expense insurance is especially popular. Unfortunately, the figures do not tell the whole story.

Health insurance payments in the U.S. are grossly inadequate. One set of statistics shows up this inadequacy. In 1969 personal expenditures for medical care added up to $42 billion, of which health insurance covered only $12.6 billion, 30% of the total. A comprehensive health insurance plan should take care of at least 75% of medical bills if people are to budget intelligently for illness and accidents in advance. Australians pay 10% of their medical expenditures out-of-pocket; Swedes, 25%; Frenchmen, 20%. In contrast, even our highly touted Medicare plan barely takes care of 50% of health expenses for people over 65 years of age.

Not only is health insurance in the U.S. inadequate, but it is hopelessly fragmented. There is a wide variance in the benefits provided by the 1,800 private carriers of health insurance. Some plans offer comprehensive coverage but at high costs; others exclude poor-risk patients; some return a scandalously low amount in benefit payments for the premium dollar. Medical bills may be paid by commercial insurers, nonprofit groups such as the Blue Cross Plan, federal insurance plans, the Veterans Administration, local tax money, workmen's compensation, a union health center, or a prepaid group practice plan. In addition, there are at least 15 publicly funded programs providing medical care.

The public, government, and organized medicine are all looking for a way out of this maze of medical financing arrangements. Everybody, including the AMA, agrees that government intervention is necessary—the only question is to what extent. The answer to that question is highly controversial, as witness the raft of health insurance legislation that has poured into the Congressional hoppers in the past few years, differing widely in costs and benefits. Health insurance plans have been proposed by the White House, key Congressional leaders, the AMA, the AHA, and the Health Insurance Association of America (HIAA). Each has features that are highly distasteful to one or another segment of society—union leaders could hardly be expected to see eye to eye on medical care financing with trustees of the AMA.

National Health Insurance Proposals

The essential features and an analysis of the leading national health insurance plans follow:

The National Health Insurance Partnership Act sponsored by President Nixon would require employers to pay most of the basic health insurance costs for their employees; would subsidize coverage for the poor and near poor; and would encourage everyone to enroll in a health maintenance organization (HMO; a comprehensive group practice organized to provide care to a geographic area and reimbursed through a pre-negotiated, fixed, periodic payment.) Medicaid would be replaced by insurance subsidies for the poor and near poor. Medicare would continue to cover those over 65 years of age. All costs of catastrophic illness between $5,000 and $50,000 would also be covered. It is estimated that this plan would increase the federal government's health expenditures from $3 billion to $5.5 billion the first year and that employer-employee premium costs would rise from the current $13 billion to $20 billion by 1974. The Nixon plan would have a moderate impact on doctors because it is intended to entice more of them into prepaid group practices. Some legislators feel that the Nixon proposals, because of coinsurance and deductible factors, do not go far enough and would only cover about 50% of the average person's annual medical costs. The health insurance industry can be expected to support the president's programs since they would mean more business for private insurers. The weakest part of the Nixon plan is its reliance on HMO's for cost and quality controls. There is absolutely no consensus at this time on whether they will be accepted by patient or doctor. Indeed, the specific features of these organizations have yet to be spelled out.

At the liberal end of the national health insurance spectrum is the Health Security Act, popularly known as the Kennedy Plan. Senator Edward M. Kennedy (D, Mass.) has advanced a proposal that would provide almost total "cradle-to-grave" medical care with no coinsurance or deductibles. The entire plan would be financed through payroll taxes and general federal revenues and would replace Medicaid and Medicare. The sponsors envision true compulsory national health insurance designed to reorganize the health service system and to rigidly control costs and quality of care. Private health insurers would be completely frozen out under this program, which would cost, according to various estimates, between $57 billion and $77

Medical manpower

Physicians' fields in 1970
Total Physicians in U.S.* 334,028

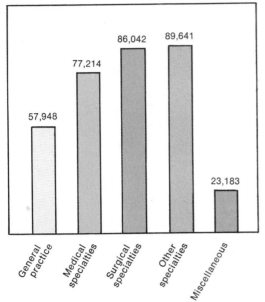

Of the 334,028 total number of physicians in the United States in 1970, 252,897 were engaged in various specialties. Some controversy exists within the profession on the question of whether there are too many specialists. Some feel that there are far too many, but others believe that the addition of a family specialist to replace the general practitioner and better coordination among specialists can result in an overall improvement in patient care. Between 1950 and 1970 the ratio of physicians to the total population has improved slightly. In 1950 there were 141 physicians per 100,000 population (1 for each 711 persons), while in 1970 there were 158 (1 for each 632 persons).

*Excludes temporary foreign physicians totaling 4,148.
Source: Center for Health Services Research and Development

Physician manpower has improved slightly in relation to population growth

Physicians in thousands

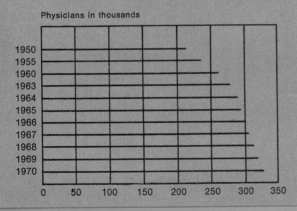

Population in hundreds of thousands

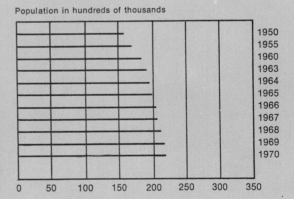

Physicians per 100,000 population

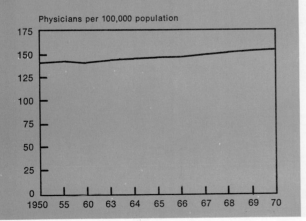

Population per one physician

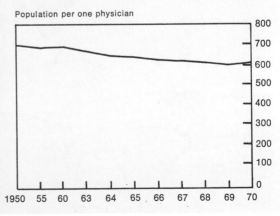

Source: American Medical Association

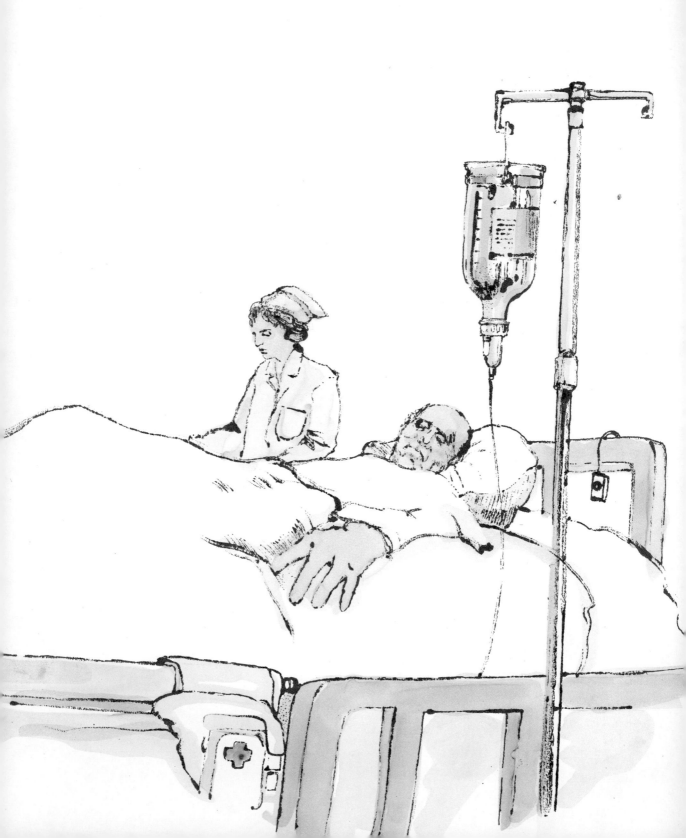

billion yearly. Doctors would be greatly influenced by passage of the Kennedy Plan because first monies would go to prepayment groups and salaried doctors in institutions. If any money is left over after reimbursing doctors who accept per capita compensation for treating patients, fee-for-service physicians would be paid according to a fixed fee schedule. This is an extreme measure that would create tremendous demands for medical manpower which simply is not available. The vast majority of physicians are not in favor of practicing prepaid medicine, and no plan has any chance of success without the co-operation of the medical profession. Another weakness of the Kennedy proposal is the certain abuses under a plan without deductible features. No country in the world has been able to make such a utopian scheme work. Great Britain is currently backtracking from financing complete care and, as a start, is instituting first dollar payments by patients for prescriptions. The Kaiser Foundation-Permanente Medical Care Program in the U.S. has had to take similar measures to prevent over-utilization and underfunding of its programs.

The AMA is sponsoring Medicredit, designed to continue the present system of health service by helping Americans to pay their health insurance premiums through a system of income tax benefits. This would be a voluntary plan for anyone under 65 years of age; Medicaid would be absorbed by the government's paying the premiums for the poor, and Medicare would continue to function for those over 65. Coverage for catastrophic illnesses is provided in the bill. The estimated cost to the government for subsidizing all or part of private health insurance premiums is $14.5 billion in the first year of operation. Medicredit is at the opposite extreme from the Kennedy proposals. Doctors would not be affected at all by the AMA plan since there would be no change in the present delivery system, which is heavily weighted toward fee-for-service medical care. The bill's lack of medical quality and cost controls insures little chance for its passage through a reform-minded Congress.

The HIAA has introduced a Health Care Program that has the modest price tag of $3.2 billion for the first year of operation. Financing would be through income tax deductions and government contributions. Funds are provided for increasing medical manpower through liberal loans to medical students and to subsidize doctors willing to practice in areas of short supply. The plan's primary purpose, however, is to help finance existing types of health care coverage, and would thus be a bonanza to the health insurance industry. It would do nothing to alter doctors' modes of practice, and the prospects for passage of legislation are poor.

The latest entry into the national health insurance sweepstakes is the AHA's Ameriplan which had not been introduced into Congress by fall 1971. The plan calls for the establishment of public or private health care corporations in each community to provide comprehensive care to a defined population. A "standard benefits package" would be available to all on a voluntary basis and would be paid for by an individual or his employer. Uncle Sam would foot the bill if the subscriber were poor, needy, or aged. Medicaid and Medicare would be eliminated. The plan provides catastrophic-illness benefits and has coinsurance and deductible features. The Health Care Corporation would "negotiate with and pay providers on an equitable basis for services rendered." The estimated cost is about the same as the current $70 billion health bill. At present, many features of the plan are vague, and it has been greeted coolly by organized medicine. A serious drawback is the corporate structure, which would require enabling legislation by all 50 state legislatures.

It seems clear that, for the U.S. public, national health insurance is an idea whose time has come, and, being an election year, 1972 may be the time for action. It is unfortunate that some of the leading proposals have been clouded by political feuding in Washington, D.C. It can only be hoped that Congress will present a healthier product than the last time our lawmakers delivered a major health bill. Almost everyone agrees that the Medicare-Medicaid program is in serious trouble.

U.S. Rep. Wilbur D. Mills (D, Ark.), chairman of the House Ways and Means Committee, probably will be the key man in the passage of a national health insurance bill. He is knowledgeable in both what the public wants and what the national treasury can afford, and, if the legislation can be disengaged from political infighting, Mills may be able to combine the best features of all the proposals into a workable and effective measure.

Regardless of the innumerable rewritings that will take place as it wends its way through the halls of Congress, the bill should not lose sight of the fundamental principles of national health insurance:

1. National health insurance should be universal and compulsory. People are not all ra-

Foreign physicians in the U.S. and allied health manpower

The number of graduates of foreign medical schools licensed to practice in the United States has climbed steadily from 308 in 1950 to 3,016 in 1970. Of the 1970 total, 2,830 were licensed by examination and 186 by endorsement of credentials. Many foreign physicians enter the U.S. as visitors or temporary workers with the intention of changing their status to permanent residents. In 1970 some 31.4% of the interns and residents enrolled in approved programs were graduates of foreign medical schools.

In addition to physicians, the health care field encompasses several other professional and supporting occupations. These totaled 2,074,036, or 1,039 per 100,000 population at the beginning of 1970.

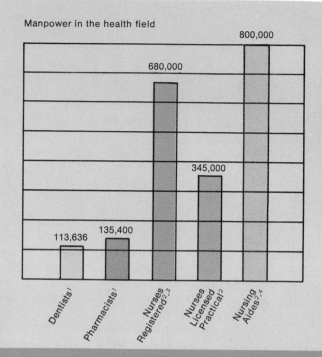

Manpower in the health field

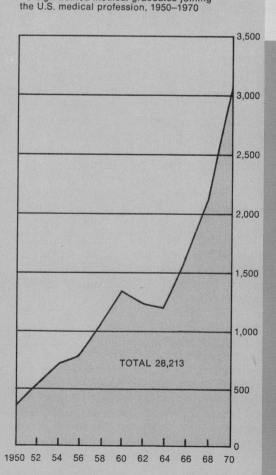

Foreign-trained medical graduates joining the U.S. medical profession, 1950–1970

TOTAL 28,213

1950 52 54 56 58 60 62 64 66 68 70

Source: *Journal of the American Medical Association*

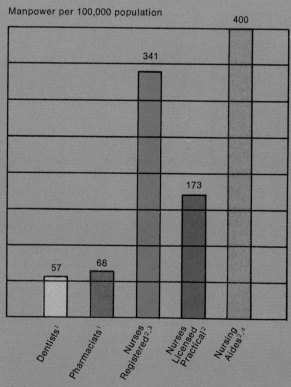

Manpower per 100,000 population

[1] Includes active and inactive individuals in 1968.
[2] Early 1969 estimates which include only those in practice.
[3] The American Nurses Association's 1966 inventory reported 285,791 inactive registered nurses.
[4] Includes home health aides, orderlies, and attendants.
Source: American Medical Association

tional or in the same wage earning class, and we would only compound the present chaotic health insurance system if individuals are allowed to join on a voluntary basis, or if the plan provides different categories of benefits.

2. A large part of the cost of the program should be borne by the federal government and come out of general tax funds. The cost of comprehensive care will certainly be several hundred dollars per family, which would not hurt the $50,000-a-year man if deducted from his salary, but may be an extreme hardship if taken out of the paycheck of a low-income worker.

3. National health insurance should cover at least 75% of a family's total medical expense in order to be meaningful and equitable to the lower-income groups.

4. There must be built-in quality controls. It would be unthinkable for the government to underwrite the shoddy medical care that now exists in some quarters.

National health insurance for our pluralistic society will of necessity be quite different from insurance programs in other countries. Centralization of services and socialization of the medical profession are not likely to accompany universal health insurance here. In the U.S., hospitals have sprung up in jerry-built fashion so that duplication and overlapping of facilities are widespread. The majority of these hospitals have fewer than 100 beds and are individually managed. Relatively few of them have full-time

staffs, as in England and Sweden, providing medical care to a geographic area. The more centralized hospital systems in socialistic countries enable them to deliver excellent health services, but at the cost of less free choice of doctor by patient. And many doctors working for a fixed salary under a socialized system function less well than if there were greater incentives for performance.

Quality of Medical Care

Medical care *costs* cannot be divorced from the *quality* of medical care. Patients are interested not only in how much they are paying for their care but what they are getting for their money. As it assumes an increasing share of the nation's health bill, government can also be expected to concern itself more with medical care quality. In the past, insufficient weight has been given to the relationship between the quality and the cost of medical care. And yet, more stringent controls over the quality of medical practices would go a long way toward lessening the need for medical manpower and facilities as well as containing costs.

Changes in the present methods of providing health care are inevitable. But the nation's good health will also depend upon eliminating poverty, rejuvenating the inner cities, purifying our polluted environment, and providing better education for the disadvantaged. It is clear that this must be a job not only for physicians but for all Americans.

"Prepare for a shock, Mr. Fletcher"

Your Vanishing Privacy
by Ralph Nader and John Spanogle

**Ralph Nader is the well-known lawyer and consumer advocate;
John Spanogle is professor of law at the University of Maine.**

Information about private citizens is being gathered today at an astonishing rate. Dossiers on millions of Americans are compiled by government and by employers and made available through private investigators to finance institutions, banks, insurance companies, and other mass merchandisers. On the basis of these dossiers, individuals may be granted or denied credit, insurance, and jobs. But few people realize the extent of the information that is collected about them or the range of uses to which it is put.

The legitimate need for information in our society cannot be denied. Both citizens and institutions profit from the planning and policy-making made possible by relevant data. But the increasing demand for information, along with the development of more efficient means of gathering, storing, and retrieving data through computer technology, has led to a tendency by some government and private organizations to seek more and more sensitive facts about people. The implications of the "information industry" extend beyond the immediate possibility of unjustly losing a job, failing to secure life insurance, or being denied credit to buy a car. They extend to the parameters of human behavior and the stifling of individual initiative when a person believes that the people and institutions with which he must deal on a daily basis may have access to personal details of his or her life.

A significant number of Americans feel their privacy is being invaded. In late 1970 Louis Harris & Associates conducted a survey, asking the public whether they thought "people are trying to find out things that are none of their business?" One out of three surveyed said "yes."

And Americans do have cause for concern. They are far more subject to credit-economy investigation than citizens of the Soviet Union. The development of sophisticated information systems has not been accompanied by equally efficient safeguards for those whose personal lives may be recorded. Individuals have little control over what is known about them and even less over who knows it.

The Lack of Protection for Privacy Rights

As new demands for more information have been made, protections of privacy rights have been generally inadequate or ignored. For example, under the recently enacted financial recordkeeping law, the United States government can require every bank and other financial institution to make a reproduction of each check a depositor draws and to keep these reproduc-

tions for up to six years. This could provide a veritable wealth of information on an individual. But the act contains no protections for the depositor. It does not limit in any way a bank's use of these reproductions. The bank can, if it wishes, sell them to any of the dossier-creating organizations that are in the business of selling information on people to anyone claiming "a legitimate business need" and willing to pay for the information, such as credit bureaus and inspection agencies. The bank can also sell them to another dossier-keeper, the employer.

The cooperation shown by banks in giving personal information to such agencies in the past demonstrates that they value the individual's privacy very little. In May 1970 a Federal Bureau of Investigation (FBI) agent contacted the cashier of a southeastern Pennsylvania bank to obtain information about an account maintained there by a locally based organization known as the National Black Economic Development Conference, headed by Muhammed Kenyatta. The bank made available for review by the FBI agent copies of the group's checking account statement for several months and microfilms of the checks drawn on the account. The FBI agent then inspected the checks and prepared a long report listing the face information on all the specific checks, identifying to whom the check was drawn, the amount, and the notation as to the purpose of each payment that Kenyatta or his associates had written on them. According to the newspaper the *Philadelphia Inquirer,* the records were given to the inspector without a subpoena or any other court test of whether due-process requirements for a police search had been met.

If an investigator can discover to whom checks are written, and for how much, or what is charged on credit cards, he can discover an individual's recreational habits, the charitable and political causes to which he contributes, his saving habits, and, in general, his style of living. At that point, a citizen's personality is virtually laid bare to minute inspection by strangers.

The cooperation that banks give to investigators is not limited to the FBI. Some banks will hand out information to credit bureaus and inspection agencies as well. They will tell private investigators how much money is in a depositor's checking account, what amounts he has borrowed from them over the past years, and what they think of his payment habits. Further, there is nothing in the present law to prohibit banks from letting these private investigators see microfilms of a depositor's checks.

"They're following me because I applied for a credit card."

"Morning, boss!"

Investigations That Violate Your Privacy

Most Americans believe that they are never subjected to such investigations. They couldn't be more wrong. Anyone who has ever applied for credit or insurance or been employed has almost certainly been investigated by at least one private firm.

If you have borrowed money, a credit bureau probably has the information on how much you borrowed, from whom, for what, and how you paid it back. If you filled out a loan application form, they probably also know your income and net worth. If the agency is particularly zealous, the dossier may also include your IQ scores on high school tests. All of this information is for sale to anyone claiming to be a potential creditor, or a potential insurer, employer, or landlord, and others. The number of people affected by credit bureaus is great. The members of the Associated Credit Bureaus of America (ACBA), for example, have files on 105 million Americans. Credit Data Corp., not a member of ACBA, has files on another 27 million people.

If you have bought insurance other than group insurance, an inspection agency was probably hired by the insurance company to compile a dossier of intimate information about you. This information included not only such expected information as your job, length of time on your present job, marital status, health, any criminal record, and any lawsuits, but also such tidbits as your drinking habits (how often, how much, with others or alone, and even what beverages), your net worth, present salary, domestic troubles, reputation, manner of living, associates, recreation habits, and standing in the community. At least one report form seeks to know what social and religious clubs you belong to. They all want to know whether there is "any criticism of character or morals." The agency's investigator must also state whether he recommends that the insurance be declined.

The inspection agency puts the information into a file and saves it. The agency may use it again in an investigation for another client. In fact, the agency will probably make this personal information available to anyone who has $5 and calls himself a "prospective employer."

These agencies affect a surprisingly large number of people. For example, Retail Credit Co. of Atlanta, Ga., has approximately 45 to 50 million dossiers and investigates 35 million people each year.

If you have been employed, your employer most likely has a file on you. It may only contain the length of time on the job and the salary.

But it may also contain periodic evaluation reports on your work or even the results of tests on your intelligence, aptitudes, interests, and personality traits.

Employment application forms constitute an invasion of privacy in many instances. How many of the questions on it are really relevant to your ability or competence? It is still common to ask about race, creed, community activities, and organizational memberships. You may be asked not only where you live but also with whom, not only whether you are a veteran but if not, also why not. You may be required to list all arrests whether or not they have any relationship to job requirements and hazards. You may be fingerprinted even when you have no past arrest record and the job presents no substantial opportunity for crime against the employer. Each of these presents a serious invasion of privacy, intruding on your personality in an area of no legitimate concern to the employer.

If the information in the file is startling, so too are the ways in which the file may be used. An employee expects his file to be used for internal purposes, such as determining promotions, and he may be aware that some of the information may be passed on to a prospective employer. He doesn't expect this information to be given to his local credit bureau or the inspection agency. However, a study by the National Industrial Conference Board showed that about 50% of employers were willing to give the credit bureaus information about salary, quality of work, and reason for leaving.

Disclosure of reason for leaving creates special problems. The *Wall Street Journal* has reported that department stores in many cities have formed "mutual protective associations" through which they trade the names of former workers who were fired for suspected theft. The stores are not willing to subject their suspicions to the normal tests of due process through criminal prosecutions because managers fear that such prosecutions would be "bad publicity." This fear, however, does not prevent them from branding an employee a thief on the basis of their untested suspicions and publicizing this suspicion to any one who may employ him. At least one corporation has experimented with such a system on a computerized basis for nationwide blacklisting.

Use of files is not the only way employers may violate your privacy. One company has closed-circuit televisions on some of its employees all day, and another has bugged the telephones its employees use. There are many cases in which employees have been discharged because they refused to let the employer search their personal belongings. Refusal to take a lie detector test has also caused firings.

Anyone who has used a tax-preparation service has reason to wonder who knows about his financial situation. The Federal Trade Commission (FTC) has charged two tax-return services, H & R Block and Beneficial Finance Co., with selling information about taxpayers to the Pennsylvania Life Insurance Co. and to a list broker and with using the information to solicit potential borrowers. The FTC also charged that the firms sold income information to help pinpoint the best potential life insurance customers and those who might need loans at vacation time or back-to-school time. This additional use of confidential information was not disclosed to the taxpayers.

The most startling invasion of your privacy is probably that perpetrated by the Federal Housing Administration (FHA). According to Senator Mark O. Hatfield (R, Ore.), if you have ever applied for an FHA loan, the FHA has on file an estimate of the prospect that your marriage will last. That is bad enough, but Senator Hatfield also reports that the FHA has added an ingenious twist to make some money from its investigations: the agency will sell its assessment on your marital stability for $1.50.

How Information Is Obtained

Most information is collected without the knowledge of the subject. The employer's file is the only one in which most of the data is obtained from the person considered—when a job applicant fills out a form or takes tests.

If the credit bureau can avoid it, it does not deal with the subject at all in compiling its file. Credit investigators gather information from creditors, employers, newspapers, and public records. Most of this information is subject to some form of objective verification. However, the procedure is weighted against the subject: a premium is placed on derogatory information that "shows" that the bureau can identify bad risks.

Some computerized credit bureaus also obtain information directly from the computers of member merchants. This can create problems because an error in the merchant's account statement can be passed through the credit bureau's computer to other potential credit grantors without being discovered. In some instances, the use of the computer by a credit bureau can help protect privacy because the expense of input and storage limits the amount of data that can be handled economically. Credit Data Corp., for example, does not list such information as IQ scores, which noncomputerized agencies sometimes file. On the other hand, the use of computers may compel the deletion of explanatory material because of the prohibitive cost of coding it in computer language. For example, potential creditors do not get the full picture of any prior payment dispute or the context or explanations necessary to present the consumer's side of the dispute.

In contrast to the credit bureau data, the inspection agency deals in information that is inherently unverifiable, including family relationships, reputation, morals, and the character of both the subject and his neighborhood. It gets this information and these estimates through what is called "the neighborhood check," in which the investigator talks to neighbors, the building superintendent, or neighborhood grocery store personnel. In small towns, the local postmaster, chief of police, or town clerk may be sources of information. The legal term for this information is hearsay; laymen call it gossip. As with credit bureaus, the file is considered to be particularly valuable if it contains derogatory information.

Each inspection agency investigator must make

10 or 15 of these reports each day if he is to meet his quota, so you can imagine what degree of care he can take to protect your reputation. One inspection agency imposes an even more unsavory requirement on its investigators. Each inspector is required to list daily the percentage of cases in which he found "protective" (i.e., adverse) information and in which he has recommended that insurance or employment be denied.

The FTC criticizes this practice in staff guidelines: "In our view practices such as maintaining quotas on the development of protective or adverse information by investigators and recording the percentage of cases in which an investigator has recommended that the applicant be denied should be discouraged. Such practices are clearly inconsistent with the [Fair Credit Reporting] Act's policy of accurate reporting because they tend to put pressure on the investigator to write as many adverse reports as possible." The FTC has not, however, attempted to enforce this part of its own guidelines against the inspection agency.

The basic problems of the inspection report are illustrated by the story of "Charlie Green" (pseudonym), as told to the U.S. Senate Committee on Banking and Currency. Green was refused many jobs during a four-year period be-

"I guess they're O.K."

cause of an inspection agency preemployment report that (1) detailed how he had spit at a neighbor, (2) stated that his landlord at the same location disliked him, and (3) included the statement "said to have been dishonorably discharged from the Army."

Charlie's side of the story was quite different. The "abused" neighbor was an elderly crank who complained about many young couples and even demanded that Charlie take off his shoes in *his own* apartment so as not to make noise; further, he said he never spat at her. The landlord wrote that Charlie was "a perfectly satisfactory tenant." But the true test was the conflict over Charlie's discharge. Charlie had been honorably discharged from the Army and had the papers to prove it.

Charlie's side of the story was never heard, nor was he ever informed of the charges. In fact, for most of the four years, he never knew there was such a report or who had made it.

The Easy Availability of Personal Information

The consequences of making information easily available that is not only highly personal, but also subject to error or misinterpretation have only begun to be disclosed. One example is cited by Arthur R. Miller in his recent book 'The Assault on Privacy'. Miller reports on the case of a data bank on migrant children, which was designed to help the school placement of these children by recording past school experience. When asked whether there were restrictions on the use of this information, the California director of migrant education said that information from the files would be released to anyone who had access to individual school records and to persons identifying themselves as prospective employers. He also said that he would include in this released report derogatory information such as negative character traits.

The young subjects of this information blitz may indeed find easier placement in schools. But in future years a student may be haunted by the fact that an eighth-grade teacher reported that he was slow in math or a discipline problem —a report that may or may not be true and that may or may not be relevant.

The information kept in government files is often available to private recordkeepers. The methods of transferring the information vary from situation to situation. Alan F. Westin has written at length about the information "buddy system," in which private investigators and government investigators casually exchange intimate information but do it orally so that there are no records of the exchanges. Such a "buddy system" allows employers to gain access to FBI files in exchange for FBI access to the employer's files. In other words, what goes into the government files may also be known to private investigators.

Examples of the availability of governmental files to private investigators are the Sept. 23, 1969, *Look* magazine article on Mayor Joseph L. Alioto of San Francisco and the Aug. 9, 1968, *Life* magazine article on U.S. Representative Cornelius E. Gallagher (D, N.J.). These articles show how writers who are regarded favorably by government agents can have access to confidential, personal information of a highly damaging nature, so that their stories can state the substance of these files or even quote from them. The leaks may violate confidentiality or secrecy laws, but there are no prosecutions when the leak is politically approved.

The best illustration of this problem was the letter written by FBI Director J. Edgar Hoover to Trans World Airlines (TWA) Board Chairman Charles C. Tillinghast, Jr., about a TWA employee. The employee was a pilot who had dared to criticize the FBI's handling, or mishandling, of an airplane hijacking incident. Hoover then wrote the pilot's employer, revealing certain derogatory information about the pilot's service record in the U.S. Air Force—an act which probably violated not only the pilot's constitutional rights but also Air Force regulations about disclosure of personnel records.

Sometimes, however, both the givers and the recipients of illegally disclosed government information files are prosecuted. In a recent New York City case, four policemen, two government clerks, Retail Credit and several other investigation agencies, and American Airlines were all indicted on felony charges of using bribery or taking bribes to obtain confidential information from the New York City police department files. The payments ranged up to $30,000 and the information reportedly was used in preemployment reports by the agencies. All the agencies were allowed to plead guilty to a misdemeanor, and the felony charges were dropped. Retail Credit paid a fine of $4,000. The other fines were similarly small, and they could all be written off as a cost of doing business with no assurance that the agencies would stop violating the confidentiality of the files in the future.

What Can Be Done

There are ways in which employees of governmental and private inspection agencies can stop these routine invasions of privacy. For example, they can refuse to participate. When the officials of California's Alameda County decided to stage an early morning mass raid on the homes of people on the county welfare rolls, one social worker, Benny Max Parrish, refused to go. Even though he based his refusal on the grounds that the raids were an unconstitutional violation of his clients' privacy, he was fired. Five years later, the California Supreme Court upheld Parrish, stating that the raids were unconstitutional without search warrants and noting that the raids were prohibited by the federal rules that governed the federally aided welfare programs. Parrish was ordered reinstated with back pay, and Alameda County officials stopped making such raids.

Parrish's five-year fight established for other governmental workers the right to refuse to follow unconstitutional orders if they will only stand up to their administrators. The concept was being used in 1971 by two California social workers who refused to furnish intimate data on their clients related to psychiatric treatment, style of living, and use of alcohol or drugs. The data was to be stored in a state department of social welfare computer that they have contended has insufficient safeguards to protect the privacy of the individuals involved.

But you don't have to be an agency employee to thwart these privacy invaders. Bill Gold of the *Washington Post* suggested one course of action in his column, "The District Line." He received a letter stating: "One Tuesday, a man knocked on our door and introduced himself as an insurance investigator. He wanted information about one of our neighbors . . . Do you have any suggestions as to how this kind of request ought to be handled?" We agree with his answer: "Tell them about as much as you'd want somebody to tell about you."

One attempt to deal with the problem of consumer investigations was the Fair Credit Reporting Act, enacted in 1970. The act deals with the problem of an inaccurate consumer report. It requires that a creditor, insurer, or employer must notify you of the existence of a report and the name of the consumer reporting agency that made it whenever they take adverse action due to the report. The law gives you the right to go to the agency and learn the "nature and substance of all information" in the agency's file, except medical information and the sources of "investigative" information (i.e., gossip). Also you have a right to find out what is in your file even if you have not had an adverse report, but

you may have to pay $1 to $5 for the agency's time. If you dispute the accuracy of the information in your file the agency must reinvestigate and reverify or delete the disputed item. The combination of these provisions gives you a fighting chance to discover that an inaccurate report about you is being circulated and to have it corrected.

There are two basic problems regarding consumer investigations—whether for credit, insurance, or employment. One is that the report may be inaccurate; the other is that, accurate or not, the use of a dossier may violate the individual's privacy. Even its advocates admit that the Fair Credit Reporting Act attacks only the problem of the inaccurate report and does very little to protect a person's privacy from these professional intruders.

In the House of Representatives U.S. Rep. Leonor K. Sullivan (D, Mo.) sponsored a bill that would have attacked the privacy problem, but at the crucial time she could not get a quorum of her subcommittee to consider it.

An individual may believe that a truthful description of his marital troubles or a list of his social clubs is no one's business but his own. However, he cannot get the information deleted or control its dissemination. The Fair Credit Reporting Act stops short of privacy questions. For this reason, we feel that the Fair Credit Reporting Act is inadequate and in need of reform.

Reforming the Fair Credit Reporting Act

There are four distinct problems regarding invasions of privacy by a consumer reporting agency. These are: (1) who may have access to the information, (2) what information may be gathered, (3) how the information may be gathered, and (4) when an investigation may be conducted.

After the information is on file, who should have access to it? Under the Fair Credit Reporting Act, anyone claiming to be a prospective employer can get an inspection agency or credit bureau report. In other words, the act offers no practical limitations on access.

A common problem arises when you disclose information for a limited purpose. One example is the use of information from taxpayers' returns by H & R Block and Beneficial Corp. A second example is information given to a mortgage lender. You may be willing to give the lender information about your income and savings because you seek a large amount of credit. This does not mean that you want this information passed on to prospective employers or to a neighbor who is a merchant and sells you a $15 item on credit. There is, however, nothing in the Fair Credit Reporting Act that allows a borrower to limit the use of the information once it has been given to the mortgage lender.

What can be done to control the availability of these dossiers? An Oklahoma statute requires that any agency that sells reports must first mail a copy of the report to the subject before mailing it to the employer, insurance company, or creditor. We suggest a similar but even stronger approach. Before mailing out any report, the agency should be required to obtain your express consent to a particular release. This would recognize the individual's interest in preserving the privacy of his own personality. It would allow him to decide whether any particular transaction was worth the invasion of his privacy by the other party.

Even if the information in the file is completely accurate and available only to creditors, insurers, and employers, there may be some intimate information that you consider irrelevant to the legitimate needs of employers or the credit insurance industry and wish to keep to yourself. For example, if you buy nongroup life insurance to protect your family, an inspection agency may examine your entire life in detail. One part of that examination concerns your club life. The scope of this examination is suggested by the club life questions in the manual of one such agency, Retail Credit: "Specific names of civic, social, fraternal, or church organizations in which applicant is active or interested should be covered. Not only are they important to the grade of risk; but [they] become a valuable lead to sources of information."

Does anyone want a company delving that deeply into his private life in order to allow him to buy something from them? Insurance company underwriters indicate that many of them do not use this information; nonetheless, it is collected by the inspection agencies, reported by them, and put into their files.

However, the Fair Credit Reporting Act gives no protection to anyone who feels such a file violates his privacy. The law allows an individual to have information deleted if it is inaccurate, but not if it violates his sense of privacy. In fact, even if you ask an agency what is in your file, you may be told only the information that would adversely affect your insurance application. All the other information that might infringe on privacy but is not specifically "derogatory" may not be mentioned.

What should be done? Anyone who is investigated should know what the questions are before they are asked. In other words, before he commits himself to a transaction requiring an investigation, he should know the extent to which his private life will be scrutinized and have the choice of whether to enter into the transaction or not. If loss of privacy is part of the price of the transaction, then that price should be fully disclosed before you buy. The Fair Credit Reporting Act, on the other hand, requires no such disclosure except for investigative reports (the kind that involve a neighborhood check). Even then, disclosure of an investigation need not be made until three days after the investigation has been ordered. Since agency procedures require all investigative reports to be completed within four days after they have been ordered, most protests would be too late.

The methods used to gather information also have ominous implications for privacy. Credit bureaus gather their information from employers, newspapers, and credit grantors who are members of the bureau. They also frequently use the "welcome wagon" woman as an investigator in disguise. She visits a home to find out the buying "needs" of the owner so that he can be dunned by the right merchant. The banker who has litigated about revealing bank accounts to government agencies on the ground that it is confidential information will still breach that confidence and reveal the approximate amount in an account—and much more about its activity —to a credit bureau or agency upon request.

Each of these investigating methods is an invasion of privacy, but the most serious invasion is the neighborhood check by inspection agencies. The entire purpose of this investigation method is to find out what you do while you are in your own home. It is accomplished by questioning your neighbors and enlisting them to spy on you, creating a kind of surveillance of your home that is the hallmark of totalitarian regimes. For most people the only place where they can feel completely free to discard their social roles and express their own personalities is at home.

The Fair Credit Reporting Act does not require your consent to this invasion of your home life. Its only provision is that you be warned about it—after the investigation is ordered and you have already signed the insurance contract.

Under what circumstances may information about an individual be gathered at all? This question involves the right of people to speak and act freely, since a private investigation may be used in an attempt to silence or intimidate. Neither the Fair Credit Reporting Act nor any other federal law effectively controls the conditions or uses of such investigations.

Clearly, the Fair Credit Reporting Act is insufficient to deal with the privacy violations of consumer reporting agencies. What is needed is a Privacy Protection Act that would require the consent of the individual to any investigation or dissemination of information about him that occurs in connection with a business transaction. Further, this should be a knowledgeable consent, made only after the scope of the questions, the information, and the method of gathering facts have been fully revealed.

Conclusion

The threats to privacy posed by private investigators and their files will increase dramatically in the next five to ten years. Until now, technology has been a major limiting factor on the amount of information that could be placed in computerized files. In the past the costs of computer storage have forced agencies either (1) to reduce the information stored to a minimum and to use management discretion to rigorously weed out irrelevant information (which does protect your privacy) or (2) simply not to computerize the files. But there will be less such automatic technological limitation in the late 1970's. Indeed, it may become more expensive to make relevancy studies than to store irrelevant but intrusive information. For this reason we need statutory protection either on the federal or state level, and we need it before storage technology has already established new patterns of business thinking on relevancy.

If we are not able to assert our collective right to privacy, and to protect it effectively from privacy investigators, we can only expect to live increasingly in the shadow of our dossiers. The effects of a well-oiled information system may not be felt immediately, as in the case of the TWA pilot, but in that instance (as well as in others) open opposition to established interests led to surreptitious snooping. The danger to 1st Amendment freedoms is clear.

And one need not be a public figure to attract an investigation. It can happen to anyone. The California migrant child, or any student, will be haunted by his eighth-grade teacher's evaluations, which can be gathered by a private agency and noted in a preemployment report. The same will happen both to those who dissent from established political dogma or join groups who protest current policies and to those who do not.

Thus, it is not enough to protect our freedom of speech from arrest and prosecution if an information-gathering system can deny employment, insurance, and credit to either the dissenter or the ordinary. The magnitude of such a threat raises the question of whether the present reporting system can be adequately "reformed" or whether Congress must probe deeper and determine whether the utility of such reports is outweighed by the social costs. If consumer reporting agencies are not willing to undertake reforms that will disclose the entire "privacy price" of their participation in your transaction with business, more decisive reforms may be necessary, such as limiting the types of information they may gather and sell or even prohibiting personality investigations completely. In any case, legislation is needed now, before new technology provides the means to allow the files on you to become even more pervasive and intrusive.

Events of the Year 1971

ADVERTISING.

ADVERTISING. As 1971 came to a close, some experts were predicting an advertising volume increase in the United States of as much as 4%. However, predictions made in the fall by organizations representing the nine largest carriers of national advertising were not so optimistic. Network television expected to end 1971 with $1.47 billion in national advertising dollars, a decline from the medium's actual result in 1970, which was $1.65 billion. Spot television also forecast a drop to $1.04 billion from $1.2 billion. Direct mail looked to a $2.8-billion year, which would be off from the 1970 figure of $2.85 billion. On the other hand, six media were expecting gains. Newspapers anticipated a rise from $1.08 to $1.2 billion, magazines from $1.19 to $1.25 billion, business publications from $807.4 million to $810 million, network radio from $48.4 million to $49.9 million, spot radio from $350 million to $365.8 million, and outdoor advertising from $145 million to $160 million. The nine media thus expected to end the year with a combined $9.14-billion worth of national advertising, a decline from the 1970 actual total of $9.32 billion.

Critics and regulators multiplied their attacks on marketers in 1971. An *Advertising Age* editorial assailed the Federal Trade Commission (FTC) for "getting pretty picayune" in demanding that General Electric Co. provide substantiation for an advertising claim that its air conditioner provides "the clean freshness of clear, cool mountain air." The editorial said, "This is the kind of tortured action on the part of the FTC that has businessmen tearing their hair out wondering in what directions the commission is going to move next."

The FTC moved in many directions. It challenged the ITT Continental Baking Co. for claiming that its Wonder bread "helps build strong bodies 12 ways," and it got that company to agree to devote 25% of its media advertising budget for one year to FTC-approved advertisements for its Profile bread. In another move against claims of "uniqueness," the FTC called on the Amstar Corp. to devote 25% of its advertising for a year to correct the claim that its Domino and Spreckels sugars are different from other refined sugars in that they assimilate faster into the body and enable professional athletes to perform better. The FTC said Domino and Spreckels were endorsed by the National Football League and major league baseball because they were paid by Amstar and not because of superior quality and nutritional value as represented. The FTC further indicated it planned to

A group called Help Unsell the War used a dramatic ad (below) to promote peace. The U.S. Army staged a major "soft sell" ad campaign to garner recruits (right).

MEDALS FOR PEACE
Thousands of Viet Nam veterans marched in Washington this April—against the war. Hundreds turned in their hard-won medals. Because medals were meant to be worn proudly and these men could no longer feel proud. Could anything tell us more loudly and clearly that it's time not just to "wind down" the war, but to end it completely?

Strike one blow for peace. Write or wire your Congressman. Urge him to work for total withdrawal this year.

LIVE AND WORK IN EUROPE

Today's Army now offers 16 months or more in Europe. Guaranteed. Ask today about enlisting in Armor, Artillery or Infantry. If you want to live and work where tourists only visit.

Today's Army wants to join you.

Red and white beach pants are one of a series of products sold to the public to spread the fame of the Coca-Cola Co.
COURTESY, THE COCA-COLA CO.

take a broad look at testimonial advertising where the endorsement was based primarily on "monetary consideration" and not on personal use, preference, or familiarity with the product.

Breakfast cereal companies, which had been charged in 1970 by independent food researcher Robert B. Choate, Jr., with selling products containing "empty calories," were the subject in 1971 of an FTC study that reportedly charged them with increasing prices from 15% to 25% to provide for high profits and high advertising expenditures. Meanwhile, Choate reported in July that the industry had been "upgrading" its breakfast cereal formulations and that some companies were taking the lead in fortifying some of their previously low-ranking cereals. In November Choate, in a speech in Minneapolis, Minn., said that several cereals have improved in nutritional value over the preceding 15 months. (*See also* Magazines; Newspapers. *See in* CE: Advertising.)

AEROSPACE. In 1971 the United States dropped out of the fast-paced international race for a supersonic transport aircraft (SST). Foes of the SST in Congress, led by Senator William Proxmire (D, Wis.), cited high costs, air pollution, and noisy sonic booms as the main reasons for the SST's unpopularity. Despite arguments to the contrary by champions of the SST, Congress scrapped the program. However, Aleksandr F. Aksyonov, deputy minister of civil aviation of the Soviet Union, scoffed at fears over the possible environmental hazards of the SST. As an instance, he said, because the fast jets burn essentially the same fuel as subsonic jets, he did not believe their emissions would add a significant burden to the atmosphere.

The TU-144, the Soviet entry in the SST race, was on display after it flew to the Paris Air Show last May. It was expected to be in commercial operation by late 1973. The Anglo-French SST,

the Concorde, flew from Toulouse, France, to Cayenne, French Guiana, late in the summer, setting a claimed speed record for a transatlantic flight. During the 5,000-mile flight the Concorde averaged about 1,120 mph. The U.S. Boeing 747, currently the largest jetliner in the worldwide commercial operation, cruises at about 650 mph.

More Superjets Take to the Air

The DC-10 entered airline service in August. Built by the McDonnell Douglas Corp., the DC-10 could accommodate from 250 to 345 passengers. It also boasted of drastically reducing noise and air pollution. The DC-10 reportedly enters and leaves airport areas with scarcely more than a hum and a "whoosh," without leaving a smoke trail. Each of its three General Electric CF6 engines produces more than twice the thrust of those on conventional four-engine transports and generates much less noise because of sound-absorbing materials.

The Lockheed L-1011 underwent flight testing in 1971. Scheduled for commercial operation in 1972, the L-1011 TriStar would carry up to 400 passengers at speeds of more than 600 mph. The 178-foot-long TriStar is a trijet, like the DC-10.

Lockheed's Money Problems

Early in the year there was considerable question whether the Lockheed Aircraft Corp. would be in business long enough to build a fleet of L-1011's. In January the Defense Department asked Lockheed to take a $200-million loss on cost overruns incurred on the C-5A, the giant military transport Lockheed was building. To compound problems, Rolls-Royce, Ltd., British contractor for the L-1011's engines, went into bankruptcy in February. The British government quickly took over

One version of a heavy-lift helicopter (HLH) was designed by the Boeing Co.
COURTESY, THE BOEING CO.

This F-4 fighter jet has been used by the U.S. Air Force in the Indochina war. There was some speculation in 1971 that F-4's might be phased out by the services and replaced with a newer fighter.
COURTESY, U.S. AIR FORCE

operation of Rolls-Royce but ensured engine production only if Lockheed could resolve its money problems.

Lockheed was finally rescued in August by the U.S. Senate, which agreed—by only one vote—to back a $250-million loan to the aircraft company. The government-guaranteed loan was to be repaid by the end of 1974.

Military Aircraft

Lockheed again experienced trouble when, in October, the U.S. Air Force "stood down," or temporarily grounded, its fleet of 47 C-5A's. Plagued with engineering problems since the inception of the C-5A program, several of the giant transports had such recent troubles as a cracked wing and a torn-away engine. Despite the setbacks, Air Force spokesmen continued to praise the C-5A, trusting that its flaws would be remedied eventually.

In 1971 the U.S. and the Soviet Union reduced their bomber forces while continuing their missile race, according to the International Institute for Strategic Studies. The institute's findings showed that the U.S. Air Force cut back its B-52 bomber force from 405 to 360 aircraft. The Soviet force of MYA-4 Bison and TU-20 Bear bombers was put at an estimated 140 planes.

The aging B-52 was expected to be replaced by the B-1 bomber. Flight trials of the B-1 were set for 1974. Compared to the B-52, the B-1 would have a higher speed, larger bomb capacity, quicker reaction launch, and the ability to operate from less costly bases. However, congressional opposition to expensive defense projects rose considerably in 1971. Supporters of the B-1 feared the bomber would suffer the same fate as the U.S. supersonic transport.

Two aircraft companies—Fairchild Hiller Corp. and Northrop Corp.—competed for the Air Force

A new passenger jet, the DC-10, was put into service in the summer of 1971. The plane was noteworthy for its relatively low levels of air and noise pollution.
COURTESY, MCDONNELL DOUGLAS CORP.

contract on the AX, a new attack fighter-bomber. The winner of the competition would get the contract to produce 600 of the aircraft. Each company is to build two prototype test models for evaluation in late 1972 at Edwards Air Force Base in California. The competition was part of the Defense Department's "fly-before-you-buy" attitude aimed at eliminating the wasteful cost overruns of recent years.

Meanwhile, the controversial F-111, built by General Dynamics Corp., gained some advocates in 1971. Its supporters felt the F-111 was the best aircraft yet developed for night and bad-weather strikes deep within enemy territory. However, the Air Force temporarily grounded its F-111's in late April because of a rash of crashes.

The McDonnell Douglas F-15 was scheduled to make its first test flight in 1972. The F-15 is a single-seat, all-weather fighter powered by two turbofan engines. High-ranking Air Force officers were banking heavily on the F-15 as a means for the U.S. to regain the air superiority it was starting to lose in the Vietnam war.

The U.S. Navy sought to replace its aging McDonnell Douglas F-4 Phantom fighter with the Grumman F-14, a variable-swept-wing aircraft. Late in 1971 the Senate gave its permission for continuing development of the F-14. However, the Grumman Aerospace Corp. was experiencing cost problems with the F-14, citing a $2-billion cost rise since the program was first contracted in 1968.

Helicopters

The world's largest helicopter, the Soviet MIL V-12, was publicly unveiled at the 1971 Paris Air Show. A heavy-duty transport helicopter, the MIL V-12 could vertically raise a 55,000-pound payload. Operating as a STOL (short takeoff and landing) craft, it could carry 66,000 pounds. Forty-one feet high, the MIL V-12 has a fuselage 122 feet long, and a rotor-tip span of some 220 feet.

The U.S. Army encouraged development of a heavy-lift helicopter (HLH) that could manage a 23-ton payload. In the meantime, an interim HLH —the improved Sikorsky CH-54B—entered production in 1971. The CH-54B was capable of hauling 12.5 tons of personnel or equipment.

The Sikorsky HH-3, the "Jolly Green Giant" of the Air Force, assumed a new role as an aerial fire truck in Alaska. Alaskan Air Command officials said the "rainmakers," fitted with water-filled fiber glass buckets, were available for local military and civilian emergencies. (*See in* CE: Aerospace articles.)

AFGHANISTAN.
Attempts to develop effective parliamentary government in Afghanistan were thwarted in 1971 by squabbles between the government and the legislature. The 1969 elections had returned members who were unfamiliar with parliamentary methods. Among other incidents, the legislature had refused to pass bills the government

Sheep were traded at very low prices in Afghanistan during a severe drought. Grain and water shortages forced sheep farmers to glut the market, and prices plummeted.

considered essential. Finally, Afghanistan's king, Mohammed Zahir Shah, intervened with a threat of dissolution in order to secure passage of the essential legislation.

On May 17 Afghanistan's prime minister, Noor Ahmad Etemadi, resigned after being continually frustrated in his efforts to modernize the administration and bring the country forward. Abdul Zahir was confirmed as his successor on June 9. Zahir made earnest efforts to reach a good understanding with the legislature. The king assured him that the wishes of the deputies would be respected, and agreed to withdraw press censorship.

The economy was severely affected by the most serious drought in Afghanistan's history. People crossed into Pakistan and Iran in search of food. The government responded with massive relief operations. (*See in* CE: Afghanistan.)

AFRICA.
The patterns established in recent years were substantially repeated in Africa during 1971—an assortment of abortive coups, slow but visible economic growth, the continuation of white dominance in the south, and the maintenance, elsewhere, of one-party states. Echoing the nationalism of the past decade, the Democratic Republic of the Congo (Kinshasa) changed its name to the Republic of Zaire on October 27, and Sierra Leone became a republic on April 19.

Over a dozen countries reported unsuccessful

A Tanzanian government official (left) assures Masai elders that the government will administer Masai territory with a strong emphasis on local interests and needs.

attempts at overthrowing their regimes. The only successful coup occurred in Uganda, where President Milton Obote, who had been in power since 1962 and who had sought to make his land a pillar of socialism, was displaced by Maj. Gen. Idi Amin on January 25.

The Sudan went through three days of turmoil in July as a coup by leftist forces was reversed by a successful countercoup. Maj. Gen. Gaafar Mohammed al-Nimeiry, who had seized power in 1969, had earlier in 1971 called for the ending of Communist subversive activities. On July 19 the Communists, who had considerable influence in the country, took control of the state only to be quickly defeated by al-Nimeiry, who forthwith hanged the leading Communist, Abdel Khalek Mahgoub, and arrested hundreds of the revolutionaries.

In Morocco, during a lavish birthday party for King Hassan II, with hundreds of guests, the palace was attacked. Ninety-seven guests and defenders were killed and 130 wounded. The coup ostensibly was staged to fight corruption. When it was put down with the support of loyal troops, Hassan struck quickly, and summary executions, including those of ten high army officers, followed.

In the aftermath of the unsuccessful invasion of Guinea, in November 1970, by disaffected Guineans led by Portuguese officers, the government announced that 92 persons were sentenced to death on January 24. Other countries that experienced aborted coups or plots included Sierra Leone, Mali, Malagasy Republic, Kenya, Somalia, Chad, Zambia, Congo (Kinshasa), and Egypt.

Organization of African Unity (OAU)

Although no unusually dramatic step was taken, the OAU did reaffirm earlier positions when the African states assembled in June 1971. Because of disagreements over the coup in Uganda, the original meeting place for the conference (Kampala, Uganda) was rejected, even though former President Obote had built a $17-million meeting hall to house the delegates. However, ten days before the conference, the OAU's Council of Ministers had accepted General Amin's new Ugandan regime.

The OAU's eighth Assembly of Heads of State and Government was held in Addis Ababa, Ethiopia, on June 21 to 23. In perhaps its most significant action, the assembly rejected the "outward diplomacy" of South Africa. Dialogue with that nation was rejected by a 28 to 6 vote. Those believing that more could be gained by talking with the white-dominated land than by the present ineffective policy of opposition included Ivory Coast, Gabon, Lesotho, Malagasy Republic, Malawi, and Mauritius, with abstentions recorded

Senegal's President Léopold Senghor (in car, right) is host to France's President Georges Pompidou during a good-will visit.

by Upper Volta, Dahomey, Niger, Togo, and Swaziland. All others bitterly denounced what seemed an unnecessary concession and one unlikely to change South Africa's program of apartheid.

Intra-African Unity

On September 1 a loose union made up of Egypt, Libya, and Syria, called the Confederation of Arab Republics, received overwhelming popular approval in referendums. Also, several small but functional meetings indicative of African cooperation took place during the year. The first all-African seminar on the human environment in Africa was held in Addis Ababa in August, with 33 countries in attendance. Meeting for the first time in ten years, the second conference on hydrology in the economic development of Africa met for ten days in September. Jointly sponsored by the OAU and the United Nations (UN) Economic Commission for Africa (ECA), it attracted 34 African countries and 60 international experts.

The ECA also brought together eight Western industrial nations and African states on October 1 to discuss a proposed trans-African highway from Mombasa, Kenya, to Lagos, Nigeria. On July 19 the first scientific advisory panel set up by the OAU began work in Addis Ababa.

The Economy

At a conference of the Association of African Central Banks, in Rabat, Morocco, it was noted that, taken as a whole, during the UN Development Decade the average annual per capita growth of the gross domestic product in Africa had been less than 2%. Of the 25 countries listed by the UN with unusually low per capita incomes, 16 were in Africa.

The Algerian government on February 24 took 51% control of French-owned oil holdings; the French had controlled two thirds of Algerian oil production, with an investment since 1954 of $1.35 billion. France paid the lowest price in the world for this oil and was supplied with 30% of its needs. With unsuccessful talks having gone on since 1969, the Algerians seized the companies and demanded the payment of tax arrears. The French preferred 100% nationalization and a just compensation. On June 30 a ten-year accord (amplified on September 21) was signed by Sonatrach (the Algerian oil trust) and the Compagnie Française des Pétroles, one of the two main companies whose assets had been taken. The latter was to receive a $50-million indemnity to be paid over a seven-year period, and in turn would pay back taxes of $27 million.

External Relations

African nations, led by Tanzania, played an important role in the admission of the People's Republic of China to the UN and the expulsion of Taiwan. Twenty-six voted for the resolution and 15 opposed it.

On September 13 Togo became the sixth African state in less than a year to recognize the Peking government, the others being Equatorial Guinea, Nigeria, Cameroon, Sierra Leone, and Ethiopia. The last, after a visit to Peking by Emperor Haile Selassie I in October, received an $84-million loan for farm development. The Chinese, in August, had also provided the Sudan with a $35-million loan for highways, bridges, and a textile factory.

Southern Africa

No fundamental shift in attitude or power occurred during the year in southern Africa. The reaching out for "dialogue" with other African states, though rebuffed by the OAU, was moderately successful in a handful of countries.

On August 16, the first black head of state ever to visit South Africa, President H. Kamuzu Banda of Malawi, was given a warm diplomatic reception. Delegates also came from the Malagasy Republic and the Ivory Coast, and contacts were made with Uganda. (*See also* individual countries by name; International Relations. *See in* CE: Africa; countries by name.)

AGNEW, SPIRO T. In contrast to his strenuous vocal campaigning for conservative, law-and-order candidates in 1970, United States Vice-President Spiro T. Agnew attempted to maintain a posture of low visibility in 1971. His major duties during the year were two low-keyed official visits—in June and July, a trip to ten nations in Asia, Europe, and Africa, and in October, a visit to Turkey, Iran, and Greece. Despite his attempts to be innocuous, the vocal vice-president remained controversial. His chief blunder was his characterization of U.S. black leaders as "querulous," but he

Vice-President Spiro T. Agnew responds to the warm applause he received at a Raleigh, N.C. political rally in October.

was also criticized for putting a U.S. stamp of approval on the authoritarian regimes of Greece and Spain.

Agnew appeared to depart somewhat from his unquestioning support of U.S. President Richard M. Nixon's policies when he voiced misgivings about the U.S.-China thaw, but whether this was personal or political was unclear. Denials of any rift between the president and vice-president over this issue were made, but the incident led to speculation that Agnew might be assuming a role of Administration spokesman to the right-wing faction of the Republican party, assuaging their uneasiness over the seemingly abrupt change in the Administration's China policy.

Agnew certainly continued to champion causes that endeared him to this faction—strongly defending Federal Bureau of Investigation Director J. Edgar Hoover and continuing his attacks on the U.S. news media. It was his popularity with this conservative constituency that appeared to be his strongest asset in quelling the intermittent speculation during the year that he would be dropped as Nixon's running mate in 1972. (*See also* Nixon.)

AGRICULTURE.

For corn belt farmers, 1971 was a year of worry and wait. The Southern corn-leaf blight that had reduced the 1970 corn crop threatened to break out anew. Blight-resistant seed was at a premium, so much so that a "gray market" was in operation throughout the farm states. But in 1971, the dry, cool summer, coupled with increased planting of resistant varieties of corn seed, resulted in a bumper corn crop.

Increased urbanization continued to cut sharply into farmlands, with about 1.5 million acres being

In 1971 the Department of Agriculture introduced a cartoon character named Woodsy Owl to help promote the cause of conservation throughout the U.S.

UPI COMPIX

FOREST SERVICE · U.S. DEPARTMENT OF AGRICULTURE

AUTHENTICATED NEWS INTERNATIONAL

In August Secretary of Agriculture Clifford M. Hardin (center) inspected effects of corn leaf blight on an Indiana farm.

taken for housing and other urban uses in 1971. California, for instance, one of the top United States farm states, was losing 375 acres of agricultural land each day to urban projects.

Subsidies paid by the federal government to farm operators totaled $3.7 billion in 1970, the most recent year such figures were available. Nine large operators, six of which were in California, received $1 million or more in subsidies. Foes of agricultural price supports in Congress tried to impose sharp cuts in the program by introducing an amendment to the 1971 farm appropriations bill that would limit any individual payment to no more than $20,000. The maximum had already been cut to $55,000 in 1970. However, after the Senate rejected the $20,000 ceiling, conferees from both houses of Congress in July agreed to retain the more generous 1970 limit. Several members of Congress and close relatives had received $5,000 or more in farm payments. Senator James O. Eastland (D, Miss.) received more than $164,000, mostly in cotton price-support payments.

A jurisdictional dispute that pitted the United Farm Workers Organizing Committee (UFWOC) and its leader, César Chavez, against the International Brotherhood of Teamsters (IBT) was ended in March. The dispute raged over which union would represent the California lettuce workers. According to the settlement, the UFWOC would have jurisdiction over the pickers, while the IBT would represent drivers and processors.

An 18-day railroad strike ending in early August affected West Coast produce and its Eastern markets. California fruit and vegetable producers estimated that they lost $35 million as a consequence of the rail walkout. California farms usually supplied about 40% of all U.S. produce.

Farm Profits and Costs

Farm income fared slightly better in 1971 than in the years before. Against the 1967 index of

100, farm prices by mid-year 1971 stood at a composite index of 113. However, there was considerable price variation among individual crops. For example, food and feed grains brought in slightly less money in 1971, whereas the prices of oil-bearing crops, cotton, and fresh fruits and vegetables were up.

The parity index of production costs paid by farmers reached 121 (1967 = 100). Those costs included commodities and services, interest paid on loans, taxes, and wages for extra help.

The parity rates that measured the overall buying power of U.S. farmers dropped to 93 (1967 = 100), as compared with 94 in 1970. The farm labor force dropped again, to 5.2 million workers, about 100,000 fewer than in 1970. Hired hands, who constituted about 30% of the farm force, put in an average 32.5 hours each week at an average wage of $1.54 an hour.

U.S. President Richard M. Nixon talked to the nation's farmers by radio on May 2, and he assured them that recent agricultural measures would improve the farmer's position in the economy. Through one such measure, the Foreign Agricultural Service, which was dedicated to expanding U.S. farm exports, received an extra million dollars in funding, bringing the total to $28.7 million. Also, the federal government began guaranteeing private farm loans, instead of acting as the lending agency. Federal insurance of loans was expected to broaden the borrowing power of the individual farmer.

Sales of most types of farm equipment during the first half of 1971 sagged even below the low levels of the prior year. Tractor purchases, for example, were down by 11%.

Real estate activity involving sales of farmland for farm uses was sluggish. The national index of farmland value per acre rose to 121 in March (1967 = 100), 3% higher than in the previous annual comparison.

A New Secretary; Crop Yields

Bumper grain crops and low government support prices cut farm income and angered farmers against the Nixon Administration's agricultural policies in the fall. In November U.S. Secretary of Agriculture Clifford M. Hardin resigned and was replaced with Earl L. Butz, whose nomination was hotly debated before confirmation in the U.S. Senate. (*See* United States.)

The 1971 corn crop was forecast at 5.3 billion bushels, 35% higher than the 1970 crop. Because of the blight threat, farmers had been allowed to increase corn acreage without losing eligibility for price supports, thus creating the record harvest.

Hay and forage reached a record high production index of 104 (1967 = 100) in 1971. All hay totaled 131 million tons. The alfalfa crop was 76 million tons.

More grain sorghums and barley were harvested in 1971 than in the year before. However, oats dropped 3% short of the 1970 crop. Despite the severe drought that plagued the Southwest during the year, the grain sorghum yield averaged 54.5 bushels per acre. The total crop was 889.8 million bushels. The barley crop was at a record high of 46 bushels per acre, with a total harvest of 469.9 million bushels.

A record wheat harvest was forecast at 1.6 billion bushels. The winter wheat crop of 1.2 billion bushels was 4% higher than in 1970. Kansas was

A Maine potato farmer is one of many forced out of business by bad weather and poor market conditions for his crop.
"THE NEW YORK TIMES"

Other Maine farmers, unable to meet mortgage or loan payments, watch their farming life come to a close at public auction.
"THE NEW YORK TIMES"

WIDE WORLD

A farm in Dallam County, Tex., shows dramatic evidence of the drought that swept the area in the summer of 1971.

responsible for about a quarter of the harvest. Durum wheat was estimated at 87 million bushels, brought in mainly from North Dakota. Other spring wheat was forecast at 377.8 million bushels. According to early indications, the acreage to be sown for 1972 wheat would exceed that for 1971, in spite of lower prices and mounting surpluses. The total production of food grains, which included wheat, rye, and rice was more than 54.5 million tons, 17% greater than in 1970.

Demand for soybeans would probably exceed the supply, even though a record soybean crop was harvested in 1971. Production rose to 1.2 billion bushels. Illinois led in soybean production with 241 million bushels, followed by Iowa with 182 million bushels.

The 1971 cotton crop was estimated at 10.7 million bales. Rain hindered the crop in the Southeast, while early drought delayed it in the Southwest. Nevertheless, the average lint yield was 444 pounds per acre, against 437 pounds in 1970. Texas continued to lead cotton production with a total of 3.1 million bales, followed by California and Mississippi.

The sugar-beet crop dropped somewhat to 25.7 million tons, 2% less than in 1970. Sugarcane, by contrast, was forecast at 25.7 million tons, 7% more than in 1970. Hawaii was the top sugarcane producer; Louisiana ranked second.

Fresh vegetables were in fairly short supply in 1971. Prices in the first half of 1971 averaged 9% higher than in the same period of 1970.

Livestock and Poultry Production

For the most part, livestock raisers enjoyed a successful year in 1971. The value of all livestock and poultry in the U.S. at the start of the year stood at a record high of $23.8 billion. Cattle and calves accounted for most of this total, at $21.1

billion. Texas, with 12.6 million head, was the leading cattle state.

Dairy cow numbers, on the decline since the 1950's, fell to 12.4 million head at the beginning of 1971. Wisconsin had the most milk cows with 1.8 million head, trailed by New York and Minnesota. Despite the price freeze on processed agricultural products in August, dairy production was expected to reach about 119 billion pounds.

Hog raisers, faced with the possibility of having to pay high prices for feed if the corn blight proved widespread, chose to drastically reduce the pig supply early in the year. However, sparked by the bumper corn crop, they were expected to increase the pig crop by 1972. By late 1971, a hundred pounds of hog was worth $19.50, up from $17.90 a year before.

Sheep and lamb production, in general, declined in 1971. However, commercial sheep and lamb slaughter during the first half of 1971 was higher than for the comparable period of 1970. An early crop of lambs, plus the drought in the Southwest, contributed markedly to the increased slaughter. In the face of low wool prices, however, shorn-wool production slumped considerably.

The poultry inventory of Jan. 1, 1971, disclosed 442.8 million chickens, excluding commercial broilers. Hen and pullets of egg-laying age totaled 335 million. Both figures exceeded the 1970 inventory. Egg output rose well above 1970 production, with layers producing an average 221 eggs each in 1971 compared with 218 the year before.

A midsummer epidemic of Venezuelan equine encephalomyelitis threatened horses and mules in Texas and nearby states. To meet the emergency, health officials inoculated many thousands of the animals against the dangerous mosquito-transmitted virus disease. (*See also* Animals and Wildlife; Veterinary Medicine.)

Canadian Farm Production

The Prairie Provinces returned to major grain production and export in 1971. As a result, the 1970 emergency program to cut the Canadian wheat surplus and encourage diversification into feed grains and livestock was terminated. The 1971 wheat harvest amounted to 507.4 million bushels, up 57% over that of the prior year. The tremendous increase was due to the planting of additional wheat acreage, 19.2 million acres. Other large harvests were 656.1 million bushels of barley and 371.4 million bushels of oats.

An increase in feed grain production was in part responsible for the upsurge in Canadian livestock raising. The number of cattle and calves inventoried on June 1, 1971, reached an estimated record high of 13.7 million head.

The Canadian government continued to support prices and give subsidies to the dairy industry in 1971. Indications early in the year forecast a more successful production of poultry and eggs in Canada than in 1970. (*See in* CE: Agriculture.)

ALBANIA. During 1971 Albania continued to pursue a policy of widening its diplomatic and trade contacts, following the example of its ally, the People's Republic of China. On February 5 Albania and Yugoslavia agreed to raise their respective diplomatic missions to embassy level despite their ideological differences and the long-disputed question of the large Albanian minority in Yugoslavia. In June Yugoslavia's President Tito appointed his country's first ambassador to Albania.

On May 6 Greece and Albania agreed to exchange ambassadors. The two countries, technically at war since 1940, had had no diplomatic relations for more than 30 years. This diplomatic rapprochement was interpreted by Albania as evidence of Greece's dropping its claim to the so-called North Epirus region in Albania.

During the year Belgium, the Netherlands, Norway, Iran, Chile, and Peru also agreed to establish diplomatic relations with Albania. Albanian-Soviet relations were marked by hostility, although somewhat ameliorated from previous years.

In November the 6th Congress of the Albanian Communist party was held. Enver Hoxha was reelected first secretary of the party and a new Central Committee of 11 members was chosen.

Albania continued to develop its economy with Chinese aid. About 33 industrial enterprises covered in the 1971–75 plan were being financed by China. Many Chinese technicians worked in the country, although their numbers had diminished during recent years. The Albanian-sponsored resolution to seat China in the United Nations was finally passed in October. (*See* United Nations. *See in* CE: Albania.)

ALGERIA. The most important event in Algeria in 1971 was the government take-over of the country's French-dominated oil industry on February 24. The take-over, achieved at the cost of ending the country's special relationship with France, put the regime of Algeria's President Houari Boumédienne in a position to prove that Algeria could become a significant industrial nation on the basis of its own natural and financial resources without French help.

The take-over occurred after negotiations with France had dragged on intermittently since July 1970, when Algeria unilaterally imposed higher prices for its oil. The situation reached a crisis point in January 1971, and, finally, in February 51% of all French oil companies' Algerian interests were taken over by the Algerian government and vested in its own national oil corporation—Sonatrach. The French companies resisted the nationalization measures and sought to prevent their application by the withdrawal of their technical staff and an attempt to blacklist Algerian oil on the international market. Algeria responded by banning oil exports to France. By the end of June, however, Compagnie Française des Pétroles had accepted its role as a minority partner in its Algerian operations in return for compensation payable over seven years. Elf-Erap, the other major French group involved, came to similar terms in late September. Full production and exports were resumed at the end of that month.

The take-over was the most important sign of a trend away from Algerian dependence on France. There were others. For most Algerians the most visible remaining evidence of this former dependence were the extensive vineyards that had long provided France with cheap wines. With the end of the grape harvest in August, a start was made on converting the "colonialist" vineyards to the growing of other food crops. In September French was eliminated as the language of the law courts, and Boumédienne promised that the "Arabization of Algerian life" would be progressively carried out.

With economic development the preoccupation of the regime, little attention was given to the political life of the country. Only the students of Algiers University demonstrated their militant opposition to the regime.

Trade and aid ties with the Soviet Union and Eastern Europe were maintained but on a muted scale. Soviet Premier Aleksei N. Kosygin underlined this continuing cooperation with a visit to Algeria in early October. (*See in* CE: Algeria.)

ANIMALS AND WILDLIFE. Some kinds of wildlife were in considerable jeopardy in 1971 because of their economic value, or in some cases, because of systematic elimination. But a growing awareness of the environmental role of wildlife by many was instrumental in winning at least a temporary reprieve for some seemingly-doomed wildlife.

Joy Adamson, author of 'Born Free', won the Joseph Wood Krutch award of the U.S. Humane Society in 1971 for her writings.

MARION KAPLAN

Pribilof Seal Slaughter

Impassioned efforts were made to halt the yearly seal harvest on the Pribilof Islands off Alaska. The seals, three- or four-year-old males, are first stunned by blows with a bat and then bled to death. In answer to an uproar over the harvest, a special board of veterinarians convened in the United States in September; they concluded that the practice was humane.

Critics questioned whether profits justified the slaughter of seals and other ocean mammals. Furthermore, some hinted that females and baby seals were being killed on the Pribilofs, too. Late in the year, congressional hearings were conducted on the Harris-Pryor bill to ban the killing of any ocean mammal by a U.S. citizen or firm, and to make the Pribilof Islands a wildlife sanctuary.

Oil Spills Threaten Wildlife Again

On January 18, two tankers collided in dense fog and spilled 840,000 gallons of oil into San Francisco Bay. The oil slick trapped thousands of seabirds and destroyed fish and shellfish along a 50-mile stretch of California coast. Students, construction workers, housewives, and retired persons worked together to save the oil-soaked grebes, loons, and other diving birds.

Several thousand birds that survived the first day were cleaned by the volunteers. For three months volunteers fed special diets to the surviving birds and played surf recordings to calm them. At the end of the effort, probably the most intensive wildlife rescue ever, about 300 seabirds were ready for return to the shore.

Campaigns to Preserve Wildlife

Thousands of young Americans staged a strong campaign to save the wild mustangs and burros of the West from extinction by hunters who sell the meat for pet food. Because they are descended from once-domesticated animals and thus are not considered native wildlife, the mustangs and burros are not protected by the Endangered Species Act. The movement to save them was begun by fourth-graders in Rosebud, Ore. It spread to Nevada, where most of the surviving 17,000 wild horses live. Within a short time boys and girls across the nation joined the movement, sending tons of protesting mail to Congress. Sixth-graders in the East even sold bumper stickers and sent the money to Washington, D.C., for lobbying expenses. Also prominent in the fight to save the mustangs was Mrs. Velma Johnston ("Wild Horse Annie"), the president of the International Society for the Protection of Mustangs and Burros. Largely as a result of her efforts and the young people's campaign, Congress passed a bill in November to establish refuges in the West where wild horses and burros would be protected as a "national heritage."

Preservation of another Western animal, the prairie dog, received public support. Thirty miles north of Santa Fe, N.M., 20 acres were set aside in 1970 by the U.S. Bureau of Land Management for a protected village of white-tailed prairie dogs. Similar villages have been preserved in seven other western states, but most of them are for black-tailed prairie dogs. Burrowing owls, quails, and badgers were quickly attracted to the New Mexico village. Also, the prairie dog tunnels aerated the soil and

A band of wild horses, numbering about 20, roams free through the Plumstead area of London. Fences and hedges proved to be no deterrent to the wanderings of the herd.
POPPERFOTO FROM PICTORIAL PARADE

The ivory-billed woodpecker was thought to be extinct until 1971, when a birdwatcher in South Carolina heard its eight-note call.

allowed rain to penetrate deep into the dry ground —demonstrating again the useful role prairie dogs play in keeping nature balanced.

In South Carolina a bird long thought extinct— the ivory-billed woodpecker—blocked the destruction of a natural wildlife sanctuary. After an Audubon Society member heard the eight-note call of the bird, a South Carolina public utility postponed timber cutting in the state-owned Santee Swamp. Not only is it possible that the woodpecker still survives there, but the swamp contains nesting areas for bald eagles and serves as the habitat for eight species that are on the endangered animal list.

New regulations for the protection of the bottle-nosed dolphin went into effect in Florida in November 1970. At least 193 of the popular ocean mammals were captured in Florida waters as recently as 1970. The new rules prohibit the capture of bottle-nosed dolphin less than six feet long, its usual length when weaned.

Even the snake found friends along the West Coast. Ecologists in California sought passage of laws to stop the profitable traffic in pet snakes. So many snakes have been taken from their natural habitats recently that mice, rats, and other small rodents are overrunning ranching areas where snakes formerly kept them in check.

Slowly increasing after near extinction, the known whooping crane population was 77 in 1971. Fifty-six birds lived in the wild, 4 were in zoos, and 17 were in captivity at the Patuxent Wildlife Research Center in Maryland.

A Bad Year for Eagles

Hundreds of bald and golden eagles, already close to extinction, were deliberately destroyed in 1971. Nearly 50, including 11 bald eagles, national emblem of the United States, were killed, 22 of them poisoned by thallium sulphate. The rancher held responsible was fined $679, the minimum fine that could be imposed.

The matter seemed ended until further investigation revealed that 770 eagles, some of which were bald eagles, were shot to death from helicopters during the past year. The pilot charged with the killings claimed that a prominent sheep rancher agreed to pay $25 per eagle.

Bald eagles were further endangered in one of their major wintering areas, a narrow strip along the Mississippi River in west-central Illinois. Logging, sand excavations, and utility lines were disrupting so much of the environment that ecologists feared that the birds would not return to winter in the area.

Virus Threatens Horses

Fast action by public health officials and the U.S. Department of Agriculture stopped a potentially disastrous epidemic of the mosquito-borne Venezuelan equine encephalomyelitis (VEE) among horses in Mexico and the U.S. By summer a massive VEE vaccination program was in operation in all states along the Mexican border and the Gulf of Mexico. So serious is the disease that veterinarians reported up to a 40% death toll among infected horses.

A quarantine was placed on every horse in Texas and surrounding states. The quarantine applied also to the Ringling Brothers and Barnum &

A dolphin was born in the aquarium at St. Petersburg Beach, Fla., in August. Births of dolphins in captivity are rare.

Bailey circus horses in Dallas, Tex. When the circus moved on to its next appearance in Arizona, the "Greatest Show on Earth" went on without horses for the first time in its history. (*See also* Environment. *See in* CE: Animals and related articles.)

ANTARCTICA.
In 1971, 10 Antarctic Treaty nations occupied 43 stations in Antarctica. Norway and Belgium, while not having bases of their own, participated in the research programs of other nations. A broad program of scientist exchange in both land and ocean research was carried out between most nations.

A study of the August 1970 volcanic eruption on Deception Island determined that it was the most violent of several eruptions that had occurred over the previous three years. It altered the shoreline, erased the three-crater island of cinder cones that emerged during the 1967 eruption, shifted the intertidal zone upward, and destroyed all subtidal life to a depth of 120 feet. Whaling was outlawed by the United States, which urged other countries, through the International Whaling Commission, to follow suit. At its meeting in Washington, D.C., in June 1971, the commission postponed action on this issue despite warnings that many species of whales were facing extinction.

Unusually warm weather hampered scientific studies during the austral summer. A high of 44°F. was recorded, causing melting of ice runways and snow cover to such an extent that supply planes were unable to land and programs were delayed for a full month. Meteorologists suggested that melting was due to black volcanic ash from the latest Deception Island volcanic eruption.

Over 200 scientists and technicians from more than 50 universities, government agencies, and industrial firms participated in the 1971 U.S. Antarctic Research Program. Logistical support was provided by ships, aircraft, helicopters, and

United States and New Zealand ships are anchored in Winter Quarters Bay in Antarctica in February 1971.
COURTESY, U.S. NAVY

more than 1,000 personnel at five permanent stations and several summer sites. Four research vessels assisted by icebreakers carried on a wide range of research studies in the seas and islands around Antarctica. (*See also* Arctic. *See in* CE: Antarctica; Polar Exploration.)

KEYSTONE

In 1971 the Tasaday, a Stone Age tribe, were found living in a rain forest on Mindinao in the Philippines.

ANTHROPOLOGY.
A rare opportunity for anthropologists and other scientists to study people living in Stone Age style resulted from the discovery in 1971 of a primitive tribe in a rain forest on Mindinao in the Philippines. Calling itself the Tasaday, the tribe numbers fewer than 100 persons. The Tasaday use paleolithic stone flake tools, wear loin cloths and leaves, and speak in a tongue related to the Malayo-Polynesian language family. Ignorant of food cultivation, they subsist on the pith of the wild palm, fish, game, and roots. Philippine officials surveying minority groups were led to the tribe by a hunter. The Tasaday had been cut off from all outside contact for at least 400 years, and possibly for 2,000 years. To protect them, the survey team asked the government to set aside the forest as a preserve.

Egyptian scientists returning from an exploratory survey in Egypt's Western Desert reported the discovery of drawings by prehistoric men in caves on Uweinat Mountain, where the Egyptian, Sudanese, and Libyan borders meet. Depicting animals in a manner resembling the paleolithic cave paintings of France and Spain, the drawings are believed to date back to 6,000 B.C. The expedition also found five animal species thought to be extinct living on the Libyan side of the mountain.

Anthropologist Richard Leakey, continuing the search for fossils of early man near Lake Rudolf in Kenya, reported a find of 16 hominid specimens, including, for the first time, limb bones. He identified specimens taken from the same level as belonging to two genera—*Homo* and *Australopithecus*—indicating that they were contemporaries; previous theories held that *Australopithecus* was an ancestor of *Homo*. Harvard University scientists announced that an *Australopithecus* jawbone fragment found in Kenya in 1967 dates back 5.5 million years, making it the oldest fossil of the human family ever found. (*See also* Archaeology. *See in* CE: Anthropology.)

ARAB EMIRATES, UNION OF.

On Dec. 2, 1971, six Trucial states in the Persian Gulf of the Middle East became one independent country, the Union of Arab Emirates. The six were Abu Dhabi, Dubai, Sharja, 'Ajman, Fujaira, and Umm al Qaiwain. The first president of the new nation was the ruler of Abu Dhabi, Emir Zaid bin Sultan al-Nahayan.

The independence proclamation made a point of declaring solidarity with "the Arab nation." The union became the 18th independent Arab country.

Great Britain had made persistent efforts to create a federation of Bahrain, Qatar, and the seven Trucial states to preserve British interests in the gulf after its military withdrawal at the end of 1971. However, Bahrain and Qatar each declared their independence separately. (*See* Bahrain; Qatar.) The seventh Trucial state, Ras al Khaima, did not join the new nation immediately but was reportedly negotiating to become a member as the year drew to a close.

The day that the new country was formed a treaty of friendship was signed with Britain. The new country's army was to be led by the armed forces of Abu Dhabi, trained in Britain.

Iran fulfilled its declared intention of occupying the gulf islands of Abu Musa and the two Tunbs (Greater and Lesser) on November 30. Representatives of the Sharja government, which controlled Abu Musa, welcomed the Iranian troops. On December 1, however, there was an unsuccessful attempt to assassinate the deputy ruler of Sharja. One Arab policeman and three Iranian soldiers were killed during the landings on the Tunbs, claimed by Ras al Khaima.

ARCHAEOLOGY.

One of the major problems with which archaeologists were concerned in 1971 was the destruction of archaeological sites and cultural contexts by man-made projects and by the activities of illicit diggers, who provided artifacts for the commercial art market. The Archaeological Institute of America and the Society for American Archaeology approved resolutions condemning the looting of archaeological sites, the smuggling of stolen antiquities, and the irresponsible purchase of stolen items by museums and private collectors. Most other professional organizations, the United Nations Educational, Social, and Cultural Organization (UNESCO), and a 17-nation committee of the Council of Europe had adopted similar resolutions.

A number of countries, hopeful of preserving their archaeological heritage, pleaded for outside aid in salvage work. Pakistan sought aid in preserving the great Indus valley site of Mohenjo Daro from the effects of a new irrigation system. Salvage excavations in Egypt around the temples of Karnak continued with international assistance. In Cambodia the country's only archaeologist was coordinating an effort to save the ancient temples and statues at Angkor Wat from the ravages of war.

Several new means for the analysis of archaeological materials were reported during the year. A technique for determining whether an animal bone came from a wild or domestic animal was described by a Columbia University team of scientists. The technique, it was felt, might prove to be a useful tool in understanding how prehistoric

These are the mummified feet of Nefer, an ancient Egyptian court musician whose 5000-year-old mummy was discovered at Saqqara, Egypt. Experts termed it one of the best preserved mummies ever found.

UPI COMPIX

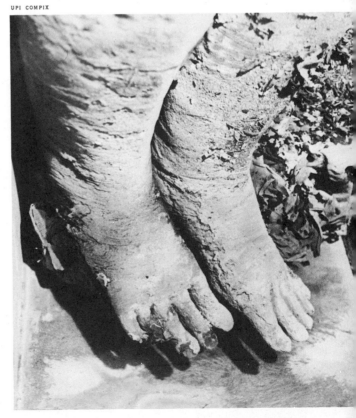

Diggers uncover the skeleton of what is thought
to be a California grey whale of the late
Pleistocene Age.

man developed from a hunting way of life to a
pastoral existence.

Of equal importance were improvements in dating techniques. Computer analysis of the results
of microscopic studies of the long-lived bristlecone
pine enabled a University of Arizona scientist to
establish a precise tree-ring chronology that extended back nearly 8,000 years. This became significant when the ages of wood samples determined
by both the tree-ring method and the radiocarbon
technique were compared. The results of such
comparisons supported other data indicating that
the amount of carbon-14 in the atmosphere was not
constant in the past, a vital assumption of the radiocarbon method of dating. The bristlecone pine
studies provided a method for converting radiocarbon ages into true dates, thus correcting and
refining the radiocarbon dating procedure.

Eastern Hemisphere

What was thought to be the oldest known hominid occupation site was reported to have been found
in East Africa during the year. Three scientists
uncovered stone artifacts sealed within a bed of
tuff (a kind of volcanic rock) east of Lake Rudolf
in Kenya. The tuff was dated more than 2.5 million years old.

In Egypt the tense political situation restricted
the activities of archaeologists to relatively urban
areas. Some 29 royal mummies of pharaohs and
their queens were X-rayed, revealing medical information and the presence of valuable artifacts.
In contrast, in Israel a great amount of digging

Archaeologists carefully search the Pepper Cave at the Ayacucho Valley site in Peru for
possible repositories of plant and animal remains.

activity occurred at more than 25 sites. In a burial site on the outskirts of Jerusalem, the first physical evidence of a crucifixion was discovered. It had long been known through literary sources, of course, that crucifixion was a commonly used method of execution in the early decades of the Christian era.

In the field of Greco-Roman studies, a number of interesting discoveries were made. A large limestone slab near the Acropolis in Athens, the capital of Greece, was identified as that upon which the ancient city's elected leaders stood to be sworn into office. A marble statue of Hercules as an adolescent and a bust of the Roman Emperor Antoninus Pius were also found in this area. Under the Yugoslav market town of Sremska Mitrovica (somewhat northwest of Belgrade, the capital), an imperial Roman city was excavated.

The entire question of whether European civilization developed independently or with the help of diffusionary influences from the lands at the eastern end of the Mediterranean was being reevaluated as a result of the newly revised radiocarbon dates. Certain European antiquities (such as Stonehenge in Great Britain and large stone tombs built in a variety of places in Europe), previously felt to have been built in imitation of similar monuments in the Near East, were now found to antedate their supposed prototypes. Although it was too soon yet to make a broad generalization that "civilization" itself was independently achieved in Europe, it was felt that the origins of even some general developments such as copper metallurgy and the domestication of certain types of animals might have been achieved independently in Europe as they were in the Near East.

Western Hemisphere

An archaeological reconnaissance was made of a portion of the right-of-way of the proposed Alaskan oil pipeline, which was to extend about 800 miles from Prudhoe Bay to Valdez, Alaska. More than 100 sites, representing a wide array of time periods and cultural affiliations, were discovered, with additional findings expected as the survey continued.

Investigation along the eastern coast of the Ungava Peninsula in northern Quebec revealed evidence of early Norse activity dated by radiocarbon technique at A.D. 1050. Remnants of a bow and iron axe, both unique for this portion of Canada, were found. The remains were believed to represent a hunting outpost of Norsemen whose major settlement was in Greenland.

Radiocarbon ages were reported for a number of human skeletal remains that had been found in California during past years. Of greatest importance was the date of 15,200 B.C. for the so-called Laguna skull, originally discovered in 1933 in Laguna Beach. The remarkably early date was the oldest yet determined for human bone in the New World.

New data and interpretations on the decline and collapse of the Mayan civilization were reported. According to a report on a symposium held on the Mayans in Santa Fe, N.M., the initial signs of slowdown appeared in Mayan culture shortly after A.D. 770, after almost 500 years of Classic-period growth in the tropical lowlands of southern Mexico and adjacent Central America. By A.D. 830 most of the ceremonial centers were seriously affected, and by A.D. 940, outlying farming villages and the great Mayan centers were almost totally abandoned.

In a worldwide study of prehistoric metallurgical processes a scientist from the California Institute of Technology demonstrated that the Mochi people of Peru were smelting, melting, alloying, and casting metals at about A.D. 200. The development of metallurgy in the Andean region between A.D. 200 and A.D. 1500 was shown to have progressed through a complex series of steps similar to the ones that occurred earlier in southwest Asia between 5500 B.C. and 3800 B.C. The parallel development and the significant time differences indicated that there was a lack of influence by Old World cultures upon New World metallurgy. (*See in* CE: Archaeology; Man.)

ARCHITECTURE. Despite the economic recession and growing inflation, many important architectural projects were completed in 1971, notably commercial and educational buildings and particularly in the United States. There were, however, some major architectural disappointments.

Perhaps the most publicized of these was the John F. Kennedy Center for the Performing Arts in Washington, D.C., The dean of U.S. architectural critics, Ada Louise Huxtable of *The New York Times,* called the white marble building, designed by U.S. architect Edward Durell Stone, "safe and sanitary kitsch," marked by "elephantine esthetic poverty," and in short, "a monumental disaster."

In 1971 the city of Chicago ironically celebrated the centenary of the famous Chicago fire—which was the reason for the city's rise as a center of American architecture—at the same time that one of the masterpieces of that period, the Louis Sullivan and Dankmar Adler Old Stock Exchange Building, was being demolished. The failure of the City Council and the city's mayor to respond to an 11th-hour public-spirited effort to save the building underlined the difficulties inherent in preserving the American architectural heritage. Another bitterly fought campaign took place in San Francisco, Calif., where voters turned down an opportunity to preserve the low-rise level of the city's skyline by voting against a proposal to limit future buildings to a six-story height.

School and University Architecture

One of the most exciting new buildings to be erected on a school campus was the huge athletics facility at Phillips Exeter Academy in New Hampshire, by the architectural firm of Kallmann and

McKinnell. On the outside of this striking building were enormous three-dimensional steel trusses supporting the roofs of the gymnasium, swimming pool, and skating rinks. The trusses had been built outside rather than inside to leave the building free of interior supports, which would have hindered the sporting activities it was designed to house.

The new gymnasium for the Japan Dental College in Tokyo by architect Shin'ichi Okada represented a very different solution to the challenge of designing an athletic building. The structure was composed of a see-through glass cage supported by concrete service towers at the ends. Facilities for the various activities were "stacked" vertically to make the most of a restricted city site. The glass cage made sports an urban event, giving pleasure not only to the participants but to outside spectators as well.

In Great Britain the first stage of a series of residential buildings was completed for Christ's College in Cambridge, England, by Denys Lasdun and Partners, adding yet another fine example of modern architecture to a town that already had more excellent modern buildings than almost any other in Britain. The new Christ's building was based on a plan of stepped construction and interlocking spaces. The building was of precast concrete and housed a series of study bedrooms, all facing toward gardens.

Office Buildings

The new headquarters of the American Can Co. at Greenwich, Conn., was designed by architect Gordon Bunshaft of Skidmore, Owings & Merrill on an impressively landscaped 175-acre site. Another new corporate headquarters was that of the Ralston Purina Co. at St. Louis, Mo., which was designed as a showplace for visitors by Hellmuth, Obata, and Kassabaum. The 15-story structure was of concrete with a pyramidal base. The new building for the City Blue Print Co. of Louisville, Ky., was designed by architect Jasper D. Ward as a sort of visual joke. The playful design featured an enormous bright blue cube at the corner. The exterior volume was broken by huge circular windows on one facade.

The Westcoast Building in Vancouver, B.C., by architects Rhone and Iredale, with engineering by Bogue Babicki and Associates, won the award for the best engineering in high-rise construction in the 1970–71 Design in Steel Award program of the American Iron and Steel Institute. The new concrete-and-glass West German headquarters for Rank-Xerox Corp., located in a suburb of Düsseldorf, was designed by German architects Hentrich-Petschnigg and Partners. The building was composed of three hexagons grouped around a central service core. The new Standard Bank Center in Johannesburg, South Africa, also by Hentrich-Petschnigg, was the largest suspended-floor structure in the world.

Civic and Cultural Buildings

The new Denver Art Museum in Colorado was one of the largest museums in the western U.S. Designed by architects John S. Sudler of Denver and Gio Ponti of Italy, the structure was composed of two six-story cubes. The main entrance, lobbies, and utility core were located where the cubes joined.

Several noteworthy new libraries were completed in the U.S. in 1971. Among these was the Mount

The study of architecture is introduced at an elementary school in Paterson, N.J. A young student designs and builds a structure utilizing three-sided forms and paper cups.

MARJORIE PICKENS FROM 'BEGINNING EXPERIENCES IN ARCHITECTURE' BY GEORGE TROGLER, PUBLISHED BY VAN NOSTRAND REINHOLD 1972

Sweden gave these crystal chandeliers to the John F. Kennedy Center for the Performing Arts, which opened in September. The center was designed by Edward Durell Stone.

Angel Abbey Library, in St. Benedict, Ore., which was designed by the famous Finnish architect Alvar Aalto and was one of his few U.S. buildings. The new Lyndon Baines Johnson Library in Austin, Tex., designed by Bunshaft of Skidmore, Owings & Merrill, was planned "to express through monumentality the importance of its historical treasures." The main mass of the tomblike library rested upon a podium and was defined by two vast 65-foot-high parallel walls, 90 feet apart and 200 feet long. The library was dedicated on May 22.

The Mummers Theater in Oklahoma City, Okla., by architect John Johansen represented a new departure in theater design. The controversial building incorporated grain-elevator tubes of brightly painted steel. The helter-skelter expressive form, akin to the stage sets of some contemporary plays, was composed of three volumes connected by "people tubes."

A new cathedral at Kasama in northern Zambia, which included residential accommodations, was designed by Julian Elliott to be built by unskilled local labor. It consisted of a conglomeration of small vaults on local oatmeal-colored brick, with the church itself roofed by a concrete shell.

A "capsule" office-apartment building in Tokyo was designed by architect Noriaki Kurokawa to nest factory-made, capsulated apartment units into 175-foot shaft frames. Each steel capsule would have built-in furniture, bathroom, and air conditioning, and would sell for $10,000 to $13,000. (*See also* Construction. *See in* CE: Architecture.)

ARCTIC. In 1971 actual production of oil and gas resources in the North American Arctic failed to materialize on the scale predicted by past exploration activities. Nevertheless, considerable progress was made during the year in resolving environmental and native land claims problems and in preparing to start work on the vast pipeline and transportation projects required to bring fuel

In March 1971, the British Royal Navy's nuclear-powered submarine *Dreadnought* became the first British sub to surface at the North Pole.

and power south to the consumer markets in Canada and the United States.

At midyear it was announced that Canada and the U.S. had signed a cooperative agreement for combating forest fires along the Yukon-Alaska border. The agreement established a ten-mile buffer zone on either side of the border where parties from both Canada and the U.S. could initiate immediate fire-fighting action without making application for formal permission or documents of any kind.

At the request of the U.S. government, exploratory discussions were held in Ottawa, Ont., during July on a proposal to pave the Canadian portion of the Alaska Highway. The discussions were the outcome of passage in December 1970 by the U.S. Congress of the Federal-Aid Highway Act that authorized the president, through the secretaries of state and transportation, to open negotiations with Canada on the subject of paving and reconstructing the Alaska Highway. The highway, built in 1942–43, is 1,523 miles long, of which 302 miles are in Alaska. Fewer than 110 miles of the Canadian portion of the highway are paved; the remainder consists of an all-weather gravel surface that badly needs paving.

Recruiting officers of the Canadian Armed Forces (CAF) visited Arctic communities during the year to interest young northerners in a career with the armed forces. Increased CAF responsibilities in Canada's north created a need to recruit people who have an intimate familiarity with local working and living conditions. (*See in* CE: Arctic Regions.)

Telephone company trucks were turned over and burned during rioting by striking telephone workers in Buenos Aires, Argentina.

ARGENTINA. On March 22, 1971, President Roberto Marcelo Levingston was overthrown after only nine months in office. Three days later the ruling junta appointed a new president, Lieut. Gen. Alejandro Agustín Lanusse, the army commander in chief. A growing antipathy between Levingston and Lanusse and the poor economic situation were the principal factors behind Levingston's fall.

Although Lanusse inherited an unstable economic situation, emphasis was placed from the outset on solving the country's political problems. In September the government announced details of the political timetable whereby elections would take place in March 1973 and the elected government would be installed on May 25, 1973. In the meantime, legislation governing the electoral process was passed, and the institutional framework of political parties formed after July 1, 1971, was settled.

Lanusse's commitment to a return to representative democracy aroused considerable opposition among certain elements of the military, and early in October a section of the army attempted to oust the president. The movement, led by Col. Manuel Alejandro García, commanding officer of a tank regiment, and supported by former president Levingston, accused Lanusse of "counterrevolution," that is, of the betrayal of the original aim of the 1966 military takeover—to put the country in order before allowing elections to be held. Support anticipated from the air force did not materialize—both the air force and the navy reaffirmed their support for Lanusse—and the revolt was largely confined to the army garrisons at Azul and Olavarría. The two garrisons were quickly surrounded by loyalist forces and in less than 24 hours the rebellion collapsed with the surrender and imprisonment of the rebel leaders and the arrest of Levingston.

Against this background of political uncertainty and experimentation, the economic situation deteriorated substantially in 1971. The expansionist policies pursued by Aldo Ferrer, who had replaced Carlos Moyano Llerena as economy and labor minister in October 1970, proved inadequate. In May Ferrer was forced to resign. (*See in* CE: Argentina.)

ARMED FORCES, UNITED STATES.

In 1971 the armed forces of the United States continued to assume the major responsibility of maintaining the security of the non-Communist world. The services remained active in the war in Southeast Asia, but on a reduced basis. (*See* Defense; Selective Service; Vietnam.)

AIR FORCE

Although faced in 1971 with continuing manpower and budgetary problems, the U.S. Air Force mission for the remainder of the 1970's remained clear: to provide airpower necessary to meet any challenge to U.S. national security. To insure accomplishment of that mission, the Air Force focused on two key goals during 1971. First, it

This is a design for the new Air Force B-1 supersonic bomber. The bomber could be put into production in the early 1980's. It would eventually replace the B-52 and FB-111.

COURTESY, U.S. AIR FORCE

sought to improve and update its hardware despite the pressures of an austere defense budget. Secondly, it began several long-range programs to retain top quality active duty and reserve forces.

In order to maintain a formidable strategic posture, the U.S. developed its triad concept—a deterrent force composed of manned bombers, land-based missiles, and sea-based missiles. With this new approach, the manned bomber element took on new emphasis in 1971 as engineering development began on the B-1. The proposed aircraft, an international jet bomber, would be able to operate from shorter runways than the aging B-52. This feat is an important part of survival, because rapid dispersal is necessary to survive surprise enemy-launched missile attacks. The aircraft was being designed to appear smaller on radar screens and thus be more difficult to see and to detect. The B-1 also was to have a higher penetration speed and a larger payload than the B-52.

The second element of the triad concept was land-based missiles. In May 1971 a second 50-missile squadron was added at Minot Air Force Base, North Dakota, bringing the total strength to 100 Minuteman III's. The Minuteman III, capable of employing the multiple independently targetable reentry vehicle (MIRV) warhead, plus substantially improved penetration aids, was replacing the older Minuteman I and supplementing the Minuteman II, currently a mainstay of the Air Force's missile force. The final element of the triad was the U.S. Navy's submarine-launched missiles, including the Polaris and the MIRV-capable Poseidon.

Perhaps the most important continuing development underway in tactical operations during 1971 concerned the F-15 air-superiority fighter. Combining power and high speed with maneuverability and ease of handling, the F-15's first flight was expected in July 1972.

In the vital area of aerospace defense, the Air Force maintained its hopes of winning production of the Airborne Warning and Control System (AWACS). A priority item, the AWACS would prove capable of detecting, identifying, and tracking high- and low-flying enemy bombers over both land and water before they could reach their air-to-surface missile launch points.

On July 13 Air Force Capt. Thomas S. Culver was convicted by an eight-man court-martial of taking part in an antiwar demonstration in London and of inciting other airmen to do likewise. Culver, stationed at Lakenheath, England, was given a reprimand and fined $1,000. (*See also* Aircraft. *See in* CE: Air Force, U.S.)

ARMY

In 1971 the U.S. Army found itself the target of criticism from many quarters. In South Vietnam, Gen. Creighton Abrams told visiting Senator George McGovern (D, S.D.) that his troops were beset with problems of racial hostility, drug abuse, low morale, soldier crime, and friction with the South Vietnamese people.

Threatened with a loss of public confidence, the Army initiated new programs to eliminate many of the traditional irritants of Army life. Kitchen police (KP) was abolished at many Army posts, soldiers were permitted to wear longer hair, programs stressing increased individual responsibility were started, and higher pay scales were planned for lower enlisted and officer grades.

Early in 1971 estimates of heroin use among soldiers in Vietnam ranged from 10 to 20%. As part of a comprehensive war against drug abuse, the Army began chemical testing of Vietnam returnees. First reports of the tests suggested an addiction rate of 4.5%, far lower than had been estimated earlier. However, the rate could not be determined exactly, and the subject generated controversy. There were also serious drug abuse problems at Army posts in the U.S. and other overseas posts. In mid-year, U.S. President Richard M. Nixon sought congressional approval for a new office to combat drug addiction and appointed Dr. Jerome H. Jaffe as his special consultant on drug abuse. In addition, the Army instituted a comprehensive program of detection and treatment of drug abusers within the Army. An "amnesty" program persuaded soldiers to voluntarily submit themselves to treatment without fear of punishment.

Racial problems among soldiers in Vietnam, Korea, Europe, Okinawa, and the U.S. focused public attention on the Army with increasing regularity throughout 1971. This was particularly disquieting because of the Army's long-standing claim of successful integration dating from 1948. Charges of promotion inequities and double standards of justice were voiced by blacks against the Army and constituted the basis for protests.

War protest within the Army was manifested in the appearance of numerous underground newspapers at Army posts and in the growing presence of groups such as the Concerned Officers Movement. A more liberal interpretation of conscientious objection by the Supreme Court (in 1970) resulted in a small but noticeable increase in the number of soldiers applying for conscientious objector status.

The Army continued the prosecution of enlisted men and officers accused of war crimes. First Lieut. William L. Calley, Jr., was found guilty, on March 29, and sentenced to life imprisonment for his role in the 1968 massacre of more than 100 Vietnamese civilians at My Lai. Calley's sentence was reduced later, upon review, to 20 years in prison. On September 22, Capt. Ernest L. Medina, also charged in the My Lai massacre, was acquitted of charges of responsibility for the deaths of the murdered villagers.

Charges of covering up other war crimes were made by Lieut. Col. Anthony B. Herbert against Brig. Gen. John W. Barnes and Lieut. Col. J. Ross Franklin. After investigation, the charges were dropped by the Army. In another action, the secretary of the Army ordered a poor fitness report expunged from the record of Lieut. Col. Herbert, thus clearing the way for his promotion. How-

In 1971 Lt. Col. Anthony B. Herbert announced his intention to resign from the Army. He said the Army harassed him after he tried to file charges on U.S. war crimes in Indochina.
WIDE WORLD

ever, in November Herbert announced his intention to resign from the Army because, he said, he was being harassed. The Army also prosecuted Col. Oran K. Henderson, charging him with covering up the My Lai massacre, but he was acquitted in December.

In 1971 several attempts were made within Congress to force troop reductions in Europe. With little fanfare, 20,000 troops were withdrawn from Korea and programmed withdrawals from Vietnam continued ahead of schedule. By November, Army troop strength in South Vietnam had dipped to 191,000.

During the year the Army began a major demilitarization and detoxification of chemical and biological warfare agents. Public protests against the overland movement of chemical and biological agents coupled with public outcry against dumping such agents at sea forced the Army to detoxify them at their storage sites. In June Robert F. Froehlke was named the new secretary of the Army by President Nixon. Froehlke succeeded Stanley R. Resor.

COAST GUARD

U.S. Coast Guard operations in South Vietnam were phased down during 1971. Shortly after January 1, the Coast Guard turned over two high-endurance cutters to the South Vietnamese navy. A few Coast Guard units remained in Vietnam, including two loran (long range navigation) stations, two cutters, and several smaller units.

In line with its role in the prevention and cleanup of oil spills, the Coast Guard conducted, in June, full-scale development tests in the Gulf of Mexico of a high-seas oil containment barrier designed and built for the Coast Guard by the Johns-Manville Corp. The Coast Guard hoped to develop an oil containment barrier that could be used to protect coastal areas from oil spills in offshore regions.

The year was a busy one for the Coast Guard in law enforcement, particularly with respect to enforcing fisheries agreements. Cutters were used off the New England coast to investigate claims that foreign fishing vessels were damaging lobster pots placed by U.S. fishermen. In August, U.S. President Richard M. Nixon signed legislation giving the Coast Guard stronger authority for enforcing fisheries agreements in the northwest Atlantic. The law matches recent changes in the International Convention for the Northwest Atlantic Fisheries—to protect fish populations in the northwest Atlantic between Greenland, Canada, and the U.S. (*See in* CE: Coast Guard, U.S.)

MARINE CORPS

Throughout 1971, the emphasis in the U.S. Marine Corps was on attaining a quality-imbued, highly motivated force of men, capable of carrying out the Corps' historic role as the nation's amphibious force-in-readiness. The most significant new items entering the Marine Corps inventory in

1971 were the AV-8A Harrier attack jet and the LVTP7 family of amphibian tracked vehicles.

For more than a decade before its commitment to the Vietnam war, the Marine Corps kept its strength at an authorized level of approximately 200,000. Concurrent with the Vietnam troop withdrawals, the Marine Corps reduced its overall size from a Vietnam high of 317,000 in 1969 to approximately 212,000 in fiscal year 1971.

The Marine Corps acquired about 59,000 new enlistees during fiscal 1971. In addition, 2,059 new officers were commissioned, and 628 Marine student pilots received their wings. Both Marine recruit training and the officer candidate course were extended, and higher standards for completion were set.

A new formal Staff Noncommissioned Officer Academy was established at Quantico, Va., and convened its first class in February 1971. Full-scale operation began in the fall of 1971 with 200-man classes lasting six weeks each.

The Marine Corps, unlike the Army and the Navy, decided during the year to maintain its traditional codes of discipline and personal appearance. Long hair continued to be forbidden, and sideburns were not permitted.

On August 12, Marine Sgt. Jon M. Sweeney, age 21, of West Babylon, N.Y., was granted an honorable discharge. The action came less than 24 hours after he was acquitted of charges of desertion and engaging in Communist propaganda while spending 18 months as a North Vietnamese prisoner of war. Sweeney testified that his unit had deserted him and left him to die in the jungle. (*See in* CE: Marine Corps, U.S.)

NAVY

For the U.S. Navy 1971 was a year of many changes. Adm. Elmo R. Zumwalt, Jr., who became chief of naval operations (CNO) on July 1, 1970, put a great deal of emphasis on the personnel situation, which had been deteriorating for a decade before reaching a crisis stage in 1970.

To this end, Zumwalt issued over 130 orders, commonly known as "Z-grams," designed to remove annoying restrictions and regulations, improve living conditions, and to reward leadership, proficiency, and responsibility in the enlisted and junior officer grades. One of the more celebrated of these was Z-gram 57, issued late in 1970, which eliminated "Mickey Mouse," or "chicken," regulations that were judged detrimental to the individual's feelings of personal worth and dignity.

The maximum sea tour for all sailors was cut to six years. Also, the continuing conversion to a personnel management program called "centralized detailing" provided a more equitable sea and shore rotation for all Navy men.

In June it was announced that by July 1, 1975, the well-known sailor suit—including bell-bottom trousers, round white cap, and jumper with neckerchief—would no longer be worn by Navy men.

The Navy's Deep Submergence Rescue Vehicle, the first of its kind in the world, ran through tests off the California coast.

The new dress uniform for the lower enlisted grades would be the same basic uniform that was being worn in 1971 by officers and chief petty officers, with variations in the hat insignia, buttons, rating badge, and other accessories that would still make a man's rank readily apparent. (*See in* CE: Navy, U.S.)

ARTS. As United States orchestras, museums, theaters, opera and dance companies, and other artistic groups floundered in financial straits, widespread national attention focused on the plight of the arts in 1971. U.S. President Richard M. Nixon took the lead in supporting federal aid to the arts by urging bipartisan congressional support for funds for the National Arts and Humanities Endowments. The U.S. Congress responded generously, voting $61.21 million for fiscal 1972, the largest amount ever allotted for federal support for this purpose. U.S. state and territorial funding for local arts councils also increased and was expected to reach $15 million in fiscal 1972, nearly twice the appropriation of $8.86 million for fiscal 1971 (exclusive of an emergency grant by the state of New York of $18 million).

Despite this ground swell of public support, total government funding would amount at best in fiscal 1972 to less than 40¢ per person. The goal of a private group, Partnership for the Arts, was U.S. government support in the amount of $200 million, which would represent a per capita figure of less than $1 and would be "a mere 10% of the annual $2 billion spent on the arts in the U.S., leaving 90% to be raised locally." The organization pointed out that $200 million was only one tenth of 1% of what the U.S. government spent on highways—in fiscal 1970 a per capita amount of more than $1,000.

In the private sector, the Ford and Rockefeller foundations continued their traditional high level of support for the arts. The Ford Foundation, for example, established in 1971 a $10 million grant program to assist 37 economically troubled opera, dance, and drama companies. The role of U.S. business in aiding the nation's cultural institutions also continued to expand.

In a glittering display of public pomp and circumstance, the John F. Kennedy Center for the Performing Arts officially opened in September in Washington, D.C. On opening night members of the late president's family, celebrities, and an impressive number of foreign dignitaries attended the official premiere performance of Leonard Bernstein's work, 'Mass'. Although critics were mixed in their reviews of both the 'Mass' and the center (a white marble edifice designed by U.S. architect Edward Durell Stone), it was obvious that the first cultural center in the nation's capital would perform an important role in U.S. cultural life.

The first of the massive U.S. cultural complexes to be built, the Lincoln Center for the Performing Arts in New York City, had its share of problems in 1971. A proposal was made to remodel the financially troubled Vivian Beaumont Theater building to include a cinemathèque with three movie theaters. The plan aroused great controversy, however, and was eventually shelved. (*See also* Architecture; Dance; Museums; Music; Painting and Sculpture; Theater. *See in* CE: Arts, The.)

ASIA.

A watershed in Asian politics was clearly marked by the actions of the People's Republic of China in 1971. The new pragmatic foreign policy inaugurated by the Peking government sent reverberations through every Asian capital, demolishing some old theories and building up some new ones. A general indication of the region's new attitude was provided by Philippine President Ferdinand E. Marcos when, in July, he opened the sixth ministerial conference of the Asian and Pacific Council in Manila, Philippines. He said that a rapprochement between the United States and China would have a definite effect on the political climate of Asia and would enable countries of the region to concentrate more on solving their economic and development problems.

China's motive might have been, as Marcos said, to shut out the Soviet Union or to check Japan's growing economic hold on the region, or both. China had always considered Southeast Asia its natural sphere of influence. As the "Ping Pong diplomacy" unfolded, China indicated its willingness to establish relations with Asian nations, including those which in the past had not recognized the People's Republic. In any event, almost all Southeast Asian governments seemed willing and ready to grasp this opportunity. (*See* China.)

The necessary climate for such a major change in attitude was provided by the U.S. government's decision to disengage itself from Asia, wind down the Vietnam war, and maintain only a low profile in the region thereafter. Southeast Asian countries that had closely identified themselves with all aspects of U.S. policy in Asia now felt obliged to change some of their fundamental assumptions. They were pushed further when the U.S. began dealing directly with China and U.S. President Richard M. Nixon announced, in July, his intention to visit China before May 1972. (The trip was later scheduled for February 1972.)

In Thailand, long a bastion of U.S. policy in the region, there was support for a dialogue with China. The Philippines sent a chamber of commerce delegation to China, which was followed by tourists and women's groups. Malaysia achieved perhaps the most spectacular successes with China—exchanging trade delegations, receiving a Communist dance troupe from Hong Kong, signing a very useful trade agreement with Peking, and, above all, practically eliminating Singapore as a middleman in the import of Chinese goods. Ironically, Malaysia had an internal Communist insurgency problem to cope with—as had Thailand—and China was widely believed to be lending tacit support to the insurgents.

Two Southeast Asian countries did not share Malaysia's enthusiasm. Singapore was clearly worried about the prospects of a peaceful and respectable China exercising a gravitational pull on the predominantly Chinese population of the island republic and thereby upsetting government plans to create a "new Singaporean identity." Indonesia, still licking the wounds of the Communist-inspired abortive coup in 1965 that had led to the suspension of diplomatic relations with China, showed cautious interest in normalizing its relations with the Peking government.

There was no doubt, however, that the region as a whole was overhauling its fundamental attitudes. The dominant mood was to see China as a friendly giant with whom it was possible to get along and desirable to trade. This rethinking promised to bring about a restructuring of the basic political forces in the region.

In the face of China's new status, the Soviet Union apparently held its own in Southeast Asia during 1971. The number of Soviet cultural and trade delegations to the region sharply increased, and Soviet sailors and Aeroflot crews became a familiar sight in more and more Asian cities. Malaysia and Singapore had established diplomatic relations with the Soviets, and the Philippines and Thailand were expected to follow suit. An insight into the thinking behind the policies of these governments was provided by Singapore Prime Minister Lee Kuan Yew when he said that "the Soviet naval capacity in the Indian Ocean and the South China Sea can be a counterpoise to China's might on the littoral countries of Asia and Southeast Asia."

The Soviets were believed to be maintaining three operations in Asian waters—a fishing fleet, a

South Vietnamese marines were airlifted
into Cambodia to aid government troops at
Pich Nil Pass in January.

space-effort support flotilla, and a potential combat force that usually comprised 20 vessels of all types. In addition to this the Soviet merchant navy emerged as an important factor in Pacific shipping, offering cut-rate prices.

At the 24th Soviet Communist party congress in March, Communist Party General Secretary Leonid I. Brezhnev scathingly attacked the West for talking in terms of a "Soviet threat" in the Indian Ocean. Soviet commentators said repeatedly during 1971 that their naval presence in the region would be long-lived.

In contrast, there were indications during the year of a lessening of U.S. influence. While U.S. initiative in normalizing relations with China directly affected all Asian governments, it also tended to erode the credibility of U.S. commitments to its old Asian allies.

Two other factors contributed to the devaluation of U.S. prestige in the region—the presidential election in South Vietnam and the admission of China to the United Nations (UN), both in October. The South Vietnamese election turned out to be a farcical one-man race, and the U.S. establishment was openly associated with events that led up to this situation. The U.S. effort to retain a seat in the UN for Nationalist China was denounced by most Asian countries. The consensus of opinion in Southeast Asia was that the UN vote constituted a humiliating defeat for the U.S., when it need only have been a victory for China.

There was speculation that President Nixon's projected visit to Peking would be preceded by the pullout of all U.S. combat troops from Asia. At a press conference in April, however, U.S. Defense Secretary Melvin R. Laird had said that the U.S. would maintain a naval and air presence in Southeast Asia after withdrawing U.S. ground troops.

ASEAN; SEATO

In March, at a summit conference in Manila, the Association of Southeast Asian Nations (ASEAN; Indonesia, Thailand, Singapore, Malaysia, and the Philippines) recognized the value of organizing concerted action among themselves on international issues and of presenting a united stand to advance their common interests. However, the China debate in the UN pointed up their divided positions. Malaysia and Singapore voted for Taiwan's expulsion, the Philippines voted against, and Indonesia and Thailand abstained. The five members were more agreed on the question of widening the association's membership. South Vietnam and Cambodia (now called the Khmer Republic) attended

Allied troops visibly
demonstrated their
feeling about the
Indochina war by
flying a peace flag
on their armored
vehicle. These men
were in operations
along the Laotian
border.

In 1971 the U.S. returned Okinawa to Japanese control. U.S. Secretary of State William P. Rogers (below, seated) signs the reversion agreement in Washington, D.C., as the Japanese ambassador to the U.S. watches. Militant Japanese students (right) protest the terms of the agreement.

RIGHT: WIDE WORLD.
BELOW: KEYSTONE

the Manila meeting as observers. This provoked deposed Cambodian ruler Prince Norodom Sihanouk to issue a statement from his sanctuary in Peking accusing ASEAN members of being "U.S. satellites."

While ASEAN managed to maintain its status as the most promising regional organization in Southeast Asia, the military-oriented Southeast Asia Treaty Organization (SEATO) continued to be overtaken by events. Its 16th annual ministerial conference in London, in April, hardly attracted any serious notice in Asia. Its resolutions were seen largely as platitudinous—that South Vietnam had further developed its capability to defend itself effectively, that the Cambodians continued to show a firm determination to resist the North Vietnam-ese, and that the U.S.-South Vietnamese invasion of Laos in February had been justified.

More relevant to Asian reality was the conference's call for external assistance to development programs in member countries and for regional cooperation; but it gave no indication of being able to pursue these objectives. Thai Foreign Minister Thanat Khoman, who had strongly criticized SEATO the preceding year, said that the organization might change its structure completely if China showed a new attitude of reconciliation in Asia. U.S. Secretary of State William P. Rogers lent weight to the idea by saying that U.S. policy was not to deny China's growing role in Asia but to encourage it.

Other Asian Highlights

The war in Indochina continued in 1971 to create an ever increasing number of refugees. It was estimated in May that over one third of the 27 million people of Indochina had been forced to leave their homes. (See Feature Article: "The Tragedy of Indochina: Ten Million Civilian Victims.")

In March the federal government of Pakistan sent troops to East Pakistan to crush the Bengali independence movement. By late June close to 6 million refugees had fled across the border into India where death, hunger, and sickness became commonplace—cholera took many lives. Meanwhile, tensions between the Pakistan government and India increased; India was accused of aiding the Bengalis. Finally, full-scale war broke out early in December. India invaded East Pakistan, the Pakistani government surrendered, and in its place in East Pakistan, the new country Bangla Desh (Bengal Nation) was established. (See also individual countries by name. See in CE: Asia; individual countries by name.)

ASTRONOMY. The most far-reaching advance in observational astronomy during 1971 was the development of speckle interferometry, a technique that permits optical telescopes to record smaller objects than ever before. Previously, the ability of astronomers to discern tiny objects had been limited not by the size of telescopes but by inhomogeneities in the earth's atmosphere that distort the incoming light. Speckle interferometry can sharpen these blurred images, permitting, for example, the 200-inch Hale reflector at Mount Palomar Observatory in California to reveal objects as small as a penny at a distance of about 100 miles. With this telescope a team from the State University of New York at Stony Brook succeeded in taking the first photographs of the disks of stars other than the sun, including the supergiants Betelgeuse and Antares.

Their results agreed with previous indirect determinations of these stars' diameters.

The recognition of two large galaxies near our own, the Milky Way, was the most surprising astronomical discovery in 1971. Named Maffei 1 and 2 after the Italian astronomer who first called attention to them, these objects had escaped detection because they were almost completely obscured by a dense cloud of dust in the Milky Way. Maffei 1 is a giant elliptical system; Maffei 2 is a spiral similar to the Milky Way. The actual identification of these objects as galaxies was carried out by a team of astronomers from the California Institute of Technology, as well as the University of California at Berkeley.

During the year many astronomers were involved in environmental studies. A group at the Univer-

Astronomers want to know more about the distribution of light in the head of a comet. Agfa contour film, newly developed, gives a finely detailed photograph of the comet (below, right)—in contrast to the old film used, which yields a dense and impenetrable picture (right).

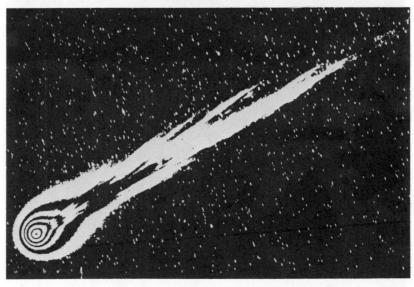

sity of Washington demonstrated that the starlight seen on a clear night is about 10% dimmer than it was a half century ago. Dust particles suspended in the atmosphere are probably responsible for this significantly great obscuration.

Venus, Mars, and Jupiter

Three planets—Venus, Mars, and Jupiter—were in the news during the year. The mapping of the surface of Venus has been achieved with a precision unimagined a few years ago. Since clouds perpetually shroud its surface, cartography can only be carried out with radar, which maps the reflective properties of the surface. For example, dense consolidated material of which mountains are composed appears "brighter" than loose powder.

On May 30 the United States launched the space probe, Mariner 9, on a 247-million-mile voyage that carried it to Mars by Nov. 13. After going into orbit around the red planet, Mariner 9 had the task of photographing much of the surface, measuring temperatures, and searching for indications of life. It was heavily handicapped in these tasks by a dust storm that had raged over the planet since September. The Soviet Union also launched two spacecraft on similar missions. On December 7 signals were received from one of the Soviet spacecraft, Mars 3, that a capsule from the spacecraft had made a successful soft-landing on Mars, an outstanding scientific feat.

An unprecedented event occurred on May 13, when Jupiter passed in front of the bright double

Radar was used to make this map of Venus, one of the best and most detailed that astronomers have been able to produce.

COURTESY, SKY PUBLISHING CORP.

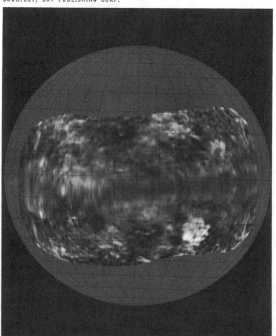

star Beta Scorpii. As these stars slowly disappeared into and then emerged from the planet's atmosphere, astronomers measured the changes in their brightness. These observations provided new information about variations in temperature and composition at different heights in the Jovian atmosphere.

"Uhuru"

Probably no artificial satellite has returned as much information per dollar as "Uhuru," which was launched in December 1970. It was designed to map the entire sky at X-ray wavelengths. Though its profuse data has only been sampled, tens of new X-ray sources have been found, the determination of positions of previously known objects has been improved, and rapid changes in the intensity of some X-ray sources have been discovered. These dramatic advances were possible because "Uhuru" could scan the sky day after day, whereas rockets (the previous method for observing X rays) could record data for only a few minutes during each flight.

Among the discoveries based on observations by this satellite were the almost certain identification of a strong X-ray source in the constellation of Cassiopeia with a supernova that erupted perhaps 1,600 years ago; the detection of X rays from Seyfert galaxies, objects that may be related to quasars (quasistellar radio sources); and the discovery that the sources Cygnus X-1 and Centaurus X-3 have rapid, periodic variations in their emissions. Only the famous X-ray source in the Crab Nebula has exhibited similar behavior. (*See also* Space Exploration. *See in* CE: Astronomy.)

AUSTRALIA. During 1971 the Liberal-Country party (LCP) government of Australia was faced with an almost continual crisis. The most important event occurred in March, when John G. Gorton stepped down as prime minister. Gorton was voted out of office by the parliamentary Liberal party after an attack on his methods of leadership by Minister for Defense Malcolm Fraser. According to Fraser, Gorton had "a dangerous reluctance to consult the cabinet" and an "unreasoned drive to get his own way." Because Fraser did not consider Gorton fit to hold the office of prime minister, he could not serve in Gorton's government, and therefore resigned.

The Liberal party met on March 10 and in a no-confidence motion on Gorton's leadership the vote was 33–33. Gorton then cast his vote against himself, breaking the deadlock. Subsequently, an election was held for party leader, and William McMahon, the minister for foreign affairs, defeated Billy Mackie Snedden, minister for labor and national service, thus becoming the new prime minister. There were three candidates for the post of deputy-leader of the Liberal party—Gorton, Fraser, and David Fairbairn. Gorton won this contest and was appointed minister for defense.

A herd of kangaroos bound over the rocks of Quamby East, a 3,000 acre ranch in Woolsthorpe, where they live in safety with sheep and cattle. The kangaroo is exploited in Australia where it is killed for its hide and fur and is heavily used by the pet food industry. There were 15 species of kangaroo native to Victoria 150 years ago. Today, only 7 species survive in Australia.

"LONDON DAILY EXPRESS" FROM PICTORIAL PARADE

Later, on August 12, Gorton was dismissed from this post by the prime minister, following an article by Gorton that was published in a Sunday newspaper. McMahon said that Gorton had reflected on the integrity of some cabinet members by alleging that they had leaked confidential material to the press.

Demonstrations; Aboriginal Land Rights

There was considerable division among the Australian people as a result of a tour of Australia by the South African rugby union team, the Springboks. Violent clashes took place between supporters and opponents of the tour, and hundreds were arrested in demonstrations against South African apartheid. The premier of Queensland, J. Bjelke-Petersen, declared a state of emergency before the Springboks toured his state.

Aboriginal land rights continued to be a thorny issue. In April the aboriginals at Yirrkala, on the Gove Peninsula in Arnhem Land, lost their test case in the Northern Territory Supreme Court. Eleven tribes had claimed legal title to the Gove Peninsula, where a Swiss-Australian aluminum company was mining. The aboriginals' legal expenses had been paid by the Methodist Christian Citizenship Council in Melbourne, and the unsuccessful proceedings took over 12 months to complete. Aboriginals believed that the Yirrkala mission station was endangered by blasting. They feared that their mission would close and their town be removed, notwithstanding the federal government's assurances to the contrary.

Foreign Affairs

The question of the recognition of the People's Republic of China replaced the Vietnam war as the major issue of Australian foreign policy. Canadian recognition of the Chinese government in 1970 sparked the controversy. Two weeks after Canada recognized the regime of Mao Tse-tung, the Canadian Wheat Board announced the sale of 98 million bushels of wheat to the Chinese, the biggest sale the board had made to a single country over a 12-month period. R. A. Patterson, the Australian Labor party (ALP) spokesman on basic industry, pointed out in Parliament that if Australia wished to compete with Canada for the wheat trade it would first have to recognize China and its 750 million people. Douglas Anthony, minister for trade and industry, said he was not prepared to sacrifice political principles to economic expediency, adding that he did not believe that diplomatic recognition was a significant factor in selling wheat to China.

In August the prime minister announced that he expected most of the 6,000 Australian troops in Vietnam to be home by Christmas, leaving a small group of trained personnel. (*See also* Commonwealth of Nations. *See in* CE: Australia.)

William McMahon, formerly foreign minister, became Australia's prime minister and leader of the Liberal party in 1971.

CENTRAL PRESS FROM PICTORIAL PARADE

Bruno Kreisky, Austrian chancellor, votes
in the parliamentary elections in which his
Socialist party won a majority.

AUSTRIA.

In the Austrian presidential election,
held on April 25, 1971, President Franz Jonas, the
candidate of the Socialist party of Austria (SPÖ),
was reelected for another six-year term. He defeated Kurt Waldheim, Austrian ambassador to the
United Nations and candidate for the conservative
Austrian People's party (ÖVP). The country continued to be governed by a Socialist minority administration, under the leadership of Chancellor
Bruno Kreisky.

Out of the 165 parliamentary seats, 81 were held
by the SPÖ, 78 by the ÖVP, and 6 by the Austrian
Freedom party (FPÖ). In order to legislate, therefore, Kreisky's government had to seek the support
of one or the other of the opposition parties in parliament. Anxious to try to achieve an overall majority, the SPÖ decided in July, with the help of the
FPÖ, on a premature dissolution of parliament and
a general election in October.

Kreisky's party gained an absolute majority of
the 183 seats contested for the new enlarged parliament in that election and could thus form a one-
party SPÖ government to take office for the next
four years. With an electoral turnout of over 90%,
the final figures were: SPÖ, 93 seats; ÖVP, 80 seats;
and FPÖ, 10 seats. The Austrian Communist party
(KPÖ) increased its support from 0.98% in 1970
to 1.35%, but under regulations excluding splinter
parties from parliament it did not gain a seat. Because the Socialists would provide the nonvoting
speaker, Kreisky's new government had an overall majority of two.

New legislation during the year included various
reforms of the Austrian criminal code and considerable emphasis on the extension of the welfare
state. Enactments included the abolition of certain
privileges for civil servants, the legalization of
homosexuality between consenting adults, and an
improvement in the legal status of illegitimate children. Stricter penalties were introduced for cruelty
to children and animals.

Austria and the People's Republic of China
agreed on mutual recognition and the exchange of
ambassadors within six months. On September 15
the Chinese ambassador presented his credentials.
(*See in* CE: Austria.)

AUTOMOBILES.

On Aug. 15, 1971, United
States President Richard M. Nixon announced a
90-day wage and price freeze program, which
had great impact on the nation's automobile industry. The surcharge increase from 3.5% to 10%
on all imported goods had a substantial effect on
cars brought in from Europe and Japan.

Prices of import cars rose a minimum of $65 as
a result of the move; in the luxury models, the
jump amounted to more than $300. Meanwhile,
the 1972 models that U.S. producers introduced in
September were held to 1971 prices. The result
was a more favorable selling position for the domestic products.

In reaction to the announcement, the auto companies changed the equipment on many 1972 models in order to decrease production costs. For
example, Ford reinstalled rubber floor mats in the
Pinto to avoid the higher cost of carpeting, which
was to have been a standard item on the 1972
model.

In certain cases, the government permitted manufacturers to charge higher prices when new equipment was made standard on 1972 models. If, for
example, power steering was an option on a 1971,
then made standard equipment on the 1972 model,
the manufacturer was permitted to include the price
of the power steering in the 1972 prices. However,
when Ford brought out its 1972 Torino and Mon-
tego lines complete with new styling, new interiors,
new suspensions, and a new frame and body construction, it was ordered to sell them at 1971 prices.

It was widely believed that auto manufacturers,
especially General Motors (GM), were informed
of the president's intentions weeks in advance of
the announcement. However, GM Chairman
James M. Roche said the company had no prior
knowledge of the president's move. The basis for
the widely held belief of prior knowledge was the
fact that GM announced its higher 1972 prices on
August 5. In the past GM had always waited until
the day before its new cars were put on public display, usually in September or October, before announcing prices. The matter was resolved when
GM agreed to sell its 1972 models at 1971 prices
for the duration of the freeze.

Import executives expressed little concern about
the effect the president's program would have on
sales. Most foreign producers believed that revaluation of currency would affect U.S. sales much
more than the president's program would. If their
currencies were revalued, then the higher cost of
their products might sizably reduce sales. In
December West Germany and Japan agreed to
revalue their currencies, in exchange for a devaluation of the dollar, but the effect of this agree-

ment on the auto market would be unclear for some time.

It was no accident that the U.S. auto industry was the one most affected by the president's program. For years U.S. car manufacturers had been losing ground to the imports. Just before the president's message, 26% of potential new-car buyers in one survey expressed the intention to buy a foreign car. By mid-1971 foreign cars were accounting for a record high percentage of U.S. sales: in July, 18.2% of sales were imports; in August, almost 22%. Annual foreign car sales showed that import sales in 1969 were 11.3% of the total; in 1970 they rose to 14.7%. Reviewing these figures, one analyst commented that the president's program prevented a "catastrophe" in the U.S. automobile market.

Nixon's economic program, which also included a proposal to repeal the 7% excise tax on new cars (later approved by Congress), provided a great boost for the U.S. auto industry. In October more than one million new cars were sold, including a higher percentage of domestic cars than in previous months, ensuring, it seemed, that new car sales would reach the ten million mark by the end of the year. Although U.S. auto company profits increased, they were "held back," according to industry spokesmen, by the price freeze. During Phase II of Nixon's economic program, which began November 15, both domestic and foreign car makers increased prices on their 1972 models.

Market Changes, Trends, and Innovations

The year 1971 was the first full year of production for the two domestic mini compacts, Vega and Pinto. The cars were selling well, but they did not have much effect on the sales of foreign cars.

It was estimated that the two cars would sell about 350,000 units each during 1971, less than the 400,000 units that GM and Ford executives had predicted and much less than the 600,000-plus expected to be retailed by Volkswagen in 1971.

By almost any measurement, 1971 was an off year for the automobile industry. A large number of models were dropped when the 1972's were introduced in September. Changes in the new models were fewer, too. Only Ford and Chrysler showed major body changes; in other models facelifts amounted to only minor cosmetic differences from the '71's. A large percentage of the new cars were virtually unchanged from the '71's.

One new nameplate, Ventura II, was added to the Pontiac model lineup. A compact-size car, offered in two- and four-door body styles, it closely resembled Chevrolet's Nova. With a wheelbase of 111 inches, Ventura II was available with six-cylinder or V-8 engines.

In other changes, Detroit cut 45 models from the 1972 lineup, dropping the total number of different models to 296. Chrysler had 20 fewer models, Ford 10, GM 9, and American Motors Corp. (AMC) 6. The introductory total was the lowest since 1962. Among the types of cars hardest hit by the cutbacks were the performance models, whose sales were severely affected by high insurance costs, and convertibles, a body style that has been fading gradually from the automotive scene for several years.

American Motors reversed an automotive trend when it improved its warranty coverage on the 1972 models with its new four-point Buyer Protection Plan. Summing up the details of the program, William V. Luneburg, AMC president, said, "If anything goes wrong [with the car] that is our fault,

Pontiac's Ventura II was the only new model introduced by U.S. auto companies in 1971.
COURTESY, GENERAL MOTORS CORP.

COURTESY, FORD MOTOR CO.

This new sports car, the deTomaso Pantera, was designed by Ghia Studios of Turin, Italy. Its distinctive features include concealed headlights, full-framed curved side glass, and a hinged rear deck that swings up for greater accessibility to the luggage area.

we'll fix it—at factory expense." "Fixing it" included a no-questions-asked policy and the use of a free loaner car if the customer's car was kept overnight for repairs. The company said that dealers' warranty claims would receive 100% reimbursement, including any claims for time spent discovering the cause of the defect. The program was seen as a breakthrough in warranty coverage, even though the length of coverage was limited to 12 months or 12,000 miles. Included in the AMC warranty for the first time were such short-life items as spark plugs, brakes, and clutch.

In all 1972 models, horsepower ratings were based on net rather than gross horsepower. This change was brought about by a California law that provided penalties for publication of any but the net figures on 1972 cars sold in that state. The net horsepower is usually a third lower than the gross, though there is no consistent method of computing an average reduction that can be applied to all engines. Net, or as-installed, horsepower rating is obtained from laboratory tests that represent actual performance of an engine with accessories and normal air-fuel mixture and timing in a car. The gross figure previously given indicated the engine's maximum capacity with only such essential accessories as oil and water pumps.

Advances in Safety and Pollution Control

General Motors brought out in its 1972 Chevrolet, Pontiac, Oldsmobile, Buick, and Cadillac model lines "2½-mph bumpers." It claimed they would protect the front of the car from damage in barrier crashes up to 2½ miles per hour, or in car-to-car crashes up to 5 miles per hour.

However, the 1972 GM bumpers did not meet the government standard proposed for all 1973 model cars. That standard required that a car's front bumpers withstand a 5-mile-per-hour barrier crash without damage to safety-related items such as lights, steering, brakes, or cooling system. The one 1972 model that was able to withstand a 5-mile-per-hour barrier crash without damage was the Swedish-made Saab 99E. Allstate Insurance Co. announced that Saab owners would be the first to qualify for a 15% discount on collision policies.

Several changes were made in the federal government's planned safety standards. The Transportation department gave some small car makers a one-year exemption from the requirement that all 1974 models have bumpers of uniform height. The deadline for air bag installation was also postponed, for safety reasons, from 1974 models to 1976 models.

Chrysler introduced an electronic ignition system on a number of its V-8 models, and Pontiac offered a similar system on its 455-cubic inch V-8 engines. The electronic ignition promised to eliminate the need for periodic engine tune-up for the life of the car, since mechanical contact points that could wear out were eliminated. It promised better spark plug operation and longer spark plug life, resulting in more complete fuel combustion. Since there was less deterioration of the fuel combustion chamber, the engine emitted fewer contaminants into the atmosphere.

In December GM announced the largest auto recall in history. Spearheaded by complaints from consumer advocate Ralph Nader and by the National Highway Traffic Safety Administration about unstable engine mountings on Chevrolets made from 1965 to 1969, GM issued a recall for almost 6.7 million cars and light trucks to make necessary repairs. (*See also* Safety.)

Automobiles

Special Report:
Cars of the Future

by Jerry M. Flint

The ferment in the United States automobile industry is greater now than at any time since World War II. The federal government has demanded the production of cars that will be safer, more damage resistant, and pollution free. As a result, styling, with all its traditional "planned obsolescence," is taking a back seat. It is the engineers who are initiating the changes today, while the stylists are busy trying to make the safer cars as reasonably attractive as they can.

The most exciting recent development is a new type of car engine, the Wankel rotary engine, invented by Felix Wankel in Germany almost two decades ago. The early versions of this engine, built for German cars, broke down. Then a Japanese manufacturer improved the design and began turning out Wankel-powered cars in volume, shipping some to the U.S. in 1971. But the Wankel future had already brightened considerably before that, when in the fall of 1970 General Motors (GM) Corp. agreed to pay $50 million for the patent rights. A year later GM's engineering force went to work to ready the Wankel for production.

The Wankel is a simple, small, lightweight engine. Potentially, it would be cheaper to build than today's car motor. It is also easier to service,

quieter, and creates less vibration. But its principal attraction is its potential role in the fight for cleaner air.

The present internal combustion engine emits carbon monoxide, unburned hydrocarbons or gasoline fumes, and oxides of nitrogen. But, then, so does the new Wankel engine. The latter, however, is a smaller engine, and there is more room under the hood for antiemission devices; furthermore, the Wankel venting system makes emissions easier to handle.

In the car engine of today, gasoline and air are mixed in a carburetor; the fumes are pumped into a combustion chamber where they are compressed by pistons, then ignited. The explosions keep the four or six or eight pistons pumping up and down, supplying the power that eventually turns the wheels.

In the Wankel the air-fuel mixture is compressed and ignited as in the piston engine, and the expansion from the burning fuel provides the force that, in due time, turns the wheels. But there are no pistons moving up and down; instead a triangular-shaped rotor revolves around a shaft in an eccentric path within the working chamber, and the spinning shaft sends power to the wheels.

The experimental Opel CD was displayed by Buick-Opel in 1971. The car is powered by a 5.4 liter engine with a Turbo-Hydramatic automatic transmission.
COURTESY, GENERAL MOTORS CORP.

According to the manufacturer, this 511 model commuter car features exceptional stability and maneuverability, as well as fuel economy.

The tips of the triangular rotor continually touch the chamber surface as it spins, forming continually changing pockets. Fuel enters an intake port and is compressed as the rotor swings around, squeezed in the narrowing space between the chamber wall and the rotor face. A sparkplug ignites the fuel, and the gases expanding against the rotor face drive it around, turning the shaft, the rotor swinging past an open exhaust port and the spent gases leaving the chamber as the cycle continues. A Wankel may have fewer than half the moving parts of a V-8 engine and take up less than one fourth the space. The first Wankel used by a U.S. manufacturer could come in a small GM car in the middle of the decade, and GM engineers already are testing their version of the engine in their smallest models.

One other engine has a future in the U.S. automotive industry—the turbine. In a turbine, air is compressed and heated in a combustion chamber and then forced through a turbine wheel that spins and creates power for the car's wheels. The turbine can use a variety of fuels, has few moving parts, is quiet, and has little vibration. But it appears to be difficult and expensive to mass-produce, and more important, it is not at its best when pulling a light load through stop-and-go traffic. Instead, the turbine engine seems likely to appear in heavy trucks and buses, quite likely before 1975.

There are other engines, too, that may see service in the future. Some are built and tested, others just fantasied—but they have been well publicized because of the public pressure for a less-polluting engine. These include: electric engines, steam engines, the Stirling engine, and the static-charge engine; and there is even a vehicle run with a super flywheel. A variety of battery-powered cars have been built, but there appears to be no relatively inexpensive power source to give a car the speed and range needed—and the power plants needed to recharge the engines of approximately 100 million electric automobiles might cause more pollution than before.

The steam-powered vehicle has been hailed by William Lear, the inventor of a number of electronic aircraft devices and developer of the Lear Jet, as a cure for auto-caused pollution. Lear has spent several million dollars attempting to develop a steam car and a steam bus, and has said at various times that it cannot be done and on other occasions that he can do it. The U.S. car manufacturers have taken note that there are some steam cars around —relics of the 1920's, plus a few they have built recently—but they insist the steam engine is too bulky, too complicated to be a practical automobile power plant.

Natural gas can be used in an automobile engine, but this clean-burning fuel already is in short supply. Most of the other engines that have been considered just do not seem practical—and despite a $50 million effort initiated by the federal government to research new engines, only the old internal combustion engine, the Wankel, and the turbine for trucks and buses seem likely to power the nation's vehicles over the next decade.

But even the internal combustion engine will be cleaner burning, and the heart of the antiemission effort is concerned with the development of devices to eliminate the three auto pollutants. By 1975 it is likely that all cars built in the U.S. will carry a catalytic converter—a mufflerlike device laced with a catalyst, such as platinum, to help burn the fumes escaping through the exhaust system. In addition, cars may require a small reactor, a furnacelike device near the engine to burn fumes. Such systems, along with air pumps and fuel injection to feed gasoline into the engine accurately, will remove the bulk of the carbon monoxide and unburned hydrocarbons. The automobile makers do not believe that their systems will meet the government's standards for clean-burning engines by 1975, but they are certain they can come so close that the car will no longer be an important source of air pollution.

The General Motors 512 experimental electric vehicle is powered by an 84-volt battery pack and has a removable canopy.

AUTO RACING.

Jackie Stewart of Scotland dominated Grand Prix auto racing in 1971. Stewart, the year's world champion driver, drove his V-8 Tyrrell-Ford to victories in the Spanish, Monacan, French, British, German, and Canadian Grand Prix races. Mario Andretti of Nazareth, Pa., captured the South African Grand Prix; Jackie Ickx of Belgium won the Dutch; Jo Siffert of Switzerland took the Austrian; Peter Gethin of Switzerland won the Italian; and François Cevert of France finished first in the United States race.

In 1971 the U.S. Auto Club (USAC) enjoyed another good year. Its new Triple Crown of 500-mile races for single-seater cars was quite successful. Defending champion Al Unser of Albuquerque, N.M., won the Indianapolis 500 again; versatile Mark Donohue of Media, Pa., won the first Schaefer 500 at Mt. Pocono, Pa.; and Unser's teammate on the Parnelli Jones-Vel Miletich racing team, Joe Leonard of San Jose, Calif., won the second Ontario 500 in California, and thereby the 1971 USAC championship. It was the steady, 37-year-old Leonard's only victory of the year on the Marlboro Championship Trail, but he was a consistently high finisher.

USAC was much less successful in splitting its championship single-seater division into three parts. George Snider of Bakersfield, Calif., won the first national dirt-track title, but the races generally suffered for lack of the accepted stars of USAC, and the road-racing division all but collapsed—only one race was held. That race, courtesy of a heavy entry of Formula A (Formula 5000) machinery from the rival Sports Car Club of America (SCCA), was won by Jim Dittemore of California, making his first Formula 5000 ride. Meanwhile, the USAC stock-car crown was won by a relative newcomer, 31-year-old Butch Hartman of South Zanesville, Ohio. Hartman's major triumph was the Pocono 500.

The Canadian-American Challenge Cup for Group Seven machinery again was the property of Team McLaren. But Peter Revson of New York City became the first American to capture the title, winning at Road Atlanta in Georgia; Watkins Glen, N.Y.; Road America in Elkhart Lake, Wis.; and Donnybrooke in Brainerd, Minn. Denis Hulme of New Zealand was victorious at Riverside, Calif.; Mosport in Ontario; and Edmonton, Alta. Team McLaren's biggest competition came from Jackie Stewart. Driving a Lola T260-Chevrolet, the amazing Scot won at St. Jovite, Que., and at Mid-Ohio. The championship went down to the final two races in California. Revson won the Laguna Seca, then finished second at Riverside to Hulme.

Two of the three manufacturers' championships in the U.S. were won by Porsche. Pedro Rodriguez of Mexico (killed later in a race at Nuremberg, West Germany) and Jackie Oliver of England won the 24 hours at Daytona, Fla., going 2,621 miles after the Ferrari of Tony Adamowicz of Torrance, Calif., and Ronnie Bucknum of Capistrano Beach, Calif., fell from the lead. David Hobbs of England and Donohue in another Ferrari were third. The Sebring, Fla., 12-hour race was won by Vic Elford of England and Gérard Larrousse of France, a triumph for Porsche. In the Watkins Glen Six Hour race, the final manufacturers' event of the season, the Porsche winning streak was broken by Andrea de Adamich of Italy and Ronnie Petersen of Sweden, who covered 677.4 miles for Alfa Romeo.

At the Indianapolis 500, Donohue led easily for the first 50 laps but eventually succumbed to gearbox trouble, 16 laps later. Bobby Unser of Albuquerque, N.M., and Joe Leonard led briefly before Al Unser took command for the second half of the race, winning it with a record-breaking average speed of 157.735 mph. Only 12 of 33 cars finished, Revson taking second; A. J. Foyt, Jr., of Houston, Tex., third; Bill Vukovich of Fresno, Calif., whose father had been the last to win back-to-back Indianapolis 500's (1953–54), fourth; and Jim Malloy of Denver, Colo., fifth.

Donohue won the Schaefer 500 with an average speed of 138.649 mph. Joe Leonard finished second, only 1.61 seconds behind, and third place went to Foyt. In the Ontario 500, Leonard charged into the lead on the 161st lap and won over Art Pollard of Medford, Ore., Gary Bettenhausen of Tinley Park, Ill., Lloyd Ruby of Wichita Falls, Tex., and rookie Steve Krisiloff of Parsippany, N.J., in that order. Leonard's average speed was 152.354 mph.

Among National Association for Stock Car Auto Racing (NASCAR) racers in 1971 there were two superstars—Richard Petty of Randleman, N.C., and Bobby Allison of Hueytown, Ala. Petty became the first NASCAR driver to have career winnings of over $1 million as he rolled to 19 Grand National victories, including the most prestige-laden race of the season, the Daytona 500. But Allison and his Holman & Moody 1969 Mercury won an unprecedented seven races of 400 miles or more, including the Southern 500 and the 500's at Talledega, Ala.; Charlotte, N.C.; and Michigan. Petty became the only three-time winner of the Daytona 500, driving his blue Plymouth with a 144.456-mph average speed and edging his Chrysler Corp. teammate Buddy Baker of Charlotte, N.C., by ten seconds. Foyt was third.

Foyt did, however, win two NASCAR races, capturing the High Life 500 at Ontario, Calif. and the Atlanta 500. In other NASCAR events Donnie Allison won the Winston 500 at Talledega; Bobby Allison beat out his brother to win the World 600 at Charlotte, then proceeded to win the Dover 500 in Delaware, the Motor State 500 in Michigan, and the Riverside Golden State 400 in California. Petty edged Bobby Allison for the Dixie 500 title in Atlanta; but Allison came back to beat Petty for the Michigan 500 and the Talledega 500, then won the Southern 500 at Darlington, S.C., and the National 500 at Charlotte. The Rockingham (N.C.) 500 went to Petty. (*See in* CE: Automobile Racing.)

AWARDS AND PRIZES.

The Nobel peace prize for 1971 went—for the first time in 50 years —to a head of government, West Germany's Chancellor Willy Brandt. Brandt was cited for achieving "eminent results in creating preconditions for peace in Europe" and for extending "his hand to reconciliation between countries that have long been enemies." The selection of Brandt was particularly noteworthy in that the outcome of his policies of East-West reconciliation was still in doubt. It was felt that the award itself would add a moral endorsement to enhance Brandt's ability to bring his policies to fruition.

The Nobel prize for literature went to a candidate who had reputedly been under consideration for a number of years—Chilean poet, diplomat, and Communist politician Pablo Neruda. He was the second Chilean and third Latin American ever to win. Neruda, whose major works to date include an epic poem about the history and geography of Latin America called 'Canto General' (General Song), was described by one member of the Nobel committee as "the poet of violated human dignity."

Simon S. Kuznets, a Russian-born United States citizen who developed the most well-known statistical measure in economics—the gross national product (GNP)—was the Nobel winner in the field of economics. Another U.S. citizen, Dr. Earl W. Sutherland, Jr., won the Nobel prize in medicine or physiology for his work in discovering how cyclic AMP (cyclic adenosine 3′,5′-mono-

phosphate) regulates the action of hormones in living organisms. In the category of physics the winner was Dennis Gabor for his discovery of holography, the phenomenon of three-dimensional photography. Gabor was a Hungarian-born scientist who became a naturalized British subject. In chemistry Gerhard Herzberg, a German-born Canadian, was honored "for his contributions to the knowledge of electronic structure and geometry of molecules, particularly free radicals." The monetary value of each Nobel prize in 1971 was just under $90,000.

Pulitzer Prizes

The winners of the 55th annual Pulitzer prizes in journalism and arts and letters were announced in May. In the category of national reporting, the Pulitzer winners were Lucinda Franks and Thomas Powers of United Press International for their 12,000-word study of the late U.S. radical activist Diana Oughton. Jimmie Lee Hoagland of the *Washington Post* won the international reporting prize for a series on South Africa's system of apartheid. The local reporting prize went to William Hugh Jones of the *Chicago Tribune* for a series of stories that revealed collusion between police officers and private ambulance drivers. Horance G. Davis, Jr., won the Pulitzer editorial award for more than 30 editorials supporting peaceful desegregation of Florida schools published in the *Gainesville Sun* (Fla.). In the category of criticism Harold C. Schonberg was cited for his distinguished music criticism in *The New York Times,* and William A. Caldwell was cited in the category of commentary for his daily column on local affairs in the *Record* (Hackensack, N.J.). The cartooning prize went to Paul Conrad of the *Los Angeles Times* (it was his second Pulitzer); the spot news photography to John Paul Filo of the *Valley Daily News* (Tarentum, Pa.) and the *Daily Dispatch* (New Kensington, Pa.) for coverage of the Kent State University student killings; and the feature photography prize to Jack Dykinga of the *Chicago Sun-Times* for his photographs illustrating a story on schools for retarded children. The staff of the *Winston-Salem Journal* and *Twin Cities Sentinel* (Winston-Salem, N.C.) received the gold medal for meritorious public service for their special coverage of local environmental problems. The staff of the *Akron Beacon Journal* (Ohio) was honored in the category of general local reporting for its coverage, under intense deadline pressure, of the Kent State tragedy.

In the category of arts and letters the Pulitzer winners were Lawrance R. Thompson for 'Robert Frost: The Years of Triumph 1915–1938' (biography); James MacGregor Burns for 'Roosevelt: The Soldier of Freedom' (history); John Toland for 'The Rising Sun' (general nonfiction); and William S. Merwin for 'The Carrier of Ladders' (poetry). There was no award in the category of fiction. In music, Mario Davidowsky was cited

Dennis Gabor won the 1971 Nobel prize in physics for his invention of holography, three-dimensional photography using lasers.

WIDE WORLD

WIDE WORLD

Dr. Earl W. Sutherland, Jr., won the Nobel prize in medicine or physiology for his research in hormones.

CENTRAL PRESS FROM PICTORIAL PARADE

Willy Brandt, chancellor of West Germany, won the 1971 Nobel peace prize for promoting a thaw between Eastern and Western Europe.

for his composition 'Synchronisms No. 6 for Piano and Electronic Sound', and in drama, Paul Zindel was honored for his play, 'The Effect of Gamma Rays on Man-in-the-Moon Marigolds'.

Awards in Literature

The National Book Awards, given for the best works of literature published in 1970, were surrounded, as usual, by considerable controversy in 1971. For the first time, nominations were made by polling booksellers, librarians, and critics across the U.S. Nevertheless, the judges in the fiction category refused to consider one of the books in the top ten selected by the poll—Erich Segal's best seller 'Love Story'. Instead, the winner in the fiction category, was, for the third time, Saul Bellow, for his most recent novel, 'Mr. Sammler's Planet'. Other recipients were James MacGregor Burns (history and biography) for 'Roosevelt: The Soldier of Freedom' (also a Pulitzer winner); Francis Steegmuller (arts and letters) for 'Cocteau', his biography of French artist, writer, and filmmaker Jean Cocteau; Raymond Phineas Stearns (science) for 'Science in the British Colonies of America' (awarded posthumously); and Lloyd Alexander (children's literature) for 'The Marvelous Misadventures of Sebastian'. Frank Jones and Edward G. Seidensticker jointly shared the translation award, Jones for his translation of Bertolt Brecht's 'Saint Joan of the Stockyards' and Seidensticker for his translation of Yasunari Kawabata's 'The Sound of the Mountain'. In poetry Mona Van Duyn was the winner for her 'To See, To Take'.

The $5,000 Bollingen prize, the most prestigious U.S. award in poetry, administered by Yale University Library and presented every two years, went to two poets, Mona Van Duyn (also a National Book Award winner) and Richard P. Wilbur. The Columbia University Bancroft prizes for books of "exceptional merit and distinction" in history (including biography), diplomacy, and international relations were announced in April. Erik Barnouw was cited for 'The Image Empire', a history of the television medium; Joseph Frazier Wall for his biography 'Andrew Carnegie'; and David M. Kennedy for his book, 'Birth Control in America: The Career of Margaret Sanger'. The awards carried a monetary value of $4,000.

Awards in Science

The highest U.S. government award for achievement in science and engineering, the National Medal of Science, went to nine recipients during the year. Among the winners were Albert B. Sabin for his general contributions "to the understanding of viruses and viral diseases culminating in the development of the vaccine which has eliminated poliomyelitis as a major threat to human health" and George E. Mueller, who directed and planned the Apollo space program that put man on the moon. For the first time since 1962 a woman was included among the recipients, Barbara McClintock, who was cited for her work in genetic research. Other winners and their fields of specialty were Robert H. Dicke (physics); Richard D. Brauer (mathematics); Allan R. Sandage (astronomy); John C. Slater (physics and chemistry); Saul Winstein (chemistry), awarded posthumously; and John A. Wheeler (physics).

In 1971 the Albert Lasker Medical Research Awards, one of the most distinguished honors in U.S. science, went to three geneticists and a researcher in hypertension (high blood pressure disease). In basic research Drs. Seymour Benzer, Sydney Brenner, and Charles Yanofsky were joint winners for their pioneering work in explaining how the basic hereditary unit, the gene, operated in transmitting inherited characteristics. In clinical research Dr. Edward D. Freis was honored for determining the dangerous effects of even moderately high blood pressure and for proving that treatment could prolong life. (*See also* Literature.)

BAHRAIN. On Aug. 14, 1971, Bahrain declared itself independent. This action followed Iran's renunciation of its claim on Bahrain in 1970 and the continued failure of British-initiated efforts to establish a federation linking the sheikhdom with Qatar and the seven Trucial states. Following independence, the ruler's title was changed to emir. The decision ended 151 years of political and military dependence on Great Britain, the 1882 treaty governing Bahrain's relations with Britain (which followed previous ones dating from 1820) being replaced by a new treaty of friendship. This contained no British commitment to defend the island but did provide for "consultation in time of need."

Egypt, Jordan, Saudi Arabia, Kuwait, Iraq, Iran, and the United States gave speedy recognition to Bahrain's independence, but the People's Democratic Republic of Yemen (Aden) denounced the move as an "imperialist and reactionary plan."

Bahrain's admission to membership in the United Nations was approved by vote of the General Assembly on September 21.

On May 11 a British-built, $155 million aluminum smelter was inaugurated. It had a potential capacity of 120,000 tons a year.

BANKS. The banking industry in the United States was in the news in 1971 because of two major events. The first was the decision by members of the International Monetary Fund (IMF) to seek a new agreement on the structure of the global monetary system. Their decision marked the end of a quarter-century of reliance on the international monetary system developed under U.S. guidance at Bretton Woods, N.H., in 1944. The second event was the anti-inflation program outlined by U.S. President Richard M. Nixon in the second half of the year. Although President Nixon's freezing of wages and prices did not officially extend to interest rates, it affected them nonetheless. Administrators of wage and price controls made it clear that they would invoke similar control over interest rates if it seemed necessary. No doubt in part because of this, the prime rate, the rate banks charged their most creditworthy customers, continued the decline it began in 1970.

One precedent-shattering development concerning the prime rate occurred in October when the First National City Bank of New York, the second largest U.S. bank, adopted a floating prime rate that would shift according to market forces. A number of other banks adopted a similar policy, and it was predicted that the practice would become widespread. The adoption of a floating prime rate marked a fundamental change in the way banks

The summer residents of Fire Island, N.Y., were serviced by a floating branch of the Security National Bank.
COURTESY, "BANKING" MAGAZINE

had been doing business since 1934. Besides making the banks more flexible and competitive in the money markets, it also removed some of the political difficulties banks had encountered in the past when they had raised their prime rate.

Perhaps because of the continued decline in interest rates, mortgage loans by commercial banks increased during the year. The Federal Reserve Board reported a 1971 first-quarter total of $74.2 billion in mortgage loans, $3.3 billion above the comparable 1970 figure. This increase in mortgage loans was reflected in a nationwide surge of home-building.

Total deposits held by commercial banks rose to a September total of $498 billion, an increase of $50 billion from September 1970. Loans outstanding also increased, with the Federal Reserve reporting a September total of $331 billion, up $29 billion from the same month in 1970.

The growing volume of paper—bills, checks, and securities—that constituted the nation's financial exchange led to banking-industry efforts to find new ways to transfer funds. One answer to the paper explosion, the bank-credit-card industry, continued to expand. By 1971 there were 1,427 banks issuing cards to 47.6 million cardholders for use with 1.1 million merchants.

The growing complexity of the banking industry, coupled with domestic economic problems, led to increased emphasis on banking legislation and regulation. There was extensive discussion in the U.S. Congress over the proposed Banking Reform Act of 1971. The act would ban interlocking directorates and other practices that represented potential conflicts of interest between banks and their customers or companies in which their trust departments held stock. There was also a great deal of attention focused on the Federal Reserve Board's proposals to implement the Bank Holding Company Act of 1970. Discussion centered largely on permissible nonbanking activities of bank holding companies. Consumer advocate Ralph Nader published a report on the First National City Bank that, among other things, charged that its allocation of loans was socially irresponsible. Nader also accused U.S. bank-regulating officials of allowing banks to violate consumer-credit laws. (*See also* Economy; Money and International Finance. *See in* CE: Bank.)

BARBADOS. At the general election in September 1971, Prime Minister Errol W. Barrow and his Democratic Labour party were returned to power in Barbados with an increased majority of 18 out of 24 seats. Barrow had previously warned the governments of the United States, Great Britain, and Guyana against intervention on behalf of the opposition—alleging that the U.S. Central Intelligence Agency had made such attempts in the past.

In December 1970 Barbados became a member of the International Monetary Fund, with a quota

in the fund of $13 million. In addition, the government announced its intention of establishing a central bank and introducing its own currency. Barbados had a tax-free budget for the first time in ten years.

Tourism, Barbados' major foreign exchange earner, suffered from rapid expansion, high prices, tougher competition from cheaper European resorts for the North American tourist trade, and apprehensions aroused by black power and other radical activities. There was evidence of an increase in black American tourism, and Barbados promoted tourism from Europe, aided by a new airline, International Caribbean Airways. (*See in* CE: Barbados.)

BASEBALL. The 1971 major league baseball season ended in dramatic fashion when the Pittsburgh Pirates dethroned the world champion Baltimore Orioles 2–1 in game seven of the World Series. Roberto Clemente of Pittsburgh was adjudged the series' most valuable player. The 37-year-old right fielder from Puerto Rico got a record-tying 12 hits, en route to a .414 average, and hit safely in all seven games.

Pittsburgh qualified for the series by beating the San Francisco Giants, three games to one, in the best-of-five divisional play-offs for the National League pennant. The Pirates lost the opener to the Giants 5–4, then took three straight by scores of 9–4, 2–1, and 9–5. Baltimore required only three games to eliminate the Oakland Athletics in the American League play-offs, winning by margins of 5–3, 5–1, and 5–3.

Prominent Newsmakers

It was a season of bizarre happenings. California Angels' outfielder Alex Johnson, American League batting champion in 1970, was suspended without pay by the Angels in June for "not hustling and not showing the proper mental attitude." However, in what was termed by some as a landmark decision, an impartial arbitration board ruled in late September that an emotional disturbance should be treated no differently than a physical ailment in baseball and ordered the Angels to restore Johnson's back pay of $29,970. The board upheld 29 disciplinary fines against Johnson, totaling an estimated $3,750. Johnson was traded to Cleveland at season's end.

Chicago Cubs' owner Philip K. Wrigley made headlines on September 3 when he took out advertisements in four Chicago newspapers in support of Cubs' manager Leo Durocher. The ad was published following a stormy clubhouse meeting in which Durocher feuded with some of his star players. Wrigley's message warned that players who let down on the job would be traded in the off-season. The Cubs, who had made a bold bid for divisional honors late in August, wound up in a third-place tie with the New York Mets, 14 games out.

KEN REGAN FROM CAMERA 5

Oakland's Vida Blue thrilled fans with his incredible pitching capacity; his final record was 24-8.

American League owners, by a vote of 10 to 2, gave Washington Senators' owner Robert E. Short permission to move his financially troubled franchise to Dallas-Ft. Worth, Tex., in time for the 1972 season. The nation's capital had been the site of an American League franchise since 1901.

Baseball's Hall of Fame at Cooperstown, N.Y., inducted eight new members in 1971: Leroy (Satchel) Paige, Dave Bancroft, Jacob Beckley, Charles (Chick) Hafey, Harry Hooper, Joseph James Kelley, Richard (Rube) Marquard, and George Weiss. Paige was named by the new Hall of Fame Committee on Negro Baseball Leagues. The other new members were chosen by the Veteran's Committee.

Baltimore's pitching staff produced four 20-game winners: Dave McNally, Mike Cuellar, Jim Palmer, and Pat Dobson. It was the second such pitching accomplishment in major league history. The 1920 Chicago White Sox turned the trick behind Urban (Red) Faber, Claude Williams, Dickie Kerr, and Ed Cicotte.

Spectacular rookie Oakland pitcher Vida Blue electrified the baseball world by winning 17 games before the All-Star break. His final record was 24–8. Three National Leaguers—Ken Holtzman of the Chicago Cubs, Rick Wise of Philadelphia, and Bob Gibson of St. Louis—pitched no-hit, no-run games. It was Holtzman's second masterpiece.

Atlanta's Hank Aaron became the third player ever to hit 600 home runs. Harmon Killebrew of Minnesota and Frank Robinson of Baltimore both delivered their 500th homers, the 10th and 11th to reach that plateau. Ron Hunt, Montreal's second baseman, set a major league record when he was hit by pitched balls 50 times.

Gen. William D. Eckert, the former commissioner who had held baseball's highest post for three years, died on April 16 at Freeport on the Bahamas. Eckert was 62.

The National League established a new attendance record of 17,333,371 as 11 of its 12 teams topped the million mark. The American League attendance dropped off somewhat from that of the preceding year, to 11,870,557.

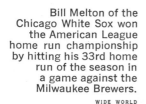

Bill Melton of the Chicago White Sox won the American League home run championship by hitting his 33rd home run of the season in a game against the Milwaukee Brewers.

WIDE WORLD

Pennant Races and World Series

A frenzied finish in the National League's West Division highlighted regular season competition. The San Francisco Giants took over first place on April 12 and stayed there for 172 days and 155 games, but it took a victory in their final game to outlast onrushing Los Angeles. The Dodgers staged a blistering rally after trailing by 8½ games early in September only to lose out by the margin of one game. The Giants beat San Diego 5–1 in their finale to preserve their one-game edge over the Dodgers, whose 2–1 defeat of Houston thereby became meaningless. Pittsburgh captured the National League East convincingly. St. Louis was runner-up, ending a full seven games behind the Pirates.

Both American League races developed into runaways. Baltimore ran up 101 victories in the East Division to shake off Detroit by 12 games. Oakland gathered the same win total in the West Division and finished 16 games in front of Kansas City.

The World Series opened in Baltimore, and the Orioles responded by winning game one 5–3. Lefthander Dave McNally survived early problems to post a three-hit win. McNally pitched hitless ball for 6⅔ innings, retiring 19 straight batters in one stretch. The Pirates, helped along by two errors, piled up a 3–0 lead in the second inning. Frank Robinson's home run off loser Dock Ellis reduced the deficit to 3–1 in the bottom of the second. Merv Rettenmund then homered with two on in the third to put the Orioles on top to stay. Don Buford hit a fifth inning homer for Baltimore's final run.

The Orioles won game two in a runaway 11–3, after rain forced postponement of the series for one day. Baltimore got 14 hits, all singles, and ran up an 11–0 lead for pitcher Jim Palmer before Richie Hebner's three-run homer put Pittsburgh on the scoreboard in the eighth. The loser was Bob Johnson.

UPI COMPIX

The Baltimore Orioles' Frank Robinson scores the winning run in the sixth World Series game against the Pittsburgh Pirates.

Dave Cash, Pirates' second baseman, makes a wholehearted but unsuccessful grab for a line drive in the first game of the World Series.

WIDE WORLD

The series moved to Pittsburgh's Three Rivers Stadium for game three and the Pirates grabbed their first victory 5–1, behind the three-hit pitching of Steve Blass. Pittsburgh led 2–1 in the seventh when Bob Robertson, after missing a bunt sign, smashed a home run with two on off loser Mike Cuellar to put the game out of Baltimore's reach. Frank Robinson's homer accounted for the Orioles' lone run.

The first night World Series game in history unfolded at Three Rivers Stadium on October 13 and a record Pittsburgh baseball crowd of 51,378 saw the Pirates beat Baltimore 4–3 to tie the series at two games apiece. The Orioles took a 3–0 lead in the top of the first inning, but 21-year-old rookie pitcher Bruce Kison came on in relief to halt Baltimore on no runs and one hit over the next 6⅓ innings. Ironically, Kison walked none but hit three batters, a World Series record. Kison was credited with the win when pinch-hitter Milt May singled home the tie-breaking run in the seventh. Reliefer Eddie Watt was the loser.

Nelson Briles handed Pittsburgh the series lead, three games to two, by pitching a brilliant two-hitter to shackle the Orioles 4–0 in game five. Bob Robertson homered off Dave McNally in the second inning to provide Briles with the only offensive support he needed.

The series switched back to Baltimore for game six and Baltimore rebounded from a 2–0 deficit to survive 3–2 in 10 innings and square the fall classic at three games apiece. Brooks Robinson's sacrifice fly in the bottom of the tenth scored the clincher to make a winner out of McNally in relief and a loser out of Bob Miller, also in relief. Clemente and Buford hit home runs.

Four-hit pitching by Blass carried Pittsburgh to baseball's pinnacle in game seven. The Pirates' 2–1 win upset earlier conjecture that the Orioles had built a long-term dynasty. Clemente's fourth-inning home run was the first hit off the loser, Cuellar. Jose Pagan's double in the eighth drove home Willie Stargell from first and boosted the Pirates' advantage to 2–0. Ellie Hendricks and Mark Belanger singled off Blass to lead off the Baltimore eighth, but the Orioles' budding rally produced only one run. Blass made it look easy in the ninth and Pittsburgh thus emerged as champion, four games to three.

Individual Stars

The Most Valuable Player awards went to Joe Torre of the Cardinals in the National League and to Vida Blue in the American. The Cy Young Awards for best pitchers were given to Ferguson Jenkins of the Cubs in the National and to Blue in the American. Rookie-of-the-year honors went to Earl Williams of the Braves in the National and to Chris Chambliss of the Indians in the American.

Ten American League pitchers won 20 or more games in 1971, highest total in the majors since 1920. Detroit's Mickey Lolich (25–14) and Oakland's Vida Blue (24–8) led the way in wins. In addition to Baltimore's big four of McNally, Cuellar, Palmer, and Dobson, the select group included Wilbur Wood of the Chicago White Sox, Jim (Catfish) Hunter of Oakland, Andy Messersmith of California, and Joe Coleman of Detroit. Blue paced the earned-run averages with 1.82. Lolich struck out 308 batters.

Minnesota's Tony Oliva won the American League batting title with .337. Bill Melton became the first White Sox player ever to grab home-run honors, belting out 33. Harmon Killebrew of Minnesota drove in the most runs, 119.

In the National League, Ferguson Jenkins of the Chicago Cubs collected a league-high total of 24 wins. It was his fifth straight 20-game season. Three other pitchers won 20—Al Downing of Los Angeles, Steve Carlton of St. Louis, and Tom Seaver of the New York Mets. Seaver was tops in both earned-run averages, 1.76, and strikeouts, 289.

Joe Torre of St. Louis hit .363 and produced 137 runs batted in for leadership in both categories. Pittsburgh's Willie Stargell hammered 48 home runs to capture the fight for individual home-run laurels from Atlanta's Hank Aaron who had 47.

The American League beat the National League 6–4 in the All Star Game at Detroit. A prodigious home run by Reggie Jackson of the American League was one of six homers in all, tying an All-Star record. Frank Robinson and Harmon Killebrew also connected for the Americans. Johnny Bench, Hank Aaron, and Roberto Clemente homered for the Nationals. Robinson's two-run home run climaxed the American League's four-run third to rub out the Nationals' 3–0 lead and bring the victory to the starter, Vida Blue. The Americans thus triumphed for the 18th time against 23 losses and one tie. The American League had lost eight straight to the Nationals.

Amateur Baseball

University of Southern California repeated as champion of the college World Series at Omaha, Neb., in 1971, thereby dominating the National Collegiate Athletic Association (NCAA) tournament for the seventh time, four more than any other school. The Trojans clinched the title with a 7–2 win over Southern Illinois University, on the eight-hit pitching of Steve Busby.

The Little League World Series title went to the Far East for the fourth time in five years, as Tainan, Taiwan (Republic of China) defeated Gary, Ind. (Anderson League), 12–3 in three overtime innings at Williamsport, Pa., before a crowd of 32,000. Taiwan worked its way to the finals by a first round 7–0 victory over the Latin American team from Caguas, Puerto Rico, and a semi-final 11–0 conquest of Wahiawa, Hawaii. Gary defeated Lexington, Ky., in the first round, and took the semi-final 7–0 from the Madrid, Spain, team of United States servicemen's sons. (See in CE: Baseball.)

BASKETBALL. The University of California at Los Angeles (UCLA), again emphasizing team balance and a clawing, pressing defense, continued its remarkable domination of United States collegiate basketball in 1971. Coached by John Wooden, who has never had a losing season, UCLA finished with a 29–1 record, losing only a midseason game to Notre Dame, and for the fifth consecutive year (a record) won top honors in the National Collegiate Athletic Association (NCAA) tournament.

It was the seventh title for the Bruins in the last eight years, perpetuating the longest dynasty in college basketball history. In these eight seasons the Bruins had a combined 221–15 record, and they were 203–7 in the seven years they won the NCAA championship. Additionally, the Bruins, as a result of their latest success, finished with 28 successive NCAA tournament victories, also a record. Sidney Wicks, chosen the player of the year by the U.S. Basketball Writers' Association, led the Bruins with a 21.3 scoring average, which ranked him 60th among the nation's major college scorers.

Only two major colleges, Marquette University and the University of Pennsylvania, were undefeated going into NCAA tournament play. Marquette, rated number one during much of the season, was upset by Ohio State 60–59 in the Mideast regionals. Pennsylvania was also eliminated, bowing 90–47 to a Villanova University team that had grown stronger as the season progressed and that reached the finals before losing to UCLA in the championship game.

The Bruins entered NCAA tournament play in the Western regionals and won their opener 91–73 over Brigham Young University. Their next tournament opponent, California State at Long Beach, champion of the Pacific Coast Athletic Association, put up a good fight but lost 57–55. The Bruins then went on to Houston, Tex., for the NCAA finals and marched to the title with victories over the University of Kansas, 68–60, and Villanova, 68–62.

The title game against Villanova was close throughout. Villanova, in the championship game for the first time in the school's history, trailed by eight points, 45–37, at the half and in the final minutes twice drew to within three points of a tie, first at 61–58 and later at 63–60. Steve Patterson, who averaged only 12.9 points for the season, led the Bruins in this game with a sensational 29-point performance, his best of the season. He sank 13 of 18 field-goal attempts and was also a major factor in the Bruins' highly successful full-court pressing defense.

The University of Evansville (Indiana) won the championship in the NCAA's college division (limited to smaller schools) by defeating Old Dominion University (Norfolk, Va.) 97–82. The University of North Carolina won the championship in the annual National Invitational Tournament (NIT) by defeating Georgia Tech, 84–66.

WIDE WORLD

Lew Alcindor (center), later Kareem Abdul Jabbar, of the Milwaukee Bucks won the Podolof Trophy for the NBA's most valuable player.

College Standouts

Johnny Neumann, a University of Mississippi sophomore, won the major division scoring title with 923 points, for a 40.1 game average. Austin Carr of Notre Dame played in six more games and scored 1,101 points, but was second to Neumann with a game average of 38.

Players chosen on the Consensus All-America team, as published in the 'Official NCAA Basketball Guide', were: Howard Porter, Villanova; Carr, Notre Dame; Neumann, Mississippi; Ken Durrett, LaSalle; Sidney Wicks and Curtis Rowe, UCLA; Jim McDaniels, Western Kentucky; John Roche, South Carolina; Dean Meminger, Marquette; and Artis Gilmore, Jacksonville.

Professional Basketball

The National Basketball Association (NBA) had its 25th anniversary season in 1971 and continued to boom in popularity. New franchises were opened in Buffalo, N.Y.; Cleveland, Ohio; and Portland, Ore., raising league membership from 14 to 17 teams and creating a new geographical alignment of four divisions, replacing the old Eastern and Western divisions.

The Milwaukee Bucks, led by Lew Alcindor (later Kareem Abdul Jabbar) and veteran playmaker Oscar Robertson, won the league title. The Bucks set several major records en route to the championship. They had a sequence of 20 consecutive victories, bettering by two the previous league record, and they had a .509 team field-goal percentage. The Bucks were the first team in the NBA's 25-year history to make good on half of their shots from the floor.

Alcindor, a 7-foot 2-inch center in his second season as a professional, was the league's dominant performer. He led the league in scoring with a 31.7 average, was second in field-goal percentage, and fourth in rebounding. He was a near-unanimous choice for the all-star team and won the Podolof Trophy, which goes to the league's most valuable player.

The combination of Alcindor and Robertson, who was acquired in a trade with Cincinnati, made Milwaukee an easy winner in the Midwest Division. The Bucks finished 15 games ahead of Chicago in the Midwest Division and had the largest winning margin of any of the four divisional champions. One champion, Baltimore in the Central Division, barely won half its games, finishing with a 42–40 record. New York was the champion in the Atlantic Division, Los Angeles in the Pacific Division. The top two teams in each division qualified for the play-offs.

Milwaukee and Baltimore advanced to the finals. Baltimore eliminated New York's defending league champions in the semifinals, winning an exciting series four games to three. New York was weakened on the boards as a result of a knee injury suffered by Willis Reed, its star center and the NBA hero of the preceding season. Milwaukee eliminated Los Angeles in five games in the other semifinal series and then breezed to the title by knocking off Baltimore in four games.

The rival American Basketball Association (ABA) also had a successful season and continued to approach the major league standards achieved by the NBA. The ABA, with 11 teams, had in excess of 2 million paid admissions and continued to sign many of the top college stars. Officials from both the NBA and ABA agreed to a merger and sought Congressional approval. However, the NBA Players Association opposed the proposed merger, and both leagues were still operating independently when the 1971–72 season began. The Utah Stars won the 1971 ABA championship.

Steve Patterson of UCLA is about to take a fall, but his team went on to beat Villanova and take its fifth straight NCAA title.
WIDE WORLD

Elmore Smith (left) of Kentucky State was considered one of the best college basketball players of the year.
PAUL WEDDLE FROM "FRANKFORT STATE JOURNAL"

1971 NCAA BASKETBALL TOURNAMENT

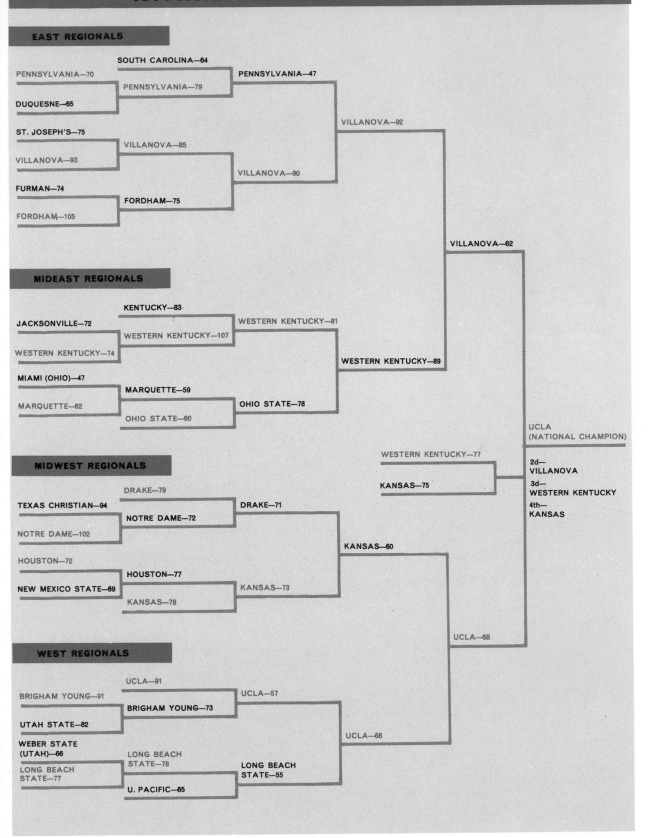

EAST REGIONALS

SOUTH CAROLINA—64
PENNSYLVANIA—70
PENNSYLVANIA—79
PENNSYLVANIA—47
DUQUESNE—65
VILLANOVA—92
ST. JOSEPH'S—75
VILLANOVA—85
VILLANOVA—93
VILLANOVA—90
FURMAN—74
FORDHAM—75
FORDHAM—105

VILLANOVA—62

MIDEAST REGIONALS

KENTUCKY—83
JACKSONVILLE—72
WESTERN KENTUCKY—81
WESTERN KENTUCKY—107
WESTERN KENTUCKY—74
WESTERN KENTUCKY—89
MIAMI (OHIO)—47
MARQUETTE—59
MARQUETTE—62
OHIO STATE—78
OHIO STATE—60

UCLA
(NATIONAL CHAMPION)

2d—
VILLANOVA
3d—
WESTERN KENTUCKY
4th—
KANSAS

MIDWEST REGIONALS

WESTERN KENTUCKY—77
KANSAS—75

DRAKE—79
TEXAS CHRISTIAN—94
NOTRE DAME—72
DRAKE—71
NOTRE DAME—102
KANSAS—60
HOUSTON—72
HOUSTON—77
NEW MEXICO STATE—69
KANSAS—73
KANSAS—78

UCLA—68

WEST REGIONALS

UCLA—91
BRIGHAM YOUNG—91
BRIGHAM YOUNG—73
UCLA—57
UTAH STATE—82
UCLA—68
WEBER STATE
(UTAH)—66
LONG BEACH
STATE—78
LONG BEACH
STATE—77
LONG BEACH
STATE—55
U. PACIFIC—65

RUK ONZE TOEKOMST NIET STUK
W'J HEBBEN REYT OP GELUK
K.L.J. BLEGEM

Demanding higher prices for their products, 80,000 western European farmers demonstrate in Brussels in March. Their banner reads: "Don't ruin our future: we have a right to be happy." The march became a near-riot in which 3,000 policemen battled the demonstrators, leaving one man dead and 140 injured. Extensive property damage also occurred.
CAMERA PRESS FROM PIX

BELGIUM. In September 1971 the Belgian government decided to dissolve parliament and to hold an early general election, which would normally have been scheduled for the spring of 1972. The election, held on November 7, gave the Social Christians 66 seats (a loss from 69 seats in 1968), the Socialists 61 (59 in 1968), and the Liberals 34 (47 in 1968). The government therefore remained in the hands of the Social Christians and Socialists, with Gaston Eyskens still premier. However, both the Social Christians and the Liberals lost seats, while the two French-speaking federalist parties, the Front Démocratique des Bruxellois Francophones and the Rassemblement Wallon, doubled their combined strength with 24 seats in the new parliament as opposed to 12 in 1968 and a mere 5 in 1965. The Volksunie (Flemish nationalists) increased their total from 20 to 22 seats.

The introduction of the value-added tax on Jan. 1, 1971, one year behind schedule, caused much apprehension because of the unique automatic link between prices and wages. Fearing unbridled inflation the government ordered compulsory price reductions and an almost universal price freeze. Moreover, parliament was invited to reactivate a World War II law providing for strict price controls. The new legislation met with opposition.

As the year progressed, signs of stagnation in the economy began to appear: industrial production slowed down, balance of trade deficits were registered, and home building declined sharply. In March, Belgian farmers demonstrated throughout the country to protest the prices policy of the European Economic Community. A mass rally of Western European farmers in Brussels on March 23 ended in rioting and considerable property damage. One farmer was killed and 140 people were hurt. (*See in* CE: Belgium.)

BHUTAN. In September 1971 the United Nations approved Bhutan's application for membership, and Bhutan announced plans for a permanent UN mission in New York City. Earlier, Bhutan for the first time had exchanged ambassadors with India, which, according to a 1949 treaty, guided the Himalayan kingdom in foreign affairs, defense, and communications. The exchange of ambassadors put relations between the two countries on a new basis befitting Bhutan's independent status. (*See also* India; United Nations.)

The country's third five-year development plan, involving nearly $47 million, was officially launched in 1971. India was again to provide the bulk of funds as well as technical personnel, mainly for the improvement of agriculture, communications, and education.

Bhutan's King Jigme Dorji Wangchuk made an official visit to India in April. He expressed satisfaction with the 1949 treaty with India and dismissed reports that Bhutan might consider seeking a revision of it.

BIOLOGY. The effects of budget cuts and of increasing public mistrust of science were felt in the biological sciences in 1971, though not as deeply as in some of the other sciences. Funding was cut so severely that the only major success reported in basic research was the synthesis of the human growth hormone (HGH).

One area where finances and interest were abundant, partly at the instigation of United States President Richard M. Nixon, was cancer research. Viruses were found to be associated with more kinds of cancers, and, for the first time, a new virus that appeared to be a distinctly human cancer virus was discovered by a team of medical scientists at the University of Southern California School of Medicine and Children's Hospital of Los Angeles.

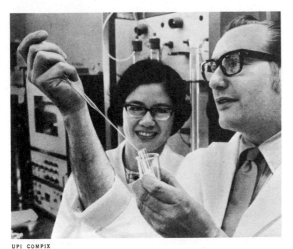

Dr. Darrell N. Ward, assisted by Dr. Wan-Kyng Liu, has discovered the structure of the hormone vital to human ovulation and conception.

Synthesis of HGH

Choh Hao Li and Donald H. Yamashiro of the University of California's Hormone Research Laboratory in San Francisco assembled 188 amino acids, one at a time, to form the single chain that constitutes the hormone responsible for human body growth. The biochemists had determined the chemical structure of the hormone in 1966 and had struggled since to reconstruct it. The technique that finally succeeded had been established in 1969 by Robert B. Merrifield of Rockefeller University in New York City.

HGH was the largest biologically active molecule yet synthesized. The only natural source for it is the human pea-sized pituitary gland. The larger supply that would now be available could be used to treat dwarfism and possibly to gain insight into other diseases involving abnormal growth, including cancer and cholesterol accumulation in the blood.

Genetic Manipulation

Several developments in 1971 demonstrated the degree of sophistication achieved by the biologist in his attempts to gain greater control over the life process. The U.S. Department of Agriculture reported that the housefly might now be controlled by using genetic manipulation to create a strain in which only males would mature. At Johns Hopkins University, Baltimore, Md., a major obstacle to efforts to develop mammalian life in a test tube was overcome. A protein substance used as a substitute for the wall of the uterus, to which mammalian eggs must attach for full maturation, permitted artificially fertilized mouse eggs to develop past the blastocyst stage for the first time.

In the field of human genetics, amniocentesis, the technique of detecting defects in fetal cells extracted from the womb, was an established tool of maternity counseling. Also, test-tube conception techniques became so sophisticated that some scientists predicted that within a year a woman would bear a child conceived in a test tube.

Interest in the moral implications of genetic manipulation increased with each innovation. Scientists, physicians, philosophers, theologians, and legislators formed centers to study and promote responsible debate on the ethical, social, and legal implications of modern science, and legislation along these lines was proposed. Considerable argument was stimulated by "Chance and Necessity," an essay by French Nobel prizewinner Jacques Monod. Monod maintained that the only conceivable conclusion he could draw from his pioneering work in unraveling the genetic code was that man's existence is the result of mere chance and that there is no point in tampering with it. (*See in* CE: Biology.)

BIRTHS. Among the births that attracted public attention in 1971 were:

To Bernadette Devlin, Roman Catholic political activist in Northern Ireland and youngest member of Great Britain's House of Commons, on August 23, a daughter.

To Abbie Hoffman, U.S. political activist, author ('Steal This Book'), and one of the 1969–70 Chicago "Conspiracy" trial defendants, and his wife, Anita, on July 20, a son.

To Paul McCartney, singer, formerly with the Beatles, and Linda Eastman, professional photographer, on September 17, a daughter.

To Svetlana Alliluyeva Peters, daughter of Soviet leader Joseph Stalin, who defected to the U.S. in 1967, and William Wesley Peters, an architect and

Svetlana Peters, daughter of the late Soviet dictator Joseph Stalin, gave birth to a 7-pound, 9-ounce girl in 1971.

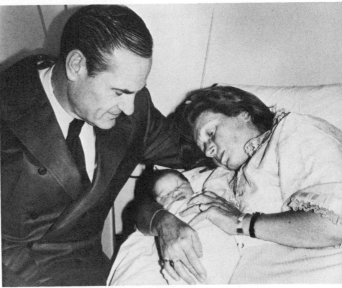

Linda Eastman, professional photographer and wife of former Beatle Paul McCartney, gave birth to a girl in September.

BOATS AND BOATING.

Boating safety took a giant step forward in 1971 when United States President Richard M. Nixon on August 11 signed into law the long-awaited Federal Boat Safety Act. Industry and government officials had worked on the measure since 1968. The final draft covers four general areas of recreational boating: it (a) provides for federal grants to states for boating safety programs; (b) authorizes the Coast Guard to set construction standards aimed at reducing accidents; (c) provides that all powerboats be registered, regardless of horsepower; and (d) provides for the collection of statistics on the sport. Under the new code, the Coast Guard is empowered to order a skipper to return to port if his boat or his physical condition are not deemed proper for navigation.

Along with the act came a rash of bills in both state and federal legislatures aimed at eliminating from waters as many pollutants as possible. The outboard industry responded by installing equipment to prevent spilling fuel overboard and by using only biodegradable oil additives.

Major Boating Competitions

On the sailing scene, Ted Hood became the first two-time winner of the biennial Marblehead (Mass.)-to-Halifax (Nova Scotia) yacht race in his 54-foot yawl *Robin*. The 2,225-mile Trans-Pacific race from Los Angeles, Calif., to Honolulu, Hawaii, was taken by *Windward Passage,* skippered by Robert Johnson of Hawaii's Lahaina Yacht Club. British Prime Minister Edward Heath took the helm of the *Morning Cloud* to lead Great Britain to victory over the U.S. yachtsmen in the Admiral's Cup series at Plymouth, England. John Kolius of Houston, Tex., won the Mallory Cup for the men's championship; Mrs. Romeyn Everdell of Duxbury, Mass., took the Adams Cup, the emblem of the women's championship; and the Sears Cup for the junior team went to the Annapolis Yacht Club of Maryland. Defending champion Earl Helms retained his Snipe Class world title, and Joerg Bruder of Brazil his Finn Class world

vice-president of the Frank Lloyd Wright Foundation, on May 21, a daughter.

To Sharon Percy Rockefeller, daughter of Senator Charles H. Percy (R, Ill.), and John D. Rockefeller IV, West Virginia secretary of state, on April 1, a daughter.

To Senator Strom Thurmond (R, S.C.), and his wife, Nancy, a former Miss South Carolina, on March 30, a daughter.

To Pierre Elliott Trudeau, Canada's Prime Minister, and his wife, Margaret, daughter of a Canadian government official, on December 25, a son.

To Michael Wilding, Jr., son of film stars Elizabeth Taylor and Michael Wilding, and his wife, Beth, on July 25, a daughter.

The last of the sidewheelers, the *Alexander Hamilton,* made its final voyage on the Hudson River in September 1971.

William Wishnick won the Sam Griffith Hennessey Trophy for the world's powerboat championship with his two boats, both called the *Boss O' Nova.*

title. Bob Mosbacher of Houston took world Soling Class honors.

The America's Cup competition impasse was erased in June when the New York Yacht Club recognized the Royal Thames Yacht Club as the challenger-of-record for the next series, which was postponed until 1974. Great Britain will conduct elimination trials off Newport, R.I., with challengers from Australia, Canada, and France to decide the eventual challenger for the New York Yacht Club's defender.

In powerboat racing, *Miss Madison,* a hometown hydroplane piloted by Jim McCormick, won the Gold Cup race in Madison, Ind., with an upset victory of 101.522 mph. William Wishnick, chairman of the Witco Chemical Co., won the Sam Griffith Hennessey Trophy for the world's championship with his two boats, both named *Boss O' Nova.* The first world inboard championship, run in Dayton, Ohio, in July, drew a record field.

Other Developments

Consumerism continued as a major theme in 1971, with boat owners and users demanding more and better service, quality, performance, and attention. Small-boat sailing continued to boom, particularly the Hobie Cats, Sunfish, and Sailfish. Also increasing in popularity were the racing hulls such as Penguin, Thistle, and Star, and planing hulls of fiber glass and molded plywood. The industry estimated that more than 44 million persons engaged in recreational boating in the U.S. in 1971; the Coast Guard estimated some 10 million less. American outboards, many assembled in Europe, Canada, and Australia, continued to dominate the world market. (*See in* CE: Boats and Boating.)

BOLIVIA. On Aug. 22, 1971, the ten-month-old government of Bolivia's president, Gen. Juan José Torres Gonzales, was overthrown by a coalition of anti-Communist forces. After four days of intense fighting, in which more than 120 were killed and 700 wounded, Col. Hugo Banzer Suárez was named to succeed Torres, who was given safe conduct to Peru. Since independence in 1825, Bolivia had seen 188 uprisings against 150 ruling governments.

The rebellion pitted military men (including a unit trained by the Green Berets of the United States Army) and disgruntled business leaders against Torres' student, labor, and hard-core radical supporters. The majority of Bolivia's population, the impoverished Indian peasants, played little part in the action. Discontent among the businessmen had many sources, including the nationalization of U.S.-owned mining and oil installations, the expropriation of the sugar industry, the expulsion of the Peace Corps, and the government's surrender to labor's demands for higher wages and greater control of working conditions. Unrest within the military stemmed mainly from fear of the growing power of the hard-core radicals.

Banzer's political power rested in a nationalist popular front, a merger of the two anti-Marxist parties, the Nationalist Revolutionary Movement (MNR) and the Bolivian Socialist Falange (FSB). The new government pledged cooperation with the U.S. and with foreign investment interests and ruled out restoration of relations with Cuba (favored by President Torres). The U.S. contributed $2,500 worth of medical supplies to the Bolivian government, to treat those wounded in the fighting.

Economic development in 1971 was slowed by the uncertainty of the political situation. In Janu-

KEYSTONE

The government of Bolivia's President Juan José Torres Gonzales was overthrown by right-wing rebel military forces in 1971.

ary a $12 million tin smelter was opened, and an antimony smelter was being financed by a Czechoslovak state firm. Foreign credits of $42 million were forthcoming for aid construction of a 350-mile Santa Cruz–Argentina gas pipeline. In September the Banzer regime announced its intention to seek $100 million in economic aid. (*See in* CE: Bolivia.)

In an unsuccessful effort to defend La Paz, miners loyal to General Torres arm themselves with sticks of dynamite.

UPI COMPIX

BOTSWANA. In 1971 Botswana continued to strike a balance between its economic dependence on South Africa and its political allegiance to black Africa. Following Botswana's ban on Rhodesian tobacco and beer, South Africa increased its exports to Botswana, remaining the country's main trading partner. A large part of Botswana's trade deficit continued to be made up from customs revenue from South Africa and foreign aid, chiefly from Great Britain. Game park tourism, with South Africa as the main customer, developed rapidly, though the economy remained dominated by huge mining projects. The copper-nickel Shashe mining project was absorbing more than half of the budget allocated for Botswana's 1970–75 national development plan. Diamond production began at Orapa in July.

Domestic pressure increased for Africanization of the civil service, and in August police command was transferred to the country's first African commissioner. Work permits were granted less freely to foreigners, who were encouraged by the government to seek citizenship.

In the realm of foreign affairs, Botswana's president, Sir Seretse Khama, remained opposed to British arms sales to South Africa. Sir Seretse announced support for the admission of the People's Republic of China to the United Nations, despite the presence of a Taiwanese agricultural aid mission in Botswana. (*See in* CE: Botswana.)

BOWLING. In 1971 the 7th World tournament of the Fédération Internationale des Quilleurs (FIQ) was held in the United States for the first time, at the Milwaukee Arena. More than 30,000 spectators attended the eight-day competition in which the U.S. won five of the eight first-place gold medals.

In Detroit, Mich., the site of the 68th annual American Bowling Congress (ABC) tournament, the classic (professional) five-man championship was captured by Chester Iio Investments of Houston, Tex., which totaled 3,081 in a roll-off to decide the title. In other classic competition, Bill Zuben, Wilmington, Mass., and Barry Warshafsky, Watertown, Mass., led the doubles with 1,357; Vic Iwlew, Kalamazoo, Mich., won the singles with 750; and Gary Dickinson, Fort Worth, Tex., topped the all-events competition with 2,000.

The ABC's regular division champions were: team, Carter Tool & Die Corp., Rochester, N.Y., 3,238; doubles, Tony Maresca, Mesa, Ariz., and Bill Haley, Tempe, Ariz., 1,330; singles and all events, Al Cohn, Chicago, 738 and 2,063, respectively. The Booster five-man competition (for teams averaging 850 pins and under) was led by Bay Jewelers, Norfolk, Va., which rolled 2,856.

The prestigious ABC Masters tournament crown was won by Jim Godman, Lorain, Ohio. Emerging from the loser's bracket, Godman averaged 229 for 40 games, a record in the tournament's 21-year history.

UPI COMPIX

After greeting the winners of the 7th World tournament of the Fédération Internationale des Quilleurs, United States President Richard M. Nixon bowls a strike himself.

Open-division champions of the 52d annual Woman's International Bowling Congress (WIBC) tournament, conducted in Atlanta, Ga., were: team, Koenig & Strey Real Estate, Wilmette, Ill., 2,891; doubles, Dotty Fothergill, North Attleboro, Mass., and Millie Martorella, Rochester, N.Y., 1,263; singles, Ginny Younginer, Winnsboro, S.C., 667; and all events, Lorrie Koch, Carpentersville, Ill., 1,840. For the second consecutive year, Millie Martorella triumphed in the WIBC Queens tournament.

Eddie Lubanski, a longtime Detroit standout, was elected to the ABC Hall of Fame. Shirley Garms, Island Lake, Ill., and Tess Small, Wisconsin Rapids, Wis., were elected to the WIBC Hall of Fame.

In one of the top professional events, Mike Limongello, North Babylon, N.Y., and Paula Sperber, Miami, Fla., were winners of the first U.S. Open, successor to the National All-Star tournament. Johnny Petraglia, Brooklyn, N.Y., captured the $25,000 first prize in the Firestone Tournament of Champions, the year's richest.

In collegiate competition, Harding College of Searcy, Ark., won the National Association of Intercollegiate Athletics team title, while Steve Rumbaugh of West Virginia State took the all-events crown. In the Association of College Unions-International championships, Roger Dalkin of Georgia Tech won the men's all events, while the same honor in the women's division went to Barbara Duns of Mesa College, San Diego, Calif. (*See in CE: Bowling.*)

BOXING. The world heavyweight boxing championship was settled beyond all dispute on March 8, 1971, when Joe Frazier of Philadelphia, Pa., won a unanimous 15-round decision over Muhammad Ali (Cassius Clay) at Madison Square Garden in New York City. Although Frazier had been accepted as official champion by all 50 of the United States and by Europe and the Orient after he stopped Jimmy Ellis of Louisville, Ky., in four rounds in New York City in February 1970, the general public would not accept him as champion until he had proved himself the master of Ali. The last appearance of Ali as champion had been in March 1967, but the title was declared vacant after he had refused to join the U.S. armed forces. Frazier's victory was convincing, as he floored Ali in the final round to receive the decision of the two judges and the referee. Frazier did not fight again in 1971, but Ali had two more fights during the year, stopping Ellis in 12 rounds at Houston, Tex., in July, and defeating Buster Mathis of Grand Rapids, Mich., in 12 rounds, also at Houston, in November.

Bob Foster of Albuquerque, N.M., successfully defended the world light-heavyweight championship four times, beating U.S. challenger Hal Carroll in four rounds, Ray Anderson in 15, Tommy Hicks in eight, and Brian Kelly in three. The World Boxing Association (WBA) light-heavyweight champion, Vicente Rondon of Venezuela, beat Jimmy Dupree of the U.S. in six rounds, Piero Del Papa of Italy in one, Eddie Jones of the U.S. in 15, Gomeo Brennan of the Bahamas in 13, and Doyle Baird of the U.S. in eight.

Carlos Monzon of Argentina retained the middleweight championship, beating Nino Benvenuti

Rocky MacDougall (right) retained his Canadian featherweight title in a split decision over Billy McGrandle in July.

of Italy in three rounds and Emile Griffith of the U.S. in 14. The junior middleweight title changed hands during the year. After retaining it by drawing with José Hernandez of Spain, Carmelo Bossi of Italy lost it in Tokyo to Koichi Wajima of Japan.

In a surprise upset, José Napoles of Mexico dropped the welterweight championship in four rounds to Billy Backus of the U.S. but later recaptured it, stopping Backus in eight rounds. Napoles

retained the championship in later bouts, stopping Jean Josselin of France in five rounds and Hedgemon Lewis of Los Angeles in 15. Bruno Arcari of Italy retained the World Boxing Council (WBC) junior welterweight crown, outpointing João Henrique of Brazil, and then stopping Enrique Jana of Argentina in nine rounds and Domingo Barrera Corpas of Spain in ten. Nicolino Loche of Argentina successfully defended the WBA junior welterweight crown, stopping Barrera Corpas in two rounds.

Ken Buchanan of Scotland, who had won the WBA lightweight title by beating Ismael Laguna of Panama, was recognized by the WBC and British Boxing Board of Control after defeating Ruben Navarro of Mexico in Los Angeles. When he successfully defended the championship against Laguna again in New York City, the WBA and the New York State Athletic Commission recognized him as champion, but the WBC and the British Boxing Board of Control declared the title vacant because Buchanan had declined to meet Mando Ramos of Mexico. Ramos was matched for the WBC title against Pedro Carrasco of Spain in Madrid, Spain; an uproar followed after Nigerian referee Samuel Odubote disqualified Ramos in the 12th round after he had knocked Carrasco down four times. Later the WBC declared the championship fight "null and void." Japan lost the WBC and WBA junior lightweight titles in 1971. Yoshiaki Numata, after retaining the WBC version against Rene Barrientos of the Philippines and Lionel Rose of Australia, was beaten in ten rounds by Ricardo Arredondo of Mexico. Hiroshi Kobayashi had earlier retained the WBA version of the title by beating Arredondo, but lost the championship in

In an unanimous decision Joe Frazier (right) defeated Muhammad Ali to win the heavyweight championship of the world.

ten rounds to Alfredo Marcano of Venezuela in an unexpected defeat.

Japan lost another title when Antonio Gomez of Venezuela took over the WBA featherweight crown at the expense of Shozo Saijo. But Japan's Kuniaki Shibata, who had won the WBC championship from Vicente Saldivar of Mexico, retained it by knocking out Raúl Cruz of Mexico in the first round. Ruben Olivares of Mexico regained the bantamweight championship from Chucho Castillo of Mexico and then retained it against Kazuyoshi Kanazawa of Japan in 14 rounds and Jesus Pimentel of Mexico in 11. Masao Ohba of Japan retained the WBA flyweight championship, defeating Betulio Gonzalez of Venezuela and Fernando Cabanela of the Philippines. Erbito Salavarria of the Philippines was later involved in a controversy, after drawing with Gonzalez, when the WBC disqualified him for allegedly drinking from a bottle of "sugar water." The title was awarded to Gonzalez pending further investigation.

Henry Cooper of England lost the European heavyweight title on a hotly disputed 15-round decision to Joe Bugner of England; the British and Commonwealth championships were also at stake. Cooper, who had first won the British title in 1959, announced his retirement in the dressing room following the bout. (*See in* CE: Boxing.)

WORLD BOXING CHAMPIONS
As of Dec. 31, 1971

Division	Boxer
Heavyweight	Joe Frazier, U.S.
Light Heavyweight	Bob Foster, U.S. Vicente Rondon, Venezuela*
Middleweight	Carlos Monzon, Argentina
Junior Middleweight	Koichi Wajima, Japan
Welterweight	José Napoles, Mexico
Junior Welterweight	Bruno Arcari, Italy Nicolino Loche, Argentina*
Lightweight	Ken Buchanan, Scotland
Junior Lightweight	Ricardo Arredondo, Mexico Alfredo Marcano, Venezuela*
Featherweight	Kuniaki Shibata, Japan Antonio Gomez, Venezuela*
Bantamweight	Ruben Olivares, Mexico
Flyweight	Betulio Gonzalez, Venezuela Masao Ohba, Japan*

*Recognized as champion by World Boxing Association.

BRAZIL. On Jan. 16, 1971, the Swiss ambassador to Brazil, Giovanni Enrico Bucher, was freed by his guerrilla kidnappers. Bucher was kidnapped in Rio de Janeiro on Dec. 7, 1970. The kidnappers killed a Brazilian security agent accompanying the ambassador and left leaflets identifying themselves as members of the Popular Revolutionary Vanguard, a guerrilla organization that was responsible for three similar kidnappings since 1969. The authorities and the whole country were extremely shocked by this new abduction of still another foreign diplomat.

In 1969 a Vanguard leader had been killed by the police in an ambush in the city of São Paulo. An avowed Maoist, he was the author of 'Minimanual of the Urban Guerrilla', in which he advocated all kinds of terrorism, including assault on financial institutions, police stations, and the kidnapping of foreign diplomats to be used in exchange for the release of imprisoned revolutionaries. This manual apparently was extensively read in Brazil and abroad. Another Vanguard leader had died allegedly of a heart attack while being taken into custody by the police on Oct. 23, 1970, and so it was generally believed that the organization had been disbanded.

The kidnappers of Ambassador Bucher informed the authorities by indirect means that they wanted the release of 70 prisoners (68 Brazilian and 2 foreign) as ransom for the ambassador. The released prisoners were to be flown to Chile, Algeria, or Mexico. After the government of Chile had been consulted and agreed to receive the 70 prisoners, Brazil's president, Gen. Emílio Garrastazú Médici, signed a decree on January 13 banishing them from Brazil. They were then flown to Santiago, Chile, where they arrived on January 14; two days later Ambassador Bucher was released.

At the beginning of 1971 some action was taken by the courts of justice against the vigilante groups known as the "death squads." On January 29, two policemen were sentenced to 65 years in jail on charges of murder. The men were said to be the first members of the squads so sentenced. On March 9, 15 more policemen were indicted on charges of murder. At about the same time a military court sentenced to death by firing squad a man convicted of fatally shooting a policeman. This was the first instance of such a sentence since the restoration of the death penalty in September 1969.

In June the federal court of appeals declared unanimously that civil courts instead of military courts would henceforth try cases arising from death squad executions. The military courts continued to try persons accused of subversive activities. In fact, on July 9, 16 persons accused of such activities were sentenced to from two to four years in jail by a military court.

As unfavorable criticism of the Brazilian authorities continued in the country and abroad, it was extended to include alleged inhuman treatment of the Indian population, especially in the Amazon Basin.

Many problems plagued Brazil in 1971. Farmers (below) left their homes to find relief from drought. The first of 70 political prisoners (right) released by Brazil arrive in Santiago, Chile. They were exchanged for the Swiss ambassador to Brazil, Giovanni Enrico Bucher, who had been kidnapped by guerrillas.

RIGHT: WIDE WORLD
BELOW: "THE NEW YORK TIMES"

The authorities acknowledged that although there had been cases of murder of Indians and the stealing of their lands in the preceding 20 years, with the connivance of some officials, the responsible parties had been duly prosecuted in the courts of law. In May 1970 a three-man surveying team was sent by the International Committee of the Red Cross to investigate the matter. After traveling approximately 14,000 miles in the hinterland of Brazil, with permission from the government, they reported on February 23 that although the Indian population in Brazil was in danger of extinction, nowhere had they seen evidence of massacre or signs of physical ill-treatment.

On February 21 Brazilian consul Aloysio Dias Gomide (kidnapped by the terrorist group known as Tupamaros in Montevideo, Uruguay, on July 31,

1970) was released. It was reported that the terrorists received payment of between $250,000 and $1 million from the consul's wife. She had raised the money privately, the Brazilian government having declared that it would not pay ransom for the kidnapped consul. (*See in* CE: Brazil.)

BULGARIA. The major event of 1971 in Bulgaria was the tenth congress of the Bulgarian Communist party held in Sofia, the capital, from April 20 to 25. In his speech to the congress Bulgarian Communist Party First Secretary Todor Zhivkov emphasized his country's firm friendship with the Soviet Union as a cornerstone of Bulgarian policy.

Zhivkov presented an optimistic picture of the economy, forecasting that during the sixth five-year development plan (1971–75) national income would rise almost 50%. Once again the Soviet Union was providing substantial aid in support of the plan. In the past 25 years Bulgaria had received more than $2 billion from the Soviet Union, more aid than any other Eastern European Communist country.

The party congress discussed and approved the draft of a new constitution to supersede that of 1947 and elected a new 147-member Central Committee, which reelected the old 11-member Politburo. The new constitution, adopted by the party congress and by the National Assembly, was submitted on May 16 to a national referendum and approved by 99.7% of the electorate. In place of the old Presidium of the National Assembly, the new Council of State of 22 members was the "supreme organ of State power." The new constitution downgraded the position of national minorities by giving them only "the right to study their mother tongues."

A new National Assembly was elected June 27 and met on July 7. Georgi Traikov was reelected as its speaker. Zhivkov, who resigned as premier,

At the site of the first reactor block, men
work to complete construction of
Bulgaria's first atomic station.

was elected to the position of chairman of the
newly created Council of State (in effect, president), and Stanko Todorov was elected premier.
(*See also* Communist Movement; Europe. *See in*
CE: Bulgaria.)

BURMA.
Steps toward political change were
taken in Burma in 1971 when the ruling Burma
Socialist Program party (BSPP) held its first congress at midyear. To broaden the BSPP from a
cadre-oriented party into a people's party, new
members were admitted. The drafting of a new
constitution was planned, and the 15-man Revolutionary Council was reorganized to include civilians
for the first time. Gen. Ne Win formed a new
government, retaining the post of prime minister.

Political and ethnic rebels continued to control
about 45% of Burma's territory. A coalition of
rebel groups, the United National Liberation Front,
elected Mahn Ba Zan of the Karen minority their
leader. The coalition included insurgents operating
from Thailand, led by former Burmese Prime Minister U Nu. The Burmese army launched successful raids against rebels in various areas.

A four-year development program was to be inaugurated in October in an attempt to end Burma's
chronic economic stagnation. During the year
cooperatives were replacing the state-run "people's
shops," which by their inadequate distribution of
goods allowed the black market to thrive.

Diplomatic relations with the People's Repub-
lic of China were enhanced by a visit to Peking
by Ne Win. Burma's refusal to accept further
United States aid terminated the aid program in
June. West Germany and Japan made loans to
Burma for offshore oil exploration. (*See in* CE:
Burma.)

BURUNDI.
As 1971 began the government of
Burundi was endeavoring to put into effect programs called for by President Michel Micombero
in November 1970. These included measures to
improve conditions for Burundian peasants, to increase communication between the government
and the people, and to begin promulgating a constitution that would legalize Micombero's military
regime. The constitution provided for strong presidential powers, a one-party system dominated by
the ruling Unity and National Progress party, and
an independent judiciary. A referendum on the
constitution, promised for 1971, had not yet been
held by late fall.

Burundi established diplomatic relations with
Romania in February. During a state visit to
Burundi by Ethiopian Emperor Haile Selassie I
in April, an agreement for cultural and scientific
cooperation was signed. Burundi, Rwanda, and
the Congo (Kinshasa) agreed to joint exploitation
of waterpower in their territories. The United
Nations (UN) Development Program provided
Burundi aid for water research around Lake Tan-
ganyika, and Burundi joined a UN-sponsored project to explore and develop the Kagera River basin
to Lake Victoria. Burundi's national airline began
operations in April with three planes given by
France. (*See in* CE: Burundi.)

BUSINESS AND INDUSTRY.
The plodding
economic recovery of 1971—slowest of any of the
five postwar recoveries by almost any criteria—
took place against a background of continuing inflation, persistent unemployment, corporate upheaval, prolonged strikes, and an international
monetary crisis. The biggest business news of the
year came on August 15, when United States President Richard M. Nixon announced a group of administrative decisions and legislative proposals designed to curb inflation, stimulate the U.S. economy, and redress its competitive edge in world
markets. His actions included a 90-day freeze on
wages and prices; cancellation of a U.S. pledge to
redeem foreign claims against the dollar in gold;
and imposition of a 10% surcharge on most dutiable imports. (This effectively raised the prices
on foreign goods in the U.S. market by 10%, thus
giving U.S. producers a better chance to compete
with imports.) Nixon also announced that he
would ask the U.S. Congress to repeal the 7%
excise tax on automobiles, thus assuring U.S. consumers a price cut on 1972 models, and to enact a
10% investment tax credit on new U.S.-built capital equipment. In effect, this would be a $3-billion
tax cut and a strong incentive for U.S. industry to
begin replacing outmoded equipment. (*See* Congress, U.S.)

The day after the president's announcement, the
New York Stock Exchange registered a spectacular
burst of approval. The Dow-Jones industrial average of stock prices soared almost 33 points for a
new record. The enthusiasm, however, dampened

Special Report: White-Collar Crime

by Lawrence R. Zeitlin

Several years ago the nation was shocked to learn that the grandmotherly head cashier of a small bank in Pennsylvania had embezzled over $2 million over a period of years. The money was not used for gambling or high living but to make loans and cash grants to friends. Several years earlier the public was similarly startled by the disclosure that a purchasing agent for a large printing equipment manufacturer had defrauded his organization of $1.8 million by depositing checks drawn to nonexistent suppliers in dummy bank accounts controlled by the thief himself. More recently, securities thefts from brokerage firms and financial institutions have reached such a peak (estimates for 1970 vary widely from $12 million to $200 million) that Assistant United States Attorney Andrew J. Maloney remarked: "Stock stealing is so easy that I don't know why anyone robs banks anymore."

Business-related thefts of this sort, rather than being isolated instances, appear to be merely the tip of an iceberg of white-collar criminality that threatens to change the whole character of American business and possibly the character of the nation itself. Indeed, the practice of stealing from one's employer is so widespread that neither the criminal nor the illegal nature of much employee activity is usually recognized as such. The large-scale crimes, while newsworthy, are virtually swamped in the aggregate by those smaller thefts that go unnoticed. Xerox Corp., for example, states that almost half of all office copying work is of a personal nature, totally unrelated to the employees' work activities. This kind of seemingly minor loss costs business over $200 million per year. Similarly, 12% of business telephone calls are in reality personal calls; retail employees steal an average of over $10 million a day in cash and merchandise, amounting to over $3 billion a year; and kickbacks and illegal referrals cost business over $5 billion a year. Finally, the largest overall cost to business is loss or theft of employee time. When the total cost per year of employee dishonesty is estimated, the figure invariably exceeds the $10 billion mark. This overall estimated loss is about double the yearly figure of five years ago, and it is growing at an accelerated rate.

White-collar crime can be viewed as that group of criminal activities engaged in by members of a business organization for individual and private purposes. These crimes occur in all areas of business—in the front office, in sales, in distributive activities, in production, and, of course, in finance.

Four types of illegal activity make up the bulk of these offenses: larceny, embezzlement, illegal business practices, and theft of time.

Larceny

Direct theft of business property by employees constitutes the most obvious of the white-collar crimes. The stealing of money, goods, and services from employers has certainly been going on as long as there has been an employee-employer relationship. But only in recent years has the white-collar criminal had as many opportunities for large-scale theft as his blue-collar brother. With the exception of cash, which most businesses treat with due respect, the typical white-collar, non-sales employee formerly confined his thefts to office supplies and telephone calls. These thefts do constitute a considerable drain on corporate resources but seem almost trivial in the individual case.

The increase in financial and securities transactions by the nation's banks and securities brokers has been a windfall for the white-collar thief. Massive, well-organized thefts of stock and bond certificates are perpetrated by brokerage house employees (with possible assistance from the underworld). Lax security measures, confusion in busy brokerage offices, and indifferent bookkeeping almost invite theft.

Embezzlement

Embezzlement is defined in law as the appropriation to one's own use of that which is entrusted to one for another. Embezzlement is closely allied to larceny, the chief difference being that in embezzlement the property comes lawfully into the possession of the offender, and in larceny it does not. The scale of embezzlement ranges from the office manager who takes a few cents out of the petty-cash box to the bank teller who misappropriates millions of dollars. The common and, in most cases, disturbing factor in such crimes is that the offending employee is usually one of the most trusted members in the company—and often one with great seniority.

In the last few years a new kind of embezzlement has become a serious business problem. "I could steal a company blind and leave its books looking balanced," boasted one employee. His method—electronic embezzlement. His accomplice—the company's own computer. An increasing number of business transactions that formerly were recorded on ledger pages are now being translated into magnetic impulses that are stored in a computer. It is a simple matter for a crook with technical know-how to fleece a company and fool its auditors. Corporate executives rarely question the reliability of financial results that emerge from the complex million-dollar machines. They simply forget that the computer does whatever the operator directs and there is nothing to stop it from working quite efficiently for the imaginative embezzler.

Illegal Business Practices

Illegal business practices are more difficult to document than overt theft or embezzlement. Many such practices—kickbacks to suppliers, for example—have gone on for so long that they are regarded as quasi-legitimate. One firm, experienced in the detection and prevention of white-collar crime, uncovered more than $100-million worth of business dishonesty during 1970 alone. Supervisors and executives were responsible for over 60% of those dishonest acts.

It is certainly easier to juggle accounts, take kickbacks, and pass trade secrets to competitors from an office than to drive away from a factory with truckloads of stolen merchandise. A trusted supervisor does not have to break into the office and crack the safe; he has already been given the key and the combination. In most cases the key is symbolic. Most executives, and in fact many lower-level employees, have valuable information about their company's future plans, acquisitions, stock issues, products, and so forth, that are worth thousands, even millions of dollars to competitors. The exchange of a few discreet words over lunch and a couple of pages of copied documents would hardly seem to constitute a criminal act, yet such actions account for the largest single portion of the $10-billion annual business loss due to white-collar crime.

Theft of Time

Theft of time is so prevalent that it is simply not considered a crime. Recent figures indicate that the average white-collar worker, when paid for an 8-hour day, puts in only about 5¾ hours of productive work. A carefully controlled study revealed that when a worker is allowed to quit work and go home when he accomplishes a "fair" day's work, yet still be paid for the full day, a full week's work can be accomplished in slightly over three days.

The almost horrendous loss to American business from white-collar crime might make one conclude that for the dishonest employee, crime pays. But does it really? As a matter of fact—considering the time and effort involved in planning the average theft of merchandise or other business dishonesty, the risk of detection and firing, and the real, if small, risk of prosecution—the actual return on white-collar crime is poor.

as many investors took a wait-and-see attitude, but improved after Nixon's announcement of "Phase II" of his new economic program. (*See* Economy; Stocks and Bonds.)

Major Business Events

The $3.3-billion RCA Corp. suddenly announced in September a decision to abandon the computer business. As a result, the company sustained a tremendous loss of about $250 million, which it wrote off in its third-quarter report. RCA's retreat from computers followed a similar pullout by General Electric Co. a little more than a year earlier. Both companies conceded their inability to compete with International Business Machines Corp. (IBM), which had long dominated the market.

International Telephone & Telegraph Corp. (ITT), one of the biggest and best known of the conglomerates, received a setback in its expansion plans from the U.S. Department of Justice. The department decided that ITT could only go through with its acquisition of Hartford Fire Insurance Co. if it agreed to rid itself within two years of other subsidiaries producing an equal amount of business. In essence, the decision signaled to other huge companies that the only way they could make significant acquisitions was to divest themselves of other assets and remain the same size.

Leon H. Sullivan became the first black man ever to hold a position on the board of directors of the General Motors Corp.
UPI COMPIX

A number of young people have gone into business making handcrafted products, especially those with appeal to a youthful market. Denise Rinas and Barry Kleinman make leather purses in their New York City workshop; they call their company Minimal Leather. In their first quarter of operation they grossed about $10,000.

RUSSELL REIF
FROM PICTORIAL PARADE

Divestiture, in fact, was far more common during 1971 than acquisition. Monsanto Chemical, Avco Corp., Union Carbide, and W. R. Grace & Co. were only a few of the companies that sold inadequately performing subsidiaries in order to seek maximum return on investment.

These and other cost-cutting measures combined with slightly higher sales and prices to boost corporate profits in many industries. Overall, corporate profits in the second quarter jumped to about a $46-billion annual rate, after taxes. In other words, U.S. corporations had begun earning money at about the same rate they earned in early 1969 before the economy slid into recession.

Troubled Industries

Although almost all sectors of the economy were suffering to some degree from the recession, several key industries were particularly troubled. The defense and aerospace industries were perhaps in the worst shape as a result of sharp reductions in defense spending and over-capacity in air travel. The Nixon Administration conceded that there could be no early solution to these problems when it asked Congress to approve an Administration bill to shore up its largest defense contractor, Lockheed Aircraft Corp., with a $250-million federally guaranteed loan. The aerospace combine had sustained losses totaling nearly $500 million in the past few years, and opponents of the loan held that the government was rewarding Lockheed for bad management. (*See* Aerospace.)

U.S. machinery manufacturers, suffering from their worst recession in a decade, were particularly angered by the failure of the U.S. Department of Commerce to rule on U.S. participation in supplying the giant truck plant the Soviet Union planned to build. Iron curtain countries, it seemed, were eager to buy U.S.-built machine tools, and U.S. manufacturers were eager to sell them. License applications to export several hundred million dol-

lars worth of equipment were filed by late September. But Mack Trucks, Inc., which was to orchestrate U.S. participation in the new truck plant, told the Soviets in September that it would be unable to participate because the U.S. government had not yet approved its role.

The auto industry, however, appeared during the fourth quarter to be recovering briskly from its mini-recession. Prior to the Nixon announcement, autos appeared to be a disaster area. Assaults on product safety by consumer advocate Ralph Nader, on auto pollution by ecologists, on auto advertising claims by the Federal Trade Commission, and on U.S. markets by small, cheap imported cars had all taken a heavy toll. The inventory of leftover 1971 models was 1.5 million cars, the biggest pileup ever. By late September, however, sales had picked up and production was quickly increased. The new industry mood was described by one auto executive as one of "unbridled enthusiasm." (*See* Automobiles.)

The increase in auto production began to show up in late September in the orders for steel for November delivery. Auto companies had built up a huge backlog of steel in anticipation of a steel strike. That strike was averted on August 1 by a three-year contract that gave steel workers a wage package worth something more than 30% above previous wage levels. It was followed 24 hours later by an 8% increase in the price of steel products. (*See* Metals.)

Other wage negotiations were not as smooth. The worst was probably the West Coast shipping strike that began July 1 and lasted into the fall. Companies all along the coast were forced to lay off workers as the shipping strike caused supplies to be interrupted and shipments to pile up. In October President Nixon invoked the Taft-Hartley law providing for an 80-day cooling-off period. (*See* Labor Unions; Ships and Shipping. *See in* CE: Industry, American.)

A Cambodian soldier approaches a burning house in Saang, Cambodia, after an attack by the Viet Cong in January.
UPI COMPIX

CAMBODIA. At the beginning of 1971 the "Vietnamization" of Cambodia was so complete that what the Cambodians did or did not do hardly seemed to matter; the conduct of the war was largely in the hands of the Vietnamese (South and North) and the United States. The fighting in Cambodia was only secondary to the main war—which was in Vietnam—and the Cambodians were used as supplementary forces.

The Communists ushered in 1971 with a spectacular show of strength. On the night of January 21–22 a guerrilla squad made a daring raid on the international airport at Phnom Penh, the capital, turning almost every plane in Cambodia's small air force into a rubble of twisted steel. At least 39 Cambodians were killed before the Communists withdrew, losing one or two of their own men. Simultaneously, they shelled central Phnom Penh for the first time since the war began. U.S. military analysts saw the unexpected Communist attack as a direct response to the widening U.S. involvement in Cambodia.

The U.S. involvement was wide open in 1971. On the ground American soldiers appeared only in civilian clothes and only as advisers directing Cambodian troops in combat. However, in the air U.S. planes were out in force. In January, as battles raged to free Phnom Penh's lifeline to the seaport of Kompong Som (formerly Sihanoukville) from Communist control, the U.S. committed its Strategic Air Command B-52 bombers in widespread raids. In early March the U.S. sent in a giant air armada of 1,000 planes to sweep over Laos and Cambodia in support of ground troops.

South Vietnamese troops, though officially allies of the Cambodians, continued to cause much unrest in Phnom Penh. They were 18,000 strong, with their principal base in Neak Leung, a ferry point 35 miles southeast of Phnom Penh. Their reported atrocities against Cambodians made the Phnom Penh government highly resentful. A joint Cambodian-South Vietnamese military commission was set up to inquire into allegations of burning, looting, and rape by the South Vietnamese against civilians in Neak Leung and neighboring areas, but the South Vietnamese authorities maintained that these charges were exaggerated. In August the Cambodian high command said it was working out plans for the withdrawal of South Vietnamese troops from Neak Leung, but the objective was still unrealized by the end of the year.

Early in the year the government in Phnom Penh came under a sudden threat of collapse. On February 8, shortly after he finished a three-hour speech to a National Assembly committee on the military situation, Premier Lon Nol suffered a stroke that paralyzed his right side. Being the only universally respected figure in post-Sihanouk Cambodia, Lon Nol was the indispensable unifying force in the government. He was later flown to Honolulu, Hawaii, for treatment and remained there for two months. During that period Deputy Premier Lieut. Gen. Sisowath Sirik Matak acted as premier. But Sirik Matak, with a reputation as a canny politician, had powerful enemies. In March there were reports that a group of army officers had tried to stage a coup and restore the monarchy. One or more generals, a colonel, and a dozen other officers were said to have been involved. The acting premier was able to crush the plot in time.

But the issue of succession defied settlement. On returning to Phnom Penh in April, Lon Nol formally resigned. On April 21, one day after

Premier Lon Nol of Cambodia suffered a stroke in February and resigned his office in April. He was made titular premier in May and was appointed to rule by decree in October.

WIDE WORLD

submitting his resignation, Lon Nol received a mandate from Chief of State Cheng Heng to form a new government, but on April 29 Lon Nol submitted his final resignation. At the same time, however, he was placed in command of the armed forces and Deputy Premier Sirik Matak was made second in command.

There were reports that the U.S. favored Sirik Matak as premier. Cheng Heng offered the job to him, but in a surprise move—interpreted by analysts as calculated to consolidate his position—Sirik Matak declined on April 30. This led to unsuccessful attempts by some others to form a government. Eventually the ailing Lon Nol was again asked to become the titular premier, with Sirik Matak as his "premier-delegate" wielding the real authority. The announcement of this compromise was made in the National Assembly and was made official by an announcement from the office of Cheng Heng. On October 18 it was announced that Lon Nol would rule by decree and that the National Assembly would be abolished.

During a three-week visit to the U.S. in August, Sirik Matak met U.S. President Richard M. Nixon in Washington, D.C. Their talks centered mostly around U.S. aid to Cambodia. According to the U.S. embassy in Phnom Penh, the country needed the absolute minimum of $200 million in military aid alone during the year. This was in addition to substantial economic aid, which Cambodia needed to avoid bankruptcy.

The economic situation was dangerous indeed. The riel was down to 200–220 to the U.S. dollar from the official rate of 55. A headlong flight of capital from the country only intensified following the death sentence passed on two Chinese merchants in August on charges of "economic sabotage." There were reports that government presses were turning out large stacks of new money to pay the soldiers, whose number had increased from 35,000 at the time of Sihanouk's deposition in March 1970 to approximately 170,000.

In September the government circulated a letter to interested countries calling for a preliminary meeting on an international special fund to finance Cambodia's imports. It was looking for at least $25 million in hard currency. The U.S. was reportedly willing to provide the bulk of this but wanted other developed countries to contribute at least token amounts. However, few others seemed interested. In late October the government devalued the riel as part of a stringent anti-inflation program to improve the economy. (*See also* Asia. *See in* CE: Cambodia.)

CAMEROON. International opinion was deeply stirred by the conspiracy trials held in Yaoundé, the capital of Cameroon, in January 1971. A tribunal passed the death sentence on six men accused of attempting to overthrow the government. Among them were Ernest Ouandie, leader of the illegal opposition party, the Union of the Cameroon Peoples (UPC), and Albert Ndongmo, Roman Catholic bishop of Nkongsamba. President Ahmadou Ahidjo denounced what he termed a "vile smear campaign" being waged against his government over the trials. However, Pope Paul VI and United Nations Secretary-General U Thant intervened on behalf of the condemned men.

Ndongmo's sentence was finally commuted, but Ouandie was publicly shot at Bafoussam, in the home territory of the dissident Bamileke population. This action was presumably taken as a public demonstration of the government's power. (*See in* CE: Cameroon.)

CAMPING. Although there were no official statistics available, indications were that camping participation declined in the summer of 1971. State and national parks and forests reported about 10% fewer visitors.

In contrast to the decline in campground use, many areas reported an increase in backpacking into remote areas, especially by young people of high school and college age. It was anticipated

Approximately 30,000 members of the National Campers and Hikers Association of the United States held their annual convention in Brantford, Ont., in 1971.

"TORONTO STAR"

that the increasing interest in wilderness camping would lead eventually to the rationing of such use if the natural character of the environment was to be maintained.

The number of campground facilities continued to increase. Figures from 1970 showed that there were more than 462,000 sites (not campgrounds, but sites within campgrounds) in private operation and more than 247,000 sites provided by various public agencies.

A new development was the trend toward reservations being accepted in public campgrounds. Until recently, all public facilities were operated on a first-come, first-served basis. Now a number of states, including Florida, California, and Oregon, have introduced a reservation system in their state-park campgrounds. The National Park Service experimented with reservations in a selected few of the national parks in 1971.

In the realm of organized camping (children's summer camps), major interest in 1971 was focused on legislation. After six years of effort, the Youth Camp Safety Act was passed by the United States Senate; however, the bill failed to pass in the House of Representatives. The basic purpose of the act would have been to safeguard the health and well-being of children attending summer camps by establishing safety regulations at the federal level. (*See in* CE: Camping.)

CANADA. In 1971 Canadians shifted their attention from the terrorist crisis of the previous October in Quebec to the urgent problem of relations with the United States. The economic measures imposed by U.S. President Richard M. Nixon on August 15 created immediate difficulties for Canada. (*See* Canadian Economy.)

Canada's first reaction to the Nixon announcement was to make strong representations to Washington, D.C., claiming exemption from the 10% import surcharge that the U.S. had imposed to help correct its unfavorable trade balance. Canada made two principal points in asking relief: the Canadian dollar was not overvalued in relation to the U.S. dollar, and Canada had not imposed any discriminatory trade barriers against U.S. exports.

On August 20, interrupting a visit to Yugoslavia to return to Canada and deal with the crisis, Prime Minister Pierre Elliott Trudeau provided a further argument. The proposed restrictions would not help to solve the difficulties of the U.S. economy; on the contrary, they would weaken the Canadian economy so that it would not be able to absorb U.S. exports.

Negotiations to resolve the crisis continued through 1971, climaxed by Trudeau's meeting with Nixon in December, from which emerged some promise of a solution by early 1972.

Within Canada, an Employment Support Bill, introduced in Parliament in early September, represented the Trudeau government's first measure to counteract the effect of the surcharge. It provided

$80 million over the next seven months for the relief of injured companies. The grants were not to compensate for lost sales, but to allow production and employment to be maintained. If the surcharge should last a year, the export loss might be $900 million and 90,000 jobs might be in danger. However, in December the U.S. announced that the surcharge would be rescinded.

Ever since World War II, Canada and the U.S. had enjoyed a high degree of economic cooperation. The ending of this "special relationship" by U.S. action posed a grave dilemma for Canada. It was to be hoped that this dilemma could be resolved without imperiling the confidence and friendship that had marked Canadian-U.S. relations in modern times.

Parliament

The ruling Liberal party lost a little ground in the House of Commons in 1971. Out of 11 by-elections held since the general election in 1968, the New Democratic party had captured five seats, the Conservatives three, and the Liberals three (all in Quebec). Two of the New Democratic victories occurred in 1971. Party standings in the 264-seat House after the latest by-election on November 8 were: Liberals 150; Conservatives 71; New Democratic party 25; Social Credit (Ralliement des Créditistes) 13; Independents 2; Independent Liberal 1; and two vacancies.

The Trudeau government's legislative program for the 1970-71 session consisted of 68 bills. The government replaced its original weapon against the Quebec terrorists, the War Measures Act, with the less drastic Public Order (Temporary Measures) Act, 1970, which expired on April 30, 1971. At that time the government proposed the creation of a joint parliamentary committee to recommend legislation to deal with terrorism.

An important innovation in economic development was embodied in the Canada Development Corporation Act, establishing a public corporation capitalized at $2 billion, which would initiate and finance large-scale Canadian-owned enterprises. The new body was given power to create companies, merge them, purchase them in order to prevent foreign take-overs, and acquire successful public enterprises.

Pollution received more attention in 1971. Pollution of the air and of navigable waters were dealt with in legislation paralleling the Canada Water Act (1970). A packaging and labeling bill was approved that would bring about uniform standards and ensure accurate statements on packages. Veterans' pensions and unemployment insurance benefits were increased. Old-age pensions were readjusted; the basic pension was frozen, but guaranteed income supplements were provided in case of need.

Two pieces of major legislation were introduced in 1971 but were not likely to win approval before 1972. Debate on tax reform proposals, which

Soviet Premier Aleksei N. Kosygin is attacked in Ottawa, Ont., by a right-wing Hungarian protester.
"TORONTO STAR"

were put forward by Finance Minister Edgar Benson in 1969, began after the summer recess, but progress was slow. A new Competition Act, creating a powerful tribunal to review mergers and take-overs, also came under discussion.

Foreign Affairs

Canadian foreign policy took a new direction in 1971 when closer relations were established with the Soviet Union. The approach was initiated by Prime Minister Trudeau in May when, accompanied by his wife of less than three months, he paid an 11-day official visit to the U.S.S.R. The Canadian party traveled from the Arctic cities of Murmansk and Norilsk in the north to Tashkent and Samarkand in the south. Trudeau emphasized that the common northern location of the two countries provided many opportunities for them to learn from each other in the fields of industry, science, and technology. The two countries signed an agreement in which they promised to hold high-level talks at least once a year on matters of mutual interest and to look into the possibilities of increasing Soviet-Canadian trade. An agreement was also concluded for the exchange of scientific information on development in the Arctic. Trudeau's visit was returned by Soviet Premier Aleksei N. Kosygin, who visited Canada for eight days beginning on October 17. His tour began in Ottawa, the capital, where he held talks with ministers and visited industrial plants, then moved on to Montreal, Que., and to British Columbia. A four-year renewable agreement to expand relations between the two countries in many fields was signed by Kosygin during his visit. His stay in Ottawa was somewhat marred by anti-Soviet demonstrations and a physical attack on him by one demonstrator; Kosygin was not harmed.

Another distinguished visitor whose presence in Canada symbolized the healing of old quarrels was Foreign Minister Maurice Schumann of France. Schumann's round of talks with Canadian ministers on subjects ranging from the international monetary crisis to Canada's involvement in French-speaking Africa showed that relations between France and Canada had improved markedly since 1967, when the late French President Charles de Gaulle had been severely reprimanded by Prime Minister Lester Pearson for exclaiming "Long live free Quebec" in Montreal.

In early November President Tito of Yugoslavia and his wife arrived on a six-day tour of eastern Canada. The visit returned the one that the Trudeaus had undertaken in Yugoslavia in August, but that had been cut short by the economic crisis. Tito signed a scientific and technical agreement with Canada, and the two countries agreed to investigate the possibilities of a direct air link between them.

The first Canadian ambassador to the People's Republic of China, Ralph Collins, took up his post early in 1971. His counterpart in Ottawa, Huang Hua, an experienced diplomat, arrived in Canada some time afterward. Later, following China's admission to the United Nations, Huang Hua was also appointed as China's permanent representative in that world body. In July, Jean-Luc Pepin, Canada's minister of industry, trade, and commerce, led a trade mission to Peking, in the first of a series of visits between the two countries by commercial groups. Pepin announced that more Canadian grain sales to China were planned, and that the two countries were anxious to diversify their trade. China was especially interested in selling metals, light manufactures, and textiles to Canada.

Trudeau played an active role in the Commonwealth Prime Ministers Conference held in Singapore in January. At this meeting, Trudeau attempted to mediate between Britain and the African member states in the clash of views that developed over Britain's proposed sale of arms to South Africa. An agreement was worked out under which Britain agreed to consult with Commonwealth states on the proposed sale, and an eight-member study group, which included Canada, was set up to consider the security of trade routes in the Indian Ocean and the South Atlantic. Following the withdrawal of Nigeria in February, the group collapsed, leaving the issue a potentially explosive one in the Commonwealth association. Even so, Trudeau's success as a mediator was probably responsible for preventing a walkout of African members.

Defense

A White Paper on defense, issued in August, confirmed Canada's partnership with the U.S. in North American defense arrangements, as well as its continued participation in the North Atlantic Treaty Organization (NATO). Surveillance and control over Canadian territory were reemphasized as the chief functions of Canada's integrated defense forces, however. They would have the responsibility of ensuring that regulations such as those passed in 1970 relating to pollution in the Arctic are enforced. The report also suggested a more active role for the defense forces in supporting the civil power, a function that had been successfully performed during the 1970 Quebec crisis.

The White Paper went on to outline changes in Canada's contribution to North American defense. The two squadrons of Bomarc nuclear-tipped missiles located in eastern Canada would be phased out of service, but 48 interceptor aircraft carrying nuclear weapons would be maintained at three Canadian bases. U.S. tanker aircraft were to be allowed refueling facilities at Goose Bay, Labrador, and U.S. Strategic Air Command training exercises could be held in Canadian airspace if nuclear weapons were not carried. Canada would take over and operate the radar station at Melville in Labrador, which U.S. forces were vacating.

The Canadian air force in Europe would abandon its nuclear strike role at the end of the year, according to the White Paper. The strength of the Canadian forces was set at 83,000 by the end of the fiscal year 1972–73, and the freeze on military spending imposed in mid-1969 would be lifted at the same time. (*See also* Commonwealth of Nations; Trudeau. *See in* CE: Canada.)

CABINET

Communications Minister Eric W. Kierans resigned in April 1971, charging that Canada's whole industrial and tax policy made unnecessary concessions to resource development. He called for

THE CANADIAN CABINET

Members of the Canadian Cabinet at the close of 1971, listed in order of precedence, were:
Prime Minister . . Rt. Hon. Pierre Elliott Trudeau
Leader of the Government in the
  Senate . . . . . . Hon. Paul Joseph James Martin
Secretary of State for
  External Affairs . . . . Hon. Mitchell Sharp
Minister of Public Works . . . . Hon. Arthur Laing
President of the Queen's Privy Council
  for Canada . . . Hon. Allan Joseph MacEachen
President of the Treasury
  Board . . . . Hon. Charles Mills Drury
Minister of Finance . . . . Hon. Edgar John Benson
Minister of Industry,
  Trade, and Commerce . . . Hon. Jean-Luc Pepin
Minister of Regional
  Economic Expansion . . . Hon. Jean Marchand
Minister of Energy, Mines,
  and Resources . . . . . Hon. John James Greene
Postmaster
  General . . Hon. Joseph Julien Jean-Pierre Côté
Minister of Justice and Attorney General
  of Canada . . . . Hon. John Napier Turner
Minister of Indian Affairs and Northern
  Development . . . . Hon. Jean Chrétien
Minister of Labour . Hon. Bryce Stuart Mackasey
Minister of National
  Defense . . . . . . Hon. Donald Stovel Macdonald
Minister of National Health
  and Welfare . . . . Hon. John Carr Munro
Secretary of State
  of Canada . . . . Hon. Gérard Pelletier
Minister of the Environment . . . Hon. Jack Davis
Minister of
  Agriculture . . . . . Hon. Horace Andrew Olson
Minister of
  Veterans Affairs . . . . . Hon. Jean-Eudes Dubé
Minister of Consumer and Corporate
  Affairs . . . . Hon. Stanley Ronald Basford
Minister of
  Transport . . Hon. Donald Campbell Jamieson
Minister of State for
  Urban Affairs . . . . Hon. Robert Knight Andras
Minister of Supply and
  Services . . Hon. James Armstrong Richardson
Minister of Manpower
  and Immigration . . . . . . Hon. Otto Emil Lang
Minister of National
  Revenue . . . . Hon. Herb Gray
Minister of
  Communications . . . . . . Hon. Robert Stanbury
Solicitor General
  of Canada . . . . Hon. Jean-Pierre Goyer
Minister of State for Science and
  Technology . . Hon. Alastair William Gillespie
Minister of
  State . . . . Hon. Martin Patrick O'Connell

more emphasis on social needs. Kierans had been one of six major candidates defeated by Pierre Elliott Trudeau in the 1968 contest for leadership of the ruling Liberal party. Trudeau had invited all six into his original Cabinet, but only Justice Minister John Turner retained a first-rank portfolio in 1971 with acknowledged prospects of succeeding Trudeau as prime minister.

The Kierans resignation led to a number of minor changes in the Cabinet lineup. Robert Stanbury was promoted to the communciations portfolio; as minister without portfolio, he had been responsible for the new agency Information Canada. Trudeau brought in Martin O'Connell, a political scientist, to oversee Information Canada, the Canadian Broadcasting Corp., and citizenship matters.

Another new member of the Cabinet in 1971 was Alastair Gillespie, a Toronto management consultant who became minister of state for science and technology, responsible for policy advice and the expenditure of government funds on research, and for the coordination of research efforts in all fields influenced by government.

Jack Davis, who had been minister of fisheries and forestry, became minister of the environment

Robert Stanfield (left) was leader of the opposition in 1971. Mitchell Sharp (below, left), minister of external affairs, met in January with Abdelkrim Lazrak, then finance minister of Morocco.

LEFT: PETER BREGG FROM CANADIAN PRESS. BELOW: CHARLES MITCHELL FROM CANADIAN PRESS

in a reorganization of departmental functions. The same series of changes resulted in the creation of a Ministry of State for Urban Affairs under Robert Andras. Jean-Pierre Côté resumed the position of postmaster general, a portfolio he had held earlier, before it was merged briefly and unsuccessfully with the Communications Department under Kierans.

PROVINCES

Voters in three more Canadian provinces turned to younger leaders in 1971, completing a remarkable recoloring of the Canadian political map that had begun in 1966. Only British Columbia, under the Social Credit government of W. A. C. Bennett, 71, remained in the certain control of an experienced administration.

Joseph Smallwood, 70, Liberal premier of the isolated island province of Newfoundland, was the last of the older leaders to be rejected during the year. However, a curiosity of Canada's parliamentary system made it technically possible for Smallwood to stay in power, at least briefly, despite the fact that he won only 20 of the Newfoundland legislature's 42 seats in the October 28 election. Smallwood was obliged to give up power to Progressive Conservative leader Frank Moores only if he formally resigned or was defeated in a vote in the legislature. Since the Progressive Conservatives had won 21 seats, they could defeat Smallwood only if they gained the support of Tom Burgess, leader of the New Labrador party; Burgess had won a seat with a campaign protesting alleged ill-treatment of Labrador, a resource-rich part of Newfoundland on the Canadian mainland.

In the eight provinces between Newfoundland and British Columbia, general elections or party leadership changes since 1966 had brought younger men into every premier's chair. The average age of the eight premiers in 1971 was 40, and seven were lawyers. Although three of the administrations were Liberal, three Progressive Conservative, and two New Democratic party, all revealed essentially similar tendencies, especially in the direction of improved government housing and other social programs.

Western Provinces

The Prairie Provinces of Saskatchewan and Alberta both turned out the incumbents in 1971 elections. In Saskatchewan, Allan Blakeney led his New Democrats to a sweep over the Liberal party under Ross Thatcher. The New Democrats won 45 seats, the Liberals 15. In his campaign, Blakeney attempted to associate the Thatcher government with the unpopular agricultural policies of the federal Liberal administration, but post-election analysis put more blame on Thatcher's outspoken confrontations with teachers, public employees, and unions over their wage demands.

Alberta had been ruled since 1935 by the Social Credit party, led by active fundamentalist Baptist ministers who got blanket support from rural strongholds. The first crack in the Social Credit grip occurred in 1967, when the Progressive Conservatives under a new leader, Peter Lougheed, won six seats. In the general election of Aug. 30, 1971, the Lougheed forces captured 49 seats to 25 for Social Credit and 1 for the New Democrats. Nominally a conservative like his Social Credit opponents, Lougheed played down his more liberal views during the campaign but was expected to direct an active administration in the fields of economic and social policy.

Blakeney's victory in Saskatchewan gave Canada its second New Democratic party (NDP) government, marking the first time that two socialist provincial governments have held power at the same time. The other NDP government, that of Ed Schreyer in Manitoba, pushed through a major legislative program in 1971. It reduced the drinking age to 18 from 21, introduced government-sponsored legal aid, created a provincial lottery, and limited foreign ownership of trust and loan companies. Schreyer's government also outlawed certain sales practices as part of a consumer-protection program.

Ontario

The governing Progressive Conservatives in Ontario changed leaders well in advance of the autumn election. William Davis succeeded Premier John Robarts at a leadership convention February 12. In the succeeding eight months, Davis put his stamp on the government. One of his first notable actions was to halt an enormous expressway project in the Toronto area that would have uprooted hundreds of homes.

Davis followed this with the introduction of 86 items of legislation that lowered voting and drink-

"EDMONTON JOURNAL"

Peter Lougheed, Alberta's new premier, is cheered by supporters after defeating the party that had held power for 36 years.

ing ages to 18 from 21, reformed welfare programs, extended government services in remote northern areas, provided for loans and grants to Canadian-owned businesses, curbed pollution, and extended civil rights guarantees. He received a rousing vote of confidence in the October 21 election, when his party won 78 seats in the 117-seat legislature, a gain of 10.

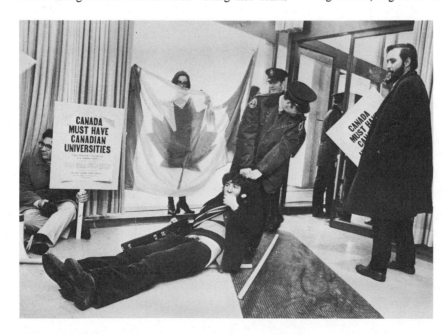

Canadian students sit in at the Canadian immigration office in Toronto, Ont., demanding a ban on the hiring of U.S. teachers at Canadian universities.

"TORONTO STAR"

Quebec

After the upheavals of 1970 that had culminated in two political kidnappings and a murder, forces working actively for the separation of Quebec from the rest of Canada marked time in 1971. The repercussions of federal government action sending troops into Quebec to quell the activities of the terrorist Quebec Liberation Front (FLQ) continued to be felt. Civil rights groups, academics, and the media across Canada argued that the federal use of the War Measures Act to deal with the situation had been repressive and totally unnecessary. They drew support from repeated verdicts in Quebec courts dismissing charges against members of the outlawed FLQ.

Premier Robert Bourassa's Liberal provincial government, faced with 8% unemployment and lagging industrial development, sought to reestablish confidence in the Quebec economy. Bourassa traveled in Europe and the U.S. to promote investment opportunities in his province. One major success was signaled in his announcement of a ten-year, $6 billion plan to develop the hydroelectric power, resources, and tourist potential of the giant James Bay watershed at the southern tip of Hudson Bay.

In June Bourassa and other premiers tentatively negotiated a formula for amending of the Canadian constitution and repatriating it to Canada from Great Britain. Reaction to the formula in Quebec forced Bourassa to veto the plan, however, and late in the year his government was negotiating with Ottawa to resolve the critical constitutional issue of control over social programs.

Atlantic Provinces

The economic problems common to all the provinces were most severe in the seaboard provinces of Newfoundland, Prince Edward Island, Nova Scotia, and New Brunswick during 1971. Unemployment rates ranged between 7% and 9½%, and promised investments moved ahead slowly. A major drilling program continued off the Nova Scotia coast in anticipation of oil and natural gas strikes. One gas find was announced on tiny Sable Island in June. A federal study indicated potential reserves of 56 billion barrels of oil and 336 trillion cubic feet of natural gas, approximately ten times the reserves lying beneath the Gulf of Mexico.

CANADIAN ECONOMY.

In Canada the most important economic event in 1971 was the August 15th announcement by United States President Richard M. Nixon of a wide-ranging series of economic measures, which were viewed as a major threat to the Canadian economy. The country's political leaders and businessmen assessed the Nixon program as potentially disastrous to Canadian trade and to Canada's long-range industrial policy.

That policy had been based on a progressive move away from exports chiefly of natural-resource materials to steadily increasing exports of manufactured goods. During the 1960's Canadian manufacturers had developed specialized production facilities and economies of scale based on relatively free access to the large U.S. market. The Nixon program erected three barriers to this long-term strategy. The first was the 10% U.S. surcharge, which applied against about $3 billion of Canada's annual exports to the U.S. The second was the proposed U.S. business tax credit of 10% for purchases of U.S.-produced machinery. The tax credit would act in combination with the surcharge to set up a virtual embargo on Canadian sales of many machinery items for a period of at least a year. Finally, the Nixon proposal for tax deferrals by U.S. exporting corporations raised the prospect of increased U.S. competition in Canada and in other markets, together with a potential mass withdrawal of U.S.-owned production facilities from Canada. In response to the Nixon program the government proposed various emergency measures to aid affected industries and workers, including personal and corporate tax cuts and a $498-million pump-priming program. (*See* Canada.)

Long before the U.S. action Canada had been deeply divided on the entire question of U.S. domination of the Canadian economy. As the year ended, the debate focused sharply on whether Canadian industrial policy could remain viable in its existing framework—and whether the federal government should directly intervene in order to curb foreign investment.

Apart from the long-term policy concerns, the immediate effect of the Nixon program was to retard the economic recovery that had begun late in 1970, following two years of firm fiscal and monetary restraint. Canada's gross national product in real terms in the first half of the year advanced at an annual rate of 5.5%, almost double the 1970 rate. Other statistical indexes also substantiated the evidence of recovery.

After containing price increases more successfully than any other free-enterprise industrial nation in 1970, Canada slipped back into the worldwide trend of chronic inflation in 1971. Consumer prices rose at an annual rate of 5% during the first eight months of the year. With most industrial plants in the nation operating well below capacity, there was room for significant improvement in labor productivity. Labor costs per unit of output grew at a rate of 3.2% in the first half of 1971, compared with 5.3% in 1970. However, new wage settlements were still being made at relatively high rates; their annual compounded increase in the first half was 7.8%.

Economic policy at all government levels during the year was clearly expansionary, but it failed to arrest serious unemployment in the country. After peak unemployment of 6.8% in September 1970, the rate moved down only gradually during the next

Gaston Bourdon, mayor of Mont-Laurier, Que., speaks to 4,000 worried demonstrators facing unemployment because of the planned shutdown of two wood processing plants in the area.
STUDIO IMPACT

six months but began rising later in the year, reaching a new high of 7.1% in September. The figures remained stubbornly high despite the fact that new jobs were being produced at an annual rate of 2.8% in the first half. Particularly hard hit were teenagers. The unemployment rate in the 14–19 age bracket exceeded 15% on a seasonally adjusted basis in August. The comparable midsummer rate for older workers declined to less than 6%.

CENTRAL AFRICAN REPUBLIC.
The unpredictable behavior of Central African Republic President Jean-Bedel Bokassa continued to be a disruptive factor in the political life of the country in 1971. Bokassa reshuffled his government several times during the year, concentrating ever wider powers in his own hands and brutally suppressing the slightest opposition.

The country's relations with France remained chaotic. In June and September the government expelled various French personnel without any convincing reason. Bokassa demanded sovereignty in monetary matters from France but expressed the wish that the Central African Republic remain within the franc area.

One incident kept the president in the international limelight for several months, the "two Martines" affair. A teen-age Vietnamese girl by the name of Martine claimed to be his daughter, born while he served with the French forces in Indochina. When a "true" Martine was found and accepted as his real daughter, Bokassa placed the "false" Martine under house arrest, accused of espionage. However, he later relented and decided to pardon the "imposter," eventually adopting her. (*See in* CE: Central African Republic.)

CEYLON.
The most significant event of 1971 in Ceylon was an armed rebellion against Prime Minister Sirimavo Bandaranaike's left-wing coalition government by the People's Liberation Front, or "Che Guevarists." The rebels were led by Rohana Wijeweera, a graduate of the revolutionary Lumumba University in Moscow. Participants were mainly unemployed college graduates, school dropouts, and young Buddhist monks. The People's Liberation Front and the Maoist section of the

Ceylonese soldiers stand beside crude arms captured from rebels who threatened the government of Mrs. Bandaranaike.
CAMERA PRESS FROM PIX

Communist party wanted extreme radical measures taken, such as the complete nationalization of the press, farms, and banks.

The rebellion, which had been well planned and armed, began in March with an attack on the United States embassy in Colombo, the capital, in which a police inspector was killed. Some university students blew themselves up trying to make bombs. In early April attacks were made on several police stations and public buildings, and several individuals were murdered. The government, which had already declared a state of emergency, called out the armed forces. The outnumbered army was short of arms and ammunition, and the government appealed to foreign countries for supplies. These were quickly furnished by Great Britain, India, the Soviet Union, Yugoslavia, Pakistan, and the U.S. and included some helicopters. The revolt was crushed, and at least 1,200 people were killed, 60 of them from the army and police; 14,000 were taken into custody. (*See in* CE: Ceylon.)

CHAD. In August 1971 the regime of President François Tombalbaye survived an attempted coup that was immediately suppressed. Despite appeals for national reconciliation launched in January and in April, serious political tensions remained within the Progressive party, the country's only legal political party.

Rebellion continued throughout the year in the central and northern areas of the country. Abba Sidick, the leader of the illegal opposition party, the Chad National Liberation Front (FROLINAT), refused to negotiate with Tombalbaye. Operating from Tripoli, Libya, with the help of the Libyans, he continued to direct the movement in the armed struggle it had been engaged in since 1965.

After the failure of the August coup, Tombalbaye accused Libya of interfering in his country's affairs and broke off diplomatic relations with that government. (*See in* CE: Chad.)

CHEMISTRY. The controversy whether or not polywater is indeed a heavy, viscous, polymeric form of pure water continued to rage among colloid chemists in 1971. A Bell Telephone Laboratories scientist suggested that the minute samples of alleged polywater may have been contaminated by the aerosol sweat cloud that surrounds everyone. Research on polywater has been stymied, moreover, because no one has discovered how to make sizable quantities of it.

Molecules in Outer Space

An increasing variety of molecules have been discovered in the ultrahigh vacuum of outer space. A team of University of Illinois chemists and astronomers detected the first four-element molecule ever found in interstellar space. Formamide, consisting of carbon, hydrogen, oxygen, and nitrogen, was found in two stellar clouds directed toward the center of the Milky Way galaxy. The scientists used the 140-foot radio telescope at Green Bank, W.Va., to make their discovery.

Where and how space molecules are formed has not yet been determined. However, scientists are hopeful that when the concentrations of molecules in outer space and the equilibrium existing between them are learned, they will have some answers to these intriguing questions. As of 1971, radio astronomers have detected a number of molecules in the Milky Way, including carbon monoxide, formaldehyde, formic acid, water, hydrogen cyanide, methanol, and ammonia.

Chemical combinations have also been found in the interstellar space of other galaxies. Using the facilities of the California Institute of Technology, one scientist discovered that neutral hydroxyl radicals (OH) exist in two distant galaxies.

New Way to Prepare Superpure Metals

A team of scientists at the National Aeronautics and Space Administration (NASA) center in Cleveland, Ohio, developed a radiochemical method for preparing ultrapure metals. In the method, which has produced 99.998% pure copper, metal salt solutions are bombarded with high-energy electrons to precipitate the metal.

Disposal of the experimental Lopac bottle presents few environmental problems—it burns without polluting the air, is safely breakable, and is recyclable.

The radiochemical technique has also been used to synthesize compounds by selective oxidations (electron losses) and reductions (electron gains). For example, pure anhydrous (water-free) ferrous chloride is difficult to make because water and ferric chloride always contaminate it. However, the NASA team made the compound by bombarding a toluene solution of ferric chloride with electrons, causing a chemical reaction that stops with a pure precipitate of toluene-insoluble ferrous chloride.

A Chemical Pest Control; New Compounds

Pheromones, organic chemicals secreted by some insects as attractants, have been recently put to pest-control uses, especially against the gypsy moth. As recently as 1970, gypsy moth larvae ate the leaves from nearly a million acre of trees in the Northeast.

The female gypsy moths' own sexual pheromone —chemically identified as *cis*-7,8-epoxy-2-methyl-octadecane—has been used by United States Department of Agriculture scientists to lure the male moths into traps. The efficacy of the program will not be known until 1972, however.

Two new compounds that might prove useful in the manufacture of drugs and agricultural chemicals were synthesized recently by chemists of E. I. du Pont de Nemours & Co. Classed as cyanocarbons, they are diiminosuccinonitrile and diaminomaleonitrile. Both can be used to synthesize polyimides, which are commercially useful polymers. (*See in* CE: Chemistry.)

CHESS. Beginning in May 1971 the elimination series to determine the challenger for the world chess championship, held by Boris Spassky of the Soviet Union, was played. In the first round, eight participants were reduced to four: Bobby Fischer of the United States, who beat Mark Taimanov of the Soviet Union by winning six straight games; Tigran Petrosian of the Soviet Union, who defeated Robert Huebner of West Germany; Bent Larsen of Denmark, who defeated Wolfgang Uhlmann of East Germany; and Victor Korchnoi of the Soviet Union, who beat Yefim Geller, also of the U.S.S.R. In the semifinals Fischer defeated Larsen, again winning six straight games, and Petrosian beat Korchnoi.

The final playoff match, held in October in Buenos Aires, Argentina, between Fischer, an eight-time U.S. champion, and Petrosian, a former world champion, was followed closely by chess fans throughout the world. Fischer won the first game of the match, extending his winning streak begun in playoff rounds in Spain during 1970 to 20 games, a number unprecedented in the history of the grandmaster chess championships. The streak ended as Petrosian took the second game. The next three games were draws. However, Fischer then took the next four games, to win the match by a score of 6½ to 2½. Fischer was the first U.S. player to challenge the world champion

KEYSTONE

Bobby Fischer of the U.S. won the playoffs for the world chess championship and will face reigning champion Boris Spassky in 1972.

since the world playoffs were instituted in 1948. He will meet Spassky in a 24-game title match sometime in the spring of 1972.

The U.S. Chess Open Championship was held during August at Ventura, Calif. Among the record 398 entrants were 8 international grand masters, 3 international masters, and 27 U.S. masters. After seven rounds, Larry Evans, international grand master and former U.S. champion, emerged as the winner. (*See in* CE: Chess.)

CHILE. Events in Chile in 1971 centered around the economic and social reforms introduced by Chile's Marxist president, Salvador Allende Gossens. Allende's intention was to change the structure of Chilean society along socialist lines but within a framework of due process of law.

The most far-reaching reforms were directed at the organization of the economy. The government declared its intention to create a state-owned sector to include all 200 or so key industries; a mixed area where the state would own a majority interest but would allow private participation; and a private area of small- and medium-sized enterprises. In practice, the new government expropriated companies in many industries not included in the "key industry" list. Usually the government obtained control over private companies by purchasing shares through direct negotiations with the former owners, but seizures by workers followed up by government intervention were not uncommon. The process of expropriation was sometimes resisted through legal means, and several companies were ordered returned to their private owners.

A number of United States-owned companies were obtained by the government, and in September

"Land or death" is the slogan of a Chilean peasant group that has seized privately owned farms. On Chile's National Day of Voluntary Work, President Salvador Allende Gossens does his part by wielding a hammer.

RIGHT: "THE NEW YORK TIMES."
BELOW: CAMERA PRESS FROM PUBLIX

Allende announced the takeover of U.S holdings in the large copper mines. The legal basis for the expropriation was a constitutional amendment passed unanimously by the Congress in July. It authorized the president to deduct from the adjusted book value of the U.S. investment "excess profits" earned by those companies since 1955. The amendment did not define the term "excess profits," but the president declared that any return in excess of 10% of book value would be deducted.

In most cases, this meant no compensation would be paid to the owners. In response, U.S. Secretary of State William P. Rogers announced that if no compensation were paid, U.S. aid to Chile would be suspended.

In agriculture the government accelerated the process of expropriating large land holdings, usually according to the provisions of the agrarian reform law passed by the previous government. Sometimes, however, expropriation was carried out by illegal seizures by peasants, often with the active support of armed political bands. The Allende government denounced these seizures.

The government's economic policies were guided by political as well as economic considerations. The short-term effects of its policies were reasonably successful, in that industrial production rose, unemployment fell, and inflation was reduced, but indicators of future growth were less favorable.

Politically, there was little change. In April Allende's ruling coalition received 50.8% of the votes in the municipal election, a rousing popular endorsement that greatly strengthened the Allende government. However, pro-government candidates later lost a by-election for Congress. At year's end relations between Allende's ruling coalition and the major opposition party worsened, mostly over Allende's proposal to replace the bicameral Congress with a "People's Assembly." Tension reached a climax in December when a women's march mainly protesting food shortages set off violent street clashes between government and anti-government forces. Allende then declared a state of emergency to cope with the crisis, the worst since he took office.

Although Chile's relations with the U.S. were strained, they improved with various Communist countries, including the U.S.S.R. and Cuba. Cuba's Premier Fidel Castro was warmly welcomed during his visit in late fall. (*See in* CE: Chile.)

CHINA, PEOPLE'S REPUBLIC OF.

In 1971, as moderate leaders in China continued to seek a return to normalcy from the turbulance and disruption of the "cultural revolution," more rational domestic and foreign policies prevailed. Premier Chou En-lai, one of the most durable and resilient figures in Chinese politics since the forming of the Chinese Communist party in 1921 and the architect of China's foreign policy since the conclusion of the cultural revolution, emerged as a central figure in the events of the year.

The most dramatic of these events were those that led to a thaw in Sino-American relations. The thaw seemed to begin on February 25 with United States President Richard M. Nixon's State-of-the-World message to the U.S. Congress, in which he declared that "there would be no more important challenge to the U.S. in the 1970's than that of drawing the People's Republic of China into a constructive relationship with the world community. . . ." On March 15 the U.S. Department of State lifted its ban on travel by U.S. citizens to China. Then came a surprise Chinese invitation to the U.S. table tennis team to visit China, and on April 10, a team of 15 U.S. players accompanied by U.S. correspondents went to China for a week's stay. Receiving the U.S. visitors in a dramatic and unprecedented manner, Premier Chou stated that there was "a new page in the relations of the Chinese and American people."

To strengthen his policy of seeking normal ties with China, President Nixon announced on April 14 a series of measures to remove trade barriers. Early in May these were implemented when the U.S. government removed curbs on the use of dollars in trade with China and granted authorization to U.S. vessels and aircraft to transport commodities en route to China to ports and airfields not on Chinese territory. On June 10 Nixon lifted the 21-year embargo on most nonstrategic items and permitted all imports from China under general license. The climax in seeking improved relations came in July, just after President Nixon's national security affairs adviser, Henry A. Kissinger, had returned from a secret visit to China where he had extensive talks with Premier Chou. Nixon made a dramatic statement over U.S. television and radio networks that, in order "to seek the normalization of relations between the two countries" and as "a journey for peace," he had accepted Premier Chou's invitation to visit China at an appropriate date before May 1972. Although this announcement did not reveal the content of the Chou-Kissinger secret talks, it constituted one of the major events of the year in international relations. It signified a sudden and major change in U.S. policy in Asia.

The radical reversal of U.S. policy—felt to have added prestige and respectability to China—caused shock and anger to the Nationalist Chinese government in Taiwan, jolted U.S. allies in Asia, and fed the fear of Soviet leaders concerning the possible making of a Sino-American deal against the Soviet Union. In mainland China the people had been urged for years by the government to unite and defeat the "U.S. aggressors and all their running dogs." Thus the announcement of Nixon's forthcoming visit evoked surprise, curiosity, and ideological confusion. Belatedly, Chou revealed that it was the decision of the revered Communist

An historic meeting took place in Peking in July. Henry Kissinger (left), national security adviser to U.S. President Richard M. Nixon, met with Premier Chou En-lai to arrange Nixon's visit to China, to take place in February 1972.

WIDE WORLD

KEYSTONE

A vast irrigation project in Shensi Province, built by the People's Popular Front communes, has reclaimed hundreds of thousands of acres for cultivation.

Party Chairman Mao Tse-tung to invite the U.S. table tennis team and, in an ideological journal, Chou's invitation to Nixon was justified by citing the precedent of Mao's earlier policy of negotiating with enemy Nationalist Chinese leaders during the civil war in the 1940's.

It was speculated that the thaw in Sino-American relations might have precipitated a power struggle within the Chinese leadership, as the extremists regarded Chou's invitation to Nixon as an abandonment of the revolutionary principles proclaimed by China. Signs of leadership struggle and political crisis were made evident by a number of actions shortly before the scheduled annual October 1 National Day celebration. These included reports of unusual troop movements and the suspension of army leaves, the canceling of military and commercial flights in September, and the cancellation of the National Day parade in Peking, the capital. On this auspicious occasion Chairman Mao and top leaders had for the previous 21 years customarily lined up in order of precedence to display unity, deliver speeches, and review military and mass parades. The sudden cancellation of this traditional celebration gave rise to speculation on the state of health of Chairman Mao

and his heir apparent, Defense Minister Lin Piao, and on the possibility of political unrest.

If Mao or Lin were ill or dead, it would create a serious problem of succession and necessitate the reshuffling of top positions and power roles. The foreign ministry in Peking confirmed that for reasons of economy the annual October 1 parade had been canceled, and at the same time declared that Chairman Mao was in perfectly good health. No mention, however, was made of Defense Minister Lin. On September 29 Radio Peking announced that National Day celebrations would take place but would be limited in scope. Thus for the first time since 1949 the Chinese celebrated National Day without their top leaders taking the traditional salute in Peking and party spokesmen making important pronouncements. Also, Peking's three major journals published no editorials to define or redefine the policies of the party and government, and no photos of Mao or Lin appeared in the journals for the occasion. Premier Chou, however, appeared at a National Day celebration with U.S. Black Panther party co-founder Huey P. Newton. On October 8, without Lin, Mao reappeared in public for the first time in two months, to greet Ethiopia's Emperor Haile Selassie I on his visit to Peking. Knowledgeable observers believed that with the notable reduction of the cult of Mao and the unusual absence of Mao and Lin, the "Supreme Commanders of the Nation and Army," from the National Day celebration, Mao's central role in Chinese politics was diminishing and Lin was losing in his rivalry with Chou for leadership.

These unusual developments in Peking caused concern in the U.S. On October 2 U.S. Secretary of State William P. Rogers, speaking to newsmen in New York City, expressed the hope that events in China did not "signal any change in the possibility of President Nixon's visit to Peking." Three days later the White House and Radio Peking simultaneously announced that, through direct and secret contacts between Chinese and U.S. officials, the two governments had agreed to have Kissinger return to Peking at the end of the month with a team of ten specialists to make concrete arrangements for President Nixon's visit to China. The announcement indicated that Chou's position in the hierarchy had been retained and evidently enhanced.

Economic Developments

Political turmoil and emphasis on ideological indoctrination during the cultural revolution retarded economic advancement. The gross national product for 1970 was estimated by some sources to be between $75 and $90 billion, although Premier Chou said that it was about $120 billion. The New China News Agency claimed that for the tenth year a bumper grain harvest was expected in 1971, and that the country was now self-sufficient in grain. During the year Chou announced the inception of China's fourth five-year plan (1971–75).

The recovery of the domestic economy resulted in an increase of China's foreign trade to more than $4.2 billion in 1970, about equal to the previous record years of 1966 and 1959. Non-Communist countries remained the chief trading partners of China, accounting for some 80% of its total foreign trade. Japan continued to be the largest trading partner, followed by Hong Kong and West Germany. To increase exports, trade fairs were held and trade missions dispatched to a number of countries including Ceylon, Malaysia, Sudan, Morocco, Romania, Yugoslavia, France, Italy, and the Scandinavian countries. Several important trade agreements were signed during the year, in particular with Malaysia, Italy, and Peru.

Foreign Affairs

As the moderates among the Chinese leadership took greater control over domestic affairs, they also began to assert their influence in achieving China's big-power position in foreign affairs by means of conventional diplomacy. Early in 1971 Chinese diplomats who had been recalled during the cultural revolution were being sent back to their posts in more than 40 countries. Following the recognition of the People's Republic as the sole legal government of China by Canada and Italy in late 1970, more than ten other countries recognized China by October 1971. In July the arrival in Canada of Huang Hua, one of China's most experienced and trusted diplomats, as the first ambassador of the People's Republic to Canada, attracted considerable attention.

China's bid for leadership in the Third World of developing nations was clearly demonstrated by the joint communiqué against great-power chauvinism signed on June 9 by Premier Chou and Romania's leader, Nicolae Ceausescu, who visited China in June. In signing the document Chou stated that "we will always stand together with oppressed countries and peoples in firmly opposing power politics of superpowers."

Although the thaw in Sino-American relations was the most important event in 1971, there also had been an improvement in Sino-Soviet relations with the exchanges of new ambassadors and the conclusion of a new trade agreement toward the end of 1970. However, the talks to settle various border issues stalled over the question of the scope of negotiations. China wanted to limit the discussion relating to border disagreements and sought Soviet acknowledgement in principle that the Russians had gained much of their Far Eastern territories through "unequal treaties" under the czarist regime. The Soviet Union simply refused to discuss the question of legitimacy of territories under its control but wanted to expand the talks to include economic, cultural, and political matters. China's demand for an immediate pullback of troops on both sides of the border met no response. Consequently, tensions on the borders intensified with heavy deployment of troops on both sides. (*See also* Communist Movement.)

In March China launched a bitter ideological attack on the Soviet Union. The exchange of polemics between the two Communist giants continued practically throughout the year. In the midst of this conflict, the Soviet Union became extremely sensitive about U.S. overtures to China and about China's invitation to President Nixon. Ten days after the announcement of Nixon's planned trip to China, the Soviet Communist party newspaper *Pravda* published a long article accusing the Chinese leadership of splitting activities in world Communism, and warned that U.S.-China contacts should not be used to put pressure on the Soviet Union.

Farm products from China's local communes are brought to the nearest town, where they are sold on the open market at food stalls.
UPI COMPIX

KEYSTONE

The Chinese women's militia trains for coastal defense in Fukien Province. The women work during the day and stand sentry duty on the coast at night.

China's Entry into the United Nations (UN)

The proposal for admitting mainland China into the UN, which had been an issue since the founding of the People's Republic in 1949, became an overriding item of the 26th General Assembly in 1971. The central issue became whether to replace Taiwan (Nationalist China) with the People's Republic or admit China and still let Taiwan keep a seat.

In his State-of-the-World message of February 25, President Nixon declared that the U.S. policy was to find a solution that would admit China without expelling Taiwan, and that China should not be allowed to dictate the terms of its participation in the UN. In April a U.S. Presidential Commission on the question, headed by Henry Cabot Lodge, formally recommended a two-China doctrine as U.S. policy. When Nixon announced on July 15 his projected visit to China, the U.S. holding action against the entry of China into the UN came to an end for all practical purposes. On the same day Albania submitted a resolution to the General Assembly proposing the expulsion of Taiwan and the seating of China as one of the five permanent members on the Security Council. On August 2 Secretary of State Rogers formally announced that the U.S. would support the admission of China into the UN while opposing the expulsion of Taiwan. The reaction of China to the U.S. two-China policy was immediate and outspoken, calling the formula absurd. The Chinese foreign office declared on August 20 that China would not take a seat at the UN unless Taiwan were expelled.

The coincidental timing of Henry Kissinger's second trip to China to resume talks with Premier Chou in October, during the final phase of the General Assembly debate on the China issue, evidently made many UN delegations anticipate the eventual normalization of relations between the U.S. and China. Their votes on the issue certainly reflected this expectation. On October 25 the General Assembly defeated the resolution sponsored by the U.S.—which asked that the proposal for Taiwan's expulsion be treated as an important question requiring two-thirds majority—by 59 votes against 55 votes, with 15 abstentions. The Albanian-sponsored resolution expelling Taiwan and admitting China was then adopted by a vote of 76 in favor, 35 against, and 17 abstentions, thus admitting the People's Republic on its own terms.

China called the vote a victory of the people of the world. On November 2, Chiao Kuan-hua, vice-minister of foreign affairs, was named head of China's delegation to the General Assembly and Huang Hua, China's ambassador to Canada, was appointed deputy to Chiao and Permanent Representative on the Security Council. In China's debut speech in the UN Chiao attacked the U.S. for its policies in Asia, demanding the immediate withdrawal of U.S. forces from Vietnam, Cambodia, and Laos and from the Taiwan Strait. (*See in* CE: China, People's Republic of.)

CITIES AND URBAN AFFAIRS. Critical revenue shortages continued to plague American cities in 1971 as "the urban crisis" widened and deepened. Municipalities for the fiscal year 1970, as reported by the Bureau of the Census, spent $1.5 billion in excess of their receipts, a gap between expenditures and revenues greater than in previous years. Expenditures increased by 12% from the preceding year, whereas revenues increased by only 10%.

The greater financial deficit occurred despite the fact that many cities in the United States curtailed or failed to increase essential services such as police protection, education, health services, garbage collection, and welfare. Moreover, the financial plight of the central cities in metropolitan areas was understated by these statistics because they included municipalities in suburbia. These figures substantiated the vocal claims of the nation's mayors about the worsening of municipal finances. The need for urban services increased while the tax base eroded, with the influx of poor minority group population—mainly black—and the exodus of middle-class and upper-income whites to the suburbs.

Although mayors, especially of the larger cities, increased their pressures for more federal and state aid, most of the increase in funds for cities came from their own sources. Municipal sources of revenue provided an increase of 11% while federal and state moneys to cities increased by only 8%. A report by a special commission appointed by the National Urban Coalition stated that "most cities by 1980 will be preponderantly black and brown and totally bankrupt."

The financial plight of the cities and the prospect that it would worsen rather than improve led the Administration of U.S. President Richard M. Nixon, in response to intense pressures, public and private, to propose a "revenue sharing" program. The Administration's revenue sharing plan would provide state and local governments with a total of $16 billion of federal funds. Of this amount $6 billion would be new money, that is, above that which state and local governments were already receiving for specific programs.

The revenue sharing plan, as proposed, had two major elements: One was "general revenue sharing," which entails the granting of unencumbered funds for state and local use. The second was "special revenue sharing," which calls for providing state and local governments with funds for specified program areas within which localities would have flexibility in expenditures. General revenue sharing would represent a step in the direction of closing the revenue gap of state and local governments, estimated at $10 billion for 1971. The revenue gap has increased despite the increase in state and local taxes, mainly from property and consumer taxes—which, during the past two decades, rose from $105 to $380 per capita; and despite the increase in state and local government debt from $19 billion in 1948 to $135 billion in 1969. Federal revenues, more so than state and local revenues, increase with national economic growth and, therefore, can more readily meet new expenditure requirements.

Special revenue sharing would provide state and local governments with greater discretion than they now have under categorical grant programs. In place of 130 separate grant programs, $11 billion of shared revenues would be placed under six broad headings within which local priorities could be followed. The six categories would be: rural community development, urban community development, education, manpower training, law enforcement, and transportation. The direct recipients of shared revenues under the Administration plan would be the general-purpose units of government: states, counties, cities, and towns.

Opposition to the president's plan was dramatized in a statement by Senator Adlai E. Stevenson III (D, Ill.), in which he attacked it on the following grounds, among others:

1. That it would violate two principles "vital to our federal system—(a) each level of government should be held accountable for funds raised and spent, and (b) national moneys should be used to meet national objectives and not widely scattered."

2. The plan would "not bring new life to local government—it will embalm the status quo . . . . Many of our larger states are patchworks of local

Avoiding frustrating traffic and subways, New Yorkers took to the motorcycle, praising its speed, comfort, economy, and convenience.

"THE NEW YORK TIMES"

governmental units. Some of these are too small and too weak to be effective; others overlap, causing a nightmare of confusion and conflict . . . . There are over 6,000 units of local government in Illinois alone. To pour tax dollars indiscriminately into outmoded creaking and complex state machinery, irrespective of need or purpose, would do little to help. It might be harmful."

3. Improvement is needed, but it would be more important for the Administration to pull the nation out of the recession than to obtain its revenue sharing program, because a full employment economy would generate "revenues far greater than revenue sharing would bring."

By the end of 1971 state and local governments were still beset with financial crisis and the prospects for an early solution of any kind seemed dim. Revenue sharing remained in committee as the 1st session of the 92d Congress was adjourned; the Administration had pushed for its passage early in the year, but by late summer the program was eclipsed by the president's new economic program. (*See* Economy; Nixon.)

The focus of national attention on the financial distress of the cities and the debate on the Administration's proposals for revenue sharing led to the consideration of alternatives. Among the alternatives certain to be considered are: (1) extension of state income taxes and increased tax rates, with credits for state income-tax payments in the federal income tax; (2) imposition of a federal consumption tax such as the "value added" tax—a tax on a product at each stage of fabrication and sale—which would be regressive but could raise substantial revenue; (3) allocation of all costs of welfare, including present and possible future public medical costs, to the federal government; (4) allocation to state governments of all costs of public education (the 1971 decision of the California Supreme Court declaring unconstitutional the use of the property tax for local public education, because of the educational inequities it generated, may accelerate this decision); and (5) increase of federal grant-in-aid programs with improved distribution of funds to assure adequate flow to the most needy areas.

Urban conditions during the year showed little evidence of improvement. Although the summer of 1971 did not bring widespread riots and flames in its wake, some cities still experienced serious incidents. Increasingly it was Chicanos, Puerto Ricans, and American Indians who revolted, rather than blacks. In contrast to 19 major disorders in the first eight months of 1970 (through August) there were, according to the Department of Justice, 11 for the same period in 1971; and 32 serious disturbances in 1971 compared with 49 in 1970. The consensus of observers seemed to be not that living conditions have improved for minority groups but, rather, that the blacks have found more productive ways to express their frustration and alienation. Blacks and other minority groups were increasing their community organization efforts and political activity to bring about change within the system. Other factors in the decrease in violent revolt were the increased sophistication of police and government officials in dealing with episodes and more reasoned coverage of episodes by the mass media.

In general, then, decreased riots and arson cannot be interpreted to mean that conditions have improved or that frustration and hostility have diminished. On the contrary, a Harris survey reported on Oct. 4, 1971, that the attitudes of blacks were becoming increasingly hostile towards whites, even while white perceptions of blacks were im-

Made of soft flexible plastic, this portable Instant Playground for New York City children will be put into use as a result of efforts by the State Urban Development Corporation, the State Council on the Arts, and the Police Athletic League. The equipment can be erected by one man in 15 minutes.

"THE NEW YORK TIMES"

The city of Toronto, Ont., closed Yonge Street—a major thoroughfare—to traffic for a week. Large numbers of pedestrians gathered and enjoyed the occasion.

FRANZ MAIER

proving with the deterioration of distorted stereotypes from the past. Guerrilla warfare—aimed particularly at the police—and bombings increased, and pent-up inner city hostility continued to be a major threat to the viability of American society. (*See* Race Relations.)

As to the actual conditions within cities the evidence was that they had probably worsened. According to the Federal Bureau of Investigation (FBI) violent crimes increased by 11% during the first six months of 1971—murder, forcible rape, aggravated assault, and robbery. The FBI also reported that 80 law enforcement officers were killed in the first eight months of 1971 compared with 67 for the corresponding period of 1970. (*See* Crime.)

Moreover, a task force of the National Urban Coalition reported that the condition of American cities generally worsened in the three years following the Kerner Commission report. The 12-member task force, of which Senator Fred R. Harris (D, Okla.) and New York City's Mayor John V. Lindsay were cochairmen, issued a report entitled "The State of the Cities," which assessed the progress made since the 1968 report of the National Advisory Commission on Civil Disorders. The National Urban Coalition report concluded that the races have become more polarized and that American institutions, public and private, were losing the confidence of the public. Sol M. Linowitz, the coalition chairman, stated that ". . . the cities have not cooled off. The basic causes that sparked the tragic ghetto rebellions of the 1960's are still there —worse than ever, in most cases. And the people are angry." The finding was that the Kerner Commission recommendations for improvement in housing, employment, welfare, and education have, in the main, not been carried out. Comparing the situation with that at the end of 1967, the coalition report stated: "Housing is still the national scandal it was then. Schools are more tedious and turbu-

lent. The rates of crime and unemployment and disease and heroin addiction are higher. Welfare rolls are larger. And, with few exceptions, the relations between minority communities and the police are just as hostile."

Another indication of the worsening quality of life in urban America was a Gallup Poll that found that public discontent increased between 1969 and 1971. Most Americans continued to express satisfaction with their condition of life; however, dissatisfaction with jobs, income, and housing increased during the past two years, and dissatisfaction with the future facing the person and his family also increased. The level of dissatisfaction of blacks was without exception higher than that of whites in 1971. Dissatisfaction with their jobs was 25% for blacks compared with 9% for whites; with family income, 57% for blacks compared with 33% for whites; with housing, 46% for blacks compared with 19% for whites; and with children's education, 29% for blacks compared with 26% for whites. (*See also* Political Parties. *See in* CE: City.)

COIN COLLECTING. The major event of 1971 for coin collectors in the United States, and in many other countries, was the release of the President Dwight D. Eisenhower-Apollo 11 dollar. This coin, the first metallic dollar issued by the U.S. since 1935, was made available in three forms: .400 fine silver clad proofs at $10.00, .400 fine silver clad regular strikes at $3.00, and copper-nickel clad (no silver) for circulation. The two premium-priced coins were available only from the U.S. Mint during 1971 but were to be struck again with 1972 dates, as were those for regular circulation.

After having produced only 2,150,000 John F. Kennedy half-dollars in 1970, all for use in special "mint sets" for collectors, the mint began striking the coins for circulation in 1971. However, those

COURTESY, THE COIN AND CURRENCY INSTITUTE, INC.

The Hall of Fame for Great Americans issued a medal honoring Booker T. Washington, black leader and educator. One side bears his portrait; the other, ex-slaves, books, and buildings.

COURTESY, U.S. TREASURY

The new "one dollar" coin honors the late President Dwight D. Eisenhower, with a profile of him on one side and the bald eagle, symbolizing the Apollo 11 spacecraft, on the other.

dated 1971 do not contain any silver, being composed of copper-nickel outer layers bonded to pure copper cores.

Other countries issuing commemorative coins during the year included Austria (three: Chancellors Karl Renner and Julius Raab, and the 200th anniversary of the Vienna Bourse [stock exchange]); Canada (silver and nickel dollars for the centennial of British Columbia's entry into the confederation); Czechoslovakia (centennial of birth of Nikolai Lenin); East Germany (Wilhelm Konrad Roentgen, discoverer of X rays); Haiti (discovery by Columbus); Isle of Man (first coinage since 1839 depicting a Manx cat); Israel (atomic theme for 23d anniversary of independence); Italy (centennial of Rome as capital); Malaysia (dedication of Bank Negara Malaysia); Philippines (visit of Pope Paul VI); Portugal (500th anniversary of birth of explorer Vasco da Gama); the Arab sheikhdom of Ras al Khaima (Dwight D. Eisenhower); Egypt (Gamal Abdel Nasser); Vatican City (eight coins, 8th year of reign of Pope Paul VI); West Germany (Konrad Adenauer); and Western Samoa (two: Capt. James Cook and visit of Pope Paul VI).

Numismatic organizations and publishers continued to encourage young people to take up the hobby. The enrollment of new members in the American Numismatic Association (ANA) included about 17 juniors for each 100 adults during the year ending June 30, 1971. The association

encouraged juniors to join by waiving the admission fee, by offering several annual awards for achievements, and by publishing a quarterly magazine for them in addition to a special page in its regular monthly, *The Numismatist*.

The annual August convention of the ANA, held in Washington, D.C., drew a record attendance of over 10,500. Noted numismatists from Canada, Mexico, and several other countries took part in the scheduled activities of the five-day convention. The ANA manifested its appreciation for federal government cooperation and participation by bestowing an honorary membership on U.S. President Richard M. Nixon. Bureau of the Mint Director Mary T. Brooks and Bureau of Engraving and Printing Director James Conlon spoke at the educational forum, provided displays throughout the convention, and took part in other activities.

Related to numismatics, especially its commercial aspects, was the attempt made in July 1971 to establish public trading in gold coins as a commodity. In Los Angeles the West Coast Commodity Exchange announced and opened trading in contracts for 200 ounces of gold (in coins), and reported a volume of $3.2 million the first day. (*See also* Hobbies; Postal Service; Stamps. *See in* CE: Mint, U.S.; Money.)

COLLEGES AND UNIVERSITIES. During 1971 college and university campuses in the United States were notable for the absence of violent dissent and disruptions. Only a few demonstrations and incidents of violence marred the general calm, and the response to a call for a nationwide student strike in May was limited. Many factors contributed to the change in student attitudes, including the rate at which the U.S. was pulling out of Vietnam, the Selective Service System reforms, increased student participation in university affairs at the policy-making level, and student disillusionment over the limited achievements of violent protest. Fear of repression was also a factor, as was the national economic situation, which adversely affected educational funding and the job market for college graduates. Student concern for social change remained acute but was tempered by the realization of the complexity of social and economic problems.

With campus unrest at a minimum, the primary concern of educators turned toward the growing financial crisis in higher education. While national economic inflation continued to drive the operating costs of educational institutions upward, their income did not keep pace. As a result, many private institutions were forced to raise tuition, which in turn led to a drop-off in applications for enrollment for the fall of 1971. Applications to the high-priced Ivy League colleges decreased significantly. Enrollment at the less expensive, publicly supported state colleges and universities increased. Many state-supported institutions, however, suffered cutbacks in funds as legislators reacted to previous campus violence and to national inflation.

A survey of public universities by the National Association of State Universities and Land-Grant Colleges revealed that many such institutions were operating on "standstill" budgets that did not allow for inflationary costs. Contributions to colleges and universities from private individuals and foundations also decreased, as did endowment income, as a result of inflation. The financial plight of higher education was also affected by cutbacks in support by the federal government, including reductions in student grants and construction funds.

In addition to the worsening economic situation, there were other factors in the changing pattern of higher education. Many young people questioned the value of higher education; others, no longer subject to the draft, preferred to work or to travel before committing themselves to college. There was also a trend among youths toward working with their hands, with a resultant upsurge in enrollment at vocational and technical institutions. An adverse reaction to technology, and unemployment in such professions as engineering, contributed to a decline in enrollment at some science-oriented institutions, and large-scale unemployment among recent graduates with doctoral degrees was considered a factor in the leveling off of graduate school applications. At the same time, graduate enrollment in law and medicine increased substantially.

Although enrollment at private colleges and universities declined, the total number of students in higher education increased from 7.9 million in the 1970–71 school year to an estimated 8.4 million in the 1971–72 school year. About 70% of them were registered in state institutions. The enrollment of blacks and other minority groups rose during the 1970–71 school year.

Hard-pressed colleges and universities took a variety of steps to economize, including faculty reductions, the elimination of some departments and programs, cutbacks in maintenance, and sharing programs, facilities, and faculty members with neighboring institutions of higher education. Groups of colleges formed consortiums for the joint purchase of supplies, for sharing academic personnel, and for admissions. Some state institutions set quotas for out-of-state students, largely under pressure from legislators and taxpayers; educators considered this trend a threat to their ability to attract top-ranking students and teachers and out-of-state alumni contributions. Many educators, particularly at higher-priced institutions, feared that tuition increases necessitated by the economic situation would drive away less affluent students.

With the national emphasis on the racial integration of white colleges, the country's private, all-black colleges faced severe hardships. Their best students and faculty members continued to be lured away by integrated institutions, and some previous financial contributors, tending to equate all-black institutions with black separatism, held back funds. The Carnegie Commission on Higher Education recommended that federal aid to black colleges be tripled. By mid-1971, however, most black colleges had not been able to qualify for increased federal aid offered in 1970 because they could not raise the required matching funds.

To ease financial pressure on students and the threat of pricing themselves beyond the reach of many young people, several institutions introduced tuition innovations during 1971. Yale University offered a deferred tuition plan, accepted by more than 22% of its 1971 undergraduates, which allowed students to spread tuition payments over a number of years after graduation; the cost to the student is based on a percentage of future earnings. A similar plan was offered on a limited basis by Duke University. Beloit College initiated a tuition plan based on the ability of the student's parents to pay.

Students sit on the roof terrace of the new Academic Wing of the University of Pennsylvania Museum. Designed by Mitchell/Giurgola Associates, Architects, it contains an Education section, the Department of Anthropology, a 50,000-volume library, a restaurant, and the University Museum's collections.

AUTHENTICATED NEWS INTERNATIONAL

Kent State University held services in memory of the four students killed by National Guardsmen in antiwar demonstrations in 1970. Flowers were placed at the Victory Bell on campus.

WIDE WORLD

There were accelerating trends during 1971 toward reducing the length of higher education programs and toward "external degree" plans that allow students of any age to do their degree work without attending campus classes. Both plans help to cut the cost of education for students and institutions, and to free higher education from the tradition of the four-year college. The concepts were supported by reports from the Carnegie Commission on Higher Education and from the U.S. Department of Health, Education, and Welfare, which called for new ways of making higher education more flexible and more accessible to persons unable to attend regular college programs.

The California state colleges initiated a three-year college program in the fall of 1971, and several other institutions, including major universities, were considering the plan. California and New York offered external-degree programs in 1971 in which individual programs were pursued using correspondence study, television courses, and equivalency examinations. New York's Empire State College opened as an institution without a campus but with centers around the state for counseling, tutoring, and testing.

Twenty colleges and universities, both public and private, joined in the University Without Walls (UWW) program sponsored by the Union for Experimenting Colleges and Universities and supported by the U.S. Office of Education and the Ford Foundation. The UWW plan emphasized off-campus learning through the use of community resources and teaching by nonacademic experts; each participating institution applied the UWW concept in its own way. (*See also* Education.)

COLOMBIA. Despite President Misael Pastrana Borrero's plans to ease unemployment and introduce urban and agrarian reforms, his National Front coalition government faced increased opposition and serious social unrest in 1971. A state of siege was declared throughout Colombia on February 26, following student demonstrations in Cali in which eight people were killed. At the end of April, another series of student uprisings resulted in the closing of five universities. Peasants took over numerous landholdings when promises of land reform did not materialize. On March 25, four West German technicians and four Colombian officials were kidnapped by guerrillas, but they were freed two days later after a battle between the guerrillas and the Colombian army. Continued clashes between guerrillas and the government marked the rest of the year.

On June 1 all but one of the 12 cabinet ministers resigned to enable Pastrana to reshuffle his coalition with new ministers chosen mainly from the right wings of the Conservative and Liberal parties. The National Popular Alliance (Anapo), the strong political group of the former president, Gen. Gustavo Rojas Pinilla, was officially announced as a political party on June 13. Rojas described his goal as establishing a "Colombian socialism."

Colombia's economic situation continued to be grave, as coffee prices fell, heavy rains damaged crops, living costs rose steadily, and import expenditures increased. (*See in* CE: Colombia.)

COMMONWEALTH OF NATIONS. At the 1971 meeting of the Commonwealth heads of government, held in Singapore, economic anxieties over Great Britain's proposed membership in the European Economic Community (EEC) were only equaled by the confrontation over policy toward white supremacist southern Africa. It was the first major Commonwealth conference to convene outside London, and also the largest, with all 31 members represented. Only the skill of Chairman Lee Kuan Yew, prime minister of Singapore, aided by older members, prevented its degeneration from a unique "body of friends" into a United Nations-type forum for prepared national propaganda. At the insistence of African nations, attention was centered on southern African problems, particularly the sale of arms to South Africa. Great Britain's Prime Minister Edward Heath insisted that his nation must act in its own interests; this view met with vigorous denials from some Afro-Asian members. However, the British position was maintained that legal obligations under the Simonstown naval agreement included the supply of limited categories of equipment for the defense of sea-lanes threatened by the Soviet naval buildup in the Indian Ocean. Three factors emerged from the conference: the agreed value of the association and the need for its existence; agreement that no member should dictate policy to another; and the need to revert to the "no vote, no veto" informality and privacy of early Commonwealth meetings.

Africa

Repercussions of the South African dispute were felt by African leaders who returned home to pressure for and against a policy of "dialogue." Though denounced by a divided meeting of the Organization of African Unity, H. Kamuzu Banda, president of Malawi, made history in August as the first black head of state to visit South Africa (returning South African Prime Minister John Vorster's 1970 visit). Malawi's Joseph Kachingwe became the first black ambassador to South Africa, and Zambia became more amenable to Malawi's stand, opening a mission there, followed by visits from the foreign and trade ministries.

In Sierra Leone the government moved left toward accommodation with Guinea. Nigeria and Ghana, though competing for African leadership, remained bound by domestic problems: Nigeria, despite peace, faced the problems of its return to civilian government and the absorption of a swollen army; Ghana remained bowed by the burden of its external debts and the resultant political and economic frustrations.

UPI COMPIX

Bengali demonstrators wearing death masks picket the Pakistani cricket team in London.

East African leaders, most vehement against South Africa, faced increasing domestic problems. President Milton Obote of Uganda was deposed in January while on his way home from the Commonwealth conference and took refuge in Tanzania, while Maj. Gen. Idi Amin, head of the armed forces, took over Uganda's administration. His revolution to the right altered the East African balance of power, though Tanzania refused to recognize the new regime and reports of border fighting between Uganda units and Chinese-led Tanzanians were widespread later in the year.

The Commonwealth heads of government meeting convened in Singapore in January and grappled with a number of controversial issues.

FOX PHOTOS FROM PICTORIAL PARADE

Construction of the Tanzam railway continued with the aid of a Chinese loan of over $400 million and the import of 13,000 Chinese personnel by June 1971. Zambia and Tanzania agreed to repay equal shares of about $6.9 million a year, beginning in 1985. Zambia in 1971 experienced economic deterioration through a fall in copper production and prices, and the loss of foreign confidence and exchange with the expansion of nationalization. Former Zambian Vice-President Simon Kapwepwe formed a new opposition party against the alleged corruption and the tribal discrimination of President Kenneth Kaunda's administration. He demanded immediate elections, a new constitution, and economic independence. A decline in corn production resulted in the humiliation of having to buy 1.5 million bags from Rhodesia. (*See* Africa; Rhodesia.)

The British government sent several missions to Rhodesia under Lord Goodman in the hope of reaching a settlement with Prime Minister Ian Smith's regime. In November it was announced that a tentative settlement had been reached. The terms of the settlement provided for some hope of eventual devolution of political power to the black Rhodesian majority and some guarantees against racial discrimination. The Organization for African Unity, however, called the agreement an "outright sellout," although Britain claimed it was the best that could be hoped for. During the year no major guerrilla incidents occurred in Rhodesia, and the country's independence day was celebrated by the biggest military parade there since World War II. Rhodesia's economy prospered both by agricultural diversification and major nickel discoveries, but remained limited by scarcity of foreign exchange.

Other Countries

In April 1971 a conference on Far Eastern defense was held by representatives of Australia, Malaysia, New Zealand, Singapore, and Great Britain in London. A five-power defense agreement was made (effective from November 1971), to replace the Anglo-Malaysian defense agreement and to establish an integrated air defense system for the area and an air defense council responsible for its operation.

In August a South Pacific Forum was held in New Zealand, with Australia, Fiji, Western Samoa, Tonga, and Nauru present. The meeting concentrated on inter-regional trade, the population explosion in relation to resources, and joint diplomatic representation. (*See also* individual countries by name.)

COMMUNICATIONS.
In 1971 the Federal Communications Commission (FCC) seemed to be edging away from its policy of tight control over the United States telecommunications and broadcasting industries, as evidenced by the positions it took on two major communications issues. The de-

cisions reached indicated that the FCC would place more stress than it ever had previously on the principle of competition within these industries.

The first of the two FCC decisions hastened the hookup of the computer industry with the communications industry by allowing competition in microwave and other specialized communications systems. On May 26 the FCC ruled that virtually any company could offer such communication service provided that it could meet the financial and technical specifications. Microwave transmission, for example, could be used for both voice and data transmission, but the greatest growth was expected in the area of data transmission. By the end of the decade it was expected that the microwave transmission industry would outstrip telephone communications.

The second of the major FCC decisions concerned community antenna television, or as it was more widely known, cable television. On August 5 the FCC sent what it called a "letter of intent" to the U.S. Congress that outlined the rules the FCC wished to use to govern cable television. Basically, the FCC wanted the cable television market expanded and was planning to permit cable television firms for the first time to "import" distant signals into major U.S. cities:

In sending its letter the FCC intended to give Congress time to hold hearings and to formulate possible legislation. The FCC did not expect to put its new rules into effect until Congress approved them. Strong opposition to the expansion of cable television was expected by the FCC from existing television networks. In addition, a stand on the issue was expected from the White House Office of Telecommunications Policy.

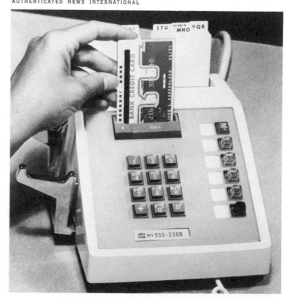

Automation comes to dialing, with Bell Laboratories' new plastic card that does the job in appropriately equipped telephones.
AUTHENTICATED NEWS INTERNATIONAL

MISS PEACH

By Mell Lazarus

YESTERDAY I CAME TO A SPIRITUAL DECISION...

—I GOT TO THINKING HOW, IF I CALLED UP MY MINISTER, AND TOLD HIM OF MY FEARS AND LONGINGS, HE WOULD POINT THE WAY FOR ME, AND LEAD ME ON THE PROPER PATH TO A LIFE OF SERVICE TO OTHERS, FULFILLMENT, AND A RICHER UNDERSTANDING OF THE MEANING OF CREATION, AND THE MARVELLOUS REWARDS THAT COULD BE MINE FOREVER AFTER.

THAT'S BEAUTIFUL, IRA! WHAT HAPPENED ??

THE PHONES WERE OUT OF ORDER.

© FIELD ENTERPRISES

Satellites

In May delegates to a third plenipotentiary conference on the International Telecommunications Satellite Organization (Intelsat) finally reached agreement, after more than two years of negotiations, on arrangements to run a global satellite communication system. As a result of their deliberations, U.S. ownership and management was to be reduced to a maximum of 40%.

During a six-year transition period, the Communications Satellite Corp. (Comsat), the U.S. quasi-public corporation that had been running Intelsat, was to be phased out and replaced by a secretary-general and an international board of directors. Comsat would continue to handle the technical functions during this time.

Telephone and Telegraph Developments

A new era in trans-Pacific communications was opened in September when the American Telephone and Telegraph Co. and telephone companies of countries in the Pacific region announced plans for a vastly expanded communication system. The first phase of the plan was expected to be completed by 1974.

In September it was also announced that telephone and telegraph service was being restored between the People's Republic of China and the U.S. The service had been suspended in 1968 by the Chinese.

In the U.S. there was some improvement in telephone service in 1971, according to the FCC, which had been studying complaints about poor telephone service since May 1970. The FCC said that New York City; Chicago; Boston, Mass.; and Miami, Fla., had "aggravated service difficulties" in 1969 but that services had improved in 1970 and 1971, though New York City continued to be plagued by poor telephone service.

Despite this general improvement, however, some telephone services had deteriorated since 1966, according to the FCC report. About 2% of long-distance calls dialed by an operator could not be completed on the first attempt in 1971; in comparison the figure in 1966 was only 1.4%. Similarly, in 1966, 2.9% of directly dialed calls could not be completed immediately; in 1971 the figure had risen to 3.2%.

Little public inconvenience was apparent as a result of a strike by more than 600,000 members of the Communications Workers of America and other unions against the Bell telephone system, which began on July 14 and ended in nearly all locations six days later. Telegraph workers were also out on strike during the year. The last of the telegraph unions settled in September after striking since June 1. It was the longest strike in the 127-year history of the telegraph industry.

COMMUNIST MOVEMENT.

The rivalry between the Soviet Union and the People's Republic of China for dominance of the world Communist movement remained an influential and divisive factor in Communist affairs in 1971. Through Communist party congresses and leadership meetings the Soviets endeavored to strengthen the movement's unity and consolidate domestic support, with limited success. The expanding role of China and Chinese Communism in world affairs, nationalist and polycentrist factions within the movement, and distrust of Communist intentions by many Third World political powers were obstacles to unity, as in the past.

Soviet Unification Efforts

A major Communist event during 1971 was the 24th Congress of the Soviet Communist party, held in Moscow in the spring. It was attended by 101 foreign delegations and representatives of 90 countries, but was boycotted by China and the pro-Chinese parties of Albania, Thailand, Burma, and Malaya and the right-wing Communist parties of the Netherlands and Iceland.

While the primary task of the congress was ratification of a new Soviet five-year plan emphasizing consumer priorities, the occasion was used by Soviet Communist Party General Secretary Leonid I. Brezhnev to expound a party line based on centrist policies. These included an avoidance of both excessive re-Stalinization and renewed de-Stalinization; the prohibition of both leftist and

185

rightist deviation from the party line; and the necessity of submerging party differences in order to combat anti-Soviet nationalism and bourgeois ideologies with a united front. Brezhnev declared that economic concessions could be made to the people to maintain domestic support and that some diversity within the Communist movement could exist, but that all ideological dissent or anti-Soviet activity must be suppressed. Most delegates to the congress supported the Soviet call for solidarity, but several refused to join in Brezhnev's criticism of Chinese Communism, and the Romanian and Italian leaders renewed their demand for the independence of each party and country.

Following through with their consolidation efforts, Soviet leaders attended Communist party congresses in Bulgaria (April), Czechoslovakia (May), East Germany and the Mongolian People's Republic (June). These efforts were offset by the visit of Romanian Communist Party General Secretary Nicolae Ceausescu to China, North Vietnam, and North Korea, which dramatically stressed Romania's neutrality in Communist affairs; by the announcement that United States President Richard M. Nixon planned to visit China; and by the failure of a pro-Soviet coup in Sudan. Summoned to a conference with Brezhnev in the Crimea, Soviet-bloc leaders (excepting Ceausescu, who did not attend) expressed alarm over these events. Subsequently, Soviet denunciations of the Chinese increased, and Soviet leaders undertook a diplomatic offensive aimed at improving relations with the West and with the Arab world.

Chinese Communism

Although the ideological rift between Soviet and Chinese Communism led to no reported border clashes during 1971, border negotiations were stalemated and the propaganda war continued. Each side accused the other of deviation from Marxism-Leninism. The Soviets repeatedly charged Chinese party leaders with turning China into an armed camp.

The 50th anniversary of the Chinese Communist party, on July 1, was marked quietly in Peking. In late 1970 the rebuilding of party organizations in China's provinces had begun. Party structures had been dismantled during the "cultural revolution" of the 1960's.

China proceeded rapidly to break out of the self-imposed diplomatic isolation of the cultural revolution period. In addition to moving towards a détente with the U.S. and accepting United Nations (UN) membership, the Chinese launched a worldwide diplomatic offensive aimed, according to Premier Chou En-lai, at forming a "united front" of lesser powers to resist the hegemony of the U.S. and the U.S.S.R. This drive included the establishment of diplomatic relations with many nations and was consistent with the Chinese commitment to anti-imperialist liberation movements and to anti-Soviet Maoist parties in various nations.

Communism in Europe

Various diplomatic exchanges and cooperative agreements between China and the nationalist-oriented Communist governments of Romania and Yugoslavia led to speculation that the Peking government was attempting to form a pro-Chinese entente in the Balkans, with Albania—China's long-time European ally—as a third member. Like the Chinese, the Albanians continued to move out of their diplomatic isolation. Yugoslavia, beset by internal problems, remained nonaligned. Soviet leader Brezhnev held talks in Belgrade with Yugoslavia's President Tito, who pointedly reaffirmed Yugoslavian independence; Brezhnev conditionally accepted the idea of noninterference in Yugoslavian affairs and thus had to hedge on his doctrine of limited sovereignty for Communist states.

While maintaining its independence from the Soviets in foreign affairs, Romania nonetheless

Luigi Longo, secretary of the Italian Communist party, spoke at the party's 50th anniversary celebration in Livorno.
KEYSTONE

Czechoslovakia's leaders visited Sofia, Bulgaria, in January. Gustav Husak (center), Czechoslovak Communist party general secretary, and Lubomir Strougal, Czechoslovak premier, ride with Todor Zhivkov, Bulgarian Communist party first secretary.

KEYSTONE

showed willingness to compromise by participating in East European Communist bloc organizations, and by joining them in denouncing Israel for the Middle East impasse. Romania hosted a meeting of the Council for Mutual Economic Assistance (Comecon), which adopted a long-range plan for economic integration of the Soviet bloc.

The complete restoration of hard-line, pro-Soviet Communism in Czechoslovakia was signaled with a declaration at the 14th congress of the Czechoslovak Communist party that "normalization" had been achieved. An estimated 80,000 Soviet troops remained stationed in the country, and Czechoslovak party affairs were closely supervised by the Soviets. The Communist parties of East Germany and Poland came under new leadership as a result of economic deterioration. In Poland Edward Gierek, who assumed party leadership from Wladyslaw Gomulka in December 1970, reorganized the party apparatus and shifted economic priorities toward consumer needs. The Polish regime also took steps to improve relations with the Roman Catholic church. At the 8th congress of the East German Communist party Erich Honecker took over leadership of the party, replacing Walter Ulbricht, who had led the party for nearly a quarter of a century. Honecker acknowledged Soviet hegemony.

The popularly elected Marxist government of Chile—the first in the Western Hemisphere—was admired by nonruling Communists in Western Europe and held up as a model for emulation by the Soviets. (*See in* CE: Communism.)

COMPUTERS. The major event of 1971 in the United States computer industry was the startling announcement by RCA Corp. that it was withdrawing from computer manufacturing. The decision to withdraw cost RCA an estimated $250 million,

which it wrote off in its third quarter report for 1971. This write-off was responsible for a tremendous loss to the corporation of $231 million for the quarter and of $188 million for the first nine months of the year.

The RCA decision not to compete any longer with International Business Machines Corp. (IBM), in spite of RCA's position as one of the largest and strongest companies in the U.S., shook the very foundations of the computer industry. In the judgment of most observers, many customers would probably desert the remaining smaller companies in favor of IBM, which controlled 70% of the computer market—mainly because they feared

Computer graphics have become increasingly popular in recent years. One such graphic is designed on a "display/memory" panel.

COURTESY, OWENS-ILLINOIS INC.

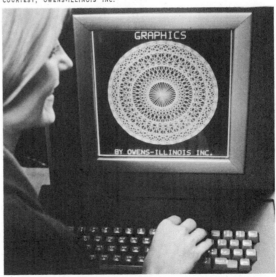

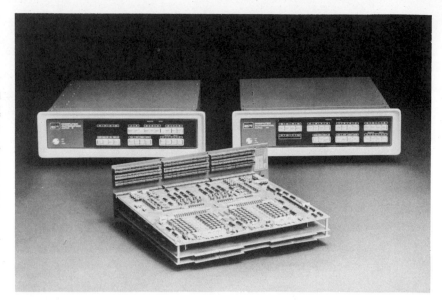

The Alpha 8 (left) and the Alpha 16 (right) are the finished versions of the Naked Mini (foreground). They comprise a new series of minicomputers, compact and relatively inexpensive.

COURTESY, COMPUTER AUTOMATION, INC.

that they might be left with an "orphan" computer and no source of parts or services if its makers went out of business or merged.

In general, the computer industry, like other U.S. industries, was affected by the lagging economic recovery. Despite IBM's domination of the market, a number of independent manufacturers, who were offering equipment that could directly replace IBM's but at much lower prices, were doing quite well. In an effort to regain its lost market IBM continued the aggressive price-cutting policy

A new computer technique reduces an electroencephalogram to a single sheet (from an average of 150 pages) that can easily be read by clinicians. The technique was developed at the University of California at San Diego School of Medicine.

AUTHENTICATED NEWS INTERNATIONAL

that it had begun in 1970. It also began shipping to customers the first of its miniaturized or minicomputers, the System 3 model 6, a small, general-purpose machine, and the System 7, developed for such specialized applications as process control, data acquisition, and laboratory instrumentation.

The minicomputer market, dominated by two companies, Digital Equipment Corp. and Data General Corp., remained one of the fastest areas of growth in the industry. Minicomputers had a number of distinct advantages. They were less expensive (prices ranged from $3,000 to $25,000 in comparison to a minimum of $100,000 for larger computers), and since they were smaller and more quickly built, they were able to reflect technological advances more rapidly than larger computers. They could also be used for a great variety of tasks where larger machines were too cumbersome. One of the most important areas of use for minicomputers was in running machinery in factories.

Progress also continued during the year on some of the supercomputers. Illiac IV, the giant array processor conceived at the University of Illinois and built in the laboratories of Burroughs Corp., was nearing completion. A prototype of the Staran IV, made by Goodyear Aerospace Corp., was installed as part of the air traffic control equipment at the Knoxville, Tenn., airport by the Federal Aviation Administration. When fully developed, Staran IV would be able to keep track of hundreds of aircraft, isolate those on collision courses, and provide information for display—all at perhaps 200 times the speed of conventional machines.

Considerable interest arose in 1971 in networks of interconnected minicomputers—said to be as effective in many applications as a single, large computer and much less expensive. There were also some significant developments in plasma display panels. The panels, invented in 1966, were flat and only about a half inch thick. They were potentially much less expensive than the cathode-ray tubes currently in use to display information from the computer. Another development was the completion, after an eight-year development period, of a computer called Symbol, which had a unique characteristic—a high-level programming language implemented directly in the hardware. (*See in* CE: Computers.)

CONGO, DEMOCRATIC REPUBLIC OF THE (Kinshasa).

On Dec. 5, 1970, Joseph D. Mobutu, president of the Democratic Republic of the Congo, announced an amnesty for all rebels who returned to the country by Jan. 31, 1971. A number of former opponents of the state responded, among them Christophe Gbenye, minister of the interior in the governments of Patrice Lumumba and Cyrille Adoula. Gbenye had left Kinshasa, the capital, in 1963 to become one of the leaders of the pro-Lumumbist uprising against the government of that time, and in the following year he had proclaimed himself president of the Congolese People's Republic. He had subsequently lived in Uganda, Egypt, and Sudan. On his return he announced his support for the policies of Mobutu. Others who took advantage of the president's offer included Michel Mongali, another former minister in Adoula's government, Nicolas Olenga, and Casimir Bagira.

Following demonstrations at the University of Lovanium at Kinshasa in June, almost the whole student body of about 3,000 was conscripted into the army for two years. Students of the Official University of the Congo who, in sympathy, volunteered to undergo the same training were drafted for seven years. Lovanium was temporarily closed and renamed the University of Kinshasa. In July a number of East European diplomats, accused of instigating the troubles, were given 48 hours to leave the country.

Relations with Portugal so improved toward the end of the year that some guerrillas based in Kinshasa moved their headquarters to Zambia. In October the country changed its name to the Republic of Zaire. (*See in* CE: Congo, Democratic Republic of the.)

CONGO, PEOPLE'S REPUBLIC OF THE (Brazzaville).

Political developments in the People's Republic of the Congo in 1971 revolved around two main axes. They were unconditional adherence to the revolutionary line laid down by the leadership in Brazzaville, the capital, and the strengthening of ties with the People's Republic of China.

In February and in June, changes in the cabinet were made, and in March several members of a "gang of counter-revolutionaries" were arrested, accused of having circulated leaflets inciting civil war. They were later tried and sentenced by a military court in Brazzaville. In April, Capt. Kibouala Kaya was relieved of his position as political commissar for the army and head of the armored corps for alleged "subjectivist and tribalist attitudes." In May, upset by the attitude of the police force, the government merged it with the army. (*See in* CE: Congo, Republic of.)

CONGRESS, UNITED STATES.

The 92d Congress began its first session Jan. 21, 1971, with the Democratic party firmly in control. The Democrats held 254 seats in the House of Representatives against 180 for the Republicans and 1 vacancy—a gain of 9 Democratic seats from the 91st Congress. In the Senate the Democrats held a 55 to 45 edge, a loss of 2 seats.

The 91st Congress adjourned January 2 after the longest session since the Congressional session of 1950. The House ended its session with eulogies to retiring Speaker John W. McCormack (D, Mass.), who had spent 42 years in Congress, 9 of them as speaker.

When the House reconvened, former Democratic Majority Leader Carl Albert (Okla.) was sworn in as speaker. Rep. Hale Boggs (La.), former majority whip, succeeded Albert as majority leader, and Rep. Thomas P. O'Neill, Jr. (Mass.), succeeded Boggs as whip. Rep. Olin E. Teague (Tex.) was elected chairman of the Democratic caucus, succeeding Rep. Dan Rostenkowski (Ill.).

Senate Democrats reelected Senator Mike Mansfield (Mont.) as majority leader and Senator Frank E. Moss (Utah) as chairman of the Senate Democratic caucus. Both were unopposed. Senator Edward M. Kennedy (Mass.) suffered a surprising political blow when he was defeated for reelection

In March Gen. Joseph D. Mobutu, president of the Democratic Republic of the Congo, made an official visit to Paris.

as assistant Senate majority leader by Senator Robert C. Byrd (W.Va.).

The Republican House leadership in the 92d Congress was Rep. Gerald R. Ford (Mich.), minority leader; Rep. Leslie C. Arends (Ill.), minority whip; and Rep. John B. Anderson (Ill.), chairman of the House Republican Conference. Republican Senate Majority Leader Hugh Scott (Pa.) defeated Senator Howard H. Baker, Jr. (Tenn.), 24 to 20 to win reelection. Senator Robert P. Griffin (Mich.) was elected minority whip without opposition.

Senator Allen J. Ellender (D, La.) became president pro tempore of the Senate during January, upon the death of Senator Richard B. Russell (D, Ga.). The post is held by the senator with the longest continuous service. Ellender became a senator in 1937.

The start of the 1971 session marked the third successive year in which the party opposed to the president has controlled Congress. The result was an uneven record of partisan disputes and cooperation with the White House. Senator Mansfield and Speaker Albert often took the position that it was the responsibility of Congress to give serious consideration to the legislative proposals of President Richard M. Nixon, possibly making revisions but keeping essentials. However, there were major challenges to the president on foreign policy and on a number of domestic issues.

Possibly the most important legislation of the 92d Congress was passed the fastest. Moving rapidly to give state legislatures a chance to ratify it before the 1972 presidential elections, Congress approved the 26th Amendment to the Constitution. The amendment stated that "the right of citizens of the United States, who are 18 years of age or older, to vote shall not be denied or abridged by the United States or by any state on account of age." The measure passed the Senate, 94–0, March 10; the House, 400–19, March 23. Rapid approval by the states allowed 18-year-olds to vote in the 1971 off-year elections. (*See also* Supreme Court, U.S.)

A presidential request for a two-year extension of the draft law was made January 28, but action was not completed until late September. The issue became linked with efforts to set a timetable for ending the war in Vietnam, to cut U.S. troop strength in Europe, and to set military pay scales high enough to attract an all-volunteer army. The draft law expired June 30, and there was a period in late summer when no men could be drafted. In the end, Congress extended the draft for two years. It raised pay scales by a total of $2.4 billion a year —about $1.5 billion more than the president requested. Whether the raise would be large enough to attract an all-volunteer army by the time the draft law expired in 1973 was uncertain. In an effort to keep a measure of control on foreign policy, Congress ordered that not more than 130,000 men be drafted in the fiscal year ending June 30, 1972, and 140,000 in the following fiscal year. Thus there would have to be another request to Congress if any significant expansion of the armed forces was required. Congress approved an Administration request to authorize an end to student deferments for youths beginning college in 1972 or later. The law called on the president to fix a "date certain" for withdrawal of all U.S. forces from Indochina, contingent only on release of all American prisoners of war. The provision was a victory for the Administration. The Senate had previously passed a more stringent proposal by Mansfield calling for a withdrawal nine months after the prisoner release.

Another major foreign policy fight centered around the foreign aid bill. Late in the session, the Senate surprised itself and the nation by voting 41–27 to kill the foreign aid bill. Opposition grew from the objections of some Republicans and Southern Democrats to the expense, the feeling of some liberals that aid had evolved into a military program leading to conflicts like that in Vietnam, and anger over the United Nations (UN) vote to expel Nationalist China from the UN General Assembly. The foreign aid program finally was salvaged, but it took until the final minutes of the session. The Senate again attached a Mansfield

In 1971 the first two girl Senate pages were sworn in. Senator Charles Percy (R, Ill.) sponsored Ellen McConnell (left), and Senator Jacob Javits (R, N.Y.) sponsored Paulette Dessel (right). These are the first girl pages in the history of the Senate.

UPI COMPIX

House Speaker Carl Albert charged that President Nixon withheld an unprecedented $20 billion in funds provided for state and local programs.

Rep. Wilbur Mills (D, Ark.) was instrumental in pushing through a measure for increased Social Security benefits.

amendment, this time calling for withdrawal of U.S. forces from Indochina within six months. The provision was dropped after an adverse test vote in the House.

Congress finally authorized $2.75 billion for foreign aid. The Administration had asked for $3.6 billion. A number of provisions indicated Congressional determination to have an increasing voice in foreign affairs. The foreign aid bill put a ceiling of $341 million on U.S. operations in Cambodia and limited the number of employees for the foreign aid program to 285. It barred transfer of other funds to Cambodia without Congressional approval. (The limit did not apply to U.S. support of Vietnamese operations within Cambodia.) It also required periodic Congressional authorization of State Department activities, and suspended aid to Pakistan and Greece. In a novel use of appropriations power, aid funds were frozen until after April 30, 1972, unless the president released approximately $2 billion in domestic project funds which he had frozen.

Even this did not end the foreign aid dispute. Congress always passes twin money bills—one authorizing spending and one specifically providing the money. For foreign aid, Congress simply approved continued spending at last year's level until Feb. 22, 1972. Meantime, it will try to work out a new appropriations bill at the start of its next session.

The Senate approved a treaty returning Okinawa and the southern Ryukyu islands to administrative control of Japan. Under the 1951 treaty ending the state of war that began in World War II, the U.S. was to maintain control as long as strategic conditions made it necessary. The new treaty provides that the U.S. may retain military bases on Okinawa.

The domestic legislative picture changed radically in August. President Nixon acted dramatically to slow persistent inflation at home and an increasingly grim prospect for the nation's import-export balance. Using the authority Congress gave him over his objection in 1970, he announced a temporary wage-price freeze, to be followed by a longer-range system of wage and price controls. The president had already shifted his position on wage-price authority early in 1971, when he told Congress it was acceptable but unnecessary. On that basis, Congress renewed the authority through April 30, 1972. After imposing the freeze, the president asked for and obtained control authority effective through April 30, 1973.

Congressional leaders also expressed support for the president's decision to devalue the dollar, thus cutting the price of American goods abroad and increasing the price of imports in the U.S. They promised action early in 1972 on an Administration request to increase the price of gold, set at $35 an ounce since 1934.

A tax reduction bill requested by the president to stimulate the economy was altered in many respects, but achieved substantially all of the presidential objectives. The final version cut taxes by an estimated $15.8 billion over three years. Personal income tax exemptions were increased from $650 to $675 per person for 1971 taxes, payable 1972. It was to be $750 for 1972 taxes, payable

Walter Fauntroy (at podium) is the first Congressional delegate to the U.S. Congress from Washington, D.C., in a century. The swearing-in ceremony was attended by Mayor Walter Washington of the District of Columbia (second from left) and Mrs. Martin Luther King, Jr. (right).

in 1973. The percentage standard deduction was increased from 14% to 15%, effective in 1972. The 7% excise tax on autos was repealed, retroactive to August 15, and the 10% excise tax on trucks was repealed, retroactive to September 23. Businesses were authorized to deduct from their taxes 7% of their spending for new machinery and equipment, retroactive to orders placed on or after April 1. (The president had requested 10%.) Companies were allowed to defer taxes on up to 50% of the export volume of corporations they set up to handle international sales. Companies also were allowed to accelerate tax depreciation of assets by as much as 20% over previous guidelines. A tax credit for sending children to college was killed, but a "baby-sitter" deduction of up to $4,800 a year was authorized for working couples and single persons with incomes up to $18,000 a year. A plan to let taxpayers deduct a small amount to finance presidential and Congressional campaigns was passed, but the starting date was postponed until after the 1972 elections. (*See* Political Parties.) A bill to set up a nationwide system of federally assisted day-care centers for children of working mothers was vetoed by the president.

Relief for the unemployed commanded considerable attention. Congress passed a $5.6-billion public works and Appalachian regional development bill, which the president vetoed because it contained an emergency program of public works to provide employment. Such a plan, many economists feared, might provide an extra push for the economy at a time when it was so brisk that the added buying power would prove inflationary. Congress sustained the veto and passed a substitute $4.4-billion program without the emergency public works feature. Congressional acceptance of the veto was facilitated by the president's approval of a measure for creation of up to 200,000 emergency jobs in public service—a measure he originally opposed. Under the $2.25-billion program, the federal government would pay up to 90% of wages for emergency jobs in schools, hospitals, parks, police and fire departments, and social service agencies. The rest would be paid by state and local governments. The plan would run for two years.

Congress passed a 10% Social Security increase, with taxes increased to pay for it beginning in January 1972. The Administration had asked for a 6% increase.

The Administration received a setback when Congress refused further funds for development of a supersonic transport plane, ending several years of controversy. In an unrelated action, a bill was passed guaranteeing Lockheed Aircraft Corp. $250 million in loans to carry it through development of its 400-passenger Tristar airliner.

After rejecting two Nixon appointments to the Supreme Court in previous sessions, Congress approved late in 1971 two nominees who were generally regarded as conservatives. The new associate justices are William H. Rehnquist and Lewis F. Powell, Jr. Congress also confirmed Earl L. Butz as secretary of agriculture despite objections of some Democrats and some farm groups.

For the first time in its history, the Senate voted in May to employ girls as pages and women as elevator operators and police officers. The first three pages confirmed by the Senate were Julie Price, Bartlesville, Okla.; Paulette Desell, Schenectady, N.Y.; and Ellen McConnell, Dundee, Ill. All were 16 when nominated by their senators. Pages were paid $7,380 a year.

Each Congress lasts for two years. Bills introduced in 1971 and pending at the end of the session were to be available for action in 1972. Proposed constitutional amendments providing for direct election of the president and vice-president were in committees of both houses. If passed, time required for ratification by the states would almost certainly prevent their affecting the 1972 elections. A constitutional amendment prohibiting discrimination based on sex was passed by the House and pending in the Senate judiciary committee. An amendment that would permit prayer in public schools—banned by a court decision on freedom of religion—was killed in the House. (*See in* CE: Congress of the United States.)

MEMBERS OF THE CONGRESS
OF
THE UNITED STATES

2d Session, 92d Congress*

THE SENATE

President of the Senate: Spiro T. Agnew

State	Senator	Current Service Began	Current Term Expires
Ala.	John Sparkman (D)	1947	1973
	James B. Allen (D)	1969	1975
Alaska	Theodore F. Stevens (R)	1969	1977
	Mike Gravel (D)	1969	1975
Ariz.	Paul J. Fannin (R)	1965	1977
	Barry M. Goldwater (R)	1969	1975
Ark.	John L. McClellan (D)	1943	1973
	J. W. Fulbright (D)	1945	1975
Calif.	Alan Cranston (D)	1969	1975
	John V. Tunney (D)	1971	1977
Colo.	Gordon Allott (R)	1955	1973
	Peter H. Dominick (R)	1963	1975
Conn.	Abraham Ribicoff (D)	1963	1975
	Lowell P. Weicker, Jr. (R)	1971	1977
Del.	J. Caleb Boggs (R)	1961	1973
	William V. Roth, Jr. (R)	1971	1977
Fla.	Edward J. Gurney (R)	1969	1975
	Lawton Chiles (D)	1971	1977
Ga.	Herman E. Talmadge (D)	1957	1975
	David H. Gambrell† (D)	1971	1972
Hawaii	Hiram L. Fong (R)	1959	1977
	Daniel K. Inouye (D)	1963	1975
Idaho	Frank Church (D)	1957	1975
	Len B. Jordan (R)	1962	1973
Ill.	Charles H. Percy (R)	1967	1973
	Adlai E. Stevenson III (D)	1971	1977
Ind.	Vance Hartke (D)	1959	1977
	Birch E. Bayh (D)	1963	1975
Iowa	Jack Miller (R)	1961	1973
	Harold E. Hughes (D)	1969	1975
Kan.	James B. Pearson (R)	1962	1973
	Robert Dole (R)	1969	1975
Ky.	John Sherman Cooper (R)	1957	1973
	Marlow W. Cook (R)	1969	1975
La.	Allen J. Ellender (D)	1937	1973
	Russell B. Long (D)	1948	1975
Maine	Margaret Chase Smith (R)	1949	1973
	Edmund S. Muskie (D)	1959	1977
Md.	Charles McC. Mathias, Jr. (R)	1969	1975
	J. Glenn Beall, Jr. (R)	1971	1977
Mass.	Edward M. Kennedy (D)	1962	1977
	Edward W. Brooke (R)	1967	1973
Mich.	Philip A. Hart (D)	1959	1977
	Robert P. Griffin (R)	1966	1973
Minn.	Walter F. Mondale (D)	1964	1973
	Hubert H. Humphrey (D)	1971	1977
Miss.	James O. Eastland (D)	1943	1973
	John C. Stennis (D)	1947	1977
Mo.	Stuart Symington (D)	1953	1977
	Thomas F. Eagleton (D)	1969	1975
Mont.	Mike Mansfield (D)	1953	1977
	Lee Metcalf (D)	1961	1973
Neb.	Roman L. Hruska (R)	1955	1977
	Carl T. Curtis (R)	1955	1973
Nev.	Alan Bible (D)	1954	1975
	Howard W. Cannon (D)	1959	1977
N.H.	Norris Cotton (R)	1955	1975
	Thomas J. McIntyre (D)	1963	1973
N.J.	Clifford P. Case (R)	1955	1973
	Harrison A. Williams, Jr. (D)	1959	1977
N.M.	Clinton P. Anderson (D)	1949	1973
	Joseph M. Montoya (D)	1965	1977
N.Y.	Jacob K. Javits (R)	1957	1975
	James L. Buckley‡	1971	1977
N.C.	Sam J. Ervin, Jr. (D)	1954	1975
	B. Everett Jordan (D)	1958	1973
N.D.	Milton R. Young (R)	1945	1975
	Quentin N. Burdick (D)	1960	1977
Ohio	William B. Saxbe (R)	1969	1975
	Robert Taft, Jr. (R)	1971	1977
Okla.	Fred R. Harris (D)	1964	1973
	Henry Bellmon (R)	1969	1975
Ore.	Mark O. Hatfield (R)	1967	1973
	Robert W. Packwood (R)	1969	1975
Pa.	Hugh Scott (R)	1959	1977
	Richard S. Schweiker (R)	1969	1975
R.I.	John O. Pastore (D)	1950	1977
	Claiborne Pell (D)	1961	1973
S.C.	Strom Thurmond (R)	1955	1973
	Ernest F. Hollings (D)	1966	1975
S.D.	Karl E. Mundt (R)	1949	1973
	George McGovern (D)	1963	1975
Tenn.	Howard H. Baker, Jr. (R)	1967	1973
	William E. Brock III (R)	1971	1977
Tex.	John G. Tower (R)	1961	1973
	Lloyd M. Bentsen (D)	1971	1977
Utah	Wallace F. Bennett (R)	1951	1975
	Frank E. Moss (D)	1959	1977
Vt.	George D. Aiken (R)	1941	1975
	Robert T. Stafford§ (R)	1971	1977
Va.	Harry F. Byrd, Jr.♦	1965	1977
	William B. Spong, Jr. (D)	1957	1973
Wash.	Warren G. Magnuson (D)	1944	1975
	Henry M. Jackson (D)	1953	1977
W.Va.	Jennings Randolph (D)	1959	1973
	Robert C. Byrd (D)	1959	1977
Wis.	William Proxmire (D)	1957	1977
	Gaylord Nelson (D)	1963	1975
Wyo.	Gale W. McGee (D)	1959	1977
	Clifford P. Hansen (R)	1967	1973

*Convened January 1972.
†Appointed as interim successor to the late Richard B. Russell (D) until November 1972 election.
‡Party designation: Conservative Party (of New York).

§Appointed as interim successor to the late Winston L. Prouty (R); elected to his own term in January 1972.
♦No party designation (Independent).

THE HOUSE OF REPRESENTATIVES *

Speaker of the House: Carl Albert

Alabama
Jack Edwards, 1 (R)
William L. Dickinson, 2 (R)
† 3
Bill Nichols, 4 (D)
Walter Flowers, 5 (D)
John Buchanan, 6 (R)
Tom Bevill, 7 (D)
Robert E. Jones, 8 (D)

Alaska
Nick Begich (D)

Arizona
John J. Rhodes, 1 (R)
Morris K. Udall, 2 (D)
Sam Steiger, 3 (R)

Arkansas
Bill Alexander, 1 (D)
Wilbur D. Mills, 2 (D)
John Paul Hammerschmidt, 3 (R)
David Pryor, 4 (D)

California
Don H. Clausen, 1 (R)
Harold T. Johnson, 2 (D)
John E. Moss, 3 (D)
Robert L. Leggett, 4 (D)
Phillip Burton, 5 (D)
William S. Mailliard, 6 (R)
Ronald V. Dellums, 7 (D)
George P. Miller, 8 (D)
Don Edwards, 9 (D)
Charles S. Gubser, 10 (R)
Paul N. McCloskey, Jr., 11 (R)
Burt L. Talcott, 12 (R)
Charles M. Teague, 13 (R)
Jerome R. Waldie, 14 (D)
John J. McFall, 15 (D)
B. F. Sisk, 16 (D)
Glenn M. Anderson, 17 (D)
Robert B. Mathias, 18 (R)
Chet Holifield, 19 (D)
H. Allen Smith, 20 (R)
Augustus F. Hawkins, 21 (D)
James C. Corman, 22 (D)
Del Clawson, 23 (R)
John H. Rousselot, 24 (R)
Charles E. Wiggins, 25 (R)
Thomas M. Rees, 26 (D)
Barry M. Goldwater, Jr., 27 (R)
Alphonzo Bell, 28 (R)
George E. Danielson, 29 (D)
Edward R. Roybal, 30 (D)
Charles H. Wilson, 31 (D)
Craig Hosmer, 32 (R)
Jerry L. Pettis, 33 (R)
Richard T. Hanna, 34 (D)
John G. Schmitz, 35 (R)
Bob Wilson, 36 (R)
Lionel Van Deerlin, 37 (D)
Victor V. Veysey, 38 (R)

Colorado
James D. (Mike) McKevitt, 1 (R)
Donald G. Brotzman, 2 (R)
Frank E. Evans, 3 (D)
Wayne N. Aspinall, 4 (D)

Connecticut
William R. Cotter, 1 (D)
Robert W. Steele, Jr., 2 (R)
Robert N. Giaimo, 3 (D)
Stewart McKinney, 4 (R)
John S. Monagan, 5 (D)
Ella T. Grasso, 6 (D)

Delaware
Pierre S. du Pont IV (R)

Florida
Robert L. F. Sikes, 1 (D)
Don Fuqua, 2 (D)
Charles E. Bennett, 3 (D)
Bill Chappell, Jr., 4 (D)
Louis Frey, Jr., 5 (D)
Sam Gibbons, 6 (D)
James A. Haley, 7 (D)
C. W. (Bill) Young, 8 (R)
Paul G. Rogers, 9 (D)
J. Herbert Burke, 10 (R)
Claude Pepper, 11 (D)
Dante B. Fascell, 12 (D)

Georgia
G. Elliott Hagan, 1 (D)
Dawson Mathis, 2 (D)
Jack Brinkley, 3 (D)
Benjamin B. Blackburn, 4 (R)
Fletcher Thompson, 5 (R)
John J. Flynt, Jr., 6 (D)
John W. Davis, 7 (D)
W. S. Stuckey, 8 (D)
Phil M. Landrum, 9 (D)
Robert G. Stephens, Jr., 10 (D)

Hawaii
Spark M. Matsunaga (D)
Patsy T. Mink (D)

Idaho
James A. McClure, 1 (R)
Orval Hansen, 2 (R)

Illinois
Ralph Metcalfe, 1 (D)
Abner J. Mikva, 2 (D)
Morgan Murphy, 3 (D)
Edward J. Derwinski, 4 (R)
John C. Kluczynski, 5 (D)
George Collins, 6 (D)
Frank Annunzio, 7 (D)
Dan Rostenkowski, 8 (D)
Sidney R. Yates, 9 (D)
Harold R. Collier, 10 (R)
Roman C. Pucinski, 11 (D)
Robert McClory, 12 (R)
Philip M. Crane, 13 (R)

John N. Erlenborn, 14 (R)
‡ 15
John B. Anderson, 16 (R)
Leslie C. Arends, 17 (R)
Robert H. Michel, 18 (R)
Tom Railsback, 19 (R)
Paul Findley, 20 (R)
Kenneth J. Gray, 21 (D)
William L. Springer, 22 (R)
George E. Shipley, 23 (D)
Melvin Price, 24 (D)

Indiana
Ray J. Madden, 1 (D)
Earl F. Landgrebe, 2 (R)
John Brademas, 3 (D)
J. Edward Roush, 4 (D)
Elwood Hillis, 5 (R)
William G. Bray, 6 (R)
John T. Myers, 7 (R)
Roger H. Zion, 8 (R)
Lee H. Hamilton, 9 (D)
David W. Dennis, 10 (R)
Andrew Jacobs, Jr., 11 (D)

Iowa
Fred Schwengel, 1 (R)
John C. Culver, 2 (D)
H. R. Gross, 3 (R)
John Kyl, 4 (R)
Neal Smith, 5 (D)
Wiley Mayne, 6 (R)
William J. Scherle, 7 (R)

Kansas
Keith G. Sebelius, 1 (R)
William Roy, 2 (D)
Larry Winn, Jr., 3 (R)
Garner E. Shriver, 4 (R)
Joe Skubitz, 5 (R)

Kentucky
Frank A. Stubblefield, 1 (D)
William H. Natcher, 2 (D)
Romano Mazzoli, 3 (D)
M. G. (Gene) Snyder, 4 (R)
Tim Lee Carter, 5 (R)
William P. Curlin, Jr.§, 6 (D)
Carl D. Perkins, 7 (D)

Louisiana
F. Edward Hebert, 1 (D)
Hale Boggs, 2 (D)
Patrick T. Caffery, 3 (D)
Joe D. Waggonner, Jr., 4 (D)
Otto E. Passman, 5 (D)
John R. Rarick, 6 (D)
Edwin W. Edwards, 7 (D)
Speedy O. Long, 8 (D)

Maine
Peter N. Kyros, 1 (D)
William D. Hathaway, 2 (D)

Maryland
William O. Mills♦, 1 (R)
Clarence D. Long, 2 (D)
Edward A. Garmatz, 3 (D)

Paul Sarbanes, 4 (D)
Lawrence J. Hogan, 5 (R)
Goodloe E. Byron, 6 (D)
Parren Mitchell, 7 (D)
Gilbert Gude, 8 (R)

Massachusetts
Silvio O. Conte, 1 (R)
Edward P. Boland, 2 (D)
Robert Drinan, 3 (D)
Harold D. Donohue, 4 (D)
F. Bradford Morse, 5 (R)
Michael Harrington, 6 (D)
Torbert H. Macdonald, 7 (D)
Thomas P. O'Neill, Jr., 8 (D)
Louise Day Hicks, 9 (D)
Margaret M. Heckler, 10 (R)
James A. Burke, 11 (D)
Hastings Keith, 12 (R)

Michigan
John Conyers, Jr., 1 (D)
Marvin L. Esch, 2 (R)
Garry Brown, 3 (R)
Edward Hutchinson, 4 (R)
Gerald R. Ford, 5 (R)
Charles E. Chamberlain, 6 (R)
Donald W. Riegle, Jr., 7 (R)
James Harvey, 8 (R)
Guy Vander Jagt, 9 (R)
Elford A. Cederberg, 10 (R)
Philip E. Ruppe, 11 (R)
James G. O'Hara, 12 (D)
Charles C. Diggs, Jr., 13 (D)
Lucien N. Nedzi, 14 (D)
William D. Ford, 15 (D)
John D. Dingell, 16 (D)
Martha W. Griffiths, 17 (D)
William S. Broomfield, 18 (R)
Jack H. McDonald, 19 (R)

Minnesota
Albert H. Quie, 1 (R)
Ancher Nelsen, 2 (R)
Bill Frenzel, 3 (R)
Joseph E. Karth, 4 (D)
Donald M. Fraser, 5 (D)
John M. Zwach, 6 (R)
Bob Bergland, 7 (D)
John A. Blatnik, 8 (D)

Mississippi
Thomas G. Abernethy, 1 (D)
Jamie L. Whitten, 2 (D)
Charles H. Griffin, 3 (D)
G. V. (Sonny) Montgomery, 4 (D)
William M. Colmer, 5 (D)

*Numbers after names indicate Congressional districts; where no number is given, congressman is elected at large.
†Vacancy caused by the death of George Andrews (D), Dec. 25, 1971.
‡Vacancy caused by the resignation of Charlotte T. Reid (R) in October 1971 upon her appointment to the Federal Communications Commission (FCC).
§Elected in December 1971 to fill unexpired term of the late John C. Watts (D).
♦Elected in May 1971 to fill unexpired term of Rogers C. B. Morton (R).

Missouri
William Clay, 1 (D)
James W. Symington, 2 (D)
Leonor K. Sullivan, 3 (D)
William J. Randall, 4 (D)
Richard Bolling, 5 (D)
W. R. Hull, Jr., 6 (D)
Durward G. Hall, 7 (R)
Richard H. Ichord, 8 (D)
William L. Hungate, 9 (D)
Bill D. Burlison, 10 (D)
Montana
Richard G. Shoup, 1 (R)
John Melcher, 2 (D)
Nebraska
Charles Thone, 1 (R)
John Y. McCollister, 2 (R)
Dave Martin, 3 (R)
Nevada
Walter S. Baring (D)
New Hampshire
Louis C. Wyman, 1 (R)
James C. Cleveland, 2 (R)
New Jersey
John E. Hunt, 1 (R)
Charles W. Sandman, Jr.,
2 (R)
James J. Howard, 3 (D)
Frank Thompson, Jr.,
4 (D)
Peter H. B. Frelinghuysen,
5 (R)
Edwin B. Forsythe, 6 (R)
William B. Widnall, 7 (R)
Robert A. Roe, 8 (D)
Henry Helstoski, 9 (D)
Peter W. Rodino, Jr.,
10 (D)
Joseph G. Minish, 11 (D)
Florence P. Dwyer, 12 (R)
Cornelius E. Gallagher,
13 (D)
Dominick V. Daniels,
14 (D)
Edward J. Patten, 15 (D)
New Mexico
Manuel Lujan, Jr., 1 (R)
Harold L. Runnels, 2 (D)
New York
Otis G. Pike, 1 (D)
James R. Grover, Jr., 2 (R)
Lester L. Wolff, 3 (D)
John W. Wydler, 4 (R)
Norman F. Lent, 5 (R)
Seymour Halpern, 6 (R)
Joseph P. Addabbo, 7 (D)
Benjamin S. Rosenthal,
8 (D)
James J. Delaney, 9 (D)
Emanuel Celler, 10 (D)
Frank J. Brasco, 11 (D)
Shirley Chisholm, 12 (D)
Bertram L. Podell, 13 (D)
John J. Rooney, 14 (D)
Hugh L. Carey, 15 (D)
John M. Murphy, 16 (D)
Edward I. Koch, 17 (D)
Charles Rangel, 18 (D)
Bella Abzug, 19 (D)
William F. Ryan, 20 (D)
Herman Badillo, 21 (D)

James H. Scheuer, 22 (D)
Jonathan B. Bingham,
23 (D)
Mario Biaggi, 24 (D)
Peter A. Peyser, 25 (R)
Ogden R. Reid, 26 (R)
John Dow, 27 (D)
Hamilton Fish, Jr., 28 (R)
Samuel S. Stratton, 29 (D)
Carleton J. King, 30 (R)
Robert C. McEwen, 31 (R)
Alexander Pirnie, 32 (R)
Howard W. Robison,
33 (R)
John H. Terry, 34 (R)
James M. Hanley, 35 (D)
Frank Horton, 36 (R)
Barber B. Conable, Jr.,
37 (R)
James F. Hastings, 38 (R)
Jack F. Kemp, 39 (R)
Henry P. Smith III, 40 (R)
Thaddeus J. Dulski, 41 (D)
North Carolina
Walter B. Jones, 1 (D)
L. H. Fountain, 2 (D)
David N. Henderson, 3 (D)
Nick Galifianakis, 4 (D)
Wilmer (Vinegar Bend)
Mizell, 5 (R)
Richardson Preyer, 6 (D)
Alton Lennon, 7 (D)
Earl B. Ruth, 8 (R)
Charles Raper Jonas,
9 (R)
James T. Broyhill, 10 (R)
Roy A. Taylor, 11 (D)
North Dakota
Mark Andrews, 1 (R)
Arthur A. Link, 2 (D)
Ohio
William J. Keating, 1 (R)
Donald D. Clancy, 2 (R)
Charles W. Whalen, Jr.,
3 (R)
William M. McCulloch,
4 (R)
Delbert L. Latta, 5 (R)
William H. Harsha, 6 (R)
Clarence J. Brown, 7 (R)
Jackson E. Betts, 8 (R)
Thomas L. Ashley, 9 (D)
Clarence E. Miller, 10 (R)
J. William Stanton, 11 (R)
Samuel L. Devine, 12 (R)
Charles A. Mosher, 13 (R)
John F. Seiberling, Jr.,
14 (D)
Chalmers P. Wylie, 15 (R)
Frank T. Bow, 16 (R)
John M. Ashbrook, 17 (R)
Wayne L. Hays, 18 (D)
Charles J. Carney, 19 (D)
James V. Stanton, 20 (D)
Louis Stokes, 21 (D)
Charles A. Vanik, 22 (D)
William E. Minshall, 23 (R)
Walter E. Powell, 24 (R)
Oklahoma
Page Belcher, 1 (R)
Ed Edmondson, 2 (D)

Carl Albert, 3 (D)
Tom Steed, 4 (D)
John Jarman, 5 (D)
John N. Happy Camp,
6 (R)
Oregon
Wendell Wyatt, 1 (R)
Al Ullman, 2 (D)
Edith Green, 3 (D)
John Dellenback, 4 (R)
Pennsylvania
William A. Barrett, 1 (D)
Robert N. C. Nix, 2 (D)
James A. Byrne, 3 (D)
Joshua Eilberg, 4 (D)
William J. Green, 5 (D)
Gus Yatron, 6 (D)
Lawrence G. Williams,
7 (R)
Edward G. Biester, Jr.,
8 (R)
John H. Ware III, 9 (R)
Joseph M. McDade, 10 (R)
Daniel J. Flood, 11 (D)
J. Irving Whalley, 12 (R)
R. Lawrence Coughlin,
13 (R)
William S. Moorhead,
14 (D)
Fred B. Rooney, 15 (D)
Edwin D. Eshleman, 16 (R)
Herman T. Schneebeli,
17 (R)
H. John Heinz III¶, 18 (R)
George A. Goodling, 19 (R)
Joseph M. Gaydos, 20 (D)
John H. Dent, 21 (D)
John P. Saylor, 22 (R)
Albert W. Johnson, 23 (R)
Joseph P. Vigorito, 24 (D)
Frank M. Clark, 25 (D)
Thomas E. Morgan, 26 (D)
** 27
Rhode Island
Fernand J. St. Germain,
1 (D)
Robert O. Tiernan, 2 (D)
South Carolina
Mendel J. Davis††, 1 (D)
Floyd Spence, 2 (R)
Wm. Jennings Bryan Dorn,
3 (D)
James R. Mann, 4 (D)
Tom S. Gettys, 5 (D)
John L. McMillan, 6 (D)
South Dakota
Frank E. Denholm, 1 (D)
James Abourezk, 2 (D)
Tennessee
James H. Quillen, 1 (R)
John J. Duncan, 2 (R)
LaMar Baker, 3 (R)
Joe L. Evins, 4 (D)
Richard Fulton, 5 (D)
William R. Anderson, 6 (D)
Ray Blanton, 7 (D)
Ed Jones, 8 (D)
Dan Kuykendall, 9 (R)
Texas
Wright Patman, 1 (D)
John Dowdy, 2 (D)

James M. Collins, 3 (R)
Ray Roberts, 4 (D)
Earle Cabell, 5 (D)
Olin E. Teague, 6 (D)
W. R. Archer, 7 (R)
Bob Eckhardt, 8 (D)
Jack Brooks, 9 (D)
J. J. Pickle, 10 (D)
W. R. Poage, 11 (D)
Jim Wright, 12 (D)
Graham Purcell, 13 (D)
John Young, 14 (D)
Eligio de la Garza, 15 (D)
Richard White, 16 (D)
Omar Burleson, 17 (D)
Robert Price, 18 (D)
George H. Mahon, 19 (D)
Henry B. Gonzalez,
20 (D)
O. C. Fisher, 21 (D)
Bob Casey, 22 (D)
Abraham Kazen, Jr.,
23 (D)
Utah
K. Gunn McKay, 1 (D)
Sherman P. Lloyd, 2 (R)
Vermont
‡‡ Richard W. Mallary (R)
Virginia
Thomas N. Downing, 1 (D)
G. William Whitehurst,
2 (R)
David E. Satterfield III,
3 (D)
Watkins M. Abbitt, 4 (D)
W. C. (Dan) Daniel, 5 (D)
Richard H. Poff, 6 (R)
J. Kenneth Robinson,
7 (R)
William Lloyd Scott, 8 (R)
William C. Wampler, 9 (R)
Joel T. Broyhill, 10 (R)
Washington
Thomas M. Pelly, 1 (R)
Lloyd Meeds, 2 (D)
Julia Butler Hansen, 3 (D)
C. G. (Mike) McCormack,
4 (D)
Thomas S. Foley, 5 (D)
Floyd V. Hicks, 6 (D)
Brock Adams, 7 (D)
West Virginia
Robert H. Mollohan, 1 (D)
Harley O. Staggers, 2 (D)
John M. Slack, 3 (D)
Ken Hechler, 4 (D)
James Kee, 5 (D)
Wisconsin
Les Aspin, 1 (D)
Robert W. Kastenmeier,
2 (D)
Vernon W. Thomson, 3 (R)
Clement J. Zablocki, 4 (D)
Henry S. Reuss, 5 (D)
William A. Steiger, 6 (R)
David R. Obey, 7 (D)
John W. Byrnes, 8 (R)
Glenn R. Davis, 9 (R)
Alvin E. O'Konski, 10 (R)
Wyoming
Teno Roncalio (D)

¶Elected in November 1971 to fill unexpired term of the late Robert J. Corbett (R).
**Vacancy caused by the death of James G. Fulton (R), Oct. 6, 1971.
††Elected in April 1971 to fill unexpired term of the late L. Mendel Rivers (D).
‡‡Elected in January 1972 to fill unexpired term of Robert T. Stafford (R).

CONSTRUCTION.

Inflationary costs within the United States construction industry—one of the nation's largest sectors of economic activity—continued to be of special concern during 1971 as they had been the previous year. As a result, in February, U.S. President Richard M. Nixon suspended the Davis-Bacon Act, which required that construction workers on most federal and federally aided construction projects be paid wages that the U.S. Department of Labor determined to be "prevailing" in the particular area. The prevailing wage usually was defined as the local union scale, which in many places was higher than rates paid for similar work performed by nonunion labor. Consequently the Davis-Bacon Act had discouraged competitive bidding on many federal projects, with regard to wages, by establishing a uniform local floor on these costs.

The suspension of the Davis-Bacon Act soon prompted labor and management leaders in the construction industry to participate more closely with the federal government in moderating wage and benefit settlements. In March Nixon reinstated the Davis-Bacon Act at the same time that he issued an executive order establishing a Construction Industry Stabilization Committee. The committee was set up to review all wage and benefit adjustments incorporated in collective bargaining agreements judged to be acceptable by local craft dispute boards. By early September the committee had

IVEY FROM BEN ROTH AGENCY

approved more than 500 settlements, and the level of wage increases had dropped sharply.

Cost pressures, however, remained high in the construction industry. Although wage and benefit increases during the first half of 1971 were smaller than in 1970, they still averaged as much as 14% over the life of the contract, compared with 8.3% in all industries. Construction materials also contributed to the general rise in construction costs during 1971. Wholesale prices of lumber, paint, iron and steel products, plumbing fixtures, and other materials in August averaged 8% above 1970 levels. Wholesale prices in all industries were up no more than 4%. In August, Nixon announced his sweeping new economic program involving a 90-day freeze on all wages and prices. (*See* Business and Industry; Economy.)

About 30% of all new construction outlays during the first eight months of 1971 were for publicly owned facilities erected for federal, state, or local governments. Another 30% was for private structures such as shopping centers, factories, and offices. The remainder was for housing, which was undergoing its biggest boom in 20 years. (*See* Housing.)

Efforts to bring more blacks and members of other minority groups into the construction craft unions continued to yield little success. The Chicago Plan, stressing voluntary efforts to open up the construction trades to minority groups, was dismissed by the Nixon Administration as a failure, though the Philadelphia Plan, involving a mandatory approach, had greater success. The unions'

An inflatable greenhouse covering one acre is located near Wooster, Ohio. Inflatable structures developed by Goodyear were being marketed by Environmental Structures, Inc.

COURTESY, THE GOODYEAR TIRE & RUBBER CO.

desire to maintain their select position in the labor market, the poor state of the economy, and the Administration's reluctance to vigorously enforce the civil rights laws were among the reasons cited for the lack of progress in this area.

Some exceptionally large projects continued under way in 1971 as developers sought to make the most of the economies of large-scale output in the face of rising construction costs. Work continued on the Sears Tower in Chicago, the world's tallest building (1,450 feet), and on the twin towers of the World Trade Center in New York City, the world's largest private office development (10 million square feet) of its type. (*See also* Economy. *See in* CE: Building Construction.)

CONSUMER PROTECTION. During 1971

consumers in the United States concentrated heavily on improving the enforcement of consumer protection laws already enacted. American industry continued to be the main target of consumer ire, but the federal regulatory agencies, especially the U.S. Federal Trade Commission (FTC) and the U.S. Food and Drug Administration (FDA), also came in for their share of criticism for inefficiency in enforcing the various consumer protection laws and for tending to have an industry, rather than a consumer, point of view. The new laws that consumer lobbies sought to have enacted were mostly concerned with improving enforcement, giving the consumer a better chance to make use of the courts, or eliminating loopholes in existing legislation. The shift in emphasis from legislation to enforcement doubtlessly reflected consumer disappointment at the slow pace of reform and continuation of the threat to life, health, and pocketbook from business practices the public thought had been outlawed.

As individuals, consumers continued to show their frustration by their sales resistance in the face of Madison Avenue's best efforts. Growing numbers of Americans, especially the young, rebelled against what they called the junk culture and simply refused to buy. More consumers than ever before sought to utilize their opportunities for what they felt was a more rational method of product selection, by consulting the reports of independent testing and evaluating organizations. The circulation of the magazine *Consumer Reports,* for example, reached two million in 1971, just double its 1965 circulation. The cooperative movement exhibited new growth during 1971 in the areas of food, housing, credit, and group health insurance. (*See* Cooperatives.)

Consumer protest groups proliferated at every level. By the end of 1971 the Consumer Federation of America, Inc. (CFA)—the umbrella organization founded in 1967 whose member groups included 196 area, state, and regional consumer organizations, cooperatives, and labor unions—could speak for an estimated 30 million individual consumers. At its two-day national assembly in Washington, D.C., in January, the CFA adopted as its top national priorities: an independent consumer advocate in the government, U.S. Congressional sanction of consumer class actions, and reforms in auto insurance. Next in order of importance came lower prices and interest rates, more economical health services delivery, and opposition to high tariffs.

Ralph Nader's Crusade

Consumer advocate Ralph Nader's crusade in behalf of the U.S. consumer continued to flourish and expand in 1971. His efforts and those of the hundreds of students, engineers, lawyers, and scientists who had flocked to his standard—working for little or no pay to attack shoddy merchandise, inefficient service, or neglect of consumer safety—had coalesced into an organization in 1969, the Center for Study of Responsive Law in Washington, D.C. In the past Nader had supported the

Ralph Nader (right) and U.S. Rep. Benjamin S. Rosenthal (D, N.Y.) discuss a bill to create a Consumer Protection Agency. Rosenthal had originally cosponsored the bill but voted against it after key amendments broadening the agency's powers were defeated in committee.

WIDE WORLD

effort financially through foundation money, supplemented by his earnings from writing and lecturing. In 1971, however, Nader went to the public for financing, asking, by direct mail and newspaper advertisements, for donations of $15 or more. He hoped to receive $1 million.

The Nader groups included the Center for Auto Safety; Consumer Action for Improved Foods; the Aviation Consumer Action Project; public interest research groups in Washington, D.C., Connecticut, and Ohio; and a corporate accountability research group. The last was a clearinghouse where people who worked for corporations and government agencies could "blow the whistle" on their employers' wrongdoings in confidence. There were also student groups in seven states, with other groups in the process of formation. In 1971 Nader traveled to Japan, France, and Great Britain to help set up similar groups there.

By the end of the year, the Nader organizations had published major reports covering auto safety, the Interstate Commerce Commission, the FTC, the FDA, air pollution, water pollution, defective cars, and self-regulation in the medical profession. Also published were reports on the U.S. Department of Agriculture, antitrust enforcement, and occupational safety. A major undertaking announced for 1972 was a one-year study of the workings of the U.S. Congress. During the year the central group streamlined its staff to make it less dependent on students and volunteers. Its main thrust was redirected toward political action.

Industry's Response

In general, U.S. business sought to restore consumer confidence by showing a genuine concern for the barrage of criticism in 1971. The National Council of Better Business Bureaus, many of which were accused of having deteriorated into mere window-dressing operations, announced a major overhaul of member organizations. The council also joined with three major advertising groups in a National Advertising Review Board to undertake self-policing of ad content. Individual advertisers also began enriching the information content of their ad copy. Whirlpool Corp., which had started a "Cool-Line" in 1967 for toll-free calls to company headquarters from purchasers of its products, logged about 20,000 such calls in 1971, and other appliance manufacturers set up similar services. Chrysler Corp. created an Office of Public Responsibility and appointed the auto industry's first official ombudsman, "Your Man in Detroit," to deal directly with buyer complaints. Some grocery chains started dating perishable items so that customers could tell how fresh the items actually were, and a few also began experimenting with nutritional labeling as an aid to customers.

It was clear that the vanguard of industry was awakening to a need for action in 1971, but not all businessmen recognized the consumer revolt. Much of this negative reaction to consumerism was directed at the most visible independent consumer spokesman, Ralph Nader. For example,

Elliot Richardson, U.S. secretary of health, education, and welfare, appeared before the Senate Commerce Committee in July to propose the conversion of the Food and Drug Administration into a new Consumer Safety Administration. The new agency would have authority over household products as well as food and drugs.
UPI COMPIX

A New York City supermarket manager explains the system of unit pricing used by his store. A New York City ordinance made unit pricing mandatory. Middle-income shoppers made the greatest use of the system, which helps shoppers determine the relative values of different-sized packages of the same product.

"THE NEW YORK TIMES"

James M. Roche, chairman of the board of General Motors Corp., refused to confront Nader in a debate over company policies, saying that business should avoid the "adversary culture." C. W. Cook, chairman of the board of General Foods Corp., represented another negative industry point of view when he said that "the economic cost of industry's response to consumerists' pressure would either raise consumer prices to a prohibitive level or inhibit our ability to generate required profits—or both—with possible permanent damage to this nation's productive mechanism."

Government Response

All levels of government—federal, state, and local—found it politically opportune to respond in some way to consumer dissatisfaction during the year. Although not regarded as a strong consumer advocate, U.S. President Richard M. Nixon in February upgraded the President's Committee on Consumer Interests, making it the Office of Consumer Affairs. The new office was charged with analyzing and coordinating the consumer activities of all federal agencies and departments; advising the Administration on consumer policy; and directly handling consumer complaints.

Nixon also outlined a special consumer program to Congress in February. He proposed empowering the FTC not only to represent consumers as their advocate, in court and before other federal agencies, but also to seek preliminary injunctions to stop apparently unfair practices; and giving the U.S. Department of Health, Education, and Welfare, the power to establish and enforce safety standards for consumer goods. The president also

called for higher penalties for fraud and deception; class-action suits that would permit access to federal courts for consumers suing for damages (but only after successful prosecution of the offender by the federal government); identification coding of all drug tablets and capsules to cut down on errors; more explicit guarantees and warranties couched in simpler language; and a study of ways to improve handling of small claims and voluntary settlements.

Little consumer legislation was actually enacted by Congress in 1971, but it was clear that Congress, under pressure from consumer lobbies, was ready to go even farther than the president in pushing through strong consumer legislation. In October the House of Representatives overwhelmingly passed a bill to create an independent agency to represent the interests of consumers. (*See also* Congress, U.S.)

The various federal regulatory agencies made strenuous efforts during the year to refute accusations that they represented the industries they were supposed to regulate rather than the public. The FTC, for example, sought to broaden its rules so that they would cover entire industries. The commission undertook a major study of the advertising industry and at midyear was asking more manufacturers to produce proof of their advertising claims. The FTC also began insisting that some major advertisers whose ads had created a lasting false impression on the public devote a percentage of future advertising space to correcting that impression.

The FDA completed in 1971 a major reexamination of prescription drugs being sold; in November 1970 it had published a list of 369 that were ineffective or probably ineffective. A review and revision of the list of food additives "generally regarded as safe" was completed. The FDA's new Bureau of Product Safety started work in 1971 on reducing the annual 30,000 deaths and 20 million injuries from accidents involving consumer products by identifying more than 140 hazardous toys and banning them from the market. It also prepared regulations requiring "childproof" packaging for dangerous household items (such as liquid drain cleaners and furniture polish).

The U.S. Department of Commerce set a new strict flammability standard for children's sleepwear. By July 30, 1973, pajamas, nightgowns, bathrobes, and other sleepwear in sizes up through 6X had to be flame resistant. And finally, after long prodding by consumer groups, the General Services Administration (GSA), the federal government's civilian purchasing agent, published its first list of brand names of the products it buys. The list, which included 350 products used by the government, was to be updated quarterly as a service to consumers. (*See also* Advertising; Automobiles; Drugs; Food; Insurance; Safety. *See also* Feature Article: "Your Vanishing Privacy.")

COOPERATIVES.
In 1971 cooperatives continued to thrive in the United States. The young people on farms responded to programs offered by farmer cooperatives, programs that emphasized the value of working for common goals through cooperation. The young in the U.S. higher educational system turned to cooperation as an alternative to the things they regard as wrong in their society and as a less expensive way to get through college. Housing cooperatives were the major cooperative enterprises for students. In addition to being less expensive, these afforded the participants an oppor-

tunity to work together in running a house or apartment. Other ventures included dining co-ops, bike co-ops, grocery store co-ops, and book co-ops.

Elsewhere, farmer co-ops continued as the nation's prime example of the worth of cooperative enterprise. Together, farmer co-ops did about one third of the business on farms in the U.S.—or more than $17-billion worth. Much of the credit needed to carry on this business is derived from a farmer-owned cooperative credit system called the Farm Credit System. Farmers borrowed $13.6 billion through the system in 1971.

Group health cooperatives, where people prepay for complete medical care, grew rapidly as the result of the high cost of medical care. Approximately $75 billion was spent on medical care in the U.S. in 1971. (*See in* CE: Co-operative Societies.)

COSMETICS.
In the spring and summer of 1971 an allover suntan was safe enough, but in the fall, the cosmetics industry began offering preparations designed to make female complexions reflect the healthy glow of an outdoor life. Pomades and fingertips replaced powder and brushes as appropriate implements, for color was now to be dabbed on cheekbones, with the effect a glazed rather than a matte finish. Lipstick, which previously had been offered in subdued tones, became brilliantly colored, but by remaining transparent avoided the harsh look of the 1930's. The new cosmetic colors were attuned to the new deep, rich tones of fashion and were coordinated for cheeks, eyes, lips, and nails. Nail polish echoed the rich shades of the lipsticks and lip color was intended to complement or match eye shadow. Eyebrows were plucked and drawn into a curve, with lashes shaggy or spider-like.

Members of a food cooperative in Boston, Mass., make their purchases at a wholesale market. About 1,200 Bostonians belonged to 17 co-ops, most of them set up in the past two years.

ALBIE WALTON

There were also major changes in hair styles, from curls and waves in the spring to a healthy, natural look in the fall, with hair cut medium-long and often parted in the middle. Back-combing finally disappeared.

The continuing "consumer revolution" had its effects in the U.S. cosmetics industry. On March 25 the industry, in response to consumer concern about the safety of ingredients used in cosmetics, submitted a proposal to the U.S. Food and Drug Administration offering to reveal their secret ingredients for safety evaluation. Another reflection of consumer concern was the increased interest in pure, allergen-free products and in natural or organic products—vegetable beauty baths, avocado moisturizers, and wheat-germ-oil lipsticks. In December *Consumer Reports* magazine suggested that women stop using vaginal deodorant sprays, which can be painful and dangerous. The manufacturers of these sprays had insisted that they were cosmetics, not drugs; thus the sprays had not been tested by the federal government.

COSTA RICA. In 1971 Costa Rica's trade relations worsened because of a balance of payments deficit. There was an overall deficit of $9.6 million in 1970, compared with a previous surplus of $18 million.

In an effort to improve the financial situation, a dual rate of exchange was reintroduced in June, and customs guarantees were required on some imports from other countries in the Central American Common Market (CACM). However, to prevent a complete breakdown of the CACM, the customs restrictions were later dropped. After a series of meetings were held, a Commission for the Normalization of the Common Market was set up to regulate relations between Costa Rica, Nicaragua, El Salvador, and Guatemala.

A large coffee surplus and no immediate prospect of increasing sales to Western countries prompted the development of trade relations with Eastern Europe. The Soviet Union offered $200 million in credit to be used only to buy Soviet machinery, equipment, and manufactured goods.

The possible establishment of a Soviet Embassy in Costa Rica became a major political issue. President José Figuéres Ferrer favored the idea, believing that it would strengthen the Costa Rican export drive. However, because of strong opposition the government decided to suspend establishment of the embassy. (*See in* CE: Costa Rica.)

CRIME. Bombings in the United States continued to present a serious crime problem in 1971. On January 7 in Pomona, Calif., a fire bomb caused $50,000 damage to the Camp Fire Girls headquarters; on January 8 a small bomb exploded outside the Soviet cultural building in Washington, D.C.; and on March 1 a bomb exploded in the U.S. Capitol. On April 27 in Washington, D.C., Federal Bureau of Investigation (FBI) agents arrested a

ARNOLD SACHS FROM PICTORIAL PARADE

This wall in the U.S. Capitol building was damaged by a bomb blast in March. An anonymous phone call predicted the explosion.

19-year-old girl, Leslie Bacon of Atherton, Calif., as a material witness in the bombing of the Capitol. A federal grand jury in New York City on June 24, 1971, returned an indictment that charged Miss Bacon with having conspired to fire-bomb a Manhattan bank. Six other persons were named in the indictment as co-conspirators.

Some airplane hijackings in 1971 involved fatal shootings. On July 23 a Trans World Airlines (TWA) jet, with 55 passengers and a crew of 5, left New York City's La Guardia Airport for Chicago. A hijacker placed a gun at the back of a stewardess, Idíe Maria Concepcion, and forced her to accompany him to the cockpit, where he ordered the captain, Albert R. Hawes, to take the plane to Milan, Italy. Upon being informed that the plane was not equipped for such a flight, the hijacker agreed to return to La Guardia Airport, where, upon landing, he took the stewardess and a driver as hostages on a nine-mile shuttle to John F. Kennedy International Airport. As the hijacker, hold-

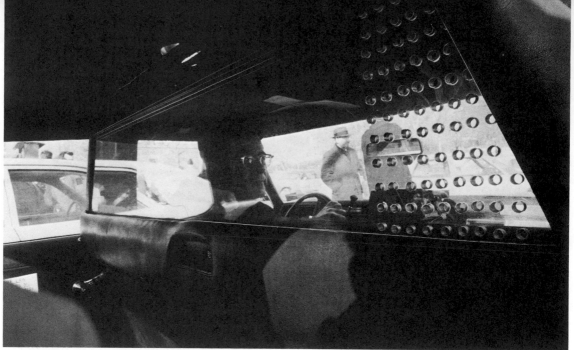

By order of the Police Department's hack bureau, all New York City taxis now have nonmovable bulletproof partitions, armored backs for front seats, and locked cashboxes.

ing a gun at the back of the stewardess, approached a waiting TWA jet, an FBI agent, using a rifle with a telescopic sight, shot and killed him. From papers found in his possession, the man was identified as Richard A. Obergfell, 26, of Passaic, N.J. The Federal Aviation Administration stated this was the first fatal shooting of a hijacker in the U.S.

Sheriff's deputies search for buried murder victims along the Feather River near Yuba City, Calif. The bodies of 25 transient farm workers were uncovered in May and June.

At O'Hare International Airport in Chicago on June 11, a TWA jetliner was taking on passengers when a stewardess turned away a man because he did not have a boarding pass. This man, later identified as Gregory White, 23, of Harvey, Ill., pulled a .38-caliber revolver and demanded that he be flown to North Vietnam and be given $75,000 in cash as well as a machine gun. At this point, a passenger on the plane, Howard L. Franks, 65, a Darien, Conn., executive, moved and the hijacker fired two shots, killing Franks. A deputy federal marshal, Joseph Zito, donned a TWA uniform and succeeded in climbing into the plane for the purpose of aiding the crew. While the plane was en route to New York City, shots were exchanged between the hijacker and Zito and a crew member. Upon landing at Kennedy Airport, the plane was met by police and FBI agents. Shots were exchanged between the officers and the hijacker. One shot, fired by an FBI agent, struck the hijacker in the left arm. White was taken into custody, and on June 29 in Chicago, he pleaded not guilty to federal charges of kidnapping and hijacking. He also faced assault charges in New York City.

In November a hijacker of a Northwest Airlines plane demanded a ransom of $200,000 and four parachutes, which he was given when the plane landed in Seattle, Wash., and discharged its passengers. Then, somewhere en route to Reno, Nev., the hijacker evidently parachuted from the plane. A ground search uncovered no evidence of him.

In testimony before the U.S. Senate Permanent Subcommittee on Investigations in June 1971, Attorney General John N. Mitchell stated that by "conservative estimate" more than $500-million worth of securities had been stolen in the preceding two years, much of it by organized crime. Counterfeiting of securities also became serious.

Crime rates on U.S. college campuses were rising, according to surveys conducted in 1971. Campuses, once relatively free of crime, were experiencing grand larceny, armed robbery, assault, murder, and rape.

There were several instances of multiple killings during the year. In Cleveland, Ohio, on the night of March 6, a long-smoldering grudge between two motorcycle gangs broke into the open, and 5 persons were killed and more than 20 injured. In California, during May and June, the dead bodies of 25 transient farm workers were found buried in the soft earth of peach orchards along the Feather River just outside the Sacramento Valley farming center. The bodies appeared to have the same type of deep lacerations about the heads and puncture wounds in the chests. On July 12 Juan V. Corona, a 37-year-old Mexican-American farm-labor contractor, was indicted in Yuba City, Calif., by the Sutter County grand jury and charged with the murders.

In Detroit, Mich., on June 14, the police received a call from a woman who reported she had found her husband seriously wounded in a house at 1790 Hazelwood and had taken him to a hospital. "There's a bloodbath in that house," she said. Upon entering, the police found seven persons— three young men and four young women—shot to death. In the house were found five handguns and five long guns, including a sawed-off shotgun, as well as instruments used by heroin addicts.

The longest criminal trial in California history ended in Los Angeles on Jan. 25, 1971, when Charles M. Manson and three young women who were members of his hippie "family" were found guilty of five murders that took place in August 1969 at the home of actress Sharon Tate and of the murders of Mr. and Mrs. Leno LaBianca that took place in their home in the Los Feliz district of Los Angeles. On March 29, Manson, Susan Atkins, 22, Patricia Krenwinkel, 23, and Leslie Van Houten, 21, were sentenced to death in the gas chamber. On October 12 Charles (Tex) Watson, whose testimony stated that he shot or stabbed six of the victims, was convicted of first degree murder and sentenced to the gas chamber.

On November 13, Aubran W. Martin, 23, was sentenced to death for his part in the murder of United Mine Workers official Joseph A. Yablonski and Yablonski's wife and daughter. Four others implicated in the murder remained to be tried.

After three trials that ended inconclusively, Black Panther party co-founder Huey P. Newton was finally freed of charges of manslaughter on December 15. (*See also* Race Relations.)

On February 26 a federal jury in Brooklyn, N.Y., acquitted Joseph Colombo, Jr., and Joseph Ianacci on charges that they had conspired to melt U.S. silver coins into more valuable ingots. A third defendant, David Lennard, was found guilty of the same charge. A witness, Richard W. Salomone, 27, a former coin dealer, had originally implicated the defendants but recanted his testimony and was arrested after the trial for perjury.

On March 5 Joseph Colombo, Sr., the reputed head of one of New York's five organized crime Mafia-type families, was arrested with five other persons in connection with the theft three years earlier of $750,000 in jewels in Nassau County, N.Y. Three days later, Colombo was released from the

A Federal Bureau of Investigation (FBI) agent (at fence) takes deadly aim at a hijacker approaching a trans-Atlantic jet at the John F. Kennedy International Airport in July. The hijacker, who was holding a stewardess as hostage, had demanded to go to Italy.

WIDE WORLD

Nassau County Jail, and within a few hours he joined a group of demonstrators from the Italian-American Civil Rights League in picketing the FBI offices in New York City. On March 11 Colombo, Sr., was sentenced by a State Supreme Court to serve one to two and a half years in prison following conviction on perjury charges.

On June 28 the second annual Unity Day rally of the Italian-American Civil Rights League was held in Manhattan's Columbus Circle. As the senior Colombo, the unofficial leader and chief promotor of the league, moved through the crowd, joking and posing for photographers, shots rang out. Colombo crumpled to the ground from gunshot wounds in the head and neck and was rushed to a hospital. Almost immediately a second volley of shots struck and killed Colombo's assailant, identified as Jerome Johnson, 24, a black photographer who only seconds before had been filming Colombo. Johnson's killer disappeared, although police were present as he shot the photographer three times.

In Attica, N.Y., on September 9, one of the worst prisoner uprisings in U.S. history broke out at the state correctional facility. When it was over, 38 men—9 hostages and 29 prisoners—were dead (5 more died later). (*See also* Police; Prisons; Prisons Special Report. *See in* CE: Prisons and Punishments.)

CUBA. During 1971 Cuba continued to enjoy political stability though little economic progress was made. For the sixth consecutive year sugar production fell short of the official target. The Soviet Union continued as Cuba's principal trading partner, and the two countries again signed trade and payment agreements. Relations between the United States and Cuba remained unchanged, but the U.S. watched closely for signs of any Soviet military buildup in Cuba. There were, however, growing indications that many Latin American countries wished to end the diplomatic and commercial isolation imposed upon Cuba by the Organization of American States (OAS).

Premier Fidel Castro called for a year of productivity as the economic situation continued to deteriorate. The 1971 sugar crop amounted to 5.9 million metric tons against a target of 7 million; the 1970 harvest was 8.5 million metric tons against a 10-million ton goal. Coffee, citrus fruit, and tobacco crop production were lower than in 1970 mainly because of a severe drought. Large numbers of Cubans were conscripted for harvesting, and Deputy Prime Minister Raúl Castro threatened to send 6- to 16-year-old school dropouts to work in the cane fields. Cigars and cigarettes were added to the rationed list, which, since 1962, has covered almost all food and manufactured goods.

Soviet economic aid to Cuba was estimated at $500 million per year, and the total Cuban debt stood at $5.7 billion. In October Soviet Premier Aleksei N. Kosygin visited Havana, Cuba's capital. He reportedly discussed United States President Richard M. Nixon's planned visits to Peking, People's Republic of China, and Moscow and reassured Castro of the Soviet Union's continued support of the Castro government.

The U.S. continued to seek assurances that the Soviet Union still adhered to the agreement of 1962 forbidding the installation of offensive-weapons systems in the Caribbean area. Estimates put at least 7,000 Russian technicians in Cuba, and the U.S. watched closely visits by the Soviet navy to Cuban waters.

On September 1 the Cuban government suspended the refugee airlift between Havana and Miami, Fla. Since 1965 about 246,000 people had arrived in Florida through the twice-daily, five-day-

Premier Fidel Castro of Cuba addresses the final session of the 13th Congress of Sugar Workers. A new National Union of Sugar Workers was created at this meeting.
KEYSTONE

per-week flights. U.S. officials reported that more than 127,000 others remained on the waiting list to leave. Cuba's decision to end the flights was seen as a move to prevent the loss of skilled personnel. However, on September 23 it was announced that the airlift would be temporarily restored.

Four Cuban fishing boats were seized off Florida in February for fishing in U.S. waters. They were exchanged in July for 13 Americans held by Cuba for allowing their boats to violate the jurisdictional waters of Cuba. In December U.S.-Cuban tension heightened when Cuba seized in international waters a ship owned by Cuban exiles and captained by a naturalized U.S. citizen. Cuba claimed the vessel was actually a U.S. spy ship.

Relations with Latin American governments improved in 1971. Peru and Bolivia were considering the resumption of diplomatic ties with Cuba. The governments of Chile and Cuba, having restored diplomatic relations in late 1970, signed a technical and scientific cooperation agreement in August. At an OAS meeting held in San José, Costa Rica, in April, there was considerable pressure on the U.S. to end economic sanctions. In late 1971 Castro made a visit to Chile where he was warmly received by Chile's democratically-elected Marxist president, Salvador Allende Gossens. It was Castro's first visit to another Latin American nation since he became premier.

Cuban support for guerrilla movements in Latin America appeared to cool. Official policy was directed toward change in other Latin nations through constitutional means to repeat the Chilean success. (*See in* CE: Cuba.)

CYPRUS. Renewed tension, prompted by failure to reach accord, marked the relations between Greek and Turkish Cypriots in 1971. The Turks sought autonomous control of their own communities. The Greeks tried to achieve agreement on a government in which they, as the majority, would control the whole island nation.

In June the Greek government proposed to President Makarios that a Turkish Cypriot be named a minister in the Cyprus cabinet. The Turkish government encouraged this proposal because this minister's role would embody a concession to the Turkish Cypriots. The Athens government hinted that its troops would be withdrawn from Cyprus if Makarios refused the proposal. He did refuse, risking a solitary confrontation with Turkey.

To counter this refusal, Greece and Turkey threatened an imposed solution in which each nation would annex its own respective ethnic community. In an effort to block that move, Makarios went to the United Nations and the U.S.S.R. for their support.

On September 1, 1971, Gen. George Grivas traveled secretly from Greece to Cyprus. This trip, forbidden by the Greek government, greatly heightened tension in Cyprus. General Grivas was

President Makarios cuts through the ribbon to officially open the Cyprus International Fair in September.

leader of the Greek Cypriot extremists who sought Cyprus' union with Greece. Cypriot newspapers claimed that the general intended to renew his old struggle. Military reprisal by Turkey was feared. (*See in* CE: Cyprus.)

CZECHOSLOVAKIA. Throughout 1971 Czechoslovakia's situation remained fundamentally unchanged—Communist Party General Secretary Gustav Husak consolidated his position and Soviet troops continued to occupy the country. The resultant political apathy among the people contributed to the country's economic stagnation.

At the beginning of the year the federalization program, designed to create Czech and Slovak states within the republic, became a meaningless formal arrangement when the federal government was given powers to override decisions of the separate Czech and Slovak governments. Husak undertook the change, including a return of most economic decision-making to the central government, as part of his economic efficiency plan.

The purge of those considered politically "unreliable" continued. At the congress of the Slovak Communist party, which met in May, it was announced that 17.5% of the party membership in Slovakia had been purged as "right-wing opportunists." The total expelled from the party throughout Czechoslovakia was given at more than 300,000, about 20% of party membership.

The 14th Czechoslovak Communist party congress was held in Prague, the capital, May 25–29. It was considered the first official party congress since 1966; the dramatic "14th congress," organized the day after the Soviet-led invasion in August 1968, had been stigmatized as illegal. The congress seemed to complete the transformation of Czechoslovakia's President Ludvik Svoboda, who had been one of the heroes of the 1968 reforms, into a "loyal" Soviet supporter. In his opening speech, with Soviet Communist Party General Secretary Leonid I. Brezhnev in the audience, Svoboda thanked the Soviet Union for its "assistance" in 1968. Husak, in his speech, also spoke of the inevitability of the Soviet intervention.

In November the first national elections in seven years were held. The 99.8% vote for the party slate was viewed by the Czechoslovak leadership as an endorsement of the party's pro-Soviet line.

The wrath of the diehards in the Czechoslovak party leadership during the year was directed mainly against the intellectuals, who were blamed for the ideological infection that caused the 1968 crisis. Expulsions from the journalists' union were reported with continuing regularity. The Historical Institute of the Czechoslovak Academy of Sciences had virtually ceased to exist, and more than 230 historians were either driving trucks or working in factories or on the railways. In July the historian Jaroslav Sedivy and the former head of the Czechoslovak film industry, Alois Polednak, were convicted and sentenced for subversion. The remarkable reputation of the Czechoslovak cinema disintegrated, and censorship in the theater was used to mutilate works not only by Molière and Shakespeare, but also by the Marxist playwright Bertolt Brecht. A play on the French commune was banned entirely. A new Union of Czech Journalists was set up in May, and a committee was later established to prepare the formation of a new Actors' Union. Perhaps the most obvious manifestations of the regime's thirst for revenge were the persecution of the chess champion Ludek Pachman and the retrial of the journalist Vladmir Skutina, sentenced in February to two years imprisonment for criticizing government policy and brought back in July to receive an additional sentence of 26 months for similar offenses.

The languishing state of the Czechoslovak economy was a reflection of the country's general condition. The 7.5% increase in industrial production reported in 1970 meant very little when adjusted to rising prices. Wages rose by 3.6% in 1970, and the cost of living went up by 1.4%. A 3% rise in savings was recorded. Husak's need to win workers' support made it difficult to adopt policies aimed at containing wage inflation. Pressures from the Soviet Union seemed directed toward a return to old priorities in economic management. The economic development plan for 1971–75, made public in April, forecast an expansion of heavy engineering and a doubling of machine-tool production, but there was some effort made to improve the supply of consumer goods, and the directives for 1971–75 indicated an emphasis on further improvements.

In foreign policy the government cautiously followed the Soviet lead. It was thought that Husak's visit to the Soviet Union in January included some discussion of the consequences of the treaties concluded in 1970 by West Germany with the Soviet Union and with Poland as part of West German Chancellor Willy Brandt's *Ostpolitik* (Eastern policy), aimed at lessening East-West tension. In the case of Czechoslovakia, however, talks with West Germany on the normalization of relations proceeded slowly. (*See in* CE: Czechoslovakia.)

DAHOMEY. In striking contrast with the atmosphere of political unrest that had disrupted Dahomey's domestic affairs in previous years, 1971 was a year of calm. The foundation of this stability was the "troika" political arrangement worked out in 1970 under which the country's three most influential civilian politicians agreed to rotate the presidency among themselves every two years. While one politician served as president, the other two formed an advisory "presidential council." In 1971 Hubert Maga was the country's president.

With political calm, attention could be focused on the economy. The 1971 budget, a record $35 million, provided for the implementation of various social and educational projects, including the completion of the University of Dahomey. Among the year's economic improvements were an increase in agricultural exports, the completion of a cement plant, and initial work on a cotton mill and a cashew nut processing factory. In May the government concluded a nine-year agreement with the Shell Oil Co. for oil prospecting. Although offshore petroleum exploration had begun in Dahomey in 1965 and some oil deposits had been discovered, no actual exploitation had yet taken place. (*See in* CE: Dahomey.)

DANCE. In 1971 Ted Shawn's immeasurable contribution to dance in the United States was honored at a party celebrating his 80th birthday, given by the Dance Collection of the New York City Public Library and the Museum of Performing Arts at Lincoln Center. Shawn, who made his debut as a dancer in 1911, was very probably the first American male dancer to make an international reputation in the 20th century. He choreographed major innovative works, produced the first all-male group dance in modern times, and presided over the building of the first theater built for dance, the Ted Shawn Theater near Lee, Mass., the site of Shawn's world-famous Jacob's Pillow Dance Festival. His marriage to Ruth St. Denis, also a celebrated dancer, led to the founding of the Denishawn schools and companies, the most influential organizations in dance in the U.S. from 1915 to 1931. Products of Denishawn included Martha Graham, Doris Humphrey, and Charles Weidman.

Dancers of the City Center Joffrey Ballet rehearse a movement from 'Trinity' before their opening performance in London in May. Their appearance at the London Coliseum marked the first time the famous American company had danced on a London stage.

CENTRAL PRESS FROM PICTORIAL PARADE

Major Dance Events in the U.S.

Dance festivals continued to function as showcases for many U.S. companies. The 39th year of the Jacob's Pillow Dance Festival included performances by the Northeast Regional Ballet Festival, with 11 member companies represented. The 24th year of the American Dance Festival, sponsored by Connecticut College at New London, Conn., featured modern dance, including the first East Coast appearance of one of California's leading dancers, Bella Lewitzky, and her company. The New York Dance Festival, held annually in the open-air Delacorte Theater in New York City's Central Park, offered examples of ballet, modern dance, ethnic dance, and the avant-garde by numerous groups in programs free to the public.

In Washington, D.C., the John F. Kennedy Center for the Performing Arts was inaugurated with Leonard Bernstein's 'Mass', for which Alvin Ailey provided the choreography and dancers. The American Ballet Theatre (ABT), the Center's official dance troupe, played an inaugural season followed by Ailey's American Dance Theater, the National Ballet of Washington, D.C., and an Afro-Asian Dance Festival.

To its repertoire the ABT added several new works—Agnes de Mille's 'A Rose for Miss Emily', Michael Smuin's 'Schubertiade', and Dennis Nahat's 'Mendelssohn Symphony'. Eliot Feld returned to the ABT as a choreographer following the disbanding of his own group, the short-lived American Ballet Company, which could not survive financial difficulties.

The Brooklyn Academy of Music presided over the final New York City season of Feld's company, featuring premieres of the choreographer's 'Romance', 'Theatre', and 'The Gods Amused'. The Academy also offered a well-received Afro-Asian Dance Festival featuring national groups from Senegal, Cambodia, Iran, Morocco, and Sierra Leone.

The major addition to the repertory season of the New York City Ballet was a polished version of Jerome Robbins' 'The Goldberg Variations', which was an instant hit. The City Center Joffrey Ballet increased its repertoire by eight ballets. Revivals of George Balanchine's 'Square Dance', Ailey's 'Feast of Ashes', and Stuart Hodes' 'Abyss' were presented. The Joffrey premiered 'Reflections', 'Valentine', and 'Kettentanz' by Gerald Arpino (the company's principal choreographer); Ailey's 'The Mingus Dances'; and Margo Sappington's 'Weewis'. Joffrey II, the organization's junior group, appeared on tour and for invited audiences in New York City.

The ANTA Theater in New York City featured the City Center American Dance Season with the Alvin Ailey American Dance Theater, the Dance Theatre of Harlem, and Pearl Lang, Louis Falco, Paul Taylor, Alwin Nikolais, Eleo Pomare, Erick Hawkins, Don Redlich, and their companies. Later in the year, the Ailey troupe, after extensive tours, gave a late fall season at the New York City Center.

Dance Events in Europe

In Great Britain the Royal Ballet, which had undergone a major change of structure in 1970 under its new artistic director Kenneth MacMillan, had a busy year. In the early part of the 1970–71 season at Covent Garden in London, Robbins mounted his enormously successful 'Dances at a Gathering'. Other works added to the regular repertoire in-

George Balanchine introduced a satirical work called 'PAMTGG' for the New York City Ballet. The title is taken from the commercial theme, "Pan Am Makes the Going Great."

The Dance Theatre of Harlem and the New York City Ballet combined forces for a one-time performance of 'Concerto for Jazz Band and Orchestra' in May.

cluded the successful revival of Sir Frederick Ashton's 'Creatures of Prometheus', a revival of 'Swan Lake' (an amalgamation of previous productions), and MacMillan's 'Anastasia'. The new Royal Ballet touring group, which was successful in the English provinces, featured such works as Dame Ninette de Valois' 'The Rake's Progress', Ashton's 'Symphonic Variations', and Balanchine's 'Apollo'.

Ballet Rambert enlarged its repertoire as well as its activities. Norman Morrice, the company's director, contributed two new works, 'The Empty Suit' and 'That Is the Show'. Works were also created by dancers in the company, and several pieces were added to Ballet Rambert's very popular children's show, 'Bertram Batell's Sideshow'.

The London Contemporary Dance Theatre, Britain's first company based on Martha Graham's techniques, also expanded its repertoire. The two most important works from Robert Cohan, the artistic director, were 'Consolation of the Rising Moon' (to guitar music arranged and played by John Williams), and a mixed-media work, 'Stages', that employed several levels, projections, and moving objects.

The Netherlands was once again a main focus for creative work. One of the major offerings in the Netherlands Dance Theater repertoire was the nude ballet 'Mutations', which was a spectacular hit during the company's London season. (*See in* CE: Ballet; Dance.)

DEFENSE. The major strategic development of 1971 was the Soviet's Union's imminent displacement of the United States as the global superpower, self-confidently increasing its military strength and political influence throughout the world. America's belief in its need or ability to fulfill a global military role had been declining since it first realized that it was unlikely to win the Vietnam war, and the cumulative effects, combined with continuing domestic problems, had created a snowballing loss of willpower. This was symbolized by the U.S. Senate's rejection in October of the 25-year-old foreign aid program, later restored in a truncated form.

As the U.S. retreated, the Soviet Union sought to replace American with Soviet influence. Historic treaties signed with Egypt and India represented the first pledge of Soviet military support to major regional powers outside the Soviet sphere of control in Europe, Cuba being a special case. Unlike the U.S. strategy of the early 1950's, the Soviet expansion remained cautious, confined to those areas of fairly well-defined Soviet interest: the Middle East, Cuba, and India. As in Europe, the Soviets seemed to follow a stepping-stone strategy, securing one country before moving on to the next; acquiescing in their allies' suppression of local Communist parties, the Soviets concentrated on diplomatic alignment rather than internal control.

In the Middle East there was a growing number of Soviet instructors and advisers: 15,000–20,000 in Egypt; 1,500 in Algeria; 1,000 in Syria; and, until the failed coup, 1,000 in the Sudan. They were supported by the Soviet navy, whose helicopter cruisers *Moskva* and *Leningrad* could act as commando carriers in conjunction with the 15,000-man naval infantry, the Soviet equivalent of the U.S. Marines.

U.S. Policies

U.S. Secretary of Defense Melvin R. Laird made a posture statement in March, describing the new American strategy as one of "realistic deterrence." The position of the Administration of U.S. President Richard M. Nixon was that the U.S. could not financially support forces able to do more than fight a major conventional war in Europe for a matter of days, or a small limited war for clearly defined objectives elsewhere. The first line of defense would therefore be local troops, with American equipment and training. Only in areas of exceptional value to the U.S. would combat units be stationed, composed primarily of aircraft with tactical nuclear weapons able to delay an enemy attack long enough for a decision on intervention. With the introduction of intercontinental ballistic missiles and the projected Undersea Long-Range Missile System, overseas bases would no longer be required for the strategic striking force. The bases would be confined to a few major storage depots for heavy equipment and to refueling points facilitating the air and sea transport of the strategic reserve based in the U.S.

With the ending of the draft scheduled for July 1973 (after almost being killed by the Senate in 1971), and a fiscal 1972–73 budget of $80 billion that would buy less than the budget for 1964, American forces would be reduced to 2.5 million or less. The Army's total of 12 divisions (3 armored, 1 air cavalry, 4 mechanized infantry, 2 infantry, and 2 airborne), plus 1 air cavalry, 1 airborne, and 3 independent infantry brigades, and 5 armored cavalry regiments, would be reduced to about 11 divisions. Of these a nominal 4 (2 armored and 2 infantry) would be retained in West Germany, with about half the men in the 1st in-

U.S. servicemen board a plane for home at Bien Hoa Air Base near Saigon, South Vietnam.

ABOVE AND BELOW: WIDE WORLD

Louis Smoyer (left), chief of the National Warning Center, located in Colorado, shows a reporter the emergency warning tape that was erroneously transmitted to all U.S. radio and TV stations on February 20. The alert (below) was followed by a cancellation 40 minutes later.

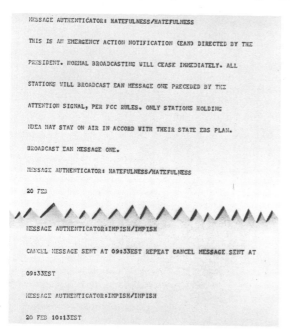

fantry division remaining in South Korea. In South Vietnam a mixed force totaling about one division (16,000 men) would replace the current 2 divisions and 2 brigades. The 72,000-man force in Japan and Okinawa was being reduced, probably to about one division. Similarly, the 18,400-man total in the Philippines would drop, giving a maximum deployment in Southeast Asia of 2 divisions once the one in South Vietnam was withdrawn.

The remaining 6 to 8 divisions would be based in the U.S.

To utilize its helicopter experience against tanks, the Army was experimenting with a new Tricap (triple-capable) divisional formation, using 330 troop-transport helicopters, gunfire support, and the Cheyenne helicopter armed with 3,000-meter range TOW antitank missiles. Combining one tank, one helicopter, and one infantry brigade, the divisional strength would be 12,000 to 13,000, instead of 16,000.

Recruitment would clearly be the Army's greatest problem, especially in view of Congressional resistance to raising pay scales. However, Congress finally approved a $2.4-billion pay increase, 75% going to men in the lower ranks of service. Army morale continued to be a major problem. Officers were being "fragged" (attacked with fragmentation grenades) by their own men, and the use of both "soft" and "hard" drugs was increasing. Capt. Ernest L. Medina's acquittal of charges of complicity in the My Lai massacre and the reduction of First Lieut. William L. Calley's sentence to 20 years did little to dispel the Army's opinion that these men were scapegoats or the public's concern that the traditional standards of military conduct were declining.

Under Chief of Naval Operations Elmo R. Zumwalt, Jr., Navy morale seemed to be improving, though the number and capabilities of its ships declined. Partly, this reflected the retirement of some World War II vessels, which were replaced by fewer, more powerful vessels, resulting in a drop from 886 to 714 ships and 770,000 to 623,000 men and women between mid-1969 and mid-1971.

As the organization most suited to the Nixon-Laird strategy, the U.S. Marine Corps would remain at the current level of 3 very large divisions (19,000 men each), and each division with 1 tank and 1 surface-to-air missile (SAM) battalion having 24 Hawk missiles. Integral artillery and air support was supplied by 3 air wings of 540 combat aircraft, chiefly 14 squadrons of F-4 Phantoms, 12 attack squadrons with A-6A and A-4 planes, 1 squadron with AV-8A Harrier V/STOL close-support aircraft, 45 AH-1 Cobra gunship helicopters, and 15 squadrons of helicopters. The reserves formed a complete division with its air wing.

The U.S. Air Force shared the Navy's problem of obsolescence, with over half of its 6,000 combat planes being more than 10 years old. The major requirement was for a new strategic bomber, the B-1, at $25–30 million each, now that only 70 instead of 82 FB-111's were being added to the Strategic Air Command (SAC), saving $103 million. Orders for the F-111D's, with the expensive Mark II avionics system, were held at 96, giving a total F-111 procurement of 538 instead of the 1,700 planned. SAC was reduced to 150 B-52 C/F's (2 squadrons being based in Southeast Asia) and 210 B-52 G/H's, with 90 planes in storage. The air defense forces of the North American Air Defense Command (NORAD) had been reduced, and the Nike Hercules SAM batteries decreased to 27, but the Air National Guard was reequipping with F-101, -102, and -104 fighters in place of their obsolete F-84's and RF-84's.

Two significant political events reflected the disenchantment with America's global role and consequent military involvement. The June publication, despite Administration attempts to stop it, of the so-called Pentagon papers produced a sense of betrayal. Commissioned by former U.S. Secretary of Defense Robert S. McNamara in 1967 to trace the history of the Vietnam war, the study—leaked by one of its authors, Daniel Ellsberg—was extremely one-sided, based only on Department of Defense files. Its impact came from the revelation that Presidents John F. Kennedy and Lyndon B. Johnson had never properly determined the objectives of the Vietnam war; that both men had been poorly served by their military advisers and had consistently misled the public on the nature and scope of the war. Ironically, only John A. McCone, director of the Central Intelligence Agency (CIA) in the years of escalation, had repeatedly questioned the assumption that increasing applications of American airpower and men could win a war of attrition. Undersecretary of State George Ball had tried to suggest, as long ago as 1965, that any war in South Vietnam would inevitably be lost and that a defeat would damage the U.S. far more than a compromise solution. (*See* Law Special Report.) The reaction to these disclosures strengthened the isolationist element.

North Atlantic Treaty Organization (NATO)

In 1971 NATO faced the prospect of Mutual and Balanced Force Reductions against a worsening military balance vis-à-vis the Warsaw Pact. Total U.S. forces fell to 2.7 million, with a target of 2.5 million, while the Soviet Union's grew by 70,000 to almost 3.4 million.

American forces in Europe had fallen to 300,000 from 434,000 in 1962, while the number of Soviet divisions had risen to 31 from 26 in 1967. Since U.S. infantry divisions contained 16,000 men against the Soviet Union's 10,500, a more accurate assessment was in terms of divisions equivalents. In Northern and Central Europe there were 8 armored and 16 infantry, mechanized, and airborne NATO divisions to 28 Warsaw Pact armored and 37 infantry divisions, of which 19 and 22 were Soviet. (*See also* Armed Forces, U.S.; Disarmament; Selective Service.)

DENMARK. In 1971 Denmark's deteriorating economic situation was a major topic of public debate. Despite strict financial controls and increased taxation, inflation in the country was running at about 8% by mid-1971. The balance of payments situation also continued to worsen.

On September 21 in a general election, Premier Hilmar Baunsgaard's "bourgeois" party coalition government was defeated. A Social Democratic minority government then took office under Jens Otto Krag, with the support of the leftist Socialist People's party. Krag's new government had an effective majority of one in the parliament, but Krag resisted suggestions that a broad coalition government should be formed.

The Social Democrats had fought the election on a program directed toward a guided economy and, specifically, had campaigned for the establishment of a council to direct capital into industries primarily engaged in export or in competition with imported goods in an attempt to tackle the serious balance of payments problem. Taking up office after an interval of three and a half years (he had been premier from 1962 to 1968), Krag declared that his government would be judged on its economic achievements. At the opening of the new parliament in October, the government's first step was to announce a temporary 10% surcharge on two thirds of the country's imports. However, in view of considerable opposition pressure, the proportion of total imports exempted was raised from some 35% to about 42% and later to 50%.

Denmark's negotiations for entry into the European Economic Community (EEC) were linked to Great Britain's entry, so that following the decision of the British parliament on October 28 to join the EEC, it only remained for Denmark to vote on the matter. It was agreed, however, that whether or not the needed majority was achieved in the parliament the matter would be the subject of a referendum in 1972. (*See in* CE: Denmark.)

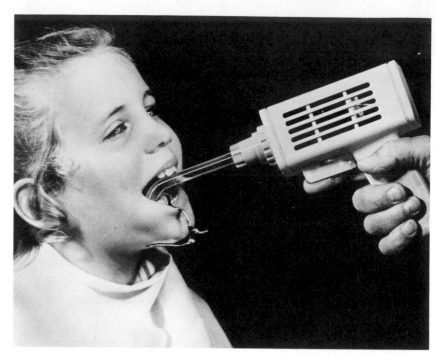

A new technique to fight tooth decay was launched by the New York State Health Department. Teeth are painted with a plastic adhesive; then the oral gun directs a beam of ultraviolet light to harden the plastic, which forms an invisible protective covering over the teeth.

COURTESY, EASTMAN DENTAL CENTER

DENTISTRY. The filler of holes became a teacher in 1971, as new knowledge that could mean a cavity-free future for mankind began to have dramatic impact on all levels of dental practice. Private practitioners, community health-education programs, and dental schools adopted new methods of preventive dentistry and began reeducating the public in techniques for keeping teeth free of plaque, the bacterial substance that clings to teeth and initiates caries (tooth decay).

It was now well established that caries and other dental diseases could be controlled through a daily program of plaque removal, the use of fluorides to make tooth enamel caries-resistant, the application of newly developed seals to biting surfaces to close microscopic holes that fluorides and brushing cannot protect, and the adoption of a diet low in sugar. No program of preventive dentistry, however, would be completely successful until all aspects of it become as simple as fluorides put in drinking water.

Research toward this end was under way, much of it through the National Institute of Dental Research in Bethesda, Md., which proposed a five-year plan to improve dental research in the United States. Studies being considered would investigate alternative methods of administering fluoride therapy; the development of more-permanent tooth sealants; sugar substitutes, dietary supplements, and trace elements as inhibitors of caries; more-effective methods of tooth cleansing; and whether or not immunizations against caries is possible.

One substance currently under investigation held promise of helping to solve the problem of the development of plaque and gingivitis (inflammation of the gums). A 0.2% solution of chlorhexidine gluconate used as a mouth rinse twice daily was found to effectively prevent plaque formation. Complete inhibition of plaque might be achieved through use of this substance provided it could reach all tooth surfaces. (*See in* CE: Dentistry.)

DISARMAMENT. The strategic arms limitation talks (SALT) between the United States and the Soviet Union, which began in 1969, continued through 1971. Progress was achieved in identifying many key issues, but negotiations eventually were stymied over the question of the scope the initial agreement would take—exactly what weapon systems should be covered. In May there was a significant breakthrough when the U.S. government and the Soviet government simultaneously announced that a decision had been made to concentrate in 1971 on working out an agreement to limit the deployment of the ABM (antiballistic missile) system. They also agreed that they would consider certain measures with respect to the limitation of offensive strategic weapons. The establishment of this negotiating framework was regarded as a favorable augury for fruitful negotiations. Intensive discussions were undertaken in Helsinki, Finland, and in Vienna, Austria, to translate this understanding into concrete agreements.

On September 30 the U.S. and the Soviet Union signed two agreements, concluded by the U.S. and Soviet SALT negotiators in parallel with the principal SALT negotiations, designed to reduce the risk of nuclear war. One agreement concerned the avoidance of an accidental outbreak of nuclear war. It covered three broad areas: a pledge by both sides to take steps to guard against accidental or unauthorized use of nuclear weapons; arrangements

Soviet Foreign Minister Andrei Gromyko and U.S. Secretary of State William P. Rogers sign two agreements designed to prevent accidental nuclear war and to modernize the "hot line."

for rapid communications should the danger of nuclear war arise from such nuclear incidents or from detection of unidentified objects on missile-warning systems; advance notification of certain planned missile launches. A second agreement provided for modernization of the Washington, D.C.–Moscow direct communications link, or "hot line," taking into account recent technological developments.

The Geneva disarmament conference—the United Nations (UN) Conference of the Committee on Disarmament (CCD)—the world's principal forum for negotiating multilateral arms control agreements—was the focal point for continuing discussions on control of chemical and biological weapons. In August substantial success was achieved when the U.S. and the Soviet Union, as cochairmen of the CCD, presented a joint draft text of a convention prohibiting the development, production, and stockpiling of biological weapons and toxins. The draft convention was later forwarded to the UN General Assembly for its consideration.

In May the U.S. ratified, with a clarifying statement, Protocol II of the Treaty for the Prohibition of Nuclear Weapons in Latin America. This protocol was designed for ratification by the nuclear powers who pledged to respect the denuclearized status of Latin America.

In March Leonid I. Brezhnev, general secretary of the Soviet Communist party, proposed a conference of the five nuclear powers to negotiate nuclear disarmament and also called for a world disarmament conference. At the same time Brezhnev reiterated Soviet readiness to participate in a general conference on European security and suggested a mutual reduction of armaments and forces in central Europe. (See Europe.) The European security conference proposal was greeted favorably by the North Atlantic Treaty Organization (NATO), but the proposal for a five-power nuclear conference was rejected by the People's Republic of China at the end of July. In rejecting the Soviet proposal, China repeated its desire for a general meeting of all nations of the world to discuss the prohibition and destruction of nuclear weapons.

DISASTERS OF 1971.

Among the catastrophes that occurred in the world in 1971 were:

Air Disasters

May 23 Rijeka, Yugoslavia. A Yugoslav TU-134 twinjet charter plane en route from London crashes and burns on landing, killing 78 persons, most of whom are British tourists.

July 3 Hakodate, Japan. A Japanese YS-11 turboprop airliner approaching Hakodate Airport in fog and rain hits a mountainside and kills all 68 persons aboard.

July 30 Morioka, Japan. A Japanese Air Force F-86 jet fighter collides with a Japanese Boeing 727 passenger plane; all 162 persons aboard the airliner die, though the student pilot of the F-86 parachutes to safety. The collision is the world's worst air disaster.

Survivors gather in the ruins of Bingol, Turkey, after an earthquake nearly devastated the town on May 22. At least 1,000 persons were killed; more than 95% of the buildings were destroyed. Rescue operations were hampered by the rough terrain.

The Panamanian tanker *Texaco Caribbean* sinks into the Strait of Dover after colliding with a Peruvian ship; eight men were killed.

Aug. 11 (?) Irkutsk, U.S.S.R. A Soviet TU-104 twinjet commercial airliner explodes on take-off from Irkutsk Airport, killing all 97 persons aboard.

Sept. 4 Juneau, Alaska. A U.S. 727 commercial jetliner beginning an approach into Juneau Municipal Airport slams into a bare mountainside; all 111 persons aboard die in the worst single-plane accident in U.S. air history.

Dec. 24 Near Pucallpa, Peru. A Peruvian Lockheed Electra turboprop passenger plane crashes in a mountainous jungle area; of the 92 persons aboard one survivor is found.

Fires and Explosions

Feb. 3 Near Brunswick, Ga. A munitions manufacturing complex is rocked by a blast thought to have been caused by magnesium trip flares; 25 persons are killed and more than 100 injured.

Feb. 16 Bangkok, Thailand. An explosion and fire wreck one wing of the Imperial Hotel and cause the death of at least 25 persons.

Dec. 14 Mufulira, Zambia. Nine freight cars loaded with explosives blow up and kill 29 persons.

Dec. 25 Seoul, South Korea. A fire in the plush 22-story Taeyonkak Hotel, believed to have started in a second-story coffee shop, causes a 12-hour holocaust that takes the lives of at least 157 persons and injures 100 others, in the worst hotel fire in history.

Marine Disasters

May 22 Vancouver, B.C. The Norwegian cruise ship *Meteor* is severely damaged by an explosion and fire as it comes through the Strait of Georgia; all passengers are successfully evacuated but 32 seamen are lost.

June 12 Manila Bay, Philippines. An excursion boat capsizes in stormy weather; 54 persons are drowned or missing and presumed dead.

Aug. 6 Persian Gulf. An Iranian motorboat transporting Iranian laborers for illegal entry into Kuwait strikes a submerged rocky shelf and sinks; an estimated 300 passengers are drowned.

Nov. 9 Atlantic Ocean. Encountering a severe storm about 600 miles off the French coast, the 9,400-ton French freighter *Maori* breaks up and sinks; 39 crewmen are lost.

Nov. 21 Central Philippines. A 30-ton wooden cargo vessel ferrying passengers between the islands of Leyte and Cebu runs into turbulent water and goes to the bottom; about 100 of some 200 persons aboard are drowned or are missing and presumed dead.

Mining and Tunneling Disasters

Oct. 30 Hunedoara, Romania. The collapse of a mine settling tank causes a landslide that traps a crew of miners working underground; 51 persons die and 88 others are injured.

Dec. 1 Keelung, Taiwan. A mine explosion 7,260 feet underground kills 41 miners; 7 others are missing and 4 seriously injured.

Dec. 11 Port Huron, Mich. Deadly methane gas explodes and rips through a tunnel being built 250 feet under the surface of Lake Huron; 22 workers in the tunnel die, 9 others are injured.

Natural Disasters

Jan. 4 Midwestern United States. A huge storm piles snow into 12-foot drifts, stranding thousands of motorists along a 1,000-mile belt through Iowa, Illinois, Nebraska, Wisconsin, Kansas, Minnesota, and Michigan; 37 deaths are attributed to the storm.

Jan. 29 Zambezia region, Mozambique. Torrential rains accompanying a cyclone inundate lowland areas and threaten 500,000 trapped residents with starvation; estimates of the final death toll range from 500 to 1,000 persons.

Feb. 6 Tuscania, Italy. Two earthquakes strike within hours to destroy the ancient city of Tuscania and many of its priceless art treasures; the city and 23 surrounding small towns suffer at least 20 fatalities, 120 other persons are injured, and the homeless number 4,000.

Feb. 9 San Fernando Valley, Calif. An earthquake hits the Los Angeles area, bringing death to 65 persons (many of them patients at a veterans hospital) and injuring about 1,000 others in the nation's most costly disaster to date, with damage estimated at upward of $1 billion.

Feb. 21 Louisiana and Mississippi. Twisters rip through the ill-famed "Dixie Tornado Alley" hitting Mississippi with violent fury; 115 persons die with 500 others injured; property damage amounts to more than $7.5 million.

March 19 Near Canta, Peru. A light earthquake triggers an avalanche of water, mud, and rocks that roars down a mountain slope and overruns a mining camp; as many as 600 persons are believed buried in the avalanche.

April 29 Salvador, Brazil. Three days of heavy rains, floods, and landslides leave more than 150 persons dead, 10,000 others homeless, and damages amounting to around $6 million.

May 22 Bingol, Turkey. The second quake in Turkey within ten days, centered in the eastern province of Bingol, destroys 90% of the provincial capital of Bingol and wreaks havoc on more than 300 mountain villages and hamlets; the official death toll is given as 1,000 persons.

Aug. 5 Western Kyushu, Japan. Typhoon Olive moves across part of Kyushu Island, leaving at least 135 persons dead or missing and presumed dead.

Aug. 17 Hong Kong. Typhoon Rose drenches Hong Kong with 12 inches of rain, destroys about 40 fishing boats, capsizes a ferry (drowning 88 persons), and grounds another 26 oceangoing vessels; official death toll is about 90 persons, some 200 are injured.

Sept. 9 Uttar Pradesh, India. The worst floods in 11 years force the evacuation of 35,000 persons; 300 persons perish.

Sixteen persons were killed and at least 99 injured when the City of New Orleans passenger train was derailed in southern Illinois.

WIDE WORLD

Oct. 23 South Vietnam. Typhoon Hester tears into five northern provinces, flattening 17,000 homes, and damaging another 40,000 with its 140-mile-per-hour winds; 89 persons die.

Oct. 29–30 Eastern India. A 16-foot tidal wave, preceded by a cyclone, devastates a river-laced area of eastern Orissa state; officials estimate that 10,000 to 25,000 persons are dead, with tens of thousands homeless and facing starvation.

Railroad Disasters

May 27 Near Wuppertal, West Germany. A two-coach train is rammed head-on by a freight; 46 persons die.

Aug. 4 Near Belgrade, Yugoslavia. A passenger train collides with a freight; at least 40 persons perish; 100 others are injured.

Traffic Accidents

May 10 Chongpyong, South Korea. A bus plunges off a roadway into a reservoir; at least 60 persons are drowned, 14 others survive.

Aug. 18 Near Casablanca, Morocco. A bus falls into a deep gorge, bringing death to 45 persons and injuring 30 others.

Sept. 13 Thelwall, England. Fog on M-6, a major superhighway, causes a massive pileup of 200 cars and trucks; at least 10 persons die, 61 others are hospitalized.

Miscellaneous

Jan. 2 Glasgow, Scotland. The end of a closely contested soccer game brings fans rushing out of their seats to the exits; a steel crowd barrier collapses and 66 persons are trampled or crushed to death and at least another 100 are injured.

DOMINICAN REPUBLIC. As President Joaquín Balaguer finished his fifth year in office in 1971, the economy was growing at around 6% annually. At the same time, newspapers reported the island full of political terrorism, corruption, and misery. Terrorism reportedly was led by an anti-Communist, government-backed organization, *La Banda* (The Band). Main targets of the group of militant youths were the Popular Dominican Movement (MPD), the Dominican Revolutionary party (PRD), and groups in city slums that oppose the government. Balaguer denied that such a group existed, but the Roman Catholic church and the Autonomous University of Santo Domingo joined public outcries against *La Banda*.

On June 30 Balaguer announced that former General Elías Wessin y Wessin had been arrested as the leader of a right-wing military group that tried to overthrow the government. The general was exiled to Spain.

Social services accounted for $106.6 million, or 41% of the total 1971 national budget. The gross national product (GNP) rose for the fifth year, import taxes increased, and the 1971 sugar harvest projection indicated a 140,000 ton increase over the 1970 record of 1.2 million tons.

The enactment of a "quickie" divorce law, patterned after Mexico's abandoned one, was expected to attract many foreign visitors. (*See in* CE: Dominican Republic.)

DRUGS. The problem of drug abuse continued to be a crucial one in the United States in 1971. Focal point of the drug-abuse concern was the increasing number of Vietnam veterans who returned home slaves to the deadly heroin habit. But the

Rescue workers remove the bodies of persons killed in an earthquake in Tuscania, Italy. At least 20 were killed and 120 injured.
KEYSTONE

problem was more widespread. U.S. President Richard M. Nixon, in declaring Drug Abuse Prevention Week for October, summed it up in part as follows:

Not so long ago it was easy enough to regard the tragedy of drug abuse as 'someone else's problem'. But recent years have brought that tragedy home—often very literally—to all Americans. We have learned that 'drug abuse' refers not only to the crime-prone heroin addict that is the disease at its deadliest, with over 1,000 heroin fatalities annually in New York City. The term also refers to the suburban housewife dependent on tranquilizers and diet pills; to the student leaning on amphetamines to help him cram for exams; even to pre-teens sniffing glue.

It has become a problem that touches each of us. Its manifestations are many and varied, but all grow from a common root—psychological and physical needs unmet through legitimate social channels—and all feed on common ignorance of the profound harm the drug abuser does to himself and society. Drug abuse is nothing less than a life and death matter for countless Americans, and for the moral fiber of this Nation. The drive to meet this threat must command from us our very best—our attention, our energies, our resources and our prayers.

As the panic over drug abuse spread to many segments of society, so did the fight against drugs spread. By the end of 1971 it involved government at all levels, the armed forces, schools, civic and youth clubs, ghetto and street cultures, and even former addicts. Business and industry, where narcotics joined alcohol as a personnel problem, set up test, treatment, and search programs. The mass media through articles, ads, and spot announcements by prominent athletes sought to turn off America from escape by drugs.

In June the president created the Special Action Office for Drug Abuse Prevention headed by a Chicago psychiatrist, Dr. Jerome H. Jaffe. Included in the president's proposed $371-million budget for drug abuse control was provision for crash research to find a blocking agent to help heroin addicts kick the habit.

At an international level the United Nations and the World Health Organization continued efforts to halt drug traffic. Meanwhile, curtailment of the opium poppy in Turkey as a cash crop had adverse effects on the Turkish national economy. Also, the smuggling and illicit sale of heroin, hashish, and marijuana throughout Southeast Asia corrupted individuals and governments while addicting American servicemen. The processing of narcotics in southern France for shipment to the U.S. brought with it international discord and distrust, as did the bulk shipment of amphetamines and other

JEFF TAYLOR FROM UPI COMPIX

Drugs seemed easily available in Quang Tri province in Vietnam. A U.S. soldier openly makes a purchase from a Vietnamese woman.

dangerous drugs from U.S. pharmaceutical firms to Mexico, for packaged reentry into the U.S.

While the use of LSD and glue sniffing declined, a new and sometimes fatal fad invaded the junior-high group as boys and girls got their kicks from aerosol sprays inhaled from paper bags and balloons. Dirty needles spread hepatitis and endocarditis (inflammation of the heart lining) among addicts who took their "stuff" by vein, and mainlining (direct injection) of amphetamines became more widespread. Alcohol continued to be the most common American choice for escape, but a cure for that habit was no closer. Methadone, another addictive drug, remained the controversial preferred treatment in weaning heroin addicts. But in late November, federal researchers announced that a new drug, EN-1639A, was close to clinical testing as a harmless, nonaddictive antagonist to heroin. With the announcement came a warning, perhaps a keynote to an effective battle against drug abuse. Dr. William R. Martin, chief of the federal research center at Lexington, Ky., stated that no antidote, however helpful, can cure the psychological or physiological factors that lead victims to addiction in the first place.

The debate on marijuana continued in 1971. In November the governor of Illinois granted clemency to 41 prisoners jailed under old marijuana laws. At the Midwest Research Center a urine test was developed to determine marijuana count in drivers suspected of being too "high" to handle their cars. Marijuana will also be part of a Department of Transportation study in which coroners

Women harvest the 1971 opium crop in Turkey, which was expected to produce about 125 tons of opium. Almost half that total is sold on the black market—much of it to U.S. soldiers in Vietnam. The U.S. government offered Turkey $5 million a year to stop opium production.

from 35 states will submit tissue and fluid samples from dead-on-arrival drivers; through testing, the researchers hope to pinpoint the role of drugs in fatal car crashes.

In October the FDA began a vast study of the effectiveness of nonprescription drugs. The first target was mood pills. About 200 tranquilizers and sleeping pills consist of a weak antihistamine and minute amounts of a nervous-system depressant, while the more than 60 patent "pep" pills contain caffeine, in about the same amount provided by one cup of coffee—according to Dr. Charles C. Edwards, FDA commissioner.

New on the drug market were rifampin, an antibiotic for use against tuberculosis, and a broad-spectrum antibiotic, Minocin, approved for use against the drug-resistant and often deadly staphylococcus bacteria. Minocin required ten years of testing and a $10-million investment by Lederle Laboratories, whose researchers found it also effective against gonorrhea, typhus, cholera, Rocky Mountain spotted fever, and certain types of dysentery. The *Journal of the American Medical Association* reported a combination vaccine for immunity against measles, mumps, and German measles. Two anticancer drugs were approved for use on skin diseases, one for actinic keratosis, the other for severe psoriasis.

An old synthetic female hormone DES (diethylstilbestrol) was cited in October as an effective "morning-after" birth control pill (recommended for emergencies only). In November the FDA restricted its use in preventing miscarriages, after studies linked the hormone to vaginal cancer in young women whose mothers were treated with it while pregnant with them.

In November the FDA also issued a warning on the use of hexachlorophene, citing studies showing its use had resulted in brain damage in monkeys.

Hexachlorophene was a common ingredient in many personal hygiene products.

From 1763, when the Royal Society of London heard a report on willow bark (which contains salicylic acid) as a fever cure, until 1971 when aspirin, a salicylate, was a best-selling drug, little was known about its action. However, researchers have now found that aspirin can block synthesis of prostaglandins, the hormone-type substances produced throughout the body, which can cause fever and headache. The research was expected to aid development of more effective aspirin relatives and the understanding and control of prostaglandins. (*See also* Medicine. *See in* CE: Drugs.)

EARTH SCIENCES. Plate tectonics, the theory that the earth's crust consists of a small number of rigid but slowly moving plates, gained further acceptance in 1971, providing a basis for unifying the often divergent fields of earth science. Petrologists were investigating "petrotectonic assemblages," rock groups identified with specific earth plates. The rock scientists knew that rocks held the record of past geologic events, although not always candidly. Petrotectonic assemblages, they believed, would produce evidence of the boundaries held by earth plates in the distant past.

In search for causes of plate movement, earth scientists pondered several tectonic energy sources. One cause could be the heat released by the decay of radioactive elements in the earth's mantle, the layer beneath the crust. Since hot rocks in the mantle could behave as a fluid, thermal convection currents in the mantle might move the overriding crustal plates. Another possibility could be the weight of the forward part of the colder, denser plate driving downward into the warmer, less dense mantle at the ocean trenches. If it did so, it would pull the rest of the plate along with it. A third possibility, recently advanced by William Jason Morgan of Princeton University, assumed that convection occurred far down in the earth's lower mantle. As molten lava rose along mid-ocean ridges through nearly two dozen 60-mile-wide "flues," or thermal hot spots under the plates, it would push the overriding plates and fill gaps left from the movement.

Crustal Drilling

The drilling ship *Glomar Challenger* continued its ambitious program of deep-sea drilling in 1971. During the year it bored into seabed rocks from the Caribbean Sea to the central Pacific Ocean and up to the Bering Sea. Cores from one of the drill sites produced evidence that the sea floor spread more rapidly away from the East Pacific Rise—three inches a year—during the early Tertiary Period some 65 million years ago than the present rate of spread—slightly more than two inches a year.

The deepest holes yet drilled have pierced only five miles of the earth's crust. But several new drilling techniques promised to deepen the penetration. Soviet technologists, for example, have devised a turbine-powered drilling system capable of penetrating almost ten miles of rock. It features pipes of aluminum alloy instead of steel. At the Los Alamos Scientific Laboratory in New Mexico, engineers were experimenting with an electric rock-melting device. In addition, they planned to test a small nuclear reactor capable of melting rocks to a depth of 18 miles. (*See* Oceanography.)

Earthquakes

Earth wobble was cited as a factor in major earthquakes. This was the opinion of Charles A. Whitten, chief geodesist of the U.S. National Ocean Survey, an agency of the National Oceanic and Atmospheric Administration. The north-south polar axis on which the earth spins zigzags in a circle around the north pole. This movement, called the Chandler wobble, may be as much as six inches a day, for a total of up to 72 feet every 14 months. In addition, the wobble reaches its peak every seven years. When it does, according to Whitten, it acts with other forces to set off earthquakes. Partner forces include the pull exerted by the sun and moon and the crustal shifts accompanying subsurface strains. Findings in 1971 seemed to corroborate the theory. Earthquake energy released in 1971 surpassed that of any year since 1964, when the great Alaskan quake took place.

On February 9 an earthquake with the moderate Richter-scale strength of 6.5 struck the area north of Los Angeles, taking dozens of lives and causing $1 billion in damage. Most of the deaths occurred in a complex of 50-year-old hospital buildings not designed to withstand earthquakes.

Seismologists intensified their efforts toward an earthquake warning system for fear that major shocks in heavily populated areas, such as the quake-prone West Coast, would result in large losses of life. Scientists at the National Center for Earthquake Research (NCER) at Menlo Park, Calif., discovered that in the days preceding recent tremors near San Francisco, the entire Bay area tilted toward the epicenter of the shocks. Although reluctant to consider the finding an earthquake predictor, the researchers felt that further examination of the phenomenon was warranted.

Discovering an impending earthquake was one matter, but preventing it was a far more difficult task. However, earth scientists who gathered at the annual meeting of the American Geophysical Union, at Washington, D.C., discussed the use of hydrostatic pressure to control earthquake activity. Of special interest was an NCER study of an oil

A snow tractor carries a large radar antenna that will be used to study the interiors of glaciers. The antenna, called the Radio Echo Sounding System, was developed by the Canadian government.
CHARLES MITCHELL FROM CANADIAN PRESS

field at Rangely, Colo., where strategic injection of water drove oil to the surface. As water was evacuated from the wells, subsurface pressure dropped as much as 800 pounds per square inch. In the meantime, tremor activity that ordinarily took place along a fault under the oil field subsided. Thus, if high pore pressure in the oil reservoir rocks could trigger earthquakes in some circumstances, then relief of that pressure through pumping might lessen the odds of a tremor.

Geysers that fascinate thousands of tourists every year might be natural earthquake warning systems. Seismologists learned that geysers, such as Old Faithful at Yellowstone National Park, do not perennially erupt with clocklike regularity. Instead, they speed up their eruptions when crustal stresses begin to mount. Then they slack off after the earthquake occurs. Old Faithful, for instance, sped up its intervals of eruption in the early 1960's until it spouted every 65½ minutes in 1963. Then it dropped off to an eruption rate of once every 67 minutes in 1964, coincident with the Alaskan shock.

Moon Findings

Evidence obtained by the three-day Apollo 15 moon mission in the Hadley Rille area at the edge of the Mare Imbrium (Sea of Rains) tended to confirm the view that the moon's "seas" had been scooped out by the impacts of giant meteorites. Astronauts David R. Scott and James B. Irwin toured the area with their lunar rover vehicle to collect about 170 pounds of rock from the Apennine Mountains.

Perhaps the most astonishing discovery of the Apollo 15 mission was the finding of well-defined rock layers in the upper part of Hadley Rille. Up to 10 layers were found in the rille's wall, suggesting

the basin was flooded by a series of lava flows, one piling atop another.

Instruments on the Apollo spacecraft in lunar orbit detected highly radioactive areas on the moon. Scientists speculated that subsurface rocks had melted into lava by the heat of radioactive decay. As a result, the moon could have a cold core and still show volcanic activity.

Basalt collected from the rille's rim was 3.36 billion years old. This contrasted with the Apollo 14 basalt sample from the Fra Mauro crater region that proved to be 500 million years older. Scientists previously thought the entire Mare Imbrium had been covered with lava generated from the impact heat of a huge meteorite. The range in basalt ages, however, suggested another volcanic cause.

Soviet scientists at a January meeting in Houston, Tex., disclosed some of the data amassed by the unmanned Luna 16 moon probe. Their analysis of lunar soil returned by the probe indicated all the moon's "seas" were alike in origin and makeup. Glassy grains among the Luna 16 samples were thought to be 4.45 to 4.65 billion years old, as old as the solar system.

Data telemetered from the moon continually surprised scientists in 1971. In October Rice University scientists were convinced they detected signs of water on the moon. Based on the information sent by ion detectors on the moon, the water vapor allegedly vented through fissures and spread over a hundred square miles. Venting was associated with minor moonquakes.

Trends in Geography

In 1971 geographers paid added attention to human needs—where man lived and how he interacted with his physical environment. Preliminary plans for the 22d International Geographical Congress

Cuts made in this California hillside clearly show slippage above the San Andreas fault.
"LOS ANGELES TIMES"

showed that geographers were keenly interested in environmental ecosystems. The August 1972 gathering was to be held in Montreal, Que.

Geographic resources were under consideration by U.S. policy planners involved with the problems of maritime jurisdiction and the uses of the seas and seabeds. Mapmaking research by geographers, aided in part by the valuable data telemetered by the Earth Resources Technical Satellite, would undoubtedly be a key element in resolving such issues as the extent of national claims in territorial waters and the determination of continental shelf boundaries. (*See also* Space Exploration. *See in* CE: Earth; Geology; Maps; Moon.)

ECONOMY.

On Aug. 15, 1971, against a background of highly inflationary pressures, an increasingly high unemployment rate, and mounting international financial difficulties, United States President Richard M. Nixon abandoned his previous "game plan" for the economy and boldly acted to provide a new set of economic policies for the country. His object was to boost lagging confidence in the nation's economic prospects.

Using the power available to the president under the Economic Stabilization Act of 1970, he instituted a 90-day freeze on wages and prices (including rents and excluding raw agricultural products), imposed a 10% surcharge on a wide range of imported products, and suspended the convertibility of dollars into gold, thus allowing the dollar to "float" in relation to other currencies. Nixon also recommended to the U.S. Congress additional measures to stimulate economic activity that required legislative action. These included the elimination of the 7% excise tax on automobiles (retroactive to mid-August); the establishment of a one-year 10% investment tax credit on new machinery and equipment provided it was made in the U.S. (also retroactive to mid-August), to be followed by a permanent 5% investment tax credit; and early implementation (January 1972) of the reductions in personal income taxes contained in the 1969 Tax Reform measure, which had been scheduled to take effect in January 1973.

The immediate reaction to the president's startling announcement was rousing approval from all quarters, as indicated by the spectacular rise recorded in the stock market the day after the president's speech. A new record was achieved on the New York Stock Exchange when the Dow-Jones industrial average soared almost 33 points in one day. Enthusiasm abated somewhat as skeptical investors sat back to see how the president's program would actually work—in particular, whether the voluntary compliance the president requested would be effective in reducing prices, and more important, what would happen after the freeze ended. Confidence was somewhat revived with the president's announcement of "Phase II" of his economic program, which began on November 14, after the expiration of the 90-day freeze.

Phase II

The aim of Phase II was to allow some flexibility in the rigid economic controls of Phase I without bringing on a resurgence of rampant inflation. Nixon hoped to achieve a decrease in the rate of inflation to an annual 2 to 3% by the end of 1972. To accomplish this goal, the only permissible increases in wages were to be those supported by a rise in productivity, with the cost-of-living index taken into account. Price increases were to be permitted only when justified by a rise in costs.

The president established several executive committees to deal with the actual implementation of Phase II; most prominent were the Price Commission and the Pay Board, both coordinated by the Cost of Living Council (which had been established in Phase I under the chairmanship of U.S. Secretary of the Treasury John B. Connally, Jr.). The Price Commission as set up was composed of seven members chosen by the president from the general public. Their announced goal was to maintain an overall average price increase of 2.5% a year. The Pay Board was in reality the key committee established. It had 15 members, chosen by the president in equal numbers from the labor, business, and public sectors. After initial balking by organized labor's chief spokesman George L. Meany, mainly over the issue of whether the Cost of Living Council would have a veto over the Pay Board, the Pay Board's autonomous status was established, and labor agreed to participate. (*See also* Labor Unions.) The Pay Board established a permissible average wage increase of 5.5%.

However, in their first two cases, the board approved a contract in the soft coal industry providing for a 15% wage increase for the first year and a contract for railway signalmen calling for a 46% increase over 42 months. The board justified the actions as part of "getting the last cows through the gate and then closing it," in effect allowing those last labor groups who were still involved in settling 1971 bargaining issues to achieve a settlement equal to those that had gone before. One of the board members said that "once the stragglers are pushed aside and the gate is closed, then 1972 must and will become a 5.5% year, and 1973 must be a 5.5% year or less."

The Price Commission did not allow the soft coal producers to pass on the additional costs of the higher wages to the consumer, approving only about 9% as a basis for price increases. The railway signalmen's contract was still subject to review. Nevertheless, these cases aroused concern about how effective Phase II controls actually would be in controlling inflation.

One major issue of contention affecting the Pay Board was the question of retroactivity—whether workers scheduled to receive pay increases during the Phase I freeze could collect back pay. Labor wanted retroactivity, the Administration did not. This issue was settled in December when Congress

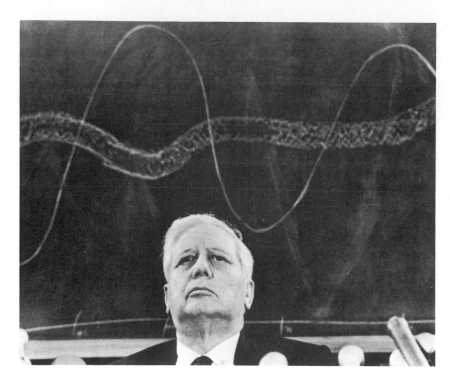

In January Secretary of the Treasury David M. Kennedy discusses Administration plans to revive the economy by cutting business taxes. Kennedy, a "lame duck" at that point, was replaced by John Connally in February.
WIDE WORLD

voted to permit retroactive pay raises under certain conditions—if prices, taxes, or government appropriations had already been made in anticipation of raises or if the raises were not "unreasonably" inconsistent with Pay Board standards.

At the same time Congress, with strong bipartisan support, extended the authority of the president to establish economic controls under the Economic Stabilization Act to April 30, 1973 (also including additional authority to regulate interest rates and dividends). Congress also enacted the tax-cut bill requested by the Administration, incorporating repeal, retroactively, of the automobile excise tax, provision for a 7% tax credit for business equipment purchases, and an earlier effective date for the scheduled increase in personal income tax exemptions.

The Monetary Crisis

While these measures were being put into effect in the domestic economy, Treasury Secretary Connally was pursuing a hard bargaining policy in foreign trade. The U.S. 10% import surcharge, which effectively made foreign goods more expensive in the U.S., was widely resented, particularly by Japan, Canada, and the industrial nations of Western Europe, whose economies were heavily dependent on trade with the U.S. These countries were also angered by the unilateral decision by the U.S. to abandon the monetary system the U.S. itself had been instrumental in setting up in 1944. The uncertainty created by the monetary crisis and the new trade barriers was heightened when Denmark became the first country to react to the U.S. surcharge by enacting an import surcharge of its

own. Fears were aroused that the outcome of the crisis might be a worldwide trade war.

However, in December, after almost four months of bargaining in various bilateral and multilateral forums, a compromise agreement was worked out on the basic issues. The U.S. agreed to devalue the dollar 8.57% in return for a realignment of other major currencies. Nixon also agreed to drop the 10% surcharge in exchange for trade concessions in the European Economic Community, Canada, and Japan, its major trading partners.

It was hoped that a major benefit to the U.S. economy of the devaluation, the first undertaken by the government since 1934, would be a rise in U.S. exports. This would reverse the trend of the first three quarters of 1971, which showed a steady deterioration in the U.S. trade balance. The Nixon Administration anticipated that a secondary effect of the devaluation would be an increase in jobs that would help cope with the high rate of unemployment, which had stubbornly averaged around 6% in 1971.

Third-Quarter Economic Results

Nixon's innovative economic program represented a sharp break with U.S. tradition, particularly for a Republican president whose party had long been philosophically opposed to government interference in the economic sphere. The compelling circumstances that led to Nixon's decision to take such drastic action could be seen in the third-quarter economic statistics released by the U.S. Department of Labor.

The Consumer Price Index at the end of the third quarter was 122.6, based on the 1967 established average of 100. However, if the 1957–59 average of 100 were still in use the country's index would have stood at a staggering 142.1. Corporate profits rose slightly in the third quarter of 1971. Pretax profits were at a seasonally adjusted annual rate of $83.6 billion, about a 0.3% increase over the second quarter. The comparable figure for September 1970 was $78.5 billion.

Total consumer credit outstanding at the end of the third quarter was $130.64 billion. Of that total, consumer installment debt outstanding climbed $999 million, exceeding the previous record increase of $947 million in October 1968. The record expansion of credit was mainly attributable to record auto sales. Auto sales were at high levels in September because of the introduction of new models, the price freeze, and the expected repeal of the 7% automobile excise tax. Another bright spot in the economy was housing, which was undergoing a long-awaited boom, spurred in part by Administration policies that eased interest rates on mortgages. (*See* Automobiles; Housing.)

The growth in the gross national product (GNP), the country's total output of goods and services, slowed in the third quarter of 1971. Although total output rose $16 billion to a GNP of $1.059 trillion seasonally adjusted, the real GNP, based on 1958 dollars to strip away the effect of inflation,

DON WRIGHT FROM THE "MIAMI NEWS"

President Nixon's new economic policies, announced in August, were confusing to some Toronto merchants who put up signs notifying American customers that their money could not be used to purchase merchandise until rates of exchange were re-established.

"TORONTO STAR"

rose at a 2.9% annual rate in the third quarter, down from 4.8% in the second quarter and 8% in the first quarter of 1971.

Outlook for 1972

In general, the new Nixon economic policy appeared to be working. In October and November 1971 the cost-of-living rise was limited to 0.2%. The rise was attributable to a large extent to price increases on those items exempt from the freeze. For the period of August through November, approximately the period of the freeze, the cost-of-living index increased at a seasonally adjusted rate of about 1.7%. The rate for the previous six months had been 4.1%. The Nixon Administration referred to the statistics as "heartening" and indicated that it felt the economic stabilization program was working.

Based on the encouraging year-end statistics, the economic forecasts for 1972 were optimistic. In the early months of 1972 the price increases permitted under Phase II would begin to take their effect but it was predicted by government economists that the overall average increase in the cost of living for the first four or five months of 1972 would be small. (*See also* Banks; Business and Industry; Employment; Money and International Finance; World Trade. *See in* CE: Economics.)

ECUADOR. The main political events in Ecuador in 1971 were a short-lived revolt by the head of the military academy, Gen. Luis Jácome Chávez, and a renewal of the so-called tuna war with the United States. The unsuccessful revolt led to preventive detention for General Jácome and prompted the dismissal of the minister of defense, Jorge Acosta Velasco; President José María Velasco Ibarra retained support of most of the military.

Early in the year Ecuador seized a number of U.S. tuna fishing boats more than 12 miles from the Ecuadorean coast but well within the 200-mile limit claimed by Ecuador. In retaliation, the U.S. suspended military sales to Ecuador, which then expelled the U.S. military mission from the country. In the fall there were further seizures of U.S. tuna boats.

President Velasco repeatedly announced his intentions to set up a plebiscite to reinstate constitutional rule but, owing to failure to arrange talks between the minister of the interior and leaders of other political parties, plans for elections in 1971 were abandoned. On June 25 it was announced that presidential and congressional elections would be held on June 4, 1972. The electorate would also be asked either to approve proposed reforms to the 1946 constitution or to delegate the matter to Congress.

The June 1972 elections would give immediate effect to constitutional order, but the Supreme Court would replace Congress until Aug. 10, 1972. On Aug. 31, 1972, President Velasco would hand over the presidency to the Ecuadorean citizen elected (according to the 1946 constitution, both president and vice-president must be Ecuadorean by birth). The political situation remained complex and uncertain as the various parties began to prepare for the elections against a background of popular unrest due to the sharp rise in living costs, increasing unemployment, and economic stagnation. (*See in* CE: Ecuador.)

Women relatives of the crews of U.S. tuna boats seized by Ecuador meet with Bolivar Valladores, Ecuador's consul general in Los Angeles. They demanded the return of the men, who had been fishing in waters under territorial dispute.
WIDE WORLD

EDUCATION. In contrast to recent years, student dissent was muted during 1971 and events in the field of education were dominated by the actions and policies of the United States government, by court decisions, and by a nationwide crisis in the financing of education at all levels. Racial desegregation in public schools remained a major issue; the use of busing to achieve school integration was the subject of a landmark Supreme Court decision, as was federal aid to nonpublic schools. The financial plight of public and private schools alike, intensified by national economic inflation, was a growing concern of educators and public officials.

School Desegregation and Busing

In January the Administration of U.S. President Richard M. Nixon issued the first government figures on the extent of school integration achieved in the South under federal court orders. These revealed that 38.1% of Southern black students were enrolled in predominantly white schools; that 43.5% were in predominantly black schools; and that 18.4% were in all-black schools. The accuracy of these figures in reflecting actual desegregation within schools was challenged by the biracial Southern Regional Council, which reported that in many "desegregated" schools classes remained racially segregated, and that blacks were often excluded from school organizations and were subject to intimidation. Both the council and the National Education Association (NEA) reported that in some school districts black teachers and administrators were dismissed or demoted when integration was carried out. The federal General Accounting Office accused the Nixon Administration of giving desegregation funds to ineligible schools, including private white "segregation academies." Although these criticisms reflected serious problems, desegregation in Southern schools was the rule rather than the exception for the first time.

The busing of students to achieve racial balance in schools erupted into a major national issue during 1971 as a result of opposition from both Northern and Southern whites, and a conflict between Nixon Administration policies and a Supreme Court ruling. President Nixon had long made known his opposition to massive school busing and his preference for neighborhood schools. In April this policy appeared to be undermined when the Supreme Court ruled unanimously that desegregation in schools, including neighborhood schools, must be achieved even by "bizarre" methods, and that busing was a legitimate means to that end. The court also ruled that school districts could be redrawn to achieve racial balance. (*See also* Supreme Court of the U.S.)

Using the court's decisions as a guide, school administrators and officials of the Department of Health, Education, and Welfare (HEW) worked out plans for new desegregation measures; many of them were approved by federal courts and included busing and use of federal funds to finance busing.

"VANCOUVER SUN"

This student received a 100,000-volt lesson in the laws of electricity from a Van de Graaff generator.

On August 3, a month before schools were due to open under the new plans, President Nixon publicly denounced an HEW plan for the Austin, Tex., schools for involving too much busing. He repeated his opposition to busing, warned federal officials that busing to further desegregation in the South should be held to the minimum required by law, and later attempted to withdraw federal funds from busing programs. Furthermore, Chief Justice Warren E. Burger of the Supreme Court issued an opinion declaring that the court's ruling did not require racial balance in all schools within a district and did not mandate busing.

These actions created disagreement among federal agencies charged with implementing school desegregation as to what the federal policy was, and angered the Southern school administrators, who were caught between the conflicting federal positions and also faced with local anti-integration pressures. Alabama's Gov. George C. Wallace, a potential threat to Nixon's reelection in 1972, deliberately challenged Nixon's sincerity by ordering several county school boards to ignore court-approved desegregation plans; a federal judge directed schools to ignore the governor's orders.

The city of Pontiac, Mich., was the center of a furious controversy involving school busing to promote desegregation. White parents demonstrated in a futile attempt to halt the federally ordered busing, and a number of women were arrested.

When schools opened in the fall public resistance to busing and desegregation was more marked in the North and West than in the South, where school districts went ahead with desegregation with a minimum of disruption. In Boston, Mass., a previously approved busing plan was scrapped when both white and black parents refused to honor it. White antibusing protestors in Pontiac, Mich., dynamited a number of buses; and a boycott of schools by both Chinese and whites in San Francisco, Calif., was only one of a number of such incidents. Pressure for desegregation in the North continued to grow, but there were serious obstacles, including segregated housing patterns, the tradition of neighborhood schools, and the flight of whites to the suburbs—which rendered racial balance in urban schools more difficult.

The Dilemma Over Aid to Parochial Schools

In an important and long-awaited ruling issued in June, the Supreme Court held that public aid to church-related schools below the college level was unconstitutional. The ruling was made on test cases involving Pennsylvania and Rhode Island laws that allowed public funds to be used to pay for certain teachers' salaries and/or teaching materials in parochial schools. Both laws were held to violate the 1st Amendment's required separation of church and state, and the 14th Amendment's equal-protection provisions. In another, related ruling the court decided that federal aid for academic building construction at private colleges, including church-related colleges, was constitutional. The ruling on direct lower-school aid did not invalidate cooperation between public and parochial schools

in matters such as released time for public school students to attend religious instruction.

The court's ruling was a further blow to the financially troubled Roman Catholic school system, which enrolled about 86% of the nation's private school pupils. Rising costs, decreasing enrollment, and the necessity to pay lay teachers to make up for a decline in religious instructors, continued to force the closing of parochial schools. As an alternative to direct aid to parochial schools, several states passed legislation providing tax credits for partial tuition refunds to the parents of parochial-school children. An experiment in which parochial and public schools shared data and such facilities as laboratories, auditoriums, and vocational training equipment was carried out in three major cities under Ford Foundation sponsorship.

Public School Financing Crisis

Public schools throughout the nation also faced severe financial problems. The causes included increasing costs due to inflation, rapidly rising teachers' salaries, and demands for services, coupled with a growing refusal of taxpayers to vote more funds for schools. Also contributing to school-budget deficits were increasing vandalism, the costs of court-ordered busing, and the conversion of heating systems to meet antipollution standards. Another factor in the cities was erosion of the tax base by the flight of whites to the suburbs. Schools across the country were forced to lay off teachers and other employees, cut back on maintenance, transportation, and services, and discontinue instruction in areas such as driver training, the arts, sports, and even foreign languages.

To finance public schools, many educators and state and federal officials proposed greater federal aid to the schools and a reform of state school-financing methods. In January an NEA report showed that while public education costs continued to rise the share contributed by the federal government had dropped to only 6.9% in 1970–71. Although the U.S. Congress passed a record-high $5.1 billion education appropriation in late June, the economy-seeking Nixon Administration did not use all of the funds. An Administration order to cut back on the federally funded school-lunch program in the fall met with widespread opposition and was rescinded.

An important development in education during the year was a drive to equalize school taxes. A study group funded by the U.S. Office of Education indicated that the traditional method of financing schools through local property taxes was obsolete, and courts in California and Minnesota found that this financing method was unconstitutional because it discriminated against low-income-area schools and pupils. The California ruling declared that the state must spend the same amount per pupil in all areas, regardless of local tax bases. Many states began to reexamine their tax structures and explore alternative means of school financing, such as statewide levies that would fund schools on a statewide, rather than a local, basis.

The financial crisis in the schools affected teachers through personnel cutbacks and by increasing the size of classes where layoffs occurred. In addition, the number of surplus teachers had doubled by the fall of 1971. However, openings for teachers dealing with special problems of the poor and the handicapped were available.

Innovations in Education

The operation of year-round school programs as a means of expanding curricula, accommodating more students without crowding, and making more efficient use of existing facilities gained in popularity in 1971. Another growing innovation was "performance contracting," under which businesses contracted to run entire schools or to take over special teaching functions within schools; they were paid according to the progress made by pupils. This system was also used in a number of programs for disadvantaged children and dropouts, some of which were sponsored by the federal Office of Economic Opportunity (OEO).

There was a further trend toward more informal, less structured education on the high school level, aimed primarily at students alienated from traditional school systems. On the adult level "external degree" programs, independent study plans, and life-experience credits were promoted by an increasing number of educators and institutions as a means of relieving both students and institutions of financial burdens and providing education for persons otherwise unable to attend regular colleges.

Record enrollments at vocational schools during 1971 resulted from a rapidly growing demand for skilled labor, unemployment at the professional level, disaffection with colleges and universities, and the inability of college graduates to find jobs. State and federal funding for vocational education increased. (*See* Colleges and Universities.)

Eric Hamburger leads a group of five- and six-year-olds in an exercise of the imagination. He and two friends work with children at municipal, church, and private day-care centers and camps in New York. The teachers make use of the principles of dramatic improvisation.

"THE NEW YORK TIMES"

EGYPT. The year 1971 was one of significant changes in Egypt. The nation entered into a confederation with Libya and Syria on September 1, and at the same time changed its name from the United Arab Republic to the Arab Republic of Egypt. The government undertook a diplomatic offensive aimed at implementing a Middle East settlement by the end of the year, but nevertheless increased its military preparedness. Major upheavals in the government and in the Arab Socialist Union (ASU), Egypt's only political party, left President Anwar el-Sadat in a stronger position as the country's leader and as successor to the late president, Gamal Abdel Nasser.

With the Egyptian-Israeli truce along the Suez Canal due to expire on February 5, Egypt began the year by preparing for war on the home and military fronts. On February 4 President el-Sadat announced a 30-day extension of the cease-fire and offered to reopen the canal in exchange for a partial pullback of Israeli forces on the Sinai Peninsula. The proposal was aimed at breaking the stalemate in Middle East negotiations and was viewed by Egypt as a first step toward an overall settlement. In later statements el-Sadat declared that under such a partial pullback Egyptian forces would cross the canal, but that Egypt would accept a neutral zone on the peninsula between Israeli and Egyptian forces. During February Egypt informed United Nations (UN) mediator Gunnar V. Jarring that it agreed to accept the principle of a peace treaty with Israel, in exchange for an Israeli agreement to withdraw from all Arab territory captured in the 1967 war.

Although the truce was not extended in March, el-Sadat repeated his proposals and pledged to continue diplomatic efforts for a peaceful settlement. These efforts included contacts between el-Sadat and United States President Richard M. Nixon, who supported el-Sadat's pullback proposal. Almost immediately after the lapse of the truce the Soviet Union began large-scale shipments of new air defense equipment to Egypt. (*See also* Middle East; U.S.S.R.)

The New Arab Confederation

On April 17 el-Sadat and the leaders of Libya and Syria, meeting in Benghazi, Libya, signed an agreement to unite their nations under a confederation. The plan provided for a presidential council of the three nations' presidents, a national assembly for the confederation, a combined military command, an ideology of "democratic socialism," and a no-compromise policy against Israel.

The union, named the Confederation of Arab Republics, was proclaimed in Syria on August 20. The plan had been ratified by Egypt's National Assembly late in April and was approved by over 99% of Egypt's voters on September 1. In October the presidential council named el-Sadat its first president and chose Cairo, the capital of Egypt, as the confederation's capital. Subsequently ministers of the confederation nations met to plan the amalgamation of economic, financial, and military affairs.

The Aswan High Dam, officially opened on January 15, provides full control of the Nile River, and its power station produces 10 billion kilowatt hours of electricity annually. The $1-billion project, backed by the Soviet Union, now meets 50% of Egypt's power needs.

UPI COMPIX

Egypt's Political Upheaval

President el-Sadat's Suez proposals, his closer relations with the U.S., and the Arab confederation plan stirred opposition in the ASU, led by Egypt's pro-Soviet vice-president, Aly Sabry. In the spring Sabry succeeded in obtaining a vote against the confederation in the ASU's executive committee, and el-Sadat's later presentation of the issue to the full ASU central committee was greeted by disruptions. El-Sadat then obtained secret emergency powers and the backing of the armed forces in the event of a recurrence of such a blatant challenge to his authority. The central committee eventually voted unanimously in favor of confederation.

El-Sadat dismissed Sabry as vice-president on May 2. On May 13 a number of government ministers and ASU officials resigned in another attempt to challenge el-Sadat, but el-Sadat immediately created a new government under the premiership of Mahmoud Fawzi. Sabry and other dissident members of the government and the ASU were arrested following an announcement May 14 by el-Sadat of an attempted coup. El-Sadat won popular acclaim by declaring a ban on certain secret police surveillance and by ordering free elections for a reorganization of the ASU. After trials in the fall, Sabry and others were given life terms in prison for conspiring to seize power.

Following the attempted coup el-Sadat dissolved the ASU's central committee and turned over its functions to the National Assembly, with instructions to draft a new constitution for Egypt. In July new elections were held for the ASU and for professional and trade unions. The ASU then gave el-Sadat a broad mandate for dealing with Israel on both the diplomatic and military fronts, endorsed confederation with Libya and Syria and friendship with the Soviet Union, adopted a ten-year economic program, and condemned Jordan for its campaign to control Palestinian guerrillas. Jordan's Premier Wasfi el-Tal was assassinated in Cairo in November by Palestinian guerrillas.

In spite of the ouster of pro-Soviet leftists from the government and the ASU, Egypt and the Soviet Union signed a 15-year treaty of friendship and cooperation on May 27. The treaty barred each country from interference in the internal affairs of the other and provided for continued Soviet aid to Egypt's armed forces. Nonetheless, Egypt backed the Sudanese government's repression of a Communist coup in July, and in August President el-Sadat declared that Egypt would resist Communism in the Arab world and that the country needed national unity rather than class struggle. El-Sadat's political independence apparently strained relations with the Soviets, and in October el-Sadat visited Moscow and joined Soviet leaders in condemning anti-Communist and anti-Soviet moves among the Arabs. The Soviets agreed to increase military aid to the Arabs.

El-Sadat's ouster of the leftists had occurred just

WIDE WORLD

El Qantara, in the occupied Sinai, has been a ghost town since Israeli forces evacuated all Egyptian citizens in January 1969.

after a visit to Egypt by U.S. Secretary of State William P. Rogers. Contacts between Egypt and the U.S. continued throughout the year, but by midsummer Egypt had grown disillusioned with U.S. attempts to mediate with Israel. To spur mediation efforts, el-Sadat set December 31 as a deadline for peace efforts. In the fall Egyptian armed forces were placed on alert, el-Sadat took personal command of the military, and Egypt undertook a political offensive against Israel in the UN. In December the UN General Assembly passed a resolution calling on Israel to "respond favorably" to the withdrawal proposal presented by UN mediator Jarring earlier in the year.

New Internal Policies; the Economy

In September el-Sadat further pursued governmental reorganization by dissolving the National Assembly and announcing new elections to be held in October. On September 11 Egypt's voters almost unanimously approved a new constitution that strengthened individual freedoms, protected ownership of private property and small businesses, provided guarantees against arbitrary arrest, granted freedom of worship within the official Islamic state, and gave equal rights to women. The constitution also provided for a strong president with powers to appoint ministers and to dissolve the new People's Assembly. A new cabinet was formed under Mahmoud Fawzi on September 19.

During the year the government took steps to remove travel restrictions, release political prisoners, and restore confiscated property to former owners. A law was drafted guaranteeing foreign businesses from nationalization.

The el-Sadat government initiated economic reforms to decentralize authority, cut down on bureaucratic inefficiency, and stimulate production.

A ten-year development program aimed at doubling the national income was launched, and an international bank for foreign trade was planned to finance Egypt's foreign commerce and to attract investments from other Arab nations. To encourage investment, customs-free zones were proposed for the importation of materials for foreign-owned projects. Egyptian banks were reorganized to permit specialization in various branches of the economy. The management of reclaimed desert lands, previously operated at a loss to the government, was reorganized to allow large-scale production units that could function as separate companies. Greater autonomy in industrial management and reforms in labor benefits were also planned. (*See also* Israel; Jordan; Sudan. *See in* CE: Egypt.)

ELECTRONICS.

Much of the news in electronics in 1971 centered on reducing costs of devices already developed rather than on developing new ones. The electronics industry in the United States was hard hit by poor business conditions, reductions in government spending, and foreign competition. Many electronics companies that depended on receiving government contracts for the major portion of their business resorted to cutting back their work force in order to survive. Emphasis thus shifted from government work to equipment aimed at the consumer and commercial markets.

This hand-held Busicom calculator from Japan operates on one integrated circuit and adds, subtracts, multiplies, and divides.

COURTESY, BUSICOM

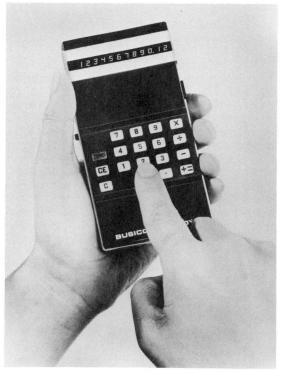

To achieve the low costs needed to compete in these markets, companies installed labor-saving production machinery. For example, RCA Corp. redesigned its color television sets to use hybrid microcircuits that were more easily built on an automated production line than previous circuits. General Electric Co. introduced a new packaging method for semiconductor devices, a plastic strip that carried the devices through basic production, testing, and insertion in equipment. In another cost-cutting move, semiconductor integrated circuits were being made still more complex to hold more circuitry, thus avoiding the cost of interconnecting less-complex integrated circuits.

A new generation of electronic watches hit the market in 1971. Earlier electronic watches used a tuning fork oscillator for the basic timing and were accurate to one minute per month. The new watches used a quartz piezoelectric crystal as the oscillator, an integrated circuit as a divider, and either a conventional dial mechanism driven by a small electric motor or a direct numeric readout display. The oscillator, in many designs, vibrated at 16,384 cycles per second and the integrated circuit divided this in half 14 times to bring it down to one pulse per second. One of the first quartz-crystal watches was introduced by a Japanese company, Seiko, and was based on integrated circuits made by a U.S. company, Intersil, Inc. It was accurate to one half second per day.

In the audio field, the big newsmaker was quadrasonic, or "four track," sound, in which the two speakers of stereo sound were increased to four, surrounding the listener with sound to give him a more realistic feeling of actually "being there."

Two competing approaches to quadrasonics emerged: the "purist" approach, in which four separate sound tracks were recorded from four microphones and then played back separately to four speakers, and the "matrix" approach, in which two specially encoded channels were fed into a decoder where they were electronically adjusted and then split up and fed to the four speakers. Of the two approaches, the purist approach was more realistic but the matrix approach was cheaper.

Electronic calculators dropped in price during the year as competition increased and as manufacturing costs decreased. In late 1970, for example, small hand-held calculators were selling for $400. By mid-1971, prices had dropped to the $200 range. The goal of most calculator manufacturers was to produce a calculator that sold for under $100. Such a calculator would have a large potential market in average family use for such tasks as checking bills, income tax, and homework. One dramatic development that suggested the goal was near was the single-chip calculator introduced by Japan's Busicom Corp. All the calculator's logic circuitry was on one integrated circuit chip. A similar single-chip calculator was also announced by Texas Instruments. (*See also* Computers. *See in* CE: Electrons and Electronics.)

EL SALVADOR. In 1971, the maintenance of the five-member Central American Common Market (CACM) was of special concern to El Salvador, the most industrialized and densely populated of the member countries. Since the war with Honduras in July 1969, and the subsequent border closing with that nation, El Salvador has been fortunate in establishing alternate trade routes to its markets in Nicaragua and Costa Rica. Continuing favorable agricultural and marketing conditions, combined with vigorous public and private efforts, have done much to reduce if not eliminate the ill effects of the war.

Thus far, telephone, telegraph, and postal links have been reestablished between El Salvador and Honduras, and all traffic across the border is permitted except that which has originated in either of the two countries. In efforts to further reduce these border barriers and strengthen the CACM, the foreign minister of El Salvador joined counterpart representatives from CACM countries, except Honduras, at several meetings in 1971. (*See in* CE: Salvador, El.)

EMPLOYMENT. As the United States economy remained sluggish in 1971, the unemployment rate continued to be high, hovering around 6% for most of the year. It was the highest jobless rate since 1961. About five million Americans were out of work at any one time during the year.

There were a number of groups that were particularly affected by the unemployment crisis—returning Vietnam war veterans, scientists and engineers, and recent college graduates. Among veterans, those who found it hardest to get jobs were the untrained in their early 20's, members of minority groups, and those who did not get honorable discharges. Scientists and engineers were affected mainly because of the sharp cutback in U.S. government spending on defense and scientific research. The shortage of jobs for these highly trained specialists was thought by some to be at the worst level since the depression years of the 1930's. And for the second subsequent year, there was a decline in job opportunities for college graduates. Those in the class of 1971 who found it most difficult to find employment were graduates with degrees in engineering, mathematics, and science.

The rise in unemployment was directly attributable to the anti-inflation policies of the Administration of U.S. President Richard M. Nixon, which had resulted in a slowdown of the economy. As the Administration shifted to a new phase of its economic game plan in 1970 to revive the economy, expansionist policies were instituted, but the unemployment rate remained stubbornly high. Nixon established a target of reducing unemployment to a 5% rate by the end of 1971. His "full employment" budget for fiscal 1972 was designed to help accomplish this goal by basing government expenditures on what the government would receive in taxes if the economy were operating at full employment, which was defined as one in which there was only a 4% unemployment rate.

Gary, Ind., steel workers rushed to the Indiana Employment Security Division to sign up for benefits following continued layoffs and news that U.S. Steel would recall only 30% of its force.
UPI COMPIX

Employment

NEWSWEEK PHOTO BY JEFF LOWENTHAL © NEWSWEEK, 1971

When the Burlington Northern railroad was formed by a merger, 60 clerks from one of the merged lines found themselves with nothing to do; however, their job security was protected by a strong union. They sat all day and read or knitted, saying they would have preferred work.

In March, in the wake of increasing criticism of his economic policies by Democratic members of the U.S. Congress, Nixon proposed a program to permit states and municipalities to use federal funds to create temporary jobs in the public service sector. This represented a full turnabout in the president's policies. Only a few months earlier, in December 1970, Nixon had vetoed a similar program passed by Congress as "inappropriate and ineffective." The president also announced appropriation of more than $100 million for various specific programs for the unemployed, including $64 million to provide more summer jobs for urban youth; $1 million for a pilot program to help Vietnam veterans go to school or get on-the-job training; and $42 million for retraining scientists.

Through midyear the Administration sought to view the economic statistics in the most optimistic terms, although, at times, its interpretations contradicted those provided by the Bureau of Labor Statistics (BLS), the government agency responsible for compiling the monthly economic indicators. Thus the Administration became subject to the charge that it was manipulating the meaning of the statistics for political reasons in order to keep the American public in the dark about just how badly the economy was doing.

On August 15, however, the BLS's more negative interpretation of the state of the economy was borne out when Nixon suddenly abandoned his previous economic game plan and announced a new economic policy, which included a 90-day wage and price freeze to curb inflation and to stabilize the economy. After the freeze ended in November, Phase II of Nixon's program began, continuing the wage and price controls, although with some degree of flexibility.

In general, the new economic program appeared to be reviving the economy as reflected in the favorable economic indicators at the end of the year. However, the unemployment rate remained close to 6%. In September, in fact, the first full month of Nixon's new economic program, the number of major cities with "substantial unemployment" (6% or higher for a minimum of two months) rose to 64, the highest number in ten years. Thus it remained unclear how long it would take before an economic upturn would actually begin to reduce unemployment. Nor was it clear how well the specific programs Nixon had instituted to help the unemployed would work. The public service employment bill, which the president had proposed in March and Congress had passed in July, was originally expected to create some 150,000 to 200,000 jobs. By early October, however, only about 6,000 people had been hired, and it appeared that only 130,000 jobs would eventually be created. (*See also* Economy; Labor Unions.)

ENGINEERING PROJECTS.

A wide variety of engineering construction projects were begun or completed throughout the world in 1971, many undertaken by the developing nations, which sought to lay the foundation for economic growth by first creating the necessary infrastructure. The most important of these projects was doubtlessly Egypt's Aswan High Dam, which after nearly $1 billion of expenditure and more than a decade of work, was finally inaugurated in 1971. An increasing concern of the industrial nations was the environmental aspect of new projects, chiefly the need to preserve natural environment against further encroachment by steel and concrete.

BRIDGES

Discussion on the box-girder method of bridge construction continued in 1971. The technique came under question when portions of both the Milford Haven Bridge in Wales, Great Britain, and of the West Gate Bridge over the Yarra River in Melbourne, Australia, collapsed during construction in 1970. As a result the British government had restricted traffic on 42 box-girder bridges. A British royal commission inquiry on the West Gate Bridge collapse was critical of the British consulting engineers. They, however, upheld the method,

The 15-mile twin span Sunshine Skyway Bridge connects two Florida cities, St. Petersburg and Bradenton. A link to Miami is planned.

KEYSTONE

and one spokesman attributed failure, if and when it occurred, to human error rather than to faulty design concept. In September Britain's Department of the Environment announced that it would implement the royal commission's recommendations for tightening safety rules in the construction of box-girder bridges. The adoption of adequate safety rules was given added urgency by the collapse in November of a box-girder bridge under construction in Koblenz, West Germany.

Work began on a number of cable-stayed structures during the year. It seemed likely that structures of this type would be increasingly preferred to suspension bridges in view of their improved rigidity, economy of cables, and simplified anchorings. Among cable-stayed structures under construction in 1971 were the Zarate-Brazo Largo viaducts, each three miles long, on two branches of the Paraná River north of Buenos Aires, Argentina, and the Bratislava Bridge in Bratislava, Czechoslovakia.

Although large bridges with triangulated girders had been virtually abandoned in Europe for aesthetic reasons, they were still fairly popular in the United States. Among those under construction were the four-mile-long Chesapeake Bay Bridge on the East Coast and the Auburn-Forest Hill Bridge north of Sacramento, Calif.

The longest viaduct in Europe (19,909 feet) was being built in Sweden between Kalmar and the island of Öland. Other structures of outstanding length that came in service included, in the Netherlands, the bridges at Katerveer (main span 494 feet), Deventer (center span also 494 feet), and Heteren (15 spans with lengths varying between 157 feet and 396 feet); and in Japan, the Nagoya-Ohashi Bridge (main span 577 feet) and the Amakusa Bridge (main span 525 feet).

In Europe new, sophisticated building techniques were being employed for crossing distances of between 80 and 100 feet. One technique, developed in West Germany, seemed particularly promising since it required only a limited amount of equipment. The deck was prefabricated in successive sections on one bank of the space to be crossed, and then jacked progressively into its final position. (*See in* CE: Bridge.)

DAMS

On January 15 the Aswan High Dam in Egypt was officially inaugurated by the presidents of Egypt and the Soviet Union. The overall cost of the 364-foot-high dam, which took 11 years to build, was just under $1 billion. There were some critical reports that the dam—the largest of its kind ever built—was not living up to the expectations anticipated for it in terms of land reclamation and water supply and that the dam was in fact creating myriad problems, among them, erosion and a rise in water-borne disease.

In South Africa the Hendrik Verwoerd arch dam on the Orange River (height 280 feet) was com-

A big new dam across the Haiho river in China will prevent disastrous flooding. Heavy rain has menaced the area for centuries.

pleted during the year. In Morocco building began of the Koudiat-El-Rhorfa earth-and-rock-fill dam (height 230 feet) on the Loukkos River. In Tanzania construction was started on the Great Ruaha River earth-and-rock-fill dam (height 131 feet).

In Hong Kong work was started on the High Island Reservoir, formed by two 200-foot-high rock-fill dams across the narrow sea passage separating High . Island from the Saikung Peninsula. One dam was to be 1,500 feet long, the other 1,000 feet long. Construction involved digging 75-foot-deep trenches underwater. In Turkey construction began on two dams in 1971, the Karakaya arch-gravity dam (height 590 feet, volume 1.8 million cubic yards) and the Karababa straight-concrete buttress dam (height 394 feet, volume 4.8 million cubic yards). Both dams were on the Euphrates River.

Major dam projects were also under way in Asia —in Iran, Japan, India, and the U.S.S.R. Difficulties with construction, changes in the schedule, and other economic priorities put off to 1976 the completion of the Soviet 886-foot-high Inguri River arch dam, the highest of its type.

In Australia the Talbingo earth-and-rock-fill dam (height 530 feet, volume 19 million cubic yards) on the Tumut River was completed, part of the vast Snowy Mountains project. It had an earth-fill core sloping upstream.

In Europe the major completion in 1971 was that of Austria's Schlegeis arch-gravity dam (height 426 feet, crest length 2,378 feet, volume 1,255,680 cubic yards). Work was also under way on massive projects in Spain and Switzerland.

In Montana the Libby concrete-gravity dam on the Kootenay River (height 420 feet, volume 3.75 million cubic yards) was near completion. Its 90-mile-long reservoir would eventually extend 42 miles into British Columbia along the Kootenay Lake. Construction began on the Pyramid earth-fill dam (height 381 feet, storage 183,000 acre-feet) and on the Cascadia rock-fill dam (height 255 feet, volume 2.5 million cubic yards) on the South Santiam River, in Oregon. (*See in* CE: Dam.)

ROADS

Highway engineering projects proliferated in 1971 as in previous years. The transcontinental network of European high-speed roads was being extended, and, as before, the developing countries continued to build routes running from areas of production to centers of distribution.

Most European countries completed important parts of their highway programs. France brought into use in October 1970 the last stretch of its 626-mile-long expressway linking Lille, near the Belgian border, with Marseilles, the major port on the French Mediterranean coast. West Germany also completed the last few miles of its Ruhr expressway, an important route through the heavily populated and heavily industrialized Ruhr Basin. The Brescia-Piacenza highway in northern Italy was completed during the summer of 1971. Part of it was built with concrete as a test for future highway construction in Italy. In June 1971 the 14-mile-long Prague-Mirovice section of Czechoslovakia's Prague-Brno-Bratislava highway was opened, which would eventually be linked up with another expressway that, in turn, would run to the Austrian border. In Britain, several new sections were added to existing highways.

In Cameroon the 70-mile-long Waza-Maltan road was opened during the year. Work also progressed on the all-weather road between Nairobi, Kenya, and Addis Ababa, Ethiopia. Kenya still had about 100 miles of its section to complete.

In Pakistan two important projects were completed. The first was a section of an express highway that would ultimately run from Karachi, the chief seaport and industrial center of West Pakistan, to Lahore, the capital of that region. The second major project completed was the Karakorum Road from Pakistan to Sinkiang in the People's Republic of China. The road, almost 200 miles long, rose in several places to some 9,000 feet. In 1971 the government of Malaysia announced that several major reconstruction projects on major roads had been completed.

In Peru a four-lane express highway replaced Tupac Amaru Avenue, which led from Lima, the capital, into the Canta valley. In Brazil a major road-widening project took place along more than three miles of the famous Copacabana Beach in Rio de Janeiro. Traffic along the new six-lane highway would be computer-controlled. The road project was part of an extensive urban-renewal program. In El Salvador an important highways project, La Cuchilla-Km35, was completed. The eight-mile-long highway formed part of the Central American Highway System. (*See in* CE: Roads and Streets.)

TUNNELS

Projects for tunneling flourished with undiminished vigor in 1971. Some 72 countries were considering underground transportation systems, of which 22 were in Europe. The demand for tunnels for water supplies and drainage systems increased.

Work began in Amsterdam, Netherlands, and in Brussels, Belgium, on new subways. In Italy work continued on the $40-million Gran Sasso D'Italia tunnel forming part of the four-lane *autostrada* linking Rome with the Adriatic. Two special boom-type tunneling machines were in use, each costing $1 million. It was claimed that though machines of this type had been used before, these two were the largest ever employed in tunneling.

At Lucerne, Switzerland, Swiss engineers employed a novel method for boring twin tunnels on the route of National Highway 2. Twin pilot tunnels were driven with a conventional mole, the tunnel being enlarged to a full diameter of 34.5 feet using a tunneling machine equipped with two cutting units, which enlarged the pilot first to about 25 feet in diameter and then to full size. In Britain work on a cable tunnel under the River Severn continued with the use of two hard-rock tunneling machines. Considered one of the most difficult tunneling projects of the century, the tunnel was to be completed at the end of 1972.

In the U.S. work continued on the tunnel drive at Straight Creek in Colorado. The tunnel cross section was approximately 42 feet by 44 feet. Immensely difficult ground conditions in this mountain region slowed down the work. In Alabama progress was made on a $47.5-million contract for a twin-tube tunnel under the Mobile River. In Mexico in the Federal District construction began on the main outfall tunnel that was to form part of a new main drainage system. The tunnel was to be about 32 miles long and about 21 feet in diameter. (*See in* CE: Tunnels.)

ENVIRONMENT. From around the world in 1971 came reports of an increasing environmental crisis, indicating that solutions could not be reached by single nations but must be met by international planning and control. Air and water pollution and the disposal of wastes were growing problems for the world's great cities. New York City, Los Angeles, Houston (Tex.), Rome, Tokyo, Singapore, and many other cities were smog-ridden or beset by other serious environmental difficulties.

Along the shores of the great oceans and lakes, beaches were being closed one by one because they were no longer safe for swimming. (The United States alone closed 91.) Far out on the high seas, accumulations of floating garbage and oil were sighted daily by mariners. The Soviet Union was struggling with pollution from mills and factories that threatened to ruin its rivers and lakes. The once-blue Mediterranean was described as a sick sea, poisoned by wastes from every country that surrounded it. The Sea of Galilee, the North Sea, and the Rhine River were filling up with sewage or other poisons. Mercury, lead, and other chemicals from pesticides were being found in greater numbers of fish and other food sources. Foresters in

This underwater tunnel section is part of the Bay Area Rapid Transit (BART) System, which will consist of 75 miles of elevated and subway lines linking San Francisco, Alameda, and Contra Costa counties in California. The tunnel portion of the system was completed in 1971.

COURTESY, BAY AREA RAPID TRANSIT DISTRICT

several countries reported trees dying from polluted air. Even the world's deserts, invaded by too many people in new modes of transportation, were in trouble.

All these reports pointed up the importance of the first international Conference on the Human Environment to be held in Stockholm, Sweden, in June 1972 under the sponsorship of the United Nations (UN). Representatives from 131 countries and several world organizations will meet to deal with the vast environmental problems that threaten eventual biological death to the planet earth. The conference is not expected to provide final answers for global problems, but first steps will be taken toward international agreements involving marine pollution, soil conservation, and environmental monitoring. One organization to be represented is the new Scientific Committee on Problems of the Environment (SCOPE), set up by the International Council of Scientific Unions, a confederation of 16 nongovernmental scientific institutes. Its function is to offer independent advice to the UN, especially through conferences such as this one.

Water Pollution

In a move toward international cooperation in pollution control, environmental officials of the U.S. and Canada met in August to ratify 14 resolutions toward implementing water quality standards in the Great Lakes. Under the agreement, the International Joint Commission of the two countries would have authority to monitor a 3,000-mile-long area from Duluth, Minn., to Massena, N.Y., near the St. Lawrence River. Earlier the commission had recommended that the phosphate content of household and industrial detergents be reduced immediately and replaced entirely by the end of 1972. It also recommended that the U.S.

spend some $1.5 billion and Canada $250 million for waste-treatment facilities to remove phosphates from sewage.

The problem of phosphates in detergents was intensified in the fall when the U.S. government said phosphate substitutes could be more harmful than the phosphates they replaced. In the late 1960's it was revealed that phosphates in detergents could be dangerous pollutants to rivers and streams because they promoted the growth of algae that used up oxygen in water and thus killed off other forms of aquatic life (eutrophication). The federal government was even considering legislation to outlaw phosphate-containing detergents. (The sale of phosphate laundry products was restricted in four states—Indiana, Maine, New York, and Connecticut—and in several major cities—Chicago; Miami, Fla.; and Akron, Ohio.) However, in September the government changed its position and warned consumers that the substitute chemicals could create health hazards greater than the ecological dangers inherent in phosphates. The leading substitutes included NTA (nitrilotriacetic acid) and various caustic carbonates and silicates. These might cause irritation to eyes, nose, and throat, and possibly more serious ailments. However, some conservationists feared that the government's decision might have been influenced by detergent industry lobbyists.

Recognizing that the U.S. was accountable for more than one fourth of the wastes dumped into the oceans, Congress began considering laws that would give the Environmental Protection Agency (EPA) power to halt dumping of radiological, chemical, and biological wastes. A rigid permit system would be established for disposing of all other materials. According to a study made by the Council on Environmental Quality, the dumping of

Feeling that the Manhattan-to-Queens subway tunnel project is a safety hazard for children and an environmental menace, demonstrators wrote protest slogans on fences bordering the construction site. The subway will go through the southern part of New York City's Central Park.
"THE NEW YORK TIMES"

industrial wastes into the Atlantic and Pacific oceans and the Gulf of Mexico had more than doubled during the 1960's, and sewage sludge dumping increased by half. Another government report estimated that one fourth of all DDT manufactured to date is in the world's oceans.

Scientists of the National Oceanic and Atmospheric Administration reported that although the oceans might be able to assimilate current levels of sewage and solid wastes, they cannot break down the loads of persistent pesticides, heavy metals, and hydrocarbons. Instead of being absorbed by the seas, these elements are being absorbed by marine life through the aquatic food chain. During the year amounts of mercury at levels thought to be toxic to humans were found in the livers of Alaskan fur seals that live in the open Pacific 50 to 100 miles from coastal areas. The mercury was found after the livers were used in the manufacture of iron supplement pills for human beings. Catfish and bass caught off the southern California coast and around the New York City area not only contained high amounts of lead but showed a high incidence of skin ulcers, malformations, and genetic changes as a result of poisons that cannot be dissipated by the oceans.

British scientists reported that examination of the carcasses of thousands of seabirds that have been dying along the coasts of the Irish Sea contained the highest levels of polychlorinated biphenyls (PCB) on record. PCB is a group of poisonous industrial chemicals that, like the persistent pesticides, remain permanently in the oceans and, through the food chain, collect in the livers of seabirds and seals. Although the use of PCB is banned in Great Britain and is declining in the U.S., the Food and Drug Administration in September reported finding high levels of biphenyls in breakfast cereals that had been packed in recycled cardboard. Other foodstuffs found to be contaminated with PCB and then withdrawn from the market included eggs, chickens, and turkeys. In 1968 PCB contamination of cooking oil killed five persons in Japan.

The EPA reported that oil spills during 1971 around the globe totaled between 5 million and 10 million tons, much of it deliberate dumping. Only five years before, the average was about a half-million tons annually. In the Gulf of Mexico, an oil production platform that burst into flames and killed four workmen on Dec. 1, 1970, burned until April 12, 1971. Two tankers collided near the Golden Gate Bridge in San Francisco, Calif., on January 18, spilling more than a million gallons of bunker oil into the bay. Five days later another tanker hit a rock ledge at the mouth of New Haven, Conn., harbor; then through gashes in the vessel 385,000 gallons of fuel oil poured out into Long Island Sound. Britain also had to battle oil slicks in the English Channel after a tanker sank in the Strait of Dover; oil soaked the beaches of Kent and Sussex, exacting heavy death tolls of seabirds in

A forest fire in the Everglades left desolate remains near the Tamiami Trail between Naples and Miami, Fla.

some areas. In August 230,000 gallons of oil flowing from valves carelessly left open on a U.S. Navy tanker formed a slick 100 yards wide and several miles long off the California coast. It left patches of tarlike scum and fouled the private beach of U.S. President Richard M. Nixon at San Clemente. In September the San Francisco Bay suffered a second big oil spill when pipes being used to unload a tanker broke apart and sent 15,000 gallons of crude oil into the bay.

To detect oil spills before they spread out and become unmanageable, the National Aeronautics and Space Administration (NASA) developed sensors that when placed in satellites can spot and track slicks on a global basis. For local detection the same device can be used in airplanes. Scientists also reported success in identifying differences in petroleum from different parts of the world. Under tests, every consignment of oil was found to have its own compositional features that are as typical and persistent as a fingerprint. Oil from Kuwait, for example, has a completely different "fingerprint" from Texas oil. Through use of these "fingerprints," it is expected that laws against illegal oil discharges and spills will become easier to

Giant cooling towers were installed at the Paradise steam-powered generating plant in southern Kentucky after the Tennessee Valley Authority found that warm water discharged from the plant into the Green River Reservoir forced fish away from the area.
WIDE WORLD

enforce because offenders will not be able to conceal their identity.

Air Quality Standards

A number of amendments to the Clean Air Act became law in the U.S. on January 1, 1971. A major provision was the requirement that new motor vehicles be virtually pollution-free by 1975. (Car exhaust fumes account for about 80% of all atmospheric contamination in U.S. cities.) The law requires reduction of carbon monoxide and hydrocarbon emission by 90%.

The EPA, under provisions of the Clean Air Act, in April announced national air standards that would limit permissible amounts of six major air pollutants by 1975. The EPA said there would need to be "drastic" changes in power-generating practices and in "commuting habits" of persons in metropolitan areas. States had until Jan. 1, 1972, to submit plans for meeting standards for the six pollutants. The EPA would then either accept the proposals or impose its own.

Pollution from Fuel and Power

Four lawsuits filed in May and June signaled the beginning of what may become the biggest environmental controversy in U.S. history. The outcome may determine just how much destruction of the nation's environment will be tolerated in satisfying the ever increasing demands for electrical energy, and how much open space and clean air can be traded off to provide power for urban light and heat. The suits concerned the construction of six huge coal-fired generating plants on the great Colorado Plateau reaching from southern Nevada to northern New Mexico.

The decision to build these plants came more than a decade before when a consortium of 23 public and private organizations involved in electrical power needs sought generating sites long distances from cities in the Southwest. The first plant was completed at Farmington, N.M., in 1963, and the pollution from it has been extremely high. The gray plume from the plant's smokestacks has been tracked by planes for 215 miles, and it was visible to Gemini 12 astronauts 170 miles out in space. When the other five plants reach full operation, what is now the cleanest and most scenic area of the U.S. may be completely obscured by yellow haze with particles of sulfur and nitrogen raining down upon several Indian reservations and six national parks, including the Grand Canyon.

The lawsuits seeking to block further development of the power plants were filed by the Native American Rights Fund, a group of Navajo Indians, leaders of the Hopi tribe, the National Wildlife Federation, the Environmental Defense Fund, and the Sierra Club. They asked the U.S. District Court in Washington, D.C., to try all the cases together and issue an injunction barring federal agencies from further cooperation with the power complex until the National Environmental Policy Act of 1969 is complied with. The suits charged that laws providing for the protection of fish and wildlife, national parks, recreation areas, and historic and cultural sites had been violated.

To obtain coal for the power plants, strip mining was started on Arizona's Black Mesa, creating additional controversy. Black Mesa is a highland of hundreds of square miles of valleys and dry washes with islands of great forest and grass, where the Navajos raise livestock and the Hopis have their villages. The coal is spread thin over a 64,000-acre mining lease. To mine the coal requires extensive stripping, which destroys vegetation and leaves huge expanses of bare earth. The power companies promise that Black Mesa will be returned to the Indians "in as good condition as received, except for ordinary wear, tear, and depletion incident to mining operations." They have agreed to grade the land back into shapes that blend with the surrounding terrain and to replant native vegetation. Conservationists, however, point to disastrous results of strip mining in states east of the Mississippi River and say that land ripped apart can never be restored and is damaged permanently. Some fear that the scarring left by earth movers in northern New Mexico and Arizona is only the beginning of continuous stripping all the way north to Montana and the Dakotas.

Saving the Big Thicket

Another attempt to save a large natural area from destruction involved land in Texas. Scientists from 27 states formed a committee in an effort to preserve 200,000 acres of the Big Thicket, a wilderness in eastern Texas, and set it aside as a national park. Originally consisting of 3.5 million acres of thick woods, the Big Thicket has been reduced to 300,000 acres by lumber interests that have cut much of its pine and oak.

Migrating birds use the Big Thicket as a refuge, and owls, whooping cranes, and bald eagles nest there. A holly tree more than 13 feet in circumference, believed to be the world's largest, still survives. The world's tallest variety of cypress and many rare ferns, orchids, mosses, and lichens grow in the Big Thicket.

Administrative and Judicial Decisions

Conservationists won a considerable number of battles against industrial incursion in various parts of the U.S. in 1971. After several years of controversy, President Nixon on January 19 ordered a halt to further construction of the Cross-Florida Barge Canal. A total of $50 million already had been spent and nearly one third of the project was completed, but the president followed the recommendations of the Council on Environmental Quality because, as he said, "the project would endanger the unique wildlife of the area."

A U.S. District Court decision in Arkansas blocked construction of a dam on the Cossatot River in a rugged Ouachita Mountains area. The decision gave strength to the National Environmental Policy Act which forbids alteration of the environment without preparation of satisfactory impact statements justifying the changes. In Maine the state's Environmental Improvement Commission during the summer denied an application for construction of a $150-million oil refinery on Sears Island in Penobscot Bay.

A federal judge in the fall barred further construction on the $387-million Tennessee-Tombigbee waterway through Alabama and Mississippi until it could be determined if the Administration-backed project would damage the environment. The project would create a series of locks in the Tombigbee River that would permit water traffic from the Gulf of Mexico to the Tennessee River at the juncture of Tennessee, Mississippi, and Alabama.

Regulating Feedlots

New laws were put into effect in 1971 to control one of the growing pollution problems connected with livestock raising—the operation of feedlots. This operation involves contract feeding of cattle for several farmers in an area. Large numbers of beef animals are concentrated in one place, where automatic feeding and watering lowers the cost of preparing them for market. In the decade between 1960 and 1970 the number of cattle handled by feedlots doubled from 12 million to 24 million. Because of the high concentration of animals, waste runoffs from feedlots have become major pollutants of streams in beef-producing states, contributing as significantly to water pollution as factories do in industrialized states.

The new laws regulated distances of feedlots from homes and waterways and established systems of permits based on lot size. Dumping of drainage water or manure into streams was prohibited, and waste control systems were required in some states. Preliminary studies in some areas indicated that further regulations may be required to prevent seepage of wastes from feedlots into water tables.

Neighborhood recycling projects, like this one in New York City, collect garbage to sell to companies that have recycling programs.
RUSSELL REIF FROM PICTORIAL PARADE

The Civic Auditorium in Portland, Ore., features a distinctive block-square fountain park. The man-made waterfalls, terraces, and the shrubbery provide a pleasant and restful enclave, surrounded by high grassy knolls that keep out city noise and turmoil.

International Action

In 1971 there were a number of noteworthy environmental activities internationally. The Council of Europe, meeting at Strasbourg, France, in December 1970 passed a Declaration on the Management of the Natural Environment of Europe that stressed the interdependence of continental land-use systems, regardless of national frontiers. This theme was expressed again at a UN conference on pollution held near Helsinki, Finland, in July, attended by conservationists from all major countries.

The British Royal Commission specified several priorities for action, including the urgent need for studies of river and coastal water pollution. In France plans were made for a central Environmental Research Institute to coordinate the work of several specialist institutes. In Yugoslavia, through the Federal Council for Coordination of Scientific Activities, a scientific investigation of the Adriatic Sea was started. The Japanese government in May established national standards for acceptable levels of noise recommended by the Living Environmental Council. The West German government opened its Bavarian Forest National Park, covering 30,000 acres along the mountainous frontier with Czechoslovakia.

Other Developments

Other conservation and antipollution activities included President Nixon's April request that Congress add 14 areas to the nation's wilderness system, four of which were located in states that previously had no such areas—Ohio, Utah, Louisiana, and Virginia. The first U.S. Earth Week was observed April 18–24; observances were mainly local and included such activities as "bike days" and cleanup campaigns. Conservationists in West Virginia in June took bold legal action to try to abolish all strip-mining in the valuable Coal River Valley watershed, a 35-mile area where 30 to 40 operators are active. In July the governors of Washington, Oregon, and Idaho joined conservationists to prevent construction of hydroelectric dams in the last wild stretch of the Snake River in Hells Canyon.

The U.S. Forest Service introduced an antipollution companion to Smokey the Bear; he is Woodsy the Owl, a cartoon character whose slogan is "Give a hoot—Don't pollute." Oregon became the first state to require by law a deposit (5¢) on all soft-drink and beer containers. The objective was to encourage recycling and halt littering by making containers valuable enough that they would not be discarded. (*See also* Animals and Wildlife. *See in* CE: Conservation.)

EQUATORIAL GUINEA. Severe political and economic instability plagued the country in 1971. Late in 1970, President Francisco Macías Nguma condemned Portugal for the invasion of the Republic of Guinea; his action was the signal for brutal reaction against the white colonists of Equatorial Guinea. Of 7,000 Europeans in the country in 1968, only a few hundred now remained. They were mostly Spanish and Portuguese and owned or controlled nearly all the agricultural and commercial enterprises. Consequently the people of Equatorial Guinea found themselves bereft of thriving cocoa and lumber industries and without many of the goods sold by the departed shopkeepers. The nation's problems were compounded by an autocratic leader, legions of secret policemen, bands of undisciplined soldiers, and the Juventud, a militant youth squad.

Libya provided $1 million in January, and some aid was given by the Organization of African Unity. Spain regularly provided direct financial assistance and bought the cocoa crop of its former colony.

In September Equatorial Guinea made international news when a U.S. embassy official in the country was found murdered. His colleague was later charged with the murder.

ETHIOPIA. The serious threat of the rebels of Eritrea Province continued in Ethiopia in 1971. Fear of the rebels and their backers—certain Arab insurgent organizations and the governments of Syria, Iraq, and the People's Democratic Republic of Yemen (Aden)—led to a declaration of martial law in December 1970 in that northern province.

In May students in Addis Ababa, the capital, staged a protest against increased prices, which was brutally repressed. Economic difficulties included

Emperor Haile Selassie I wears both traditional and modern clothing. His garb reflects the contradictions of Ethiopia.

CAMERA PIX FROM KEYSTONE

a fall in coffee prices and significant increases in external freight charges.

Favorable economic developments included two new hydroelectric plants due for completion by 1972, a new tire plant, and a cement plant that would more than double existing production. An assistance program for small farmers, with credit for fertilizers and improved seeds, was planned to reach an estimated one million farmers (representing 4 million people) in 13 years. Also during 1971, the fifth National Highway Program, with a heavy concentration on feeder roads to complement the major highway pattern, was submitted for financing to the World Bank. An important proposal to define and guarantee the customary rights of the tenant farmers, who make up over 80% of the population, was presented to the parliament but its passage was blocked by conservative forces.

The only remaining United States military base in Africa, the tracking station at Asmara, was visited by Gen. William C. Westmoreland in June. During the year Emperor Haile Selassie I visited Spain, Burundi, Rwanda, and the People's Republic of China. (*See in* CE: Ethiopia.)

EUROPE. Two events of major significance marked the year 1971 in Europe: the determination of the conditions under which Great Britain might become a member of the European Economic Community (EEC), or Common Market, and Britain's acceptance of those conditions, and the successful negotiation of a draft agreement on the status of Berlin by the four wartime powers—the Soviet Union, the United States, France, and Britain. Although the trend toward Western European unity was temporarily set back by the monetary and trade crisis instigated by United States President Richard M. Nixon's new economic policy in August and the four powers had not formally signed the Berlin agreement by the end of the year, the trend of events was nevertheless regarded with optimism. A start had been made toward resolution of one of the most troublesome problems of the postwar situation, and a major step had been taken toward a new political and economic alignment for the future.

European Integration

The negotiations between the six EEC countries —France, West Germany, Italy, Belgium, the Netherlands, and Luxembourg—and Britain on the conditions under which Britain might enter the Common Market were terminated successfully in June. Perhaps the most expeditiously achieved agreement was that dealing with Britain's future institutional position in the EEC. In such bodies as the Council of Ministers, the Executive Commission, and the European Parliament, Britain was to be on an equal footing with France, West Germany, and Italy. On the industrial tariff question the agreement provided that duties between Britain and the EEC would be reduced by 20% annually over a period of five years with virtually duty-free British access to the

British Prime Minister Edward Heath (at right, above) was cordially received at the Élysée Palace in Paris when he arrived in May to talk with French leaders about England's entry into the EEC. At home (above, right, and facing page) British citizens were divided on the issue.

Common Market within three years. As for the common external tariff of the Common Market, Britain was to apply it according to a somewhat similar schedule. With regard to the EEC budget, the ceiling on Britain's payments was to rise gradually over five years with another two-year adjustment period in 1978 and 1979.

Despite the fact that these conditions were relatively favorable to Britain, there remained a lack of enthusiasm on the part of the British public about entering the Common Market. In the period since 1967, when British EEC membership was vetoed for the second time by France's President Charles de Gaulle, the British had cooled perceptibly towards such a possibility. In June 1966, opinion polls indicated that 66% of the electorate would support membership; in May 1971 support had dropped to 20%. However, in the government White Paper on the subject, Prime Minister Edward Heath insisted that there was no alternative to membership, that if membership were rejected in spite of the very favorable terms that had been offered, Britain might never be given another chance.

On October 28 Parliament voted on the issue,

and the government managed to achieve an impressive majority in favor of EEC entry, 356 votes to 244. Thus if all followed as planned, Britain would become a formal member of the EEC on Jan. 1, 1973, and, after the five-year transition period, a fully qualified member.

In the wings, while Britain and the six EEC members were coming to terms, were the other three announced candidates for EEC membership: Ireland, Denmark, and Norway. It was the prevailing opinion that once the British case was settled favorably, these three countries would have no trouble in making satisfactory arrangements for membership. Nevertheless, there were internal obstacles in these countries as there had been in Britain.

As the EEC expanded and augmented its influence, it undercut other European regional economic organizations, the most important of which was the European Free Trade Association (EFTA). Established as a less ambitious alternative to the EEC in 1959, EFTA seemed doomed to dissolution in view of the defection of its most important member, Britain, as well as the probable defection of two others, Norway and Denmark. No doubt other

EFTA members would eventually seek some sort of association with the EEC, either full membership, associate membership, or a treaty relationship.

The chief regional economic organization among Communist states, the Council for Mutual Economic Assistance (Comecon), continued to foster the expansion of economic cooperation among its members—the U.S.S.R., East Germany, Czechoslovakia, Poland, Hungary, Romania, Bulgaria, and the Mongolian People's Republic. In July 1971, Comecon delegates (including representatives from Yugoslavia, an associate member) met for their annual session and endorsed the "Comprehensive Program," a lengthy document that set out the principal goals and methods for achieving economic integration, stage by stage, over a period of 15 to 20 years. One of the chief obstacles impeding economic integration of Comecon members, however, was the fear smaller countries had of losing their national identity in view of their obvious discrepancy in size and power with the Soviet Union. (*See also* Communist Movement.)

The Monetary Crisis

As steps were being taken to expand the EEC, a policy inimical to European unity was being pursued by the U.S. in an attempt to solve its own economic difficulties. This was Nixon's introduction of restrictive trade measures: a special 10% surcharge on most imported goods, a tax credit for domestic industry that would provide an advantage over European and other foreign competitors, and an effort to "float" the dollar, forcing major European and Japanese currencies to revalue their currencies upward against the dollar.

The policy constituted a sharp change from earlier U.S. attitudes, which politically had been uniformly benevolent toward European unity and economically had included zealous efforts to lower trade barriers and to liberalize trade. One immediate effect of the new U.S. policy was to produce a national, rather than a joint, EEC response among the six members on monetary matters. France and West Germany for some time were sharply divided on the appropriate response to the U.S. initiative. The result was to complicate and delay efforts to establish a firm parity among the EEC currencies and to create a European monetary union. Even more injurious was the prospect of European retaliation to the U.S. measures, which began to take on the aspect of grim reality when Denmark instituted an import surcharge of its own in October. The specter of a trade war that might accentuate trends within the EEC and in the U.S. toward increased protectionism, specialized preferences, and closed economies increased the necessity for a solution to the monetary crisis.

Thus in December, after almost four months of uncertainty, a compromise agreement was reached on the basic issues. The U.S. agreed to devalue the dollar by 8.57% in exchange for a realignment of the other major currencies. The U.S. also announced that it would drop the 10% import surcharge in return for trade concessions by the EEC, Japan, and Canada. Although these compromises removed the major points of contention between the U.S. and the other key industrial nations, they still left unresolved major monetary matters to be settled in the future. (*See* Money and International Finance.)

Despite the fact that the monetary crisis had temporarily clouded U.S.-European relations, the U.S. made clear its long-term commitment to Europe as a cornerstone of U.S. foreign policy. Although U.S. Secretary of the Treasury John B. Connally argued for a greater sharing of the U.S. defense burden by its European allies, the Nixon Administration twice defeated attempts during the year, led by U.S. Senator Mike Mansfield (D, Mont.), to unilaterally decrease U.S. troop commitments in Europe. Nevertheless, it was obvious to Europeans that they had to make greater efforts to increase their own defense spending, and in December European members of the North Atlantic Treaty Organization (NATO) announced that they would budget an additional $1 billion in 1972, thus reducing the U.S. financial commitment to NATO.

To underline further the friendship and reliance of the U.S. on its European allies, President Nixon at year's end embarked on a series of highly pub-

licized consultations with France's President
Georges Pompidou, Britain's Prime Minister Heath,
and West Germany's Chancellor Willy Brandt.
These and other consultations undertaken by Nixon
with members of the Western alliance were viewed
as a concerted display of unity and strength among
U.S. allies before Nixon's major summit meetings
with Soviet and Chinese leaders, scheduled for
1972.

East-West Events

In September, after almost 17 months of continuing negotiations, the four wartime powers—the
U.S.S.R., the U.S., Britain, and France—signed an
agreement on the draft text of an accord determining the future status of the city of Berlin. The draft
agreement confirmed West Berlin's cultural, economic, and juridical links to West Germany, providing for "unimpeded" movement between West
Germany and Berlin, for restoration of periodic
visits by West Berliners to East Berlin and East Germany, and for the right of West Berliners to travel
on West German passports. The major Western
concession to the Soviet Union was permission for
the Soviets to establish a consulate office in West
Berlin. Once the preliminary agreement on Berlin
was reached between the "big four" powers, East
Germany and West Germany began negotiating on
the final details of the accords. East Germany's
basic insecurity in the prospect of increased contacts with West Germany created a long delay in
completing the negotiations, but in December the
two Germanys formally completed the detailed
agreements. However, the four powers still had to
sign the formal agreement before the treaty would
become effective. It was not expected that this
would occur until the spring of 1972.

Despite the delay, the positive trend of events
augured well for Chancellor Brandt's *Ostpolitik*
(Eastern policy), which had as its goal the "normalization" of West Germany's relations with Eastern
Europe. Brandt had made ratification of the 1970
West German-Soviet nonaggression pact conditional on the satisfactory outcome of the Berlin
negotiations, but the Soviet Union demanded that
the nonaggression treaty be ratified first. On December 13 Brandt's government began the process
of ratification by submitting to the West German
parliament the draft legislation necessary to put
both the Soviet and the Polish nonaggression treaties into effect. With these obstacles apparently
being cleared away, progress toward achieving
Brandt's other goals could continue, including the
establishment of diplomatic relations by West Germany with Czechoslovakia, Hungary, and Bulgaria,
and the creation of some sort of formal relationship
with East Germany.

In a larger sense, the conclusion of the Berlin
agreement would also mean the removal of a long-
standing source of East-West friction and thus be
a further step toward the achievement of a permanent détente. With the Berlin agreement, the stage

would be set for the long-discussed European security conference, an idea supported most vigorously by the Soviet Union and its allies in the
Warsaw Pact.

Although the U.S. had in the past been opposed
to the convening of such a conference, claiming
that it would be a means for the Soviet Union to
legitimize its control over Eastern Europe and to
gain official recognition for the East German regime, NATO came out in favor of the conference
with the condition that it be held only after the
Berlin accord was concluded. Thus, in December
U.S. Secretary of State William P. Rogers announced that the U.S. would also favor a European
security conference once the Berlin agreement was
concluded but wanted it to include discussions on
the question of mutual troop reductions in NATO
and Warsaw Pact countries. Earlier, NATO had
appointed a representative to begin exploratory
talks with the Soviet Union on the subject of mutual
troop reductions. However, the Soviets had not
received the NATO representative by the end of
the year, leaving it unclear whether the Soviet attitude would be favorable on this question. Nevertheless, it appeared that with ever growing support
for the European security conference, though not
for its agenda, it would take place, with preliminary
discussions probably in 1972 and the actual conference in 1973. (*See also* individual countries by
name; International Relations. *See in* CE: Europe.)

FAIRS AND SHOWS. The world's multibillion-dollar fairs and shows industry continued
to flourish with buoyant growth in 1971 despite
widespread inflation, rising labor costs, lagging
production, and relatively high unemployment.
More than 75% of the estimated 14,000 fairs held
throughout the world drew over one billion visitors
and reported generally favorable results. Revenues were up 10% to 14% on entertainment features, food and beverage grosses rose more than
8%, and attendance was up 1½% to 5% over
1970. Some fairs reported higher gross revenues
despite attendance losses. This fact was attributed
to increased prices of admissions, particularly at
fairs in the United States.

The U.S. 1976 Bicentennial Exposition, after
nearly a year of civic controversy over site selection, became a prize for the state of New Jersey,
even though a presidential commission had previously approved Philadelphia, Pa., for the project.
The new site, including a 362-acre tract on the
Delaware River waterfront, is part of Pennsauken
township, north of Camden, N.J. Perhaps the
most ambitious proposal of the planners of the
$600-million fair (originally estimated to cost $1.5
billion) was for the construction of three man-
made concrete islands that would connect with the
southern tip of Petty's Island at Camden and extend downstream under the Benjamin Franklin
Bridge, adding an additional 125 acres. Philadel-

phia's share would be Penn's Landing, a 50-acre site on the west bank of the Delaware. Philadelphia's apparent disenchantment with the project, which it had fought so vigorously to win for itself, would thus confer almost complete suzerainty of this 1976 world's fair to New Jersey. Efforts to gain parity control were, at year's end, being actively made by New Jersey with the Philadelphia Bicentennial Corp. Proposals called for building the major expositions on Petty's Island and on the floating concrete islands, while Philadelphia's Penn's Landing site would house most of the exposition's historical exhibits. Selection of the new site was promulgated by economic as well as urban regional development considerations.

The leading fairs in North America were the Canadian National Exhibition, Toronto, Ont., which recorded 3,210,000 people in 1971, and the state fair at Dallas, Tex., with 3,134,646 visitors. Still holding third position was the Ohio State Fair, Columbus, with 2,182,125 persons. Some of the fairs around the world which drew one million or more in attendance were the Indiana State Fair, Indianapolis; Rand-Easter Show, Johannesburg, South Africa; Fair of Rome, Pacific National Exhibition, Vancouver, B.C.; and the Royal Easter Show, Sydney, Australia.

Approximately two billion people visited an estimated 17,000 amusement facilities in 1971, filling coffers to more than $4 billion. Nearly 25% of the total world attendance and gross business was accounted for at over 2,000 amusement and fun parks in North America alone.

In the fall Walt Disney World was opened to the public. Situated on a 27,500-acre site near Orlando, Fla., it is a bigger version of southern California's Disneyland. Included among its many attractions are Cinderella Castle, the Haunted Mansion, the Hall of Presidents, the Mickey Mouse Review, the Grand Prix Raceway, and Blackbeard's Island.

Rodeos were popular in North, Central, and South America, where an increasing number of these shows were featured at fairs and agricultural

Giant hexagonal shapes mark the impressive entrance to Ulster 71. The 17-week exhibition in Northern Ireland was Great Britain's biggest fair in 20 years.
AUTHENTICATED NEWS INTERNATIONAL

Wandle Robert, an exceptionally tall
10-year-old shire stallion, won first prize
in his class at the London Harness Parade.

and livestock expositions. Efforts to promote rodeos in Europe were, for the most part, dismal failures. Promoters had their share of problems in the U.S. as well, because of the relentless efforts of humane societies to wipe out rodeos wherever they occurred. The equine disease that hit the southwest U.S. and Central and South America and that brought about an embargo on the shipment of horses by the U.S. Department of Agriculture on July 14, 1971, was another crippling blow to many rodeo shows, which were forced to cancel contract dates. The disease, found to be Venezuelan equine encephalomyelitis, caused the deaths of thousands of horses. Most of the world's 665 circuses closed their season with better-than-average returns, with indoor events emerging more successfully than outdoor and tented shows. (*See also* Veterinary Medicine. *See in* CE: Fairs and Expositions.)

FAMILIES. Perhaps the most startling statistic in United States family life in 1971 was the rising divorce rate. Throughout the 1960's the rate of divorce among the nation's approximately 50 million families had held at a steady rate of 10 divorces for every 1,000 marriages. In 1970 and 1971, however, the rate suddenly soared to 14 for every 1,000 marriages, a rise of 40%. This rise was largely attributed to the more liberalized divorce laws passed in the late 1960's in several states, particularly in the two most populous, New York and California.

The role of women in U.S. family life was undoubtedly in the process of change in 1971. The emergence of a new women's liberation movement was felt to be a factor in this process, but to what degree was unknown. What was obvious, however, was that women were becoming more aggressive in asserting their rights.

One area in which women's rights were expanding was that of abortion. In 1971 the question of abortion was considered for the first time by the U.S. Supreme Court. A U.S. District Court judge had held a District of Columbia law that permitted abortion "only when necessary for the preservation of the mother's life and health" to be unconstitutional because it was vague. The Supreme Court reversed the decision, said that the statute was not vague, and put the burden of proof on the government to show that a given abortion performed by a doctor did not fall within the exception to the statutory ban. The court also ruled that "health" as a justification for abortion could include mental as well as physical health.

Only three states—Alaska, Hawaii, and New York—permitted abortion for any reason if performed by a doctor. Thirteen other states permitted abortion to save a mother's life, protect her mental or physical health, or prevent birth of a physically or mentally defective child—or in cases of rape or incest. All other states still outlawed abortion for any reason except to save a mother's life. In one of those states, Florida, a woman, 23, was sentenced to two years' probation for having an abortion; the condition of her probation was that she marry the man with whom she had been living or that she return to live in her parents' home.

Adoption

The legal problems of adoption were very much in the news during the year. One case, that of "Baby Lenore" in New York City, focused national attention on the question of whether the natural mother had any rights to her child once she had relinquished it for adoption. Baby Lenore's mother had given her to an adoption agency, which had then placed the child with a couple for adoption. A month after the natural mother had surrendered the child, she changed her mind, deciding she wanted the child back. A long court battle ensued with the result that the New York court ordered Lenore to be returned to her natural mother. Refusing to give up the child, the adoptive parents fled with her to Florida where, in another legal action, a Florida court awarded custody of Lenore to her adoptive parents.

In another precedent-setting case, a couple had been ordered by a New Jersey court to relinquish their adopted daughter because they did not believe in a supreme being and had no religious affiliation. However, the New Jersey Supreme Court reversed the decision and granted the adoption, ruling that the adoption could not be denied solely because the adoptive parents were atheists.

Fatherless Families

The U.S. Bureau of the Census in 1971 produced a research report about black families without fathers. Of the approximately 4.7 million black families in the United States, 1.3 million, or 28%, were headed by mothers alone. Of all the white families in the United States (some 46 million), only 9% were without fathers.

However, in more than 60% of the black families without fathers, the mother worked and supported her offspring; less than half were on welfare or otherwise dependent. The incidence of families bereft of fathers was also related to income. In the lower income brackets there were the greatest number of fatherless families, among blacks as well as whites. (*See also* Race Relations; Social Services; Women.)

FASHION.
In the world of fashion 1971 was a year of contrasts, with fashion changing swiftly and subject to many contradictions. The world of high fashion, or haute couture, continued to encounter growing competition from the ready-to-wear market, whose biannual showings attracted more and more international buyers. In August haute couture was dealt a shattering blow by the sudden announcement by one of the most influential couturiers, Yves Saint Laurent, that he had shown the last of his public couture collections

An award-winning British designer, Alan Paine, showed striped, rib-knit sweaters for men in the popular short length.

JOHN ADAMS STUDIOS

AGIP FROM PICTORIAL PARADE

Romantic designs were definitely a part of the fashion picture of 1971. This hat, resplendent with veil and flowers, was shown in Paris.

and would henceforth devote his creative efforts to designing ready-to-wear clothes for his own boutiques. Among the young, there was a continued trend to refuse dictated fashion and to create individual, "make your own fashion" looks.

The year's first fashion fad appeared on the scene in the winter days of late 1970 and early 1971—ironically enough, the shortest of shorts, "hot pants." They were seen in their most chic guise only half-concealed under a shaggy, bear-type fur coat to mid-calf, known as the midi, which covered the top of the inevitably high boots, higher heeled than the previous year. Hot pants worn in London soared to thigh top, but in Paris they were modestly lengthened to mid-thigh. In New York City, where long skirts had never been considered attractive or very practical and were only worn by a small set—the intellectual types—shorts were quickly adopted as an alternative, though often taking on the above-knee Bermuda-shorts aspect. Hot pants could be in anything from cotton to leather or mink or satin sprinkled with rhinestones for evening.

When not in shorts, fashionable young women kept up the antiestablishment fashion direction, following whims and picking up inspiration right and left, floating around swathed in long-fringed wool shawls or in Far Eastern robes. They created casual and often humorous fashion of their own. The 1971 spring collections showed hems fluctuating in length anywhere from mid-calf to knee level. The result was that the hemline ceased to be a point of controversy, with individual taste prevailing. The couturiers produced their own version of shorts, more or less concealed under front-buttoned or slit skirts, and they freely indulged in charade and folklore looks that were poorly received by the press and fashion buyers alike. On the last day of the showings Saint Laurent enlivened the rather dull fashion atmo-

In 1971 Christian Dior's collections included flowered hot pants for evening and polka-dot ones for daytime (left), an afternoon suit featuring a white flannel blazer (below, center), and a crepe culotte dress with slit sides (below). Valentino showed a black velvet coat and pants outfit (below, left), the coat featuring an ermine collar.

TOP LEFT: SPORT AND GENERAL FROM PICTORIAL PARADE
FAR LEFT: WIDE WORLD
BELOW LEFT: A.F.P. FROM PICTORIAL PARADE
BELOW: "LONDON DAILY EXPRESS" FROM PICTORIAL PARADE

sphere with a surprise revival of the 1940's. The fashion critics went into an uproar, strongly criticizing Saint Laurent for reviving all the vulgarity of that period—heavily padded shoulderlines, dagger-pointed lapels, long piped jackets over shortened low-pleated skirts, artificial flowers at a tightly draped hipline, silver fox stoles, boxy coats, ankle straps, and wedge-soled shoes. The press scorned his collections to such a point that in July many journalists were not invited to see the fall-and-winter Saint Laurent collection, which turned out to be his last. Nevertheless, Saint Laurent's 1940's revival had its effect. As it turned out, the tailored style came back, with a slightly lifted shoulderline and wider, more pointed lapels, and the blazer became a mainstay of U.S. fashion in the fall.

An important trend that Paris couturier Emanuel Ungaro helped launch, top ready-to-wear firms developed, and the young generation rapidly adopted was the layered look of garment over garment—vest over blouse, shirt over pullover or T-shirt. Layered dressing became a new way of life with the utmost freedom to choose and to mix. Besides adding garment to garment, the new fad was to coordinate and combine patterns and prints: stripes for the skirt, flowers for the blouse, and perhaps wry pop art patterns for the sweater. Another fad among the young were unisex G.I. fatigues, from khaki to olive drab, battle dress badges and insignias complete. Genuine work clothes, including the ever-present blue jeans, and rugged workman's shoes were another unisex fashion expression.

The fall-winter lines of the top designers represented a return to haute couture and an emphasis on elegance. The hemline was stabilized at knee level, the basic suit was reinstated, and dresses as such made a comeback. Boxy-shouldered jackets, or "chubbies," often in fake fur, were everywhere, worn over skirts or pants. There were lots of gay plaids and tartans for coats and skirts, both long and short. The fall evening scene was very feminine and romantic. Again from Saint Laurent were tiered frills, flounces, and even bustles, tight bodices, and a general fin de siècle atmosphere—the Gay Nineties all over again. The "little black dress" made a comeback in the U.S., as did hats and rhinestone jewelry.

Men's Fashions

The keynote in men's fashion on the international scene in 1971 was classic elegance. It was an evolution rather than a revolution, following the usual mode of change in men's fashion. Frills and frippery began to disappear from both day shirts and evening dress shirts. Shorter, classic sweaters were favored, body-fitting and finished at waist level. Blazers, never unfashionable, were given new interest by woven or knitted fabrics.

In suits the single-breasted, two-button with slightly wider lapels and deeper flaps to the pockets, and deeper side or back vents based on the hacking jacket, emerged as the universally accepted style for business. Pure wool worsted remained the most popular choice, but blended materials, particularly double-knits, made great inroads. The decline of the traditional suit continued, especially in the U.S., where knitted fabrics and casual jackets and slacks were being worn more and more for business and leisure.

In conventional suit patterns, the elegant classics enjoyed a revival: chalk stripes, with more color and wider spacing; pinstripes; neater herringbones; and bird's-eye weaves. The big, bold, geometric patterns favored by Italian designers gained some acceptance in the U.S. but little or none elsewhere. No appreciable change took place in the top four suit colors—gray, blue, brown, and green, usually in that order. The acceptance of colored shirts for business wear continued, with a move toward multicolored patterns and colored motifs and more discreet stripes on contrasting color grounds. Cotton shirts made a comeback.

In shoes the rounded toe and slightly lower heel superseded the pointed toe and high heel, but high boots with high heels were worn by younger men. The lace-up shoe made a reappearance. The decline of the standard hat continued unabated in 1971. (*See also* Cosmetics; Furs. *See in* CE: Dress; Fashion.)

FIJI. During its first year of independence, 1971, Fiji demonstrated its determination to play a positive role in the Pacific area by joining the South Pacific Commission and participating in the South Pacific Forum and the South Pacific Conference. Diplomatic missions were established in London; Canberra, Australia; and New York City.

The government attempted to promote economic growth through a five-year development plan that will stress agriculture, forestry, rural development, and tourism in order to narrow the income gap between urban and rural populations. A 28-day dock strike produced serious shortages and resulted in price control measures and a wage increase. Further economic diversification is urgently needed for increased job opportunities, as half the population is under 19 years of age.

Talks in London between Great Britain and other Commonwealth of Nations countries resulted in promises of a continuing British market for sugar and satisfactory price agreements until 1974. The Fiji government announced that it would purchase the holdings of the Colonial Sugar Refining Co. of Australia upon its withdrawal from Fiji in 1972. (*See in* CE: Fiji Islands.)

FINLAND. Early in 1971 the economic policy of Finland's five-party coalition cabinet was debated in parliament where, on March 17, the Communists rejected it. As a result, Prime Minister Ahti Karjalainen (Center party) reorganized the cabinet, leaving the three Communist ministers outside. It was especially the Stalinist wing of the Communist party that had sabotaged cooperation within the coalition, demanding wage increases and urging unified workers' action in the factories. The Social Democrats, representing the largest group in parliament, preferred a more cautious and conciliatory line, fearing moves that might weaken and split the coalition.

Karjalainen's new coalition included Social Democrats and members of the Center, Swedish People's, and Liberal parties. It had a nonsocialist majority of 9–8 and the support of 108 of parliament's 200 members.

The situation within the Communist party, with the minority Stalinist leader, Taisto Sinisalo, fighting the more moderate chairman, Aarne Saarinen, had been closely followed by the Soviet government. The Soviet deputy foreign minister, Vassili Kuznetsov, paid a secret visit to Helsinki, the capital, in December 1970, and relations were also discussed by Finland's President Urho K. Kekkonen during an unofficial visit to the Soviet Union in February 1971. A change of Soviet ambassadors in Helsinki occurred in May, with Viktor Maltsev succeeding Aleksei Beliakov, a high party official who had come to Finland the preceding year but who, after Kuznetsov's visit, spent only a part of his remaining time in the role of ambassador.

In the international field, Finland continued its search for commercial arrangements with the European Economic Community compatible with its neutrality policy. Agreements were signed on April 20 for the delivery of Soviet natural gas to Finland and for a second Soviet nuclear power station. (*See in* CE: Finland.)

FISH AND FISHERIES. In 1971 the world fish catch continued to decline, following a trend established in the preceding two years. This decline was mainly evident among the more technically advanced nations, while the catch of the developing nations continued to rise. This difference within

Fishermen from Provincetown, Mass., in their small boats (below) are finding it difficult to compete with the giant fishing boats of many nations that have been working the U.S. Atlantic coast. The catch (above) is sorted by the crew of one such small boat.

ABOVE AND BELOW: "THE NEW YORK TIMES"

an overall downward trend was indicative of two factors that continued to control world fisheries development.

First, there was reluctance on the part of established fishing nations to undertake the very heavy capital investment necessary for large modern vessels, when traditional fishing grounds were liable to closure by unilateral action and many popular fish species were showing signs of maximum exploitation. Second, the many technical aid programs operated by the UN Food and Agricultural Organization (FAO), together with nationally sponsored aid-plus-credit programs, were beginning to show results in less-developed nations. At the same time, a number of such nations were undertaking their own development plans, often with foreign advisers or in joint ventures with other countries.

The United States continued to import much of its fish products, and imports rose by 26% to 84,000 tons, while the home catch fell. The U.S. still led the world in tuna purse seining and during the year the biggest-ever tuna boat, *Apollo,* 259 feet long, was commissioned, with another superseiner of 202 feet, the *Quo Vadis.*

The U.S. Bureau of Commercial Fisheries became the National Marine Fisheries Service and continued to explore the use of space hardware and satellites to seek out fish shoals as part of a spin-off from the space/defense program. Techniques included infrared photography, image intensifiers, and color-sensitive photography to distinguish oil slicks from fish shoals.

Alarm mounted during the spring over the discovery of a dangerous level of mercury contamination in tuna caught in certain U.S. waters. After withdrawal of suspected cans, the public was reassured. (*See also* Ecuador; Food. *See in* CE: Fisheries.)

FLOWERS AND GARDENS. One of the results of mounting public concern over environmental problems during 1971 was the development of outdoor garden laboratories in many schools across the United States. The labs were designed with the help of the U.S. Soil Conservation Service to suit the land area available and the school's curricula. The labs enabled students to participate in tree planting, observe decay organisms at work, test soils and pond water, survey land areas, and study the effects of weather on plants. Some labs were large enough to contain nature trails; others reproduced in miniature different natural areas, including plant and animal life.

The results of a three-year research program by the University of Nebraska, in cooperation with the Rocky Mountain Forest and Range Experiment Station, showed that plants and trees could be effectively used to reduce noise pollution from automotive sources. The most efficient noise reduction was achieved by a broad belt of trees and shrubs close to the noise source, in conjunction with soft surfaces such as tall grass or plowed fields. Research at the Connecticut Agricultural Experiment Station indicated that leaves absorb considerable amounts of high-frequency sound; that foliage, stems, and soil all help to reduce sound transmitted near the ground; and that dense foliage helps to quiet the noise of high-speed traffic.

In other research developments, a chemical compound known as benzimidazole proved to be effective in protecting plants from ozone, a primary component of smog. A new biodegradable insecticide called Zectran was developed to combat budworms, which damage conifers in North America.

During 1971 the gypsy moth, a serious tree defoliator, spread to epidemic proportions in the northeastern U.S. Dutch elm disease killed the

The 1972 All-America Selections of winning flowers included (from left to right), Circus petunia, with large double deep-salmon and white blooms; Summer Carnival hollyhock, a large flower with a single row of petals framing the double centers; and Carved Ivory zinnia, featuring large blooms.

COURTESY, ALL-AMERICA SELECTIONS

300-year-old Whittier Elm in Haverhill, Mass., made famous by John Greenleaf Whittier's poems. Damage to conifers in Glacier National Park, caused by industrial pollutants, led conservationists to file suit against the Anaconda Aluminum Co.

The All-America Rose awards for 1972 were won by Apollo, a sunrise-yellow hybrid tea, and Portrait, a deep-pink hybrid tea. All-America gold medals for 1971 went to Peter Pan Plum and Peter Pan Pink, both F1 hybrid dwarf double zinnias. Other All-America Selections for 1971 included Queen of Hearts, a hybrid *Dianthus chinensis;* Southern Belle, an F1 *Hibiscus moschetus;* Little Darling, an F1 hybrid snapdragon; Silver Puffs, a dwarf double pink hollyhock; and Early Extra Sweet, an F1 hybrid sweet corn.

A Pacific Coast nursery introduced a new ever-green magnolia able to withstand cold to −5° F. The U.S. Department of Agriculture released a new lilac called Cheyenne, hardy in extreme cold; its flowers are a delicate light blue. A new fall-bearing red raspberry named Heritage was introduced by a New York state agricultural experiment station. Green Ball, a green cauliflower, was developed at Michigan State University from a cross between cauliflower and broccoli.

Scientists at the Texas Agricultural Experiment Station discovered a restorer gene that makes possible the hybrid breeding of sunflowers for the first time. An experimental compound, designated 6706, was found to produce pure white blossoms on ornamentals by preventing coloring in flowers and plant foliage. The Lunar Receiving Laboratory at Houston, Tex., reported that a fine powder ground from moon rocks promoted the growth of vegetable seedlings and other plants. (*See in* CE: Flower, Fruit, Garden, and Plant articles.)

FOOD. Shoppers were wary of the safety of many foods in 1971. In June a New Yorker died of botulism from a can of specialty potato soup. The Food and Drug Administration (FDA) admitted that the plant that made the soup had not been inspected in four years. With only 212 inspectors available for 60,000 canning plants, the FDA pleaded that it needed more inspectors for better surveillance.

In August the Campbell Soup Co., largest in the United States and long associated with wholesome food, recalled nearly a quarter million cans of its chicken vegetable soup because of a tainted taste. This action was taken before the company found botulin in one day's output of the soup from the same modern Texas plant. Then on August 31 Campbell recalled 48,000 cans of a meatless vegetable soup. The company said no botulin was found in the meatless soup, but FDA inspectors urged the recall after discovering some bulging cans, a suspicious sign of bacterial activity. In October the National Canners Association, smarting under the publicity the canning industry was receiving, called for more stringent federal regulation of canneries.

A July report by a group working for consumer advocate Ralph Nader charged the U.S. Department of Agriculture (USDA) with laxity in protecting buyers from bad meat, diseased poultry, and pesticide-containing farm products. The report did concede that USDA inspectors generally performed well in checking meat subject to federal inspection. But state inspection, technically accountable to the USDA, was usually so remiss that meat from sick or dying animals could easily find its way into stores.

The FDA strongly urged consumers in May not to buy swordfish because it contained dangerously

The first shipment of foodstuffs from the People's Republic of China in more than 20 years arrived at the Wo Kee Co., in San Francisco, Calif., in June. The ban on imports to the U.S. from mainland China was lifted June 10, 1971.

UPI COMPIX

high levels of mercury. However, tests of canned tuna in 1971 revealed a lower mercury content than shown in earlier tests.

Hunger continued to blight the lives of at least 15 million of the hard-core poor in the U.S. Another 10.5 million, less poor, still needed federal food stamps and other aid to subsist. In 1971 families with less than $30 a month income could be eligible for free food stamps.

The Federal Trade Commission (FTC) charged some food companies with exaggerated advertising. The agency said that Swift & Co. claimed its baby foods were common-cold fighters and appetite improvers and possessed "exclusive and unique dietary qualities." The FTC also charged that Ocean Spray Cranberries, Inc., wrongly claimed its cranberry drink was more nutritious than orange or tomato juice. The FTC was trying to impose "affirmative disclosure," corrections of false ads, upon guilty firms. In one such case, the ITT Continental Baking Co. agreed to prepare disclaimers to its advertising, which once stated that two slices of its Profile bread before meals would help dieters lose weight.

In June the FTC said that breakfast-cereal prices were too high because of excessive profits and costly advertising. By August those prices were beginning to drop, because of competition and not FTC pressure, according to the major producers. In 1970 many dry cereals were charged with containing only "empty calories." However, no drop in their sales was noted during 1971. (*See* Advertising.)

The FDA urged saccharin users to limit intake of the artificial sweetener to a gram a day. Before the proposal, saccharin was "generally recognized as safe." Now, it was only provisionally viewed as a safe substance.

The product of an African berry may someday replace the present artificial sweeteners. The "miracle berry" is such a powerful sweetener that it can mask the sour taste of at least four lemons. (*See also* Agriculture.)

FOOTBALL.

The sixth annual Super Bowl football game was played in New Orleans, La., on Jan. 16, 1972, before a crowd of 81,023. The Dallas Cowboys of the National Conference soundly defeated the Miami Dolphins of the American Conference, 24–3, to win their first National Football League (NFL) title. The Cowboys were led by former Navy Heisman trophy winner Roger Staubach, who threw two touchdown passes, and Duane Thomas, the silent running back, who scored on a three-yard run to put the game out of reach. Miami's lone score came on a 31-yard field goal by Garo Yepremian.

Divisional Races and Play-offs

The biggest story in the NFL during the regular 14-week season was the sensational rise of the Washington Redskins. George Allen, a veteran

WIDE WORLD

Tom Slade (dark jersey) of Michigan is hit by Mike Simone of Stanford in the first quarter of the Rose Bowl for 1972. Stanford won 13–12.

coach fired by the Los Angeles Rams following the 1970 season, was brought in to take over the moribund Redskins and was given the dual position of general manager and head coach. As he had done in Los Angeles, where he had also built winning teams, Allen immediately started trading future draft choices, concentrating on an effort for instant success. Allen engineered a series of 19 separate transactions, giving up 24 draft choices and 12 players, and in exchange he acquired 21 new players. The results were sensational. Despite an early-season injury to regular quarterback Sonny Jurgensen, the Redskins won their first five games. They then tapered off somewhat but finished with a 9–4–1 record, only their second winning season since 1956.

Eight teams reached the play-offs—the six divisional champions (three from each of the NFL's conferences), plus the second-place team in each conference with the best won-and-lost record. The divisional champions were Dallas, Minnesota, and San Francisco of the National Conference, and Miami, Cleveland, and Kansas City of the American Conference. Washington and Baltimore were the "wild card" qualifiers.

Dallas, which advanced to the Super Bowl for the second successive season, was led by quarterback Staubach, who was not installed as a regular until mid-season. The Cowboys closed their regu-

George Blanda, quarterback for the Oakland Raiders, kicks a field goal during the game in which he achieved an all-time pro scoring record of 1,609 points in 22 seasons.

lar Eastern Division season with a string of seven consecutive victories and once again had a barbed-wire defense keyed by Bob Lilly, a mammoth tackle who earned all-pro honors for the seventh year. Following Dallas and Washington in the Eastern were Philadelphia, St. Louis, and the New York Giants.

Defense was also emphasized by the Minnesota Vikings, who had an 11–3 record and retained their title in the National's Central Division. The Vikings ranked 17th in the league in scoring and employed a rare and often ineffective three-quarterback tandem of Gary Cuozzo, Bob Lee, and Norm Snead; but they were the toughest team to score against, yielding only 139 points, second lowest total ever given up by one team during a 14-game season. Alan Page, a tackle, was the Vikings' defensive star and was chosen, in an Associated Press poll, as the NFL's most valuable player, the first defensive player to win this coveted honor. Runners-up to Minnesota were Detroit, Chicago, and Green Bay. The San Francisco 49ers had to struggle to win the National's Western Division

championship, barely finishing ahead of the Los Angeles Rams, who beat out Atlanta and New Orleans for second.

The Miami Dolphins, an expansion team started only six years earlier, were the surprise winner in the American's Eastern Division. They were 10–3–1 and won the divisional title with an assist from the New England Patriots, who upset Baltimore on the last Sunday of regular-season play. The New York Jets tied the Patriots for third place, and hapless Buffalo finished a distant last. Cleveland, coached by Nick Skorich, captured the title in the American's Central Division, the weakest of the NFL's six groupings. The Browns finished with a 9–5–0 record. Pittsburgh was second, Houston third, and Cincinnati fourth. Kansas City's Chiefs, a perennial power, repeated as champions in the American's Western Division and had an outstanding passing combination in quarterback Len Dawson to Otis Taylor, a wide receiver who led the American Conference in yardage gained by receptions. Oakland, San Diego, and Denver were runners-up.

The first round of the play-offs, a total of four games, were scheduled as television doubleheaders on the weekend of December 25–26 and attracted a large viewing audience. However, the Christmas Day schedule also drew considerable criticism in the press, with some sportswriters claiming that Christmas Day, which fell on a Saturday, should have been sacred and was not the time for televising football games. In the Christmas Day pairings Dallas routed Minnesota, 20–12, and Miami eliminated Kansas City, 27–24. The Miami-Kansas City struggle went into a second overtime and was the longest game in professional football history, lasting 82 minutes and 40 seconds. Miami broke the 24–24 tie on the strength of a 37-yard field goal by Yepremian. The next day San Francisco and Baltimore won their first-round matches. The 49ers eliminated Washington, 24–20, and scored the decisive touchdown when tackle Bob Hoskins recovered a fumble, on a punt attempt, in the end zone. The Colts defeated Cleveland, 20–3, and were led by their defensive unit which intercepted three passes, recovered two fumbles, and blocked two field goal attempts.

A week later Miami and Dallas qualified for the Super Bowl. Miami defeated Baltimore's defending NFL champions, 21–0, and Dallas defeated San Francisco, 14–3. Both Miami and Dallas led all the way and had strong games from their defensive units.

Standout Players; A Gridiron Tragedy

Five NFL players rushed for 1,000 yards or more, with Floyd Little of Denver leading with 1,133. Others to reach the 1,000-yard plateau were rookie John Brockington of Green Bay, 1,105; Larry Csonka of Miami, 1,051; Steve Owens of Detroit, 1,035; and Willie Ellison of Los Angeles, 1,000. Ellison also broke the NFL single-game rushing record with a 247-yard performance. Kicking specialists dominated the scoring and were the only players to score more than 100 points. The leaders were Yepremian of Miami, who was first in the American Conference with 117 points, and Curt Knight of Washington, who led in the National Conference with 114. The NFL total attendance for the regular 182-game schedule was 10,362,448, bettering the record of 9,884,580 which had been set the preceding year for the same number of games.

Tragedy struck on October 24 when Chuck Hughes, 28, a wide receiver with the Detroit Lions, died of a heart attack during a game against the Chicago Bears. Hughes collapsed in mid-stride on the Bears' 15-yard line and did not regain consciousness, becoming the sixth fatality in professional football history.

College Football

Nebraska's Cornhuskers of the Big Eight Conference were No. 1 again in 1971 and seldom had there been a more clear-cut winner of the nation's collegiate football championship. With two weeks remaining in the regular season, there were six undefeated teams among the top ten in the wire-service polls. But at the finish—after the bowl games—only Nebraska was undefeated and untied. The Cornhuskers, moreover, knocked off two of these previously unbeaten teams. On Thanksgiving Day Nebraska protected its No. 1 rating by defeating second-ranked Oklahoma, 35–31, in a game that was nationally televised and billed as the year's "game of the decade." Five weeks later Nebraska finished its season by whipping second-ranked Alabama, 38–6, in the Orange Bowl. It was the second successive national title for Nebraska and enabled the Big Eight to score a rare grand slam; the second- and third-ranked teams in the polls were Oklahoma and Colorado.

Aside from Nebraska the only undefeated team in the Associated Press' top 20 was Toledo, ranked No. 13. Toledo finished with a flawless 12–0 record and with a whopping 28–3 victory over Richmond in the Tangerine Bowl. It was Toledo's 35th successive triumph, the longest winning streak in college football.

Oklahoma, which used the wishbone and had a superior running quarterback in Jack Mildren, set National Collegiate Athletic Association (NCAA) records in team rushing and total offense. The Sooners had a total-offense game average of 565.5 yards and gained an average of 472.4 yards rushing. Oklahoma capped its season with a convincing 40–22 win over Auburn in the Sugar Bowl.

In the East, Dartmouth and Cornell were the co-champions of the Ivy League, both with 6–1 conference records. Cornell won its first five con-

The two top college teams in the nation met on Thanksgiving Day with Nebraska defeating Oklahoma 35–31. Running back Jeff Kinney (35) led the ground attack for Nebraska.

DICK SRODA

Chuck Hughes, 28-year-old Detroit Lions receiver, collapsed and died during a game with the Chicago Bears on October 24. He had not been involved in the preceding play, and it was determined later that he had suffered a heart attack.

ference games, and Dartmouth its first four. Columbia dealt Dartmouth its only loss, 31–29, but Dartmouth recovered and the following week defeated Cornell, 24–14. Both teams then finished with victories, Dartmouth defeating Princeton, 33–7, and Cornell whipping Pennsylvania, 41–13. Cornell's Ed Marinaro was the nation's leading ground gainer with 1,811 yards and a 209-yard game average, both new one-season NCAA records. Harvard defeated Yale, 35–16, in their traditional game, the 88th in the series. Penn State, an independent, won the Lambert Trophy, symbolic of Eastern supremacy. The Nittany Lions captured their first 10 games, stretching their winning streak to 15 before losing to Tennessee. Lydell Mitchell, a running back, was the Penn State star and scored 29 touchdowns, an NCAA record. Penn State defeated Texas, 30–6, in the Cotton Bowl. Army beat Navy in a 24–23 thriller, the first one-point margin game in the 72-game series; and Massachusetts and Connecticut were the co-winners in the Yankee Conference.

Texas won a record-breaking fourth consecutive championship in the Southwest Conference, barely edging Arkansas which finished second. Houston, still playing an independent schedule, finished with a 9–2 season record, and Memphis State won the title in the Missouri Valley Conference.

Alabama, which went through its regular season undefeated, won the Southeastern Conference title for the tenth time, a record. The Crimson Tide had a perfect 7–0 conference record and was led by Johnny Musso, a running back who set a school and conference record by scoring 100 points. Auburn and Georgia tied for second with 5–1 records, and Mississippi and Tennessee tied for fourth with 4–2 marks. Auburn's star quarterback Pat Sullivan won the Heisman Memorial Trophy Award.

North Carolina's Tar Heels won the title in the Atlantic Coast Conference with a perfect 6–0 league record and 10–2 overall, its best record since 1963. Richmond won top honors in the

Southern Conference, with William and Mary finishing second. Western Kentucky was the undisputed champion in the Ohio Valley Conference, winning six of seven conference games.

Michigan's Wolverines won the Big Ten title with a flawless 8–0 conference record, swept through its regular 11-game schedule undefeated, but then lost to Stanford in the Rose Bowl, 13–12. Michigan set seven school offensive records and had a superior defense, especially against the rush, and was led by running back Billy Taylor, who became the Wolverines' all-time leading ground gainer— breaking records previously set by Tom Harmon and Ron Johnson. Taylor finished his collegiate career with 3,079 yards rushing. Northwestern was second in the Big Ten with a 6–3 record, with Ohio State, Illinois, and Michigan State finishing at 5–3 and in a third-place tie. Michigan State's Eric Allen, who rushed for 350 yards against Purdue, a single-game NCAA record, also set three one-season Big Ten records: most yards rushing, 1,203; most points scored, 110; and most touchdowns, 18.

Notre Dame, which was expected to be among the nation's top-three teams, experienced a disappointing season and finished with an 8–2 record. Undefeated Toledo won an unprecedented third consecutive title in the Mid-American Conference.

In the rugged Big Eight Conference Iowa State's Cyclones were fourth behind Nebraska, Oklahoma, and Colorado and closed their regular season with a 54–0 shutout over Oklahoma State, their most one-sided victory since 1959. The feature game in the Big Eight was the Thanksgiving Day match up between Nebraska and Oklahoma.

In the Far West Stanford's Indians, led by quarterback Don Bunce, won the Pacific Eight championship with a 5–1 conference record. Arizona State won its third successive title in the Western Athletic Conference with a 7–0 record. Idaho, with a 4–1 record, won the title in the Big Sky Conference. (*See in CE: Football.*)

FOREIGN POLICY, UNITED STATES.

Startling new departures in foreign policy marked the year 1971 in the United States. The decision by President Richard M. Nixon to resume at least limited relations with the People's Republic of China led directly to that country's admission to the United Nations (UN) and ended two decades of implacable Sino-U.S. hostility. News of Nixon's plans to visit Peking, China's capital, coupled with the subsequent announcement of his new economic policy, created apprehension among U.S. allies and trading partners. Accordingly, the president arranged a series of top-level meetings with foreign leaders, including a projected visit to Moscow.

Congressional Action

In Congress one of the most hotly debated pieces of legislation during the year was the Mansfield amendment, introduced by Senate majority leader Mike Mansfield (D, Mont.). It set a fixed date for the withdrawal of U.S. forces from Indochina. Passed twice by the Senate, the amendment was watered down in House-Senate conference both times, only to appear a third time as a rider to a foreign aid bill. But it was eliminated from the bill in a Senate-House conference December 16. Another Mansfield amendment also created controversy. Offered first in May and then in November, the amendment would have reduced the number of U.S. troops in Europe from 300,000 to 150,000, but it was defeated both times.

The biggest surprise of the first session of the 92d Congress was the Senate's vote on October 29 to kill the $2.9-billion foreign aid program proposed for fiscal 1972. The defeat was engineered by an unusual coalition–conservatives who saw the program as a giant giveaway and liberals who believed that it placed too much emphasis on military assistance. President Nixon called the rejection of the program an irresponsible and dangerous action. By the end of the session, however, it was

"I need a key to get out of here . . . ah, there's the key. Now I'll have to get a ladder . . . Well, the ladder is attached to the wall. Now I need a screwdriver. . . ."

clear that foreign aid was not as dead as it had appeared to be earlier. The Senate divided the foreign aid package into economic assistance and military assistance bills—an approach proposed by Nixon in April—and passed both bills by wide margins. The House repassed its version of the original foreign aid bill and took it to conference with the two new Senate bills. When conferees disagreed on the Mansfield amendment for withdrawal of troops from Indochina, both houses passed continuing resolutions to extend aid at existing levels into early 1972.

U.S.-China Relations

President Nixon provided a hint of things to come in his February 25 message to Congress on foreign policy. The U.S., he said, was "at the end of an era" in its relations with other countries. "The postwar order of international relations—the configuration of power that emerged from the Second World War—is gone," he added. "With it are gone the conditions which have determined the assumptions and practice of United States foreign policy since 1945."

Despite that statement, few persons would have guessed that Nixon would announce, as he did on July 15, that he planned to go to Peking before May 1972 "to seek the normalization of relations" between the U.S. and China and "to exchange views on questions of concern to the two sides." Nixon revealed that arrangements for his trip had been worked out a few days earlier in secret talks between Chinese Premier Chou En-lai and presidential assistant Henry A. Kissinger in the Chinese capital.

Further details of the Nixon visit were announced in Washington, D.C., and Peking on November 29–30. It was revealed that the China trip would begin Feb. 21, 1972, and include visits to Shanghai and Hangchow. The president, Kissinger said, was scheduled to meet with both Chou and Communist Party Chairman Mao Tse-tung; their discussions were to be of "a free-wheeling nature" so as to permit either side to raise any topic it considered urgent.

U.S.-Soviet Relations

At a White House news conference on October 12, President Nixon disclosed that he would visit the Soviet Union "in the latter part of May 1972" for discussions with Soviet leaders on "all major issues, with a view toward further improving . . . bilateral relations and enhancing the prospects of world peace." Nixon emphasized that his visit to Moscow had no connection with his visit to Peking. "Neither trip is being taken for the purpose of exploiting what differences may exist between the two nations," he said.

Two agreements between the countries demonstrated the improvement in Soviet-U.S. relations. One dealt with the prevention of nuclear accidents and the other with the modernization of the Wash-

George Bush (right), U.S. ambassador to the United Nations (UN), and his aides listen intently as Nationalist China resigns from the UN. Bush had supported seating both Chinas, a policy which was unacceptable to most of the members of the UN, including Nationalist China itself.
UPI COMPIX

ington-Moscow "hot line" for emergency messages. (*See* Disarmament.)

Diplomacy with Allies

In addition to the Peking and Moscow visits, President Nixon arranged a series of meetings with major U.S. allies. The schedule included talks with Prime Minister Pierre Elliott Trudeau of Canada in Washington on December 6; with President Georges Pompidou of France in the Azores, December 13–14, and also with Premier Marcello Caetano of Portugal during that time; with Prime Minister Edward Heath of Britain in Bermuda, December 20–21; with Chancellor Willy Brandt of West Germany in Key Biscayne, Fla., December 28–29; and with Premier Eisaku Sato of Japan in San Clemente, Calif., Jan. 6–7, 1972. These consultations, Kissinger explained on November 30, would be undertaken to assure U.S. allies that their interests would not be impaired by Nixon's talks in Peking and Moscow.

Vietnam

The president's diplomatic initiatives had the effect of drawing attention away from the war in Indochina, which appeared to be winding down in 1971 in any event. Nixon announced on April 7 that he intended to withdraw 100,000 U.S. troops from Vietnam between May 1 and December 1 and that "American involvement in this war is coming to an end." On November 12, he ordered a further withdrawal of 45,000 troops by Feb. 1, 1972, at which time the number of U.S. military personnel in South Vietnam would be down to 139,000. In regard to future cutbacks, Nixon said that the next announcement would be made before February 1, and would depend on (1) the level of enemy activity, particularly the infiltration rate; (2) progress of the Vietnamization program; and (3) progress "that may have been made" on freeing U.S. prisoners of war and gaining a cease-fire.

Late in December the U.S. subjected North Vietnam to the heaviest bombing since the bombing-halt agreement of 1968. In answer to North Vietnam's protests, the U.S. said that the North had broken the agreement by attacking U.S. planes over Laos and by its buildup of war matériel. (*See also* United Nations; Vietnam.)

FOREST PRODUCTS. The world's production of lumber, pulpwood, and other forest products continued its steady rise both in volume and value in 1969. In constant 1960 dollars the total value of the world's production in 1969 was $48.4 billion, compared with $45.5 billion in 1968 and $33.9 billion in 1960.

Of the 1969 total, $16.3 billion represented the value of sawn wood (lumber, railway sleepers, and boxboards). The value of pulp products (paper and paperboard) was $20.7 billion; of panel products (veneers, plywood, particle board, and fiberboard) $6 billion; and of all other wood products $5.4 billion. Of the 2,184,739,000 cubic meters (1 cubic meter = 35.31 cubic feet) of wood cut from the world's forests in 1969, 1,219,428,000 cubic meters were removed for industrial uses, the remainder being cut for fuel wood, charcoal, and other domestic and nonindustrial purposes.

The Soviet Union ranked first in the production of sawn wood in 1969, with a reported total of 116,290,000 cubic meters. Second was the United States with 88,359,000 cubic meters, followed by Japan with 41,969,000 cubic meters and Canada with 27,297,000 cubic meters.

In the U.S., criticism of the practice of clear-cutting (nonselective removal of all trees from an area) by the Sierra Club and other conservationist groups led to special hearings on the subject before Congressional committees. Legislation was introduced to declare a moratorium on clear-cutting on federal lands. Representatives of the U.S. Forest Service and of the forest industries explained, however, that the practice is necessary in the management of certain types of forest, which can reproduce themselves only on open ground with full sunlight. (*See in* CE: Lumber; Wood.)

FRANCE. During 1971 Georges Pompidou consolidated his authority as president, as was clearly demonstrated in his press conferences in January and September. The September conference, in particular, affirmed that his interest, like that of his predecessor, Charles de Gaulle, was in foreign affairs.

Foreign Affairs

In the wake of the world monetary crisis and the financial measures announced by United States President Richard M. Nixon on August 15, President Pompidou held a press conference September 23 to outline and justify French policy decisions dealing with the crisis. Pompidou defended France's reliance on gold as a basis for a new international monetary system and suggested the development of a common European defense against speculative money inflows.

Pompidou also made clear his views on the subject of Franco-German relations, against the background of West German Chancellor Willy Brandt's *Ostpolitik* (Eastern policy) and the détente in Europe. He indicated strong support for Brandt's policies and seemed to indicate full acceptance of the economic repercussions of the Eastern policy—increased trade and economic ties between Western Europe and the Soviet bloc.

Pompidou showed himself a convinced European. He stated in January that he favored a Europe comprising "a confederation of states that

have decided to harmonize their policies and to integrate their economies." It was in the light of this statement that his talks with Great Britain's Prime Minister Edward Heath took place in May. Despite the delays, the arguments, and the breakdowns that had characterized previous negotiations at this level in the past, the meeting between Pompidou and Heath finally paved the way for Britain's entry into the Common Market. This dramatic change in French policy was realized during negotiations in June when France finally worked out an agreement on the question of the status of sterling and thus removed a major obstacle to Britain's entry into Europe. On this occasion Pompidou's attitude diverged significantly from that of De Gaulle.

The year was one of intense diplomatic activity. In February Pompidou made a ten-day tour of French-speaking black Africa, visiting Mauritania, Senegal, Ivory Coast, Cameroon, and Gabon. In pursuit of France's efforts in the sphere of international friendship, Premier Jacques Chaban-Delmas and Foreign Minister Maurice Schumann visited a number of countries, including Yugoslavia, Poland, Iran, Romania, Bulgaria, Switzerland, Canada, Spain, and the Scandinavian countries.

France's relations with the People's Republic of China continued to develop. In July 1971 Alain Peyrefitte headed a parliamentary mission to Peking, China's capital, and in return, on September 29, a nine-member Chinese government delegation arrived in Paris for a two-week visit. This was the

In October, during the subway strike in Paris, citizens lined up at the river bank in Charenton le Pont, a suburb of Paris, waiting to board ferry boats that would take them to the city.

KEYSTONE

first visit by any member of the Chinese government to any West European country since Mao Tsetung's government took over in 1949 (with the exception of the conferences on Indochina in 1954 and 1962 in Geneva, Switzerland).

The visit of Communist Party General Secretary Leonid I. Brezhnev at the end of October was the occasion for lengthy discussions between the French and Soviet leaders. A ten-year economic agreement was signed, designed to facilitate industrial cooperation and encourage the important long-term contracts. In the political sphere Pompidou emphasized that France was still a member of the Western bloc, but reaffirmed his support for the European security conference proposed by the Soviet Union with considerably more enthusiasm and emphasis than many of his Western allies. The French and Soviet leaders signed a document listing the basic principles that would guide future cooperation. These included the inviolability of current European frontiers, noninterference in the internal affairs of other states, equality, independence, and the renunciation of force or the threat of force.

Both sides attached great importance to the normalization of the Berlin problem as an essential step toward the convocation of a European security conference. Pompidou's action in delaying his reply to Brandt's proposal for an unofficial Franco-German "summit" meeting until the end of the Soviet visit suggested that the German question figured prominently in discussions between the French and Soviet leaders. The meeting with Brandt thus did not take place until early December. Later in the month Pompidou flew to the Azores for meetings with President Nixon, during which they agreed on a basis for a settlement of the international monetary crisis. (*See* Europe; Money and International Finance.)

Domestic Affairs

During the year the French political scene was characterized by immense activity on the part of the various forces comprising the Gaullist majority, each proclaiming its desire for autonomy and renewal. A notable event was a speech by Valéry Giscard d'Estaing, finance minister and president of the Independent Republicans, that was interpreted by some as a proclamation of his candidacy for president.

While there was considerable dissent in the ranks of the majority, there was no less disarray on the opposition side. The tactics and strategy of the Communists and Socialists would doubtlessly depend to a large extent on the outcome of talks between the leader of the reorganized Socialist party, François Mitterand, and Georges Marchais, deputy secretary-general of the French Communist party. However, Mitterand and his party seemed unwilling to enter negotiations before 1972. The Radical party congress in mid-October was dominated by a personal battle between the current party chairman,

Maurice Faure, and Jean-Jacques Servan-Schreiber. The latter finally was elected the new chairman of the party.

The economy of 1971 underwent a mild recession, intensified in part by the trade and monetary crisis. The government policy was to ask for voluntary wage and price restraints to cope with the inflation. Social unrest prompted a new wave of strikes, and the government continued its efforts to deal with the long-term situation. Premier Chaban-Delmas declared that he had not abandoned the construction of a "new society." In June the National Assembly approved a landmark bill drafting municipal reform and reorganization, and four bills aimed at upgrading technical and professional education. A draft bill on regional reform also made positive headway. (*See in CE: France.*)

FUEL AND POWER. Compared with 1970, which was highlighted by an international oil supply interruption and a fuel and electric power supply crisis in the United States, the year 1971 was relatively calm for fuel producers. The Trans-Arabian pipeline, carrying oil from Saudi Arabia to the Mediterranean, was reopened on January 29 after being out of service 270 days. Tanker rates dropped from their high levels of 1970 as the need for emergency movement of Middle East oil around Africa to Europe subsided, declining so far that some tankers were laid up. The coal supply in the U.S., which had been seriously interrupted by wildcat strikes, adjustments to the 1969 Federal Coal Mine Health and Safety Act, and diversions to the export market, was nearly back to normal condition. And, unlike 1970, there were also few "brownouts"—voltage cutbacks and power-supply difficulties in the electric industry caused by excessive power loads.

The international oil markets, however, were subjected to severe shocks during the year from a series of new price agreements between the oil-exporting countries and the companies producing oil in those countries. The agreements were the result of a concerted effort by the oil-exporting countries to increase their share of revenues from the oil.

Several administrative actions and pronouncements by the federal government during the year were of significance for U.S. fuel and power industries. In June U.S. President Richard M. Nixon sent an Energy Message to the U.S. Congress that included a program for increased funding of research and development in sulfur dioxide control technology; provision for the construction of a fast-breeder nuclear reactor by 1980; an expanded pilot-plant program in cooperation with industry to develop commercial coal gasification; accelerated oil and gas leasing on the federally owned outer Continental Shelf; and increased imports from Canada through agreement with that country. The most significant action taken on these proposals was the U.S. Department of the Interior announcement of a five-year schedule of lease sales for the outer Continental Shelf.

The general 90-day, wage-price freeze announced by Nixon in August and the actions taken at its expiration included in their scope fuel and electricity prices. Those prices that had been caught by the freeze at seasonal lows, however, were permitted to be raised to normal winter levels of the previous year. In other government action the Federal Trade Commission announced that it was undertaking an exhaustive investigation of concentration and competition in the energy industries. The Environmental Protection Agency issued national air quality standards for a variety of pollutants and announced that it intended to abolish the use of lead additives in gasoline for 1975 light-duty model vehicles.

COAL

World coal production in 1971 was expected to show a modest increase. In 1970 demand exceeded production in many countries, thus reducing stockpiles, but this seemed unlikely in 1971. A notable feature was the increase in Canada's coal exports, which went almost exclusively to supply Japan's steel industry.

World hard coal production in 1970 was an estimated 2.4 billion short tons, a significant increase over the 1969 level. Most of the increased output came from the U.S., the Soviet Union, Poland, Australia, Canada, and the People's Republic of China. The greatest advance in the 1970 estimates was, once again, for China.

The U.S. coal industry in 1971 was expected to exceed its 1970 sales, which had been the highest in 21 years. This rise was due to a 5.5% increase in demand from the electric power industry, which consumed a record 322 million short tons in 1970. In the first half of 1971, total coal output was up by 6.2% over the corresponding period in 1970. Bituminous coal production in 1970 was 587 million short tons, an increase of 5% over 1969. Anthracite production continued to fall, with a 9.5% reduction in output to 9.5 million short tons. (*See in* CE: Coal.)

ELECTRICITY

Total electric power supplies in the major industrial countries increased at a slower rate in 1971. There was continued recovery in orders for nuclear stations. In conventional electricity production, coal firing declined and oil increased, despite the rise in oil prices. Production growth in individual countries during 1969–70 was: Japan 11.3%; France 8.2%; the Soviet Union 7.4%; West Germany 7.3%; Canada 7.0%; the U.S. 5.5%; and Great Britain 0.3%.

Great Britain led among countries taking a positive interest in the development of breeder reactors, followed by France, West Germany, and the Soviet

A prototype fast-breeder nuclear reactor was being built in 1971 at Dounreay, Scotland. The reactor will produce more plutonium than it uses as fuel.
KEYSTONE

Union. Although the U.S. had no significant project under way in the breeder field, the budget of the Atomic Energy Commission (AEC), approved by Congress in August 1971, included a credit of some $2 billion for the construction of a breeder before 1980.

There was general agreement that breeders on an industrial scale would have to have a capacity of at least 1,000 megawatts. In view of the scientific and technical problems, development would be difficult and costly. In May 1971 French and West German electric companies signed a declaration expressing their intention to cooperate in producing breeders on an industrial scale. Italy's national electrical company later announced its intention of joining the project.

In the U.S. the revival in orders for nuclear power stations, evident in 1970, speeded up. In the first half of 1971 total capacity ordered was 12,820 megawatts, compared with 7,600 megawatts in the corresponding period in 1970. The number of reactors in service, under construction, or on order, reached 119. The problem of reconciling environmental goals with power needs during the

Engineers study pressure and temperatures of a geothermal steam well in Sonoma County, California. Geothermal steam is being studied as an alternative to the traditional fossil fuel sources (which cause air pollution) and nuclear power sources (which are potentially very dangerous).

WIDE WORLD

year was underlined by a federal court decision in July that required the AEC to give more weight than it had in the past to environmental factors in granting construction and operating licenses for nuclear power plants. The AEC complied with the court ruling by issuing new regulations in September requiring all utilities that had received permits or licenses since 1969 to file an environmental justification for those plants, together with comprehensive cost-benefit studies of the environmental impact of the plants.

In Great Britain, West Germany, France, Switzerland, Canada, Japan, and the Soviet Union a variety of nuclear power plants were completed or under construction in 1971. The U.S., Great Britain, and Japan ranked highest in the world in total nuclear power capacity.

In thermoelectricity the most impressive project of the year was that begun in East Germany. With its ultimate capacity of 3,860 megawatts, it would be the most powerful thermoelectric station in Europe.

A number of major hydroelectric projects were announced in developing countries—the Philippines, Malaysia, and Tanzania—as well as in the Soviet Union, France, Italy, and Australia. Egypt's Aswan High Dam, which was brought into full service in 1970, was officially dedicated Jan. 15, 1971. The station had a total capacity of 2,100 megawatts, and would have an annual mean output of nearly 10 billion kilowatt-hours. (*See also* Nuclear Energy. *See in* CE: Electric Power.)

GAS

Natural gas reserves in the U.S. continued to decline. New production failed to keep up with increased demand. Producers complained of a lack of financial incentive to add to the gas supply, but users argued that producers were attempting to force the price of gas upward by leaving some supply untapped in the face of increasing demand. The federal government, which regulated the industry, still had to rely on industry production figures in its assessment of the situation. Prominent members of Congress and others, however, began exploring the possibility of making their own independent survey.

In 1970, for the third consecutive year, the reserves of 66 major U.S. interstate pipeline companies declined. Production rose in 1970 by 4.8%, compared with 6.5% in 1969. Texas and Louisiana accounted for 73.7% of the total of marketed natural gas production in 1970, Oklahoma accounted for 7.3%, and New Mexico 5.2%. Imports in 1970 increased almost 13% over the 1969 figure.

It was expected that the demand for gas would continue to increase. Five possible solutions that were being explored to cope with this expected increase were higher rates for gas; new discoveries; use of substitutes; manufacture of gas; and increased imports. The Federal Power Commission

did increase gas prices in a number of regions and freed small producers from price regulation. It also directed some sales from the industrial market to the residential market. A number of new discoveries were made, the most significant in the Canadian Arctic. Research also continued on various methods of obtaining gas. Moves were under way to increase imports, mainly from Canada, but in November Canada announced that it did not have gas supplies for export.

PETROLEUM

The most important development affecting the international oil industry during 1971 was the series of meetings between the principal oil companies and members of the Organization of Petroleum Exporting Countries. In February, after a month's negotiation under a threat of an embargo on oil exports, the oil companies signed an agreement with the Middle East member countries, increasing the total taxes on Middle East crude oil. In April negotiations with Libya under a similar embargo threat led to an agreement raising the total oil taxes in that country. Both agreements also contained provisions for further escalation through 1975. Similar tax increases were imposed by Nigeria, Algeria, Venezuela, and Indonesia in separate negotiations between each of these countries and the companies producing oil within their territories.

Because of the complexities of the specific tax provisions and their application to different grades of oil, their effect on the price of crude oil varied widely, ranging from a few cents to as much as 90¢ per barrel. The impact of these increases on the prices of refined products in different parts of the world also varied, but consumers quickly felt the effect. Prices on a wide variety of petroleum products increased in Europe and the Far East. In the U.S., where prices were determined largely by domestic market conditions, the price impact was confined to heavy fuel oil.

The one consolation Europe had was the confirmation of the existence of large reserves of oil in the North Sea. Limited production began in June from the giant Ekofisk oil-field discovery in the Norwegian portion of the North Sea. Other discoveries were made during 1971 in the Danish and British portions, and also in the territorial waters of Spain in the Mediterranean Sea. Another large field, Kingfish, located in the Bass Strait in Australia, came into production in April.

In the U.S., industry and the public were preoccupied with the problems of national energy supply. The National Petroleum Council drew attention to the growing overdependence of the U.S. on the importation of crude oil and the reduced development of domestic sources of oil and gas. The secretary of the interior acknowledged the need for an energy policy, but controversy raged on its possible scope, the relevance of a multi-energy approach, and the role of nuclear energy. Meanwhile, the issues of pollution and conservation remained paramount. There was no resolution of the trans-Alaska pipeline controversy by the end of the year.

At the beginning of 1971 the world total proven and probable oil reserves increased to some 620.7 billion barrels, enough for 33 years at current rates of consumption and discovery. The Middle East accounted for the largest share of the world reserves with 55%; the U.S.S.R., Eastern Europe, and China together had 16.1%; and the U.S. 7.5%. During 1970 world production increased by 9.6% above 1969. The Middle East dominated production with its share of some 23% a day. (*See in* CE: Fuel; Petroleum articles.)

FURS. The fur industry in the United States turned in one of its poorest years on record in 1971, with business across the board falling further below the severely depressed levels of 1970. Economic difficulties in the country, employment problems, uncertainties arising from President Richard M. Nixon's measures to stem inflation and recession, and a concentrated antifur campaign mounted by conservationist and humane societies all combined to hand the industry its big setback. In sharp contrast to the U.S. scene, the European fur industry continued to show prosperity, especially in West Germany, Switzerland, and Italy.

Paris and the other fashion centers of the world endorsed furs in 1971, probably more so than in many years. This was mainly in connection with fashion's return to a look of elegance following several seasons of concentration on novelties and costumes. However, even this strong impetus

Creed's of Toronto, Ont., designed this $12,000 full-length beige chinchilla coat. The honey-colored skins came from a rare new breed of chinchilla.

"TORONTO STAR"

failed to lift the U.S. business out of the doldrums. One bright area, however, as a result of the Paris collections, was the greater use of fur as trimming on cloth coats and in small scarves and boas to be worn over suits and ensembles. This included furs from silver fox to sable.

Poor business brought about further depletion in the ranks of mink ranchers in most of the producing countries throughout the world. Probably the only exception was the breeders in the Soviet Union, where economic factors seldom cause changes in state-operated industries. The U.S. Department of Agriculture reported at midyear that there were 2,227 ranches producing mink in 1970, a drop of 20% from the preceding year. By the end of 1971, unofficial estimates were that the year would show a similar percentage decline. (*See also* Fashion. *See in* CE: Furs.)

GABON. Perhaps the most important event in Gabon in 1971 was the visit in February of France's President Georges Pompidou, who was on a tour of five African nations. French influence and aid continued to dominate the country's economy, though some successful attempts were made to attract other foreign investment.

In a speech on Gabon's 11th anniversary of independence, Gabon's President Albert-Bernard Bongo defended his "open door" investment policy against the charge that it was a guise for neocolonialism, pointing out how successful his policies had been in developing the economy. Export earnings, mainly from timber, oil, and manganese, exceeded import costs in 1970 by 73%. In the country's second five-year plan (ending in 1976) the emphasis was on developing agriculture.

In June President Bongo reorganized his government. Among his changes was the appointment of Georges Rawiri as foreign minister. (*See in* CE: Gabon.)

GAMBIA, THE. In 1971 The Gambia continued to make significant progress in developing its economy. The president, Sir Dawda Jawara, announced that the budget had been balanced without outside aid for the fifth year. Good prices were obtained for the peanut crop, and it seemed likely that the 1967–71 development plan would achieve its objectives, including the expansion of the port and airport in Bathurst, the capital. An agreement was reached with Senegal over the proposed Gambia River Basin project aimed at integrating agricultural development with Senegal. The tourist industry, which catered chiefly to Scandinavians, continued to expand. Great Britain remained the chief source of aid and main trading partner.

Relations with Senegal improved with the signing of a joint defense agreement in March. In July, President Jawara visited Egypt, Sudan, and France. France agreed to extend cultural and economic aid. (*See in* CE: Gambia.)

KEYSTONE

Bocar Ousman Semegah-Janneh, the new
high commissioner for The Gambia, prepares
to present his credentials at Buckingham Palace
in London on May 5.

GERMANY. In September 1971, after 17
months of negotiations between the governments of
the United States, Great Britain, France, and the
Soviet Union, an agreement governing the status of
Berlin was concluded. The effect of this agreement
between the Western Allies and the Soviet Union
was to complete the first step leading to unimpeded
transit between West Germany and West Berlin and
for visits by West Berliners to East Berlin and East
Germany.

The "big four" power agreement was based on
principles agreed upon earlier, but details were to
be developed by "competent German authorities."
Egon Bahr, state secretary of West Germany, and
Michael Kohl, his East German counterpart, met to
work out details of increased communication and
easier transport between West Germany and West
Berlin. Ulrich Müller, an official of the West Berlin Senate, and Gunter Kohrt, East German state
secretary, met to discuss travel of West Berliners
to East Berlin and East Germany. In December
formal agreement was reached between the two

Germanys on the details for the Berlin-access and
the travel agreements. Once the four powers approved the detailed agreements, the Berlin accord
was to come into effect. It was not anticipated that
this would occur until spring 1972.

East Germany

On May 3 Walter Ulbricht resigned as first secretary of the Communist party. At the 16th plenary
session of the Central Committee, he said that age
and ill health prompted his decision. He recommended as his successor Erich Honecker, a member
of the Central Committee. The committee elected
Honecker unanimously.

In June Honecker was appointed chairman of
East Germany's National Defense Council, a post
formerly held by Ulbricht. The latter retained his
position as chairman of the Council of State and
was also named honorary chairman of the party.
Both these positions were largely ceremonial.

The power transition appeared to be smooth, but
when Ulbricht resigned as East German party chief,
it was widely speculated that he had really been
forced out by Soviet pressure aimed at eliminating
his stubborn opposition to improvement of Mos-
cow-Bonn relations. Honecker's speech before the
East German Communist Party's 8th Congress
in June provided substantial support for this speculation. He dropped the Ulbricht demand that West
Berlin be considered a "special political entity."
Unlike his predecessor, Honecker expressed his
wishes for the success of the four-power negotiations on Berlin.

East Germany continued to be affected by shortages of basic consumer goods and even staples such
as butter, meat, and coffee. However, because of
the government's fear of violent public protests
against economic problems, the leadership took
pains to avoid broad-scale price increases on foods.

West Germany

The nonaggression treaty between the U.S.S.R.
and West Germany negotiated by federal Chancellor Willy Brandt in 1970 had paved the way for the
four-power agreement on the status of Berlin. This
agreement was another facet of Brandt's policy of
easing tension between Germany and Eastern Europe. The treaty and his efforts toward achieving
European unity won him the Nobel peace prize of
1971.

Not long after the four-power agreement was
signed in September, Brandt went back to the Soviet
Union to discuss mutual troop and arms reduction
in Europe with Soviet Communist Party General
Secretary Leonid I. Brezhnev. (*See* Europe.)

The West German opposition party, the Christian Democratic Union (CDU), expressed concern
that Brandt was too eager to get agreement from the
Russians. Rainer Barzel, newly elected party chairman in October and probable opponent to Brandt
in the 1973 elections, hinted that he might oppose
the necessary parliamentary approval of the treaties

10 JAHRE ANTIFASCHISTISCHER SCHUTZWALL

10 Jahre
sicherer
Schutz
des Friedens
und des
Sozialismus

WIDE WORLD (BOTH)

The West German Navy displays its new small U2 submarine (right) that carries a crew of 22 and can hold 16 torpedos. East German leaders (left) celebrated the 10th anniversary of the Berlin Wall with a parade. The sign in the background reads "10 years of anti-fascist protective wall—10 years of secure protection of peace and socialism."

gained by Brandt in 1970 with the Soviet Union and Poland. Kurt Kiesinger, Brandt's predecessor as chancellor and Barzel's predecessor as CDU party chairman, voiced the opinion that Germany was making most of the concessions and the Soviet Union reaping most of the benefits.

In October Andrei Gromyko, Soviet foreign minister, suggested that Bonn ratify the Soviet-West German nonaggression treaty before the Soviets would sign the final protocol of the Berlin accords —rather than six months after as had been the understanding. Despite initial resistance, Brandt completed negotiations between the two Germanys on the detailed agreements in December, and submitted both the Soviet-West German and the Polish-West German nonaggression treaties to the German parliament for ratification.

Chancellor Brandt's Social Democratic party (SPD) coalition government lost slightly in most 1971 parliamentary elections, narrowing its majority to only four. There appeared to be a possibility that Brandt's efforts at international conciliation might be stifled. However, the removal of Kiesinger by his party, and the virtual elimination of the small rightist parties in these elections, seemed to lessen that possibility.

In his first policy statement to the Bundestag in 1969 Chancellor Brandt had put the main emphasis on the need for electoral reform. By 1971 a great deal of legislation to this end had been prepared, although the chancellor's objectives were far from being realized.

Educational reform was still very much in the planning stage. The aim was the creation of a democratic, adaptable educational system, offering equality of opportunity and attention to the special needs of individuals. This was to be attained by the introduction of comprehensive education— there were already experimental comprehensive schools in various parts of the country—by extending the school leaving age to 16 and improving vocational training. At a cost of about $8.4 billion 200,000 places were to be created for new secondary school students in the next four years.

In May the federal government approved a divorce-law reform bill that based the grounds for divorce not on the guilt of husband or wife, but on the evidence of a broken marriage. After the divorce each partner was to be put on the same legal footing, and the husband would not have to support his wife financially if she could adequately provide for herself. The bill was expected to become law by the summer of 1973. The government also planned to reform the law on abortion. Grounds for legal abortion were to be ill health or poor social circumstances of the mother, pregnancy resulting from rape, or the probability of an abnormal child.

By mid-year the economic boom of recent years had clearly passed its peak. In the fall there were reports of short-time working and layoffs in certain industries, particularly in the steel industry.

Economic difficulties were blamed to a large extent on the 10% import surcharge imposed by the U.S. government in August. The May "floating" of the mark, mainly in order to stem the inflow of dollars, had the effect of an upward revaluation of about 10%. Finance Minister Alex Möller resigned in May, but his leaving was not connected with this decision. He felt that he could not persuade some of his cabinet colleagues to trim their budget estimates. His post was taken over by the economics minister, Karl Schiller, who thus became economics overlord.

Schiller indicated that West Germany was going to adopt a less pliant attitude in international fiscal policy. In September at Brussels, Belgium, Josef Ertl, farm minister, warned West Germany's partners in the European Economic Community, primarily France, that Bonn would continue taxing farm imports and subsidizing farm exports until perhaps 1980.

In December, in the general realignment of currencies that came about as part of the settlement of the international monetary crisis, West Germany's mark was pegged at a new parity of 3.2225 marks to the dollar, a revaluation of more than 13.5% (including the effect of U.S. devaluation). The new official rate ended the seven-month float of the mark. (*See in* CE: Germany.)

GHANA.
The year 1971 was a difficult one for Ghana. World prices for cocoa, the mainstay of the economy, fell in 1971; at the same time the country's share in the world cocoa market continued to decrease. To help cocoa farmers, a five-year cocoa rehabilitation project, financed by a World Bank loan, was announced in June.

In July, Ghana's President Edward Akufo-Addo spoke of unemployment in the ever expanding labor force as another major national problem. He condemned strikers and general labor unrest, viewing the solution to Ghana's economic difficulties in terms of the development of labor-intensive agriculture and local production to ease the pressure on foreign exchange. In August, Finance Minister J. H. Mensah announced an austerity budget banning luxury imports to help cope with the economic crisis, which he blamed on excessive government expenditure, misdirected investment, and the burden of repaying foreign debt.

Economic difficulties only added to the increased political frustration felt by a growing number of Ghanaians with Prime Minister Kofi A. Busia's government. Major complaints centered around the government's intolerance of criticism and its refusal to allow a free press to operate. Another issue that added to Busia's unpopularity was his support for the Ivory Coast's proposals for dialogue with South Africa, which he later qualified in view of Ghanaian hostility to the idea. Busia, however, condemned the sale of British arms to South Africa. (*See also* Commonwealth of Nations.)

Ghana was among the African countries that quickly recognized Maj. Gen. Idi Amin's coup in Uganda. During a visit by Israel's foreign minister, Abba Eban, in June, Ghana expressed support for Israel's right to a secure existence. Also in June, an agreement was signed with the Ivory Coast on a joint commission on cooperation in cultural and technical affairs. (*See in* CE: Ghana.)

GOLF.
When Lee Trevino sank his final putt in the 1971 British Open at Southport, England, he completed an achievement without parallel in the history of championship golf. Nineteen days earlier he had beaten Jack Nicklaus in a play-off for the United States Open at Ardmore, Pa., and in between had won the Canadian Open as well. Only Bobby Jones (1926, 1930), Gene Sarazen (1932), and Ben Hogan (1953) previously had won the British and U.S. opens in the same year and none of them faced as severe competition as Trevino had in both events. Week after week during the early summer Trevino played excellent golf and when he came to Ardmore he exuded much confidence. After three rounds he was four strokes behind a young amateur, Jim Simons, who stayed within a stroke of the pace until the 72d hole, but he finished strongly. In the play-off round the following day, Nicklaus made three costly mistakes, twice taking two shots to escape from a bunker, and Trevino's steadiness gained him the title by three strokes.

The magic was still upon Trevino at the British Open. In his first round he shot a 69 and seven times in the first nine holes he needed only a single putt. He finished his second round with an eagle and afterward was never caught; yet just when Trevino seemed to have the championship won easily his drive to the 71st was trapped in a sand dune and he took a seven. His partner and closest rival, Lu Liang Huan of Taiwan, whose courtly manners and fine play had made him a favorite with the crowds, also had a dramatic finish. His second shot to the last hole was violently hooked but bounced from a spectator's head back to the fairway from where he was down in two more. This bit of freakish play meant that Trevino had to finish with a four to win. He did so, and Lu settled for second. Tony Jacklin, who had lost his U.S. title at Ardmore and had been out of form for some time, gave a courageous performance, finishing third, two strokes behind Trevino. Nicklaus shared fifth place with Charles Coody, who had beaten him in the Masters at Augusta, Ga.

Coody's triumph at the Masters was one of the surprises of the year. He had not been outstand-

Lee Trevino won the U.S. Open championship in Ardmore, Pa., in June. In 1971 he became the first golfer in history to win the U.S., British, and Canadian championships in the same season.

WIDE WORLD

ingly successful on the tour, but he opened this tournament with a 66. With a round to go he was even with Nicklaus who, having won the Professional Golfers' Association of America (PGA) championship at Palm Beach Gardens, Fla., in February, was bent upon the professional "grand slam." But it was Coody, not Nicklaus, who finished with a solid 70 and performed expertly under great pressure—similar to that which had destroyed him two years earlier in the same tournament. Nicklaus tied for second with John Miller, one of the brightest young golfers to arrive on the scene in years. Later Coody beat Nicklaus in the World Series of Golf at Akron, Ohio. Nicklaus, however, had a great year, winning, in addition to the PGA, the Australian Open; the Dunlop tournament, in Australia; the Tournament of Champions, at Rancho La Costa, Calif.; the Byron Nelson Classic, at Dallas, Tex.; and the Walt Disney World Open, at Orlando, Fla. His triumph in the last pushed his year's winnings total to a record $244,490.

On the international front, teams from Great Britain had one of their most successful years. In the Walker Cup match at St. Andrews, Scotland, Michael Bonallack led the British to a memorable victory (13–11) over a powerful U.S. team that included several outstanding young players, of whom Steve Melnyk, Lanny Wadkins, and Allen Miller turned professional later in the year. The Americans had some consolation the following week at Carnoustie, Scotland, when Melnyk beat Simons, a fellow American, 3 and 2 in the final of the British Amateur championship. In the U.S. Amateur championship, Gary Cowan of Canada, winner in 1966, finished in spectacular fashion by holing a number 9-iron shot out of the rough to the last

green for an eagle; he had needed a par 4 to beat Eddie Pearce.

Proof that British golfers had lost their fear of Americans came in the Ryder Cup matches at St. Louis, Mo. One of the strongest teams ever to represent the U.S., including, for the first time, Arnold Palmer, Nicklaus, and Trevino, won 18½–13½, but it was a close call for the Americans.

Nicklaus and Trevino represented the U.S. in the World Cup at Palm Beach Gardens and won an easy 12-stroke victory with a score of 555. Nicklaus was the individual scoring leader with a 17-under-par 271.

In women's golf JoAnne Gunderson Carner, who had won the U.S. National Amateur title five times before turning professional, had a great triumph in the U.S. Women's Open. Sixteen-year-old Laura Baugh became the youngest winner of the U.S. Amateur championship. (*See in* CE: Golf.)

GREAT BRITAIN AND NORTHERN IRELAND, UNITED KINGDOM OF.

The predominant issues in Great Britain in 1971 were the nation's proposed entry into the European Economic Community (EEC), inflation, industrial unrest, and a situation approaching civil war in Northern Ireland. To these was added, in November, a settlement of the Rhodesian question by which the former colony's independence, unilaterally declared six years before, was to be recognized.

The decennial census, held on April 25, 1971, showed an increase in Britain's population (including the Isle of Man and the Channel Islands) of 2,653,818. The first returns, published on August 18, put the total population at 55,521,534.

Most large cities showed a decline in population. The biggest loss, of more than 600,000, was in Greater London.

Domestic Affairs

Negotiations on Britain's application for membership in the EEC, which had opened on June 30, 1970, were completed on all the main issues on June 23, 1971. Subject to the enactment by Parliament of consequential legislation, Britain would become a member of the EEC on Jan. 1, 1973. Under the terms negotiated, Britain would adopt the common external tariff, the common agricultural policy, and the rules of the EEC by transitional stages over a period of five years. Industrial tariffs would be eliminated by five annual cuts of 20%. Alignment to EEC agricultural price levels would be carried out over five years, and Britain's practice of deficiency payments to farmers would be phased out. Britain's contribution to the EEC budget would start at 8.64% in the first year, rising to 18.92% in the fifth year.

The question of Britain's entry into the EEC split the political parties as well as dividing public opinion. Prime Minister Edward Heath secured a more emphatic declaration of support than had been expected from the Conservative party, which voted 8 to 1 in favor of entry. Encouraged by so much support from the constituency rank and file, Heath decided to make the crucial vote in the House of Commons on October 28 a free vote. The Labour party, particularly in the trade unions and among the party workers, had swung heavily against entry into Europe. Recognizing the strength of this feeling, former Prime Minister Harold Wilson himself switched to the anti-European wing of the party, arguing that his previous revival of the British application had been conditional on satisfactory terms. He was joined by most of his former cabinet colleagues in rejecting the terms negotiated by Geoffrey Rippon. A number of former Labour party ministers, however, remained firmly convinced that the terms for entry were satisfactory and ought to be accepted. Although the Labour party pressured its members of Parliament to vote against EEC entry, on October 28, 69 Labour members voted for entry. There were 39 Conservative members of Parliament voting against entry, but the government won with a majority of 112 (356 votes to 244).

Inflation caused considerable labor unrest in 1971, as the government and employers sought to reduce the rate of annual wage increases from 15% at the turn of the year to below 10%, with an unofficial target of 7%. The strike record, calculated on the number of working days lost, was the worst since 1926, the year of the general strike. But there was some decline in the number of strikes, and the situation continued to improve into the fall. The two most important and longest work stoppages were in the Post Office (47 days) and in the Ford Motor Co. (9 weeks).

An airport was scheduled for their locality, but villagers in Stewkbury, England, intended to resist the plan by any means necessary.

Foreign Policy and Defense

On November 24, after a year of negotiations, Heath's government reached agreement with Prime Minister Ian Smith's regime in Rhodesia on a basis for the recognition of that country's independence, which Smith had declared unilaterally more than six years before. The following day, the foreign secretary, Sir Alec Douglas-Home, having conducted the concluding stages of the negotiations himself in Salisbury, Rhodesia, flew home to announce the terms of the agreement to a divided Parliament.

Neither the Labour nor Liberal party opposition were in any way convinced that the terms fell within the five principles previously accepted by all parties in Parliament as obligatory for an honorable settlement. Points of criticism included the time scale for African majority rule (estimated by many at between 60 and 100 years), the lack of effective external guarantees, and inadequate assurances of an end to racial discrimination. The Liberal party threatened to use its six members of Parliament to delay government legislation on the EEC if its demands on Rhodesia were not met. The Liberal party council called for a referendum on the settlement together with amnesty for politi-

Members of the Irish Republican Army go through training outside of Belfast, Northern Ireland. They wear stocking masks to conceal their identities.

SIPAHIOGLU FROM JOCELYNE BENZAKIN

cal prisoners in Rhodesia and an end to censorship and restrictions on political activity.

The government halted its predecessor's policy of withdrawal from "east of Suez" in 1971. A new five-power defense agreement between Britain, Australia, New Zealand, Malaysia, and Singapore came into effect on November 1. This included an integrated air defense system for Malaysia and Singapore. The British commitment to stations

Joe Cahill, leader of the Irish Republican Army's Provisional wing, was denied entry to the U.S. in September. He had planned a fund-raising tour.

P. MICHAEL O'SULLIVAN

east of Suez was to be six frigates or destroyers, one submarine, a battalion group, a detachment of Nimrod maritime reconnaissance aircraft, and Whirlwind helicopters. In October the defense secretary, Lord Carrington, announced a decision to build two destroyers and four frigates. It had earlier been decided to keep the aircraft carrier *Ark Royal* in service until the late 1970's. Partly because of the demands made on the army in Northern Ireland, four new battalions were formed. At the January meeting of Commonwealth heads of state and of government in Singapore, the proposed sale of British arms to South Africa was condemned by nearly all the African members.

The Economy

Stagflation—the anomalous combination of inflation with industrial stagnation and high unemployment—continued to trouble the Conservative government in 1971. With record exports being reported month after month (reaching nearly $2 billion in September) and imports somewhat depressed, a visible trade surplus averaging $50 million a month was recorded during the first nine months of the year. Therefore, with the addition of invisible earnings it seemed possible that the balance of payments surplus for 1971 might come to $2 billion. But this brought little joy to the public and little credit to the government, for it was offset by continuing inflation, with prices in the autumn about 10% above those of the preceding year; this was largely accounted for by wage inflation.

Stagnation persisted in industry. In the first half of the year total output was down by 1.75%, and up by only 1% by the end of the summer in spite of a substantial stimulus from the easing of taxes and credit restrictions. Unemployment continued to rise, reaching 970,022 in November, representing 4% of the work force, and an increase of over 45% compared with the preceding year. In the worst hit areas the unemployment rate reached 8.6% in Scotland and 10.2% in Northern Ireland. The uneasy state of the economy was reflected in the collapse of a number of business enterprises, most spectacularly two in which the government was heavily committed by its Labour predecessors—Rolls-Royce and Upper Clyde Shipbuilders.

Northern Ireland

A relative lull in the feud between Ulster Protestants and Roman Catholics in the winter of 1970–71 was the prelude to a succession of planned attacks by the Irish Republican Army (IRA) and its extremist Provisional wing against the British army. As the situation deteriorated into a form of sustained urban guerrilla war in Belfast, the capital, in Londonderry, and from time to time in other cities, the Northern Ireland government with the approval of the British government in Westminster resorted on August 9 to the internment of IRA leaders and militants. This proved the signal for even more violent attacks on troops and police, with the bombing and machine-gunning of police stations, military posts, pubs,

shops, hotels, offices, and industrial premises. The IRA, taking the law into its own hands in the Catholic areas, was said to have shot or maimed alleged collaborators. Young women had their hair cut off and were tarred and feathered for associating with British troops. Statistics released by the army on November 9 stated that 36 British soldiers, 2 members of the Ulster Defense Regiment, and 9 policemen had been killed, and 171 soldiers injured. The army reported that at least 76 civilians had died, of whom 33 had been shot by soldiers. The worst of the incidents occurred after the introduction of internment. By the fall the number of British troops in Northern Ireland had risen to 13,600.

Political pressure for more rigorous action against the IRA led to the resignation of Maj. James Chichester-Clark as prime minister of Northern Ireland on March 20. Brian Faulkner was elected leader of the Unionist Parliamentary party on March 23, and took over as prime minister, declaring that his main task was to restore law and order. Meanwhile, the Ulster government persisted with a reform program that included introducing one-man one-vote suffrage in local elections, the appointment of parliamentary and local ombudsmen, housing allocation on a points system, special grants for socially deprived areas, a

Continuous outbursts of protest, hostility, and violence occur in Belfast as government soldiers patrol the streets.

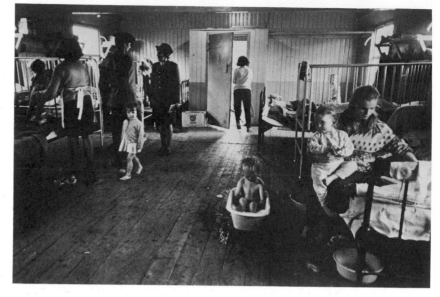

Catholics whose homes
were burned during
riots in Belfast
seek temporary shelter.
P. MICHAEL O'SULLIVAN

declaration of equality of opportunity in employment, steps to avoid sectarian discrimination in official contracts, and penalties under the Prevention of Incitement to Hatred Act. The reform program, however, was overshadowed by the intensification of the drive against the IRA. A committee under Sir Edmund Compton, formerly the British parliamentary commissioner for administration (ombudsman), was set up to investigate allegations that prisoners had been tortured during interrogation. It found that although there had been some ill-treatment of detainees, there was no evidence of physical brutality by either the British army or the Royal Ulster Constabulary. (*See in* CE: Great Britain and Northern Ireland, United Kingdom of.)

Protestants burnt their homes as they moved out of the predominantly Catholic Farrington Gardens section of Belfast, Northern Ireland, in August.
WIDE WORLD

GREECE. The year 1971 marked both the 150th anniversary of Greece's war for independence from the Turks and the fourth year in power for Premier George Papadopoulos' military regime. Although the resumption of United States military aid in 1970 had led to speculation that the slow "liberalization" of the regime would speed up, a report to the U.S. Senate Foreign Relations Committee early in March indicated that the junta had not significantly moved toward restoring parliamentary government, and that the U.S. Department of State and embassy officials had seemingly been supporting the regime by issuing misleading statements concerning the easing of repressive junta policies. In August the U.S. House of Representatives voted to cut off all military aid to Greece until free elections were held or until the president determined that such aid was vital to national security, but the Senate did not pass such an amendment. Vice-President Spiro T. Agnew's week-long visit to Greece in October was widely criticized as indicating official U.S. support.

In January the government denied the International Committee of the Red Cross access to political prisoners on the grounds that 305 political prisoners had been released at the end of 1970 and promises had been made to release about 400 more within four months. The Léros Island prison camps were closed down in April and 234 Communists released. The remaining 50 prisoners were sent to remote villages under "enforced residence." About 25 other non-Communist opponents of the regime were released from enforced residence. A private study later found that by September there were still at least 340 men and women, including prominent citizens, either in jail for, or awaiting trial on charges of, antiregime activities. One was Christos Sartzetakis, the judge whose investigation of the 1963 assassination of left-wing Deputy Gregory Lambrakis was the subject of the popular motion picture 'Z'. In September Lady Amalia Fleming, wife of the late Sir John Fleming (who discovered penicillin), was one of five people sentenced for an alleged plot to free a would-be assassin. Her sentence of 16 months was later suspended, and she was forcibly deported from her native Greece.

Greek exiles in London attempted to unify their opposition to the junta by forming the National Resistance Council and circulating, in March, a blacklist of some 2,000 persons who have collaborated with the regime. The leaders of the two largest opposition parties, now banned, issued a statement on March 23 denouncing the regime and indicating that an alternative to military rule did still exist. One day earlier, 133 prominent Greeks had signed a statement deploring the suspension of democracy and personal liberty under the junta. Both statements came at the same time that official celebrations were being held of the anniversary of the 1821 war for independence.

Throughout the year Premier Papadopoulos held

KEYSTONE

Lady Amalia Fleming was deported from Greece for her role in a plan to free Alexander Panagoulis, imprisoned as a would-be assassin.

talks with former members of parliament about the possibilities of restoring parliamentary government. However, late in August, the premier reshuffled his cabinet to strengthen his own position by downgrading his two most powerful colleagues and dispersing other coup collaborators to new administrative areas throughout the country as regional governors. In a speech August 28, Papadopoulos said that the 8 million Greeks were not yet ready for a return to democracy and that the reorganization was designed to develop political maturity through decentralization.

In May Greece and Albania agreed to resume diplomatic relations. The two countries had been technically at war since 1940, since no peace treaty was signed in 1945. (*See in* CE: Greece.)

GUATEMALA. In 1971 Guatemala celebrated the 150th anniversary of its independence in a year marked by political strife, a chronic problem for the republic since its founding. For the last ten years the country had been wracked by violence from both leftist and rightist elements. Although Guatemala's President Carlos Arana Osorio had declared, upon becoming president on July 1, 1970, that he would pacify the strife-torn country, Guatemala continued to suffer widespread outbreaks of terrorism. A declaration of a state of seige in November 1970 had given the government broad powers to deal with the extremists, and it responded to the latest incidents with harsh, repressive measures, aided, some knowledgeable observers said, by rightist terrorist organizations intent on destroying the government's enemies. During late 1970 and early 1971 there were some 1,600 arrests and between 700 and 1,000 deaths attributable to the action of the military, the police, and rightist vigilante groups. During the same period there were reportedly 25 to 30 additional assassinations attributable largely to guerrillas with leftist— Castroite or Maoist—sympathies.

The killing attributed to rightist elements reached its height in the spring of 1971. The government had some success in reducing the activities of the leftist rebel movement, but peace still did not come. In the summer, renewed violence, mostly perpetrated by rightist elements, led to agitation against the government's continued use of repressive action. In the fall there were vigorous student protests and a call for peace by clergymen, and in November the government lifted the state of siege.

Despite political strife, the economy continued to expand. The national development plan for 1971–75 was initiated. (*See in* CE: Guatemala.)

GUINEA. In 1971 Guinea's domestic affairs were dominated more and more by President Sékou Touré's increasingly suspicious attitude toward the outside world, following the attempted invasion of his country in November 1970, for which Portugal was held responsible by the United Nations (UN) Security Council despite that country's denials of guilt. The unsuccessful invasion was followed by a wave of arbitrary and hasty trials in Conakry, the capital. In January 9 people were sentenced to death for conspiracy and some of them hanged within hours of the verdict. Many others, including the archbishop of Conakry, were sentenced to life imprisonment. However, these strong measures did little to dispel the president's fears, and in April he declared that he had escaped an attempt on his life. In September, a UN commission of inquiry, dispatched at the urgent request of President Touré, filed a report without making recommendations.

It was announced by the government that a large number of alleged conspirators were to stand trial by giving evidence on Guinea radio; judgment would be passed by the people of Guinea after hearing the broadcasts. The trial by radio opened at the end of July and ended on October 3, with 120 people giving testimony. No verdicts had been announced at year's end. (*See in* CE: Guinea.)

AGIP FROM PICTORIAL PARADE

Guinea's President Sékou Touré, fearing an invasion, was granted a UN commission of inquiry, which filed its report in the fall.

GUYANA. In 1971 the government of Prime Minister Forbes Burnham implemented its announced policy of gaining control of Guyana's natural resources by tightening its hold on the bauxite supply. Guyana took over the Demerara Bauxite Co., a Canadian-owned operation that represented a major source of export earnings. The government agreed to pay $53.5 million for the installations over a 20-year period. However, the smaller United States-owned Reynolds Metals Co. mine and the extensive British-owned sugar industry were not touched.

The influence of foreign-owned banks was to be minimized by the Guyana Cooperative Bank, the beginning of a wholly indigenous banking system. New regulations required higher deposits by foreign insurance firms. The External Trade Bureau was operating as the new state import agency and rapidly eroding the functions of the private sector.

The government exchanged diplomatic relations with the Soviet Union and entertained a trade mission from the People's Republic of China. (*See in* CE: Guyana.)

HAITI. The death of President François Duvalier on April 21 dominated political and economic events in Haiti during 1971. Duvalier, who had ruled the country for 14 years, was succeeded as president-for-life by his 20-year-old son, Jean-Claude, whose chief lieutenants were his sister, Marie-Denise; her husband, Col. Max Dominique; Gen. Claude-Louis Raymond, army chief of staff; and Luckner Cambronne, the minister of the interior and national defense.

The new government's immediate task was to

consolidate the support of the armed services. To this end, the powers of the late president's unofficial militia, the Tonton Macoute, were curbed. Plans were announced in May for the formation of a 567-man force, the "Leopards," to fight internal subversion. (In November it was reported that the U.S. was supplying military instructors for the Leopards.) Plans for merging the army with the Tonton Macoute were shelved during the year.

Steps were also taken to promote political liberalization and to ensure economic growth. A total of 38 political prisoners, sentenced to death or imprisonment by the former president, were reprieved, and several prominent exiles allowed to return. A five-year development plan announced in May concentrated on expanding farm production and undertaking public works projects. A program was announced to overhaul the road network, almost entirely neglected since 1934, and the legal minimum wage was to be raised by 40%, the first increase in 20 years. The Péligré hydroelectric plant was inaugurated in July.

There were indications in the fall that the United States was preparing to resume financial aid to Haiti, suspended since 1963. It was reported that the government would be allowed to buy U.S. materiel to equip two army battalions. U.S. officials also came to Haiti to reorganize the customs and postal services. The minister of finance, Édouard Francisque, visited Washington, D.C., in August to discuss the granting of credits for development purposes with representatives of the Inter-American Development Bank and other international financial institutions. A delegation from these institutions visited Port-au-Prince, the capital, in September. A further sign of confidence in the new regime was the granting by the International Monetary Fund of standby credit of $3 million in foreign currency over a period of 12 months.

Industrial production showed a small increase, mainly because of 50 processing installations put in by U.S. companies over the previous two years, which created over 8,000 new jobs.

A considerable increase in U.S. visitors to Port-au-Prince also was reported. (*See in* CE: Haiti.)

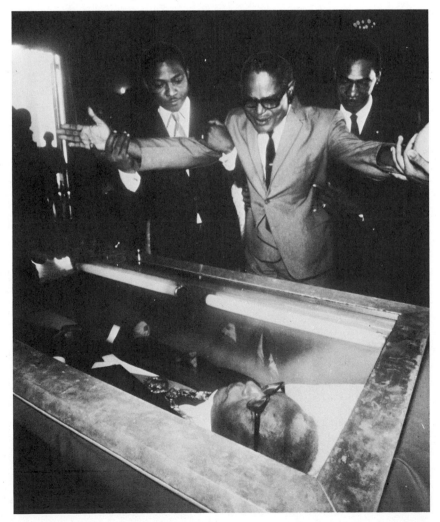

President François (Papa Doc) Duvalier lies in state in Haiti's presidential palace while mourners pay their final respects.

KEYSTONE

Emir Ahmad bin Ali bin Abdullah al-Thani, of Qatar.

AUTHENTICATED NEWS INTERNATIONAL

Nicolae Ceausescu, General Secretary of the Romanian Communist party.

HEADS OF GOVERNMENT

Although not all of those listed were official heads of state, they controlled the government as of Dec. 31, 1971.

COUNTRY	LEADER
Afghanistan	King Mohammed Zahir Shah
Albania	Communist Party First Secretary Enver Hoxha
Algeria	President Houari Boumédienne
Arab Emirates, Union of	President, Emir Zaid bin Sultan al-Nahayan
Arab Reps., Confederation of	President Anwar el-Sadat
Argentina	Lieut. Gen. Alejandro Agustín Lanusse
Australia	Prime Minister William McMahon
Austria	President Franz Jonas
Bahrain	Emir Isa Bin Salman al-Khalifa
Barbados	Prime Minister Errol W. Barrow
Belgium	Premier Gaston Eyskens
Bhutan	King Jigme Dorji Wangchuk
Bolivia	Col. Hugo Banzer Suárez
Botswana	President Sir Seretse Khama
Brazil	Gen. Emílio Garrastazú Médici
Bulgaria	Communist Party First Secretary Todor Zhivkov
Burma	Gen. Ne Win
Burundi	President Michel Micombero
Cambodia	Deputy Premier Sisowath Sirik Matak
Cameroon	President Ahmadou Ahidjo
Canada	Prime Minister Pierre Elliott Trudeau
Central African Rep.	President Jean-Bedel Bokassa
Ceylon	Prime Minister Sirimavo Bandaranaike
Chad	President François Tombalbaye
Chile	President Salvador Allende Gossens
China, People's Rep. of	Communist Party Chairman Mao Tse-tung
Colombia	President Misael Pastrana Borrero
Congo, Dem. Rep. of the	President Joseph D. Mobutu
Congo, People's Rep. of the	President Marien Ngouabi
Costa Rica	President José Figuéres Ferrer
Cuba	Premier Fidel Castro
Cyprus	President Makarios
Czechoslovakia	Communist Party General Secretary Gustav Husak
Dahomey	President Hubert Maga
Denmark	Premier Jens Otto Krag
Dominican Rep.	President Joaquín Balaguer
Ecuador	President José María Velasco Ibarra
Egypt	President Anwar el-Sadat
El Salvador	President Fidel Sánchez Hernández
Equatorial Guinea	President Francisco Macías Nguma
Ethiopia	Emperor Haile Selassie I
Fiji	Prime Minister, Ratu Sir Kamisese Mara
Finland	Prime Minister Ahti Karjalainen
France	President Georges Pompidou
Gabon	President Albert-Bernard Bongo
Gambia, The	President Sir Dawda Jawara
Germany, East	Communist Party First Secretary Erich Honecker
Germany, West	Chancellor Willy Brandt
Ghana	Prime Minister Kofi A. Busia
Great Britain	Prime Minister Edward Heath
Greece	Premier George Papadopoulos
Guatemala	President Carlos Arana Osorio
Guinea	President Sékou Touré
Guyana	Prime Minister Forbes Burnham
Haiti	President Jean-Claude Duvalier
Honduras	President Ramón Ernesto Cruz
Hungary	Communist Party First Secretary Janos Kadar
Iceland	Premier Olafur Johannesson
India	Prime Minister Indira Gandhi
Indonesia	President Suharto
Iran	Shah Mohammed Reza Pahlavi
Iraq	President Ahmed Hassan al-Bakr
Ireland	Prime Minister John Lynch
Israel	Prime Minister Golda Meir
Italy	Premier Emilio Colombo
Ivory Coast	President Félix Houphouet-Boigny
Jamaica	Prime Minister Hugh L. Shearer
Japan	Premier Eisaku Sato

Lieut. Gen. Alejandro Agustín Lanusse (above), president of Argentina. Jean-Claude Duvalier (right), president of Haiti.

ABOVE: A.F.P. FROM PICTORIAL PARADE.   RIGHT: UPI COMPIX

Jordan	King Hussein I
Kenya	President Jomo Kenyatta
Korea, North	Premier Kim Il Sung
Korea, South	President Park Chung Hee
Kuwait	Sheikh Sabah as-Salim as-Sabah
Laos	Premier Souvanna Phouma
Lebanon	President Suleiman Franjieh
Lesotho	Prime Minister Chief Leabua Jonathan
Liberia	President William R. Tolbert
Libya	Col. Muammar el-Qaddafi
Luxembourg	Premier Pierre Werner
Malagasy Rep.	President Philibert Tsiranana
Malawi	President H. Kamuzu Banda
Malaysia	Prime Minister Abdul Razak
Maldives	President Ibrahim Nasir
Mali	Lieut. Moussa Traore
Malta	Prime Minister Dom Mintoff
Mauritania	President Moktar Ould Daddah
Mauritius	Prime Minister Sir Seewoosagur Ramgoolam
Mexico	President Luis Echeverría Alvarez
Monaco	Prince Rainier III
Mongolian People's Rep.	Communist Party First Secretary Yumzhagiyin Tsedenbal
Morocco	King Hassan II
Nauru	President Hammer de Roburt
Nepal	King Mahendra
Netherlands	Premier Barend W. Biesheuvel
New Zealand	Prime Minister Sir Keith Holyoake
Nicaragua	President Anastasio Somoza Debayle
Niger	President Hamani Diori
Nigeria	Maj. Gen. Yakubu Gowon
Norway	Premier Trygve M. Bratteli
Oman	Sultan Qabus bin Said
Pakistan	President Zulfikar Ali Bhutto
Panama	Brig. Gen. Omar Torrijos
Paraguay	President Alfredo Stroessner
Peru	President Juan Velasco Alvarado
Philippines	President Ferdinand E. Marcos
Poland	Communist Party First Secretary Edward Gierek
Portugal	Premier Marcello José das Neves Alves Caetano

Qatar	Emir Ahmad bin Ali bin Abdullah al-Thani
Rhodesia	Prime Minister Ian D. Smith
Romania	Communist Party General Secretary Nicolae Ceausescu
Rwanda	President Grégoire Kayibanda
Saudi Arabia	King Faisal
Senegal	President Léopold S. Senghor
Sierra Leone	President Siaka Stevens
Singapore	Prime Minister Lee Kuan Yew
Somalia	Maj. Gen. Mohammed Siad Barre
South Africa	Prime Minister John Vorster
Spain	Generalissimo Francisco Franco
Sudan	Maj. Gen. Gaafar Mohammed al-Nimeiry
Swaziland	King Sobhuza II
Sweden	Prime Minister Olof Palme
Switzerland	President Rudolph Gnägi
Syria	Gen. Hafez al-Assad
Taiwan	President Chiang Kai-shek
Tanzania	President Julius K. Nyerere
Thailand	Premier Thanom Kittikachorn
Togo	President Étienne Eyadema
Tonga	Premier Prince Tu'ipelehake
Trinidad and Tobago	Prime Minister Eric Williams
Tunisia	President Habib Bourguiba
Turkey	Prime Minister Nihat Erim
Uganda	Gen. Idi Amin
U.S.S.R.	Communist Party General Secretary Leonid I. Brezhnev
United States	President Richard M. Nixon
Upper Volta	President Sangoulé Lamizana
Uruguay	President Jorge Pacheco Areco
Venezuela	President Rafael Caldera
Vietnam, North	Premier Pham Van Dong
Vietnam, South	President Nguyen Van Thieu
Yemen Arab Rep. (Sana)	President Abdul Rahman al-Iryani
Yemen, People's Dem. Rep. of (Aden)	President Salem Ali Rubaya
Yugoslavia	President Tito
Zambia	President Kenneth Kaunda

Roosevelt (Rosey) Grier, former football player for the Los Angeles Rams, relaxes with his needlepoint work.

HOBBIES.

Rapid growth of the hobby industry and its increasing differentiation from the toy industry highlighted 1971. Macy's New York City store on Herald Square opened a huge hobby department with more than 5,000 items from 200 manufacturers. Macy's also employed many experts in macrame, leathercraft, metal art, candlecraft, sculpturing products, flowermaking kits, bead-making kits, rock jewelry, etc., to show purchasers how to work with the materials.

Model airplane kits were popular in 1971, especially World War I and II military planes as well as later jet models. Flying models continued to grow in popularity and model rockets continued to be in demand. New rocket features included a mid-ejection recovery system that causes a slower descent and minimizes damage to the rocket; some rockets are equipped with parachutes.

Newly designed in 1970, the Puffer Kite began to catch on in 1971. It flies by creating a turbulence in the air, much like an airplane wing, the lift being derived from the flow of a breeze over the top of the kite.

Candle-making kits enjoyed great popularity. Kits provide materials and instructions for making candles of assorted shapes, sizes, colors, and scents. Special translucent molds permit the hobbyist to see what he is making. Paint-by-numbers kits are perennially popular and becoming more sophisticated with the production of more original-looking end products. Macrame kits sold very well. The hobbyist did creative tying in yarn, making such articles as belts, sashes, hanging planters, pillow covers, wall hangings, and rugs.

An organic food company in Houston, Tex., developed an herb kit containing 24 seeding pots, a growing tray, potting mix, and eight different kinds of herb seeds. Instructions tell how to grow, dry, and use the herbs in cooking, healing, scenting, and beauty aids. (*See also* Toys and Games. *See in* CE: Hobbies.)

HOME ECONOMICS.

What the housewife should or should not buy at the supermarket was a central concern in home economics in 1971. Throughout the United States, laundry detergents, canned soups, the week's advertised "special," and small home appliances came under scrutiny. During the year the discount supermarket, which had been a West Coast phenomenon a few years before, appeared in hundreds of suburban areas. These new stores could offer shoppers lower prices than the major food chains by reducing labor costs, increasing volume, eliminating trading-stamp promotions, reducing the variety of brands and sizes offered, leaving stock in its shipping crates, and, in some cases, having customers bag their own groceries.

Shoppers could save about 7% by shopping at a discount store but would have the same problems deciding what to buy wherever they shopped. In the course of the year, for example, the federal government urged the removal of phosphates from laundry detergents, then questioned the safety of the additives recommended as phosphate substitutes, eventually banning one of them called NTA, and finally endorsed phosphates as the safest possible additive and even urged states and local governments to rescind their antiphosphate laws.

A new security system for the home involves a TV camera at the door that will project a picture of callers.

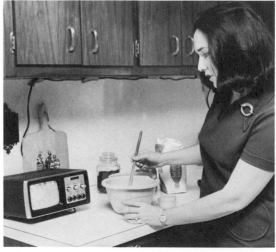

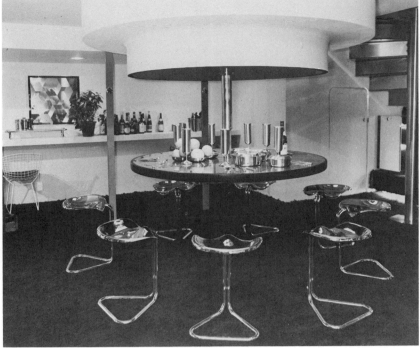

This all-steel table retracts into the ceiling. It can be lowered, set for dinner, then retracted complete with dirty dishes until guests are gone. The table was a popular exhibit at the 1971 Ideal Home Exhibition in Great Britain in March.

FOX PHOTOS FROM PICTORIAL PARADE

Inspection procedures being maintained in food-processing plants came under question when soup canned by two well-known processors was found to contain botulism, a poison usually associated with home canning. Home economists reassured housewives of the rarity of such contamination, warned against buying dented or bulging cans, and advised that boiling destroys the toxin.

As a result of "hundreds" of complaints, the Federal Trade Commission (FTC) ruled that, under penalty of prosecution and a $5,000 fine, stores advertising specially priced items must make the items "readily available for sale at or below the advertised prices." An FTC study showed that in some stores 11% of the "specials" were not available when the shopper got to the market.

Small home appliances, particularly such speciality items as bacon ovens, egg cookers, and fondue makers, continued to be in great demand. As these appliances became more and more complicated the problems of warranty and repairs of them came under study. Legislators sought means of widening the FTC's powers to insure service and to enforce warranties. (*See in* CE: Home Economics and Management.)

HONDURAS. Presidential elections were held in Honduras on March 28. Ramón Ernesto Cruz, a lawyer and diplomat and leader of the National party, narrowly won over Jorge Bueso Arias, his Liberal party opponent. Bueso Arias was minister of economy in a previous administration and helped draft the terms of Honduras' entry into the Central American Common Market (CACM). The presidency was decided by only about half of the 900,000 eligible voters. This was the highest proportion of voter abstention ever recorded in a Honduran general election, and also was the first direct election of a president since 1932.

In January both major parties had agreed to a national unity plan whereby representation of all elective parties would be divided equally to give 32 deputies each to the National and Liberal parties in a 64-member national assembly. The presidential nominees of both parties joined incumbent President Osvaldo López Arellano in announcing the plan. The post of president of the national assembly went to the National party as the victor in the March elections; the Liberal party was allowed to select the president of the supreme court. The plan also stipulated equal party representation on the supreme court and in the cabinet.

As president-elect, Cruz pledged that he would seek a peaceful solution to Honduras' border dispute with El Salvador and spoke in favor of retaining the border observer force of the Organization of American States (OAS). Cruz began his six-year term as president on June 6, replacing López Arellano who had held the office since 1965. López Arellano, a former army general, retained the key post of armed forces chief. On November 22 the United States agreed to cede the two small Swan Islands to Honduras. (*See also* El Salvador. *See in* CE: Honduras.)

HORSE RACING. Not in decades was thoroughbred racing in the United States stirred as it was in 1971 by the early-season exploits of Canonero II. Kentucky-bred and Venezuelan-owned and raced, the 3-year-old son of Pretendre

Canonero II (foreground, left), guided by jockey Gustavo Avila, won the 97th Kentucky Derby in Louisville on May 1. Jim French (second from right) came in second.

won both the Kentucky Derby and Preakness Stakes, but finished fourth in the Belmont Stakes. He thus failed to become the first winner of the Triple Crown since Citation accomplished the feat in 1948.

The large bay annexed the Kentucky Derby at Churchill Downs, in Louisville, Ky., by almost four lengths in the slow time of 2:03⅕, after coming from far off the pace. In the shorter Preakness, at Pimlico, in Baltimore, Md., Canonero II raced head and head with Eastern Fleet to the eighth pole and then drew away to win by 1¼ lengths in track record time of 1:54 for the 1³⁄₁₆ mile.

Before a crowd of 81,036 at Belmont Park in Elmont, N.Y., the largest crowd ever jammed into a U.S. racetrack, Canonero II led for one mile in the Belmont Stakes. He then yielded to the successful Pass Catcher in the one-and-a-half mile classic that was broadcast worldwide. The monumental race virtually brought everything to a standstill in Venezuela.

Other early-season stars of the 3-year-old division were Hoist the Flag, Executioner, Eastern Fleet, Good Behaving, Jim French, and Bold Reasoning. They tired later in the year and were replaced by Run the Gantlet, Bold Reason, Tinajero, and West Coast Scout. Run the Gantlet won five consecutive turf stakes against older horses, including the United Nations, Man o' War, and the Washington (D.C.) International. Bold Reason captured four stakes, including the Travers on dirt and the American Derby on turf. Tinajero won

several stakes in the U.S. after arriving in mid-year from Puerto Rico where he was practically unbeatable.

Forked Lightning Ranch's Ack Ack, racing exclusively in California, was by far the most consistent handicap performer. Numbered Account dominated the two-year-old filly division and Riva Ridge was supreme in the two-year-old male ranks. There was no standout in the three-year-old filly division.

In harness racing, Albatross paced the two fastest race miles in the history of the sport—identical trips in 1:54⅘—in the $52,865 Tattersalls pace at the Red Mile in Lexington, Ky., October 2, for trainer-driver Stanley Dancer. No harness horse had ever covered a mile that fast in a race, but Steady Star had preceded this performance with his incredible 1:52 time trial one day earlier. The year was also distinguished by the driving heroics of 31-year-old Herve Filion of Angers, Que., who surpassed his own world record of 486 victories in a single season, set in 1970, by winning well over 500 races in 1971. In passing the 500 milestone, Filion earned his fourth consecutive North American race-winning championship.

The Trotter of the Year award went to Speedy Crown, winner of the $129,770 Hambletonian at Du Quoin, Ill. He also was the fastest trotter of 1971 with a race mile victory of 1:57⅕ at Lexington, Ky., in early October, for trainer-driver Howard Beissinger. (*See also* Animals and Wildlife. *See in* CE: Horse.)

HOSPITALS. United States hospital costs jumped again in 1971. However, they were checked somewhat by the new economic policy instituted by U.S. President Richard M. Nixon in mid-August. At the start of the year the cost of providing care for a patient each day in a community (nonfederal, short-term, general and special) hospital stood at $81.01. The American Hospital Association (AHA) estimated that by the end of 1971 the same care would cost a patient $93.26 a day.

Hospital costs rose in large part because of the increasing number of skilled workers needed. At the beginning of 1971, there were 292 employees for every 100 patients, contrasted with 280 workers per 100 patients the year before. Community hospital expenses continued their upward trend. During 1970, for example, hospital expenses totaled $19.6 billion—a 17.7% increase over the preceding year.

Toward a National Health Policy

The latest health-cost statistics merely reinforced what many already knew: hospitalization imposed a major financial burden on the patient. As a result, considerable debate in Congress surrounded proposals for a national health policy. There was little doubt that the nation's hospitals would play a significant part in whichever way the health care delivery system was restructured.

Of the several health plans broached, the one offered by the AHA, called Ameriplan, was centered around health care corporations (HCC). Each HCC would be responsible for registered individuals in a particular locale. Both federal and private funding would be utilized.

President Nixon presented his own plan that would provide mandatory health insurance for workers. They and their employers would pay for it. The federal government would pay for similar coverage for the poor. Private insurance companies would be called upon to underwrite and administer the plan.

A national health scheme presented by Senator Edward M. Kennedy (D, Mass.) would provide "cradle-to-grave" nationalized insurance coverage for all U.S. residents. Half of its cost would be paid from general tax revenues, the remainder from payroll taxes. (*See* Feature Article: "The Health Care Crisis.")

Hospitals in Place of the Doctor's Office

A growing number of people, especially the poor, were forsaking the physician's waiting room for the hospital emergency room, even for treatment of ailments not meriting emergency attention. Also, ghetto dwellers and other poor persons were often served by huge public hospitals as far as 20 miles away from them.

A survey of 57 nonprofit hospitals in Detroit, Mich., revealed that their boards were controlled by rich and socially prominent persons. Critics suggested that these board members might be unresponsive to the needs and problems of those served by the institutions. More realistic consumer representation on hospital boards was called for. (*See* also Medicine; Nursing; Social Services. *See in* CE: Hospitals.)

HOUSING. The long-awaited housing boom arrived in 1971. Throughout the year, housing was the brightest spot in an otherwise dull economic picture. Private-housing starts in the period from January to August ran an impressive 36% ahead of 1970's showing in the same period. By October 1971, a new annual record of just over 2 million starts had been achieved.

Throughout most of 1971, buyers snapped up new homes as fast as builders could erect them. One reason was that builders increasingly found ways to meet the huge demand for homes priced below $30,000 and even below $20,000. The housing industry did this by producing its own version of the compact car. There were many more town houses and "fourplexes" (four condominium apartments in one structure designed to look like a large single-family home). The floor area of the average unit also decreased 12%, and homes contained fewer extras such as air conditioning, basements, and two-car garages.

A second reason for the housing boom was the fact that mortgage money was more plentiful and down-payment requirements more liberal. The federal government took several steps during the year to ensure that there would be adequate mortgage funds at moderate rates. United States President Richard M. Nixon's new economic policy instituted in mid-August also helped the industry by controlling rapidly escalating building costs.

Federal government housing programs dominated the market in 1971 as they did in 1970. In single-family homes, for example, 51% of all new homes sold were financed with mortgages insured by either the Federal Housing Administration (FHA) or the Veterans Administration.

It was estimated that 750,000 apartments were started in 1971, nearly one third more apartments than in any previous year. Ironically, relatively few of these new units were built where they were most needed, in New York City and Washington, D.C. However, in Chicago; Atlanta, Ga.; Houston, Tex.; Denver, Colo.; and San Diego, Calif., apartment starts ran between 50% and 100% ahead of 1970.

The federal government's widely publicized program Operation Breakthrough, designed to enlist U.S. industry in seeking a solution to the nation's housing crisis, was receiving mixed reviews. In its general goal, it was successful in that it lured many companies into the field of factory-built or industrialized housing, including some of the nation's largest industrial corporations—Westinghouse Electric Corp., General Electric Co., Olin Corp.—and many more. But industrialized hous-

Factory-built homes are shipped by train from Battle Creek, Mich., to Seattle, Wash., as part of the government's Operation Breakthrough.

ing was still an infant industry. Only about 50,000 units were produced in 1971, although this total was expected to increase dramatically in the next few years. By 1980, in fact, George Romney, U.S. secretary of housing and urban development (HUD), predicted that some 70% of the nation's housing would be produced in the factory. In terms of actual demonstration units built, however, Breakthrough was a disappointment. By year-end, it was expected to be still at least six months away from completion of a mere 2,500 units.

The program was credited, however, with breakthroughs in at least two important areas, building codes and union antipathy. By the end of 1971, many states had passed legislation that allowed a state building inspector to certify a house design as acceptable for any town in the state. This was a major improvement that made feasible the emergence of a truly national housing market. The construction unions were also cooperating. In July 1971 the laborers' union (the largest in the building industry) signed national contracts with several companies, following the earlier lead of the carpenters' union. (*See also* Construction. *See in* CE: Housing.)

HUNGARY. The government of Hungary in 1971 continued its program of controlled reform with several steps that put Hungary in the forefront of liberalization among Communist-bloc countries. On April 25, general elections were held in which, for the first time under Communist government, candidates not officially endorsed by the party appeared on the ballot. Seats in 49 of the 352 parliamentary districts were contested, as well as in 3,016 of 68,865 local council districts. Three deputies were forced into runoff elections. Communist Party First Secretary Janos Kadar, Premier Jeno Fock, and other top government leaders were unopposed. All candidates had to support the Communist party program, but a quarter of the seats in the National Assembly were won by nonparty members. About 98% of all eligible voters, including 18-to-21-year-olds who voted for the first time, cast ballots. Legislation passed in February gave additional revenue and responsibilities to 1,800 municipal councils in an effort to improve the efficiency of local government.

The first international bonds issued by a Communist country since World War II were offered by Hungary during the year. The $25-million Eurobond issue was sold to a number of London banks. The proceeds were to be used to modernize roads and build hotels and other facilities to promote the tourist trade. Another indication of Hungary's efforts to strengthen economic ties with non-Communist nations came when it was disclosed that the government had requested that the International Monetary Fund send a mission to Budapest, the capital.

Foreign Minister Janos Peter met with Pope Paul VI in Rome on April 16. It was the first time an official of the Hungarian Communist government and the pope had met. Joseph Cardinal Mindszenty, archbishop of Esztergom and primate of Hungary, ended a self-imposed exile of 15 years in the U.S. Embassy in Budapest when he arrived in Rome on September 28. (*See in* CE: Hungary.)

ICE HOCKEY. The Montreal Canadiens resumed their customary dominance of the National Hockey League (NHL) in 1971, rebounding to win their third Stanley Cup in four years. The Canadiens had finished third in the East Division, behind the Boston Bruins and the New York Rangers, then upended the Bruins, 1970 cup champions, in seven games in the first round of the play-offs. They then beat the Minnesota North Stars in six games in the semifinals, then took the cup by winning the final game of a seven-game series with the Chicago Black Hawks on Chicago ice. The sweep of the 1971 cup was accomplished largely through the outstanding play of Kenneth Dryden, former star goalie at Cornell University. The 23-year-old star had been studying law at McGill University in Montreal and playing part-time for the Montreal Voyageurs, a Canadien farm club in the American Hockey League.

Chicago breezed through the season to win the West Division title. The team then earned its way to the finals by eliminating the Philadelphia Flyers and the New York Rangers.

Individual honors went mostly to Boston. Phil Esposito, the Bruin's rangy center, won the Art Ross Trophy as the season's top point scorer—76 goals and 76 assists. Boston's Bobby Orr, runner-up to Esposito in points, took the James Norris Memorial Trophy as the NHL's best defenseman, and the Hart Trophy as the most valuable player. Boston's left wing, John Bucyk, won the Lady Byng Trophy for skill combined with sportsmanship. Ed Giacomin and Gilles Villemure of New York shared the Vezina Trophy for allowing the fewest goals—177. The Calder Memorial Trophy for distinguished play among the rookies went to Gilbert Perreault, Buffalo Sabres center.

The first team all-stars, picked by writers and sportscasters, included Giacomin, goalkeeper; Orr and J. C. Tremblay (Montreal), defense; Esposito, center; and Ken Hodge (Boston) and Bucyk, wings. The second team included Jacques Plante (Toronto), goalie; Brad Park (New York) and Pat Stapleton (Chicago), defense; Dave Keon (Toronto), center; and Yvan Cournoyer (Montreal) and Bobby Hull (Chicago), wings.

Other Pro Developments

The Springfield Kings won the play-offs in the American Hockey League, with the Portland Buckaroos clinching the Western League title. The Charlotte Checkers took the Eastern League crown; the Port Huron Flags, the International League; and the Omaha Knights, the Central League.

In the fall it was announced that a newly formed World Hockey Association, a 12-member pro circuit, would compete against the veteran NHL. Franchises were granted to Chicago, New York, Miami, St. Paul, Ohio (Dayton and Columbus), Milwaukee, San Francisco, Los Angeles, Calgary, Edmonton, and Winnipeg.

Amateur Ice Hockey

The Soviet Union won the Group A amateur world championship in 1971 for the ninth successive year, with the European title going to Czechoslovakia. Switzerland won the Group B tournament, Romania the Group C. Boston University took the National Collegiate Athletic Association championship. (*See in* CE: Ice Hockey.)

Ed Giacomin, goalie for the East, holds the puck on his fingertips as he makes a save off the stick of Gordon Berenson (7) of the West, in the first period of the All-Star game in Boston in January. The West won 2–1.

WIDE WORLD

ICELAND. General elections on June 13, 1971, resulted in the defeat of the coalition of the Independence and Social Democratic parties that had governed Iceland since 1959. On July 13 a new coalition of left-wing parties, which controlled 32 of the 60 Althing (parliament) seats, was formed. The new cabinet consisted of Premier Olafur Johannesson and two other ministers from the Progressive party, two ministers from the Communist-led People's Alliance, and two from the Liberal and Leftists Union, a Communist splinter group. The leftward swing in voting was attributed to discontent with the deterioration of the island's economy since 1967—a result of several poor fishing seasons, severe inflation, two currency devaluations, and increasing taxes.

The new coalition announced as its goals the extension of Iceland's fishing limits from 12 to 50 nautical miles by Sept. 1, 1972, the gradual phase-out over a four-year period of the 3,700-man North Atlantic Treaty Organization (NATO) base at Keflavik, tax reform, wage increases, and new housing. The government also announced that Iceland would not seek to join the European Common Market. There was some speculation that the closedown of the Keflavik base would lead to Iceland's withdrawal from NATO.

An important cultural event occurred in April when Denmark returned several manuscripts of the Icelandic sagas which had been taken to Copenhagen, Denmark, in the 18th century. (*See in* CE: Iceland.)

ICE SKATING. The Netherlands' racers dominated men's speed skating again in 1971, with Ard Schenk retaining the overall title in the world championships at Göteborg, Sweden, in mid-February. Schenk won three events—the 1,500-meter, 5,000-meter, and 10,000-meter, breaking the world mark in the latter race with a time of 15 minutes 1.6 seconds. The 500-meter sprint was won by a Norwegian, Dag Fornaess. Göran Claesson of Sweden was overall runner-up, with Kees Verkerk of the Netherlands finishing third.

In the women's world speed championships at Helsinki, Finland, February 6–7, Nina Statkevich (U.S.S.R.) snared the women's overall, although she won only one event, the 1,500-meter. Stien Kaiser of the Netherlands won the 3,000-meter race and overall runner-up honors. The two shorter events—the 500-meter and 1,000-meter—were won by Americans Anne Henning and Dianne Holum, respectively.

Later in the month the new International Skating Union (ISU) sprint championships, held at Inzell, West Germany, proved a popular innovation. Anne Henning, 15-year-old speedster from the United States, twice broke the 500-meter world standard for women. Her best time was 42.75 seconds. Ard Schenk set a world mark of 1:18.8 for the 1,000-meter at Inzell. In March Schenk set world records of 7:12.1 in the 5,000-meter and

Dianne Holum of the United States won the women's world speed skating title for the 1,000-meter in Finland, in February.

14:55.9 in the 10,000-meter, and Erhard Keller of West Germany established a new world standard of 38.42 in the 500-meter.

Figure and Dance Skating

Nearly 120 skaters from 16 nations competed in the 1971 world ice-dance and figure-skating championships at Lyons, France, February 23–28. In the men's division Ondrej Nepela of Czechoslovakia edged Patrick Péra of France in an exciting freestyle duel. Nepela, a Bratislava student, became the first Czech to win the title since it was inaugurated in 1896. Third place went to a Russian, Sergei Chetverukhin.

Beatrix Schuba of Austria was awarded the women's title for an outstanding performance in figures, although her free-skating program was no better than mediocre. A runner-up in two previous seasons, she was the first Austrian to win in 45 years. Julie Holmes of California narrowly defeated Canadian Karen Magnussen for second. The outstanding freestyle performer was Janet Lynn of Illinois, fourth overall.

Both the pairs and ice-dance titles were retained by Russians by slender margins. Aleksei Ulanov and Irina Rodnina barely defeated their compatriots, Andrei Suraikin and Ludmila Smirnova, for their third successive win in the pairs, with Americans Ken Shelley and Jo Jo Starbuck a close third. Husband and wife Aleksandr Gorshkov and Ludmila Pakhomova won their second ice-dance victory by a 5–4 margin over West German brother and sister Erich and Angelika Buck. James Sladky and Judy Schwomeyer of the U.S. finished in third place.

CHRIS HANEY FROM CANADIAN PRESS

Kenneth Shelley and Jo Jo Starbuck of the United States won the North American figure skating championship in Canada in February.

Important Rule Changes

The ISU's 34th biennial congress in Venice, Italy, June 1–4, adopted several long-sought changes in ice skating championships, to become effective on Sept. 1, 1972. Separate medals were approved for figures and for each of the distances covered in speed skating. Previously titles were recognized only for overall performance in figures and freestyle, and for combined titles in speed skating.

Under the new figure skating rules, compulsory figures were reduced from six to three, counting 40%; a new short program of compulsory moves with prescribed free-skating elements was adopted (20%); and free-skating was awarded the remaining 40%. The admittance of Luxembourg to membership brought the ISU total to 31 nations. (*See in* CE: Skates and Skating.)

INDIA. As 1971 began, India was in the grip of election fever; the president had dissolved the Lok Sabha (House of the People) on Dec. 27, 1970. Conscious of the winds in her favor, Prime Minister Indira Gandhi sought to increase her parliamentary majority by going to the polls a year ahead of the end of her term. She also sought to separate central and state elections so that the emphasis would not be on local problems but on the need to provide a central government stable and strong enough to introduce rapid social change. But Mrs. Gandhi herself became the main issue of the elections. The Jan Sangh, the Swatantra party, and the Opposition Congress formed a "grand alliance" to oust her.

Polling took place between March 1 and March 10. Fifty-five percent of the electorate exercised their franchise. Suspense was heightened because ballot counting was begun only after voting had been completed throughout the country. Even as the first results came in it was apparent that Mrs. Gandhi and the Ruling Congress party had won a landslide victory. The Congress secured more than two thirds of the seats in the Lok Sabha although it had contested only 441.

The party position on May 15 (with the strength in the previous House shown in parentheses) was the Ruling Congress 349 (223); Communist Party of India (Marxist) 25 (19); Communist Party of India (CPI) 24 (24); Dravida Munnetra Kazhagam (DMK) 23 (25); Jan Sangh 22 (33); Opposition Congress 16 (63); Telengana Praja Samiti 10 (0); Swatantra party 7 (35); Muslim League 3 (0); Samyukta Socialist party 3 (17); Revolutionary Socialist party 3 (0); Kerala Congress 3 (0); Praja Socialist party 2 (15); smaller parties and unattached members 23 (43); Bharatiya Kranti Dal 1 (10); nominated 2; vacant 5; total 521. The "grand alliance" parties were practically wiped out from the Lok Sabha.

Elections were also held for three state assemblies, those of West Bengal, Orissa, and Tamil Nadu. In West Bengal there was a keen fight between a Ruling Congress-led front and an alliance led by the Communist (Marxist) party. The former gained the support of a few smaller parties, claimed 141 of the 277 assembly seats, and formed the government under Ajoy Mukerjee. In Orissa a coalition of Swatantra, Utkal Congress, and Jharkhand formed the government, the Ruling Congress securing only 51 out of 139 seats. In Tamil Nadu, the Ruling Congress left the field open to the DMK in return for the party's support of Congress in the national election. DMK secured 184 out of the 234 assembly seats.

Mrs. Gandhi was formally reelected leader of the Congress parliamentary party, and was sworn in as prime minister for a third time on March 18. In her 14-member cabinet were 7 newcomers—C. Subramaniam, Moinul Haq Chandhury, U. S. Dikshit, Raj Bahadur, S. S. Ray, Mohan Kumaramangalam, and H. R. Gokhale. The latter three were lawyers who had gained reputations for radicalism.

The new government moved quickly on some of its election promises. The 24th Constitution Amendment bill was introduced in July to restore to Parliament the right to amend the constitution, even the chapter on fundamental rights. The bill was passed early in August by the Lok Sabha by 384 to 23 and by the Rajya Sabha (Council of States) by 177 to 3. The 25th Constitution Amendment bill was also introduced in Parliament with the object of keeping out of the courts' purview payments made for acquisition of property.

The massive popular vote in favor of Mrs. Gandhi acted as a gravitational pull on large sec-

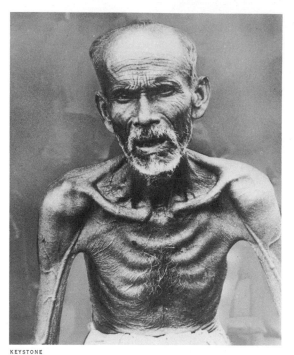

tions of the Opposition Congress in many states. As a result the Opposition Congress governments fell in two states, Mysore and Gujarat, which came under president's rule in March and May. Punjab followed suit in June. In Uttar Pradesh, the chief minister, T. N. Singh, was defeated in a by-election that led to the fall of his coalition ministry. This paved the way for a Ruling Congress government to be sworn in under Kamalapati Tripathi. In Kerala the Ruling Congress, which had supported a CPI-led ministry, formally joined the government in September. In Rajasthan, Mohanlal Sukhadia stepped down from the chief ministership for unstated reasons, and Barkatullah Khan took over. In Andhra Pradesh, K. Brahmananda Reddy made way for P. V. Narasimha Rao to help the Telengana Praja Samiti to merge in the Congress and give up its demand for separate statehood.

The decennial census placed the population of India on April 1 at 546,955,945 (males 283,055,-987; females 263,899,958), an increase of 24.57% over the 1961 figure. The sex ratio was 932 females per 1,000 males; the literacy rate (including the age group 0–4) 29.35%. The urban population was 19.87%; the percentage of workers to

Millions of Bengali refugees from East Pakistan fled to India during the year. A man in a Calcutta refugee camp (above) reflects the common conditions of hunger and despair. Children line up (below) to receive food from a relief organization.

Too weak to walk, an old woman is carried from Pakistan in a small litter. A makeshift tricycle carries refugees as they flee to India.

total population was 33.54%, composed of cultivators (42.87%), agricultural laborers (25.74%), and other workers (31.37%). There were 142 cities with populations above 100,000 and 2,779 towns of population between 5,000 and 100,000. The first ten cities were Calcutta (7,040,345), Bombay (5,931,989), Delhi (3,629,842), Madras (2,470,288), Hyderabad (1,798,910), Ahmedabad (1,746,111), Bangalore (1,648,232), Kanpur (1,273,042), Poona (1,123,399) and Nagpur (866,144).

Parliament adopted a medical-termination-of-pregnancy bill. Abortion was made legal if a doctor certified that pregnancy would cause mental or physical damage or resulted from a failure of family planning methods.

Pakistani Crisis and Its Effect on India

Within a week of the new Parliament's meeting in Delhi, negotiations broke down in Pakistan between President Agha Mohammed Yahya Khan and Sheikh Mujibur Rahman, who had won a sweeping victory in elections held in 1970 in East Bengal. His Awami League was outlawed, and the military regime took repressive action against the East Bengal people's agitation. This resulted in a massive migration of refugees into India. By November the total number of East Bengali refugees was estimated at some ten million. More than 7 million were said to have sought shelter in West Bengal, the remainder in Tripura, Assam, and Meghalaya.

Large amounts of money and energy had to be spent to provide food, shelter, and medical aid for the refugees. A massive outbreak of cholera had to be combated. The relief expenditure as well as the general political uncertainty led to a rise in prices. In West Bengal, the strain on the state administration, combined with interparty confrontation, led to a political deadlock. President's rule was proclaimed in the state on June 29.

Diplomacy, War, and a New Nation

Soon after the crisis in East Bengal (or Bangla Desh—"Bengal nation"—as it came to be called in India) Parliament adopted a resolution recording the "profound conviction that the historic upsurge of the 75 million people of East Bengal will triumph," and assuring them that their struggle had the wholehearted sympathy and support of the people of India. Mrs. Gandhi took the position that the Pakistani government should reach a political solution with the leaders who had won the election in East Bengal and thus create conditions under which the refugees could return to their homes. She wrote to numerous heads of government, including the premier of the People's Republic of China, explaining India's point of view and sent emissaries to several countries. However, the effort to mobilize international pressure on Pakistan yielded no conclusive result.

On August 9, after a trip by Soviet Foreign Minister Andrei A. Gromyko to New Delhi, the capital, a 20-year treaty of peace, friendship, and cooperation was signed with the Soviet Union. Its operative clause called for consultations between the two countries in the event of an attack or threat of attack on either. Later in the year Mrs. Gandhi visited Moscow. In November she had talks with United States President Richard M. Nixon in the White House. The discussions centered mainly on the troubles in Pakistan.

After heightened tension and various border incidents in the late fall, full-scale war broke out between Pakistan and India on December 3, with each side accusing the other of aggression. India invaded East Pakistan along with the Mukti Bahini, the Indian-supported and trained East Bengali guerrilla forces. In a few days time the Pakistani army, outmanned and cut off from its source of supplies, and the central government in East Pakistan surrendered to the Indian forces.

Village women of India line up to cast their votes in the national election in March.

Thus with India's help the new nation of Bangla Desh was born. Ravaged by the troubles of the past nine months, Bangla Desh faced an uncertain future, but India, which was the first to recognize the new nation, pledged its assistance.

During the struggle the U.S. government supported Pakistan (as did China), thus angering India and souring U.S.-Indian relations. India, however, had the support of the Soviet Union, particularly in the United Nations, where Soviet vetoes prevented the Security Council from arranging a ceasefire and mutual troop withdrawals between the two belligerents. (*See* Pakistan; United Nations.)

The Economy

For the fourth successive year food production increased. The 1970–71 grain harvest was estimated to be 107.8 million metric tons (8% higher than the preceding year). National income at constant prices was estimated to have expanded by 5 to 5.5%. However, the growth rate of industrial production was slowing down: the increase had been 7.1% in 1969, 4.5% in 1970, but 1.5% in the first quarter of 1971. Although a survey of the Reserve Bank of India stated that the economy was in a better position than ever before to attain a high and sustained rate of growth, there was unrest because of a steep rise in prices. The annual budget of the Union government, presented on May 28, placed revenue receipts at $4.97 billion (including

$238 million as the central government's share of new taxation) and revenue disbursements of $4.8 billion. Along with capital receipts of $2.7 billion (including $588 million from foreign aid) and expenditures of $3.2 billion, the deficit was estimated at $296 million. With an additional expected rise in defense expenditure this burden threatened to cause a serious recession unless enormous amounts of foreign aid were forthcoming. A preliminary survey by the Ministry of Finance put the total cost of supporting the refugees at around $840 million. Of further concern was the strain on the road and rail system caused by the movement of large stocks of supplies to refugee camps. By late October depletion of food supplies and other essential commodities had increased the rate of inflation from 5% to 7% and sent prices spiraling beyond the means of ordinary Indians. With the establishment of Bangla Desh in December, however, the refugees began returning home, thus easing the burden on India.

On October 16 the Indian government nationalized 214 coking coal mines in Bihar state. This action and talk of further nationalization created a discouraging investment climate.

The introduction of the U.S. 10% import surcharge was expected to affect about 21% of India's exports to that country, which was India's largest trading partner, but Nixon dropped the surcharge on December 20. (*See in* CE: India.)

INDIANS, AMERICAN.

Public health gains, growing pride in Indian heritage, and a more liberal interpretation of race combined to register a population gain of more than 50% among American Indians from 1960 to 1970. Figures released by the United States Bureau of Census in 1971 showed a total of 792,730 Indians, against 523,591 ten years before. Health service reports of Indians showed a four-year gain in life expectancy, from ages 60 to 64 years, in the period 1950–67. Between 1950 and 1968 death rates from tuberculosis dropped 75% and the infant mortality rate fell from 63 to 31 deaths per thousand live births.

Another factor in the population gain, according to Bureau of Census officials, was that previously an individual had to have 26% Indian blood to register as an Indian, while in 1970 racial determination was left to the individual. Also taken into account was the growing pride in Indian heritage spurred by an increasingly effective Indian rights movement.

One target for the Indian demands for rights in 1971 was the Bureau of Indian Affairs (BIA). Secretary of the Interior Rogers C. B. Morton caused a furor among Indian leaders when he abruptly shifted the control of the BIA from Commissioner Louis R. Bruce to newly appointed Deputy Commissioner John O. Crow, a career BIA employee. Subsequently William H. Veeder, an outspoken critic of U.S. Indian policy and an expert on Indian water rights, was asked to transfer to Arizona and two other BIA employees were transferred out of Washington, D.C. The move brought protests from a number of Democratic U.S. senators. Militant factions charged that the moves were designed to deprive Indians of a voice in their own affairs. Morton later amended the power shift, restoring authority to Bruce.

There were 50 Indians in the 100 top jobs in the BIA. During the disagreement Crow pointed out that it is not possible in all cases to find Indians qualified to meet the Civil Service requirements. Later the National Tribal Chairmen's Association requested that the BIA be transferred from the Interior Department to direct White House control. Veeder was not transferred, and U.S. President Richard M. Nixon asked for a "shake-up" of the bureau that would give more control to Indians.

A group of Indians covered Plymouth Rock with sand (above) to protest whites' treatment of Indians throughout the nation's history. Another Indian protest had a definitely contemporary theme—the lack of decent housing that Indians can afford. A group of Indians in Chicago (left) occupied a Nike missile site that the Army had recently vacated to dramatize their housing grievances.

ABOVE: UPI COMPIX. LEFT: PAUL E. SEQUEIRA FROM RAPHO GUILLUMETTE

On December 14 the Alaska Native Claims Settlement Act was finally passed by Congress. The Act provided for $962.5 million compensation and 40 million acres of land to settle century-old Indian, Eskimo, and Aleut land claims in Alaska. In the intervening years before settlement, the discovery of great oil fields and other minerals had greatly increased the value of the land.

Housing continued to be a prime problem for American Indians during the year. In June, after a 19-month occupation of old federal prison grounds at Alcatraz Island, off San Francisco, Calif., 15 Indians who remained were ousted. A few days later they and others seized an abandoned Nike missile site near Richmond, Cal., but they were soon removed. Indians occupying a 640-acre abandoned army communications center near Davis, Calif., were given deed to the land. At Redding, north of San Francisco, a 61-acre site with buildings will be turned over after two years supervision by a community group. In Chicago Indians occupied an old Nike missile site, asking jobs and housing. The occupants, about 50, were removed; housing was found for several in the Uptown Chicago area, but the others went from one temporary shelter to another. At Shiprock, N.M., the largest housing project ever built on a reservation got under way with cooperation from Fairchild Camera & Instrument Corp. and the federal government. The corporation plant there employs about 800 Indians. The $5 million project will house 1,500.

Tourism remained the hope of many tribes. The Utes dedicated a $2.5-million resort at Bottle Hollow, Utah. Hunting, fishing, and wild mustang roundups under Indian supervision were expected to net excellent profits in addition to the income from the lodge. On the Mescalero Indian Reservation in New Mexico an Indian-run ski resort, opened two years ago, attracted approximately 300,000 winter sports enthusiasts. (*See in* CE: Indians, American.)

INDONESIA.

The year 1971 was a watershed in Indonesia's domestic and foreign affairs. Domestically, for the second time since the proclamation of independence in 1945 and for the first time since 1955, the country elected a parliament. Although the election was heavily influenced by the government, the election procedure itself marked a gradual return to the concept of the popular ballot and set the pattern for future political development. In foreign affairs perhaps the most significant development was Indonesia's quiet movement toward a closer relationship with Japan, not only in the economic sphere but also in military affairs.

There was also a healing during the year of the post-World War II breach between Indonesia and the Netherlands, which had ruled Indonesia for almost 350 years. In 1971, for the first time in Indo-Dutch history, a reigning monarch of the Netherlands visited Indonesia. Queen Juliana's journey was a spectacular success, and it signaled the dawn of a new relationship between the two countries.

Domestic Affairs

In the first test of public support for President Suharto, who assumed power in 1965, Indonesians went to the polls July 3 to elect a parliament. Of the 460 seats, 360 were to be filled by the election, the remainder, by government appointment.

The tone of the campaign was set by the army's decision not to align itself with any of the existing political parties in the race, but to back a government-created "non-party" organization, Sekber Golkar (the Joint Secretariat of Functional Groups). Golkar, a loose coalition of civil servants ranging from village headmen to the country's president, became the dominant political machine virtually overnight. It was clearly the biggest, best organized, most heavily financed, and most aggressive group in the campaign. Opposition parties accused the government of intimidating villagers into joining Golkar, and some critics charged that the balloting was not a general election but an election of generals.

The outcome of the election was predictable, but even the government was surprised by the extent of Golkar's victory—65% of the popular vote, which resulted in 227 seats. With the addition of the government appointees to parliament, Golkar emerged with an absolute majority in the legislative body. This ensured Suharto's reelection to a new five-year presidential term in 1973 since the parliament would take part in the election process. Despite the election's obvious shortcomings, some observers felt that the modest step forward to popular rule was no small achievement in a country with limited democratic traditions and with a chaotic political history.

Foreign Affairs

The highlight of the year, which received relatively little attention abroad, was the agreement reached between Japan and Indonesia to "exchange military experiences." Under the terms of the understanding, Japan expressed its willingness to send military instructors to Indonesia and to permit Indonesian army officers to go to Japan for military study and training.

During the year, Indonesia made repeated efforts to restore a dialogue with the People's Republic of China and to normalize diplomatic relations, which were suspended in 1967 after Indonesia accused China of playing a role in the abortive Indonesian Communist putsch of 1965. Indonesia made plain that although it sought a revival of Sino-Indonesian relations, it did not intend to do so at the expense of its integrity and self-respect, and that the Chinese regime would have to halt its subversion against Indonesia, ranging from propaganda attacks to financing Indonesian Communist exiles in China. However, China rebuffed Indonesia's overtures.

The Economy

The economy continued its recovery from the devastating Sukarno years. Prices remained remarkably stable in 1971, and the country's balance of payments showed nearly 20% improvement in exports.

The government continued to welcome private foreign investment, which had increased to more than $1.5 billion since the Suharto government announced its open door policy in 1967. Private U.S. and Japanese companies maintained the lead as the heaviest investors. The Inter-Governmental Group on Indonesia, the "Indonesian aid club" composed of Japan and various Western nations, extended Indonesia a new credit of $640 million at favorable terms. In the wake of the world monetary crisis, Indonesia devalued its currency, a decision long favored by Indonesian economists to spur exports.

In outlining a 25-year development plan for the country, President Suharto, for the first time, put stress on the need for a vigorous birth control program. He expressed the fear that population growth would wipe out the country's economic gains. However, the paramount economic development of the year was the start of offshore oil production. During 1971 Indonesia produced about one million barrels of onshore crude oil daily. With the start of offshore oil production, the amount of oil produced was expected to double by the end of 1972. Many observers viewed this development as another step toward the emergence of Southeast Asia as one of the world's major oil-producing regions. (*See in* CE: Indonesia.)

INSURANCE.

The controversial "no fault" automobile insurance plan received much attention in 1971 from government and insurance company officials, as well as the general public. "No fault" insurance enables the victim in an auto mishap to collect promptly from his own insurance company, no matter which driver was judged to be at fault. The plan went into effect in Massachusetts early in the year, and later in Delaware.

Life

By the close of 1970, nearly 140 million Americans owned life insurance policies with legal reserve life insurance companies, which accounted for $1.4 trillion of protection. This was an increase of $118.2 billion of coverage over 1969. The average amount of life insurance held by the American family increased by $1,400 in 1970 and stood at $20,900 in 1971. Life insurance benefit payments increased to $16.4 billion in 1970, up 6% over the preceding year. Of this amount, benefits to living policyholders totaled $9.4 billion.

New life insurance bought during 1970 amounted to $193.7 billion worth of protection,

an increase of $34.4 billion over the preceding year. Men continued to be the most frequently insured: 86% had some type of life insurance protection, compared with 74% of women. Americans bought about two thirds of their new life insurance in 1970 on an individual basis to meet individual or family needs, rather than receiving similar coverage as part of a group.

The most significant action in the life insurance business in 1971 came at midyear with the introduction of the concept of variable life insurance. Essentially, a variable life insurance policy would pay benefits above a guaranteed minimum that would either rise or fall depending on the result of the investment of its premiums in the stock market. Widespread controversy developed over the plan, which, according to some observers, would have a powerful impact on the nation's securities markets—particularly on mortgage and bond markets—if insurers withdrew their investment funds from these markets to put funds into the stock market.

Health

In the United States during 1971, the large majority of health care expenses were financed through private health insurance. However, during the year the topic of national public health insurance continued to be debated strongly.

At the end of 1970 the number of persons protected by some form of private health insurance in the U.S. stood at 181.5 million. During the year health benefit payments totaled $17.3 billion. Of this amount, insurance companies paid $9.1 billion while the remaining $8.2 billion came from Blue Cross, Blue Shield, and other plans.

The general trend of health insurance has been to provide protection against a wider spectrum of health care expenses, and also toward coverages that have been broadened to reflect changes in the economic environment. The fastest-growing type of health insurance—major medical—encompasses virtually all types of medical expense, both in and out of the hospital, as prescribed by a physician.

In 1971 the nation's health system continued to be strained by a number of interrelated factors including shortages of doctors and other medical personnel, poorly distributed health care facilities, and high and rising costs. A number of proposals by different groups were suggested as means of bringing quality medical care within the reach of all Americans. These ranged from proposals for full federal subsidy of all health expenses to plans that would offer partial subsidy and tax incentive measures. (*See also* Feature Article: "The Health Care Crisis." *See in* CE: Insurance.)

INTELLIGENCE OPERATIONS.

In 1971 the world's major spy drama was once again enacted in Great Britain where Soviet intelligence operations suffered a severe setback with the expulsion of 105 Soviet officials in September. The accused U.S.S.R. spies included 12 counselors, 7 of the 12 first secretaries from the embassy, trade delegates, and other representatives. A short time after the expulsion an announcement from the British Foreign and Commonwealth Office revealed that information leading to the crackdown came from a defecting agent of the Soviet Committee for State Security (KGB). He was subsequently identified as Oleg Lyalin, 34, who had been granted asylum, bringing with him "certain information and documents including plans for the infiltration of agents for the purpose of sabotage."

As a result of the shake-up the number of Soviet representatives in various categories was limited to the number left after the expulsion. In addition, the British government stipulated that any future expulsions for spying would reduce the representation further on a one-to-one basis. At the time there were more than 550 Soviet representatives in the country, whereas there were only 110 British citizens in Moscow.

After denying British charges, the U.S.S.R. retaliated by expelling four diplomats and a British businessman and barring 13 other Britons from reentry into the Soviet Union. Further, several official trips (including a planned 1972 visit by Foreign Secretary Sir Alec Douglas-Home) were canceled and a number of cultural and economic exchange programs were suspended.

Soviet espionage suffered another blow in October when Anatol Chebotarev, a friend of Lyalin and a member of the Soviet trade mission in Brussels, Belgium, defected to the West and was given asylum in the United States. News reports stated that he had given valuable reports about KGB agents to the North Atlantic Treaty Organization. In November the Belgian government admitted that

Great Britain expelled 105 Soviet citizens living in London for spying. British intelligence made a film of a Russian (left) picking up information left for him. Several Russians board a ship for home (below).

it had quietly ousted some 30 suspected Soviet spies after Chebotarev's disclosures. In December a new twist occurred when Chebotarev left the U.S. to return to the Soviet Union, thus raising the question that his defection might have been a Soviet ploy to outwit Western intelligence.

In the U.S., Richard Helms, head of the Central Intelligence Agency (CIA) since 1966, gave his first public address since taking office. Speaking to the American Society of Newspaper Editors in Washington, D.C., Helms emphasized that the organization does not function as a watchdog over American citizens. Stressing the importance of the CIA as a peacetime organization, he cited the 1962 Cuban missile crisis as a past example and declared the intelligence operation vital to any international arms limitation agreement. He pointed out the People's Republic of China as an important target for current intelligence operations.

In May there were press reports of presidential plans to overhaul U.S. intelligence operations. The Administration was reportedly irritated with two recent failures of the Pentagon's Defense Intelligence Agency, a 3,000-man operation that costs taxpayers an estimated $500 million a year. One was the breakdown in operations preceding the unsuccessful raid to release U.S. prisoners at Sontay, North Vietnam, in November 1970; the other, the lack of knowledge of North Vietnamese resistance to the South Vietnamese invasion of Laos in February and March. Another news item of note was a reported break in direct liaison between the CIA and the Federal Bureau of Investigation (FBI) after a disagreement with FBI Director J. Edgar Hoover. The allegation was denied by the FBI.

INTERIOR DECORATION.

During 1971 United States design seemed to have successfully challenged that of Europe, which had captured a nice piece of the market. Leaner styling, away from the plumper Italian designs, was evident in such seating units as those by Andrew I. Morrison and Bruce R. Hannah for Knoll International. The upholstery for the spare-looking chairs, benches, and sofas is a sling locked into slots in the stretchers that join the tubular end pieces. More of the country's top furniture designers, including Wendell Castle and John Mascheroni, started designing for mass production in order to make good designs available at lower costs. Stable prices and more punctual deliveries aided U.S. firms as costs of labor and materials rose in Europe, an excise tax was imposed on imports, and dock strikes slowed deliveries from abroad considerably. The U.S. showrooms also presented more complete furniture groupings instead of so many isolated pieces—and many reported that retail sales were showing their best gains in several years.

Architect Ludwig Mies van der Rohe—who died in 1969 and whose famed Barcelona chair set a standard of elegance for more than four decades—was back in the news. A wood-framed sofa he de-

COURTESY, ELECTROHOME

Using spun aluminum and plexiglass, Electrohome designed this Futuristic 711 stereo with matching speakers. Tape space is also provided.

signed nearly 50 years ago was reintroduced. It is trim, bolstered, and being manufactured in walnut, teak, or rosewood with either fabric or leather upholstery.

One trend of the year was a wider use of colors. Another was the use of travel motifs in design. Robert Sonneman designed a chandelier of polished aluminum that looked like a cluster of shiny hubcaps, and George Kovacs introduced a panel of lights resembling a railroad switch. The Simmons Co. had a firm that makes dune buggies produce a mirror-bright finish for the metal frame of a new sofa bed. For carpeting patterns, Glen Kauffman incorporated road-sign arrows; Edward Fields, gears; and Milo Winter, cloverleaf highways. Seating, however, went all the way with the transportation craze. Charles Stendig designed a chromed-steel and hardwood chair that resembles a tractor seat; Veli Maijo, a bicycle chair that looks something like a home exercise machine; J. Wayne Burris, an upholstered chair similar to an airplane seat; and Selig, several chairs reminiscent of the automobile bucket seats.

The Water-Bed Hassle

The water bed's popularity seemed to continue to grow, and several versions of both a water pillow and a water bag appeared on the market. Several cities, however—including Los Angeles, Calif., and Portland, Ore.—outlawed the sale of electrically heated water beds until they had been tested and approved by such recognized testing organizations as Underwriters' Laboratories. In New York City the Buildings Department's Bureau of Water, Gas, and Electricity also recommended that heated water beds not be sold until proven safe.

Early in February in Santa Clara County, Calif., two water beds with improper heating elements burned, though no one was injured. The gravest danger feared by some authorities is that, since water is an excellent conductor of electricity, someone may be electrocuted if a bed should burst. Even with unheated beds, there may be some danger in case water soaks nearby loose wiring. Another danger for either heated or unheated types that approach 12 inches in thickness is that of sheer weight. Water weighs 62.5 pounds per cubic foot, whereas most post-World War II housing has been built to support a "live" load of only 40 pounds per square foot.

Supporters of the beds, however, were quick to point out that hospital versions had been used successfully for several years to provide comfort to patients with bed sores and to paraplegics. Most advertising claimed that the gentle undulations provide a more relaxing and restful night's sleep than do conventional beds—and some advertising contained frankly erotic overtones in an effort to intrigue an even larger market.

The Year's Highlights

Chicago's International Home Furnishings Market that opened the design year early in January showed little work that was actually innovative, though much that seemed new. On the other hand, the Museum of Modern Art (MOMA) in New York City presented "Recent Acquisitions: Design Collection" that contained many pieces that were not so recent but certainly more creative. Among the 70 objects on display, which had been selected from those most recently acquired for the prestigious MOMA's permanent collection, were Poul Cadovius' and Charles Mauro's Cube-in-a-Tube (a chrome-plated steel building block for expandable display units), Leonardi Cesare's Dondolo rocking chair, and Achille and Piergiacomo Castigioni's Toio standing lamp.

Early in the year one of the oldest and best art schools in the U.S., Parsons School of Design in New York City, celebrated its 75th anniversary. The school, best known by the public for the popular Parsons' table that was introduced in the 1920's, had trained such influential designers as Anita J. Moller, William Pahlmann, Bertha Schaefer, and John Wisner.

On March 14 the only major museum-sponsored showing of furnishings and decorative arts in the U.S., "California Design XI," opened at the Pasadena Art Museum. The triennial exhibition presented about 350 jury-screened items for domestic use that had been designed or manufactured in California during the preceding three years.

This $2,800 water bed comes with stereo radio, color TV, and light fixtures built into the foam rubber and plywood units surrounding it. "Pleasure Island," as designer Aaron Donner calls it, was the most expensive water bed available.

MICHAEL ROUGIER,
LIFE MAGAZINE © TIME INC.

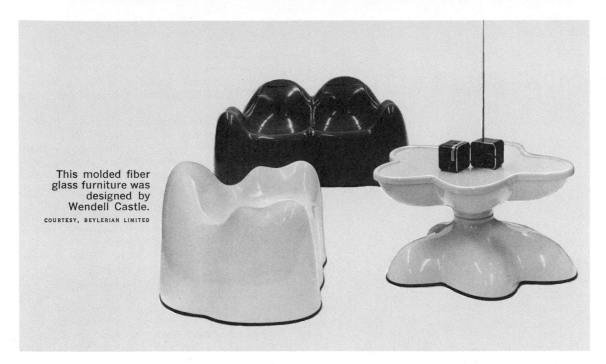

This molded fiber glass furniture was designed by Wendell Castle.

COURTESY, BEYLERIAN LIMITED

The American Institute of Interior Designers celebrated its 40th anniversary on July 8. The Home Furnishings Council, an association of various industry groups, sponsored "Debut '72," a promotion held by many stores in 43 U.S. cities between September 26 and October 9. More than 250 manufacturers participated—with displays emphasizing coordinated room settings, and a sweepstakes featuring an unfurnished four-bedroom home as top prize. On October 22 the weeklong fall home-furnishings show opened at the Southern Furniture Exposition Building in High Point, N.C. (*See in* CE: Interior Decoration.)

INTERNATIONAL RELATIONS. The most dramatic development on the international scene in 1971 was the end of the isolation of the People's Republic of China and its recognition as a major, legitimate force in international relations. This shift in the position of China was made possible by the thaw in relations between the United States and China after a period of nearly 22 years of animosity, exacerbated by two bitter wars—in Korea and Vietnam—where each had viewed the other as the implacable and ultimate enemy. The thaw was highlighted by the extension of a Chinese invitation to the U.S. table tennis team for a visit in April, followed by a relaxation of the U.S. embargo on trade with China in May, and was climaxed in July by U.S. President Richard M. Nixon's public acceptance of an invitation to visit China (later the visit was scheduled for February 1972).

What the outcome of Nixon's talks with China's leaders would be was a matter of intense speculation. It was obvious, however, that any trade and cultural agreements would be a mere prelude to the real issue—the power balance in the wake of continuing U.S. withdrawal from Indochina.

The reasons for the reversal in U.S.-China relations were in fact viewed by some observers in terms of traditional balance of power strategy. China was certainly concerned with its strained relations with the Soviet Union, and the U.S. seemed anxious to pit the two Communist superpowers against each other in an attempt to further U.S. interests.

With the U.S.-China thaw and the recognition of the People's Republic as the legitimate government of China by more than 60 countries, it was obvious that China could not be kept out of the United Nations (UN). The U.S. attempt to end its long campaign of opposition to the admission of China with a face-saving "two-China" policy—ad-

Two U.S. scientists visited China after the thaw in Sino-American relations began in 1971. Ethan R. Signer (right), a molecular biologist, and Arthur M. Galson, a plant physiologist, stressed China's desire for increased communication with other countries.

WIDE WORLD

BEHRENDT—HET PAROOL, AMSTERDAM, FROM BEN ROTH AGENCY

Talks ahead . . . .

mitting China but retaining Taiwan—was un-equivocally rejected. In part, no doubt, this was because of a general erosion of U.S. influence, but it also was because China appeared to the small and weak states in the UN as a useful counter-weight to both U.S. and Soviet power. China's entry into the UN indeed further enhanced its prestige and strengthened its position as a spokes-man and defender of Third World interests.

China's new position in world affairs had myriad effects on the foreign policies and alignments of other nations. The Soviet Union, although it had long championed China's admission to the UN, viewed China's friendly relations with the U.S. with intense suspicion. The lengthy polemical harangues that ensued between Chinese and Soviet UN representatives in late 1971 underlined con-tinuing Chinese-Soviet enmity. U.S. relations with its loyal allies in Asia became cooler. The quick about-face in U.S. policy had left these countries, which had been loudly proclaiming their anti-Communist stance, in an awkward position and they quickly began reassessing their roles in the more fluid international situation. Japan, which had long viewed itself as the major ally of the U.S. in the Far East, was particularly piqued when the U.S. did not consult with it prior to re-versing its policy on China.

Another source of international dissension in 1971 was Nixon's new economic policy—an at-tempt to improve the U.S. trade balance by im-posing a 10% surcharge on U.S. imports and by demanding that foreign currencies be revalued to improve the opportunities for U.S. exports. When Denmark retaliated shortly after with its own sur-charge, the specter of an international trade war loomed reminiscent of the 1930's. The trade and monetary crisis pointed out the necessity of a new international agreement to replace the 1944 Bretton Woods agreement. It was obvious that if the in-ternational monetary market was to function with stability—a basic prerequisite for the continuation of trade—Europe, Japan, and the U.S. would have to compromise to work out a new framework. In December a monetary agreement was reached. (*See* Money and International Finance.)

European Unity

The trend toward unity in Western Europe was greatly strengthened when the European Economic Community (EEC) and Great Britain reached an agreement on terms for its entry. However, this trend toward unity received a major setback when attempts to form a common bargaining stance

Protesting the harassment of Jews in the Soviet Union, thousands of Jews accompanied by many gentiles marched silently through London to the Soviet Embassy.

"THE TIMES", LONDON, FROM PICTORIAL PARADE

toward U.S. demands broke down because of the pressure of national economic interests. Although eventually a joint monetary policy was achieved, the disagreement cast doubt on the ability of the separate states of Western Europe to meld together into a viable force that would be able to play an independent role in world affairs.

The trend toward the easing of relations between East and West Europe continued, however, spearheaded in large part by the *Ostpolitik* (Eastern policy) of West Germany's Chancellor Willy Brandt. The "big four" powers—Britain, France, the U.S., and the Soviet Union—reached agreement on a new status for Berlin, guaranteeing access to it by West Germany, but final details implementing the agreement were not completed by the end of the year. The North Atlantic Treaty Organization insisted that a genuine agreement on Berlin was the indispensable condition for a European security conference, which the Soviet Union repeatedly championed during the year as a means of reducing troop levels and creating a buffer zone between East and West. (*See* Europe; Germany.)

East-West Relations

The general relaxation of East-West tension continued, making possible a decline in the abrasive confrontations of recent years. Instead of competing in a buildup of strategic arms, U.S.-Soviet competition tended to take different forms—diplomatic, political, economic, and cultural—but neither power was averse to seizing any opportunity to increase its advantage short of war. (*See also* Disarmament.)

In the Middle East, the Soviet Union continued to send additional arms to Egypt, and Israel responded by calling on the U.S. to live up to the Nixon pledge that military parity would be maintained. The U.S. sought to use the arms request

as a lever to press Israel into concessions for a limited settlement, but Israel rejected the U.S. approach. (*See* Middle East.)

In the confrontation between Pakistan and India, which eventually erupted into full-scale war, the great powers were also involved. The Soviet Union was allied with India, China was allied with Pakistan, and the U.S., which first appeared to be neutral, eventually took the side of Pakistan. However, the threat of nuclear war restrained the great powers from direct intervention and limited their role to diplomacy. Whether the tensions aggravated among them by the India-Pakistan war would be permanent, remained to be seen. (*See* India; Pakistan. *See* in CE: International Relations.)

IRAN. On Oct. 12, 1971, Iran's Shah Mohammed Reza Pahlavi placed flowers on the tomb of Cyrus the Great at Pasargadae, inaugurating a spectacular celebration of the 2,500th anniversary of the Persian monarchy. At ancient Persepolis an "imperial camp" of modern hotels disguised as vast tents, built for the occasion, housed dignitaries from all over the world; the hotels remained as tourist facilities afterward. In addition to the lavish banquets and parades marking the occasion, a centenary committee raised, by public subscription, sufficient funds to build over 2,500 schools and an equal number of electrical facilities for rural communities.

On the eighth anniversary of Iran's land reform movement the Shah promised to build new rural roads and irrigation works and to expand the rural handicrafts industry. In September, under the reform program, farmers became owners of the land they tilled; the move was aimed at increasing agricultural production and the purchasing power of farmers.

Iranian women weave portraits of U.S. President Richard M. Nixon. Portraits of a number of world leaders were made especially for Iran's lavish 2,500th birthday celebration.

JOCELYNE BENZAKIN

KEYSTONE

The year 1971 marked the 2,500th anniversary of the Persian empire. In October a massive pageant was held at Persepolis. Hundreds of musicians dressed in period costumes were a colorful and impressive part of the celebration.

Early in 1971 public opinion turned against the continuing student demonstrations over various grievances and student attacks on the monarchy. Although the students won some concessions, the government restored discipline and outlawed the Confederation of Iranian Students, an organization of some 5,000 Iranians studying abroad. Some students were thought to be influenced by Maoist-led terrorists, who engaged Iranian forces in sporadic guerrilla warfare in northwestern Iran during the year.

New developments in transportation included the inauguration of a 215-mile Turkish-Iranian railway in September, and an Iranian-Kuwaiti transit agreement. Iran and the U.S.S.R. signed a measure designed to reduce pollution of the Caspian Sea. Iranian resorts on the Caspian had been damaged by industrial wastes, pesticides, and oil spillage carried by wind and currents from Soviet sources. During the year Iran recognized the People's Republic as China's legal government and restored diplomatic relations with Egypt (severed in 1960) and with Lebanon (broken off in 1969). Iran was one of six Persian Gulf oil-exporting nations to reach a new agreement with western oil interests,

under which the Gulf nations increased their share of oil revenues. On November 30 Iran seized three small but strategic islands in the Persian Gulf also claimed by two Arab emirates. Iraq immediately broke off diplomatic relations with Iran. (*See in* CE: Iran.)

IRAQ. A somewhat more relaxed atmosphere prevailed in Iraq during 1971 as a result of an easing of political and economic restrictions by the government late in 1970. The state of emergency that had been in effect since the monarchy was overthrown in 1958 was lifted, some political prisoners were released, taxes and import restrictions on some consumer goods were eased, and reforms were made in the court system. In January the government enacted a law providing for the establishment of a national legislature of about 100 members, and announced a ten-year campaign against illiteracy.

The failure of the Iraqi government to provide the Kurdish minority with economic aid, promised under the 1970 settlement of their differences, led to growing Kurdish discontent in 1971. Kurdish leaders accused the government of delaying a census of Kurdish areas in order to dilute the population with non-Kurdish peoples before determining where Kurdish administrations were to be set up. The Kurdish Democratic party was strengthened by uniting with the Kurdish Revolutionary party.

Iraq's foreign policy in 1971 reflected apparent attempts to break out of its isolated position in the Arab world and to win back the respect of Arab radicals, lost by its failure to aid Palestinian guerrillas during Jordan's 1970 civil war. Iraq's ruling Ba'athist party launched a propaganda campaign aimed at preventing a peaceful Arab-Israeli settlement, resumed criticism of the Egyptian government, and condemned the "vacillation" of some Palestinian leaders. Iraq closed its border with Jordan and broke off relations with King Hussein's government following Jordanian moves against Palestinian guerrillas. The expulsion of three British diplomats from Iraq on vague spying charges was seen as a move to gain the favor of Arab radicals.

Other events served to increase Iraq's isolation. Iraq's support of an unsuccessful pro-Communist coup in Sudan led Sudan to break relations with Iraq. A territorial dispute with Iran erupted in border clashes, and finally a break in relations when Iran seized three small islands in the Persian Gulf also claimed by two Arab emirates. Iraq also denounced Syria for prosecuting Syrian politicians who had supported Iraq's Ba'athist regime.

Iraq and the Soviet Union signed trade agreements. Also, new agreements with foreign oil interests increased Iraq's earnings from its oil exports. (*See also* Iran. *See in* CE: Iraq.)

IRELAND. Shock waves from the bitter, bloody battle in Northern Ireland rattled the foundation of John Lynch's ruling party in the Irish Republic in 1971. The prime minister's policy for peaceful unification of his long-divided homeland backfired on many fronts.

The rift between militants and moderates in his

Ireland's Prime Minister John Lynch stressed the importance of Catholic participation in the Northern Ireland talks.

own Fianna Fail party climaxed in September with the formation of a new group, the Republican Unity party. The founder was Kevin Boland, a former minister in the Lynch government. In Parliament there was continued criticism of Lynch's Northern Ireland policy, and from opposition parties—Fine Gael and Labour—there were steady demands for results in the negotiations with British officials. Lynch was criticized particularly for allowing the rebel Irish Republican Army (IRA) to operate freely from Dublin, the capital.

Meetings between Lynch, his foreign minister, Patrick J. Hillery, and the British proved futile. In September talks with Prime Ministers Edward Heath of Great Britain and Brian Faulkner of Northern Ireland, Lynch asked for full rights for the Roman Catholic minority in the north and condemned the internment policy instituted there in August. He gained no ground, and the chief result was a steady weakening of his position at home. Part of his failure was attributed to his request in August for abolition of the Northern Ireland government. He had also backed the withdrawal from parliament of the combined Northern Ireland opposition parties and had supported their civil disobedience campaign.

Another of Lynch's approaches to a united Ireland was support for the removal of the strictly Catholic precepts that permeate law in the republic—for example, bans on divorce and on contraceptives. Attempts to introduce a bill to legalize contraceptives were defeated in 1971. But there was widespread rebellion over the issue. In May about 50 Irish women's liberationists from Belfast invaded Dublin for a demonstration. They carried with them supplies of smuggled contraceptives, samples of almost every known means, and they threw a number of devices at the feet of customs officers.

Joseph Brennan, the minister of labor, added another black mark to Lynch's government in April when he stopped unemployment pay for unmarried men (some 12,000), bringing about vehement protest and the resignation of rural deputy Joe Leneghan. Unemployment rose, factory shutdowns increased, and the balance of payments situation worsened in 1971. Tourism felt the pinch of inflation and fear of the strife in the north. However, the growth rate registered just under 3% and the 6% ceiling on wage increases imposed in 1970 was well observed. Strikes, the plague of Irish economy in late 1970 and early 1971, dwindled. Farmers, disgruntled with increased costs and inadequate income, staged a boycott of farm-machinery buying.

On May 11 Sean Lemass died; he had served as prime minister from 1959 to 1966. Also during the year 89-year-old President Eamon De Valera traveled to Lourdes, France, and Prime Minister Lynch visited the United States as the guest of President Richard M. Nixon.

Moshe Dayan, Israel's defense minister, made inspection tours of army positions. One of his stops was in the Mount Hermon area on the Syrian border.

Successful on the international level were Foreign Minister Hillery's negotiations for Irish entry into the European Economic Community (EEC). He won many concessions in the talks, including special terms for Irish industry. However, the question of entry provoked widespread controversy and major campaigns on the issue were expected to precede the planned 1972 referendum, required before the Irish Republic can enter the EEC. (*See in* CE: Ireland.)

ISRAEL. As 1971 began, the mood in Israel was strangely ambivalent. The sudden alarm about a possible outbreak of fighting on Dec. 30, 1970, was symptomatic of the general uneasiness about the intentions and capabilities of President Anwar el-Sadat of Egypt. Prime Minister Golda Meir had told the Israeli parliament on December 29 that there was a broad basis of understanding between Israel and the United States on most of the outstanding issues and that Israel had agreed to resume talks (which had been broken off on Sept. 6, 1970) through the United Nations (UN) special representative Gunnar V. Jarring. Nevertheless, the Israeli defense forces were placed on alert that day in view of evidence of a possible Egyptian attempt to cross the Suez Canal.

At the same time the country appeared unusually relaxed, confident, and accustomed to the quasi peace that had existed since August 1970. Confidence was reinforced by the report that Defense Minister Moshe Dayan had brought back from Washington, D.C., after talks in mid-December with U.S. President Richard M. Nixon and his secretaries of state and defense. The U.S., in Dayan's opinion, still treated the Suez Canal as part of the front line of the cold war.

Dayan's confident assessment of the military and diplomatic situation was qualified by the increasing impact of Israel's domestic politics on foreign policy discussions. Dayan's proposed Suez Canal peace initiative—linked to a limited Israeli withdrawal from the canal—received no support from the cabinet or the Israeli press. Moreover, during Dayan's U.S. talks American officials so carefully avoided the subject that Dayan returned home convinced that the U.S. was not really interested in a limited solution to the Egyptian-Israeli conflict. The issue of choosing a successor to Mrs. Meir had begun to influence domestic politics, and the powerful anti-Dayan lobby in the Israeli press helped to write off Dayan's initiative.

The government presented to Jarring a list of suggestions for a Middle East settlement. The 14 suggestions largely restated the familiar Israeli position but did not insist on direct negotiations and did not negate the general principle of an ultimate withdrawal from occupied territories.

All this was overshadowed, however, by the events that followed. On Feb. 4, 1971, President el-Sadat announced a 30-day extension of the cease-fire and his willingness to negotiate the opening of the canal in return for a substantial Israeli withdrawal. The offer took Israeli officials by surprise and Israeli public opinion saw it as an Egyptian seizure of the political initiative. Before the cabinet had fully recovered from this shock, it received a further unpleasant surprise in the form of a letter from Jarring that said in effect that the time had come, if headway was to be made, when he must formulate the steps to be taken by Egypt and Israel. This assumption angered the Israeli government, and it refused to answer the Jarring questions except in the form of a reply addressed directly to the Egyptian government, which the Egyptian authorities, for their part, refused to accept. When the actual Egyptian and Israeli answers to Jarring's communication were published much later, it became evident that neither had provided direct replies. On February 9, Mrs. Meir told the parliament that Israel was not prepared to consider the canal opening "on Sadat's terms." Egypt pronounced this a rejection of the Egyptian offer.

The Rivka Hospital in Petah Tiqwa, Israel, suffered extensive damage during an Arab rocket attack.

Public opinion in Israel began to reflect restlessness at the lack of initiative shown by the Israeli government. A public opinion poll at the end of February showed a more than 50% vote for Dayan as the successor for the premiership—more than three times the vote cast for his nearest rival. But once again—as in the preceding year—all Israeli attention became suddenly focused on a largely artificial "crisis" in Israel's relations with the U.S. Reports in the press and radio spoke of the "erosion" of U.S. support for Israel. In vain did Defense Minister Dayan point out on March 16 that Israel's military position was "stronger than it had ever been" and that Israel was receiving U.S. military supplies on a level never before achieved.

Despite the publicity focused on U.S. policy, nothing changed very much, and by the beginning of April attention was preempted by the convention of the Israel Labor party in Jerusalem, the capital, attended by 3,000 delegates. The convention was concerned with social realities at home as well as with foreign policy. It wanted to know government intentions concerning the 500,000 underprivileged persons in the country. It deliberated on the underrepresentation of Oriental Jews in the higher grades of the civil service and on the growing conflict between organized religious interests and the state. These questions were driven home by the discontent of organized labor and by new expressions of unrest, such as the demonstrations of the Black Panthers, a group of militant young Oriental Jews.

Then the nation's attention returned once more to relations with the U.S. and the prospect of a limited settlement with Egypt. On May 6 U.S. Secretary of State William P. Rogers and Joseph J. Sisco, assistant secretary for Near Eastern and South Asian Affairs, arrived in Israel. The first round of their talks with Mrs. Meir ended in a deadlock. But, in a private session between Dayan and Sisco, a formula was agreed upon that was acceptable to Mrs. Meir and Rogers. Sisco then submitted the proposal to President el-Sadat in Cairo, Egypt. Meanwhile, however, the situation in Cairo had undergone drastic change. Leading members of the cabinet, the armed forces, and the president's office had been arrested and charged with treason. It became evident that until the Egyptian president had consolidated his political position, no real advance in a settlement between Egypt and Israel would be possible.

Israel was also increasingly concerned with other matters. Figures released in Jerusalem showed that in the four years since June 10, 1967, about 125,000 new immigrants had arrived in Israel, 45,000 from Europe, 35,000 from the Western Hemisphere, 41,000 from Asia and Africa, and 3,500 from Australasia. It was a substantial number, though not quite as large as had been anticipated or publicized; 80% of the immigrants were under 50 years of age and a very high proportion were highly skilled. Included in the total was an unpublicized but considerable number of Russian Jews who had been allowed to leave the Soviet Union. They represented, however, only a small proportion of the 2.25 million Jews whose condition as a national minority within the Soviet Union became a major issue in Israeli politics and of much concern to the Israeli government. At the same time that a worldwide campaign on behalf of Soviet Jewry received active support and encouragement from the Israeli government, there were indications of moves by both Israel and the Soviet Union to resume diplomatic relations, which had been broken off in June 1967. Some progress was made during the summer but by fall the issue seemed to have lost momentum.

Much the same happened to the U.S. peace initiative. Assistant Secretary Sisco returned once more to Israel (July 28–August 6) and proposed a Suez disengagement not unlike that advocated by Dayan but both Israeli and Egyptian positions had hardened. The Egyptians insisted on a military presence on the Sinai side of the canal in the wake of an Israeli withdrawal. The Israeli government rejected this demand. Other differences centered on the nature and extent of the cease-fire and on the Egyptian demand that the partial Suez settlement be linked to a total Israeli withdrawal. Added to these differences was Israel's rejection of the UN Security Council resolution of September 25 calling on Israel not to change the character of Jerusalem and to rescind all steps hitherto taken by the Israeli government.

Following Rogers' speech to the UN General Assembly on October 4, Israeli criticism of the "erosion" of U.S. support was renewed, only to be corrected by Mrs. Meir's informal visit to Washington, D.C., for talks with President Nixon on December 2. These talks, in the shadow of the assassination of Jordan's Prime Minister Wasfi el-Tal in Cairo on November 28, led once more to Mrs. Meir's conceding much that the U.S. had asked for. At the same time, however, Israel received increased U.S. aid.

It was not the Arab situation or relations with the U.S. that remained foremost in Israeli consciousness at the end of the year. For the first time since the establishment of the state in 1948 internal differences and divisions caused the government the greatest concern. The government was also involved in a crisis of confidence. Both the minister of justice, Yaakov Shimshon Shapiro, and the deputy finance minister, Zvi Dinstein, were involved in a public inquiry into the practices of a government-sponsored oil corporation in the occupied Sinai Peninsula. There were specific charges that involved a million-dollar mining and drilling equipment theft, government funds manipulation, and attempts by high-ranking government officials to conceal corruption. On November 14 the cabinet decided, reluctantly, to set up a judicial commission of inquiry to conduct public hearings into the affairs of the Netievei Neft oil company.

On November 21, the cabinet announced that on Jan. 1, 1972, Lieut. Gen. Haim Bar-Lev, chief of staff of the Israeli defense forces, would step down from that position, to be succeeded by Maj. Gen. David Elazar. Bar-Lev, who took over the defense forces position on Jan. 1, 1968, was expected to become a member of the cabinet.

There was evidence of widespread discontent, charging that Mrs. Meir's administration had failed to consider the home front adequately in its concentration on defense and foreign policy. The question was put forth for the first time whether under these conditions Mrs. Meir would remain in office, as had been expected, until 1973. Suddenly, the question of the succession was no longer academic and the establishment front was closing ranks to keep out the most popular candidate who was not part of the establishment—Defense Minister Dayan. (*See also* Middle East. *See in* CE: Israel.)

ITALY. The future of Italy's shaky left-center coalition government of Christian Democrats, Social Democrats, and Socialists appeared to rest on the outcome of the nation's 1971 presidential election. The new chief of state was chosen in December by a joint session of the 952-member na-

Protesting a new system of awarding scholarships, students try to occupy the Public Instruction Ministry in Rome.
UPI COMPIX

tional parliament and 58 representatives from the country's 20 regional assemblies.

As the leading partner in the coalition and Italy's largest single party, the Christian Democrats were determined to name one of their own leaders to replace outgoing President Giuseppe Saragat, a Social Democrat. But the faction-ridden Christian Democrats not only had less than a majority of votes but could not unite behind one candidate. The party was divided between a large conservative wing backing Senate President Amintore Fanfani, a former premier, and a small left wing backing Foreign Minister Aldo Moro, also a former premier. Finally they compromised and elected Giovanni Leone, a senator, on the 23d ballot.

The Italian president was constitutionally a figurehead, with main executive power in the hands of the premier. Rivalry for the post lay in the fact that shortly after taking office in January 1972 the new president would designate a successor to Premier Emilio Colombo, a Christian Democrat.

It was a troubled year for Premier Colombo, as the country was plagued by the worst economic recession since the post-World War II recovery. A million workers were out of jobs, while the nation's industrial growth came to a virtual standstill and prices kept rising. In September the government moved against inflation by reviving retail price controls. Some critics charged that production costs and wholesale prices were ignored, and they called for a parallel wage freeze.

The Italian labor movement reacted to the economic crisis with numerous work stoppages. In a nationwide general strike on April 7 the unions demanded long-promised social reforms. In the next month talks were held between labor and political leaders on legislation to provide more low-cost housing, improved public health services, and a more equitable tax structure. Modified housing and tax reforms were enacted by parliament later in the year. In November leaders of Italy's three major labor federations—both Communist and non-Communist—announced an agreement to merge their organizations early in 1973.

The neofascist Italian Social Movement (MSI) made impressive gains at the expense of the conservative Christian Democrats in scattered local and regional elections in June. They polled 14% of the vote compared with 5% in the 1970 regional elections. The shift to the MSI was seen as a backlash against the Christian Democrats, whom the MSI had accused of being soft on crime, Communism, and labor strife. Alarmed at the rightist resurgence, a Communist-led coalition organized a series of antifascist demonstrations, including a march of nearly 100,000 persons in Rome, the capital, late in November.

It was disclosed in March that an ultra-rightist plot to overthrow the government in December 1970 was being investigated. Incriminating documents and explosives had been seized in police

The 25th anniversary of Italy's becoming a republic was celebrated with a military parade, while some groups picketed against the army.

raids on the homes and offices of right-wing extremists in several cities. Several persons were arrested but Prince Junio Valerio Borghese, head of the militarist National Front and leader of the alleged plot, could not be found. In December eight persons were arrested on a bomb-plot charge. The ultra-leftist Workers Power movement was under police investigation. Pointing to repeated street clashes that had been taking place between right-wing and left-wing extremists, Premier Colombo had earlier warned that Italian democracy was seriously in danger.

Italy's new divorce law, which went into effect in December 1970, was ruled constitutional by the nation's Constitutional Court in July. But in June, divorce opponents had collected 1,370,000 petition signatures—far more than the necessary 500,000—to force a national referendum on repeal of the

Striking taxis surround the statue of Emperor Marcus Aurelius in Rome's Capitol Square. The drivers were demanding more traffic lanes for public transportation.

highly controversial law sometime early in 1972. The referendum was expected to be bitterly contested and to cause increased strain within the nation's governing coalition, with the anti-divorce Christian Democrats on one side and the Socialists on the other.

In February, despite a half year of demonstrations and an 18-day general strike, the residents of Reggio Calabria finally lost the struggle to have their city named the capital of the Calabrian region at the southern tip of Italy. The regional assembly voted instead to place the capital in the smaller city of Catanzaro. In a compromise engineered by Premier Colombo, however, the assembly agreed to hold its meetings in Reggio Calabria.

In July, after a seven-year investigation, a parliamentary commission issued a report that labeled Italy's top Mafia leaders "bloody criminals, killers, drug dealers." The report described Mafia ties with government officials. Nationwide arrests of Mafia suspects followed. Earlier in the year a number of suspected Mafia chiefs had been rounded up and exiled to Filicudi, a small island off the north coast of Sicily. Protesting that their tourist trade would be ruined, the 200 residents of Filicudi had abandoned their homes and fled the island, vowing not to return until the *mafiosi* were removed.

In October Italy signed a three-year trade agreement with the People's Republic of China, the first by any member of the European Common Market.

The two countries agreed to most-favored-nation treatment, extending to each other tariff and customs terms that are as good as those existing with any other nation. Italy had recognized the People's Republic of China in November 1970. (*See in* CE: Italy.)

IVORY COAST. President Félix Houphouet-Boigny's offer to open a dialogue with the South African government kept the Ivory Coast in the forefront of African current affairs throughout 1971. In April the president held a major press conference at which he renewed the proposals he had outlined the preceding year and explained his intentions in greater detail. The issue of dialogue with South Africa was one on which black African states were deeply divided, the majority remaining steadfastly opposed to any rapprochement with that nation. But President Houphouet-Boigny was not to be deterred. An official delegation from the Ivory Coast visited South Africa in October, and a future visit by the president himself was considered likely.

In February President Georges Pompidou of France was given an exceptionally warm welcome on his visit to the Ivory Coast. During the spring antigovernment agitation developed among the students at Abidjan University, and in April the president ordered the university closed. It was reopened in May. (*See also* Africa. *See in* CE: Ivory Coast.)

JAMAICA. The long-threatening crisis in the Jamaican banana industry seemed destined to come to a head early in 1971, but both the representatives of the industry and their carrying and marketing agents agreed to make new attempts to solve their difficulties. Future prospects for the sugar industry appeared uncertain in light of Great Britain's expected entry into the European Economic Community. Some of the smaller cane factories, continued with government support, experienced considerable losses.

Electricity, water, transportation, and telephone services were unable to meet existing needs in 1971. Long negotiations over rates, franchises, and financing slowed down plant modernization and the expansion of services.

An election was widely predicted for early 1972 as the government neared the end of its five-year term. Both major parties, the Jamaica Labor party, currently in power, and the People's National party, in opposition since independence, clearly regarded the election as crucial, and there was a noticeable heightening of political activity. (*See in* CE: Jamaica.)

JAPAN. In 1971 an analysis of the October 1970 census showed clearly that the population of Japan had over the preceding five years continued its massive migration to the city. Urban population accounted for 72% of the total and rural population for 28%.

Fears of environmental disruption provided some legitimate reasons—as well as political excuse—for massive opposition by local farmers, supported by radical students, to the construction of the new Tokyo International Airport, at Narita, east of Tokyo. On July 27, workers backed by 2,000 riot policemen braved a hail of missiles to seize a corner of expropriated land to be used for the main runway. Some 175 protesters, including 20 women, were arrested. On September 16 three riot policemen were killed at the site as the last four plots of land were expropriated.

Meanwhile, Japan's airways were being crowded beyond margins of safety. On July 30 an All-Nippon Airways Boeing 727 jet airliner with 155

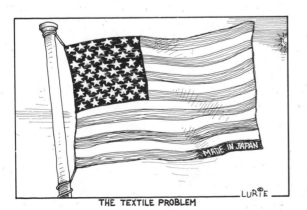
THE TEXTILE PROBLEM

passengers and a crew of 7 aboard collided in mid-air over Morioka with a Self-Defense Force (SDF) jet fighter. It was the worst air accident in history in terms of loss of life, and the surviving SDF pilot and his instructor were arrested for involuntary manslaughter of the 162 victims.

Relations with United States, China

On June 17 Japan and the U.S. signed an agreement whereby the island of Okinawa would revert to Japan in 1972, after 27 years of U.S. occupation. The nine-article pact was signed by Foreign Minister Kiichi Aichi at the premier's official residence in Tokyo and simultaneously by U.S. Secretary of State William P. Rogers in Washington, D.C. In the fall radical youths staged heavy riots to protest the treaty. On November 10 the U.S. Senate ratified the treaty, 84–6, and the Japanese lower house of the Diet (parliament) did likewise. Final agreements were still under debate and consideration at year's end.

Meanwhile, deteriorating Japanese-American economic relations were greatly complicated by the abrupt announcement on July 15 that U.S. President Richard M. Nixon would visit Peking, People's Republic of China, before May 1972. Premier Eisaku Sato, in his administrative speech to the Diet on January 22, had expressed hope for increased economic and cultural contact with China. He added that he also hoped the "Government of the People's Republic of China" would meet Japan halfway. It was the first time he had used the official name for the regime in a public statement. The China issue, however, had always been (as numerous Japanese pointed out in July and after) not simply a matter of diplomatic recognition, but one of the most sensitive issues in domestic Japanese politics. Even government spokesmen admitted that Japan's postwar foreign policy, having given priority to relations with the U.S. and having neglected mainland China, was shaken to its very foundations by the sudden Nixon announcement.

On July 17 Premier Sato, in a policy statement presented to both houses of the Diet, welcomed the proposed Nixon visit to Peking: "The Government intends to improve relations between Japan and China with care, based on the understanding that the attitude of the People's Republic of China will have great influence on the easing of tensions in the Far East." He added, however, that it was "most important" for Japan to maintain and promote amicable relations "with the Republic of Korea and Nationalist China [Taiwan] and other neighboring nations."

On July 21 Premier Sato told the Diet that he was prepared to visit Peking to normalize relations with China. On September 16, however, Chinese Premier Chou En-lai, in a meeting with a group of Japanese representatives, said that China would welcome the visit of a *new* Japanese prime minister, if he came with due respect for "Chinese principles."

Under severe pressure from the opposition, the Sato government tried valiantly to project an image of smooth coalition diplomacy with the U.S. On August 7 the U.S. announcement favoring admission of China to the United Nations (UN) and opposing Nationalist China's expulsion was officially greeted in Tokyo as little different from Japan's basic posture. American strategy, the Sato government stated, was in line with agreements reached in consultations on China policy between the two countries.

On September 22 Premier Sato announced that Japan would co-sponsor the two U.S. resolutions, one admitting China to the UN and one designed to preserve the membership of the nationalist regime on Taiwan. In October the UN members voted to admit China and drop Taiwan from their membership. Sato came under considerable criticism at home, being held responsible for Taiwan's ouster. His government turned back three no-confidence motions in the Diet.

On August 15 President Nixon's announcement of a dollar defense plan (including a 10% surcharge on imports) dismayed government leaders, plunged foreign-exchange transactions into utter confusion, and sent Tokyo stock-market prices into a tailspin. At first the government affirmed a policy of keeping the yen-dollar parity unchanged, but Japan stood to suffer a huge loss (over $1.2 billion in exports annually) with the import surcharge. Kakuei Tanaka, international trade and industry minister, reported that in fiscal 1970, Japan's exports to the U.S. totaled $6 billion (more than 30% of total exports). Already the U.S. had suffered a $1.4 billion deficit in trade with Japan during the first half of 1971. Vice-minister of international trade and industry, Yoshihiko Morozumi, nevertheless regarded the U.S. import surcharge as a clear case of violation of the General Agreement on Tariffs and Trade (GATT).

The Tokyo stock exchange was thrown into semi-panic on August 19 when massive sell orders flooded the chamber following rumors of an imminent revaluation of the yen. The day's decrease in average stock price was the third largest in the history of the market. Following a one-day record $1.2 billion purchase of dollars (to protect yen parity) by the Bank of Japan on August 27, the Finance Ministry decided to float the yen temporarily, effective August 28. On September 1, according to International Monetary Fund (IMF) calculations, the value of the yen shot up more

Japan's Emperor Hirohito and Queen Elizabeth II of England rode through London in an open landau on October 5 when he arrived for a state visit.

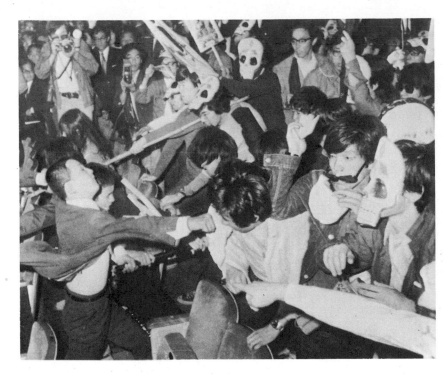

A scuffle broke out between antiwar protesters and management supporters at a shareholders' meeting of Mitsubishi Heavy Industries in Tokyo. The company is Japan's largest manufacturer of weapons.

than 6% from 360 to the dollar to about 338 on the Tokyo foreign exchange market.

On September 10 Japan and the U.S. ended their two-day cabinet-level discussions in Washington, D.C., without resolving any major differences, including the nations' policies on realigning world currency parities. The Japanese delegation stressed that the surcharge, if prolonged, would encourage protectionism throughout the world and threaten the free trade system, which had been crucial to postwar expansion of commerce. On September 14, in Ottawa, Ont., Foreign Minister Takeo Fukuda urged that Canada and Japan—the U.S.'s number one and number two trading partners accounting for 42% of all imports into the U.S.— should ally in the face of U.S. economic measures.

The stridency in Japan-U.S. relations fell off slightly when Finance Minister Mikio Mizuta returned to Tokyo from Washington, D.C., where he had attended the Group of Ten ministers' meeting on September 26 and the annual meeting of the IMF September 27–October 1. The path had been cleared, Mizuta reported, for an eventual multilateral realignment of currency parities toward the end of the year. In Mizuta's absence, however, U.S. special envoy Anthony Jurich, on September 30, had given Japan what amounted to an ultimatum: either Tokyo would replace voluntary restraints on textile exports with a government-level agreement, or strict import quotas would be unilaterally imposed by the Nixon administration on October 15.

Finally, on October 15 Japan (together with Taiwan, South Korea, and Hong Kong) agreed to limit exports of man-made fibers for three years

(to an increase of 5% per year) and woolen goods (1% per year) over a period of three years. In the pact, initialed by Minister Tanaka and special envoy David M. Kennedy, the U.S. in turn agreed to remove the 10% import surcharge on textiles, for Japan and all other countries, retroactive to October 1.

On December 18 President Nixon announced that the U.S. dollar would be devalued by 8.57%. At the same time the Japanese yen was revalued upward a total of 16.88% in relation with the U.S. dollar. The yen was thus valued at 308 per dollar. Two days later President Nixon signed a proclamation that removed the 10% surcharge on all imports.

The Emperor's Trip Abroad

On September 26 Emperor Hirohito, Empress Nagako, Foreign Minister Fukuda, and their party arrived in Alaska for a brief refueling stop on their way to Copenhagen, Denmark. For the first time in Japanese history a reigning Emperor had left his nation. And for the first time a U.S. president met a Japanese ruler—President and Mrs. Nixon had traveled all the way from Washington, D.C., for the pleasant, informal chat. The Imperial party also visited Denmark, Belgium, France, Great Britain, the Netherlands, Switzerland, and West Germany. (*See in* CE: Japan.)

JORDAN. Events in Jordan during 1971 were dominated by conflicts between Jordanian authorities and Palestinian guerrillas using Jordan as a base of operations against Israel. In a series of actions from January to July the Jordanian army

Jordanian Prime Minister Wasfi el-Tal (left) attends a meeting of the Arab Defense Council on November 27, the day before he was assassinated in the lobby of a hotel in Cairo, Egypt.
WIDE WORLD

succeeded in regaining control over areas of northwestern Jordan where the guerrillas had established themselves. As a result, the guerrilla movement was seriously weakened, and Jordan became politically isolated within the Arab world.

From the beginning of the year armed clashes between the Jordanian army and the Palestinian guerrillas erupted periodically. Following the kidnapping of several soldiers by the guerrillas on January 7, the army launched a drive against guerrilla bases north of Amman; fighting in the north and in Amman continued until January 14, when a truce arranged by outside Arab observers went into effect.

The truce called for implementation of a pact that had ended civil war between the army and the guerrillas in September 1970, for the withdrawal of guerrillas to bases outside towns and cities, for a release of prisoners, and for free guerrilla movement in Jordan. Divisiveness within the guerrilla movement was indicated by the condemnation of the truce by the left-wing Popular Front for the Liberation of Palestine (PFLP). The army's action led Kuwait to suspend its annual $45-million subsidy to Jordan at first, but it was reinstated in March.

Skirmishes between the army and the guerrillas occurred in February, and in mid-March the guerrillas briefly closed down the airport at Amman, Jordan's capital. Late in March fighting broke out in Irbid and spread to Amman and the Syrian-Jordanian border region. Jordan and Egypt both called for Arab summit meetings to end the conflict. Many Arab governments supported the guerrillas, and Egypt allowed the Voice of Assifa and other guerrilla radio programs to resume broadcasting; their broadcasts from Cairo, Egypt, had

been suspended in 1970 for criticizing Egyptian President Gamal Abdel Nasser's acceptance of Middle East peace initiatives by the United States government.

Fighting continued into April, with the guerrillas launching an offensive aimed at the ouster of Jordanian Prime Minister Wasfi el-Tal, who was accused of planning to eliminate the guerrilla movement. Jordan's King Hussein I declared that Jordan would not succumb to pressures from other Arab states and warned the guerrillas to evacuate Amman; Jordanian troops surrounded the city. Through Syrian mediation another truce was arranged and guerrilla forces left Amman. After the evacuation the government declared a general amnesty under which 435 guerrillas were freed from Jordanian prisons. In searches of former guerrilla-held sectors of Amman, the Jordanian army discovered large quantities of hidden weapons.

Following their removal from Amman and other cities, the guerrillas established themselves in tunnels and bunkers in the hills west of Jarash. The guerrilla movement, however, was weakened by the successes of the Jordanian army, by the political impact of Middle East peace efforts, by its failure to score major military gains against Israel, and by its disagreement on objectives. The PFLP and other left-wing factions continued to assert that revolution against moderate and conservative regimes within the Arab world was more important than the destruction of Israel, which was the goal of Al Fatah and other more moderate guerrilla groups. At a meeting in Cairo in March the Palestine National Assembly, comprising Palestinian guerrilla groups, froze all organizational changes and projects for unity; the meeting was boycotted by the PFLP.

A new round of conflict began in June, with the government accusing the guerrillas of acts of sabotage against Jordan's economy, and the guerrillas charging the government with trying to exterminate them. In mid-July the Jordanian army, in a major offensive, drove the guerrillas from their remaining strongholds in inhabited areas and cut their supply routes, effectively disbanding the guerrilla movement within Jordan. Many guerrillas escaped to Lebanon and Syria, where they subsequently announced plans to carry on their war against Israel; a number of guerrillas were reported to have fled to Israel to surrender. In support of the guerrillas the governments of Iraq, Libya, Algeria, and Syria suspended diplomatic relations with Jordan; also, Iraq and Syria closed their borders with Jordan, forcing Jordan to direct all its imports through the port of Aqaba on the Red Sea.

During the summer Jordan released some 2,000 guerrillas captured in the July offensive and announced that nonsubversive guerrilla groups would be allowed to operate against Israel from Jordan. Moderate guerrilla groups were offered a narrow strip of land along the Jordanian-Israeli cease-fire line as a base of operations. In September Egypt and Saudi Arabia attempted to arrange negotiations between Jordan and the guerrillas; the PFLP held out against any reconciliation with King Hussein.

In November Jordan's Prime Minister el-Tal was assassinated in Cairo, presumably by Palestinian guerrillas. Hussein appointed Ahmed al-Lawzi as his successor and vowed that the hardline policies against guerrilla activity in Jordan would continue.

Several political innovations were made by King Hussein during the year. In March he decreed a two-year extension of the term of the parliament's house of representatives; in September he appointed a new senate and announced the establishment of a one-party political system in Jordan.

From early in the year Jordan took a tough stand on Arab-Israeli peace negotiations in the United Nations, insisting on the return of Jerusalem to Jordanian control and the withdrawal of all Israeli forces from Arab lands. Jordan rejected an Israeli offer to compensate Jerusalem Arabs for land lost when Israel became independent. (*See also* Middle East. *See in* CE: Jordan.)

KENYA. Other events in Kenya in 1971 were overshadowed by the worst drought in half a century. The drought brought famine to Kenya's North Eastern Province, where it was estimated that as many as 250,000 people were affected. The government brought in large quantities of food.

In foreign affairs the government's main fear was the possibly adverse impact the military coup in Uganda would have upon the East African Economic Community to which Kenya, Uganda, and Tanzania belonged. Although Tanzania was hostile to the new Ugandan regime, Kenya adopted a moderate attitude.

CAMERA PRESS FROM PICTORIAL PARADE

England's Princess Anne, president of the Save the Children Fund, visited a home for orphaned boys in Kenya.

The Kenyan government, however, took an overtly critical line concerning relations with South Africa. In January, Kenya's Vice-President Daniel Arap Moi rejected Great Britain's attempted justification for supplying arms to South Africa. He maintained that Britain could not ensure their use solely for maritime defense and questioned the existence of any threat to the security of the trading route around South Africa. In May, Kenya's President Jomo Kenyatta joined with Nigeria's head of state, Maj. Gen. Yakubu Gowon, in a joint statement condemning the proposal made by a number of other African countries to hold a dialogue with South Africa.

The question of British Asians who left Kenya for Britain also remained contentious. Arap Moi announced that any of these people who were refused entry to Britain would not be readmitted to Kenya. However, President Kenyatta reassured foreign nationals that these decisions did not indicate any general censure of Britain and publicly emphasized that Kenya needed and welcomed skilled expatriates.

An attempt at reconciliation was made in the political sphere in March when Oginga Odinga, former vice-president of Kenya, was released after 18 months of detention. In September Odinga was readmitted to the Kenya African National Union (KANU) political party, which had been split by his resignation from the government five years previously. (*See also* Africa; Commonwealth of Nations. *See in* CE: Kenya.)

KOREA.

In 1971 the rival regimes of South Korea and North Korea agreed to discuss plans for reuniting the families of some 10 million of their citizens who were separated by the division of Korea in 1945 after World War II. Preliminary negotiations began on September 20. The unprecedented talks, first proposed by the South Koreans on August 12, were ostensibly between the Red Cross societies of South Korea and North Korea. They were held in a cordial, even friendly atmosphere, and the leaders of the two delegations expressed hope that the talks would be the first step toward reunification of the two Koreas.

South Korean President Park Chung Hee was reelected to his third term on April 27. He defeated Kim Dae Jung, candidate of the New Democratic party, by almost one million votes out of a total of some 12 million. Park's inauguration on July 1 was attended by Japanese Premier Eisaku Sato and United States Vice-President Spiro T. Agnew.

The May 25 National Assembly elections in South Korea gave President Park's ruling Democratic Republican party a greatly reduced majority.

The opposition New Democrats more than doubled their representation. Opposition gains were seen as the result of resentment against alleged one-man rule by Park and suspicions of corruption.

On June 3 Kim Chong Pil, vice-president of the Democratic Republican party, was appointed prime minister of South Korea by President Park. Kim, a retired general and mastermind of the 1961 coup that brought Park to power, was widely considered Park's heir apparent.

Troops were used to suppress student demonstrations protesting compulsory military training in South Korean universities. The demonstrations began in April in Seoul, the capital, during the presidential election campaign. They erupted again in October and spread to other cities.

There were reports during the year that South Korea was planning a complete pullout of its nearly 50,000 troops in South Vietnam. This was a result of concern that a possible rapprochement between the U.S. and the People's Republic of China and the continuing U.S. military withdrawal from Vietnam would isolate South Korea. In December Korea's uneasiness in the face of shifting international alignments was underlined when President Park declared a state of emergency. He claimed that North Korea was preparing to attack, but U.S. government spokesmen dismissed his claim as unfounded. Park's domestic opponents viewed the move as an attempt to strengthen his regime.

Students in Seoul, South Korea, protested against compulsory military training in June. The demonstration ultimately resulted in a full-scale battle with police.

CAMERA PRESS FROM PICTORIAL PARADE

As part of a government program, an orchestra of Young Pioneers performs at a summer camp in Wonson, North Korea. The prominent portrait depicts Premier Kim Il Sung.

The South Korean government announced early in the year that its economic plan for 1972–76 envisioned an annual growth rate of 8.6%, a marked slowdown from the growth rates of each year since 1966. Details of the new five-year plan included self-sufficiency in major food grains, development of the chemical industry, and steep increases in commodity exports. As part of an effort to expand its export markets South Korea began a new policy of trading with "nonhostile" Communist countries. The first such trade deal was a shipment of clothing to Czechoslovakia late in the year. Plans emerged in mid-year for Japanese participation in financing a subway in Seoul and of South Korea's first integrated steel mill.

The North Korean budget for 1971, announced at the April session of the Supreme People's Assembly in Pyongyang, the capital, envisioned a 17% increase in revenues and a 21% increase in expenditures over 1970. The budget reflected the new six-year development plan approved at the ruling North Korean Workers' (Communist) party congress in November 1970. At the congress Premier Kim Il Sung had been reelected the party's secretary-general. (*See in* CE: Korea.)

KUWAIT. Kuwait's third general election in its decade of independence was held in January 1971 to choose members for the 50-seat National Assembly. Unlike the 1965 election, it was conducted without government interference; as a result, a range of Kuwaiti political views was represented in the legislature for the first time. A ten-member opposition bloc within the assembly was formed by supporters of the radical Arab Nationalist Movement and independents. An Arab Nationalist legis-

lator was included in the new cabinet. Opposition attacks on government corruption and mismanagement were apparently effective in encouraging some reforms during the year.

In foreign affairs, Kuwait declared its support for the new federation of Egypt, Libya, and Syria, and established diplomatic relations with the People's Republic of China. Relations with Nationalist China were subsequently severed. Kuwait suspended its annual $45-million subsidy to Jordan for the second time in January, in reaction to Jordanian army actions against Palestinian guerrillas. After an appeal by Jordan's King Hussein I the subsidy was reinstated in March.

Kuwait's sluggish economy was expected to benefit from increased oil revenues as a result of a new agreement between Western oil interests and Persian Gulf oil producers, including Kuwait. A transit agreement with Iran provided Kuwait with new access to the Soviet Union, Turkey, and other nations. (*See also* Iran. *See in* CE: Kuwait.)

LABOR UNIONS. Organized labor in the United States made new gains in 1971 despite the slowdown in the national economy. Spurred by membership increases in public employee, teacher, and service industry unions, labor's representation of American workers rose. Hard bargaining and strikes in a number of industries resulted in large contract settlements during the year but helped to bring on action by U.S. President Richard M. Nixon to freeze wages and prices for 90 days, beginning August 15. Unions reacted angrily to the wage freeze and their strong dissent brought labor's criticism of President Nixon and the Republican Administration to a new high.

George Meany, president of the AFL-CIO, clashed with U.S. President Richard M. Nixon over the Administration's economic policies.

In November the American Federation of Labor–Congress of Industrial Organizations (AFL-CIO) held its biennial convention in Miami Beach, Fla. President Nixon addressed the convention in an attempt to win support for his post-freeze Phase II economic program, but his effort met with little apparent success.

During the year James R. Hoffa relinquished the presidency of the International Brotherhood of Teamsters (IBT) after he failed to win parole from federal penitentiary sentences for convictions of jury tampering and other charges. He was succeeded by Frank E. Fitzsimmons, acting IBT president. President Nixon visited a Teamsters' executive board meeting to congratulate Fitzsimmons, and Secretary of Labor James D. Hodgson visited an IBT convention in Miami Beach, signifying government willingness to accept the Teamsters under Fitzsimmons equally with other unions. In December President Nixon commuted Hoffa's sentence, after he had served 57 months.

George Meany, president of the AFL-CIO, and Fitzsimmons moved to reestablish relations between the federation and the IBT, once the largest union in the AFL-CIO but independent since its expulsion in 1957. Meany and Leonard Woodcock, president of the United Auto Workers (UAW), also began working together more closely, thawing the cool relations existing between the AFL-CIO and the UAW since it withdrew from the federation in 1968.

Meany and Lane Kirkland, secretary-treasurer, were reelected for two-year terms at the Miami Beach convention. Meetings there focused primarily on economic and social policies of the Nixon Administration, and the sharp criticism had political overtones.

In November Aubran W. Martin was sentenced to death after his conviction in the 1969 slayings of United Mine Workers (UMW) official Joseph A. (Jock) Yablonski, his wife, and daughter. Martin was the first of five defendants to be tried.

Inside Labor

Membership in U.S. labor unions and public and professional associations increased by more than half a million between 1968 and 1970, according to a biennial Bureau of Labor Statistics (BLS) report released in 1971. Labor unions claimed an all-time high of 20.7 million members in 1970, including 1.3 million in Canada. The U.S. figure was 465,000 higher than that of the previous BLS census. However, union membership as a percentage of the U.S. labor force slipped from 23% in 1968 to 22.6% in 1970.

The increase in membership over the 1968–70 period continued an upward trend begun in the mid-1960's, but the latest increase failed to match the gains in 1964–66 and 1966–68. In part the increase of only 465,000 compared with 1.1 million and 1 million in the previous periods, was a result of the tighter economy.

In manufacturing, where unionization had been strongest, total membership declined by 44,000. But unions in nonmanufacturing, particularly in service fields, added 361,000 new members. Unions of state and local government employees, including teachers, added 143,000 members.

Generally labor closed ranks during the year. More unions began exploring the possibility of mergers as interunion rivalries and jurisdictional disputes declined. New "no raid" agreements were reached between AFL-CIO unions and unions outside the federation.

More bargaining coalitions were formed to confront managements having operations that cut across industry and union lines. In the new labor spirit of solidarity for a common cause, the National Education Association, a professional organization, and the American Federation of State, County, and Municipal Employees formed a loose alliance for mutual assistance.

Labor and Government

Organized labor's relations with the Nixon Administration continued to deteriorate in 1971. Unions blamed Nixon's policies for high unemployment and for the "economic stagnation" in the country. They condemned Nixon Administration efforts to "control statistics" on the state of the economy and on unemployment through changes within the BLS. The unions opposed proposals for a new and stronger transportation labor law that would bar railroad strikes and require some form of arbitration.

Labor leaders officially criticized President Nixon's announced plans to visit the People's Republic of China as a rejection of "friendly" Nationalist China. The president's effort to wind down the war in Vietnam virtually ended the hawks vs. doves split in labor and was about the only White House policy to have any noticeable labor support.

The most outspoken opposition strongly criticized the "unfairness" of the president's wage-price freeze, complaining that while wages were frozen, prices were still rising and other inflationary factors in the economy were ignored. In October organized labor's representatives considered refusing to go along with the Phase II controls program. When they agreed to cooperate, it was partly because President Nixon had assured labor that the tripartite Pay Board, composed of public, business, and labor members, would function independently. Another factor was labor's reluctance to take an obstructionist position and risk blame for the continuing inflation.

Labor made its furthest shift from traditional free trade policies. Worried about rising imports and their impact on U.S. jobs, unions advocated tariff barriers against imports from countries with lower labor costs and demanded broad-scale measures to protect U.S. workers.

Collective Bargaining

As 1971 began, some 5 million workers looked ahead to deferred wage increases negotiated in 1968 or 1969. These raises averaged 4.9% to 7.8% in manufacturing industries but 10.8% in trucking and construction industries.

Nearly 5 million workers were under contracts that terminated in 1971 and hard bargaining took place during the year. Through September wage increases rose "at an unprecedented pace," according to the Bureau of National Affairs, Inc. (BNA), a private reporting service. In major industries, settlements tended to follow the pattern set in UAW bargaining with the auto industry in 1970, with raises averaging about 31% over three years. BNA figures for first-year raises showed a median increase of 37.3¢ an hour for all industries. The nine-month figure was 9.4¢ an hour above that for a comparable period in 1970.

Settlements and Strikes

Despite the strikes that occurred, peaceful settlements in what was expected to be a particularly

Striking drawbridge operators in New York City closed off the bridges and then left their posts, causing massive traffic jams. The operators asked for an improved pension plan.
"THE NEW YORK TIMES"

bad bargaining year held down lost time in labor disputes. According to the BLS, only 1.8 working days per 1,000 scheduled were lost in strikes during the first six months of 1971, the lowest total since 1966.

The United Steelworkers (USW) union was the big question mark as the year began with critical negotiations ahead in can, aluminum, steel, and nonferrous industries, and large strikes seemed possible. However, the USW settled with National Can Co. for a $1-an-hour increase over three years, a new unlimited cost-of-living adjustment clause, and other fringe gains. The union struck other can companies when they balked at similar settlements. After 28-day walkouts, the companies signed on similar terms, estimated at about 27% over three years.

Later the USW and major aluminum companies settled for about 31% over three years. Again, the unlimited cost-of-living clause was accepted by employers. The basic steel industry, determined to resist the automatic additional raises based on the government's Consumer Price Index, saw its position undercut. The White House announced that the president was "disappointed" with the trend of USW settlements.

Copper companies were encouraged to hold out against the USW, and the union struck nonferrous operations July 1. When it was the basic steel industry's turn at the bargaining table, talks went one day beyond contract deadlines and most producers shut down mills at high cost before reaching a 30–31% settlement with unlimited cost-of-living adjustments. After lingering strikes, copper companies followed the existing pattern.

The UAW extended the pattern of its automobile agreements to auto parts, farm equipment, and other allied industries, but with "great difficulties" and high costs. The union reported that the ten-week strike against General Motors in 1970 had cost $156 million and left the union deeply in debt. When talk turned to the UAW's return to the AFL-CIO, auto union officials admitted that the UAW was not in a position to pay per capita taxes to the AFL-CIO for at least a year or two.

The International Association of Machinists and the UAW, the two major unions in the aerospace industry, collaborated during the year in bargaining with major companies, demanding settlements in line with the UAW's 1970 agreements with auto companies (31% over three years) for "comparable" work. Aerospace contracts ran out in September and October, with companies protesting that they could not afford auto-level settlements. Because of the uncertainties of President Nixon's wage freeze and plans for controls, the unions did not strike when the contracts expired, but continued bargaining. In December agreement was reached between the UAW and North American Rockwell Corp. for about a 30% wage increase over 34 months. The contract was expected to set an industry pattern if approved by the Pay Board.

In February the Brotherhood of Railway and Airline Clerks set an important pattern for settlements in the industry with agreements for 42% spread over 42 months, part of the money retroactive for a year. This formula appeared frequently in other railroad settlements during the year, and it was given a Nixon Administration stamp of approval when, in a dispute case, a settlement was recommended on the negotiated terms.

Two railroad strikes occurred during the year. The Brotherhood of Railroad Signalmen struck for two days against all of the country's major roads, seeking to break out of the 42% and 42-month pattern. Congressional action forced a return to work until October, when the union was free to strike again but instead continued bargaining. In November a contract was negotiated that included a 46% wage increase over 42 months. The United Transportation Union (UTU) sued to win the right to strike selectively in the industry and walked out first against two carriers and then added others until ten roads were shut down. After 18 days, the UTU settled for the 42% over 42 months, but traded concessions with the industry on work rules and other issues.

The International Longshoremen's and Warehousemen's Union struck all 24 U.S. Pacific ports on July 1, with a complex jobs dispute adding to the problems of getting a negotiated settlement. President Nixon invoked the Taft-Hartley Act's national emergency strike clause after 100 days to reopen ports for at least 80 days, after the western states and Hawaii had complained of losses mounting to billions of dollars.

However, the International Longshoremen's Association (ILA) dock strikes in Atlantic and Gulf Coast ports on October 1 were not barred by the presidential action. The strikes, which closed down most major Atlantic and Gulf ports, did not end until late November when restraining orders (later extended to Feb. 16, 1972) were finally issued at the government's request under the Taft-Hartley Act's provisions.

In the coal industry, the UMW struck soft coal operations in 20 states on Oct. 1 after contract negotiations bogged down. By the end of the month, the issues had narrowed but questions of the impact of the wage freeze slowed progress toward a settlement. In November a new three-year contract was agreed upon but negotiators admitted that the pay increases were not compatible with the Pay Board's guidelines. Meanwhile, railroads that depend on coal freight revenue suffered heavy losses.

The new quasi-public Postal Service signed its first negotiated labor contract with seven unions representing some 650,000 employees. The corporation estimated the cost at more than $1 billion over two years, but many locals across the country complained that the increases were not satisfactory.

The first nationwide telephone strike in 25 years began July 14 and was settled a week later when the Communications Workers of America (CWA) and Bell System companies agreed on raises estimated by the CWA at 33.5% over three years, with a cost-of-living clause and other gains for some 500,000 employees. New York locals refused the settlement and remained on strike through December; service continued but repair and installation work was slowed. Striking locals charged that Bell had brought in "strikebreaking" supervisors from outside the city to augment nonstriking personnel.

The United Telegraph Workers (UTW) struck Western Union for eight weeks before settling nationally for 21% over two years. One CWA local in New York balked at the UTW pattern and held out for two months before settling close to the national terms.

In construction, settlements began at a high level but a controls program under the Construction Industry Stabilization Committee, established in March, brought the level of wage increases down substantially in the second and third quarters of the year. Government reports indicated a reduction from settlements at about 15% a year to 10.8% a year on the average. The government's ultimate goal was a 6% average. The BNA reported

median settlements of 70¢ an hour in construction in the third quarter of 1971, 24.9¢ an hour under the figure for the same period of 1970.

In soft goods, the Amalgamated Clothing Workers of America settled with the Clothing Manufacturers Association for 60¢ an hour over three years for 125,000 workers nationally. (*See also* Business and Industry; Economy; Employment. *See in* CE: Labor.)

"You're out of luck, mister—the railways are on strike."

Residents of a Chicago suburb jam into a rapid transit station after a nationwide railroad strike interrupted commuter train service in the area.

RIGHT: ULUSCHAK—"EDMONTON JOURNAL," CANADA, FROM BEN ROTH AGENCY. BELOW: HOWARD LYON FROM "CHICAGO SUN-TIMES"

Special Report:
The Four-Day Week

by Riva Poor

"Four days, 40 hours" is an extremely simple innovation in work scheduling that has made a tremendous impact on the employees and the profits of companies that have tried it. It is a simple plan because it is merely a rearrangement of work hours that trades longer workdays for longer weekends. It is an innovation, because rearranging is a new way of dealing with work scheduling. The most important thing about 4 days, 40 hours is that it works. Companies that use it report higher profits. Employees who experience it report they like having a long weekend every weekend of the year. In January of 1970, hardly one firm a month was converting to it. By January 1971 one firm a day was converting. By fall 1971, as the number of firms on four-day approached 1,000, over five firms a day were converting.

In order to explain why the four-day week creates more profits for almost any firm that tries it, it is important first to explain that the term "4 days, 40 hours" refers to innumerable possible rearrangements in work scheduling. Although the most frequent rearrangement at this time is the four ten-hour days referred to in 4 days, 40 hours, this variation is by no means the only one. Three-day weeks, three-and-a-half day weeks, and four-and-a-half-day weeks occur. Also, there are variations such as four days on, four days off (an eight-day week pattern), five days on, five days off, and even seven days on, seven days off. Further, the manpower schedule and the number of days that a firm is open per week do not necessarily coincide. While some firms are open only three days or four days a week, other companies are open as many as seven days a week but have their manpower scheduling on a four-day or three-day basis.

The key to the concept of 4 days, 40 hours is the idea of breaking out of the habit of thinking that workweeks have to be five days long, as though a five-day week were a God-given, immutable fact of life. Under the old way of thinking, managers viewed their scheduling problem as one of how to fit the work into the standard workweek pattern.

The innovation is the idea of starting with the work itself and building the schedule around the work. The breakthrough means that firms are setting the goal of optimizing work scheduling—they are looking at how to make the workweek work for the firm instead of against it. This new way of looking at things enables a firm to develop an appropriate schedule when it looks at the problem of how to optimize production.

Because firms are in effect individualizing their scheduling, it is not amazing that the benefits they report as a result of converting to 4 days, 40 hours are quite different at different firms. The firms, obviously, start with different problems and different goals. Banks use the longer day to create longer customer hours, bringing them more customers without increasing their payrolls. Computer operations are able to have computers manned 24 hours a day, using two shifts (of 12 or 12½ hours each) rather than three shifts; thereby they cut down on information transfer problems and improve the timing of auxiliary work that used to create costly idle-machine time. Batch processors obtain longer production runs on fewer setup times, meaning lower unit costs for their production runs. Firms that require seasonal overtime are able to offer employees two-day weekends when they are working overtime, instead of the one-day weekends that overtime used to lead to. Firms that had two shifts a day find that they can eliminate the undesirable night shift and put all their people onto the prime daytime shift by staying open more days a week for longer hours per day.

In some cases, increases in productivity gained through rearranging have been so great that firms have reduced the number of hours in the workweek in addition to rearranging the hours. A paint manufacturer that had made 15 batches of paint a week on five-day now makes 16 batches on four-day and has reduced its workweek to 36 hours. Absenteeism, tardiness, turnover, and so on, are reported to be vastly reduced.

The industries trying the four-day week include every major type, with new variations turning up daily. So far, there appears to be no kind of enterprise for which the innovation cannot work with the exception of those that may already be on an optimum schedule.

There are a few cases where firms trying four-day have reverted to their original five-day schedules. This is similar to the reversions to six-day when the five-day week was newly tried.

While companies report diverse benefits in using the four-day week, employees are much more uniform in their reactions. Basically they like having a long weekend every weekend of the year. They report that the repackaging of nonwork hours makes their leisure time more useful. People can accomplish more with longer spans of nonwork hours. They can travel longer distances; they can go visiting or camping; they can apply themselves in more concentrated fashion to hobbies or household projects, or both. They also have time to accomplish personal errands on the weekend.

Furthermore, with fewer trips to work each week, there is a slight reduction in the number of the nonwork hours that have to be devoted to getting to and from work, and there is a reduction in the monetary cost of commuting. Also, since the longer workday frequently takes employees out of customary rush hours, they frequently find commuting quicker and less irritating than before.

Female workers report they are able to get their housework done on one of the weekend days and still get a two-day weekend. Mothers frequently find it easier to arrange for baby-sitters when fewer days are involved, and a number of women report this easing of the baby-sitting problem permits them to join the work force for the first time.

Attitudes towards the four-day week appear to grow more positive with increased experience. In March 1971 the Gallup Poll reported that 38% of Americans favored four-day. (Probably none in the sample had experience with four-day, and certainly some of the sample were not part of the labor force.) In April *The Machinist,* a union paper, reported from an informal poll of its union members that about 50% favor four-day. Workers asked by management to vote whether they want to try four-day at their own firm generally vote 75% in favor. After employees have experienced four-day on a trial period, they generally vote more than 90% in favor of retaining it.

(*Parts of this article are adapted from the book '4 Days, 40 Hours: Reporting a Revolution in Work and Leisure', Riva Poor [editor], Bursk and Poor Publishing, Cambridge, Mass., 1970.*)

RON VILLANI—EB, INC.

"We need a vacation——these three-day weekends are killing us."

LANDMARKS AND MONUMENTS.

The effects of environmental pollution on landmarks and monuments received attention from United States President Richard M. Nixon and from the United Nations (UN) during 1971. In a message to Congress on environmental problems, Nixon proposed the formation of a "world heritage trust" to preserve natural, cultural, and historic objects.

A report by UN experts declared that industrial pollution from the plain of Athens was causing corrosion and cracking in the marble of the Parthenon. Damage from pollutants over the past 40 years was estimated to be greater than the total pollution during the previous 2350 years.

Worldwide concern was stirred by the shelling of the Cambodian temple of Angkor Wat early in 1971. The 12th-century temple, a Cambodian national treasure and part of the ruins of the ancient city of Angkor, was hit by Cambodian army artillery in an attack on Communist forces occupying the building. Heavy damage was reported to the temple's southern side.

Work was begun in 1971 on the removal of temples from the island of Philae in Egypt. The temples were to be dismantled to save them from inundation by waters backed up behind the Aswan High Dam. They are to be reassembled on a nearby island. Reconstruction of the 2000-year-old Temple of Taffeh, also saved from the high dam's waters, was begun in the Netherlands. The temple was a gift to the Dutch from Egypt.

A monument to space exploration (above) was presented to the European bureau of the United Nations (UN) in Geneva, Switzerland. A gift of the Soviet Union, the monument consists of a titanium tower bearing an inscription honoring space heroes, and a bronze sculpture by Yuri Neroda, who stands below it. A pavilion of Les Halles, the former central market of Paris, is torn down (right). Some of the pavilions were saved by the government when the old market was cleared away.

ABOVE: KEYSTONE. RIGHT: A.F.P. FROM PICTORIAL PARADE

In France orders for the demolition of the 19th-century cast-iron pavilions of Les Halles, the former central market of Paris, led to a mass campaign to preserve some of the structures. The 12 pavilions were among the first large cast-iron structures to be built. The French government decided to remove a few of the pavilions to another site for use as museums.

A substantial increase in appropriations for Great Britain's Historic Buildings Council resulted in grants for the preservation of 46 historic sites. These included the medieval Great Hospital at Norwich, the 14th-century Compton Castle in Devon, and a defensive redoubt at Harwich. England's oldest chapel royal, the 12th-century Chapel Royal of St. Peter ad Vincula at the Tower of London, was restored during the year.

Purchase by the city of Rome of the Villa Doria Pamphili and its 230-acre park tripled the amount of park land available to Romans. In Poland a campaign was launched to raise funds for the rebuilding of Warsaw's ancient royal palace, destroyed during World War II. An international team of experts met in Indonesia to draw up plans for stabilizing the monument of Borobudur on the island of Java. The structure, which has sculptured terrace walls and which may date from the 8th century, has been weakened by seismic shocks. (*See also* National Park Service.)

LAOS.

The most important event of 1971 in Laos was the Lam Son 719 operation in February and March. About 20,000 South Vietnamese troops, with massive United States air support, attempted to cut the Ho Chi Minh Trail, the complex communications and supply network running through Laos and linking North Vietnam with Communist forces in South Vietnam, southern Laos, and Cambodia. The operation demonstrated how closely the fate of Laos depended on that of its neighbors and greatly lessened the impact of negotiations—aimed at a separate settlement of the Laotian problem—that continued between Prince Souvanna Phouma, head of the Laotian government, and his half brother Prince Souphanouvong, president of the pro-Communist Neo Lao Hak Sat (Laotian Patriotic Front—the political wing of the Pathet Lao). At the end of June Prince Souphanouvong, with the support of his North Vietnamese allies, proposed an immediate cease-fire throughout the country. The suggestion was rejected by Prince Souvanna Phouma on the advice of the U.S., which wished to retain the possibility of bombing the Ho Chi Minh Trail.

The deteriorating military situation throughout the country, together with the difficulties of recruiting locally, led to the recruitment, at first kept secret but later officially admitted by the U.S., of Thai reinforcements estimated toward the end of the year at some 8,000 men. Military setbacks, together with uncertainty about future U.S. involvement in Indochina, caused growing uneasiness in govern-

WIDE WORLD

A South Vietnamese soldier hitches a ride on a U.S. helicopter that is removing troops from Laos. Antiaircraft fire from below was intense, and the chopper was overladen.

ment circles and increasing optimism in the Neo Lao Hak Sat.

The Lam Son 719 operation, which was launched on February 8, led initially to increased pressure by the extreme right wing on Prince Souvanna Phouma to abandon official neutrality in favor of open alignment with the anti-Communist regimes in South Vietnam, Cambodia, and Thailand. After a month the campaign failed at the strategic intersection of Tchepone, without the Trail having been completely cut at any point. This development strengthened Souvanna Phouma's position on the need for continuing official contact with North Vietnam, the People's Republic of China, the Soviet Union, and the Neo Lao Hak Sat.

The lull in military operations proved short-lived. Early in the year North Vietnamese forces had begun to harass the Long Cheng base, headquarters of Gen. Vang Pao's force of mountain tribesmen supported by the U.S. Central Intelligence Agency (CIA), and the base was saved only by the urgent dispatch of several battalions of Thai reinforcements. By March the outskirts of the royal capital, Luang Prabang, were seriously threatened.

At this delicate juncture for the anti-Communist forces, Prince Souphanouvong on May 8 dispatched his special envoy to the Laotian government, Prince Tiao Souk Vongsak, with a message proposing an immediate general cease-fire, to include the cessation of U.S. bombing throughout the country and the reopening of talks between the two main political groups. There was no immediate reply from the government, and the proposals were renewed in a later message according to an announcement made on June 25 by the North Vietnamese delegation at the Paris peace talks.

South Vietnamese reinforcements move into Laos to aid a heavily besieged Vietnamese unit in March.
WIDE WORLD

Meanwhile, the North Vietnamese and the Pathet Lao had increased their military pressure by taking the Dong Hène area of mid-Laos and, more importantly, almost the entire Bolovens Plateau including the town of Paksong in the south. However, the dry season was drawing to a close and as in preceding years the military initiative returned to the anti-Communist forces, because the rains hampered the mobility of the Communists.

Government troops encountered little resistance in driving the North Vietnamese back from the immediate outskirts of Luang Prabang, and during July Vang Pao's special forces, airlifted by U.S. helicopters, took control of the Plain of Jars and established there four artillery bases manned by Thai forces. Dong Hène was recaptured and government forces advanced to the outskirts of Muong Phalane, which they had lost in January. At the end of July, in another helicopter operation, the town of Saravane, located near the Ho Chi Minh Trail, was recaptured after being held by the North Vietnamese since June 9, 1970.

During this time Prince Souvanna Phouma had replied to the cease-fire proposals, suggesting neutralization of the Plain of Jars, with talks to be held alternately there and at Vientiane, the Laotian administrative capital. The counterproposals implicitly rejected the idea of an immediate general cease-fire, in accordance with the wishes of the U.S.

forces who sought to obtain a limited cease-fire in the north while retaining the possibility of daily bombing of the Ho Chi Minh Trail in the south. They were accordingly rejected by the Communists, who sought principally a cessation of U.S. bombing of the Trail, and early in August Prince Souk Vongsak returned to Samneua in the north, headquarters of the Neo Lao Hak Sat.

Even before U.S. President Richard M. Nixon's projected visit to Peking, China, was announced in July, Prince Souvanna Phouma had proposed the appointment of an ambassador to Peking, where for several years Laos had been represented by a subordinate diplomat. Although by mid-November the Chinese had still not replied, the Vientiane government continued its efforts to normalize relations.

The government's chief worries nevertheless continued to be military ones. By mid-September government forces had succeeded in recapturing Paksong, but at the cost of a six-week campaign with a total of 1,200 dead, wounded, or missing; at the end of the month, in a final rainy-season operation, they recaptured the former base of Muong Suy to the north of the Plain of Jars. But, with the approach of the dry season, the initiative returned to the other side. In mid-December Communist troops, estimated at 15,000, recaptured the Plain of Jars and six major artillery fire bases. (*See also* Cambodia; Vietnam. *See in* CE: Laos.)

LATIN AMERICA. During 1971 there was increasing frustration among Latin American governments because of the "low profile" policy toward the region adopted by United States President Richard M. Nixon. At the majority of meetings of official hemispheric organizations, delegates pressed for greater U.S. interest in the region and easier access for their products to the U.S. market.

Some governments, particularly those of Peru and Chile, sought development aid from sources other than the U.S. The Soviet Union and China showed increased interest in expanding their influence in Latin America. There were also signs that Japan was intensifying efforts to expand trade and investments there; this was demonstrated by the announcement in April of a program involving investments of approximately $300 million for petroleum prospecting in three countries: Colombia, Peru, and Ecuador.

The sense of frustration was reflected in the increasingly left-wing course pursued by Chile and Peru (and by Bolivia prior to the overthrow of President Juan José Torres Gonzales on August 22) and also in the nationalistic foreign policies adopted by some governments, even by those friendly toward the U.S., such as that of Brazil. Indeed, Brazil appeared to be determined to press its lead-

ership among Latin American countries, as shown by the succession of visits by foreign ministers of neighboring countries between July and September, and the granting of development loans to Uruguay, Bolivia, and Ecuador.

The greatest imponderable in inter-American relationships in 1971 was the effect of policies pursued by the government of President Salvador Allende Gossens in Chile. The U.S. government was seriously aggrieved by the prompt resumption of diplomatic relations with Cuba in 1970 and the nationalization of the copper industry in the fall of 1971. The U.S. announced that it would suspend foreign aid to Chile if it failed to compensate U.S. companies for the takeover of their installations. Chile had also presented a bill for compensation to replace profits it claimed were unjustifiably taken out of the country. The Soviet Union appeared ready to give Chile the technical and financial aid withdrawn by the U.S.; Soviet missions advised on the restructuring of the copper industry and offered a loan for the purchase of Ilyushin aircraft after the U.S. Export-Import Bank withdrew a previous credit offer for the purchase of Boeing jet airliners.

Neighboring governments became increasingly uncertain over Chilean intentions. However, in

A guerrilla group was operating in the rugged, mountainous terrain of Guerrero state, Mexico. They kidnapped wealthy landowners and exchanged them for money.

Cuba's Premier Fidel Castro (left) is welcomed to Chile by President Salvador Allende Gossens (right) in November. The trip was Castro's first to another Latin American country since 1959.
WIDE WORLD

July, August, and September Allende visited Argentina, Ecuador, Colombia, and Peru, and official communiqués published during the visits stressed his government's support for Latin American economic integration, noninterference in other countries' internal affairs, and friendship toward nations in the hemisphere.

Organization of American States

The General Assembly of the Organization of American States (OAS) met in San José, Costa Rica, in April. During its sessions, motions were submitted calling for an end to trade barriers and restrictions throughout the world, a huge increase in development aid to Latin American countries, and the introduction of preferential arrangements for exports from developing countries to the rest of the world. The governments of Brazil and Paraguay pressed for a declaration outlining coordination in antiterrorist measures, but failed to achieve the necessary two thirds majority. Many countries complained of unfavorable trading conditions with the U.S. The Brazilian representatives stressed that Latin American exports were not increasing in line with world trade, and many governments were concerned about the decline in U.S. development aid in recent years. U.S. Secretary of State William P. Rogers said that he understood these problems and that the U.S. Congress would be asked to adopt some preferences for imports from Latin America. The presence at the assembly of United Nations (UN) Secretary-General U Thant led to considerable speculation that it would in time become similar to the UN General Assembly. It was considered not to be a body that could impose binding policy resolutions on its members, but a general forum offering useful opportunities for unofficial bilateral meetings.

The attack on U.S. protectionist policies was renewed at the meeting of the Special Latin American Coordinating Committee (CECLA) in Argentina in September, after the U.S. dollar crisis in August. The delegates agreed to adopt a common front against the suspension of the convertibility of the U.S. dollar into gold, and to demand the immediate withdrawal of the 10% surcharge imposed on all imports (except raw materials, petroleum, and some foods) announced by President Nixon as part of a package of measures to stabilize the U.S. economy. These motions were to be submitted to the Inter-American Economic and Social Council (IA-ECOSOC) meeting held in Panama City, Panama, in the same month. The U.S. refused to comply with them but made it clear that Latin American countries would be exempted from the 10% cut in development aid included in President Nixon's August measures.

The import surcharge was greeted with much concern by many Latin American governments. Mexico calculated that half its exports would be affected, although the surcharge would not apply to products covered by quotas, such as textiles and sugar. Respectively 85% and 98% of Argentina's and Uruguay's exports would be liable to increased tariffs; but the Brazilians were confident that theirs would not be adversely affected. About 27% of all Latin American exports were expected to be involved. However, Nixon rescinded the surcharge on December 20.

The problem of Cuba was also considered at San José. Chile and Bolivia advocated the lifting of the quarantine that was imposed by the OAS in 1964 at the behest of the Venezuelan government; however, Cuban Premier Fidel Castro stated that his government was not prepared to join the organization. Meanwhile, there were increasing signs that

Julian Beck and Judith Malina, founders of the Living Theater, were arrested in Ouro Prêto, Brazil, along with 13 other members of their group, for possession of marijuana.

MANCHETE FROM PICTORIAL PARADE

Cuba's long isolation from the Latin American fold was ending. Although it was increasingly difficult for the U.S. to maintain its economic blockade, in view of its current attempts to arrive at a détente with the Soviet Union and China, the U.S. still appeared to be determinedly resisting Cuba's admission to the OAS. Relations between Cuba and Chile grew closer during the year. The foreign ministers of the two countries exchanged visits in July and August. In the fall Castro himself made

a 25-day visit to Chile where he was enthusiastically received by supporters of Chile's Marxist president, Allende. It was Castro's first visit to another Latin American country since he became premier in 1959. On his return to Cuba Premier Castro made brief stopovers in Peru and Ecuador.

Peru was considering the reopening of diplomatic relations with Cuba and in July signed an agreement to sell large quantities of fishmeal to Cuba.

Bolivian troops in La Paz take to the streets to put down student resistance to the country's new regime. Hundreds of students were imprisoned and at least four were killed.

WIDE WORLD

Trinidad and Tobago, Guyana, Panama, and Barbados were also reported to be ready to establish diplomatic and commercial links if Venezuela took a favorable attitude. The increasing acceptance of Cuba was partly explained by the decline in Cuban support for guerrilla movements in Latin America during the preceding two years.

Regional and Subregional Integration

Little progress was made during the year toward achieving the ultimate objective of the Montevideo Treaty of 1960, which set up the Latin American Free Trade Association (LAFTA)—complete free trade within the region by 1980. At an annual conference of the association held in Montevideo, Uruguay, in November and December 1970, only 31 tariff cuts were negotiated, compared with 989 reductions in 1968. Four industrial complementation agreements, however, were signed. The most important of these were on photographic equipment, involving Argentina, Brazil, Uruguay, Mexico, and Venezuela, and on petrochemical projects, to which all these countries were signatories with the exception of Uruguay. The United Nations Economic Commission for Latin America (ECLA) reported that the compounded problems faced by LAFTA prevented its achieving its aims; this set a formal seal on the general feeling of many observers.

Some progress was made during the year toward fostering cooperation in the joint development of the resources of the basin of the Río de la Plata. Argentina, Bolivia, Brazil, Paraguay, and Uruguay agreed early in June to establish a common fund for this purpose. A series of presidential meetings during the year stressed the need to develop the basin's water resources and transport and communications.

Territorial Waters

The claims of some Latin American countries to territorial waters up to 200 miles offshore were maintained during the year. On July 1 Brazil began to enforce a decree, issued in March 1970, increasing the limit of its waters.

U.S. fishing vessels chose to ignore the ruling, but after an exchange of protests the U.S. appeared to accept the Brazilian demands. Ecuador also made a strong protest over Californian tuna boats fishing in its waters, and this was condemned at the OAS assembly meeting in April. (*See also* articles on individual countries. *See in* CE: Articles on individual countries; Latin America.)

LAW. In 1971 several proposals were introduced in the United States Congress that would take the Legal Services program of the Office of Economic Opportunity (OEO) out of that organization and into a government-funded, independent, nonprofit national legal services corporation. The establishment of such a corporation would enable legal services programs to continue representing the in-

terests of the poor; at the same time, the corporation would maintain independence from political pressures and from administrative and policy conflicts existing in large government agencies. This would theoretically enable the collective poor to seek legal redress for wrongs committed not only by private but also by public wrongdoers.

A major prison reform movement arose in the U.S. in 1971, most notably after the uprising at the Attica State Correctional Facility in New York. Prison reformists took action in several areas, especially in individual and class action suits and in the introduction into state legislatures of prison reform legislation. Among the areas of prisoners' complaints were indeterminate sentences, prison conditions, custodial brutality, lack of rehabilitative opportunity, and prison mail censorship. (*See* Prisons Special Report.)

The U.S. jury system continued to change. Many states began to adopt 6-man juries rather than the traditional 12-man juries. The change came about as an economic measure. The work burden on the courts has steadily increased over the years, with consequent increase of time and expense in selecting more juries.

There was a possibility that another traditional aspect of the jury system might also be altered. The great majority of states required that in a criminal jury trial the jury must return a unanimous verdict. In two states, however, a less-than-unanimous verdict was permitted in trials of serious

Charles Manson and three of his followers were sentenced to death in the gas chamber on 27 counts of murder and conspiracy.

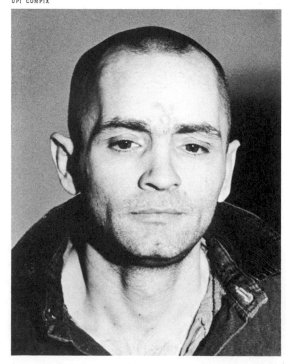

criminal cases other than capital offenses: Oregon permits a 10–2 jury verdict, and Louisiana permits a 9–3 verdict. Court cases challenging the nonunanimity rules of these two states were before the U.S. Supreme Court at year's end.

The growing number of criminal cases in the courts and the accompanying delay constantly increased both the necessity for, and the problems of defining and implementing, speedy trials. Speedy trial bills were put before the U.S. Senate and U.S. House of Representatives. If passed, such legislation would establish standardized rules applicable to all federal courts pertaining to the period of time in which criminal cases would have to be tried. If such a federal law is passed, it may become a model after which the states could fashion a uniform law for speedy trial in state criminal courts.

The narcotics laws were of special interest to Americans in 1971. As to hard drugs, the recent emphasis of the law has been on questions of criminal procedure and law enforcement (such as search and seizure questions), and of the statutory severity of penalties. Concerning marijuana, courts asked basic questions, but confusion still arose. In May 1971 the Michigan Court of Appeals upheld a state statute defining marijuana as a narcotic and, in so doing, affirmed a conviction and sentence of 9½ to 10 years for possession of two joints of marijuana. Four months later, the Supreme Court of Illinois held that the classification of marijuana under the Narcotic Drug Act was arbitrary and unconstitutional. That court considered marijuana as nonnarcotic and nonaddictive, and reversed the conviction of the defendant. (*See* Law Special Report.)

Murder charges against Bobby Seale (above) and Ericka Huggins were dropped when a New Haven, Conn., jury failed to reach a verdict in their case. Seale, national chairman of the Black Panther party, and Mrs. Huggins, a Panther organizer, had been indicted for the killing of Alex Rackley, a Panther who was suspected of being a police informer. Still under indictment at the end of 1971 was Angela Davis (left, wearing glasses). She faced murder charges in connection with a 1970 courtroom shootout in San Rafael, Calif.

ABOVE: UPI COMPIX. LEFT: WIDE WORLD

Law

Special Report:
Part One: A Summary of the Pentagon Papers

by David K. Willis

In June 1967, United States Secretary of Defense Robert S. McNamara, who had become personally disenchanted with the war in Vietnam, ordered a sweeping study of how and why the United States had become involved in the war. As a result, a team of 36 government officials worked for a year and a half to produce a 47-volume study. In final form, the study was incomplete in that it contained no information from White House files and thus reflected none of the crucial thinking of U.S. President Lyndon B. Johnson as he made final decisions. Nonetheless, the revelations based on the documents—which came to be known as the Pentagon papers—offered an unparalleled look at the interior workings of the government of a major power, its contingency plans, the private doubts behind its public utterances.

The first newspaper article based on the Pentagon papers appeared in *The New York Times* on June 13, 1971; on June 18 the *Washington Post* published an article based on the same study. During the remaining days of June and into July, 16 other newspapers published articles based on the papers, Xerox copies of which were distributed to them through anonymous channels. Daniel Ellsberg, formerly with the Rand Corp. (a government think tank), later publicly admitted "leaking" the documents to all but one of the papers. What follows is a review of some of the published highlights of the Pentagon papers, presented in chronological order.

1945–50: The First Step of U.S. Involvement

The seeds of U.S. involvement in Vietnam were sown between 1945 and 1950, according to the authors of the Pentagon papers. Washington saw the "vacuity" of French colonial policies in Indochina but, committed to retaining French friendship in opposition to the Soviet Union, ignored appeals for aid from Vietnamese nationalist leader Ho Chi Minh and refused to intervene directly.

The fall of Chiang Kai-shek in China in 1949 spurred the Administration of U.S. President Harry S. Truman into action. Following Soviet and Chinese recognition of Ho Chi Minh's government in North Vietnam in 1950, Washington recognized the rival Vietnamese regime of Emperor Bao Dai and announced some aid to the French in Indochina. The first step was taken; the U.S. was irrevocably involved.

1950–60: Opposition to a Communist Vietnam

After the defeat of the French, the Geneva conference of 1954 hammered out a set of accords dividing Vietnam into two halves and calling for reunification through elections in 1956. But U.S. President Dwight D. Eisenhower and his secretary of state, John Foster Dulles, feared a Communist victory in the elections. The reason that the elections were never held, however, was not the strenuous efforts of Washington but the objections of Ngo Dinh Diem, who had come to power in South Vietnam.

In 1958 the Eisenhower Administration established a national policy to eliminate Communist control from all Vietnam and to reunite the country under a single, pro-U.S. government. In doing so, the Administration overruled advice from the U.S. Central Intelligence Agency (CIA) that the Communists in Vietnam would stay relatively quiet if reunification elections were held.

1960–63: A "Broad Commitment"

Of the John F. Kennedy Administration, the Pentagon analysts said it took the "limited-risk gamble" of the Eisenhower years and turned it into a "broad commitment" to stop a Communist takeover of South Vietnam. Kennedy did not send ground combat troops into Vietnam but did authorize several military actions including provision

Daniel Ellsberg, a former employee of the Rand Corp., admitted that he had released the Pentagon papers to *The New York Times* and other newspapers. He justified his action with a belief in the public's right to information about the government.

for sabotage and harassment inside the north. He also greatly expanded the U.S. military advisory mission. In 1963, when Kennedy was assassinated, about 16,000 U.S. troops were in South Vietnam.

As plans for escalation developed, the Kennedy Administration was also laying other plans—for withdrawal—which were further expanded by the Johnson Administration but were never used. In August 1963 the National Security Council rejected a State Department official's view that the time had come to withdraw honorably. Secretary of State Dean Rusk is quoted as saying that "we will not pull out" but "we will not run a coup." Yet, the papers show the Kennedy Administration was intimately involved in the maneuvering that led to the downfall of Diem in November 1963.

1964–65: The Decision to Take the Offensive

Soon after Johnson succeeded Kennedy as president, secret military operations against the north were increased. When North Vietnamese patrol boats attacked one and perhaps two U.S. destroyers on the Gulf of Tonkin, the Administration held to a previously written scenario, pushed a prepared resolution through Congress, and secretly warned Ho Chi Minh to stop leading insurgencies against South Vietnam and Laos or "suffer the consequences."

On Sept. 7, 1964, the Johnson Administration reached a "general consensus" that air attacks against the north would probably have to be launched, and that they would begin early in 1965. At the time President Johnson was engaged in his campaign for the presidency against Barry Goldwater, whom Johnson portrayed as a man too willing to resort to nuclear weapons for the safety of the nation. In February 1965, just over 100 days after an overwhelming victory at the polls, Johnson launched full-scale bombing of the north. Shortly after, the president, in order to prevent a collapse in the south, secretly authorized U.S. combat troops to use offensive action. News of the change in role

from defense to offense "crept out almost by accident in a State Department release."

1966–67: The Failure of Bombing

The Pentagon analyst who wrote "The Air War with North Vietnam" section of the Pentagon papers said that it was a "colossal misjudgment" to think that Hanoi would be brought to its knees by the bombing campaign. In the summer of 1966, the analyst wrote, government councils were split on the bombing issue. Defense Secretary McNamara, his civilian advisers in the Pentagon, and the CIA, who were doubtful, opposed the Joint Chiefs of Staff and the generals and admirals in the field, who were enthusiastic. The rapid buildup of U.S. forces in the south took place in 1965 and 1966 in part because the enemy's capacity to boost its own forces was "consistently underrated."

McNamara grew less and less sanguine about the war and, convinced that the air war had no real effect on Hanoi's ability to wage war, tried in October 1966 to persuade President Johnson to cut back the bombing and to seek a political settlement. The Joint Chiefs, at the same time, told the president that the bombing was a "trump card." In April 1967, faced with fresh requests for troops, Johnson asked, "When we add divisions, can't the enemy add divisions? If so, where does it all end?"

1968: The Decision to De-Escalate

Following the enemy's Tet offensive in February 1968, President Johnson came under strong pressure from the Joint Chiefs to order national mobilization in the United States. But the pressure set off a last, intense policy debate in Washington.

The CIA bolstered advocates of de-escalation when it said that the enemy could withstand a U.S. war of attrition regardless of U.S. troop increases over the following ten months. The final result was the opposite of what the military wanted—a partial bombing halt, which Johnson announced on March 31, 1968, along with his own retirement.

Special Report:
Part Two: Legal Issues and the Pentagon Papers

by Philip B. Kurland

On a comparatively uneventful Sunday in June 1971, *The New York Times* began publication of a series of articles based on a government study of the United States involvement in the Vietnam war. It is very likely that the publication of the "Pentagon papers," as they came to be called, would have stirred only a minor flurry of interest and would soon have been forgotten. (The *Times* reported no increased sales until after the U.S. government sought to interfere with publication.) The Administration of U.S. President Richard M. Nixon, however, ensured the creation of a cause célèbre when it brought suit in the United States District Court in New York City to enjoin further publication of the documents by *The New York Times*. In response, a temporary order restraining publication was issued. Shortly after, the *Washington Post* published an article based on the same study, and the U.S. Department of Justice filed another suit in the District of Columbia and again succeeded in staying publication of further installments. But after other newspapers took up the stories, Attorney General John N. Mitchell abandoned further lawsuits and concentrated on successfully culminating the two suits he had already brought.

The cases went with extraordinary speed from the trial courts in the two separate jurisdictions to the respective courts of appeals and then to the U.S. Supreme Court, which had to call a special hearing. Speed was deemed of the essence. The cases were argued on June 26 and were decided June 30, with an opinion for every justice of the court in addition to the statement that purported to come from the court as a whole.

The Long-Term Impact of the Case

There are some cases that make for big news whose immediate and long-term effects change the face of the U.S. Constitution and its impact on the American people. There are other legal cases that are forgotten almost as quickly as they gain prominence, controversies of the day whose importance is to be found in their newsworthiness and not their effect on constitutional jurisprudence. The New York Times case of 1971 would seem to fall in the second category. The judgment in favor of the newspapers adds little legally to what has gone before.

In part, the transient importance of the decision may be attributed to the facts. In part, it may be due to the nature of the arguments that were presented. In part, it may result from the inadequacies of the opinions that were composed, necessarily, with too little deliberation and consultation.

The fact that reads against the importance of the case is the extraordinary nature of the publication. It is not likely that many government secrets will take the form of multiple volumes. There will not ordinarily be that first, partial publication on the basis of which later publications would be sought to be enjoined. A secret is obviously no longer a secret after publication and not all the king's horses, the king's men, nor the king's courts can return it to its original state.

The framing of the issues by counsel will probably make the case of only passing interest because of the questions that were not raised. It is important to remember that the case holds nothing about whether a newspaper can be punished for publishing classified government documents, although there are strong hints that it can. Nor is it concerned with the question of preventing publication of purloined documents because they were purloined. Both the government and the newspapers were content to state the question in the case not as *whether* publication can ever be enjoined, but rather as *when* publication may be enjoined. Both sides seemed in agreement that publication could not be enjoined unless publication would seriously and materially adversely affect the national security. Both sides were agreed that if publication would seriously and materially adversely affect the national security it could be enjoined. And so the case was reduced to a question of fact: would the publication of these particular papers result in such egregious harm as the government suggested or would publication be of lesser consequence that would preclude censorship?

The First Case of an Attempt at Prior Restraint

It is true that the case, in one sense, is unique. Never before had the U.S. resorted to the courts in an effort to prevent publication of a newspaper. In the one instance that reached the Supreme Court in which a state had sought to do so, the court said that an injunction would be a violation of the First Amendment. But in that case—Near *vs.*

Minnesota—the court did suggest that there were times when such prohibition might be allowed, for instance in "the publication of the sailing dates of transports or the number and location of troops." There is no basis for suggesting that the decision in New York Times Co. *vs.* United States changed either the holding or the dictum of Near *vs.* Minnesota.

The opinion of the court simply quoted from two earlier opinions—one concerned with obscenity and the other with neighborhood picketing of a real estate dealer. From the first of these the court took the sentence: "Any system of prior restraints of expression comes to this Court bearing a heavy presumption against its constitutional validity." The court went on: "The Government 'thus carries a heavy burden of showing justification for the enforcement of such a restraint.' . . . the Government (has) not met that burden."

The Individual Opinions

For Justices Hugo L. Black and William O. Douglas, however, there never could be any justification for enjoining newspaper publication. As Justice Black put it: "The word 'security' is a broad, vague generality whose contours should not be invoked to abrogate the fundamental law embodied in the First Amendment. The guarding of military and diplomatic secrets at the expense of informed representative government provides no real security for our Republic."

Justice William J. Brennan, Jr., more in keeping with the court's opinion, said, in effect, that nothing less than the threat of a nuclear catastrophe or a situation of war would satisfy him of the need for censorship. Both Justices Potter Stewart and Byron R. White were convinced that the publication of the documents would "do substantial damage to public interests." However, because it was not shown that "disclosure . . . will surely result in direct, immediate, and irreparable damage to our nation or its people," they would deny the injunction. Both acknowledged the potential validity of criminal sanctions for the same conduct that they said could not be barred by prior restraint. Throughout the opinions of both these justices, and again in the opinion of Justice Thurgood Marshall, ran the refrain that a different result might be forthcoming if the ban were sanctioned by the U.S. Congress.

The three justices who refused to join in the judgment vacating the orders of restraint were Chief Justice Warren E. Burger and Justices John Marshall Harlan and Harry A. Blackmun. Each of the three refrained from speaking to the merits on the ground that the courts had not had adequate time to consider the data necessary to an informed judgment.

Senator Mike Gravel (D, Alaska) reads aloud from the Pentagon papers at a hearing of the Public Works Committee in June. Gravel had attempted to read the papers before the full Senate, but he was prevented from doing so by the Republican leadership. He took action to demonstrate his belief that the controversial defense study should be available to the public.

WIDE WORLD

LEBANON. Although considerable domestic unrest troubled Lebanon in 1971, internal security improved as friction with Palestinian guerrillas diminished. The guerrilla movement, seriously weakened by Jordanian army actions in 1970–71, closed its offices in Lebanon in August in order to operate underground. Lebanese-based guerrillas raided Israel periodically, but both attacks and Israeli reprisals were relatively light. Lebanon sought military equipment in Europe to modernize its army; parliament approved the purchase of arms from the Soviet Union for the first time.

Strikes by Lebanese university students demanding educational reforms resulted in the temporary closing of American University in Beirut. Strikes were also called by many unions in 1971, but a general strike of all unions was avoided by a 5% wage increase and the raising of the minimum wage. The government was forced to use troops in the north to quell unrest stirred up by radical peasant groups and a leftist movement that was operating in Tripoli.

At mid-year 20% of Lebanon's labor force remained unemployed, but improving agricultural and industrial exports benefited the economy. In February Lebanon became the first Arab nation to set up a comprehensive public health system for its workers. Television censorship, lifted in 1970, was reinstated in 1971 after media criticism of the federation of Egypt, Syria, and Libya. (*See also* Jordan. *See in* CE: Lebanon.)

LESOTHO. Under the leadership of Lesotho's prime minister, Chief Leabua Jonathan, the country returned to political calm in 1971 after a year of crisis. Lesotho's king, Moshoeshoe II, was publicly reconciled with Chief Jonathan; however, pursuant to a law passed in December 1970 when Moshoeshoe resumed his role as head of state, the king was prohibited from participation in politics. In June the opposition Congress party leader, Ntsu Mokhehle, was released from prison. Despite these events, which lessened tension, the political situation remained uncertain; no date was set for new elections and no new constitution drafted. However, the fact that Great Britain had recognized the government and restored aid in mid-1970 greatly helped to legitimize and stabilize the situation.

Lesotho remained bound economically to South Africa, where 80% of its male working population was employed. The development of the diamond industry, a Holiday Inn hotel, and other projects, however, were creating more domestic jobs. (*See in* CE: Lesotho.)

LIBERIA. On July 23, 1971, William V. S. Tubman, president of Liberia since 1944, died in London following surgery. Tubman, 75, had been elected to a seventh term as president the preceding May. William R. Tolbert, 58, vice-president for 19 years, was sworn in as president the same day that Tubman died.

Thousands of Liberians poured into Monrovia,

Participating in a government program, these women of Lesotho worked to build a dam in exchange for badly needed food for their families. A fourth season of poor rainfall resulted in continued massive crop failures.

LONDON "DAILY EXPRESS" FROM PICTORIAL PARADE

the capital, to mourn the death of their "chief of chiefs." From the United States, a delegation headed by Robert H. Finch, presidential counselor, arrived on a U.S. Air Force jet. The U.S. delegation also included Rep. Charles C. Diggs, Jr. (D, Mich.); Roy Wilkins, executive director of the National Association for the Advancement of Colored People (NAACP); Samuel C. Jackson, assistant secretary of housing and urban development; and W. Beverly Carter, Jr., deputy assistant secretary of state for African affairs. Heading the list of foreign dignitaries were nine African heads of state, including Emperor Haile Selassie I of Ethiopia. (*See in* CE: Liberia.)

LIBRARIES. The annual session of the International Federation of Library Associations (IFLA) was held in Liverpool, England, in 1971. The main theme of the session was "The International Organization of the Library Profession," and papers were read on library associations in various countries at a special plenary session. Two international exhibitions were held, one of library associations and one of library technology and library suppliers. Some 750 participants from 60 different countries attended. The session was preceded by a United Nations Educational, Scientific, and Cultural Organization (UNESCO) seminar on advanced librarianship for developing countries.

UNESCO's Computerized Documentation Service (CDS), which is compatible with the computer-based documentation service of other UN organizations, became operational in 1971. A master negative microfiche will be made for all documents, so that any document can be distributed on demand, either on positive microfiche or in enlarged form. UNESCO continued to operate pilot projects for the development of library service, including one on public- and school-library development in Ceylon and one in Honduras on school libraries for Central America. In addition, UNESCO continued to send library experts to various countries under its participation program, and important books and documents were microfilmed in Algeria, Nepal, Sierra Leone, and Sudan.

Studies began on the international bibliographical control of publications, to be based on computerized national bibliographies. The British National Bibliography was prepared from the machine-readable cataloging service, in collaboration with the United States Library of Congress.

In collaboration with the International Council of Scientific Unions (ICSU), UNESCO's science section completed its feasibility study on UNISIST, a proposed world system of scientific and technical information. A report was published by UNESCO in English, French, Russian, and Spanish editions.

The Great Hall of the Lyndon Baines Johnson Library features a massive staircase, storage decks, and portraits of Johnson with other presidents.

FRANK WOLFE—COURTESY, LYNDON BAINES JOHNSON LIBRARY

The publication of the White Paper on the British Library provided the machinery for bringing the British Museum Library, the National Central Library, the National Lending Library for Science and Technology (NLLST), and the British National Bibliography into one unified national framework. This also gave authority to the plan to build a new national library opposite the British Museum in London. The NLLST continued to collect periodicals on the social sciences, and began a national microfilm collection of research materials in the humanities.

In the U.S. the Library of Congress launched a two-year experimental program under which cataloging information will be provided for publication in the books themselves. Libraries receiving these books will be able to catalog them for use more quickly, and small libraries without catalogers will be able to arrange their books more easily. Twenty-seven publishers have agreed to participate in the trial program.

The Lyndon Baines Johnson Library was opened May 22 at the University of Texas at Austin. Containing 31 million pages of documents covering 40 years of public service, 500,000 photographs, and 500,000 feet of film, it is the largest and most complete presidential collection yet assembled. Although construction of the John F. Kennedy Memorial Library at Harvard University has not yet begun, nearly 3.3 million pages of documents, excluding those classified as secret, were opened to researchers at the Federal Records Center in Waltham, Mass. (*See in* CE: Library articles.)

LIBYA. In 1971 Libya's military ruler, .Col. Muammar el-Qaddafi, vigorously pursued the cause of Arab unity. In April the leaders of Libya, Syria, and Egypt formally agreed to unite their countries in a Confederation of Arab Republics. The confederation was approved in a referendum in September, in which the 42 million people of the three countries participated, and was formally inaugurated in October. (*See* Egypt; Syria.)

The fact that Sudan did not join the confederation was a deep disappointment to el-Qaddafi. The accord of the Sudanese and Libyan leaders was confirmed, however, when el-Qaddafi thwarted a coup against Sudan's president by forcing down a British airliner en route to Sudan that held two of the coup leaders. (*See* Sudan.)

At a summit meeting of Arab leaders organized by el-Qaddafi in July, Jordan's King Hussein I was condemned for his treatment of the Palestinian guerrillas. However, only Libya, a strong supporter of the Palestinian cause, and Algeria broke diplomatic relations with Jordan over the issue. Libya also broke relations with Morocco following the premature support given by el-Qaddafi to the abortive coup there in July.

Throughout the year Libya pressed the foreign oil companies operating in Libya for improved terms. In April the companies agreed to a 90¢

price increase. In December Libya appropriated the assets of the British Petroleum Co. to protest Britain's part in Iran's takeover of three small islands in the Persian Gulf also claimed by two Arab emirates. (*See in* CE: Libya.)

LITERATURE. Almost every distinguished name in American fiction managed to publish a new novel in 1971, but the result was far from producing a new American classic. Reacting to an adverse national economy with the safety of names, book club selections, and publicity campaigns, publishing firms avoided the "serious" new novel that might lose money except if its topicality or the author's reputation might guarantee sales. So, in a year that saw former Pulitzer prizewinners like Robert Penn Warren, Bernard Malamud, Shirley Ann Grau, A. B. Guthrie, Jr., and James A. Michener contribute 'Meet Me in the Green Glen', 'The Tenants', 'The Condor Passes', 'Arfive', and 'The Drifters', respectively, readers were more likely to choose overt Gothic fluff like 'The Other' by Thomas Tryon or 'The Exorcist' by William Peter Blatty, the romance of 'Penmarric' by Susan Howatch, the mystery of Frederick Forsyth's 'The Day of the Jackal', or the nostalgia of R. F. Delderfield's 'Theirs Was the Kingdom'. This last is a successor to his very popular novel of 1970, 'God Is an Englishman'.

Saul Bellow won the 1971 National Book Award for his novel 'Mr. Sammler's Planet'.
WERNER BRAUN—CAMERA PRESS FROM PUBLIX

Former National Book Award winners for fiction fared little better. Philip Roth's 'Our Gang' and Joyce Carol Oates's 'Wonderland' kept both writers in the spotlight, but like Wright Morris' 'Fire Sermon', Jerzy Kosinski's 'Being There', and Walker Percy's 'Love in the Ruins', they competed modestly for readers' attention with the gaudier efforts of more popular writers like Morris L. West ('Summer of the Red Wolf'), Irving Stone ('The Passions of the Mind'), Arthur Hailey ('Wheels'), and Allen Drury ('The Throne of Saturn'). Mary McCarthy's 'Birds of America' and John Hawkes's 'The Blood Oranges' delighted their respective coteries; J. P. Donleavy published 'The Onion Eaters'; Wallace Stegner, 'Angle of Repose'; and William H. Gass, 'Willie Masters' Lonesome Wife'.

John Gardner won over a small following of critics with his 'Grendel', while Hortense Calisher may well have lost a few with 'Queenie'. James Jones contributed 'The Merry Month of May'; James Leo Herlihy, 'The Season of the Witch ; and John Knowles, 'The Paragon'. However, they failed to compete with the successes of first efforts like Sol Stein's 'The Magician' or former presidential aide Pierre Salinger's 'On Instructions of My Government'. Sylvia Plath's 'The Bell Jar', which received few critical accolades, made it into the best-seller lists despite obvious faults in style and the unpopularity of its mental breakdown theme. Novels by poets Karl Shapiro ('Edsel') and Sandra Hochman ('Walking Papers') failed to equal the success of James Dickey's 'Deliverance' in 1970 or of the late Miss Plath in 1971.

Nor did the addition of British novels or collections of shorter fiction offer much consolation. Doris Lessing's 'Briefing for a Descent into Hell', Anthony Burgess' 'M/F', P. G. Wodehouse's 'The Girl in Blue', and Ivy Compton-Burnett's posthumous 'The Last and the First' were each politely received by critics. Well written and generally more serious than their United States counterparts, these books still managed to be less than first-order efforts. Even the publication of E. M. Forster's 'Maurice' proved no new boon, though clearly a lasting, minor, and dated work by a major writer. The novel, which had been completed in 1914, had been withheld from publication during the writer's lifetime because of its subject matter, homosexuality, but its theme of class-consciousness proved the final, telling adverse factor. Mary Lavin's 'Collected Stories' topped the year's short-fiction lists. George MacDonald Fraser, who created Sir Harry Flashman in the novel 'Flashman: From the Flashman Papers 1839–1842' a few years ago, contributed 'The General Danced at Dawn', and Sylvia Townsend Warner 'The Innocent and the Guilty'. Margarita G. Smith brought together the previously uncollected pieces of Carson McCullers' work for 'The Mortgaged Heart', and Herbert Gold, in the tradition of 'confused realms' and the nonfiction novel, mixed essays and stories to come up with his 'The Magic Will'.

Yoko Ono, accompanied by her husband John Lennon, autographed copies of her book 'Grapefruit' in London in July.

Nonfiction

In the "anything goes" world of general nonfiction, Norman Mailer continued the observations on American life that began with 'The Armies of the Night' and turned his attention to his own inability to cope with the space program in 'Of a Fire on the Moon' and with women's liberation and Kate Millett in 'The Prisoner of Sex'. Germaine Greer's 'The Female Eunuch' and Midge Decter's 'The Liberated Woman and Other Americans' provided new and equally contrasting opposing views to male chauvinism. Dr. David Reuben wrote about sexual fulfillment in 'Any Woman Can!', and "M" about 'The Sensuous Man'. Homosexuality was looked at in Colin J. Williams and Martin S. Weinberg's 'Homosexuals and the Military', Donn Teal's 'The Gay Militants', and Arno Karlen's 'Sexuality and Homosexuality'. The Kennedy women were treated again in Gail Cameron's 'Rose' and in Mary Van Rensselaer Thayer's 'Jacqueline Kennedy: The White House Years'. The Rev. Martin Luther King, Jr., got the Jim Bishop treatment in 'The Days of Martin Luther King, Jr.'. Racism was the theme of Margaret Mead and James Baldwin's 'A Rap on Race', Imamu Amiri Baraka's (LeRoi Jones) 'Raise Race Rays Raze', Stokely Carmichael's 'Stokely Speaks', Malcolm X's posthumously edited 'The End of White World Supremacy', and George

Jackson's 'Soledad Brother: The Prison Letters of George Jackson'.

Professional football was enshrined in Myron Cope's 'The Game That Was' and attacked by both Dave Meggyesy's 'Out of Their League' and Bernie Parrish's 'They Call It a Game'. Baseball came in for more lumps with Jim Bouton's 'I'm Glad You Didn't Take It Personally' and Curt Flood's 'The Way It Is', written with Richard Carter.

Mayor Richard J. Daley of Chicago came in for praise in Bill Gleason's 'Daley of Chicago' and for blame in Mike Royko's 'Boss'. Black politicians were the subjects of both Charles Evers' autobiography 'Evers' and John Nearey's 'Julian Bond'. Loren Eiseley's 'The Invisible Pyramid' charged that the inventive genius of the nation was being poured into the space programs at a considerable sacrifice to the public. Richie Ward's 'The Living Clocks' talked about the built-in biological clocks in most organisms, and Ashley Montagu discussed the importance of skin in 'Touching'. Dee Brown offered a compelling and important Indian look at the winning of the West in 'Bury My Heart at Wounded Knee', and Samuel Eliot Morison contributed a balanced survey of the northern voyages to A.D. 1600 in 'The European Discovery of America'. F. Scott Fitzgerald continued to be a subject of interest, thanks to Sara Mayfield's 'Exiles from Paradise', Aaron Latham's 'Crazy Sundays', and Calvin Tomkins' 'Living Well Is the Best Revenge'. 'The Orangeburg Massacre' by Jack Nelson and Jack Bass examined the death of three students and the wounding of 27 others by state police in Orangeburg, S.C. Michener's 'Kent State' recalled the killings at that university, and William A. Westley investigated police methods in 'Violence and the Police'. The fouling of the American environment was the subject of a number of new books, while works like Adam Yarmolinsky's 'The Military Establishment', Morton Mintz and Jerry S. Cohen's 'America, Inc.', Richard F. Kaufman's 'The War Profiteers', Richard Harris' 'Decision', Rowland Evans, Jr., and Robert D. Novak's 'Nixon in the White House' and former President Lyndon B. Johnson's 'The Vantage Point' looked at visible and invisible government. Arthur R. Miller showed the intrusion of government agencies on individuals in 'The Assault on Privacy'. The origins of U.S. attitudes toward Asia were explained in Barbara W. Tuchman's 'Stilwell and the American Experience in China, 1911–1945' and Marvin Kalb and Elie Abel's 'Roots of Involvement: The U.S. in Asia, 1784–1971'. David Bergamini published 'Japan's Imperial Conspiracy', a book that lays much of the blame on Emperor Hirohito for Japan's World War II war crimes.

Books on the movies were numerous in 1971. There were still the reminiscences of old Hollywood with Sheilah Graham's 'The Garden of Allah', Mel Gussow's biography of Darryl F. Zanuck in 'Don't Say Yes Until I Finish Talking', Frank Capra's 'The Name Above the Title', and Ken Murray's 'The Golden Days of San Simeon', but the more serious reader went to a number of new film magazines, printed film scripts, Pauline Kael's brilliant two-part study on Orson Welles in *The New Yorker,* or to William S. Pechter's 'Twenty-Four Times a Second', Stanley Kauffmann's 'Figures of Light', John Simon's 'Movies into Film', or Rex Reed's 'Big Screen, Little Screen'. The usual accounts of movie stars' lives underwent some drastic changes in Hildegard Knef's less than plastic 'The Gift Horse' and Melina Mercouri's 'I Was Born Greek'.

U.S. Army First Lieut. William L. Calley, Jr., was the subject of several biographies, including his own 'Lieutenant Calley', as told to John Sack. Martin Gilbert completed the third volume of the definitive biography of 'Winston Churchill', begun by Churchill's son, Randolph. Queen Anne of Great Britain was the subject of an interesting study by David Green, and David Rockefeller of a very derivative book by William Hoffman. Thor Heyerdahl described his experiences in 'The *Ra* Expeditions', and Edmund Wilson his impressions of 'Upstate'. William Maxwell wrote a charming and penetrating book about his family called 'Ancestors'. Albert Einstein was the subject of a new biography by Ronald W. Clark and figured importantly in both Alexander Moszkowski's 'Conversations with Einstein' and Werner Heisenberg's 'Physics and Beyond'. O. Mannoni's 'Freud' made its U.S. appearance along with the autobiography of 'The Wolf-Man', one of Dr. Freud's most famous cases. Anna Balakian contributed a new book on 'André Breton'. Graham Greene, Edward Dahlberg, and Horace Gregory provided substantial autobiographies in 'A Sort of Life', 'The Confessions of Edward Dahlberg', and 'The House on Jefferson Street'. Biographies of Henrik Ibsen, G. B. Shaw, Ford Madox Ford, Harriet Shaw Weaver, and Brendan Behan were supplied by Michael Meyer ('Ibsen'), Stanley Weintraub ('Journey to Heartbreak'), Arthur Mizener ('The Saddest Story'), Jane Lidderdale and Mary Nicholson ('Dear Miss Weaver'), and Ulick O'Connor ('Brendan'). Other outstanding books of criticism included William Gass's 'Fiction and the Figures of Life', George Steiner's 'Extraterritorial', Robert Penn Warren's 'Homage to Theodore Dreiser', and Leslie A. Fiedler's two-volume 'Collected Essays'. James Dickey experimented with 'Self-Interviews', and Robert Duncan issued the first part of his long-awaited 'H. D. Book'.

Poetry

Hit by skyrocketing prices, American poetry seemed to divide equally into two groups: the collected and selected, and the individual volumes. Heading the first category was James Wright's 'Collected Poems' and the late Charles Olson's 'Archaeologist of Morning'. Other outstanding collections included John Malcolm Brinnin's 'Sorrows of Cold Stone: Poems, 1940–1950', Arthur Gregor's

'Selected Poems', and George MacBeth's 'Collected Poems'. Impressive individual collections were A. R. Ammons' 'Briefings', Galway Kinnell's 'Book of Nightmares', Ben Belitt's 'Nowhere But Light', Stanley Kunitz' 'The Testing-Tree', Denise Levertov's 'To Stay Alive', Robert Creeley's 'St. Martin's', John Hollander's 'The Night Mirror', and Anne Sexton's 'Transformations'. Sylvia Plath's 'Crossing the Water' was published posthumously in the U.S., as was 'Winter Trees' in Great Britain. Other new collections included Michael Benedikt's 'Mole Notes', Ted Hughes's 'Crow', Jon Silkin's 'Amana Grass', and Adrienne Rich's 'The Will to Change'.

Rare Discoveries

A 2 × 3-inch scrap of papyrus, acquired by Columbia University about 50 years ago, was found by Lawrence Feinberg to be one of the oldest written fragments of Homer's 'Odyssey'. The papyrus dates to the 3d century B.C. Feinberg, a graduate student at Columbia, identified the writing as a section of Book XII of the poem. The papyrus contains several variants from what became in the 2d century B.C. the standard version of the epic. The fragment is considered priceless.

Professor William H. Willis of Duke University found on a 3 × 3-inch piece of parchment what he believes to be the "missing link" in the evolution of the book from papyrus scrolls. Dating from about A.D. 130, the parchment is a part of Plato's dialogue 'Parmenides'. It represents the oldest instance known of Roman uncial capital letters on parchment and was part of a mixed lot bought from a Middle Eastern dealer in 1969. The text of a previously unpublished valentine, written by Elizabeth Barrett to her cousin Lizzie in 1844, was also made public. Discovered by Phillip Kelley while he was working on a catalog of Barrett letters, it was first displayed in London in 1961 as part of the centenary of the poet's death.

Troubles in the Soviet Union

Official Soviet reaction to Aleksandr I. Solzhenitsyn's award of the 1970 Nobel prize in literature continued cool. When Solzhenitsyn wrote to Soviet publishing houses in 1971 concerning his newest novel, 'August 1914', he met with no takers. The writer considered the work "the most important work of my life," and early critical response seemed to confirm his judgment in thinking it a classic. Fearful at first that manuscript circulation might result in the book's unsanctioned release to the West similar to the releases earlier of 'The First Circle' and 'The Cancer Ward', Solzhenitsyn finally allowed the book to be published in Paris. The work was conceived in 1936, when he was graduated from high school, and it opens with a Tolstoy-like kaleidoscopic description of war on the Eastern front. The first of a projected three-volume work that will carry the reader through 1918, this opening novel delineates ten days during the catastrophic

czarist campaign in East Prussia. Motion-picture script-writing techniques are introduced periodically throughout the work, whose pre-Soviet subject matter would normally guarantee it against party attack. The novel circulated in the Soviet Union as did many other underground works only in *samizdat* (typewritten copies).

An easing of restrictions seemed to be suggested by the publication of Oleg Smirnov's novel 'Troop Train' in the pages of *Novy Mir*. The work is critical of Joseph Stalin and the belief in his infallibility. It seemed nevertheless to strike a balance advocated by Communist party leader Leonid I. Brezhnev, who thought it wrong to dwell on Stalin's crimes and equally wrong to whitewash the past. Vladimir Krasilshchikov's 'The Eternal Flame', published in the pages of the conservative *Oktyabr*, became the Soviet Union's first novel attacking Nikita Khrushchev. It calls Khrushchev's downfall a victory for sound economic policy over flashy, inefficient projects. *Oktyabr* had long been critical of Khrushchev's attempts to blacken Stalin's name, and the new novel reads in many places as a parody of the anti-Stalin novels that were common during the Khrushchev regime. Despite a more than ordinary tightening of safeguards against Western news-

Germaine Greer, who teaches literature at Warwick University in England, won praise for her book 'The Female Eunuch'.

Karl Shapiro published his first novel, 'Edsel', in 1971. He had previously won a Pulitzer prize for his poetry.

men fraternizing with Russians, word leaked out that Andrei A. Amalrik was seriously ill with tubercular meningitis. Amalrik was sentenced in 1970 to three years in a restricted labor colony for his anti-government book, 'Will the Soviet Union Survive Until 1984?'.

The Year in Other Countries

In other Communist countries like Poland, the lessening of controls seemed to bespeak a rebirth of writing. The replacement of Wladyslaw Gomulka by Edward Gierek as Communist party leader was given as one reason for the reappearance in print of many writers whose work had not been seen since 1968. Antoni Slonimski published a volume of critical pieces dating back to 1918, and the once-popular journalist Stefan Kisielewski began to publish columns again. But writers were warned against presuming anything like the freedom which Czechoslovakia claimed before its invasion by the Russians in 1968. In Czechoslovakia party leader Gustav Husak continued to remove traces of the 1968 reform era by asking that factory libraries ban from distribution works by former party chief Alexander Dubcek along with works by a number of the country's best-known literary figures. These included Vaclav Havel, the late Jan Prochazka, Antonin Liehm, and Ivan Sviták. The authors' politics rather than the works' content seemed to have been the rationale of the ban as such esoteric and nonpolitical items as Vaclav Cerny's 'Medieval Drama' fell within the order. In Yugoslavia Mihajlo Mihajlov faced the possibility of a new prison sentence for having published a piece on writing in *The New York Times*.

Not all repression of writers was either European or Communist. The government of Nationalist China, situated on Taiwan, arrested writers Li Ao and Meng Hsiang-ko for questioning the legitimacy of the current regime. Li was the editor of the popular *Wen Hsing* (Literary Star) magazine before the government closed it down in 1965. In Cuba Herberto Padilla, the well-respected author of 'Rules of the Game', was arrested for conspiring with Western newsmen to embarrass the government. He had given foreign sociologists a bleak picture of life in Cuba. As recently as 1968, he had been the recipient of the Cuban government's highly regarded poetry award. In Greece, where repressive measures have now come to be expected, the extremely popular anti-government book of 1970, 'Eighteen Texts', was followed in 1971 by 'New Texts', an anthology of 20 writers attacking government policy. The various contributors ranged from moderate conservatives to Marxists, but, whereas in 'Eighteen Texts' the attacks had been oblique, in 'New Texts' they are more direct. The editor promised to follow the collection with another of the same nature. In South Africa the first book of poems in over 20 years by a black, 'Sounds of a Cowhide Drum', proved one of the more popular books in that segregated country. Written by Oswald Joseph Mtshali, the poems tell of the conflicts of an urban black's life in a white man's world.

In France, where one of the best sellers of 1970 was Jean-François Revel's attack on the political perversity of French intellectuals, 'Without Marx or Jesus', readers again found politics a favorite subject. In 1971 the near-simultaneous publication of two chapters that President Charles de Gaulle had completed for the second volume of his memoirs before his death in 1970 and a long, four-hour interview with him by Andre Malraux ('Les Chenes Qu'on Abut') highlighted French reading. On the literary front, the first two volumes of Jean-Paul Sartre's long-awaited lengthy book on Flaubert appeared under the title 'L'Idiot de la Famille'. Cast in the form of a biography similar to those he had written earlier on Baudelaire and Genet, the study was expected to run to four or five volumes and to constitute Sartre's major work. A novel by Albert Camus was also issued posthumously. Written before 'The Stranger', 'La Mort Heureuse' was discarded by its author in favor of that novel though the hero of both books is the same. Two new novels attracting attention were Michel Tournier's 'The Erl King', about the Nazis, and Julien Green's 'L'Autre'. Italians welcomed 'Satura', a new collection of poems by their leading poet, Eugenio Montale. In a new burst of energy, Montale followed the publication with a new series of poems expected to be collected soon as well.

In Spain, after a two-year silence, Juan Goytasolo, one of its leading writers, published 'Cuestiones de Conde don Julian'. The novel abandons his earlier direct realistic, sociological, and historical approach for problems of language, literature, and national character. (*See also* Awards and Prizes.)

LITERATURE, CHILDREN'S.

Although the publishing industry suffered an off year in 1971, there was little evidence of a cutback in children's books. The trend toward recognition of children's interest in social problems was evident in the many books on such topics. For younger children, there were a number of very simply written books of biography and historical fiction, and the passion for poetry was reflected in books by and for the young. The trickle of books on ecology and pollution of the environment, which had begun in 1970, grew to flood proportions in 1971.

For Younger Children

Arnold Lobel's 'On the Day Peter Stuyvesant Sailed into Town' was one of the most charming picture books of the year, a bit of history told in rollicking rhyme. 'Father Fox's Pennyrhymes', by Clyde Watson, illustrated by Wendy Watson, showed the busy activities of the fox world, with verses very much in the Mother Goose tradition. A handsome French version of Mother Goose, 'Rimes de la Mère Oie', translated by Ormonde de Kay, Jr., was illustrated in varying styles by Milton Glaser, Barry Zaid, and Seymour Chwast. The latter also was co-illustrator with Martin S. Moskof of the highly original 'Still Another Number Book', in which one page is used for "1," two for "2," and so on.

A new author, Ellen Parsons, told a realistic story of a mother and child's happy day, crowned

Arnold Adoff edited 'It Is the Poem Singing Into Your Eyes'. The book is an anthology of young poets' writing.

Arnold Lobels authored a colorful picture book, 'On the Day Peter Stuyvesant Sailed Into Town'.

by the return home of a bearded, rain-wet father, in 'Rainy Day Together'. Another real-life story was Charlotte Zolotow's 'A Father Like That', in which a child with no father envisions one so perfect that he refuses to show off at Parent-Teacher Association meetings. A Newbery and a Caldecott winner, Lloyd Alexander and Ezra Jack Keats, joined forces to produce 'The King's Fountain', the story of a timid man who learns how to ask a favor of a king. A lesson of another sort was spelled out in Peter Parnall's 'The Mountain', in which the sad effect of pollution on wilderness beauty is made clear.

'What's the Prize, Lincoln?', by Dale Fife, was the story of an ebullient and imaginative black child whose penchant for entering contests produces hilarious consequences. Mindel and Harry Sitomer's 'Circles' was an excellent example of introducing mathematical concepts to children in the primary grades. A fine example of historical writing for younger children was F. N. Monjo's 'The Vicksburg Veteran', in which the son of Union Gen. Ulysses S. Grant describes the strategy that captured Vicksburg, Miss., and gave the North control of the Mississippi River. An outstanding biography was 'Maria Tallchief', by Tobi Tobias, the life story of the great ballerina, who is part Osage Indian.

The 8-to-12 Group

Robert C. O'Brien's 'Mrs. Frisby and the Rats of NIMH', a notable fantasy, told of the remarkable laboratory rats who had developed superior intelligence and were devoted to improving their image. Another fantasy was Betty Brock's 'The Shades', in which the shadows of former residents live on in a magical garden.

In Zilpha Keatley Snyder's 'The Headless Cupid', a group of young children is initiated by an older girl into the rites of the occult in a powerful story that verges on admission of the supernatural. As potent in a different way was Jean Little's 'Kate', the story of an adolescent troubled by the breach between her father and his family, who have never quite forgiven him, a Jew, for marrying a Gentile. Another good realistic tale of 1971 was Eleanor Cameron's 'A Room Made of Windows', in which a self-centered adolescent's growing understanding leads her to accept her mother's remarriage.

One of the funniest books of the year was Francis Kalnay's 'It Happened in Chichipica', a story in which none of the engaging characters is more appealing than the whole picture of a Mexican community. Another humorous tale was Roger Drury's 'The Finches' Fabulous Furnace', a story told in a straight-faced manner about a family who discover a small volcano in the basement.

Louise Tanner's 'Reggie and Nilma' describes the bitter resentment of a black youth when he is the first to be suspected of theft in the home of a white family who have been his friends as well as his employers. A story based on the author's experience, 'Journey to Topaz', is a fictionalized account of Yoshiko Uchida's life as a member of a Japanese-American family disrupted by evacuation and relocation during World War II.

Arnold Adoff edited a stunning anthology by and for young poets, 'It Is the Poem Singing into Your Eyes'; another impressive collection was 'The Voice of the Children', compiled by June Jordan and Terri Bush. In 'The Trees Stand Shining', Hettie Jones collected poetry of the North American Indians; Richard Lewis compiled a volume of moving Eskimo poetry, 'I Breathe a New Song'.

For Adolescents

One of the most effective novels of the year was John Donovan's 'Wild in the World', the story of a young man living alone on a mountainside farm. 'The Seal-Singing', by Rosemary Harris, is set on a Scottish island, mingling fantasy and realism deftly. Other notable stories were Richard Wormser's 'The Black Mustanger', about a black cowboy just after the Civil War, and Theodore Taylor's 'The Children's War', set in Alaska during World War II.

Among the good biographies for older readers were Iris Noble's 'Emmeline and Her Daughters: The Pankhurst Suffragettes', a vivid account of the struggle to enable women to vote half a century ago; 'The Life of Malcolm X', by Richard Curtis; and Edna Barth's 'I'm Nobody! Who are You?', a perceptive life story of Emily Dickinson.

Delightful as well as informative, 'Chipmunks on the Doorstep' was the first natural science book by the distinguished author-illustrator Edwin Tunis. One of the best of the books on drugs was 'The Dope Book', by Mark Lieberman. Of the many books on dissent and rebellion, two choice ones were Robert Liston's 'Dissent in America' and 'Some Dissenting Voices', by Arthur and Lila Weinberg, the stories of six American dissenters. 'Now or Never: The Fight Against Pollution', by Daniel S. Halacy and 'Clean Air–Clean Water for Tomorrow's World,' by Reed Millard were substantive books on the environment.

In 'The Burning Thorn' Griselda Greaves compiled a fine poetry anthology, some of the selections by adolescents. 'In the Trail of the Wind' was an impressive collection of American Indian poems and orations compiled by John Bierhorst.

Awards

The National Book Award for children's literature was given to Lloyd Alexander for 'The Marvelous Misadventures of Sebastian', a romantic and humorous adventure story. The John Newbery Medal went to Betsy Byars for 'The Summer of the Swans'. The Caldecott Medal was won by Gail E. Haley for her woodcut illustrations in an African tale retold, 'A Story, A Story'.

The Canadian Library Association's award for the most outstanding children's book of the year in English was given to William Toye for 'Cartier Discovers the St. Lawrence'; the French winner was Henriette Major for 'La Surprise de Dame Chenille'. The Gibbon Medal for illustration went to Elizabeth Cleaver for 'The Wind Has Wings', compiled by Mary Alice Downie and Barbara Robertson.

The Kate Greenaway Medal of the Library Association of the United Kingdom was awarded to John Burningham for his illustrations in 'Mr. Gumpy's Outing'. The association's Carnegie Medal for literary excellence was won by Leon Garfield and Edward Blishen for their sonorous retelling of Greek mythology in 'The God Beneath the Sea'.

LUXEMBOURG. On March 31, 1971, a moderate splinter group of the Socialist party of Luxembourg broke away to form the new Social Democratic party. Henri Cravatte, former president of the Socialist party and former cabinet minister, was selected as the leader of the new party. The Socialist split began in late January when five deputies belonging to the party's parliamentary delegation resigned in opposition to the decision of the Socialist party committee to cooperate with Communist party candidates at the communal level.

The Soviet Union on July 14 signed a trade agreement with Benelux (the economic union of Belgium, the Netherlands, and Luxembourg) providing for mutual most-favored-nation status. The agreement, believed to be the first between the Soviet Union and a Western economic group, was hailed as a means to revive the sagging foreign trade of the Benelux member states. The standard of living of Luxembourg, a highly industrialized state, remained well above the average for Western Europe. (*See in* CE: Luxemburg.)

MAGAZINES. The most pressing problem in the magazine industry in 1971 was, doubtlessly, the poor economic health of most magazines. Even when the number of advertising pages went up, rising costs from labor and postal rates cut deeply into profits, causing publishers to raise rates.

Despite hard times, about 80 new magazines came out during the year. The emphasis continued to be on the journal catering to a specialized interest. Some of these new publications and their specializations were: *Audience* (the arts), *New Woman* (careers, entertainment, fashion), *Vintage Magazine* (wine), *Kids* (by and for children), and *Imani* (by and for blacks). Taking advantage of the nostalgia trend, publishers also brought out versions of old favorites: *The Saturday Evening Post* reappeared as a quarterly and *Liberty* came out again featuring work reprinted from back issues. Great Britain continued its popular magazine invasion of the United States with *Forum,* which offered serious articles on sex, and the *Grand Diplôme Cooking Course,* published over a 72-week cycle to teach its readers classic French cooking. Despite both legal and economic setbacks, the basically youth-oriented underground press and "hip" publications continued to proliferate. One expert estimated that by 1971 there were approximately 700 in existence.

The main magazine deaths were *Look,* a 35-year-old picture magazine, and *Scanlan's,* a year-old monthly journal of investigative reporting. High postal rates and low advertising revenues were blamed for *Look*'s demise. *Scanlan's* went bankrupt after a costly battle to publish a controversial issue on guerrilla warfare.

The growing demand in the journalistic field that staff have as much, if not more, to say about editorial policy as owners came to a dramatic head in 1971 at *Harper's* magazine. A disagreement between the editor, Willie Morris, and the board chairman, John Cowles, Jr., ended with Morris walking out, followed by almost the entire staff. Considerable speculation on the conflict and its wider ramifications appeared in many magazines. A similar editor-publisher dispute on the magazine *Saturday Review* resulted in the resignation of the magazine's long-time editor, Norman Cousins.

Seeking liberation of another type, women continued to harass the male-dominated magazine world. Women employees of *Time, Life, Fortune, Sports Illustrated,* and *Newsweek* reached an agreement with their managements providing for equal salaries and working conditions with men on the staff. The leading women's magazines began in earnest to introduce innovations appropriate to the new role of women in response to the increasing vocal resentment and anger of women over the stereotyped female images the magazines presented.

Another magazine trend was the rise of "personalized" journalism, symbolized best by U.S. writer Norman Mailer, who started it several years ago. Signed columns or sections of issues analyzing cur-

Capitalizing on a wave of nostalgia, a publisher reprinted *Liberty* magazine with features taken from past issues.

rent topics from a personalized point of view appeared in a variety of magazines.

One controversial sally into what might be termed "personalized" journalism was perpetrated by William F. Buckley, Jr., conservative spokesman and publisher of *National Review.* After the publication of the Pentagon papers (*see* Law Special Report; Newspapers), Buckley published in *National Review* what he first claimed to be secret U.S. government documents concerning Vietnam. He was sharply criticized by some of his journalistic colleagues, however, when he later admitted that the documents were "composed *ex nihilo*" (out of nothing). (*See in* CE: Magazines.)

MALAGASY REPUBLIC. The relatively stable government of the Malagasy Republic was beset by a number of political difficulties in 1971. In February President Philibert Tsiranana dissolved his cabinet and removed nearly all ministries from the supervision of his four vice-presidents. The most important result of this reshuffling was the demotion of First Vice-President André Resampa, who had been widely regarded as the probable successor to Tsiranana. Resampa was dismissed from his important government posts and in June was arrested on charges of high treason and collaboration with a foreign power.

In March an unsuccessful rebellion of the Maoist Monima party took place in the southern Madagascar region; the government stated that more than 40 persons were killed in the uprising, but, other sources said at least 800 were killed. About 500 persons were arrested, including Monja Jaona, leader of the party, and the party was banned. (*See in* CE: Malagasy Republic.)

MALAWI.

The main focus of events in 1971 in Malawi was President H. Kamuzu Banda's continuing attempt to find a solution to Africa's racial problems by friendly contacts with white-ruled southern Africa. In July Banda appointed Joe Kachingwe as ambassador to South Africa—the first black ever to serve in that capacity in South Africa. In August Banda became the first black head of state to pay an official visit to South Africa. During his well-received visit, he stressed that he disliked apartheid but preferred to talk with its supporters rather than to break off relations with them and thus with the black population of South Africa. In September Banda visited the Portuguese African province of Mozambique.

In November 1970 Malawi's constitution had been amended to enable Banda to become president-for-life, and in July 1971 Banda took the oath of office. In the April parliamentary elections all the Banda-approved candidates were returned unopposed. (*See in* CE: Malawi.)

MALAYSIA.

With the reopening of Malaysia's Parliament in February 1971, the country returned to parliamentary democracy after 21 months of emergency rule that had been imposed after the Malay-Chinese racial riots of May 1969. In March the Parliament approved a controversial constitu-

tional amendment bill, which made it a crime to discuss anything that "endangered racial peace" and also ensured the continued existence of special constitutional privileges for Malays, who dominated the government. These special privileges were designed to rectify economic disparities that existed between Malays and non-Malays (mostly Chinese and Indian), who dominated the economy.

The country's second development plan (1971–75) went into force during the year. It emphasized the government's aim to pursue the "restructuring [of] Malaysian society to reduce and eventually eliminate the identification of race with economic function." In the new plan the gross national product was expected to grow 6.5% each year, and nearly 600,000 new jobs were to be created. Despite a moderately high rate of growth in 1971, unemployment continued to be severe, reaching a 25-year high of 9%.

Communist subversion in the country continued to pose a threat. Government countermeasures, however, appeared to be keeping the situation well under control.

In 1971 relations with the People's Republic of China took a new turn. In May a Malaysian trade delegation paid a visit to China. A visit to Malaysia by a Chinese delegation followed shortly after, and agreement was reached for direct trade between the two countries.

The Anglo-Malaysian Defense Agreement, under which Great Britain was automatically committed to the defense of Malaysia, ended at midnight on October 31. At that time new five-power defense arrangements involving Britain, Australia, New Zealand, Singapore, and Malaysia came into force. (*See in* CE: Malaysia, Federation of.)

MALDIVES.

In 1971 Maldives continued to pursue a nonaligned policy, though this proved difficult because of unrest in nearby Ceylon and international interest in the strategic significance of the Indian Ocean. Aid from Great Britain included the support of Maldivian students overseas and a grant to finance the use of a cargo ship between Maldives and Ceylon, India, Pakistan, the Persian Gulf, and the Red Sea. This operation provided essential foreign exchange and employment for several hundred Maldivian seamen.

Britain's Royal Air Force (RAF) staging post on Gan Island (leased until 1986) continued its pivotal work in the Commonwealth defense agreement, its importance increasing as Britain began to pull out of the Persian Gulf. The RAF unit of about 600 men, with civilian support and a meteorological unit, provided service to aircraft and ships as well as maintaining an extensive air-sea search unit. (*See in* CE: Maldives, Republic of.)

Malaysian government soldiers patrol in search of Communist terrorists around a Methodist mission near Bukit Lan, on Sarawak, in August.
WIDE WORLD

Distinctive huts in the tradition of their ancestors mark the Dogons' settlement near the bend of the Niger River in Mali. The village, concealed at the foot of a cliff, was established in the 12th century, and in 1971 the people lived much as their forebears did then.

MALI. The major trends in Mali's political life during 1971 were moves toward greater liberalization in domestic affairs and toward better relations with France. Trade union activities, which had been suspended when union leaders came into conflict with government policy, were resumed in August. About 30 political prisoners were released in March after two months' detention.

In April Lieut. Moussa Traore, president of the ruling National Liberation Military Committee (CMLN), announced that an attempted coup by two members of the CMLN had been foiled. Capt. Yoro Diakité, first vice-president of the CMLN, and Capt. Malik Diallo, information officer, were both expelled from the CMLN and the army.

The military government's desire for better relations with France was evident. New agreements for cooperation between the two countries were signed in January. (*See in* CE: Mali.)

MALTA. A change of heart by the Roman Catholic church and a hard-hitting campaign by a long-time Labor party leader combined in 1971 to dislodge Nationalist party leader George Borg Olivier, who had been prime minister of Malta for nine years. Victor in the June election was Dominic (Dom) Mintoff, who edged out the opposition when his party took 28 Parliament seats against the 27 won by the Nationalists. A record 93% of the voters turned out as Malta's Catholic

hierarchy removed its ban on voting for the Laborites; previously the church had made it a mortal sin to vote for Labor.

In a flurry of post-election moves Mintoff (1) had the British-born governor-general replaced by a Maltese, (2) renegotiated the ten-year defense pact with Great Britain, made when Malta got its independence in 1964, (3) ousted the Italian naval commander of the North Atlantic Treaty Organization (NATO), (4) effected the transfer of NATO naval headquarters from Malta, (5) temporarily banned the United States 6th fleet's Malta stops, and (6) accepted financial aid from Libya to enable government operations to continue. In September, Malta agreed to allow Britain and NATO the use of its naval facilities in return for about $26 million annual rent, with half payable immediately. Britain complied with this request. However, in late December Mintoff demanded immediate payment of another $11 million. Britain refused to pay and announced that instead it would withdraw its forces and sever its 170-year military relationship with Malta.

Mintoff's chief economic action, a prime issue in the election campaign, was the announcement of reorganization of Malta's once-busy dockyards. The British-run ship repair station, traditional backbone of Malta's economy, was to be revamped with the creation of a combined Maltese government and workers corporation. (*See in* CE: Malta.)

MARRIAGES. Among the famous public figures who were married in 1971 were:

Lew Alcindor (who later changed his name to Kareem Abdul Jabbar), 24, basketball star of the Milwaukee Bucks, to Janice (later changed to Habiba) Brown, 23, teacher; May 28, in Washington, D.C.

Susan Elaine Eisenhower, 19, second oldest granddaughter of the late U.S. President Dwight D. Eisenhower, to Alexander Hugh Bradshaw, 29, British barrister; January 8, in Gettysburg, Pa.

W. Averell Harriman, 79, U.S. diplomat, former governor of New York, to Pamela Hayward, 51, former wife of Randolph Churchill and widow of theatrical producer Leland Hayward; September 27, in New York City.

Mick Jagger, 28, British rock superstar as lead singer of the Rolling Stones, to Bianca Perez Morena de Macias, 26, daughter of a Nicaraguan diplomat; May 12, in St. Tropez, France.

Jennifer Jones, 52, Academy Award-winning actress, to Norton Simon, 62, wealthy financier; May 30, aboard a yacht in the English Channel.

Dr. William H. Masters, 55, to Virginia Johnson, 46, U.S. sex researchers and coauthors of the pioneering studies "Human Sexual Response' (1966) and 'Human Sexual Inadequacy' (1970); January 7, in Fayetteville, Ark.

Famous newlyweds of 1971 included W. Averell Harriman and Pamela Hayward (above) and Mick Jagger and Bianca Perez Morena de Macias (right).

Canada's Prime Minister Pierre Elliott Trudeau and Margaret Sinclair (left) were married in March.

Dr. William Masters and Virginia Johnson (right) were married in January.

Stavros S. Niarchos, 62, Greek shipping tycoon, to Athina (Tina) Livanos, about 41, daughter of one of the first modern Greek shipowners; October 21, in Paris.

Patricia Nixon, 25, elder daughter of U.S. President Richard M. Nixon, to Edward Finch Cox, 24, student at Harvard University law school; June 12, in the White House Rose Garden, Washington, D.C.

Christina Onassis, 20, daughter of Greek shipping magnate Aristotle Onassis and stepdaughter of Jacqueline Kennedy Onassis, to Joseph Bolker, 47, U.S. real estate entrepreneur; July 26, in Las Vegas, Nev.

Pierre Elliott Trudeau, 51, Canada's prime minister, to Margaret Sinclair, 22, daughter of a Canadian government official; March 4, in North Vancouver, B.C.

George C. Wallace, 51, governor of Alabama (1963–66; 1971–) and 1968 presidential candidate of the American Independent party, to Cornelia Ellis Snively, 31; January 4, in Montgomery, Ala.

MAURITANIA.

As sole candidate of the Mauritanian People's party, the only political party permitted, Moktar Ould Daddah was reelected president of Mauritania in August 1971. Because some opposition still existed among trade unionists and students, a number of people were placed in preventive detention during a visit by President Georges Pompidou of France in February.

In August President Ould Daddah reshuffled his cabinet and admitted several young "technocrats" who had formerly been outside the party. In September some 200 civil servants who had been temporarily suspended were reinstated.

As president of the Organization of African Unity (OAU), Ould Daddah acted as mediator in disputes arising from the Arab-Israeli conflict and from the proposal by some OAU members for a policy of dialogue with South Africa. In April Mauritania signed an economic and technical agreement with the People's Republic of China. (*See in* CE: Mauritania.)

MAURITIUS.

During 1971 events in Mauritius reflected the island's strategic vulnerability in the path of Soviet naval expansion. Mauritius' foreign minister, Gaëtan Duval, held that the country could not ask Great Britain to defend it while criticizing the means of defense—the sale of British arms to South Africa. The prime minister, Sir Seewoosagur Ramgoolam, however, pledged uncompromising support for the fight against apartheid, South Africa's policy of racial separation. How this issue would be resolved was unclear, but in May Duval visited South Africa where he confidently predicted that diplomatic relations with his country would be established.

The state of emergency declared in 1968 after Muslim-Creole riots was lifted in December 1970.

A Public Order Act was then introduced and, after disturbances in April 1971, public meetings were banned. However, in December 1971 a state of emergency was again declared in the wake of a disruptive four-month dock strike that had precipitated strikes in the public sector and on some sugar plantations, on which the economy was dependent. (*See in* CE: Mauritius.)

MEDICINE.

The United States Congress drew closer in 1971 to enacting a health plan for the medical needs of the entire nation. About a dozen versions of National Health Insurance (NHI), a federally backed program of medical insurance, were pending before Congress. Although the major plans differed in the means for financing NHI, it was probable that the U.S. would join the other industrialized Western nations with a comprehensive health program in 1972 or soon after. (*See* Feature Article: "The Health Care Crisis.")

According to government spokesmen, including Elliott Richardson, secretary of health, education, and welfare, the majority of Americans by 1980 would get their medical care from Health Maintenance Organizations (HMO's). Through prepaid group medical care, HMO's would conduct regular examinations of participants, give vaccinations, and use other medical measures to foster "health maintenance." In the meantime, the federal government had already spent more than $14

This revolving wall in a California medical laboratory contains several testing units. It enables doctors and technicians to screen more than one patient at the same time.

million in planning for nationwide HMO's, centered mainly in urban areas. (*See also* Hospitals.)

Each year the U.S. populace spent an estimated $60 billion for health care. Against this, the $1.6 billion in federal funds spent for bettering the national health care delivery system seemed scant. The Association of American Medical Colleges urged government and private industry to give medical schools more money for basic health research. Some medical schools groped for ways of introducing community health problems into the medical curriculum. Johns Hopkins University, for example, was lauded for establishing an HMO serving the ghetto in East Baltimore, Md.

At the onset of 1971 a new Institute of Medicine, part of the National Academy of Sciences, was in operation. Under the leadership of Dr. Robert J. Glaser, the fledgling institute was charged with finding ways of improving health care in the nation.

The American Medical Association (AMA) met in June at Atlantic City, N.J., in a setting far more tranquil than the noisy gathering in Chicago the year before. But with younger physicians begin-

ning to shun the AMA, its membership probably contained fewer than half of all active doctors in the U.S. Some were disenchanted with it because of its traditional hostility toward government health programs. In late November, Dr. Wesley W. Hall, the AMA head, acknowledged its diminishing image and continued to call for a constitutional revamp, the first in 124 years. By December the AMA had extended unprecedented policy-making voting power to medical students.

An AMA survey in 1971 showed that the general practitioner worked an average of 52 hours each week, treating an average of 167 patients. Several years ago, general practice was raised to medical specialty status with its own certifying organization —the American Academy of Family Physicians.

Physicians continued to settle in highly populated regions, leaving the rural areas increasingly starved of doctors. In the sparsest areas, according to AMA figures, only one doctor served every 2,145 persons. By contrast, there was a doctor for every 442 persons in the most densely populated counties.

Hertford, N.C., advertises its acute need for a doctor. There was a growing shortage of physicians in small towns and rural areas throughout the United States.

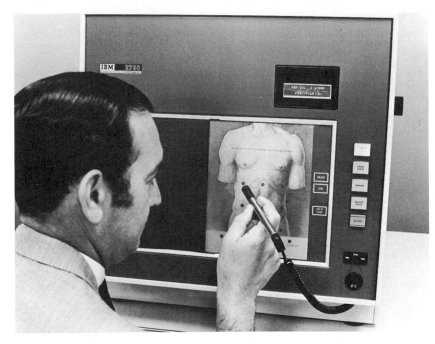

A patient uses an electronic "light pen" to show where it hurts. This is one phase of the computer-assisted Medical Examination System, developed by the International Business Machines (IBM) Corp. The system records the patient's history, his symptoms, and test results; then the computer synthesizes and summarizes all the information for the physician.

AUTHENTICATED NEWS INTERNATIONAL

Scientific debate still raged over the addictive power of marijuana. Meanwhile, a Chicago psychiatrist estimated that 1.5 million marijuana users in the U.S. were dependent upon it.

Dr. Jerome Jaffe, a pioneer in methadone use as an alternative to heroin, was appointed by U.S. President Richard M. Nixon to lead a national effort against addictive drugs. Jaffe's first task was to reduce the incidence of drug abuse among U.S. servicemen in Southeast Asia. (*See* Armed Forces, U.S.; Drugs.)

For centuries Chinese medicine had used acupuncture as a way of relieving pain and treating some ailments. In acupuncture, needles are inserted into any of some 500 points of the body, mostly, it was found, in a nerve region. Western doctors, suspecting quackery, long scoffed at the notion of abating pain through acupuncture. However, American doctors touring China in 1971 reported witnessing patients who successfully underwent major surgery with only acupuncture as an anesthetic.

If it could be shown that a fetus might develop into a retarded child, should it be aborted? Because of amniocentesis—a method of prenatal diagnosis —moral problems concerning the unborn were becoming immediate. In the procedure, amniotic fluid from around the fetus is extracted through a hypodermic syringe. The fetal cells in the fluid are then examined for certain genetic deficiencies. Although amniocentesis was not yet a standard clinical procedure, it enabled workers at the 300 or so genetic counseling centers in the U.S. to advise couples on birth defect risks.

Vitamin use reached faddish proportions in 1971 as some scientists urged the intake of huge "megadoses" of vitamins for various disorders. In one instance, Dr. Linus Pauling, a Nobel prizewinning chemist, wrote a best seller asserting that vitamin C could prevent the common cold. Controversy over the claims of vitamin-therapy proponents was expected to continue for years.

Recent surveys confirmed what many suspected —children were maturing physically at an earlier age. For example, American girls, on the average, began to menstruate at 12.5 years of age. Thirty-seven years ago, according to one study, they did so at 13.5 years. And the height of American ten-year-old boys had been increasing by about half an inch per decade between 1875 and 1965.

Considerable attention had been given to a group of hormonelike substances called prostaglandins. Since some were found to cause contractions of the uterus, they were used experimentally as contraceptives. In a so-called morning-after pill, they would prevent a fertilized egg from attaching to the uterine wall. Prostaglandins were also found to cause body fever and inflammation. Recent research suggested that aspirins derived their fever- and inflammation-reducing powers from an ability to block bodily manufacture of prostaglandins.

Several researchers in 1971 established that a substance called Australia antigen (AuA) was the major cause of serum hepatitis, a debilitating disease that sometimes resulted from transfusions of virus-infected blood. But scientists were still unsure whether AuA, so-called because it was discovered in an Australian aborigine, was the virus itself or merely its shelter. A New York researcher was working on a vaccine heavily infused with AuA in hopes of developing a hepatitis preventative. Blood banks were urged to catch contaminated blood by testing all donated blood for AuA presence.

Diabetes mellitus, the metabolic disorder that afflicted some 3 million persons in the United States, might be virus-induced, at least in some cases. Researchers believed that the Coxsackie B-4 virus, when attacking persons genetically disposed toward diabetes, damaged the pancreas where insulin—the hormone needed for normal sugar metabolism—is made.

An Ohio boy, seven-year-old Matthew Winkler, became the world's first known rabies survivor. Bitten by a rabid bat in 1970, he was released from hospital care in early 1971, free of any impairment from the disease.

CANCER

Political leaders in 1971 called for an attack against cancer on a scale rivaling the national effort that put a man on the moon. They felt such an effort would be best directed by an anticancer "superagency." It could take the form of a vastly beefed-up National Cancer Institute (NCI), part of the National Institutes of Health (NIH), or an independent National Cancer Authority reporting directly to the president of the U.S.

The proposal held high appeal, particularly because cancer—the second most frequent killer disease, claiming more than 300,000 American lives each year—invoked special fear in many. But some cancer researchers and medical educators cautioned against a ballyhooed approach, citing the unpredictability of an early cure for cancer. The issue was settled in December when President Nixon signed a bill that would pump $1.6 billion into a three-year anticancer effort. Although the program would be carried out within the NIH, a three-man presidential panel would oversee it.

The cause of the numerous forms of cancer, if indeed a single cause existed, continued to elude investigators. But many scientists were beginning to believe that viruses, known to cause some animal cancers, might also be responsible for some or perhaps all human malignancies. A stumbling block to the proof of this notion had been the inability of anyone to isolate a virus from a human tumor, grow it in the laboratory, and then cause another cancer with the extract. However, researchers in Houston, Tex., claimed to have isolated a C-type virus from a patient suffering from Burkitt's lymphoma, a type of lymphatic cancer. The finding seemed to favor the argument of those who held that a C-type virus—consisting of the genetically important ribonucleic acid (RNA)—might cause all human cancers. Later, however, NCI scientists, some of whom believed in viral human cancer, discounted the discovery by asserting that the Houston sample had been contaminated by a mouse virus.

In December University of Southern California workers found what they believed was a cancer-causing virus in a girl suffering from a muscle

One method of cancer detection involves a Thermographic Scanner Unit, developed by Great Britain's Atomic Energy Authority. Cancer creates heat in the body, and the unit can locate cancer growth by recording temperatures and translating them into different colors on a television screen.

CAMERA PRESS FROM PIX

cancer. When isolated and injected into experimental animals, the virus produced tumors. Although the work was undergoing further analysis by year's end, some felt this was further evidence linking viruses with cancer.

For several years, scientists have reported finding substances similar to B-type mouse breast cancer virus in human milk. The same viruses were also seen in human breast cancers. As a result, a Columbia University scientist cautioned women with a family history of breast cancer against nursing their babies.

Women using oral contraceptives were no more susceptible to breast cancer than nonusers, according to a British survey. Studies in the U.S., by contrast, linked breast cancers in experimental animals with the synthetic hormones in contraceptive pills.

Doctors were predicting cures, or at least long-term control, of Hodgkin's disease, once an invariably fatal cancer of the lymphatic system. Radiation of extremely high voltage was one of the recent methods used against this cancer in its early stages. In more advanced cases, NCI workers devised a multi-drug therapy that successfully kept 63% of the treated sufferers alive at least four years afterward. Evidence was also pointing toward a viral cause of Hodgkin's disease.

Some cautious claims of leukemia cures, at least for one form of the disease, were advanced in 1971. Lymphocytic leukemia, constituting four of five of all childhood leukemias, once killed almost all victims. However, clinicians at St. Jude Children's Research Hospital in Memphis, Tenn., said that nearly 60% of the children receiving the hospital's drug and radiation combination treatment between 1967 and 1968 were free of the disease for more than three years. Treatment was no longer needed in these cases, the doctors said.

Many lung cancer victims who shed the disease after treatment but continued to smoke cigarettes got the disease again. A University of Louisville Medical School study showed that 40% of the smokers suffered relapses, while only 6% of those who no longer smoked had the disease again.

HEART

In the U.S. diseases of the heart and blood vessels continued to kill more people than any other disease. They accounted for more than 5 of every 10 deaths. Among them, heart attack was the major killer, claiming more than 670,000 lives in 1971. Approximately 28 million Americans suffered from some form of heart and blood-vessel disease—nearly 21.5 million had hypertension, 3.75 million had coronary heart disease, 1.65 million had rheumatic heart disease, and 1.6 million had strokes.

In 1971 the American Heart Association (AHA) began an effort to inform people of the early signs of heart attack. In hopes of preventing needless deaths, the AHA distributed millions of pamphlets listing the warning signs and advertised recommendations for reducing the risk of heart attack. Among them were elimination of cigarette smoking, adherence to a diet low in animal fats and cholesterol, and regular medical examinations.

Major changes were necessary in the manner in which community health delivery systems responded to heart attack sufferers. This was the recommendation of reports by the Inter-Society Commission for Heart Disease Disorders (ICHD), which represented 29 medical, scientific, and nursing groups concerned with cardiovascular diseases. One ICHD report pointed out that an undetermined number of people died within two hours of the first heart attack symptoms. Thus, the more the public knew about the signs and symptoms of coronary disease, the greater would be the number of persons saved by seeking immediate medical attention. The symptoms given included oppressive chest pain and attendant nausea, vomiting, and sweating.

The National Heart and Lung Institute, part of the NIH, applied $16.4 million of U.S. funds in 1971 to the establishment of 29 research centers throughout the nation dealing with cardiovascular and lung diseases. More than a dozen of the centers would concentrate on arteriosclerosis, the hardening and thickening of artery walls. Arteriosclerosis was thought to be responsible for nearly 45% of all deaths in the U.S.

Dr. Adrian Kantrowitz, who had performed the world's second heart transplantation and the first in the U.S., implanted the first successful heart booster pump in a patient in August. The pump, a plastic balloon inserted into the aorta, was operated by a battery-powered energy source worn on a belt. It was connected to the aorta booster by a tube through the patient's body wall. As the booster contracted rhythmically, it took over much of the pumping load of the patient's weakened left ventricle, which performed most of the heart's work.

Increased use of a person's own blood vessels to replace his malfunctioning coronary arteries was evident in 1971. Coronary arteries bathe the heart with nourishing blood. When they become diseased or blocked by arteriosclerosis, a bypass could be formed around them by transplantation of veins from other parts of the body.

PUBLIC HEALTH

The U.S. Public Health Service (PHS), an agency of the department of health, education, and welfare (HEW), was reorganized in 1971 in preparation for its new role under the Emergency Health Personnel Act that was signed into law on Dec. 31, 1970. Because of the desperate need for better health care in inner-city and rural areas, the PHS enlarged its corps of commissioned health officers for service in those areas. Under the new law, physicians, dentists, nurses, and other health workers could enlist in the PHS for two-year stints. They could then be sent anywhere they are needed in the U.S.

The gonorrhea epidemic of recent years was reaching pandemic (very widespread) proportions

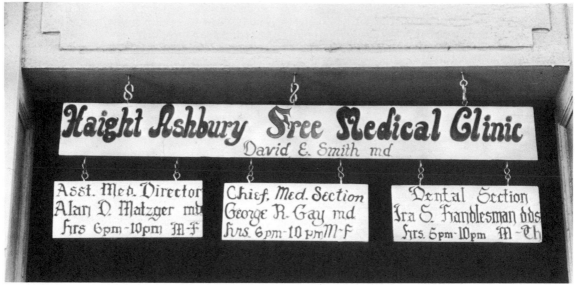

This storefront clinic in San Francisco, Calif., like many others, was set up to provide medical care for people who do not or cannot get help from conventional institutions.

in 1971. During the year ending June 30, more than 600,000 cases of the venereal disease were reported. Gonorrhea ranked first of all the communicable diseases that required official reporting. Syphilis, a more serious form of venereal disease, was on the rise for the second consecutive year. More than 23,000 cases were reported during the year ending June 30. Researchers were confident that a blood test for gonorrhea would be available soon. Also appearing imminent was an improved blood test for the detection of syphilis.

In June Polish scientists announced the successful experimental results of a syphilis vaccine. After the completion of more laboratory trials, the researchers planned to test the vaccine on humans.

Citing the waning incidence of smallpox in the U.S. and elsewhere, the PHS recommended a halt to smallpox vaccination. The agency defended its recommendation by pointing out that there was greater risk of a fatal reaction to the vaccine, although admittedly small, than of contraction of the once-dreaded viral disease. The PHS action

After receiving free medical examinations from temporary "miniclinics" in New York City's Harlem, children line up for doughnuts distributed by the Red Cross. The neighborhood medical testing was organized by Dr. Benjamin Watkins, honorary mayor of Harlem. Special attention was given to detecting cases of sickle-cell anemia and lead poisoning.

came precisely 175 years after the first smallpox vaccination was administered by Edward Jenner, a British doctor.

Apathy to other vaccines, however, was believed instrumental in the increase of other infectious diseases. The incidence of measles, for example, soared, while the number of measles vaccinations dropped off. Some public health officials blamed the national campaign against rubella (German measles) for diluting the antimeasles effort. Others ominously predicted that the dwindling number of polio immunizations might foreshadow future outbreaks of the crippler.

An estimated 400,000 U.S. children, most of whom lived in dilapidated housing in urban ghettos, suffered from lead poisoning, a potentially brain damaging ailment. Most of the cases resulted from children eating leaded-paint peelings. In August $7.5 million in federal funds were appropriated for detection and correction measures in cases of lead poisoning. However, some public health workers believed that systematic housing cleanups in high-incidence areas would be far more practical than costly lead-poisoning treatment programs.

Sickle-cell anemia detection programs were in operation in several major urban areas in 1971. Sickle-cell anemia was a genetic disorder that affected an estimated 2.5 million U.S. blacks. It caused red blood cells to take on a sickle shape and thus minimize their oxygen-carrying capabilities. The blood tests used in the detection program were designed to pinpoint carriers of the disease. An estimated 10% of all blacks in the U.S. carried the genes for sickle-cell anemia. By year's end, a federally funded campaign was begun to eradicate the disease.

SURGERY

Heart transplantations, done with some frequency since the first one in 1967, dropped off considerably in 1971. The poor success rate of the operation beyond the short term was probably responsible. Noting that his colleagues questioned the medical worth of heart transplantation, Dr. Christiaan Barnard, the South African surgeon who performed the first one, said that patients with hopeless heart disorders were no longer being referred to him.

Soviet surgeons devised an electrical method of breaking up bladder stones. In the technique, they first irrigated the patient's bladder and then pushed an electrical probe into it next to a stone. The shock wave generated by the probe shattered the stone.

Several new instruments will enable surgeons to get an internal view of diseased organs before surgery. One, called a pyelourethroscope, permitted doctors to look inside the kidney. Photographs could also be taken with the device. Similar instruments allowing an inside view of the heart and some major blood vessels were also being developed.

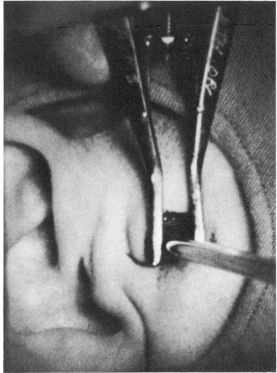

TOM HILL FROM "MEDICAL WORLD NEWS"

Using cryosurgery (a low temperature method) to relieve migraine headaches, Dr. Norman C. Cook of Canada freezes a cranial artery.

Many men were heeding calls for population control by vasectomy, the severing and tying off of the tiny sperm-carrying tubes called the vasa deferentia (singular, vas deferens). The minor operation often ended in lasting sterility. However, New York surgical researchers devised a T-shaped valve, called the Phaser, which when inserted into a vas deferens and turned to the closed position could block sperm passage. If the recipient later wished to become fertile again, the valve could be opened after another minor operation. The Phaser was still under experimentation in 1971.

Surgeons at the University of Pennsylvania in October reported the successful use of electricity to heal a bone fracture that had previously failed to knit. A low electrical current applied to the bone ends enabled them to grow together. In the opinion of the surgeons, the application of low-amperage electrical current to stubborn fractures would hasten healing and, in some cases, make bone grafts unnecessary.

Persons who suffered from excessive pathological sweating could in certain cases find relief through surgery. Mild cases were usually eased through the use of commercial antiperspirants, which for the most part contain aluminum compounds that destroy sweat gland cells. In pathologically severe cases of sweating, however, surgeons severed the nerves that controlled specific sweat glands, and thus abolished sweating in the denervated body area.

Two disorders that require surgical correction—diverticulosis and appendicitis—were found prevalent in regions of the world where people ate low-bulk foods. Diverticulosis, a disorder becoming fairly common, was characterized by outcroppings of the wall of the large intestine. Studies in the U.S., Great Britain, Australia, and France—countries where bulky vegetable fibers are removed from foods during refining—disclosed that a significant portion of the population over 40 years old suffered from diverticulosis. In areas where the incidence of diverticulosis was high, so too was the incidence of appendicitis. (*See also* Dentistry. *See in* CE: Medicine; Surgery.)

MENTAL HEALTH. The year 1971 continued to reflect a downward trend of resident populations in state mental hospitals in the United States. Many of these hospitals continued to develop and expand specialized services outside the hospital setting for particular groups of patients. For example, in Colorado elderly chronic patients in a lodge setup did their own housekeeping and engaged in a variety of group activities. In Florida a program designated as Operation Hope endeavored to locate alternative placements for patients over 65 years of age.

At the same time, special programs of inpatient care for emotionally disturbed children and adolescents were developed or expanded in at least 16 states. This was in contrast to the prevailing system that forced disturbed children under treatment in state hospitals to be mixed with adult patients. Drug addicts and alcoholics were among other groups of patients for whom specialized facilities became more available in state hospitals.

The controversy surrounding the use of amphetamines in treating hyperactive children abated during the year, with the published findings by a panel of 15 specialists in medicine and education that the use of such drugs could be supported as a therapeutically effective measure. The study, which was made under the auspices of the U.S. Department of Health, Education, and Welfare's Office of Child Development and Office of the Assistant Secretary for Health and Scientific Affairs, noted that about 3% of the nation's elementary school children fell within the category of hyperactive children with serious learning and behavioral problems. While stimulant medication may be used in the treatment of these hyperkinetic children, the panel members pointed out that other treatment methods such as behavior modification through a reward system, counseling, and the employment of special classes and teachers, should also be used.

The 25th anniversary of the founding of the National Institute of Mental Health (NIMH) was observed in June 1971. Its program is designed to encompass drug abuse and alcoholism, as well as a myriad of support activities for treatment, rehabili-

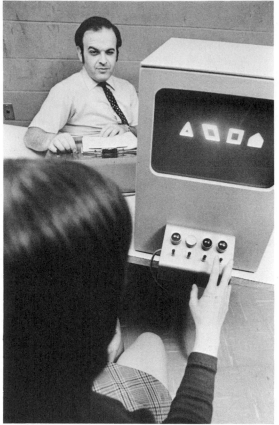

AUTHENTICATED NEWS INTERNATIONAL

Allan Berman, a psychologist, tests a subject's understanding of number concepts. He heads a center devoted to finding a link between brain disorders and juvenile delinquency.

tation, training, research, and education in a broadly conceived mental health frame of reference. Among subject areas that were given special priority during the year by the NIMH were mental health needs of minorities and children.

Accentuating a trend acknowledging that patients confined to mental hospitals have the right to treatment, a federal district court in Alabama ruled that patients involuntarily committed to a mental hospital through noncriminal procedures have a constitutional right to "adequate and effective treatment." According to Judge Frank M. Johnson, Jr., who made the ruling, the U.S. Constitution requires that adequate and effective treatment be provided because without it, the hospital is transformed "into a penitentiary where one could be held indefinitely for no convicted offense." He noted further that "the purpose of involuntary hospitalization for treatment purposes is treatment and not mere custodial care or punishment."

In 1971 social issues of the day, such as violence, hunger, the right to abortion, liberation movements, and the plight of the elderly, recurred as dominant themes in the deliberations of the various mental health professions. In May, at the annual conference of the American Psychiatric Association, the board of trustees of that organization unanimously endorsed a resolution urging "the prompt halt to the hostilities in Southeast Asia and the prompt withdrawal of American forces so as to make it possible to reorder our national priorities to build a mentally healthier nation."

METALS. World metal prices in 1971 slid to the lowest level in four years. The price collapse shifted the balance of trade in favor of the industrial nations. This widened the gap between the developing nations, which produce raw materials, and the manufacturing, consumer nations.

Early in 1971 most metals prices in the United States had risen. By the middle of the year, actual selling prices of most copper, aluminum, other nonferrous metals, and of stainless steel were lower than they had been 15 months before. Import competition, the economic recession, labor problems, and rising operational costs hurt producers. Federal efforts to improve business spending, including the import surcharge, were expected to help metals producers. The price freeze was not expected to have much adverse effect on sales. Previously, producers had been selling below listed prices to spur lagging markets.

The imposition of stricter pollution regulations and a declining market forced several smelters to cut down their copper output. Several mercury refining plants were shut down for the same reasons.

Growth in the U.S. aluminum industry was halted in 1970 by the recession. In 1971 major aluminum producers reacted by closing plants and cutting production to about 70–90% of capacity. Cutbacks in the aerospace industries reduced the demand for some metals. Two of the three producers of titanium in the U.S. shut their plants.

In contrast to the bleak economic situation was the breakthrough of a new continuous casting process for aluminum sheet. Production is about ten times faster and 50% cheaper than conventional methods. So far, continuous casting has not proved entirely satisfactory for steel production. However, a technique using powdered steel shows promise for the future. (*See in* CE: Metals.)

MEXICO. In 1971 Mexico's political and economic stability, although not seriously or permanently impaired, suffered some major setbacks. A potentially explosive situation resulted from impatience with the one-party political system and with the government's efforts to deal with the continuing national problems of poverty, unemployment, and corruption.

Domestic Events

During his first year in office, Mexico's President Luis Echeverría Alvarez showed himself to be a dynamic leader committed to reform as he set about fighting corruption, releasing political prisoners, and opening a dialogue with independent opinion. His actions endeared him to the public and the press and gained for him the respect of all but his most extreme political opponents. The latter included influential right-wing groups who seemed to believe that no corrective action was needed and that Mexico's political and economic status quo could be maintained indefinitely. It was to these groups, upset by President Echeverría's reforming zeal, that the serious political disturbances of June 10 were widely attributed.

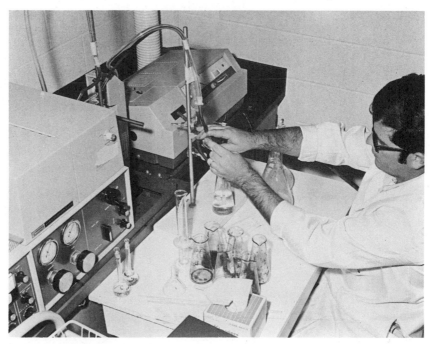

Robert Huggett and two colleagues at the Virginia Institute of Marine Science used oysters to detect heavy-metal content in sea water. Oysters will build up high concentrations of metals through their natural feeding, and will reflect in a very short time the metal content of water being studied.

The June 10 events actually had their beginning in a confrontation that occurred in May between students at the University of Nuevo León and the governor of the state, who had sponsored a law interfering with the university's autonomy. President Echeverría had eventually intervened on the side of the students; the governor had been forced to resign and the law was rescinded. On June 10 the university students of Mexico City, the capital, decided to demonstrate their solidarity with the Nuevo León students and to show that they had not forgotten the bloody government repression of the 1968 student demonstrations. Their peaceful demonstration was broken up by an armed group of young thugs who called themselves *Los Halcones* (the Hawks). In their attacks the Hawks killed at least 13 students and wounded more than 150 others while the police stood passively by. It was later discovered that members of the Hawks had been trained by the police in the use of weapons and had used police equipment in the June 10 battle. Mexico City's mayor, Alfonso Martínez Domínguez, a powerful figure in the right wing of the ruling party, was found to have connections with the Hawks.

As a right-wing attempt to discredit the president, the Hawk attack failed. With strong support from liberal forces, Echeverría reacted promptly and angrily. He instructed the attorney general to conduct an investigation, and the immediate resignations of the mayor and chief of police followed. Two months later Echeverría replaced the attorney general for having failed to prosecute persons responsible for the incidents.

With some exceptions—such as the well-known artist David Alfaro Siqueiros, who requested other Communists to cooperate with Echeverría's new administration—the extreme left also created problems. On September 27 Julio Hirschfeld Almada, a wealthy government official, was kidnapped and released only after a ransom of $240,000 was paid. On November 19 another wealthy political figure was kidnapped and then let go after payment of a large ransom and release of nine political prisoners to asylum in Cuba. Both incidents were attributed to the Movement for Revolutionary Action. This group had first been uncovered in March when 19 of its members were arrested and charged with subversion. That incident had been followed by the expulsion of five Soviet diplomats.

Economic Developments

Although 1970 had generally shown a very high rate of economic growth, with the gross national product increasing by 7.5% in real terms, that growth had actually deteriorated in the latter half of the year. This trend continued through the first half of 1971. In the second half of the year, however, various corrective government measures began to take effect. Business began to accelerate, exports increased, and inflation slowed down.

Mexico's economy was affected by the wide-ranging economic measures announced by United States President Richard M. Nixon on August 15, particularly the 10% import surcharge. Although sugar and textile quotas were excluded, about half the total value of Mexican exports to the U.S. were affected by the surcharge until President Nixon lifted it in late December. This greatly reinforced one of the stated aims of the Echeverría administration, to work for a greater degree of economic independence from the U.S. Accordingly, efforts were made to develop new trading partners. (*See in* CE: Mexico.)

A few leftist students battle with members of the rightist Hawks in Mexico City on June 10. The same day a full-scale riot broke out between the two groups, and at least 13 students were killed while police stood and watched.

WIDE WORLD

MIDDLE EAST. The conflict between the Arab states and Israel remained a predominant factor in the Middle East throughout 1971, but moves in the conflict were played out in diplomatic maneuvering and at the United Nations (UN) rather than on the battlefield. Although the cease-fire along the Suez Canal expired in the spring, and Arab-Israeli tensions remained high, the quiet along Israel's military fronts was broken by relatively few incidents. The role of the Palestinian guerrillas in Middle Eastern affairs was seriously weakened by internal disunity and by a Jordanian army campaign to control them. Arab disunity was also reflected in an unsuccessful revolt in Sudan, in rebel terrorism in Oman, and in disputes between some governments. On the other hand, Arab unity was enhanced by the formation of the Confederation of Arab Republics, binding Egypt, Libya, and Syria, and also by the joining of six Persian Gulf states into one country, the Union of Arab Emirates. Israel maintained a hard line in its approach to a settlement with the Arabs, and in doing so incurred a degree of diplomatic isolation from the United States. The U.S. increased its efforts to achieve a political solution to the Mid-East conflict.

The Arab-Israeli Conflict

Diplomatic efforts to renew indirect Arab-Israeli negotiations began early in the year; Israel had suspended previous negotiations shortly after the Suez Canal cease-fire took effect in August 1970, because of an Egyptian arms buildup. On Jan. 5, 1971, the UN special representative for the Middle East, Swedish diplomat Gunnar V. Jarring, resumed talks with Israel, Egypt, and Jordan. The basis of the talks was a commitment from both sides in the dispute to seek agreement on lasting peace, founded on the UN Security Council resolution 242 of Nov. 22, 1967. By affirming the resolution as a basis of peace talks Israel acknowledged the principle of withdrawal from occupied Arab territory, and the Arabs acknowledged the principle of recognition of Israel. On February 8 Jarring asked the Egyptian and Israeli governments if negotiations could be conducted on the basis of an Israeli commitment to withdrawal from Arab lands occupied in 1967 and Arab assurances that Israel could navigate freely through the Suez Canal; that safeguards for Israeli navigation at Sharm el-Sheikh would be provided; and that demilitarized zones would be set up in the Sinai Peninsula. These conditions were accepted by Egypt.

The initiative in promoting peace talks was taken up by Egypt on February 4, when Egyptian President Anwar el-Sadat extended the Suez cease-fire for 30 days and proposed an immediate clearance and opening of the Suez Canal in exchange for a partial withdrawal of Israeli forces from the waterway, the right of Egyptian forces to cross the canal, and the establishment of a demilitarized zone between Israeli and Egyptian forces amassed on the Sinai Peninsula.

As of mid-February, the Arab and Israeli positions on Middle East issues stood as follows: Israel accepted UN resolution 242 as a basis for negotiations; insisted on a formal peace treaty; viewed withdrawal from Arab lands as a subject for negotiations and remained adamant about holding onto all of Jerusalem and some other Arab areas for security reasons; welcomed international guarantees of a settlement but opposed imposition of an international peace; offered limited compensation to Palestinian Arabs; and demanded navigation rights to the Gulf of Aqaba. Egypt accepted UN resolution 242 as an "embryonic peace treaty"; insisted on Israeli withdrawal from all occupied Arab lands; desired a peace plan guaranteed by the UN and the "big four" powers; called for repatriation or compensation for all Palestinian Arabs displaced by Israel in 1948 and 1967; and would permit Israeli use of the Suez Canal once the commitments of UN resolution 242 had been met.

On March 7 the Suez Canal cease-fire agreement expired, but there was no immediate renewal of armed hostilities. Diplomatic moves on the Middle East situation subsequently focused on the Egyptian proposal to reopen the canal as a first step toward resolving Arab-Israeli differences. Representatives of the U.S., France, the Soviet Union, and Great Britain met to discuss peace-keeping guarantees in the event of a settlement. The U.S. had previously refused to consider guarantees on the ground that they might undercut the Jarring mission.

Lack of progress in the peace talks led Jarring to suspend his mission late in March. The U.S. persisted in efforts to promote an interim agreement based on partial Israeli withdrawal and reopening of the canal. U.S. Secretary of State William P. Rogers visited Israel and four Arab nations in May; his tour was seen as a means of maintaining the momentum toward negotiations, and further contributed to improving relations between the U.S. and the Arab states, and with Egypt in particular. Although U.S. efforts to move Israel toward a more flexible position continued throughout the year, they were largely unsuccessful. By midyear the Arabs had become disillusioned with the U.S. initiative and President el-Sadat set a December 31 deadline for a peaceful Middle East settlement.

In the fall the presidents of Senegal, Cameroon, and the Congo (Zaire), and Maj. Gen. Yakubu Gowon of Nigeria, acting for the Organization of African Unity (OAU), held talks with Israel and the Arabs in an attempt to find a basis for renewing the Jarring mission. Their findings were presented to the UN General Assembly, where diplomatic maneuvering was resumed during the fall session. In December the UN voted to resume indirect Arab-Israeli negotiations through the Jarring mission and called on Israel to respond "favorably" to Jarring's February proposals for an Israeli withdrawal commitment.

With the exception of a few isolated incidents the cease-fire along the Suez Canal was maintained

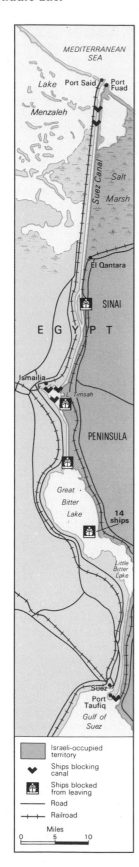

CAMERA PRESS FROM PIX

The rulers of Egypt, Libya, and Syria (above, seated, from left) sign an agreement setting up the Confederation of Arab Republics. Israel captured several Arab guerrillas (right) who fled Jordan during a crackdown on their activities. Sudanese leader Maj. Gen. Gaafar Mohammed al-Nimeiry (below, left) questions an army officer (far right) who led an abortive coup in July.

UPI COMPIX

WIDE WORLD

throughout the year in spite of the lack of a formal agreement. Renewed Soviet arms shipments to Egypt following expiration of the formal truce in March resulted in Israeli demands for more U.S. military equipment; but the U.S. withheld its aid as a means of pressuring Israel to negotiate.

The Situation in Israel

During 1971 Israeli security was improved by the virtual elimination of Palestinian guerrilla activity, stemming from Jordan's crackdown on guerrilla organizations. Guerrilla actions against Israel from Lebanon, on the Golan Heights, and on the occupied Jordanian west bank were minimal. West bank Arabs showed little enthusiasm for a return to Jordanian rule, and received no encouragement from either the Israelis or the Arabs for the establishment of an autonomous west bank Palestinian state. Under a new Israeli policy some 100,000 Arabs from outside Israel and the occupied territories were allowed to visit Israel during the summer.

Israel's most serious security problem was in the Gaza Strip, where strikes and guerrilla-type bombings occurred at a high rate throughout the year. Many of the bombings were directed at Arabs who worked for Israeli enterprises. Israeli security forces in Gaza were increased, and a security fence was under construction around the entire strip. Under another new Israeli policy a number of Gaza refugees were resettled in areas away from refugee camps.

Jordan's Campaign; Other Arab Affairs

During the first half of the year relations between the Jordanian government and Jordanian-based Palestinian guerrillas remained uneasy, following the 1970 civil war. In July the Jordanian army undertook a campaign to control the guerrillas, which resulted in their virtual expulsion from the country. Jordan was subsequently condemned by other Arab states for its action, and Arab heads of state refused an invitation from King Hussein I of Jordan to inspect the situation. Mediation between the Jordanian government and the guerrillas was attempted by a joint Egyptian-Saudi Arabian team, which proposed complete adherence by both sides to agreements made in 1970, the release by Jordan of all Palestinians held hostage, and the abolition of all underground Palestinian organizations in Jordan. In November the Jordanian prime minister, Wasfi el-Tal, who was considered by Palestinians to be responsible for the anti-guerrilla campaign, was assassinated in Cairo by four Palestinians, and shortly thereafter an attempt was made to kill Jordan's ambassador to England.

In protest against Jordan's suppression of the guerrillas, Syria and Iraq closed their borders with Jordan; during the campaign there had been clashes between Jordanian and Syrian forces. In other matters, however, the rival Ba'athist regimes in Iraq and Syria remained at odds, and Iraq in particular continued to be diplomatically isolated from the rest of the Arab world by its hard-line, anti-Israeli policies. The new regime in Oman was faced with continuing rebellion by Communist-led terrorists, while the pro-Marxist regime in Yemen (Aden) had to contend with rightist rebels. A Communist coup in Sudan in July was suppressed with the help of Egypt and Libya. Sudan severed relations with Iraq for its complicity in the coup.

The Palestinian Guerrillas

Early in the year the Palestine National Council, a parliament comprising representatives of ten Palestinian guerrilla organizations, endeavored to reduce differences between the groups by adopting a plan for the unification of guerrilla activities. The action was condemned, however, by two extreme left-wing guerrilla organizations. In July a further step toward unity was attempted when all major guerrilla organizations agreed to take part in a new 13-member executive committee of the Palestine Liberation Organization (PLO); this was the first time that the Marxist-oriented Popular Front for the Liberation of Palestine and the Iraqi-sponsored Arab Liberation Front had been willing to join the PLO council and its executive committee.

The PLO congress in July was abruptly terminated when Jordan began its campaign to control the guerrillas. As a result of Jordan's action, most of the guerrillas were dispersed to Lebanon and Syria, and in the fall they shifted their tactics from regular army action to urban guerrilla activities within Israeli-held territory. The willingness of Yasir Arafat, chairman of the PLO, to undertake reconciliation efforts with the Jordanian government led to serious dissent within the guerrilla movement, and in October an attempt was made on Arafat's life. At about the same time the PLO executive committee dismissed the commander and the chief of staff of the Palestinian Liberation Army, whose conflicts were said to endanger the army's unity.

The New Arab Federations

A loose federation of Egypt, Libya, and Syria, called the Confederation of Arab Republics, was agreed to by leaders of the three nations in April, and received overwhelming approval in national referendums held on September 1. Sudan was expected to join the federation as soon as its political affairs reached stability. Under the federation's constitution each nation retained its sovereignty and its power to make separate treaties with nonmembers. (*See* Egypt.)

In July six of the Arab emirates known as the Trucial states reached an agreement to form one nation, the Union of Arab Emirates. Impetus for the agreement was provided by Great Britain's decision to withdraw its forces from the Persian Gulf by the end of the year, and to terminate its defense treaties with the emirates. (*See also* individual countries by name.)

Rescuers worked to free trapped miners in the number 15 mine of the Finley Coal Company, after an explosion in the eastern Kentucky mine in December 1970. Thirty-eight men were killed in the disaster. In 1971 the United States Bureau of Mines prosecuted the coal company for the use of an illegal explosive fuse in the mine.

WIDE WORLD

MINES AND MINING. The economic and political uncertainties confronting the mineral industries in the United States worsened in 1971. Reduced aerospace and military expenditures led to reduced demand for metals. Despite general inflation, prices were weak and profits declined. Criticism of the environmental damage caused by mining techniques led to widespread support in several states for proposals to ban or strictly control the strip-mining of coal. Following the death of 38 Kentucky coal miners in December 1970, the U.S. Bureau of Mines was heavily criticized for failure to enforce federal mine safety standards.

Mineral market prospects were increased by U.S. President Richard M. Nixon's new economic policies and their favorable impact on residential construction and automobile manufacturing. However, many mineral prices remained at depressed levels in spite of hopes for higher demand and prices due to expected manufacturing growth. Labor strikes in the copper and coal industries resulted in production losses, although stocks on hand were sufficient to prevent serious shortages.

Gold and silver continued to make international news because of their irregular market behavior resulting from speculative trading. Markets for other metals also confounded analysts, as sharp declines occurred in prices of cadmium, mercury, antimony, and platinum. Political impediments in developing countries, notably nationalization actions in Peru and Chile, held copper supplies down, and low lead prices resulted in cutbacks in many mines.

There was a sharp drop in exploration for new ore bodies in Canada, but activity on committed mining projects continued at a high level. As rising nuclear energy requirements were anticipated, there was renewed interest in uranium in Canada and in the development of the major high-grade uranium deposits discovered in Australia.

The Soviet Union continued its intensive state mineral exploration program. It appeared that mineral production was rising steadily and that a high degree of self-sufficiency had been achieved.

Declining ore grade, new health and safety requirements, and added costs to prevent environmental damage combined to force intensive research in production technology. Advances in rock breaking and large-diameter rotary drilling were made through improved equipment design. Metallurgical research concentrated on efforts to avoid or control sulfur dioxide emission from smelters. Modernization of mine rescue techniques was a major concern, and studies to determine and control causes of mine injuries were under way. (*See also* Economy; Metals; Labor Unions. *See in* CE: Mines and Mining.)

MONACO. A $500-million land reclamation project on Monaco's Mediterranean shore continued in full swing throughout 1971. A 3,300-foot breakwater was expected to be completed by the end of the year. Upon completion of the project, later on in the decade, the area of the tiny principality is expected to increase by 20%.

The gross national product (GNP) of Monaco continued to depend heavily on tourism. According to recent estimates, tourism contributed directly 55% of the GNP while small, tourist-oriented industries added between 25% and 30%. An additional 4% of the GNP stemmed directly from the famed Monte Carlo Casino.

The International Festival of the Arts was held from July 2 through September 29. Featured groups included the London Festival Ballet, the Netherlands Dance Theater, the Comédie Française, and the Vienna Symphony. (*See in* CE: Monte Carlo.)

MONEY AND INTERNATIONAL FINANCE.

Throughout most of 1971 the non-Communist countries of the world were troubled by an international monetary crisis. The long-persisting disequilibrium in the international monetary system, focusing on the relationship between gold and the dollar, reached a dramatic turning point on August 15 when United States President Richard M. Nixon announced that he was cutting the dollar away from gold, allowing it to "float" in value, and imposing a 10% surcharge on most imports. At the same time, he announced a 90-day wage and price freeze and other measures to stimulate the U.S. economy. The resulting monetary crisis, with its depressing effect on world trade, was not resolved until mid-December, when the U.S. agreed to officially devalue the dollar in relation to gold. A major realignment of world currencies then took place.

The dollar crisis in mid-August had come like a thunderbolt, but its imminence had been indicated by the various currency crises that had occurred since 1967. The final crisis, that from April through August 1971, while centered around the dollar, was by no means exclusively a dollar crisis.

In the background were the facts that the U.S. trade balance had fallen into deficit; that large outflows of U.S. private funds for long-term investment abroad, mostly to Western Europe and Canada, had continued while foreign purchases of U.S. corporate securities had dwindled; and that U.S. military expenditures in West Germany, Japan, and Vietnam had remained heavy—all contributing to a huge U.S. balance of payments deficit. Furthermore, the uncoordinated use of monetary policies—restrictive in West Germany and expansionary in the U.S.—brought about large flows of U.S. dollars into German marks. An even more critical factor was that, beginning in April, some government officials in West Germany and the U.S. advocated exchange rate flexibility as the therapy for the world's monetary ills. This had a profound negative effect on confidence. Corporate treasurers and others entrusted with funds thus sold dollars, even when their need for German marks and other currencies was well in the future, or they postponed normal sales of such currencies for dollars. By early May these "leads and lags" had reached colossal proportions.

The Currency Float

The West German government, to protect its economy against the massive influx of dollars into its official reserves (and thus to counter an unwanted expansion of its domestic money supply), in May stopped buying dollars at a fixed price and, as a result, allowed the mark to float. The Netherlands followed suit with the guilder.

As the German mark and the Dutch guilder floated upward, they tended to become barometers of the weakening confidence in the dollar. In July and early August, events moved inexorably toward a climax as trade and investment decisions throughout the world were influenced by anticipation of a depreciation of the dollar in terms of other currencies. When the U.S. gold stock was about to fall below $10 billion—the level that had for long

The Tokyo Stock Exchange was the scene of frantic activity and much confusion in August, shortly after U.S. President Richard M. Nixon announced his new economic policies. The Japanese were strongly affected by Nixon's 10% surcharge on most imports. The surcharge was finally dropped in December as part of the resolution of the international monetary and trade crisis.

KYODO PHOTO SERVICE

been regarded as the safety minimum—President Nixon formally suspended what remained of the U.S. commitment made in 1934 to convert dollars into gold at the request of foreign governments and central banks.

The suspension of convertibility of dollars into gold and other reserve assets—special drawing rights and the reserve positions in the International Monetary Fund (IMF)—marked the end of an era. Foreign governments had to decide if they should keep their currencies pegged to an inconvertible dollar, defend themselves against unwanted dollars by allowing their currencies to float, or impose controls on dollar inflows. The U.S. thus removed the linchpin of the post-World War II international monetary system of fixed—though not immutable—parities of currencies. It was a monetary system based on a U.S. dollar of fixed gold content and supported by arrangements, under the IMF rules, to provide international liquidity and preserve convertibility among currencies.

After the U.S. move on August 15, the principal European governments kept their foreign exchange markets closed while seeking to develop some joint policy response to the U.S. steps. These efforts failed, and on August 23 the markets were reopened on an uncoordinated basis. Each government maintained the pre-August 15 parity for its currency, but all, except the French government, suspended their commitment under the IMF's basic rule to defend the previous upper limits set for permissible fluctuation of their exchange rates (1% on each side of par value).

Because of floating, the dollar became convertible only through the exchange markets and entirely at the risk of the holders. By mid-December the dollar had in effect depreciated by about 8% against the currencies of industrial countries abroad. The import surcharge was equivalent to an additional dollar depreciation of 3% to 4%. This direct and indirect depreciation was sought by the U.S. as a way of remedying the overvaluation of the dollar as evidenced by the persistent U.S. balance of pay-

"Pull yourself together, Mary! . . . You can't just stay in bed till it's all over!"

ments deficit. President Nixon's action was thus tantamount to asking other industrial nations to upvalue their currencies in order to accommodate a change in the U.S. basic balance of payments from a large deficit to a small surplus.

The principal industrial countries abroad declined to accept a reshuffling of their trade and payments to bring about a U.S. surplus. They were concerned about the consequences; the profitability of their export industries would affect domestic employment and, therefore, votes. Thus they resisted unwanted appreciations of their currencies through direct controls or through official intervention in exchange markets.

On a broader level, the floating of currencies and the relapse into restrictions on trade and payments threatened to destroy the standards of economic behavior embodied in the international "rule-book" elaborated under the auspices of the IMF and the General Agreement on Tariffs and Trade (GATT), which had governed trade and payments for the past quarter-century.

The Currency Realignments

For these compelling reasons the governments of the major Western industrial nations and Japan—the key nations involved—endeavored to resolve the crisis, finally succeeding on December 18. The basis for their agreement was the decision by the Nixon Administration to propose to the U.S. Congress a devaluation of the dollar in terms of gold through a rise in the official price from $35 to $38 per ounce "as soon as the related set of short-term measures [with regard to trade with the European Common Market, Canada, and Japan] is available for Congressional scrutiny." However, while formally postponed until January, the U.S. devaluation, entailing an 8.57% increase in the U.S. monetary gold price, immediately became the nucleus of currency realignments. Among the major currencies the pound sterling and the French franc remained unchanged relative to gold, and the Japanese yen, the German mark, the Dutch guilder, and the Belgian franc were, in effect, upvalued.

The countries that did not upvalue or devalue their currency against gold established new "central" rates in terms of the dollar. These could be changed without formal permission from the IMF. The Canadian dollar continued to float as did several other currencies. The permissible margins of fluctuation for exchange rates around the new central rates were widened to 2.25% on each side—a total spread of 4.5% against the dollar and as much as 9% for any pair of nondollar currencies.

Following the currency realignment, the U.S. import surcharge was eliminated on December 20. Although there were issues still to be settled for 1972, the whole package was welcomed as a working compromise for a situation that could have led to monetary disorder, trade protectionism, and a world recession. (*See also* Banks; Economy; World Trade. *See in* CE: Money.)

MONGOLIAN PEOPLE'S REPUBLIC. The 16th congress of the Mongolian People's Revolutionary party held in Ulan Bator, the capital, June 7–11, 1971, adopted its fifth five-year development plan (1971–75). The main aims were to continue industrialization and to increase livestock to more than 25 million head by 1975. Communist Party First Secretary Yumzhagiyin Tsedenbal told the congress that failures in the livestock industry were reducing export earnings.

In his report Tsedenbal criticized the People's Republic of China for its alleged attempts to disrupt the Socialist camp. He revealed that for the first time since 1943 the Mongolian party lists had been scrutinized and "unworthy" members excluded. By April 1 the party had 58,048 members and candidates. The congress elected a new Central Committee, which reappointed the old Politburo.

Nicolae Ceausescu, Romania's Communist party first secretary, paid an official visit to Mongolia June 21–24. His pro-Chinese attitude resulted in a cool reception. (*See in* CE: Mongolia.)

MOROCCO. In 1971 the Moroccan monarchy suffered—but survived—the only serious threat to its existence since full independence in 1956. On July 10 King Hassan II's control of the country was threatened when a group of army officers, using cadets from a military school as their dupes, attempted a coup d'etat aimed at eliminating corruption and, it appeared, deposing the king. The prime movers in the attempted coup were of right-wing persuasion, although the crowds in Rabat, the capital, quickly welcomed the coup as a potential move to the left, as did the revolutionary regime of Libya.

The attempted coup was started during a royal birthday party at the seaside palace at Skhirat. Cadets from a military training school fired wildly at the royal guests, killing 97 persons, including several ministers, army generals, civilian officials, and one foreign diplomat. Public buildings in Rabat were temporarily occupied, but order was soon restored after King Hassan, briefly detained in a room at the palace, was released and gave full powers

Mongolians vaccinate their cattle as efforts to increase the size of their livestock herds continue.
E. SCHWAB FROM THE
WORLD HEALTH ORGANIZATION (WHO)

to his minister of the interior, Gen. Mohammed Oufkir. The ostensible leader of the coup, Gen. Mohammed Medbouh, the king's personal military adviser, was killed in the shooting at Skhirat. Four generals and six other officers were later executed after summary investigation. The cadets were held in detention pending a decision on whether to bring them to trial.

After the attempted coup in July the king, in an apparent attempt to rectify the situation that had led to the coup, embarked on a long-term plan to improve his administration. The new government formed in August under the former finance minister, Mohammed Karim Lamrani, a successful businessman, was pledged by the king to fight corrupt practices that "made the rich richer and the poor poorer." Heavy penalties for corruption were promised, and there was a general reshuffle in top administrative posts. In November some evidence that corruption was being seriously tackled was provided by the arrest of six former ministers and several other high officials and businessmen.

The military threat to the monarchy posed by the attempted coup was met by the appointment of General Oufkir as minister of defense and a revision of the system of semiautonomous regional military commands to provide more direct central control over individual units. The armed forces lost nine of their 15 generals in the events of July.

In January the king had announced the uncovering of a plot by another group, the leftist National Union of Popular Forces and its sympathizers. In June 193 alleged conspirators were brought to trial and in September 5 (4 of them in absentia) were sentenced to death for treason and 6 others (3 in absentia) to life imprisonment.

The presence of a United States communications base near Rabat—officially admitted during U.S. congressional hearings in 1970—provoked some minor agitation by Moroccan opposition groups early in 1971, but Morocco's very close political and economic relations with the U.S. were not seriously impaired. King Hassan's visit to the U.S., planned for April, was postponed, but the new Moroccan prime minister made an official visit to the U.S. at the end of September. U.S. Vice-President Spiro T. Agnew stopped briefly in Morocco in July.

After the U.S., the two countries that pledged the most assistance for Morocco's five-year development plan were France and West Germany. Although the visit in October of Soviet Premier Aleksei N. Kosygin included an agreement for increased aid to Morocco, there was no suggestion that it would result in a change in the country's firm pro-Western stance. (*See in* CE: Morocco.)

MOTION PICTURES. Confirming once again the principle that there is no way of predicting what will attract motion-picture audiences, the outstanding box-office success in the United States in 1971 was 'Love Story', directed by Arthur Hiller and released late in 1970. This movie related the love affair and marriage of two college students and concluded with mawkish scenes of the girl's death from a lingering unidentified blood disease and of the too-late repentance of the boy's rich father, who had opposed the match. The entire film industry was puzzled and frustrated in its attempts to identify the formula that had worked such magic—were the members of the audience drawn by some nostalgia for their own college days, or attracted by a simple story of sentimental love at a time when films were becoming ever more explicit in their depiction and discussion of physical love? One considerable factor in the movie's success was undoubtedly the syrupy musical score by Francis Lai. The movie's theme song remained high on the popular-record charts for several months.

Other films hinted at nostalgia for some past age of innocence, when the campus was associated with clumsy experimental sexual discovery rather than revolution and dissent. Robert Mulligan's 'Summer of '42' was a more romantic treatment of the first-love theme than was Mike Nichols' caustic 'Carnal Knowledge', which subjected American sexual mores to harsh satirical examination through a story of the curious adventures of two men (Jack Nicholson and Arthur Garfunkel) from college days to maturity—in years, if not in emotions.

In a fast-paced detective movie, 'Shaft', Richard Roundtree played a black private eye and Charles Gioffi a white policeman.

COURTESY, METRO-GOLDWYN-MAYER, INC.

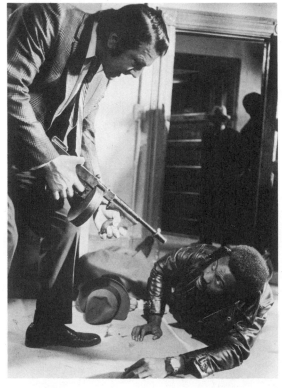

Arthur Garfunkel and Candice Bergen were two of the stars of 'Carnal Knowledge', written by Jules Feiffer and directed by Mike Nichols. Garfunkel and Jack Nicholson portray two men who do not know how to love and who exploit all the women in their lives.
© 1971 AVCO EMBASSY PICTURES CORP. AND ICARUS PRODUCTIONS, INC.

Following 'Tora! Tora! Tora!', the costly re-creation of the Japanese bombing of Pearl Harbor released at the end of 1970, massive spectacular films were perhaps less in evidence in 1971 than in preceding years. One large-scale musical was Norman Jewison's disappointingly unimaginative transfer to the screen of 'Fiddler on the Roof', the enormously successful stage production based on the Shalom Aleichem tales of Russian Jewry in the days of the pogroms.

The continuing appeal of science fiction was reflected in the surprising box-office success of a low-budget film, 'Willard', a horror story about an army of trained rats that get out of their owner's control. Walon Green's 'Hellstrom Chronicle' used documentary nature photography in a similar horrendous demonstration of the possibility of insects taking control of the world. Robert Wise's 'Andromeda Strain' employed a reportage style and convincing scientific exposition in an intelligent allegory about a noxious organism brought to earth from outer space.

Other directors dealt with present-day realities rather than the projection of a fictional future. Two especially vivid reflections of contemporary U.S. society were outsiders' views. Czech director Milos Forman turned his shrewd and comic powers of observation to the American bourgeoisie in 'Taking Off', a merciless satire of the generation gap. In this movie the parents of a runaway girl are exposed to a few of the pressures that affect the younger generation and emerge from the experience with little credit. Within the framework of a lightweight thriller, French director Roger Vadim's 'Pretty Maids All in a Row' delivered some no less accurate blows at some of the conventional values —ambition, virility, aggression—maintained in various guises in high-school society.

Dennis Hopper's second film disappointed the hopes raised by the runaway success of 'Easy Rider'. 'The Last Movie' was a highly self-conscious and very incoherent allegory. Hopper's collaborators on 'Easy Rider' both made debuts as directors in 1971, Peter Fonda with an intelligent if over-arty Western, 'The Hired Hand', and Jack Nicholson with 'Drive, He Said'.

Underground preoccupations became appreciably more politically militant in 1971. There were films that effectively discussed race conflicts (Yolande du Luart's 'Angela, Portrait of a Revolutionary'; Mike Gray's 'Murder of Fred Hampton'), women's liberation (Julia Reichert and James Klein's 'Growing Up Female'; New York Newsreel's 'Janie's Jane'; San Francisco Newsreel's 'The Woman's Film'), and Vietnam (Alan Levin's 'Who Invited Us?').

The film critics were enthusiastic about a good number of other motion pictures of 1971. One of the most highly regarded of these was 'The Last Picture Show', directed by Peter Bogdanovich. It concerned life in a small Texas town in the early 1950's. Also high on the list of critical successes were 'A Clockwork Orange', the movie version of the Anthony Burgess novel, written, directed, and produced by Stanley Kubrick; 'The French Connection', an urban crime melodrama set in New York City's seamier districts, directed by William Friedkin and starring Gene Hackman; and 'Le Boucher', written and directed by Claude Chabrol.

Other new movies favorably reviewed included 'The Conformist', a film adaption of the Alberto Moravia novel; 'Claire's Knee', a sophisticated comedy written and directed by Eric Rohmer; 'Bed and Board', directed by François Truffaut; and 'Derby', directed and photographed by Robert Kaylor, a documentary film about a youth who has his heart set on being a roller derby star. 'Such Good Friends', Otto Preminger's latest motion picture, was also released. And it would be a crime not to mention the new, and well-received, James Bond movie, 'Diamonds Are Forever'; it featured the return of Sean Connery as Bond.

The U.S. Academy of Motion Picture Arts and Sciences presented its annual Academy awards in April. 'Patton' took seven Oscars, including awards for best movie, best director (Franklin J. Schaffner), best original screenplay (Francis Ford Coppola and Edmund North), and best actor (George C. Scott, who declined the award on the principle that art should not be made competitive). The best-actress award went to Glenda Jackson for her role in 'Women in Love'; the best supporting actor and actress were John Mills for 'Ryan's Daughter' and Helen Hayes for 'Airport'. The best-musical-score award went to Lai for 'Love Story'; the top prize of best original song score was awarded to the Beatles' last film, 'Let It Be'.

The New York Film Critics' awards were announced in December. The winners were: best motion picture of 1971, 'A Clockwork Orange'; best actor, Hackman for 'The French Connection'; best actress, Jane Fonda for 'Klute'; best supporting actor and actress, Ben Johnson and Ellen Burstyn, both for 'The Last Picture Show'; best director, Kubrick for 'A Clockwork Orange'; best screenwriter, a tie—Penelope Gilliatt for 'Sunday Bloody Sunday' and Larry McMurtry and Bogdanovich for 'The Last Picture Show'.

Hollywood Items

In June it was announced that Columbia Pictures Industries, Inc., and Warner Bros., Inc., would combine their organizations and operate a consolidated motion-picture and television studio, to be located in Burbank, Calif., on the Warner lot. Both movie companies, however, intend to continue their independent operations. April 1, 1972, was the date set for the opening of the new facility.

A four-day auction late in February, of movie memorabilia taken from the Twentieth Century-Fox Film Corp. stockpile of props, netted $364,480. Motion-picture fans and furniture dealers mingled with Hollywood stars to bid for the 2,000 items. The throne used by Elizabeth Taylor in 'Cleopatra' brought $1,300. Other items from 'Cleopatra' were a pair of Roman Legion standards, which were purchased for $225 by Debbie Reynolds for her own movie museum. The teddy bear from the Shirley Temple movie 'Captain January' found a buyer willing to pay $450; and a painted long-case clock used in the motion-picture 'Laura' brought $625.

British and Canadian Films

In Great Britain, despite continuing economic difficulties, a number of distinguished new films were shown. 'The Go-Between', directed by Joseph Losey, deservedly carried off the top prize at the Cannes Film Festival in France in May, against stiff competition that included Luchino Visconti's 'Death in Venice', which won a special prize. Adapted from L. P. Hartley's novel about the lasting effects upon a young boy of his involuntary involvement in the subterfuges of a clandestine love affair, 'The Go-Between' sensitively evoked the atmosphere of a far-off summer in rural, class-ridden England. During the year another Losey film, 'Figures in a Landscape'—a hermetic study of two men on the run from some unspecified danger and making for some equally uncertain refuge—had seemed too much a virtuoso exercise.

'Willy Wonka And The Chocolate Factory' is a tale of three children who, upon entering a fantasy world in a chocolate factory, are taught some valuable lessons.

Peter Finch (left) and Glenda Jackson compete for the affections of Murray Head (center) in the motion picture 'Sunday Bloody Sunday'.
© 1971 UNITED ARTISTS CORPORATION

After 'Midnight Cowboy' John Schlesinger returned to Great Britain to make 'Sunday Bloody Sunday', from Miss Gilliatt's script. The film marked a new stage of maturity in which Schlesinger succeeded in casting off an earlier tendency to irrelevant effect. The story told of an unconventional triangle in which an egotistical young artist carries on affairs with both a middle-aged man and a divorced woman.

Several of the most important middle- and younger-generation British directors—Lindsay Anderson, Karel Reisz, John Boorman—produced no new work. However, Ken Loach followed 'Kes' with 'Family Life', an adaptation of David Mercer's television play, 'In Two Minds'—the tragic story of a young girl driven into madness by her family and others who seek to cure her. Ken Russell seemed wholly preoccupied with a desire to shock. His movie, 'The Music Lovers', was a vulgar extravaganza loosely based upon the life of Peter I. Tchaikovsky, with crude crosscutting of scenes and the use of the composer's music as a background for luridly literal sexual fantasies. 'The Devils' was a no less hysterical and ludicrous version of the story of the nuns of Loudun, France, and had the dubious distinction of being banned by a number of local and national censors.

Nicholas Roeg's second feature film, 'Walkabout', based on an Australian children's classic, related the meeting of two worlds: two schoolchildren abandoned in the desert are befriended by an aborigine boy on his "walkabout," an aboriginal initiation rite. Roeg showed himself a director of substantial gifts, able to translate stimulating and intelligent ideas into coherent and often dazzling images. Directorial debuts in 1971 included Stephen Frears' 'Gumshoe', starring Albert Finney, a tribute to Humphrey Bogart gangster mov-

ies; actor Lionel Jeffries with an elegant and lively adaptation of E. Nesbit's children's classic 'The Railway Children'; and editor Reginald Mills with a charming film-ballet, "Peter Rabbit and Tales of Beatrix Potter'. Barney Platts-Mills's 'Private Road' showed the same sympathy for ordinary, baffled, young people as did his first feature, 'Bronco Bullfrog'.

While the young film makers were operating on small budgets and dealing with intimate themes, the older generation of British directors was occupied with spectacular productions. David Lean's 'Ryan's Daughter', written by Robert Bolt and released late in 1970, was a showy melodrama set in the revolutionary Ireland of 1916.

In Canada Harvey Hart directed a vivid and effective adaptation of John Herbert's successful stage play, 'Fortune and Men's Eyes'. It was about homosexuality in prisons and was adapted for the screen by the playwright. (*See in* CE: Motion Pictures.)

MOUNTAIN CLIMBING.

In 1971 mountain climbing continued to attract more and more of the world's most adventurous and daring individuals. A characteristic of the winter 1970–71 in the Alps was the great number of winter first ascents, and especially of solo winter ascents, particularly in the Mont Blanc group. Among these were ascents of Mont Blanc itself: four Poles climbed the Bonatti-Gobbi route on the Eckpfeiler Buttress, and one of them with another climber made a diagonal route up the Brenva face; the Peuterey Arête was ascended to the Col de Peuterey by a party, who were then taken down by helicopter. An attempt on a new route left of the Walker Buttress of the Grandes Jorasses ended in the death of one of the party and the rescue of the other by helicopter.

During the year the most striking features of climbing in the Himalayas were the number of Japanese expeditions—many from universities—and the number of fatalities. The year's major event was the international expedition to Mount Everest, which was marred by the publicity given to the differences of opinion within the party, caused in part by elements of nationalistic feeling. The attempt on the west ridge was abandoned on the death of the Indian member, after which the French, Swiss, and Italian members left the expedition. The attempt on the southwest face failed. An Argentine expedition to the mountain was abandoned after its sick leader had been evacuated by the personal helicopter of Nepal's King Mahendra. A South Korean attempt on Lhotse Shar failed, as did a Japanese attempt on Pumo Ri. Makalu was climbed by the French, but the Japanese failed on Makalu II, one member dying.

In the Karakorum range in northern Kashmir, Japanese, West German, and British expeditions failed on Malubiting, Rakaposhi by the north flank, and the Ogre, respectively; but an Austrian party succeeded on Malubiting West. A Polish expedition made the first ascent of Khinyang Chhish. In the Hindu Kush in late 1970 a British party failed on Koh-i-Bandaka Sakhi. In 1971 a Yugoslav expedition made the first ascent of the south face direct of Istro Nal.

The "last great problem" of the Southern Alps of New Zealand—the Caroline face of Mount Cook—fell in the summer of 1970–71. In Alaska, a French party made the first ascent of Rooster's Comb, Ruth Amphitheatre, and Mount McKinley.

MUSEUMS. Financial problems were in the forefront of the museum world in 1971, as many institutions were forced to cut back hours and exhibits, lay off employees, or charge admission fees. The employees of New York City's Museum of Modern Art went on strike after the museum dismissed 53 employees in an effort to cut its operating expenses. Many museums in Italy remained closed for four weeks as a result of employee strikes. In England and the United States the introduction of admission fees was met with protests from the public and from the museum staffs.

In an effort to ease the plight of museums, a bill was introduced in the U.S. Congress to appropriate $40 million, to be matched by the museums, for museum services and renovation. The National Endowment for the Arts announced its largest mu-

Swiss alpinist Fritz Lotscher (below), accompanied by Jonne Kisaka of Tanzania, became the first man to cross the entire Kilimanjaro range. Their feat included climbing ten peaks.
KEYSTONE

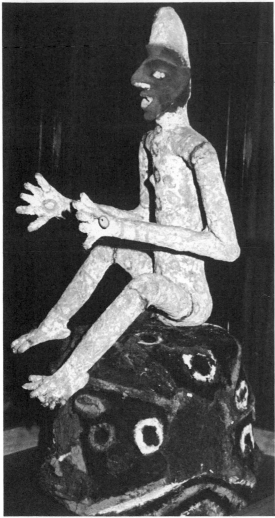

A clay headdress bearing the figure of a man
is part of the newest permanent exhibit at the
American Museum of Natural History in New
York City: a collection of artifacts from
New Hebrides and New Caledonia.

new museums in the U.S. were the Art Museum of
the University of California at Berkeley and the
Salvador Dali Museum in Beachwood, Ohio. The
Walker Art Center in Minneapolis, Minn., moved
into a new building, and plans for expansion were
announced for the Metropolitan Museum of Art in
New York City, the Art Institute of Chicago, the
Houston Museum of Fine Arts, and the National
Gallery of Art in Washington, D.C. In other parts
of the world, new museums opened in Moscow;
Courtrai, Belgium; Lisores, France; La Guaira,
Venezuela; Cesena, Italy; Kamphaeng Phet, Thaï-
land; Cape Coast, Ghana; Damietta, Egypt; and
Baghdad, Iraq.

Important recent acquisitions by U.S. museums
included 'Portrait of Juan de Pareja', by Diego de
Velásquez, for the Metropolitan Museum of Art;
J. A. D. Ingres's 'Portrait of the Marquis de Pas-
toret' for the Art Institute of Chicago; 'Guitar', a
1912 sculpture by Pablo Picasso, donated by the
artist to the Museum of Modern Art, New York
City; Correggio's 'Cardinal Bibiena' for the Minneapolis Institute of Arts; and Sandro Botticelli's
'Madonna and Child with the Young St. John' for
the Cleveland Museum of Art. The Whitney Museum of American Art, New York City, received a
bequest of nearly 2,000 works by the painter Edward Hopper.

The Boston Museum of Fine Arts returned a
Raphael portrait to Italy after claims that it had
been exported illegally were substantiated. The
United Nations Educational, Scientific, and Cultural Organization (UNESCO) adopted a convention prohibiting the illicit import, export, or transfer
of ownership of cultural property. Article Six of
that convention instituted a form of "passport" for
legally exported cultural property, making it illegal
for museums or institutions to acquire such property without the passport.

The Metropolitan Museum of Art, the British
Museum in London, the Louvre, and several other
museums found that their neolithic Anatolian pottery collections contained high percentages of for-
geries when they were tested by a thermolumines-
cence method. (*See also* Painting and Sculpture.)

seum assistance program, $1 million in grants, pri-
marily to fund purchases and exhibitions. Grants
totaling $160,000 were also made by the Endow-
ment to 16 museums for the purchase of contemporary American art.

Efforts to modify the traditional austere image
of museums showed some results in 1971. A new
Education Wing was opened at the Cleveland Museum of Art. A department of Urban Outreach
was established at the Philadelphia Museum of Art,
for the purpose of aiding local community groups
working to establish neighborhood art centers. In
New York City several large museums established
branch museums in other parts of the city.

Despite the financial crises in existing museums,
new ones continued to open. The Denver Museum
was the largest structure added. Other important

MUSIC. Achievement through international cooperation became a significant aspect of music in
1971. On United Nations (UN) Day, cellist Pablo
Casals, just prior to the celebration of his 95th
birthday, stood before representatives of world
powers in the General Assembly Hall to conduct
the first performance of his 'Hymn to the United
Nations'. A chamber orchestra, the Manhattan
School of Music Chorus, and the UN singers joined
to present the brief plea for peace, the text of which
was based on a poem by W. H. Auden. Casals also
conducted two Bach concertos and took up his cello
to play an encore, 'Song of the Birds', a folk song
of his native Catalonia; the music, Casals said, tells
that "the birds in the sky, in the space, cry out when
they fly 'Peace, peace, peace'." UN Secretary Gen-

FLETCHER DRAKE

Leonard Bernstein's 'Mass' was performed at the opening of the John F. Kennedy Center for the Performing Arts in Washington, D.C.

eral U Thant presented Casals with the 1971 UN Peace Medal at the concert.

On October 22 more than 140 musicians from 64 nations were assembled in a temporary World Symphony Orchestra at Philharmonic Hall in New York City. The project, under the direction of Boston Pops conductor Arthur Fiedler, was initiated by Walt Disney Productions in cooperation with a number of corporations and agencies.

A triumph for the Boston Pops was its 1971 European tour, the orchestra's first performances outside the U.S. The Chicago Symphony Orchestra also toured Europe in 1971; the concerts were a brilliant success, bringing rave notices in West Berlin; Brussels, Belgium; and London. Georg Solti and Carlo Maria Giulini shared conducting on the 15-city tour.

In January Pierre Boulez outlined plans for his first year as music director of the New York Philharmonic, and in September took his place as conductor of the BBC Symphony Orchestra in London. In October Lorin Maazel's appointment (effective in 1972) as chief conductor of the Cleveland Orchestra was announced. Maazel began work as associate principal conductor of the New Philharmonia Orchestra in London in January.

Death came in 1971 to the world's oldest living major composer. Igor Stravinsky, 88, the Russian-born genius who virtually ushered in the era of 20th-century music with 'Le Sacre du Printemps' in 1913, died April 6 at his Manhattan apartment. In June a festival was held at Lincoln Center in New York City in a five-day international observance of the 450th anniversary of the death of Josquin

Després. The English Bach Festival in London and Oxford honored Greek composers on the 150th anniversary of Greek independence. Also commemorated in 1971 were the 25th anniversary of the Edinburgh Festival and the 25th year of the Juilliard String Quartet, which was celebrated at Alice Tully Hall in New York City.

Two unusual new compositions introduced in 1971 were Leonard Bernstein's multimedia 'Mass', which opened the John F. Kennedy Center for the Performing Arts in Washington, D.C., and Dmitri Shostakovich's 14th Symphony, premiered at Philharmonic Hall with the Philadelphia Orchestra. A departure for the composer in both style and technique, the symphony uses a small orchestra, 2 singers, and 11 poems to carry the theme of death through the composition.

Violins made music headlines in 1971. The Paganini Concerto No. 3 in E, lost since the composer's death in 1840, was discovered in Milan, Italy, by a Polish-born violinist, Henryk Szeryng, who planned to perform and record the concerto. In London a Stradivarius was auctioned at a record price of more than $200,000. In New York City a 300-year-old Amati stolen in 1966 was recovered. The instrument, inlaid with rubies and diamonds, was made in Cremona, Italy, for Louis XIV of France. (*See in CE: Music.*)

OPERA

Sir Rudolph Bing (knighted by Queen Elizabeth II in 1971) opened his last season as manager of the Metropolitan Opera with 'Don Carlo', the opera with which he had opened his first New York season in 1950. Named to succeed Bing was Göran Gentele, who came to New York City after 22 years with the Royal Swedish Opera in Stockholm, where he had been general manager since 1963. The new post of music director at the Met will be filled by Czechoslovak Rafael Kubelik. He will assume the office in 1973, but will continue to serve as music director of the Bavarian Radio Symphony for three months a year.

In July Georg Solti made his farewell appearance at London's Covent Garden, conducting 'Tristan und Isolde', with Birgit Nilsson as Isolde. Solti, for ten years musical and artistic director of the Royal Opera, will become musical director of the Paris Opera in 1972, with Rolf Liebermann as the Opera's new administrator. Solti was replaced at Covent Garden by Colin Davis, who opened his first season with 'Fidelio.'

In the U.S. opera became a vehicle for exploration of contemporary questions. Halim El-Dabh, a composer-in-residence at Kent State University in Ohio, was commissioned by a private secondary school in Washington, D.C., to create an opera based on the 1970 confrontation at Kent in which four students were killed. El-Dabh had witnessed the incident at firsthand. His composition, 'Opera Flies' (flies, the composer said, were "the students, the insects to get rid of"), dealt with the rights of man in conflict with the need for social control. The opera was performed by high school students for the benefit of the Kent State Medical Fund to aid students injured in the shootings.

'Koanga', one of the earliest of the few operas presenting the problems of blacks, was revived by the Opera Society of Washington, D.C., in December 1970. Written by Frederick Delius in 1897, 'Koanga' deals with slavery, racism, and revolt, and makes use of Negro and Creole melodies. It was the first Delius opera staged in the U.S.

Gang violence and the motorcycle cult were the subjects of a Juilliard production, 'The Losers', with music by Harold Farberman and libretto by Barbara Fried. The anguish of a black man in a segregated society was the theme of Gian Carlo Menotti's 'The Most Important Man', presented by the New York City Opera in March. It is the story of a black scientific genius in a white African state who develops a formula that will enable his country to rule the world.

Other notable U.S. productions in 1971 included, at the Met: Massenet's 'Werther' (Franco Corelli in the title role), 'Der Freischütz', and 'Tristan und Isolde'; at the San Francisco Opera: 'Manon' with Beverly Sills; at the Chicago Lyric Opera: 'Semiramide', with Joan Sutherland and Marilyn Horne, and 'Werther', with Tatiana Troyanos as Charlotte.

The Opera Society of Washington, D.C. chose 'Beatrix Cenci', a horrific tale set in 17th-century Rome, as the first opera staged at the Kennedy Center for the Performing Arts. It was written by contemporary Argentine composer Alberto Ginastera. (*See in* CE: Opera.)

POPULAR

A number of new trends in the world of rock music were apparent in 1971—among them, disillusionment. New York City's Fillmore East and San Francisco's Fillmore West concert halls were closed down by rock promoter Bill Graham, who cited as reasons the increasingly high fees demanded by rock groups and their agents, and the difficulty of booking top talent into small theaters. Graham's move emphasized the growing disenchantment that has gone hand in hand with the commercialization of rock. Few rock festivals were scheduled in 1971, and the most highly publicized, Louisiana's Celebration of Life, was cut short following three deaths and over 100 arrests for drug abuse. The Newport Jazz Festival was also forced to close early. Thousands of young people had crashed the gates, destroying property and injuring some 300 people.

The rock opera 'Jesus Christ Superstar' was popular in 1971. Jeff Fenholt appeared as Christ in the Broadway version.
ZODIAC PHOTOGRAPHERS

The era of the supergroups seemed to be fading. Former Beatles continued to release solo albums, as did former members of Crosby, Stills, Nash, and Young. The Rolling Stones moved to southern France and Mick Jagger got married, but they came out with 'Sticky Fingers', an album with an eye-catching cover by Andy Warhol that sold very well. Jefferson Airplane lost singer Marty Balin but gained fiddler Papa John Creach. On their own label, the Airplane produced a new album, 'Bark', with a heavily political emphasis. In August a benefit concert in New York City for East Pakistani refugees was highlighted by appearances of Bob Dylan, George Harrison, Ringo Starr, Leon Russell, Eric Clapton, and Ravi Shankar.

A notable feature of rock in 1971 was the prominence of women singers and musicians. Carole King, a songwriter with many hits to her credit, released a solo album, 'Tapestry', that was a tremendous success. Her songs 'It's Too Late', 'I Feel the Earth Move', and 'Smackwater Jack' were also hits as singles. A number of other women who had previous experience as soloists and backup singers released successful albums. Among them were Melanie, Joni Mitchell, Carly Simon, Rita Coolidge, and Merry Clayton. A new rock band, Fanny, composed of four women instrumentalists and singers with a good deal of backup experience, came out with an album, 'Charity Ball', that proved once and for all that women can play hard rock too.

The soft rock trend continued. Cat Stevens, a British singer-songwriter, established a huge following in the United States through several albums and singles. James Taylor continued to be very popular. His concert at New York City's Philharmonic Hall sold out, and his movie, 'Two-Lane Blacktop', was released. The music from the album 'Jesus Christ Superstar' was performed in concert throughout the U.S., and it opened as a Broadway musical in October, to mixed reviews.

Country and western music reached wider audiences as more AM radio stations played country records. Charley Pride, one of the few black country singers, won the top male-vocalist and entertainer-of-the-year awards from the Country Music Association. Lynn Anderson won the top female singer award, and Dolly Parton and Porter Wagonner were voted top duo.

Jazz buffs were greatly saddened by the death of Louis Armstrong in July. One of the greatest jazz trumpet players of all time, he had brought New Orleans-style jazz to millions of people throughout the world. Duke Ellington toured the Soviet Union and was enthusiastically received. Earl (Fatha) Hines received the third annual James P. Johnson Award from Rutgers Institute of Jazz Studies. The National Endowment for the Arts recognized jazz as an indigenous American art form by awarding grants totaling over $20,000 to 30 individuals and organizations for projects in the field of jazz.

Former Beatle George Harrison (center) organized a benefit concert in New York City for East Pakistani (Bangla Desh) refugees, at the request of Indian sitar player Ravi Shankar. Among the many rock stars who performed were Ringo Starr (left) and Bob Dylan (right).

FRANK LEONARDO FROM KEYSTONE

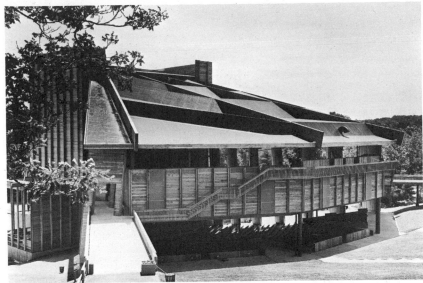

The Filene Center auditorium opened in July in the Wolf Trap Farm Park for the Performing Arts in Virginia. The park is the nation's first devoted to the arts. The center was presented to the National Park Service by Mrs. Jouett Shouse.

COURTESY, JACK ROTTIER FROM NATIONAL PARK SERVICE

NATIONAL PARK SERVICE. In 1971 the National Park Service and the National Parks Centennial Commission (created in 1970) completed plans for a series of events that would help celebrate the 100th birthday of the National Park System in the United States. When President Ulysses S. Grant signed the Yellowstone National Park Act on March 1, 1872, the world's first national park was established. Thus, it was most appropriate that Yellowstone and its neighboring park, Grand Teton National Park, Wyoming, were designated the sites of the Second World Conference on National Parks, Sept. 18–27, 1972. Since 1872, 93 countries have established close to 1,200 national parks and equivalent reserves. Sixty-three nations were represented at the First World Conference on National Parks at Seattle, Wash., in 1962.

A national symposium organized by the Conservation Foundation under contract from the Centennial Commission and the National Park Service was scheduled to be another major event of the 1972 National Park Centennial. The symposium will discuss major problems facing the National Park System and will prepare recommendations for dealing with many of those likely to be encountered in the immediate future and over a long-range period as the park system enters its second century. A distinguished array of park and other natural resource experts was slated to comprise the panel. Other Centennial events scheduled included: dedication of the American Museum of Immigration, Statue of Liberty National Monument, in New York and New Jersey, in April; dedication of Grasslands Environmental Study Area, Homestead National Monument of America, in Nebraska, May 15; a two-week teaching seminar on the environment, Rocky Mountain National Park, in Colorado (date to be announced); 100th anniversary of settlement of a boundary dispute

with Great Britain, San Juan Island National Historical Park, in the state of Washington, October 21; and the opening and dedication of Chamizal National Memorial, Texas-Mexico, in El Paso, Tex., October 28.

In 1971 Congress added Voyageurs National Park, in Minnesota, and Gulf Islands National Seashore, in Florida, Louisiana, and Mississippi, to the National Park System. Voyageurs National Park contains exceptional canoe trails. There visitors can paddle in lakes and streams where the French *voyageurs,* after whom the park is named, traveled in the 16th and 17th centuries while seeking furs and trading with the Indians. The 219,-000-acre park on the Canadian border is rich in wildlife, scenery, and history. Gulf Islands National Seashore covers 163,000 acres, 80% of which is water. It contains 52 miles of white sand beaches and the site of what was probably the first official effort at national resource conservation—President John Quincy Adams set aside Naval Live Oaks Plantation in north Florida to conserve live oaks for the Navy's wooden sailing ships.

There were two changes made in Utah during the year. Arches National Monument was changed to Arches National Park, and 79,618 acres were added to Canyonlands National Park.

On July 1, the $2-million Filene Center auditorium-amphitheater at Wolf Trap Farm Park for the Performing Arts, in Virginia, the nation's first national park dedicated to the arts, opened with a concert attended by Mrs. Richard M. Nixon. The first lady was made honorary chairman of the Wolf Trap Foundation, which manages the park's art program. The Filene Center, presented to the nation by Mrs. Jouett Shouse, of Washington, D.C., can seat 3,500 in its spacious red-cedar auditorium and 3,000 more on sloping lawns outside. Named in honor of Mrs. Shouse's parents, Mr. and Mrs. Lincoln Filene of Boston, Mass., it has a stage 88 feet high that looks over an orchestra pit large enough for a 116-piece orchestra. Though open only ten weeks in 1971, the Filene Center drew more than 330,000 visitors. Attractions ranged from the Stuttgart Ballet, the New York City Opera, and the Cleveland Symphony Orchestra to pop, jazz, and folk concerts.

President Richard M. Nixon visited Lincoln Home National Historic Site at Springfield, Ill., on August 18 to sign the legislation that brought into the National Park System the only home ever owned by Abraham Lincoln. The site, covering four city blocks, will be restored to its appearance of 1861, the year Lincoln departed for the nation's capital and the presidency.

Legislation to authorize a Gateway National Recreation Area, in New York and New Jersey, was before Congress when the president flew over New York Harbor in May to inspect the site by helicopter. The 23,000-acre park would include approximately ten miles of sand dunes and beach at Sandy Hook, N.J., now part of Fort Hancock. Jamaica Bay and four miles of ocean beach on Long Island also would be included in the park and thus quickly accessible to some 14 million people in New York City and the northern New Jersey urban complex. (*See also* Conservation. *See in* CE: National Parks articles.)

NAURU. On Jan. 23, 1971, the first elections were held in Nauru since independence in 1968; 48 candidates contested 18 available seats in the Nauruan parliament. President Hammer de Roburt was reelected by parliament for a term of three years; he was unopposed. De Roburt foreshadowed the possibility that Nauruans might in the future have to pay taxes. Predicting that the supply of phosphate, on which the national wealth was founded, would run out in about 20 years, De Roburt asked whether Nauruans ought to examine the idea of a welfare state to decide if they should contribute to it as individuals.

During 1971 Nauru planned closer diplomatic ties with Japan, and the republic decided to open a diplomatic office in Tokyo—its only two existing ones being in Melbourne, Australia, and in London. The Nauruans and the Japanese planned to exchange consuls and at the same time increase trade between their two countries. Japan was the only customer for Nauruan phosphate outside Australia, New Zealand, and Great Britain.

NEPAL. After a year of direct rule by Nepal's King Mahendra, a new cabinet headed by former Prime Minister Kirti Nidhi Bista was appointed in April 1971. Normal legislative powers were also resumed by the national assembly. The king kept

Moose roam freely in the new Voyageurs National Park in Minnesota. The park, on the Canadian border, was named after French voyageurs who hunted the area and traded with the Indians.

tight control over the administration and intervened directly in August to reinstate legislature member Ramraja Prasad Singh, who had been prosecuted by the government on sedition charges. Differences between the king and some cabinet members led to the resignation of the Bista ministry in August. Three days later Bista was reinstated by King Mahendra, but three other cabinet members were replaced.

Relations with India were improved with the signing of a new five-year trade and transit treaty in August. It provided preferential treatment for goods of either country and was expected to help diversify Nepalese trade. Industrial development was to be boosted by the treaty's provision for Indian investment in joint ventures. (*See in* CE: Nepal.)

NETHERLANDS. On April 28, 1971, 78.6% of the electorate in the Netherlands went to the polls to choose their representatives in the lower house of parliament. A total of 28 political parties took part and 14 were successful in gaining seats. The most significant features of the election were the continued decline in support for the religious parties—the Catholic People's party (KVP; down 7 seats at 35) and the two major Protestant parties, the Christian Historical Union (CHU; down 2 seats at 10) and the Antirevolutionary party (ARP; down 2 seats at 13); growing discontent with government policies; support of the main opposition; and the success of the Democratic Socialists '70 (DS '70). A breakaway group from the Labor party, the DS '70 attacked "wasteful government" and excessive taxation and won 8 seats in its first appearance at the polls.

Following the election the cabinet of the outgoing premier, Piet J. S. de Jong, remained in office for more than two months in a caretaker capacity while efforts were made to form a new ma-

ANEFO FROM PIX

A bomb exploded in the Soviet trade building in Amsterdam in April, injuring ten persons.

jority administration. In mid-May Queen Juliana asked Pieter A. J. M. Steenkamp, a leading member of the KVP, to undertake exploratory talks with other party leaders to this end. On June 22 it was announced that the queen had charged Barend W. Biesheuvel, who had been named premier on

Young members of the Amsterdam city council reflect changes in political trends in the Netherlands.

ANP

June 18, with the formation of a new coalition government. Biesheuvel succeeded in forming a five-party coalition consisting of the four former coalition partners—the ARP, the KVP, the CHU, and the People's Party for Freedom and Democracy (Liberals; down 1 seat at 16)—plus the DS '70. This gave the new government 82 out of the 150 seats in the lower house. The right-of-center cabinet comprised six members from the KVP, three from the Liberals, three from the ARP, two from the CHU, and two from the DS '70.

On September 21 Queen Juliana opened the new session of parliament. Her speech, prepared by the government, underlined the general concern over the deterioration of the economy, the chief causes of which were inflation and continuing overexpenditure. (*See in* CE: Netherlands.)

NEWSPAPERS.

The publication by *The New York Times* and subsequently by other newspapers of portions of what came to be known as the Pentagon papers, a secret United States government study of the country's involvement in the Vietnam war, and the attempt by the government to prevent such publication eclipsed the routine of U.S. journalism in 1971. At issue was the freedom of the press to report the conduct of government versus the power of that government to prevent publication of any information it opted to conceal in the

"Gosh, Chief, you should see how they control the press."

An editor of *The New York Times* (bottom) reads excerpts from the Pentagon papers after the U.S. Supreme Court allowed the *Times* to continue publication of the documents (top).

name of national security. The cause célèbre eventually involved the first instance in the nation's history where the government forcibly imposed judicial bans on political reporting. The U.S. Supreme Court resolved the question in favor of the right of the press to publish, but the 1st Amendment constitutional guarantees seemed less immutable to many as a result. (For a summary of events and a discussion of the legal issues involved in the Pentagon papers, *see* Law Special Report.)

Besides *The New York Times,* the *Washington Post,* the *Christian Science Monitor,* the *Chicago Sun-Times,* the *Los Angeles Times,* the *Boston Globe,* the *St. Louis Post-Dispatch,* and the 11-paper Knight chain published stories based on the Pentagon papers. All the newspapers based their reports on the same documents, apparently photocopies of a set Daniel Ellsberg admitted smuggling from the Rand Corp., where he had once worked as a defense analyst and consultant to the Pentagon.

The New York Times series of articles was certainly a unique journalistic coup. It was not the normal investigative reporting job that bore fruit after tireless digging. It required Herculean work but only after Ellsberg supplied Neil Sheehan of the *Times* with the raw material. After the *Times'* top editorial echelon approved the project, a six-week marathon began under stringent security. Sheehan was joined by three other top reporters: E. W. Kenworthy, Hedrick Smith, and Fox Butterfield. Less heralded than the *Times'* coup was the *Washington Post*'s accomplishment of getting an almost equally valuable appraisal of the report into print without the weeks of preparation time, shortly after the *Times* first published.

The episode of the Pentagon papers was not the only clash between the press and other news media and the Administration of U.S. President Richard M. Nixon. In February there were complaints by newsmen that the U.S. Department of Defense was placing undue restrictions on reporters to prevent them from reporting on the war in Laos. In April the American Society of Newspaper Editors charged that there had been a major increase in the past year in the number of subpoenas issued newsmen to force them to disclose their confidential sources of information. In September the U.S. Justice Department filed a friend-of-the-court brief with the Supreme Court that sought to have the court declare in certain cases under its consideration that newsmen had no constitutional right to withhold the names of their confidential sources of information or any confidential information.

In November it was disclosed that the White House had authorized a Federal Bureau of Investigation check on a well-known correspondent, Daniel Schorr, who was known to have angered the Nixon Administration with his news coverage. The White House claimed the investigation was ordered because Schorr was being considered for a job "in the environmental area," though Schorr himself said he had never been approached about such a job. During the fall Senator Sam J. Ervin, Jr., (D, N.C.) conducted hearings into the increasing antagonism between the government and the press before his Senate subcommittee on constitutional rights. Several witnesses before the committee claimed that the press and other news media were suffering intimidation and harassment by the government. (*See also* Awards and Prizes; Television and Radio. *See in* CE: Newspapers.)

NEW ZEALAND. On June 23, 1971, the New Zealand government announced to Parliament its provisional agreement to the terms under which Great Britain was expected to enter the European Economic Community (EEC) in 1973. It was the most important and most controversial agreement that any New Zealand government had been required to negotiate in decades. New Zealand had never denied that it was in Britain's interests for Britain to join the EEC. However, New Zealand fought for permission to continue selling its own dairy and meat products inside the EEC trading area or to have them phased out very gradually.

In Luxembourg, with New Zealand's Trade Minister John R. Marshall in attendance, Britain's chief EEC negotiator Geoffrey Rippon and the members of the EEC finally agreed that New Zealand butter and cheese exports to Britain would gradually decrease over a five-year period, so that in 1977 they would be 71% of current sales, with cheese sales being reduced more rapidly. At the end of the period there would be no continued guarantee for cheese trading. A review formula for butter was

agreed on (the meaning of which became a point of controversy inside New Zealand), and the EEC attempted to plan its butter-trading policies so as to avoid undercutting the efforts of New Zealand to diversify its exports.

The government announced in August that the last company of New Zealand combat troops in Vietnam would be withdrawn to the battalion in Singapore by the end of the year. A small training force was expected to remain. On November 1 a new joint defense pact linking New Zealand, Australia, Malaysia, Singapore, and Britain came into force. Britain had previously been solely responsible for defense. (*See in* CE: New Zealand.)

NICARAGUA. Early in 1971, President Anastasio Somoza Debayle, the powerful, firmly entrenched leader of the Liberal party, who is constitutionally unable to succeed himself, announced that he would step down at the end of his term, in May 1972. The president will be succeeded by a three-man junta that will govern during a two-and-one-half-year term designated as a period of constitutional reform. Such an action was made possible by an agreement between the leaders of the two major parties, the Liberals and the Conservatives, that will let the Liberals continue as the major party of the nation but at the same time will give

The volcano Cerro Negro in Nicaragua spewed smoke and ash for days in February. Three people were killed and 5,000 left homeless.

the Conservatives their strongest voice in the government in several decades. By this arrangement, rather than by the regular election of a new president and congress, a 100-man constitutional assembly will be elected early in 1972. This constitutional assembly will revise the constitution and serve as the legislative body for two and one-half years. On August 31 the country's congress voted to dissolve, thus transferring legislative authority to President Somoza. His opponents strongly criticized the move as an attempt to engineer Somoza's reelection under a new constitution.

On the economic scene there was a reversal of the recession that has plagued the nation the last few years. Although there was only a slight increase in the gross national product, this was a break in the downward trend of the economy. (*See in* CE: Nicaragua.)

NIGER. For Niger 1971 was a year of calm and stability. In February President Hamani Diori pardoned a number of political prisoners who had been involved in an attempted coup in December 1963 and in various other subversive activities.

Uranium mining operations at Arhli continued to prosper. Mining was expected to begin within five years at the Akokane site about 12 miles south of Arhli. A number of international oil companies had concessions in Niger, and although no commercially exploitable deposits had yet been found, the government remained hopeful that eventually oil would be added to uranium as a source of revenue.

President Diori made use of his country's friendly relations with Libya in seeking to promote a reconciliation between Libya and Chad. Diplomatic relations between the two countries had been broken off when Libya was accused by President François Tombalbaye of Chad of assisting rebels attempting to overthrow his government. Efforts to establish friendly relations with other predominantly Muslim countries were a major feature of Niger's foreign policy in 1971. (*See in* CE: Niger.)

NIGERIA. Under the control of a military government, the Nigerian economy began to recover in 1971 from three years of civil war. Oil production climbed to 1.5 million barrels a day, making Nigeria one of the world's top ten oil producers. Foreign investments, encouraged by the return of political stability, helped to diversify the economy.

However, dissatisfaction with the military grew following the announcement by Maj. Gen. Yakubu Gowon, head of state, that his government expected to stay in power until 1976. The high cost of maintaining a 200,000-man peacetime army was a major source of complaint, but officials felt that a rapid reduction of the size of the force would lead to increased crime and unemployment. Living costs and unemployment rose despite efforts at wage and price controls. Several labor unions protested attempts to regulate their power by calling strikes and work slowdowns in defiance of a government ban.

A cholera epidemic in the western states resulted in about 500 deaths. Poverty, hunger, and unemployment were particularly severe in the East Central state, where fighting during the civil war had been concentrated. Although many of the busi-

An Ibo village market in the East Central state of Nigeria shows signs of economic recovery two years after the bitter civil war that left the state in shambles.

JOCELYNE BENZAKIN

Joel Amamiye, one of eight men convicted of armed robbery and sentenced to death, laughs as a priest prays for him just before his execution. Thousands of people turned out to watch the eight executions in Lagos, Nigeria.

NIXON, RICHARD M. The third year of the Administration of United States President Richard M. Nixon, 1971, was one of major policy reversals and political surprises. The president stunned the nation and the world by announcing, in rapid succession, that he would visit both the People's Republic of China and the Soviet Union early in 1972, and by imposing bold wage and price controls and a 10% import surcharge to help the sagging U.S. economy.

The announcement of the trip to Peking, China, came July 15, after Henry Kissinger, the president's assistant for national security, returned from talks there with Premier Chou En-lai. At that point, Nixon's handling of the national economy was under criticism. George Meany, president of the American Federation of Labor-Congress of Industrial Organizations (AFL-CIO), and Carl Albert (D, Okla.), speaker of the House of Representatives, charged that Nixon had created an economic crisis unequaled since the depression of the 1930's. The economy was indeed in a slump: 5 million persons unemployed, the cost of living rising at a quickened 6% annually, and 25 million persons with incomes below the poverty level.

On August 15, however, the president appeared on television and announced a new block-busting economic package aimed at strengthening the economy and slowing down inflation. He wanted to strengthen the dollar by pressuring foreign governments to realign their currencies. The bold new economic plan included a freeze on wages, prices, and rents for 90 days. The president issued an invitation for the world to devalue the dollar, in effect; he announced that the U.S. for an indefinite time would not buy gold at the $35-an-ounce price fixed in the 1930's (leaving the dollar to find its own level in foreign markets).

Nixon's announcement on October 12 that he would visit the Soviet Union in late May 1972 was almost anticlimactic. Nixon would be the first post-war president to visit the Kremlin. The dates of his visit to China, February 21–28, 1972, were announced on November 29.

The president had begun 1971 with a State of the Union Message on January 22. He outlined what he called a New American Revolution, which included a federal revenue sharing plan to give $16 billion a year to state and local governments. He asked for welfare reform, a cleanup of the environment, and a comprehensive public health program. He also urged labor and management to try harder to keep their wage and price decisions in the national interest. Nixon gave no hint that he had any plans to use the authority to freeze wages and prices that Congress had given him the previous year. His message dealt only with broad domestic issues. A 65,000-word foreign policy statement issued in February stated that the nation's interests or commitments abroad would not necessarily lessen. Observers agreed there were few departures from past policy.

nesses forced to shut down during the war were reopened, few had returned to their previous levels of production or employment. An agricultural program providing $3.5 million in federal aid for food production and farm subsidies was launched by the government in an effort to increase food supplies in the East Central state. Several public executions of armed robbers took place as part of a nationwide effort to control crime.

Nigeria began to assume a more active role in international affairs during the year. Major General Gowon urged the Organization of African Unity (OAU) to take greater steps toward the liberation of African territories still under foreign control; among the military there was support for creation of an African High Command to ensure the security of all African nations. Diplomatic relations were established with the People's Republic of China and with Paraguay, and a cultural agreement was set up with Bulgaria. A delegation from the Soviet Union visited Nigeria to discuss a trade agreement. In July Nigeria became the eleventh member of the Organization of Petroleum Exporting Countries.

Chief Obafemi Awolowo, a veteran socialist and the highest senior civilian in the military government, resigned his post as minister of finance and vice-chairman of the federal executive council. The resignation was seen as a reproach to Gowon for his failure to facilitate the promised return to civilian government and for his failure to curb corruption within the government and to ease unemployment and rising living costs. (*See also* Africa. *See in* CE: Nigeria.)

President Richard M. Nixon surprised the U.S. and the rest of the world with his new policy toward China and his drastic program to bolster the American economy.

JACQUES HAILLOT FROM LIAISON

Late in January Nixon named John B. Connally, a Democrat and former governor of Texas, as his new secretary of the treasury—to the surprise of many Republicans. In February, a Gallup Poll revealed that Nixon's popularity had reached its lowest level since he took office; a bare majority of 51% of those interviewed approved of his performance. In an apparent effort to improve his image, Nixon granted a number of rare personal interviews in the next few weeks, including interviews to *The New York Times,* the National Broadcasting Co. (NBC), and the American Broadcasting Co. (ABC).

On April 7 the president addressed the nation about troop withdrawals from Vietnam. He said 100,000 troops would be withdrawn from May to December, but he did not set a deadline for complete withdrawal. He repeated his desire "to end this war—but to end it in a way that will strengthen trust for America around the world."

Throughout the year, Nixon continued to diminish the U.S. military presence in South Vietnam and said that his goal of ending the American military combat role there would be completed before his Soviet trip. "We are proceeding both on the negotiating track and on the Vietnamization track to end American involvement." However, Nixon also said that if the U.S. ended the war in Vietnam "in failure," a resurgence of isolationism would result. In line with his view of the necessity of forestalling a major U.S. military defeat in Southeast Asia, the president authorized the heaviest bombing of North Vietnam in more than three years, from December 26–30. The bombing followed a series of military reversals that cast doubt on the efficacy of "Vietnamization."

The economy remained sluggish through midsummer, and it appeared that Nixon was planning to continue with a "do little" policy. Treasury Secretary John Connally made it clearer. He said the president would not institute a wage-price review board, impose wage-price controls, ask Congress for tax relief, or increase federal spending. Another poll released in July showed Nixon's popularity still falling; only 48% of the public indicated approval.

In August, however, the president did a dramatic political about-face when he announced his new economic plan. Some diplomatic officials feared the drastic action would spark an international trade war. Some political observers felt the president had acted to keep Democrats from making an issue of the economy in the 1972 election campaign. Whatever the president's reasons, his plan was far-reaching and was described as the most comprehensive economic program since President Franklin D. Roosevelt's New Deal. Nixon's New American Revolution that he had proposed in January was shelved and all but forgotten in the wake of the excitement over his new economic policy. Nixon set up mechanisms to enforce his economic plan.

The nation apparently was pleased with Nixon's action. A Louis Harris survey released September 7 showed the wage-price freeze was supported by 73% of those interviewed.

There was strong pressure by foreign governments to remove the import surcharge. Nixon lifted the surcharge on textiles from Japan, South Korea, Nationalist China, and Hong Kong after those governments agreed to "voluntarily" restrict textile exports to the U.S. The Administration also applied pressure to encourage foreign governments to help resolve the international monetary crisis by realigning their currencies, especially West Germany and Japan. In turn, foreign governments urged Nixon to devalue the dollar, and on December 14 he announced that he had agreed to devaluate. On December 20 he fully rescinded the import surcharge. (*See* Economy.)

When Congress reconvened in the fall Nixon outlined Phase II of the economic program. He declared that he would not extend the wage-price freeze beyond the November 13 deadline, but added that he would take whatever steps necessary to "see that America is not again afflicted by the virus of runaway inflation." He set up to assist him a Pay Board and a Price Commission; the Cost of Living Council, previously organized, was given overall responsibility for the economic program. On November 8 the new Pay Board ruled that pay raises granted after the expiration of the freeze could not exceed 5.5% a year.

In September Nixon went to Anchorage, Alaska, to confer briefly with Emperor Hirohito of Japan. This was a diplomatic gesture designed to ease Japanese-American relations, which had worsened with Nixon's new economy. The meeting was the first ever between a U.S. president and a Japanese emperor, and was the first time a ruling emperor had ever been out of Japan.

With the resignations of Supreme Court Associate Justices Hugo L. Black and John M. Harlan (who both died later in the year), Nixon had an opportunity to make the court more conservative. His nominees, Lewis F. Powell, Jr., and William H. Rehnquist, were approved by the Senate in December. Thus Nixon had appointed four of the nine justices sitting on the high court.

Nixon was the eighth president in U.S. history to witness the marriage of a daughter in the White House. Nixon gave his daughter Patricia in marriage June 12 to Edward Finch Cox in a Rose Garden ceremony. (*See* Marriages.)

Although Nixon made no major foreign trips in 1971, his announcement that he would visit both major Communist powers in 1972 underscored his determination, expressed in his inaugural address, that his presidency would launch an era of negotiation instead of confrontation with the Communist world. (*See* Agnew; Foreign Policy, U.S.)

NORWAY.
After more than five years of uneasy alliance, Norway's governing coalition of four nonsocialist parties finally foundered in March 1971. The immediate cause for the collapse was an indiscretion by Premier Per Borten, who first denied, and then admitted having leaked confidential documents on negotiations with the European Economic Community (EEC) to the leader of the People's Movement Against Norwegian Membership in the EEC. Borten's own Center party wanted to continue the coalition under his leadership, but the Conservative, Liberal, and Christian People's party members of the cabinet demanded his resignation. Accordingly, Borten resigned his office on March 2.

On March 17, the Labor party, with 74 of the 150 seats in parliament, formed a minority administration under its leader Trygve M. Bratteli. Bratteli declared that his government would work for a European security conference, increased support for developing countries, and mutual diplomatic relations with North Vietnam. The government would complete negotiations with the EEC, but only on satisfactory terms (particularly in regard to the welfare of farmers and fishermen), and would do its best to combat inflation.

The September municipal elections showed a small gain for the anti-EEC Center party, which won 11.6% of the votes as against 9.3% in 1967. Both the Labor party, with 41.9% of the votes, and the Conservative party, with 17.8%, lost support slightly.

The brightest feature of the economic scene was the start of oil production on a trial basis by the Phillips Petroleum Co. at the Ekofisk field in the Norwegian sector of the North Sea. In full production, Ekofisk was expected to yield at least 300,000 barrels daily. (*See in* CE: Norway.)

NUCLEAR ENERGY.
Supporters of nuclear energy continued to hail it in 1971 as the best means of meeting the growing demand for power. At the start of the year, there were about 80 nuclear-electric plants throughout the world generating a total of 25 million kilowatts of electricity. Of these, some 20 were in operation in the United States. Opinions voiced at the Fourth International Conference on the Peaceful Uses of Atomic Energy, at Geneva, Switzerland, in September, held that the output from all nuclear plants must increase as much as ten times to satisfy energy needs.

The U.S. fell behind in construction of fast-breeder reactors, widely touted as the power producers of the next few decades. Fast breeders make more fissionable fuel than they consume. In September U.S. President Richard M. Nixon said that two fast breeders would be built for operation by 1977 and 1979. However several European prototype fast breeders were expected to be in operation by 1972.

Some progress was made toward perfection of fusion power devices, which use the principles of the hydrogen bomb for production of controlled energy. The Atomic Energy Commission (AEC) began testing a fusion device patterned after the Russian "tokamak." Fusion-produced electric power, not feasible until the 1990's, promised to be nearly pollution-free.

Glenn T. Seaborg, the Nobel prizewinner who headed the AEC for ten years, relinquished the post to James R. Schlesinger, an economist, in August. Seaborg was credited with being a leading advocate of nuclear-power development. In contrast, Schlesinger vowed to increase the AEC's regulatory role

Maj. Gen. Edward B. Giller (left) and James R. Schlesinger, head of the Atomic Energy Commission, examine deep cracks in the surface of Amchitka Island in Alaska after an underground nuclear test in November.

UPI COMPIX

over the nuclear-power industry rather than to maintain a promotional stance.

After seven years of indecision, a consortium of ten European nations agreed to build a proton accelerator potentially capable of producing an awesome 300 billion electron volts. The huge accelerator would be built on the French-Swiss border near Geneva. Great Britain, France, and West Germany were among the nations involved in the cooperative venture. (*See also* Fuel and Power. *See in* CE: Atomic Energy and Structure.)

NURSING. During 1971 registered nurses (RN's) in the United States in several areas of practice sought new ways to expand the role of the nurse in health care. More nurses were working in communities, rather than in hospitals and institutions, and so were better able to serve patients as individuals and as whole families. A new emphasis on the psychosocial needs of patients rather than just the pathological was evident.

In order for nurses to assume this larger role, the number of new postgraduate courses and specialty courses increased. The pediatric nurse associate, the nurse midwife, and the psychiatric nurse specialist were included in this new group of clinical nurse specialists. The pediatric nurse associate, for example, in addition to health maintenance, is responsible for managing common child-hood conditions and carrying out predetermined immunization plans. In some cases, the nurse will be responsible for initial screening, treatment, parent counseling, and follow-up.

During 1971 the American Nurses' Association (ANA), the professional organization for RN's, celebrated its 75th anniversary. In 1971 the ANA claimed nearly 200,000 members, 53 constituent associations (state and territorial), and 860 local district associations. To mark its 75th anniversary, the ANA held a national symposium and banquet in Washington, D.C., attended by 1,500 nurses and guests.

Continuing education for RN's was a topic of great concern in nursing during 1971. The U.S. Public Health Service (USPHS), Division of Nursing, awarded the ANA a one-year $42,000 grant to survey the programs and resources for continuing education for RN's currently available throughout the country.

The number of practicing RN's increased from 700,000 in 1970 to 723,000 in 1971. Of these, 515,000 were employed full-time and 208,000 part-time. The ratio of nurses to population also increased slightly over that of 1970—from 345 to 353 nurses per 100,000 population. The nurse shortage continued, however, and the USPHS estimated that one million nurses would be needed by 1975. (*See also* Medicine. *See in* CE: Nursing.)

OBITUARIES. Among the notable people who died in 1971 were:

Rudolf Abel, Soviet intelligence agent who was convicted of conspiring to obtain and transmit defense information from the United States to the Soviet Union, sentenced to 30 years' imprisonment in 1957, and exchanged for U-2 pilot Francis Gary Powers in 1962; November 15, Moscow, age 68.

Dean Acheson, U.S. government official who was secretary of state under U.S. President Harry S. Truman (1949–53), was considered to have been the master planner of the U.S. cold war strategy; October 12, Sandy Spring, Md., age 78.

Pier Angeli (Anna Maria Pierangeli), actress who appeared in movies during the 1950's and 1960's ('Somebody Up There Likes Me'); September 10, Beverly Hills, Calif., age 39.

Louis Armstrong. (*See* box, page 381.)

Max Beberman, U.S. mathematician who was one of the creators of "new math," which sought to develop the reasoning powers of children rather than stressing rules and formulas; January 24, London, age 45.

Hugo L. Black, associate justice of the U.S. Supreme Court (1937–71), whose landmark liberal decisions reflected his strong support for civil liberties; September 25, Bethesda, Md., age 85.

Col. Florence A. Blanchfield, retired U.S. Army nurse who, after 30 years in the Army Nurse Corps, in 1947 became the first U.S. woman to receive a commission in the regular Army; May 12, Washington, D.C., age 87.

Margaret Bourke-White, U.S. photographer, a pioneer in photojournalism, who covered World War II and the Korean War, interviewing and photographing most of the notables of the era; August 27, Stamford, Conn., age 67.

Sir (William) Lawrence Bragg, British physicist who, at the age of 25, was the youngest person ever to receive a Nobel prize when he won in the category of physics in 1915 with his father, Sir William Henry Bragg; July 1, London, age 81.

Ralph J. Bunche, U.S. black who rose in his country's diplomatic service to become the top U.S. representative to the UN, holding the title of under-secretary-general for special political affairs (1958–71), winner of the 1950 Nobel peace prize; October 11, New York City, age 67.

Leo Burnett, U.S. advertising executive whose firm, founded in 1935, had become the world's fifth largest advertising agency by the time of his death; June 7, near Lake Zurich, Ill., age 79.

Spring Byington, character actress who appeared in more than 30 stage plays and 75 films but was best known in later years for her role in December Bride, a popular television series of the 1950's; September 7, Hollywood, Calif., age 77.

Bennett Cerf, book publisher (founder of Random House) and television personality (What's My Line?) who published such major writers as James Joyce, William Faulkner, and Eugene O'Neill; August 27, Mount Kisco, N.Y., age 73.

NIKITA S. KHRUSHCHEV

TASS FROM SOVFOTO

Nikita S. Khrushchev, who emerged as leader of the Soviet Union after the death of Joseph Stalin, served his country as general secretary of the Soviet Communist party from 1953 to 1964 and as head of government from 1958 until his fall from power in 1964. His major achievements were bringing the Soviet Union out of the shadow cast by Stalin's brutal rule and initiating a foreign policy of coexistence.

Born on April 17, 1894, in Kalinovka, Kursk Province, in the Russo-Ukrainian borderland, Khrushchev began his career as a shepherd boy and then a metalworker, joining the Communists in 1918. He gradually rose through the party hierarchy to become a full member of the Politburo in 1939. It was in his native Ukraine that he established his reputation by restoring the shattered economy after World War II and by ruthlessly suppressing anti-Soviet activities. He became a trusted intimate of Stalin.

Six months after Stalin's death in 1953 Khrushchev was appointed general secretary of the Soviet Communist party. He set about raising the Soviet standard of living through new agricultural policies, beginning a massive campaign to settle the virgin lands of Central Asia. In 1956 he ushered in a new, relaxed period of de-Stalinization in Soviet life when, in a speech at the secret 20th party congress, he denounced Stalin and his ruthless policies. In 1958 Khrushchev assumed supremacy over the collective leadership that had ruled since Stalin's death and embarked on an active foreign policy. He visited the United States and began enunciating a policy of coexistence with Western capitalism. This policy met with strong criticism, particularly from China, and eventually culminated in a worsening of Sino-Soviet relations. Soviet relations with the U.S. also deteriorated when he attempted to install missiles in Cuba in 1962 but later improved as underlined by the signing of the limited nuclear test ban treaty in 1963.

Khrushchev's fall from power came suddenly in October 1964. Although his resignation was officially attributed to ill health, Western analysts felt that it was a result of his unsuccessful domestic—particularly agricultural—policies, his excessive anti-China zeal, and his failures in foreign policy. Khrushchev spent his retirement quietly. His death on September 11 at the age of 77 received little publicity in the U.S.S.R.

UPI COMPIX

IGOR STRAVINSKY

Igor Stravinsky was regarded as the most influential and original composer of the 20th century. His works created a revolution that vastly expanded the world of musical thought.

Stravinsky was born near St. Petersburg (later Leningrad), Russia, on June 17, 1882. His first youthful compositions, in a Russian nationalist style, so impressed Sergei Diaghilev that he commissioned Stravinsky to write a ballet score. The result was 'The Firebird' (1908), which secured Stravinsky's reputation—which was then permanently assured by the innovative masterpieces 'Petroushka' (1911) and 'The Rite of Spring' (1913).

World War I and the Russian Revolution made Stravinsky an exile and led to a change in his style. His works of the next 30 years reflected a concern with the techniques of classical music but always redefined in a uniquely Stravinskian manner. In the 1950's the composer once again surprised the musical world when he turned to serialist compositional techniques. At the time of his death at the age of 88 on April 6 in New York City, Stravinsky had created more than 100 works that had already influenced four generations of composers.

Gabrielle (Coco) Chanel, French couturier who created many popular fashion designs for women, including the famous Chanel suit, and the perfume Chanel No. 5, which became the foundation of her fashion empire; January 10, Paris, age 87.

Thomas E. Dewey, U.S. politician who twice ran, in 1944 and 1948, as the Republican party's candidate for president, and also served three terms as governor of New York; March 16, Bal Harbour, Fla., age 68.

Thomas J. Dodd, U.S. senator (D, Conn., 1959–70) whose career foundered in 1967 when the Senate censured him for misusing campaign funds for personal expenditures; May 24, Old Lyme, Conn., age 64.

François (Papa Doc) Duvalier, dictator of Haiti from 1957, whose ruthless policies kept his countrymen in abysmal poverty and fear; April 21, Port-au-Prince, Haiti, age 64.

Fernandel (Fernand Joseph Contandin), French comedian who played in almost 150 films during his very successful 40-year career; February 26, Paris, age 67.

Sir (William) Tyrone Guthrie, British theatrical producer, director, and author who helped found the Stratford, Ont., Shakespeare Festival and the Tyrone Guthrie Theatre in Minneapolis, Minn.; May 15, Newbliss, Ireland, age 70.

John M. Harlan, associate justice of the U.S. Supreme Court (1955–71), a conservative who believed in a sharp dividing line between federal and state authority; December 29, Washington, D.C., age 72.

Henry D. (Homer) Haynes, partner of the comic country-music team of Homer and Jethro; August 7, Hammond, Ind., age 51.

Van Heflin, actor who starred in more than 50 films and won an Academy Award in 1942 for his supporting role in 'Johnny Eager'; July 23, Los Angeles, age 60.

George Jackson, prison inmate who, while serving time for a 1960 robbery, became a symbol for many blacks in their anger against the judicial system after he was charged with the killing of a guard at Soledad Prison in 1970; author of 'Soledad Brother' (1971); killed in an escape attempt August 21, San Quentin, Calif., age 29.

Bobby Jones (Robert Tyre Jones, Jr.), U.S. champion golfer who was the only man ever to win golfing's "grand slam"—the U.S. Open, the British Open, the U.S. Amateur, and the British Amateur tournaments—a feat he accomplished in 1930; December 18, Atlanta, Ga., age 69.

Paul Karrer, Swiss chemist, recipient of the Nobel prize in chemistry in 1937; June 18, Zurich, Switzerland, age 82.

Nikita S. Khrushchev. (*See* box, page 379.)

Sean Lemass, Irish patriot and politican who served as his country's prime minister (1959–67); May 11, Dublin, Ireland, age 71.

Nathan F. Leopold, convicted slayer, with Richard Loeb, of 14-year-old Bobby Franks in 1924; spared a death sentence, Leopold became a model prisoner and when released on parole in 1958 served in various humanitarian activities; August 29, San Juan, Puerto Rico, age 66.

Joe E. Lewis, well-known nightclub comedian; June 4, New York City, age 69.

Ted Lewis (Theodore Friedman), popular entertainer and bandleader who was known by his favorite line, "Is everybody happy?"; August 25, New York City; age 80.

Charles (Sonny) Liston, heavyweight boxing champion of the world from September 1962 until February 1964; found dead January 5 (although he apparently died a week before), Las Vegas, Nev., age 38.

Harold Lloyd, bespectacled comedian who starred in numerous films in the 1920's; March 8, Beverly Hills, Calif., age 77.

György Lukács, Hungarian Marxist philosopher, writer, and critic, who was a major figure in the history of European Communist thought and a defender of humanistic values; June 4, Budapest, Hungary, age 86.

Diana Lynn (Dolly Loehr), actress known for her roles in light-comedy films during the 1940's; December 18, Los Angeles, age 45.

Jim Morrison (James Douglas), U.S. rock musician who was lead singer of the Doors, and who also wrote many of the group's songs ('Light My Fire'); July 3, Paris, age 26.

Audie Murphy, U.S. war hero who was his country's most decorated World War II soldier (28 decorations including the Medal of Honor); he later took up an acting career, playing himself in the film version of his autobiography, 'To Hell and Back'; appeared in some 40 movies in the 1950's and early 1960's, but at the time of his death was engaged in business activities; May 28, near Roanoke, Va., age 46.

Ogden Nash, U.S. poet who was the nation's best-known writer of humorous poetry; May 19, Baltimore, Md., age 68.

Allan Nevins, U.S. historian, pioneer in the techniques of oral history, winner of two Pulitzer prizes for his historical writings; March 5, Menlo Park, Calif., age 80.

Reinhold Niebuhr, leading U.S. Protestant theologian, and activist in many liberal causes; June 1, Stockbridge, Mass., age 78.

J(ames) C(ash) Penney, U.S. merchant who founded the J. C. Penney department store chain; February 12, New York City, age 95.

Lieut. Gen. Lewis B. (Chesty) Puller, the U.S. Marine Corps' most decorated veteran, winner of 56 medals; October 11, Hampton, Va., age 73.

Elmo Roper, U.S. public-opinion analyst who first developed the scientific poll for political forecasting; April 30, West Reading, Pa., age 70.

Carl Ruggles, U.S. composer, a major pioneering figure in 20th century American music ('Sun-Treader'); October 24, Bennington, Vt., age 95.

Richard B. Russell, U.S. senator (D, Ga.) from 1933 until his death, leader of Southern senators in their fight against civil rights legislation; January 21, Washington, D.C., age 73.

David Sarnoff, U.S. executive who launched television in America in 1939 and was the long-time head of the Radio Corp. of America; December 12, New York City, age 80.

George Seferis, pen name for Giorgos Seferiades, Greek poet, diplomat, and scholar who was awarded the Nobel prize for literature in 1963; September 20, Athens, Greece, age 71.

Spyros P. Skouras, U.S. movie magnate who headed the Twentieth Century-Fox Film Corp. from 1942 until 1969; August 16, Mamaroneck, N.Y., age 78.

AGIP FROM PICTORIAL PARADE

LOUIS ARMSTRONG

Louis Armstrong, known affectionately as "Satchmo," was a trumpeter and singer who was considered to be one of the most influential creators of American jazz music. Born on July 4, 1900, in New Orleans, La., he made his way from an orphanage in that city to concert stages on five continents.

Armstrong played with pickup bands in New Orleans until, at 22, he joined "King" Oliver and his Creole Jazz Band in Chicago. He then played with Fletcher Henderson's band in New York City but returned to Chicago to lead his own groups, the Hot Five and the Hot Seven, at the Dreamland Cafe. It was during these golden days of jazz in the 1920's that Armstrong attained his finest performances and produced the recordings that were to become classics: 'My Heart', 'Cornet Chop Suey', and 'Potato Head Blues'.

Armstrong's popularity had spread to Europe by the 1930's, and he made his first trip abroad in 1932. Following that were appearances in the Middle East, in the Orient, Africa, South America, and the Soviet Union. Always included in Armstrong's programs were his fans' all-time favorites, 'When the Saints Go Marchin' In' and 'Sleepy Time Down South'. He died on July 6 in New York City at the age of 71.

Arthur B. Spingarn, a white U.S. attorney and leader in the struggle for equal rights for blacks as a founder (1909) of the National Association for the Advancement of Colored People (NAACP); December 1, New York City, age 93.

Wendell M. Stanley, U.S. virologist, recipient of the 1946 Nobel prize for chemistry for his pioneering work into the nature of viruses; June 15, Salamanca, Spain, age 66.

Igor Stravinsky. (*See* box, page 380.)

Theodor H. E. Svedberg, Swedish physical chemist who was awarded the Nobel prize for chemistry in 1926; February 26, Stockholm, Sweden, age 86.

Igor E. Tamm, Soviet physicist who was one of the developers of the hydrogen bomb for the

PETER L. GOULD

WIDE WORLD

WIDE WORLD

WIDE WORLD

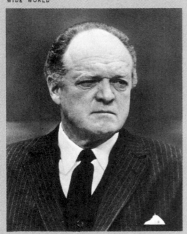

UPI COMPIX

Thomas E. Dewey (above, left); Ogden Nash (above); Hugo L. Black (above, right); Van Heflin (left); Bennett Cerf (right)

WIDE WORLD

WIDE WORLD

Gabrielle (Coco) Chanel (far left); Ralph Bunche (left)

U.S.S.R., a winner of the Nobel prize for physics in 1958, and also a liberal critic of many Soviet government policies; April 12, Moscow, age 75.

Dick Tiger (Richard Itehu), Nigerian boxer who was both world middleweight (1962–63; 1965–66) and light heavyweight (1966–68) champion; December 14, Aba, Nigeria, age 42.

Arne Tiselius, Swedish biochemist, who was awarded the 1948 Nobel prize for biochemistry; October 29, Uppsala, Sweden, age 69.

William V. S. Tubman, Liberian statesman who served as president of his country from 1944 until his death, making his administration the longest in Liberian history; July 23, London, age 75.

Aleksandr T. Tvardovsky, Soviet poet who, as editor of the leading independent Soviet literary journal *Novy Mir* (New World) from 1950–54 and 1958–70, was responsible for publishing such major Soviet works as Ilya Ehrenburg's 'Thaw' (1954) and Aleksandr I. Solzhenitsyn's 'One Day in the Life of Ivan Denisovich' (1962); December 18, Moscow, age 61.

Whitney M. Young, Jr., U.S. black champion of civil rights who served as executive director of the National Urban League from 1961 until his death; March 11, Lagos, Nigeria, age 49.

OCEANOGRAPHY.

The Deep-Sea Drilling Project on the ship *Glomar Challenger* continued in 1971 to provide data for the study of the age and structure of the earth. The project, sponsored by the United States National Science Foundation, has provided evidence supporting the theory of continental drift and sea-floor spreading, and has helped to fill in many details of these processes. The project's scientists found that the crust of the northern Pacific Ocean is being thrust under the continent of North America at the rate of 2 inches per year. The floor of the Pacific has been moving northward across the equator for at least 30 million years; over the past 100 million years the central Pacific crust apparently has moved as much as 1,800 miles.

Core materials that were obtained from a drilling site off the California coast now make up a complete sedimentary record of fossilized microscopic marine life spanning the last 26 million years. By studying these fossils, scientists will be able to chart the climatic variations that occurred in the area. Other research in the Pacific provided new insights into the formation of the Isthmus of Panama.

The crust of the Caribbean Sea was found to be 2½ times thicker than that of normal ocean basins; it is composed of granite, a material previously thought limited to the continental crust. The Mediterranean floor has been affected by the drifting of Europe and Africa. Sediment recovered off the coast of Portugal showed that the Iberian block and the continent of Africa broke away from Europe more than 130 million years ago.

These discoveries were in part made possible by the perfection of new drilling techniques. The project's scientists have developed a device that enables them to relocate a drilling hole under thousands of feet of water. When a drill bit is worn out, it can be replaced and the drilling continued at the same site to greater depths. The Deep-Sea Drilling Project may now be extended until 1975 in order to study the Mediterranean, the Black Sea, and the polar regions. Drilling had been scheduled to be completed in August 1972.

In other technological developments, four volunteers at the University of Pennsylvania's Institute for Environmental Medicine lived for 24 days at simulated depths to 5,000 feet, using neon as the primary atmospheric gas. It is hoped that further research will lead to the widespread use of neon, which is readily available, has no narcotic effect, does not distort voices as badly as helium, and seems to be superior to both helium and nitrogen for avoiding the "bends," the single greatest hazard to deep-sea divers. In July three diver-scientists

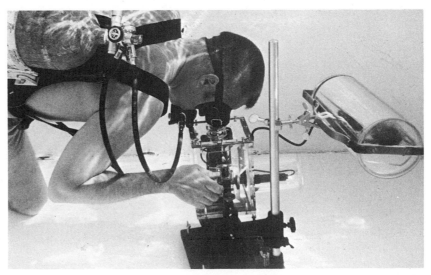

Scientists at the University of California at Santa Barbara devised a submarine microscope that enabled divers to observe firsthand the effects of pollution on marine life.

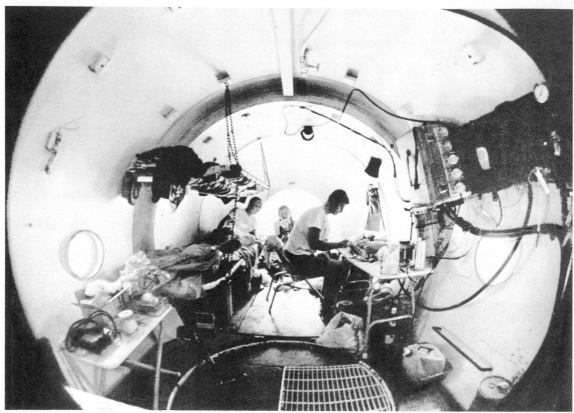

Two biologists and a nurse spent six days in a "hydro-lab" with an interior of 8 feet by 15 feet. They were studying ways to protect the human body underwater.

working in an underwater lab on the sea floor were able to operate independent of a surface personnel support team. During the five-day experiment, air, water, and electricity were supplied by an unmanned barge.

Pollution of the oceans continued to be of major concern in 1971. Representatives of 35 countries met in London in June to discuss organizing international machinery that could produce "periodic, comprehensive reports on the health of the oceans." The Pacem in Maribus conference, which met in July with representatives from more than 30 nations, called for international legislation to control pollution of the oceans. Jacques Cousteau, a pioneer undersea explorer, told a U.S. Senate subcommittee that unless the industrialized countries of the world cooperate to save them, the world's oceans will be unfit for any form of life within 50 years. Earlier in the year, U.S. Defense Secretary Melvin Laird banned the dumping of obsolete gas and explosive weapons into the ocean. (*See in* CE: Oceanography.)

OMAN. The resources and efforts of Oman's new government were almost equally directed in 1971 toward modernization of the nation and subduing Communist-led rebels in Dhofar province. Major military offensives against the rebels and increasing rebel attacks on government-controlled areas intensified the civil war and diverted national resources from needed development projects.

During 1971 Omani officials toured Arab capitals to obtain support for their admittance to the Arab League and the United Nations (UN). Their admittance was opposed by Yemen (Aden), which claimed Oman was still a British colony; by Imam Ghaleb, an exiled religious leader who claimed the right to rule Oman; and by the rebel leadership. Oman became a member of the league in September and of the UN in October. Oman supported the proposed federation of Persian Gulf emirates (which was officially formed on December 2) but declined to join because the country needed to devote its resources to internal modernization.

Massive demonstrations by striking workers, who protested the employment of foreigners and sought better wages and working conditions, were put down by troops in Muscat and Matrah in September. A government grievance committee was established.

As part of Oman's development program, contracts were let to West German and Belgian firms for road construction and port expansion. The first hospital in inner Oman was opened at Nizwa in August, and Oman's first hotel began operating in Muscat in June.

PAINTING AND SCULPTURE. The 90th birthday of Pablo Picasso, perhaps the world's greatest living artist—certainly the most famous and probably the richest artist who ever lived—was celebrated in 1971 with several major exhibitions. In New York City a double show of the artist's work was mounted by two galleries: the Saidenberg Gallery featured works from 1901 to 1924; the Marlborough Gallery had works dating from 1924 to 1971. On October 21, four days before Picasso's actual birthday, the Louvre in Paris opened an exhibition in honor of the artist in its main gallery, the first time such a presentation had been accorded to a living artist.

The 500th anniversary of the birth of Albrecht Dürer, the outstanding artist of Renaissance Germany, was also the occasion for several major exhibitions in 1971. The largest of these was the loan exhibition held at the German National Museum in Nuremberg, West Germany. Although some of the artist's most famous paintings were too delicate to transport, a representative selection of his work was assembled. Works by Dürer's contemporaries were also exhibited, thus putting him into the perspective of his own time. The show included prints and drawings as well as paintings. The National Gallery of Art in Washington, D.C., mounted an exhibition of prints and drawings by Dürer from North American collections. Almost every Dürer drawing in a North American collection was included. An exhibition of Dürer prints was shown at the Philadelphia Museum of Art in Philadelphia, Pa., early in the year, and in the fall, the Museum of Fine Arts in Boston, Mass., had a Dürer exhibition showing the differences in individual prints made from the same plate.

The Art Year in Europe

The many difficulties involved in organizing loan exhibitions were highlighted by the show "Art in Revolution" organized by the Arts Council of Great Britain and held at the Hayward Gallery in London in early 1971. The show was originally planned to chronicle avant-garde Russian art of the 1920's. The Soviet government promised to lend a large number of important items. However, when it was discovered that works by Eleazar Lissitzky and Kasimir Malevich from private sources in the West were to be included, Soviet officials threatened to withdraw the promised loan. The Ministry of Culture refused to participate in the show unless the work of these artists, which had met with official disapproval, was excluded. The paintings were removed, and this, of course, changed the character of the exhibition—at the last minute emphasis had to be shifted from painting to architecture and the theater. Part of the exhibit later traveled to New York City.

Later in the summer the Hayward Gallery was the scene of a retrospective exhibition devoted to the English op artist Bridget Riley. The exhibition included many of her most recent paintings in which she had begun to experiment with color. The retrospective was also seen in Hanover and Düsseldorf, West Germany; Berne, Switzerland; and Turin, Italy.

The Queen's Gallery at Buckingham Palace in London held an exhibition devoted to Dutch paintings in the British Royal Collection. Included were 6 Rembrandts and almost 100 other master-

The Whitney Museum held an exhibit, "Two Hundred Years of North American Indian Art," consisting of over 300 works of art from 57 Indian tribes. A mask (left) and a carved feast bowl (right) were among the pieces shown.

The lost original of Raphael's painting,
'Portrait of Lorenzo de Medici, Duke of Urbino',
painted in January 1518, was found and
positively identified.

pieces. The exhibition was confined to the 17th century, the golden age of Dutch painting.

In the spring London's Victoria and Albert Museum held an exhibition entitled "The Ceramic Art of China" to mark the 40th anniversary of the Oriental Ceramics Society. It was the first such large-scale show since 1935. The exhibition traced the development of Chinese ceramics through 3,000 years, from the unglazed earthenware of the Neolithic period to the sophisticated, elegant porcelain of the 18th century.

The Royal Academy in London featured the work of the Vienna Secession, an Austrian movement in architecture and the decorative arts roughly corresponding to Art Nouveau, in its winter exhibition for 1971. The Tate Gallery show "Léger and Purist Paris" was devoted to the work of a single decade, 1918 to 1928, in Paris. More than half the works were by the artist Fernand Léger, who celebrated the machine age in his mechanical-looking compositions of figures and objects. Other works included were by Picasso, Georges Braque, Juan Gris, and their contemporaries.

The Tate Gallery was also the scene of a very popular show of works by the American pop artist Andy Warhol. Confined to work done since 1961, the exhibition included his famous themes of soup cans and Brillo boxes. The show had been previously seen in Pasadena, Calif., and in Paris, and later went to the Whitney Museum of American Art in New York City.

As always, many provocative art exhibitions were held in Paris. The Musée des Arts Décoratifs held a show devoted to "20th Century Pioneers," covering the works of four great architects of the period: the Spaniard Antonio Gaudí, the Frenchman Hector Guimard, and the Belgians Victor Horta and Henry van de Velde. The show included sculptures, photographs, and audiovisual aids.

The first of a series of exhibitions, each to be devoted to a single famous work of art, was held at the Louvre. The subject was the painting 'The Turkish Bath', by J. A. D. Ingres. Intended to document the work as fully as possible, the show included preliminary studies, drawings, photographs, sources, and material showing the painting's influence on later works.

"A Thousand Years of Japanese Theater" was the title of an exhibition held in January at the Musée de l'Homme. Devoted to the evolution of the Japanese theater to the present day, it included prints, doll masks, and costumes.

The Armenian S.S.R. (one of the Soviet republics) lent an exhibition of Armenian art to the Musée des Arts Décoratifs. It included almost 500 objects—tools, pottery, jewels, ceramics, bronzes, and models of architecture—from the Paleolithic period to the present day. Armenian art formed a vital link between Asian and Western art. In return the French government lent an exhibition of 100 French impressionist masterpieces to the Soviet Union. The whole collection, which included important works by Édouard Manet, Claude Monet, Pierre Auguste Renoir, and Edgar Degas, was shown in Leningrad and in Moscow. Later in the summer the same canvases were lent to the Museum of the Prado in Madrid, Spain.

The Art Year in the U.S.

Again U.S. museums mounted a number of large and important exhibitions. "Zen Painting and Calligraphy" was one of the major exhibits displayed in Boston in late 1970 to celebrate the centennial year of Boston's Museum of Fine Arts. The largest show of Zen Buddhist painting and calligraphy ever assembled, it included more than 80 Chinese and Japanese paintings borrowed from temples, museums, and private collections in Japan. Two of the items in the exhibition were classified by the Japanese government as national treasures, and most of the works had never been seen outside of Japan.

Another major exhibition was "Four Americans in Paris: The Collections of Gertrude Stein and Her Family" at the Museum of Modern Art in New York City. The show later traveled to Baltimore, Md.; San Francisco, Calif.; and Ottawa, Ont. There were 224 paintings, drawings, prints, and sculptures, many of which had never before been seen in the U.S. Included were works by Henri Matisse, Picasso, and Gris. The major show in the fall of 1971 at the Modern was a retrospective of the work of the late U.S. artist Barnett Newman.

To mark the occasion of its 50th anniversary the Phillips Collection in Washington, D.C., mounted an exhibition of the works of Paul Cézanne, which was also seen in Chicago and in Boston. A fine group of paintings was borrowed to complement the Phillips' Cézanne collection.

The Baltimore Museum of Art celebrated the centennial of the birth of Matisse after the fact (he was born in 1869) with an important exhibition of his drawings from the museum's own superb collection. About one third had not been seen previously in the U.S. The exhibition later traveled to San Francisco and Chicago.

Another French painter, Francis Picabia, a pioneer of abstraction whose work was little known by the general public, was the subject of a show at the Solomon R. Guggenheim Museum in New York City in late 1970. It was the first American retrospective of Picabia's work. The Guggenheim mounted a major retrospective exhibition of the work of the Dutch painter Piet Mondrian in the fall of 1971.

The Whitney Museum organized the most important exhibition ever held of the work of the influential modern American artist Georgia O'Keeffe. The show consisted of over 110 paintings, water-colors, and drawings selected from some 50 years of her creative career. The show was seen in New York City in late 1970 and then moved on in 1971 to Chicago and San Francisco.

Another important show organized by the Whitney was the comprehensive exhibition of the work of the great American realist Thomas Eakins. It was the first major Eakins show in New York City in 53 years. In the fall of 1971 the Whitney opened a major exhibition of the work of the American realist Edward Hopper, selected from the collection the artist had bequeathed to the museum. Most of the works had not previously been reproduced or exhibited.

At the Philadelphia Museum of Art an exhibition devoted to multiple art pointed the way to future directions in collecting. A multiple was defined by the museum as "a work of art designed by the artist to be produced in sizable or even unlimited editions, hence aimed at the collector whose income is limited." The artist created a prototype that was then mass-produced in a factory. The show included work by Marcel Duchamp, Warhol, Claes Oldenburg, and Victor Vasarely. The catalog to the exhibition was itself designed as a piece of multiple sculpture.

The sculpture 'Split Ring', by Clement Meadmore, was one of many contemporary works exhibited in Van Saun Park, Paramus, N.J. The size of the exhibit, and the scale of the pieces, was remarkable. The sculptures, by 58 contemporary artists, were spaced over a half mile area.

"THE NEW YORK TIMES"

Art Sales

In general prices for works of art rose steeply in 1971 for only the rarest and finest specimens; mediocre examples generally fetched no more than they did two years before. Fine drawings and prints rose in price, but silver did not. New high prices were paid for modern American paintings and sculptures ($75,000 for a Roy Lichtenstein; $45,000 for an Oldenburg). In general the market in impressionist paintings was noticeably quieter than in recent years, but a painting by Henri Rousseau was sold for $775,000, the highest auction price ever paid for a 20th-century painting.

Perhaps the biggest event of the art sales year was the sale of Titian's 'The Death of Actaeon' to a London dealer for about $4 million. Shortly afterward, the painting was resold to the J. Paul Getty Museum in Malibu, Calif., but when the National Gallery in London announced its interest in acquiring the painting, the granting of an export license was delayed. Attempts to raise the money to keep the painting in Britain met with success.

Many of the possessions of the late Anna Thomson Dodge, widow of the U.S. automotive pioneer, were sold during the year. A highlight was the sale of a Louis XVI writing table that once belonged to Czarina Maria Fedorovna of Russia. It went for the highest price ever paid for a single piece of furniture, $415,800.

In May the Metropolitan Museum of Art in New York City revealed that it had been the purchaser of Diego Rodríguez de Silva y Velásquez's painting of his assistant Juan de Pareja, which had been sold for a record $5.5 million in November 1970. In October a portrait of Lorenzo de Medici was revealed to be an authentic Raphael. (*See also* Museums. *See in* CE: Painting; Sculpture.)

PAKISTAN.
The year 1971 opened in Pakistan under the shadow of the tragic cyclone and tidal wave disaster of November 1970. The enormous difficulties of restoring communications and aid to the stricken areas were gradually overcome by relief efforts of Pakistani authorities, with the aid of generous assistance from abroad. Further loss of life due to disease and starvation was averted, though the initial number of dead was estimated at about 300,000. A plan for the rehabilitation of distressed areas and for such protection against future disasters as could be devised was worked out with the support of the World Bank.

The cyclone, which had caused serious disruption of Pakistan's economy, had major repercussions on an already uneasy political situation. In the general elections in December 1970, the East Pakistan Awami League led by Sheikh Mujibur Rahman had won 167 of East Pakistan's 169 seats (out of a National Assembly total of 313), and 288 out of the 300 seats in the East Pakistan Provincial Assembly. Thus the league was in a very strong position to realize its six-point program for a reduc-

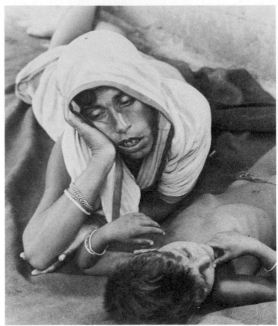

Only one among millions of Bengali refugees, this mother helplessly watches as her child dies in a refugee camp.

tion in centralized power and maximum regional autonomy for the East despite the fact that its support amounted to only 41% of the fully enfranchised adult electorate. Long-held grievances concerning West Pakistan's alleged exploitation of the more populous and, in earlier years, more productive East seemed at last on the point of rectification through political power.

On Feb. 13, 1971, Pakistan's President Agha Mohammed Yahya Khan announced that the National Assembly would meet on March 3. On February 15 former foreign minister Zulfikar Ali Bhutto, leader of the Pakistan People's party, the dominant party of West Pakistan, declared that he would boycott the National Assembly failing a prior agreement between East and West on a constitutional formula. In the East, propaganda against the central government was intensified. The civil authorities and defense forces were accused of treating the cyclone disaster with heartless indifference, of stealing relief supplies and embezzling overseas funds. As a result the political atmosphere in East Pakistan grew very tense.

It had been generally assumed that Sheikh Mujibur Rahman would become prime minister of Pakistan and would institute a constitution granting East Pakistan regional autonomy and control over its foreign trade, foreign exchange, and foreign aid. On March 1, President Yahya Khan postponed the National Assembly meeting to avoid a political confrontation between East and West. In response Sheikh Mujib called a general strike in East Pakistan. Violent clashes erupted between East Pakistanis and government forces, resulting in more than 150 deaths. Yahya Khan set a new opening date of March 25 for the Assembly and warned the sheikh that he would use the army to prevent the country's disintegration. In reply the sheikh demanded the immediate transfer of power to the elected representatives of the people, the withdrawal of martial law, the return of troops to their barracks, and an inquiry into alleged massacres.

By March 10 the populace in East Pakistan had accepted Awami League leadership as its government and was complying with the league's directives. On March 15, in a desperate effort to avert disaster, Yahya Khan arrived in Dacca, the East Pakistani capital, for new talks with Sheikh Mujib. He offered to set up a commission "to inquire into the circumstances which led to the calling out of the Army in aid of civil powers in East Pakistan." This the sheikh rejected. The National Assembly meeting was indefinitely postponed, and Yahya Khan returned to West Pakistan. On March 26 full-scale war erupted in the East, and a clandestine radio station announced the formation of the "sovereign independent people's republic of Bangla Desh" (Bengal Nation). Yahya Khan announced the outlawing of the Awami League, a total ban on political activity in both wings of the country, and complete press censorship. The Awami League was denounced as a treasonous movement aiming

for complete secession. The sheikh and many of those who were elected to represent the Awami League were arrested and charged with treason.

Thereafter the situation became extremely confused, with conflicting reports coming from the military authorities, the clandestine radio, and the foreign press. Communications were disrupted and food-deficit areas accustomed to receiving supplies from the outside faced starvation. There were reports from East Pakistan that the Pakistani army was slaughtering the civilian population in massive numbers. The Indian government announced that by April 21, a total of nearly 260,000 Hindu and Muslim refugees had fled across the border into India. By August 10 the number was put at 7.5 million, and by early December estimates were as high as 10 million. The Pakistani authorities stated that the maximum number was 4 million. Guerrilla activities by the East Pakistani "Liberation Army" erupted sporadically.

In August the central Pakistan government issued a White Paper asserting that the Awami League had planned an uprising for March 26, and thus attempted to justify Yahya Khan's ruthless suppression of the Bengali independence movement. However, the situation continued to worsen, with the brutal slaughter and persecution of the Bengalis by the Pakistani army only serving to arouse world sympathy for the Bengalis.

In April young Bengali students met secretly in East Pakistan to make crude grenades as the Pakistani crisis erupted into war.

UPI COMPIX

Broadly speaking, the Muslim world supported the view that the East Pakistan tragedy was a domestic matter. Of the superpowers, the People's Republic of China and the United States also took this view. The U.S. continued to supply arms and other military equipment to the Pakistani government until November. The Soviet Union, anxious for good relations with both Pakistan and India, tried to hold a balance; however, after signing a friendship treaty with India in early August, the U.S.S.R. increasingly took the side of India, particularly in its demand for the return of the refugees to East Pakistan.

By the fall tensions between Pakistan and India were continuing to mount as witnessed by the increasing number of border incidents. Finally, full-scale war broke out on December 3 with each side accusing the other of aggression. India invaded East Pakistan along with the Mukti Bahini, the Bengali guerrilla forces that India had trained and supplied with arms. Despite attempts by the United Nations to bring about a cease-fire, in two weeks' time India had achieved military superiority, surrounding the Pakistani army and securing its surrender as well as that of the Pakistani government in East Pakistan. In its place the new independent nation of Bangla Desh was proclaimed. In the face of the humiliating defeat, Pakistan's President Yahya Khan was forced to resign. Bhutto, the foreign minister and head of the People's party, became the new president. On December 20 Sheikh Mujib was released from jail but held under house arrest. Bhutto met with the sheikh in an attempt to work out some political arrangement in which East and West Pakistan would still be united, but without apparent success. (*See* India; United Nations. *See in* CE: Pakistan.)

Rebel soldiers of Bangla Desh, training to fight the West Pakistan Army, are met with friendly greetings from a villager.

CAMERA PRESS FROM PICTORIAL PARADE

PANAMA. In 1971 Panama's military government, dominated by Brig. Gen. Omar Torrijos, continued to rule with considerable support in spite of charges of oppression. To broaden the popular base of the government, two leftists who had been removed from the cabinet by Torrijos in 1970 were restored to important cabinet posts in April. A few weeks later President Demetrio Lakas indicated Panama's willingness to renew diplomatic relations with Cuba and other Communist countries.

In June representatives of Panama and the United States began a series of meetings to negotiate a new Panama Canal treaty to replace the 1903 treaty currently in effect; a draft treaty was rejected by Panama in 1970. Progress on the negotiations, reported in October, indicated that Panama sought and would obtain commercial concessions and increased legal jurisdiction within the canal zone, as well as cession of some canal zone territory—in return for U.S. rights to operate, defend, and improve the canal for a specific time period.

The Panamanian government announced in February that it would terminate the services of U.S. Peace Corps volunteers in May 1971. The U.S. personnel were to be replaced by Panamanians and international volunteers. (*See in* CE: Panama.)

PARAGUAY. In 1971 Paraguay's President Alfredo Stroessner, who first took office in 1954, continued to govern the country firmly with the backing of the Colorado party, the small business oligarchy, and the army. There were, however, further clashes between the government and the Roman Catholic church; they increasingly viewed each other as antagonists—the church charging the government with political, economic, and social injustices, the government charging the church with interference in political affairs.

General tension within the population continued to develop, mainly because of the low rate of increase in the gross national product. In the past, government policy was more concerned with basic infrastructure projects than with development and employment. However, late in 1970 Paraguay's first five-year development plan was published, calling for greater emphasis on increasing the rate of economic growth, with a planned annual growth rate of 6%.

The government's long-standing policy of maintaining price stability was not successful in 1971, and the government was obliged to grant a general 10% increase in minimum wages. The taxation of both personal and company income was finally introduced in March after Congress had exhibited one of its rare shows of resistance to President Stroessner's wishes, but the business oligarchy succeeded in postponing its implementation. (*See* in CE: Paraguay.)

PEOPLE OF THE YEAR. During 1971 the following people were brought before the public eye, some through laudable accomplishments, others through questionable ones. For other notable persons of 1971 see individual biographies by name.

F. Lee Bailey defended in court **United States Army Capt. Ernest L. Medina,** who was charged with bearing responsibility in the My Lai murders, and later acquitted. Bailey also survived unhurt a helicopter crash at Logan International Airport in Boston, Mass.

Romana A. Banuelos was nominated for the post of treasurer of the U.S. by U.S. President Richard M. Nixon. Shortly afterward, in a raid on a food company in Los Angeles owned by Mrs. Banuelos, 36 Mexican workers were arrested for illegal entry into the U.S. Mrs. Banuelos denied having knowledge that illegal aliens were in her employ. Her nomination was later confirmed.

The **Rev. Philip F. Berrigan** and five others were indicted on federal charges of plotting to kidnap President Nixon's national security adviser Henry A. Kissinger. The five were **Sister Elizabeth McAlister, the Rev. Joseph R. Wenderoth, the Rev. Neil R. McLaughlin, Anthony Scoblick,** and **Eqbal Ahmad.** Two others were added in a later indictment, **John Glick** and **Mary Scoblick,** the wife of Anthony Scoblick.

Derek Curtis Bok was elected president of Harvard University. Bok, who was dean of the Harvard Law School, succeeded Nathan M. Pusey.

Archie Bunker captured the hearts of millions of television viewers who watched All in the Family on Saturday evenings. Archie, portrayed as a lovable bigot by Carroll O'Connor, shared the spotlight with his wife Edith (Jean Stapleton), his daughter Gloria (Sally Struthers), and his son-in-law Mike (Rob Reiner).

A warrant was issued charging cartoonist **Al Capp,** of "Li'l Abner" fame, with a morals offense against a 20-year-old co-ed at Eau Claire State University in Wisconsin. Capp, who was on that campus for a lecture, denied the charges.

One of the more celebrated letters of the year was written by **U.S. Army Capt. Aubrey Daniel III,** the man who prosecuted First Lieut. William L. Calley, Jr. Daniel got Calley a life sentence, but when President Nixon intervened to lessen the punishment, Daniel wrote him a letter criticizing his action.

In embattled Northern Ireland, 19-year-old **Martha Doherty** had her head shaved and was tarred and feathered as punishment for dating a British soldier. The incident took place in Londonderry's Catholic Bogside district amid the taunts of 80 women who shouted, "Soldier lover! Soldier lover!" A few days later, inside the protection of Ebrington Barracks, Miss Doherty was married to her soldier sweetheart, Pvt. John Larter, 18.

A movie might have cost **Eddie (Popeye) Egan** his pension rights as well as his job on the New York City police force. Egan, a narcotics detective whose fast-moving career was portrayed in 'The French Connection', was instructed to turn in his badge and weapons less than 12 hours before his retirement from the force was to begin. The official reasons given for his dismissal included his not accounting for small amounts of heroin confiscated while on duty and his failure to turn up as a prosecution witness at certain trials. Egan himself blamed police department officials who he said were irritated at his becoming a celebrity.

A 106% pay raise was recommended by a British House of Commons committee for **Queen Elizabeth II.** If approved by Parliament, the queen's salary will reach $2.45 million per year. Prince Philip, Queen Mother Elizabeth, and Princess Margaret were also recommended for pay increases, designed to meet inflationary pressures.

Bandleader **Duke Ellington** made a highly successful five-week tour of the Soviet Union. When the U.S. Department of State heard that Ellington was losing weight, it ordered a dozen T-bone steaks flown immediately to Minsk, the tour's second stop. Ellington vigorously denied that he was wasting away on Russian cooking, claiming he had actually put on weight.

Daniel Ellsberg, a former employee of the think-tank Rand Corp., admitted "leaking" the Pentagon papers to the press. (*See* Law Special Report.) He was indicted by two federal grand juries in Los Angeles—once in June on two counts and then in December on 12 criminal charges, including conspiracy. Indicted on four counts, including conspiracy, was **Anthony J. Russo, Jr.,** a former colleague at the Rand Corp. Ellsberg defended the right of the American people to know about the workings of their government.

Americans **Richard Fecteau** and **Mary Ann Harbert** had good reason to celebrate in 1971. Both were released from captivity by the People's Republic of China. Fecteau spent 19 years in prison after being charged with spying during the Korean War; he was at that time a civilian employee of the U.S. Army. Miss Harbert and a male companion,

RUSSELL REIF FROM PICTORIAL PARADE

DENNIS BRACK FROM BLACK STAR

John Kerry (above), Rabbi Meir Kahane
(above, right), Ruby Keeler (right),
and Frank Sinatra (far right).

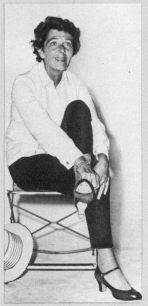

WIDE WORLD

CENTRAL PRESS FROM PICTORIAL PARADE

Gerald Ross McLaughlin, were arrested in 1968 when their yacht was stopped while sailing in Chinese waters north of Hong Kong. Peking officials said that McLaughlin took his life in 1969. The Chinese also announced that another prisoner, **John T. Downey,** was to have his life sentence commuted to five years. Downey was on the plane with Fecteau when it was shot down by the Chinese.

At the Vatican, **Sister Fiorella** was given a special assignment: let no women into St. Peter's Basilica wearing miniskirts, see-through blouses, or other clothes of a revealing nature. Sister Fiorella did a good job, turning away thousands of females considered immodestly clad. But the task became too demanding after a while and she was relieved of her post, suffering from nervous exhaustion.

Southern novelist **Jesse Hill Ford** came into prominence after his novel about racial injustice, 'The Liberation of Lord Byron Jones', was highly praised. His book made the point that whites in the South could get away with homicide provided their victims were black. The citizens of his hometown of Humboldt, Tenn., both white and black, did not care much for the novel and many grew to dislike the author, too. Then, ironically, Ford found himself in court in 1971 to answer a first-degree murder charge. His victim was a black soldier, Pvt. George Henry Doaks, Jr., who, according to the writer, was trespassing on his property, parked in a car on the driveway after dark. Ford, edgy from threatening telephone calls to his home and his family, fired two warning shots, hitting and killing Doaks. Ford was acquitted.

A former silversmith, **Jeanne M. Holm,** became the first woman to achieve the rank of general in the U.S. Air Force. At a Pentagon ceremony Brigadier General Holm received her silver star from Air Force Secretary Robert C. Seamans, Jr., and Lieut. Gen. Robert J. Dixon.

Billionaire recluse **Howard Hughes,** a hermit

Daniel Ellsberg (above, left),
Capt. Aubrey Daniel (center),
Martha Doherty (above), and
Lee Trevino (left).

with the resources of Midas, the influence of Mohammed, and the mystique of the abominable snowman, has been seen in recent years by only five male secretary-valets and has run his considerable empire from the ninth floor of the Desert Inn in Las Vegas, Nev. A mystery man with a vengeance, Hughes made headlines in 1971 because holes appeared in the heretofore impermeable curtain of corporate secrecy surrounding him. Rumors spread concerning heavy investment losses, where he was keeping himself, and even if he were still alive. On Thanksgiving Eve 1970, he had abruptly flown to a hideaway in the Bahamas under extraordinary secrecy. Hughes was reportedly still living in the Bahamas at the close of 1971. A New York City publisher was planning to bring out Hughes's autobiography in 1972.

Trunk murderess **Winnie Ruth Judd,** who in 1931 was convicted of killing one of two friends whose bodies were found stuffed in trunks, had her life sentence commuted by Arizona Gov. Jack Williams. Mrs. Judd, sentenced to hang for her crime, was spared when she was granted a sanity hearing just 72 hours before she was to die. She was expected to be paroled. Also freed from prison was **Edgar H. Smith,** who was released from Trenton State Prison in New Jersey after spending 14 years on death row. Smith was put on four years' probation. He was convicted in 1957 of murdering a teen-age girl.

After many turbulent months in which his militant campaign against the treatment of Jews in the Soviet Union brought him frequently into conflict with the law, **Rabbi Meir Kahane** moved his wife and children to Jerusalem in July and began to commute between Israel and the U.S. As head of the Jewish Defense League, which he organized in 1968, Kahane had been arrested repeatedly during the year and was under a suspended five-year sentence for conspiring to make a bomb.

Ruby Keeler returned to Broadway for the first time since 1929, when she appeared in 'Show Girl'. She was given the star role in 'No, No, Nanette' and received rave notices from the critics.

Antiwar activist **Jane Kennedy** was paroled from the Detroit House of Correction where she was sent after taking part in a raid on the Dow Chemical Co. plant in Midland, Mich. She was charged with helping to destroy computer tapes on defoliants.

The Vietnam Veterans Against the War came up with a persuasive and eloquent spokesman in **John Kerry,** 27, winner of a Silver Star, a Bronze Star Medal, and three Purple Hearts. A former U.S. Navy lieutenant junior grade, discharged in 1969, Kerry appeared before the Senate Foreign Relations Committee to plead the case against U.S. involvement in Vietnam.

Rumors persisted that Chinese defense minister **Lin Piao,** who disappeared from public view in 1971, had died aboard an airplane that crashed in the Wentenkhhan area of Mongolia. He had been considered the heir apparent to Communist Party Chairman Mao Tse-tung, but according to some sources he had dropped from Mao's good graces.

Great Britain's **Sir Laurence Olivier** became the first actor to be made a peer. Lord Olivier therefore became a member of the House of Lords.

Jacqueline Kennedy Onassis emphatically denied a published report that she had a marriage contract with her second husband that specified an outlay of $600,000 per year for her use, as well as separate bedrooms.

When columnist for *The New York Times* **James (Scotty) Reston** was felled by acute appendicitis in China, he underwent surgery in a Peking hospital. The operation was a success and the Chinese acupuncture technique, employed to fight postoperative pain, was termed effective.

After more than three decades in show business, singer-actor **Frank Sinatra** retired from public life at 55. He thought he might do some writing and perhaps teach, too.

Harvard University psychologist and social planner **B. F. Skinner** wrote a book 'Beyond Freedom and Dignity', which stirred great controversy. Skinner revealed that he had little faith in individual man, or in freedom of choice, thus bringing down on his head a storm of antagonism.

U.S. golfer **Lee Trevino** was, as usual, always willing to clown and trade quips with the fans. But in 1971 he moved up the ladder to become one of the best players in the game, winning the U.S., Canadian, and British open tournaments.

Twiggy, the much-publicized teen-age fashion model of the late 1960's, returned to the spotlight. She made her first movie, 'The Boy Friend'.

Captured by the Viet Cong and then reported as dead, **Catherine M. (Kate) Webb** nevertheless returned to tell all about it. The United Press International correspondent was released unharmed three weeks after being seized in Cambodia.

PERU. To mark Peru's 150th anniversary of independence from Spain, President Juan Velasco Alvarado on July 28, 1971, delivered an address in which he described his government's long-term social goals and ideology. Peru's three-year-old government has been called a blend of "capitalism and Communism," a cooperative society that evolved after a military coup seized the government in October 1968. President Velasco described his government's model as a "social democracy."

Two organizations were created in 1971 to further cooperative developments. The National System of Support for Social Mobilization was designed to assist in establishing cooperative enterprises in agriculture, fishing, mining, and other industries. The Corporación Financiera de Desarrollo (COFIDE) was set up to channel public and private investment into development.

In line with this plan, a mining law introduced on June 9 granted workers 10% of profits and participation in the management of mining companies. Also in June, the Peruvian government signed a 35-year contract authorizing the Occidental Petroleum Corp., a United States firm, to begin oil exploration. The contract assigned 50% of any oil produced to the state-owned Petroperú company. On September 20, the Tenneco Oil Co. and the Union Oil Co. of California signed a similar 30-year contract. Also in September, Peru and the Soviet Union signed an agreement for the construction of a $54 million fishing port at Paita.

In November Peru established diplomatic relations with the People's Republic of China. It became the third Latin American nation to do so. In December Peru also recognized Albania.

On November 10, the government placed all television and radio stations under state control, the most sweeping state intervention in broadcasting in Latin America outside Cuba. Under the law, employees of stations would receive one quarter of all profits each year. (*See in* CE: Peru.)

PHILIPPINES. President Ferdinand E. Marcos faced serious opposition in 1971 as political, economic, and social problems in the Philippines intensified. Much of the nation's wealth was concentrated in the hands of a very small percentage of the population, while the average per capita income was under $200 per year, with very high rates of inflation and unemployment. Maoist organizations such as the New People's Army and the Patriotic Youth gained increasing support from intellectuals and students.

In January a strike by bus drivers in Manila over gasoline price increases was supported by students and led to riots in which four were killed and many injured. In August a political rally of the opposition Liberal party was disrupted by a grenade attack in which 10 were killed and nearly 100 injured. President Marcos blamed the attack on Communists who were attempting to mount an insurrection, and he suspended all rights of habeas

A newsboy holds up a Manila newspaper announcing the suspension of the writ of habeas corpus in the Philippines in August.
WIDE WORLD

corpus for persons arrested for crimes of rebellion. Marcos accused Senator Benigno Aquino, a leader of the opposition party, of providing Communist subversives with guns and ammunition, but Aquino challenged him for proof. Senator José W. Diokno resigned from the president's Nationalist party over the suspension of habeas corpus and claimed that the military was responsible for the grenade attack. Habeas corpus was later restored in most provinces.

On Mindanao traditional hostility between Moslems and Christians flared again, particularly in Lanao and Cotabato provinces. An attack by armed Christians on a Moslem mosque left 61 persons dead.

Elections in November were the bloodiest in Filipino history as nearly 200 people were killed in political violence during the campaigning. The opposition party won six of eight contested Senate seats, and the new mayor of Manila was a staunch Marcos foe. (*See also* Anthropology. *See in* CE: Philippines, The.)

PHOTOGRAPHY. The greatest international exhibition of photographic equipment held during 1971 was Photo Expo 71 in Chicago, which attracted 79,500 visitors. A few novelties were shown, but most of the exhibits had already appeared at the 1970 Photokina in Cologne, West Germany.

Kodak introduced a new, fast Super 8 film, balanced for artificial light, that made it possible to take motion pictures at light levels as low as seven footcandles. Agfa introduced Agfacontbur, a film that produced a line along areas of strong tone change. Repeated copying onto this material could result in a picture with a multitude of lines, resembling an abstract painting. It could be used for pictorial effect, but its chief value lay in technical and scientific fields. It was for this that Agfa re-

ceived the international Interkamera Medal for technical progress.

At Photo Expo 71, Edith Weyde revealed a new developing process using silver halides. Minute quantities acted as an image-intensifying catalyst, thus providing a high emulsion speed with a low silver content. The economy achieved was obvious, especially in view of continually rising silver prices.

Following the introduction in 1970 of Kodak's Magicube, a flashcube fired mechanically instead of by electricity, many firms began making plans to manufacture cameras incorporating this system. This was especially true in Japan, where Minolta, Ricoh, Konishiroku, Fuji, and Sedic were all negotiating with Kodak. In the rush to Magicube, General Electric's Hi-Power Cube, a development of the battery-operated cube giving twice the normal amount of light, was receiving comparatively little attention, although the new 400 series of Polaroid cameras incorporated it. The Polaroid 400's used a flashgun with an unusual system of adjustable louvers in a shield that varied the amount of light reaching the lens according to the distance of the subject from the camera.

Nippon Kogako, in conjunction with the Japanese National Geography Department, produced a marine camera capable of working at a depth of 650 feet. The camera body was separate from the control unit and was housed in a pressure-resistant cover. The lens was designed to compensate for the difference in the way light refracts in water and in air.

Tungsten halogen lamps were introduced, especially for use in enlargers. In ordinary incandescent lamps, tungsten evaporates from the filament and is deposited on the glass, causing blackening. In the halogen lamps, the evaporated tungsten combines with iodine to form a compound that does not deposit on the glass but is decomposed by the filament; the tungsten is redeposited on the filament and the iodine is released for recycling. The constant light made these lamps particularly valuable for color printing.

West Germany and Japan continued to lead the world in the production of photographic equipment. Both reported good business in 1971. Japanese camera production rose 25.4% in value. (*See in* CE: Photography articles.)

PHOTOGRAPHY EXHIBITIONS.

In November 1971 the photography gallery Light opened on Madison Avenue in New York City, bidding for attention from fine arts lovers who frequented the area. The opening exhibition contained the work of 13 photographers, including the well-known Aaron Siskind and Harry Callahan.

The Latent Image gallery in Houston, Tex., celebrated its 1st anniversary during the year. Social commentary was the theme of an exhibit of the works of Lewis Hine, culled from the archives of the National Child Labor Committee. Latent

Image also mounted a show called "Seen in Passing: Photographs from Automobiles"—containing works by Garry Winogrand, Joel Meyerowitz, and Lee Friedlander, among others.

The Floating Foundation of Photography used a purple-and-white boat to bring photography exhibits to a number of boat landings in the New York City area. The aim of the foundation was to bring photography to those who could not attend conventional exhibits—particularly the very young and the very old, mental patients, and prisoners. (The foundation utilized lectures and workshops, in addition to its floating shows.) One show for 1971 was Lawrence Selzman's "Neighbors on the Block," a study of the aged on New York's West Side.

As usual, the Department of Photography of the Museum of Modern Art in New York City arranged a number of important photo exhibits. One such show featured the work of Walker Evans, known for his evocative photos of America in the 1930's. In the summer the museum mounted a retrospective of the work of Manuel Alvarez Bravo

'Warsaw' was one of the photographs in an exhibition of the work of Dr. Roman Vishniac. The show, which opened in October 1971, was held in the Jewish Museum in New York City.

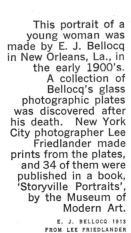

This portrait of a young woman was made by E. J. Bellocq in New Orleans, La., in the early 1900's. A collection of Bellocq's glass photographic plates was discovered after his death. New York City photographer Lee Friedlander made prints from the plates, and 34 of them were published in a book, 'Storyville Portraits', by the Museum of Modern Art.

E. J. BELLOCQ 1913
FROM LEE FRIEDLANDER

of Mexico; death was one of the persistent themes of the works on view.

The Museum of Modern Art also produced a show called "The Artist as Adversary"—with a total of over 400 works, 56 of them photographs and a number of others mixed-media collages employing photographs in part. The exhibit was designed to focus on the evils of war, racism, and poverty. Photographers on exhibit included Jacob Riis, Dorothea Lange, Robert Capa, David Douglas Duncan, Elliott Erwitt, and Jerry Uelsmann.

Also in New York City, the Museum of Contemporary Crafts produced a show called "Photo Media." Conventional photographic prints were included along with more unorthodox works, such as photographic jewelry, gum prints on cloth, and photo designs that were incorporated into the frame as well as the print.

About 500 works by W. Eugene Smith were displayed in a retrospective at the Jewish Museum in New York City. Many of his moving photographs of people gained widespread circulation in the pages of *Life* magazine. The Jewish Museum also mounted an exhibit of the work of Dr. Roman Vishniac, falling into two distinct categories—scientific photographs of enlarged microscopic phenomena on the one hand, and finely detailed portraits of East European Jews in the 1930's, on the other hand.

"Edward Weston: Nudes and Vegetables" was the provocative title of a show at Witkin Gallery in New York City. About 60 works by the French photographer Brassaï were displayed at the Robert Schoelkopf Gallery in New York City; Paris night life, street scenes, and portraits of other artists were included, covering the years 1932–58.

The photography world mourned the death of photo-journalist Margaret Bourke-White in August. She was 67. She had a long association with *Life*, which began when she snapped the cover photo for the first issue. Her World War II pictures received wide recognition, and she was thought to be the first woman to fly with a bombing mission in combat. (*See in* CE: Photography articles.)

PHYSICS. For nearly a century, physicists have been engaged in a search for truly elementary particles, the ultimate building blocks out of which all matter is constructed. By the early 1900's it had become clear that atoms were not the basic particles, and since that time physicists have recorded more than 200 particles that are more fundamental than the atom. These were called elementary, even though there were reasons to suspect that they, too, were not the basic constituents of matter.

The year 1971 saw a series of experiments that appeared to support this suspicion, at least as re-

The main accelerator of the National Accelerator Laboratory is four miles in circumference. The laboratory, located near Batavia, Ill., was opened in 1971.

gards one of the most important of the particles, the proton. The experiments showed that when a proton is bombarded by various other particles at high energy, the probability of producing new particles in the collision does not depend on the energy of the bombarding particle in a complicated way, as it does at low energies, but in a relatively simple way called scaling. This scaling relation was first reported in 1969 in experiments in which electrons were the bombarding particles. In 1971 results of experiments at Brookhaven National Laboratory, Upton, N.Y., and at the Stanford Linear Accelerator Center, Stanford, Calif., indicated scaling is also exhibited when the bombarding particles are pi mesons or gamma rays.

One possible explanation of scaling is that the protons are made of distinguishable subparticles, which experimenters named partons, and that the incoming particles bounce off a parton rather than the whole proton. Experiments continued during the year at the Stanford Linear Accelerator Center in an attempt to find out more details about the possible existence of partons and to determine precisely the role they might play in such collisions.

Nuclear physicists in 1971 took several steps toward the use of beams of accelerated heavy ions in experimental work. Elements heavier than helium form heavy ions when most or all of their electrons are stripped from the atom, leaving an essentially bare nucleus. For years physicists had probed the structure of atomic nuclei by striking them with single particles such as neutrons, protons, and electrons. But by using nuclei to strike

other nuclei the physicists hoped to be able to study complexities of nuclear structure that could not be reached by single-particle probes. This process might enable them to manufacture superheavy elements—those with atomic numbers of 114 or higher. Beams of accelerated nuclei also permit striking a nucleus against a stationary proton; physicists hoped that this might elucidate properties of the undisturbed nucleus that are altered beyond recognition when a nucleus is the target and a high-energy proton is the probe.

In various parts of the world, physicists were building special machines to accelerate atomic nuclei. Others sought to adapt existing proton accelerators to handle heavy nuclei as well. An important achievement of that kind was attained in August by the Bevatron accelerator at the Lawrence Radiation Laboratory in Berkeley, Calif.

Plasma physicists continued their efforts to achieve controlled thermonuclear fusion through new devices that could confine a dense enough and hot enough plasma of ions and electrons long enough for a significant number of nuclear fusions to take place. At the Los Alamos Scientific Laboratory, Los Alamos, N.M., the first section of the Scyllac plasma machine was completed and tested. The completed Scyllac was to be a doughnut-shaped ring 15 meters in circumference. It would heat plasma by a magnetic implosion called a theta pinch. This method will permit it to work with denser plasmas than a "tokamak" (a Soviet fusion reaction machine) can now use. (*See in* CE: Physics.)

POLAND. Throughout 1971 Edward Gierek, first secretary of the Polish Communist party, consolidated his position both within the party and the country as a whole. Former party leader Wladyslaw Gomulka, who was replaced by Gierek following riots over economic policies in December 1970, was gradually removed from other positions. In February he was suspended from the party's Central Committee, its highest body, and in May he resigned his seat in the Council of State, the country's nominal ruling body. Although he retained his seat in parliament, he was reported to be seriously ill. Gierek's chief rival for the party leadership, Mieczyslaw Moczar, was relieved of his key position in the Secretariat of the party's Central Committee after being appointed chairman of the Supreme Control Chamber, a considerably less influential position. In December the party's sixth congress was held in Warsaw, the capital. A new Central Committee of 115 members was elected, and it appointed a new Politburo. Only 3 of the new Politburo's 11 members had taken their seats before December 1970. Moczar and Jozef Cyrankiewicz, the former premier, were both dropped as Gierek emerged in a much stronger position.

Gierek instituted a series of moderate reforms to help ease the economic tensions that had led to the 1970 riots and to strikes during the early part of 1971. In June a new five-year economic plan was instituted, providing for a shift from emphasis on investment in heavy industries to emphasis on production of consumer goods. Premier Piotr Jaroszewicz, speaking at a session of the Central Committee, outlined planned increases in investment in light industry and consumer goods, food and animal production, and increases in imported consumer items. The new plan promised special emphasis on housing; a 25% increase was envisioned. Polish families in recent years have had to wait as long as five years for apartments. Smaller increases were planned for heavy industries.

Relations between the state and Poland's influential Roman Catholic church came closer to normalizing as Premier Jaroszewicz talked in March with Stefan Cardinal Wyszynski, primate of Poland. In October Aleksander Skarzynski, director of the Office for Religious Affairs, met with Pope Paul VI at the Vatican. (*See in* CE: Poland)

POLICE. Violent attacks on police officers continued to present a major problem in the United States in 1971. In Dallas, Tex., on February 15, five sheriff's deputies were taken captive during a routine burglary investigation. They were driven to a swampy area where three officers—Samuel Garcia Infante, 32; William Don Reese, 31; and A. J. Robertson, 55—were shot and killed in execution style. A fourth officer was wounded and a fifth escaped a barrage of bullets by jumping down an embankment to safety.

Two Riverside, Calif., policemen were ambushed and slain by shotgun blasts on April 2 when they responded to a burglary report that turned out to be false.

In Philadelphia, Pa., patrolman John McEntee, 25, was shot to death on February 21. McEntee, a member of the force for two years, was found slumped over the steering wheel of his patrol car in a ghetto area. On the next day Joseph Kelly, 45, a veteran of 16 years on the force, was found shot to death inside his patrol car about ten miles from the earlier slaying.

In Baltimore, Md., on January 14, a criminal-court jury convicted Black Panther party member Marshall E. Conway of first-degree murder in the ambush slaying of city patrolman Donald Sager. The jury also found Conway guilty of the near-fatal shooting of a second policeman and of wounding a third policeman, who had chased him after the first two shootings.

On June 5 four heavily armed men were arrested during a holdup of a black social club at 3802 Park Avenue in the Bronx section of New York City. Two of the men arrested were Richard Moore and Edward Josephs, who were among the 22 original defendants in the 1970–71 Black Panther conspiracy case. The district attorney's office announced that the .45-caliber machine gun used by Moore and Josephs in the Bronx holdup had been

Sister Cornelia (called Sister Fuzz) joined the Pontoon Beach, Ill., police force to help with local drug problems.

Patrolman William Phillips of New York City testified before the Knapp Commission in October. He said that every plainclothes policeman in New York City was involved in graft.

identified as the gun used in the shooting of two policemen on May 19.

It has been a rather common occurrence for police officers to be attacked by onlookers during confrontations with suspects. However, in New York City on June 20, in an area where many Greeks and Italians reside, an angry crowd attacked two men after one had shot a police officer. The shooting occurred when the suspects had been stopped for a traffic violation near 31st Avenue and Broadway in Queens. A crowd gathered and shouted, "A cop has been shot . . . Let's get them." Several punches had been thrown before other policemen arrived and prevented the crowd from further venting its anger on the suspects, who were arrested and charged with attempted murder, robbery, and felonious assault. The wounded officer, William Beschel, 22, was shot in the left ankle and back and was hospitalized. At the time of the incident seven New York City policemen had been killed in the line of duty in 1971.

On July 1, the Commission to Investigate Alleged Police Corruption in New York City, headed by Whitman Knapp, a Wall Street lawyer, made public an interim report on its 11-month inquiry. The Knapp Commission report revealed widespread corruption in the New York City Police Department—corruption that extended beyond narcotics, gambling, and prostitution to many other areas of the city's life. The Knapp Commission was created by Mayor John V. Lindsay in May 1970, following public charges of widespread police corruption and allegations that high officials in the Lindsay administration had not acted when informed of specific acts of venality. At a news conference

on July 1, 1971, Knapp stated that the mayor, "as chief executive officer of this city, cannot escape responsibility for a situation that develops in a department as important as the police department." He also asserted that the former police commissioner, Howard R. Leary, "has a lot to answer for for failing to provide leadership in this field."

In April 1971 three former New York City policemen had told the New York State Commission of Investigation about their involvement in heroin traffic. The commission had charged that corruption was one reason why enforcement of heroin laws in New York City had been a failure. Two of the police department's top corruption investigators, Supervising Assistant Chief Inspector Joseph McGovern and Inspector Donald F. Cawley, stated that in recent years corruption in narcotics enforcement had been the largest single graft problem within the department.

Early in 1971 the Knapp Commission issued subpoenas to 21 policemen in the investigation of a $25,000 burglary of meat in January from the Great Plains Packing Co., Inc., of New York City. An anonymous informant reported that he had seen uniformed policemen loading the stolen meat into radio patrol cars. The owner of the burglarized company, James E. Reardon, was a former New York City policeman who had been associated with Harry Gross in a $20-million-a-year bookmaking scandal in the 1950's. Reardon, who resigned from the force in 1947, was convicted of perjury in 1952 for lying to a Brooklyn grand jury that was investigating Gross and his alleged bribe payments of $1 million a year for police protection. (*See also* Crime. *See in* CE: Police.)

POLITICAL PARTIES. For the first time, citizens between the ages of 18 and 20 will be able to vote in a United States presidential election in 1972. The 26th Amendment to the U.S. Constitution became effective after the Ohio state legislature became the 38th to vote ratification on June 30, 1971. The amendment was ratified three months after its passage by the U.S. Congress. U.S. President Richard M. Nixon immediately hailed enfranchisement of the young voters. "Some 11 million young men and women who have participated in the life of our nation through their work, their studies, and their sacrifices for its defense are now to be fully included in the electoral process of our country," he said. "I urge them to honor this right by exercising it."

In addition to these 11 million, the U.S. Census Bureau estimated that 14 million people between the ages of 21 and 25 will be eligible to vote in a presidential election for the first time in 1972. Polls suggested that the ratio of Democrats to Republicans was somewhat larger in this huge bloc than in the general population, but great numbers classified themselves as independents.

Opinions varied widely on how many young people would vote. Traditionally young persons are less likely to register and vote than their elders. Labor unions, civic groups, and liberal organizations launched intensive voter registration campaigns.

An almost equally important question was where students would vote. Some guidelines on voter eligibility were established in the 1970 federal Voting Rights Act, but registration was governed by a maze of state and local regulations. These could exclude an estimated 2 million student voters because of residency requirements. Many students argued that if they could not vote where they attend college, they could not vote at all. As the presidential campaign approached, court decisions had given students the right to vote in many, but not all, campus towns.

Republican Party

President Nixon was almost certain to be the 1972 presidential nominee of the Republican party. The party selected Senator Robert J. Dole of

Three potential Democratic candidates for president met at a dinner sponsored by the Liberal party of New York (left); they were Senator Edmund Muskie (left), Senator George McGovern (second from right), and New York City's Mayor John V. Lindsay (right). They are shaking hands with Alex Rose, Liberal party chairman. Another person often mentioned as a potential candidate was Senator Edward M. Kennedy (above); however, he stated on a number of occasions that he would not run.

ABOVE AND LEFT: WIDE WORLD

Kansas at the beginning of 1971 as chairman of the Republican National Committee. He succeeded Rep. Rogers C. B. Morton (R, Md.) who was named secretary of the interior. Dole told the committee he would begin work immediately on the reelection of President Nixon. He also termed Vice-President Spiro T. Agnew the best available running mate for the president in 1972. The Republican National Committee selected San Diego, Calif., just 55 miles from the president's western residence in San Clemente, Calif., as the site for the party's 1972 convention August 21–24.

President Nixon stated his campaign theme early in 1971 when he told a Republican fund-raising dinner that the issue would be achievement of "minimum goals—peace and prosperity without war." The president was expected to avoid having his name entered in primary elections wherever possible. In some instances it was expected that stand-in candidates pledged to support the president might be nominated. First to announce such an effort was Senator Robert Taft, Jr., of Ohio.

One opponent for the Republican nomination emerged in early, preconvention campaigning. Rep. Paul N. McCloskey, Jr., of California announced he intended to enter primaries in at least two states: New Hampshire and California. He said he would seek delegates pledged to his nomination on a platform of ending the war in Vietnam on the sole condition of the release of prisoners of war. He also promised "to restore truth in government, to achieve a return to the historical Republican moral commitment on social issues rather than the present 'Southern strategy', and restoration of judicial excellence and independence."

Democratic Party

The Democratic National Committee voted to hold the party's presidential nominating convention in Miami Beach, Fla., the week of July 9. It was the second time since the Civil War that the Democrats chose to meet in a state of the old Confederacy. The other occasion was in 1928, in Houston, Tex.

A wide-open field of contenders for the Democratic presidential nomination emerged by the beginning of 1972. Among the avowed or prominently mentioned candidates were: Senator Edmund S. Muskie of Maine, vice-presidential candidate in 1968 and leader in many preference polls; Senator Hubert H. Humphrey of Minnesota, the Democratic presidential candidate in 1968; Senator George S. McGovern of South Dakota, an outspoken liberal who has made a last-minute bid for the presidential nomination in 1968; Mayor John V. Lindsay of New York City, a former liberal Republican who switched his allegiance to the Democratic party in 1971; Senator Henry M. Jackson of Washington, who assailed what he termed the Democratic left, insisted on law and order as a significant issue, and urged support for a negotiated settlement rather than an unconditional with-

WIDE WORLD

U.S. Rep. Paul N. McCloskey, Jr. (R, Calif.), said that he would challenge President Richard M. Nixon for the Republican presidential nomination in 1972 if the Indochina war were not wound down substantially.

drawal from Vietnam; Rep. Wilbur D. Mills of Arkansas, chairman of the tax-writing House Ways and Means Committee, generally viewed as a conservative; Rep. Shirley Chisholm of New York, the first black woman to seek the presidency; Senator Edward M. Kennedy of Massachusetts, who repeatedly stated that he would not be a candidate, but whose name recurred just as frequently; and former Minnesota senator Eugene McCarthy, who mounted the principal challenge to the nomination of Senator Humphrey in 1968. McCarthy indicated he was interested in an effort to gain the Democratic nomination. He also indicated that he thought a third party should be formed if necessary to get an antiwar candidate into the 1972 presidential race.

Gov. George C. Wallace of Alabama, who took office in January 1971, indicated in late summer he would again seek the presidency, as he did in 1968. He expressed interest in entering presidential primaries in North Carolina, Tennessee, and Florida. Thus a three- or four-party presidential contest in 1972 appeared a distinct possibility, with threats of splinter parties from both the Democratic left and right.

Party Reform

Both parties acted to make their 1972 conventions more representative of the voting public. A Republican committee on delegates and organization drafted recommendations that urged states to seek equal representation of men and women in their delegations and to see that voters under 25 are represented "in numerical equity to their voting strength within the state." It also began work on a recommendation for black delegates. The reform proposals were requests to the state organizations rather than mandatory rules.

Two Democratic committees, set up after the storm of the 1968 convention, completed their work, and their major recommendations were approved by the Democratic National Committee. Among the proposed rules for the convention were the abolition of the unit rule that allows an entire delegation's vote to be cast as a bloc by the state chairman, the opening of delegate selection to broader participation by blacks, women, and young voters, and the requirement that no delegates be selected before 1972. According to rules adopted for conduct of the convention, floor demonstrations would be banned, nominating and seconding speeches would be limited to 15 minutes and three speakers, favorite-son candidates would be banned unless sponsors could produce a nominating petition guaranteeing at least 50 votes (not more than 20 from any one state), and the delegates' position on the convention floor and on roll calls would be decided by lot. A battle developed over selection of a temporary chairman for the credentials committee, which will determine the issues on which challenges to any delegation will be decided. Mrs. Patricia Harris, a black lawyer and former ambassador to Luxembourg, was chosen over Senator Harold Hughes of Iowa, who had the backing of militant party reformers.

Finances

Planning for the campaign was clouded by the state of party finances. The Democratic party was about $9.3 million in debt at the beginning of 1971; most of this deficit was a holdover from the 1968 presidential campaign. The Republican party, on the other hand, was solvent as the year opened.

The difficulties of campaign financing led to a tax-law change that could revolutionize political fund raising. Congress authorized each taxpayer to allot $1 of his income tax to the party of his choice, to be used to finance presidential campaigns. President Nixon let it be known through legislative and administrative aides that he was bitterly opposed to the plan. To avoid a threatened veto, Congress made the provision effective with tax returns filed in 1973, rather than in 1972.

Elections

Off-year elections in 1971 provided only scant evidence of voters' probable performance in 1972. Two 19-year-old mayors were elected in November —Ron Hooker, a write-in candidate, in Newcomerstown, Ohio, and Jody Smith in Ayrshire, Iowa. Indiana University student support appeared to be decisive in electing a recent law school graduate, Francis X. McCloskey, 32, as mayor of Bloomington, Ind. Three self-proclaimed radicals gained election to the Berkeley, Calif., city council in April; and a bloc of four students was chosen to serve on the Madison, Wis., city council. In both cases, university student votes were important factors.

In Kentucky, Democrat Wendell Ford was elected governor, returning his party to control of a statehouse they normally held until the election of a Republican in 1967. Democrat William Waller, a white moderate, defeated Charles Evers, black mayor of Fayette, for the governorship of Mississippi. Evers polled a surprisingly light 21% of the vote, although about 30% of Mississippi's registered voters are black.

A black candidate for mayor of Cleveland, Ohio, Arnold R. Pinkney, ran second in a three-way race won by Republican Ralph J. Perk, who concentrated his campaign in white enclaves of the city.

Carl Stokes, mayor of Cleveland, Ohio, until November 1971, proposed a "black political strategy for 1972." He said that this strategy might include running a black candidate for president.

UPI COMPIX

The Republicans also won easily in Indianapolis, Ind., where Richard Lugar was elected to a second term.

In Gary, Ind., black Mayor Richard G. Hatcher easily won a second term; the community has been under Democratic control since 1938. Other black mayors were elected in Englewood, N.J.; Kalamazoo, Mich.; Berkeley, Calif.; East St. Louis, Ill.; and Benton Harbor, Mich.

Like the evidence of black political power, the evidence on effectiveness of law and order campaigns was inconclusive. Democrat Frank L. Rizzo, a former police commissioner, was elected mayor of Philadelphia, Pa., despite fear of many blacks that his law and order campaign might mask racist attitudes. Mayor Richard J. Daley of Chicago was elected to a fifth term. In Boston, Mass., Mayor Kevin H. White defeated Rep. Louise Day Hicks, who ran on a law and order campaign, by a wide margin. Both were Democrats.

POPULATION.

The United States Census Bureau continued to analyze the results of the 1970 census during 1971. The resident population on April 1, 1970, was 203,184,772, an increase of 13.3% over the 1960 census total of 179,323,175. Two major patterns of population movement—each an extension of an historic trend—are discernible in the 1970 totals. Americans continued to move out of predominantly rural counties and into urban areas; and more than 75% of the decade's population growth occurred in the 243 Standard Metropolitan Statistical Areas, with the bulk of that gain taking place in the suburban areas around these centers. The official center of population of the U.S. moved further west, to a point in a farmer's field about five miles southeast of Mascoutah, Ill.

The black population of the U.S. increased 20% over that of 1960. There were 22.6 million blacks in the U.S. in 1970; they made up 11.1% of the total population. Blacks continued to migrate to metropolitan areas, with one third of the total black population residing in 15 cities, although about 53% still lived in the South. The black population in suburban areas rose 42%, but black suburbanites made up only about 4% of the black population.

The second-largest minority group, persons of Spanish-speaking origin, comprised 9.2 million people, about 5% of the total population. The count of American Indians in the census was 792,730, with more than half in five states. Oklahoma, with 98,468, had the largest Indian population, followed by Arizona, 95,812; California, 91,108; New Mexico, 72,788; and North Carolina, 44,406.

The proportion of the population 65 years of age and older increased from 16.6 million (9.2%) in 1960 to 20 million (9.9%) in 1970. Florida contained the highest percentage of the elderly (14.5) of any state.

The 1970 census also showed that the number of housing units increased at a faster rate than the population. Total housing units increased 17.4%, from 58.3 million in 1960 to 68.7 million in 1970. Another indication of the trend toward suburban living was the sharp difference between the growth rate of housing for central cities of metropolitan areas and for their suburban fringes. Since 1960 the gain in the suburbs totaled 5.5 million units (a 31% increase), in contrast to a 10% gain in the central cities and a 14% gain outside of metropolitan areas.

Fewer housing units were overcrowded in 1970, census information indicated. The number of units with more than one person per room declined from 6.1 million in 1960 to 5.2 million in 1970. The data also showed a big drop in the number of units lacking basic plumbing—only 6.9% in 1970, as compared with 16.8% in 1960.

The Census Bureau calculated a number of social midpoints which can be used to compare the average family of 1970 with that of 1950. The average family was more likely to have two children than three, and the children were likely to be older—about 17 and 19. The father was likely to be about 45 and the mother almost 42, each about a year older than in 1950. Median family income was $9,870 as compared with $3,300 in 1950. However, the current figure converted into equivalent 1950 dollars would be $6,100. This gain in income occurred because more wives were working and husbands' earning power had increased. Both parents were likely to have finished high school, a considerable advance over 1950, when the average was nine years of schooling.

But members of minority groups were not as well off as the rest of the nation. Blacks and Spanish-speaking Americans on the whole had considerably fewer years of schooling than the average for the whole population—little more than a grade school education. They were also younger: the median age for the whole population was 28; for blacks, 21.2; and for Spanish-speaking people, 20. Members of minority groups were far less likely to be white-collar workers or to earn $10,000 or more per year. Census officials were concerned that, in spite of special efforts, the census count of the nation's black population was probably less complete than that of the white population.

A national coalition was formed in August to lobby for a national policy of stabilizing population growth. Cochairmen Milton S. Eisenhower and former Senator Joseph D. Tydings announced three objectives of the coalition: legislation declaring the official national policy of the U.S. to be one of stabilizing the population through voluntary means; funding the full amount authorized by the Family Planning Services and Population Research Act of 1970 for birth control services and research in order to develop a safe, totally effective contraceptive for both men and women; and the implementation of federal population education programs. (*See in* CE: Census; Population.)

Population

Special Report:
American Attitudes Toward Population Growth

by John D. Rockefeller III

There is a good chance that several trends may soon bring the birthrate of the United States down to a level eventually consistent with a zero rate of population growth. I believe that we ought to take steps to encourage this development. It is not inevitable, and if it comes it may not last—many concepts in our society stand in its way.

The dominant ethic of the nation involves expansion, conquest, progress, accumulation, innovation, and untrammeled growth—not growth of human numbers alone, but growth in every material aspect of our existence. We have evolved sets of institutions, laws, political ideologies, and social norms that take this perpetual growth as their unexamined, primary axiom.

Industrial man has too often acted as if seized by a demon directing him to plunder the earth in a quest to increase his satisfactions, but all the while denying himself any true enjoyment for fear that the rate of increase may diminish tomorrow. At the root of the explosion of numbers, the despoliation of the environment, the threat of military catastrophe, the breakdown of our sense of community and belonging is the extraordinary increase in man's power to manipulate the external, material world.

We have characteristically reacted to the growth of technology as though it were a free gift of the gods, to be employed according to the whim and fancy of the instant, without regard to consequences. Much that we have done with technology—to improve health, lengthen life, spread knowledge, and increase the security of daily existence—can be applauded. But we have failed to see that with the new "goods" we have acquired hosts of new "bads" and, more important, that in accepting new powers we must accept new responsibilities.

It is not easy to question the assumptions on which we have built our lives—particularly if those assumptions seem so natural that we are hardly aware of them. However, we have learned of late to beware of things we have formerly taken for granted—for example, the air that we breathe. Now thoughtful persons are raising questions about our way of life that did not come to mind a few decades ago. One of those questions is the desirability of continuing population growth.

Many people believe that the world already faces a scarcity of vital natural resources. As our numbers increase, so do our demands upon those resources. We will not survive as a society in the long run without resolving the issue of balance between numbers and the life-support system of our finite planet. It also appears that we will not survive the stresses that our ethic of perpetual expansion puts on the social fabric, as well as on the external environment. Those institutions that weave our social fabric—health, legal, educational, and welfare systems, for instance—clearly have to find new ways of meeting society's needs. But I strongly believe that the resistance to change within most of our people-serving institutions is partly traceable to our demand that they create new ways to serve us even as they must serve ever increasing numbers of people. My point is quite simple. What I am trying to convey here is the warning that in many parts of the world potential gains in the quality of life will be offset in meeting the basic needs of ever increasing numbers of people.

However desirable it may be to stop—or slow—our growth, let me refer to the many basic features of our society that stand in the way of reaching, and maintaining, a rate of simple population replacement.

1. As a nation we have an ideological addiction to growth, for reasons that, as I suggested earlier, no longer apply.

"They've come up with a cause that George finds irresistible."

NORRIS FROM "VANCOUVER SUN," CANADA

2. Our social institutions, including many of our laws, are basically pro-natalist in outlook. These include the images of family life and women's roles projected in television programs; the child-saves-marriage theme that permeates women's magazines; the legal restrictions on contraception, sex education, and abortion; tax disabilities that are imposed on single people and working wives; and many others.

3. The Commission on Population Growth and the American Future found a totally unsatisfactory level of understanding of the role of sex in human life and considerable misunderstanding of the reproductive process and its control.

4. The population issue has taken on racial overtones. We must recognize the failure of our society to bring racial minorities and the poor into the mainstream of American life, where they would have developed a stake in slower population growth. Statistics prove that the white middle-class majority bears the primary responsibility for population growth, contrary to much popular opinion.

5. If it should happen that in the next few years the birthrate falls to replacement levels or below, we are likely to observe a strong counterreaction. In the U.S. in the 1930's, and in several foreign countries, the response to this development has been a cry of anxiety over the national virility, spirit, and health.

In spite of the above "pro-growth" factors, I believe our current population cannot grow forever. Any growth rate, even our current rate of 1% per year, would lead to physical absurdity if continued indefinitely. Simple arithmetic shows that continuation of current U.S. population growth rates for 1,300 years would result in one American per square foot of the entire land area of the country. Obviously we will stop short of this. Where? One American per square yard? If that is too many people, where short of that will we stop? It is clear that we *shall* stop, and the question is how and when we choose to do it.

I am not trying to suggest that our population is going to stop growing immediately. Our past high birthrates produced a record 31 million babies in the 1950's, who are beginning now to enter their child-bearing years. The baby boom that produced them is bound to echo in rising numbers of births in this decade and beyond. What I do want to urge is that we move toward reproductive habits that are ultimately consistent with a balance of births and deaths.

Concern over the effects of population growth has been mounting. Two thirds of the people interviewed in a 1971 survey by the Commission on Population Growth and the American Future felt that U.S. population growth is a serious problem. Half or more expressed concern over the impact of population growth on the use of natural resources, on air and water pollution, and on social unrest and dissatisfaction.

PORTUGAL. In 1971, after more than two years in office, Portugal's Premier Marcello José das Neves Alves Caetano firmly established himself as undisputed national leader. While some measures toward liberalization of his regime were taken, Caetano continued to deal harshly with dissent both in Portugal and in the African colonies of Angola, Mozambique, and Portuguese Guinea, where guerrillas had been fighting for independence for several years.

In July the National Assembly approved constitutional reforms granting the overseas colonies greater autonomy in administrative and financial matters. Further constitutional reforms were passed later abolishing press censorship and granting freedom of religion. However, press censorship could be reinstated in certain states of emergency, such as the imposition of martial law.

The activities of urban guerrilla groups caused increasing concern. A bomb detonated on the eve of an important North Atlantic Treaty Organization (NATO) meeting in June disrupted communications in Lisbon, the capital. Government security forces launched a determined drive to eradicate the responsible groups, and 31 persons accused of membership in such groups were brought to trial in October.

Hundreds of persons were killed during the year in Angola, as the war for independence there entered its 11th year. The White Fathers, an order of Roman Catholic priests, were ordered to leave Mozambique after two members had been expelled for supporting Frelimo, the Mozambique Liberation Front. Two other priests were brought to

Black African rebels continued their struggle to wrest control of Mozambique from Portugal.

Involved in a colonial war, a force of black rebel guerrillas was fighting the Portuguese for control of Portuguese Guinea.
"THE NEW YORK TIMES"

trial in Portugal for expressing support for the independence of African colonies. In February the Rev. Mario Pais de Oliveira was acquitted of charges of subversive activities. The Rev. Joaquim Pinto de Andrade, who had spent the last ten years in prison or under restricted residence for his support of Angolan rebels, was sentenced to three years in prison for his rebel sympathies.

Just prior to a meeting between Premier Caetano and United States President Richard M. Nixon in mid-December in the Azores, the U.S. announced that an agreement had been reached with Portugal whereby the U.S. would provide up to $436 million in aid in exchange for retention of its military base in the Azores until 1974. (*See also* Africa; *See in* CE: Portugal.)

POSTAL SERVICE. Major changes in the United States postal system were launched in 1971, as the semi-independent U.S. Postal Service (USPS) took over direct responsibilities for operation from the old Post Office Department on July 1. Postmaster General Winton M. Blount, who had been appointed in 1968, served as the chief executive officer of the USPS until he resigned in October. On December 7 Elmer T. Klassen was named his successor.

While the changeover was designed to end the historic political importance of the post office as a source of patronage jobs, it also represented a major effort to place the agency on a sound economic basis, utilizing modern technology and marketing techniques to improve deteriorating services. The key features of the new system included authority for the USPS to engage in direct collective bargaining with labor unions on wages, hours, working conditions, and other matters; to set its own budget; and to develop rate schedules on a businesslike basis. An independent Postal Rate Commission was also created.

The U.S. Congress relinquished its authority over postal rates and employee wages in July, when the USPS became an independent establishment within the executive branch of the federal government. The USPS is directed by an 11-member board of governors; nine members are appointed by the president with the approval of the Senate. These nine are empowered to select the chief executive officer who, along with his deputy, completes the board's membership.

The USPS assumed its responsibilities amid labor troubles, court challenges, squabbles over proposed rate increases, and charges that the USPS was even more inefficient than the old Post Office Department. However, by the end of 1971 a number of precedents had been set, including the signing of the first collective-bargaining agreement in postal service history. The two-year contract between the USPS and seven major unions representing 650,000 of the system's 750,000 employees called for raises totaling $1 billion, and guaranteed that no employee would be laid off because of technological changes during the life of the pact. The contract also permitted the USPS to begin implementing plans to increase the introduction and use of automated classifying and sorting equipment to speed up the processing of mail. The USPS encountered a different type of labor problem when officials of the predominantly black National Alliance of Postal and Federal Employees accused the service of discriminatory practices—locating the new automated processing facilities in suburban areas that offered little or no low-income housing, and bypassing blacks in promotions.

The mail service also met court challenges over efforts to raise postage rates in order to cut deficits that had reached $2.6 billion by June 30, 1971. The increases, which were effective May 16, were expected to produce an additional $1.45 billion by the end of June 1972. The cost of a first-class letter rose from 6¢ to 8¢ an ounce, and airmail went from 10¢ to 11¢ an ounce. Proposals to increase other classes of mail were challenged in court suits charging the USPS with exceeding its authority to increase rates. The USPS is authorized to change rates only after submitting a proposal to the Postal Rate Commission and getting its recommendations, but can institute increases on a temporary basis pending the commission's decision.

The USPS began putting into effect plans designed to improve its efficiency and public image, while cutting costs wherever possible. A major realignment of the service's internal management merged 15 regions into 5, each headed by a regional postmaster general. Three operating staffs were created to cover the areas of mail processing, customer services, and specialized support for postal activities. An Office of Consumer Affairs was organized, reporting directly to the postmaster general, in an effort to deal more adequately with individual complaints.

New services inaugurated included a "facsimile mail" project between Washington, D.C., and New York City—permitting important documents to be sent quickly through electronic transmission of written material over telephone lines. New service standards were also announced that were designed to provide overnight delivery for 95% of all airmail to cities within the 600-mile radius of the point of origin, and next-day delivery of 95% of local first-class mail deposited before 5 P.M. There was also a crackdown on the distribution of pornographic materials through the mail, as officials utilized a new federal law that permitted individuals to have their names taken off mailing lists for such materials. (*See also* Labor Unions. *See in* CE: Postal Services articles.)

POWELL, LEWIS F., JR. United States President Richard M. Nixon, in a television and radio address to the nation on October 21, named Lewis F. Powell, Jr., to a seat on the U.S. Supreme Court, along with William H. Rehnquist. (*See* Rehnquist.) Powell was a conservative Democrat and corporate lawyer from Richmond, Va., who was widely respected in legal circles and was viewed as an eminently qualified candidate. In contrast to Rehnquist, Powell met little opposition in the U.S. Senate and was easily confirmed by an 89 to 1 vote on December 6.

In naming Powell and Rehnquist, President Nixon emphasized that they fulfilled his desire to give the court a more conservative cast. Powell was known to be critical of some of the court's recent decisions expanding the rights of the accused and took a hard line on various law and order controversies. His stand on civil rights, however, was considered moderate. While he was chairman of the Richmond school board, blacks were admitted to white schools in 1959 with none of the bitter disruption that marked integration in other Virginia districts. He also helped to establish the Legal Services to the Poor of the Office of Economic Opportunity.

Born Sept. 19, 1907, in Suffolk, Va., Powell attended Washington and Lee University in Lexington, Va., where he graduated Phi Beta Kappa and was first in his class at law school. He received his master's degree from Harvard Law School. From 1937 until he resigned to take the seat on the Supreme Court, he was with a prominent Richmond law firm. He was a past president of the American Bar Association. (*See also* Supreme Court of the U.S.)

PRISONS. The simmering discontent inside United States prisons was brought forcefully to the public's attention by two spectacularly violent developments in 1971. First, a nationally known black inmate was killed along with five other men, authorities reported, during a desperate attempt to

The new U.S. Postal Service faced a variety of customer complaints and problems in 1971. Some dilemmas were easily solved, such as that of three-year-old Lori Ann Pfaff of La Crosse, Wis.

WIDE WORLD

escape over the high walls of the California State Prison at San Quentin. Then, a few weeks later, a massive uprising at the Attica State Correctional Facility in upstate New York was suppressed at the cost of the lives of 32 inmates and 11 of their hostages.

Just after breakfast on September 9 at Attica, a group of inmates refused to line up for a work detail. Such strikes, which occur fairly often in prisons, usually end quietly. However, the Attica revolt spread rapidly and soon about 1,200 inmates had joined it, captured more than 30 hostages, and established control over a cellblock and the sizeable yard facing it.

The inmates advanced 30 demands, a substantial number of which had been made many times under less dramatic circumstances at most other prisons. All but two of the demands were approved rather readily by Russell G. Oswald, the state commissioner of corrections. However, the commissioner flatly declined to remove the institution's superintendent, or warden, Vincent R. Mancusi, on the ground that it would be a bad precedent to fire an official under duress. The inmates also sought full amnesty from prosecution for any criminal acts arising from the riot, but New York Gov. Nelson A. Rockefeller said a total amnesty was beyond his constitutional authority.

A group of outside negotiators, many of them prominent figures largely sympathetic with the inmates, could not resolve the deadlock. They asked Rockefeller to visit the prison, but—in a move for which he was later criticized by some—he refused. Finally, on September 13, about 1,000 state police, sheriff's deputies, and guards stormed the facility and overpowered the inmates. In the first confusing hours after the assault, the statement was made that a number of hostages had been killed by the inmates with knives during the attack. Actually, the hostages had died from gunshot wounds and were presumably caught in the fire of their rescuers (the inmates had no guns). The 32 inmates were also killed by gunshots from the invading force.

George Jackson was one of three black inmates (the "Soledad brothers") charged with the 1970 murder of a white guard at the Correctional Training Facility at Soledad, Calif. The three inmates were transferred to San Quentin to await trial. On August 21, Jackson was being searched at the Adjustment Center at San Quentin after visiting elsewhere in the prison with a young attorney when, guards said, he drew a pistol and ordered a number of the inmates freed from their cells. Three unarmed guards and two prisoners were killed. Authorities reported that Jackson rushed toward the prison's north wall and was shot down by a guard on a gunwalk about 20 feet above the ground. Others, including his mother and the surviving "Soledad brothers," Fleeta Drumgo and John Clutchette, charged that Jackson was intentionally murdered. The lawyer, who could not be found, was charged with smuggling the pistol to Jackson.

PIEROTTI FROM BEN ROTH AGENCY

Several broad questions were raised in the wake of the Attica and San Quentin events. Nearly half of the prisoners in California were nonwhites, and black and Spanish-speaking Americans made up about 85% of the population at Attica. Some considered these statistics—for which parallels could be found in most prisons in the country—to be evidence of racial discrimination, and for them George Jackson and the inmates of Attica symbolized the oppression of the poor and minority groups by the criminal justice system. For others, including prison officials, the events in California and New York were signs of increasing militancy and political activity among inmates. It was also thought somewhat ominous that both Attica and San Quentin were considered to be among the better-run prisons in the U.S.

Other disorders in 1971 were small-scale versions of the two big outbreaks. For example, more than 60 inmates were hurt when guards at the Florida State Prison in Raiford fired on a striking group that was protesting overcrowding, a parole system it considered harsh, and other conditions. About 200 inmates rioted at the Essex County Jail in Newark, N.J., complaining of overcrowding, high bail requirements, and other matters. There were uprisings, for similar reasons, at a New Orleans prison. There was rioting at the Idaho Penitentiary in Boise; two buildings were burned and two prisoners injured. There were politically motivated strikes in the federal facilities at Lewisburg, Pa., and Danbury, Conn. (*See also* Crime. *See in* CE: Prisons and Punishments.)

Prisons

Special Report:
Prison Reform

by Joseph R. Rowan

On Jan. 18, 1971, *Time* magazine, in an article titled, "The Shame of the Prisons," stated: "Since 1967, four presidential commissions, dozens of legislative reports and more than 500 books and articles have pleaded for prison reform. But the system remains as immutable as prison concrete, largely because life behind the walls is still a mystery to the public." By the end of 1971, however, a spate of violent crises in prisons throughout the United States had stimulated public interest in the penal system, and the possibility of effective prison reform had a better chance than it might have had otherwise.

Basically, the public, because it is uninformed, wants punishment. This would not be the situation if more administrators in the correctional field spoke frankly regarding their problems and needs. The greatest single need in the entire delinquency and crime field is for a better-informed and involved public, which will then support sound policies for handling offenders and provide the machinery to do the job. When informed and involved, the public usually makes the right decisions.

Involving the Public

Formally developed citizen advisory bodies representing business, industry, agriculture, law, labor, the media, education, and the professions must be involved on a solid two-way basis in the various prisons and corrections departments if greater public understanding and support are to come about. Yet, few prisons and departments of corrections have such groups. No administrator can "go it alone," and this must be more fully recognized—and changed.

Prisons need the involvement of not only formally established representative advisory groups but also a variety of individual volunteers who are properly screened, trained, and supervised. Volunteers have given and will continue to render invaluable service to the prisoner, the prison, and the public. The prisoner has faith in them; volunteers are outsiders who are not paid and who offer hope for the future because the help they give will better prepare the prisoner for release. The prison gets tangible help for its educational, recreational, counseling, employment, and other programs and greater public support from the people with firsthand experience with the system. The public benefits because both the prisoner and the prison have been helped by volunteers.

Involving the Inmate

An indication that rehabilitation frequently is only a good phrase to use in discussions or as "window dressing" is borne out by the fact that very few prisons allow inmate participation or inmate advisory councils. No one is talking about having inmates run prisons, but two wardens of prisons that had riots or disturbances in 1971 attested to the merits of formally involving inmates in their own plight. Unfortunately, these institutions did not start their programs until they were demanded by inmates as the terms for ending a disturbance.

Other wardens, however, have had inmate advisory or participating councils operating for years with strong administration and staff support. Generally, changes recommended by the inmates have been in line with the thinking of the administration and have been implemented. Overall, wardens who voluntarily established councils and those who were forced into having them say that operating the prisons was much better afterward because the inmates felt involved and, therefore, supported common goals and objectives.

Interaction, instead of reaction and overreaction, must be one of the major objectives of prison reform. Offenders must be treated as men. Lack of respect for their dignity is a major problem that must be overcome by communication. The question of whether they deserve dignity must be faced. Just simply talking with offenders tells them that we think they are important enough people. "If I talk with you, you are my equal" gets across to the inmate, and when it does he is a lot less likely to want to do away with the system. The objective must be talking with prisoners, not to them.

If true prison reform is to be brought about, the philosophy of the American taxpaying public must be: "You can hate the crime, but not the criminal." Offenders generally expect to be treated firmly but fairly. A review of demands made by prisoners following riots and disturbances shows that they are not "pie in the sky" requests, but matters that pertain to the basic necessities of life and that are related to their need to be treated as men—as human beings. If prison administration does not involve inmates, the inmates will involve administration. It is better to have discussion on the table rather than under it. If people are talking about their problems, they are less likely to be acting them out.

The Prisoner Has Changed

Prisons today have a higher percentage of hard-core offenders than they had in the past. Increased use of probation and parole, even though it falls far below recommended standards in many states, has meant that the kind of prisoner who formerly helped to stabilize the prison population is no longer there. The percentage of racial minority inmates from ghetto environments has also increased to the point where in some states they constitute the majority race in the prison. Greater consciousness of racial prejudices on the part of these persons, and the resulting stronger feelings of militancy, has produced a more violent and demanding prisoner who feels he is a "political prisoner," a victim of a society that has not treated him like others.

Another more activist-minded person has appeared on the prison scene in the form of the middle- or upper-class offender who has entered the prison for offenses connected with protests or drug use. Challenging the establishment, including the prison system, has been a hobby of some of them. A "merger" has taken place in prison. The political activist has been influenced by the criminal and learned his ways, and the criminal has learned political activism. The result is that the days of running "smooth prisons" are over. As time goes on more prisoners are going to be asking more questions and the system will be challenged more. Wardens will be a lot better off when they recognize this more fully.

The System Has Not Changed

But while the prisoner has changed, the system has not. Most prisons are located out in the country. Many of them were located politically on a "pork-barreling" basis, sometimes because of a need for employment in the area and sometimes

On the second day of the Attica revolt, inmates confront Russell G. Oswald, state commissioner of corrections (below, far left). Lawyer William Kunstler (right) was one of the mediators for the prisoners.

RIGHT AND BELOW: WIDE WORLD

because a legislator got them located in his area to repay some favor received. This approach must be changed. Prisons must be located in urban or near-urban areas so that the public can be involved in them, and vice versa, and so that minority employees are more likely to be hired. Recent efforts to relocate minority-group employees in outlying communities that will not accept them have failed miserably.

The need for minority staff would not be an issue in prisons if no prejudices existed. The training of present guards in interpersonal relationships, race relations, and what makes prisoners "tick" could do much to eliminate prejudice. Such training has been started in some prisons but, basically, we still have guards who guard rather than cor-

In October approximately 50 inmates of the Parish Prison in New Orleans, La., staged a sit-down strike. They were seeking repairs for a damaged portion of the facility.

WIDE WORLD

rectional officers who correct. Correctional officers should also be paid a living wage. Facilities that pay competitive wages to officers do exist, and few, if any, complaints from inmates in these institutions are heard regarding brutality, harassment, or not being treated as men. Better wages have also proven to be a major factor in attracting better qualified officers.

The prison of today has four camps—the administration, custody staff, professionals, and inmates. Only one camp must exist psychologically if prisons are really to succeed. At the best institutions, we find good coordination among the various groups but this must be further improved by accelerated participation of both staff and inmates. To accomplish this, sound staff training and inmate involvement are required, preceded by agreement on a philosophy of mutual involvement. The latter constitutes the biggest hurdle. Superimposing programs upon staff and inmates with little, if any, prior involvement by them is all too commonplace.

Just and Natural Goals

The prison of today, as in the past, is an unnatural setting. It must be "naturalized." This means modernizing vocational and academic programs in line with today's needs and paying minimum or union wages for prisoners' services. It also means providing opportunities for decision-making on the part of the prisoner and opportunities to make mistakes so that offenders can learn from them in prison rather than out in the community. Prisons today reward conformity rather than the assumption of responsibility. Paying the going wage to prisoners will cost no more, and possibly less in the long run, than the staggering toll that the continued criminal behavior of the man who has learned nothing in prison now places on society—in terms of welfare payments, loss of wages, insurance costs, losses to victims of crime, high prosecution expenses, and the costly matter of returning the man to prison.

The goal of the prison and criminal justice system must be to effect the best possible protection of the public and of long-range economies. This means returning to the streets a better person than the one who entered prison. Involvement of prisoners, treating them as human beings, educating and reeducating them in terms of society's present needs, and at the same time maintaining an atmosphere of healthy discipline, are the ingredients necessary to reduce returns to prison. The atomic and space programs were goal-oriented efforts and achieved their objectives because they were. In prison reform basic honesty regarding goals has been lacking or confused. If effective prison reform is to be achieved, the public will have to influence prison officials to establish clear-cut goals, or prison officials will have to pursue a vigorous and sound approach that involves and informs the public.

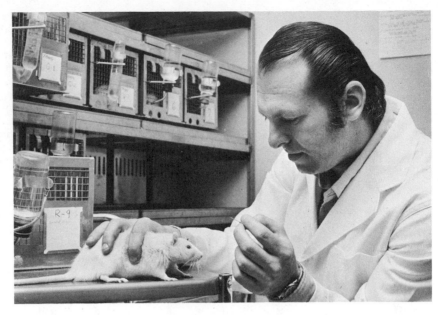

Seeking to learn more about how to control depression in man, Dr. Russell C. Leaf of Rutgers University administers an anti-depressant to a rat. The drug inhibits the animal's natural instinct to kill mice, making it tame, curious, and not at all aggressive.

AUTHENTICATED NEWS INTERNATIONAL

PSYCHOLOGY. Behavioral therapy was a top psychological research item in 1971. A popular form of this therapy, called systematic desensitization, has been recently used to treat phobias. A sufferer is taught to relax through suggestion, muscle exercises, or hypnosis. Then the problem that usually invokes fear is presented in a step-by-step way. The number of anxiety-arousing cues is raised until the patient can deal comfortably with the feared object or situation, such as an airplane flight.

Vienna, Austria, the city from which Sigmund Freud was expelled in 1938 during the Nazi regime, was the site of the 27th meeting of the International Psychoanalytic Association in July. Freud, the founder of psychoanalysis, was coldly treated in the past by the Viennese medical world. Austrian officials at the gathering tried to clean the slate by praising Freud's accomplishments. However, the belated praise came at a time when psychoanalysis was being harshly criticized for failing to acknowledge that human aggression might have social roots rather than the deeply personal basis believed by Freudians.

Animal studies first revealed that lithium carbonate, in current use to treat the manic phase of manic-depressive psychosis, also lessened aggressive behavior. To test for similar effects in man, psychiatrists at a Connecticut prison gave the drug to 12 healthy inmates with a long history of violence. For comparison, they were also given a placebo (inactive pill) during alternate four-week periods. The psychiatrists noted a significant reduction in aggressive behavior by the prisoners during the lithium periods.

A research report on operant conditioning and its effect on body control drew considerable attention during the 1971 meeting of the American Psychological Association. According to the study, subjects were hypnotized and then told to make one of their hands cold and the other one warmer. As an aid, the subjects were offered such images as one hand immersed in ice water while the other was on a hot stove. All the hypnotized were able to effect changes in hand temperature, which in some cases varied from nearly 13°F. colder to about 4°F. warmer. The study added to the growing evidence that people can to some degree control their body functions.

To describe human personality, psychologists have long contrasted certain traits—introversion versus extroversion, for example. Now another personality dimension has been found—internal control of behavior versus external control. That is, an "internal" person believes that his own actions—hard work and perseverance, for instance—determine reward and success. By contrast, an "external" person feels these result from chance, or "the breaks." This newly emerging concept of personality appears to have relevance in educational programs. In one example, disadvantaged children identified as "internal" usually did better scholastically than their "external" counterparts. This supposedly learned state underscores the importance of relating reward or progress to the individual's own achievements early in life.

Is United States society on the way to unisex? Recent findings showed that sexual roles assumed by young men and women were becoming less distinct. This view came from a study of Rorschach, or inkblot, tests during the last ten years. Younger subjects of both sexes often saw the figure in the sex-role part of the test as a female entity. In the classical interpretation, males reacting in this way were thought of as feminine, or even homosexual. Psychologists were quick to note, however, that the Rorschach was not the sole test used for personality evaluation. (*See also* Education; Mental Health. *See in* CE: Psychology.)

Author Erich Segal suns himself at Cannes, France, in May. His book 'Love Story' was a worldwide best seller.

PUBLISHING, BOOK.

Although book production continued to rise in 1971, spiraling costs cut publishers' profit margins to the danger point. But when prices were raised, sales fell. The success of the paperback increased sales resistance to the higher-priced hardback, and fiction, the traditional breadwinner of general book publishing, was hardest hit.

The number of titles issued in the United States in 1970 jumped to 36,071 from 29,579 in 1969. The increase not only indicated a strong growth in new editions and reprints in both hardcover and paperback—from 26% of total titles in 1969 to about 33% in 1970—but it also reflected improved listing procedures adopted by *Publishers' Weekly,* which reported the figures. New titles and new editions published in 1971 were expected to exceed 36,000. The number of paperback titles issued jumped from 7,079 in 1969 to 9,279 in 1970, with sales increasing as much as 27% in some book- stores. Total publishers' receipts were estimated at $2,933,000,000 for 1970, and despite continuing economic uncertainty, they were expected to top $3 billion in 1971. Book prices continued to rise: the median price for a novel in 1971 appeared to be $6.95, compared with $5.95 in 1970.

If the future of publishing could be determined by the number of people reading books, the outlook would be promising. A Gallup Poll reported in February that 26% of all adults surveyed had read a complete book in the preceding month, the highest percentage reported since the poll had begun in 1958. The themes these readers seemed to be interested in were economic analyses, biographies and current affairs, and social concerns, notably consumer protection and environmental controls. Books by or about American Indians appeared to be replacing the earlier profusion of publications by and about blacks. Interest in Jewish themes persisted, and books on all aspects of life in China, Japan, Germany, and Latin America received increasing attention. Interest in fiction books dealing with sex appeared to be diminishing.

Figures released in February indicate that the top-ten nonfiction best sellers for 1970 outsold the best-selling fiction list almost four to one, even though for the second year in a row there were few "how to" books on the list. The top-selling nonfiction work, Dr. David Reuben's 'Everything You Always Wanted to Know About Sex but Were Afraid to Ask', outsold Erich Segal's 'Love Story' 906,484 copies to 406,044.

Works by well-established novelists dominated a list of best-selling fiction in 1971. Best sellers included 'The Day of the Jackal', by Frederick Forsyth; 'Wheels', by Arthur Hailey; 'The Drifters', by James A. Michener; 'The Exorcist', by William Peter Blatty; 'Message from Málaga', by Helen MacInnes; 'The Other', by Thomas Tryon; 'The Bell Jar', by Sylvia Plath; 'The Passions of the Mind', by Irving Stone; 'The Winds of War', by Herman Wouk; and 'Rabbit Redux', by John Updike.

Nonfiction best sellers for 1971 represented a wide range of interests and included 'Bury My Heart at Wounded Knee', by Dee Brown; 'The Female Eunuch', by Germaine Greer; 'Stilwell and the

Chicago newspaper columnist Mike Royko wrote 'Boss: Richard J. Daley of Chicago', which became a quick best seller in 1971.

Thousands of demonstrators from the Puerto Rico Independence movement demonstrated before the hotel where the National Governors conference was in session, chanting "Yankee go home."

American Experience in China, 1911–1945', by Barbara W. Tuchman; 'Future Shock', by Alvin Toffler; 'Honor Thy Father', by Gay Talese; 'The Last Whole Earth Catalog', edited by Stewart Brand; 'Beyond Freedom and Dignity', by B. F. Skinner; 'Any Woman Can!', by Dr. David Reuben; 'The *Ra* Expeditions', by Thor Heyerdahl; and 'The Pentagon Papers', by *The New York Times* staff. (*See also* Literature. *See in* CE: Books and Bookmaking.)

PUERTO RICO. The controversy over the future status of Puerto Rico continued in 1971. Small but growingly militant groups of nationalists agitated for complete independence from the United States, while the government supported steps that could lead to Puerto Rico's becoming the 51st state. In August it was announced that a referendum would be held to determine if the government should ask Congress to give Puerto Ricans the vote in U.S. presidential elections.

In March the conflict erupted into violence on the San Juan campus of the University of Puerto Rico when radical students led riots protesting the Reserve Officer Training Corps (ROTC) program on the campus, long regarded as a symbol of American presence. The university was temporarily closed down following the deaths of two policemen and one student.

The controversy over the use of the island of Culebra, a municipality of Puerto Rico, by the U.S. Navy for target practice came closer to resolution in 1971. A compromise agreement was signed that surrendered the Navy's control over most of the island. Protest from residents of the island continued, and consequently there was a promise from the Defense Department that the Navy would seek a new location for its target practice.

Plans by two U.S. companies to exploit copper deposits in the central mountain region were slowed down when a report filed with the director of the Environmental Quality Board indicated that the smelting plant would endanger a national park. (*See in* CE: Puerto Rico.)

QATAR. On Sept. 3, 1971, Qatar, a sheikhdom on the west coast of the Persian Gulf, declared itself independent. With this act, it ended all former treaty arrangements with Great Britain, which were first concluded in 1868 and subsequently renewed in 1916. Qatar's ruler, Emir Ahmad bin Ali bin Abdullah al-Thani, then signed a new treaty of friendship with Britain.

Qatar's application for membership in the United Nations was approved, and the country was also admitted to the Arab League. The Qatari government announced support, in an official statement, of the proposed six-member federation of neighboring Persian Gulf emirates, which came into being in December. (*See* Arab Emirates, Union of.)

The country's economy was dominated by oil, which provided the chief source of government revenue. During the year work progressed on a new fertilizer plant, one of several projects underway aimed at diversifying the economy. In 1970 the population was estimated at 130,000.

Mrs. Whitney Young, Jr., accepts a posthumous Doctor of Laws degree for her husband from President William J. McGill of Columbia University in June. Young, executive director of the National Urban League, died in Nigeria in March.
WIDE WORLD

RACE RELATIONS.

American race relations entered a new era in 1971. Confrontations and violence subsided as other issues, from war to economics, crowded racial conflict off the front pages of daily newspapers. Yet race relations during the year presented a complex pattern of both gains and retrogressions.

Employment; Housing

The United States Census Bureau announced that nonwhites had made significant advances in employment during the 1960's. Only 16% of the nonwhite labor force had white-collar employment in 1960. But by 1970 it had increased to 28%. There was also upgrading in blue-collar employment. Although the portion of the nonwhite labor force in service occupations declined during the decade from 32% to 26%, the total of craftsmen, foremen, and operatives climbed from 26% to 32%. These trends continued, although at a slower pace, into the 1970's. The nation experienced serious unemployment in many sectors throughout 1971, but workers from racial minorities suffered the most. U.S. Department of Labor statistics in October estimated the total unemployment percentage at 5.8%, but among black Americans the unemployment figure was 11%. These figures recorded neither those underemployed nor those who needed but no longer were seeking work, categories where blacks have been disproportionately numerous.

Many factors contributed to these racial disparities, but the major cause was blatant discrimination. Little improvement in eradicating discrimination was recorded during the year. In October leaders of Spanish-speaking minorities filed suit against four federal agencies for allegedly discriminatory employment practices; they claimed that Latins comprised 7% of the nation's population but only 2.9% of its federal employees. The Administration's principal initiative involved extending "the Philadelphia plan" to five other major cities. Upheld as legal by the Third U.S. Circuit Court of Appeals, this plan fixed quotas of minority employ-

ment on federal construction projects. It had scant effect, however, because minority workers were shifted from other projects to federal work.

Not surprisingly, then, black income continued to lag far behind that of whites. While the median black family income went from $4,000 to $6,191 between 1960 and 1970, the racial differential expanded as the median white family income climbed from $7,252 to $9,794. Roughly one quarter of black families by 1971 received over $10,000 in annual income, but one fifth still received less than $3,000. Defining poverty as a family of four with

Rep. Shirley Chisholm (D, N.Y.) told newsmen that she would announce her candidacy for the presidency on Jan. 1, 1972.
WIDE WORLD

an income of less than $3,968 in 1970, the census reported that approximately 25.5 million Americans were living in poverty, including one in every three blacks (7.7 million), but only one in ten whites (17.7 million).

In January U.S. President Richard M. Nixon opposed any efforts of the federal government "to force integration in the suburbs" as "counterproductive, and not in the interest of better race relations." Nevertheless, the Department of Justice brought suit in scattered cities against racial discrimination by developers, apartment owners, and real estate dealers. The Department of Housing and Urban Development (HUD) offered guidelines to prevent racial and religious designations in newspaper advertisements for housing and to limit development grants to communities that agreed to plan for low- and medium-income housing. The Supreme Court was also active in rendering decisions involving racial discrimination in housing and other areas. (*See* Supreme Court of the U.S.)

Political Power

The effects of increased black political power were evident throughout the nation in 1971. In his January inaugural address, Georgia Gov. Jimmy Carter asserted that "the time for racial discrimination is over"; and at his inauguration in the same month South Carolina Gov. John West pledged to eliminate any "vestige of discrimination" from state government. At the national level the possibility of a black candidate for vice-president was seriously discussed. Although presidential aspirant Senator Edmund Muskie (D, Me.) publicly doubted that the Democratic party could win in 1972 if a black joined the ticket, many observers disagreed with him. U.S. Rep. Shirley Chisholm (D, N.Y.), the only black woman in Congress, later announced her intention to run for president. Other black leaders favored supporting a single black candidate and presenting a united front to win blacks more federal jobs and high appointments.

The growth in the number of black elected officials was also impressive. By April there were at least 1,860 such officials compared to approximately 1,500 in 1970 and only 475 in 1967. This figure still constituted only about 0.3% of the country's elected officials. Yet recent gains were particularly notable in the South, where 711 elected blacks held office in 1971 compared to 563 in 1970. Black mayors won elections in Benton Harbor, Mich.; Berkeley, Calif.; East St. Louis, Ill.; Engle-

Draped in a blue flag bearing the Black Panther emblem, the casket of slain "Soledad brother" George Jackson was carried from St. Augustine's Episcopal Church in Oakland, Calif., on August 28.
WIDE WORLD

wood, N.J.; and Kalamazoo, Mich. The first black commissioner in the history of Chattanooga, Tenn., won election; the Rev. Walter Fauntroy won the first District of Columbia seat in the House of Representatives; and Richard Hatcher, who in 1967 won election as the first black mayor of Gary, Ind., easily won reelection. However, blacks lost by substantial margins in mayoralty elections in Boston, Mass.; Baltimore, Md.; Cleveland, Ohio; and Minneapolis, Minn.; and Charles Evers lost decisively in his gubernatorial bid in Mississippi.

Also symptomatic of growing political strength and sophistication was the Black Caucus (formed in 1967), comprising all black members of the U.S. House of Representatives. In January the 12 boycotted President Nixon's State of the Union address because of his "consistent refusal to hear the pleas and concerns of black Americans." They were then invited to meet with the president in March. When they did so, they introduced a 32-page booklet of recommendations concerning race relations. When the president later rejected the proposals, his relations with the Black Caucus, all of whose members are Democrats, remained strained.

Racial Tensions; Trials

Extreme tensions continued between largely white police forces and black communities. In February there were four days of racial violence in Wilmington, N.C., that involved 600 National Guardsmen and led to the death of two persons, one a 19-year-old black youth killed by a policeman. In June there were similar disturbances in Jacksonville, Fla., and Columbus, Ga. Racial disturbances also erupted in Newburgh, N.Y., and Lubbock, Tex. An 18-year-old black girl was shot to death

from a passing car in Drew, Miss., and three whites were charged with the murder. Another young black girl was killed in Butler, Ala., while participating in a demonstration. In Jackson, Miss., 11 members of the militant black Republic of New Africa were charged with killing a policeman in a gunfight that broke out during a police raid of the group's headquarters. And in Darlington, S.C., an all-white jury found three whites guilty of rioting against busing; they had destroyed two school buses.

Racial tensions combined with the frustrations of incarceration to produce a wave of prison disorders. In August George Jackson, the best-known of three black convicts called the "Soledad brothers," was shot to death as he attempted to escape from California's San Quentin Prison. Seven others were later indicted for five additional deaths that occurred during the episode. But it was the September revolt in New York State's Attica Correctional Facility that thrust prison tensions into world view. (*See* Prisons.)

Racial tensions also flared in the armed forces. Racial incidents among U.S. servicemen increased in South Vietnam and West Germany. At Travis Air Force Base in California, black airmen became incensed by the detention of three blacks (but no whites) following an interracial altercation. In the riot that ensued, one fireman died, ten airmen were hurt, and 97 were arrested.

Black militants were involved throughout the year in court trials. In January seven black gang members were acquitted of charges in the sniper shooting of a Chicago detective. In May four blacks were found guilty and one acquitted of possession of weapons in a New York City trial in-

The Chinese community in San Francisco, Calif., opened four "neighborhood schools for quality education" in September. The Chinese objected to school busing that would scatter their children about the city and that would, they felt, destroy Chinese cultural closeness.

WIDE WORLD

volving an alleged plot to kill policemen. Black Panther leader David Hilliard, after being freed of charges of threatening the president in a speech, was sentenced in July to one-to-ten years in prison on an assault charge growing out of a 1968 police and Black Panther shoot-out. In January two Black Panthers were arrested following an exchange of gunfire with police in Winston-Salem, N.C., and 13 Black Panthers were arrested in Memphis, Tenn., after a housing dispute. In May, 13 Panthers were cleared of charges involving a New York City bomb plot; in June, 12 were cleared of charges of murdering a Detroit, Mich., policeman; and in August, 12 more were cleared of charges of attempting to murder New Orleans police. In New Haven, Conn., the national chairman of the Black Panthers, Bobby Seale, and a local Panther leader had murder charges against them dismissed. Finally, Huey Newton, a co-founder of the organization, had his third trial for the killing of an Oakland, Calif., policeman end in a mistrial with a hung jury in December; charges were finally dropped.

The repeated acquittals of the Black Panthers during 1971 quieted some fears that members of the organization would not be able to receive fair trials in the U.S. In June the Supreme Court furthered this trend by unanimously reversing the draft conviction of Muhammad Ali, the former world heavyweight boxing champion. The high court decided that the Selective Service System erred when it refused Ali conscientious objector status. Moreover, in August, 14 law enforcement officials were indicted in Chicago on charges of conspiring to obstruct justice in connection with a 1969 police raid on an apartment in which Panther leaders Fred Hampton and Mark Clark were killed.

None of this court action received the publicity accorded the trial of Angela Davis in San Rafael, Calif. Miss Davis was charged with murder, kidnapping, and criminal conspiracy growing out of a courtroom shoot-out in 1970 in which four persons were slain. Pre-trial hearings in her case dragged on throughout the year.

Education

The greatest changes in education during 1971 occurred at the college level. In 1964, about 200,-000 blacks attended college, with 51% in predominantly black institutions. Seven years later, almost 400,000 blacks attended college, with only about one third in black institutions. This increase was faster than the growth rate of white college enrollment and was especially sharp in the South. Yet blacks still represented only 7% of the nation's undergraduates and 2% of graduate students.

More controversy and less progress was recorded at the elementary and secondary school levels. Desegregation made headway in the South, with the percentage of black children attending mostly white schools in the fall of 1970 reaching 38% compared with 28% in the North. However, it was also true that many southern districts experienced "massive firings" of black teachers and administrators in retaliation; that white private school enrollment in the South from 1968 to 1971 had risen from roughly 300,000 to 500,000 (4% of the region's public school enrollment); that only 23 of these private schools had lost their tax exemption privileges by March; and that both private and official evaluations determined that the $75 million emergency school aid to southern districts for 1970–71 had often been misused. (*See* Indians, American.)

UPI COMPIX

William H. Rehnquist was nominated and approved as a new associate justice of the Supreme Court.

REHNQUIST, WILLIAM H. On Oct. 21, 1971, United States President Richard M. Nixon nominated William H. Rehnquist and Lewis F. Powell, Jr., to fill two vacant seats on the U.S. Supreme Court. (*See* Powell.) After a concerted effort by U.S. Senate liberals to defeat the nomination, Rehnquist was finally confirmed on December 10 by a vote of 68 to 26.

Appointed by Nixon in 1969 as assistant attorney general, Rehnquist served Attorney General John N. Mitchell as a chief interpreter of the U.S. Constitution and U.S. statutes. He had helped prepare many of the controversial legal documents issued by the Nixon Administration and had been the Administration's hard-line spokesman on police handling of demonstrations and government surveillance of suspected subversives. Thus Senate opponents of Rehnquist contended that he had a negative record on racial justice and a "dangerous hostility" to individual liberties and to civil rights.

Rehnquist was born Oct. 1, 1924, in Milwaukee, Wis. After graduating from Stanford University Law School first in his class, he served as law clerk to the late Supreme Court Justice Robert H. Jackson. Prior to becoming an assistant attorney general, he practiced law for 16 years in Phoenix, Ariz., where he was an active supporter of Sen. Barry M. Goldwater (R, Ariz.). (*See also* Supreme Court of the U.S.)

RELIGION.

In the world of religion, 1971 might be marked as the year of the rediscovery of Jesus Christ, particularly in North America and Western Europe. The shock waves of the preceding decade were still being felt. Church concerns about poverty, racial oppression, war, and ecumenism still remained important agenda items. Frequently denominations and church groups found themselves embroiled in controversies because of their espousal of activist causes. There were also serious quarrels between theological liberals and conservatives in some major denominations.

In a nationwide survey of clergymen in the United States released by George Gallup, Jr., and John O. Davies, Jr., the American Institute of Public Opinion cited figures showing that religion in the U.S. had fallen on unhappy days. Of the clergy who were polled, 59% of the Protestant ministers, 61% of the Roman Catholic priests, and 63% of the rabbis said that religion as a whole was losing its influence on American life. About 75% of the general public also held to that view. Churchgoing, while remaining fairly constant among Protestants and Jews, fell off sharply among Catholics, with the largest drop among young Catholics in their twenties. The report also showed that nearly four in ten young Protestant and Roman Catholic clergymen under the age of 40, and six in ten young rabbis, have seriously considered leaving the religious life. The survey also indicated a gap between the general public and Protestant and Catholic clergymen in terms of what are considered the top problems facing the nation. The public placed the Vietnam war and the state of the economy at the top, while the clergymen felt the top-ranking problems were indifference to spiritual values, sin and immorality, and polarization of attitudes in the nation.

There was a positive side on the survey's balance sheet that indicated some optimism for the future of religion. Younger clergymen were more inclined to say that the changes now going on would help improve Christianity. The movement toward Protestant-Catholic unity was backed by solid majorities in all age groups. The survey revealed no evidence that there was a general turning away from basic beliefs, even among those considering leaving professional church life.

The Jesus Movement

Underscoring the revival of interest in the spiritual was the burgeoning of the Jesus movement led by the "Jesus people." This move away from "secular" Christianity was significant because it was not led by conservative churchmen who had in the past been critical of the church's emphasis on social and political issues. While the movement had its start in California, it spread across the U.S., Canada, and overseas so rapidly that it would be diffi-

Members of a group called Children of God sing for inspiration before going out to convert other young people to Christianity. They were part of a growing "Jesus movement."
WIDE WORLD

cult to single out one specific cause or person for the rise of the movement. Robert S. Ellwood, a professor at the University of Southern California, stated that the direction of religion among youth in the late 1960's was apparently toward Eastern mysticism, along with the use of "mindblowing" drugs. However, drugs and meditation "didn't deliver what they promised," according to Ellwood, and youth were focusing on one man—Jesus. Through him they felt they were reaching infinity without drugs or meditation. Arthur Blessitt, a California evangelist and leader in the Jesus movement, said that youth have become disillusioned with the dreams of material utopia and are "turning on" with Jesus.

Tied in with the Jesus movement was the increasing frequency of religious themes in popular entertainment. 'Jesus Christ Superstar', a rock opera, attracted overflow crowds to churches and theaters. Although some churchmen criticized the opera as irreverent, the large majority of church youth applauded it as an expression of their faith. The Broadway musical 'Godspell', based on the Gospel of Matthew, was equally popular despite criticisms from conservative church groups.

Greater Voice for Blacks

Black Christian assertiveness manifested itself to an increasing degree on the U.S. religious scene. There were calls for a black Roman Catholic archbishop in Washington, D.C., and there was growing participation and influence in high-echelon Protestant councils. The National Black Catholic Clergy Caucus, together with a black nuns' caucus and a black lay caucus, demanded greater recognition in decision-making processes. The rise of black Catholic militancy was accompanied by the charge that the Roman Catholic church has had a "racist history" in the U.S.

Similarly, black Protestant church leaders declared that American blacks have been "scarred" in the past five years by the failure of progress to end discrimination and injustice. At a caucus in Cincinnati, Ohio, black Christians agreed to make every effort to establish black Christian identity. Black Christians, according to a variety of churchmen, asserted repeatedly that blacks have given Christianity a great deal more than Christianity has given them.

JUDAISM

No major changes occurred in the distribution pattern of the Jewish populations in 1971. There was an increased immigration flow to Israel from the Soviet Union (about 5,000 as against 1,000 in 1970), from Western Europe, and from North and Latin America, but the total, reported at about 40,000, did not exceed the figure for the preceding year.

The cease-fire in Israel, maintained throughout the year, and the disarray in the Arab world turned attention away from the Israeli-Arab conflict. World Jewry, deeply identified as ever with Israel's

PAUL CONKLIN FROM PIX

About 700 people were arrested during a demonstration in which they blocked a busy intersection in Washington, D.C. They were protesting Soviet harassment of Jews.

anxieties, breathed more easily. An intensification of the fight for greater freedom for Soviet Jewry, therefore, came at an opportune time. There were two major developments: the growing protest by the Jews of the Soviet Union themselves and the change in the reaction of the Soviet authorities. Soviet Jews became increasingly articulate and bold in defending their constitutional rights, including the right to emigrate, and they engaged in many daring acts of defiance unthinkable a few years ago. They were supported by world Jewry, which by various forms of open protest—highlighted by the World Conference of Jewish Communities on Soviet Jewry held in Brussels, Belgium, in February 1971—attempted to awaken the conscience of the world at large.

The rather inept conduct of the Soviet authorities in holding a series of political trials of Jews charged with attempting to hijack a plane and anti-Soviet activity (in Leningrad, Riga, Kishinev, and elsewhere) gave public opinion a specific issue on which to focus. These trials made clear in a concrete and tragic form the plight of Soviet Jewry, and on this issue U Thant, secretary-general of the United Nations, Pope Paul VI, and heads of state

The biennial convention of the Lutheran Church, Missouri Synod, was held in Milwaukee, Wis., in July. The Rev. Jacob A. O. Preus, president of the Synod, urged that the Bible be studied to settle doctrinal disputes.
UPI COMPIX

were willing to make themselves heard, and thus for the first time world public opinion became acquainted with the seriousness and magnitude of the problem. The Soviet authorities, who for decades had refused their Jewish citizens the right to emigrate, apparently reached the conclusion that attempts to stifle dissident Jews by all forms of oppression were self-defeating and finally decided to allow some Jews to depart. This affected not only elderly Jews who were allowed to join their families in Israel but also some of those who were causing trouble. There were no means, however, of knowing what proportion of Soviet Jews wished to leave the country.

Another critical area of Jewish collective concern was Latin America, containing some 25 Jewish communities ranging from 500,000 strong in Argentina to a few dozen families in Honduras and Nicaragua (the Jewish population in all Latin American countries was estimated at about 813,-000). These communities feared the prospect of being buffeted between left and right in the developing revolutionary situations. In Chile (estimated Jewish population 35,000), following the 1970 electoral victory of President Salvador Allende

Gossens, a Marxist, a number of Jews left the country. They were prompted not by fear of potential anti-Semitism but by fear of the effect of socialist reforms on the economic class to which they belonged (as had happened in Cuba); as time went on some of them returned to Chile.

One of the most important achievements of Western and Israeli collective scholarship was the completion in 1971 of a 16-volume 'Encyclopaedia Judaica', edited by Cecil Roth (who died in Jerusalem in 1970) and Geoffrey Wigoder. Important research projects in the field of Jewish studies were undertaken at the universities of Israel, in the U.S., and in Western Europe, and there was a steady stream of books and monographs relating to all aspects of Jewish learning.

PROTESTANTISM

Data gathered during 1970 and issued in 1971 by the National Council of Churches showed only a tiny increase in total U.S. church membership over the previous report, up only three hundredths of 1%. The Southern Baptist Convention showed an increase, and remained the single largest Protestant body, with 11.5 million members.

The death, in June, of Reinhold Niebuhr was a major loss for liberal Protestants. Niebuhr, one of the giants of modern Protestant thought, taught at New York City's Union Theological Seminary for 32 years. His deep analyses of the philosophical and social implications of pride, power, and politics in human life affected a generation of ministers and their ministry.

Women continued to advance in prominent church positions. The leading example in 1971 was the election of Lois H. Stair of Waukesha, Wis., as the first female moderator of the general assembly of the United Presbyterian Church.

The Lutheran Church-Missouri Synod held its biennial convention in Milwaukee, Wis., in July and a controversy over doctrinal purity took up much time. The conservatives, led by the church's president, the Rev. Dr. Jacob A. O. Preus, decried the so-called liberal "drift" in their churches.

Efforts to start new denominations grew stronger during the year. The Federation for Authentic Lutheranism tried to organize a church home for right-wing members of Lutheran churches who do not like social action and who take the Bible literally. Also, representatives from some independent Presbyterian groups met to organize a new church should the Presbyterian Church in the U.S. (Southern Presbyterian) join with the more liberal United Presbyterian Church in the U.S.

In a more positive manner, representatives of nine major Protestant denominations met in Denver, Colo., to assess the Consultation on Church Union (COCU). The tenth annual plenary session of the group heard progress reports on the proposed plan to unite into one church the nine denominations and their 25 million members. The denominations included were: the African Methodist Episcopal Church, the African Methodist Episcopal Zion Church, the Christian Church (Disciples of Christ), the Christian Methodist Episcopal Church, the Episcopal Church, the Presbyterian Church in the U.S., the United Church of Christ, the United Methodist Church, and the United Presbyterian Church in the U.S.

A new Bible translation, 'The Living Bible', was issued in 1971. Containing all books of the Old and New Testaments, it seeks through simplified modern English to make the scriptures more easily understood.

ROMAN CATHOLICISM

The third international synod of the Roman Catholic Church met in Rome, Sept. 30–Nov. 6, 1971. Its agenda had been published as early as January and the two themes it proposed to deal with—the priestly ministry and justice in the world—became the focus for discussion and dissension throughout the year. The debate on the priesthood was concerned with its relevance to the contemporary world, namely whether there should be part-time priests having other jobs, and whether a priest could or should engage in political activities. An-

The 25th general synod of the Anglican Church of Canada opened in Niagara Falls, Ont., on January 25. The Right Rev. Edward W. Scott was elected primate of Canada.

"NIAGARA FALLS REVIEW"

In San Diego, Calif., the Rev. Victor Salandini, research director for the United Farm Workers Organizing Committee, says a mass using a corn tortilla. Though threatened with suspension for the practice, which violates church canon law, the priest felt that the Mexican workers would be better served by a mass related to their culture and customs.

other topic inevitably raised was the question of celibacy.

In this debate, the U.S. seemed to take over the lead from the Netherlands, largely through the activities of the National Federation of Priests' Councils (NFPC). At its annual conference in Baltimore, Md., in March, it voted overwhelmingly in favor of an immediate end to the obligatory link between the priesthood and celibacy. In July, after a discouraging reply from the bishops, the NFPC repeated its plea and criticized the bishops for being unwilling even to discuss the matter. A sociological survey, prepared by National Opinion Research Center of Chicago, had discovered that "the majority of priests do not accept the present position on obligatory celibacy . . ."

At Geneva, Switzerland, in April, a meeting of elected representatives of European priests took place. Their discussions were more wide-ranging than those of the NFPC, but they passed a motion in favor of ordaining to the priesthood men who were already married. Again, surveys had shown a shift of opinion among the clergy. One in Italy in late 1970 had shown that about 40% of priests were in favor of a relaxation of the celibacy ruling and that 15% might marry if it were abolished. One third of Spanish priests declared themselves in favor of optional celibacy. At the conclusion of the synod, 107 bishops endorsed a declaration that opposed any change in the celibacy rule as it now stands; 87 bishops advocated a somewhat liberal viewpoint that would make for some exceptions.

The other document prepared for the synod, on justice in the world, received a more general welcome. The ground was prepared by an Apostolic Letter published on May 14 in which Pope Paul VI drew attention to a number of pressing problems and saw the task of the church as setting down some of the conditions for a more human future. It dealt with the effects of urbanization and the new loneliness which it can bring. It showed itself not unaware of the demands of the women's liberation movement, and spoke of the "new poor," the fringe members of society, the handicapped, and the maladjusted. The synodal document took up these themes and stressed the interdependence of the developed nations and the third world. It also expressed the need for development of a theology of revolution and noted that "young people manifest a growing skepticism toward any doctrinal message that turns out to be unable to achieve the liberation of man."

Meanwhile, there was increasing diplomatic activity between the Vatican and Eastern Europe. The first visit of a Communist head of state to the Vatican took place in March with the meeting between the pope and President Tito of Yugoslavia. The change of leadership in Poland brought hope for improved church-state relations there and meetings between Polish and Vatican representatives justified this confidence. The Hungarian foreign minister also visited the pope, Archbishop Casaroli visited Moscow, and there were talks with the Czech government on church affairs.

Efforts to reunify the Roman Catholic church with the Anglican Communion achieved a major milestone in 1971. On December 30 the Anglican-Roman Catholic Commission announced that agreement had been reached on essential teachings on communion.

RETAIL TRADE. Although inflation and a poor economic climate persisted in 1971, retailers had hopes for a greater sales volume. The year began with promise, as retail chains' sales in January rose 7.9% over January 1970. Sales mounted steadily during spring and summer. By June sales rose to a record total of $33.11 billion (seasonally adjusted); this figure was 8% above that for June 1970. There were substantial gains all over the United States in the sales of both durable and nondurable goods.

Unusually warm weather slowed October sales. Nonetheless, they were about 10% above those of a year earlier. Durable-goods sales were 20% higher and nondurables sales 6% above those of the preceding year. Except for a 4% drop in drugstore sales, sales in all major groups rose. The new economic program announced in August had produced no great difference in business except in car sales, which showed a huge increase. It remained to be determined how Phase II and the Christmas season had affected total sales figures for the year.

Doubtlessly, the year's most dramatic improvement was in clothing. American retailers reported increases in men's apparel sales of from 47.5% to 80% in June over the same month last year. One of the best sellers in men's wear was double-knits, particularly slacks. Dresses were the surprise seller in women's wear. In 1970 women had expressed displeasure with skirt lengths by not buying, according to retailers. There was much more choice in 1971, and the hemline ceased to be of major importance to women. All types of sportswear, particularly "hot pants," also did well nationwide.

A new development benefiting the cash-paying customer was initiated. A company based in Delaware County in Pennsylvania offered the cash buyer a discount if he bought in a member store. The consumer could get a discount of 5% to 15%. The company did not charge its consumer members a membership fee; instead, participating merchants who issued cash certificates forfeited 7¢ for each redeemed 5¢ certificate, or "chit." The chits could be cashed at the company whenever $10 or more was saved by the member. A similar program in Los Angeles charged its members a fee of $10 to $25 a year.

Retail businesses that joined the cash-discounts organizations were relatively small firms. They found that less money was spent on advertising under the cash-discount plan. They were glad to rid themselves of the burdensome paper work necessary to the credit business. Also, the plan helped attract new customers. It tended to pry cash purchases from customers who otherwise would use credit.

The U.S. Federal Trade Commission (FTC) continued to challenge leasing deals in which large retailers in shopping centers were maintaining veto power over leases of other tenants. The FTC argued that these retailers were able to keep out discount stores. It charged that the veto power was also used unfairly to force smaller stores to join merchants' associations; advertising that featured price competition was shunned by these associations.

Complaints were issued against some of the largest department stores in some eastern metropolitan areas. The FTC charged that provisions in their leases "tend to eliminate, discourage, and hinder discount store operations in the shopping centers." (*See also* Consumer Protection. *See in* CE: Trade.)

RHODESIA. Published in April 1971, the 'Economic Survey of Rhodesia 1970' showed once again that sanctions against the country were having an adverse effect. Particularly serious was the continuing shortage of foreign exchange in spite of efforts made to beat the sanctions by exporting minerals. Mineral production increased during the year by nearly 10%, and in the agricultural sector wheat and dairy produce also showed an upward trend. The wheat crop was sufficient to satisfy 50% of the country's requirements. At the same time the quantities of corn and cotton to be marketed fell sharply, and there was an 8% decline in the production of flue-cured tobacco. Secret tobacco sales continued, however, and there were hopes that the crop might contribute significantly to the country's export earnings.

The growth in the black African population pre-

Two young men, easily identified in red jackets with the legend "monitor," were part of a supermarket patrol on the lookout for shoplifting and purse snatching. The store employing the monitors, in Boston, Mass., experienced a 90% drop in offenses.
WIDE WORLD

JAN KOPEC—CAMERA PRESS FROM PICTORIAL PARADE

The Rhodesian Women's Reserve is trained in
radio, weaponry, and first aid. It consists
of women between the ages of 18 and 61.

sented further problems as employment opportunities diminished. With 60% of the African population under the age of 20, the prospect of increased African unemployment was serious.

An issue often discussed in 1971 was the prospect of reaching an agreement with Great Britain. The Commonwealth sanctions committee called on all the governments represented at the Commonwealth prime ministers' conference in Singapore in January to cut postal and telegraphic communication with Rhodesia and to improve measures to detect sanctions violators; however, there were almost immediate indications that the British Conservative government was about to make a further attempt to reach a settlement. In spite of persistent optimistic rumors of early talks, however, the countries' prime ministers showed little evidence of abandoning their basic positions. Hopes of a reconciliation rose higher with the news that Lord Goodman had visited Salisbury, the capital, in June as a special envoy of Britain's foreign secretary, Sir Alexander Douglas-Home. This visit was followed by several others later in the year. In late November it was announced that an agreement had been reached between British Foreign Secretary Douglas-Home and Rhodesian Prime Minister Ian D. Smith providing for a settlement to the constitutional dispute. The agreement provided some hope of eventual devolution of political power to Rhodesia's blacks, but the Organization of African Unity characterized its specific provisions as a "sellout." The agreement was not to become effective until both countries officially accepted it.

Meanwhile, the Rhodesian government continued to pursue policies that increased racial segregation. Early in the year, Rekayi Tangwena, the unofficial chief of the Tangwena tribe, wrote a letter to the *Times* of London calling on Britain to rescue his people, who were being driven from their land by the Rhodesian government because it now formed part of a European-owned ranch. By mid-January the government claimed that after nearly five years' resistance it had completed the task of evicting the rebellious tribesmen.

The government, too, met with success in another area. In February the Roman Catholic bishops, who in 1970 had led the opposition to the Land Tenure Act, agreed under protest to call on church schools in European areas to apply for permission to admit African pupils.

The banned African nationalist groups Zimbabwe African Peoples' Union (ZAPU) and Zimbabwe African National Union (ZANU) played little part in the country's affairs during 1971. Talks between the liberation committee of the Organization of African Unity and representatives of ZAPU and ZANU in Dar es Salaam, Tanzania, in January on merging were inconclusive but later talks between ZANU and ZAPU resulted in a decision to merge October 1 to form the Front for the Liberation of Zimbabwe (FROLIZI). (*See in* CE: Rhodesia.)

ROMANIA. During 1971 Communist Party General Secretary Nicolae Ceausescu devoted himself further to defining the Romanian brand of Communism to other countries of the Communist bloc. On April 1, in Moscow, he addressed the 24th Congress of the Communist Party of the Soviet Union and stressed once more that the Romanian Communist party was "against any interference in internal affairs of other parties." Later, the Soviet radio commented, in Romanian, that "proletarian internationalism and bourgeois nationalism were irreconcilable." Ceausescu answered that charge on May 7, in a speech celebrating the 50th anniversary of the Romanian Communist party, when he said that there was "no contradiction between the concern for the prosperity of a socialist homeland and the principle of internationalism."

From June 1–24, Ceausescu paid state visits to the People's Republic of China, North Korea, North Vietnam, and the Mongolian People's Republic. In Peking, China, he discussed world affairs with leaders Mao Tse-tung, Lin Piao, and Chou En-lai. Both sides reaffirmed their "revolutionary friendship and fighting unity."

With the single exception of Yugoslavia, Romania remained the one East European people's democracy with important national minorities, the largest groups being the 1,600,000 Hungarians and the 377,000 Germans. In a talk in May Ceausescu said that peoples of minority nationalities had no other place to go, and therefore had to remain and help the Romanian people build a socialist state. On June 23, speaking at the Hungarian national assembly, Zoltan Komocsin, a member of the Communist party's politburo in Hungary, remarked that cooperation with Romania was difficult because of the difference in views on China. He added: "We are fundamentally interested that the inhabitants of both our country and of Romania, including the Hungarian minority living there, should come to understand that the fate of our peoples is inseparable from socialism." Paul Niculescu-Mizil, a member of the Romanian party's politburo, pointed out in an article published on July 9 that Komocsin's assertions had caused "amazement" in Bucharest, the capital, because of its implications for the Transylvanian issue involving the Hungarian minority in Romania.

A consequence of Ceausescu's oriental travels was that he was not invited by Soviet Communist Party General Secretary Leonid I. Brezhnev to the meeting of leaders of seven Communist states held in August in the Crimea. Commenting on this absence, a Czechoslovak periodical stated that Romania would eventually pay for its political acrobatics; and a publication in Moscow warned Romania that neutrality toward China could not be tolerated in a Communist ally of the Soviet Union.

Ceausescu's reaction to his relative isolation within the Communist bloc was the launching of a nationwide campaign to reinstill Communist discipline. On July 6 he had presented to the Romanian Communist party executive committee 17 propositions aimed at "improving political and ideological activity in the spirit of Marxism-Leninism." Three days later, at a mass rally, he explained why it was necessary to stamp out bourgeois influence in Romania. On November 3–5 an enlarged meeting of the central committee of the Romanian Communist party discussed and adopted the 17 propositions. It was probably Ceausescu's hope that after such a drive toward puritanical Marxism-Leninism it would be difficult for Romania's Warsaw Treaty allies to mount an ideological offensive against it. (*See in* CE: Rumania.)

RUBBER. Figures released in 1971 by the International Rubber Study Group (IRSG) showed world production of natural rubber in 1970 estimated at 2,895,000 metric tons, a new record and an increase of 9,000 metric tons over 1969. (One metric ton equals 2,204 pounds.) Production for the first six months of 1971 was estimated at 1,410,000 metric tons, up 62,500 metric tons compared with the corresponding period in 1970. The *Rubber Statistical Bulletin*, published by the IRSG, began using metric tons in its reporting in March 1970. Other 1971 estimates included natural rubber supplies, 3,090,000 metric tons; synthetic rubber supply, 5,170,000 metric tons; consumption of natural rubber (manufactured products), 3,050,000 metric tons; consumption of synthetic rubber, 5,050,000 metric tons.

Malaysia was the largest producer of natural rubber (1970 estimate: 1,276,000 metric tons), and the United States was the largest producer of synthetic rubber (1970 estimate: 2,232,000 metric tons).

The disposal of rubber tires after they are no longer serviceable is a major ecological problem. Goodyear Tire and Rubber Co. used ground-up tire scraps to make an artificial turf that is very resilient and can be dyed green to resemble grass. The Columbian Division of Cities Service Co. announced that a small percentage of finely ground-up rubber from tires can be substituted for the oil feedstock used in manufacturing carbon black.

Other suggestions included grinding old tires to make pads for the floors of cow barns, thermally treating ground-up tires to produce oils and other usable materials, and using old tires to construct artificial reefs to encourage fish breeding. (*See in* CE: Rubber.)

RWANDA. Rwanda underwent a crisis in 1971 when it became embroiled in a dispute between Uganda and Tanzania. Uganda's president, Gen. Idi Amin, accused Rwanda of attending a Tanzanian-sponsored conference in April aimed at finding ways to reverse Amin's overthrow of former Ugandan president Milton Obote. In July Amin accused Rwanda of allowing passage to anti-Amin guerrillas from Tanzania. In retaliation, he closed the Uganda-Rwanda border, cutting Rwanda's only reliable trade route to the sea. The border was finally reopened in August after Rwanda agreed to prohibit anti-Amin activity.

Rwanda's relations with its other neighbors reached a high degree of cooperation during the year. In February joint plans were established with the Democratic Republic of the Congo for the development of hydroelectric power. In June Rwanda joined with Burundi and Tanzania in the United Nations Kagera River project. Rwanda's trade continued to be mainly with Belgium, but it was also party to the Second Yaoundé Convention, which took effect in January and continued the association of 18 African states with the European Economic Community. (*See in* CE: Rwanda.)

SAFETY. The safety movement in the United States was significantly advanced in 1971 by the implementation of the Occupational Safety and Health Act (OSHA). The law, which went into effect on April 28, was designed to protect more than 57 million employees in over 4 million businesses. The legislation was made applicable to all businesses affecting commerce, with the exception of mining and railroads, which are covered by separate federal regulations. The U.S. Department of Labor was put in charge of the administration and enforcement of the act, along with the Occupational Safety and Health Review Commission, a quasi-judicial body whose members are appointed by the president. Research, training, and related functions will be the responsibility of the National Institute for Occupational Safety and Health.

In 1970 there were more than 16 million motor vehicle accidents of all kinds, involving 27.7 million drivers and resulting in an estimated $4.7 billion in property damage. Efforts were increased in 1971 to improve highways, tighten safety standards for automobiles, and maintain programs for recalling vehicles that might have defective parts. The federal government continued to play an important role in reducing automobile accident injuries and fatalities. The Department of Transportation, for example, pressed for devices to give occupants of an automobile better protection in an accident. New standards will require vehicles manufactured after Aug. 15, 1975, to have passive (air bag) protection for occupants involved in collisions. In cars manufactured after Aug. 15, 1973, an ignition interlock system will be required that will prevent the car from starting until the front-seat occupants buckle their safety belts.

Americans, with more and more free time at their disposal, have been expanding their recreational activities and at the same time meeting with new hazards. Efforts to make recreational vehicles safer have centered on the problems presented by snowmobiles. An increasing number of states have passed legislation limiting the use of snowmobiles. With their accelerating popularity, snowmobiles were blamed for 102 deaths during the year, compared with 82 the preceding year.

The thrust of many of the new laws was to prohibit the use of snowmobiles in certain areas and to keep them off the highways.

Water safety also became a high priority issue. The Federal Boat Safety Act, designed to protect the 44 million people who go boating every year, was signed into law in 1971. During the past five years approximately 7,000 people have been killed in boating accidents. In addition, the total number of drownings each year has increased, to an estimated 7,300 in 1970.

One of the most important and most neglected aspects of safety received long overdue attention in 1971: the protection of the individual (as a consumer) in his home. New safety standards were developed, and existing ones upgraded, for such household products as lawn mowers, glazing materials used in building, flammable fabrics, and safety closures for packaging of hazardous products. Standards were also being developed for children's toys, infants' furniture, and backyard equipment.

The National Safety Council reported that 114,000 people lost their lives as the result of accidents in 1970, down 1% from 1969. In motor vehicle accidents, 54,800 people were killed, down 2% from the preceding year. (*See in* CE: Safety.)

Rows of shallow, lengthwise grooves were carved into the concrete on a stretch of Route 22 at New Smithville, Pa. This technique was thought to reduce accidents on wet curves.

North American Rockwell developed an energy-absorbing bumper system.

SAUDI ARABIA.

During 1971 Saudi Arabia played a major role in promoting stability and unity within the Arab world. With British forces scheduled to be withdrawn from the Persian Gulf emirates late in 1971, King Faisal dispatched his foreign affairs adviser to the emirs to urge them to join a proposed Persian Gulf federation to keep stability in the area.

Closer ties with Egypt were formed by Faisal's exchange of visits with Egyptian President Anwar el-Sadat, and the two leaders jointly attempted to mediate differences between Jordan and the Palestinian guerrillas, who had been subdued by the Jordanian army in July. Saudi Arabia hired 3,200 Egyptian teachers for Saudi schools during the 1971–72 academic year. Faisal continued to pay an annual subsidy to Jordan. He visited Iran, Nationalist China, Japan, and the United States, and he received diplomatic visits from U.S. Vice-President Spiro T. Agnew and U.S. Secretary of State William P. Rogers.

Improved relations with Yemen (Sana) led to the signing of an agreement to facilitate the transportation of goods between the two countries and an agreement for cultural, educational, and technical cooperation; relations with Yemen (Aden) were poor. Saudi Arabia's strained relations with Syria were eased when Syria allowed a trans-Arabian oil pipeline to be repaired; stoppage of the line had cost Saudi Arabia an estimated $1.5 million a week in revenues. Saudi Arabia lifted its ban on the importation of Syrian goods.

Agreement was reached with Lebanon to build a third jointly owned Saudi-Lebanese oil refinery in Lebanon. In the spring the government's ministry of oil and mineral wealth announced the discovery of valuable deposits of gold, silver, copper, and zinc in Saudi Arabia's central and western regions. In July work was begun on the construction of the longest highway in the Middle East—an 812-mile road that is to link Saudi Arabia's Red Sea coast with the port of Dammam on the Persian Gulf. The project, which will span the central desert, is scheduled for completion in 1976. The new Jizan dam in western Saudi Arabia, under construction since 1967, was put into operation in March.

Saudi Arabian Airlines began weekly flights to Istanbul in August and ordered new jet airliners to provide expanded service to Mecca during the pilgrimage season. Saudi Arabia and Iran signed their first trade agreement in April. (*See also* Middle East. *See in* CE: Saudi Arabia.)

SCIENCE.

Prospects of generous United States funds for science seemed rosier in 1971 than they had been for half a decade. The fiscal 1972 science budget submitted to Congress by U.S. President Richard M. Nixon earmarked $16.7 billion for basic research, up nearly 8% over the prior year's funds. Dr. Edward E. David, Jr., President Nixon's science adviser, assured the scientific community of future U.S. generosity toward science.

The National Science Foundation (NSF), overseer of the direction taken by basic research in the U.S., expanded its role by establishing a program called Research Applied to National Needs (RANN). About $81 million was to be used by RANN to explore social, environmental, and health problems. But the RANN appropriation was eventually slashed to $30.6 million. And, in Oc-

"I hate to say this, but, even under our brutally slashed research budget, I've made an important discovery."

tober, the NSF suffered a disappointing $30-million cut in its science education budget.

The *Journal of the American Medical Association* decided to follow customary scientific usage and publish only metric measurements in its articles, beginning in January 1973. In July Maurice H. Stans, U.S. secretary of commerce, asked Congress to permit total national adoption of the metric system. The first such proposal had come from John Quincy Adams in 1821. Conversion was expected to cost industry between $10 billion and $40 billion over a recommended 10-year period. However, in 1971 Congress still appeared unreceptive to the metric system.

Are there intelligent beings in outer space? Maybe, said some scientists interested in communication with extraterrestrial intelligence (CETI). At a September CETI meeting, participants felt that the best way of determining whether thinking beings indeed lived in outer space lay in analyzing radio waves of extraterrestrial origin for possible information content. (*See in* CE: Science articles.)

SELECTIVE SERVICE. In September 1971, after seven months of debate, the United States Congress finally approved legislation extending the Selective Service law through June 1973. Because Congress had not acted by the end of June when the old law expired, the government's authority to draft men into the military temporarily lapsed for the first time since 1948. No one was drafted in July, August, or September, but conscription was resumed after the new law was enacted. The total draft for 1971 was slightly less than 100,000 men.

The legislation was one of the most controversial measures before Congress during the year. Attempts to limit the extension of the draft to one year instead of two were defeated by only two votes in the House and six votes in the Senate. Efforts to abolish conscription altogether were rejected by larger margins, as were proposals to place other limitations on U.S. President Richard M. Nixon's war policy.

Congressional debate on the draft was entwined with debate on the war in Indochina. Just as an increasing number of congressmen had become disaffected by the war, so had they turned against the draft. A principal reason that the bill was tied up for so long in Congress was a disagreement between the House and Senate over whether a timetable should be set for the withdrawal of U.S. troops from Southeast Asia. (*See* Congress, U.S.) The final legislation, however, set no precise date for the withdrawal. In the end, President Nixon was given generally the law he wanted: a two-year extension of conscription, permission to end deferments for college undergraduates, increases in pay for servicemen, and no important restrictions on his defense policy (although the law did set ceilings on the total number of men who could be drafted).

The bill's pay increases for servicemen amounted to $2.4 billion a year. The purpose of the massive

JAMES SWEEN

A demonstrator displays an anti-draft sign during a massive march for peace in Washington, D. C., on April 24, 1971.

pay increase, in addition to raising servicemen's wages to a level more comparable to what they could expect to earn as civilians, was to attract enough volunteers into the military so that the draft would no longer be needed.

A number of reforms were included in the new legislation. The Selective Service System was permitted to call men on a national rather than a local basis. This meant that men with the same lottery number would stand the same chance of being drafted regardless of the location of their draft boards. The law lowered the minimum age for membership on a draft board to 18 and set a maximum age for membership at 65. New procedures established by the law also gave each potential draftee the right to appear in person before Selective Service appeal boards, to present witnesses on his behalf before local or appeal boards, to request that a quorum be present during his appearance, and to request a written statement explaining any adverse ruling by the board.

In March, the U.S. Supreme Court ruled (in an 8–1 vote) that men were entitled to be classified as conscientious objectors only if they opposed all wars. For several years the court had been broadening the meaning of conscientious objection, but the 1971 ruling put an end to that process. Despite the decision, the number of men who applied for conscientious objector status and the number of men who were granted such a classification increased over 1970.

In August, the Selective Service System held its third annual draft lottery. The lottery established the order in which men born in 1952 would be subject to the draft.

SENEGAL.
In January 1971 several bomb and incendiary attacks were carried out in Dakar, Senegal's capital, by extreme left-wing elements. In February Dakar University was closed after disturbances there, and trouble broke out again in March and April. However, in October tensions lessened, and several imprisoned trade unionists were released. There were plans for freeing former President Mamadou Dia, serving a life sentence for alleged conspiracy.

During the year President Léopold S. Senghor made determined efforts to establish closer links with neighboring states, particularly Mauritania and The Gambia. Relations with Guinea became progressively worse. Guinea's President Sékou Touré claimed that Senegalese territory was being used as a base by forces planning aggression against his country. Senegal's refusal to repatriate Guinean insurgents and the arrest of five Guinean spies in Dakar further aggravated the situation.

Disputes of this kind had paralyzed the Organization of Senegal River States (Guinea, Senegal, Mauritania, and Mali) to the extent that Senegal resigned from the organization in late 1971. (*See in* CE: Senegal.)

SHIPS AND SHIPPING.
A major maritime disaster of 1971 was the burning on August 28 of the 11,232-ton *Heleanna,* a Greek ferryboat, in the Adriatic Sea. The vessel had been billed as the largest ferryboat afloat. Carrying more than 1,100 passengers and crew, the *Heleanna* caught fire after an explosion in the kitchen. Twenty-four persons died. The vessel's smoldering hulk finally ran aground near the port of Brindisi, Italy.

Demetrios Antypas, captain of the *Heleanna,* was arrested and charged with homicide and neglect. According to officials, the vessel lacked adequate fire-fighting and lifesaving equipment.

Reopening of Suez Canal Considered

The Suez Canal, blocked to shipping traffic since the Arab-Israeli war of June 1967, could be cleared in four months, asserted Mashour Ahmed Mashour, chairman of the Egyptian Canal Authority, early in 1971. As a result of the Arab-Israeli hostilities, the canal was littered with destroyed bridges, sunken vessels, and heavy military equipment. A plan for raising these obstructions included the use of polystyrene beads pumped into structural spaces to provide buoyancy. The Canal Authority also planned to widen and deepen the canal.

The *Höegh Hill* was the world's biggest ore/oil carrier. Built by Kawasaki Heavy Industries of Japan, it could transport vast quantities of ore or oil.
KEYSTONE

Import Surcharge Revoked

On September 1, in response to loud complaints, the United States Treasury Department reversed its decision of a few days earlier to impose a 10% surcharge on all imports that had not yet arrived in the U.S. by August 16. The surcharge, part of U.S. President Richard M. Nixon's new economic program, had been severely criticized by importers whose merchandise was still in the holds of ships or otherwise en route on August 16.

An estimated $1.5 billion worth of merchandise was affected. The Treasury Department conceded that placing a surcharge on these goods could have forced some importers into bankruptcy. The surcharge was lifted on December 20.

Shipbuilding Highs and Lows

The world's largest tanker, the 372,400-ton *Nisseki Maru,* was launched in Kure, Japan, in April. The cost of the tanker, owned by the Tokyo Tanker Co., was $26.4 million. The ship was to operate between Persian Gulf ports and Japan and was scheduled to make ten trips yearly.

At the first of the year 49 large merchant ships were on order in U.S. shipyards. The total tonnage of these vessels was 1,608,800 tons. In June the Bureau of Domestic Commerce of the U.S. Department of Commerce estimated the value of all shipbuilding in the U.S. at $3.1 billion. This was a 15% increase over 1970.

On the other side of the Atlantic, one of Great Britain's major shipbuilders, the Upper Clyde Shipbuilders, announced in June that it would be forced to liquidate. The company, which had earlier received financial support from the British government, was denied further public aid. Although the firm had orders on hand worth more than $216 million, it was trying to recover from orders taken at a loss in recent years. It was also being sued for $4.8 million for late delivery of the luxury liner *Queen Elizabeth 2,* which had gone into service in 1969. (*See in* CE: Ship and Shipping.)

A 45-ton, five-bladed propeller (above) was made for the *Doctor Lykes,* which upon completion would be the world's biggest dry cargo commercial ship. The *LASH Italia* is a transport vessel that carries lighters, or barges, already loaded with freight. The lighters can be loaded and unloaded in deep water away from docks, thus generating some thorny labor disputes with longshoremen. LASH stands for "lighter aboard ship."

ABOVE: AUTHENTICATED NEWS INTERNATIONAL. RIGHT: "THE NEW YORK TIMES"

SIERRA LEONE. After several months of political unrest in Sierra Leone, an unsuccessful army coup occurred on March 23, 1971. On the day of the coup two abortive attempts were made to assassinate Prime Minister Siaka Stevens. Guinean armed forces then entered Sierra Leone at Stevens' request to safeguard his government, in accordance with a defense agreement signed on March 26 by which the armies of the two countries "became one."

On April 19 diamond-rich Sierra Leone, celebrating its 10th anniversary of independence, declared itself a republic. Stevens was sworn in April 21 as president, and Sorie Ibrahim Koroma, appointed vice-president, automatically became prime minister and leader of the House. John Akar, Sierra Leone's ambassador to the United States, resigned his post April 22, accusing Stevens of taking upon himself "sweeping dictatorial powers" domestically.

Political turmoil, along with a general recession in the world diamond market, depressed the nation's economy. The departure of many officials impaired the efficiency of the administration. The closing of rutile mining operations proved a setback for developing other mineral assets. (*See in* CE: Sierra Leone.)

SINGAPORE. On Jan. 2, 1971, Dr. Benjamin Sheares was installed as president of Singapore. He had been elected by Parliament on Dec. 30, 1970, for a four-year term, succeeding President Yusof bin Ishak, who died on Nov. 23, 1970. During January Singapore was host to the year's conference of Commonwealth of Nations heads of state and of government. (*See also* Asia; Commonwealth of Nations.)

At midnight on October 31, the 152 years of British military dominance in Singapore came to an end. The 14-year-old Anglo-Malayan treaty terminated, and in its place a five-power defense arrangement— involving Great Britain, Australia, New Zealand, Malaysia, and Singapore as equal partners—came into force. The new arrangement provided for the physical presence of British, Australian, and New Zealand (ANZUK) forces— ground, air, and naval in Singapore and air defense in Butterworth, northwestern Malaysia—with an Australian in command. There also came into force a five-power Integrated Air Defense System with full responsibility for Malaysia-Singapore air defense. The windup of the huge British Far East Command bases meant the reversion of nearly one tenth of Singapore's land area to the Singapore government.

In domestic politics the creation of the People's Front and the National party of Singapore gave the republic 15 political parties, although only a handful were active. There was no opposition in Parliament, and the People's Action party of Prime Minister Lee Kuan Yew occupied all 58 seats. (*See in* CE: Singapore.)

SKIING. Highlighting the ski world in 1971 was a controversy that threatened to eliminate leading skiing nations from competition in the 1972 Winter Olympics at Sapporo, Japan. The conflict flared when the International Olympic Committee (IOC) declared several Alpine skiers ineligible because they had accepted payment for coaching. The skiing nations promptly threatened to boycott the Olympics if any athlete was barred for professionalism. The crisis was resolved in July, however, when the IOC cleared ten athletes after it was brought to light that they had had permission from their national federations and that no racing had occurred. Membership in the International Ski Federation (FIS) in 1971 rose to 50 nations, most of which possessed their own recognized holiday ski centers.

Alpine Racing

Major interest in a year without biennial world championships switched to the fifth annual Alpine World Cup series, contested in a four-month circuit in North America and Europe. Overall winners in the 23 men's and 24 women's events were 20-year-old Gustavo Thoeni, an Italian, and 17-year-old Annemarie Proell, an Austrian. Although finishing second in the slalom and in the giant slalom, and 13th in the downhill, Thoeni topped

Bernhard Russi of Switzerland placed second in the Lauberhorn World Cup Downhill Race in St. Moritz, Switzerland, in January.
UPI COMPIX

Annemarie Proell, 17, of Austria was the overall women's division winner of the fifth annual Alpine World Cup series.

three Frenchmen—Henri Duvillard, Patrick Russel, and Jean-Noël Augert—in the final standings. Miss Proell won both the downhill and giant slalom, with Michèle Jacot and Isabelle Mir of France finishing second and third overall. Tying for slalom honors were Britt Lafforgue of France and Betsy Clifford of Canada.

In a new Canadian-American Ski Trophy series, based on World Cup lines, victors were Lance Poulsen and Karen Budge, both of the United States. Something of a record was chalked up by an American family, the Cochrans—Bob, 19, and his three sisters, Marilyn, 21, Barbara Ann, 20, and Lindy, 18. All except Lindy (who was on the training squad) made the U.S. national team, a distinction that was crowned by an invitation to the White House on April 12.

Spider Sabich of Kyburz, Calif., won the world professional championship at Vail, Colo., March 20–21. He also won the Lange Cup and prize money totaling $21,188 during nine North American meetings.

For the first time, the biennial world championships in ski-bobbing were held outside Europe, at Reno, Nev., late in March. Joseph Estner of West Germany won the men's title; Gertrude Geberth of Austria, the women's.

Nordic Events

Interest in the year's Nordic skiing events centered chiefly on preparation for the 1972 Winter Olympics. Outstanding among the ski jumping meets was the annual Four Hills Tournament at Oberstdorf and Garmisch-Partenkirchen, West Germany, and Innsbruck and Bischofshofen, Austria. Overall winner was the Czechoslovak, Jiri

Raska, 1968 Olympic gold medalist, with his first victory in nine attempts. Ingolf Mørk of Norway and Zbynek Hubak of Czechoslovakia finished second and third, respectively. Jerry Martin, U.S. champion, broke the North American mark for 90-meter hills by 5 feet with a leap of 345 feet at Iron Mountain, Mich.

In the 79th Holmenkollen meeting near Oslo, Norway, in March, Gerhard Grimmer of East Germany won the 50-kilometer cross-country marathon; Osmo Karjalainen, a Finn, the 15-kilometer. Another Finn, Rauno Miettinen, won the Nordic combination, with the 80-meter Holmenkollen jump going to Mørk. Women's cross-country honors also went to the Finns.

Dieter Speer became the first East German to take the individual title in the world biathlon championships in Finland early in March. The U.S.S.R. recaptured the team title from Norway, the sixth Soviet victory since the meets began in 1958. (*See in* CE: Skiing.)

SOCCER.

During 1971 outbreaks of violence in the world of soccer seemed to fall off slightly, probably because of better crowd control rather than any change in spectators' attitude. Nevertheless, there were days of tragedy. At Ibrox Park, in Glasgow, Scotland, 66 people were killed in January when barriers collapsed under the surge of fans near the end of a game. A riot in Haifa, Israel, later in the year, when a Jewish team was playing an Israeli-Arab team, led to a wave of arrests and the injury of approximately 20 people. In Buenos Aires, Argentina, when the local Boca Juniors met Sporting Crystal of Peru, 19 players were removed from the game after a brawl.

England again won the British Isles championship, played over eight days in May. Even though their final performance in beating Scotland 3–1 at Wembley, London, was convincing enough, they were far from impressive in the tournament.

Ajax of Amsterdam followed their compatriots Feyenoord when they took the premier European Cup competition trophy back to the Netherlands after defeating the Greek team Panathinaikos 2–0 at Wembley, before 90,000 people.

For the second year in a row the European Cup-winners' Cup went to an English team. Chelsea beat Real Madrid in a replayed game in Athens, Greece, on May 21, after the two teams had tied in a contest a couple of days before. Leeds United became the fourth English club in succession to win the European Fairs' Cup—the last under its title of Fairs' Cup—when it defeated Juventus of Turin, Italy.

During the year Pelé, the great Brazilian forward, bowed out of international soccer. His last game was played amid fantastic scenes of adulation from the 200,000 fans in the Maracaña stadium in Rio de Janeiro, Brazil, on July 18, when Brazil drew 2–2 with Yugoslavia. Jimmy Greaves (West Ham), one of England's most prolific scorers, retired at the end of the season; and players from all over the world turned out for a final testimonial for Lev Yashin, the legendary Moscow Dynamo

The Football Association Cup Final at Wembley, England, was won by Arsenal with a final score of 2–1 against Liverpool.

SPORT & GENERAL FROM PICTORIAL PARADE

goalkeeper, who played for 50 minutes for the Moscow Select XI on May 27. Francisco Gento, the famed Real Madrid winger, also retired, after 18 years at the top. And Bulgaria's World Cup player Georgi Asparoukhov was tragically killed in a traffic accident in June.

SOCIAL SERVICES. Shifting, sometimes contradictory, attitudes toward social welfare services were evident in the United States during 1971. After a decade of expansion and liberalization of welfare programs, several states moved to reduce benefits and tighten eligibility, and national welfare rolls began to decline; U.S. President Richard M. Nixon's controversial welfare reform legislation was stalled in Congress. A comprehensive federal program of subsidized child care was passed by Congress but vetoed by President Nixon. At the same time, however, there was a boost in Social Security benefits and the start of Congressional debate on a national health care program.

For the second year, attention was focused on welfare reform legislation. A measure setting a $1,600 national income floor for a family of four had been passed by the House of Representatives in 1970, but was blocked in the Senate. President Nixon, who had originally proposed the reform in 1969, reiterated his support in the 1971 State of the Union Message, calling it one of "six great goals" for action in the 92d Congress. On June 22 the House of Representatives passed a new welfare reform bill by a vote of 288–132. But again, the legislation received a less enthusiastic reception in the Senate. It suffered a further setback when Nixon, as part of his new economic policy budget restrictions, called for a one-year postponement in the starting date of the new welfare program—to July 1, 1973. As a result, final action on the measure was put off until 1972.

As passed by the House, the welfare reform bill was in some ways more ambitious than the 1970 version and in other ways more restrictive. Its key section provided for replacing the existing federal-state welfare structure with two programs: the Family Assistance Plan (FAP) and the Opportunities for Families Program (OFP). These would shift the major burden of costs from states to the federal government and would provide a nationally uniform system of minimum cash grants to families who met federal standards of eligibility.

Even though welfare reform with its proposed boost in Social Security did not become law, an across-the-board increase in Social Security benefits did go into effect in 1971. Congress in March approved a 10% hike in Old Age, Survivors, and Disability benefits, retroactive to Jan. 1, 1971, for 27.4 million persons. This raised the minimum monthly payment to individuals from $64 to $70.40 and to couples from $96 to $105.60. The measure also provided a 5% increase in special benefits payable to individuals 72 years old and over who were not insured for regular benefits.

The increases were to be financed by raising the base wage on which payroll taxes are assessed. That wage, $7,800 in 1971, was to go up to $9,000 in 1972. The tax rate would remain the same—5.2% each for employers and employees and 7.5% for self-employed individuals covered by Social Security. The law set up a table of gradual future rate increases for employers and employees, reaching 6.05% in 1987.

The effect of the changes for wage earners was that the maximum tax in 1972 would be $468, compared with $405.60 in 1971. By 1987 the maximum under the law would be $544.50. All rates were to be subject to future readjustments in order to guarantee enough revenue for the Social

More than 1,000 New York City welfare families were placed in hotels, whose operators sometimes collected high rents for dirty, rundown, and unsafe facilities.

"THE NEW YORK TIMES"

Security Trust Fund, and they were to go up if Congress approved further benefit increases as part of welfare reform. The welfare reform bill that passed the House of Representatives would raise payroll taxes to 5.4% in 1972, 6.2% in 1975, and 7.4% in 1977. In addition, the tax base would be lifted to $10,200 in 1972 and automatically after that whenever there was an increase in benefits because of increases in the cost of living.

While the future federal role in welfare remained uncertain, many states moved in 1971 to cut back public assistance programs. A survey by *The New York Times* indicated that at least 19 states—including California and New York, which had two of the most liberal welfare programs—had acted to tighten relief rolls and cut costs. The steps came as total national spending for welfare reached $16.3 billion in the fiscal year ending June 30, 1971, an increase of 27% over the preceding 12 months and four times the outlay of 1961. At the end of fiscal 1971 a total of 14.3 million persons were on welfare, 17% more than a year before.

Some of the methods employed by states to stem the welfare tide included: a requirement that able-bodied recipients take nonpaying public works jobs and pick up their checks in person rather than by mail; stiffer eligibility rules and more rigid investigations to screen out ineligibles; lower grants to families with outside incomes; and a requirement that relatives of welfare recipients share support costs when possible.

For the first time in three years, the total number of persons on state welfare rolls showed a decrease. Declines were reported in May, June, and July, after average monthly increases of about 2% earlier in the year. A spokesman for the U.S. Department of Health, Education, and Welfare said that several factors appeared to be contributing to the apparent leveling off of welfare caseloads, the most notable being the determined efforts of many states to cut back.

In a ruling that was interpreted as another setback to liberalized welfare, the U.S. Supreme Court held, 6–3, that welfare caseworkers may insist on going inside recipients' homes to check on their eligibility, and may halt payments to persons who refuse to admit them. On the other hand, the court held unanimously in another decision that states cannot deny welfare benefits to needy persons solely because they are aliens.

In December the court voided two Illinois welfare rules that restricted benefits. In the first case, the court said that the state must provide benefits for dependent children, ages 18 through 20, who are attending college. Two mothers receiving Aid to Dependent Children (ADC) had appealed after their children's payments were stopped. In the second case, the court voided a state regulation that a mother on ADC must identify the father of her children to the state, so that attempts may be made to collect support from him.

The role of social-welfare programs in the U.S. was underscored during the year by a report issued by the Census Bureau. It said that the number of persons in the nation living at the poverty level had increased 5% in 1970, reversing a 10-year downward trend. The Bureau reported that there were 25.5 million poor persons in the U.S. at the end of the year, an increase of 1.2 million over 1969. A major factor in this rise was unemployment. Although poor whites outnumbered poor blacks 17.5 million to 7.7 million, one Negro in three lived in poverty, compared with one white in ten, according to the report. The poverty level, which is adjusted periodically to reflect changes in the cost of living, was defined as $3,968 for a family of four in 1970. (*See also* Feature Article: "The Health Care Crisis." *See in* CE: Social Security.)

SOMALIA.

Maj. Gen. Mohammed Siad Barre and the Supreme Revolutionary Council (SRC) showed no signs of relinquishing power in Somalia in 1971. On Oct. 21, 1970, Siad had formally declared Somalia a socialist state. A campaign to eliminate "tribalism" began with a law abolishing the traditional payment of bloodwealth compensation for homicide and of the office of government-salaried chief. In another measure, censorship boards were to be set up to cover the news and entertainment media.

The outstanding event of 1971 in Somalia was the conference of East and Central African heads of state, held at Mogadishu, the capital, October 18–20. In internal affairs the emphasis on national self-reliance continued, with "self-help" programs in operation throughout the country.

The interior of the country suffered from a severe drought that lasted until March. Relief was organized with Soviet and Chinese aid.

In May the vice-president of the SRC, Maj. Gen. Mohammed Ainanshe Guleid, was arrested with several associates on charges of treason. Their trial began on September 27. (*See in* CE: Somali Republic.)

SOUTH AFRICA.

The dramatic seizure of a leading clergyman by the security police was an act representative of the expanding political repression in South Africa in 1971. On the morning of January 20 the Anglican dean of Johannesburg, the Very Rev. Gonville Aubrey ffrench-Beytagh, 59, was taken from his home and put in solitary confinement. He was released on bail, and was later charged with 10 offenses under the 1967 Terrorism Act. On November 1 he was convicted and sentenced to five years imprisonment, partly for distributing money to banned organizations. He had given money to wives and children deprived of support because the government had jailed or banned their husbands and fathers for illegal political activity.

Raids on church and student organizations were made in February in major cities. Many clerics

MICHAEL IRWIN

Gonville A. ffrench-Beytagh, dean of Johannesburg's Anglican cathedral, was sentenced to five years in prison for fighting apartheid.

were expelled from the country. In October during a roundup of clergy and intellectuals, one of the detainees, Ahmed Timol, plummeted to his death from the tenth floor of the Johannesburg security police headquarters.

Despite the government's overall repressive policies, flexible enforcement of legislation allowed it to remain effective and efficient. In June it set aside the eight-year arrest without trial of Helen Joseph; she was 66 years old and had cancer. In March the Anglican bishop of Zululand, the Rt. Rev. Alpheus H. Zulu, was arrested for failure to produce his pass book. Authorities later withdrew the charges. The number of executions by hanging decreased to 80, down from 117 in 1970.

In parliament the Nationalist party, under the leadership of Prime Minister John Vorster, proposed tough new laws apparently as a concession to the *verkrampters* who did not leave the party. The *verkrampters* are supporters of the hard-line policies of Albert Hertzog, who had left the Nationalist party in reaction to Vorster's *verligte* (enlightened) policies. One of the new bills made it an offense even to talk about censorship cuts made in films.

In April the education minister announced in parliament that the state-controlled South African Broadcasting Corp. would operate the country's first television service. When fully operational in 1975, it would have four channels in color: one intended for blacks in urban areas, one in English for urban whites, one in Afrikaans for whites in rural areas, and one for blacks in the Bantustans, or homelands. Hertzog rejected television as a symbol of "Western degeneracy" and declared that it would lead to the destruction of apartheid, the policy of racial segregation.

Race Relations

The Orange Free State attorney general withdrew charges against 5 white men and 14 black women in January. They had been charged under the Immorality Act. The only Progressive member of parliament, Helen Suzman, sought to abolish this miscegenation law because of the havoc it brought. Convictions under the act averaged two a day.

A new law made it possible to have a tribal language proclaimed as the official language of a tribal territory and to permit its being used as an official language outside the territory. The government announced its intention to hasten the consolidation of the scattered portions of the tribal homelands to form contiguous units. Provisions were made under the Bantu Homelands Citizenship Act for the issuance of tribal citizenship papers to blacks living away from their designated tribal areas. These papers would entitle a black to citizenship only in his own Bantustan. The Bantu Homelands Constitution Act of 1971 empowered the state to grant limited self-rule to a homeland on the Transkei pattern by proclamation and without recourse to Parliament.

The new Ministry of Bantu Administration and Development was formed to centralize control of blacks in white urban areas. This new control, coupled with the existing law prohibiting blacks from being in a place not assigned to them by whites, would make it easier to move and exploit the black labor force.

The government disenfranchised mulatto voters, except for representation in the powerless Coloured Persons' Representative Council. This removal from the voter rolls was associated with "parallel development," the new name for the policy of racial segregation as applied to mulattoes ("separate development" designated the segregation of blacks).

The large Indian community became alarmed at the sudden increase of raids and detention of Indians. However, the Chinese had somewhat less cause for alarm. Some were allowed to live in white communities after the government canvassed prospective neighbors for their consent and found little resistance.

Foreign Affairs

At the request of the United Nations Security Council the World Court at The Hague in June ruled 13 to 2 (Great Britain and France dissenting) that South Africa should withdraw its administration from South-West Africa (Namibia). South Africa rejected the court's opinion as being politically motivated. A South African offer to hold a plebiscite in the territory was rejected by the UN Council for Namibia.

Zambia accused South Africa of pursuing into Zambian territory terrorists who had set land mines that killed two white South African policemen. The incident occurred in the Caprivi Strip, a narrow projection of South-West Africa that separates Zambia from South Africa. South Africa denied the accusation and charged Zambia with harboring terrorist forces.

Great Britain finally decided to risk the ire of black Africa and sell South Africa military equipment. (*See* Commonwealth of Nations.)

It was revealed that Vorster had been in contact with Zambian President Kenneth Kaunda since 1968. On April 21 Vorster accused Kaunda of being a "double-talker" for publicly condemning apartheid while privately meeting with South African diplomats. Kaunda countered that Vorster was annoyed because he would not meet with him.

Two notable visits by blacks to South Africa were those of H. Kamuzu Banda, president of Malawi, and U.S. Rep. Charles Diggs, Jr. (D, Mich.). Banda was well received by the whites because his visit was contrary to a basic principle of the Organization of African Unity (OAU)—that South Africa be shunned. Diggs was popular with the blacks because his visit was intended to discover the nature of their condition. Arthur

Chito Kachingwe was the first black child to attend the previously all-white Pretoria Convent school. She is the daughter of Joe Kachingwe, Malawi's ambassador to South Africa.

UPI COMPIX

Ashe, black American tennis champion, was denied entry into the country despite the urgent request by the U.S. State Department that he be admitted.

The Economy

Defense spending was increased by $83.2 million to $445.6 million. Attempts were made to slow inflation caused by excessive consumer expenditure and low savings. Measures taken to reduce consumption included raising the income tax and sales tax and increasing excise duties. Public works spending was cut. Demands for higher wages were discouraged, although imposition of a wage or price freeze was rejected.

About 17% of the almost entirely black labor force was unemployed. Because of the critical skilled-labor shortage, the government conceded to pressure to allow blacks to work at some skilled trades. Also because of the labor shortage and at the prompting of American investors—notably a subsidiary of Polaroid Corp., which sold equipment used in producing identification photos for the blacks' pass books—the government allowed some firms to pay equal wages to blacks doing the same work as whites.

With more imports and no compensating increase in exports, the balance of payments deficit grew worse—for the first nine months of 1971 it was $1.4 billion, compared to $953 million for the same period in 1970. But more than $1 billion in foreign investments and gold sales to the International Monetary Fund and on the free market greatly reduced the disparity. (*See in* CE: South Africa.)

SPACE EXPLORATION.
Tragedy marred the end of an otherwise highly successful Soviet space mission in 1971. The three cosmonauts of Soyuz 11 were found dead upon returning to the earth on June 30 after their 23-day mission aboard the Salyut 1 space station. Proponents of manned spaceflight were, however, elated by the extremely successful United States Apollo 15 lunar mission in the following month.

The success of Apollo 15 notwithstanding, the U.S. space program continued to decline. There was a 15.7% drop in employment in the aerospace industry between March 1970 and March 1971, and further reductions were predicted. The U.S. National Aeronautics and Space Administration (NASA) also was required by Congress to reduce its payroll by 1,500 employees on October 1.

NASA gained its fourth administrator on May 1. James C. Fletcher, former president of the University of Utah, accepted the position after it had been offered to and declined by a number of prominent men in the aerospace field. While gaining an administrator, the agency lost astronaut Walter Cunningham, who resigned on August 1 to become a vice-president of Century Development Corp., a non-space company in Houston, Tex. Neil A. Armstrong, the first man to walk on the moon, also

A 24,000-pound nose cone was explosively split into four panels to check for proper ejection of the panels in a space-like environment.

resigned from NASA. After little more than a year as the agency's deputy associate administrator for aeronautics, Armstrong on October 4 became professor of engineering at the University of Cincinnati. His fellow Apollo 11 astronaut, Edwin E. Aldrin, Jr., returned to duty with the U.S. Air Force.

In Europe, interest in space continued to increase. The budget for the European Launcher Development Organization (ELDO) was fixed at $88 million. It included approval for the development of the Europa 2 space carrier vehicle. Generally, the Western European space organizations seemed to be relying more on ELDO and the European Space Research Organization (ESRO) and less on cooperation with NASA.

Cooperation between the U.S. and the Soviet Union, on the other hand, increased considerably during the year. The two nations exchanged lunar soil samples for analysis in each other's scientific institutions.

Flights of Apollo 14 and Apollo 15

Apollo 14 continued the success of the U.S. lunar landing series, which had been marred only by the failure of Apollo 13. The crew of Apollo 14

Bright sunlight reflected off the Apollo 14 lunar module on the moon, creating a circular flare photographed by the astronauts.

COURTESY, NASA

consisted of Alan B. Shepard, Jr., America's first man in space; Stuart A. Roosa, a rookie astronaut on his first mission; and Edgar D. Mitchell, also on his first mission. Lifting off from Kennedy Space Center January 31, the mission soon proved to be exciting. After achieving parking orbit, the "Kitty Hawk" command module was unable to dock with the "Antares" lunar module. For almost two hours the crew attempted to join the two. Finally, on the sixth try, the two craft achieved a "hard dock" and the mission proceeded, entering lunar orbit on February 4.

With Shepard at the controls the lunar module landed on February 5 within 60 feet of its designated target in Fra Mauro. After about 5½ hours Shepard and Mitchell left the module and spent 4 hours and 49 minutes on the lunar surface. They set up the Apollo Lunar Surface Experiments Package (ALSEP) approximately 500 feet west of the spacecraft, collected 43 pounds of rocks and soil, and deployed a solar wind experiment and a laser beam reflector. For the first time in the Apollo program, a two-wheeled cart was used to carry tools, scientific instruments, and rocks and soil samples.

A second five-hour period of exploration on February 6 found Mitchell and Shepard struggling toward the rim of Cone Crater with their cart loaded with photographic equipment and a magnetometer. However, they never reached the rim because the condition of the soil impeded their progress to the extent that they might not have had enough oxygen left in their portable life support systems to get back to the spacecraft.

For the first time, geologists on the earth had the

opportunity of studying a man-made seismic event on the moon by means of two seismometers on the lunar surface. After Shepard and Mitchell had successfully lifted off from the moon and rejoined Roosa in the command module, the 5,200-pound lunar module was deliberately crashed into the moon at a velocity of 3,850 miles per hour. The moon reverberated for about one and a half hours after the impact.

In summary, the Apollo 14 mission largely succeeded in its objective of evaluating the role of man in lunar exploration and the implantation of scientific instruments on the moon. It also succeeded in returning about 100 pounds of lunar rocks and soil samples to the earth. Further, it demonstrated the high degree of accuracy with which spacecraft could be returned to a predetermined location on earth. On February 9 at 4:05 P.M. EST, Kitty Hawk landed, only four nautical miles from the recovery ship USS *New Orleans*. Its crew was the last to be quarantined for two weeks in the Lunar Receiving Laboratory at the Manned Spacecraft Center in Houston.

Later in the year, America's manned spaceflight program produced its most spectacularly successful mission since the first landing of man on the moon. Apollo 15 lifted off from Kennedy Space Center on July 26. For this mission the command module ("Endeavor") weighed 2,640 pounds more than usual. The lunar module ("Falcon") was 2,470 pounds heavier as it included a 480-pound lunar roving vehicle, folded up and stored in the descent stage. The crew consisted of David R. Scott, a veteran of the Gemini 8 and Apollo 9 missions;

Alfred M. Worden, an astronaut making his first space mission; and James B. Irwin, also making his first space mission. They wore a new type of spacesuit that permitted greater mobility and flexibility on the moon.

After only minor problems on the journey the lunar module landed on the moon on July 30 near the Hadley Rille at the base of the Apennine Mountains. The next day Scott and Irwin extracted the lunar roving vehicle from its storage bay and set off on their first exploration of the surface. The astronauts checked out the rover and found that the front wheels did not steer. While annoying, the situation was not serious, since the car was designed to steer with the rear wheels as well. The astronauts then traveled five miles in the rover, driving to the edge of Hadley Rille and then up the slope of St. George Crater. On this first exploration, they spent 6½ hours collecting samples, taking photographs, and deploying scientific instruments.

On August 1, the two again left the lunar module and climbed aboard their lunar rover for the slopes of the Apennine Mountains. The high point of this exploration was the discovery of a rock later dubbed the Genesis rock, which appeared to be about 4.15 billion years old (plus or minus 200 million years). The oldest rock previously returned from the moon was about 3.8 billion years old.

After a third excursion in the lunar rover, to the northern edge of Hadley Rille, Scott and Irwin on August 2 lifted off to rejoin Worden in orbit in the command module. With them were over 170 pounds of lunar rocks and soil samples, and hundreds of invaluable photographs in black and white and in color. The docking was accomplished without problem.

On August 4 the crew ejected into lunar orbit a subsatellite from the scientific instrument bay of the service module. Weighing 78.5 pounds, the satellite contained instruments that would gather data on the moon's gravitational field, the earth's magnetosphere, and the moon's magnetic field. The next day Worden left the command module and took a 16-minute "walk" in space to the instrument bay to recover film from its cameras. On August 7, Apollo 15 splashed down in the Pacific Ocean, only 6.6 miles from the planned impact point.

Soviet Manned Space Flight

On April 19 the U.S.S.R. launched an unmanned space station, Salyut 1, which was placed into a near-circular orbit of about 133 by 120 miles. Four days later Soyuz 10 was launched with cosmonauts Vladimir Shatalov, Aleksei S. Yeliseyev, and Nikolai N. Rukavishnikov on board. Its objective seemed to have been to rendezvous and dock with Salyut 1. After some difficulty the docking was achieved, and the two craft stayed joined for 5½ hours. During this period the cosmonauts checked

On the Apollo 15 mission, astronaut David R. Scott studied the area as part of the extravehicular activity on the surface of the moon. He had emerged from the lunar roving vehicle (right).
COURTESY, NASA

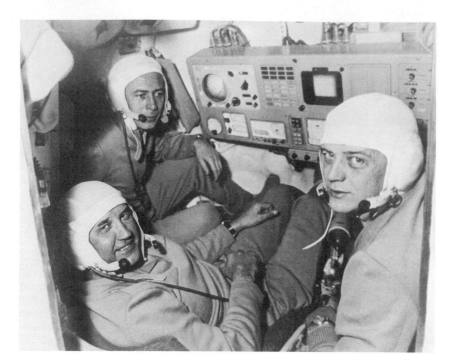

Three Soviet cosmonauts were found dead inside their spacecraft at the end of the Soyuz 11 mission. Georgi T. Dobrovolsky (from left), Vladislav N. Volkov, and Viktor I. Patsayev had set a new endurance record of 23 days in orbit.

KEYSTONE

out the systems within the Salyut but did not enter it. Soyuz 10 returned to earth on April 25.

The ill-fated Soyuz 11 mission began with a perfect lift-off on June 6. The crew consisted of Georgi T. Dobrovolsky, Vladislav N. Volkov, and Viktor I. Patsayev. On June 7 Soyuz 11 docked with the Salyut. The crew then moved into the Salyut. Twice in the next several days the joined vehicles were lifted into higher orbits.

During the third day of the mission, the crew began wearing special pressure suits to maintain muscle tone and to counteract the debilitating effects of weightlessness on the cardiovascular system. Medical and biological experiments were prominent among those conducted by the crew. Among the former was a special instrument for studying human adaptation to weightlessness and another for determining bone density. Typical of the latter was the hatching of tadpoles under conditions of weightlessness and their preservation at varying stages of development. In addition, plants such as flax, cabbage, and onions were grown in special solutions.

On June 24, after 18 days in orbit, the crew set a new endurance record, breaking the 17-day, 17-hour record set by their fellow cosmonauts of Soyuz 9 a year earlier. The crew continued to perform its experiments and maintain a rigid physical training program for the duration of the mission. At no time was there any indication of illness or lack of adaptation to weightlessness.

The crew reentered the Soyuz 11 on June 29, undocked from Salyut, and returned to earth. The spacecraft made a smooth landing in the assigned area, but when a rescue group opened the hatch they found all three cosmonauts dead.

It was later reported by the Soviet government that the cosmonauts had died when their reentry craft suddenly lost cabin pressure. Since there was no rupture of the cabin structure itself, the failure was thought to have been in a pressure seal of the hatch or perhaps a valve.

Unmanned Satellites and Probes

The fall of 1970 and 1971 generally found an increase in activity with military satellites. The Soviet Union, for example, clearly demonstrated that it had an advanced reconnaissance satellite capable of matching U.S. counterparts in longevity, if not in quality and quantity of intelligence sensed and transmitted.

Belatedly, the U.S. Air Force began studies with the aerospace industry to develop a maneuverable inspection satellite, a weapon system in which the U.S.S.R. had a clear lead. The studies were to determine the feasibility of developing a satellite capable of making changes in its orbital plane and rendezvousing with an enemy satellite to determine whether it was armed with a nuclear warhead.

As early as 1968, the U.S.S.R. proved with Cosmos 248, 249, and 252 that it had under development a "killer" satellite with rendezvous and inspection capabilities. In October 1970 the U.S.S.R. again demonstrated that it had such a weapons system, perhaps now operational. On October 23, Cosmos 374 was launched from Plesetsk. Within four hours, it was maneuvered into close proximity to Cosmos 373, which had been launched three days earlier. Suddenly, Cosmos 374 appeared as a number of fragments on radar tracking screens monitoring the event. It occurred as both satellites were almost over Leningrad. On October 30, Cosmos 375 was launched into an orbit closely resembling that of Cosmos 374. In less than four hours after launch it also passed near Cosmos 373, over Leningrad, and, just as suddenly, fragmented.

As 1970 drew to a close, several significant events took place in the field of interplanetary probes. The Soviet Union's incredible Lunokhod 1 continued to amaze scientists and engineers with its technological longevity. For months the unmanned eight-wheeled vehicle traveled back and forth within its landing area, making tests of the lunar soil and measuring radiation. In early October it had finally exhausted its fuel supply and could no longer move about.

On Dec. 15, 1970, the Soviet Union's Venera 7 rendezvoused with Venus, after having been launched on August 17. It ejected a landing pod as had the earlier Veneras 4, 5, and 6. However, this pod had been built to withstand pressures as great as 2,645 pounds per square inch and temperatures as high as 986° F. The trip to the surface took 36 minutes and 32 seconds. Once there, the pod's instrumentation telemetered data to the earth for 23 minutes. It reported a stable temperature of 887° F. and a pressure of about 1,136 pounds per square inch.

A number of probes were fired toward Mars by the U.S. and U.S.S.R. in May. After initial failures by each country the Soviet Union successfully launched Mars 2 and Mars 3 on May 19 and May 28, respectively. Mars 2 went into orbit around the planet on November 27. A capsule was launched from the probe and crashlanded on Mars, thus becoming the first manmade object on the planet. Mars 3 went into orbit shortly after and ejected a capsule that soft-landed on the planet and sent back radio and television signals.

Mariner 9 was successfully launched by the U.S. from Cape Kennedy on May 30. On November 13 the probe entered into orbit around Mars but a raging dust storm prevented it from sending back clear television signals. (*See also* Astronomy. *See in* CE: Space Travel.)

SPAIN. During most of 1971 in Spain the position of Generalissimo Francisco Franco and his government seemed stronger than it had been for some time. The struggle for power within the Spanish establishment, caused by the court-martial of 15 Basque guerrillas in Burgos toward the end of 1970, ended in stalemate. But the Opus Dei faction of the administration increased its power, and the army, though incensed at having been used as a convenient scapegoat for conducting the Burgos trials, prudently withdrew from open conflict with the government.

The sense of security felt by the Franco government was such that the emergency measure that enabled the police to make arrests without warrants (imposed for six months on Dec. 14, 1970) was allowed to expire on June 14. On October 1, on the occasion of the 35th anniversary of Franco's coming to power, the government's confidence was further illustrated by the declaration of a wide amnesty releasing some 3,000 people from jail.

Although there was an increase in the number of industrial strikes over the year compared to 1970, a greater measure of freedom was given to workers in the form of the long-awaited labor organization reform law that came into effect on March 11. By this law the structure of the "syndicates" (representing the branches of industry and trade) was retained under the control of a member of the cabinet, to be known as the minister for syndical relations;

Generalissimo Francisco Franco (in car, right) escorts Ethiopia's Emperor Haile Selassie I on an official visit to Madrid in April.

CIFRA FROM PIX

but management, technicians, and workers would be allowed to set up independent associations within each syndicate. Workers would also be allowed to hold meetings in the shop or factory under specified conditions.

Speculation continued in 1971 over whether Franco would retain absolute power for much longer. It was rumored in the international press that pressure, particularly from the United States, was being put on Franco to at least appoint a prime minister to take over some of his responsibilities. The rumors did not abate because Franco gave increasing importance to the position of Prince Juan Carlos of Bourbon. In July it was decreed that in the event of Franco's absence from Spanish territory or illness his functions would be directly entrusted to the prince, who was given the rank of captain general in October. But Franco gave no positive indication of retiring from the political arena himself.

In the field of foreign affairs, Spain showed a marked interest in Latin America. Minister of Foreign Affairs Gregorio Lopez Bravo visited Argentina, Chile, Uruguay, Paraguay, and Brazil in March and April, formulating new policies of eco-nomic and cultural cooperation and signing several agreements. In June and July he held talks with leading officials in Colombia, Venezuela, Peru, Bolivia, and Ecuador. After years of strained relations, a movement was begun during 1971 to improve contacts with the Soviet Union.

Spain's economic situation was particularly frustrating. After experiencing rapid growth up until 1969, the economy was considered "overheated" and the brakes on expansion were applied toward the end of that year and the early part of 1970. In 1971 the authorities were struggling to reactivate the economy once more; a condition of "stagflation"—an inflationary price spiral combined with a stagnant rate of growth—had settled in.

Tourism continued to increase. In the first half of the year, the number of tourists rose by 21.7% and revenue by 22.7% compared with the same period in 1970. (*See in* CE: Spain.)

SPORTS CHAMPIONS OF 1971.

Archery. World champions (target): men's individual—J. Williams (U.S.); men's team—U.S.; women's individual—E. Gapchenko (U.S.S.R.); women's team—Poland.

On June 5 in Hempstead, Long Island, N.Y., Cornell won the first National Collegiate Athletic Association lacrosse championship, beating Maryland 12–6.

"THE NEW YORK TIMES"

Vasily Alekseyev, 28, of the Soviet Union, was the world champion weight lifter in the super-heavyweight division. He weighs 315 pounds and is 6 feet 1 inch tall.

A.F.P. FROM PICTORIAL PARADE

Badminton. All-England Open championship: men's singles—R. Hartono (Indonesia); women's singles—E. Twedberg (Sweden); men's doubles—P. Gunalan, Ng Boon Bee (Malaysia); women's doubles—N. Takagi, H. Yuki (Japan); mixed doubles—S. Pri, U. Strand (Denmark).

Billiards (Pocket). World professional champion: R. Williams (Great Britain). World amateur champion: N. Dagley (Great Britain). European single pocket: L. Dielis (Belgium).

Bobsledding. World champions: 2-man—M. Armano, G. Gaspari (Italy); 4-man—R. Stadler, M. Forster, K. Schaerer, P. Schaerer (Switzerland). European champions: 2-man—P. Bader, H. Floth (West Germany); 4-man—I. Panturu, N. Neagoe, P. Hristovici, G. Maftei (Romania).

Canoeing. World champions: men's kayak singles, 500 meters—N. Kakol (U.S.S.R.), 1,000 meters—H. Siedziewski (Poland), 10,000 meters—V. Tsaryev (U.S.S.R.); men's kayak pairs, 500 meters—L. Andersson-R. Peterson (Sweden), 1,000 meters—J. Kurt-D. Sienov (East Germany), 10,000 meters—A. Kostyenko-V. Konyonov (U.S.S.R.); men's kayak fours, 1,000 meters—U.S.S.R., 10,000 meters—Romania; women's kayak singles, 1,000 meters—L. Pinayeva (U.S.S.R.); women's kayak pairs, 1,000 meters—G. Höllösy-A. Pfeffer (Hungary); women's kayak fours, 10,000 meters—U.S.S.R.

Cross-Country. International senior champions: individual—D. Bedford (Great Britain); team—Great Britain.

Curling. World champion: Canada.

Cycling. World professional champions: men—sprint, L. Loeveseijn (Netherlands); pursuit, D. Baert (Belgium); motor-paced, T. Verschuren (Belgium); road, E. Merckx (Belgium); women—sprint, G. Tsareva (U.S.S.R.); pursuit, T. Garkuchina (U.S.S.R.); road, A. Konkina (U.S.S.R.). Pan-American Games champions: men—sprint, L. King (Trinidad); individual pursuit, M. Rodriguez (Colombia); team pursuit, Colombia; time trial, J. Lovell (Canada); road-team time trial, Cuba; road, J. Howard (U.S.). World amateur champions: men—sprint, D. Morelon (France); pursuit, M. Rodriguez; motor-paced, H. Gnas (West Germany); road, R. Ovion (France).

Fencing. World champions: men—foil, V. Stankovich (U.S.S.R.); épée, G. Kriss (U.S.S.R.); saber, M. Maffei (Italy); team—foil, France; épée, Hungary; saber, U.S.S.R.; women—foil, C. Demaille (France); team—foil, U.S.S.R.

Gymnastics. Pan-American Games champions (men): all-around—J. Rodriguez (Cuba); floor exercises—J. Crosby (U.S.); side horse—J. Rodriguez; rings—J. Crosby; long horse vault—J. Cuervo (Cuba); parallel bars—J. Elias (U.S.); horizontal bar—J. Rodriguez. Pan-American Games champions (women): all-around—R. Pierce (U.S.); floor exercises—L. Metheny (U.S.); side horse vault—R. Pierce; uneven bars—R. Pierce; balance beam—K. Chase (U.S.). European champions (men): combined exercises—V. Klimenko (U.S.S.R.); floor exercises—R. Khristov (Bulgaria); side horse—N. Andrianov (U.S.S.R.); rings—M. Voronin (U.S.S.R.); long horse vault—N. Andrianov; parallel bars—G. Carminucci (Italy); horizontal bar—K. Koste (East Germany).

Handball. European champions (indoor): European Cup—men, V. F. L. Gummersbach (West Germany); women, Kiev Spartak (U.S.S.R.).

Judo. World champions: lightweight—T. Kawaguchi (Japan); light middleweight—H. Tsuzawa (Japan); middleweight—S. Fujii (Japan); light heavyweight—F. Sasahara (Japan); heavyweight

Li Ching-kuang, a powerful player on China's team in the 31st World Table Tennis Championships, helped defeat Japan.

—W. Ruska (Netherlands); unlimited weight—M. Shinomaki (Japan). European champions: lightweight—J. J. Mounier (France); light middleweight—R. Hendel (East Germany); middleweight—G. Auffray (France); light heavyweight H. Howiller (East Germany); heavyweight—W. Ruska (Netherlands); unlimited weight—V. Kuznyetsov (U.S.S.R.).

Karate. European champions: individual—D. Valera (France); team—France.

Sailboat Racing. World championships: boat class, Albacore—J. Langmaid (Canada); Canoe—J. Biddle (Great Britain); Dragon—P. Sundelin (Sweden); Fireball—J. Caig (Great Britain); Flying Dutchman—R. Pattisson (Great Britain); G.P. 14—A. Read (Great Britain); Hornet—L. Wrobel (Poland); Moth—J. Fauroux (France); O.K.—T. Jungblut (West Germany); Star—D. Conner (U.S.); Tempest—G. Foster (U.S.); Tornado, catamaran—I. Fraser (Great Britain); 4-7-0—Van Essen (Netherlands); 5-0-5—D. Farrant (Great Britain); 5.5 meters—T. Turner (U.S.). European champions: Dragon—P. Sundelin; Finn—B. Binkhorst (Netherlands); Soling—P. Elvström (Denmark); Hornet—D. Derry (Great Britain); 4-7-0—J. Follenfant (France); 5.5 meters—R. Symonette (Bahamas); Star—J. Schoonmaker (U.S.).

Speed Skating. World champions (men): overall—A. Schenk (Netherlands); 500 meters—D. Fornaess (Norway); 1,500 meters—A. Schenk; 5,000 meters—A. Schenk; 10,000 meters—A. Schenk. European champions (men): overall—D. Fornaess; 500 meters—A. Schenk; 1,500 meters—D. Fornaess; 5,000 meters—D. Fornaess; 10,000 meters—P. Guttormsen (Norway). European champions (women): overall—N. Statkevich (U.S.S.R.); 500 meters—L. Titova (U.S.S.R.); 1,000 meters—L. Titova; 1,500 meters—N. Statkevich.

Squash Racquets. World champions: men's singles—G. Hunt (Australia); team—Australia. British Open champions: men's singles—J. Barrington (Great Britain); women's singles—H. McKay (Australia).

Table Tennis. World champions: men's singles—S. Bengtsson (Sweden); men's doubles—T. Klampar, I. Jonver (Hungary); women's singles—Liu Hui-ching (China); women's doubles—Liu Hui-ching, Cheng Min-chin (China); mixed doubles—Chang Shin-lin, Liu Hui-ching (China); men's team—China; women's team—Japan. British Commonwealth champions: men's singles—T. Taylor (Great Britain); men's doubles—A. Hydes, T. Taylor (Great Britain); women's singles—J. Shirley (Great Britain); women's doubles—K. Matthews, P. Piddock (Great Britain); mixed doubles—A. Hydes, P. Piddock. English Open champions: men's singles—T. Klamper (Hungary); men's doubles—S. Bengtsson, B. Persson (Sweden); women's singles—M. Alexandru (Romania); women's doubles—M. Alexandru, E. Mihalca (Romania); mixed doubles—A. Stipancic (Yugoslavia), M. Alexandru; men's team—Great Britain; women's team—West Germany.

Tobogganing. World champions: men—K. Brunner (Italy); women—E. Demleitner (West Germany).

Trampoline. European champions: men—P. Luxon (Great Britain); women—N. Dull (West Germany).

Volleyball. Pan-American Games champions: men—Cuba; women—Cuba.

Water Skiing. World champions: men—slalom, M. Suyderhoud (U.S.); figures, R. McCormick (U.S.); jumping, M. Suyderhoud; overall, G. Athans (Canada); women—slalom, C. Freedman (U.S.); figures, W. Stahle (Netherlands); jumping, C. Weir (U.S.); overall, C. Weir; combined teams—U.S. European Cup winners: men—slalom, R. Zucchi (Italy); figures, R. Zucchi; jumping, H. Klie (West Germany); overall, R. Zucchi; team—Italy.

Weight Lifting. World champions: flyweight—Z. Smalcerz (Poland), 749¼ lbs; bantamweight—G. Chetin (U.S.S.R.), 815¼ lbs.; featherweight—Y. Miyake (Japan), 854 lbs.; lightweight—Z. Kaczmarek (Poland), 969¾ lbs.; middleweight—Y. Kanygin (U.S.S.R.), 1,052¼ lbs.; light heavyweight—B. Pavlov (U.S.S.R.), 1,091 lbs.; middle heavyweight—D. Rigert (U.S.S.R.), 1,195¼ lbs.; heavyweight—Y. Kozin (U.S.S.R.), 1,217¼ lbs.; super heavyweight—V. Alekseyev (U.S.S.R.), 1,400¾ lbs.; team—U.S.S.R. U.S. champions: flyweight—P. Moyer, 589 lbs; bantamweight—F. Dominguez, 666 lbs.; featherweight—E. Hernandez, 765 lbs.; lightweight—J. Benjamin, 860 lbs.; middleweight—R. Knipp, 1,008 lbs.; light heavyweight—M. Karchut, 1,008 lbs.; middle heavyweight—R. Holbrook, 1,096 lbs.; heavyweight—G. Deal, 1,157 lbs.; super heavyweight—K. Patera, 1,305 lbs. Pan-American Games champions: flyweight—J. Romero (Colombia), 661 lbs.; bantamweight—R. Chang (Cuba), 755 lbs.; featherweight—M. Mateos (Mexico), 771 lbs.; lightweight—P. Rodriguez (Cuba), 865 lbs.; middleweight—R. Knipp, 992 lbs.; light heavyweight—M. Karchut, 1,041 lbs.; middle heavyweight—P. Grippaldi (U.S.), 1,091 lbs.; heavyweight—G. Deal, 1,173 lbs. European champions: flyweight—Z. Smalcerz (Poland), 732¾ lbs.; bantamweight—I. Földi (Hungary), 809¾ lbs.; featherweight—J. Wojnowski (Poland), 876 lbs; lightweight—W. Baszanowski (Poland), 991¼ lbs.; middleweight—V. Kurentsov (U.S.S.R.), 1,019¼ lbs.; light heavyweight—G. Ivanchenko (U.S.S.R.), 1,102 lbs.; middle heavyweight—D. Rigert, 1,184½ lbs.; heavyweight—V. Yakubovsky (U.S.S.R.), 1,234 lbs.; super heavyweight—V. Alekseyev, 1,388¾ lbs.; team—U.S.S.R.

Wrestling. World freestyle champions: light-flyweight—E. Javadi (Iran); flyweight—M. Ghorbani (Iran); bantamweight—H. Yanegida (Japan); featherweight—A. Abdulbekov (U.S.S.R.); lightweight—D. Gable (U.S.); welterweight—Y. Gussov (U.S.S.R.); middleweight—S. Tediashvili (U.S.S.R.); light heavyweight—R. Petrov (Bulgaria); heavyweight—S. Lomidze (U.S.S.R.); super heavyweight—A. Medved (U.S.S.R.). World Greco-Roman champions: light flyweight—S. Zoubkov (U.S.S.R.); flyweight—P. Kirov (Bulgaria); bantamweight—E. Kazakov (U.S.S.R.); featherweight—M. Markov (Bulgaria); lightweight—S. Damjanovic (Yugoslavia); welterweight—V. Igumenov (U.S.S.R.); middleweight—I. Hegedus (Hungary); light heavyweight—V. Rezyanov (U.S.S.R.); heavyweight—N. Martinescu (Romania); super heavyweight—P. Svensson (Sweden).

STAMPS. Collectors were busy in the spring of 1971, when most of the regular issue United States stamps, postal cards, booklets, and envelopes with new postal rates were released. New postage included 8¢ versions of the Dwight D. Eisenhower stamp and the flag stamp, 9¢ and 11¢ airmail stamps, a 16¢ issue honoring U.S. journalist Ernie Pyle, a 6¢ Paul Revere postal card, and a 60¢ special-delivery stamp.

A 21¢ international airmail stamp was issued in conjunction with the National Philatelic Exhibition (NAPEX) in Washington, D.C. When the U.S.

Hiroe Yuki of Japan (right) returns the birdie hit by Noriko Takagi in a match at the 12th Canadian Open Badminton championships in Montreal, Que., in April. Miss Yuki won the women's singles event.

"MONTREAL GAZETTE"

Two stamps (top) were part of a series of eight issued by the new state of Bangla Desh, formerly East Pakistan. The U.S. historic preservation series in 1971 commemorated the San Francisco cable car (center) and the 400th anniversary of San Juan, Puerto Rico (bottom, left). A stamp honoring Emily Dickinson (bottom, right) was included in the series commemorating American poets.

Postal Service became operative July 1 an 8¢ stamp was issued showing its emblem.

Great Britain's long-awaited "Decimalization Day," February 15, marking the introduction of decimal currency, came during a postal strike. As a result, the low-denomination decimal stamps were issued with little notice. (The higher denominations had been issued in 1970.)

Three major exhibitions were held in 1971. In May Japan held its first international stamp show in Tokyo to mark the centenary of that nation's first stamp. Cape Town, South Africa, was the site of an exhibition in May in conjunction with the tenth anniversary of the Republic of South Africa. The largest exhibition was in Budapest, Hungary, in September to mark the centenary of the country's first stamps. The British Museum showed a portion of the Tapling collection (early Hungarian issues), the first time the collection had left the museum.

Plans were completed for Interphil 76, an international stamp show to be held in Philadelphia, Pa., in 1976 as part of the bicentennial celebration of the American Revolution. A series of stamps to commemorate the revolution was inaugurated July 4 with the issue of the Bicentennial Commission's insignia, a five-pointed star in a rosette. America's oldest national stamp collectors organization, the American Philatelic Society, observed its 85th anniversary in the fall.

H. R. Harmer of New York City ended sales of the Dale-Lichtenstein collection, finishing a three-year series of auctions with receipts totaling more than $3 million. Harmer also sold the airmail collection of the late Henry M. Goodkind of New York City and a mint copy of a 1918 U.S. 24¢ airmail stamp with an inverted center, which brought $31,000. The Joseph Silkin British collection was sold for $145,085 in London. An imperforate pane of one hundred 8¢ U.S. flag stamps sold for $15,560 after being cut into pairs and blocks. The plate number block of 20 brought $3,600.

Leaders of the Bengali movement in East Pakistan, who embarked on an eventually successful struggle for independence, issued a set of stamps in July. Doubt existed about the status of the stamps at that time, because Bangla Desh was not recognized as independent and was not a member of the Universal Postal Union.

The U.S. Postal Service began selling, at post offices in Rhode Island and Phoenix, Ariz., a souvenir folder of U.S. stamps issued in 1970. These $2 folders, containing all U.S. stamps of the previous year, have been offered for some time, but only from Washington, D.C. If sales are good, other post offices may handle the folders.

The Bureau of Engraving and Printing installed Andriotti gravure presses, and a commemorative marking the 150th anniversary of Missouri statehood (tied in with former President Harry S. Truman's birthday) was the first stamp printed on it. (*See in* CE: Stamp and Stamp Collecting.)

STATE GOVERNMENTS, UNITED STATES.

Rising costs of services, especially welfare, and attempts to establish a federal-state revenue sharing program were among the major concerns of state governments in the United States in 1971. Problems of providing adequate education remained pressing, state taxes were generally increased, and scandal embarrassed several states. However, environmental interest was still high, 18-year-olds were given the right to vote, and new measures were enacted to protect consumers and combat drug abuse. Forty-nine states held regular legislative sessions and more than a dozen held special ones.

Revenue Sharing and Welfare in Congress

Plans to share federal revenues with state and local governments and demands for welfare reform dominated federal-state relations in 1971. President Richard M. Nixon called for both in January. His program included some $5 billion in "general revenue sharing" during the first year of operation and $11 billion in "special revenue sharing." The money would be distributed to states according to population, with "no strings attached." States and cities would split the funds about equally. Some officials doubted that the money would go to the states and cities that needed the most help; defenders of the poor said their needs would

not be met; and civil rights leaders wanted stronger provisions against discrimination. The national wage-price freeze announced in August overshadowed the issue, and the revenue-sharing debate slowed down. Revenue sharing remained in committee as Congress closed its session for 1971. It was expected to become a major issue again in 1972.

In June the House of Representatives for the second time in two years passed a welfare reform bill with a federally guaranteed income for poor families. The bill was sent to the Senate where it was still being considered by the Senate Finance Committee by the end of the session. Its enactment would mean a large shift of welfare responsibility from the states to the federal government, possibly a complete take-over. Meanwhile, Congress passed a public employment bill to provide 150,000 jobs on state and local government rolls, with the federal government paying 90% of the wages, states and localities the remaining 10%. (*See also* Social Services.)

Finances

State budgets stood at record highs in 1971 to keep pace with population increases and higher costs in general. Financial pressures reflecting social needs preoccupied the states, and well over half of the state legislatures increased taxes in

A young voter fills out a card to indicate her political party preference at the 18-year-old Voter's Fair sponsored by the New York Democratic Committee in New York City's Central Park.

1971. Pennsylvania and Rhode Island voted new personal income taxes; Connecticut adopted a new 6.5% sales tax, highest in any state; New York, Tennessee, and Texas increased general tax rates; and Alabama, Connecticut, Florida, and West Virginia broadened sales tax coverage. Personal income tax rates were raised in Arkansas, Delaware, Iowa, Massachusetts, Michigan, Montana, and North Dakota, and corporate income taxes were increased in Delaware, Iowa, Michigan, Montana, New Hampshire, New York, North Dakota, and Tennessee. Taxes were raised on motor fuel in 10 states, on alcoholic beverages in 9, and on tobacco in 13.

State tax collections in the 1971 fiscal year totaled $51.5 billion, up 7.3% from 1970. Of the new total, $15.5 billion was from general sales and gross receipt taxes; $14.1 billion was from selective sales taxes; $10.1 billion was from individual income taxes; $3.4 billion was from corporation net income taxes; and $5 billion was from motor vehicle and other licenses.

Data compiled in 1971 showed that state revenues from all sources reached $88.9 billion in fiscal 1970, up 14.6% from the preceding year. General revenue (excluding state liquor store and insurance trust revenue) was $77.8 billion, up 15.5%. Total state expenditure was $85.1 billion. General expenditure, excluding outlays of state liquor stores and insurance trust systems, totaled $77.6 billion, 14.2% above the preceding year. Of general revenue, 61.7% came from state taxes, 12.3% from charges and miscellaneous revenue (including education charges), and 24.8%—$19.3 billion —came from the federal government.

The largest state outlays were $30.9 billion for education, $13.5 billion for highways, $13.2 bil-

New York's Gov. Nelson A. Rockefeller explains how state and local spending have increased proportionally over federal spending for domestic purposes (right). The governor became the center of an intense controversy (above) after he sent armed law officers into Attica State Correctional Facility to put down a prisoner rebellion.

ABOVE AND RIGHT: WIDE WORLD

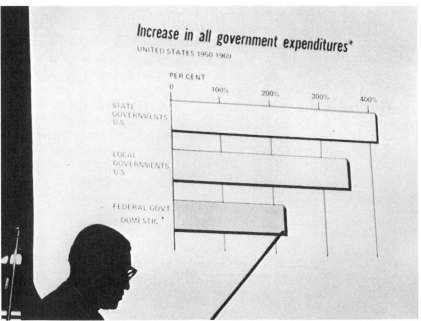

lion for public welfare, $4.2 billion for hospitals, and $1.2 billion for other health items. Largest proportionate increases from the preceding year were these: health (other than hospitals), up 23.5%; welfare, 21.6%; education, 13.7%; hospitals, 11.4%; and highways, 7.7%. From the federal government the states received $4.6 billion for education, $4.4 billion for highways, $7.8 billion for public welfare, and $508 million for health and hospitals.

Administrative and Reapportionment Matters

Nine states consolidated executive departments within the governmental framework or centralized administrative offices. Iowa, Vermont, and Arkansas proposed constitutional amendments to increase gubernatorial terms from two to four years. (Only five states would retain two-year terms.)

Legislative reapportionment became an important issue as a result of the 1970 census and by mid-autumn 28 legislatures had redistricted. Challenges to reapportionment had been lodged in 16 others. Indiana and Wisconsin established annual legislative sessions, raising to 33 the number of states requiring them.

Welfare and Health

Legislatures adopted varied forms of welfare trimming during 1971. Four states—Hawaii, New York, Connecticut, and Rhode Island—voted one-year residency requirements for eligibility for welfare payments, but, in the summer, federal courts held the Connecticut and New York laws unconstitutional.

New York also adopted a 10% reduction in payments to some 1.6 million welfare recipients and required recipients to pick up their relief checks at state unemployment offices and take jobs if they were available. California adopted measures that were expected to cut state welfare costs by some $250 million.

In other welfare-related legislation, Iowa adopted a law authorizing financial aid to persons adopting hard-to-place children; Florida strengthened child-abuse laws and passed a "no fault" divorce law; and Idaho, Alabama, Florida, Kentucky, Maine, and New Jersey reduced taxes for the elderly. Pennsylvania agreed to provide free public education for all of its retarded children.

Education

Increases in state appropriations for education were general throughout the nation as costs continued to rise. The California Supreme Court on August 30 ruled that the state's system of public school financing—based primarily on local taxes—was unconstitutional because of imbalances in the amounts raised by rich as against poor communities. (*See also* Education.) Hearings on the matter were ordered by the court. Because other state laws are similar to California's, the outcome could be far-reaching. Michigan and Minnesota, after

GOVERNORS OF THE STATES

(With Party Affiliations and Current Terms)

State	Governor
Ala.	George C. Wallace (D), 1971–75
Alaska	William A. Egan (D), 1971–72
Ariz.	Jack Williams (R), 1971–75
Ark.	Dale Bumpers (D), 1971–73
Calif.	Ronald Reagan (R), 1971–75
Colo.	John A. Love (R), 1971–75
Conn.	Thomas J. Meskill (R), 1971–74
Del.	Russell W. Peterson (R), 1969–73
Fla.	Reubin Askew (D), 1971–75
Ga.	Jimmy Carter (D), 1971–75
Hawaii	John A. Burns (D), 1970–74
Idaho	Cecil Andrus (D), 1971–75
Ill.	Richard B. Ogilvie (R), 1969–73
Ind.	Edgar D. Whitcomb (R), 1969–73
Iowa	Robert Ray (R), 1971–73
Kan.	Robert Docking (D), 1971–73
Ky.	Wendell Ford (D), 1971–75
La.	John J. McKeithen (D), 1968–72
Me.	Kenneth M. Curtis (D), 1971–75
Md.	Marvin Mandel (D), 1971–73
Mass.	Francis W. Sargent (R), 1971–75
Mich.	William G. Milliken (R), 1971–75
Minn.	Wendell R. Anderson (D), 1971–75
Miss.	William Waller (D), 1972–76
Mo.	Warren E. Hearnes (D), 1969–73
Mont.	Forrest H. Anderson (D), 1969–73
Neb.	James Exon (D), 1971–75
Nev.	D. N. O'Callaghan (D), 1971–75
N.H.	Walter R. Peterson (R), 1971–73
N.J.	William T. Cahill (R), 1970–74
N.M.	Bruce King (D), 1971–75
N.Y.	Nelson A. Rockefeller (R), 1971–75
N.C.	Robert W. Scott (D), 1969–73
N.D.	William L. Guy (D), 1967–73
Ohio	John J. Gilligan (D), 1971–75
Okla.	David Hall (D), 1971–75
Ore.	Tom McCall (R), 1971–75
Pa.	Milton J. Shapp (D), 1971–75
R.I.	Frank Licht (D), 1971–73
S.C.	John C. West (D), 1971–75
S.D.	Richard F. Kneip (D), 1971–73
Tenn.	Winfield Dunn (R), 1971–75
Tex.	Preston E. Smith (D), 1971–73
Utah	Calvin L. Rampton (D), 1969–73
Vt.	Deane C. Davis (R), 1971–73
Va.	Linwood Holton (R), 1970–74
Wash.	Daniel J. Evans (R), 1969–73
W.Va.	Arch A. Moore, Jr. (R), 1969–73
Wis.	Patrick J. Lucey (D), 1971–75
Wyo.	Stanley K. Hathaway (R), 1971–75

studying the California decision, instituted procedures to determine the equity of their educational financing.

State aid to parochial schools suffered a setback in June when the U.S. Supreme Court declared unconstitutional state programs to reimburse church-related schools. Some 36 states already had adopted varying aid programs.

Crime, Drugs, and Environmental Matters

Connecticut increased penalties for making bombs. New York set a maximum penalty of life imprisonment for bombing an occupied building.

Reductions of marijuana penalties were approved in Colorado, Idaho, Illinois, Indiana, Florida, Massachusetts, Nevada, and Missouri. A number of other states made provisions for easier access to treatment for drug addiction.

Connecticut created a Department of Environmental Protection and 12 other states enacted new ecological measures. Pennsylvania and New Mexico declared preservation of the environment a "right" of the people. Four states—Connecticut, Indiana, Maine, and New York—acted to limit phosphates, as did the city of Chicago. Oregon passed a law requiring deposits on beer and pop bottles and prohibiting cans with pull-tab tops. States bordering on Lake Michigan sought means

Ronald Weaver, symbolically dressed, picketed against the proposed state income tax outside the state capitol in Harrisburg, Pa.

WIDE WORLD

of preventing the lake's "death," wanting it to avoid the fate of Lake Erie.

Prison Reforms

Authorities remained aware that deplorable conditions existed in many prisons; nevertheless, they were shocked by the violence of the September prison riot at New York's Attica State Correctional Facility. (*See* Law; Prisons; Prisons Special Report.) They agreed that more money was needed for long overdue prison reforms, but because money was generally not available for welfare requirements in most states, few expected adequate funds for modernizing prisons.

Some progress occurred, however. Pennsylvania announced a "bill of rights" for prisoners; Mississippi agreed to end its armed trusty system —one that had been accused of much brutality; and Indiana authorized pre-release centers for prisoners. Arkansas approved a work-release program, and Washington allowed inmates to adopt a constitution and elect a resident governmental council at the Walla Walla prison facility.

The 18-Year-Old Vote

The U.S. Supreme Court in December 1970 had upheld an earlier act of Congress lowering the voting age to 18 for federal elections. However, this ruling did not apply to state and local elections. The 26th Amendment to the U.S. Constitution solved this problem and qualified voting at age 18 in all elections. Congress approved the amendment in March and in record time the 38 states that were required to make it effective acted.

A problem arose involving college students— should they vote at home or in their college towns? By autumn state officials in almost half the states had issued opinions, and more than half of these appeared to support the constitutional rights of students to vote in their college towns. However, many students in the 18-to-20 age group complained that they were harassed or discouraged when they attempted to register in college towns. Legislation was introduced in Congress to establish the students' rights.

Other Laws

Pennsylvania established a state lottery; Delaware, Florida, Illinois, and Oregon passed versions of "no fault" auto insurance. Michigan and Vermont gave 18-year-olds full legal rights; and North Carolina and Washington reduced the age of majority to 18, except for buying alcoholic beverages.

State Scandals

The year 1971 produced major state scandals in Illinois and Texas. Illinois discovered that its late Secretary of State Paul Powell, a Democrat, had left an estate of some $3 million, much of it stashed in old shoeboxes. He apparently had maintained questionable financial ties with racetrack,

Alabama's Gov. George C. Wallace maintained his stand against school busing. He ordered the transfer of a white pupil from a black school.

trucking, banking, and insurance interests. In another Illinois scandal, evidence made available to a federal grand jury showed that several prominent politicians had bought racing stock at bargain prices and then sold it at profits totaling thousands of dollars. (Racetracks are regulated by the state in Illinois.) Best known of those involved was former Gov. Otto Kerner, a Democrat, now a U.S. Court of Appeals judge. Kerner and several aides were indicted on a number of counts.

The Texas scandal followed the collapse of a $100-million insurance and banking empire, headed by Houston magnate Frank W. Sharp, after investigations by the Securities and Exchange Commission (SEC). The SEC said that Gov. Preston Smith, a Democrat, and Elmer Baum, state Democratic chairman, each made a $62,500 profit on stock in a Sharp life insurance company which they bought in 1969 with money loaned them by one of Sharp's banks. Sharp pleaded guilty in June to making false bank entries and selling unregistered securities. A dozen other prominent political figures later were indicted by grand juries in the case.

Party Strengths

Twenty-nine state governors were Democrats and 21 were Republicans at the start of 1971. The November election of a Democratic governor in Kentucky to succeed a Republican raised the majority affiliation to 30. Democrats had the edge in all four major regions of the U.S., except in the Northeast, where 6 Republicans and 3 Democrats were in governors' offices. Democrats had majorities in both legislative chambers of 23 states. Republicans had majorities in 16.

In the remaining states (except Minnesota and Nebraska, whose legislators are elected without party designation) one house was controlled by one party, the other by the opposition. Only four states had legislative elections in 1971, and party control remained unchanged in three. (*See* Political Parties. *See in* CE: State Governments.)

STOCKS AND BONDS. The United States stock market was unusually erratic in its performance for 1971. The general trend, however, was positive and upward. The Dow-Jones industrial averages (DJI), the most closely followed stock-market indicator, rose from 838.92 on January 4, the year's first day of trading, to an average of 890.20 on December 31. This was a total gain of 51.28 points, compared with the 1970 gain of 38.56 points and the 1969 decline of 143.39 points.

The number of shares traded on the New York Stock Exchange (NYSE) during the year was the greatest in history. A total of 3.89 billion shares were traded, compared to 2.937 billion in 1970.

The DJI high for the year, 950.82, occurred on April 28. The year's low, 797.97, occurred on November 23. Analysts attributed the November slump to public uncertainty over Phase II of U.S. President Richard M. Nixon's new economic program. Another record, the greatest rise in the DJI during a single day's trading of securities, was established on August 16, when the DJI jumped 32.93 points, from 856.02 to 888.95. On the same day an all-time high of 31,730,000 shares of stock were traded on the NYSE.

Thefts of securities were of particular concern to brokers in 1971. In August the National Crime Information Center reported that $494.2 million in securities had been stolen in the U.S. during the first

The TV-like IBM 3670 can automatically supply a stockbroker with data and directly route his orders to the floor of the proper exchange.

six months of the year. This was an increase of $90 million over the combined totals for 1969 and 1970.

A device developed by Astrophysics Research Corp. was designed specifically for the detection of securities thefts. It consisted of an alarm system that could be activated in the presence of a special substance affixed to the surface of all securities handled by the brokerage firm. Persons leaving the firm's premises would be required to exit through a passageway equipped with the detection system's sensors. The New York brokerage firm of Hornblower & Weeks–Hemphill, Noyes announced plans to install the system.

In February William J. Casey was named by President Nixon as chairman of the Securities and Exchange Commission, the federal agency responsible for regulation of the brokerage industry. A well-known New York City tax and corporate attorney, Casey was a graduate of Fordham University and of the law school of St. John's University.

In August William McChesney Martin, Jr., former chairman of the Federal Reserve Board and one-time president of the NYSE, presented to the exchange a list of recommendations for reorganiz-ing the nation's securities industry. Chief among his suggestions was that the NYSE, the American Stock Exchange, and all the regional stock exchanges be integrated into a single, nationwide organization.

Among his other suggestions were that financial institutions such as insurance companies, pension funds, and mutual funds, as well as brokers affiliated with such institutions, be barred from membership in the organization; that Congress grant stock exchanges immunity under the provisions of the antitrust laws; that the management of the NYSE adopt a corporate form; that exchange memberships be converted into shares; and that voting power be transferred from individuals to member firms. (*See also* Business and Industry; Economy; Money and International Finance. *See in* CE: Stocks and Bonds.)

SUDAN. In 1971 an abortive coup took place in Sudan. On July 19, army officers allied with the Sudan Communist party (SCP) seized power and arrested Maj. Gen. Gaafar Mohammed al-Nimeiry, the prime minister. The three leaders of the coup

Conflict between the Northern-dominated Sudanese army and the Southern-based black rebels continued in 1971. These rebel soldiers carry a light machine gun and sacks of cassava through the bush. Israel aided the rebels during the year.

were Maj. Hashem al-Ata, Maj. Farouk Osman Hamadallah, and Lieut. Col. Babakr al-Nur Osman. All had been members of al-Nimeiry's government but were dismissed in 1970 for their Communist sympathies and their opposition to the proposed federation with Libya and Egypt. On July 22 a jet carrying al-Nur Osman and Hamadallah from London to Khartoum, the Sudanese capital, was forced by Libyan planes to land in Benghazi, Libya, where they were taken prisoner. On the same day, troops commanded by Sudanese Defense Minister Maj. Gen. Khaled Hassan Abbas attacked the presidential palace, where al-Nimeiry was being held prisoner. After heavy fighting the counter-coup, aided by Libyan and Egyptian aircraft, succeeded in restoring al-Nimeiry to power.

The coup attempt climaxed eight months of growing tension between al-Nimeiry and the SCP. In February he had accused the SCP of sabotaging the country's unity and asked the people to help him "destroy" it. In the aftermath of the coup al-Nimeiry purged his administration of known SCP sympathizers and set up a single political organization, the Sudan Socialist Union. The officers who had participated in the coup were brought to trial and executed, as was SCP General Secretary Abdel Khalek Mahgoub, one of the most respected Communist figures in the Arab world. The executions caused strong protests from Soviet bloc countries, which had previously given Sudan a great deal of economic aid.

The aid given al-Nimeiry by Libya and Egypt made it almost certain that he would press for Sudan's entry into the Arab federation formed by Libya, Egypt, and Syria, in spite of objections from rebels in southern Sudan who wished to strengthen ties with black Africa. The civil war was still being waged in the southern provinces, and after 15 years came no closer to being settled, though al-Nimeiry entered into negotiations with the exiled leaders of the southern secessionist movement, the *Anyanya*.

Following al-Nimeiry's criticism of the suspected role of European Communists in the July coup, it was expected that he would attempt to strengthen economic and political ties with the West. (*See in* CE: Sudan.)

SUPREME COURT OF THE UNITED STATES.
The 1970–71 term of the United States Supreme Court was marked by a turn toward judicial caution, away from the judicial intervention that had characterized the court during the previous decade. This shift, and a tendency to put delimiting interpretations on liberal decisions of the previous court, was attributed to the influence of Chief Justice Warren E. Burger and Justice Harry A. Blackmun, both appointees of U.S. President Richard M. Nixon. After the end of the term Justices Hugo L. Black and John M. Harlan retired for reasons of health, giving President Nixon the unusual opportunity to appoint two more members. Justice Black, who was one of the court's most

ardent champions of civil rights, died on September 25; Harlan, on December 29.

A conservative cast to the court was assured by President Nixon's nominations for the two vacancies. Lewis F. Powell, Jr., a past president of the American Bar Association and a renowned conservative, was confirmed by the Senate by a vote of 89 to 1 on December 6. The nomination of William H. Rehnquist, an assistant attorney general, was approved on December 10 by a vote of 68 to 26, after considerable controversy and accusations that he was opposed to civil rights measures. (*See* Powell; Rehnquist.)

In disposing of 3,422 cases during the term, the court set a new record for cases concluded. The number of dissenting opinions—91—was the highest in a decade. The leading dissenters were Justice William O. Douglas, who filed 28 dissents, and Justice William J. Brennan, Jr., who filed 13. The court's term was prolonged for consideration of the Pentagon papers case, with adjournment not taking place until June 30. (*See* Law Special Report.)

Major Decisions on Press Freedom, Libel, and Voting Rights

At issue in the Pentagon papers case, the popular name for New York Times Co. *vs.* United States

"So let him appoint a woman to our court. We can always declare her unconstitutional."

In December the U.S. Senate confirmed the nomination of Lewis F. Powell, Jr., as an associate justice of the Supreme Court.
UPI COMPIX

and United States *vs.* the Washington Post Co. et al., was the first attempt in history by the U.S. government to prevent publication on the grounds of national security. In a brief decision upholding lower court rulings, the Supreme Court reaffirmed a 1963 ruling that "any system of prior restraints of expression comes to this Court bearing a heavy presumption against its constitutional validity" and declared that the government had failed to justify restraint in this case. As a result, an injunction against publication of a secret Pentagon study of the Vietnam war was lifted.

In several cases heard during the term the court broadened the constitutional protection that the press had against libel suits. In Rosenbloom *vs.* Metromedia, Inc., it ruled that the press is protected from private individuals involved in public matters who seek damages for libelous news stories about them; the individual must prove calculated malice, falsity, or recklessness in order to collect damages. Rulings on Monitor Patriot Co. *vs.* Roy and on Ocala Star-Banner Co. *vs.* Damron held that the press cannot be sued by public officials, or candidates, for publishing inaccurate charges of criminal behavior.

A challenge to the Voting Rights Act amendments of 1970, by which Congress lowered the voting age in federal and state elections from 21 to 18, was provided by Oregon *vs.* Mitchell. The court held that Congress has final power of supervision over presidential and congressional elections. However, ratification of the 26th Amendment to the Constitution, authorizing 18-year-old voting in all governmental elections, virtually cancelled the effect of the court's ruling. In related challenges to the Voting Rights Act, the court upheld the ban on the literacy test and the right of Congress to outlaw residency requirements of more than 30 days in presidential and congressional elections.

Civil Rights Decisions

The nationwide controversy over the busing of students to achieve school desegregation came before the court in Swann *vs.* Charlotte-Mecklenburg Board of Education, in which a federal court order to use busing was challenged. The Supreme Court ruled unanimously that busing is a constitutional means to achieve school integration and may be ordered by lower courts. In setting guidelines for desegregation, the court did not demand complete racial balance in all schools. In a related case, North Carolina Board of Education *vs.* Swann, the court held void a state law prohibiting the involuntary busing of pupils for purposes of desegregation only.

The right of a community to close its publicly owned recreational facilities rather than comply with desegregation orders was upheld by the court in Palmer *vs.* Thompson. Blacks in Jackson, Miss., had sued to have the city's swimming pools reopened, but the court held that since both blacks and whites were denied the pools there was no basis for a suit under equal-protection laws.

In another civil rights action, the court ruled that suits for damages against individuals who conspire to deny civil rights may be heard in federal courts. Previously such suits reached federal courts only if official misconduct was involved. The case was Griffin *vs.* Breckenridge, in which four blacks sued two whites for assault and intimidation.

Another case, Griggs *vs.* Duke Power Co., involved 13 blacks who had been denied promotion because they had failed tests that were unrelated to jobs. The court held that under the equal-employment section of the 1964 Civil Rights Act, employers are prohibited from using tests that discriminate against blacks by testing for qualifications unrelated to work performance. In its first sex discrimination ruling based on the same law, the court held that companies could not deny jobs to women solely because they were the mothers of very young children. The case was Phillips *vs.* Martin Marietta Corp.

Religion, Housing, Welfare, and Citizenship

One of the most important questions before the court during the term entailed federal or state aid to church-related schools. The separation of church and state required by the 1st Amendment was the basis of several decisions in this area: in Lemon *vs.* Kurtzman the court held that a state cannot use public funds to reimburse church-related schools for teachers' salaries and instructional materials; in Tilton *vs.* Richardson the court upheld a federal law providing for grants to church-related colleges and universities for the construction of buildings used for nonsectarian purposes. It held void a section of the law allowing sectarian use of such buildings after 20 years.

The right of a majority of voters to block low-rent public housing in their community was sustained by the court in James *vs.* Valtierra and Shaffer *vs.* Valtierra. The cases involved a challenge by welfare families to the constitutionality of a California referendum law. The court held that the law was consistent with democratic procedures and was not inherently discriminatory.

The Constitution's protection of "persons" as well as "citizens" was emphasized in Graham *vs.* Richardson. The case dealt with a Mexican migrant to Arizona who was denied welfare for failing to meet state citizenship requirements. The court ruled that states cannot deny equal protection to all persons in their jurisdictions. New York State's requirement that caseworkers must inspect welfare homes as a condition for continuing aid was upheld by the court in Wyman *vs.* James. The taxpayers' right to know how public funds are spent was cited. In another citizenship case, Rogers *vs.* Bellei, the court ruled that persons born abroad of one U.S. parent may have citizenship revoked by Congress if they fail to live in the U.S. for five years before their 28th birthdays.

Military Draft and Armed Forces Rulings

Among the prominent draft cases considered by the court was boxer Muhammad Ali's appeal from a lower court conviction for refusing military induction. Ali, formerly known as Cassius Clay, had been denied conscientious objector status by his draft board. In Clay *vs.* United States the court overturned the conviction in a ruling that held Ali qualified as a conscientious objector by reason of sincerity and religious training, and that his request for exemption had been improperly handled.

Two other appeals before the court involved men who had unsuccessfully sought conscientious objector exemptions on the grounds that the Vietnam war is unjust. In its rulings, the court declared that men must oppose participation in all wars, rather than selected wars, in order to qualify for such an exemption. The cases were Gillette *vs.* United States and Negre *vs.* Larsen.

In the case of Relford *vs.* Commandant, U.S. Disciplinary Barracks, Fort Leavenworth, the court further defined a previous ruling that servicemen could be tried by courts-martial only for service-connected offenses. Ruling on Relford, the court held that an offense against property or a person, civilian or military, committed on a military base is "service-connected" and therefore may be prosecuted in a court-martial.

Juvenile Justice, Abortion, Capital Punishment, Criminal Law, and Due Process

The problem of justice for juveniles who commit crimes came before the court in McKeiver *vs.* Pennsylvania. A teen-ager charged with various

Since taking his post as chief justice of the Supreme Court in 1969, Warren E. Burger has worked for judicial reform in the nation's courts.

WIDE WORLD

acts of juvenile delinquency, McKeiver—as well as juveniles in other cases—petitioned for trial by jury. The court ruled that juveniles have no right to jury trials and stated that requiring such trials would end the "intimate, informal protective" proceedings of the juvenile court system.

The court rendered its first decision on the constitutionality of anti-abortion laws in a case challenging the District of Columbia's abortion statute. In its ruling the court upheld the statute, which permits abortions only to protect the life and health of the mother. However, the decision qualified the application of the law by stating that "health" referred to psychological as well as physical well-being.

Capital punishment was an issue in a number of cases decided during the term. McGautha *vs.* California challenged the right of juries to impose the death sentence without detailed guidelines from the court; Crampton *vs.* Ohio alleged that capital punishment was unconstitutional unless separate hearings for guilt and punishment were provided. In a single ruling covering both cases, the court held that juries have "untrammeled discretion" to impose the death penalty, and that both Ohio's single-hearing court procedure and California's dual-hearing procedure were constitutional.

North Carolina's law providing for life imprisonment if the accused pleads guilty to first-degree murder, but for the death penalty if he pleads not guilty and a guilty verdict is found by the jury, was challenged in North Carolina *vs.* Alford. The defendant claimed that he pleaded guilty only to avoid the death penalty and sought post-conviction relief on the grounds that his plea was involuntary. The court rejected his claim, holding that the plea was voluntary and that Alford had been competently represented.

On the grounds that it is unconstitutional to carry out death sentences imposed by juries made up entirely of persons who favor capital punishment, the court set aside the death penalties of 39 persons awaiting execution. The convictions remained standing.

The Warren court's landmark decision in Miranda *vs.* Arizona was significantly narrowed in 1971 when the court ruled that a suspect's statement could be used in court to contradict his testimony, even if the same statement is inadmissible as evidence. In other decisions, the court held that citizens could sue federal agents in federal courts for damages resulting from illegal search and arrest; declared that a state could not suspend a driver's license for failure to pay a traffic-accident judgment if the driver had gone into bankruptcy; ruled unconstitutional state "financial responsibility" laws that revoke the licenses of uninsured drivers involved in accidents, regardless of fault. The court upheld state hit-and-run laws requiring drivers involved in accidents to stop and give their names and addresses. (*See also* Congress, U.S.; Law. *See in* CE: Supreme Court of the U.S.)

SWAZILAND. In 1971 Swaziland celebrated its third year of independence and the fiftieth year of the reign of its ruler, King Sobhuza II, in an atmosphere of stability and progress. Race relations between the Swazi and foreign whites continued to be good although there were increased attempts to replace foreign participation with Swazi in various economic enterprises.

The mining industry continued to expand. South Africa's Rand Mines, which controlled the coal industry, investigated the possibility of a new mine near Manzini, as progress continued on a proposed rail link with South Africa.

The government's delicate relationship with South Africa, which surrounds Swaziland geographically, was underlined in January with the arrival of Leonard Nikane, a South African wanted in his own country on terrorist charges. He was refused refugee status, declared a prohibited immigrant, and held in jail. The government was unable to return him to South Africa for fear of repercussions from the Organization of African Unity, or to send him to another African country because of South Africa's overfly rights, or to free him because of rumors that he had come to assassinate the king. (*See in* CE: Swaziland.)

SWEDEN. The year 1971 was marked by a depressed economy and labor troubles in Sweden. The first union-sponsored strike since 1966 occurred in February. Members of the Confederation of Professional Associations and the Federation of Civil Servants struck following lengthy bargaining, in which the union sought wage hikes ranging from 18% to 23%. Shortly afterward, other white-collar workers from the Central Organization of Salaried Employees joined in the strike. Eventually, some 50,000 state and municipal employees were on strike or locked out. The strike/lockout lasted for six weeks; the government, in an unprecedented move, then passed a six-week back-to-work law covering all labor and banning strikes and lockouts.

A labor dispute affecting 830,000 blue-collar workers ended in June when an agreement was reached after seven months of talks. The agreement gave workers an increase in wages and benefits totaling 28% over the following three years.

Restrictive fiscal policies were in effect throughout the year because of a depressed economy. Adding to the internal woes of high unemployment were the import charges adopted by two countries that had been important export markets, Denmark and the United States.

Sweden's Social Democratic government declared in March that full membership in the European Economic Community (EEC) was not a "realistic possibility." The announcement came at a time when restrictive economic measures were pushing unemployment to the highest level in years and when three important trading partners—Great Britain, Denmark, and Norway—announced intentions of joining the EEC.

There were changes of leadership in two of Sweden's main political parties. The Conservative party in November 1970 had elected Gösta Bohman to replace Yngve Holmberg, and in June the Centre party replaced its retiring leader, Gunnar Hedlund, with Thorbjörn Fälldin.

Preparations were under way throughout the year for the United Nations Conference on the Human Environment, scheduled to meet in Stockholm in June 1972. (*See in* CE: Sweden.)

SWIMMING. The year 1971 was a good one for competitive swimmers. International matches provided the last tune-up for the 1972 Olympic Games and, for the first time ever in any sport, a United States team competed in East Germany. The Soviet Union also broke precedent when it en-

Two alleged Croatian terrorists (center) were arrested in Stockholm, Sweden, in April. They were charged with shooting the Yugoslav ambassador to Sweden, who later died.
UPI COMPIX

Mark Spitz of the Arden Hills, Calif., swim club broke his own world record by swimming the 200-meter butterfly in 2:03.89.
WIDE WORLD

tered the Santa Clara international meet in California, marking the initial U.S. appearance of a Soviet swim team. Australia, a perennial swim power, sent a strong team to London for the 14-nation Coca-Cola international meet; it outscored the U.S. 122–121; and it also entered the Santa Clara international. World record barriers were shattered on 25 occasions.

U.S. Competition

The U.S. male swimmers completely dominated the 1971 Pan-American Games at Cali, Colombia, winning 14 gold medals out of 15 races, plus 9 silver and 2 bronze. The U.S. women were barely able to outscore a strong Canadian team, winning but 8 of 14 races, with 9 silver and 5 bronze medals

to the Canadians' 6 gold, 5 silver, and 3 bronze medals.

The highlight of the Pan-American Games was the feat of Frank Heckl, six feet five inches tall, a 195-pound 20-year-old from Cerritos, Calif. He won six gold medals and one silver, and also anchored the men's 800-meter freestyle relay that lowered the world mark to 7:45.82.

In 1971, U.S. swimmers broke the world records for individual events on nine occasions and snapped five world relay marks. The U.S. Amateur Athletic Union (AAU) long-course (outdoor) championships in Houston, Tex., August 25–28, produced five world records and seven U.S. records. Tom McBreen, 18-year-old University of Southern California sophomore from San Mateo, Calif., chipped

WORLD SWIMMING RECORDS SET IN 1971 (through September 15)

	Event	Name	Country	Time		
MEN	200-meter freestyle	Mark Spitz	United States	1 minute	54.2	seconds
	200-meter freestyle	Mark Spitz	United States	1 minute	53.5	seconds
	400-meter freestyle	Tom McBreen	United States	4 minutes	02.08	seconds
	800-meter freestyle	Graham Windeatt	Australia	8 minutes	28.6	seconds
	100-meter backstroke	Roland Matthes	East Germany		56.71	seconds
	200-meter backstroke	Roland Matthes	East Germany	2 minutes	05.6	seconds
	100-meter butterfly	Mark Spitz	United States		55.01	seconds
	200-meter butterfly	Mark Spitz	United States	2 minutes	03.89	seconds
	200-meter butterfly	Hans Fassnacht	West Germany	2 minutes	03.3	seconds
	800-meter freestyle relay	National team	United States	7 minutes	45.82	seconds
	800-meter freestyle relay	National team	United States	7 minutes	43.33	seconds
	400-meter medley relay	National team	United States	3 minutes	50.41	seconds
WOMEN	100-meter freestyle	Shane Gould	Australia		58.9	seconds
	200-meter freestyle	Shane Gould	Australia	2 minutes	06.5	seconds
	400-meter freestyle	Karen Moras	Australia	4 minutes	22.6	seconds
	400-meter freestyle	Shane Gould	Australia	4 minutes	21.2	seconds
	800-meter freestyle	Ann Simmons	United States	8 minutes	59.37	seconds
	1,500-meter freestyle	Cathy Calhoun	United States	17 minutes	19.2	seconds
	1,500-meter freestyle	Shane Gould	Australia	17 minutes	19.5	seconds
	200-meter butterfly	Karen Moe	United States	2 minutes	18.6	seconds
	200-meter butterfly	Ellie Daniel	United States	2 minutes	18.4	seconds
	400-meter freestyle relay	National team	United States	4 minutes	00.66	seconds
	400-meter medley relay	National team	United States	4 minutes	27.33	seconds

Shane Gould of Australia won the women's 400-meter freestyle at the Santa Clara International Swim meet. Her time was 4:21.2.

five tenths off the 400-meter freestyle record, lowering the mark to 4:02.08.

Mark Spitz, veteran 20-year-old from Indiana University established himself as the "world swimmer" of 1971, as he lowered his own 100-meter butterfly world standard to 55.01 seconds. Two days later he regained, for four days, a world mark for the 200-meter butterfly by clocking 2:03.89 in a preliminary heat.

Olympian Ellie Daniel, 21-year-old University of Pennsylvania sophomore, from Elkins Park, Pa., lowered not only the listed world 200-meter butterfly women's mark of 2:19.3 but also a pending mark of 2:18.6 set at the Los Angeles Invitational three weeks earlier by Karen Moe, 18, Santa Clara University freshman. Miss Daniel was timed at 2:18.4.

The U.S. unveiled a bright new star at Houston. Cathy Calhoun, 13, a junior high school student from El Monte, Calif., lowered Olympic champion Debbie Meyer's 1,500-meter freestyle world record by seven tenths of a second to 17:19.2 (later lowered by Australia's Shane Gould to 17:00.06). En route, her 9:09.6 surpassed Miss Meyer's U.S. 800-meter freestyle mark (again lowered by Miss Gould to 8:59.3 in December).

European and Commonwealth Competitors

A team from Australia made a spring tour of Europe and achieved its greatest success by edging the U.S. team at the Coca-Cola International meet in London's Crystal Palace, April 30–May 1. Shane Gould, a 14-year-old from Ryde, gave the Commonwealth nation its brightest hours since the 1956 Olympics. Miss Gould equaled the oldest women's record in the book when she was timed in 58.9 for the 100-meter freestyle. Her time was ratified by the Fédération Internationale de Natation Amateur (FINA) and was made official. The following day Miss Gould lowered the 200-meter freestyle to 2:06.5, erasing the world record held by U.S. swimmer Debbie Meyer; she later brought it down to 2:05.8.

Another of Australia's great teen-agers, Karen Moras, 17, continued the world record onslaught as she surpassed the last of Miss Meyer's records, ripping 1.7 seconds from the 1970 400-meter freestyle mark to 4:22.6. Miss Moras' record was to last less than 90 days, because at the Santa Clara international meet on July 9, Miss Gould further lowered the time for 400 meters to 4:21.2.

In March, during Australia's summer season, Graham Windeatt, 17, from Sydney, broke still another of the U.S.-held world records. His 800-meter freestyle time of 8:28.6 was two tenths faster than the mark held by Mike Burton.

In the fall the swimming season was highlighted by a series of international matches between the

Tears of joy overwhelm U.S. swimmer Kaye Hall when she learned she had won the women's 100-meter backstroke and set a new world and Olympic record of 1:06.2 in October.

U.S. and the swimming powers of Europe, namely, East Germany and the Soviet Union, with the Americans lowering world marks on seven occasions. On September 3 and 4 at Leipzig, East Germany, a select U.S. team of 12 men and 12 women swimmers, plus 6 divers, swamped its host before capacity crowds of 6,000 daily.

Mark Spitz lowered the 200-meter freestyle standard he shared with Don Schollander, when he won the event in 1:54.2. East Germany's Roland Matthes, 21, lowered both of his backstroke world records, slashing his 100-meter time to 56.71 seconds and his 200-meter to 2:05.6. His victories saved the East German men from a complete shutout. The men's U.S. 400-meter medley relay team regained its world record from East Germany, blitzing the old mark by 4 seconds as it was timed in 3:50.41.

From Leipzig the U.S. swimmers moved on to Minsk, U.S.S.R., where they competed in a triangular meet on September 9–11 against Great Britain and the Soviet Union. Again the Americans swamped their rivals as they scored 342 points to the Soviet's 205 and Britain's 141.

Mark Spitz, by more than one half second, lowered his pending 200-meter freestyle time set at Leipzig to 1:53.5. An hour later Spitz, joined by Jerry Heidenreich, Fred Tyler, and Tom McBreen, ripped, by more than two seconds, the 4 x 200-meter freestyle relay record set by the U.S. team at the American Games. The quartet was timed in 7:43.33.

The U.S. girls also did well. On September 9, in the 4 x 100-meter freestyle relay, a very young national team of Linda Johnson, 17, Deena Deardurff, 14, Shirley Babashoff, 14, and Kim Peyton, 14, replaced the old world mark held by the East Germans with a new time of 4:00.66. The following day, Sue Atwood, Claudia Clevenger, Ellie Daniel, and Linda Johnson lowered the world record for the 4 x 100-meter medley relay by one tenth of a second to 4:27.33. The old record was also held by the U.S. team.

The nine-minute barrier in the women's 800-meter freestyle was finally shattered. At Minsk, on September 11, Ann Simmons, 18, from Lakewood, Calif., a freshman at Long Beach City College, stroked 16 lengths of the pool and recorded 8:59.37, the fastest ever by a woman and faster than a world record by 1960 Olympic champion John Konrads, who a dozen years ago in 1959 set a world mark of 8:59.6 for that distance. (*See in* CE: Swimming.)

SWITZERLAND. In a nationwide referendum on Feb. 7, 1971, male citizens of Switzerland granted women the right to vote in federal elections for the first time. Several cantons (states) refused to allow women to vote in local and cantonal matters, however. Women represented 55% of the 3.5 million voters in Switzerland. The first issue on which women were able to vote was the June 6 referendum on a proposed constitutional amendment to protect the environment.

Women also voted in the parliamentary election of October 31, the major political event of the year. The political composition of parliament had varied little since 1919, but with the participation of women and the redistribution of seats by cantons according to the 1970 census, the election took on a new dimension. Eleven women were elected to the parliament, and one was named to the Council of States (upper chamber), but the traditional political makeup of the legislature remained unchanged.

The economic scene was marked by the continuance of boom conditions and by a serious labor shortage. The Swiss franc was revalued upward 6.6% in May; the result of the international monetary realignment in December was a total upward revaluation of 12.18% for the Swiss franc.

In November the Federal Council set up a commission to determine the conditions under which Switzerland might become a member of the United Nations (UN). Meanwhile, the UN Economic and Social Council made Switzerland a member of its Economic Commission for Europe.

Earlier in the year the Swiss supreme court

In February Swiss women were finally given the vote and this Swiss citizen entered the polling station for the first time in her life.

UPI COMPIX

A riot broke out between students and police in Zurich, Switzerland, on May Day. The students had been picketing the consulates of Greece and Spain.

authorized federal tax officials to supply the United States Internal Revenue Service with information concerning dealings with Swiss banks of a U.S. citizen under investigation for tax fraud. (*See in* CE: Switzerland.)

SYRIA. Under the government of Gen. Hafez al-Assad, which seized power late in 1970, Syria undertook internal political reforms and worked to end its diplomatic isolation in the Arab world during 1971. In February al-Assad decreed the establishment of a 173-member People's Council, Syria's first legislative body since 1966. In appointing the council, al-Assad broadened the base of the government by giving representation to Socialists, Communists, Nasserites, and independents, in addition to the ruling Ba'athist party. Syria's head of state, Ahmed al-Khatib, resigned to become speaker of the council; al-Assad assumed the powers of the presidency on February 22.

A series of amendments to the provisional constitution of 1969, also effected in February, provided that a "president of the Republic" should replace the head of state and hold office for seven years; gave the president broad authority to appoint top officials and to dissolve the People's Council; provided a two-year term for the People's Council, and declared its functions to include the drafting of a permanent constitution and the nomination of a president from among the leaders of the Ba'athist Party Regional Command.

In a national referendum held on March 12 al-Assad was elected president of Syria by over 99% of the vote; he was the only candidate. A new cabinet was formed in April, completing the reorganization of the government promised by al-Assad. At an international Ba'athist meeting in August the party's new leaders elected al-Assad secretary-general of the party.

In April al-Assad and the leaders of Egypt and Libya signed an agreement providing for the unification of their nations under a Confederation of Arab Republics. Syria's People's Council approved the agreement, and on September 1 the confederation was overwhelmingly endorsed by the voters of the three nations. Under the confederation, which is based on an ideology of "democratic socialism" and on an uncompromising stand against Israel, each state retains its sovereignty and its United Nations seat.

During the year Syria resumed diplomatic relations with Tunisia and Morocco, undertook a rapprochement with Lebanon, and permitted the repair of an oil pipeline to Saudi Arabia, which had been closed down for nine months. Syrian relations with Saudia Arabia subsequently improved.

In July skirmishes occurred along the Syrian-Jordanian frontier, and Syria closed its border with Jordan in protest over a Jordanian campaign to subdue the Palestinian guerrillas. Following further border clashes in August and Jordan's refusal to allow Syrian mediation of the dispute with the Palestinians, Syria severed relations with Jordan. The area around Dera'a in southern Syria became the center of the guerrilla movement after the Palestinians were forced to flee from Jordan.

Syria continued to oppose a political settlement of the Arab-Israeli conflict, and announced in March that a joint Syrian-Egyptian military command had been formed. In a speech in October al-Assad declared that Syria had 250,000 men under arms to fight Israel. Several incidents erupted along the Syrian-Israeli border in the fall.

The Syrian economy suffered from a trade recession during 1971 as a result of severe drought conditions the year before. In negotiations with the Western-owned Iraq Petroleum Co., Syria won an increase of over 50% in the royalties to be paid by the firm for the right to pipe oil across Syria. During the year Syria's first phosphate plant was opened at Khunaifis; a cotton yarn factory, built with Chinese aid, began operations at Hama; and East Germany was awarded contracts to develop cement plants at Damascus, Aleppo, and Hama. Although relations with Iraq remained strained, the final section of the Baghdad–Damascus highway was opened in September. The al-Assad regime lifted Syria's ban on the importation and showing of films from certain Western nations.

Syria's third five-year economic development program went into effect during 1971. However, an unexpected increase in the annual population growth between 1960 and 1970 required greater investment in development than had originally been planned. (*See also* Egypt. *See in* CE: Syria.)

TAIWAN. On Oct. 25, 1971, the United States two-China policy—supporting the admission of the People's Republic of China into the United Nations (UN) while preserving Nationalist China's membership—was defeated. The UN General Assembly voted to expel the Nationalist government (the Republic of China, located on Taiwan, or Formosa) in favor of the People's Republic. Together with the announcement in July of U.S. President Richard M. Nixon's planned visit to Peking and the lifting of the 21-year-old embargo on American trade with the People's Republic, this was the cause of much uncertainty over the future of Taiwan. The UN vote was a particular blow to the island's ruler, President Chiang Kai-shek. Concern was expressed for the eventual fate of the U.S. treaty to defend Taiwan against attack. The U.S. Senate Foreign Relations Committee voted to repeal a 1955 resolution granting discretionary power to the president to use force in defending Taiwan from an attack by China, but the full Senate later voted (43-40) to retain it.

Some economic difficulties were anticipated, especially affecting the acquisition of long-term investments in heavy industry. Land values dropped and the Taiwan dollar depreciated against the U.S. dollar by several points. The stock market fell and a number of frightened businessmen fled the country. Although exports rose to an all-time high of $1.9 billion in the first half of 1971, the total number of new foreign investments dropped 40% from 1970. American investments fell from $44.8 million to $23.2 million.

President and Madame Chiang Kai-shek walk past public officials in the Taipei City Hall after attending ceremonies observing the 60th anniversary of the Republic of China.

CAMERA PRESS FROM PIX

The Penghu Bay Bridge was opened on March 26; it became the longest inter-island bridge in the Far East. It links two large islands in the Formosa Strait.

The UN decision damaged the Nationalist government's claim to be the rightful government of all of China. The justification for maintaining a police state and the expense of the world's sixth largest army became questionable. As a result, political reformers became more active than they had been for some years. Reformers demanded a new single government for Taiwan and its islands, a single executive branch, greater representation for younger people in the government, and a more democratic system.

The government took no action against the reformers as it would have done a year previously. The ruling Kuomintang party stated that more young people must be brought into the government and the party. A number of political prisoners were released—another indication of the government's liberalized policies. (*See also* China, People's Republic of; Foreign Policy, U.S.; United Nations. *See in* CE: Formosa.)

TANZANIA.

Events in Tanzania in 1971 were strongly influenced by a coup in neighboring Uganda in which leftist President Milton Obote was replaced by an army general. Apparently fearing a precedent, Tanzania's ruling TANU party, headed by President Julius K. Nyerere, issued a document reaffirming its commitment to socialism and stepped up its socialization program. A massive campaign to educate the masses politically was begun, and the formation of a people's militia was announced. Under a hastily passed act aimed at ending exploitation by landlords, the government nationalized a large number of buildings. The seizures primarily affected Tanzania's propertied Asian businessmen, reducing their ability to provide collateral for credit; in turn, the nation's entire trade and credit structure was damaged, and racial tensions were increased.

Tanzania refused to recognize the new regime in Uganda, its partner (with Kenya) in the East African Community (EAC), and gave refuge to Obote. Uganda accused Tanzania of fostering pro-Obote guerrillas. Tanzania prevented Ugandan officials of the EAC, nominated by the new regime, from taking up their duties in Arusha in northern Tanzania. As a result, Uganda closed its border with Tanzania and expelled several Tanzanian officials. Armed clashes occurred along the border during the summer and fall. The incidents threatened the future of the EAC, which was set up in 1967 to create an East African common market. (*See also* Africa; Uganda. *See in* CE: Tanzania.)

These men were accused of plotting against the Tanzanian government and sentenced to death. They sit handcuffed before a crowd.

TELEVISION AND RADIO. Virtually all countries had some radio service and all industrialized nations except South Africa had television in 1971—and the South African government promised to introduce TV by 1975. Television and radio sets in use throughout the world numbered more than 881 million, according to estimates compiled by *Broadcasting* magazine and *Broadcasting Yearbook*. Television sets totaled about 241,740,000 and radio sets approximately 640 million. The United States accounted for about 36%, or 87 million, of the world's television sets, followed by Japan with 30 million, and the U.S.S.R. with 28 million.

More than half, or about 336 million, of the world's radio sets were in use in the U.S. No nation of any size was without some form of radio service, although in a few cases receivers hooked to loudspeakers were still used for community listening to broaden the range of broadcasts, which in some countries came from booster and relay stations as well as from direct broadcasting stations.

There were approximately 6,380 television stations, including satellites and repeaters, throughout the world in 1971, according to *Broadcasting*. No area had gained or lost significantly since 1970. About 2,100 were in the Far East, 2,000 in Western Europe, 1,013 in the U.S., 905 in Eastern Europe, 175 in South America, 80 in Canada, and 35 in Africa. In many countries, viewers were offered a choice of several programs; in others, only one or two were available. In the U.S., it was estimated that 17% of all TV householders could receive ten or more stations, 57% could receive seven or more, 90% could receive four or more,

and 97% could receive at least three stations.

As of Oct. 1, 1971, estimates indicated that more than half—50.1%—of U.S. television households were equipped with color television sets. The total was put at 31 million color-TV homes. The three networks—American Broadcasting Co. (ABC), Columbia Broadcasting System (CBS), and National Broadcasting Co. (NBC)—transmitted virtually all of their programs in color. So did most of the 1,013 stations, whether affiliated with the networks or not.

Satellites

A major accomplishment was achieved in May 1971 when an international conference, first assembled in 1969, finally reached agreement on the form of organization for permanent administration of the International Telecommunications Satellite Consortium (Intelsat). Some 80 nations participated in the conference, held in Washington, D.C., and a dozen others, including the U.S.S.R. and other Communist countries, were represented as observers and were invited to join. One of the goals of the conference, which had approached agreement previously only to fail at the last moment, had been to reduce the role of the U.S., which through the Communications Satellite Corp. (Comsat) had managed Intelsat since 1964. This objective, shared by the U.S., was reached in the final agreement by providing for the creation of a 12-member board of directors on which voting rights would be assigned in proportion to each country's use of the current Intelsat system. On this basis, the U.S. was calculated to have a 38.28% ownership in the $500-million organiza-

The Electric Company, a new experiment in educational television from the Children's Television Workshop, focuses on helping to teach reading to second, third, and fourth graders. The adult performers are (left to right) Judy Graubart, Morgan Freeman, Lee Chamberlin, Rita Moreno, Bill Cosby, and Skip Hinnant.

COURTESY, THE CHILDREN'S TELEVISION WORKSHOP

tion, Great Britain 10.86%, and the following countries lesser percentages in descending order: Australia, Japan, Canada, France, Italy, Germany, Pakistan, Spain, Israel, and the Philippines.

The U.S. networks frequently used satellites to bring in coverage of overseas events for their news programs and to send their own coverage of special events to other countries. Two of the year's most extensive satellite arrays were set up for coverage of the U.S. Apollo 14 moon mission in February and the more extended Apollo 15 mission in late July and early August. Both included color television pictures from the surface of the moon. For Apollo 15 there was extensive live coverage of the astronauts at work on the moon and, for the first time, of the blast-off of a space capsule from the lunar surface and of its docking with the command ship in orbit. Some 20 satellite earth stations in the U.S., Latin America, Europe, the Western Pacific, and the Middle East were employed in getting the live pictures to stations around the world.

Responding to an invitation from the Federal Communications Commission (FCC), eight U.S. companies submitted proposals for operating their own complete domestic satellite systems. But by November 1971 the FCC had not yet adopted a basic domestic-satellite policy.

Cable Television (CATV)

In 1971 CATV finally received tentative clearance to move into big cities. It seemed to be on the verge of a major expansion that could eventually lead to what many broadcasters felt would be a serious erosion of their own audiences.

Broadcasting estimated in mid-1971 that there were 2,500 operating CATV systems in the U.S.

serving an average of 2,000 homes each, and that another 2,200 systems had been approved but not yet built. In addition, some 1,400 applications for systems were pending before local governments. CATV systems had been authorized in all states and were operating in all but Connecticut. On the average, ten channels of programming were offered to subscriber lists ranging from fewer than 100 homes to more than 47,000, for a San Diego, Calif., system. The average subscriber fee was about $4.95 per home per month after installation charges that averaged $20 per home.

Programming Trends

The most fundamental change in programming in the U.S. in 1971 evolved from the FCC's so-called prime-time access rule. From October 1, TV stations in the top 50 markets were required to give up a half-hour a night on weekdays, and an hour on Sundays, of programming formerly supplied by the networks. The FCC's purpose was to increase the diversity of sources of programming by making it necessary for stations to program these periods on their own initiative or to seek programming from syndicators or other non-network sources. In actuality, the ruling affected all network affiliates; the networks considered it economically unfeasible to supply programs that would not be seen in the top 50 markets.

On the whole, the plan was not a success. For the first year, the FCC permitted stations to present old movies and re-runs of old network series in the periods turned back by the networks. This was the sort of programming that most stations used, augmented by some new musical, variety, and games programming of the same basic type that was developed by syndicators to fill the network

The Hallmark Hall of Fame presented Arthur Miller's 'The Price', on February 3, starring George C. Scott (left), Colleen Dewhurst, and Barry Sullivan.

COURTESY, NBC

Sylvia Sidney (left), Helen Hayes (center), Mildred Natwick (right), and Myrna Loy (rear) played four elderly women who indulged in playing practical jokes in an ABC-TV movie, 'Do Not Fold, Spindle or Mutilate'.

UPI COMPIX

void. Occasionally purely local news or entertainment programming was offered. The reaction of audiences was not particularly encouraging. Estimates for specific time periods compiled by *Broadcasting* in November indicated that fewer people were watching the new "local" programming than had watched programming by the networks in 1970, although the audiences of network programs later in the evening were substantially larger than the year before.

The concern with ecology and minority-group problems that had distinguished the new programming on all three TV networks in 1970 clearly had not been well received, according to the A. C. Nielsen Co. and other rating-service measurements. As a result, in 1971 the networks tended to concentrate their efforts on entertainment rather than on series with a "do-good" theme. Westerns, mysteries, and comedy-variety programs were once more the norm. Like news and public affairs, ecological, sociological, and other fundamental issues increasingly were dealt with in documentaries and "specials." The success of this blend of programming was pointed up by estimates published by *Broadcasting* in November. Average family viewing was totaling over 11 hours a day, an increase of more than half an hour a day over the previous year.

One of the most spectacular developments of the year was the controversy centering on 'The Selling of the Pentagon', a special dealing with the public relations activities of the Department of Defense, produced by CBS News and broadcast on CBS-TV early in 1971. Angered supporters of the Department of Defense contended that the program made false accusations and distorted the words of Pentagon spokesmen. A House of Representatives committee voted to subpoena inter-office papers and other non-broadcast material related to the program, which CBS had consistently refused to submit. The upshot was considerable debate over broadcast journalists' responsibilities under the 1st Amendment to the Constitution. Finally, after a dramatic confrontation, the House refused to cite CBS for contempt and instead referred the issue back to the Interstate and Foreign Commerce Committee, whose leaders then declared the issue dead. CBS officials received numerous honors from journalistic societies and other organizations both for the program and for their refusal to knuckle under to pressures to discredit it.

Sports remained a major feature of broadcasting in 1971. Radio and TV networks and stations paid an estimated $40.4 million for rights to cover major-league baseball during the year, according to *Broadcasting,* and more than $66.2 million for professional and collegiate football rights. These prices represented a $2.6-million increase for baseball, but, in an indication that football prices may have peaked, there was a small decline—about $54,000 in college-game rights.

Programming for children came increasingly into the limelight. Action for Children's Television (ACT), one of the most vocal advocates for better programming, continued to insist that commercials be banned from programs directed at children and

COURTESY, CBS

The CBS television series All In The Family starred Carroll O'Connor (in chair) and Jean Stapleton (left) as Archie and Edith Bunker.

that, in addition, stations be required to present at least 14 hours a week of programming aimed at different age groups. While that issue was awaiting FCC resolution, all three TV networks introduced new, and for the most part widely acclaimed, programs for children in the fall of 1971.

In noncommercial broadcasting, Sesame Street, the TV series produced by the Children's Television Workshop for the preschool audience, again was one of the most widely talked-about programs. As it opened its third season, it had an older-audience counterpart, The Electric Company, also produced by the Workshop but aimed at helping second, third, and fourth graders with reading problems. The Public Broadcasting System's (PBS) lineup of adult programming—in which The Great American Dream Machine was the standout hit of 1971 but which also included a variety of dramatic presentations and programs on the arts and public affairs—appeared to be attracting increasingly larger audiences, though not on a scale to rival those of the commercial networks.

Radio

Radio continued to serve the varying needs of the public. Except for the relatively few radio stations devoted to all-news and a somewhat larger number devoted to all-talk (primarily through the device of telephone call-in and answer-back programs), the majority dispensed the music they thought their audiences would like best.

A survey conducted by the National Association of Broadcasters and the Recording Industry Association of America indicated that middle-of-the-road music—roughly identified as popular standards ranging from contemporary versions of The Beatles' hits to such old-timers as 'Stardust'—was the dominant form in the U.S., presented at some time during the day by 82% of all radio stations. (*See in* CE: Radio; Television.)

TENNIS. A deepening conflict of interest between the International Lawn Tennis Federation (ILTF), world governing body, and the commercial World Championship Tennis (WCT), controlled by Texan Lamar Hunt, highlighted tennis news in 1971. Hunt's 20-tournament world championship was organized in 1971 in opposition to the Grand Prix series, instituted in 1970 by the ILTF. Efforts to create a schedule satisfactory to both sides failed. So did attempts to formulate mutually satisfactory conditions of entry into the traditional events for the 32 WCT contract players, which included such outstanding stars as Rod Laver, John Newcombe, and Ken Rosewall of Australia and Arthur Ashe of the United States. The result was that the ILTF, at its July 1971 meeting, decreed that all players not accepting the authority of its national associations were barred from ILTF events as of Jan. 1, 1972. In addition, ILTF clubs were forbidden to allow their courts to be used by such players. In effect, professionals would now be designated as "contract professionals" or "independent professionals."

Another important change in the tennis competition format involved the Davis Cup. Since the inception of the cup matches in 1900, the winning nation remained out of the next year's competition and defended the trophy in the challenge round at a site of its own choosing. In 1971 the Davis Cup nations abolished the challenge round and ruled that the defending nation must play through from the start.

Among important events of the year, only the Wimbledon championships, with total attendance of 298,880, remained independent of sponsorship. The trend of increasing prize money and commercial sponsorship was otherwise maintained. Rod Laver, leading money winner in 1970 with a record $200,000, passed that total in the first six months of 1971. There was also a move to bring women's prize money earnings closer to those commanded by the men. Pioneering the trend was a series of women's tournaments sponsored by Gladys M. Heldman, publisher and editor of the U.S. magazine *World Tennis*. Of the players taking part, mostly Americans and a few Australians, Billie Jean King topped the list with prize money in excess of $100,000, record earnings for a woman.

Davis Cup Competition

In the last of the challenge rounds in the all-amateur Davis Cup competition, the U.S. defended against the challenge of Romania. With many leading players now turned professional and consequently ineligible, the standard of the competition suffered as compared to earlier years. Australia, represented in every challenge round from 1946 to 1968, fell in the early matches, with India winning the Eastern Zone final 3–2 against Japan. Brazil won the American Zone, downing Mexico 3–2 in the final.

In the European Zone A, Czechoslovakia took the final 3–2 from Spain, and Romania downed West Germany 5–0 in the European Zone B. In interzone play Brazil bested Czechoslovakia 4–1, and Romania outclassed India 4–1. Romania then qualified to meet the U.S. with a 3–2 win over Brazil. In the challenge round the U.S. outplayed Romania, 3 matches to 2, and became the first nation to win the trophy 23 times.

Other Major Tournaments

The Australian championship was won by Ken Rosewall, who also took the South African title. Rod Laver beat Czech Jan Kodes in the Italian championships (part of the WCT series), and the German championships went to a Spaniard, Andres Gimeno, in a victory over Hungarian Peter Szoeke. The French championships in Paris lacked an impressive field, and Kodes emerged a strong winner. Newcombe won the Wimbledon singles crown for the second year, but lost in the U.S. Open at Forest Hills, N.Y., to Kodes, who went on to beat Ashe before losing to Stan Smith in the finals.

John Newcombe of Australia won the men's singles crown at Wimbledon. He also won the doubles titles in Australia and Italy, with another Australian, Tony Roche.

Billie Jean King won the U.S. Open tennis championship after defeating 16-year-old Chris Evert in the semifinals. It was Miss Evert's first loss in 46 matches.

Newcombe and Tony Roche (Australia) won the doubles titles in Australia and Italy; Roy Emerson and Laver were victors at Wimbledon. Newcombe paired with Roger Taylor of Great Britain to take the U.S. title as a result of a tie-break sequence, the strict legality of which was questionable.

Australian Evonne Goolagong was the most successful woman player of the year, winning the French and Wimbledon titles and finishing in the runner-up spot to Margaret Court in the Australian and South African championships. Chris Evert, a 16-year-old from Fort Lauderdale, Fla., was another top woman player. She took a leading role in winning the Wightman Cup at Cleveland, Ohio, for the U.S. against Great Britain, 4–3. She then went on to win the Eastern Grass Court championship at South Orange, N.J. She continued her winning ways until upset in the semifinals of the U.S. Open. Mrs. King and Rosemary Casals won the German and Wimbledon doubles, Mrs. Court and Miss Goolagong the Australian and South African titles. Miss Casals then paired with Australian Judy Dalton to win the U.S. doubles.

In collegiate play, Jimmy Connors, University of California at Los Angeles (UCLA), won the National Collegiate Athletic Association singles crown in four sets. The university also took the doubles title and the team title with 35 points. (*See in* CE: Tennis.)

TEXTILES. In general, the world textile situation was anything but satisfactory in 1971. Most countries showed reduced consumption and production of fibers, yarns, and fabrics, as international uncertainty gave rise to escalating costs for raw materials, labor, and transportation.

In the United States there was much concern throughout the year about stemming the flow of imported textiles from Asian countries. On October 15 the U.S. government announced that Japan, Taiwan, Hong Kong, and South Korea had agreed to limit exports of synthetic and wool textiles. In return, the U.S. agreed to lift the 10% import surcharge, imposed in August, for the category of textiles. Under the quota agreement, Japan will be allowed only a 5% increase a year in man-made fiber exports to the U.S. for the next three years, while Taiwan, Hong Kong, and South Korea will be allowed a 7½% increase a year for five years. Many textile lobbyists were concerned that U.S. business would not be helped much, as the quotas were not strict enough; but many others expressed fears that other countries would retaliate by imposing quotas on U.S. imports.

Textile research and machinery development was very intensive in 1971. Considerable attention was given to improving fire- and crease-resistant finishes. A high-speed process for making patterned carpets was designed to do the work of 10 to 15 conventional looms. A new open-end spinner for synthetic carpet yarns was claimed to have five times the productive capacity of conventional systems. Fundamental research to improve the strength and easy-care properties of cotton paved the way for impressive commercial results in bedsheet manufacture.

In February the People's Republic of China reduced prices of raw silk by 5%, but investors' confidence was undermined by upheavals in market conditions. (*See in* CE: Textiles.)

THAILAND. The beginnings of a major foreign policy shift were noteworthy in Thailand in 1971. Like other Asian countries closely allied with the United States, the Thai government began reviewing its options in line with U.S. President Richard M. Nixon's doctrine encouraging Asian nations to take a greater role in their own defense.

The shift apparently began in December 1970 when Thailand signed its first trade pact with the Soviet Union. Relations with the People's Republic of China, however, were the crucial issue of the year. Foreign Minister Thanat Khoman, long considered the architect of Thailand's pro-U.S. posture, emerged early in 1971 as an articulate proponent of a "real dialogue" with China. He said, "We want to stop being the enemy." At a May press conference he spoke of "the People's Republic of China"—the first time any ranking Thai leader had referred to China by its official name.

The foreign minister's new China policy, however, seemed to split the Thai cabinet into two camps. Some ministers argued that it was too early to think of a rapprochement with China. They discounted prospects of any meaningful trade with China, which, they pointed out, was actively supporting Communist insurgents in northern Thailand. There were no tangible moves to put Thanat's idea into practice. In October the deputy premier and strong man of the cabinet, Gen. Praphas Charusathien, said that Thailand would watch how China behaved in the United Nations before considering diplomatic relations with the Peking government.

Meanwhile, the U.S. remained the dominant influence in Thailand. Complaints came early in the year that Thailand had not received the increases in U.S. military and economic aid necessary to help meet its new responsibilities under the Nixon doctrine. The U.S. in 1971 provided about $75 million in military aid. It was also felt that sales of U.S. rice under the food-for-peace program had cut deeply into the Thai rice markets of Indonesia and South Korea. These complaints were followed by U.S. assurances of substantial aid. In April there were reports from Washington, D.C., that Thailand would be made the center of U.S. air power in Southeast Asia.

The government announced in July its decision to lower the annual growth-rate target from 7.5% to 5% in the third five-year plan, to start in October. The change was attributed to the need for increased expenditures on defense and security, but it strengthened the impression that the economy was facing problems largely because of the de-escalation of the Vietnam war and the growing U.S. pullback.

The experimental democratic government of Thailand ended abruptly November 17 when a Revolutionary Council, headed by Premier Thanom Kittikachorn, took over in a military coup. As paratroopers moved into the capital city of Bangkok and martial law was imposed, Thanom abolished the constitution, dissolved the national parliament, disbanded the cabinet, and assumed absolute power.

The new Revolutionary Council would have the power to handle all civil and military matters. The council said that domestic troubles (strikes, terrorism, student unrest, northern insurrection, and obstruction by the parliament) as well as a disturbing international situation made the coup necessary. Foreign Minister Thanat, who earlier in the year had attempted to improve relations with China, was ousted. (*See in* CE: Thailand.)

THEATER. In 1971 some concerted measures were taken to arrest the decline of the American theater. The standard curtain time for Broadway shows was moved from 8:30 P.M. to 7:30 P.M., in an attempt to suit the convenience of theatergoers. A new "limited gross agreement" was introduced, whereby, under certain conditions, Broadway producers who were willing to keep their

Morris Carnovsky as Prospero (left), Jess Richards as Ariel, and David Hurst as Caliban (right) starred in a production of Shakespeare's 'The Tempest', at the 17th American Shakespearean Festival at Stratford, Conn.

MARTHA SWOPE

ticket prices low could obtain concessions from the theatrical unions, thus reducing expenses and, it was hoped, enabling small-scale productions to survive. "Middle theaters," not big enough for Broadway and not small enough for off-Broadway, became increasingly prominent, widening the range of possible economic arrangements. The Theater Development Fund, a foundation-supported philanthropy that purchases tickets for resale (at low prices) to students and others, made its presence felt; also, more productions seemed to be offering student discounts than ever before.

Broadway

Artistically, 1971 was not a distinguished year for the theater in the United States. The surprise sensation of the Broadway season was a revival of 'No, No, Nanette', billed as "the new 1925 musical," starring Ruby Keeler; it set off a much-publicized "nostalgia boom." Late in the year came another sensation: 'Jesus Christ Superstar', a big rock-musical version of the Gospel story, based on a best-selling record album. In spite of unfavorable reviews, it was a tremendous hit.

Other musicals aroused less excitement, including (late in 1970) 'Two by Two', a vehicle for Danny Kaye with a score by Richard Rodgers, based on 'The Flowering Peach', Clifford Odets' play about Noah and his Ark; and (in April 1971) 'Follies', an innovative experiment in wryly ironic nostalgia, produced by Harold Prince in association with Ruth Mitchell and directed by Prince and Michael Bennett, with brilliant scenery by Boris Aronson and spectacular costumes by Florence Klotz.

Straight plays on Broadway also fared badly. At the end of 1970, Neil Simon, Broadway's most successful comedy writer, offered an uncharacteristically somber work, entitled 'The Gingerbread Lady', about an alcoholic female nightclub singer; it was not enthusiastically received. Because Simon turned to serious drama, there was not one really successful new Broadway comedy during the 1970–71 season. 'And Miss Reardon Drinks a Little', Paul Zindel's play about three unhappy sisters, disappointed many who had admired his previously produced play, 'The Effect of Gamma Rays on Man-in-the-Moon Marigolds'. 'The Philanthropist', by Christopher Hampton, an intelligent British comedy about an overly complaisant English don, was highly praised but sparsely attended. 'All Over', by Edward Albee, about a group of friends and relations who are waiting for a famous man to die, was generally found to be somewhat bloodless, in spite of the fine acting of Colleen Dewhurst and Jessica Tandy as the dying man's mistress and wife, respectively. 'Lenny' by Julian Barry, an evocation of the late comedian, social critic, scatologist, and drug addict, Lenny Bruce, was admired mostly for Tom O'Horgan's phantasmagoric staging and for Cliff Gorman's galvanic performance in the title role. The fall season of 1971 began with 'Solitaire/Double Solitaire', by Robert Anderson, a pair of scrupulous but rather subdued one-act plays. Both plays dealt with marriage, though the first was science-fiction oriented and did so only peripherally. In November Neil Simon returned to comedy with 'The Prisoner of Second Avenue', and Harold Pinter's enigmatic London success, 'Old Times', came to Broadway. There were two notable classic revivals on Broadway in 1971: Molière's 'School for Wives', starring Brian Bedford, and the Royal Shakespeare

Melvin Van Peebles' bitter musical, 'Aint Supposed to Die a Natural Death', starred Ralph Wilcox and Barbara Alston.

BERT ANDREWS

Company's acrobatic and brilliant production of William Shakespeare's 'Midsummer Night's Dream', directed by Peter Brook.

Off-Broadway

The New York Drama Critics' Circle Award for the best U.S. play of 1970–71 went to an off-Broadway production, 'The House of Blue Leaves', by John Guare, a grim farce combining high jinks and deep agony, about an amateur songwriter who dreams of becoming famous in Hollywood. Another notable off-Broadway play was 'The Trial of the Catonsville Nine' by the Rev. Daniel Berrigan, an account of the trial of nine antidraft civil-disobedience activists in which Father Berrigan was a defendant. A popular off-Broadway musical was 'Godspell', a rock version of St. Matthew's gospel, with music and lyrics by Stephen Schwartz. There were successful off-Broadway revivals of 'Waiting for Godot', by Samuel Beckett (directed by Alan Schneider), 'Long Day's Journey into Night', by Eugene O'Neill (directed by Arvin Brown, with a cast that included Robert Ryan, Geraldine Fitzgerald, and Stacy Keach), and 'One Flew Over the Cuckoo's Nest', by Dale Wasserman. 'Cuckoo's Nest', a dramatization of Ken Kesey's novel of the same name, failed on Broadway several seasons ago; the revival was particularly popular with young people. Claire Bloom had a personal triumph in a repertory of two plays by Henrik Ibsen, 'A Doll's House' and 'Hedda Gabler'.

In the avant-garde, the Performance Group, under the direction of Richard Schechner, presented a new environmental-participational work entitled 'Commune', concerned with the U.S., the career of convicted murderer Charles Manson, and other matters. Even more participational was an import from Los Angeles called 'The James Joyce Memorial Liquid Theater', directed by Steven Kent and presented in New York City at the Solomon R. Guggenheim Museum. Billed as "an experiment in making people feel good," it involved games, sensitivity exercises, dancing, and various forms of body contact; every ticket buyer was individually hugged and kissed by members of the ensemble. It was described by one critic as "the first of the feelies" and was widely considered an event to be enjoyed rather than taken seriously. But it was innovative in the extent to which it transformed the traditional relationship between performer and spectator.

As in recent years, permanent, nonprofit theater organizations contributed a great deal to the New York City theater scene. Black theater, for instance, has been largely the product of permanent off-Broadway organizations. Two plays by Ed Bullins were produced in 1971: 'In New England Winter', at the Henry Street Playhouse, and 'The Fabulous Miss Marie', at the New Lafayette Theatre. The Henry Street Playhouse also offered 'Black Girl', a naturalistic first play by J. E. Franklin. The Negro Ensemble Company presented, among other plays, 'The Dream on Monkey Mountain', a dense fantasy on black-white themes by the Trinidadian poet-playwright Derek Walcott—this play had previously been done by the Center Theatre Group of Los Angeles.

The Public Theater of the New York Shakespeare Festival, which now comprises several auditoriums of different shapes and sizes under one roof, had a tremendously productive season in 1970–71. It introduced two notable plays by new young U.S. playwrights: 'Subject to Fits: A Response to Dostoyevsky's "The Idiot"', by Robert Montgomery, and 'The Basic Training of Pavlo Hummel', by David W. Rabe, a play about a U.S. soldier in Vietnam. Other Public Theater presentations included a one-man show, 'Jack MacGowran in the Works of Samuel Beckett', and a one-woman show, 'Here Are Ladies', in which Siobhan McKenna performed work by Irish writers, including a superb rendition of Molly Bloom's monologue from James Joyce's 'Ulysses'. The Public Theater began its 1971–72 season with 'Sticks and Bones', another play by Rabe. Meanwhile, in its open-air summer home in New York City's Central Park, the Shakespeare Festival offered a musical version of Shakespeare's 'Two Gentlemen of Verona', adapted by John Guare and Mel Shapiro, with music by Galt MacDermot, the composer of 'Hair'.

The 1970–71 season of the Chelsea Theater Center, in Brooklyn, N.Y., featured two new plays by British playwrights. 'Saved', by Edward Bond,

ZODIAC PHOTOGRAPHERS

John Guare's 'The House Of Blue Leaves' won the New York Drama Critics' Circle award for the best American play of 1971.

'Lenny' opened on Broadway in the spring. Cliff Gorman (center) received widespread acclaim for his portrayal of Lenny Bruce, the comedian whose life ended in a tragic early death.

MARTHA SWOPE

was a grim piece of naturalism—in its most famous scene, a baby was shown being stoned to death onstage. 'AC/DC', by Heathcote Williams, was a baffling expression of the electronic age. The 1971–72 season began with the U.S. premiere of 'The Screens', by Jean Genet. The American Place Theater opened its 1971–72 season in new, custom-built quarters—the first completed result of the New York City Planning Commission's policy of encouraging the building of theaters in new office buildings in the theater district.

Repertory Theater

The Repertory Theater of Lincoln Center in New York City aroused little enthusiasm with its main-stage productions; the general consensus was that the work done in the Repertory Theater's second auditorium, the Forum, was far more interesting. The Forum productions included a revival of Harold Pinter's 'Birthday Party', the U.S. premiere of 'Play Strindberg', by Friedrich Dürrenmatt (a parody of August Strindberg's 'Dance of Death'), and 'Scenes from American Life', a sardonic comedy by A. R. Gurney, Jr., about the decline and fall of Buffalo, N.Y. In 1971 a plan was made public for the remodeling of the Vivian Beaumont Theater, the headquarters of the Repertory Theater of Lincoln Center. Under this proposal, the Forum would have been demolished and replaced by three film theaters and a film library, to be administered by Henri Langlois of the Cinémathèque Française in Paris; a new Forum would have been built in an unused scenery-storage area elsewhere in the building. The plan evoked furious

opposition from many prominent members of the theatrical community who were incensed at the idea of destroying the Forum and who claimed that the use of the storage area to build a new auditorium would prevent the Repertory Theater from ever operating in true rotating repertory. The proposal was withdrawn, and the result of the controversy was an outpouring of financial support for the Repertory Theater.

Outside of New York City, the Charles Playhouse in Boston, Mass., closed its doors late in 1970 after 14 years of existence, and the professional repertory company of Princeton University's McCarter Theatre suspended operations for at least a year in April 1971. For its 1970–71 season, the American Conservatory Theatre of San Francisco, Calif., retrenched somewhat, performing in only one theater instead of in two simultaneously; but its season was generally a successful one, highlighted by Ellis Rabb's modern-dress staging of Shakespeare's 'Merchant of Venice'.

The Arena Stage in Washington, D.C., resisted the tendency toward retrenchment by opening a second auditorium with the U.S. premiere of 'The Ruling Class', a savage comedy by the British playwright Peter Barnes. The Arena also offered the U.S. premiere of 'Moonchildren' by Michael Weller, a witty, perceptive, and powerful comedydrama about a group of very bright U.S. college students and the mysterious emptiness of their lives. The play was written by a U.S. playwright who now lives in England. With two theaters, a high standard of acting and production, and a program almost equally balanced between new plays and

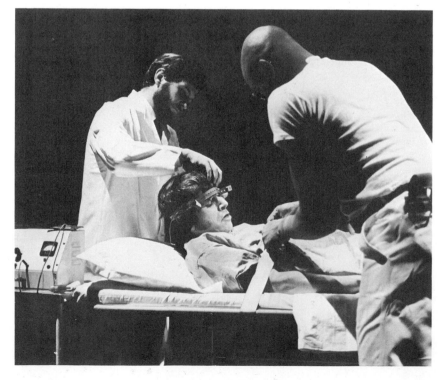

William Devane, as Randle Patrick Murphy, is prepared for an unnecessary lobotomy in 'One Flew Over The Cuckoo's Nest', a play about terrifying events in a mental institution. The play was based on the novel by Ken Kesey.

ZODIAC PHOTOGRAPHERS

revivals, the Arena looked more and more like the leader among U.S. resident professional theaters.

The Tyrone Guthrie Theatre in Minneapolis, Minn., under its new artistic director, Michael Langham, reversed a steep decline in attendance in 1971. The Seattle Repertory Theater had the biggest success in its history—a production of Shakespeare's 'Richard II', starring Richard Chamberlain. The Long Wharf Theater of New Haven, Conn., one of the most enterprising of the resident companies, offered the world premiere of Anderson's 'Solitaire/Double Solitaire'; this production subsequently appeared at the Edinburgh International Festival of Music and Drama in Scotland, and then transferred to Broadway. The American Shakespeare Festival Theater in Stratford, Conn., mounted a successful revival of 'Mourning Becomes Electra', by Eugene O'Neill, featuring Jane Alexander. (*See in* CE: Drama.)

TOBACCO. The United States tobacco crop forecast for 1971 was 1.8 billion pounds from 850,840 acres. This estimate showed a slight decrease in yield per acre from the final 1970 figures of 1.9 billion pounds from 898,330 acres. The 1971 flue-cured acreage was reduced to 536,170 acres, with the crop expected to be 1.1 billion pounds, a yield of some 90 million pounds less than the previous year. North Carolina continued in its dominant position in the flue-cured class.

In 1970 larger crops in the developing countries took world tobacco production to 4.6 million tons, a 2% increase over the preceding year, but more than 3% below the record crop in 1967. The Food and Agricultural Organization (FAO) of the United Nations confirmed that Latin America was a leader in increased output for 1970, with developing countries overall returning a 5% uplift. Tobacco production in the developed countries remained static in spite of a 7% increase in Europe.

Although all types of tobacco recorded increased output, the flue-cured and burley crops did less well than other types because of smaller crops. A 30% increase in the Greek crop of oriental tobacco was offset by a further decline in Turkish crops following reduced plantings.

Cigarette consumption increased in the majority of developed countries in spite of increased publicity about the effect of smoking on health. Two notable exceptions were the U.S. and Great Britain, where declining leaf consumption in cigarettes continued—partly because of the increased application of leaf-saving techniques and the growing use of filter tips.

The Federal Trade Commission reported total sales of cigarettes in the U.S. went up in 1970, because of an increase in population, but per capita consumption went down from 199.3 packs in 1969 to 198.5 packs. Also, the cutback in cigarette smoking by adults has been somewhat offset by increased use by teen-agers.

Cigarette advertising was increasingly restricted in various countries, but the FAO thought it too early to assess the effect of this and other anti-smoking moves. World demand for cigars and cigarillos was static, and the popularity of pipe tobacco continued to wane. (*See in* CE: Tobacco.)

TOGO. In September 1971 President Étienne Eyadema announced that the army was ready to relinquish its control and that he had vetoed a recommendation by Togo's only political party that he should be the sole presidential candidate in the 1972 election. It later transpired that a referendum was to be held on Jan. 9, 1972, and that he expected to be confirmed in office. Later in September a radio broadcast announced that in reaction to the president's speech the people had indicated that the army's mission was far from complete. The president therefore reconsidered his decision and "in the superior interests of the people" agreed to remain in office.

In March 27 people had been given prison terms for complicity in a plot to overthrow the president in August 1970.

On October 25 Togo voted in favor of the Albanian resolution in the United Nations to admit China and expel Taiwan. In December President Eyadema visited France and discussed the possibility of increased aid. (*See in* CE: Togo, Republic of.)

TONGA. With an annual population growth of about 3%, Tonga in 1971 had to provide for an ever increasing proportion of landless unemployed. As there were limits to the number of bananas and coconuts that could be produced for export, the government looked to commercial fishing and the international shipping trade for sources of income. A record budget provided for the establishment of small-scale labor-concentrated industries; and an exploratory oil well was scheduled to be sunk. For educational improvements, the government looked to the United Nations Development Programme and to the University of the South Pacific in Fiji.

The sixth and largest meeting of the Pacific Islands Producers' Association in Nukualofa, the capital, revealed the poor state of the New Zealand banana market and considered possibilities for a regional copra-crushing mill and a shipping line. Participation in the Asian Coconut Community, the South Pacific Forum (a top-level August meeting of South Pacific states in Wellington, New Zealand), and the 11th South Pacific Conference demonstrated a belief in regional cooperation.

TOYS AND GAMES. A rising tide of consumer interest in the need to protect children from unsafe toys led the Toy Manufacturers Association to develop a set of principles to guide the United States industry in 1971. Action by the U.S. Food and Drug Administration to ban certain hazardous toys was a strong force in getting manufacturers to develop safety principles and to spend $100,000 developing safety specifications for toys. Three states also introduced legislation to promote fair packaging and labeling of all toy products.

Reflecting the general business decline in 1971, the first quarter showed a 7.6% decline in orders received as compared with the same period of 1970. However, the value of shipments at the manufacturer's level was up 5.1%, indicating rising costs. The long-term upward trend in toy industry growth was slowing but still strong. Sales increased from $992 million in 1961 to $2.26 billion in 1970 and were expected to reach $3 billion by 1975.

Bicycles were extremely popular in 1971 because of a greatly increased interest in ecology and physical fitness. Many shops reported their inability to supply demand. Impetus to bicycle riding was given by widespread construction of special bicycle paths by cities and suburbs. A rising number of bicycle accidents caused the Bicycle Institute of America to set safety standards for manufacturers. The standards included the addition of reflective materials, a limit on the height of rear saddle supports, limit on handlebar width, plus specified strength of frame, fork, head tube, and seat post.

A growing interest in old and antique toys was apparent in 1971 with the publication of Joseph J. Schroeder's nostalgia book, 'The Wonderful World of Toys, Games and Dolls, 1860–1930'.

A booming business in old and antique toys was reported by the antique toy store, Second Childhood, on Bleecker Street in New York City's Greenwich Village. Toys that once sold for $5 brought $60 to $80.

Dolls, the permanent leader in the toy field, featured Bizzie Lizzie, a battery-operated housekeeper doll that irons on her ironing board and cleans with a carpet sweeper and feather duster. Then, there was Kim, a 5½-inch doll with hair that grows. Among new doll accessories were makeup and hairstyling sets, nontoxic washable cosmetics for all kinds of hair styles, and costumes featuring hot pants. Wigs could be changed from blonde to brown to red with washable tints. The demand for black dolls increased greatly.

Riding toys included a polystyrene jet plane on a stand like a hobby horse. The child "flies" it by shifting his weight around, making the plane dive, bank, spin, and climb. Many vehicles, either gas- or electric-powered, such as the Power Buggy, were popular. The small child's car has a rechargeable battery, "mag" wheels, wide oval tires, simulated tachometer, fuel gauge, dual exhausts, taillights, and dual shift for forward or reverse driving. The Snow-Droplane is a new type of sled with molded construction of double-wall polystyrene that looks like a tiny hydroplane. The Sno-Bob utilizes a frame like a bicycle's and has skis.

Children leap and bounce on a 30-foot-square inflated plastic air mattress at a playground in London. Terry Scales, a former art student, designed the mattress to be safe; if punctured, it emits a slow, hissing stream of air instead of exploding.

"LONDON DAILY EXPRESS" FROM PICTORIAL PARADE

UPI CQMPIX

A West German store capitalized on the interest in "ping pong diplomacy" by selling paddles picturing Mao Tse-tung and Richard M. Nixon.

Among educational toys was Plus N' Minus, which teaches basic addition and subtraction. Using color-coded tiles with numbers, the child sets up a problem, presses a lever, and the answer appears on a screen. A toy electronic computer forecasts weather, diagnoses illness, and analyzes intelligence tests. The popular Sesame Street television program inspired The Alphabet Set, which teaches children to associate letter shapes and sounds—for example, the white "E" on the white egg. With the Ernie and Bert set, children play with their television friends.

Variations of word games appeared in 1971. RPM is a revolving word game like Scrabble, except that the circular board rotates three times per minute, adding the factor of speed to skill. Play on Words is a new word-building game using 13 letter cubes which are placed in a grid. The cubes are rolled in a dice cup, and a sand timer clocks word formation. (*See in* CE: Toys.)

TRACK AND FIELD. Youth showed the way to five new world track and field records in the Americas in the pre-Olympic year of 1971. Three countries shared in the record-shattering performances, an unusual turn of events in a region where the sport is normally dominated by the United States.

The assaults got under way in June with a pair of world bests at the U.S. National (Amateur Athletic Union—AAU) championships at the University of Oregon. Rod Milburn, 21-year-old South-

ern University star, started it off on June 25 by clipping 0.2 second off the 120-yard high-hurdle mark of 13.2 set by Martin Lauer of West Germany in 1959. The next day, 20-year-old John Smith, University of California at Los Angeles (UCLA), nipped 0.2 second from the 440-yard sprint mark of 44.7 chalked up by Curtis Mills in 1969. Smith's teammate, Wayne Collett, tied the old mark.

A week later, in the U.S.-Soviet Union World All-Star meet at Berkeley, Calif., Pat Matzdorf (U.S.) pulled off the biggest surprise of the U.S. track-and-field year by erasing the 7 feet 5¾ inches high-jump mark of Valeri Brumel (U.S.S.R.) set in 1963. Matzdorf's leap of 7 feet 6¼ inches had been duplicated by Ni Chih-chin of the People's Republic of China in 1970, but the mark was never accepted because China was not a member of the world track organization.

Two more record setters established new standards at the quadrennial Pan-American Games in Cali, Colombia, in August. The U.S. dominated the meet, but the record-setting performances went to other nations. Don Quarrie, 20-year-old Jamaican, matched the 1968 record of Tommie Smith (U.S.) in the 200-meter dash around a turn in 19.8. Another major surprise was the record-shattering performance of 19-year-old Pedro Perez, a virtually unknown Cuban, who erased the 1968 mark of Viktor Saneyev (U.S.S.R.) with a brilliant hop, step, and jump performance of 57 feet 1 inch.

Two world-record performances by Jay Silvester, one of the older U.S. athletes, were discus tosses of 230 feet 11 inches at Lancaster, Calif., in May, and

Australian Kerry O'Brien breaks the record for the two-mile (indoor and outdoor) with a time of 8:19.2.

SHEEDY & LONG FOR SPORTS ILLUSTRATED © TIME INC.

229 feet 9½ inches at Ystad, Sweden, in June, well above Silvester's own world standard of 224 feet 5 inches. Neither mark was expected to be recognized, however, because the meets lacked official sanction.

Four U.S. national records were bettered. Steve Prefontaine, University of Oregon, chalked up a new mark of 13:30.4 in 5,000 meters, and Sid Sink, Bowling Green State, established a new standard of 8:26.4 in the 3,000-meter steeplechase. In less familiar distances Marty Liquori, Villanova, set a new 2,000-meter best at 5:02.2, and Juris Luzins, a U.S. Marine Corps officer, covered 1,000 meters in 2:17.7.

No major records were produced at the U.S.A.-Pan Africa track meet in Durham, N.C., in July, which did much to foster goodwill both on and off the track. The Africans showed unusual strength in the longer runs and considerable promise in other events.

Indoor Track and Field

Indoors, new world bests (there are no official world records indoors) were set in two field events. Al Feuerbach, Pacific Coast Track Club, outperformed Randy Matson, outdoor record holder and Olympic champion, with a heave of 68 feet 11 inches in the shot, and Kjell Isaksson (Sweden) reached a new height of 17 feet 7¾ inches in the pole vault.

On the track the outstanding performance was the new mark by Kerry O'Brien (Australia) of 8:19.2 for the two-mile event, .8 second under the previous indoor low and 0.6 second under the outdoor record. Kerry Pearce (Australia) and Frank Shorter (U.S.) ran the same race in 8:20.6 and 8:26.2 respectively, with Shorter's time becoming a U.S. indoor record. In the same San Diego meet, Jim Ryun, 23-year-old world-record holder at one mile, 1,500 meters, and 880 yards, matched the record time of 3:56.4 for the mile set by Tom O'Hara in 1964. Later in the year, however, he fell victim to an allergy and withdrew from further competition.

Other indoor bests were record clockings of 5.9 seconds for 60 yards by Mel Pender, Jean-Louis Ravelomanantsoa, Jerry Sims, Willie McGee, and Herb Washington; a record-tying 6.8 for 70 yards by Pender; 9.3 for 100 yards by Quarrie; a record-tying 30.4 for 300 yards by Carl Lawson; two 54.4 timings for 500 yards by Lee Evans; 2:20.4 for 1,000 meters by Tom Von Ruden; 3:09.4 for the mile relay by the Pacific Coast Track Club; and 9:39.8 for the distance medley relay by the University of Pittsburgh.

Paced by Liquori's wins in the mile and two-mile, Villanova won its second indoor championship at Detroit, Mich., in March, with Wisconsin taking its fifth straight Big Ten indoor title in Madison, Wis., earlier in the month. The Pacific Coast Track Club was outstanding in the AAU indoor championships in New York City in February, winning 4 of the 16 events.

Outdoor Championships of 1971

In the National Collegiate Athletic Association (NCAA) outdoor championships in Seattle, Wash., June 17–19, UCLA won, amassing a total of 52

At the U.S.-Russian track meet in Berkeley, Calif., American Pat Matzdorf set a new world high-jump record by clearing the bar at 7 feet, 6¼ inches.
WIDE WORLD

Running the mile at the International Freedom Games in Philadelphia, Pa., Marty Liquori crosses the finish line in 3:54.6, ahead of Jim Ryun.

points to 41 for Southern California and 38 for third-place Oregon. The meet was highlighted by Liquori's third consecutive sub-four-minute mile, Sid Sink's steeplechase performance, and a new collegiate hammer record of 227 feet 10 inches by Jacques Accambray, a French student at Kent State.

The AAU championships in Eugene, Ore., June 25–26, featured the world record-breaking performances of John Smith and Rod Milburn, the fifth sub-four-minute mile of Liquori, and a record-tying time of nine seconds in 100 yards by Dr. Delano Meriwether. The Southern California Striders topped the club performances with three wins—the 220- and 440-yard dashes and the 440-yard hurdles.

In the U.S.-Soviet meet at Berkeley in July, the U.S. men's team defeated the Russians 126–110. The U.S. women lost 76–60 to the visitors.

Villanova won its 11th IC4A title in 15 years in Philadelphia, Pa., in May by a single point, edging Maryland 32–31 by winning the final event, the mile relay. In other outdoor competitions, Alvaro Mejía, 30-year-old Colombian, won the 75th annual Boston Marathon in Massachusetts in April by a five-second margin. His time of 2:18.45 barely edged Pat McMahon of the Boston Athletic Association and was well above the 2:10.30 record established by Ron Hill in 1970.

The national AAU decathlon championship held in Porterville, Calif., in mid-June was captured by

Rick Wanamaker, 6 feet-9 inch former Drake University basketball player, with 7,989 points. Russ Hodge, Southern California Striders, who led most of the way, finished second with 7,958 points.

In overseas action, a Harvard-Yale team beat Oxford-Cambridge at the Crystal Palace in England in June. It was the 12th U.S. triumph in the 23d meeting of the series, which began in the 1890's. World marks were broken by Uwe Beyer, a West German, with a hammer throw of 245 feet 8¾ inches at Stuttgart, West Germany, in July, and by Emile Puttemans of Belgium in the two-mile run in 8:17.8 at Edinburgh, Scotland, in August.

Women's Competition; Other Developments

Female athletes established a number of world-best marks in 1971. Hildegard Falck (West Germany) set a record of 1:58.3 for the 800 meters at Stuttgart in July. At the national AAU women's championships at Bakersfield, Calif., also in July, Tennessee State's 440-yard women's team (D. Hughes, D. Wedgeworth, M. Render, I. Davis) set a new standard of 44.7 seconds for the event, followed by the Atoms Track Club of Brooklyn, N. Y., (G. Fitzgerald, L. Reynolds, D. Hooten, C. Toussaint), who had won in the mile relay with a timing of 3:38.8. In August a West German team broke the women's world record for the 4 × 800-meter relay in 8:16.8 at Lubeck, West Germany, followed by new marks in the women's discus (210 feet 8½ inches) by Faina Myelnik (U.S.S.R.); the 1,500 meters (4:09.6) by Karin Burneleit (East Germany); and the 4 × 400-meter relay (3:29.3) by the East Germans at Helsinki. Miss Myelnik later improved her discus mark with a 212 feet 9¼ inches toss at Munich, West Germany, and Ilona Gusenbauer of Austria shattered the ten-year-old high-jump mark for women with a leap of 6 feet 3½ inches in Vienna, Austria. A British team shaved 0.2 second off the 800-meter relay with a timing of 1:33.6 in Paris in October.

A move to rename the AAU and to redefine the term "amateur" was tabled at the organization's meeting of the board of governors at Lake Placid, N.Y. in October. (*See in* CE: Track and Field Sports.)

TRANSPORTATION. The trend toward consolidation of different forms of transportation continued during 1971. Worldwide, traffic showed signs of recovery from the 1970 recession. There were further advances in technology and its applications. With Congress refusing to provide funding, the United States supersonic transport program effectively ended, but the Anglo-French Concorde and the Soviet Tupolev TU-144 supersonic passenger aircraft underwent successful tests. Other technological improvements tested during the year included advanced forms of railway traction and tracked hovercraft.

Railways began to benefit from the large capital investment of recent years; the movement of persons and goods by rail increased, although the railways' proportion of total traffic failed to gain. Over 790,000 miles of railways were in operation throughout the world in 1971, of which about one tenth were electrified. New lines were built mainly in less developed countries, while in the more advanced countries existing lines were improved to allow far higher speeds. Coordination of railways with other forms of transportation, especially through piggyback and roll-on/roll-off services, continued. Nevertheless, inflation and rising costs resulted in large deficits on most railway systems.

The trucking industry's share of overall freight movements rose by a higher proportion than that of most other forms of transportation. Statistics for bus transportation were sparse, but the trend was for passenger traffic to decrease in urban areas while long-distance traffic rose. Several countries tried to improve mass road transportation by increasing subsidies to public transportation services.

There were new installations of pipelines for natural gas and other purposes, but the major development was in the chemical industry. More producers and consumers integrated their separate ethylene grids and pipelines, and many other chemical feedstocks were being moved by pipeline. The phenomenon was worldwide. In the U.S. a liquid

In the fall this huge pipeline began carrying water from northern California over the Tehachapi mountains to southern California.

ammonia pipeline network was being extended, and in Texas no fewer than 25 products were being carried by long-distance lines.

At the beginning of 1971 the world's natural-gas pipelines were estimated to total more than 930,000 miles, and there were several projects for extensions and additions. The biggest were in the U.S.S.R., where major new projects included the construction of long-distance, large-diameter lines from the Siberian and Central Asian areas. A 700-mile extension to the Trans-Canada system was under construction, together with an extension to the gas reserves in the Painted Mountains of the Yukon.

Oil pipeline projects under way included 6,000 miles in the Soviet Union to take West Siberian oil to the Pacific. Canada embarked on an extensive program to carry gas and oil exports to the U.S. In the U.S. the new 1,300-mile Explorer line from refineries on the Gulf of Mexico to the Chicago market came into service. Approval was still awaited for construction of the 800-mile, 48-inch-diameter crude-oil line from the North Slope of Alaska to Valdez on the Gulf of Alaska.

Seaborne trade improved in 1970, with most major ports reporting increased traffic. London dealt with 59.5 million tons of cargo, an increase of 1.5 million tons over 1969, while Great Britain's ports as a whole handled 16.6 million tons of unit traffic on both lift-on and roll-on services. This was nearly half that handled by all northwestern European ports together. There was an 18.9% increase in freight passing through the Port of New York's six marine terminals in 1970. However, in 1971 both East and West Coast ports in the U.S. were hit by prolonged strikes. (*See* Labor Unions.)

Intercity ton-miles moved on U.S. inland waterways in 1970 exceeded the previous record of 300 billion ton-miles and represented about 16% of all intercity freight traffic. The St. Lawrence Seaway in 1970 experienced its best year since its opening in 1959, with 71,113,000 tons of cargo and 9,115 ship transits. Oceangoing ships carried 20.1% and lakers 79.9%. Traffic through the Panama Canal totaled 116,143,000 metric tons in fiscal 1970, of which 74,877,000 tons crossed the isthmus from the Atlantic to the Pacific and 41,266,000 tons went in the opposite direction. The chief cargoes were coal and coke and petroleum products from the Atlantic and ores and lumber from the Pacific. In January 1971, U.S. President Richard M. Nixon ordered a halt, for environmental reasons, to the construction of a canal across north Florida that would have linked the Atlantic with the Gulf of Mexico.

Extensive building programs were under way at many major ports in North America. In New Orleans, La., a $37-million new master plan was drawn up, the first stage of which was to be completed by 1972. Additional facilities were to be provided in stages over the next 25 years. The Port of New York Authority continued its construction program. At Port Newark, N.J., a 40-acre com-

COURTESY, LOCKHEED AIRCRAFT

Lockheed produced a wide-body commercial jet liner. The L1011 TriStar houses RB.211 engines made by Rolls Royce, is 178 feet in length, and has a passenger capacity of 250 to 400.

bination container-break bulk terminal with 2,058 feet of berths was completed, while at Elizabeth, N.J., five-vessel berths at the south end of the Elizabeth Marine Terminal were under construction and a 3,870-foot wharf was completed. By the end of 1973 there would be 16,850 feet of berthing space at Elizabeth, capable of accommodating 25 modern container ships. The total cost of these facilities was estimated at $170 million. With the completion of its modernization program, the port of Seattle, Wash., became the container gateway on the Pacific to Alaska, Hawaii, and the Far East.

AIRLINES

An acutely cost-conscious, belt-tightening atmosphere characterized the U.S. scheduled-airline industry in 1971, and losses continued to plague much of the industry. For the first six months of 1971 the U.S. scheduled airlines reported a net loss of $132.4 million, compared with a net loss of $58.1 million for the first six months of 1970. These figures represented the combined results for the domestic and international operations of 12 major airlines and the operations of 9 local-service airlines.

Airline management, operating within the framework of a strictly regulated industry, faced certain limits in the options open to it in trying to achieve an economic turnaround. But even though regulation closed the door to certain management options, there were some major initiatives put into effect by management, including the following: over a 12-month period airline employment was reduced by 15,000; in many cases delivery of new aircraft was postponed and in some cases orders were canceled; cutbacks were made in food serv-

ice; and, in the toughest move of all, the airlines reduced flight frequency.

The airlines became the major form of common carrier intercity passenger service—in terms of passenger miles—by following the philosophy of providing more and more convenient service. Yet by the early fall of 1971 there were some 700 fewer daily scheduled airline flights than at the same time in 1970. It should be noted, however, that the reduction in flight frequency did not diminish total airlift capability for either passengers or cargo. Total airlift capability was actually expanded through the increased use of advanced technology and wide-body jets. These new jets carried at least twice as many passengers as the conventional jets.

Mounting cost pressures were the major cause of decline in airline earnings, and the most serious pressure continued to be generated by labor costs. Airline labor costs account for nearly one half of the industry's cash expenses. The airline industry differs from other labor-intensive industries, in that airline labor is highly skilled and highly paid. The average annual income for airline employees in 1971 reached $12,300, compared with about $7,000 for employees in manufacturing.

In the airline industry, as in other basic transportation industries, mounting labor cost pressures have been accompanied by the threat of costly strikes. When such work stoppages have occurred, they have usually inconvenienced large segments of the general public and have worked economic hardship on the carriers and their employees. Consequently, in 1971 the airlines joined the rail industry in presenting to the U.S. Congress legislative proposals designed to alter the collective bargaining

Charter flights, which were increasingly popular, sometimes left travelers stranded if the operating company suffered financial difficulties. American, British, and Canadian charter passengers wait in the London office of Seaglair Canada Ltd., demanding either a flight to New York City or a refund for their tickets.
KEYSTONE

process. The proposals, according to the industry, recognized the collective bargaining rights of employees, while also recognizing the public service characteristics of rail and air transportation. The key to the new approach was a greater flexibility under which appropriate government agencies could intervene to head off costly strikes.

The airlines' campaign to reduce air pollution in 1971 was carried out on two principal fronts. First, the new generation of jets being put into service by the airlines, although larger, was powered by engines that were quieter than any before. They were also virtually smokeless. Second, the airlines continued the antipollution retrofit of engines powering jets already in their fleets. This involved the retrofit of hundreds of two-engine and three-engine short-range and medium-range jets. Their engines, as originally built, produced highly visible smokelike plumes. After five years of testing, financed by the airlines, manufacturers produced new burner cans (a part of the jet engine) effective in virtually eliminating the visible smoke plumes. At a cost of $30 million, the airlines voluntarily undertook a refitting of such engines. By late 1971 the refitting was half completed. It was to be completed by December 1972. This refitting, plus the introduction of the advanced-technology jets, meant that the scheduled-airline fleet would be virtually smoke-free by the mid-1970's. (*See in* CE: Airlines.)

RAILROADS

The U.S. railroad industry underwent major changes in 1971, including introduction of a new intercity passenger setup, modernization of some long-controversial employee work rules, and the coming together with other surface modes in support of comprehensive transportation legislation.

On May 1 the National Railroad Passenger Corporation assumed responsibility for operating most of the nation's intercity rail passenger service. With government and railroad funds providing the initial financing, Amtrak—as the corporation was known—had the ultimate goal of becoming a profitable operation. It began by a substantial paring of uneconomic routes. The original Amtrak network—to be expanded as demand warranted—connected 114 major U.S. cities with 184 daily trains. (For map, *see* United States.)

Another major development involved work rules. Agreement on significant changes was reached in May with the 40,000-member Brotherhood of Locomotive Engineers (BLE). In August the 165,-000-member United Transportation Union (UTU) accepted these changes, subject to ratification by the membership. In both cases, the industry granted a 42% wage increase over a 42-month period—the largest increase in railroad history.

The new rules were designed to enable the railroads to capitalize on modern technology and provide more efficient service. One important change eliminated the traditional 100-mile day as a standard basis of pay for train crews and provided that road crews, like other employees, be paid on a time basis. Under the old rule, on-train employees received a full day's pay for a trip of 100 miles. In modern railroading, a 100-mile run can be made in as little as 2½ hours.

Settlement with the UTU came only after a series of selective strikes that eventually closed down ten railroads accounting for 48.1% of the nation's total rail ton-miles. Earlier in the year, the nationwide rail system had been shut down for two days by the 13,000-member signalmen's union in a dispute over wages. That strike was halted by emergency legislation enacted by Congress, and the dispute was settled late in the year.

In the legislative field, the railroads continued to press for governmental action to help them solve major problems pinpointed in a sweeping prospectus prepared for the industry in 1969–70 by a special study group called America's Sound Transportation Review Organization (ASTRO). Some of the proposed solutions were incorporated in a bill introduced in Congress as the Surface Transportation Act of 1971. The Association of American Railroads, the American Trucking Associations, and the Water Transport Association joined in support of the bill.

Railroad freight traffic totaled an estimated 745 billion ton-miles, a decrease of 2.5% from 1970. Passenger-miles declined, while commuter traffic continued its moderate increase for the sixth straight year.

Despite the decline in freight traffic, inflation, and the consequent increase in costs of operation,

the rate of return on net investment—stimulated by rate increases—rose to 2.35% for the first half of 1971, compared with 1.87% for that period of the previous year. Even so, this was far below the 6% the Interstate Commerce Commission (ICC) had said the railroads must attain in order to provide needed service improvements.

The railroads spent an estimated $1.25 billion for new equipment and other plant facilities in 1971 and an additional $2.5 billion for operating materials and supplies. Railroads operated 27,000 locomotives, 1,770,000 railroad and private freight cars, and 10,000 passenger cars during the year. (*See in* CE: Railroads.)

TRUCKS AND TRUCKING

The trucking industry in the U.S. continued to grow in 1971 at about the same pace as in 1970. The combined revenues of ICC-regulated trucking companies, numbering about 15,000, rose to more than $14 billion. Trucking continued to be the

An experimental 150-mph passenger train was unveiled in Great Britain in June. It was expected that the first such train would be put into official use in Britain in 1975–76.
KEYSTONE

foremost common carrier, accounting for more than half of the revenues of all ICC-regulated transportation.

The total number of commercial, farm, and private trucks in operation in 1971 reached a record of about 18.8 million. Highway-use taxes paid by the trucking industry increased proportionately: trucking companies paid a total of more than $5.5 billion in federal, state, and local road-use taxes in 1971.

As trucking use increased, so, too, did the demand for new trucks. In 1971 there were near-record sales of all types of trucks, including diesel-powered models. Truck-trailer sales were also substantial, though below the record level of 1969.

Containerization of cargo—particularly of goods moved internationally—continued to grow during the year, as shippers increasingly came to realize its advantages in simplifying the shipping process and reducing the cost of transferring cargo from one mode of transportation—land, sea, or air—to another. Container sizes remained unstandardized, but the trucking industry was hopeful that agreements on realistic uniform sizes could be achieved by manufacturers and shippers. In addition, international accords—intended to facilitate customs clearance—were in the final draft stages.

Government permission to use larger equipment was sought by the transportation industry as a whole during the year. The trucking industry's continuing need for relief from the restrictions imposed upon it by size and weight limits prompted the continuing development of data to support the industry's position in the various states.

Other trucking industry developments in 1971 included efforts to further computerize billings, tariffs, scheduling, and terminal operations. Emerging federal safety and pollution standards were leading to revised equipment designs. (*See in* CE: Transportation; Truck.)

TRAVEL. Figures released in 1971 revealed a record number of world travelers in 1970—approximately 167 million persons, who spent a record $15.5 billion. The International Union of Official Travel Organizations (IUOTO) said the number of tourists increased 9% and spending increased 11% over that of the previous year.

Two major factors influenced travel in 1971—air fares and the general economy. Europe was the biggest travel bargain for Americans, and the lure of a cheap vacation there resulted in a slump at other traditional resorts. The growing affluence of Western Europeans and low air fares brought record numbers to the United States. Officials said the number of Britons visiting the U.S. in 1971 should increase 30–40% over 1970; smaller increases were expected from other countries (981,-000 Europeans visited the U.S. in 1970). Some charter flight fares for European groups were about $100 for the round trip.

In June a price war broke out among interna-

tional airlines. The price cuts began when the Belgian government ordered its Sabena airlines to adopt a student fare of $220 round trip between New York City and Brussels. Most international carriers offered similar rates. American youth, mostly college students with dim prospects for jobs at home, took advantage of the fares and flocked to Europe in record numbers. Some airlines decided to extend the low fares to others, and by fall a full-scale fight in the 108-member International Air Transport Association (IATA) erupted. West Germany's Lufthansa announced plans for a $210 round-trip, off-season fare from New York City. Air Canada and Air France followed with comparable fares, and Swissair set a $180 round-trip rate for groups who take a $70–$149 ground package (hotel, meals, sightseeing). Irish Aer Lingus announced an equally tempting plan, and others also considered undercutting.

Pan American Airways and Trans World Airlines, both in the red and anticipating more losses on the European run, were fighting the new rates. All of the new lower fares were to take effect after Feb. 1, 1972, when current IATA fare arrangements expired. Talks were held throughout the year and, in December, the IATA finally ratified an agreement on transatlantic fares that represented a compromise between the lowest and highest proposed prices. It was to take effect April 1, 1972.

Starting his walk around the world in 1969, Canadian Elzear Duquette, 61, reached the French Riviera in June 1971.

A.F.P. FROM PICTORIAL PARADE

Temporary camps were set up in London to provide adequate inexpensive accommodations for the increasing number of young foreign visitors.

KEYSTONE

Charter flights from the U.S. came under attack by the Civil Aeronautics Board (CAB) in September when it filed suit in federal court in Brooklyn, N.Y., against five travel agencies, seeking an injunction to stop what it called illegal charter flights to Europe. By law, only persons who have been members for six months of a bona fide "affinity" organization chartering an airliner are eligible for such trips. Fares usually are about half those for scheduled flights. The CAB had been accused of not enforcing the rules, and complaints arose that there was a charter "underground," often unscrupulous, flourishing in the New York City area. Indeed, hundreds of Americans, mostly students, were stranded in Europe during the summer after "vouchers" for return charter flights were not honored. On December 30, CAB proposed a new rule that would make charter flights available to anyone, regardless of group affiliation.

By mid-1971 some 20 countries had approved a new World Tourism Organization (WTO). The body would come into existence after 51 ratifications and would be designated as a participating agency of the United Nations Development Programme and have a central role in promoting worldwide tourism.

Israel was enjoying its biggest tourist boom. In the first quarter of 1971, tourism receipts totaled $28 million. Visitors in mid-summer were up 37% from 1970 (100,000 were expected in July alone), and about half were non-Jewish. The U.S. continued to be the largest source of tourists.

Interest in travel to the People's Republic of China increased markedly after it appeared diplomatic relations would improve. However, it was not expected that the bamboo curtain would be opened suddenly. There was some cleanup activity at Peking's Museum of the Chinese Revolution and at T'ien An Men Square, a 98-acre park, but this was mainly because of an expected increase of official visitors, not tourists.

In 1971 Americans again were the greatest travelers and biggest spenders ($6.2 billion in foreign travel in 1970), but the economy made them more bargain-conscious. London, Paris, Rome, and other traditional European destinations remained popular, and the number of U.S. visitors to Spain and Portugal continued to increase because of low-cost hotels. Demand was slack for the Caribbean, Puerto Rico, and Hawaii, as well as for Japan and the Orient, as many persons had visited Japan for Expo 70. In the U.S., tourism was down in Florida, California, and New York City, but up in the Pacific Northwest.

Americans visiting Europe experienced some difficulty converting U.S. dollars into other currency following the August decision of U.S. President Richard M. Nixon to let the dollar "float" in relation to foreign currencies. Exchange rates fell. A total of 13.2 million tourists visited the U.S. in 1970—9.8 million from Canada, over 1 million from Mexico, and the remaining 2.2 million from overseas.

HOTELS AND MOTELS

While hotel/motel occupancy rates in the United States plummeted to the lowest level in almost 35 years, continued heavy construction of motor hotels brought the industry to the brink of overbuilding in 1971. Hotel occupancy dropped to 51% in early 1971 and remained near that point throughout the year, the lowest since the 1930's. Motel and motor hotel occupancy, a few percentage points higher, also reflected the depressed state of the U.S. lodging industry. Industry leaders attributed the declines in occupancy to a slack in the national economy, curtailment in business travel, sharply lower convention and business-meeting attendance, and the lure of low-priced travel overseas.

Significant new hotel construction in the U.S. included the opening of the 1,904-room Sheraton-Waikiki, the largest convention-resort hotel in the world, in Honolulu, Hawaii, and breaking of ground for the $30-million, 750-room convention hotel, McCormick Inn, on Lake Shore Drive in Chicago. The first new hotel built in New York City since 1965, the 46-story, 640-room Park Lane, on Central Park South, opened its doors to the public in mid-1971. At the same time two hotels containing 2,000 rooms were slated for demolition there. Industry observers noted that New York City has had less new hotel construction since 1945 than any other major U.S. city.

American hotel companies continued aggressive expansion abroad during the year. Most properties were of the luxury or first-class type and the average number of rooms reflected the trend toward building larger establishments each year. In recent months Sheraton opened a 476-room hotel in Stockholm, Sweden, the largest in Scandinavia.

Motel chains also expanded overseas during 1971. The first Howard Johnson's hotel in Europe was opened in Amsterdam, the Netherlands, and construction began on the first European Trave-Lodge motor hotel in Liège, Belgium.

TRUDEAU, PIERRE ELLIOTT.

With a characteristic flair for dramatic action, Canada's Prime Minister Pierre Elliott Trudeau, 51, provided the country with one of its most unexpected events of 1971—his marriage to Margaret Sinclair, 22. Trudeau flew unannounced from Ottawa, Ont., to North Vancouver, B.C., on March 4 to be wed in a Roman Catholic ceremony. Mrs. Trudeau traveled with her husband on an 11-day state visit to the Soviet Union in May, but she did not attempt to match his hectic schedule of travel later in the year as she awaited the birth of their first child. The arrival of their son on December 25 was the first birth to the wife of a Canadian prime minister in 102 years.

Trudeau had intended to visit President Tito of Yugoslavia and Prime Minister Edward Heath of Great Britain in August, but returned hastily from Europe to deal with the threat to Canada posed by the far-reaching economic program of U.S. President Richard M. Nixon. It appeared that Nixon's policies—in particular, a 10% surtax on imports—might aggravate the serious unemployment situation in Canada, already the chief target of Trudeau's critics.

The prime minister's personal popularity remained high among Canadians. He was received enthusiastically during election-style tours of widely separated areas of the country. At the same time his government's standing was set back during the year. A step toward reform of Canada's constitution—embodied in a tentative charter negotiated during June in Victoria, B.C.—was vetoed by the province of Quebec. The policy of spending hundreds of millions of dollars to develop slow-growth regions of Canada was showing few measurable results. The administration did, however, push through legislation on unemployment insurance, old-age security, and tax reform.

Trudeau apparently lost ground with Canada's press. It was also alleged that he displayed arrogance in confrontations with the opposition parties in the House of Commons. (*See also* Canada; Canadian Economy.)

TUNISIA.

President Habib Bourguiba's precarious state of health and the problem of his succession continued to dominate Tunisian political life in 1971. On his triumphant return to Tunisia in June after several months' absence, the president made it clear that he had no intention of "becoming merely a figurehead" or of delegating any of his power. On the republic's 14th anniversary in July he declared: "I still have the strength to lead the country and I am determined to carry on with the job I began years ago."

The president was increasingly concerned at the growing movement in favor of liberalization among some sectors of the Neo-Destour Socialist party (the government party). Ahmed Mestiri, leader of the liberal wing, was dismissed from his post as minister of the interior and over the course of the year was gradually ousted from any position of influence in the country.

The conflict between conservative and liberal elements dominated the 8th congress of the government party held at Monastir in October. During the debates, Mestiri advocated liberalization under the guidance of President Bourguiba, while others such as Mohammed Masmoudi spoke against this idea. Prime Minister Hedi Nouira, a conservative, was presented to the congress as President Bourguiba's successor. Nouira was named secretary general of the party. He then formed a new cabinet with himself as prime minister and Masmoudi as foreign minister. (*See in* CE: Tunisia.)

TURKEY.

In 1971 Turkey was plagued by crises that included the forced resignation of its government, the establishment of a new coalition, and martial law in major provinces. The difficulties stemmed from continued terrorism and the failure to enact far-reaching social reforms.

Prime Minister Suleyman Demirel and his six-year-old conservative government resigned on March 12 in the face of a threatened coup by Turkey's four top military leaders, who said they would seize power unless a new government "above party politics" was established to halt civil unrest and to initiate reforms. The demands followed

Textile workers in Turkey went on strike in January. A currency devaluation in 1970, followed by other stringent economic measures, had antagonized Turkish workers in many industries.
BEYNELMILET BASIN FROM KEYSTONE

growing military dissatisfaction with Demirel's handling of left-wing terrorism. The situation reached a climax March 4 when four United States airmen were kidnapped by the radical Turkish People's Liberation Army. (The airmen were released unharmed five days later.)

After Demirel's resignation, President Cevdet Sunay began talks with military and political leaders. Following a week of conferences the president selected a former law professor, Nihat Erim, a moderate and a member of the Republican People's party, as the new prime minister. Erim resigned from his party to satisfy military demands. On April 7 his new coalition government received a decisive vote of confidence in the National Assembly, 321 to 46.

Violence and student rioting continued, and Turkish police were unable to control the unrest. Consequently, the government on April 26 declared martial law in 11 of Turkey's 67 provinces, including the cities of Istanbul, Izmir, and Ankara, the capital. There were still individual acts of violence, including the kidnapping and murder of Israeli consul general Ephraim Elrom in May.

A crisis developed on October 5 when the Justice party (that of ousted Prime Minister Demirel and the largest group in parliament) withdrew its five cabinet ministers from the government. Erim took the move as an expression of no confidence, and he and his cabinet resigned three weeks later. President Sunay refused to accept the resignation, however, saying Erim had the "full support" of parliament and the military. Erim and his cabinet then agreed to remain. On December 3, however, another crisis erupted because of conservative opposition to Erim's reform program. Erim resigned but remained in charge of a caretaker government.

On December 11 he announced formation of a new cabinet, which later received a strong vote of confidence from the National Assembly, 301 to 45.

In foreign affairs, Erim's government recognized the People's Republic of China but reaffirmed loyalty to the West, particularly during the October visits of U.S. Vice President Spiro T. Agnew and Great Britain's Queen Elizabeth II. In response to international pressure, Turkey agreed to ban the cultivation of the opium poppy and the production of opium throughout the country by June 1972. (*See in* CE: Turkey.)

UGANDA. On Jan. 25, 1971, a military coup led by Maj. Gen. Idi Amin overthrew the government of Uganda's socialist president, Milton Obote, while Obote was out of the country. The takeover grew out of resentment of Obote's socialization program and his tribal policies, which had favored his own Lango tribe.

Ruling by decree after dissolving Parliament, Amin dismissed local officials of the Obote regime, released many political prisoners, and banned political activity for two years. He appointed a new, tribally balanced civilian cabinet, then recruited the new ministers into the army and made them swear allegiance to his regime. The army acclaimed Amin president in February. In May he severely curtailed Obote's program to nationalize business.

To promote national unity Amin allowed the body of the Baganda tribal king to be returned for burial in Uganda; exiled by Obote, the king had died in England in 1969. Amin refused, however, to restore tribal kingship offices.

Amin strengthened the army by several thousand men. However, intertribal fighting erupted within

Uganda's new ruler, Maj. Gen. Idi Amin (driving jeep), rides triumphantly through the streets with his troops.
CAMERAPIX FROM KEYSTONE

the army, military discipline weakened seriously, and the senior officer corps was depleted by desertion and death. In addition to these problems, Obote, in refuge in neighboring Tanzania, retained considerable support among leftist African governments that refused to recognize Amin's regime. Amin repeatedly accused Tanzania, Sudan, and others of aiding pro-Obote guerrillas, but his allegations were seen as attempts to divert attention from internal affairs.

Tanzania's refusal to recognize Amin led him to close the Ugandan-Tanzanian border in July. In August fighting erupted on the border. The dispute with Tanzania threatened to disrupt the East African Community (EAC). In the fall there was some indication that Ugandan-Tanzanian relations were easing. (*See also* Tanzania. *See in* CE: Uganda.)

UNION OF SOVIET SOCIALIST REPUBLICS (U.S.S.R.).

The central event of 1971 in the Soviet Union was the 24th congress of the Soviet Communist party, which met in Moscow, the capital, in April. It was a relatively peaceful gathering, and consolidation was its principal theme. The main issues dealt with economic policy, emphasizing centralized control, more efficient labor discipline, and technological progress. The congress also approved the strengthening of party control, through grass roots party units, over "institutes engaged in scientific research, educational establishments, and establishments engaged in cultural and enlightenment work and in medical care." This decision occurred against the background of criticisms of the Soviet system by some scientists who showed remarkable solidarity on occasions when the authorities decided to stifle particularly irritating criticism.

The nation's most prominent scientist, Andrei Sakharov, known for founding the Soviet Committee for Human Rights in November 1970 together with other outstanding Soviet scientists, took up the cudgel on behalf of Soviet Jews. At the end of 1970 Sakharov appealed to President Nikolai V. Podgorny for clemency on behalf of the two Jews sentenced to death in the Leningrad hijacking trial. In March 1971 he wrote to the Ministry of Internal Affairs protesting against violations of human rights in the case of a group of Jews arrested during a demonstration at the office of the chief prosecutor. And in May he joined with other members of the Soviet civil rights movement in addressing an appeal to the Supreme Soviet, criticizing the persecution of Soviet Jews and the authorities' reluctance to allow exit permits to those wishing to emigrate to Israel.

The Soviet authorities were well aware that the Jews presented them with a special problem. Many Soviet Jews felt a greater loyalty to Israel, the Jewish state they did not know, than to the Soviet Union, whose anti-Semitic tendencies they could not forget. For some, emigration to Israel was mainly a means of escaping to the West. The Soviet authorities found it difficult to admit that there were large numbers of people within their system who openly stated their preference for living outside it. The possible effect on Arab opinion of large-scale emigration from the Soviet Union to Israel had also to be considered, yet repression did not seem the answer either. This was partly because Soviet society had become less tolerant of repression since Joseph Stalin's death, and partly because of Soviet concern for world public opinion, a taste of which Premier Aleksei N. Kosygin got during his visit to Canada in October. He explained there that the Soviet government had to draw the line at allowing Jews who had recently received an expensive education to take their skills to Israel. Nevertheless, the Soviet authorities, from time to time, granted exit permits, usually to the most persistent would-be emigrants, in the hope of decapitating the protest movement. Throughout 1971 there was a considerable increase in the number of Jews allowed to leave, notably from the Georgian Soviet Socialist Republic.

In a sense, Soviet scientists occupied a privileged position since the regime could not do without them. Other intellectuals were less fortunate. The 5th congress of the Union of Soviet Writers, which took place in June 1971, illustrated the ascendancy of conformist views in literature. The secretary, Georgi Markov, devoted a considerable part of his keynote address to the role of the Russian language in unifying the various nationalities of the Soviet Union; he produced all the old slogans about the proper function of literature as serving the aims of the party. Dissenters and critics of the system were dismissed by Markov as "a few died-in-the-wool idlers," who would have to face the consequences of "their parasitic way of life." Ironically, the death on December 18 of Aleksandr T. Tvardovsky, former editor of *Novy Mir,* was the occasion for public grief among the Communist party leadership. Tvardovsky had been a nuisance to the government in sponsoring a number of "liberal" authors, in particular Aleksandr I. Solzhenitsyn

(who made a rare public appearance to attend his friend's funeral). Almost the entire Soviet leadership signed a eulogizing obituary in *Pravda,* which, however, failed to mention Tvardovsky's long editorship of *Novy Mir.*

The supremacy of the party in the Soviet power structure covered more than control over official literary establishments. At the 24th party congress, Communist Party General Secretary Leonid I. Brezhnev emerged as the most powerful man in the Soviet Union, thus confirming yet again the importance of the position at the head of the party. Four new members were added to the Politburo— all of them Brezhnev supporters: Viktor Grishin, the secretary of the Moscow city party organization; Dinmukhamed Kunayev, the first secretary of the Communist party in Kazakhstan; Fyodor Kulakov, the party secretary responsible for agriculture; and Vladimir Shcherbitsky, the chairman of the Ukrainian Council of Ministers. In the powerful Central Committee, which was elected by the congress, 44.5% of the membership (107 out of 241) were party officials; the party retained a firm grip on the direction of affairs, and Brezhnev enjoyed its confidence.

The evolution of the power game in the Soviet

Once again the May Day celebrations in Moscow lacked their former military emphasis. Soviet marchers paraded through Red Square, along with trucks carrying pictures of Communist leaders.

"LONDON DAILY EXPRESS" FROM PICTORIAL PARADE

Former Soviet leader Nikita S. Khrushchev is carried to his final resting place in Moscow in September. His son Sergei (center) is among the pallbearers.
WIDE WORLD

Union, from the revolutionary élan of Lenin's day, through the crude simplicities of Stalin and the uncertainties of the collective leadership, to the current situation, was recalled by the death of Nikita S. Khrushchev in September 1971, which passed almost unnoticed in his own country. Khrushchev's very real achievements were obscured by some failures and by his eccentric style of public behavior. But the collapse of his agricultural reforms, the failure of economic reorganization, and the inglorious outcome of the Cuban missile adventure must be set against the dilution of the Stalinist practice of government by fear.

The Economy

The ninth five-year plan, for the period 1971–75, was published in February 1971. It made some concession to the consumer by targeting an increase of 44–48% in the production of consumer goods as against an increase of only 42–46% in gross industrial production. Also, the growth rate of heavy industry was slightly reduced, thus giving light industry a somewhat higher priority.

Those economists who had hoped for a complete departure from the old overcentralized pattern of management were disappointed, but some of the ideas advocated by Yevsei G. Liberman of Kharkov University and others, seemed to have taken root since 1965. The main thesis of the reformers was that profit and profitability should be the principal yardstick in stimulating economic performance and determining its efficiency (although in February Liberman felt obliged to publish a paper rejecting the view that his proposals should ever have been regarded as an attack on the primacy of centralized planning). At the beginning of 1971 over 44,000 industrial enterprises, accounting for 95% of profits in industry, had gone over to the new method of planning and management based to some extent on Liberman's ideas.

In the agricultural sector, the new five-year plan predicted an annual average grain harvest of 195 million tons as against an annual average of 163 million tons in the period 1966–69. Massive investments in farming were intended to bring about a growth in labor productivity of 21% for state farms and 39% for collective farms, and this was expected to lead to a 12% reduction in the agricultural labor force. (In 1971 about 33% of the total Soviet labor force worked in agriculture, compared to 4% in the United States.) These trends in agricultural planning were related to the comparatively poor results achieved in the eighth five-year plan, and although the record harvest of 1970 helped to redress the statistical balance, the agricultural gross output in the years 1966–70 rose only by 21%, instead of the 25% originally laid down.

Despite the difficulties experienced in agriculture, the economic outlook in 1971 did not cause undue concern. The increase in productivity (an annual average of 4.5% in recent years) seemed to be keeping pace with the West and the forecast that real wages would go up by 31% in the period of the ninth plan appeared to be reasonably realistic. For the immediate future it appeared that steps were being taken to reduce the pressures that defense expenditure had exerted for so long on the Soviet economy. The significance of the strategic arms limitation talks (SALT) in this context was self-evident.

The initial stages of the latest plan period went well. An increase of 3% in the number of employed was reported for the first half of 1971, bringing the labor force in industry and management to 91,300,000. Some of the wage increases forecast in the plan directives were partially implemented—beginning on July 1 wages for railway workers were raised, pay for workers in agriculture went up, and the income of collective farmers also rose. Minimum old-age pensions and disability pensions were also raised.

Consumer satisfaction was one of the party's main preoccupations, and a special decree published on October 29 again called for a rapid increase in the output of consumer goods. It promised that, by comparison with 1970, production of goods in "mass demand" would go up by 90% during the ninth plan. On November 24 Premier Kosygin informed the Supreme Soviet that it had been decided to raise the growth rate of consumer goods production in the plan to 49% compared with the 44–48% of the original directive.

Foreign Policy

Soviet diplomacy was very active in 1971, particularly in the second half of the year, although most of the activity seemed to have been designed to consolidate the nation's international position and to underpin the precarious stability of the international system in areas where this would serve the Soviet national interest. The most urgent target remained the convening of a European security conference, which had been high on the Soviet Union's list of priorities since 1966. The environment for such a conference depended on the status of East Germany, the settlement of the Berlin issue, and the ratification of West Germany's treaties with the Soviet Union and Poland, concluded in 1970. With the signing of the first stage of the four-power agreement on Berlin in September 1971 and the subsequent detailed agreement worked out between the East Germans and the West Germans in December, the climate became favorable. During Brezhnev's visit to Paris at the end of October, French President Georges Pompidou agreed that a preparatory meeting for a European security conference should be called in Helsinki, Finland,

as soon as possible. At the end of November, Walter Scheel, the West German foreign minister, went to Moscow to discuss the timing of the preparations.

Brezhnev's visit to Paris was perhaps the most interesting of the many diplomatic journeys undertaken by Soviet leaders during 1971, mainly because President Pompidou, although ready to support moves for a European security conference, made it quite clear that a formal Franco-Soviet friendship treaty was not under consideration. However, the Russians did get an agreement under which the Renault firm was to supply machinery and services worth about $230 million for the construction of a big truck plant on the Kama River. A more general ten-year agreement on economic and technical cooperation between the Soviet Union and France was also signed.

From Paris, Brezhnev went to East Berlin, and soon after his visit, there was marked progress in the Berlin negotiations. In November during a visit to Moscow by a Polish delegation led by First Secretary Edward Gierek much emphasis was put on early ratification of the treaties concluded in 1970 by the Soviet Union and Poland with West Germany. Brezhnev repeated this demand in his speech to the Polish party congress in December. Soviet relations with the new Polish leadership, which took power at the end of 1970, had developed without difficulties, despite the refurbished economic policies put into effect in Poland. In February 1971 the Soviet Union granted the Poles economic aid amounting to $500 million. An agreement projecting an increase of 12% in trade with Czechoslovakia was concluded in November, and the Soviet leadership appeared to be content with the policies pursued in that country by Communist Party General Secretary Gustav Husak.

Soviet leader Leonid I. Brezhnev (second from right) and West German Chancellor Willy Brandt (left) hold talks in a very relaxed atmosphere in Oreanda, U.S.S.R.

FRED IHRT FROM STERN MAGAZINE

The ashes of the three Soyuz 11 cosmonauts are carried through Moscow's Red Square during the state funeral held in July.

CAMERA PRESS FROM PICTORIAL PARADE

Brezhnev's journeys in the fall also included a visit to Belgrade, Yugoslavia, where he was given a cordial reception by President Tito, and there were no signs that the Russians had tried to exploit the internal differences that were troubling Yugoslavia.

Kosygin's visit to Canada was disturbed by Jewish protests against the treatment of Jews in the Soviet Union and by a young Hungarian refugee who tried to assault him physically in Ottawa, Ont. He was less troubled in Cuba and Scandinavia. Great Britain was the Western country least liked by the Soviet Union in late 1971, following the expulsion of 105 Soviet officials from Britain. The British government also decided to cut the number of Soviet officials in Britain.

In the Middle East the Soviet Union continued to give general support to the Arab cause (although some Arab governments, notably Libya, criticized the Soviets for supporting India in its war with Pakistan in December). In May a new treaty between the U.S.S.R. and Egypt was signed, recording Soviet approval of President Anwar el-Sadat's regime almost immediately after the elimination of Aly Sabry, who had been regarded as Moscow's special contact in Cairo. The treaty placed great emphasis on mutual consultation, and this was understandable in the light of Egypt's military dependence on the Soviet Union. Elsewhere in the Middle East, the Soviets watched helplessly in July while the Sudanese government carried out the destruction and liquidation of the Communists who

had supported an abortive coup against the regime of Maj. Gen. Gaafar Mohammed al-Nimeiry. *Pravda* and other Soviet newspapers carried reports of worldwide protests against the mass arrests and executions of Communist leaders, but the Soviet government remained relatively cool, obviously pursuing its established policy of ideological flexibility in Arab affairs.

Asia provided the Soviet Union's major foreign policy preoccupations in 1971. The dramatic rapprochement between the U.S. and China certainly created a new dimension, and the initial Soviet reaction was almost hysterical, expressing itself in accusations charging the Romanians with organizing an anti-Soviet bloc under Chinese and U.S. patronage. Romania's rejection of the Soviet note containing these accusations was quite unambiguous and was unanimously endorsed by the Romanian Communist party's Central Committee when it met in August. The Soviet friendship treaty with India was perhaps a more rational reaction, and when it was signed in August the Bangla Desh crisis and the subsequent war were still some months away. In that event, the Soviet Union aligned itself with India against Pakistan, while China gave some political backing to the other side. In the United Nations the U.S.S.R. was able to frustrate all attempts to force a cease-fire resolution through the Security Council. Indian Prime Minister Indira Gandhi's visit to Moscow at the end of September had been useful in strengthening the special relationship between India and the Soviet Union. India's military victory against Pakistan, achieved with Soviet diplomatic support and in the teeth of U.S. and Chinese diplomatic opposition, must have strengthened the Soviet Union's position in Southeast Asia. But a difficult situation could have arisen for Soviet diplomacy had the Indians been less successful in the field.

Soviet foreign policy was faced with a new pattern by the U.S. initiative regarding China. Although they had not really come to terms with this spectacular development, Brezhnev and his colleagues did pursue fairly consistent policies right across the world. They moved toward the strengthening of the territorial status quo in Europe; they managed to keep the East European situation in a reasonably stable condition; they maintained their influence in the Middle East; they became the paramount external influence in the Indian subcontinent; and they asserted the global range of the Soviet Union's interests as a world power by challenging U.S. naval power in the Mediterranean, by deploying Soviet naval capability over a wider area, and by maintaining diplomatic contacts with many countries at the highest level. (*See in CE: Russia.*)

UNITED NATIONS (UN).

The year 1971 was highlighted in the UN by the decisions to select a new UN secretary-general and to seat the People's Republic of China in place of Nationalist China and the attempts to settle the Middle East problems and to deal with the war between India and Pakistan. Membership in the UN increased to 132 nations with the admission of Bahrain, Bhutan, Oman, Qatar, and the Union of Arab Emirates.

A New Secretary-General

On January 18 Secretary-General U Thant announced that he had no intention of serving be-

yond his second term, which would end December 31. The Burmese delegate had served since 1961 and was in failing health. Despite delegates' persistent hopes that he might change his mind, U Thant remained adamant. On September 16 he offered some valedictory thoughts to newsmen. He stated that the drafters of the UN charter "were overly obsessed with political and military conflict." He understood their concern with international security, but he believed that it would be more useful to authorize the secretary-general to bring to UN attention "global threats to human well-being other than those to peace and security." He cited as examples his own warnings about the consequences of excessive population growth and the problems for man that arose from a deteriorating environment, and he referred to his attempts to deal with "great humanitarian emergencies" resulting from natural disasters and refugee problems —like those caused in 1971 by the flight of some ten million people from East Pakistan into India.

By the time the 26th UN General Assembly opened on September 21 under the presidency of Adam Malik, foreign minister of Indonesia, the search for a successor had narrowed to five current and former UN delegates. The UN Charter required the Assembly to appoint the secretary-general from among candidates nominated by the Security Council, a procedure requiring the nominees to have the support of all five permanent Council members. The Security Council met in private sessions December 17, 20, and 21 in efforts to agree, but only at its third meeting did it select Kurt Waldheim, an Austrian career diplomat, and send his name to the General Assembly. The Council vote was 11–1 with 3 abstentions, the People's Republic of China among them, and the General Assembly endorsed the choice on December 22. Waldheim was sworn in immediately for a five-year term beginning Jan. 1, 1972.

Swedish UN troops guard a train that had been attacked by Baluba rebels in the Congo (Kinshasa). The train was carrying food parcels.

Chinese Representation

Since 1961 the United States had taken the lead in having the Assembly designate the matter of admission of the People's Republic of China as an "important question," requiring a two-thirds majority for passage. This parliamentary tactic helped insure that Nationalist China (Taiwan) would keep its seats in both the Assembly and the Security Council. However, the dramatic change in relations between the U.S. and China during 1971 resulted in a reversal of U.S. policy. On August 2, U.S. Secretary of State William P. Rogers announced that the U.S. would support a resolution to seat the People's Republic in the UN.

The parliamentary scenario in 1971 was very much like that of previous years, with the U.S. seeking to designate the issues "important," although this time with the object of keeping the Nationalists in. The Chinese government repeatedly stated that it would not sit in a UN that still accorded a place to the Taiwan regime. The U.S. argued, however, that a UN seeking to become more nearly universal by admitting the People's Republic would be ill-served by expelling the Nationalists.

When the vote came on the issue on October 25, it was quite decisive. The Assembly first rejected the U.S.-sponsored "important question" resolution by 59–55 with 15 abstentions. It then went on to adopt a resolution sponsored by Albania, Tanzania, and others, to "restore" the "lawful rights" of the People's Republic, to recognize its representatives as the only legitimate representatives of China to the UN, and to immediately expel those of Nationalist China. The vote was 76 in favor, 35 opposed, with 17 abstentions. The permanent members of the Security Council, except the U.S. and Nationalist China, whose delegates walked out of the Assembly Hall just before the final vote, voted with the majority. Analysts later attributed the crushing defeat for the U.S. resolution to the momentum generated by the Albanian and Tanzanian sponsors of the opposing proposal, to adverse reaction to U.S. "arm twisting" tactics, and to a general feeling that U.S. President Richard M. Nixon's announced visit to China in the near future suggested the need for other nations to also repair their fences with the People's Republic as soon as possible.

Threats by some members of the U.S. Congress to curtail UN funds in reprisal for the adverse vote were roundly condemned by others who remembered past U.S. criticism of the Soviet Union and France for withholding UN funds because of UN operations of which they disapproved. Reduced contributions did in fact further jeopardize the UN financial situation, which, U Thant reported in September, was close to bankruptcy.

The Middle East

In January, responding to a request of Gunnar V. Jarring, the secretary-general's special representative for the Middle East, both Egypt and Israel prepared memoranda outlining their respective positions on Middle East questions. Israel indicated that it would withdraw from territories beyond frontiers delineated in a future peace treaty, but not until it could sign a binding agreement with the Arabs. Egypt insisted that Israel had to withdraw from all Arab territory occupied in the 1967 war. It also suggested a UN peacekeeping force with the "big four" powers (U.S., Great Britain, France, and the Soviet Union) participating.

The cease-fire between the two belligerents lapsed on February 5, but Egypt agreed to a 30-day extension in response to an appeal by U Thant and, possibly, to reports that the U.S. would undertake talks with the other powers about guaranteeing a Middle East settlement. (Such talks did begin on February 12, but by late fall it was apparent that U.S.-led efforts to compose the differences between the two sides had not been fruitful.)

On February 8 Jarring sent a memorandum to Israel asking it to withdraw from Egyptian territory in exchange for security provided through demilitarized zones, special arrangements in the Sharm el-Sheikh area, and the right to freely navigate through the Suez Canal. He simultaneously asked Egypt to commit itself to a peace arrangement with Israel based on the 1967 Security Council resolution requiring "termination of all claims or states of belligerency and respect for and acknowledgement of the sovereignty, territorial integrity, and political independence of every state in the area. . . ." Egypt was willing to accept these specifications, but added that lasting peace was impossible unless Israel withdrew from all Arab land it occupied. Israel did not reply directly to the memorandum, but stated that the Egyptian reply opened the way for significant negotiations. However, it again ruled out total withdrawal from occupied territories. On December 13 the General Assembly, by a vote of 79–7, with 36 abstentions, adopted an Egyptian-supported resolution calling on Israel to resume the indirect talks and to "respond favorably" to Jarring's memorandum of February 8. Israel indicated in advance that it found the resolution unacceptable.

Discussions about clearing the Suez Canal and reopening it took place in February and April, but also failed. Each side in effect regarded as preconditions for negotiations concessions that the other side thought depended upon a final settlement.

Another source of controversy was Israel's "master plan" for Jerusalem. The plan called for constructing housing projects to accommodate 122,000 Israelis in the former Jordanian sector of the city and on the nearby hills. On September 25, by a vote of 14–0 with 1 abstention, the Security Council called on Israel "to rescind all previous measures . . . and to take no further steps in the occupied section of Jerusalem which [might] purport to change the status of the city, or which would

Nationalist China's delegation walks out of the UN (above) just before the vote to unseat them. Some delegates react with glee (left) to the seating of the People's Republic. Huang Hua (below, right) of China meets George Bush of the U.S.

prejudice the rights of the inhabitants. . . ." U Thant, acting on a Council request that he report on the situation, on October 27 asked certain delegates to look into conditions in Jerusalem. By mid-November, however, it was clear Israel would not permit the UN to check on Israeli housing and population policies in the Arab sector of Jerusalem. Israel had indicated that it regarded the resolution as "devoid of any moral foundation." On December 20, the General Assembly voted 53–20 with 46 abstentions that Israel should rescind policies leading to the annexation of Arab lands, the deportation of its Arab residents, and establishment of Israeli settlements.

India-Pakistan War

After an increasing buildup in tension between India and Pakistan through most of the year, caused by the West Pakistani-dominated central government's brutal suppression of the Bengali independence movement in East Pakistan, full-scale hostilities broke out on December 3, with both India and Pakistan accusing the other of aggression. India considered its military movements a means of "liberating" the Bengalis of East Pakistan, some ten million of whom had previously fled to India.

On November 29 Pakistan had requested UN observers to examine the border clashes with India,

UNICEF PHOTO BY H. CHANDRA

Over 34 tons of medical supplies for Pakistani refugees are unloaded at Calcutta, India. The supplies were provided by UNICEF.

Council deadlocked, the issue was shifted to the Assembly and on December 7, the Assembly, by a vote of 104–11 with 10 abstentions, adopted a resolution asking for an immediate cease-fire and mutual withdrawal and urging that "efforts be intensified in order to bring about . . . conditions necessary for the voluntary return of the East Pakistan refugees to their homes."

Meanwhile, on December 6, India recognized as independent the Bengali state of Bangla Desh. On December 9, Pakistan accepted the cease-fire on condition that India do so also, but India delayed its response. On December 13, the Security Council was again prevented by a Soviet veto from adopting a resolution calling for a cease-fire and mutual troop withdrawal, and on December 17, Pakistan accepted unconditionally a cease-fire imposed by India after the latter's military victory.

Other Matters

Among other events during the year the UN made progress in harmonizing international trade law, maintained its voluntarily financed peace-keeping force in Cyprus, and celebrated 1971 as the International Year for Action to Combat Racism and Racial Discrimination.

It also unsuccessfully pressed South Africa to modify its apartheid policies. The International Court of Justice delivered an advisory opinion on June 21, affirming the illegality of South Africa's continued presence in Namibia (South-West Africa) and asserting South Africa's obligation to withdraw its administration from the territory immediately. In 1971 the United Nations Educational, Scientific, and Cultural Organization (UNESCO) celebrated the 25th anniversary of its founding. (*See in* CE: United Nations.)

but U Thant, apparently unwilling to act on his own initiative, relayed the request to the Security Council. Because of two Soviet vetoes on December 5, however, the Council was unable to adopt a resolution calling for a cease-fire. Nor was the Soviet Union able to command a majority for its own draft resolution merely asking Pakistan to "take measures to cease all acts of violence," without calling for a cease-fire by India. With the

Cellist Pablo Casals, 94, conducts a 150-piece orchestra at the UN playing his composition 'Hymn to the United Nations'. The work was commissioned by Secretary-General U Thant.

UPI COMPIX

UNITED STATES. Abrupt changes in the nation's economic and foreign policies put the United States on a new course both at home and abroad in 1971. Long on record as being opposed to government control of the economy, President Richard M. Nixon introduced a comprehensive federal program of wage, price, and rent controls in order to combat inflation. At the same time, he initiated measures to redress the adverse U.S. balance of payments—an effort that led, at the end of the year, to the devaluation of the dollar.

The Nixon Administration's relations with Congress improved considerably in 1971, although little was done to achieve the "six great goals" of the "New American Revolution" outlined in the president's State of the Union Message on January 22. The goals proposed by Nixon were welfare reform, full prosperity in peacetime, restoration and enhancement of the environment, improved health care, strengthening of state and local governments through revenue sharing, and reorganization of the federal government. The president explained that he was asking "not simply for more new programs in the old framework"; it was his intention "to change the framework of government itself—to reform the entire structure of American government so we can make it again fully responsive to the needs and the wishes of the American people."

Congressional Action

Congress approved a one-year extension (through April 1973) of the Economic Stabilization Act of 1970, under which the president may impose wage, price, and rent controls. Congress also cleared the president's tax bill, cutting personal and business taxes over a period of three years in an effort to stimulate the economy. The bill repealed the 7% automobile excise tax, gave business a 7% investment tax credit, and raised the personal income tax exemption from $650 in 1970 to $675 in 1971 and $750 in 1972. Nixon signed the bill only after the House-Senate conferees had removed a provision establishing federal financing for the 1972 presidential election campaign. He had threatened to veto the measure if the provision were not deleted.

In other action, Congress approved a new military draft bill, a $250-million loan to the ailing Lockheed Aircraft Corp., and an end to the supersonic transport (SST) subsidy. All of these developments overshadowed traditional social service issues, as most of the president's domestic recommendations were bogged down in Congressional committees for most of the year. But Congress did clear a bill appropriating more than $1 billion to fight cancer and another establishing day-care centers for children of working parents. Nixon vetoed the day-care bill on the ground that it would tend to weaken the family structure. He had previously vetoed two other bills—one providing $5.6 billion for public works and regional development, and one raising benefits for certain retired District of

Columbia municipal employees. The vetoes were upheld in all three cases.

In 1971, two of President Nixon's three major appointees encountered opposition in the Senate, but all were confirmed. The president had been embarrassed and angered when the Senate, in 1969 and 1970, rejected two successive nominees to fill a vacant U.S. Supreme Court seat. William H. Rehnquist and Lewis F. Powell, Jr., were nominated to the Supreme Court by Nixon on October 21 to fill the seats vacated by retiring Justices Hugo L. Black and John M. Harlan. Powell, a lawyer from Richmond, Va., drew little opposition and was confirmed on December 6 by an 89–1 vote. Rehnquist had a more difficult time. As an assistant attorney general, he was involved in the efforts of the Department of Justice to handle the May 1971 protest demonstrations in Washington, D.C. Consequently, liberals asserted that he was insensitive to the rights of dissenters. After a short-lived filibuster, Rehnquist won Senate confirmation by a vote of 68–26 on December 10.

The toughest confirmation battle involved Earl L. Butz, nominated to replace Clifford M. Hardin as secretary of agriculture. Butz found himself caught in the economic discontent gripping farmers and their representatives in Congress during a lean year for agriculture. His close ties to corporate farming interests made many members of Congress fear that he would be unwilling to use government policy to protect the small family farmer. Although the nomination put many Midwestern Republicans in the uncomfortable position of choosing between loyalty to Nixon and the wishes of their large farmer constituencies, Butz was confirmed 51–44 with only four Republican senators voting against him.

New Economic Policy

President Nixon's announcement of a new economic policy was the major event on the U.S. domestic scene in 1971. Nixon ordered without warning on August 15 an immediate 90-day freeze on wages, prices, and rents and suspended the tra-

THE 11 EXECUTIVE DEPARTMENTS

(December 1971)

Secretary of State............William P. Rogers
Secretary of the Treasury......John B. Connally
Secretary of Defense..........Melvin R. Laird
Attorney General.............John N. Mitchell
Secretary of the Interior....Rogers C. B. Morton
Secretary of Agriculture..........Earl L. Butz
Secretary of Commerce.......Maurice H. Stans
Secretary of Labor..........James D. Hodgson
Secretary of Health,
  Education, and Welfare...Elliot L. Richardson
Secretary of Housing and
  Urban Development.........George Romney
Secretary of Transportation......John A. Volpe

UPI COMPIX

This billboard was sponsored by two men in Seattle, Wash. It dramatizes the city's extremely high rate of unemployment and the exodus of many people from the area.

ditional convertibility of the dollar into gold, in effect freeing the dollar for devaluation against other currencies. These were the two major points in a program that included a 10% surcharge on dutiable imports, a $4.7 billion reduction in federal expenditures, a reduction in federal personnel, and a request for Congressional action to end automobile excise taxes and to enact tax incentives for industry. The wage-price freeze was the first to be imposed in the U.S. since the controls ordered by President Harry S. Truman in 1951 to combat inflation generated by the Korean War.

Phase II of the new economic policy was unveiled in October and took effect in November. In a television address on October 7, Nixon asserted that the freeze had been "remarkably successful" because the American people had "shown a willingness to cooperate in the campaign against inflation." He said the program of wage and price restraints would be continued after the freeze, and announced new administrative machinery for Phase II—a Price Commission, a Pay Board, and a Government Committee on Interest and Dividends. The Cost of Living Council established in Phase I would continue to operate under the chairmanship of Secretary of the Treasury John B. Connally, Jr.

On the day the president spoke, the White House issued a text of explanation of the Phase II program. It stated that the Cost of Living Council had proposed an interim goal of a 2–3% annual inflation rate by the end of 1972—about half the rate prevailing before the freeze. In addition, it

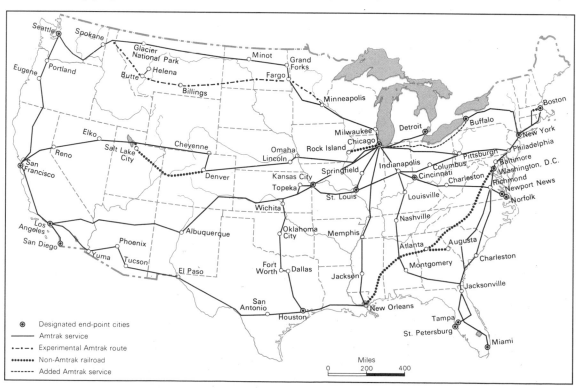

Designated end-point cities
Amtrak service
Experimental Amtrak route
Non-Amtrak railroad
Added Amtrak service

Miles
0   200   400

President Nixon receives a warm welcome in Mobile, Ala., in May. He journeyed there to dedicate the opening of construction on the Tennessee-Tombigbee waterway.
WIDE WORLD

disclosed that a Committee on the Health Services Industry and a Committee on State and Local Government Cooperation would be set up to assist the Cost of Living Council in its work. Members of the various Phase II bodies were appointed by Nixon later in the month.

While Americans generally took the 90-day freeze and Phase II in stride, foreign countries were alarmed by the implications of the 10% import surcharge and the new non-convertibility of the dollar into gold. The international monetary system, which for a quarter-century had hinged on U.S. readiness to exchange dollars for gold at the rate of $35 an ounce, seemed in danger of drifting into chaos. Then, after meeting with French President Georges Pompidou in the Azores, Nixon announced on December 14 that the U.S. was prepared to devalue the dollar by a small amount as part of an international agreement to realign the major world currencies.

Only four days later, representatives of the world's ten leading non-Communist industrial nations announced agreement on a new set of exchange rates after two days of talks in Washington, D.C. The so-called Group of Ten concluded that the dollar would be devalued by 8.57% in terms of gold, the West German mark would be revalued upward by 4.6%, and the Japanese yen would be revalued upward by 8%. Other currencies were revalued in smaller amounts, but the net effect was a dollar devaluation of nearly 12%. The realignment of exchange rates was expected to produce, within three years, an improvement of about $9 billion in the U.S. balance of payments—an amount roughly equal to the 1971 U.S. deficit in trade, tourism, and long-term investment. For its part, the U.S. consented to remove its 10% surcharge on imports (effective December 20) and delete a "buy-American" clause in the new 7% investment tax credit.

FBI and Pentagon Papers

Government practices in the interrelated areas of information acquisition and intelligence received considerable attention in 1971. In the first half of the year, the Federal Bureau of Investigation (FBI) and its director, J. Edgar Hoover, were accused by several members of Congress and others of monitoring the activities of persons not involved in or suspected of any crime. A prime source of material for these charges was provided in some of the 800 documents stolen from the bureau's Media, Pa., office in March. A self-styled Citizens' Commission to Investigate the FBI, which claimed credit for the burglary, distributed copies of the documents, a few at a time, to selected newspapers and members of Congress.

The first set of stolen documents to be made public dealt with investigations of students, blacks, and New Left groups. Among the 14 items in the set were an order from Hoover to investigate all student groups "organized to project the demands of black students" and a paper noting the plans of an Idaho Boy Scout leader to take his troop to visit the Soviet Union. The document that attracted the most attention, however, was a newsletter from the FBI's Philadelphia, Pa., office. Increased interviewing of persons identified with the New Left was necessary, the newsletter said, because "it will enhance the paranoia endemic in these circles and will further serve to get the point across there is an FBI agent behind every mailbox." Some of those interviewed, moreover, "will be overcome with the overwhelming personalities of the contacting agents and volunteer to tell all—perhaps on a continuing basis."

A second, more far-reaching controversy involved publication of the so-called Pentagon papers. At issue was the publication, first by *The New York Times* and later by several other newspapers, of excerpts from a 7,000-page "History of the United States Decision-Making Process on Vietnam Policy" commissioned by Robert S. McNamara when he was secretary of defense under President Lyndon B. Johnson. The study was classified as "top secret" and consisted of a critique of U.S. Indochina policy up to 1968, plus texts of relevant documents.

Much of the ensuing uproar centered on the "top secret" label the study carried and, by extension, on the integrity of the classification system itself. Nixon Administration officials contended that disclosure of the documents was not only unauthorized but also harmful to the defense and diplomatic interests of the U.S. Press executives generally took the position that the study dealt with events long past and thus constituted an historical treatise that the public was entitled to read. The information that appeared in print, they further asserted, was not damaging to national interests.

Legal action initiated by the Department of Justice interrupted in four newspapers the publication of articles quoting from the Pentagon papers. A flurry of appeals followed, culminating in a 6–3 decision by the U.S. Supreme Court on June 30 upholding the right of *The New York Times* and the *Washington Post* to resume publication of their respective series. Restraining orders against the *St. Louis Post-Dispatch* and the *Boston Globe* were lifted by federal district judges the same day. Although the Supreme Court was more divided than

its margin of decision would indicate, it generally agreed with the newspapers that the 1st Amendment to the Constitution ruled out prior censorship of the press.

Having lost its battle to block publication of the Pentagon papers, the government prepared to prosecute the man accused of distributing them to the press—Daniel Ellsberg, a former analyst for the Rand Corp. and one of the authors of the study. A federal grand jury in Los Angeles indicted Ellsberg on June 28 on charges of violating the Espionage Act and of stealing government property.

Prison Riots

The explosive conditions inside the nation's prisons were dramatized in 1971 by a number of violent incidents. Forty-three persons died at the Attica State Correctional Facility in Attica, N.Y., when about 1,000 state troopers, sheriff's deputies, and prison guards staged an air and ground assault to put down an uprising by 1,200 inmates. In an earlier incident, three prisoners and three prison guards were killed during an escape attempt at the California State Prison at San Quentin. Black militant George Jackson, who had acquired fame as one of the three "Soledad brothers," was shot to death as he dashed across the prison yard. (*See* Prisons Special Report).

Race Relations and Antiwar Protests

Black Panthers, who had long maintained that they were the victims of a police conspiracy and could not expect justice under the U.S. legal system, might have had some second thoughts in 1971. Thirteen Panthers were acquitted May 13 in New York City of plotting to bomb police stations, department stores, and other public places throughout the city. Less than two weeks later, a Connecticut state judge dismissed all murder and kid-

A construction worker who survived a tunnel explosion is aided by rescue workers. Seventeen men died in the blast, which took place in Port Huron, Mich., in December.

UPI COMPIX

"J. Edgar? Some of us boys down in Congress would like to discuss your possible .. er .. retireme . . ."

OLIPHANT FROM
THE LOS ANGELES TIMES SYNDICATE

nap charges against Black Panthers Bobby G. Seale and Ericka Huggins. The pair had been on trial for six months in New Haven in connection with the 1969 slaying of Alex Rackley, a former Panther. Charges were dropped after the jury announced that it was hopelessly deadlocked. In other cases, 12 Detroit Panthers were cleared of murder and conspiracy charges; two more mistrials were declared in the manslaughter case involving Huey P. Newton, a Black Panther party co-founder, and charges against him were dismissed; and Illinois State's Attorney Edward V. Hanrahan and 13 law-enforcement officers were indicted on charges of conspiring to obstruct justice in connection with a police raid resulting in the deaths of two Panthers in Chicago in 1969.

Until late December, the pace of antiwar protest slowed markedly in 1971. The chief demonstration against the war occurred in Washington early in May. Leaders of the so-called Mayday movement threatened to bring activity in the capital to a halt by blocking streets and bridges. Although some disruption of traffic occurred, the demonstrators fell far short of their announced goal. More than 7,000 of them were detained in mass arrests that were sharply criticized by civil liberties spokesmen.

When the U.S. intensified its bombing of North Vietnam in late December, antiwar groups throughout the nation responded with protests and demonstrations. Especially active were the Vietnam Veterans Against the War. On December 27 a group of 15 veterans seized the Statue of Liberty for a day and 25 others occupied the Betsy Ross house in Philadelphia for an hour. The next day 87 veterans were arrested in Washington, D.C., for blocking the entrance to the Lincoln Memorial. One spokesman for the veterans said, "We, as a new generation of men who have survived Vietnam, are taking this symbolic action at the Statue of Liberty to show support for any person who refuses to kill." (*See also* Foreign Policy, U.S.; Nixon. *See in* CE: United States.)

UPPER VOLTA. The military regime that had ruled Upper Volta since 1966 showed definite signs during 1971 of yielding to a return to civilian rule. In February President Sangoulé Lamizana appointed a civilian, Gérard Kango Ouedraogo, prime minister—a step that was regarded as a definite stage in the return to normal constitutional government. Of the remaining 15 cabinet posts, only 5 were held by members of the military.

President Lamizana's policy of strict austerity began to show positive results; the budget was balanced, and the national debt of more than $10 million inherited from the previous administration was paid off. In October President Lamizana visited France, where he stressed the importance to his country of French cooperation and aid. After talks with France's President Georges Pompidou, he obtained a significant increase in French economic assistance. (*See in* CE: Upper Volta.)

URUGUAY. In 1971 political activity in Uruguay was again dominated by the long-standing conflict between the executive and legislative branches of government over methods of suppressing the Tupamaro guerrillas. Cabinet changes and ministerial resignations, forced by opposition censure motions on the special security measures imposed in June 1969, were a prominent feature of political life. In January, following the guerrillas' kidnapping of the British ambassador, Geoffrey Jackson, President Jorge Pacheco Areco requested the suspension of individual constitutional guarantees for 90 days, but the legislature authorized only a 40-day suspension. Then in July the legislature voted to annul the 1969 security measures. These were immediately reimposed by presidential decree, but the legislature nearly succeeded in impeaching the president for his action.

On February 21 the Tupamaros freed a Brazilian diplomat, Aloysio Dias Gomide, after 206 days in captivity when his wife paid a ransom of at least $250,000. On September 6, 106 guerrillas escaped from the Punta Carretas prison via a tunnel. Included in their number was the founder of the Tupamaros, Raúl Sendic. Soon afterward the British ambassador was released.

Presidential elections were held on November 28 after a good deal of maneuvering by splinter groups. The traditional political picture showed a marked change, with the emergence of a left-wing alliance known as the Frente Amplio (Broad Front), led by Gen. Liber Seregni. The coalition's platform included land reform, nationalization of the banks, and government control of export industries, based on the lines of development in Chile. The Frente Amplio got less than 19% of the votes. President Pacheco failed to win a simultaneous plebiscite that would have allowed for an amendment of the constitution permitting him to succeed himself in office. Pending a recount, his protégé in the Colorado party, Juan Maria Bordaberry, seemed to have won the presidency, narrowly defeating the National party candidate, Wilson Ferreira Aldunate. (*See in* CE: Uruguay.)

VENEZUELA. The key political issues of 1971 in Venezuela were the role of foreign investment in the economy and the definition of policy relating to the use of government resources. Late in 1970 a new banking law was passed as the first of a series of measures designed to provide a new framework for foreign investors in Venezuela. It stipulated that banks with foreign shareholding of more than 20% could no longer accept savings deposits, issue negotiable deposit certificates, or sell foreign exchange acquired from the Central Bank. This measure was followed by a bill that placed domestic oil products under the control of the state oil company and by the establishment of

a committee to define the role of foreign and local capital in future economic development.

The oil reversion law passed by the Venezuelan Congress allowed the government to take over the underdeveloped parts of oil concessions held by foreign companies and to assume ownership of the producing and processing equipment of foreign companies upon the expiration of their concessions. A gas nationalization law provided for state retention of gas obtained from Venezuelan deposits and specified that companies formed to process and transport the gas must be Venezuelan-owned unless a special law was passed for an individual case. These developments seemed to reflect the general trend toward economic nationalism in Latin America. The oil and gas laws provoked a wave of criticism; however, a midyear speech by the finance minister emphasized that foreign investment would be actively encouraged in all other sectors of the economy.

Criticism of the government's use of public funds continued in 1971, as there were fears that extra revenue from higher oil prices and taxes would be absorbed by higher expenditures. Kidnappings and student violence were also sources of concern in 1971. (*See in* CE: Venezuela.)

VETERINARY MEDICINE. Two major outbreaks of animal disease affected the United States in 1971—Venezuelan equine encephalomyelitis (VEE) in Texas and African swine fever in Cuba. Both had been classed as exotic diseases in the U.S. because neither had ever occurred there, and thus considerable concern was expressed over the real or potential threat they posed to the highly susceptible equine and swine populations. Another

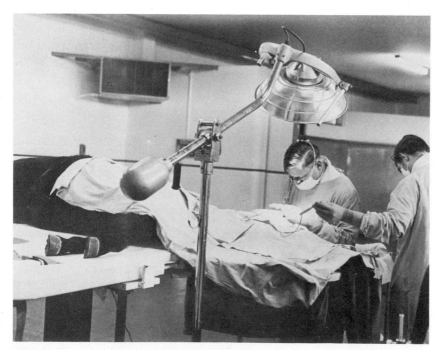

An eye surgeon from Sydney, Australia, performed a cataract operation on a seven-month-old racehorse. The operation is a delicate one for horses, as it is for people.

subtype of the VEE virus had been detected in Florida in 1962 but appeared then not to be a threat to either man or animals.

The disease had spread rapidly toward other states by mid-July, when Secretary of Agriculture Clifford M. Hardin declared the VEE outbreak a national emergency, thus making possible the transfer of $5 million from other agricultural programs for use in combating it. An experimental vaccine developed at Fort Detrick, Md., as a potential countermeasure in biological warfare, had been tested in South and Central America, but its use in the U.S. had not been permitted because the risk of establishing and perpetuating the disease had not been fully assessed. With other exotic animal diseases, such as foot-and-mouth disease of cattle, the official policy had been one of eradication by slaughter, but this approach was considered ill-advised for VEE, and it was quickly decided to vaccinate all horses that might be endangered.

Beginning in Texas and extending as far as California and Florida, more than 2 million horses in 19 states and the District of Columbia were vaccinated during a two-month period. A commercial vaccine was licensed and marketed, and the U.S. Animal Health Association, representing all state veterinarians, urged that all horses in the country be protected. Meanwhile all horses in the affected and high-risk areas were put under quarantine, and several nations placed an embargo on horses from the U.S.

Another approach to controlling the disease was the eradication of the mosquito vector by aerial spraying. By late July approximately 2.2 million acres in Texas had been sprayed with insecticide. Together with vaccination and additional sanitary precautions, these measures appeared to have had the disease under good control by early fall.

African swine fever had never been reported in the Western Hemisphere until June 1971, when an outbreak in Cuba was attributed to virus present in meat brought in from Europe. By late July approximately 30,000 hogs had been slaughtered in an attempt to control the disease, and plans calling for depopulation of all swine—perhaps 500,000—in the province of Havana were announced. The mortality rate among affected hogs was said to be 100%, and because of its proximity the possibility of the disease spreading to the U.S. caused great concern among livestock disease officials there.

The disease resembled a virulent form of hog cholera, and a mistake or delay in diagnosis would have been costly because all swine in countries where it had not appeared would be highly susceptible. No vaccine had been developed to prevent the disease, which could be spread by virus in pork products or on clothing. This prompted customs officials to perform even more rigid inspections at all U.S. ports of entry and to tighten security with regard to casual migrants from Cuba. (*See also* Agriculture; Animals and Wildlife. *See in* CE: Diseases, Plant and Animal; Zoo.)

VIETNAM. With United States forces withdrawing from South Vietnam in 1971 at a steady rate under the program of Vietnamization, South Vietnamese government troops provided most of the security under an umbrella of U.S. air and artillery support. The North Vietnamese and Viet Cong were able to avoid large-scale military action, postponing engagements in which the government's assumption of primary defense responsibilities would be tested. In 1971 the main action was initiated by the South Vietnamese, with the battleground in neighboring Laos, in line with the policy of Vietnamization. However, the efficacy of this policy was called into question late in the year with the control of the Plain of Jars in Laos reverting to the enemy, a deteriorating military situation in Cambodia, and the resumption from December 26 to 30 of the heaviest U.S. bombing raids on North Vietnam since 1968. The bombing was an apparent effort to forestall any possibility of an American defeat.

On February 8 the South Vietnamese government announced the launching of Operation Lam Son

South Vietnamese soldiers interrogate a woman suspected of being a Viet Cong guerrilla, in the U Minh forest area southwest of Saigon.

WIDE WORLD

American medic Anthony Lopez tries to revive a South Vietnamese youth aboard a helicopter. Lopez was part of a "Dustoff" team specializing in medical evacuations by chopper.
WIDE WORLD

719, a heavy, multi-unit invasion of the southern Laotian panhandle, an area long under Communist control and used by them as a staging and logistics base for operations within South Vietnam. The stated objective of the operation was to interdict North Vietnamese supply routes along the Ho Chi Minh Trail, upsetting their plans for further offensive action and thus permitting the safe and continuing withdrawal of U.S. forces from South Vietnam. U.S. ground units were not themselves involved, but as many as 20,000 government troops were involved in the thrust at one time, most of them highly trained, well-motivated elite forces, who operated under extensive U.S. air support and artillery positioned along the border, whenever possible.

A month after the drive began, U.S. President Richard M. Nixon labeled it successful enough to guarantee that American troop withdrawals could be continued through the end of the year. For the South Vietnamese forces inside Laos, however, it was a bruising, sometimes humiliating series of battles with a determined, well-equipped enemy.

On March 24 the operation was terminated, with the South Vietnamese forces badly scarred, some in disarray, and others virtually wiped out as effective battle units. Official government losses were announced as 1,160 killed in action, 4,271 wounded, and 240 missing (casualties thus represented an acknowledged 28% of the committed force).

According to the South Vietnamese government, 13,815 North Vietnamese soldiers were killed during the operation. It was also claimed that the incursion force destroyed or captured 100 enemy tanks, nearly 300 vehicles, 176,246 tons of ammunition, 6,500 weapons, and more than 65 million gallons of gasoline. While some of the claims were considered suspect, it was evident that the North Vietnamese would be further pressed to resupply

their forces in South Vietnam, while still being subjected to intensive raids by U.S. B-52 strategic bombers.

Assessments of Lam Son 719 varied. It was, clearly, a controversial operation. It was described by detractors as a rout of the South Vietnamese, who did not penetrate as deeply as planned, could not retain possession of key objectives (such as the junction village of Tchepone), and failed to destroy as much enemy material and supplies as had been hoped. Others insisted the operation succeeded in inflicting appreciable damage on the North Vietnamese before the spring monsoon and consequently forestalling future large-scale enemy attacks in the still-contested areas within the northernmost provinces of South Vietnam. In the sense that the situation below the demilitarized zone became more secure, with less need for U.S. combat power, the operation did succeed, facilitating the continuing U.S. troop pullout. South Vietnamese military officers, however, did not conceal their view that the costly price of the operation, in casualties and dispirited troop morale, was too high to permit the U.S. military phaseout. President Nguyen Van Thieu came under personal attack from some of his usually loyal officer corps for approving the Laotian invasion, one of the few instances in which the military seriously challenged the president's leadership.

South Vietnam

An extended period of several years of relative political stability in South Vietnam was broken in 1971 by a general election in which President Thieu's maneuvers left him unopposed for a second term. Although the balloting was a mere referendum on Thieu's leadership, it produced a heavy voter turnout but belied the growing discontent and war-weariness of the South Vietnamese people. For them the year ended with a sense of resignation and little chance for political or military alternatives. A crisis of important dimensions appeared imminent. But Thieu's controls over the military and the bureaucracy, plus the inability of the dissidents and the disaffected to mount sustained and effective opposition within the ostensibly democratic political system, placed the president in a near-dictatorial position.

On August 29 elections were held for the lower house of the National Assembly. The reconstituted legislature was to have 159 seats, 22 more than in the previous makeup. Only 40 deputies won re-election, and 22 of them were members of the opposition. Seventy-nine assemblymen were defeated. A total of 1,252 candidates ran for assembly seats. Individuals running on antigovernment platforms scored their greatest successes in the larger cities and in the five northernmost provinces. As a party, the biggest gains were registered by the militant religious-political An Quang Buddhists, who again became the strongest force against President Thieu; 24 of their members won election. Forty-eight avowedly pro-government candidates were elected, a number far short of a majority.

The presidential election was held on October 3. It became controversial when President Thieu forced through the legislature an election-reform bill that had the ultimate effect of eliminating all

opposition. Although it was obvious the measure was highly restrictive by making it extremely difficult for aspirants to qualify, President Thieu said that he assumed there would be at least three others challenging him: Vice-President Nguyen Cao Ky, Gen. Duong Van Minh, and a candidate of the coalition opposition. The operative clause within the new law required that anyone seeking nomination for the presidency be qualified only by collecting the endorsement of at least 40 deputies and senators or 100 city and provincial councillors. There were a total of 135 deputies, 60 senators, and 554 councillors. Most of the eligible endorsers were pro-government, and the simple arithmetic of winning eligibility discouraged opposition. General Minh termed the election-reform measure "unconstitutional," a view shared by a large number of even cynical South Vietnamese.

Vice-President Ky received the endorsement of 102 councillors, as required under the election-reform law, but the signatures of 40 of them were not certified by the government because it claimed those local officials had previously endorsed Thieu —whose own endorsement was made by 15 senators, 89 representatives, and 452 councillors, numbers which represented a virtual exclusion of any other hopeful. Ky was thus eliminated from the race. The Supreme Court considered the case on

South Vietnamese students overturn a police jeep that had been firebombed during a demonstration in September. They were protesting the upcoming one-man presidential election.

appeal and reinstated Ky's candidacy. At this point, Ky declared the court's ruling "was even more illegal" than the original decision to rule him off the ticket. He refused to run, despite the urgings of American officials (who feared that a one-man race would be inimical to their stated goal: to "insure the Vietnamese a choice in their elected officials through democratic methods"). Instead, he proposed that both Thieu and he resign and that new elections be held within 90 days under the administration of a caretaker government.

After Ky's invalidation as a candidate, but prior to the Supreme Court's overruling decision, General Minh decided to withdraw from the race. With Minh out of the race, and Ky refusing to be reinstated as a candidate, Thieu was without opposition.

Thieu's uncompromising position led to bitterness, frustration, and, sometimes, violent protest. Students in Saigon, the capital, Da Nang, and Hue staged demonstrations that were directly aimed at opposing Thieu but that, increasingly, acquired a marked anti-American flavor as well. Scores of U.S. vehicles were burned in the weeks prior to the

This hamlet near the Da Nang airbase was hit by two Viet Cong rockets, destroying 100 homes and killing five civilians.

WIDE WORLD

election. Disabled veterans joined in the anti-Thieu protests, three of whom burned themselves to death, a macabre form of protest that was practiced in the months before the assassination of President Ngo Dinh Diem in 1963.

On election day itself, extensive violence was launched by the North Vietnamese and Viet Cong. Communist action was reported to have been at its highest level in more than 18 months. There were 92 separate shellings and ground attacks on government positions, six times the daily average. Communist long-range gunners rained shells indiscriminately on practically every large South Vietnamese city, including Saigon.

Despite the level of enemy action and the disorders against a one-man presidential race, the October 3 election turnout was surprisingly high. Final official figures showed that 87.7% of the 6,331,918 eligible voters cast ballots. Of those voting, President Thieu won the support of 94%. Vice-President Ky declared there was "brazen rigging beyond imagination." He was joined by other anti-Thieu forces in similar charges. The Senate, however, voted 37 to 8 against establishing a commission to investigate the charges. Three weeks after the balloting, the Supreme Court ruled the election legal, turning down last-ditch attempts for an invalidation.

During the year, the U.S. continued withdrawing its ground combat forces and sizable air units from South Vietnam, in line with President Nixon's statement of September 16 that the main U.S. objective "is to end the American involvement just as soon as that is consistent with our overall goal, which is a South Vietnam able to defend itself against a Communist take-over and which includes, from our standpoint, our primary interest in obtaining the release of our POW's."

In April 1969 there were 543,400 U.S. servicemen in South Vietnam, the highest level reached during the war. The U.S. force at that time included 112 infantry, armor, and armored cavalry combat-maneuver battalions. They bore the brunt of the action against the North Vietnamese and Viet Cong. Gradually, the force levels were reduced as part of Vietnamization, in which South Vietnam's forces would ultimately bear the sole ground combat responsibility. In November President Nixon announced that 45,000 more U.S. soldiers would be withdrawn by Feb. 1, 1972, reducing the number remaining to 139,000 men.

South Vietnamese military strength remained at a level of 1.1 million men, with the regulars backed up by regional and popular forces totaling 520,000 men. Even with the withdrawal of American (as well as South Korean, Australian, New Zealand, and Thai units), the South Vietnamese would enjoy a seemingly superior numerical position, confronting an enemy force of 240,000 (including 100,000 North Vietnamese regulars, 40,000 Viet Cong main force troops, and 100,000 guerrillas and logistical support forces).

North Vietnam

The de-escalation of the war hardly gave any respite to North Vietnam in 1971. The leadership remained united and stable, but the unexpected rapprochement between the People's Republic of China and the U.S. worried the government. Devastating floods in September and October disrupted the program of economic recovery. In addition, President Nixon ordered a resumption of direct bombing of the north in December.

The North Vietnamese government was believed to be chary of committing new replacements to South Vietnam, employing what was termed an "economy of force" strategy. By their own admission, the North Vietnamese had lost more than a half million men in an effort to reunify the country under their banner.

In February the government announced its decision to hold general elections for the first time in seven years. Polling took place in April, for the people's councils as well as for the fourth National Assembly, and 99.8% of the electorate were reported to have voted. There were 529 candidates running for 420 seats.

The first session of the new National Assembly was held in June. In a move described as showing the stability of the leadership, 83-year-old Presi-

dent Ton Duc Thang was reelected along with Premier Pham Van Dong, the National Assembly standing committee chairman, Truong Chinh, and the vice-premier and defense minister, Vo Nguyen Giap. This meant continuation of the collective leadership provided by the triumvirate that had held the reins of power since the death of Ho Chi Minh in 1969 and that consisted of Communist Party First Secretary Le Duan, Pham Van Dong, and Truong Chinh. Despite speculation about ideological differences between Le Duan and Truong Chinh and about a continuous power struggle for the mantle of Ho, the triumvirate remained apparently united with no hint of any crisis.

There were signs that the North Vietnamese government was genuinely worried about the possibility of the China-U.S. thaw leading to an Indochina deal behind its back. It lost no time in pointing out that "the destiny of Vietnam is decided by the Vietnamese." It appeared that the Hanoi government was perhaps more disgusted at the prospect of being betrayed by China than at what it called President Nixon's attempts to divide the Communist world. Several summit-level contacts between the Chinese and the North Vietnamese followed. China hastened to state publicly that there was no question of its seeking a deal with the U.S. After a visit to Peking, the Chinese capital, by the North Viet-

A disabled South Vietnamese veteran is arrested by police for participating in a protest demonstration. He blocked traffic by sitting in the middle of a street in downtown Saigon.
WIDE WORLD

Trying to overrun a South Vietnamese position at Quang Tri, Viet Cong infantrymen charge through exploding mortar shellfire.

namese special adviser at the Paris peace talks, Le Duc Tho, China specifically condemned the idea of an international conference on Indochina on the model of the 1954 Geneva conference and emphasized that the unconditional withdrawal of U.S. troops was a precondition to ending the war.

There were hopes of a more positive contact between the North and the South in May when the South Vietnamese agreed to release 570 disabled war prisoners under terms laid down by the Hanoi government, which included a sea rendezvous under Red Cross flags and a 24-hour cease-fire. Soon after the agreement, however, Saigon officials said all but 13 of the prisoners had refused to return to North Vietnam. Denouncing this as an example of "odious treachery of the U.S. and Saigon administration," Hanoi called off the deal.

For the most part, the North Vietnamese attitude toward the U.S. remained tough throughout 1971. In a newspaper interview in Paris in May, Xuan Thuy, Hanoi's chief peace negotiator, listed Nixon's "three great errors": Vietnamization, the coup against Prince Norodom Sihanouk in Cambodia, and the Laos invasion. However, in July Hanoi backed a major new peace offer by the Viet Cong that said if the U.S. set a deadline for withdrawing all troops, then all U.S. prisoners would be released. American reaction generally was that the plan was aimed at embarrassing the U.S.

Widespread leakage of the Pentagon papers in the U.S. in midyear came as a propaganda windfall for North Vietnam. The episode received wide publicity in North Vietnam's news media, which stressed the dominant impression that the Pentagon revelations had given, namely that North Vietnam was more sinned against than sinning. (*See* Law Special Report.)

The North Vietnamese government described the floods of September and October as "unprecedented over the past 70 or 80 years." It was believed they caused more damage to the country than three years of U.S. bombing. Among the worst hit areas was the heavily populated Red River basin north of Hanoi. The main rice-producing areas were flooded. Also destroyed were some coal mines, besides railways, roads, electric cables, and houses. South Vietnam's surprise offer of aid to help flood victims was described by Hanoi's official news agency as "a perfidious trick used to scrape up the wealth of our countrymen in the South."

The floods undoubtedly put severe strains on the economy and at least temporarily reversed the encouraging trend set by two fortuitously good harvests earlier. All hopes of 1971 being a record year like 1970 were washed away. However, emergency measures such as planting short-term rice and turning playgrounds and office compounds over to cultivation were expected to hasten recovery.

On the industrial front all figures continued to be given in percentages. It was evident, however, that the government was particularly interested in the key industries of electricity, coal machinery, and building materials. (*See in* CE: Vietnam; Vietnam Conflict.)

WEATHER. Man's efforts to intervene in atmospheric events continued to mature during 1971. The National Oceanic and Atmospheric Administration (NOAA), of the United States Department of Commerce, and other private and federal institutions achieved significant successes in weather modification experiments.

The cooperative "lake effect" snowstorm modification project has for several years attempted to redistribute the heavy snows dumped by waterlogged clouds on the downwind shore of Lake Erie. The year's effort was expected to seed lake storms upwind from heavily populated Buffalo and Niagara Falls, N.Y., with the object of spreading the heavy lee-shore snowfall over a larger area.

At the request of the governor of Florida, a cloud-seeding project was mounted there to mitigate the devastating drought and fires that raged in the spring. Although the project was run as a scientific experiment, good operational results were obtained. An estimated 50,000 to 100,000 acre-feet of water were added to southern Florida's natural rainfall by the NOAA experiment.

Other weather modification efforts included lightning and hail suppression, snowpack augmentation along the western slope of the Rocky Mountains, and experimental cloud-seeding to alleviate the crushing drought that gripped the southwestern U.S. (particularly Texas) during much of the spring and summer. Atlantic Hurricane Ginger was repeatedly seeded by Project Stormfury aircraft in late September; but an evaluation of seeding effects was yet to come.

Inadvertent modification of the atmosphere was also the subject of much activity in 1971. In 43 U.S. cities, National Weather Service stations were designated Air Stagnation Advisory Offices, designed to provide timely information on air pollution potential to control agencies, which can then take appropriate pollution abatement action.

The first major eastern storm of the 1970–71 winter came in with the New Year and smothered the Atlantic seaboard from Virginia to Vermont with heavy snows. A few days later a massive snowstorm struck the Midwest, followed by a cold wave over much of the nation that produced such record temperatures as −39° F. in Arizona.

Meanwhile, a cold wave over western Europe brought ice, snow, and bitter cold. Ten persons were reported dead in Rhone Valley blizzards, and in Mouthe, France, near the Swiss border, temperatures plunged to a record −30°F.

Severe drought struck Florida's Everglades National Park in April. This is the cracked bed of a canal that normally has a water level of 18 to 36 inches.
WIDE WORLD

This U.S. cloud cover map for September 9 shows Hurricane Fern just east of southern Texas and heavy cloud concentration over Florida.

COURTESY, NOAA

The 1971–72 winter season began in the U.S. before the "official" end of summer. On Sept. 16, 1971, heavy snows began along the Rocky Mountains and brought a foot and a half of snow and unseasonably cold temperatures to the high plains and foothills.

The tornado death toll for 1971 had by summer almost doubled the 1970 figure—141 deaths, against the 1970 total of 73. The worst came on February 21, when disastrous Mississippi Delta tornadoes struck Louisiana, Mississippi, and Tennessee, killing 115 persons, injuring more than 2,000, and causing an estimated $19 million in property damage.

Despite a slow start the Atlantic hurricane season produced some memorable storms for the eastern and Gulf coasts of North and Central America. Beth brought wind damage and flooding rains to Nova Scotia in mid-August, and Doria, which struck the U.S. coast below Cape Hatteras on August 27, brought torrential rains and flooding from North Carolina into New England.

Edith struck Honduras with winds up to 170 miles per hour, then regained its spent hurricane strength over the Gulf, turned northward, and crossed the Texas-Louisiana coast in September. Ginger, one of the largest hurricanes (in area) and one of the longest-lived in recent years, struck the North Carolina coast September 30, causing severe wind and water damage. Heidi, working with an extratropical low-pressure system, brought disastrous rains to Pennsylvania, Maryland, New Jersey, and New York in September, and set off a rare tornado near Washington, D.C.

The Pacific tropical cyclone season was active, as usual. Typhoon Wanda in April killed 26 persons in the Philippines and badly damaged some farm lands. Typhoon Harriet stopped the war in coastal Indochina with torrential rains and high winds over the demilitarized zone and surrounding areas. Typhoon Olive killed 78, injured 200, and ravaged the land with floods and high winds on its progress across southern Japan and South Korea. In August, Typhoon Rose killed more than 90 persons, injured more than 200, and displaced about 2,500 in Hong Kong and surrounding areas. (*See in* CE: Weather.)

WESTERN SAMOA. The government of Western Samoa embarked on its second five-year development plan in 1971. Deficit budgeting and a substantially oversubscribed national development loan provided needed capital. New Zealand offered a generous grant to continue educational, administrative, and technical assistance and to help finance important works. The first New Zealand aid mission discussed projects that might be suitably assisted from the Colombo Plan allocation, extended in 1970 to include the South Pacific.

Great Britain offered an interest-free loan for the purchase of British materials and equipment, and the Asian Development Bank provided loans for a pilot beef project and a feasibility study for a hydroelectric plan. Volunteer service from abroad temporarily relieved the shortage of trained manpower. Regional and Commonwealth of Nations ties were strengthened by participation in meetings of the Commonwealth heads of government, the Pacific Islands Producers' Association, the South Pacific Forum, and the South Pacific Commission and Conference. (*See in* CE: Samoa.)

WEST INDIES. Economic and political problems were major concerns in the West Indies during 1971, although the unrest attributed to black power movements in recent years was not as overt as it had been in 1970. Tourism, a major source of income for many Caribbean island nations, was slack because of the general world economic situation and the fears of many tourists that stemmed from the violence of 1970. Those countries affiliated with the Commonwealth of Nations were concerned about the effect Great Britain's expected entry into the European Economic Community would have on their economies, which are still heavily dependent on agricultural exports such as sugar and bananas. Unemployment in most of the West Indian nations was between 20 and 40%, with little hope of improvement foreseen.

Elections held in several countries indicated a growing dissatisfaction with the ruling governments, many of which had been in power for as long as 25 years. In Trinidad and Tobago Prime Minister Eric Williams was elected to his fourth consecutive five-year term, and his party, the People's National Movement (PNM), won all 36 seats in Parliament. However, the opposition had withdrawn from the race and urged the people to boycott the election until a number of election reforms were instituted. The voter turnout for the May election was only about one third of the eligible voters. In Antigua, Prime Minister Vere Bird and his Antiguan Labor Party, in power for over 20 years, were defeated by George Walter, a former labor leader, and the Progressive Labor Movement, which won 13 out of 16 seats at stake in Parliament. William Bramble, chief minister of Montserrat for 18 years, was defeated in the general elections by his son, Austin Bramble, whose new party won all seven elected seats in the Legislative Council.

Robert L. Bradshaw, nicknamed "Papa," won his fifth consecutive five-year term as Prime Minister of St. Kitts-Nevis in May. Anguilla refused to participate in the elections, although the St. Kitts-Nevis government refused to recognize its claims to secession from the three-island federation in 1967. In June Anguilla agreed to accept the status of a British colony, but Bradshaw rejected this solution in spite of the passage of the Anguilla Act by the British Parliament in July.

A special meeting of Commonwealth Caribbean heads of government met in late July in Grenada to discuss the formation of a new East Caribbean state. Representatives of Guyana, Dominica, Gre-

nada, St. Lucia, St. Vincent, St. Kitts-Nevis, and Antigua attended. Forbes Burnham, prime minister of Guyana, persuaded the governments of all countries attending, except Antigua, to accept the Grenada Declaration, which called for the formation of a constituent assembly during 1972, and a new constitution linking the partners under a relatively strong central government by March 1973. In spite of the agreement, many voiced doubts about the adequacy of a union that did not include Trinidad and Tobago, Barbados, or Antigua.

Three officers and six soldiers were convicted in March of participating in the army mutiny of 1970 in Trinidad and Tobago. They were given prison sentences ranging from 2 to 20 years.

In the Virgin Islands of the United States the U.S. Immigration and Naturalization Service began a drive in March to oust aliens who had entered the islands without a permit, or who had remained after their permits had expired. (*See in* CE: West Indies.)

WOMEN. Information gleaned during 1971 from the 1970 United States Census demonstrated the growing extent of the American woman's involvement in the nation's labor market. The figures also went a long way toward explaining why the women's liberation movement, undoubtedly stronger in the U.S. than in any other country,

Marchers for women's liberation proceed down Fifth Avenue in New York City in August. One picket sign calls for the first U.S. woman president.

PETER GOULD

Patricia Bozell (left), sister of conservative columnist William F. Buckley, attacked feminist Ti-Grace Atkinson for saying that the Virgin Mary had been "used" in the birth of Jesus. Mrs. Bozell is a devout Roman Catholic.

sparked numerous judicial, legislative, and executive actions during the year and why women found it necessary to form their own political caucus. U.S. Rep. Shirley Chisholm (D, N.Y.) announced plans to seek the Democratic presidential nomination in 1972.

Women at Work

According to the census figures, 31.2 million U.S. women were working or actively seeking work; they represented 37.5% of the total labor force of 81.7 million and 42.6% of the female population. The fact that married women made up the largest portion of the labor force taking or seeking jobs represented a major shift in the character of the labor force; in 1960 only 30% of all working women were married. In 1970 18.4 million married women, or 40.8%, were working and 10.2 million of these women had children under 17 years of age. In fact, 49.2% of mothers with school-age children and 30.3% with preschool-age children were working. The percentages of working married women were highest among those whose husbands earned between $5,000 and $10,-000 a year, and whatever their husband's earnings or children's ages, the more education women had the more likely they were to be working.

Despite their increasing role in the labor force, women were not achieving an increased share of earnings. A 1960 survey of ten occupations found that men's earnings for the same work exceeded women's by 19%. Subsequent surveys in 1965 and 1970, after the passage of the 1964 Civil Rights Act, which called for equal pay for equal work, showed the percentage had dropped by only one point.

None of the several reports on women's earnings indicated that actual employer discrimination was the cause of the wage differentials. The discrepancies were most often ascribed to "role differentiation," "consumer preference," or other phrases that meant basically that some jobs were traditionally men's jobs and others women's jobs, and that women's jobs received less remuneration. This type of discrimination was documented in a report by the Equal Employment Opportunity Commission, which charged that the hiring and placement policies of the American Telephone and Telegraph Co. made it "the largest oppressor of women workers in the United States."

Women in Court

Whether or not statistics could prove sex discrimination, actual experiences of women seeking their rights in court could. The highest courts of California and New Jersey held that women had the right to work as bartenders. An Ohio statute designed to "protect" women was challenged by the U.S. Department of Justice when it brought action against Libbey-Owens-Ford and the United Glass and Ceramic Workers union, contending that the company and union discriminated against women by agreeing to treat them differently from men with regard to hiring, training, promotion, and pay. The U.S. Supreme Court ruled unanimously that employers cannot deny jobs to women on the sole ground that they have small children, unless this ground also is used to deny employment to men. The court also held that an Idaho law was unconstitutional because it stated that men were to be preferred over women as administrators of the estates of deceased persons.

Women in Politics

The principal new thrust of the women's liberation movement was into politics and centered around the formation in July of the National Women's Political Caucus, with the announced goal of placing women in half of all government offices in the U.S. The caucus' immediate aim was the election of women or candidates who opposed racism and war and espoused such women's demands as liberalized abortion laws, support for child-care centers (which was included in a legislative package vetoed by U.S. President Richard M. Nixon in December), and an amendment to the Constitution prohibiting legal discrimination on the basis of sex, which Congress failed to pass for the 48th consecutive year.

WORLD TRADE. The year 1971 was a critical one in which the world trade and monetary system that had contributed so much to the expansion of trade and economic growth since World War II underwent its most serious trial. The drastic and far-reaching measures that United States President Richard M. Nixon announced on August 15 to deal with the stagnant U.S. economy included a number of restrictive trade measures, the most prominent of which was a 10% surcharge on imports (except those already governed by quota restrictions) as well as a suspension of the U.S. government commitment to sell gold for the dollar to foreign governments. (*See* Money and International Finance.)

As part of a comprehensive program, the principal purpose of the surcharge was to help provide a temporary relief for the U.S. balance of payments while the U.S. sought more fundamental changes in the monetary system. The surcharge primarily affected the major Western European industrial nations, Canada, and Japan, whose economies were strongly dependent on their export trade, chiefly to the large U.S. market. The position taken by these nations was that although the U.S. was admittedly in a serious balance of payments situation, the surcharge, as a trade restricting measure, was clearly inappropriate, since the major U.S. problems were mainly in the area of capital movement and foreign investment rather than in international trade. There was a general feeling that the surcharge, if not removed within a short time, would have far-reaching repercussions on the world economy. It represented a culmination of the increasing trend of protectionist practices and

sentiments that had characterized U.S. trade policy in the last decade. Fears that the restrictionist attitudes would proliferate were partly realized when, in October, Denmark introduced a similar temporary 10% surcharge on most of its imports.

Efforts to resolve the monetary crisis finally achieved success in December. The U.S. agreed to officially devalue the dollar in return for the promise of trade concessions by its major trading partners—the European Economic Community (EEC, or Common Market), Japan, and Canada. A major realignment of world currencies then took place and, following the currency realignment, President Nixon officially eliminated the surcharge on December 20.

European Economic Community

While the monetary and trade crisis was occurring, another event of great significance was taking place—the expansion of the EEC with the British government's successful negotiation and Parliament's acceptance of the conditions for Great Britain's entry into the Common Market. This event represented a fundamental change in the European economic alignment for the future.

For more than ten years, successive British governments had professed a desire to join the EEC. Early in 1970 Britain, for the third time, and in concert with Denmark, Norway, and Ireland, lodged an application for membership, and negotiations on the terms of entry began in mid-1970. At the outset, Britain stressed that while it was prepared to accept membership and the decisions flowing from it, it was important to obtain fair terms that would take account of its particular in-

Ann Kerr (foreground, right), a former member of Parliament, leads a delegation of women opposed to Great Britain's entry into the EEC. They marched on the Foreign and Commonwealth Office in London in January. Many British citizens were hostile to the Common Market.

CENTRAL PRESS FROM
PICTORIAL PARADE

terest and situation and that of the Commonwealth, and the impact upon existing trading arrangements, particularly in the period of transition.

By June 23, 1971, Britain and the EEC were able to reach agreement on the major outstanding questions. One of the key points was the five-year transition period agreed upon for the alignment of Britain's industrial tariffs and its agricultural policies with the EEC. Another was Britain's contribution to the budget, which was to amount to 8.64% of the total in the first year, rising by steps to 18.92% in the fifth year. Special arrangements were made for the Commonwealth. New Zealand was promised guaranteed dairy exports in 1977 equal to not less than 71% of the 1971 level. The EEC undertook to safeguard the interests of Commonwealth sugar producers after contractual agreements expired in 1974. In the Common Market institutions Britain was to have the same representation and voting weight as France, West Germany, and Italy, with English to be used as one of the working languages.

Following the publication by the British government of a White Paper setting out the terms agreed in the negotiations and the political and economic considerations in favor of their acceptance, the debate was opened in the country on the question of entering the EEC on those terms negotiated by the Conservative government. The trade unions and a faction of the Labour party, largely dwelling on the inadequacy of the safeguards offered to New Zealand and the question of sovereignty, strongly opposed entry on those terms, while the Conservatives were generally in favor. When the vote was taken in the House of Commons on the EEC entry issue, Labour members of Parliament, in defiance of the party whip, joined the Conservatives and voted for it, and the motion was carried by a comfortable margin. The way was thus opened for resuming discussions with the EEC on further details and for the necessary legislative action. Actual entry was expected to occur on Jan. 1, 1973.

Parallel to the British negotiations, talks were opened between the EEC and the other applicants for membership as well as with members of the European Free Trade Association which for various reasons did not wish to become members of the EEC but desired to establish some forms of cooperation. There was general agreement that all such arrangements should come into effect at the same time. Progress on negotiations was accelerated after the settlement of the British case, but there still remained major problems to be settled at the end of 1971, and it was not a foregone conclusion that these would be solvable. In Denmark only 39% of those questioned in a poll at the end of the year were in favor of membership, 27% were not in favor, and 34% were undecided. In Norway the special terms demanded by that country's fishing interests remained at sharp odds with the EEC's negotiating position, and thus the majority of Norwegians were opposed to membership in late 1971. (*See also* Denmark; Europe; Great Britain; Ireland; Norway.)

Japan's car export business continued to boom. Some 1,900 cars were loaded onto the *Kanagawa Maru* in Yokohama and sent to Canada and the United States.
KEYSTONE

The General Agreement on Tariffs and Trade

Although the world monetary and trade crisis and Britain's negotiations on entry into the EEC dominated the headlines, routine international trade pursuits continued mostly unaffected. The General Agreement on Tariffs and Trade (GATT) organization plodded on, with its tariff study and its stock-taking of nontariff trade barriers, preparing for further international action toward liberalizing trade—action which might resume once the dust had settled from the stormy crisis of 1971. The GATT made further progress in its attempts to increase contacts with Eastern European Communist countries when Romania, after three years of discussion, was finally admitted as a full contracting party. The significance of this was the particularly liberal terms under which full GATT treatment was accorded to a Communist economy—in exchange for Romania's agreement to increase its imports from GATT countries at a rate not slower than that of total imports laid down in its five-year plans. Similar discussions with Hungary gained impetus soon after the settlement with Romania.

The General System of Preferences in favor of developing countries, which had been formulated in the Organization for Economic Cooperation and Development and agreed upon in the United Nations Conference for Trade and Development, received the approval of GATT, the EEC, and a number of other developed countries. In GATT the "mini Kennedy round," a long-drawn-out series of tariff negotiations among developing countries, was concluded in October. Sixteen of the some 20 participants agreed on tariff concessions which they proposed to grant, on a preferential basis, to each other.

International Policies

New international trade agreements were worked out during the year for a number of major products—including coffee, tin, and sugar. Agreements attempted for wheat and copper, however, were not successful.

The International Coffee Organization met in London during Aug. 16–30, 1971, to fix quotas and price ranges for the 1971-72 coffee year under the International Coffee Agreement (ICA). About 98% of the coffee moving in world trade was shipped by members of this pact. The initial overall export quotas were set at a total of 47 million bags versus the 1970–71 final total of 49.5 million bags. These downward adjustments were triggered by declining market prices early in the 1970–71 season.

The new price floors and ceilings agreed upon represented a victory for Brazilian coffee growers in a dispute with African producers. Thus African robusta coffee, traditionally the lowest-priced type, would be able to undersell Brazilian arabicas in 1971–72 by a much smaller margin than in 1970–71. The large competitive edge in 1970–71 for

OSRIN FROM "CLEVELAND PLAIN DEALER"

robustas caused Brazil to cut prices and to embark on an aggressive selling policy. At the London meeting Brazil indicated that it would leave the ICA rather than accept demands by African producers, backed by France and other EEC nations, to undersell Brazilian coffee by 4¢ to 5¢ per pound. The final price ranges, as well as the figure for total quotas, were a compromise between the producing and consuming members of the ICA.

The Fourth International Tin Agreement (ITA) became effective July 1, 1971, for a five-year period. Major objectives of this pact, which was similar to its predecessors, were to: prevent surpluses or shortages of tin; prevent wide tin price fluctuations; increase export earnings of tin-producing nations; secure fair prices for consumers while allowing a remunerative return to producers; and take steps (such as increasing or decreasing export quotas of its producer members) to alleviate serious supply or shortage problems. Of the world's tin-consuming countries, 22 signed the new ITA, including West Germany and the U.S.S.R. for the first time. However, the U.S., the world's largest user of tin, remained outside the pact.

Strong demand for tightening world sugar supplies in late 1971 drove the world free market price of sugar up to 7½¢ per pound, well above the International Sugar Agreement (ISA) ceiling of 5¼¢ per pound and the highest in more than seven years. Most world trade in sugar was protected by such measures as the U.S. sugar quota law, the British tariff preferential for Commonwealth producers, and other forms of subsidies. The rest of the world sugar trade, accounting for 10% to 15% of world output, moved through the so-called world free market. It was in this market that the ISA attempted to stabilize prices through an export quota system. Attempting to halt the upsurge in world sugar prices, the International Sugar Organization (ISO) on December 21, 1971, suspended all ISA quotas, effective Jan. 1, 1972.

The Growth of World Trade

The value of world trade increased by 11% to 12% in 1971 over the 1970 level, but, because of the general increase in world prices, this represented an increase in the volume of trade of only 7%—somewhat less than in recent years. The growth in world trade, as measured by the total value of individual countries' exports, was dependent to a large extent on the rate of growth of world industrial production and demand for imports. Although world industrial production grew quite rapidly during 1969, there was virtually no growth in 1970 after the first quarter. Expansion was renewed early in 1971.

The growth in world trade in 1970 and in 1971 was not shared evenly between the industrial countries and the primary producers—those developing countries whose exports were mainly unrefined agricultural commodities and mineral products. In the boom in trade in 1969, primary producers' exports increased by 12%—almost as fast as those of industrial countries. In 1970, however, the growth rate of their exports fell to 9.5% compared with 15.5% for industrial countries. Primary producers' exports benefited from the revival of world industrial production and import demand in 1971, and their exports were then growing but still not as rapidly as those of industrial countries. (*See also* Economy; Textiles. *See in* CE: International Trade.)

YEMEN ARAB REPUBLIC (Sana). The
ending of the civil war in 1970 led to a general improvement in Yemen's diplomatic position in 1971. A British nonresident ambassador to Sana, the capital, was appointed in January and an Iranian nonresident ambassador in February. In January it was announced that the recent rains had alleviated the worst effects of the three-year drought, but the economic situation remained critical. On February 26 Premier Muhsin al-Aini resigned to enable a caretaker government to supervise elections to the Consultative Council. Of the council's members no more than 20% were appointed by the president and the remainder elected by popular vote in March.

On April 21 the five-man Presidential Council resigned, and it was agreed that in the future it should have only three members. Former Premier Ahmed Mohammed Noman was asked to form a government on May 3, but he resigned on July 20, saying he was unable to shoulder the burdens of Yemen's financial problems. There were signs of tension between the civilian and the military authorities, with the latter accusing the former of poor administration and corruption.

On August 24 Maj. Gen. Hassan al-Amri, commander in chief of the armed forces, formed a new government. However, he was forced to resign on August 29 and was exiled from Yemen after he had shot a Yemeni photographer. The incident arose from a case of mistaken identity caused by a faulty telephone connection in which the victim, not realizing he was speaking to the premier, had exchanged insults with him. The premier then had the photographer brought to him, had him beaten, and then killed him. Al-Aini, who had been appointed ambassador to Paris, returned to form a government on September 18. Adeni nationalist Abdullah Asnag was appointed finance minister. (*See also* Middle East. *See in* CE: Yemen.)

YEMEN, PEOPLE'S DEMOCRATIC REPUBLIC OF (Aden). During 1971 a number of
changes were made in the government of Southern Yemen, in accordance with provisions of the new constitution proclaimed on Nov. 30, 1970. Under the constitution the nation's name was changed to the People's Democratic Republic of Yemen. A 101-member Provisional Supreme People's Council (PSPC) was formed in April, comprised of representatives of the ruling National Liberation Front (NLF), workers, peasants, soldiers, and women. Intended to allow wider participation of the people in the government, the PSPC was to act as the nation's legislative body and to draft laws for the election of a permanent council. Legislative powers were officially transferred from the NLF to the PSPC in May.

The PSPC appointed a new Presidential Council in August, with former president Salem Ali Rubaya as chairman. In a subsequent policy statement the government promised to promote a progressive Arab front and "brotherly" relations with liberal Arab and socialist states, to further economic development, and to grant equal rights to women.

Periodically throughout the year government troops clashed with members of a self-styled national deliverance army, who the government claimed were mercenaries backed by Saudi Arabian, United States, and other western interests. Attacks on the government were regularly broadcast by the clandestine 'Voice of the Free South', which accused the government of subservience to the Soviet Union and the People's Republic of China. (*See in* CE: Aden; Yemen.)

YOUTH ORGANIZATIONS. In 1971 youth
organizations in the United States stepped up their campaigns to increase membership. There were strong efforts to take a more active part in the fight against pollution and other environmental ills.

Boys' Clubs of America

Change as an instrument of progress, rather than as a goal in itself, was a prime consideration for the Boys' Clubs of America during 1971. At meetings, conferences, seminars, and workshops throughout the country, and at the 65th annual national convention at Atlanta, Ga., in mid-May,

The national theme for 4-H clubs in 1971 was "4-H Bridges the Gap," expressed in a colorful motif designed to appeal to young people.

reevaluation and possible revision of Boys' Club philosophies were thoroughly discussed.

During National Boys' Club Week (March 28–April 3), a record number of Boys' Clubs and several million citizens joined in saluting the 111th birthday of the national youth guidance organization. U.S. President Richard M. Nixon, in a ceremony that has become traditional, installed Pelton H. Stewart, 18, of the Columbia Park Boys' Club, of San Francisco, Calif., as the 26th annual "Boy of the Year." Stewart, who received a $4,000 Reader's Digest Foundation Scholarship, enrolled at Howard University in Washington, D.C.

Boy Scouts of America

In 1971 the Boy Scouts of America entered the third year of its eight-year Boypower '76 plan, designed to bring into the organization one third of the boys in the U.S. Norton Clapp, chairman of Weyerhaeuser Co., Seattle, Wash., was elected president at the 61st annual meeting held in Atlanta, Ga.

New means of bringing Scouting to boys in ghettos and other hard to reach areas were used. Storefront Boy Scout "centers" and motor vans provided meeting places for Scout units lacking facilities. More than 16,400 non-Scouts enjoyed a week or more of camping as guests of host troops, and 62% of these boys later became Scouts.

Through the project Save Our American Resources (SOAR) the Boy Scouts set off a nationwide campaign of action to improve environmental quality, intensifying conservation efforts that have always been a part of Scouting. Every pack, troop, and post was asked to participate in a year-round conservation effort and to devote as much time as possible to the problems of soil conservation, air and water pollution, and elimination of litter. The high point of the project was Keep America Beautiful Day, when more than 2 million Scouts and leaders, joined by representatives from other groups, picked up a million tons of rubbish from 200,000 miles of roadsides and 400,000 acres of land. (*See in* CE: Boy Scouts of America.)

Camp Fire Girls

Changing morals and family relationships, drugs, race prejudice, school problems, and dissent were among the principal topics discussed by Camp Fire Girls at the AWARE '71 conferences held in Washington, D.C., Denton, Tex., and Davis, Calif., during June and July. For the 1,100 girls and boys who participated, the conference was an active, open-ended experience in decision-making on current issues.

The Camp Fire Quadrennial for volunteers and staff, held in Seattle, Wash., October 30–November 2, was not designed as a passive, listening conference, but as a laboratory where participants could find better means of improving Camp Fire's impact on communities throughout the nation. (*See in* CE: Camp Fire Girls.)

4-H Clubs

For the nation's 4 million Head-Heart-Hands-Health (4-H) youth, 1971 was a year of progress and achievement. At the annual National 4-H Conference, held in Washington, D.C., in April, more than 230 delegates were guests at the White House. President Nixon spoke briefly to the group, and Mrs. Nixon was named a new "partner-in-4-H," receiving an engraved plaque bearing her citation. The conference delegates consisted of four or five 4-Hers from each of the 50 states, the District of Columbia, Puerto Rico, the Virgin Islands, and Guam. They spent most of their week in daily discussion seminars, considering five current concerns of both youth and adults: environment, education, respect for others, mind and body, and changing life-styles.

A second major 4-H event was the Golden Anniversary National 4-H Congress, held in Chicago late in the year. The congress was attended by about 1,600 award-winning teens from across the nation. The week-long occasion also marked the 50th anniversary of the National 4-H Service Committee, a nonprofit and nongovernmental volunteer group of citizens who sponsor the congress and perform many other functions to support 4-H.

National 4-H Week was observed October 3–9, with the year-round theme, "4-H Bridges the Gap." Emphasis was placed on improving communications between youth and adults, and between people of different creeds, cultures, religions, political viewpoints, and educational levels. (*See in* CE: 4-H Clubs.)

Future Farmers of America

In 1971 the Future Farmers of America (FFA) helped 47 foreign agricultural students find farms in the U.S. where they could learn about American farming methods through actual experience. The FFA arranged also for 22 of its members to spend the summer months living and working on European and Latin American farms.

The 44th National FFA Convention, held in Kansas City, Mo., attracted more than 13,387 members and guests. Many national awards were presented during the convention. The highest awards, Star Farmer and Star Agribusinessman of America, went to Lonney Eastvold, 22, of Hartland, Minn., and Wayne Robert Morris, 19, of Fullerton, Calif., respectively. Each received a check for $1,000 in recognition of their accomplishments. Bill Cofield, 18, of Woodland, Ala., earned the National FFA Public Speaking Award, speaking on the topic "A Miracle in Our Time." (*See in* CE: Future Farmers of America.)

Future Homemakers of America

Many innovative changes were put into effect in 1971 to bring the organization of Future Homemakers of America (FHA) into line with changes in the home economics education program and society in general. Early in the year the national headquarters was moved to new offices in the American Home Economics Association building in Washington, D.C., in order to accommodate additional staff and program services.

The annual national meeting was held in Kansas City, Mo., in July, with an attendance of 1,500. Delegates discussed such subjects as ecology, drug abuse, racial prejudice, and other current problems. Marsha Bowen, a high school senior from Spanish Fork, Utah, was elected national president for 1971–72.

Girls Clubs of America

Reflecting a growing public interest in improving opportunities for girls and women, Girls Clubs of America in 1971 started the second phase of a $5-million expansion goal. Total membership of girls from 6 to 18 years of age reached 115,000, an increase of 15%. Twenty-three new Girls Clubs were organized, bringing the total number of club centers open after school and on weekends to 195.

At the 26th annual Girls Club conference, held in Memphis, Tenn., April 11–14, more than 60 girls represented their Girls Clubs along with approximately 250 adult delegates. Ten new members were elected to the national board of directors, and 14 outstanding members were awarded over $6,000 in college scholarships.

Girl Scouts of the United States of America

During 1971 the Girl Scouts continued working on their two major objectives for the decade of the 1970's: Eco-Action, a nationwide ecological endeavor, and Action '70, a program designed to increase awareness of prejudice and to take action to build better relationships among persons of all ages, religions, races, and nationalities.

Across the country, local Girl Scout groups pursued the national goals of Action '70 in their own ways—by sharing projects with people of different ethnic and economic backgrounds, with children in the inner cities or in rural disadvantaged areas, with physically or mentally handicapped persons, with the elderly, and with children of migrant workers.

New and better ways for extending and maintaining Girl Scouting in low-income urban and rural areas were begun in 1971 when 21 Girl Scout councils received matching-fund grants from the Julie Eisenhower Fund for this purpose. The $81,000 gift from President Nixon's daughter represented her share of profits from a crewel embroidery kit that she designed and that was offered to the public through *Family Circle* magazine. (*See in* CE: Girl Scouts.)

Junior Achievement

In 1971, Junior Achievement (JA) continued its work as a practical business education program for high school students of all socioeconomic backgrounds. Fostering a laboratory, learn-by-doing approach, the program entered its 51st year of operation with 156,000 members ("Achievers") who created and operated 6,900 miniature business enterprises with the direct aid of 23,000 businessmen and women in over 1,000 U.S. communities.

Two thousand Achievers from all 50 states, Puerto Rico, and two foreign countries attended the 27th JA conference at Indiana University, in Bloomington, in August. Guided by 200 volunteer graduate Achievers, the conference worked to develop understanding between business and youth.

Young Men's Christian Association

In 1971 a study of the Young Men's Christian Association (YMCA) revealed that 17 people out

JOHN SHEARER, LIFE MAGAZINE © TIME INC.

The Boy Scouts made a determined effort to attract urban youths of the 1970's, like Hector Melendez of New York City.

of every 1,000 in the U.S. were registered members of the YMCA at year's end 1970, compared to 1.4 per 1,000 in 1870. During the year there were 5.5 million members registered for various programs and activities.

Traditional YMCA programs, including water safety, camping, and a vast youth program, continued in 1971, along with expanded work in drug abuse and ghetto problems.

Robert W. Harlan, appointed national executive director in 1971, pointed out that "youth want to be meaningfully involved in institutional life. They want to be part of YMCA program-planning and decision-making activities." A new metro centers program, launched in three cities, was designed as a direct response to this desire. Metro centers were being organized, staffed, and run by young people. (*See in* CE: Young Men's Christian Association.)

Young Women's Christian Association

During 1971 the national board of the Young Women's Christian Association (YWCA) of the United States underwent a major reorganization. This entailed both a reordering of priorities in order to work toward the YWCA's one imperative —the elimination of racism wherever it exists and by any means necessary—and a restaffing pattern.

The new structure, effective September 1, while calling for a reduction in staff, allowed for increased specialized services to community and student associations and emphasized the use of staff teams cutting across the responsibilities of nine units of work: world relations, program concerns and public policy, youth constituencies, membership-leadership, organization development, financial development, communications, and the data center and the convention and conference office. In addition, there was continuing participation in the United Service Organizations (USO). (*See in* CE: Young Women's Christian Association.)

YUGOSLAVIA. The adoption by the Federal Assembly of 20 major and several minor constitutional amendments, as part of a fundamental reform of Yugoslavia's entire federal structure, was the main event of 1971. Relations with the Soviet Union improved toward the end of the year despite Yugoslavia's rapprochement with the People's Republic of China. Links with Western countries continued to develop.

Domestic Affairs

Disagreements between Serbian and Croatian leaders in February and March about the powers of the big banks and trading corporations in Belgrade, the capital, and the status of Kosovo, the autonomous province within Serbia, culminated in accusations of bad faith and intrigue. On April 6 the Croatian Communist Party's Central Committee accused federal agencies of spreading false rumors about Croat leaders' alleged links with pro-Soviet Croat émigré groups in West Germany. The assassination in Stockholm of the Yugoslav ambassador to Sweden by two Croat extremists on April 7 (he died on April 15) heightened the tension. Liberal Communists feared that the assassination would be used as a pretext by conservative forces to sabotage federal reform. The situation calmed down after a meeting April 28–30 of top party leaders from all the republics at President Tito's island residence of Brioni. A communiqué issued at the meeting called for increased unity and an end to regional rivalries.

The draft constitutional amendments were unanimously approved by Yugoslavia's second congress of self-management in Sarajevo on May 8. All five chambers of the Federal Assembly in Belgrade on June 30 adopted the amendments to the 1963 constitution. Under these amendments, the federal government retained responsibility for defense, foreign affairs, and internal economic policy, including development. All other powers, including the power to initiate investment projects, were transferred to the republics and municipalities. Heading the Yugoslav state was a collective presidency of 22 members, three from each republic and two each from Voyvodina and Kosovo, Yugoslavia's autonomous provinces. Within this presidency, which was responsible for the formulation and supervision of broad domestic and foreign policies, each republic had a right to veto decisions against its national interest. On July 29 the Federal Assembly endorsed all the selected members of the collective presidency. The assembly elected the 79-year-old Tito president of the republic for a further five years and first chairman of the new presidency. It also elected a new federal government under Džemal Bijedić.

Economic Affairs

The new government was obliged to give its immediate attention to the rapidly deteriorating economic situation. Following Yugoslavia's 20% devaluation of the dinar on January 23, exports rose by only 6.3% during the first nine months of the year, while imports were 21% higher than in the corresponding period of 1970. In November inflation was running at the rate of 17% annually and demand was 6% higher than available supplies. The credit squeeze introduced by the out-going government of Mitja Ribičič was followed by a total price freeze on November 26. The slow pace of the reform of the foreign trade system provoked bitterness in Croatia, which earned 40% of Yugoslavia's total foreign exchange income but was allowed to retain only a small portion of it. On December 1 Tito attacked Croat party leaders for allowing a strike of Zagreb University students and called for a purge of "antisocialist" and "nationalist" elements. Seven leading members of the Croa-

tian Communist party then resigned. Disagreements among party leaders about fundamental economic and political issues forced Tito to postpone the party's annual conference.

With an excellent grain harvest, record tourist earnings, and substantial hard-currency remittances from Yugoslav workers in Western Europe, the balance of payments deficit diminished at the year's end. But the prospect of an economic recession in West Germany, forcing some of those workers to return home to join the 300,000 unemployed, remained a worry.

Foreign Affairs

President Tito's visit to Italy in March marked the end of the brief quarrel over the status of some of the territory awarded to Yugoslavia after World War II. His visit to Pope Paul VI at the Vatican on March 29 demonstrated the satisfactory state of relations between Yugoslavia and the Roman Catholic church. Relations with the Soviet Union, Bulgaria, and Hungary worsened in the summer. In June and July the Yugoslav press criticized the Soviets for supporting anti-Tito Yugoslav refugees in the Soviet Union and Western Europe. The visit to Peking, China, of Yugoslavia's foreign minister, Mirko Tepavac, in June provoked criticism from the Warsaw Pact press. News of maneuvers by Warsaw Pact armies in southern Hungary in the summer and signs of increasing Soviet pressure against Romania led to close consultations between

Belgrade fashion designer Aleksandr Joksimović introduced his "Vela Nigrinova" collection in a February showing. Members of the diplomatic corps were invited. Fashion shows are generally more common to the U.S. and Western Europe than to Communist nations.

EASTFOTO

Yugoslavia's President Tito (left) exchanges views on international relations with Egypt's President Anwar el-Sadat in Cairo. Tito visited Egypt in February.
EASTFOTO

Romania and Yugoslavia in August. Tito also had talks with President Nicolae Ceausescu of Romania in November. Yugoslavia emphasized its readiness to defend itself by announcing that it would hold massive defense exercises in October. On September 22 Leonid I. Brezhnev, the Soviet Communist party general secretary, began a three-day visit to Yugoslavia, which resulted in an agreement to establish closer interparty links. Brezhnev reaffirmed, with some significant qualifications, Yugoslavia's right to its "independent road to socialism"

expressed in the Belgrade declaration of May 1955, which had been signed by Nikita S. Khrushchev.

In October and November Tito visited India, Iran, Egypt, Canada, Great Britain, and the United States, where his nonaligned foreign policy met with the full support of U.S. President Richard M. Nixon. To help Yugoslavia's foreign trade position, the U.S. government undertook to help double Yugoslavia's exports to the U.S. The U.S. government also supported private U.S. capital investment in Yugoslavia. (*See in* CE: Yugoslavia.)

The Zastava-101, a new Yugoslav automobile, was unveiled in April in Belgrade.
EASTFOTO

Yugoslavia

Special Report:
A Political Experiment

by Alfred Friendly, Jr.

Yugoslavia's political course has been like a soap opera with a never-ending series of teasers. The questions are intriguing, but the program, after a run of 26 years, is still decades away from producing definitive answers. Can a Communist country work with a market economy? Can a loyalty to the Yugoslav federation supersede ethnic allegiances that are reinforced by historic, religious, linguistic, and economic differences? Can a strategic Balkan country stay nonaligned and resist Soviet pressure alone?

The Yugoslav answer, built on faith and a record of surprising achievement, has been that 21 million South Slavs can bicker, experiment, and still survive. Their society neither fully capitalist nor exclusively Communist, the Yugoslavs have found their own way. In a quarter century of development they have reconstructed a war-ravaged country while discarding doctrines, alliances, and even

leading Communist politicians in a search for a system that would match their unique problems.

The first ruling Communist party to break with the Soviets, President Tito's followers have also broken with everything orthodox Communist theory holds dear. They let banks and bankers operate under a minimum of central control, financing businesses whose directors are responsible, not to bureaucrats, but to their own employees. Their trade with the West outstrips their commerce with the Soviet bloc; their borders are open; their progress is reasonably free.

Holding pragmatism as their only dogma, they embarked in 1971 on perhaps the most remarkable experiment yet: a sweeping administrative decentralization that was designed to do in political terms what economic reforms in 1965 promised but had not delivered. Deciding that the concentration of federal power was too tempting a target for quarrelsome politicians, they dissolved that power and created a new constitutional order that attempted to accommodate the demands of those who wanted more regional autonomy with the demands of those who wanted power to remain centralized. It remains to be seen how this new constitutional arrangement will work.

A New Constitutional Order

Characteristically, it was President Tito who opened the new phase with a speech in September 1970, announcing his desire to be succeeded as president of the federation by a collegial body uniting the most authoritative politicians in the country in a group that would transcend petty regional loyalties. "It has often been said abroad that Yugoslavia will break apart when I disappear," he said. "I have thought that the [succession problem] could lead to a grave crisis. So that our socialist community should not experience such danger, which many would like to see befall it, we must perform this reorganization."

The change was easier ordered than accomplished. Making the switch from one-man rule to a 23-man presidency chaired by Marshal Tito also involved institutionalizing new relationships between an already weakened central government and the country's six republics and two autonomous provinces. Bosnia-Herzegovina, Croatia, Macedonia, Montenegro, Serbia, Slovenia, and the Serbian autonomous provinces of Kosovo and the Voyvodina had been moving toward political autonomy ever since the 1965 economic changes began to dissipate federal control over Yugoslavia's finances.

The negotiations to create this new constitutional order were supposed to be completed by May 1971, but were delayed and finally brought to an acrimonious halt by the oldest disagreement in Yugoslavia —the rivalry between the country's two largest ethnic groups, the Serbs and the Croats. That rivalry was the result of centuries of torturous separate existences for two groups of Slavs who look and speak alike but who have, over the centuries, magnified their cultural, historical, and economic differences to the point where they behave toward each other with almost the same enmity as the Roman Catholics and Protestants of Northern Ireland.

For 500 years the Serbs, rallying around their Orthodox church, lived as a rebellious but captive people under the Turks. During roughly the same period, the Roman Catholic Croats were dominated by Hungary and then by the Hapsburgs, suffering under feudal rule and later profiting from the advent of the Industrial Revolution that had only dim echoes in Serbia. When the end of World War I permitted the creation of a unified nation on Yugoslav soil, the Serbs, who were poor, unlettered farmers for the most part, became linked with the richer, more tranquil areas in the north. From the beginning the Serbs dominated the new entity, but the marriage was an unequal and stormy one. Following the establishment of a Communist government after World War II, Serb-Croat distrust was theoretically appeased by the Communist policy of "brotherhood and unity," but in fact Serb-Croat enmity was only submerged, not suppressed.

Regionalism vs. Centralism

The distrust began to blossom again after January 1970, when the Croatian League of Communists made itself the most ardent advocate of republican autonomy and the strongest critic of the dominant role of Serbia in Yugoslavia's affairs, which had been maintained even under Titoism. The call to battle was the decision that Milos Zanko would no longer represent Croatia at the Communist party's standing federal conference. Zanko was a leading spokesman for central rule, who had President Tito's blessings in urging continued federal control of Yugoslav economic development. Initially, his removal was hailed as a victory for the country's liberals—the men who believed in releasing local energies in a quasi-laissez-faire economy—in their struggle with the stuffy, orthodox (and Serbian) bureaucrats who wanted to go on running the whole show, even badly.

Praise or success or self-confidence, however, shortly went to Croatian heads. For once they, and not the Serbs, were riding a winning political horse, pushing Yugoslavia toward a modern economy, a participatory democracy, and above all, an equitable division of power and wealth among the country's various nationalities.

What looked equitable to Croats, however, looked like neo-separatism to the Serbs. What Croats first called "romantic nationalism"—public singing of the Croatian anthem, teen-agers' shoulder patches bearing the republic's emblem, noisy invocations of long-dead Croatian heroes—looked to Serbs like provocative excesses. Several incidents exacerbated the situation to the point where each group accused the other of linking its campaign to Yugoslavia's enemies abroad.

This infighting was what brought negotiations on the new constitutional order to a halt and essentially paralyzed the government. Without effective central rule, economic order crumbled. The inflation rate soared to 14% a year, and the trade deficit increased to nearly $1 billion.

The Solution?

To save his political experiment and his country from disorder, President Tito, always a reluctant autocrat, weighed in with his full prestige and, by threatening a purge, restored a semblance of order to the fractured party and civil administration. Behind closed doors and in public, he hammered home one theme: that Serbs and Croats were lost unless they worked together.

His message appeared to have gotten through in May 1971, when hard bargaining began in earnest to resolve the outstanding questions on the economic side of decentralization, the root of much of the friction. In short order, negotiators came up with workable compromises that slashed the huge federal role in past investments, much of which previously had gone to Serbian projects—without regard for their economic viability—and handed future obligations and revenues to the republics.

Among other changes, the banking system was reorganized to give a fairer share to the Croats, who generated 27% of the gross national product but controlled only 17% of the country's banking assets. Formal acceptance of the new changes was achieved in June 1971.

The way in which the partial denouement was accomplished, however, begged a fundamental question. President Tito had imposed the solution, but without the 79-year-old leader would lesser men find their own way to agreement? With power so decentralized that the federation retained supervision only over foreign and defense affairs, regulation of the common, internal market, and aid to the underdeveloped regions, would the republics not tend to drift away from each other?

Yugoslavs and many foreigners who had watched the developments were optimistic about the country's chances of surviving when the Tito era ended. With the republics forced to operate on their own revenues, development might slow down, but they should also become more cautious and responsible. With government brought one level closer to the people, the chances of "self-management socialism" —the Yugoslav formula for giving every citizen a say in his economic and political fate—should improve. And meanwhile, the League of Communists, supposedly standing above regional interest, would supply the unifying force to counterbalance the clash of local concerns.

The evidence submitted by the pessimists, however, remained. The League had already split into at least six rival elements. Self-management was a nice theory, but the facts were that technocrats were increasingly dominating the economy, dictating to their workers' councils, not consulting them. Serbs were unreconciled to their loss of dominance, and old-school functionaries were flirting with the

Soviet Union, which would like nothing better than an excuse to reimpose its brand of order on a Yugoslav experiment that had gotten out of hand. Soviet Communist Party General Secretary Leonid I. Brezhnev went to Yugoslavia in September 1971, not to put his blessing on the innovators, but to remind long-time admirers of Stalin that they retained a powerful friend in case of need. The Yugoslavs' convincing military posture made direct Soviet intervention highly unlikely, but soldierly resolve might not be enough to preclude internal dissension.

The Future

To assure stability, it is obviously necessary to build a new political consensus. On this score, the League of Communists has been more talkative than effective. The talk has concerned the need to equalize opportunities for workers throughout the country, but the huge regional disparities remain. No amount of local self-help could quickly reverse this trend in the undeveloped south where average per capita income is about $200, one fifth that of the industrial north. And under the decentralization measures, the rich regions are tacitly encouraged to think of themselves first. Here are the seeds of future conflict and here, the pressure for a system that might produce a more equitable (and inevitably more centralized) allocation of national resources. As such pressure mounts, perhaps the euphoria of regional autonomy will again subside.

Yugoslavs have shown before that they hold no doctrine permanently sacred. They prefer theories that work to models that do not. Thus the soap opera goes on and the questions remain. And the only promise is that the answers produced, when they are produced, will be Yugoslav answers, no one else's.

Women plant the fields of the Beograd agricultural-industrial combine near Belgrade.
EASTFOTO

ZAMBIA. President Kenneth Kaunda and his United National Independence party (UNIP) faced a number of serious economic and political problems during 1971. While all major areas of the economy in Zambia had been successfully nationalized in the preceding two years, its dependence on copper as an export increased in spite of a drastic decline in copper prices. Economic sanctions operating against Rhodesia, Zambia's neighbor to the south, also hampered the Zambian economy as traditional oil supply routes through Rhodesia were cut off and copper for export had to be shipped north through Tanzania. Food shortages became severe as corn production declined and imports were held up in Mozambique by the Portuguese, who accused the Zambian government of taking part in the kidnapping of several Portuguese workers from Mozambique. As the shortage continued, larger quantities of food had to be imported.

In January President Kaunda set up a commission of inquiry to investigate charges of tribal bias in the government. This was followed in May by an all-out attack on tribalism during the UNIP conference. President Kaunda stated that he would abolish the system whereby members of the party's central committee were virtually assured of cabinet posts. He then induced the conference to approve a new constitution for the party that would ensure the election of its central committee on a national rather than a tribal basis. Arising out of these changes and following the publication of the findings of the tribalism inquiry, at the beginning of June the president dismissed three ministers. In August Simon Kapwepwe, formerly vice-president of Zambia, resigned as minister of local government and culture and announced the formation of the United Progressive party (UPP). The new party, which drew support primarily from members of the Bemba tribe, the largest in Zambia, attempted to form a coalition with the traditional opposition party, the African National Congress (ANC), in order to press for an immediate general election. However, fundamental differences in viewpoints between the socialist UPP and the conservative ANC prevented the coalition from materializing. In September the government detained 75 key members of the UPP, although Kapwepwe himself was not arrested. The national council of the UNIP in October urged the introduction of a one-party system of government.

President Kaunda, who had long been a harsh critic of the white-controlled nations of southern Africa, was forced to modify his policies somewhat when the severe food shortages made it necessary to import corn from Rhodesia. Zambian business interests urged him to go further in lifting trade restrictions and resuming some of Zambia's traditional economic ties to the south. In April South African Prime Minister John Vorster announced that Kaunda had previously asked him for aid in preventing military aggression by Rhodesia and Portugal. The government denied the accusation

UPI COMPIX

More than 750 Zambian students demonstrated at the French embassy in Lusaka in July. They were protesting France's decision to permit the building of Mirage jets in South Africa. The French flag was torn down from the building and later destroyed.

and published correspondence between Kaunda and Vorster that appeared to clear Kaunda of the charge. In July, however, the president was criticized by university students protesting the French sale of arms to South Africa. After the government banned demonstrations against the French Embassy, students took over Zambia University in Lusaka, the capital. Government troops then forced the university to close temporarily. (*See also* Africa. *See in* CE: Zambia.)

ZOOS. In 1971 zoos continued the trend toward more spacious open air enclosures, and the traditional "cage" zoo was becoming out of date. Safari parks, where visitors can drive their cars among herds of animals, were opened in many parts of the world. The three new parks opened in Great Britain were at Knowsley Hall near Liverpool, Woburn Park in Bedfordshire, and Blair Drummond in Scotland.

Zoological buildings became more sophisticated, and air conditioning, scarcely used a few years ago, was used widely in many leading zoos. In Munich, West Germany, a fully air-conditioned building to house the cats was opened and a new idea adopted at Frankfurt was a glass fence outside the enclosure for great apes. In San Diego, Calif., a unique cable-suspension exhibit for birds of prey was constructed using vinyl-covered mesh.

The Hogle Zoo in Salt Lake City, Utah, opened a museum of human stupidity that displays items thrown into the enclosures by visitors. This idea has been adopted by several European zoos in an effort to shock visitors into better behavior.

The breeding of animals in captivity is of great value to the continued survival of many species, and animals thought of as impossible to breed a few years ago are now bred regularly in leading zoological gardens. Perhaps the most interesting zoo birth was a white rhinoceros at Hanover, West Germany—probably the first specimen ever to be conceived and born outside Africa. The first pacarana (a South American rodent) in Europe was born in Zurich, Switzerland, during the year.

Birds of prey are notoriously difficult to breed in captivity, but in Topeka, Kan., an American golden eagle was bred for the first time. An unusual birth at Chester, England, was a white red lechwe calf, which grew well and mixed with the rest of the herd. In Bristol, England, the first gorilla birth in Great Britain was recorded. The breeding of an elephant in captivity is considered a rarity, but in Portland, Ore., ten of them have been bred in the past nine years.

Apart from breeding rare animals in captivity, zoos aided conservation by providing collection boxes to be used for contributions to the World Wildlife Fund. The city of Frankfurt in West Germany made gifts of equipment to East African wildlife organizations. The Lincoln Park Zoo in Chicago received a pale titi monkey that is believed to be the first ever shown in captivity, and in Rome the only pair of pardel lynx in captivity was received.

The financially troubled zoo in St. Louis, Mo., was guaranteed further existence when, in April, suburban residents of that city decided to help save it by voluntarily taxing themselves. Admission to the zoo has been free.

Incidents of zoo animals being mistreated were prominent in 1971. In August, three teen-age youths were charged with having killed and tortured animals at the children's zoo in Harrison, N.Y. In the following month the Children's Barnyard in New Brunswick, N.J., was closed after a rash of brutal acts took place whereby animals were either killed, mutilated, or stolen.

At New York City's Central Park Zoo, a policeman killed a polar bear after the animal had seized the hand of a man who had thrust it through the bars of the cage. At first, attempts were made to free the man by poking the bear with a stick and by trying to scare it by firing two shots in the air. However, these attempts proved futile, and the bear was then shot in the chest. (*See also* Animals and Wildlife. *See in* CE: Zoo.)

Weighing 100 pounds at birth, Mazinda, a male white rhino born at the Whipsnade Zoo, is the first white rhino born in Great Britain, and only the second known to have been born outside Africa.

CALENDAR FOR 1972

JANUARY

1 Saturday. New Year's Day. Major football bowl games. Yellowstone National Park Centennial Year begins.
2 Sunday. Save the Pun Week begins.
5 Wednesday. Twelfth Night.
6 Thursday. Twelfth Day, or Epiphany.
7 Friday. Millard Fillmore's birthday.
9 Sunday. Richard M. Nixon's birthday.
13 Thursday. Stephen Foster Memorial Day.
15 Saturday. Birthday of Martin Luther King, Jr.
16 Sunday. Super Bowl football game. Jaycee Week begins.
17 Monday. Benjamin Franklin's birthday.
19 Wednesday. Robert E. Lee's birthday.
27 Thursday. Wolfgang Amadeus Mozart's birthday.
30 Sunday. Franklin D. Roosevelt's birthday. International Clergy Week begins.

FEBRUARY

1 Tuesday. National Freedom Day. American Heart Month, American History Month, and Boy Scouts of America Anniversary Celebration begin.
2 Wednesday. Candlemas. Groundhog Day.
3 Thursday. Winter Olympic Games begin.
6 Sunday. National Children's Dental Health Week and National Crime Prevention Week begin.
7 Monday. National Pay Your Bills Week begins.
12 Saturday. Abraham Lincoln's birthday.
13 Sunday. National Negro History Week begins.
14 Monday. Saint Valentine's Day.
15 Tuesday. Susan B. Anthony Day. Chinese New Year begins. International Pancake Race. Shrove Tuesday. Mardi Gras.
16 Wednesday. Ash Wednesday. Lent begins.
22 Tuesday. George Washington's birthday.
29 Tuesday. Purim. Leap Year Day.

MARCH

1 Wednesday. National Weights and Measures Week, Red Cross Month, Return the Borrowed Book Week, and Save Your Vision Week begin.
5 Sunday. American Camping Week begins.
6 Monday. National Housing for Handicapped Week begins.
9 Thursday. Amerigo Vespucci's birthday.
12 Sunday. Girl Scout Week begins.
15 Wednesday. Andrew Jackson's birthday. Ides of March.
17 Friday. Saint Patrick's Day.
19 Sunday. Camp Fire Girls Birthday Week, National Poison Prevention Week, and National Wildlife Week begin. Swallows return to San Juan Capistrano.
26 Sunday. Palm Sunday.
30 Thursday. Passover.

APRIL

1 Saturday. April Fools' Day. Anti-Noise Month, Cancer Control Month, National Laugh Week, and New Homes Month begin.
2 Sunday. Easter Sunday.
4 Tuesday. National Cherry Blossom Festival begins.
6 Thursday. National Artichoke Week begins.
9 Sunday. Sir Winston Churchill Day. National Hostility Week and Pan American Week begin.
13 Thursday. Thomas Jefferson's birthday.
16 Sunday. National Coin Week and National Library Week begin.
18 Tuesday. Earth Week begins.
23 Sunday. National YWCA Week and Secretaries Week begin.
27 Thursday. Ulysses Simpson Grant's birthday.
28 Friday. National Arbor Day.
30 Sunday. Daylight saving time begins.

MAY

1 Monday. Law Day. Loyalty Day. May Day. Mental Health Week, National Tavern Month, and Senior Citizens Month begin.
2 Tuesday. Clean Waters for America Week begins.
6 Saturday. Birthday of the first postage stamp.
7 Sunday. Humane Sunday. Mother-in-Law Day. National Be Kind to Animals Week begins.
8 Monday. Harry S. Truman's birthday. National Salvation Army Week begins.
13 Saturday. Let's Go Fishing Week begins.
14 Sunday. Mother's Day. National Transportation Week and Police Week begin.
16 Tuesday. Small Business Week begins.
19 Friday. Shavuot, or Feast of Weeks.
20 Saturday. Armed Forces Day.
21 Sunday. Whit Sunday, or Pentecost.
22 Monday. National Maritime Day.
27 Saturday. Indianapolis 500-mile race.
29 Monday. John F. Kennedy's birthday. Memorial Day celebrated.

JUNE

1 Thursday. Fight the Filthy Fly Month, Model Rocketry Month, National Ragweed Control Month, and National Rose Month begin.
3 Saturday. Jefferson Davis' birthday.
4 Sunday. National Humor Week begins.
5 Monday. United Nations Conference on the Human Environment begins.
11 Sunday. Kamehameha Day, Hawaii. National Root Beer Week begins.
12 Monday. National Little League Baseball Week begins.
14 Wednesday. Flag Day.
18 Sunday. Father's Day. Battle of Waterloo Anniversary. Amateur Radio Week begins.
24 Saturday. National Rooster Crowing Contest.
25 Sunday. National Music Camp, Interlochen, Mich., opens for the season.
27 Tuesday. Freedom Week begins.
29 Thursday. Old Milwaukee Days begin. Peter Paul Rubens' birthday.

JULY

1 Saturday. National Barbeque Month and National Hot Dog Month begin.
2 Sunday. National Safe Boating Week begins.
4 Tuesday. Independence Day. Calvin Coolidge's birthday. Louis Armstrong's birthday.
6 Thursday. John Paul Jones's birthday.
10 Monday. Total eclipse of the sun. Democratic National Convention begins, Miami Beach, Fla.
11 Tuesday. John Quincy Adams' birthday.
12 Wednesday. Orangeman's Day, Northern Ireland.
14 Friday. Bastille Day, France. Woodrow Wilson (Woody) Guthrie's birthday.
15 Saturday. Saint Swithin's Day.
17 Monday. Luis Muñoz-Rivera's birthday.
18 Tuesday. Antibigot Day.
19 Wednesday. Anniversary of the first women's rights convention.
20 Thursday. Moon Day. Tishah b'Ab, or Fast of Ab.
24 Monday. Simon Bolivar's birthday. Hurricane Supplication Day, Virgin Islands.

AUGUST

1 Tuesday. Beauty Queen Week and National Clown Week begin.
4 Friday. Coast Guard Day. Lizzie Borden Liberation Day.
6 Sunday. Hiroshima Day.
7 Monday. National Smile Week begins.
10 Thursday. Herbert C. Hoover's birthday.
14 Monday. Victory Day. Atlantic Charter Day.
15 Tuesday. Assumption of the Virgin Mary. Sir Walter Scott's birthday.
19 Saturday. National Aviation Day.
20 Sunday. Benjamin Harrison's birthday.
21 Monday. Republican National Convention begins, San Diego, Calif.
22 Tuesday. Anniversary of the death of England's King Richard III.
26 Saturday. Olympic Games (summer) begin. Women's Equality Day. Woman Suffrage Day.
27 Sunday. Lyndon B. Johnson's birthday.
30 Wednesday. Huey P. Long Day, Louisiana.

SEPTEMBER

1 Friday. American Youth Month and Bourbon Month begin.
2 Saturday. Mustache Day.
4 Monday. Labor Day.
6 Wednesday. Be Late for Something Day.
7 Thursday. Utah State Fair begins.
9 Saturday. Rosh Hashanah, or Jewish New Year.
10 Sunday. National Hispanic Heritage Week begins.
15 Friday. William Howard Taft's birthday.
17 Sunday. Citizenship Day. Expectant Fathers Day. Constitution Week begins.
18 Monday. Yom Kippur, or Day of Atonement.
22 Friday. American Indian Day.
23 Saturday. Kiwanis Kids' Day. National Tie Week begins. Sukkot, or Feast of Tabernacles, begins.
24 Sunday. Gold Star Mother's Day. Press Sunday. Schwenkenfelder Thanksgiving, Pennsylvania. National Dog Week begins.
28 Thursday. Confucius' birthday, Republic of China.
29 Friday. Michaelmas.

OCTOBER

1 Sunday. National Employ the Physically Handicapped Week, National 4-H Week, National Pharmacy Week, and National Restaurant Month begin. Simchat Torah, or Rejoicing of the Law.
2 Monday. Child Health Day. Mohandas K. Gandhi's birthday.
4 Wednesday. Rutherford B. Hayes's birthday.
5 Thursday. Chester A. Arthur's birthday.
7 Saturday. State Fair of Texas begins.
8 Sunday. Fire Prevention Week begins.
9 Monday. Columbus Day celebrated. Leif Ericson Day. Thanksgiving Day, Canada.
11 Wednesday. Eleanor Roosevelt's birthday.
14 Saturday. Dwight D. Eisenhower's birthday.
15 Sunday. Black Poetry Week begins.
22 Sunday. National Cleaner Air Week begins.
23 Monday. Veterans Day celebrated.
29 Sunday. Standard time begins.
30 Monday. John Adams' birthday.
31 Tuesday. Halloween.

NOVEMBER

1 Wednesday. All Saints' Day. March Against Muscular Dystrophy begins. National Model Railroad Month begins.
2 Thursday. James K. Polk's birthday. Warren G. Harding's birthday.
5 Sunday. Guy Fawkes Day, Great Britain.
7 Tuesday. Election Day.
9 Thursday. Spiro T. Agnew's birthday.
10 Friday. Christmas Seal Campaign begins.
12 Sunday. Asparagus Week, Diabetes Week, and World Fellowship Week begin.
13 Monday. National Children's Book Week and National Stamp Collecting Week begin.
17 Friday. National Farm-City Week begins.
19 Sunday. Bible Week begins. James A. Garfield's birthday.
20 Monday. Robert F. Kennedy's birthday.
21 Tuesday. International Aviation Month and League of Elderly Gentlemen Week begin.
23 Thursday. Thanksgiving Day.

DECEMBER

1 Friday. Hanukkah, or Feast of Lights, begins.
2 Saturday. Whirling Dervish Festival, Turkey.
3 Sunday. National Mimicry Week begins.
5 Tuesday. Martin Van Buren's birthday.
6 Wednesday. Saint Nicholas Day.
7 Thursday. Pearl Harbor Day.
8 Friday. Feast of the Immaculate Conception.
10 Sunday. Human Rights Day.
11 Monday. Nobel peace prize presentation.
14 Thursday. National Junior Frisbee Championships, Las Vegas, Nev.
15 Friday. Poinsettia Week begins.
16 Saturday. Ludwig van Beethoven's birthday.
17 Sunday. Pan American Aviation Day. Wright Brothers Day.
23 Saturday. Feast of the Radishes, Mexico.
25 Monday. Christmas Day.
26 Tuesday. Boxing Day, Great Britain.
28 Thursday. Woodrow Wilson's birthday.
31 Sunday. New Year's Eve.

New Words

This New Words section consists
of two parts. The first part is a
list of new words that achieved
some currency during the year,
as determined by the editors
of the Merriam-Webster
dictionaries. The second part is
an essay on new words and new
meanings of established words.

ABCDE
FGHIJK
LMNOP
QRSTU
VWXYZ

New Words from

Merriam-Webster
REG. U. S. PAT. OFF.

The following list of new words and new meanings has been prepared by the permanent editorial staff
of G. & C. Merriam Company of Springfield, Massachusetts, publishers of
Webster's Third New International Dictionary and *Webster's Seventh New Collegiate Dictionary* and
other dictionaries in the Merriam-Webster Series.

A

academagogue *n* : an academic dema-
gogue

Afro-Saxon *n* : a Negro who accepts
the values of white society

ageism *or* **agism** *n* : prejudice or discrimination against elderly people

Agnewism *n* : a derogatory and usually alliterative phrase or epithet (as
"supercilious sophisticates")

agripolitics *n* : political activism by
farmers that is directed against legislation detrimental to their interests

air art *n* : art consisting of inflatable
plastic forms

antinatalist *n* : an advocate of population control—**antinatalist** *adj*

aqua bed *n* : WATER BED

arcology *n* : an immense supercity consisting of a mile-high structure on
land or sea and containing hundreds
of thousands of people living in one
complete system—**arcological** *adj*

aromatherapy *n* : massage of the body
and face with a preparation of fresh
herbs and fruit extracts

B

bartendress *n* : a female bartender

bird dog *n, specif* : a pari-mutuel bettor
who tries to find out what horsemen
are betting so as to bet in like manner

black herring *n* : something (as anti-
white bigotry or Negro militancy) that
distracts the attention especially of
Negroes from the real problems and
issues of racial inequality

black paper *n* : a written declaration

of reactionary or traditionalist viewpoints

body language *n* : the gestures and
mannerisms by which a person un-
wittingly communicates his feelings
to others

brawn drain *n* **1** : the migration of
unskilled workers from their native
country in order to secure employment **2** : the migration of amateur
athletes from their native country in
order to accept substantial college
scholarships

bundled *adj* : having equipment (as a
computer) and supporting services
included in a single price—compare
UNBUNDLED

C

cache *n, specif* : a high-speed auxiliary
memory for a computer

canidrome *n* : a track for dog racing

cherrypick *vb* : to register new voters in an area where they are likely to be of the registrar's own party

cherry reds *n pl* : hobnailed boots with steel toes

chunnel *n* : a railway tunnel that passes under a channel of water

clean *adj, specif* **1** : free from drug addiction **2** : being without drugs in one's possession

cluttervision *n* : a diluted effect from seeing TV commercials for several different products within a relatively short period (as a half hour)

cold rodder *n* : one who races snowmobiles

condomarinium *n* : a condominium whose units are luxury boats instead of apartments

crazies *n pl* : apolitical radicals who behave irrationally and often destructively

creepy-bopper *n* : a preteen-ager who is an ardent fan of monster movies

cryotorium *n* : a storage facility for human bodies subjected to cryonics

Custerism *n* : bravado displayed in a last-ditch situation

D

desexegration *n* : the elimination of separate male and female fashions in favor of the unisex look

dew *n, specif* : MARIJUANA

drop shop *n* : a dry-cleaning shop that sends its customers' clothes elsewhere to be cleaned

E

earth art *n* : art consisting of an environmental object (as a field or hill) that is modified by the artist—**earth artist** *n*

ecclesiactivist *n* : a clergyman who is a political activist

ecocide *n* **1** : the willful destruction of the natural environment **2** : a usually chemical agent that destroys all life in a particular environment (as a lake)

ecofreak *n* : an ecology zealot

ecumene *vb* : to engage in ecumenical activities

Eurotech *n* : a European technologist who works on international projects

F

flock shooting *n* : the aiming of a sales promotion toward a wide consumer market

fragging *n* : the throwing of a fragmentation grenade at one's own overly aggressive military leader

G

gasbaggery *n* : meaningless verbosity ⟨political *gasbaggery*⟩

geep *n* : a hybrid between a male goat and a ewe

geriactor *n* : an elderly actor

ghost drawing *n* : an outline drawing of a picture in which congruent figures are identified by numbers or letters

glasphalt *n* : a mixture of asphalt and crushed glass used to surface roads

graphotherapy *n* : changing a person's character by changing his handwriting

grasshopper *n, specif* : one who smokes marijuana

grinder *n, specif* : a drill field

gross out *vb* : to offend or insult someone by the use of obscenities or crudities

guiche *n* : a curled lock of hair at the side of the head

H

homeling *n* : a member of the home team (as in football)

hot line *n, specif* : a telephone service by which usually unidentified callers can talk confidentially about personal problems to a sympathetic listener

hot pants *n pl* : very short shorts

I

imploit *vb* : to take measures that will offset the exploitation of natural resources—**imploitation** *n*—**imploiter** *n*

instant mail *n* : a subscriber service that transmits facsimile letters, documents, or photographs over telephone lines

Isro *n* : an Afro hairstyle worn by Jewish youths

J

Jesus Freak *n* : a member of a fundamentalist youth group whose lifestyle includes communal living, Bible study, street preaching, and abstinence from drugs

jive *n, specif* : MARIJUANA

job action *n* : a temporary refusal (as by policemen) to work as a means of enforcing compliance with demands

job bank *n* : a computerized job placement service for the unemployed

juvenician *n* : a physician who specializes in adolescent medicine

K

kiddielash *or* **kidlash** *n* : a negative reaction against young political activists and protesters

L

lactocrat *n* : a scientifically trained dairyman who operates a highly automated dairy farm

lip printing *n* : the using of the impression of the lips on a surface as a means of identification

longage *n* : SURPLUS ⟨a teacher ∼⟩

M

maxi-bopper *n* : a middle-aged person who dresses in the current fashions of young people

mediamorphosis *n* : the slanting of news reports by the news media

mixi *n* : an ensemble consisting of a short skirt and a calf-length coat

mule *n, specif* : a smuggler of marijuana from Mexico into the United States

musicotechnocrat *n* : a specialist in the electronic production or modification of music

N

night minister *n* : a clergyman who seeks out and helps people (as derelicts and prostitutes) who frequent the streets at night

Nixonism *n* : the principles and policies advocated by or associated with Richard M. Nixon and his administration—**Nixonian** *n or adj*—**Nixonite** *n or adj*

nonresidential college *n* : a college that does not require its students to be in residence

P

parajudge *n* : a paraprofessional court official who decides minor cases (as traffic offenses, loitering, and drunkenness) in order to free a judge for serious cases

peekapoo *n* : a hybrid between a pekinese and a poodle

physician-advocate *n* : a physician who protects the interests of subjects in research experiments

pop wine *n* : wine artificially flavored with fruit juice

pseudocide *n* : one who leaves a suicide note but does not try to kill himself

psychenautics *n* : the study of the unconscious levels of the psyche especially with the aid of hypnosis—**psychenaut** *n*—**psychenautic** *adj*

psychological autopsy *n* : an investigation of the psychological and emotional health of a recently deceased person

Q

quadplex *n* : a building that contains four separate apartments

R

right on *interj* : used to express hearty approval especially of a statement or position

S

scriptography *n* : a list of published film scripts

sexism *n* : prejudice or discrimination against women—**sexist** *adj or n*

shuck *vb* **1** : DECEIVE **2** : SWINDLE—**shuck** *n*

skyboat *n* : a round fiber glass boat attached to a large plastic balloon for traveling on water or in air

skyburb *n* : a suburb having outsize streets that can be used as taxiways for private planes

sky-hitching *n* : travel by securing free rides on airplanes

snake *n, specif* : a long narrow printed list of scheduled performances

snopolo *n* : polo played in the snow by players on snowmobiles

soul jockey *n* : a Negro disc jockey who regularly plays soul music

spaghetti Western *n* : a motion picture with a western United States setting filmed in Italy

spear block *vb* : to block a football opponent by ramming him with one's head—**spear blocking** *n*

stagflation *n* : inflation characterized by stagnant consumer demand and severe wage-price inflation

street worker *n* : an adult who seeks out and tries to help local teen-agers who are in or are headed for trouble

studentism *n* : behavior characteristic of students

stun gun *n* : a pistol-sized gun that fires small wood or lead pellets

stylostatistics *n* : the stylistic analysis of linguistic data especially by means of a computer

suedehead *n, chiefly Brit* : a rowdy whose hair is cut very short

superfecta *n* : a system of betting on races in which the bettor must pick the first, second, third, and fourth horses in this sequence in a specified race in order to win—compare TRIPLE

T

telediagnosis *n* : the diagnosis of physical or mental ailments through televised intercommunication between doctor and patient

trank *n* : TRANQUILIZER

transatlantese *n* : English marked by a mixture of British and American idioms

transsex *vb* : to change one's sex

trash *vb, specif* : to vandalize (as commercial or government buildings) especially as an act of protest ⟨five stores were *trashed* during the riot⟩—**trasher** *n*

triple *n, specif* : a system of betting on races in which the bettor must pick the first, second, and third horses in this sequence in a specified race in order to win—compare SUPERFECTA

tripsit *vb* : to act as companion to a person under the influence of LSD

U

unbundled *adj* : having equipment (as a computer) and supporting services separately priced—compare BUNDLED

uni-age *n* : the state of not being distinguishable (as by hair or clothing) as to age

up front *adv* : in advance ⟨actors demanding $1 million *up front*⟩

urbicidal *adj* : destructive to cities

V

vamp *vb, specif* : to put under arrest—usually used with *on*

vegeburger *n* : a sandwich containing vegetable protein as a meat substitute

vertiport *n* : a small airport for vertical-takeoff aircraft

video music *n* : recorded music accompanied by film

W

water bed *n* : a bed whose mattress is a plastic bag filled with water—called also *aqua bed*

watercycling *n* : the sport of operating a pedal boat

wholesaling *n* : the fixing of a horse race by tranquilizing all but one horse

workaholic *n* : an employee who works harder and longer than required so as to avoid being laid off—**workaholism** *n*

workfare *n* : a welfare program designed to encourage people to work

workship *n* : an award to a qualified college student that involves part-time employment at the college

Special Essay:
The Evolution of New Words

by Simeon Potter

In 1971 some new words came into the language, and a number of old ones took on new meanings. The connotation of *pollution* (etymologically "letting loose") was certainly extended when used to include aircraft noise, and *environmental pollution* came to cover every conceivable form of defilement. *Antitechnology* became a cult that gathered worldwide momentum. One new and potent detector of atmospheric pollution was *lidar,* a kind of light-radar; strictly, laser detection and ranging. It registered atmospheric impurities in the neighborhood of factories and workshops by bouncing back laser beams from smoke particles, water droplets, and gas molecules, and measured their intensity by means of a *photomultiplier.*

The film card, or microfiche, was further developed to produce the *microbook,* a film card bearing the image of up to a thousand pages, and by the end of the year not merely single volumes but whole libraries were being reproduced in this way. Moreover, computers also grew smaller and smaller. *Multipurpose minicomputers,* it was predicted, would soon become part of the furniture of every reputable business house. *Informatics* (borrowed from the Soviets) became a comprehensive expression embracing every species of information retrieval, especially the information services provided by public libraries and research centers.

Liveliness in word creation was especially manifest in the formation of derivatives expressing fresh nuances and refinements of meaning. These derivatives reflected an increasing linguistic awareness and sensibility. *Activism,* for instance, echoing the German *Aktivismus,* indicated a particular type of activity that (aside from its philosophical implications) indicated the doctrine and practice of vigorous action or involvement to achieve political ends. *Confidentiality* became closely associated with confidence in the legal sense of Latin *fidentia,* as of something held in trust, and referred more particularly to the safeguarding of secret information and the protection of individual privacy. *Criticalese,* modeled on *journalese,* proved a useful term to describe the style and jargon adopted by professional critics.

Deviance was something more circumscribed than deviation. Applied to persons, it denoted the quality of being deviant in behavior, whereas deviation signified any departure from the norm. *Divisiveness* became fashionable among advocates of reconciliation and peaceful settlement of disputes. They attributed divisiveness to their opponents who, they said, fostered division, dissension, and discord. *Societal,* an important adjective in social and environmental studies, referred specifically to relations among human beings living in a community.

Many blends were too frivolous to last, but *atomitats,* or atomic habitats, were being built in deadly earnest. *Reprographic,* pertaining to reproduction photography, covered the whole area of photocopying and mechanical duplication. The prefix *tele-,* in addition to its Greek signification "far off, remote," came to be short for television. A *teleplay* was one written specially for the magic box, and *telegenic,* synonymous with *videogenic* (both adjectives modeled on *photogenic*), denoted that indefinable and highly desirable quality possessed by persons who looked well on the television screen. In some quarters psychological warfare was telescoped to *psywar,* more lethal perhaps than all the forces of propaganda and counterpropaganda put together. *Agitprop* (Russian *agitatsiya propaganda*) was sometimes employed without Communistic undertones. *Guestimate,* for guesswork estimate, probably went up in status. Another blend that had apparently come to stay was the verb to *splurge,* signifying to indulge in a spending spree and to be ostentatiously extravagant. Was it a blend of *splash* and *surge?* Nobody could say for sure. Someone somewhere had thought it up on the spur of the moment, and like many another onomatopoeic monosyllable, it was suddenly on everybody's lips.

An almost unnoticed importation from the Romance languages was the use of the suffix *-phone* to denote speakers of a particular language, irrespective of nationality. For example, *Francophone Africa* was used as a neat and unambiguous label for all the French-speaking people of that continent.

The most notable abbreviations were *demo* for demonstration, and *lib* for liberation; the latter only in *women's lib,* designating the new movement for emancipation and "equal pay for equal work." As an abbreviation for vegetables on the menu, *veg* remained somewhat marginal.

In spite of numerous protests by traditionalists, *hopefully* gained ground as an attitudinal or sentence-modifying adverb meaning "as is to be hoped" or "if our hopes are fulfilled." The new use clearly emanated from the German *hoffentlich* (older *hoffen-lich,* the dental being phonetically intrusive) either by way of American Yiddish or Pennsylvania Dutch. For the time being, it showed no signs of superseding the primary sense "full of hope and expectation" (German *hoffnungsreich* or *hoffnungsvoll*), as in that oft-quoted (not to say mis-quoted) peroration to Robert Louis Stevenson's 'El Dorado': "To travel hopefully is a better thing than to arrive, and the true success is to labour."

Another more subtle innovation was *non-event,* signifying an incident that turned out, "in any event," to be of no significance whatever, however much it had been previously apprehended as a thing of enormous importance. *Timely* became an *in-word.* Any remark, warning, or change might be described as timely—a delightfully noncommittal and innocuous epithet, and therefore useful. Another novel in-word was *mismatch,* applied without opprobrium to any kind of unworkable or unsuitable union. The deverbative noun *mix* threatened to oust *mixture* completely. Among colloquial words that rose unexpectedly in dignity were *hunch* and *ploy.* A *hunch* came to mean any kind of immediate knowledge, intuition, or presentiment. A *ploy* (aphetic form of *employ*) came to denote any kind of stratagem or artifice, especially in sport or debate, by which one might gain an advantage over an opponent.

Reprints from the 1972 Compton's

This section consists of four new or fully revised articles from the 1972 edition of Compton's Encyclopedia. The articles are reprinted here to help the reader keep his home reference library complete and up-to-date.

The following are reprinted:

ANIMAL BEHAVIOR

BIOLOGICAL CLOCKS

MAPS AND GLOBES

MOTION PICTURES

Contact between monkeys is necessary for their welfare. When monkeys engage in grooming—a contact activity—they remove dirt and parasites from each other's hair. Grooming is a type of cooperative behavior.

Compton's Encyclopedia

ANIMAL BEHAVIOR

ANIMAL BEHAVIOR. Man has always been fascinated by the amazingly varied behavior of animals. Ancient man observed the habits of animals, partly out of curiosity but primarily in order to hunt and to domesticate some animals. Most people today have a less practical interest in animal behavior. They simply enjoy the antics and activities of pets, of animals in zoos, and of wildlife. But in modern times animal behavior has also become a scientific specialty. The biologists and psychologists who study animal behavior try to find out why animals act in the specific ways they do and how their behavior helps them and their offspring survive. Some of them feel that the behavior of animals provides clues to the behavior of man.

A great deal of fanciful "animal lore" has arisen over the years in the mistaken belief that animals behave for the same reasons as man. The view that nonhuman things have human attributes is called *anthropomorphism*. An example of anthropomorphism is found in the following passage written by the 1st century A.D. Roman author Pliny the Elder:

> The largest land animal is the elephant. It is the nearest to man in intelligence; it understands the language of its country and obeys orders, remembers

duties that it has been taught, is pleased by affection and by marks of honor, nay more it possesses virtues rare even for man, honesty, wisdom, justice, also respect for the stars and reverence for the sun and moon.

Undeniably, the elephant can be taught to perform certain tasks, but no one today seriously believes that it reveres the sun and the moon.

Animal behavior can be studied in natural settings or in the laboratory. Often, laboratory experiments are designed to test notions based on outdoor observation. The study of animal behavior from the viewpoint of observing instinctive behavior in the animal's natural habitat is called *ethology*. A contrasting viewpoint on behavior, practiced in the United States particularly, has concentrated mainly on learning processes, behavioral development, and the influence of behavior on an animal's internal workings—the action of nerve impulses and hormones, for example. Both approaches have contributed important information about the behavior of animals.

This article was contributed by Ethel Tobach, Curator of the Department of Animal Behavior, American Museum of Natural History (New York City).

399a (Vol. 1)

What Is Behavior?

Simply defined, animal behavior is anything an animal does—its feeding habits, its reproductive actions, the way it rears its young, and a host of other activities. Behavior is always an organized action. It is the whole animal's adjustment to changes inside its body or in its surroundings.

The group activities of animals are an important aspect of animal behavior. Bees, for example, communicate with each other about food, and birds may flock during migratory flights. Group activities are often adaptations to a new set of circumstances. Without adaptation, a species could not survive in an ever-changing environment.

Behavior can also be thought of as a response to a stimulus—some change in the body or in the environment. All animals, even those too small to be seen without a microscope, respond to stimuli.

How an Animal Reacts to a Stimulus

All but the simplest animals receive a stimulus—light, sound, taste, touch, or smell—through special cells called receptors. These receptors may be located in many places on or in the body. For example, fish have taste buds over much of their body, sometimes even on the tail. These buds enable fish to taste the water they swim through and thus to detect nearby food. Cats, which prowl the dark, rely on sensitive touch organs associated with their whiskers.

A stimulus is a signal from the animal's body or its environment. It is a form of energy—light waves or sound vibrations, for example. At the receptors, however, the incoming energy is changed into nerve impulses (*see* Nerves). In complex animals these impulses may travel either to the brain or through reflex arcs to trigger the hormone or muscle actions of a response (*see* Brain and Spinal Cord; Reflexes).

Conditioning—A Way of Modifying Behavior

The behavior of many, perhaps all, animals can be modified by a kind of training called *conditioning*. Two types of conditioning have been studied—*classical* conditioning and *operant* conditioning. The first type was discovered by the Russian physiologist Ivan Pavlov; the second, by the American psychologist B. F. Skinner.

In classical conditioning, an animal can be made to respond to a stimulus in an unorthodox manner. For example, a sea anemone can be conditioned to open its "mouth" when its tentacles are touched—a response that it does not ordinarily make to this stimulus. When undergoing such conditioning, an animal is repeatedly offered two different stimuli in timed sequences. The first, called the *neutral*, or *conditioned*, stimulus, does not usually cause the animal to respond in the desired way. In the sea anemone experiment, touch is the neutral stimulus. The second, called the *unconditioned* stimulus, does cause the desired behavior. In this experiment, squid juice is the unconditioned stimulus because it will cause the sea anemone to open its mouth. In classical conditioning, the neutral stimulus is followed by the unconditioned stimulus. The unconditioned stimulus may be given while the neutral stimulus is being delivered or afterward. The sea anemone was touched first, then given squid juice. After hundreds of such trials, it opened its mouth when touched even though no squid juice was offered.

In operant conditioning, an animal is given some type of reward or punishment whenever it behaves in a certain way—for example, whenever it pushes a lever, presses a bar, or moves from one place to another. The reward or punishment, called a *reinforcement*, follows the action. Food or water may be used as rewards; an electric shock, as a punishment. Rewarding the animal increases the probability that it will repeat the action; punishment decreases the probability. Operant conditioning has been used not only with animals but also in programmed instruction and teaching machines (*see* Teaching Machines).

Role of the Nervous System in Behavior

An important relationship exists between an animal's nervous system and its ability to respond to environmental changes. Animals with a fairly simple nervous system, such as ants, respond in a relatively fixed, or *stereotyped*, fashion as compared with animals that have a more highly developed and specialized nervous system, such as rats. A rat can link

Because of *imprinting*, this duckling has formed a bond with a decoy. Imprinting occurs when a baby bird follows the first large object it encounters. If imprinted by a nonliving "parent," the little bird will follow it even when an adult bird is present. Although this form of animal behavior is most often studied in birds, it also occurs among other kinds of animals.

By courtesy of Eckhard H. Hess, University of Chicago

AN EXPERIMENT IN ANIMAL BEHAVIOR

Negative phototaxis—the movement of an organism *away* from light—can be demonstrated in a simple experiment. The experiment requires a blowfly larva, a sheet of black paper, and either two flashlights or a desk lamp with two bulbs that can be positioned and lighted independently. The larva may be obtained from sites where the blowfly breeds, such as garbage cans. The experiment should be performed away from the house in a garage or other enclosure.

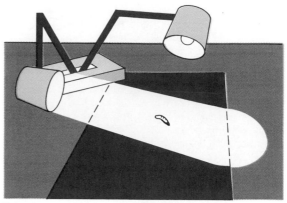

Turn the second bulb on and the first bulb off. The larva will change course to avoid the light.

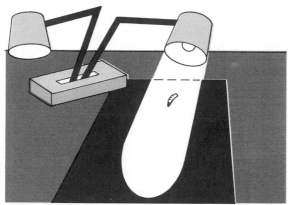

Place the larva on the black paper and place the lamp bulbs at right angles to each other and at about a 30-degree angle to the paper. Since the blowfly larva generally avoids light by keeping its light-sensitive head end in its shadow, the larva will probably move away from the light.

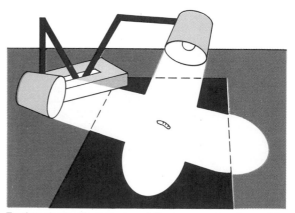

Further phototactic responses of the larva can be observed by turning both bulbs on and by moving one bulb farther from the paper while both are on. In some instances, however, the larva will move *toward* the light or will not move at all. When the larva is close to pupation, it has a positive phototaxis and leaves its dark quarters to pupate in the light. When ready to pupate, it does not respond to light.

up, or integrate, different stimuli from the environment and can store and use the information from past experience to solve simple and complex problems far better than an ant can. However, the rat does not do as well as a higher mammal, such as a chimpanzee.

For example, a rat, an ant, and a chimpanzee can each learn a complicated pattern of responses to reach food. The rat is trained to run a maze—a number of pathways toward a goal, all but one of which end in blind alleys—to find food. Then the rat begins at the end of the maze and must learn to run the course backward in order to reach food placed at the starting point. The rat takes less trials to learn the maze backward than forward. An ant given the same training cannot benefit from its past experience. It must learn the backward path as though it were a new one. The chimpanzee shows the greatest learning ability of the three. When the chimpanzee solves a problem, such as discriminating between two geometric shapes, it can do so by generalizing from a "set to learn." That is, after it has learned that it can obtain food by making the correct choice between the two shapes, it easily makes the correct response on the next try. A rat requires a number of trials before it can associate "shape" with "food."

The Evolution of Behavior

Behavioral scientists arrange living things according to the complexity of their behavior and the extent to which it can be modified. They have found that animals with more complex body and nervous systems have more complex and more modifiable behavior. In addition, however, the behavioral patterns that

have evolved among living things are particular ways of adapting to their environments—the places where they develop and reproduce. For example, though all animals feed, there are evident differences in the way they feed. Marine worms sift sand for edible organisms. An army ant stings a beetle and brings it back to the colony's bivouac, where it is dismembered by other members of the colony. A chimpanzee peels a banana before eating it.

It is possible to observe living animals and find out why they act as they do, but can anyone know how extinct animals behaved? There are fossil remains of extinct animals, but behavioral patterns cannot be left as fossils. Yet, equipped only with such fossil remains, scientists can get inklings about the behavior of extinct species. They achieve this by studying living species in the laboratory or in their natural habitats to determine their behavioral similarities and differences. Then they try to uncover the relationship between the structure of the body parts of these species and the particular function of each body part. Thus, if particular characteristics of

399c (Vol. 1)

the structure of a wing or a leg, for example, can be identified with a particular activity of a living animal, a scientist studying the evolution of behavior can make plausible guesses about the possible function of fossil bones. He can then develop notions about the possible behavior of extinct species that were ancestors of certain living animals.

For example, by studying the different groups of passerine, or perching, birds, researchers have identified the evolutionary relationships among them. One way is to use tail flick as a *taxonomic character* —a structural trait employed in analyzing the relationships among different species. Perching birds flick their tails in a particular way as they move through trees. By analysis of the extent of tail-feather spread during a tail flick and the direction and amount of tail movement, evolutionary relationships can be seen among such passerines as cardinals, buntings, weaverbirds, waxbills, and finches.

Evolutionary relationships among species may also be studied by analyzing different behavioral patterns. Among the most important behavioral patterns are *orientation, social organization,* and *communication.* All species exhibit each of these. However, within species considerable variation exists in the stimuli to which individuals respond, the age at which they respond, and the patterns of their response.

Orienting Behavior

An animal orients by adjusting its posture and position in space. It does so in relation to the source of different forms of energy in its environment. These forms include light, heat, and chemicals in the air or water, pressure, electric current, air or water currents, gravity, radiation, and magnetic fields.

Orienting behavior may take the form of a *tropism* —an action in which the animal simply orients its body toward or away from the source of energy without changing location. Plants can also respond in this way. However, the orienting response may take the form of a *taxis*—a movement toward or away from the source of energy by swimming, flying, or locomotion. As a rule, only animals are capable of such responses. Still another type of orienting response is called a *kinesis*—an increase or decrease in an animal's activity, but in no particular direction.

Prefixes are usually added to the root words tropism, taxis, and kinesis to indicate the kind of energy to which the organism is responding. For example, *geo*tropism is response to gravity; *photo*taxis, response to light. Prefixes may also indicate the type of response made. Thus *klino*kinesis refers to turning activities. In addition, the direction or intensity of a response may be described as positive, if directed toward a stimulus, or negative, if directed away from it.

Orientation makes it possible for an animal to feed, to exhibit social behavior, and to avoid obstacles and barriers. Some organisms, such as the bat, use sonar—reflected sound—to locate prey and to avoid obstacles. Some fish can navigate through tight

George Holton—Photo Researchers

Penguins space themselves in a way that ensures a place for them and their young in a crowded rookery. The behavior through which an animal claims an area and defends it against others of its species is called *territoriality.*

crevices by detecting changes in their electric field. Electronic instruments enable researchers to detect and record the sound frequencies and electricity emitted by different species (*see* Bioengineering; Bionics).

When foraging for food, the honeybee orients to the odor of flowers and the polarization of light. It also responds to cues from the sun's position off the horizon. This type of activity is called *sun compass orientation.* On returning to the hive the bee performs certain "dances"—a variety of motor patterns—that vary with the distance and direction of the food. These dances stimulate the other bees to travel the path of the returning bee. (*See also* Bee.)

Fish and birds also exhibit compass orientation when homing or migrating. However, scientists are not sure that animals navigate in the same way as man. When humans navigate, they use such instruments as the sextant to find the altitude of the sun and stars and a chronometer for timekeeping. It has not yet been demonstrated that homing and migrating animals can "shoot an azimuth" and "tell time." (*See also* Navigation.)

Some animals are known to return to the areas where they were born or spawned. The salmon, for example, upon reaching sexual maturity responds to the chemical characteristics of the stream in which it was spawned. The hormonal changes associated with sexual maturity are a cause of this new sensitivity. The stickleback moves from salty to brackish

(Vol. 1) 399d

L. David Mech

Durward L. Allen

Among social animals, dominance and submissiveness develop as a way of controlling breeding and territories. Two foxes engage in a mock battle for dominance (above). Among wolves, dominance denotes leadership as well. Alpha, or dominant, wolves usually lead the attack against prey (left). Even in an attack such as this, however, a healthy, fully grown moose will escape from the wolves.

water to reproduce. Its behavior is related to endocrine gland responses to seasonal fluctuations in light. Similar hormonal changes in birds lead to migration and reproduction. These cyclic changes in behavior due to hormonal regulation are considered evidence of a "chronometer" that might enable migrating or homing animals to correlate changes in visual cues during compass orientation with changes in internal rhythms and thus make navigation possible. (*See also* Biological Clocks; Hormones.)

Social Behavior

All living things relate to other members of their species. In an amoeba, the relationship occurs only during the short time it takes the animal to split into two animals. In other species, such as the social insects, the relationship is so necessary that they cannot survive as individuals. This is true also of humans, who are dependent on others until they reach maturity.

Social organization of some kind is common to all animals. However, the type of organization varies with the nervous system of the species. And in true social organization, animals of the same species react *to each other*.

Conspecifics, or animals of the same species, may at times be close to each other without exhibiting social behavior. For example, mollusk larvae may respond to changes in the intensity of light by swimming to the water surface. The resultant grouping, called an *aggregation*, stems from a common response to a physical aspect of the environment. But a response is truly social only when it is a response to visual, chemical, auditory, or other stimuli emanating from a conspecific. As a result of such stimuli, animals may approach each other to form a bond or to fight. Although dissimilar, both reactions are examples of social behavior.

The type of bond formed by conspecifics is a measure of their nervous and hormonal systems. Organisms with relatively simple systems may respond to each other only as long as they give off attractive or offensive stimuli. For example, a worm will approach another worm during the reproductive state because certain chemicals are released. Once mating has occurred, they have nothing further to do with each other. A goby will remain near its eggs only as long as the hormonal state of the fish and the chemical and visual features of the eggs remain the same. Once the fry, or young, hatch, the fish responds to them as it would toward any small fish and tries to eat them. The goby does not recognize the fry as its own offspring.

Although orientation, changing hormonal levels, and other processes play a part, social bonding depends primarily on a mutual exchange of stimulation and food between animals. The give-and-take stimulation of a pair or a group is fundamental to the organization of social groups.

The Army Ant Colony—
An Example of a Social Group

An army ant colony consists of many thousands of workers and a queen. The queen is capable of laying large batches of infertile eggs when she is fed sufficiently. These eggs hatch into workers, females incapable of sexual reproduction. However, at a certain stage of the queen's development she produces a brood of males and females capable of reproducing and starting new colonies.

The colony has a two-phase cycle of activity. The *nomadic phase* lasts about 18 days. By late afternoon or early evening, the larger workers cluster and leave the bivouac area where they spent the previous night. They move out over many yards in the area around the bivouac. As they crawl, they lay a chemi-

399e (Vol. 1)

Leonard Lee Rue III

O. S. Pettingill, Jr.—National Audubon Society

Many animals fiercely protect their young and even their unborn offspring from harm. Others become quite wily when danger is present. Here, birds of different species behave very differently when their eggs are threatened by predators. The sparrow hawk meets threat with threat by brandishing sharp, hooked claws (left). The piping plover bluffs a wing injury to distract the predator's attention away from the eggs (above).

cal trail. Other ants in the colony travel over the trail, and as the trail becomes more frequently traveled the concentration of chemical stimuli on it becomes stronger. The entire colony, queen and all, eventually move out from the bivouac along the trail. The ants range over large areas, preying on other insects and their young.

Army ants take in considerable food during the nomadic phase. The queen receives a good deal of it. She does not usually forage but is able to feed on the booty brought back by medium-size workers. They return to the bivouac to lick the queen for the highly attractive chemicals she exudes. (Chemicals

that attract or repel conspecifics and heterospecifics, members of other species, are called *pheromones*.) The exchanges of food and secretions between the queen and the workers produce a strong bond that keeps the colony together. The queen's increased food intake enables her to lay a batch of eggs. However, this affects her relationship with the workers. She becomes less stimulating to them, and their foraging, therefore, begins to decrease. Now the colony enters the other phase of its cycle—the *statary phase*. The number, frequency, distance, and area of foraging decreases considerably. The level of the entire colony's activity drops to a minimum.

In a "nest building" ceremony, an egret with a stick in its bill entices its mate off the nest so that it can brood the eggs. The stick was probably filched from the nest of the squawking spoonbills. Without the appropriate display by its partner, the brooding mate would be reluctant to leave the nest. Many animals use displays to communicate with other members of their species.

Helen Cruickshank—National Audubon Society

(Vol. 1) 399f

Wild animals usually run away when a man or any other possible enemy comes too close. However, an animal that cannot flee will attack when the enemy breaches its *critical zone*. Lion trainers rely on this behavior in circus acts. When a trainer steps into the caged lion's critical zone, it moves toward him. To stop the attack, the trainer steps back from the zone and the lion halts or turns around. Whips, guns, or other "punitive" devices used by the trainer are for show purposes only.

After about 21 days the eggs hatch, and the larvae emerge. These squirming, active young are an intense source of stimulation to the workers. The workers are "driven" out of the bivouac and the nomadic phase starts again. They are now attracted by the pheromones of the larvae and the queen. When the workers return from foraging, they drop their booty and feel and handle the larvae with their antennae and legs. As a result of this excitation, the number and frequency of raids again increase. The colony travels great distances, the larvae are fed, and the queen is "overfed." At this point, the colony consists of the queen, workers, and larvae.

About 18 days after the eggs have hatched, the larvae enclose themselves in cocoons and become pupae. At about the same time, the queen lays her next batch of eggs. Now the colony consists of the queen, workers, pupae, and developing eggs. However, the pupae and the eggs offer little stimulation for the workers, and the statary slowdown begins. But the queen continues to secrete pheromones that bind the colony. (*See also* Ant; Insects.)

Close Bonds Among Animals

Animals with complex nervous systems, ranging from some fish to mammals, may form *monogamous* bonds. The mates of such species stay together for a breeding season or even for a lifetime. Their social ties are not restricted by the time-bound, immediate stimulation that simpler animals need. However, monogamous pairs must be able to discriminate their mates from other conspecifics. This requires the intricate action of an advanced nervous system.

Some birds and many mammals band in large groups, such as herds and families. These groups include adult males and females and offspring of different ages. The offspring in most mammalian groups remain with the group until they reach sexual maturity. The females frequently remain until the group splits up. Some socially bonded groups of mammals consist of an older male, a number of younger males, many females, and immature offspring. Among the howler monkeys and some other mammals, the younger males band together into a marginal "bachelor" group until each establishes himself as the "older male" in a new social group.

Not all mammals maintain elaborate group arrangements. Many live fairly solitary lives, coming together only for mating. Afterward, the female remains with the litter until the young become juveniles or are sexually mature. In some instances, the mating pair stay together until the young are born. Beavers behave in this way. In other instances, the male and the female separate immediately after mating. This is true of many other rodents.

The Prairie Dog Coterie— A Complex Social Group

The prairie dog is a rodent that maintains an elaborate social organization. Bond formation among prairie dogs depends on the exchange of auditory, visual, and chemical stimuli. The coterie—the social unit of the prairie dog—is maintained in a network of burrows occupying a fairly restricted area.

Prairie dog pups are *altricial* at birth—that is, they are so undeveloped that they need adult aid for survival. When the pup is born, its mother is attracted to the helpless young organism. She licks the pup as it emerges from the birth canal, thus replenishing the salts she lost before and during birth. While licking the pup, she breaks the sac in which it developed as an embryo and thus stimulates its breathing response (*see* Embryology). The pup, still wet from birth, is attracted to the warmth of the mother's body. Moments after birth, the mother and her offspring are exchanging highly attractive stimuli,

399g (Vol. 1)

quickly forming a social bond. As the pup nurses, it relieves the pressure in the mother's milk gland. Again, the exchange of stimulation strengthens the bond between the mother and her offspring, thus helping to ensure the infant's survival.

As the pup matures, other stimuli become attractive. When it is able to see and hear, the pup begins to recognize the relationship between stimuli that occur at the same time. Soon it leaves its burrow and encounters other adults that it stimulates. From birth, the prairie dog is constantly nuzzled and licked by its mother. When it emerges from its burrow, it is handled similarly by other prairie dogs.

These behavioral patterns maintain prairie dogs in a well-organized *life space*. There, the family unit reproduces, finds shelter, and feeds. Being grazers, prairie dogs check the growth of tall grasses that would prevent them from easily spotting predators. At the same time, their grazing habits encourage the dominance of fast-growing plants. Thus, the social organization of prairie dogs influences the ecological balances in their environment (*see* Ecology). Limited grazing space soon forces maturing prairie dogs to seek new areas. When they enter the burrows of another coterie their odor marks them as strangers, and they are rejected. Pairs of rebuffed animals band together to form new coteries.

The Chimpanzee Family

The chimpanzee is one of the great apes. It lives in a family unit even more complex than that of the prairie dog. The chimpanzee family moves as a group through familiar feeding and resting areas. It has also evolved effective ways of defending itself against predators or from belligerent chimpanzees attempting to mate with the family's females.

When a chimpanzee has been attacked or has spotted a predator, it lets out an intense cry that raises the level of excitement of the other members of the family. They scream at the predator, throw rocks and other objects, and scamper off. As they flee, the females and the youngest chimpanzees are surrounded by the juveniles and the young males. The largest males guard the group. Thus, the action of a single chimpanzee serves as a signal that affects the behavior of the rest of the family.

Animal Communication

Communication in the animal world takes many forms. These include chemical, visual, and audible signals. Attacked insects, for example, secrete a pheromone that so excites their conspecifics that they either attack or escape from the predator. Flocks of birds behave similarly, except that sounds rather than chemicals trigger the response. Vocalization also evokes social responses in the porpoise, an aquatic mammal. Porpoises communicate by means of whistles and other sounds. When a porpoise is born, females may be attracted by the mother's whistles. They swim to the baby and nuzzle it. The mother does not attack other females at this time. Possibly,

this experience with many adult porpoises in the earliest days of infancy helps form the tight social bond of porpoises.

Reciprocal stimulation affects the behavior of any animal, whether briefly or for a long time. Each organism is the source of environmental changes that affect other organisms. For example, after an amoeba ingests a food particle, it excretes a metabolic by-product that changes the chemical characteristics of the environment. If another amoeba is nearby, it tends to approach the first, though it will not do so if the chemical concentration is too intense. A sexually mature male cricket *stridulates*—rubs its legs together and produces a sound—whether or not another cricket stimulates it. However, it is more likely to stridulate when it hears another cricket.

When one animal can prompt an anticipated response in another, it displays a more advanced type of communication. For example, in an experiment a chimpanzee was trained to obtain a banana by pulling on a rope attached to a weight. Then the experimenter increased the weight so that one chimpanzee could not raise it but two could. If the second

A baby monkey seems contented with its mother (left). In the laboratory a baby monkey was "reared" by two "mothers"—one of wire, the other of wire and cloth (bottom). The baby would cling to the soft mother when resting or scared, even if it had been nursed by the wire mother.

Regional Primate Research Center, University of Wisconsin

(Vol. 1) 399h

chimpanzee had already been trained to pull the rope, the first was able to stimulate it to do so by gesture, vocalization, and shoving. The two would then pull together and get the banana. In this case, the consequence of the second chimpanzee's behavior was in some way anticipated by the first.

The directed activity of one animal toward another for the solution of a problem or the attainment of a planned goal is evident only in advanced species. Furthermore, man is the only species capable of transmitting ideas through a complex system of speech and writing. The study of the evolution of language has given rise to a science called *semiotic*. This science attempts to understand the similarities and the differences among the many forms of communication.

Heredity and Behavior

The evolutionary principle of selective adaptation holds that a species survives when it is able to adapt to environmental changes and when it is able to transmit to its offspring the genetic information that makes such adaptations possible. But how do genetic processes contribute to the development of behavioral patterns? Which behavioral patterns are hereditary? Which must be learned by each new generation?

Notions about animal behavior can be tested in laboratory experiments. A test box can be designed to deliver food, electric shocks, or other kinds of reinforcement. The consequent behavior of the animal is measured electronically and recorded on graph paper. A white rat is in the test box shown here.

399i (Vol. 1)

Elio Elisofon, *Life* © Time Inc.

In an effort to answer such questions, behavioral scientists have designed a number of experimental approaches. In one type of experiment, closely related species with distinctly different behavior patterns are hybridized. For example, two species of parakeets that practically share a natural habitat but do not interbreed were crossed in the laboratory. The parakeets of one species ordinarily tuck nesting material under their tail feathers. The others carry it in their beaks. The hybrid female offspring made inadequate tucking motions with the nesting material, and the twigs fell out from their feathers. However, all the hybrids carried the nesting material successfully in their beaks. Scientists felt that since all the hybrids performed some part of the tucking behavior, it was probably the earlier form of behavior in the evolution of these species.

The relationship between heredity and behavior has fueled an old but continuing controversy in the behavioral sciences. Some scientists believe that genetic processes underlie every kind of behavior, while others think that the environment can modify genetically influenced behavior. In one type of experiment testing these views, animals with different genetic backgrounds are reared in the same environment. In another type, animals with the same genetic backgrounds are raised in different environments.

Cross-fostering is used to rear species with different genetic backgrounds in the same environment—that is, the young of one species are raised by a female of another species. In one cross-fostering study, a female great tit reared a baby chaffinch with her own babies. Great tits and chaffinches are closely related birds that feed in different ways. The great tit holds food under its feet; the chaffinch does not. A chaffinch hatched by a great tit did not use its feet during feeding, while its nestmates did. Its feeding behavior remained typical for its species, although it had no opportunity to observe other chaffinches.

However, when a great tit was reared in isolation, though it too demonstrated species-typical behavior by holding its food down, it did so very clumsily. Only after repeated tries did its performance improve. This experiment showed that experience may be important even in genetically determined behavioral patterns.

Manipulation of the physical environment was used to study the subspecies of deer mice. One subspecies lives in the forest, is a climbing animal, and has a longer tail and larger ears than the other, a prairie subspecies that lives in grassy fields. The two subspecies were reared in the same laboratory and then released in a room containing artificial grass and wooden posts with flat tops. Although neither subspecies had experienced its species-typical environment, the forest deer mice organized their life space around the "trees," and the prairie deer mice settled under the "grass." However, when prairie deer mice were bred in a laboratory for more than a dozen generations, they no longer showed a preference for the field. The environment eventually so altered

Frank and John Craighead

The behavior of large animals in their natural environment can be studied by means of telemetric devices. This grizzly bear was tranquilized and fitted with a radio transmitter (top left). When the drug wore off, the bear was released (top right). Radio signals from the bear's transmitter permitted its subsequent movements to be followed and plotted on a map (bottom left).

the genetic processes of these experimental animals as to change their species-typical·behavior.

Birdsong patterns are species-specific and have, therefore, been regarded as genetically determined. Studies of the development of species-typical song patterns have helped clarify the relative roles of heredity and experience in the development of such patterns. For example, some meadowlarks were reared where they could hear other meadowlarks singing, while others were raised where they could hear redwing blackbirds. The meadowlarks reared with the redwings developed significantly untypical songs.

The response patterns of birds are so varied that the contributions made by genetic processes and by the auditory and other experiences of a bird during singing are hard to separate. It may be that in the course of its development a bird produces certain sounds that are a function of its peculiar body makeup. These sounds may be the fundamental vocalization of its species. Additional experience with hearing and producing its own song, as well as hearing those of others in a social setting, may yield the "dialect," or song pattern, associated with the species. However, genes do not carry this pattern as such. Rather, they carry the code for the biochemical

processes that develop certain body systems which, aided by experience, will affect the animal's behavior in its typical environment. (*See also* Animals; Biology; Genetics; Psychology.)

BIBLIOGRAPHY FOR ANIMAL BEHAVIOR

Books for Younger Readers

Freedman, Russell and Moriss, J. E.   Animal Instincts (Holiday, 1970).

Freedman, Russell and Moriss, J. E.   How Animals Learn (Holiday, 1969).

Hyde, M. O.   Animal Clocks and Compasses (McGraw, 1960).

Mason, G. F.   Animal Baggage; Animal Habits; Animal Homes; Animal Tools; Animal Weapons (Morrow, 1947–61).

Selsam, M. E.   The Language of Animals (Morrow, 1962).

Simon, Seymour.   Animals in Field and Laboratory: Science Projects in Animal Behavior (McGraw, 1968).

Books for Advanced Students and Teachers

Barnett, S. A.   Instinct and Intelligence (Prentice, 1967).

Bixby, William.   Of Animals and Men (McKay, 1968).

Carthy, J. D.   Animals and Their Ways (Doubleday, 1965).

Chauvin, Rémy.   Animal Societies (Hill, 1968).

Dröscher, V. B.   The Mysterious Senses of Animals (Dutton, 1965).

Gilbert, Bil.   How Animals Communicate (Pantheon, 1966).

Life (Periodical).   Animal Behavior (Time, 1965).

(Vol. 1)   399j

BIOLOGICAL CLOCKS

Enthusiasts grab for grunions as the fish swim ashore for their semimonthly spawning. A clocklike rhythm associated with lunar tides brings the grunions to the California coast from March through July.

BIOLOGICAL CLOCKS. People who have to get up at a certain time in the morning often awaken just before the alarm goes off. A "biological clock" seems to tick off the nighttime hours and "ring" an alarm in the brain to start the waking process.

With the possible exception of viruses and bacteria, every form of life seems to have an internal means of measuring time. These internal "clocks" do not require the intricate action of muscles or nervous systems since they are found in most one-celled plants and animals. They are probably "wound" by basic biochemical events within the cells.

Why do living things need biological clocks? One reason is that such clocks regulate the sequence of tissue and organ formation during the development of many kinds of life. A plant that produced flowers before it grew roots would die. A newly born baby with teeth but no stomach would starve. Another reason is that biological clocks synchronize the natural rhythms—the times of activity and rest—of both *diurnal* (daytime) and *nocturnal* (nighttime) animals to ensure that peak activity occurs when food or prey is available. Whether the biological clock within an organism is a single master rhythm or a myriad of associated rhythms is not yet known.

Clocklike Rhythms in Nature

The rhythmic activity of most living things at certain times of the day and night offers strong support for the existence of biological clocks. When scientists first studied these rhythms, they dealt mainly with *sleep movements*, the rhythmic leaf movements of plants. Many plants go through a rhythmic daily cycle—their leaves are extended during the day and droop or are folded at night. When such plants were kept under laboratory conditions of constant darkness or low intensity light, the sleep movements continued for days. Under these conditions, however, the *frequency*, or time required to complete a cycle, of the rhythm was not exactly 24 hours. Afterward

it was learned that the daily rhythms of many living things continued when they were subjected to similar laboratory conditions. For most organisms, the frequency of the persistent rhythm varied from 23 to 27 hours. Since these rhythms had a frequency not exactly 24 hours long, they were called *circadian* rhythms, from the Latin words *circa*, meaning "about," and *dies*, meaning "daily."

Circadian rhythms were known to naturalists centuries ago. The great 18th-century Swedish botanist Carl von Linné grew a garden that told time. He planted flowers that opened or closed their blossoms an hour apart around the clock (*see* Linné).

Mice have exhibited circadian rhythms under constant laboratory conditions. Normally, these nocturnal animals begin running on an exercise wheel in their cage at about dusk and then run intermittently throughout the night. During the day they sleep. When their cages are darkened and temperature is held constant, they maintain this circadian pattern in the laboratory, often week after week.

Colonies of the microscopic alga *Gonyaulax polyedra* illuminate ocean waves at certain times of the year. The algae are luminescent at night, especially if the water is agitated, and relatively nonluminescent during the day. Under constantly dark laboratory conditions, this circadian rhythm of luminescence and nonluminescence continues. Since so many other living things have displayed circadian patterns in the laboratory, it seems probable that almost all forms of life would do so if similarly tested.

Characteristics of Circadian Rhythms

Certain similarities can be found in the circadian rhythms of most organisms. For one, frequencies are so precise that the start of each daily activity can

This article was contributed by Karl C. Hamner, Professor of Botany, University of California at Los Angeles.

163a   (Vol. 3)

often be predicted almost to the minute. In addition, circadian rhythms will *entrain*, or adjust, to an artificial light-dark cycle if the imposed cycle does not vary too much from a 24-hour length. If a test animal is exposed to 11 hours of light and 11 hours of dark in each cycle, its rhythm will entrain to the 22-hour cycle; if it is exposed to 13 hours of light and 13 hours of dark, its rhythm will adjust to the 26-hour cycle. In all the cases studied, however, the imposed cycle has never had a carry-over effect. Even though an organism has been subjected to artificial cycles for weeks, the regular circadian rhythm returns when the artificial one is removed, and the organism is placed in constant conditions.

A single exposure to light during an extended dark period may *phase-shift* any circadian rhythm. Because of the exposure, the rhythm may reach its peak at a different time of day. For example, a test mouse on a 26-hour cycle in a dark laboratory may begin running its exercise wheel at 10 P.M. on a specific evening. But if a light is turned on briefly afterward, the mouse may start running the wheel again at about 10 P.M. on the following night. This is a phase-shift of the circadian rhythm because ordinarily the running activity should begin at 11 P.M. the following night. However, the frequency of the rhythm does not change. A 26-hour cycle will remain a 26-hour cycle as long as the light is not flashed constantly.

Another characteristic of circadian rhythms is that their frequencies are not affected by temperature. This is true not only for warm-blooded animals but also for cold-blooded animals and plants, whose temperatures change with the surroundings. At cold and hot temperatures alike, circadian rhythms maintain the same frequency.

If circadian rhythms are the basis of biological clocks, they certainly have distinct advantages as timepieces. Through their entrainment feature, circadian clocks would adjust daily to the natural 24-hour cycle of earth rotation, regardless of the rhythm's natural frequency. Through their phase-shift feature, the clocks in travelers who jet across many time zones would adjust within days to new light-dark cycles. Since such clocks are temperature-compensated, they would not be affected by wide-ranging temperature changes.

Biological Clocks and the Seasons

Plants and animals in the temperate zones respond in various ways to the amount of daylight in 24-hour periods. This response to day length is called *photoperiodism*. It controls many activities, among them the migration of birds, the hibernation of animals, and the flowering of plants. The ability to respond to day length is linked to an *endogenous*, or inner, light-sensitive circadian rhythm.

In the temperate zones, day lengths during the natural 24-hour cycle vary with the seasons. In

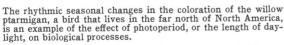

The rhythmic seasonal changes in the coloration of the willow ptarmigan, a bird that lives in the far north of North America, is an example of the effect of photoperiod, or the length of daylight, on biological processes.

During the short days of winter the ptarmigan maintains its white feathers amidst its snowy environment (top left). In early spring, as the days lengthen, the bird molts and starts to grow darker feathers (top right).

By the beginning of summer, after day length has reached its peak, the bird has dark feathers (bottom), blending into the summer foliage. By autumn, as the days grow shorter, the process reverses.

Charles Ott—Photo Researchers

(Vol. 3) 163b

winter and spring, the period of light lengthens; in summer and autumn, it shortens. Organisms in these zones undergo alternate 12-hour phases of light sensitivity. During one 12-hour phase, decreasing exposure to light induces a short-day reaction. For example, deciduous trees under the influence of the shorter days of autumn drop their leaves. During the other 12-hour phase, increasing exposure to light induces a long-day reaction. Deciduous trees grow leaves again during the lengthening days of spring. Although this description has been greatly simplified, it indicates that through their sensitivity to changes in the duration of light, living things can measure day length to determine the season and the time spans within a season.

The relationship of this "time sense" to circadian rhythms is easily demonstrated. Florists, for example, often "trick" greenhouse plants into producing blossoms out of season by exposing them to unseasonal periods of artificial light.

Some scientists are not certain that the biological clock of any organism is completely endogenous. They think that even under the most constant laboratory conditions living things are aware of the earth's rotation and that this has an effect on the "balance wheel" of their clocks. However, many scientists believe that such geophysical factors are not essential to the functioning of biological clocks and that the clocks are probably endogenous.

Biological Clocks and Animal Navigation

During their annual migrations, some birds fly over vast stretches of water or fly at night when landmarks are not visible. The golden plover, for example, leaves Alaska in late summer and flies to its winter home in Hawaii. Flying over water for more than 2,000 miles, the bird requires pinpoint navigational accuracy to reach the tiny group of islands. Any significant error would cause it to become lost in the Pacific Ocean. Insects also have this direction-finding ability. The food-laden honeybee, for instance, makes a "beeline" for its hive.

Studies show that the direction-finding ability of animals depends on "sightings" of the sun or stars and on the functioning of an internal clock that senses the time of day with some accuracy. The internal clock is vital for navigation because the positions of the sun and stars are never fixed in the sky. An animal relying on them for navigational purposes would have to know the time between one such position and another in order to maintain its course (see Navigation).

A variety of experiments have demonstrated that animals use the sun and stars for direction finding and must therefore possess the internal clock they need to navigate. In one such experiment scientists captured birds migrating southward at night and brought them to a planetarium. When the star pattern of the local sky was projected on the planetarium ceiling, the birds collected at the south wall, indicating a desire to continue their southward migration. When the pattern was rotated 180 degrees, the birds flocked to the north wall, clearly showing that they determined direction by the position of the stars.

In another experiment, birds migrating in the daytime were caught and put into an outdoor cage where they could see the sun. They indicated the direction in which they wished to fly by fluttering motions in the cage. When placed indoors and exposed to a light bulb, they moved in the normal direction of migration only when the light bulb was in the same position as the sun. Whenever the light bulb was moved to a different position, the birds changed their direction accordingly. (See also Migration of Animals.)

Somewhat similar experiments were performed with honeybees. In one test, honeybees were trained to obtain food at a fixed direction from the hive. They were then flown from their New York hive to one in California where they could get food from any of a group of trays encircling the hive. The bees flew in the direction at which they expected to find food, but it was not the same as the one in which they had been trained to go in New York. Calculations revealed that the difference between the new and the old direction corresponded to the three-hour difference in standard time between the two states. (See also Bee.)

Another experiment showed the relationship between internal clocks and direction finding. Birds and bees trained to feed at a certain site were exposed to artificial light each day until midnight and

A person's biological rhythms are synchronized with his local day-night cycle. If he travels quickly across many time zones, the rhythms still operate by the old local time and are out of phase with the new. A few days are required for adjustment.

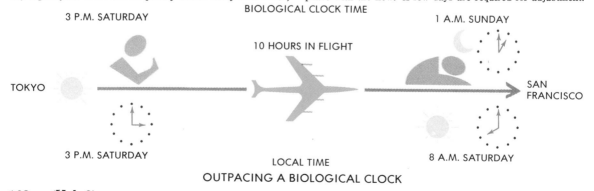

BIOLOGICAL CLOCK TIME

3 P.M. SATURDAY

10 HOURS IN FLIGHT

1 A.M. SUNDAY

TOKYO

SAN FRANCISCO

3 P.M. SATURDAY

LOCAL TIME

8 A.M. SATURDAY

OUTPACING A BIOLOGICAL CLOCK

163c (Vol. 3)

SOME BIOLOGICAL RHYTHMS IN MAN

WAKE-SLEEP CYCLE
The rhythm of wakefulness and sleep is tied to the daily 24-hour period of the earth's rotation.

BODY HEAT
The heat of the body varies throughout the day. However, body temperature falls to its lowest point during the very early morning hours.

OXYGEN INTAKE
Regulated by a control center in the brain, oxygen intake increases during the body's normal peak hours of activity, even in the absence of activity.

HEARTBEAT RATE
The heartbeat rate, about 70 beats a minute, dips somewhat between the evening and early morning hours.

ADRENAL GLAND OUTPUT
The secretion of cortisone and other adrenal hormones involved in metabolism is low during sleeping hours but increases before waking to ready the body for normal activity.

KIDNEY EXCRETION
Sodium, potassium, and other metabolic wastes are usually removed from the blood by the kidneys during the afternoon hours.

BLOOD CELL COUNT
White blood cells called eosinophils are most numerous during the early morning hours when most other rhythms are at their lowest levels. Thus the eosinophil rhythm is *out of phase* with man's typical activity rhythms.

REPRODUCTION
The reproductive cycle is not a daily rhythm. Eggs are released from the ovaries of the female about once every 28 days, in phase with the lunar cycle.

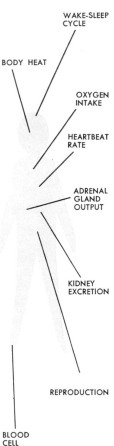

WAKE-SLEEP CYCLE

BODY HEAT

OXYGEN INTAKE

HEARTBEAT RATE

ADRENAL GLAND OUTPUT

KIDNEY EXCRETION

REPRODUCTION

BLOOD CELL COUNT

Most human body rhythms are *circadian*—that is, they occur approximately every 24 hours. With a few exceptions, these rhythms reach their peaks of activity during the day.

then kept in the dark until noon. This artificial light-dark cycle reset their internal clocks. When they were released in natural daylight after a week under artificial conditions, they went in the wrong direction to feed. Scientists could predict the error in direction simply by calculating the extent to which the internal clocks of the birds and bees had been reset.

Biological Clocks and Behavior

Since most one-celled organisms have biological clocks that regulate such things as cell division and chemical content, every cell in a many-celled organism probably has them too. However, because of the complex interaction between the central nervous system, the endocrine glands, and the muscles of man and the advanced animals, the biological clocks of only special cells probably control the time-oriented behavior and responses of the whole organism. For example, researchers studying birds assumed that only the retina of the eye perceived changes in day length during the daily cycle, a change which prepares many birds for reproduction. But the experimenters were surprised to learn that though photoperiod is ordinarily perceived by the eye, eyeless birds could also respond to changes in day length. When their heads were hooded, however, the eyeless birds could no longer perceive such changes.

The response of birds to photoperiod seems to depend on *encephalic photoreception*—the illumination of special nerve tissue either just below the eye sockets or at the edge of the brain. When encephalic photoreception combines with the circadian rhythms of the receptor cells, a hormone is released into the blood. This hormone is then carried to the anterior pituitary gland, where it stimulates other hormonal secretions that are sent to the sex organs. Thus, while the growth, behavior, and general activity of the entire organism relies on endocrine gland activity, the initial perception of changes in light and dark is made by a few nerve cells near the eye sockets. These, in turn, influence the entire endocrine system. (*See also* Hormones; Reproduction and Reproductive Organs.)

Biological Clocks in Man

Most, if not all, organisms have more than one circadian rhythm. Human circadian rhythms include the sleep-wake cycle, glandular secretion, the highs and lows in body temperature, and the excretion of urine. Many studies of persons living for a time in Arctic regions, where continual daylight can be experienced in summer, have confirmed the existence of these rhythms. Confirmation has also been provided by studies made in caves under artificial conditions.

What happens when human circadian rhythms— many of which involve vital processes—are tampered with? Circadian rhythms are known to rephase when a person flies across many time zones in a day. On reaching his destination, the traveler is under a new local time, but it takes a few days for his body to get used to it. Studies of airline pilots and stewardesses who often travel across many time zones revealed that some of their body functions became irregular.

Scientists wonder what effect future space flights will have on astronauts compelled to live for a long time under artificial conditions. They are not sure that individual circadian rhythms will continue to run in phase and cannot predict the consequences if they run out of phase. (*See also* Space Travel.)

Books About Biological Clocks

Bünning, Erwin. The Physiological Clock (Springer, 1967).
Life (Periodical). Time (Time, 1966).
Moore, Shirley. Biological Clocks and Patterns (Criterion, 1967).
Selsam, M. E. How Animals Tell Time (Morrow, 1967).
Ward, Ritchie. The Living Clocks (Knopf, 1971).

MAPS
AND GLOBES

MAPS AND GLOBES. The location of any place or feature on the earth's surface can be shown on a map or globe. A map is usually drawn on a flat surface; a globe on a spherical surface; but both are drawings or pictures, at a greatly reduced size, of what is on all or part of the earth. Maps and globes of the moon, the planets, or the sky as seen from the earth may also be made.

No one map can show everything. The features on each map are selected to fit its particular purpose. A map therefore differs from an aerial photograph, which shows all visible objects without regard to their relative importance. A map, unlike an aerial photograph, can locate not only visible features, such as seacoasts, rivers, roads, and towns, but also invisible, underground features, such as subways and geological rock layers. It can also locate abstract features, such as boundaries and grid lines, which do not appear on photographs.

A map shows how the various features on the earth's surface are arranged or distributed. A map can also show the distribution of any phenomenon or relationship—such as population density, crop production, or rainfall—that has some spatial variation. Thus a map not only shows where things on earth are but may also be a valuable geographic tool for understanding how and why the surface of the earth varies from place to place.

Types of Maps and Globes

Political maps emphasize man-made, or cultural, features, such as the boundaries and location of nations, states, provinces, counties, and cities. *Physical* maps emphasize natural features, such as mountains, plains, rivers, lakes, and seacoasts. However, both man-made and natural features are shown on most political and physical maps. Political maps, for instance, usually show important bodies of water, and

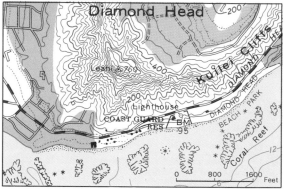

By courtesy of NASA

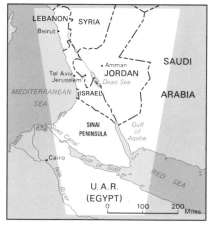

By courtesy of (right top) R. M. Towil Corp., Honolulu; (right center) U. S. Coast and Geodetic Survey

MAPS AND AERIAL PHOTO-GRAPHS COMPARED. The above aerial photographs and map show a very small portion of the earth's surface—the Diamond Head crater and promontory in Honolulu, Hawaii. The upper photograph is an oblique view of Diamond Head; the lower photograph is a vertical view. The space photograph and map at left show a much larger portion of the earth's surface—the area stretching northeastward from the Sinai Peninsula at the eastern end of the Mediterranean Sea.

physical maps usually show the most important boundaries and cities.

The typical classroom or atlas map is a *general-purpose* map that combines physical and political features. For specialized purposes use is made of *thematic* maps—maps that show only one or a few kinds of information. Thematic maps are also classified into maps emphasizing natural features and maps emphasizing cultural features.

Physical thematic maps may show the distribution of rocks and minerals, landforms, weather or climate, vegetation, soils, or such geophysical phenomena as magnetic declination. Cultural thematic maps may show the distribution of population, language, religion, land use, transportation, or manufacturing.

The moon is the only body in the universe, other than the earth, whose surface features have been mapped in detail. Since Mars has an atmosphere, it has been possible to make simple maps of its weather and climate. The other planets either are hidden by thick atmospheres or are too far away to permit mapping. But maps locating the stars—as seen from the earth—have been made for many centuries. In fact, the people of ancient civilizations knew the "geography" of the constellations better than that of the earth. Maps of the heavens, or star charts, do not locate the sun, the moon, and the planets, because unlike the stars their relative positions, viewed from the earth, vary widely from day to day and month to month.

This article was contributed by William M. McKinney, Professor of Geography, Wisconsin State University at Stevens Point.

A globe is actually a special kind of map—a map drawn on a sphere. Globes provide the same kinds of information that ordinary maps do. Political globes are more popular in the home, physical-political globes in the classroom. Among the newer types of globes are those that have raised relief and show the colors of natural vegetation. The colors are not strictly realistic, however, because they show full summer foliage for the entire earth, even though summer alternates between the northern and southern hemispheres.

Globes are sometimes made with slate surfaces for easy marking with chalk. Some slate globes have the continental outlines; others are entirely blank. Slate globes are useful for studying the earth's grid system —latitude and longitude—and for drawing great circles or other lines of mathematical geography. They also permit any lines or features on the earth's surface to be drawn at will.

Globes of bodies other than the earth are also available. Those of the moon have been the most popular, especially since the side of the moon away from the earth was first photographed in 1959. One of the most common nonterrestrial globes, the celestial globe, is like a star chart. But it shows the locations

TYPES OF MAPS. Road maps—one of many kinds of *thematic maps*—are probably the most widely used type of map in the United States. Shown here is a section of an Illinois road map distributed by a major oil company (top left). Also illustrated are sections of a *political map* of France (top right) and *physical relief maps* of the Philippines (bottom left) and of central Wisconsin (bottom right).

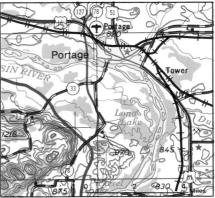

By courtesy of U. S. Geological Survey

1:100,000,000
One inch equals 1580 miles
0   500   1000
Miles

1:10,000,000
One inch equals 158 miles
0   50   100
Miles

1:1,000,000
One inch equals 15.8 miles
0   5   10
Miles

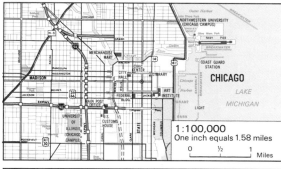

1:100,000
One inch equals 1.58 miles
0   ½   1
Miles

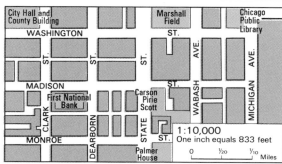

1:10,000
One inch equals 833 feet
0   1/20   1/10
Miles

of the stars by wrapping the so-called celestial sphere —or view of the entire heavens as seen from the earth—around a globe.

Since the earth is practically a sphere, a globe represents it best. A globe shows the earth as it actually looks when seen from outer space. Only on a globe can distances, directions, and the shapes and sizes of areas on the earth be shown accurately. Only on a globe can locations be shown in their true relationships to one another. A map, being flat, invariably lacks one or more of these desirable characteristics. Why, then, are maps used at all?

One reason is that globes are far more costly than maps. Indeed, globes large enough to show much detail are so expensive that only a few have been made, and these can be seen only in special exhibits. Moreover, globes, especially large ones, are difficult to carry and to store. Another disadvantage of globes is that they permit the viewer to see only one half of the earth's surface at a time. And areas toward the edge of the half he sees are foreshortened and distorted in appearance.

Although maps, unlike globes, represent the earth as flat rather than round, they have a number of advantages as compared with globes. Maps are less costly than globes because they can be produced more rapidly and require less expensive materials. Maps can be conveniently folded or rolled for carrying or laid flat for storing. On maps the entire surface of the earth can be seen at one time.

A useful compromise between a map and a globe, provided that not too much of the earth has to be shown, is the spherical map, or globe section. This is a cutaway disk having the same curvature as a larger globe. It is usually large enough to show an entire continent. A spherical map shows the shape of the earth accurately but is much cheaper to produce and much easier to carry and store than a globe.

A relief model resembles a map but is not flat. Relief models give a naturalistic, three-dimensional impression of the hills and valleys in the areas shown.

Map Scale

The scale of a map indicates how much smaller it is than the areas on the earth it depicts. Map scale is the mathematical relationship, or ratio, between the size of features on the earth and the size of corresponding features on the map. The simplest of the devices put on a map to indicate this relationship is the *graphic scale*, a ruled line or bar that is usually marked off in miles or kilometers. Any distance on the map can be marked off and measured on the graphic scale.

Another type of map scale is the *verbal scale*, so called because it is indicated on the map by words

A PROGRESSION OF MAP SCALES. These maps are centered on Chicago, Ill. The scale of each map is ten times as large as that of the map above it. The topmost map—like a far-off view—has the smallest scale and shows the largest area. The bottom map—like a closeup view—has the largest scale and shows the smallest area. The area shown by each map is indicated by the small box in the map above it.

96 (Vol. 13)

such as "16 miles to the inch" or "one inch equals 16 miles." Such a scale can be used by multiplying the number of inches between two places on the map by the number of miles indicated on the scale.

A third kind of map scale works best with the metric system of measurement. This is the *representative fraction*, or *fractional scale*, which simply states the degree of reduction. A scale that reads "1/1,000,000," for example, indicates that the distance between features on the earth is one million times as great as their distance on the map. A more common method for indicating the degree of reduction is the ratio. In the ratio 1:1,000,000 (read "one to one million"), the "1" refers to units of measurement on the map, the "1,000,000" to the same units of measurement on the earth's surface. In this instance, one centimeter on the map represents one million centimeters, or ten kilometers, on the earth's surface.

The representative fraction and ratio are harder to use with the English than with the metric system of measurement. The simple ratio 1:1,000,000, for example, is transformed into an awkward verbal scale of "15.78 miles to one inch." The simpler verbal scale of "one mile to one inch" has the awkward ratio 1:63,360 (because there are 63,360 inches in a mile). Many United States government maps have been printed with ratio scales that are compromises between the metric and English systems. These include such scales as 1:62,500 (almost one inch to one mile) and 1:250,000 (almost one inch to four miles).

Maps are sometimes classified by their relative reductions. The degree of reduction is smallest on a *large-scale* map, largest on a *small-scale* map. If one inch represents no more than about four miles, a map is generally considered large scale. If one inch represents from about 4 to about 16 miles, a map is generally considered medium scale. Maps on which one inch represents more than 16 miles are generally considered small scale. A large-scale map, which can show a large amount of detail, is like a close-up of the earth's surface. A small-scale map, which can show only a small amount of detail, is like a far-off view of the earth's surface.

There is no ideal map scale. The map scale chosen in any given instance is a compromise between two

COMPARING MAP SCALES. Miles and kilometers are portrayed graphically by these two map scales. Each scale is also described verbally and by the use of a ratio.

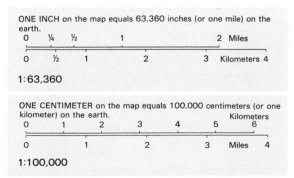

ONE INCH on the map equals 63,360 inches (or one mile) on the earth.

1:63,360

ONE CENTIMETER on the map equals 100,000 centimeters (or one kilometer) on the earth.

1:100,000

HOW TO MEASURE DISTANCE ON A MAP. To measure the distance between two points on a map—for example, Antlers, Okla., and Wright City, Okla.—ticks are marked on a paper strip placed between the two points. Then the paper is placed along the graphic scale with one tick at zero. At the other tick the distance can be estimated.

conflicting aims—the representation of as much detail as possible and maximum areal coverage.

Location

If a map is to locate places, some sort of grid system, or network of lines crossing each other at right angles, is needed. The latitude and longitude grid system is commonly used on small-scale maps, particularly those that show all or large parts of the earth. This grid system locates places by noting the intersections of meridians, or north-south lines, with parallels, or east-west lines. Meridians go from the North Pole to the South Pole; parallels go around the earth parallel to the equator (*see* Latitude and Longitude). The index of a typical atlas, or bound collection of maps, lists the location of thousands of places by their latitude and longitude.

Another, less precise, method for locating places divides a map into a rectangular grid similar to the squares of a chessboard. In this system, the vertical rows may be lettered "A," "B," "C," etc., and the horizontal rows may be numbered "1," "2," "3," etc. (or vice versa). If the location "C 3," for example, accompanied a place-name listing, this would indicate that the place listed could be found on the map somewhere within the area in both the "C" and "3" rows. This simple and convenient alphanumeric grid is used on almost all road maps. When used on atlas maps, it is often keyed to the boxed areas formed by lines of latitude and longitude.

The Range and Township grid system is used mainly on maps of central and western North America to locate and describe tracts of land. The areas shown on these maps are generally divided into six-mile squares called townships and one-mile squares called sections (*see* Lands, Public).

Two other kinds of grids are often used on government maps. These are the military grid systems, which cover the whole world, and the plane coordinate systems, one for each state of the United States. The lines of the two systems are straight and form perfect squares on the map, unlike the often gradually curving lines of latitude and longitude. Since the earth's curvature is ignored, these lines do not correspond exactly to the more familiar north-south meridians and east-west parallels. They therefore have a special "Grid North," whose direction usually differs somewhat from that of the more common geographic and magnetic norths. Each square in a military grid is identified by a specific code based on an international system of military grid zones.

HOW TO LOCATE A PLACE ON A MAP. To locate the village of Adams, Mass., for example, Adams would be looked up in the place-name index for the map of Massachusetts on page 159 of this volume. Opposite the village's name is the symbol B 2, signifying that Adams can be located on the map where the row down from "B" overlaps the row right from "2."

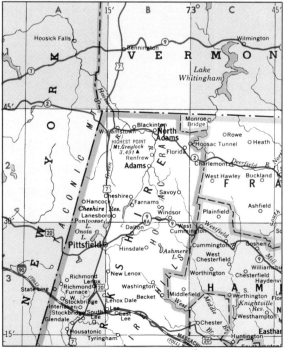

© Hammond Incorporated

98   (Vol. 13)

Direction

A map is usually printed with geographic, or true, north at the top, or away from the reader. However, it is not always convenient to follow this convention. In some cases the area being mapped will fit on the sheet better and can be shown at a larger scale if a direction other than north is at the top. For this reason, it may be misleading to think of north as "up" and south as "down."

A map can be positioned so that any feature represented on it lies in the same direction as the direction of the actual feature. This process, known as *orientation*, aligns north on the map with north in the real world. If magnetic north is shown on a map, the map can also be oriented by aligning it with north on a magnetic compass. An inconvenience in orienting a map is that the names printed on it may then have to be read at a severe slant or even upside down. (*See also* Directions.)

In a process resembling orientation, a globe can be placed so that it is aligned with the earth. This is known as *rectification*. When a globe is rectified, its axis is parallel to that of the earth and its own location is on top. Rectification is useful in studying and demonstrating various earth-sun relationships. For example, if a rectified globe is placed in direct sunlight and its north pole is turned directly toward geographic north, the globe will be illuminated exactly as the earth itself is at that particular moment. A rectified globe can thus show the changing shadow lines of sunrise and sunset as the earth rotates.

A globe is usually mounted on its axis and held within a circular or semicircular meridian ring. The axis is tilted at $23\frac{1}{2}$ degrees from the vertical to simulate the actual tilt of the earth's axis with respect to the plane of the earth's orbit around the sun. A globe with a cradle mounting, however, may be freely moved in any direction. A cradle-mounted globe has a horizontal, or horizon, ring. A cradle mounting permits easy viewing of any part of the globe and is necessary if the globe is to be rectified.

Map Symbols

Maps have a special language of their own—one that communicates more to the reader than a view of the earth itself can. This is the language of map symbols. Although aerial and space photographs give a startling view of the earth as it is, they are not as informative as maps are. Features are not named or identified in aerial and space photographs; hills and valleys are not always apparent; and the untrained person cannot easily distinguish some features—for example, he may confuse a highway with a railroad or a school with a factory. These distinctions can be learned, but learning the symbolism of the printed map is easier and faster.

Indeed, the trend of modern mapping has been to replace pictorial symbols with more abstract ones. Medieval and early Renaissance maps used drawings of actual features—chains of mountains, castles and churches, harbors filled with ships—all greatly exaggerated in size so they could be read. Such artwork was decorative and easy to understand, but it produced maps that were cluttered and imprecise. Gradually, maps were simplified as pictures were replaced by symbols. A road became a thick line or two closely parallel thin lines; a city, a dot or a small circle; a swamp, a group of tiny tufts. Nevertheless, common map symbols still often resemble, or at least suggest, the features on the earth that they represent.

Some exaggeration in size still remains, especially on small-scale maps. Otherwise, the symbols for any but the largest features might not be readable. For instance, a city's actual size does not necessarily correspond to the size of its circle on the map; a river is usually drawn wider than scale; and the parallel lines of road borders may be drawn many times farther apart than strict adherence to the map scale would require. That is why the dimensions of an actual feature cannot always be determined by measuring its symbol on the map.

Each type of map has its own set of symbols. Topographic maps have symbols showing elevation. Weather maps have symbols showing precipitation and cold fronts. Road maps have symbols showing pavement types and various tourist attractions.

Maps vary in the number of different symbols they use. For example, a map may use just one symbol to represent all roads, or it may use one symbol for paved roads and another for unpaved roads. Similarly, a map may use one symbol to represent all cities, or it may use different symbols for cities of different sizes. As map scales get smaller, the symbols used are less detailed. That is why the wiggles and turns of such features as roads and rivers are simplified on small-scale maps.

The symbol for a given feature or type of feature tends to be similar on different maps. Boundaries, for example, are generally represented by some form of dashed line. Railroads are often represented by thin black lines with tick marks; cities, by dots or small circles. Water features are usually colored blue, contour lines brown. Such similarities in symbols are known as conventions. In addition to or instead of the conventional symbols, a map may use its own symbols, identified on its *legend*.

Map symbols can be classified in terms of their form. There are point, line, and area symbols. Among the point symbols are those used for such features as buildings, mountain peaks, and towns. Line symbols include those used for roads, rivers, and boundaries. An area symbol is a color, shading, or design printed over an entire portion of the map surface. Area symbols are often used on political maps to distinguish the areas of nations, states, or provinces. Each of these political units may be overlaid with a different color. On large-scale maps, a city may cover so much space that its dimensions are also indicated by an area symbol.

Bright area colors tend to obscure the other symbols and the map lettering. In addition, the use of

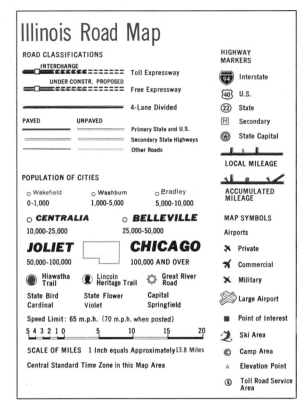

MAP SYMBOLS. This typical map legend explains the meaning of the symbols used on a highway map of Illinois.

different colors for the different areas on a map may also give the mistaken impression, especially to young children, that the actual areas represented are colored. One way to avoid these difficulties is to color brightly only a thin strip on or along each political boundary, leaving the rest of the map clear or in light color. General physical maps, such as topographic and school-atlas maps, ordinarily use subdued "natural" colors. Blue is used for water, and the land surfaces are often colored in various tones of green, yellow, and brown in an effort to duplicate their actual appearance. A limited amount of color overprinting, usually black or red, may be used for lettering and to indicate boundaries and the works of man.

Relief

The usual map, drawn on a flat surface, is better suited to showing distances in the two horizontal dimensions than in the vertical dimension. However, map makers have devoted a good deal of thought to the problem of showing this third dimension, known as *relief*.

During the period of pictorial symbolism, individual hills, mountains, and ranges were sketched on maps. This produced a cluttered map and did not show the bases and the summits of the mountains in their correct horizontal distances and directions from each other. But this so-called molehill method was easy to understand. An improved version survives today in

(Vol. 13) 99

the landform sketches used in physical geography.

The most realistic way of sketching mountains is to draw rill marks, or the natural paths carved by running water, on the mountainsides. During the 19th century, relief maps were produced by drawing such line symbols as they might appear from above. The results were called *hachures*. Like rill marks, hachures run from the top of a slope toward the bottom. But unlike rill marks, they are drawn practically straight. Varying the widths of hachure lines to indicate varying degrees of slope gives the illusion of natural light and shadow on the sides of hills and valleys. Hachures thus offer a realistic impression of the land surface.

But so many hachures have to be drawn that, like the pictorial molehills, they tend to clutter a map. Moreover, they provide no information on specific elevations, though some elevations may be indicated by placing spot heights at key locations.

The best answer to the problem of showing relief on maps has been found in *contour lines*. These are lines connecting places of equal elevation. The first contour maps did not show elevations above sea level but below it. They were drawn during the 18th century to show the depths of navigation channels in rivers and harbors. Perhaps the navigators who used them were already aware enough of the natural contour lines revealed by the levels of high and low tide to mentally picture similar lines revealing hazardous shoals and rocks beneath the water surface.

Contour lines are based on mean sea level (the average between high and low tide). Thus the shoreline of the ocean is the zero contour line. If the sea were to rise ten feet, the new shoreline would follow the ten-foot contour; if it rose another ten feet, the shoreline would follow the 20-foot contour; and so on.

If mapped over a sufficiently large area, a contour line will meet itself to form a closed loop. A number of such loops nestled within each other in a small area usually indicates a hill. The nestled loops of a hollow have tiny hachure lines on their insides to show that they are *depression contours*. Contour lines never break in two. The only contour lines that cross each other are those of an overhanging cliff. Contour lines never cross the shoreline of a still body of water. They cross rivers at right angles, with their bends pointing upstream. Closely spaced contour lines indicate a steep slope, or gradient. Contour lines spaced far apart indicate relatively flat land.

Unlike hachures, contour lines enable the map reader to estimate the elevation of any point within a narrow limit. This limit, termed the *contour interval*, is the vertical distance between two successive contours. For ease in reading, every fifth contour line is usually printed heavier and its elevation labeled. It is known as an *index* contour. United States maps usually give contour values in feet, but the maps of most foreign nations give them in meters. Contour maps, like hachure maps, give some spot heights, often those of summits, lakes, and road junctions.

Despite their precision, contour lines have the dis-

advantage of running around slopes rather than up and down them. Only in a few places—old shorelines, for example, or areas where a canyon has been cut through horizontal rock layers—can natural contour lines be found.

Area symbols also are used to depict relief. One method employs color tints to show various ranges of elevations. Land below sea level is usually shown in dark green, low elevations above sea level in medium green. As elevation increases, light green, yellow, and orange brown are used successively. The highest elevations are usually shown in brown, red, or white. Since the boundaries or lines between these colored areas are actually contours, *layer-tint*, or *hypsometric*, maps are drawn and read much like contour maps. The adoption of hypsometry for the International Map of the World in 1909 did much to popularize this method of showing relief.

A major drawback to the use of colors in this way is that they are often misconstrued to signify vegetation rather than elevation. And while it is true that in many regions low-lying plains are normally green with vegetation and mountains do have yellow-brown barren slopes, in desert areas this situation is often reversed. There, the low-lying land may be barren and yellow brown and the mountains forested and green.

The wide and usually varying contour interval for each color is another drawback of the layer-tint map. A typical sharp break between colors is the 5,000-foot contour. On maps of the United States, this break in color gives the impression that the Rocky Mountains begin at that contour. In reality, the 5,000-foot contour usually lies out on the western Great Plains, and the mountains usually begin at a higher elevation and as much as a hundred miles farther west. Another difficulty is that wider contour intervals are used with increasing elevation in order to limit the number of colors. Thus, all lands more than 10,000 feet above sea level are often indicated by just one color symbol, and much of

A RELIEF MODEL. This is a three-dimensional plastic relief model of Oahu, Hawaii. It has a horizontal scale of 1:250,000 and a vertical exaggeration of only two times.

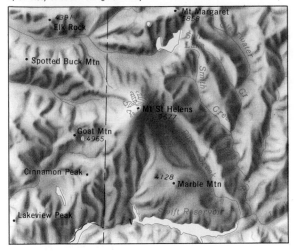

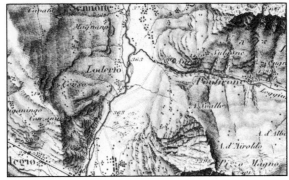

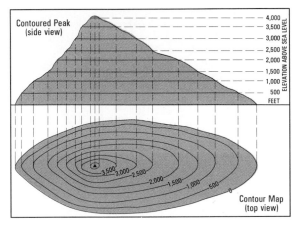

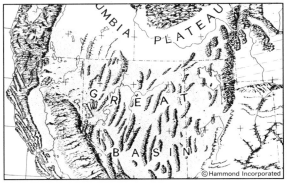

WAYS OF SHOWING RELIEF ON MAPS. At the top left is a section from a 1968 United States Geological Survey map of the state of Washington which uses shaded relief. At the top right is a section from an 1858 Dufour map of Switzerland, which shows relief by means of hachures and oblique shading. At the bottom right is a section from a 1932 Lobeck map of the United States, in which landform sketches are used to show relief. The diagram at the bottom left illustrates how contour lines show relief by joining points of equal elevation.

the sharp and rugged relief above this height is lost.

Solutions to some of these mapping problems are provided by *shaded relief*. This is actually a modernized version of the hachure maps. Subtle and detailed shading is secured by rubbed pencil coloring and the airbrush. The hill and mountain slopes that face the reader are darkened to give the effect of shadow. The untouched farther slopes then stand out in bright, illuminated contrast. Shaded relief is so convincing that it is being used increasingly, sometimes by itself but more often in combination with contour lines and hypsometric coloring.

A three-dimensional relief model, or molded-relief map, is an even more striking way of portraying differences in elevation. During the late 19th century some relief models were made, sometimes of cast iron but more often of plaster. But their cost, weight, or fragility limited their use. Modern plastics eliminated these difficulties. Maps can now be printed on plastic sheets and then molded into relief models. A number of such molded-relief maps, based on large- and medium-scale topographic maps, have been made. Some small-scale models have been made of states, nations, continents, and the entire earth. Molded-relief globes have also been produced. Molded-relief

maps make it easy to grasp the relationship between contour lines and relief. They have also proved particularly helpful in teaching geography to blind persons.

The relief on such models, except on those with very large scales, is purposely exaggerated. If the *vertical scale*—the scale used for the elevations—were the same as the horizontal scale, the relief of many landforms would hardly show. The degree to which vertical dimensions are increased is known as *vertical exaggeration*. A drawback of the great vertical exaggeration used in small-scale relief models of large areas is that mountains are greatly misshapen and overgeneralized.

Statistical Mapping

Any kind of data that can be expressed numerically and varies in quantity from place to place can be mapped. This is the basis for statistical mapping. Point, line, and area symbols are used in statistical maps.

Dot maps derive their name from one of the best-known point symbols used in statistical maps. On dot maps, each dot stands for a certain number of real units. Dot maps showing agricultural and population distributions are especially popular. The legend of a typical population map might specify that each dot represents 1,000 persons. This numerical value and the actual size of each dot are chosen so that the areas having the lowest population density appear very light, while those having the highest density appear very dark.

In order to show more than one set of data on a map, the type of point symbol can be varied. Small squares or triangles can be used instead of dots, or red and blue dots can be used along with black dots. Yellow or other light-colored dots are less desirable, because they do not give as great an impression of density as the stronger colors do.

Where the units represented by the dots are highly concentrated, as in cities on a population-density map, other point symbols can be used. Circles, drawn so that their diameters represent the size of the population, are usually employed in such instances. These circles can be combined with dots to permit the reading of parts of the map that might otherwise be solid masses of black dots. Circles shaded to look like spheres are sometimes used to show concentrations.

Just as contour lines can be drawn on a map to connect places having the same elevation, the same can be done in mapping other data. In fact, lines on maps were used in this way long before the introduction of contour lines. As early as 1701, the British scientist Edmund Halley drew lines to connect places of equal magnetic declination.

During the 19th century scientific atlases did much to popularize the use of such line symbols, particularly to show climatic data. Isobars, isotherms, and isohyets showed, respectively, the geographic distribution of atmospheric pressures, temperatures, and precipitation. So many types of lines were created to show the distribution of data that the general term *isoline* was coined to describe them.

The conclusions that can be drawn from the spacing of isolines resemble those drawn from the spacing of contour lines. For example, when isobars are spaced closely together on a weather map, meteorologists speak of this as a steep pressure gradient.

Statistical information is ordinarily reported for political units—nations, states, counties, and so on. Such data may be employed to make maps which indicate by a distinct color or pattern the average condition—average income or average population density, for example—in the areas occupied by these units. These maps are known as *choropleth* maps.

Choropleth maps are easily prepared, since both the outlines of the political units and the necessary statistical data are readily available. However, the use of averages may give the mistaken impression that conditions are the same over the entire area of a polit-

ical unit and then change suddenly at its boundaries. But sharp breaks are more likely to occur well within a statistical area rather than at its borders. This is true, for example, for the population density of the Great Plains states, each of which is more densely populated in the east and more sparsely populated in the west. Such distinctions are missed in choropleth maps that treat the states as units.

However, choropleth maps may be refined by using data for a larger number of smaller units, such as counties. Choropleth maps based on data for a large number of areas can be converted into isoline maps by assigning each area's average value to a point in the center. If desired, the areas between the isolines can be shaded in a manner similar to that used in hypsometric maps.

Data presented on statistical maps is often difficult to visualize. To help make it more understandable, *statistical surfaces* have been devised. Such surfaces give the illusion of hills and valleys over the mapped region. But these "hills and valleys" represent quantitative variations other than variations in elevation. Thus, on a statistical surface of population density, cities appear as mountains, towns as hills, and rural areas as nearly flat plains.

The *cartogram* is another statistical mapping de-

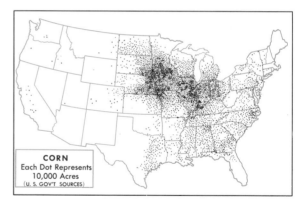

CORN
Each Dot Represents
10,000 Acres
(U. S. GOV'T SOURCES)

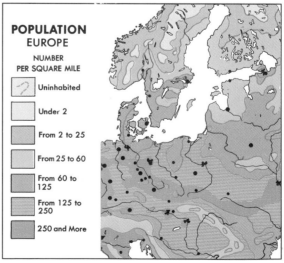

POPULATION
EUROPE

NUMBER
PER SQUARE MILE

Uninhabited

Under 2

From 2 to 25

From 25 to 60

From 60 to 125

From 125 to 250

250 and More

STATISTICAL MAPS. Place-to-place quantitative variations can be shown by dots, as in the corn-acreage map of the United States at top left. Place-to-place variations in average conditions can be shown by layer tints, as in the population density map of Europe at bottom left and the precipitation map of Japan at top right. The magnitude of movements between places can be shown by varying widths, as in the map of rural traffic volume in western Idaho at bottom right.

102 (Vol. 13)

vice. In a cartogram the relative sizes of the political units represent not their actual areas but statistical data. Thus, a cartogram of world population distribution would show heavily populated India as far larger than sparsely populated Australia even though India's area is less than that of Australia.

Map Projections

If the earth were flat, there would be no problem in representing its surface on a flat sheet of paper. If the earth were a cone or a cylinder, it could be drawn upon a conical or cylindrical surface that could then be cut and unrolled to form a flat map. But the earth is a sphere, and a spherical surface cannot be flattened.

The transfer of a spherical surface to a flat surface is known as a *projection*. When a sphere is represented upon a flat surface, there is always some distortion—distortion of distances, distortion of direction, distortion of the sizes or shapes of areas. Some projections distort shape and direction badly but show the relative sizes of areas correctly. These are known as *equal-area*, or *equivalent*, projections. Others distort size but show shapes and directions correctly. These are known as *conformal* projections. There are also *compromise* projections, in which

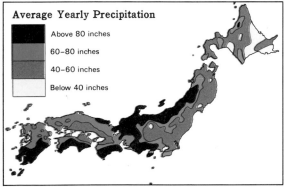

Average Yearly Precipitation

Above 80 inches

60–80 inches

40–60 inches

Below 40 inches

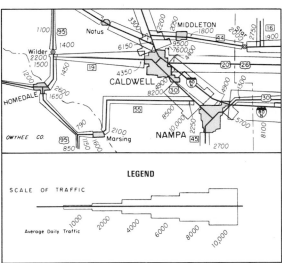

LEGEND

SCALE OF TRAFFIC

Average Daily Traffic

1000 · 2000 · 4000 · 6000 · 8000 · 10,000

area, shape, and directions are distorted, but the distortions are reasonably balanced. The basic purpose of any map projection is to transfer the earth's grid system from the globe to a map. Thus all map projections have one charactertistic in common—they show true location.

The projection chosen depends on the purposes of a particular map. Since accuracy in one property must be sacrificed to gain accuracy in another, accuracy is sought for the properties where it is most essential. Maps showing statistical distributions, for example, would probably use equal-area projections, because on a statistical map true shape is less important than other characteristics. Maps for navigators and surveyors, however, must be conformal, since on such maps true shape and direction are essential, but some distortion of size can be tolerated. Maps for most popular uses are generally compromise projections. Although cartographers still continue to devise new map projections, most mapping needs can be met by the several hundred projections already available.

Only a limited number of map projections are true projections—that is, formed by rays of light that pass through a transparent globe and project the grid lines onto a plane or developable surface such as a cylinder or a cone. Many so-called projections are actually mathematical constructions or what are technically known as *transformations*.

Map projections are often classified according to the type of surface—cylindrical, conical, or plane—onto which the globe is projected or transferred. In a *cylindrical* projection, the surface of the globe is transferred to a cylinder. The globe touches the cylinder along one line—usually the equator. Only along this tangent line is the map accurate in every respect.

When the cylinder is cut and rolled out flat, the meridians and parallels are straight and cross each other at right angles. The meridians are always the same distance from each other, though on a globe they come together at the poles. The parallels are not necessarily the same distance apart. Indeed, in the best-known cylindrical projection—the Mercator —the distance between the parallels increases as they approach the poles. But the Mercator map preserves shape and direction and is thus conformal. It was primarily designed for use in navigation, and any straight line cn it has the same compass direction throughout its length.

The Mercator is not an equal-area projection, however. The usual Mercator map—centered on the equator—greatly exaggerates the sizes of areas in the polar regions. The extensive use of Mercator maps in the classroom has given rise to many mistaken notions about the relative size of various landmasses— for example, to the notion that Greenland is larger than South America, when in reality it is only one eighth as large.

In a *conic* projection the surface of the globe is transferred to a cone. The vertex of the cone is usually placed directly over one of the poles, and

(Vol. 13) 103

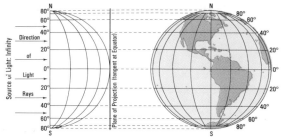

ORTHOGRAPHIC PROJECTION

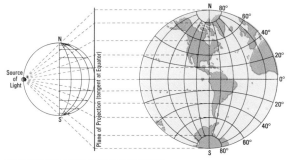

STEREOGRAPHIC PROJECTION

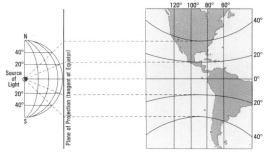

GNOMONIC PROJECTION

PROJECTIONS ON A PLANE. *Orthographic* projections (top) give a view of the earth as it might be seen from space. *Stereographic* projections (center) are used to plot ranges, since circles on the earth appear as circles on the map. *Gnomonic* projections (bottom) are used in navigation, since great circles on the earth appear as straight lines on the map.

PROJECTION ON A CYLINDER. The Mercator projection—a transformation from the simple cylindrical projection—is used for navigation, since lines of constant direction on the earth appear as straight lines on the map.

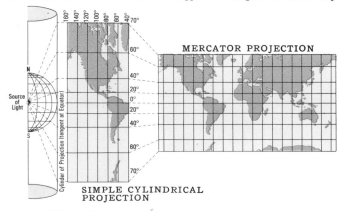

MERCATOR PROJECTION

SIMPLE CYLINDRICAL PROJECTION

the cone either touches or passes through the globe along lines of latitude called standard parallels. Only at these parallels is the map completely accurate. When the cone is cut and rolled out flat, the meridians are usually straight lines converging toward the poles and the parallels are arcs of concentric circles.

The distortions of conic projections are generally not as great as those of cylindrical projections. A conic projection is thus a good compromise, provided that not too much of the earth's surface is shown. It is used especially in maps of states, nations, and continents.

In conic projections, as in cylindrical projections, the spacing of the parallels can be varied. The simple conic, which has equally spaced parallels, distorts area and shape only slightly. The conformal Lambert conic has its parallels slightly farther apart near the edges, while the opposite is true of the equal-area Albers conic. Such conic projections as the Bonne and the polyconic do not have straight meridians.

In a *plane*, or *azimuthal*, projection the surface of the globe is transferred to a plane which touches the globe at one point. If the point of tangency is at either pole, the result is known as the polar case of an azimuthal projection; if it is at the equator, the equatorial case; if it is at any other place, the oblique case. All azimuthal maps show true direction from the point of tangency.

An entire set of azimuthal projections can be created by moving the origin of the rays of projection. If the origin is at the center of the globe, the result is a *gnomonic* projection. In the polar gnomonic projection, both the parallels and the meridians get farther and farther apart approaching the edges, and there is great distortion of size and shape. But the gnomonic projection has a quality useful in navigation—any straight line on it is a great circle, or the shortest distance between any two places on the earth.

PROJECTION ON A CONE. The simple conic projection is used in mapping small areas near the line of tangency.

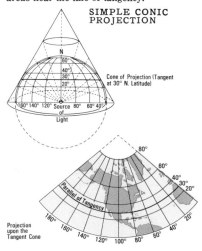

SIMPLE CONIC PROJECTION

103a   (Vol. 13)

If the origin of projection is moved to the far side of the globe, a *stereographic* projection is formed. In the polar case of a stereographic projection, the parallels are not as far apart as those of the gnomonic projection. Moving the origin of projection a little outside the globe produces a *globular* projection, with its equally spaced parallels and meridians. If the origin of projection is an infinite distance away, the result is an *orthographic* projection, which closely resembles a photograph of the globe. In the polar case of an orthographic projection, the spacing of the parallels is closer toward the edges. The polar cases of azimuthal projections, often used to show air routes across the Arctic, have been called "air age" maps (*see* Aviation). Such maps, centered on the North Pole, counter the traditional notion that the continents are strung out in an east-west direction.

Some maps of the world are so far from being true projections that it is best to consider them as transformations. These include the homolographic, the sinusoidal, and the homolosine, oval or oval-like maps whose areas of least distortion are along the equator

and a central meridian. Such maps can be split into several lobes, each having a central meridian passing through a major landmass or an ocean. These *interrupted* projections not only are equal area but also minimize the distortion of shape within each lobe.

History of Maps

The oldest surviving maps are maps from Mesopotamia made on clay tablets and maps from ancient Mediterranean cultures made on mosaic tile. The writings of ancient Greece and Rome refer to other maps, but these were drawn on perishable parchment or paper, and the originals have disappeared. Some early maps have survived, however, by being copied and recopied. Still extant are medieval copies of an ancient geography text attributed to Ptolemy of Alexandria, who lived in the 2d century A.D. Ptolemy's text contains maps drawn on a type of conic projection and information on locations and the effects of latitude.

Medieval European cartography was less advanced than that of ancient times. Many maps made in the

AZIMUTHAL
EQUIDISTANT
PROJECTION

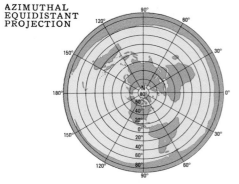

WORLD MAP PROJECTIONS. The polar case of the *azimuthal equidistant* projection (top left) shows true distance and direction along the radiating meridians but distorts area increasingly toward the edge. Both the *Mollweide homolographic* (center left) and *sinusoidal* (top right) are equal-area projections that distort shapes toward their edges. The homolographic is more true to shape in the higher latitudes, the sinusoidal in the lower latitudes. Advantage was taken of these properties in *Goode's homolosine* projection, which joined the poleward sections of the homolographic to the equatorial section of the sinusoidal. Both the homolosine projection shown here (bottom left) and the *Bartholomew regional* projection (bottom right) are "interrupted" projections, but the Bartholomew projection has the advantage of showing the relative location of the world's landmasses more accurately.

MOLLWEIDE
HOMOLOGRAPHIC
PROJECTION

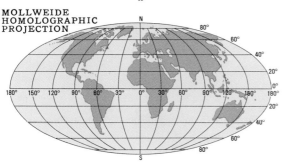

SINUSOIDAL
PROJECTION

GOODE'S HOMOLOSINE
PROJECTION

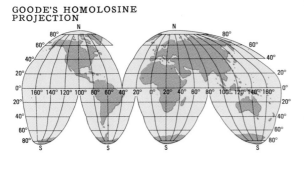

BARTHOLOMEW
REGIONAL PROJECTION

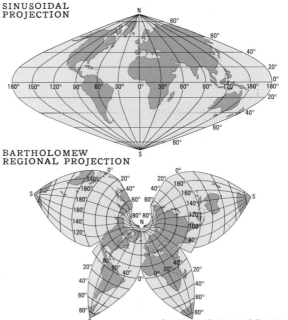

Courtesy: John Bartholomew & Son. Ltd.

(Vol. 13)   103b

Middle Ages were of the "T in O" variety. Maps of this type were bordered by a circle of ocean, and had a "T"-shaped body of water in the center that separated Asia from Europe and Africa. Asia was above the "T"; Europe, to its left; Africa, to its right. East was at the top, with Jerusalem and the Holy Land as seen from Europe the obvious center of interest.

The development of trade during the Renaissance was accompanied by the appearance of the practical sailing charts known as *portolanos*. These were first used in southern Europe during the 13th century. They showed coastlines fairly accurately and were covered with lines and compass roses giving the main directions. Improvements in practical astronomy and the development of trigonometry brought better sur-

veying methods and the mathematical tools for creating new map projections. Printing and engraving, which also originated during the Renaissance, made maps cheaper and more abundant.

Although far superior to earlier maps, the maps of the Renaissance left much to be desired. Imaginary continents and islands were drawn to fill in extensive blank areas. The unexplored interiors of known land areas were covered with fanciful detail. Borders were decorated with pretentious artwork. The latitudes of Renaissance maps were generally accurate, but the distorted shapes of some coastlines show that longitudes were not.

In the late 17th century, when newly developed astronomical techniques were used to ascertain longi-

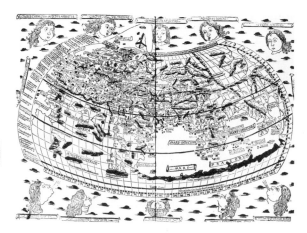

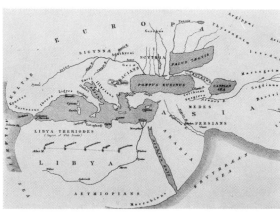

HISTORICAL MAPS OF THE WORLD. Greek maps of the 5th and 6th centuries B.C., such as those of Hecateus (top left) and Herodotus (bottom left), showed the world centered on the Mediterranean Sea. An ancient Chinese map showed the world centered on China, with other countries as small surrounding islands (bottom right). Ptolemy's map, which dates from about A.D. 150, greatly extended the picture of the known world (top right). All the continents are shown in Mercator's 1569 world map, which used the projection that bears his name (center right).

103c (Vol. 13)

tude, the relative locations of many places were accurately determined for the first time. This, combined with continued exploration of the seas, made possible the more accurate coastlines of 18th-century maps. The unknown continental interiors were largely filled in as a result of 19th-century land explorations. Scientific atlases with thematic maps now appeared. These were a great stimulus to the scholarly study of the earth. More recently, the use of power-driven presses, lithography, and photoengraving in the printing of maps has made them cheaper, more colorful, and more detailed than ever.

Many improvements in mapping coverage during the 20th century have been made through international cooperation. The pre-World War II International Map of the World (IMW) project is a prime example. Many IMW sheets, using a scale of 1 : 1,000,000 and a standard projection and set of symbols, were completed either by governmental or private agencies. The Inter-American Geodetic Survey, a joint venture between the United States and various Latin American governments, also had produced accurate maps of various areas in the Western Hemisphere by the late 1960's. Nevertheless, not all of the world has been mapped at a large scale, and even small-scale coverage on widely used maps, particularly those of the underdeveloped countries, is often not up to the best standards.

Many nations and some of the states of the United States have published atlases of high-quality thematic

OLD MAPS OF THE "NEW WORLD." The first modern world atlas, compiled and edited by Abraham Ortelius and published in 1570, included a map of the Americas (top left). Later maps of North America—for example, those made by Guillaume Delisle in 1700 (middle left) and by John Mitchell in 1755 (bottom left)—were more detailed and more accurate.

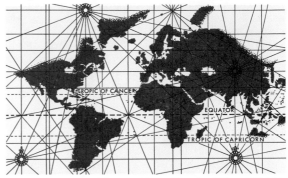

This Mercator map of the world is attributed to Edward Wright, an English mathematician who first computed navigation tables to be used with the Mercator projection. It was published in 1599. The compass roses and crisscrossing diagonal lines are in the style of the earlier portolano sailing charts.

This primitive navigation map of Wojte atoll in the Marshall Islands in the Pacific Ocean is made of sea shells fastened by plant fibers to a framework of sticks. The shells represent the islands of the atoll; the sticks are used partly for support and partly to represent wave fronts and ocean currents. Charts like this one were in use until the mid-19th century.

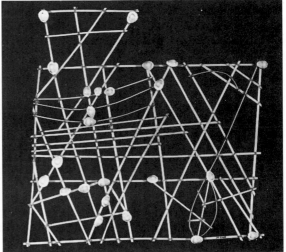

maps. For example, the National Atlas of the United States, published in 1970, contains many excellent physical, historical, and socioeconomic maps.

Map Making

Advances in science and technology continue to have significant effects upon mapping techniques. Improvements in aerial and space photography, for example, have helped improve the accuracy of modern maps. Aerial surveying has cut costs and reduced the time needed for precise mapping, and aerial photographs are used extensively to supplement ground surveying. They are especially valuable for surveying areas that are remote and not readily accessible. Much surveying is still being done, however, by the traditional land-based method of triangulation (*see* Surveying).

Pairs of aerial photographs are used in mapping relief. Taken in sequence and viewed through a special stereoscope, they produce a three-dimensional image from which contour lines can be traced.

Space photography permits large areas of the earth's surface to be seen at a glance. This helps avoid mapping errors that might otherwise result from inadequate coverage by ground and aerial surveys. Improved weather maps have been made possible by photographs of the earth's cloud cover taken from space satellites. Sightings on space satellites enable points on the earth's surface to be located more precisely. Space photographs of the moon and Mars have greatly increased the detail that can be shown on maps of their surfaces.

Electronic equipment is now used in the production of maps. Computers can be programmed to trace boundaries and coastlines, to provide printouts of map projections, and to produce a variety of statistical maps. The field plotter, one of the newest mapping devices, uses electric currents passing through conductive paper to plot the statistical gradients on isoline maps.

A great deal of new mapping, especially small-scale mapping, does not depend on the results of new surveys. It consists rather in compiling and editing data and in the design of techniques for placing this data on an existing outline map, or *base* map. The compiled data is then turned over to the designer and the draftsman who actually make the map.

Until recently, map lines were generally inked on such materials as paper, and the finished piece of art was turned over to the engraver. The earliest engraving was done by a sharp stylus on a copperplate. The engraved image was then printed from the ink that collected in the depressions. In modern photoengraving, the original map is photographed, and the negative is used to turn a specially prepared metal sheet into a printing plate.

Many professional cartographic agencies have replaced inking with a new method known as scribing. The draftsman works on a transparent plastic sheet that has been coated with an orange-red film. He draws the original map by removing portions of the

Reference to accurate and up-to-date source materials is one of the first steps in making a map. The precise map compilation being prepared here is the base for the final map.

This expert draftsman is preparing the negative for a new map by using a scribing tool. Scribing is faster and produces higher-quality linework than pen and ink.

Adhesive-backed type cut out from a preprinted list is being carefully pressed into place on this map. Lettering is one of the final steps in preparing a map for printing.

103e   (Vol. 13)

By courtesy of Replogle Globes, Division of Meredith Corp.

Flat, lens-shaped map gores are expertly stretched and smoothed into place on the curved surface of a globe shell. The best globes are handmade.

as geography, aerial photography, the natural sciences, mathematics, and statistics.

Sources of Maps

Maps can be easily and inexpensively obtained, whether for a specific use or for the building of a map library. Small-scale maps come from a great variety of sources. Oil-company road maps, usually at scales of 1: 500,000 to 1: 1,500,000, are available at most gas stations. Some show little more than the main roads and towns, but others locate points of interest and may use a shaded-relief base. Road maps issued by state and provincial governments may include additional details, such as railroad lines. Popular organizations like the National Geographic Society publish finely detailed maps of areas around the world, and school and college atlases contain small-scale, full-color thematic maps.

Among the best sources for medium-scale and large-scale topographic maps are the United States Geological Survey and the Canadian Department of Energy, Mines, and Resources. These provide complete coverage at a scale of 1: 250,000 for their respective countries. They also provide extensive coverage at larger scales (1: 62,500, 1: 48,000, and 1: 24,000 for the United States and 1: 50,000 and 1: 25,000 for Canada). Local stationery and sporting-goods stores are often outlets for these government maps.

Large-scale maps are also issued by city and county surveyors' offices, chambers of commerce, transportation companies, and printing and publishing companies. They include maps of road and street systems and of local points of interest. There are also official atlases of landownership, called plat books. Copies of rare and expensive antique maps are obtainable from stores that handle books or art supplies. (For additional information on maps and globes, *see also* Directions, subhead on road maps; Geography, subhead on maps; Graphs, subhead on statistical maps; Reference Books, subhead on atlases.)

coating with a stylus, or scribe. Since only the scribed lines transmit rays of light, the result is a negative ready for photoengraving. Scribing not only bypasses one step in the traditional photoengraving process but also permits much finer control of line widths.

A black-and-white map can be prepared from a single printing plate. For colored maps, overprinting from several plates is required. On maps with subtle gradations of color, those that depict natural vegetation, for example, the three process colors—magenta, cyan, and yellow—are blended to give a full range of colors (*see* Color).

Special techniques are required for making globes. In the most common method, an interrupted map projection of the world, divided into north-south strips called gores, is printed on a sheet of paper. When wet down, these gores can be stretched and smoothed to a round shape as each is successively pasted over a spherical shell. Each hemisphere is handled separately, and the two hemispheres are then fastened together to form the complete globe. Cardboard and plastic are better shell materials than metal, because they are lighter and more flexible. Inflatable globes of plastic or rubber have been devised for greater portability.

College courses in cartography, or the science of map making, are usually offered in the departments of geography, geology, or engineering. These courses stress mapping theory. Courses in the drafting and reproduction of maps are generally offered by vocational institutes. Cartographic theory includes such topics as the history of mapping, the interpretation of the many different types of maps, aerial mapping, map design, and the mathematical principles of surveying, map projection, and statistical presentation. Government agencies generally employ cartographers who have strong backgrounds in such related fields

BIBLIOGRAPHY FOR MAPS AND GLOBES
Books for Younger Readers

Epstein, Sam and Beryl. The First Book of Maps and Globes (Watts, 1959).

Hirsch, S. C. The Globe for the Space Age (Viking, 1963).

Hirsch, S. C. Mapmakers of America (Viking, 1970).

Moore, Patrick and Brinton, Henry. Exploring Maps (Hawthorn, 1967).

Oliver, J. E. What We Find When We Look at Maps (McGraw, 1970).

Rhodes, Dorothy. How to Read a City Map (Elk Grove, 1967).

Rhodes, Dorothy. How to Read a Highway Map (Elk Grove, 1970).

Tannenbaum, Beulah and Stillman, Myra. Understanding Maps: Charting the Land, Sea and Sky (McGraw, 1969).

Books and Films for Advanced Students and Teachers

Brown, L. A. Map Making (Little, 1960).

Greenhood, David. Mapping (Univ. of Chicago Press, 1964).

The Language of Maps, film (Encyclopaedia Britannica Films).

Neal, H. E. Of Maps and Men (Funk & Wagnalls, 1970).

Raisz, Erwin. Mapping the World (Abelard, 1956).

Raisz, Erwin. Principles of Cartography (McGraw, 1962).

Robinson, A. H. and Sale, R. D. Elements of Cartography (Wiley, 1969).

(Vol. 13)   103f

MOTION PICTURES. The medium of film is sometimes called the art of the 20th century. Young people today are called the film generation—not only because motion pictures are an important part of their cultural environment but also because so many of them have been using the medium of film to express their own ideas and interests. As inexpensive film-making equipment has become available, film making has become a craft and an art to be used in the same way that writing, painting, and other arts are used—as forms of self-expression, entertainment, and social and political commentary.

Colleges now offer advanced degrees in film and film making. Underground film makers experimenting with new techniques and subjects have pushed the boundaries of the art to new limits, and commercial film makers have been influenced by their example. Subject matter once considered taboo, such as the intimate portrayal of sexual relationships, is now treated realistically in film. The medium of film—motion pictures—is one of the most influential and important of the arts of this age.

Motion pictures were first demonstrated publicly less than 100 years ago. Since then they have become a common experience in the lives of people all over the world. Probably no other form of entertainment has received such universal popular acceptance in such a short period of time. Today motion pictures are made on every continent and in most countries, and the medium of film is an important form of international communication.

The medium of film has been put to many uses. At first motion pictures were considered only a form of entertainment and a means of studying scientific problems. Today, however, they are made by both professionals and amateurs not only for entertainment but also to supplement textbook materials in schools, explain industrial and technical processes, record scientific experiments, foster government propaganda, and advertise products. In one way or another, motion pictures—in theaters, on television, and indirectly—now influence the lives of most people.

The making of a film, whether by one person or by the production team of a commercial film studio, involves both creative and technical processes, diverse skills, and many tools. Film is an extremely versatile medium: the film maker creates with movement, color, and sound; he manipulates time and space. A film can be about anything, and its subject can be presented in a wide range of styles, including the factual, the dramatic, the narrative, the poetic, the fantastic, and the nonobjective. Film can also incorporate many other mediums—such as music, painting, drama, literature, and dance.

TOOLS OF FILM MAKING

ALL MOTION PICTURES are based on an illusion of motion made possible by a characteristic of the eye called *persistence of vision*. The image of an object remains on the retina of the eye for $\frac{1}{16}$ to $\frac{1}{10}$ of a second after the eye has stopped looking at it. When a series of pictures of an object is presented in steady, rapid succession, with the position of the object slightly altered in each picture to represent successive stages of movement, the eye blends the different pictures into one another, creating the illusion of motion.

A simple way to demonstrate the illusion of motion is to draw a line in the lower right-hand corner of each page of a pad of paper, altering the angle of each line very slightly in a single direction. If the pages are then riffled at a rather fast pace, the eye will perceive the illusion of a moving line.

In motion pictures, persistence of vision is used to create the illusion of motion from still photographs. By means of a shutter that opens and closes at high speed, the motion-picture camera photographs a series of still images (*see* Photography, Cameras and Their Operation in). Because the time lapse between images is only $\frac{1}{50}$ of a second in most cameras, the differences between images are small. The illusion of motion is provided by the projector, in which the film is moved past a light source at the same speed at which the images were photographed. Persistence of vision causes the separate images to be projected as a continuously moving scene. If there were no separations between images, the pictures would appear as a blur.

The Camera

The primary film-making tool is the camera, by which images are recorded on film. Within the camera the unexposed film is housed in a totally dark chamber, the *forward magazine*. One or both edges of the film are lined with regularly spaced perforations, or *sprocket holes*. Sprocket-driven gears grip the perforations, feeding the film into an enclosed exposure chamber. A mechanical claw pulls the film into position behind the shutter, locking the film in place. The shutter opens, exposes an image on the film, and closes. Then the claw, with an automatic pulldown movement, advances the film for the next exposure.

By means of this *intermittent motion* the film is exposed 24 times a second at sound speed. Each exposure is a single still photograph, or *frame*. As the film moves through the camera, the exposed sections are fed into the *rear magazine*, which is another totally dark chamber.

Lenses

The camera lens transmits the image being photographed to the film. Different lenses produce different

This article was contributed by Samuel Allen, author and editor of educational articles and films, and reviewed by Raymond Fielding, Professor of Communications, Department of Radio-Television-Film, Temple University, and by Lewis Jacobs, film maker, film teacher, film critic, and film historian.

504 (Vol. 14)

kinds of images. For each scene, the film maker selects a lens that will give the kind of image he wants the audience to see.

The *focal length* of a lens affects the size of the image transmitted to the film and the depth of field of the image—the relative sharpness of objects in the image. (For an explanation of focal length, *see* Lens; Photography, Cameras and Their Operation in.) A *wide-angle lens* has a short focal length and is used to obtain broad, distant views of a subject. A *long lens* has a long focal length and provides a closer view of the subject. With a *telephoto lens*, which has an even longer focal length, a close-up view of a distant subject can be obtained. The focal length of the *zoom lens* is variable —it can be increased or decreased at will. The zoom lens is particularly useful in making newsreels, documentaries, and wildlife pictures, when it is not always possible for the film maker to shoot at a distance close to his subject. It also enables him to alter the distance to his subject during one take, or shot. Zoom lenses are also used on projectors in order to fill the screen exactly.

As a lens transmits an image to film, it reduces the size of the image. During this process the lens refracts, or bends, the light rays of the image, causing some linear distortion in the photograph. A *normal lens* provides an image in which the horizontal and vertical lines appear almost straight and the objects within the frame appear in normal perspective and proportion. Other lenses are intentionally used to emphasize distortion, thereby creating special effects. A *fisheye lens* is a wide-angle lens that bends horizontal and vertical lines and distorts relationships within the frame. It is effectively used to portray such things as fantasies, dream sequences, and danger. A *multiply-*

ing lens produces a number of images of the same object side by side.

Lenses also affect how movement is perceived on film. Normal lenses appear to reproduce movement realistically. With lenses of greater focal length, movement toward and away from the camera appears to contract, or telescope, inward. With a lens of short focal length, movement appears faster than normal.

Film

The film on which images are made is a strip of cellulose acetate coated with a light-sensitive emulsion that retains images (*see* Cellulose; Photography, Cameras and Their Operation in, sections on film). Film is generally classified by its width. Most theatrical motion pictures are photographed in 35-mm. or 70-mm. (wide-screen) film. Virtually all commercial production is done in 16-mm. film. Amateur and experimental film makers often use 8-mm. or 16-mm. film. The larger the size of the film, the better the quality of the image obtained.

Film raw stock is also graded according to its sensitivity to light. A *fast*, or high-speed, *film* requires less light to retain an image than a *slow*, or low-speed, *film*. Since the grains of emulsion on fast film are larger than those on slow film, fast film generally has a grainier appearance when projected. Fast film provides a low degree of contrast between black and white tones; slow film provides a greater range of brightness and darkness.

An early Technicolor process used three separate films in the camera, each recording the image of a primary color. After development, the three negatives were printed together on a composite color print. All

Side view of a motion-picture camera (left): Film from the forward magazine is fed into a chamber behind the lens, where a film pulldown movement locks each frame in place for exposure. The film is then rewound in the rear magazine. The matte box houses filters and light modulators. Cameraman's view (right): A dissolving shutter lever enables dissolves to be made within the camera. A synchronous motor assures constant speed, which is measured by the tachometer.

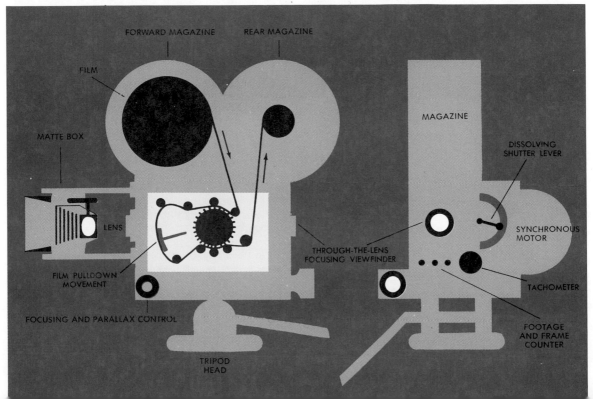

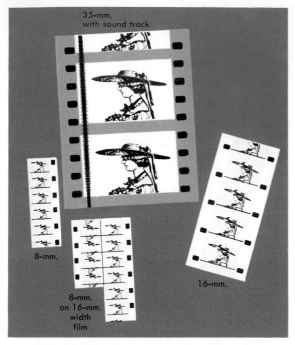

The most common motion-picture film sizes are those above, plus 70-mm., used for wide-screen projection. In production of a sound track (below), a microphone converts sound into electrical impulses. In magnetic recording, the impulses influence a magnetic field, the variations of which appear as a pattern on magnetized film. In optical recording, the impulses control the amount of light reaching sensitized film.

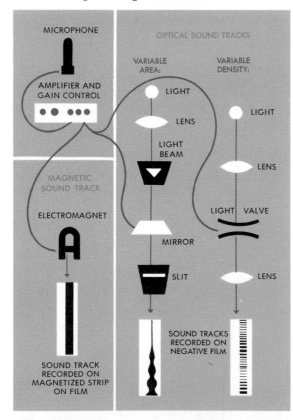

color film production today, however, is done with integral-tripack emulsions, for which only one film is needed.

Most film used in the camera is negative film: as in the negatives of a snapshot, light areas appear dark, and dark areas appear light. For projection, positive prints are made from the negative film. All 16-mm. color film used for conventional production, however, is reversal positive.

Sound Equipment

In a finished motion picture, all sound is provided by a *sound track* that is part of the film. The sound track runs the length of the film on one side, parallel to the photographed images. The sound, however, is not originally recorded on the film with the images. It may be recorded either on *magnetic tape* or on *magnetic film*. If sound is first recorded on magnetic tape, it is later transferred to magnetic film for editing and final rerecording (see Tape Recorder). The film containing the sound track is called the *sound negative*. To form the *projection print*, the sound negative and the *picture*, or *action negative*, are printed together on a single positive film known as a *composite*, or *married print*.

The Projector

The chief mechanical parts of the projector are the *picture head* and the *soundhead*. By even-paced jerks, the film is drawn from its reel, in the *upper magazine*, past the lens of the picture head. As each frame comes into position behind the lens, it is held still for an instant; a shutter opens, allowing a beam of light to pass through the film and the lens and so project the image onto the screen. When the shutter closes, the film is jerked down by the Geneva pulldown movement, and the next frame is positioned behind the lens. When the film is projected at the same speed at which it was photographed, the motion seen on the screen is exactly the same as the motion that was photographed. Slow- and fast-motion effects are produced by filming at speeds slower and faster than normal. This is called undercranking and overcranking the camera.

After passing through the picture head, the film is drawn through the soundhead, where a narrow beam of light is projected through the sound track onto a photoelectric cell. The variations in density or area on the sound track are converted by the cell into electrical impulses. These impulses are strengthened by amplifiers and then carried by wire to the loudspeakers, where they are then converted into vibrations of sound.

When film passes through the soundhead, it is moving continuously and smoothly, rather than intermittently, since any interruption or variation in speed would be heard. Because the soundhead is some distance away from the picture head on the projector, the sound track for each frame is printed exactly 20 frames ahead of the corresponding picture in 35-mm. production and 26 frames ahead in 16-mm. produc-

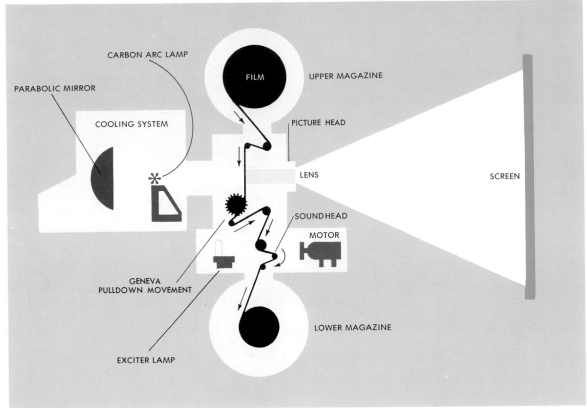

Within a projector's picture head, a Geneva pulldown movement positions and briefly stops each frame of film behind the lens. A shutter allows an arc lamp to cast an image on the screen.

Within the soundhead, the beam of an exciter lamp passes through the sound track onto a photoelectric cell, generating electrical impulses that are converted into sound.

tion. The film passes from the soundhead to a second reel that is housed in the *lower magazine*, where it is rewound.

The length of a film is measured in feet. There are 16 frames in each foot of 35-mm. film and 40 frames in each foot of 16-mm. film. Therefore, 90 feet of 35-mm. film and 36 feet of 16-mm. film will pass through the projector every minute at the standard sound projection speed of 24 frames per second. A feature-length film lasting 100 minutes is 9,000 feet long. In order to make the handling of films more convenient,

they are divided into reels; a single reel may carry up to 2,000 feet of film.

Projection booths in commercial motion-picture theaters are equipped with at least two projectors. While one reel is being shown, another can be threaded on the second projector. *Changeover cues*, such as a small dot in the corner of the picture, warn the projectionist when one reel is coming to an end and when to start the second projector. In this way a film can be presented without interruption, and the audience is unaware of the changeover from one reel to another.

CREATIVE ELEMENTS OF FILM

Whether a film is made by a large motion-picture studio, a small group of craftsmen working together, or a single individual, it is created through an important combination of four basic elements: story, direction, camera work, and editing. An individual film maker may write his own film story, plan and execute his own camera work, and edit his own film. Many experimental film makers, interested in developing new film techniques and styles, operate in this way. In a commercial studio, however, each of these jobs usually is carried out by different individuals and production crews under the overall supervision of a *producer*.

STORY AND SCRIPT

A film subject can be past, present, or future events; a family, a group of people, or an individual; and a portrayal of social conditions, an influence of an idea or a philosophy, or just a mood. The treatment of a subject may be romantic, analytical, subjective, or objective; it may be realistic, fantastic, serious, or humorous; or it may be an interpretation of a subject from a certain viewpoint.

Some motion-picture stories are originals, written specifically for the medium of film. Others are adapted from stage and television plays, novels, short

(Vol. 14) 507

stories, biographies, and other published materials; the studio or film maker buys the right to adapt these materials for the screen. Some studios employ scouts or readers to search for stories that they think might be suitable.

The adaptation of a story to film is done by a *screenwriter* or, frequently, by several writers. The *script*, or *screenplay*, is like a blueprint for the entire film production: it details all spoken dialogue or narration, visual images that will be shown on the screen, and all other sounds that will be heard on the sound track.

Structurally, the script is composed of numbered scenes and sequences. A *scene* is a continuous, unified action occurring at a single time and place. It is usually composed of a series of shots, but it may be only a single shot. (A *shot*, or *take*, is generally described as what is photographed during a single running of the camera.) A *sequence* is a group of scenes making up a dramatic unit of the film; it is comparable to an act in a play. For each shot and scene in the script, the writer specifies the action to take place, the kind of image he visualizes on the screen (such as a close-up or a distance shot), and the details of both setting and sound that he wants to have emphasized.

The script that is used in the making of a film is known as the *shooting script*. During the course of film production the script may undergo many changes at the hands of the director, the cameraman, and the film editor. A few film makers use no script at all but improvise as they go along.

THE DIRECTOR

The *director* is traditionally the person who has almost total control of the production of a film. He translates the material in the script into a motion picture. Some directors work closely with the writer in the development of the script; others write their own scripts.

The director must be able to envision the entire finished film, including sound and visual images, before photography and recording begin. In preparation for shooting the film, he works with art directors, costume designers, and other specialists in planning sets and scenes. For the shooting of a film, he chooses a cameraman whose particular skills and talents will give him the kind of photography he wants. The director controls the composition of each frame, the lighting of each scene, and the pace and rhythm of each movement. He works with the film editor to determine which shots and sequences will be used. He also decides what kinds of supportive elements, such as sound effects and music, are most suitable for the film.

Film has been called a director's medium. Many of the greatest motion pictures have been made by directors who conceived their own film stories, controlled all aspects of a film's production, and produced films in an individual, unique style. The work of an individual director frequently can be identified in various ways: by the kinds of ideas, themes, and stories he presents; by the types of visual images he uses; by the way in which the camera is used; by the styles of acting employed; and by the pace of his films.

FILM CREWS

The making of a motion picture may involve a large crew of men and women specializing in different crafts, particularly if the film is made in one of the large studios. The director may be aided by an assistant manager and a unit manager. Detailed records of shots and scenes are kept by a *script clerk*. The mounting, placing, and operating of lighting equipment are handled by *electricians*. *Grip men* are re-

For various reasons, including greater authenticity, many films are shot on location. Martin Ritt's outdoor drama 'Hud' (1963), for example, was actually filmed in Texas, the setting called for by the screenplay.

Bradley Smith—Photo Researchers

sponsible for moving scenery and camera equipment. *Propmen* take care of items used on sets, such as furniture. Studio property departments maintain large stocks of furnishings of all kinds; propmen refurbish old props for new productions and make new props according to picture requirements.

Scenery and costumes for films are the responsibility of an *art director*. If a script calls for sets that must be constructed at the film studio, *set designers* use the script as a guide to draw up blueprints and sketches.

Clothing and costumes may be especially designed by *costume designers*, or they may be rented or taken from a stock of costumes kept by the studio. The garments being used are cared for by *wardrobe supervisors*. Male and female hairstyles and makeup for the face and other parts of the body are created by *makeup artists*.

ACTORS AND ACTING

The choosing of actors and actresses has been handled in two ways by film makers. For many years, particularly in the United States, actors for leading roles were chosen primarily for their box-office appeal. They were noted as screen personalities rather than for their acting ability, and film stories were often written to suit the screen personalities of leading members of the cast. However, beginning in the 1950's in the United States, and even earlier in most European countries, acting ability became more important to many film makers. These film makers selected actors, often unknown, for their ability to portray specific roles on film. In such films the story or the message is more important than the display of personality, and the character portrayed is more important than the actor.

Many contemporary directors choose the casts for their own films. Since each director has his own way of working with actors, the actor's ability to respond to the director is usually taken into account. Some directors require that an actor conceive of his role in terms of the whole film and the ideas it presents. Other directors instruct an actor one scene at a time, without giving him an overall conception of the total film.

Acting for film requires techniques different from those required for the stage. Unlike a stage actor, the film actor has no live audience and therefore does not have to employ the exaggerated movements and overstatements of the stage actor. Because the camera can come in close on a film actor and can record his performance from all sides and distances, the best film performances are completely natural; any exaggerated gesture or statement appears superficial and false on film.

On the stage an actor goes through his role from beginning to end, usually in continuous chronological order. For film, however, the actor must be able to perform small scenes out of sequence and often days apart in time. For economic reasons the shooting schedule of a film is usually arranged so that all the scenes to be made at one location or on one set are

Studios have been used for most film making because light, sound, and temperature are controllable and equipment is readily available. Early in the 20th century, the innovative D. W. Griffith—here directing 'Intolerance' (1916)—set high standards in studio camera work.

filmed together, no matter what their order in the film. Since shots and scenes often last only a few minutes, the actor must work in short time units. He must be able to bring the character alive at once, even for brief periods, and to replay each shot and scene freshly and convincingly until the director is satisfied. There are also interruptions for changes in lighting, camera angles, lenses, and other details.

The way in which the actor's performance is seen by the film audience is finally determined by the film editor and the director in the editing process. The various shots and scenes made before the camera are fitted together into a final, complete performance. Because the actor is aware of this procedure, he tries to maintain the consistency of his role from scene to scene so that it will appear unified throughout the film.

CAMERA WORK: Shooting the Film

No matter how many people are involved in a film production, most of their efforts are aimed at creating images to be caught by the camera. The essence of film making is knowing how to compose the images to be filmed and how to use the camera to capture the images in exactly the desired way. This is the art of *cinematography*.

Most commercial films are a product of teamwork. In planning the photography for each shot, the director works closely with his chief cameraman, frequently called the *director of photography*. The chief cameraman brings to his job a knowledge of composition, film materials, optics, lighting, and color. Although he seldom operates the camera himself, he is responsible for the positioning of the camera (or cameras). Other members of the camera team may include an operating cameraman, who runs the camera, and an assistant cameraman, who loads it with film and mounts and focuses the lenses. On large productions there may be several of each.

(Vol. 14) 509

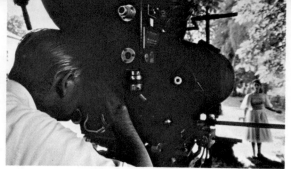

The director is responsible for all creative aspects of a motion picture, even to controlling the actual composition of each frame. Here Robert Wise carefully composes a shot of Julie Andrews in 'The Sound of Music' (1965), a film for which he won an Academy award as best director.

Although actual locations as well as full-size indoor and outdoor sets are generally used for most filming, large studios also have facilities for making and shooting scale models of various sizes for special effects, which have the appearance of reality in a completed film.

By courtesy of The Rank Organization

Some film makers—particularly pioneers in the field and modern experimentalists—have been sufficiently skilled in the techniques of cinematography to create fine films almost single-handedly. In doing their own camera work, they have often developed new techniques and photographic effects.

The kind of camera used depends on the kind of filming to be done. Large studio cameras are heavy and difficult to move. Smaller, lightweight cameras are made to be hand held during shooting, and some of them are soundproof. Hand-held cameras are usually powered by batteries, allowing the cameraman considerable freedom of movement, while studio cameras require an external power source. Generally, the larger, heavier cameras are capable of running longer without reloading than the smaller models.

Composing the Shots

A film is composed of images that change from frame to frame. In composing each shot, the film maker must consider how each image will relate to the images that precede and follow it and how he might direct the viewer's eyes exactly where he wants them. Most shots are filmed several times to make sure that the director gets what he wants; each filming of a shot is a take. The composition of a shot involves the placement and movement of people and objects in the frame, the position and movement of the camera, and the lighting of the subject to be photographed.

By the skillful placement and movement of people and objects, the film maker can overcome the two-dimensional limitations of film. The relationship of foreground to background objects provides an in-depth perspective, which can be enhanced by movement toward and away from the camera. An *extended image*, showing a portion of a person or an object emerging from the edge of the frame, suggests that the image extends beyond the boundaries of the frame.

For each shot, the film maker plans how far from the subject his camera will be, what kind of lens he will use, and the viewpoint, or angle, from which the shot will be made. Camera distance and the lens determine the relative sizes of human figures and objects in the image. A shot in which figures appear small against their background is a *long shot;* a *medium shot* shows full figures just within the limits of the frame; a *medium-close shot* shows one figure from the waist up; a *close-up,* only the face; and a *big close-up,* only a portion of the face. The master shot usually shows an entire set in order to locate and give perspective to the other shots. Because of the mobility of both the subject and the camera, the distinctions between these different kinds of shots are not always clear.

The angle of a shot depends upon the effect the film maker is trying to achieve. For example, a shot taken from above can make a figure appear insignificant; one taken from below can make a figure appear important—and often menacing. A shot may be made by moving the camera in a number of ways or from a

510 (Vol. 14)

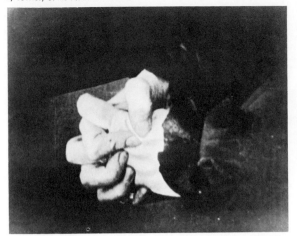

Pioneer director D. W. Griffith was responsible for developing many major film effects. For example, he exploited the use of close-ups to enhance emotional impact, as in the close-up

of wringing hands from 'Intolerance' (1916), and long- and high-angle shots, as in the spectacular Babylonian temple scene from the same film.

single viewpoint with a stationary camera. The *head*, a device mounted on the camera's tripod, allows the camera to be turned smoothly in the arc of a complete circle; this horizontal movement is known as *panning*. The head also permits the camera to be turned up or down through a 90-degree angle in a movement known as *tilting*. Panning and tilting are the basic movements of the camera from a fixed position.

So that it can be moved forward, backward, or diagonally during shooting, the camera, together with its tripod, is mounted on a *dolly*, which is any sort of cart or platform with noiseless wheels that is manually maneuvered by crew members. Shots made from a dolly are *dolly*, *tracking*, *trucking*, or *perambulator shots*. Some shots in large studios are made from power-operated *camera cranes* that can move over a wide area. The camera and the camera operator are housed in a cockpit that can be raised, lowered, and moved sideways, or horizontally. To obtain the shots they want, some film makers mount their cameras on automobiles, railroad cars, airplanes, or other moving objects. The development of lightweight, noiseless hand-held cameras in recent years has freed many film makers from dependence on mechanical mobility, and an increasing number of films involve hand-held camera work, at least in part.

Lighting

An image is exposed on film by means of the light that passes through the camera's lens when the shutter is open. How the image appears on film depends on how the subject is illuminated. Light brings out contours, creates depth and mood, and gives dramatic effect. Because images on motion-picture film are constantly changing, each shot presents particular lighting problems. By controlling the intensity, direction, and diffusion of light, the film maker models his images.

The amount and kind of light needed depend on the effect the film maker is trying to achieve and on the

film raw stock he is using. To determine the light needed, the film maker uses a *light meter* to measure the intensity of the light falling on his subject or scene (*see* Photography, Cameras and Their Operation in, section on light meters). The lighting differs for each plane of light from the foreground to the horizon. The film maker must always keep in mind that both the intensity and the quality of any light vary as the camera angle is changed.

The main source of illumination is called the *key light;* the direction from which it comes is always of major importance in composing any shot. The key light is frequently supplemented by subsidiary lighting from any direction.

The chief source of light for outdoor shooting is sunlight. Indoors, light is furnished by carbon arc lamps, incandescent bulbs, and quartz bulbs, mounted in a variety of housings. The basic indoor lights are *spotlights* and *floodlights*. Spotlights throw a beam of concentrated, intense light over a small area; they can be directed and focused at will. Floodlights disperse a soft light over a wide area and are used primarily to fill in the shadows caused by spotlights; they can also be directed by manipulation of the reflective material around the bulb.

To further soften, diffuse, and direct light, various devices are used. Outdoors, metal reflectors are positioned to direct and change the quality of sunlight. Cloths and canopies may be used to soften sunlight. Indoors, frosted glass, gelatin, silk, or gauze may be placed over the lamps or the camera's lens to modify harsh light or alter tones. Lens filters are used for the same purpose (*see* Photography, Cameras and Their Operation in, section on filters).

Special Techniques in Filming

Many techniques have been devised for overcoming problems in shooting films and for saving production costs. *Process shots* enable a film maker to combine action shots taken in one location with background

(Vol. 14) 511

shots taken in another, or with backgrounds of painted scenes or still photographs. Sometimes this is accomplished by *background projection:* the action being filmed is performed in front of a transparent screen on which a motion picture of the background is being projected from the rear. To save costs the background picture may be stock footage from a film library. Scale models are frequently used to create such special effects as earthquakes, floods, burning cities, explosions, and living dinosaurs.

In the *matte process* the foreground and the background components are photographed on different strips of film, and the desired parts of each are combined in the laboratory through either optical or bi-pack printing. The matte process is sometimes used to show an actor playing two roles in the same scene or to combine shots of studio sets with shots of scale models, paintings, or photographs. In another type of matte process, which is used infrequently, a portion of film is masked out during the shooting of a scene; then the film is removed and reshot with the already exposed portion masked out.

Other special techniques include varying the camera speed to obtain slow- and fast-motion effects and using multiple exposures of the film in order to superimpose one image upon another. Experimental film makers have devised many unusual techniques, such as showing multiple images within a single frame. The final criterion of a successful camera technique is whether it accomplishes the purpose of the film maker.

SOUND

The sound tracks of most films are made up of both *synchronous sound*—sound recorded as the film is being shot—and *postsynchronous sound*—sound recorded and added after shooting. Separate sound tracks are usually made for dialogue (the *voice track*), music, and sound effects. These tracks are later combined into the final sound track during a *mix*, or rerecording, session.

Synchronous Sound

Both dialogue and sound effects may be recorded during shooting, but sound effects are usually added later. Synchronous sound today is recorded on either magnetic film or tape. On magnetic film perfect synchronization between the picture and the sound can be achieved only if the film and the tape are moving at the same speed. Otherwise, dialogue will not correspond with the lip movements of the actors, and sound effects will not match the action in the film. Synchronous motors on both camera and recorder, as well as the same sort of perforations on both the magnetic film and the camera film, assure synchronization, or sync.

If, however, magnetic tape is used, it is impossible to run both the tape and the camera at exactly the same speed because the tape both shrinks and expands and is unperforated. Instead, a pulse-sync signal is generated by the camera and recorded on the tape along with the dialogue. This signal is used later in the laboratory to allow for proper resynchronization when the tape-recorded sound is transferred to magnetic perforated film for editing and rerecording purposes.

Recording is handled by a sound crew. While shooting is in progress, a sound engineer, called a *mixer*, watches the action and regulates the volume and the balance of voices by means of an electronic console. Other members of the sound crew adjust microphones to follow the action and to keep them out of the camera's range. In recording dialogue, the sound crew must ensure that the sound of each voice is consistent throughout the film, the direction from which voices come corresponds with the movement of the actors, and the sound perspective—the distance from which sound is heard—matches the visual perspective.

Postsynchronous Sound

Sometimes dialogue recorded during shooting is used only as a guide for a voice track made in a recording studio. The actors' scenes are projected in the studio over and over again until the actors can exactly match the timing of the synchronous track. Then their lines are newly recorded on magnetic film for inclusion in a final voice track. This process is known as *dubbing*.

Lighting is used by film makers to charge a scene with mood or dramatic effect. Sweden's best-known director, Ingmar Bergman, for example, captured a sense of foreboding in a twilight scene from 'The Seventh Seal' (1956).

In 'Suspense' (1913), director Phillips Smalley, in addition to incorporating all the typical D. W. Griffith effects, used a matte process to create the screen's first triptych.

Dubbing is also used to provide translated voice tracks for foreign films and to substitute the voices of singers for the voices of actors unable to perform the songs in a musical. For musical films in which the action of numbers of singers and dancers makes it impossible to obtain clear synchronous sound, a process called *photography to playback* is used. The music is first recorded in a studio and then played back on the film set, the performers matching their actions to what they hear.

Some films use a narrator to tell part of the story or, as in educational and documentary films, to provide information. In such films the narration is recorded separately on tape and later edited into the sound track.

Sound Effects

All film sound other than dialogue, narration, and music is called *sound effects*. Some sound effects correspond to the action in the visual image: as waves are seen breaking on the shore, the synchronous sound of breaking waves is heard. Other sound effects are used to suggest action or occurrences that are not seen in the image; such *nonsynchronous sound* can be used to expand the dimensions of what is seen. Both

Film can be edited with the help of a *Moviola*, an electronically operated machine that permits the editor to select the best shots while listening to the various sound tracks.

types of sound effects are used to heighten the sense of reality in a film—to convince the viewer that he is "there."

Sound effects are usually recorded separately in order to give the film maker complete control over what is heard. A sound-effects track is as carefully composed as a visual track to convey just what the film maker wants. After a sound-effects track is made, additional sound may be dubbed into the track if it is needed. Most standard sound effects can be obtained on tape from film-studio sound libraries. Other special or unusual sound effects may have to be created for specific uses.

Music

Music is generally used in films to support the visual images and the action. It helps create dramatic effects, emphasize rhythm, movement, and pace, and reflect and establish moods. Like some operas, some film scores contain themes or motifs that are identified with certain characters or that underlie certain scenes.

Many kinds of music for film are available on tape. When these are used, the film editor makes a music track from the tapes selected by the film maker; each selection is matched to the appropriate visual scene. Many films, however, have original musical scores composed for them. The composer may work from an edited version of the film, building his score in a series of short selections that are keyed to scenes and sequences. At other times he works with a postshooting script that indicates where music is needed. Some contemporary composers work on a film score from the beginning of filming, viewing the daily takes and building the score as filming progresses. Film composers must be aware both of how music can accentuate visual techniques and of how silences can be effectively used.

When a film score is completed, the music is performed for recording on tape. Later this tape recording is transferred to magnetic film. During the film-editing process this music track becomes part of the final sound track, which, through mixing, becomes a composite of all the tracks made for dialogue, narration, sound effects, and music.

Using an electronic console, two sound engineers, or mixers, watch the action while the filming of a scene is in progress and regulate the volume and balance of voices.

EDITING THE FILM

Editing a film consists of selecting and putting together visual images provided by the camera and aural images provided by the sound tracks to form a single, continuous film. Editing, or *cutting*, is one of the most important and creative aspects of film making. The skill and judgment of the film editor in combining and structuring thousands of shots and sounds determine whether or not the film story that emerges conveys the meaning and emotional impact intended by the writer and the director.

An individual film maker may not only write his own story and direct and shoot his own film but may also edit his own film. In film studios, however, editing is done by highly skilled professional *film editors*, who begin their work on a film by studying the script. Although editing sometimes begins only after all the shooting has been completed, usually it goes on while shooting is still in progress.

After each day's shooting, positive prints, called *rushes* or *dailies*, are made of the day's work. The director and the editor view the rushes, and the director selects from them the particular takes he wants the editor to work with. The editor uses duplicate prints of the selected takes, called *work prints*. The sound tracks he works with are also duplicates, called *work tracks*.

To enable the editor to match up the synchronous sound and visual tracks exactly, each take is identified on both the film and the sound recording as shooting begins. In one method of identifying takes, a light attached to the camera flashes, flaring up a frame, at the same time that an electronic beep sounds on the recording device. A more traditional method employs *clapper boards*, a pair of boards hinged at one end and marked with the number of the shot and the take. When shooting begins, the camera photographs the clapper boards as the identifying information is read into a microphone. Then the boards are slammed together, and the camera photographs this action at the same time as the sound is recorded. The few film makers who do not use these identification methods have to align the visual and sound tracks by eye and ear, which is very exacting work.

When the editor has aligned the photography and the synchronous sound in the order called for by the script, he is ready to cut out the takes and the shots that he wants to discard and to build up the film, shot by shot and scene by scene, from the most effective photography. How many feet of film he begins with depends on how economically the film was shot; for a feature-length film he may have to reduce hundreds of thousands of feet of film to fewer than ten thousand.

The great Russian film maker Sergei Eisenstein's 'Potemkin' (1925) deals with a mutiny aboard the warship *Potemkin* during the anticzarist Revolution of 1905. These frames illustrate the technique of montage that made him famous. Juxtaposing many shots of the massacre of civilians, he heightened the audience's emotional response.

The Museum of Modern Art

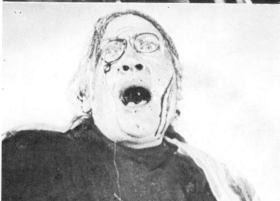

One of the basic tools of film editing is the *splicer*, on which the shots chosen by the editor are pieced together. The segments of film are joined precisely by fitting the sprocket holes in the film over metal pegs on the splicer. The final "join" is usually made with film cement. Another editing tool is the *Moviola*, an electrically operated machine on which the film may be seen and the sound tracks played either together or separately. Both the visual track and the various sound tracks can be stopped or run backward or forward at will.

Editing Techniques

The editor builds thousands of separate shots into scenes, scenes into sequences, and sequences into the full film story. By the shots he chooses and by the way he relates them to one another and cuts them together, he sets the mood, develops the action, and establishes the passage of time in each scene. The passage of time is visually indicated by the sequence of events. The normal passage of time may be interrupted by a flashback to an earlier time or a flash forward to a future time.

The most basic transition from one shot to another is the *cut:* the editor joins two shots, each of which shows different aspects of the same scene or action. The editor may compress time in a scene by *jump cutting:* to a shot showing the beginning of an action, he joins a shot showing the action being completed; what happens in between is left out. For instance, he may show an actor starting to cross a room and then show him at the other side of the room, omitting his walk through it.

The editor may also expand time by using *intercuts:* after an action has begun, he inserts shots of the action from different angles or distances, or shots showing details of the action, such as a face or an actor's hands; then he returns to the original action. He may also intercut a shot of a different setting or character; if he cuts back and forth between the original scene and the intercut scene, he is *crosscutting*. This form of parallel action is often used to create suspense. Intercutting may also be used to create a *montage sequence*—a series of brief shots that show different details of an action that occur simultaneously or that show fragments of a variety of events related to one another by the story. Montage can be used to either expand or compress the passage of time. The word "montage" in many areas of film making also means editing or cutting.

Time in a scene is also affected by the length of the shots and how rapidly or slowly they succeed one another. By progressively shortening the length of each shot in a series, the editor can create a sense of rapidly quickening time. The pace of a film can be increased by a sudden cut from one scene to an unrelated scene or by *flash cutting*, which is inserting a few almost fragmentary scenes between two longer scenes.

A change from one scene to another, or from one sequence to another, usually occurs when there is a change in the location of the action or a lapse in time or both. To link different scenes and sequences, a number of *optical effects* are used. One of these is the *fade:* the last shot in a scene gradually fades into darkness (a *fade-out*), and out of the darkness a new scene gradually appears (a *fade-in*). Another device is the *dissolve*, also called a *lap dissolve:* while one shot begins to fade out, the image of the next shot begins to appear; for a few seconds the two shots are superimposed.

In the transitional device known as the *wipe*, the last image of one scene is gradually pushed off the screen by the expanding image of the next scene. The wipe may move across the screen vertically, horizontally, or diagonally. It may move like a fan opening, burst like an exploding star in the middle of the old image, or rotate like the hands of a clock. It may begin in the center of the frame and move outward or start at the sides or at the top and bottom of the frame and move inward.

The place of these optical effects in a film is decided by the editor, who marks the film where he wants them. The technical job of creating the effect on the film is done in the film laboratory by means of an apparatus called an *optical printer*.

Editing for Sound

In building up a sound track, the editor cuts and joins segments of the work tracks just as he cuts and joins shots from the work prints to form visuals. He begins by editing the synchronous dialogue track to match the visuals, then adds nonsynchronous sounds, sound effects, and music; each of these elements may involve one or more work tracks. In preparing the sound track, the editor must determine how each sound element relates to the visual images and how it relates to previous sounds, simultaneous sounds, and the sounds that will follow it.

When all the sound tracks have been edited, the mixing is done by running all of the sound tracks in perfect synchronization through a rerecording device to produce a final sound negative for the film. A sound engineer controls the volume and balance of each component to achieve the right blend.

Revisions

A film maker may revise his work prints many times before he achieves exactly the film he wants. In a film studio the editor's first version of a film is the *rough cut*. After the director has studied the rough cut and made suggestions, the editor revises the film until he feels he has the best possible version, which is the *fine*, or *final*, *cut*. Like all work prints, the fine cut is made from duplicate film; the original film remains untouched in the film laboratory. When editing has been completed, the original film is cut to match the fine cut. From this original and the sound mix a *release*, or *composite*, print is made, containing both visuals and sound. A commercial film studio makes hundreds of such prints for distribution to movie theaters.

(Vol. 14) 515

ACADEMY AWARDS

YEAR	BEST PICTURE	BEST ACTOR	BEST ACTRESS	BEST DIRECTOR
1927–28	'Wings'	Emil Jannings	Janet Gaynor	Frank Borzage
1928–29	'The Broadway Melody'	Warner Baxter	Mary Pickford	Frank Lloyd
1929–30	'All Quiet on the Western Front'	George Arliss	Norma Shearer	Lewis Milestone
1930–31	'Cimarron'	Lionel Barrymore	Marie Dressler	Norman Taurog
1931–32	'Grand Hotel'	Fredric March & Wallace Beery	Helen Hayes	Frank Borzage
1932–33	'Cavalcade'	Charles Laughton	Katharine Hepburn	Frank Lloyd
1934	'It Happened One Night'	Clark Gable	Claudette Colbert	Frank Capra
1935	'Mutiny on the Bounty'	Victor McLaglen	Bette Davis	John Ford
1936	'The Great Ziegfeld'	Paul Muni	Luise Rainer	Frank Capra
1937	'The Life of Emile Zola'	Spencer Tracy	Luise Rainer	Leo McCarey
1938	'You Can't Take It with You'	Spencer Tracy	Bette Davis	Frank Capra
1939	'Gone with the Wind'	Robert Donat	Vivien Leigh	Victor Fleming
1940	'Rebecca'	James Stewart	Ginger Rogers	John Ford
1941	'How Green Was My Valley'	Gary Cooper	Joan Fontaine	John Ford
1942	'Mrs. Miniver'	James Cagney	Greer Garson	William Wyler
1943	'Casablanca'	Paul Lukas	Jennifer Jones	Michael Curtiz
1944	'Going My Way'	Bing Crosby	Ingrid Bergman	Leo McCarey
1945	'The Lost Weekend'	Ray Milland	Joan Crawford	Billy Wilder
1946	'The Best Years of Our Lives'	Fredric March	Olivia de Havilland	William Wyler
1947	'Gentleman's Agreement'	Ronald Colman	Loretta Young	Elia Kazan
1948	'Hamlet'	Laurence Olivier	Jane Wyman	John Huston
1949	'All the King's Men'	Broderick Crawford	Olivia de Havilland	Joseph L. Mankiewicz
1950	'All About Eve'	José Ferrer	Judy Holliday	Joseph L. Mankiewicz
1951	'An American in Paris'	Humphrey Bogart	Vivien Leigh	George Stevens
1952	'The Greatest Show on Earth'	Gary Cooper	Shirley Booth	John Ford
1953	'From Here to Eternity'	William Holden	Audrey Hepburn	Fred Zinnemann
1954	'On the Waterfront'	Marlon Brando	Grace Kelly	Elia Kazan
1955	'Marty'	Ernest Borgnine	Anna Magnani	Delbert Mann
1956	'Around the World in 80 Days'	Yul Brynner	Ingrid Bergman	George Stevens
1957	'The Bridge on the River Kwai'	Alec Guinness	Joanne Woodward	David Lean
1958	'Gigi'	David Niven	Susan Hayward	Vincente Minnelli
1959	'Ben-Hur'	Charlton Heston	Simone Signoret	William Wyler
1960	'The Apartment'	Burt Lancaster	Elizabeth Taylor	Billy Wilder
1961	'West Side Story'	Maximilian Schell	Sophia Loren	Robert Wise & Jerome Robbins
1962	'Lawrence of Arabia'	Gregory Peck	Anne Bancroft	David Lean
1963	'Tom Jones'	Sidney Poitier	Patricia Neal	Tony Richardson
1964	'My Fair Lady'	Rex Harrison	Julie Andrews	George Cukor
1965	'The Sound of Music'	Lee Marvin	Julie Christie	Robert Wise
1966	'A Man for All Seasons'	Paul Scofield	Elizabeth Taylor	Fred Zinnemann
1967	'In the Heat of the Night'	Rod Steiger	Katharine Hepburn	Mike Nichols
1968	'Oliver!'	Cliff Robertson	Katharine Hepburn & Barbra Streisand	Sir Carol Reed
1969	'Midnight Cowboy'	John Wayne	Maggie Smith	John Schlesinger
1970	'Patton'	George C. Scott	Glenda Jackson	Franklin J. Schaffner

HISTORY OF MOTION PICTURES

Motion pictures were made possible by the curiosity, the experiments, and the inventions of many men. Some were interested in how images could be projected, some in how images could be recorded on different materials, some in the phenomenon of motion itself, and some in problems of vision. Late in the 19th century their discoveries were combined by others to provide the basic tools of film. Still other men learned to use these tools and developed the art and the techniques of cinematography.

Long before anyone thought of recording moving images on films and projecting them, however, people had been fascinated by such popular entertainments as mechanical peep shows, Oriental shadow plays, and magic-lantern shows. Most of these devices told simple stories or revealed the wonders of the world by means of static drawings. Action was indicated by changes in the position of figures or objects from one picture to the next—but movement was not usually recorded, though a few experimental magic-lantern slides had intricate moving parts that did indeed suggest movement on the screen.

Inventing the Tools

The first real steps toward motion pictures were the result of experiments in the persistence of vision. Although the effects of the phenomenon had been observed for centuries, investigation of the subject was stimulated by a scientific paper presented in London, England, by Peter Mark Roget in 1824. Roget's paper, 'Persistence of Vision with Regard to Moving Objects', led investigators to try to build devices that would test his theory.

In 1832 Joseph A. F. Plateau in Ghent, Belgium, and Simon Ritter von Stampfer in Vienna, Austria, independently discovered the same method for creating the illusion of motion from a series of still pictures. They used a flat disk perforated with a number of evenly spaced slots. Around the rim of the disk on one side were an equal number of hand-drawn figures representing successive phases of movement. Holding the device with the figures facing a mirror, the viewer spun the disk and looked through the slots—and the figures reflected in the mirror appeared to move. Plateau's device, the *phenakistoscope*, and Stampfer's, the *stroboscope*, led to the invention of more elaborate devices using the same principle, such as the *zoetrope*. Such optical "toys" became popular in 19th-century homes.

The next step toward motion pictures was taken by Baron Franz von Uchatius, an Austrian military officer, who combined the revolving disk principle with the magic lantern to project a series of phased drawings on a wall or screen. Uchatius perfected his projection apparatus between 1845 and 1853. The pictures he projected could be viewed by a number of people at one time.

During the years that these men were discovering how to make pictures move and how to project them,

others were pioneering in the development of photography (*see* Photography, History of). By the middle of the 19th century, still photographs began to replace drawings on optical disks. However, due to the long exposure time required by the wet-plate process then in use, each phase of a motion had to be posed and photographed separately. By 1870, inventors in the United States and England had developed devices in which posed photographs of motion, mounted on a revolving disk, passed between a light source and a lens for projection for an audience. These mechanisms created an illusion of motion, but it was not yet possible for the photographer to capture on film the objects in motion.

By 1877 the increased speed of photographic emulsions and improved camera shutters made it possible to photograph rapid motions. The men who did this were interested in motion rather than in photography. To study the gait of a running horse, Eadweard Muybridge, an English-born photographer, set up on

(Left) The Museum of Modern Art, (right and bottom) Culver Pictures

In 19th-century homes the *zoetrope* or "wheel of life" (left), Plateau's *phenakistoscope*, or "deceiver-scope" (above), and the elaborate *praxinoscope* (below) were but three of many popular optical "toys" based on the persistence of vision. In such simple devices the capacity was limited to a brief cycle of movement, and the bands of drawings were usually of dancers, clowns, jugglers, or performing pets.

(Vol. 14) 517

Eadweard Muybridge's photographic method of tripping a battery of 12 cameras with electrical shutter controls was used in 1877 to record the motion of a running horse. In a later experiment he increased the number of cameras to 24.

a racetrack in California a row of 12 cameras that had electric shutter controls. As a horse ran by the cameras, it tripped strings that activated the shutters and exposed the plates. Within a few years Muybridge repeated the experiment using 24 cameras. In this way the first instantaneous photographs of unposed, continuous motion were made.

Muybridge's photographs were exhibited in the United States and Europe as slides projected by a magic-lantern-type apparatus. His work led to many experiments in motion photography aimed at achieving the same results with a single camera. This was first accomplished in 1882 by a Frenchman, Étienne

In 1882 the French physician Marey invented a "photographic gun" for the scientific purpose of shooting such moving objects as birds and animals.

Jules Marey, who was also studying the movement of living things. Marey invented a "photographic gun," shaped like a rifle but with a lens in the muzzle and photographic dry plates in the chamber. With only one pull of its trigger, 12 exposures were made in rapid succession. Marey later improved the gun by using emulsified paper film instead of dry plates and was able to take about 100 pictures a second. His paper film, however, could not be projected.

The next important step in taking pictures was the development of a light-sensitive emulsion on Celluloid film. This was achieved by the Rev. Hannibal Goodwin, an American amateur photographer from Newark, N. J., in 1887. A short time later George Eastman, also an American, marketed and promoted a similar transparent, flexible film to be used with the Kodak camera that he had invented. Celluloid film, though highly flammable, could be manufactured in continuous fashion, rapidly exposed by intermittent motion, quickly passed through a projecting device, and easily wound.

The first men to use Celluloid film for motion pictures were the American inventor Thomas A. Edison and his assistant William K. L. Dickson, who were trying to provide visual illustrations to supplement the sound recordings of the phonograph. By 1891 they had developed the *kinetograph*, a motion-picture camera using Eastman film. To view the film, the Edison laboratory developed the *Kinetoscope*, a peepshow type of machine in a cabinet. One viewer at a time could look at the pictures through an eyepiece. The machine ran a continuous 50-foot loop of 35-mm. film driven by sprockets. A revolving shutter allowed a brief glimpse of each image. On April 14, 1894, the first Kinetoscope parlor opened at 1155 Broadway in New York City. It was an arcade containing banks of Kinetoscope machines, which featured motion pictures of vaudeville acts, wild West and circus shows, and other entertainments. They were filmed at the "Black Maria," the world's first motion-picture studio, built by Edison at West Orange, N. J., in 1892–93. By the end of 1894, other Kinetoscope parlors had opened in the United States and Europe. (*See also* Edison.)

The success of Edison's machines inspired other experimenters to improve on his devices and to try to find a means of projecting films for large audiences. In 1895 a number of new motion-picture cameras and projection devices—some within the same machine—were demonstrated in the United States and Europe. The most successful was the *Cinématographe* —a combination camera, printer, and projector—invented by Louis and Auguste Lumière in France. They gave their first private film show in March 1895, and in December they began public showings at the Grand Café in Paris. These were almost immediately popular, and in 1896 the Lumières converted a room at the café into the world's first cinema theater. The Cinématographe spread rapidly through Europe, and in 1896 it was imported by the United States.

To meet the competition of films projected on a screen, Edison arranged to manufacture the *vitascope*, a projector developed by Thomas Armat and Charles Francis Jenkins in the United States. The Armat-Jenkins projector was the first American one to use the principle of intermittent motion, allowing each frame to remain stationary on the screen for a brief time. Like the Europeans, Edison also developed a portable motion-picture camera that could take films anywhere. On April 23, 1896, Edison's first public performance using the vitascope opened at Koster and Bial's Music Hall in New York City with films of prizefighters, dancing girls, a scene from a play, and ocean waves. With the development of the vitascope, all of the basic tools of cinematography were finally available to the film maker.

Early Films: The Silent Era Begins

The novelty of the first motion pictures quickly wore off and inspired film makers to all kinds of experiments with the camera to keep their audiences. Both the length and the variety of films had increased by the turn of the century. Film makers learned how to fake prizefights, news events, and foreign settings, and they freely borrowed one anoth-

The "Black Maria," built by the American inventor Thomas A. Edison at West Orange, N. J., in 1892, was the world's first motion-picture studio.

er's ideas and plots, since the copyright law in the United States did not apply to motion pictures until 1912. Some film makers, however, provided actual coverage of news events, such as the inauguration of President William McKinley and action at the front in the Boer War. Travelogues were filmed all over the world, filmed advertisements began to appear, and short science films were made with the aid of the microscope.

By 1905 many of the basic techniques of cinematography and film editing had been tried. At first, action was filmed only by a single camera operating from a fixed position. Gradually, film makers learned how to pan, intercut two different scenes, use the close-up, and create dissolves and other effects with their lenses.

One of the most important film pioneers was Georges Méliès, a French magician who explored all kinds of visual tricks in both shooting and editing his film. By utilizing double exposure, mattes, fades, slow and fast motion, animation, and miniature models, he created film fantasies that were the forerunners of science fiction and underground motion pictures. He was one of the first film makers to develop imagi-

The *Kinetoscope*, invented by Edison, was patented in 1893. In the following year the first Kinetoscope parlor—an arcade of peep-show machines—was opened at 1155 Broadway in New York City.

'The Giant Devil' (1902) was one of several films of ingenious theatrical conception by the Frenchman Georges Méliès, the world's first truly inventive film maker. Porter's 'Great Train Robbery' (1903), the earliest real American attempt to tell a story, remains one of the classics of the screen. 'The Starving Artist' (1907) was typical of the many short films produced by the American Vitograph Corporation that helped make the Nickelodeon Age so popular.

native storytelling at length and to use a series of related short scenes to build up a narrative. Some of his films, such as 'A Trip to the Moon' (1902), were popular throughout the world and influenced many subsequent film makers.

While Méliès staged many of his films indoors, film makers in England developed fiction films shot outdoors and pioneered the "chase" film, in which characters pursue one another through different scenes. Méliès' narrative form and the English chase were combined by Edwin S. Porter, a cameraman and director at Edison's studio. Porter's 'Great Train Robbery' (1903) abandoned a chronological sequence of events, showed different actions that occurred simultaneously, and in outdoor scenes had actors move toward and away from the camera. The camera was mounted for a time on the roof of a train. Excitement and effective continuity made the film immensely popular.

By the turn of the century, motion pictures had become an entertainment primarily for workingmen and the poorly educated. In the United States, films moved out of vaudeville houses and arcades into storefront theaters that charged a nickel for admission. The Thomas Talley Theater opened in Los Angeles, Calif., in 1902; and within a few years, there were thousands of *nickelodeons*—a name coined by two storefront operators in Pittsburgh, Pa.—all over the country. The basic fare of the nickelodeon was one- or two-reel comedies and melodramas.

The Early Film Industry

In the United States, film production was first centered around New York City and Chicago, Ill., but the varied scenery, sunny climate, and impressive land of southern California soon attracted film crews. William Selig set up a studio in a rented building in Los Angeles in 1907 and built the first permanent studio there in 1911. The producers who established the Los Angeles area as a major film center included both independent producers and members of the Mo-

tion Picture Patents Company, a trust incorporated by ten companies on Sept. 9, 1908. Until the trust was dissolved by court order in 1917, it attempted to control the American film industry by regulating the length of films, admission prices and film rental fees, salaries, and standards of production. The trust was largely responsible for limiting American film production to short melodramas and comedies.

In continental Europe, however, producers began turning out five- and ten-reel films of literary classics and made the first experiments with feature films. The French Film d'Art starred noted stage performers in famous roles. In 1912 Adolph Zukor, an independent American exhibitor, defied the trust by importing 'Queen Elizabeth', a four-reel Film d'Art production starring the French stage actress Sarah Bernhardt. In 1913 another importer presented 'Quo Vadis?', a spectacular Italian feature in nine reels. The success of such films helped weaken the control of the trust and encouraged American film makers to produce more ambitious pictures. Zukor formed the Famous Players Company, similar to the Film d'Art in presenting stage performers.

Silent Film Matures

The potentialities of silent film were developed primarily by D. W. Griffith, a young actor who began his career as a director of melodramas. In the many one- and two-reel films he produced between 1908 and 1913, he experimented with camera and editing techniques. In 1913 he defied orders to make only two-reel films by secretly filming a four-reel spectacle, 'Judith of Bethulia', and in 1915 he released the first film epic, 'The Birth of a Nation', which ran almost three hours.

Griffith developed the intercutting of parallel action, the extreme wide-angle shot, the thematic close-up, and the construction of scenes and sequences from fragmentary shots taken at different angles. He introduced both backlighting and reflectors to kill shadows. He was also one of the first film

520   (Vol. 14)

makers to plan a recorded musical accompaniment keyed carefully to the entire film. 'The Birth of a Nation' was widely popular, established film as an art form, and set new standards for American film making. Some of Griffith's other major films were 'Intolerance' (1916), 'Broken Blossoms' (1919), 'Way Down East' (1920), and 'Orphans of the Storm' (1922).

The demand of audiences for longer films and the desire of creative film makers to work in their own way led men like Griffith to form their own production companies and fostered the rise of independent producers. About 1910, the independents began promoting their leading players as stars—a practice avoided by the trust to keep down players' salaries. Noted stage actors were offered large sums to appear in films, and Griffith and others trained many performers as screen stars. To meet increased production costs, the film industry sought a new audience—the middle class—by showing films in large, comfortable theaters. The opening of the ornate Strand Theater on Broadway in 1914 ushered in the era of the "movie palace."

Contemporary with Griffith among the producers and directors of popular silent films was Mack Sennett, whose slapstick comedies employed techniques developed by Griffith. Some of Sennett's comedians —such as Charlie Chaplin, Ben Turpin, Fatty Arbuckle, Ford Sterling, and Mabel Normand—became top-ranking stars. Chaplin also became renowned as a director of his own films, in which he resisted the trend to make longer pictures; he did not make a feature-length film until 1921. He also emphasized characters in his films rather than performers.

Another noted director and producer of the time was Thomas H. Ince, who, as head of the largest studio in Hollywood, Calif., evolved the detailed script as a means of controlling every aspect of production. His organization of studio operations into an efficient, businesslike system was adopted by most other studios. He was best noted for producing exciting Westerns starring William S. Hart.

World War I and After

By the beginning of World War I, films were being made in most European countries and in Japan. When the war interrupted European film making, however, the American film industry began to dominate the world market. In the years between 1917 and 1927 the silent film reached the peak of its development. Hollywood films became increasingly expensive to make as productions became more lavish and spectacular and as the stars who drew audiences demanded enormous salaries—and sometimes part of the profits. More and more large cinemas were built,

Although the names of actors were not revealed in the early silent films, fans soon demanded to know who their favorites were—and the star system was born. By the time Mary Pickford made 'Rebecca of Sunnybrook Farm' (1917), Richard Barthelmess and Lillian Gish 'Broken Blossoms' (1919), and Stan Laurel and Oliver Hardy 'The Finishing Touch' (1928), all had an adoring public.

(Top and center) The Museum of Modern Art, (bottom) Culver Pictures

Culver Pictures

The Bettmann Archive

and the major producers expanded their distributing systems and bought entire chains of theaters.

Major studios attempted to produce a picture a week. A typical film show consisted of a feature starring big-name players, a short comedy, and a newsreel. Such spectacles as Cecil B. DeMille's 'Ten Commandments' (1923) were popular exceptions and ran for several hours. Most of the films made during this period reflected the fast pace and materialistic concerns of the nation's prosperous "flapper" era. While settings and costumes were often elaborate, film stories were often shallow. Most people went to the "movies" to see film stars, and it was often the star who saved a poor film from being a total failure. Some stars, seeking freedom from the mass-production methods of large studios, banded together to form distributing companies to market films they made in their own studios. United Artists, formed in 1919 by Griffith, Chaplin, Douglas Fairbanks, and Mary Pickford, became known for the high standards of the films it distributed.

The production of films gained momentum once more in most European countries after World War I —the most innovative and influential new film makers there appearing in Germany, Scandinavia, and the Soviet Union. Germany's films—directed by such men as F. W. Murnau, G. W. Pabst, Fritz Lang, E. A. Dupont, and Ernst Lubitsch—were often spectacular features based on history, literature, and mythology; experiments in expressionism; modern social parables; and powerful realism. The enormous production facilities of the government-run Ufa studio in Berlin enabled most films to be made indoors. Innovators at the large German studios also created new techniques in lighting and staging.

The Danish director Carl Dreyer was made famous with 'The Passion of Joan of Arc' (1928). Swedish film became known for its fine directors, such as Victor Sjöström and Mauritz Stiller.

In contrast with the Germans, Soviet film makers preferred natural settings and used the Russian people as cast members. From the start, Soviet films were closely related to the propaganda efforts of the Communist regime, and film was recognized by Premier Nikolai Lenin as the best way to reach the people. Such Soviet directors as Sergei Eisenstein, Vsevolod Pudovkin, Alexander Dovzhenko, and Lev Kuleshov produced film masterpieces inspired by revolutionary fervor. In 'Potemkin' (1925) and 'The End of St. Petersburg' (1927) montage was developed as an editing technique, influenced by Griffith's American films.

During the 1920's the avant-garde film movement became prominent in France. Much of its work was

Mack Sennett, father of American film comedy, supplied the silent screen with slapstick skits and hilarious films between 1911 and 1933. Ben Turpin, in such pictures as 'East Lynne with Variations', which satirized a popular novel of the day, and the Keystone Kops, in such comedies as 'Love in a Police Station', were great successes. The "good badman" of the wild West, William S. Hart, set the format for the cowboy picture. In one film he played three roles in an early example of the effective use of double exposure.

experimental and related to other art forms and to the impressionist, surrealist, and dadaist movements in literature and painting. Such films as 'The Andalusian Dog' (1929), by Luis Buñuel and Salvador Dali, and 'The Blood of a Poet' (1931), by Jean Cocteau, were forerunners of the underground film movement of the 1960's.

Sound Comes to the Screen

From the time of the first motion pictures many people tried to synchronize phonograph records with films without success. The year 1902 saw the introduction of subtitles—printed clues to the action inserted as separate frames. Some film exhibitors devised machines to emit sound effects behind the screen; others hired actors to read aloud during the film. In early motion-picture theaters, musical accompaniments were provided by pianists and organists, who tried to match their selections to the mood and pace of the action on the screen. Some of the more spectacular silent films were accompanied by full orchestras in many of the large theaters.

Sound films became possible through the development of the means to record sound directly on film and of the audion amplifier, which provided sufficient volume of sound for large theaters. Both of these developments were pioneered by Lee De Forest, who exhibited brief sound films to the public in 1923 (*see* De Forest; Radio). Although the public failed to respond to De Forest's sound films, electronics manufacturers continued to experiment with both sound-on-film and phonograph discs synchronized with film.

In 1926, Warner Brothers released a program using synchronized discs; it included short talking and musical films and a silent feature, 'Don Juan', with a synchronized accompaniment. A short sound-on-film comedy with spoken dialogue was released by William Fox in 1927, and later that year he also released the first sound newsreels. Public acceptance of sound came on Oct. 6, 1927, when Warner Brothers presented Al Jolson singing and saying a few words in 'The Jazz Singer'. The first full-length all-sound film was 'The Lights of New York', issued by Warner Brothers in 1928.

The success of sound revolutionized the film industry. By 1931, few silent films were being made in the United States and Europe, and synchronized discs had been abandoned in favor of the superior sound-on-film process. Theaters had to install sound projection equipment, and film studios had to find methods of soundproofing cameras and stages. Movement in most of the early sound films appeared static, because cameras had to be enclosed in soundproof boxes that were difficult to move. Eventually cameras with noiseless gears were developed; microphones were put on *booms*, or poles, which could be extended as needed; and dollies and other means of moving the camera came into even greater use.

The sound revolution ended the careers of many silent-film performers whose voices did not record well, but it also brought new performers to the screen who had stage experience in speaking roles. Playwrights who knew how to write dramatic dialogue were hired to replace silent-screen scenario writers, and many

The German director Robert Wiene's classic horror film 'The Cabinet of Dr. Caligari' (1919)—the first truly artistic film—used stylized backgrounds. 'The Last Laugh' (1925), which was directed by F. W. Murnau and starred Emil Jannings, was another great German expressionist film.

The Museum of Modern Art

National Film Archive

Typical of the swashbuckling costume epics that made Douglas Fairbanks a matinee idol, Raoul Walsh's 'Thief of Bagdad' (1924) was an elaborately plotted tale of derring-do. The German director Erich von Stroheim starred Gibson Gowland and Zasu Pitts in his masterful 'Greed' (1923), shot in California.

The Museum of Modern Art

The Museum of Modern Art

plays were filmed for the screen because they provided ready-made dialogue. New techniques had to be evolved in film editing to mix dialogue, sound effects, and music and synchronize them with pictures.

The 1930's and 1940's

During the first decade of sound film, film makers learned to use the camera and the sound track as creative elements that both supplemented and complemented each other in building the action of a story. Writers, directors, and actors learned how to create natural and convincing screen characterizations. Leading directors included John Ford, Frank Capra, King Vidor, and George Cukor in the United States; Alfred Hitchcock in England; and René Clair in France. New ways of using dialogue, camera work, and music were pioneered by Orson Welles in the highly creative 'Citizen Kane' (1941) and 'The Magnificent Ambersons' (1942).

Among the most popular sound films of the decade were musical comedies and revues. Following the first all-musical film, 'The Broadway Melody' (1929), Hollywood further developed the musical in such successes as '42nd Street' (1933) and the song-and-dance films of Fred Astaire and Ginger Rogers. The Marx Brothers, W. C. Fields, and Mae West became highly popular sound comedians.

Film makers produced a variety of different kinds of films to satisfy the growing audience of sound pictures. Gangster and suspense films, Westerns with singing cowboys, films dealing with social problems, horror stories, and films based on novels appeared in cycles throughout the 1930's. In 1939 one of the most popular films in motion-picture history, 'Gone with the Wind', was released. Walt Disney produced the first animated sound cartoon, 'Steamboat Willie', in 1928 and the first feature-length cartoon, 'Snow White and the Seven Dwarfs', in 1937. (*See also* Cartoons.)

Throughout the 1930's and in the early 1940's European film makers produced a number of serious and mature sound pictures, many of which were imported successfully into the United States. These included 'Carnival in Flanders' (1935) and 'Grand Illusion' (1937) from France; 'The Blue Angel' (1930) and 'M' (1931) from Germany; and 'Pygmalion' (1938), 'Night Train' (1940), and 'Major Barbara' (1941) from England. Important Soviet films included such historical spectacles as 'Peter the Great' (1937) and 'Alexander Nevsky' (1938).

World War II seriously curtailed film production in Europe. In England, film makers turned to the documentary film to report on the war and to strengthen morale. In England and Germany, as well as in the United States and Japan, film was used for propaganda purposes, for training armed services, and for unifying civilians.

During the war, Americans attended films in greater numbers than ever before, bringing new prosperity to the American film industry. Pictures of actual combat in newsreels led to greater realism in fictional films.

Postwar Films in the United States

The American film industry continued to prosper immediately after the war, but television had begun to reduce film audiences significantly by 1950. Not only the impact of television but also increased production costs and a court order requiring production companies to divest themselves of theater chains, as well as other controls over film distribution, created a major financial crisis in the industry. During the 1950's many studios tried to cut costs by making films abroad, where labor was cheaper. Eventually the studios began to release their films for showing on television and to make films specifically for television.

Hollywood's main attempt to attract a new audience was the introduction of wide-screen and three-dimensional films. *Cinerama*, invented by Fred Waller and introduced in 1952, required three cameras, a curved screen, and a stereophonic sound system. One 3-D process, introduced in 1953, was based on the principle of the stereoscope and required the use of special glasses (*see* Stereoscope). *Cinema-Scope*, also introduced in 1953, had been invented by

The Danish director Carl Dreyer made film history with the French production of 'The Passion of Joan of Arc' (1928), in which he successfully used frequent and extreme close-ups.

In Sergei Eisenstein's monumental 'Ten Days That Shook the World' (1927), camera placement and complex montage were employed to produce strikingly dynamic movement.

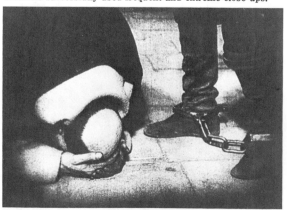

By courtesy of the National Film Archive

The Museum of Modern Art

Henri Chrétien 25 years earlier. It used one camera with a wide-angle lens to condense the image on the film and a special projector lens to spread the image out again on the screen. Other big-screen processes included *VistaVision* and *Todd-AO*. VistaVision was first used in 'White Christmas' (1954) and Todd-AO in 'Oklahoma!' (1955).

To fill their big screens, film companies produced lavish Westerns, historical and Biblical epics, and musicals. Typical of the new spectaculars were 'The Ten Commandments' (1956), 'Ben-Hur' (1959), and 'Cleopatra' (1963). Although some of the spectaculars made tremendous profits, the production costs of such films also set new records.

While major producers were making big pictures, there was a growing trend among the independent and newer film makers toward more serious, mature, and artistic pictures. Many of them worked with low budgets and with standard black-and-white 35-mm. film, and many of them experimented successfully with new film techniques and controversial subjects. They found their audience largely in the small theaters that had sprung up in major cities and university communities during the 1950's to exhibit foreign films. By 1960 some Hollywood studios were also making films for this audience.

Significant Developments Abroad

The most significant and influential developments in film making following World War II occurred in Europe. In Italy, Roberto Rossellini's 'Open City' (1945) and Vittorio De Sica's 'Shoeshine' (1946) and 'The Bicycle Thief' (1948) established a trend toward realism in film. Shunning contrived plots and entertaining stories, these directors took their cameras into the streets to make films showing the harshness of life in the aftermath of war. De Sica fused documentary and dramatic techniques to make personal statements about the world he saw around him. This use of film as a medium of personal artistic expression was further developed by such directors as Federico Fellini and Michelangelo Antonioni. In such films as 'La Strada' (1954), 'La Dolce Vita' (1959), and 'Fellini Satyricon' (1970), Fellini combined realistic plots with poetic imagery, symbolism, and philosophical ideas. Antonioni's 'L'Avventura' (1960), by dispensing with formal plot and emphasizing the nuances of human relationships, ushered in a new age of cinema. Fellini and Antonioni used film to examine both the inner lives of their characters and the society in which they lived.

In France a new generation of young film makers, called the "new wave," emerged in the 1950's. They stressed characterization rather than plot and developed new camera and acting techniques for film. Like the Italians, some of them used poetic visual images, philosophical ideas, and social commentary in their films. Jean Luc Godard—known for such films as 'Breathless' (1960) and 'Weekend' (1968)—developed new techniques with a hand-held camera and new forms of storytelling. François Truffaut drew praise

The Museum of Modern Art

In 'The Jazz Singer' (1927), directed by Alan Crosland, the novelty of sound was tested when the film's star, Al Jolson, in his motion-picture debut, both spoke and sang.

for his finely drawn characters in 'The 400 Blows' (1958) and 'Shoot the Piano Player' (1960). Other important French film makers included René Clément, Alain Resnais, and Robert Bresson.

In England, film makers continued to develop the genres of comedy, in such films as 'Kind Hearts and Coronets' (1950) and 'The Horse's Mouth' (1958), and historical fiction, as in 'Hamlet' (1948) and 'Pickwick Papers' (1953). 'Look Back in Anger' (1958) triggered a new realism that continued in such films as 'The Loneliness of the Long Distance Runner' (1962) and became known as the Angry Young Man movement. Innovative films utilizing dance, such as 'The Red Shoes' (1948) and 'The Tales of Beatrix Potter' (1971), also drew wide attention.

Individual directors in other countries also influenced contemporary film making. The Swedish director Ingmar Bergman used simple, dramatic stories and allegories to explore complex philosophical and social issues. Among his major films were 'The Seventh Seal' (1956), 'Wild Strawberries' (1957), and 'The Passion of Anna' (1970). The influence of Buñuel, a Spaniard whose films portray social injustices, began in the 1920's and continued into the postwar era with such films as 'Viridiana' (1961) and 'Belle de Jour' (1967). With 'Rashomon' (1950) the Japanese director Akira Kurosawa became the first Oriental film maker to have a significant impact in Europe and the United States. In his work he used universal themes played out in historic Oriental settings. In a trilogy on India—'Pather Panchali' (1954), 'Aparajito' (1956), and 'The World of Apu' (1959)—Satyajit Ray produced the first films that were successful abroad in interpreting life in India from a native viewpoint.

Although film making in the Soviet Union after World War II continued to be under state control, after the death of Joseph Stalin in 1953 the emphasis in some films shifted from Communist indoctrination to the problems of the individual. 'The Cranes Are Flying' (1957), directed by Mikhail Kalatozov, is an

(Vol. 14) 525

Culver Pictures

With the coming of sound, new stars replaced those of the silent screen who could not make the transition. Mae West, in such pictures as Lowell Sherman's 'She Done Him Wrong' (1933), with Noah Beery, was an instant success because of her witty dialogue, which she insisted on writing herself, and her honesty in portraying the era's concept of a liberated woman—wealthy, wicked, and with no illusions. Humphrey Bogart, Peter Lorre, Mary Astor, and Sydney Greenstreet—all with distinct screen personalities and voices suitable for talkies—were used effectively by director John Huston in his popular crime melodrama 'The Maltese Falcon' (1941), a film noted for its brilliant use of camera movement. The raspy-voiced humorist W. C. Fields was one of the new comedians who relied on the verbal joke rather than the visual ones that had provided so much mirth during the silent era. 'The Fatal Glass of Beer', with Dick Cramer as a Mountie, was one of four shorts Fields made at the Mack Sennett studios in 1932 and 1933. Fields wrote the screenplay for this film as well as for many others in which he appeared.

Warner Brothers

Culver Pictures

example. The Russians also made films based on literary classics, including the plays of William Shakespeare, and continued to produce such panoramic epics as 'War and Peace' (1965), based on Leo Tolstoi's monumental historical novel.

Film making in other Communist nations of Europe, particularly Poland and Czechoslovakia, developed more independently and stressed ideas and human situations. Among the notable Polish films were 'Kanal' (1957) and 'Ashes and Diamonds' (1958), directed by Andrzej Wajda, and 'Knife in the Water' (1963), directed by Roman Polanski. Notable Czechoslovak films included 'The Shop on Main Street' (1966), directed by Jan Kadar and Elmar Klos, and 'Closely Watched Trains' (1968), directed by Jiri Menzel.

Transatlantic Influences

Postwar European film influenced film making in the United States by presenting new techniques and subject matter and by creating a larger audience for serious and artistic motion pictures. In addition, American film producers invested money in European films and formed partnerships abroad. The films they made helped introduce European film personalities and ideas to American audiences.

When American film production began to slow down in the 1950's, foreign films were imported to fill the need for box-office attractions. At the same time, American producers seeking new markets exported their films. Today the American film industry obtains about half of its theater receipts from foreign markets, and European producers also depend on foreign markets. Coproduction of films by two or more countries is now common in Europe, and many American films are shot abroad. Most contemporary films are made with an international audience in mind.

Underground Films

Underground film is a term used today to describe a wide range of films that are usually conceived and made by a single individual as a personal statement or artistic endeavor. They are sometimes called *experimental* or *avant-garde*. Most of them differ radically from conventional films in form and content, and many differ in the techniques used in filming them.

Although some underground film makers obtain financial backing from private individuals or foundations, most underground films are made inexpensively with 8-mm. or 16-mm. equipment. Because they must be made at low cost, most of them are short. Andy Warhol's 'Empire' (1964), however, runs for eight hours. For the same reason, the use of actors and settings in underground film is limited, and for subjects many film makers use the places and people they encounter in their own lives.

The subject matter of underground films varies greatly. It includes portraits of people, landscape studies, and political protest. 'Scorpio Rising' (1963), by Kenneth Anger, is a study in contemporary violence; Bruce Conner's 'Report' (1964) restructures

526   (Vol. 14)

footage of the assassination of United States President John F. Kennedy into a poetic montage. Some underground films are abstract studies of patterns, rhythms, color, or light. Others attempt to evoke occult and supernatural experiences or, by subjecting the viewer to different kinds of filmed optical effects, explore the ways in which people see.

Underground film makers use almost any technique that occurs to them. The camera may be moved at any speed in any direction, or it may remain stationary for long periods of time. Stan Brakhage and others change the surface of the film itself by painting or scratching it or even by growing mold on it. In editing, all kinds of techniques are also used. Many small bits of film may be pieced together to create a single frame, or whole segments of different films may be joined to create a new film. Even the projection of the film becomes part of the total effect.

The contemporary underground film had its origins in the turn-of-the-century films of the French film maker Georges Méliès and in the avant-garde film movements in France and Germany during the 1920's. In France the avant-garde film movement was influenced by such artists as Man Ray, Fernand Léger, and Marcel Duchamp, who turned to film as an extension of painting, and by such professional directors as Buñuel, Cocteau, and Jean Renoir. The German avant-garde movement was an outgrowth of expres-

Victor Fleming's 'Gone with the Wind' (1939), above, the longest film released to that time, starred Clark Gable and Vivien Leigh. Fred Zinnemann's 'High Noon' (1952), top left, a film of classic economy, typified the modern Western. Robert Wise and Jerome Robbins' 'West Side Story' (1961), top right, revitalized the film musical. Indian Satyajit Ray's 'Aparajito' from the Apu trilogy (1954–59), bottom left, contributed a new clarity of style. Italian Vittorio De Sica's 'Bicycle Thief' (1948), bottom right, a poignant tragedy, spurred neorealism.

(Vol. 14)   527

Franco Pinna—Rapho Guillumette

Inspired by Petronius Arbiter's 'Satyricon', the Italian director Federico Fellini created his personal vision of decadent ancient Rome in 'Fellini Satyricon' (1970).

Authenticated News International

Though produced on a low budget, Dennis Hopper's 'Easy Rider' (1969), starring Peter Fonda, was a box-office smash and a favorite of the young.

sionist feature films, such as Robert Wiene's 'Cabinet of Dr. Caligari' (1919), and of the film experiments of the painters Hans Richter, Walter Ruttmann, and Viking Eggeling.

After the 1920's the avant-garde movement declined. Personal film making was revived in the United States in the 1940's, however, under the name *experimental film*. Notable among the film makers who began their work at that time were Maya Deren, Gregory Markopoulos, and Curtis Harrington.

By the early 1960's the availability of inexpensive motion-picture equipment made possible the widespread development of the personal film, which was described as underground. Among the leading underground film makers of this period were Robert Breer, Bruce Baillie, Scott Bartlett, Jordan Belson, Ed Emshwiller, Kenneth Jacobs, Adolfas and Jonas Mekas, Robert Nelson, Jack Smith, and Stan Van-DerBeek.

Film Awards and Festivals

The most prominent motion-picture awards in the United States are the Oscars presented each year by the Academy of Motion Picture Arts and Sciences. The academy was founded in 1927 in Hollywood and two years later began making awards for achievement

in many categories of film making. The awards for the best production, the best performances by actors and actresses, and the best film direction carry considerable prestige and often contribute to a film's commercial success.

Annual awards for film in England are made by the British Film Academy. In England, as in other European nations and in Asia, influential awards are also given by the juries of film festivals. The first film festival was held in Venice, Italy, in 1932 with government support and has been held in most years since. Its awards are among the most highly valued by film makers, but equally prestigious are the awards of the Cannes festival, established in France after World War II. Since the war, important festivals have been held annually or biannually in West Berlin; London, England; Moscow, Russia; Prague, Czechoslovakia; and elsewhere. The annual Southeast Asia festival is held in different cities in that region. Special festivals for short films, such as documentaries, are held in Scotland, France, and West Germany.

Films for most festivals are obtained by invitations to producers to enter their work. In Hollywood, films are nominated for Oscars by members of different film-making crafts, and the winners are determined by the members of the Motion Picture Academy.

Emshwiller's 'Relativity' (1966) was a 38-minute color montage of shots of animals, men, insects, and galaxies.

Ed Emshwiller

Bartlett's experimental 'Offon' (1968), a ten-minute sound film, employed electronically generated color images.

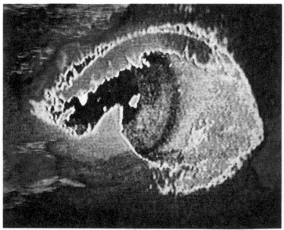

Scott Bartlett

528   (Vol. 14)

SPECIAL TYPES OF FILMS

Documentary Films

Documentary is used to describe a wide range of factual films that deal with living people, historical and contemporary events, and places and their inhabitants. Some documentaries use the camera to observe and record people in their normal environment going about their daily lives. Others take the camera inside factories to show how an industry works or use the camera to portray social conditions and their causes. Documentaries are also made of wildlife and scientific subjects and are sometimes put together from newsreel film to show historical incidents, such as battles.

Most documentary film makers use neither actors nor studio settings. After planning what kind of film they want to make, they proceed to photograph their subjects as they find them. The film maker then unifies and dramatizes his material by his editing. Many documentaries are made to present a subject from a certain viewpoint. The commentary in a documentary is usually provided by a narrator who usually is not seen in the film.

The word "documentary" was first applied to the films of Robert J. Flaherty, an American explorer, by John Grierson, a Scottish educator. Flaherty used the motion-picture camera to document the daily lives of Eskimos, South Sea islanders, and other peoples among whom he lived while filming them. His first film, 'Nanook of the North' (1922), established the form and set high standards for filming a way of life in a dramatic yet factual manner. Grierson saw in the documentary form a means of presenting modern social, economic, and political conditions to the public. Under Grierson's leadership and British government and industrial sponsorship, the British documentary movement developed. Grierson made 'Drifters' (1929), a study of North Sea herring fishermen, as a pilot film. During the 1930's a wide range of films on British products and problems was produced. Late in the decade, Grierson helped establish and became the head of the Canadian National Film Board, which produced documentaries on Canadian and world topics.

In the United States the first widely noted documentaries were 'The March of Time' news features, begun in 1935 by Louis de Rochemont for Time, Inc. They blended newsreels, news analyses, interviews, and staged scenes as a means of informing the public about world events. At about the same time, the Administration of President Franklin D. Roosevelt began using film to explain its programs. Two outstanding documentaries were made for the government by Pare Lorentz—'The Plow That Broke the Plains' (1936), about the causes and effects of the Dust Bowl, and 'The River' (1937), about flood control on the Mississippi River system. Although Congress cut off government funds for film making, Lorentz and others were later able to find private sponsors for their documentaries.

During the 1930's the documentary film was also developed in the Netherlands and in Germany. Leni Riefenstahl, who made a well-known documentary of the 1936 Olympic Games in Berlin, turned the documentary into a propaganda weapon for the Nazis.

In the United States and Europe, World War II brought documentary film makers under government sponsorship as producers of propaganda films, training films for both civilians and the military, and films to explain the war to the public. Although the scope of documentary films was expanded by the war, they failed to interest the general public in postwar years. With the growth of television in the 1950's, however, the documentary film found a large new outlet in the United States. The United Nations, private industry, and some governments continue to sponsor documentaries.

Educational Films

Since early in the development of motion pictures, the value of film as a means of instruction has been recognized. Educational films use all the available tools and techniques to teach the viewing audience. They range from films that teach physical, mental, and social skills on a simple level to films dealing with complex problems and concepts. Some provide general information or an overall view of a subject. Others furnish specific details about a single aspect of a subject or instructions on how to do a specific kind of job, such as using a microscope. An educational film may be used to create appreciation of a subject or as an exercise to help the audience learn how to do, or to remember, something.

An educational film is usually made for a particular audience—people of a certain age and educational level. The material presented must be relevant and comprehensible to its audience, and in both pictures and spoken narration it must be accurate. The organization of the film depends on how it is to be used.

Flaherty set the pattern for the documentary with his film on Eskimo life, 'Nanook of the North' (1922).

The Museum of Modern Art

(Vol. 14)   529

A film that teaches skills usually emphasizes procedures, while a film that presents a general survey of a subject may emphasize principles or historical development.

The material in an educational film may be presented by dramatization of the subject, straight exposition or demonstration, or a narration or story. Many films include maps, charts, diagrams, drawings, or animation to make subjects clear. Some are designed to stimulate discussion by presenting different sides of a problem without offering a solution.

Most educational films made for schools today are designed to fit in with the way subjects are taught and with textbook materials. Film producers work closely with educational experts in preparing their films.

Educational films are also made by industries and businesses to train people for certain jobs and to provide the public with information about how they operate and how their products are made. Medical organizations use films to teach health care, and scientists use films to record observations. Films are widely used by educational television stations to present single lessons as well as entire courses. (*See also* Audio-Visual Instruction.)

CENSORSHIP AND REGULATION

Almost since the inception of the film industry, there has existed some form of controversy over what is suitable and what is unsuitable to be shown on the motion-picture screen. Two methods have been used to control motion-picture content—self-regulation by the industry and censorship by state and local governments.

The first film censorship law was passed by the city of Chicago, in 1907, and other cities and some states followed the example. The United States Supreme Court, in 1915, took the position that films were nothing but a mere "spectacle" and therefore not entitled to the same constitutional freedoms as the press. Scandals in Hollywood, an increase in the portrayal of nudity, and controversial subject matter after World War I brought demands for regulation of the film industry. To avoid federal censorship, the industry, in 1922, formed the Motion Picture Producers and Distributors of America (now the Motion Picture Association of America) to set standards for film production. The organization's regulations, called the Production Code, were enforced after 1934 by the Production Code Administration.

During the period following World War II, new decisions by the Supreme Court and the public's acceptance of films portraying sexual intimacy, racial conflict, and other previously taboo subjects led to the liberalization of censorship and the Production Code. In a landmark decision in 1952, the Supreme Court granted to motion pictures the freedom of the press guaranteed by the 1st and 14th constitutional amendments.

Since 1952, in addition to striking down many local censorship laws on the grounds of vagueness, the Supreme Court has declared unconstitutional such criteria for film censorship as sacrilege, corruption of morals, adultery, and prejudice. Under the Supreme Court's rulings, censorship for obscenity remains constitutional, but the definition of obscenity is open to question.

After the Motion Picture Association of America began liberalizing the Production Code in 1956, bans were lifted on films depicting prostitution, kidnapping, drug addiction, abortion, homosexuality, and interracial marriage. In 1966 the association revised, modified, and considerably shortened the Production Code; approved a film containing nude scenes ('The Pawnbroker', which was directed by Sidney Lumet); and ruled that films containing controversial material must carry the qualification that they are for mature audiences only. In 1969 the Swedish film 'I Am Curious (Yellow)' was allowed through customs. This film, directed by Vilgot Sjöman, depicted frontal nudity of both sexes, as well as copulation.

In most other parts of the world as well—with the exception of Southeast Asia, the emerging African countries, and the totalitarian states—film censorship was being liberalized in the late 1960's. In Denmark all censorship of films for adults was abolished in 1969.

Books About Motion Pictures

Agee, James. Agee on Film, 2v. (Grosset, 1969).
Blum, D. C. and Kobal, John. A New Pictorial History of the Talkies (Grosset, 1970).
Brownlow, Kevin. The Parade's Gone By (Knopf, 1968).
Eastman Kodak Company. How to Make Good Home Movies (Eastman, 1966).
Fielding, Raymond. The Technique of Special Effects Cinematography (Hastings House, 1969).
Fulton, A. R. Motion Pictures (Univ. of Okla. Press, 1960).
Gordon, G. N. and Falk, I. A. Your Career in Film Making (Messner, 1969).
Griffith, Richard and Mayer, A. L. The Movies (Simon & Schuster, 1957).
Halliwell, Leslie. The Filmgoer's Companion (Hill & Wang, 1970).
Jacobs, Lewis, comp. The Emergence of Film Art (Hopkinson, 1969).
Jacobs, Lewis. The Movies as Medium (Farrar, 1970).
Jacobs, Lewis. Rise of the American Film (Teachers College Press, 1968).
Knight, Arthur. Liveliest Art (New American, 1959).
Lindgren, Ernest. The Art of the Film (Macmillan, 1963).
Pincus, Edward. Guide to Filmmaking (New American, 1969).
Renan, Sheldon. An Introduction to the American Underground Film (Dutton, 1967).
Rotha, Paul and Griffith, Richard. The Film Till Now (Twayne, 1963).
Wagenknecht, E. C. The Movies in the Age of Innocence (Univ. of Okla. Press, 1962).
Walker, Alexander. Stardom (Stein & Day, 1970).

530 (Vol. 14)

Feature Authors

Alex Gerber, M.D., Associate Clinical Professor of Surgery, University of Southern California School of Medicine, *THE HEALTH CARE CRISIS*

Walt Kelly, Comic Artist and Creator of "Pogo," *THE FUNNIES ARE RELEVANT*

Edward M. Kennedy, Chairman, Subcommittee on Refugees, Committee on the Judiciary, United States Senate, *THE TRAGEDY OF INDOCHINA: TEN MILLION CIVILIAN VICTIMS*

John V. Lindsay, Mayor of New York City, *A PROPOSAL FOR 'NATIONAL CITIES'*

Ralph Nader, Lawyer and Consumer Advocate, and **John Spanogle,** Professor of Law, University of Maine, *YOUR VANISHING PRIVACY*

Contributors and Consultants

These authorities either wrote the articles listed or supplied information and data that were used in writing them.

Stener Mørch Aarsdal, Economic Editor, 'Børsen', and Press Officer, Chamber of Commerce, Copenhagen, *Denmark*

Joseph John Accardo, Jr., Washington Columnist for several publications, *Fuel and Power* (in part)

Joseph C. Agrella, Turf Editor, 'Chicago Sun-Times', *Horse Racing* (in part)

John Anthony Allan, Lecturer in Geography, School of Oriental and African Studies, University of London, *Libya*

Gustavo Arthur Antonini, Associate Professor, Center for Latin American Studies, University of Florida, *Dominican Republic*

Alan Gordon Armstrong, Lecturer, Department of Economics, University of Bristol, England, *World Trade* (in part)

Bruce Arnold, Free-Lance Journalist and Writer, Dublin, *Ireland*

Robert M. Ball, Commissioner of Social Security, U.S. Department of Health, Education, and Welfare, *Social Services* (in part)

Kenneth de la Barre, Director, Montreal Office, Arctic Institute of North America, *Arctic*

Paul Charles Bartholomew, Professor of Government, University of Notre Dame, *Supreme Court of the United States*

John Frederick Barton, Diplomatic Correspondent, United Press International, *Nixon, Richard M.*

Howard Bass, Journalist and Broadcaster, *Ice Hockey* (in part); *Ice Skating; Skiing*

J. R. Beatty, Senior Research Associate, B. F. Goodrich Research Center, *Rubber*

Richard Herbert Beddoes, Sports Columnist, 'Toronto Globe and Mail', *Ice Hockey* (in part)

William Beltrán, Economic Research Officer, Economic Intelligence Department, Lloyds and Bolsa International Bank Ltd., London, *Argentina*

Stanley F. Bergstein, Executive Secretary, Harness Tracks of America Inc., and Vice-President, United States Trotting Association, *Horse Racing* (in part)

Clyde Richard Bergwin, retired U.S. Air Force Information Officer, Author of 'Animal Astronauts', *Aerospace*

Alan Geoffrey Blyth, Music Critic, London, *Music* (in part)

William Charles Boddy, Editor, 'Motor Sport', Full Member, Guild of Motoring Writers, *Auto Racing* (in part)

Dick Boonstra, Member of Staff, Department of Political Science, Free University, Amsterdam, *Netherlands*

Kooman Boycheff, Supervisor of Physical Education and Coordinator of Recreation, University of California at Berkeley, *Hobbies; Toys and Games*

Mary Beatrice Boyd, Senior Lecturer in History, Victoria University of Wellington, New Zealand, *Fiji; Tonga; Western Samoa*

Arnold C. Brackman, Author of 'Indonesian Communism: A History', *Indonesia*

William A. Bresnahan, President, American Trucking Associations, Inc., *Transportation* (in part)

Jack Brickhouse, Vice-President and Manager of Sports, WGN Continental Broadcasting Co., *Baseball* (in part)

D. A. Brown, Agriculture Librarian, University of Illinois, *Animals and Wildlife; Environment* (in part)

George Hay Brown, Director of the U.S. Bureau of the Census, *Population*

Major Larry Kent Brown, U.S. Air Force, *Armed Forces, United States* (in part)

William J. Brown, Chief, Venereal Disease Branch, State and Community Services Division, Center for Disease Control, Atlanta, Ga., *Medicine* (in part)

Ardath Walter Burks, Professor and Director, International Programs, Rutgers University, New Brunswick, N.J., *Japan*

Allen D. Bushong, Associate Professor of Geography, University of South Carolina, *El Salvador; Honduras*

Frank Butler, Sports Editor, 'News of the World', London, *Boxing*

Don Byrne, Washington Correspondent for 'Electronic Design' and 'Microwaves' Magazines, *Communications* (in part)

Alva Lawrence Campbell, Regional Director, Institute of Life Insurance, *Insurance*

Lucien Chalmey, Adviser, International Union of Producers and Distributors of Electrical Energy, Paris, *Fuel and Power* (in part)

Kenneth Francis Chapman, Editor, 'Stamp Collecting', Philatelic Correspondent, 'The Times', London, *Stamps*

Robin Chapman, Economic Research Officer, Lloyds and Bolsa International Bank Ltd., London, *Cuba; Haiti; Latin America; Portugal*

Robert Chaussin, Government Civil Engineer, Department of Technical Studies on Roads and Highways, Bagneux, France, *Engineering Projects* (in part)

Hung-Ti Chu, Expert in Far Eastern Affairs, United Nations Area Specialist and Chief of Asia-Africa Section and Trusteeship Council Section, 1946-67, and Professor of Government, Texas Tech University, Lubbock, 1968–69, *China, People's Republic of; Taiwan*

Donald Frederic Clifton, Professor of Metallurgy, University of Idaho, *Metals*

Max Coiffait, Correspondent, Agence France-Presse, and 'Time' Magazine, Vientiane, *Laos*

Stanley Harry Costin, London Correspondent, 'Nykytekstiili', Finland, and 'Textil Branschen', Sweden, *Fashion* (in part)

Rufus William Crater, Editorial Director, 'Broadcasting', New York City, *Television and Radio* (in part)

Norman Crossland, Bonn Correspondent, 'Manchester Guardian', *Germany*

Gloria Clare Cumper, Chairman, Council of Voluntary Social Services, and Member, Judicial Services Commission, Kingston, *Jamaica*

Krsto Franjo Cviić, Leader Writer and East European Specialist, 'Economist', London, *Yugoslavia*

Hiroshi Daifuku, Chief, Section for the Development of the Cultural Heritage, United Nations Educational, Scientific, and Cultural Organization (UNESCO), Paris, *Landmarks and Monuments*

David Keith Davies, Economic and Political Research Officer, Lloyds and Bolsa International Bank Ltd., London, *Bolivia; Spain*

Ernest Albert John Davies, Editor, 'Traffic Engineering and Control', 'Roads and Their Traffic', and 'Traffic Engineering Practice', *Transportation* (in part)

Alfred Dawber, Textile Consultant, *Textiles* (in part)

Philippe Decraene, Member, Editorial Staff, 'Le Monde', Paris, *Cameroon; Central African Republic; Chad; Congo, People's Republic of the; Dahomey; Gabon; Guinea; Ivory Coast; Malagasy Republic; Mali; Mauritania; Niger; Senegal; Togo; Tunisia; Upper Volta; West Indies* (in part)

Frances C. Dickson, 4-H Information Specialist, Extension Service, U.S. Department of Agriculture, *Youth Organizations* (in part)

Mary Ellen Dienes, Director of Research, National Legal Aid and Defender Association, American Bar Center, Chicago, *Law*

Dudley Dillard, Professor and Head, Department of Economics, University of Maryland, *Employment* (in part)

Elfriede Dirnbacher, Austrian Civil Servant, *Austria*

Jim Dunne, Detroit Editor, 'Popular Science Monthly', *Automobiles*

Raul d'Eca, formerly Fulbright Visiting Lecturer on American History, University of Minas Gerais, Brazil, *Brazil*

Herbert Leeson Edlin, Publications Officer, Forestry Commission of Great Britain, *Environment* (in part)

Wilfred A. Elders, Associate Professor of Geology, University of California, *Earth Sciences* (in part)

Harold Ellis, Professor of Surgery, Westminster Medical School, University of London, *Medicine* (in part)

Jan Robert Engels, Editor, 'Vooruitgang' (Quarterly of the Belgian Party for Freedom and Progress), *Belgium*

David M. L. Farr, Professor of History, Carleton University, Ottawa, Ont., *Canada* (in part)

Robert Joseph Fendell, New York Editor, 'Automotive News', New York City, *Auto Racing* (in part)

Melba M. Ferguson, Media Specialist, Public Affairs Division, Girl Scouts of the United States of America, *Youth Organizations* (in part)

Ronald Whitaker Ferrier, Company Historian, British Petroleum, *Fuel and Power* (in part)

Morris Fishbein, Editor, 'Medical World News', and Emeritus Professor, University of Chicago, *Medicine* (in part)

Robert Moore Fisher, Senior Economist, Board of Governors, Federal Reserve System, and Professorial Lecturer, American University, Washington, D.C., *Construction*

Jerry M. Flint, Detroit Correspondent for 'The New York Times', *Automobiles SPECIAL REPORT: Cars of the Future*

John F. Flynn, Information Branch, Division of Information, Headquarters, U.S. Marine Corps, *Armed Forces, United States* (in part)

Robert John Fowell, Lecturer, Department of Mining Engineering, University of Newcastle upon Tyne, England, *Fuel and Power* (in part)

David A. Fredrickson, Associate Professor of Anthropology, Sonoma State College, Rohnert Park, Calif., *Archaeology*

Alfred Friendly, Jr., Former Correspondent, 'The New York Times', Belgrade, *Yugoslavia SPECIAL REPORT: A Political Experiment*

Colonel James A. Fyock, Student, National War College, Fort McNair, Washington, D.C., *Armed Forces, United States* (in part)

Peter William Gaddum, Chairman, H. T. Gaddum and Company Ltd., Silk Merchants, Macclesfield, Cheshire, England, and President, International Silk Association, *Textiles* (in part)

Fabio Galvano, Correspondent, 'Epoca', London, *Italy*

Albert Ganado, Lawyer, Malta, *Malta*

Kenneth G. Gehret, Education Editor, 'The Christian Science Monitor', *Colleges and Universities; Education*

Thayil Jacob Sony George, Assistant Editor, 'Far Eastern Economic Review', Hong Kong, *Asia; Cambodia; Korea; Thailand; Vietnam* (in part)

Paul Glikson, Secretary, Division of Jewish Demography and Statistics, Institute of Contemporary Jewry, Hebrew University, Israel, *Religion (*in part)

Walter Goldschmidt, Professor of Anthropology, University of California at Los Angeles, *Anthropology*

John T. Goodman, Associate Professor of Psychiatry (Psychology), Department of Psychiatry, McMaster University, Hamilton, Ont., *Psychology*

Robert Goralski, Correspondent, NBC News, Pentagon, *Vietnam* (in part)

Laurence M. Gould, Professor of Geology, University of Arizona, and Chairman, Committee on Polar Research, National Academy of Sciences, *Antarctica*

Jarlath John Graham, Editor, 'Advertising Age', *Advertising*

The Rev. Arthur R. Green, Pastor, Good Shepherd Parish, Chicago, *Religion* (in part)

Richard D. A. Greenough, Chief English Writer, Press Division, UNESCO, Paris, *United Nations* (in part)

Anthony Royston Grant Griffiths, Lecturer in History, Flinders University of South Australia, *Australia; Nauru*

Arthur E. Grimm, Editor, 'Co-op Report', *Cooperatives*

Toni Grossi, Assistant National Public Relations Director, Junior Achievement Inc., *Youth Organizations* (in part)

Max Harrelson, Chief, United Nations Bureau, the Associated Press, *United Nations* (in part)

David Alexander Harries, Director and Chief Engineer, The Mitchell Construction Kinnear Moodie Group Ltd., *Engineering Projects* (in part)

Gerard A. Harrison, Associate Professor of Recreation, Springfield College, Springfield, Mass., *Camping*

Philip Morris Hauser, Professor of Sociology and Director, Population Research Center, University of Chicago, *Cities and Urban Affairs*

The Rev. Peter Hebblethwaite, Editor, 'The Month', *Religion* (in part)

Graham Charles Hockley, Lecturer, Department of Economics, University College, Cardiff, Wales, *Retail Trade*

Robert David Hodgson, Geographer, U.S. Department of State, *Luxembourg; Monaco*

Jerome Holtzman, Sportswriter, 'Chicago Sun-Times', *Basketball; Football*

Oscar H. Horst, Professor of Geography, Western Michigan University, *Guatemala*

Louis Hotz, formerly Editorial Writer, 'The Johannesburg Star', *South Africa*

Kenneth Ingham, Professor of History, University of Bristol, England, *Congo, Democratic Republic of the; Equatorial Guinea; Kenya; Malawi; Rhodesia; Tanzania; Uganda; West Indies* (in part); *Zambia*

Dudley Anthony Stephenson Jackson, Research Officer, Department of Applied Economics, University of Cambridge, England, *Employment* (in part)

Laurence Henry John, Producer, Science Unit, British Broadcasting Corp. (Radio), *Communications* (in part)

Bernard Solomon Katz, Public Information Specialist, U.S. Department of Defense, *Powell, Lewis F.; Rehnquist, William H.*

William A. Katz, Professor, School of Library Science, State University of New York, *Magazines*

John Arnold Kelleher, Editor, 'The Dominion', Wellington, *New Zealand*

Peter Kilner, Editor, 'Arab Report and Record', *Algeria; Morocco; Sudan*

Jon Kimche, Expert on Middle East Affairs, 'Evening Standard', London, *Israel*

Joshua B. Kind, Associate Professor of Art History, Northern Illinois University, De Kalb, *Museums* (in part)

Resa W. King, Contributing Editor, 'Business Week', *Business and Industry; Housing*

Alfred Paul Klausler, Executive Secretary, Associated Church Press, *Religion* (in part)

Jean Marcel Knecht, Assistant Foreign Editor, 'Le Monde', Paris, *France*

Ole Ferdinand Knudsen, Editor, 'Norway Exports', Oslo, *Norway*

Philip Kopper, Free-Lance Writer, Washington, D.C., *Newspapers; Publishing, Book* (in part)

Valdimar Kristinsson, Editor, 'Fjármálatidindi', *Iceland*

Miroslav A. Kriz, Vice-President, First National City Bank, New York City, *Money and International Finance* (in part)

Philip B. Kurland, Professor of Law, University of Chicago, and Editor, 'The Supreme Court Review', *Law SPECIAL REPORT: Legal Issues and the Pentagon Papers*

Geoffrey Charles Last, Adviser, Imperial Ethiopian Ministry of Education and Fine Arts, Addis Ababa, *Ethiopia*

Wilma Laws, Journalist, London, Member of International Association of Art Critics, *Painting and Sculpture* (in part)

Chapin R. Leinbach, Public Relations Officer, Air Transport Association of America, *Transportation* (in part)

Arnold E. Levitt, Senior Associate Editor, 'Chemical and Engineering News', *Chemistry*

Raymond Basil Lewry, Senior Research Officer, Lloyds and Bolsa International Bank Ltd., London, *Colombia; Ecuador*

Jerry Lipson, Public Information Officer, Commission on Population Growth and the American Future, Washington, D.C., *Postal Service*

Virginia R. Luling, Social Anthropologist, *Somalia*

Warren D. McClam, Economist, Bank for International Settlements, Basel, *Money and International Finance* (in part)

Richard Martin Michael McConnell, Chief Speechwriter, The American Bankers Association, and Washington Correspondent, 'Banking', *Banks*

Captain Terry McDonald, Chief, Public Information Division, U.S. Coast Guard, *Armed Forces, United States* (in part)

Donald L. McElroy, Associate Dean, College of Dentistry, University of Illinois, *Dentistry*

Katharine A. Mahon, Public Relations Director, Girls Clubs of America, Inc., *Youth Organizations* (in part)

Andrew J. A. Mango, Orientalist and Broadcaster, *Turkey*

Peter (John) Mansfield, formerly Middle East Correspondent, 'The Sunday Times', London, *Egypt; Iraq; Jordan; Kuwait; Lebanon; Middle East; Oman; Saudi Arabia; Syria; Yemen Arab Republic (Sana); Yemen, People's Democratic Republic of (Aden)*

Aldo Marcello, Civil Engineer, *Engineering Projects* (in part)

Edward L. Marcou, Assistant Public Relations Manager, American Bowling Congress, *Bowling*

Neville Frederic Maude, Consultant Editor, 'British Journal of Photography' and 'Photo News Weekly', and Editor, 'Photographic Processor', *Photography*

David Michael Mazie, Associate of Carl T. Rowan, Syndicated Columnist, *Social Services* (in part)

Jerome Mazzaro, Author and Professor of English, State University of New York at Buffalo, *Literature*

Raymond Spencer Millard, Deputy Director, Road Research Laboratory, Department of the Environment , Crowthorne, Berkshire, England, *Engineering Projects* (in part)

Sandra Millikin, Architectural Historian, *Architecture; Painting and Sculpture* (in part)

Marilyn M. Milow, Staff Writer, Magazines and News Features, National Board, Young Women's Christian Association, *Youth Organizations* (in part)

Stephen M. Morris, President, American Hospital Association, *Hospitals*

Molly Mortimer, Journalist on Commonwealth and International Affairs, *Botswana; Burundi; Commonwealth of Nations; Gambia, The; Ghana; Lesotho; Maldives; Mauritius; Rwanda; Sierra Leone; Swaziland; West Indies* (in part)

Olivier Mossé, Marketing Specialist, International Union of Official Travel Organisations, Geneva, *Travel* (in part)

George Saul Mottershead, Director-Secretary, Chester Zoo, England, *Zoos*

Pauline G. Mower, Information Director, Future Homemakers of America, *Youth Organizations* (in part)

Leonard M. Murphy, Chief, Seismology Division, Coast and Geodetic Survey, Environmental Science Services Administration, U.S. Department of Commerce, *Earth Sciences* (in part)

Edward Harwood Nabb, Vice-President, Union of International Motorboating, *Boats and Boating*

National Oceanic and Atmospheric Administration, Office of Public Affairs, *Weather*

Salvatore John Natoli, Educational Affairs Director, Association of American Geographers, *Earth Sciences* (in part)

Raymond K. Neal, Executive Editor, Editorial Service, Boy Scouts of America, *Youth Organizations* (in part)

John Neill, Head of Chemical Engineering Department, C. & W. Walker Ltd., *Mountain Climbing*

Bert Nelson, Editor and Publisher, 'Track and Field News', *Track and Field*

Bruce Carlton Netschert, Vice-President, National Economic Research Associates, Inc., *Fuel and Power* (in part)

Harold Stanley Noel, Editor, 'World Fishing', London, *Fish and Fisheries*

Julius Novick, Assistant Professor of English, New York University, Guest Lecturer, Drama Division, The Juilliard School, and Dramatic Critic, 'Village Voice', *Theater*

Arden W. Ohl, Instructor of Geography, Modesto Junior College, California, *Nicaragua*

Sidney Arnold Pakeman, Historian and Author of 'Ceylon', *Ceylon*

Rafael Pargas, Computer Operator, National Geographic Society, *Philippines*

Sandy Parker, Fur Editor, 'Women's Wear Daily', *Furs*

Vernon John Parry, Reader in the History of the Near and Middle East, School of Oriental and African Studies, University of London, *Cyprus*

Sheila Caffyn Patterson, Research Fellow, Centre for Multi-Racial Studies, University of Sussex, Brighton, England, *Barbados; West Indies* (in part)

Virgil W. Peterson, Executive Director, Chicago Crime Commission, 1942–70, *Crime; Police*

Thomas Fraser Pettigrew, Professor of Social Psychology, Harvard University, *Race Relations*

Eugene Edwin Pfaff, Professor of History, University of North Carolina at Greensboro, *International Relations*

David Kemsley Robin Phillips, Editor, 'World Sports', *Sports Champions of 1971*

Otto Pick, Visiting Professor of International Relations, University of Surrey, England, and Director, Atlantic Information Centre for Teachers, London, *Czechoslovakia; Union of Soviet Socialist Republics*

Frederick P. Pittera, Chairman, International Exposition Consultants Co., and Director, New Nations Exposition and Development Corp., *Fairs and Shows*

Riva Poor, President, Bursk and Poor Publishing of Cambridge, Inc., *Labor Unions SPECIAL REPORT: The Four-Day Week*

Simeon Potter, Professor Emeritus of the English Language and Philology, University of Liverpool, England, *New Words Special Essay*

Holenarasipur Y. Sharada Prasad, Director of Information, Prime Minister's Secretariat, New Delhi, *India*

Manuel Pulgar, Senior Economic Research Officer, Lloyds and Bolsa International Bank Ltd., London, *Mexico*

Howard Pyle, President, National Safety Council, *Safety*

Margaret H. Quinn, Reporter, 'Sun-Gazette', Williamsport, Pa., *Baseball* (in part)

Charles Edgar Randall, Assistant Editor, 'Journal of Forestry', *Forest Products*

Mahinder Singh Randhava, Subeditor, 'The Straits Times', Kuala Lumpur, *Malaysia; Singapore*

Robert John Ranger, Visiting Lecturer in Strategic Studies, University of British Columbia, Canada, *Defense*

Vivian Foster Raven, Editor, 'Tobacco', *Tobacco* (in part)

Randolph Richard Rawlins, Journalist and Broadcaster, Tutor, Extra-Mural Department, University of the West Indies, St. Augustine, Trinidad, *Guyana; West Indies* (in part)

Joseph Lee Reid, Research Oceanographer, Scripps Institution of Oceanography, La Jolla, Calif., *Oceanography*

A. Daniel Reuwee, Director of Information, Future Farmers of America, *Youth Organizations* (in part)

Wallace B. Riley, Computers Editor, 'Electronics', McGraw-Hill Publications, Inc., *Computers*

David Julien Robinson, Film Critic, 'The Financial Times', *Motion Pictures*

Leif J. Robinson, Associate Editor, 'Sky and Telescope', Sky Publishing Corp., *Astronomy*

John D. Rockefeller III, Chairman, Commission on Population Growth and the American Future, *Population SPECIAL REPORT: American Attitudes Toward Population Growth*

Francis John Caldwell Roe, Research Coordinator, Tobacco Research Council, London, *Medicine* (in part)

John Kerr Rose, Senior Specialist in Natural Resources and Conservation, Congressional Research Service, Library of Congress, *Agriculture* (in part); *Tobacco* (in part)

David E. Rosenbaum, Reporter, Washington Bureau, 'The New York Times', *Selective Service*

Robert L. Ross, President, Adela Development Corp., *Chile*

Joseph R. Rowan, Executive Director, John Howard Association, Chicago, *Prisons SPECIAL REPORT: Prison Reform*

Walter Rugaber, Reporter, Washington Bureau, 'The New York Times', *Prisons*

Al Salerno, Director, Press and Publications, American Heart Association, Inc., *Medicine* (in part)

Carl Fredrik Sandelin, Foreign News Editor, Finnish News Agency, and President, Society of Swedish-Speaking Writers in Finland, *Finland*

Alex Sareyan, Executive Director, Mental Health Materials Center, *Mental Health*

Albert Schoenfield, Editor, 'Swimming World', *Swimming*

William Scholz, Director, Marketing and Public Relations, American Hotel and Motel Association, *Travel* (in part)

Byron T. Scott, Executive Editor, 'Medical Opinion' Magazine, *Medicine* (in part)

Stephen Eugene Scrupski, Senior Editor, 'Electronics', McGraw-Hill Publications, Inc., *Electronics*

Peter Shackleford, Research Officer, International Union of Official Travel Organisations, Geneva, *Travel* (in part)

Mitchell R. Sharpe, Science Writer, *Space Exploration*

Harvey R. Sherman, Environmental Policy Division, Congressional Research Service, Library of Congress, *Agriculture* (in part); *Food; Tobacco* (in part)

Constant Chung-Tse Shih, Counsellor, Trade Policy Department, General Agreement on Tariffs and Trade (GATT), Switzerland, *World Trade* (in part)

Glenn B. Smedley, Governor, American Numismatic Association, *Coin Collecting*

David Lawrence Smith, Staff Member, Centre for Environmental Studies, *Environment* (in part)

John Jervis Smith, Research Officer, Economic Intelligence Department, Lloyds and Bolsa International Bank Ltd., London, *Paraguay; Peru; Uruguay*

J. Frederick Smithcors, Associate Editor, American Veterinary Publications, Inc., Santa Barbara, Calif., *Veterinary Medicine*

Kazimierz Maciej Smogorzewski, Founder and Editor, 'Free Europe', London, and Writer on Contemporary History, *Albania; Bulgaria; Europe* (in part); *Hungary; Intelligence Operations; Mongolian People's Republic; Poland; Romania*

Frank Smothers, former Director of Publications, Council of State Governments, *State Governments, United States*

Leonard M. Snyder, Associate Director, Public Relations Services, Young Men's Christian Association, *Youth Organizations* (in part)

Wallace Sokolsky, Associate Professor, History Department, Bronx Community College, the New School for Social Research, New York University, Division of Adult Education, *Africa*

Melanie F. Staerk, Editor, 'UNESCO Press', Swiss National Commission for UNESCO, *Switzerland*

Edward J. Stapleton, Public Information Director, Boys' Clubs of America, *Youth Organizations* (in part)

Robert Edward Stent, Economic and Political Research Officer, Lloyds and Bolsa International Bank Ltd., London, *Costa Rica; Venezuela*

Tom Stevenson, Garden Columnist, 'Baltimore News American', 'Washington Post', and 'Los Angeles Times', *Flowers and Gardens*

Zena Bailey Sutherland, Editor, 'Bulletin of the Center for Children's Books', University of Chicago, and Editor, Books for Young People, 'Saturday Review', *Literature, Children's*

Thelma Sweetinburgh, Paris Fashion Correspondent, 'International Textiles', Amsterdam, *Cosmetics; Fashion* (in part)

Richard N. Swift, Professor of Politics, New York University, New York City, *United Nations* (in part)

Andrew Szpakowski, Head, Section of Standards, Research and Museums, UNESCO, *Museums* (in part)

Sol Taishoff, President, Editor, and Publisher, 'Broadcasting', *Television and Radio* (in part)

Walter Terry, Dance Critic, 'Saturday Review', *Dance* (in part)

John Hunter Thomas, Associate Professor, Curator, Dudley Herbarium, Department of Biological Sciences, Stanford University, *Biology*

William Harford Thomas, Managing Editor, 'Manchester Guardian', *Great Britain and Northern Ireland, United Kingdom of*

Anthony Thompson, General Secretary, 1962–70, International Federation of Library Associations, *Libraries*

Norman Samuel Thompson, Professor of Business Education and Chairman, Department of Business Education, Eastern Washington State College, *Economy*

Dietrick E. Thomsen, Physical Sciences Editor, 'Science News' Magazine, *Physics*

Lancelot Oliver Tingay, Lawn Tennis Correspondent, 'The Daily Telegraph', London, *Tennis*

Edward Townsend, Associate Editor, 'Business Week', *Labor Unions*

James Scott Trezise, Staff Writer, 'All Hands' Magazine, *Armed Forces, United States* (in part)

Pat Tucker, Free-Lance Writer and Editor, Washington, D.C., *Consumer Protection*

Govindan Unny, Special Correspondent for India, Nepal, and Ceylon, Agence France-Presse, *Bhutan; Burma; Nepal; West Indies* (in part)

Norman Richard Urquhart, Assistant Vice-President, Commodity Section, Economics Department, First National City Bank, New York City, *World Trade* (in part)

Leslie P. Verter, Specialist in Public Information, Camp Fire Girls, Inc., *Youth Organizations* (in part)

John R. Vosburgh, Chief, Branch of Features, Division of Information, National Park Service, U.S. Department of the Interior, *National Park Service*

OUR FAMILY RECORD
FOR 1972

What we did and how we looked

This space for family group photo

Each year important events highlight the life of every family. Year after year these events may be noted in the Family Record pages of your Compton Yearbooks. You will then have a permanent record of your family's significant achievements, celebrations, and activities.

OUR FAMILY TREE

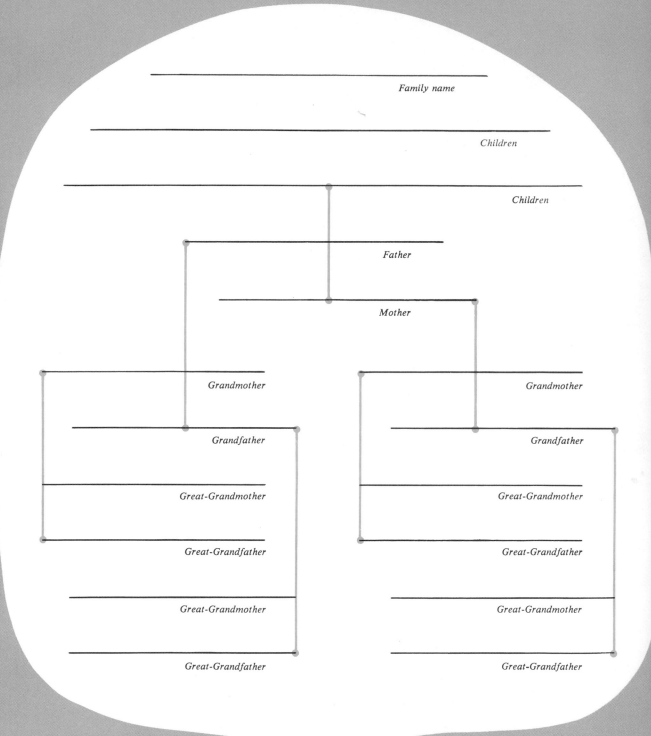

Family name

Children

Children

Father

Mother

Grandmother

Grandmother

Grandfather

Grandfather

Great-Grandmother

Great-Grandmother

Great-Grandfather

Great-Grandfather

Great-Grandmother

Great-Grandmother

Great-Grandfather

Great-Grandfather

DATES TO REMEMBER

Birthdays, weddings, anniversaries, graduations, gifts sent

JANUARY	FEBRUARY	MARCH

APRIL	MAY	JUNE

JULY	AUGUST	SEPTEMBER

OCTOBER	NOVEMBER	DECEMBER

FAMILY CELEBRATIONS IN 1972

PASTE PHOTO HERE

BIRTHDAYS

NAME ______

DATE ______

______

______

NAME ______

DATE ______

______

______

NAME ______

DATE ______

______

______

NAME ______

DATE ______

______

______

NAME ______

DATE ______

______

______

NAME ______

DATE ______

______

______

______

WEDDINGS

NAMES ______

______

DATE ______

NAMES ______

______

DATE ______

NAMES ______

______

DATE ______

ANNIVERSARIES

NAMES ______

DATE ______

______

NAMES ______

DATE ______

______

PROMOTIONS

FIRM ______

TITLE ______

DATE ______

FIRM ______

TITLE ______

DATE ______

HOLIDAYS

OCCASION _____

_____

_____

OCCASION _____

_____

_____

OCCASION _____

_____

_____

OCCASION _____

_____

_____

BIRTHS

NAME _____

DATE _____

PARENTS _____

NAME _____

DATE _____

PARENTS _____

NAME _____

DATE _____

PARENTS _____

NAME _____

DATE _____

PARENTS _____

SPIRITUAL MILESTONES

NAME _____

MILESTONE _____

_____

_____

NAME _____

MILESTONE _____

_____

_____

NAME _____

MILESTONE _____

_____

_____

NAME _____

MILESTONE _____

_____

_____

NAME _____

MILESTONE _____

_____

NAME _____

MILESTONE _____

_____

_____

NAME _____

MILESTONE _____

_____

_____

NAME _____

MILESTONE _____

_____

PASTE PHOTO HERE

SCHOOL ACTIVITIES AND ACHIEVEMENTS

NAME _____

SCHOOL _____ GRADE ____

NAME _____

SCHOOL _____ GRADE ____

SPORTS

NAME _____

SPORT _____

ACHIEVEMENT _____

NAME _____

SPORT _____

ACHIEVEMENT _____

NAME _____

SPORT _____

ACHIEVEMENT _____

NAME _____

SPORT _____

ACHIEVEMENT _____

NAME _____

SPORT _____

ACHIEVEMENT _____

CLUB ACTIVITIES

NAME _____

CLUB _____

ACHIEVEMENT _____

NAME _____

CLUB _____

ACHIEVEMENT _____

NAME _____

CLUB _____

ACHIEVEMENT _____

NAME _____

CLUB _____

ACHIEVEMENT _____

NAME _____

CLUB _____

ACHIEVEMENT _____

PASTE PHOTO HERE

PASTE PHOTO HERE

NAME _____

SCHOOL _____ GRADE ____

NAME _____

SCHOOL _____ GRADE ____

PASTE PHOTO HERE

SCHOOL PARTIES

DATE _____

OCCASION _____

_____

DATE _____

OCCASION _____

_____

DATE _____

OCCASION _____

_____

DATE _____

OCCASION _____

_____

DATE _____

OCCASION _____

_____

DATE _____

OCCASION _____

_____

DATE _____

OCCASION _____

_____

DATE _____

OCCASION _____

_____

EDUCATIONAL HONORS AND PRIZES

Scholarships, Awards, Honor Societies

NAME _____

GRADE _____

HONOR _____

NAME _____

GRADE _____

HONOR _____

NAME _____

GRADE _____

HONOR _____

NAME _____

GRADE _____

HONOR _____

GRADUATIONS

NAME _____

SCHOOL _____

NAME _____

SCHOOL _____

NAME _____

SCHOOL _____

OUR FAMILY HEALTH RECORD

DOCTOR'S NAME _____

ADDRESS _____

_____

TELEPHONE NUMBER _____

DENTIST'S NAME _____

ADDRESS _____

_____

TELEPHONE NUMBER _____

DOCTOR'S NAME _____

ADDRESS _____

_____

TELEPHONE NUMBER _____

DENTIST'S NAME _____

ADDRESS _____

_____

TELEPHONE NUMBER _____

RECORD OF GROWTH IN HEIGHT
FEET

RECORD OF WEIGHT
POUNDS

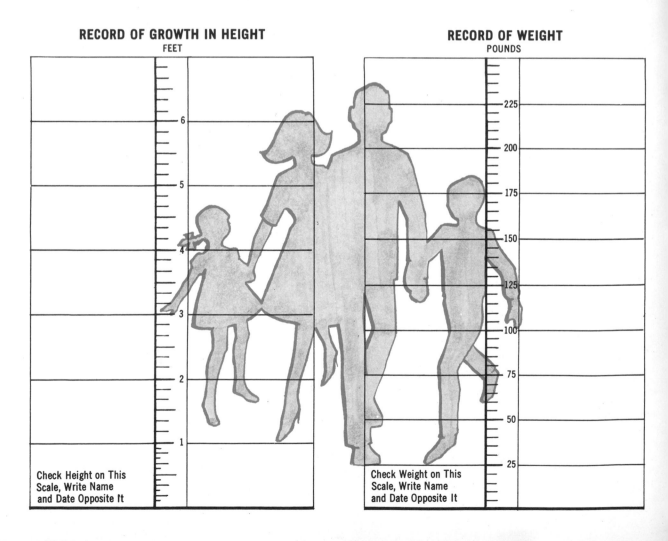

6
5
4
3
2
1

225
200
175
150
125
100
75
50
25

Check Height on This Scale, Write Name and Date Opposite It

Check Weight on This Scale, Write Name and Date Opposite It